PHILIP'S ROAD ATLAS

2021 ESSENTIAL BRITAIN & IRELAND

www.philips-maps.co.uk

First published in 2009 as *Complete Road Atlas Britain and Ireland*
by Philip's, a division of Octopus Publishing Group Ltd
www.octopusbooks.co.uk
Carmelite House, 50 Victoria Embankment
London EC4Y 0DZ
An Hachette UK Company
www.hachette.co.uk

Twelfth edition 2020
First impression 2020

ISBN 978-1-84907-522-0 spiral-bound
ISBN 978-1-84907-533-6 perfect-bound

Cartography by Philip's
Copyright © 2020 Philip's

This product includes mapping data licensed from Ordnance Survey®, with the permission of the Controller of Her Majesty's Stationery Office. © Crown copyright 2020. All rights reserved. Licence number 100011710.

The map of Ireland on pages XVI–XVII is based upon the Crown Copyright and is reproduced with the permission of Land & Property Services under delegated authority from the Controller of Her Majesty's Stationery Office, © Crown Copyright and database right 2020, PMLPA number 100503, and on Ordnance Survey Ireland by permission of the Government © Ordnance Survey Ireland / Government of Ireland Permit number 9220.

While every reasonable effort has been made to ensure that the information compiled in this atlas is accurate, complete and up-to-date at the time of publication, some of this information is subject to change and the Publisher cannot guarantee its correctness or completeness.

The information in this atlas is provided without any representation or warranty, express or implied and the Publisher cannot be held liable for any loss or damage due to any use or reliance on the information in this atlas, nor for any errors, omissions or subsequent changes in such information.

The representation in this atlas of any road, drive or track is no evidence of the existence of a right of way.

Information for National Parks, Areas of Outstanding Natural Beauty, National Trails and Country Parks in Wales supplied by the Countryside Council for Wales.

Information for National Parks, Areas of Outstanding Natural Beauty, National Trails and Country Parks in England supplied by Natural England. Data for Regional Parks, Long Distance Footpaths and Country Parks in Scotland provided by Scottish Natural Heritage.

Gaelic name forms used in the Western Isles provided by Comhairle nan Eilean.

Data for the National Nature Reserves in England provided by Natural England. Data for the National Nature Reserves in Wales provided by Countryside Council for Wales. Darparwyd data'n ymwneud â Gwarchodfeydd Natur Cenedlaethol Cymru gan Gyngor Cefn Gwlad Cymru.

Information on the location of National Nature Reserves in Scotland was provided by Scottish Natural Heritage.

Data for National Scenic Areas in Scotland provided by the Scottish Executive Office. Crown copyright material is reproduced with the permission of the Controller of HMSO and the Queen's Printer for Scotland. Licence number C02W0003960.

Printed in Malaysia

*Data from Nielsen Total Consumer Market 2016 weeks 1–52

II	Key to map symbols
III	Motorway service areas
IV	Restricted motorway junctions
VI	Route planning maps
XVI	Road map of Ireland
XVIII	Tourism and transport
XX	Distances and journey times
1	Key to road map pages
2	Road maps of Britain
161	Urban approach maps

161	Bristol *approaches*
162	Birmingham *approaches*
164	Cardiff *approaches*
165	Edinburgh *approaches*
166	Glasgow *approaches*
167	Leeds *approaches*
168	London *approaches*
172	Liverpool *approaches*
173	Manchester *approaches*
174	Newcastle *approaches*

175	Town plans

175	Aberdeen, Ayr, Bath
176	Birmingham, Blackpool, Bournemouth
177	Bradford, Brighton, Bristol
178	Bury St Edmunds, Cambridge, Canterbury, Cardiff
179	Carlisle, Chelmsford, Cheltenham, Chester
180	Chichester, Colchester, Coventry, Derby
181	Dorchester, Dumfries, Dundee, Durham
182	Edinburgh, Exeter, Gloucester
183	Glasgow, Grimsby, Harrogate
184	Hull, Inverness, Ipswich, Kendal
185	King's Lynn, Lancaster, Leeds
186	London
188	Leicester, Lincoln, Liverpool
189	Llandudno, Llanelli, Luton, Macclesfield
190	Manchester, Maidstone, Merthyr Tydfil
191	Middlesbrough, Milton Keynes, Newcastle, Newport
192	Newquay, Northampton, Norwich, Nottingham
193	Oxford, Perth, Peterborough, Plymouth
194	Poole, Portsmouth, Preston, Reading
195	St Andrews, Salisbury, Scarborough, Shrewsbury,
196	Sheffield, Stoke-on-Trent (Hanley), Southampton
197	Southend, Stirling, Stratford-upon-Avon, Sunderland
198	Swansea, Swindon, Taunton, Telford
199	Torquay, Truro, Winchester, Windsor
200	Wolverhampton, Worcester, Wrexham, York

201	Index to town plans
213	Index to road maps of Britain

Inside back cover: **County and unitary authority boundaries**

Road map symbols

- Motorway, toll motorway
- Motorway junction – full, restricted access
- Motorway service area – full, restricted access
- Motorway under construction
- Primary route – dual, single carriageway
- Service area, roundabout, multi-level junction
- Numbered junction – full, restricted access
- Primary route under construction
- Narrow primary route
- Primary destination — **Derby**
- A road – dual, single carriageway
- A road under construction, narrow A road
- B road – dual, single carriageway
- B road under construction, narrow B road
- Minor road – over 4 metres, under 4 metres wide
- Minor road with restricted access
- Distance in miles
- Scenic route
- Toll, steep gradient – arrow points downhill
- Tunnel
- National trail – England and Wales
- Long distance footpath – Scotland
- Railway with station
- Level crossing, tunnel
- Preserved railway with station
- National boundary
- County / unitary authority boundary
- Car ferry, catamaran
- Passenger ferry, catamaran
- Hovercraft
- Ferry destination — CALAIS Ferry
- Car ferry – river crossing
- Principal airport, other airport
- National park, Area of Outstanding Natural Beauty – England and Wales **National Scenic Area** – Scotland **Forest park / regional park / national forest**
- Beach
- Linear antiquity
- Roman road
- Hillfort, battlefield – with date (1066)
- Viewpoint, nature reserve, spot height – in metres (795)
- Golf course, youth hostel, sporting venue
- Camp site, caravan site, camping and caravan site
- Shopping village, park and ride (P&R)
- Adjoining page number – road maps (29)

Approach map symbols

- Motorway
- Toll motorway
- Motorway junction – full, restricted access
- Service area
- Under construction
- Primary route – dual, single carriageway
- Service area
- Multi-level junction
- roundabout
- Under construction
- A road – dual, single carriageway
- B road – dual, single carriageway (B1288)
- Minor road – dual, single carriageway
- Ring road
- Distance in miles (3)
- Congestion charge area
- Railway with station — COSELEY
- Tramway with station — LOXDALE
- Underground or metro station — M

Town plan symbols

- Motorway
- Primary route – dual, single carriageway
- A road – dual, single carriageway
- B road – dual, single carriageway
- Minor through road
- One-way street
- Pedestrian roads
- Shopping streets
- Railway with station
- Tramway with station — City Hall
- Bus or railway station building
- Shopping precinct or retail park
- Park
- Building of public interest
- Theatre, cinema
- Parking, shopmobility
- Underground station — Bank
- Metro station — West St
- Hospital, Police station — H
- Post office — PO

Tourist information

- † Abbey, cathedral or priory
- Ancient monument
- Aquarium
- Art gallery
- Bird collection or aviary
- Castle
- Church
- Country park England and Wales / Scotland
- Farm park
- Garden
- Historic ship
- House
- House and garden
- Motor racing circuit
- Museum
- Picnic area
- Preserved railway
- Race course
- Roman antiquity
- Safari park
- Theme park
- i Tourist information
- Zoo
- ✦ Other place of interest

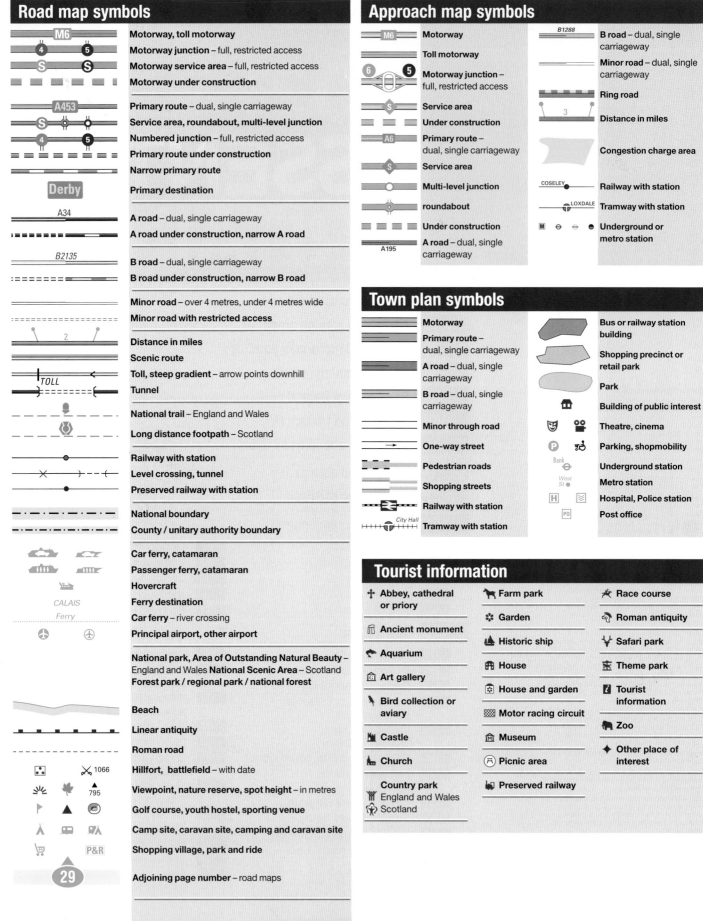

Road map scales

1 : 200 000 • 1cm = 2km • 1 inch = 3·15 miles

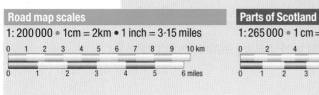

0 1 2 3 4 5 6 7 8 9 10 km
0 1 2 3 4 5 6 miles

Parts of Scotland

1 : 265 000 • 1 cm = 2.65 km • 1 inch = 4.18 miles

0 2 4 6 8 10 km
0 1 2 3 4 5 6 miles

Scottish Highlands and Islands

1 : 332 000 • 1 cm = 3.32km • 1 inch = 5.24 miles

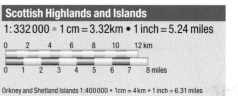

0 2 4 6 8 10 12 km
0 1 2 3 4 5 6 7 8 miles

Orkney and Shetland Islands 1:400 000 • 1cm = 4 km • 1 inch = 6.31 miles

- Motorway service area

Restricted motorway junctions

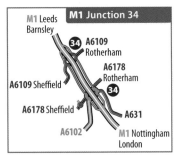

M1 Junction 34

M1 Leeds / Barnsley — 34 — A6109 Rotherham — A6178 Rotherham — 34 — A631 — M1 Nottingham London — A6102 — A6178 Sheffield — A6109 Sheffield

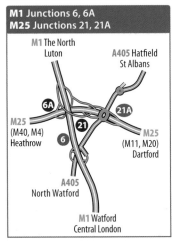

M1 Junctions 6, 6A
M25 Junctions 21, 21A

M1 The North Luton — A405 Hatfield St Albans — 6A — 21A — 21 — 6 — M25 (M40, M4) Heathrow — M25 (M11, M20) Dartford — A405 North Watford — M1 Watford Central London

M4 Junctions 25, 25A, 26

A4042 Abergavenny Cwmbran — A4051 Cwmbran — 25A — 25 — B4596 Caerleon — 26 — A4042 — A4051 Newport — B4596 — M4 Chepstow London — M4 Cardiff

M5 Junction 11A

A417 Gloucester — M5 Cheltenham (A40) — 11A — A417 Cirencester — M5 Bristol — B4641

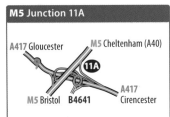

M8 Junctions 8, 9 · M73 Junctions 1, 2
M74 Junctions 2A, 3, 3A, 4

M8 Glasgow — 9 — M73 Stirling — 8 — A89 Coatbridge — 2 — A8 M8 Edinburgh — M73 — 1/4 — B7001 — A74 — B7058 — B765 — A74 — M74 Glasgow — 2A — 3 — M74 — 3A — A721 — B758 — B7071 — M74 Carlisle — A763

M1	Northbound	Southbound
2	No exit	No access
4	No exit	No access
6A	No exit. Access from M25 only	No access. Exit to M25 only
7	No exit. Access from A414 only	No access. Exit to A414 only
17	No access. Exit to M45 only	No exit. Access from M45 only
19	No exit to A14	No access from A14
21A	No access	No exit
23A		Exit to A42 only
24A	No exit	No access
35A	No access	No exit
43	No access. Exit to M621 only	No exit. Access from M621 only
48	No exit to A1(M) southbound	

M3	Eastbound	Westbound
8	No exit	No access
10	No access	No exit
13	No access to M27 eastbound	
14	No exit	No access

M4	Eastbound	Westbound
1	Exit to A4 eastbound only	Access from A4 westbound only
2	Access from A4 eastbound only	Access to A4 westbound only
21	No exit	No access
23	No access	No exit
25	No exit	No access
25A	No exit	No access
29	No exit	No access
38		No access
39	No exit or access	No exit
41	No access	No exit
41A	No exit	No access
42	Access from A483 only	Exit to A483 only

M5	Northbound	Southbound
10	No exit	No access
11A	No access from A417 eastbound	No exit to A417 westbound

M6	Northbound	Southbound
3A	No access.	No exit. Access from M6 eastbound only
4A	No exit. Access from M42 southbound only	No access. Exit to M42 only
5	No access	No exit
10A	No access. Exit to M54 only	No exit. Access from M54 only
11A	No exit. Access from M6 Toll only	No access. Exit to M6 Toll only
20	No exit to M56 eastbound	No access from M56 westbound
24	No exit	No access
25	No access	No exit
30	No exit. Access from M61 northbound only	No access. Exit to M61 southbound only
31A	No access	No exit
45	No access	No exit

M6 Toll	Northbound	Southbound
T1		No exit
T2	No exit, no access	No access
T5	No exit	No access
T7	No access	No exit
T8	No access	No exit

M8	Eastbound	Westbound
6	No exit	No access
6A	No access	No exit
7	No Access	No exit
7A	No exit. Access from A725 northbound only	No access. Exit to A725 southbound only
8	No exit to M73 northbound	No access from M73 southbound
9	No access	No exit
13	No exit southbound	Access from M73 southbound only
14	No access	No exit
16	No exit	No access
17	No exit	
18		No exit
19	No exit to A814 eastbound	No access from A814 westbound
20	No exit	No access
21	No access from M74	No exit
22	No exit. Access from M77 only	No access. Exit to M77 only
23	No exit	No access
25	Exit to A739 northbound only. Access from A739 southbound only	
25A	No exit	No access
28	No exit	No access
28A	No exit	No access
29A	No exit	No access

M9	Eastbound	Westbound
2	No access	No exit
3	No exit	No access
6	No access	No exit
8	No exit	No access

M11	Northbound	Southbound
4	No exit	No access
5	No access	No exit
8A	No access	No exit
9	No access	No exit
13	No access	No exit
14	No exit to A428 westbound	No exit. Access from A14 westbound only

M20	Eastbound	Westbound
2	No access	No exit
3	No exit. Access from M26 eastbound only	No access. Exit to M26 westbound only
10A	No access	No access
11A	No access	No access

M23	Northbound	Southbound
7	No exit to A23 southbound	No access from A23 northbound
10A	No access	No access

M25	Clockwise	Anticlockwise
5	No exit to M26 eastbound	No access from M26 westbound
19	No access	No exit
21	No exit to M1 southbound. Access from M1 southbound only	No exit to M1 southbound. Access from M1 southbound only
31	No exit	No access

M27	Eastbound	Westbound
10	No exit	No access
12	No access	No exit

M40	Eastbound	Westbound
3	No exit	No access
7	No exit	No access
8	No exit	No access
13	No exit	No access
14	No access	No exit
16	No access	No exit

M42	Northbound	Southbound
1	No exit	No access
7	No access Exit to M6 northbound only	No exit. Access from M6 northbound only
7A	No access. Exit to M6 southbound only	No exit
8	No exit. Access from M6 southbound only	Exit to M6 northbound only. Access from M6 southbound only

M45	Eastbound	Westbound
M1 J17	Access to M1 southbound only	No access from M1 southbound
With A45	No access	No exit

M48	Eastbound	Westbound
M4 J21	No exit to M4 westbound	No access from M4 eastbound
M4 J23	No access from M4 westbound	No exit to M4 eastbound

M49	Southbound	Northbound
18A	No exit to M5 northbound	No access from M5 southbound

M53	Northbound	Southbound
11	Exit to M56 eastbound only. Access from M56 westbound only	Exit to M56 eastbnd only. Access from M56 westbound only

M56	Eastbound	Westbound
2	No exit	No access
3	No access	No exit
4	No exit	No access
7		No access
8	No exit or access	No exit
9	No access from M6 northbound	No access to M6 southbound
15	No exit to M53	No access from M53 northbound

M57	Northbound	Southbound
3	No exit	No access
5	No exit	No access

M58	Eastbound	Westbound
1	No exit	No access

M60	Clockwise	Anticlockwise
2	No exit	
3	No exit to A34 northbound	No exit to A34 northbound
4	No access from M56	No exit to M56
5	No exit to A5103 southbound	No exit to A5103 northbound
14	No exit	No access
16	No exit	No access
20	No access	No exit
22		No access
25	No access	
26		No exit or access
27	No exit	No access

M61	Northbound	Southbound
2	No access from A580 eastbound	No exit to A580 westbound
3	No access from A580 eastbound. No access from A666 southbound	No exit to A580 westbound
M6 J30	No exit to M6 southbound	No access from M6 northbound

M62	Eastbound	Westbound
23	No access	No exit

M65	Eastbound	Westbound
9	No access	No exit
11	No exit	No access

M66	Northbound	Southbound
1	No access	No exit

M67	Eastbound	Westbound
1A	No access	No exit
2	No exit	No access

M69	Northbound	Southbound
2	No exit	No access

M73	Northbound	Southbound
2	No access from M8 eastbound	No exit to M8 westbound

M74	Northbound	Southbound
3	No access	No exit
3A	No access	No access
7	No exit	No access
9	No exit or access	No access
10		No exit
11	No access	No access
12	No access	No exit

M77	Northbound	Southbound
4	No exit	No access
6	No exit	No access
7	No exit	
8	No access	No access

M80	Northbound	Southbound
4A	No access	No exit
6A	No access	No access
8	Exit to M876 northbound only. No access	Access from M876 southbound only. No exit

M90	Northbound	Southbound
1	Access from A90 northbound only	No access. Exit to A90 southbound only
2A	No access	No exit
7	No exit	No access
8	No access	No exit
10	No access from A912	No exit to A912

M180	Eastbound	Westbound
1	No access	No exit

M621	Eastbound	Westbound
2A	No exit	No access
4	No exit	
5	No exit	No access
6	No access	No exit

M876	Northbound	Southbound
2	No access	No exit

A1(M)	Northbound	Southbound
2	No access	No exit
3		No access
5	No exit	No exit, no access
14	No exit	No access
40	No access	No exit
43	No exit. Access from M1 only	No access. Exit to M1 only
57	No access	No exit
65	No access	No exit

A3(M)	Northbound	Southbound
1	No exit	No access
4	No access	No exit

A38(M) with Victoria Rd, (Park Circus) Birmingham	
Northbound	No exit
Southbound	No access

A48(M)	Northbound	Southbound
M4 Junc 29	Exit to M4 eastbound only	Access from M4 westbound only
29A	Access from A48 eastbound only	Exit to A48 westbound only

A57(M)	Eastbound	Westbound
With A5103	No access	No exit
With A34	No access	No exit

A58(M)		Southbound
With Park Lane and Westgate, Leeds		No access

A64(M)		Eastbound	Westbound
With A58 Clay Pit Lane, Leeds		No access from A58	No exit to A58

A74(M)	Northbound	Southbound
18	No access	No exit
22		No exit to A75

A194(M)	Northbound	Southbound
A1(M) J65 Gateshead Western Bypass	Access from A1(M) northbound only	Exit to A1(M) southbound only

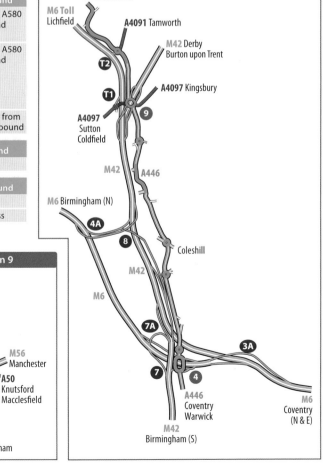

M3 Junctions 13, 14
M27 Junction 4

M6 Junctions 3A, 4A · **M42** Junctions 7, 7A, 8, 9
M6 Toll Junctions T1, T2

M6 Junction 20 · **M56** Junction 9

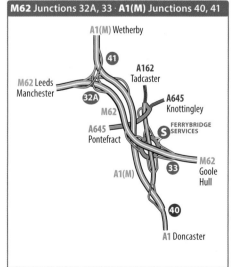

M62 Junctions 32A, 33 · **A1(M)** Junctions 40, 41

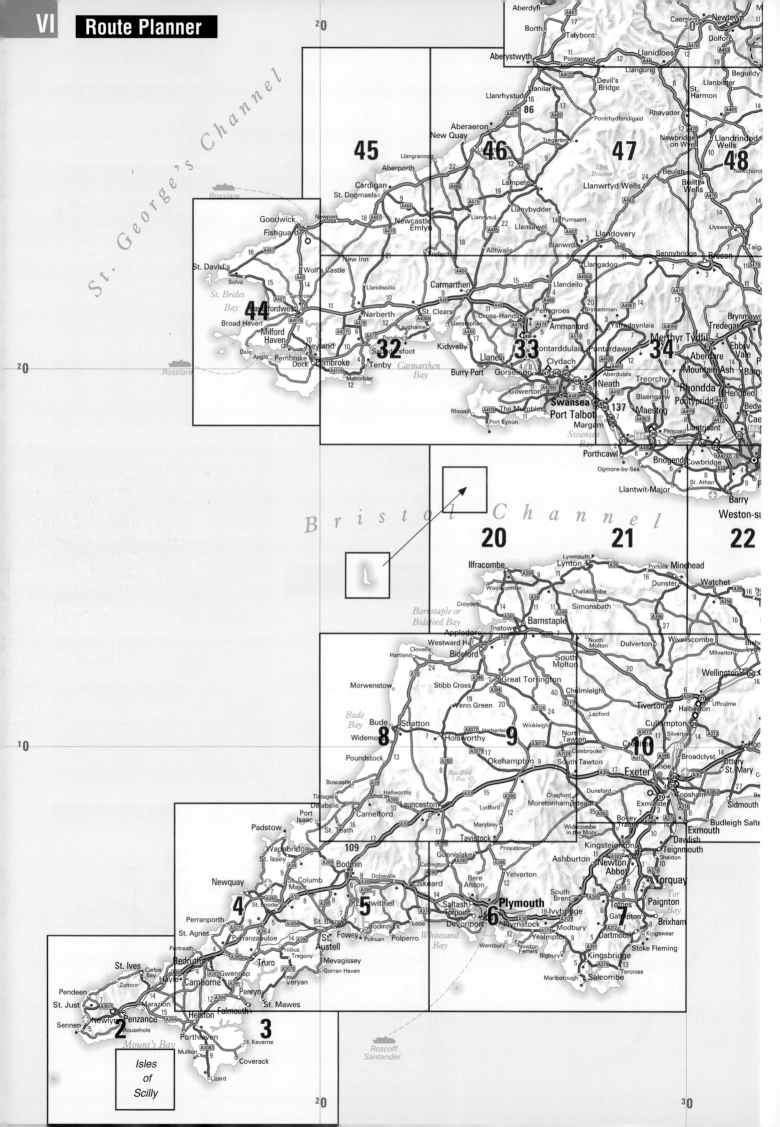

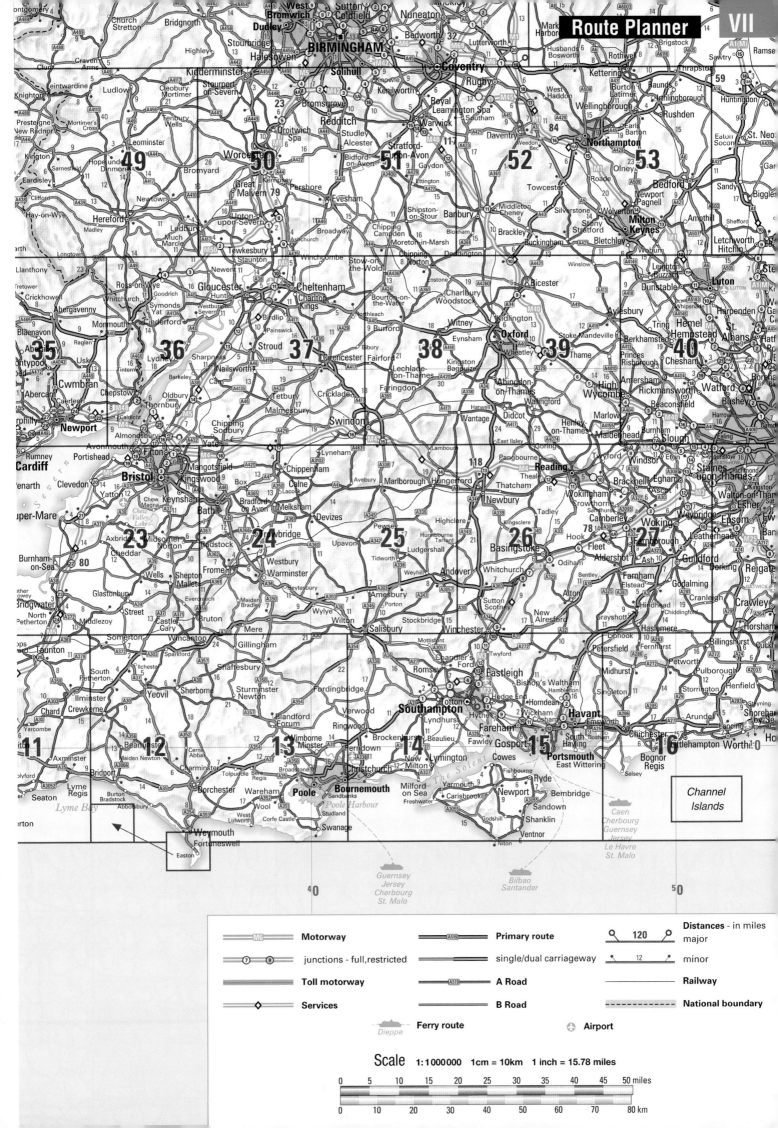

Scale 1:1000000 1cm = 10km 1 inch = 15.78 miles

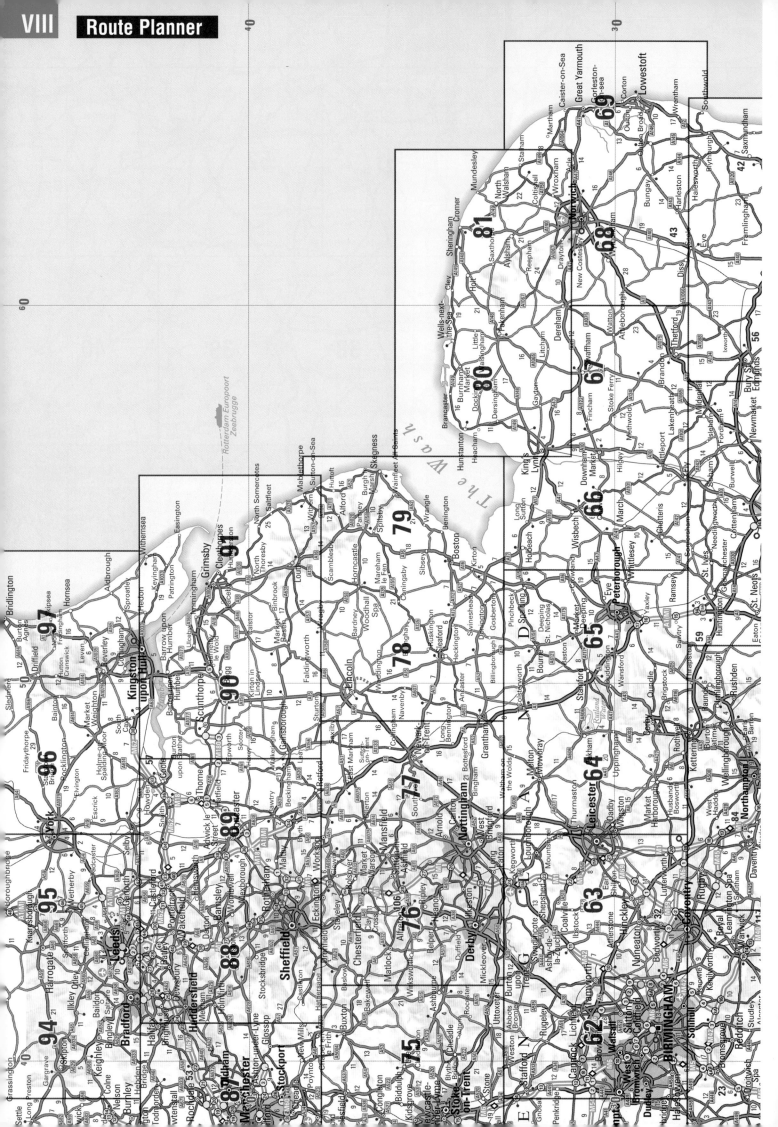

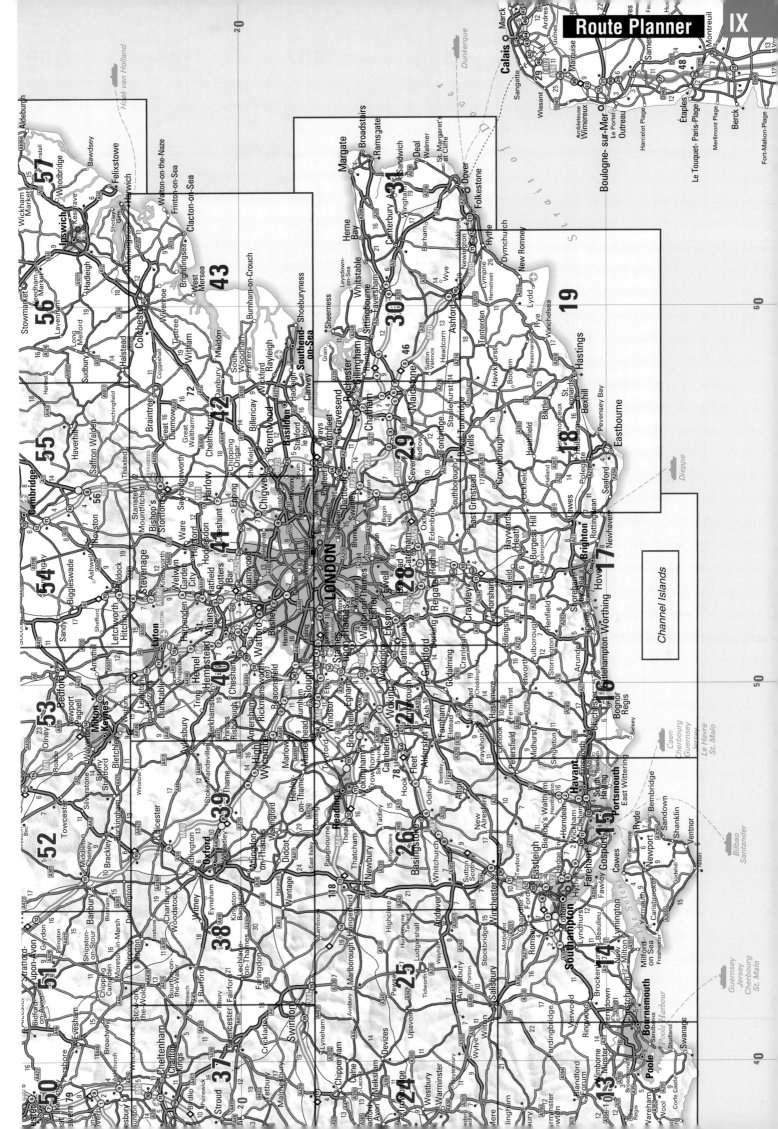

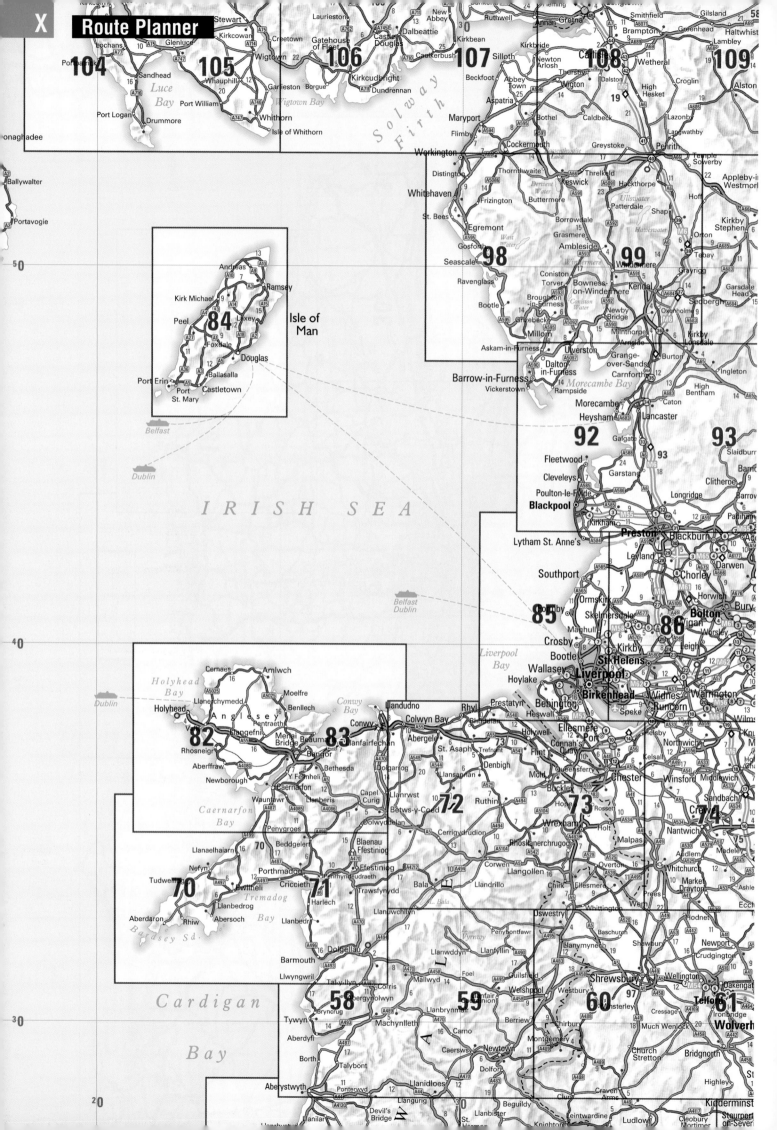

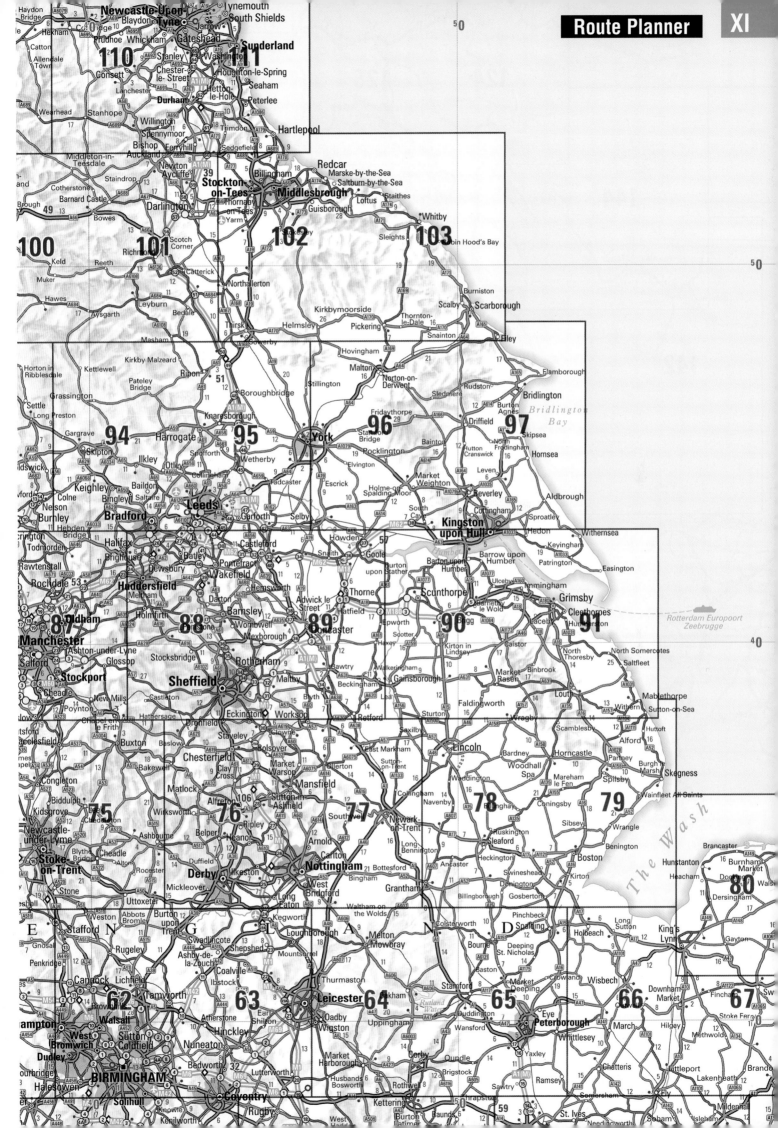

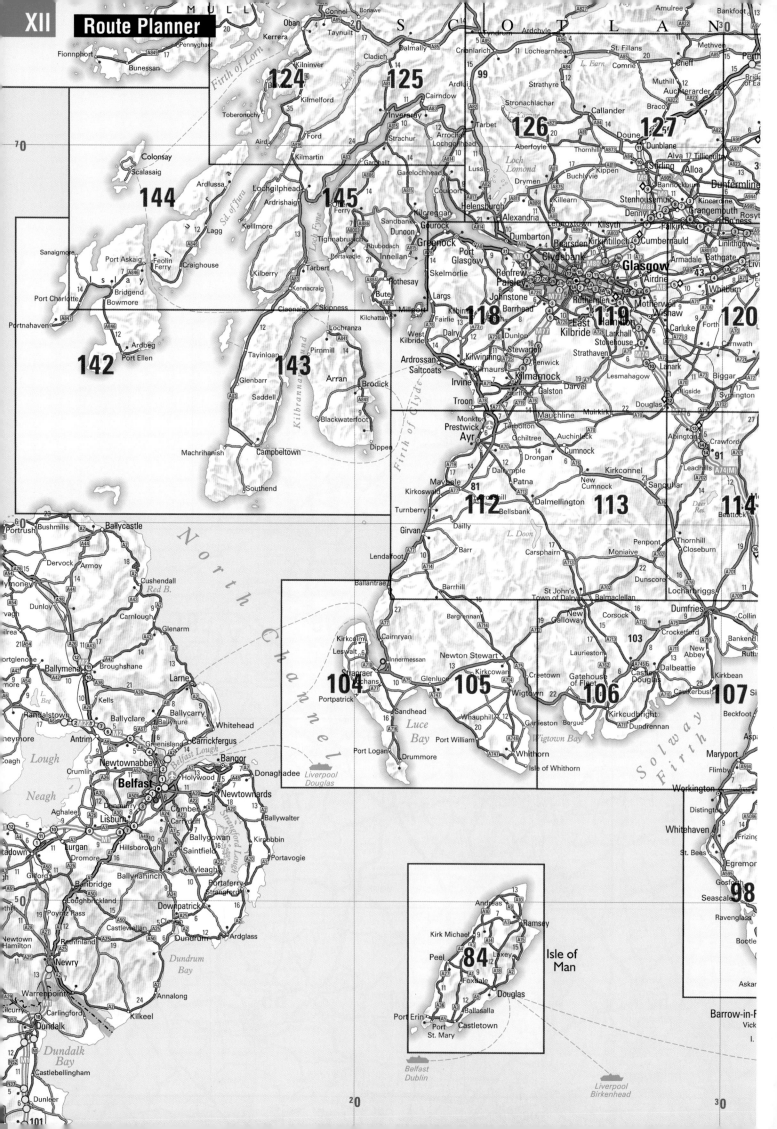

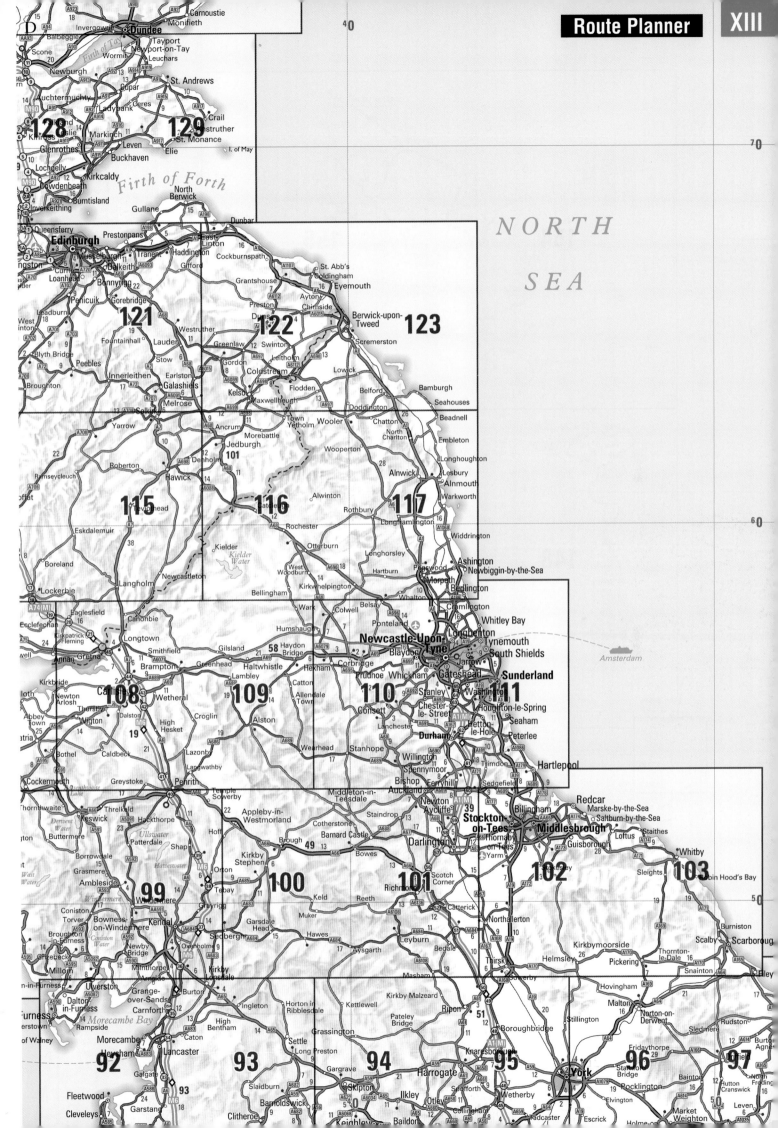

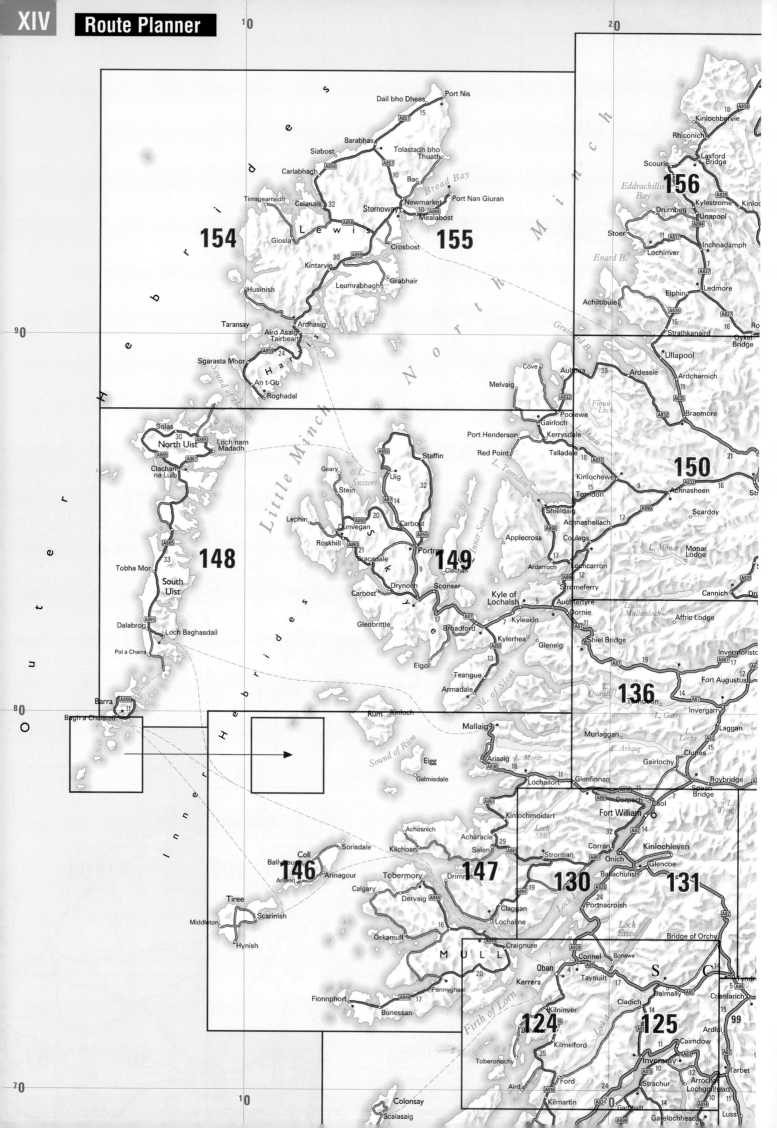

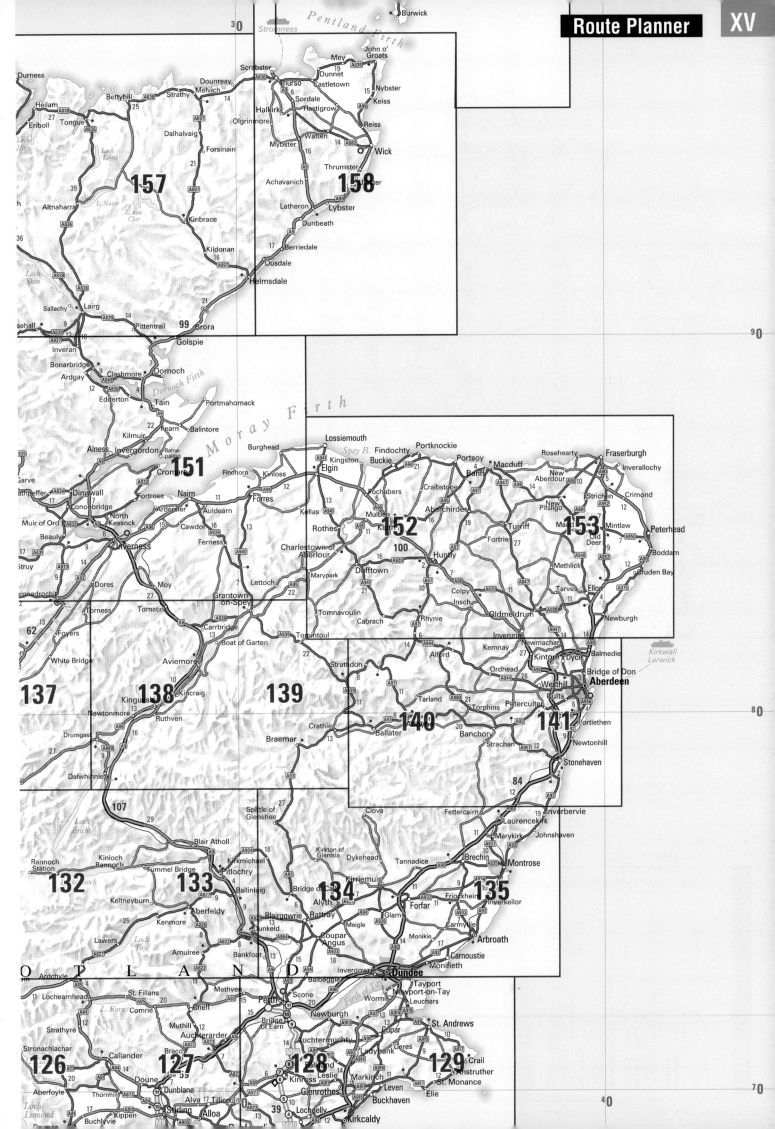

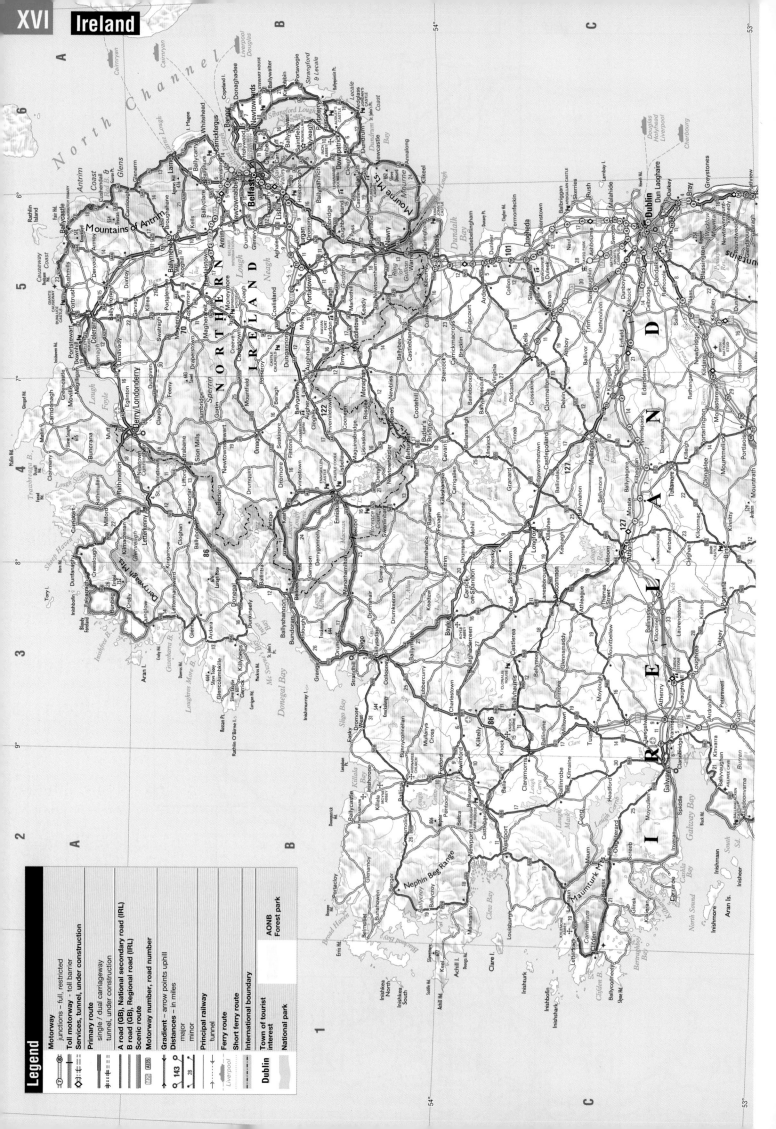

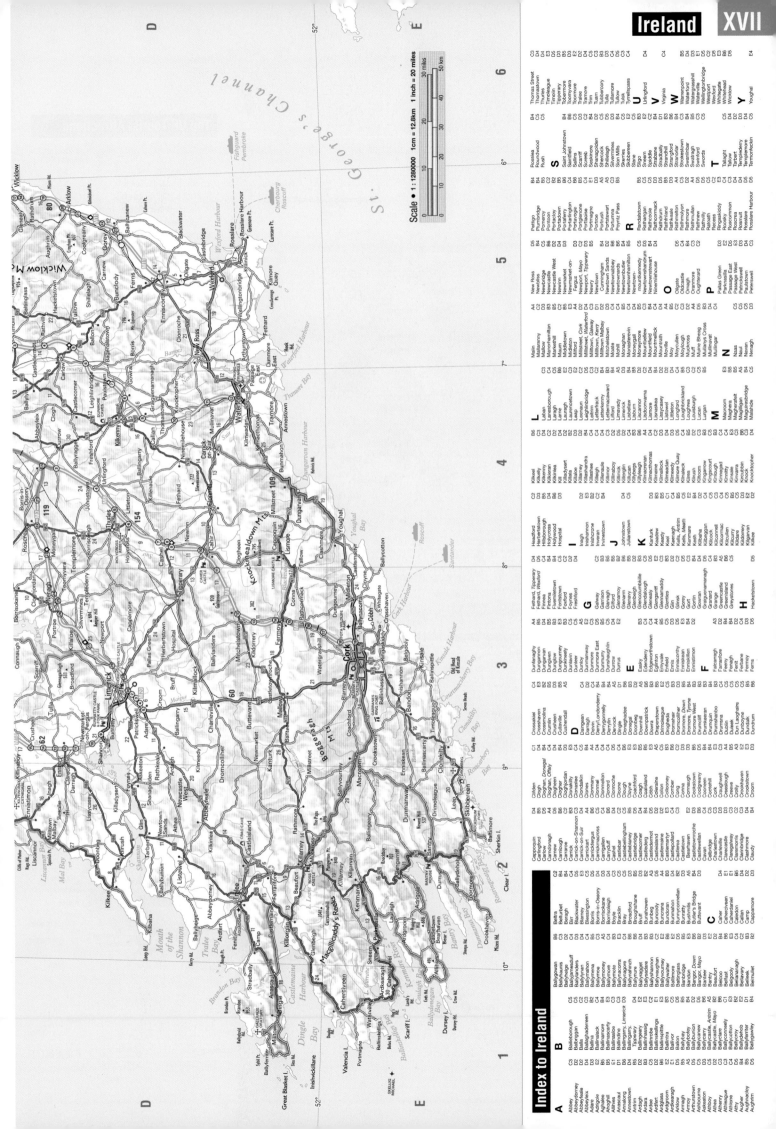

Tourism

- National Park
- Area of Outstanding Natural Beauty
- National Scenic Area
- Built-up area
- —— Long distance footpath
- ● Town of tourist interest
- ◆ Other tourist attraction
- ○ Other town

Top UK Tourist Attractions

		Visitors in millions (2018)
1.	Tate Modern, London	5.9
2.	British Museum, London	5.8
3.	National Gallery, London	5.7
4.	Natural History Museum, London	5.2
5.	Southbank Centre, London	4.5
6.	Victoria & Albert Museum, London	4.0
7.	Science Museum, London	3.2
8.	Somerset House, London	3.1
9.	Tower of London	2.9
10.	Royal Museums, Greenwich	2.5
11.	National Museum of Scotland, Edinburgh	2.2
12.	Edinburgh Castle	2.1
13.	Chester Zoo	2.0
14.	Royal Botanic Gardens, Kew	1.9
15.	Royal Albert Hall, London	1.8
16.	Scottish National Gallery, Edinburgh	1.7
17.	St Paul's Cathedral, London	1.7
18.	Royal Academy, London	1.6
19.	National Portrait Gallery, London	1.6
20.	Stonehenge, Wiltshire	1.6

Top Ireland Tourist Attractions

		Visitors in millions (2018)
1.	Guinness Storehouse, Dublin	1.7
2.	Cliffs of Moher Visitor Experience, Clare	1.6
3.	Dublin Zoo	1.2
4.	Book of Kells, Dublin	1.1
5.	National Gallery of Ireland, Dublin	0.8
6.	Glendalough Site, Wicklow	0.7
7.	Tayto Park, Dublin	0.7
8.	National Botanic Gardens, Dublin	0.7
9.	St Patrick's Cathedral, Dublin	0.6
10.	Kylemore Abbey & Gardens, Galway	0.6

Transport

———	Motorway
———	Other important road
———	Main railway
———	Main ferry route
– – –	Channel Tunnel
✈	Main airport
⛴	Main ferry port
○	Other town

Top UK Ferry ports

		Passengers in thousands (2018)
1.	Dover	11,783
2.	Holyhead	1,914
3.	Portsmouth	1,848
4.	Hull	851
5.	Harwich	676
6.	Tyne	621
7.	Plymouth	433
8.	Newhaven	380
9.	Pembroke Dock	326
10.	Fishguard	295

Top UK Airports

		Passengers in millions (2018)
1.	London Heathrow	80.1
2.	London Gatwick	46.1
3.	Manchester	28.3
4.	London Stansted	28.0
5.	London Luton	16.8
6.	Edinburgh	14.3
7.	Birmingham	12.5
8.	Glasgow	9.7
9.	Bristol	8.7
10.	Belfast International	6.3
11.	Newcastle	5.3
12.	Liverpool John Lennon	5.0
13.	East Midlands	4.9
14.	London City	4.8
15.	Leeds Bradford	4.0
16.	Aberdeen	3.1
17.	George Best Belfast City	2.5
18.	Southampton	2.0
19.	Jersey	1.7
20.	Cardiff	1.6

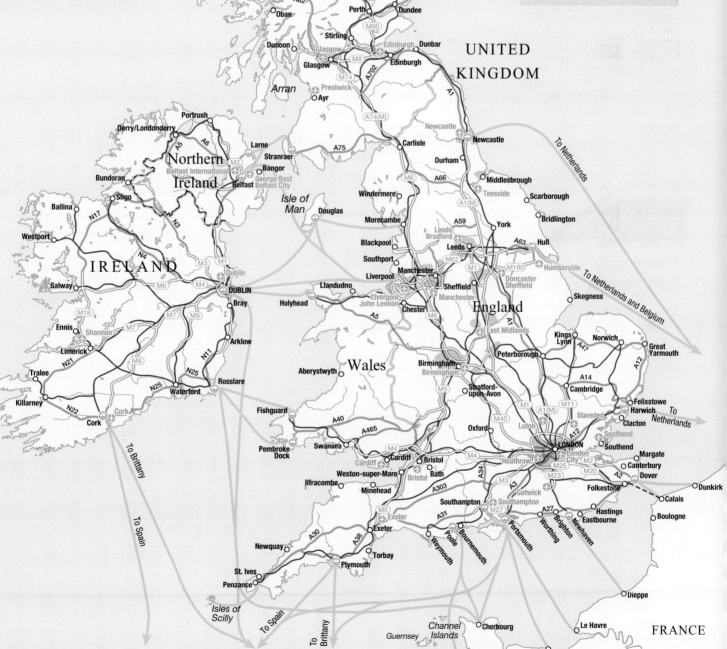

Distance table

How to use this table

Distances are shown in miles and kilometres with estimated journey times in hours and minutes.

For example: the distance between Dover and Fishguard is 331 miles or 533 kilometres with an estimated journey time of 6 hours, 20 minutes.

Estimated driving times are based on an average speed of 60mph on Motorways and 40mph on other roads. Drivers should allow extra time when driving at peak periods or through areas likely to be congested.

Map labels: John o' Groats · Kyle of Lochalsh · Inverness · Aberdeen · Braemar · Fort William · Dundee · Oban · Edinburgh · Glasgow · Berwick-upon-Tweed · Ayr · Stranraer · Carlisle · Newcastle upon Tyne · Blackpool · Leeds · York · Kingston upon Hull · Manchester · Doncaster · Liverpool · Sheffield · Lincoln · Holyhead · Shrewsbury · Nottingham · Leicester · Norwich · Great Yarmouth · Aberystwyth · Birmingham · Cambridge · Fishguard · Gloucester · Oxford · Harwich · Swansea · Cardiff · Bristol · London · Southampton · Brighton · Bournemouth · Portsmouth · Dover · Exeter · Plymouth · Land's End

Supporting

THINK!

Travel safe – Don't drive tired

Central example grid (miles / kilometres / hours:minutes):

	Dover	Dundee	Edinburgh	Exeter	Fishguard
Dundee	523 / 842 / 9:10				
Edinburgh	56 / 90 / 1:30	462 / 744 / 8:10			
Exeter	450 / 724 / 8:00	518 / 833 / 9:10	248 / 399 / 4:40		
Fishguard	230 / 370 / 4:30	399 / 642 / 7:30	460 / 740 / 8:30	331 / 533 / 6:20	
Fort William	486 / 782 / 9:30	560 / 901 / 10:20	144 / 232 / 3:30	127 / 204 / 3:10	596 / 959 / 11:00

City list for the main distance matrix (top to bottom): London · Aberdeen · Aberystwyth · Ayr · Berwick-upon-Tweed · Birmingham · Blackpool · Bournemouth · Braemar · Brighton · Bristol · Cambridge · Cardiff · Carlisle · Doncaster · Dover · Dundee · Edinburgh · Exeter · Fishguard · Fort William · Glasgow · Gloucester · Great Yarmouth · Harwich · Holyhead · Inverness · John o' Groats · Kingston upon Hull · Kyle of Lochalsh · Land's End · Leeds · Leicester · Lincoln · Liverpool · Manchester · Newcastle upon Tyne · Norwich · Nottingham · Oban · Oxford · Plymouth · Portsmouth · Sheffield · Shrewsbury · Southampton · Stranraer · Swansea · York

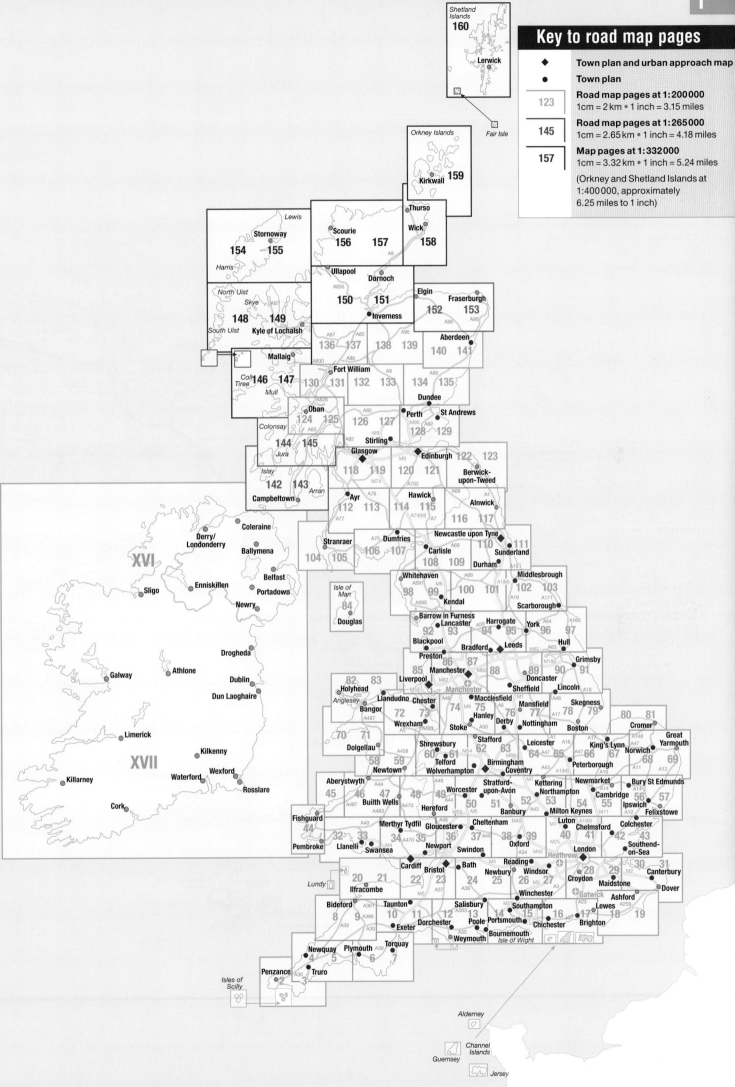

Key to road map pages

♦ Town plan and urban approach map

● Town plan

123	Road map pages at 1:200 000 1cm = 2 km • 1 inch = 3.15 miles
145	Road map pages at 1:265 000 1cm = 2.65 km • 1 inch = 4.18 miles
157	Map pages at 1:332 000 1cm = 3.32 km • 1 inch = 5.24 miles

(Orkney and Shetland Islands at 1:400 000, approximately 6.25 miles to 1 inch)

Shetland Islands **160**
Lerwick

Fair Isle

Orkney Islands
Kirkwall **159**

Thurso
Wick

Lewis
Stornoway **154 155**
Scourie **156 157** Wick **158**

Harris

Ullapool **150** Dornoch **151** Elgin **152** Fraserburgh **153**
A835
Inverness

North Uist
Skye
148 149
South Uist Kyle of Lochalsh

136 137 138 139
Aberdeen **140 141**

Mallaig
Coll Tiree **146 147** **130 131** Fort William **132 133** **134 135**

Mull
Dundee

Oban **124 125** **126 127** Perth St Andrews **128 129**

Colonsay
Stirling
144 145
Jura
Glasgow Edinburgh **122 123**
Islay **142 143** **118 119 120 121** Berwick-upon-Tweed

Arran
Campbeltown Ayr Hawick Alnwick
112 113 114 115 **116 117**

Stranraer Dumfries Newcastle upon Tyne **111**
104 105 **106 107** Carlisle Sunderland **110**
108 109 Durham

Whitehaven Middlesbrough **102 103**
Isle of Man **98 99 100 101**
84 Kendal Scarborough
Douglas

Barrow in Furness
Lancaster Harrogate York **96 97**
92 93 94 95
Blackpool Bradford Leeds
Preston **86 87 88** **90 91** Grimsby
85 Manchester Doncaster
Liverpool Sheffield **89** Lincoln
82 83 Macclesfield Mansfield Skegness **80 81**
Holyhead Chester **74 75** **76 77 78 79** Cromer
Anglesey Llandudno Hanley
Bangor **72 73** Stoke Derby Nottingham Boston Great Yarmouth
Wrexham Stafford Leicester King's Lynn Norwich **68 69**
70 71 **62 63** **64 65 66 67**
Dolgellau Shrewsbury Peterborough Bury St Edmunds
58 59 Telford Birmingham Coventry Newmarket **56 57**
Newtown Wolverhampton Cambridge **55** Ipswich
Aberystwyth **48 49** Stratford-upon-Avon Kettering **54** Felixstowe
45 46 47 Worcester **50 51** Northampton Milton Keynes Colchester
Builth Wells Hereford Banbury **52 53** Luton Chelmsford **43**
Fishguard **44** Merthyr Tydfil Gloucester Cheltenham **37 38 39** Oxford London Southend-on-Sea
Pembroke **32 33 34 35 36** Newport Swindon Reading **28 29 30 31** Canterbury
Llanelli Cardiff Bristol Bath Windsor Croydon Maidstone Dover
Swansea **20 21** **22 23 24** Newbury **25 26 27** Winchester Gatwick Ashford
Lundy Ilfracombe Bath Southampton **17 18 19**
Bideford Taunton Salisbury Portsmouth Lewes Brighton
8 9 10 11 12 13 14 15 16
Dorchester Poole Chichester
Exeter Weymouth Bournemouth Isle of Wight
Newquay Plymouth Torquay
4 5 6 7
Penzance Truro
Isles of Scilly **2 3**

Coleraine
Derry/Londonderry Ballymena
XVI
Sligo Enniskillen Belfast
Portadown
Newry

Galway Drogheda
Athlone Dublin
Dun Laoghaire

XVII
Limerick Kilkenny
Killarney Waterford Wexford
Cork Rosslare

Alderney

Channel Islands
Guernsey Jersey

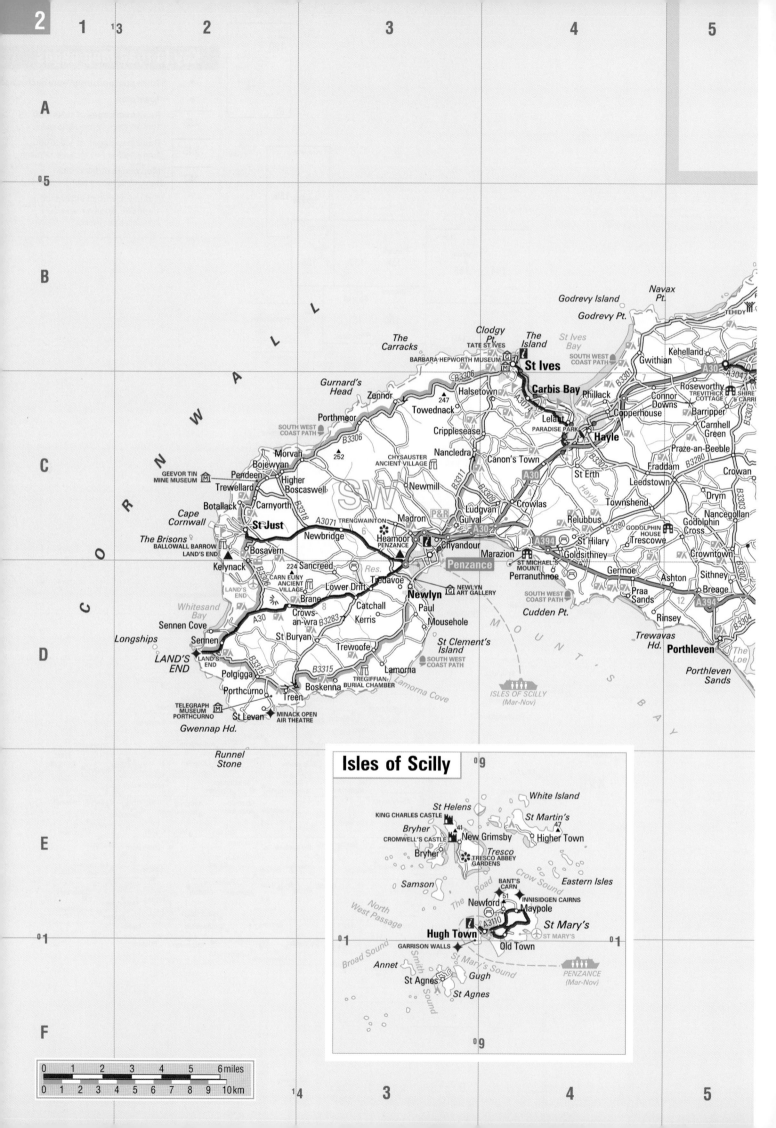

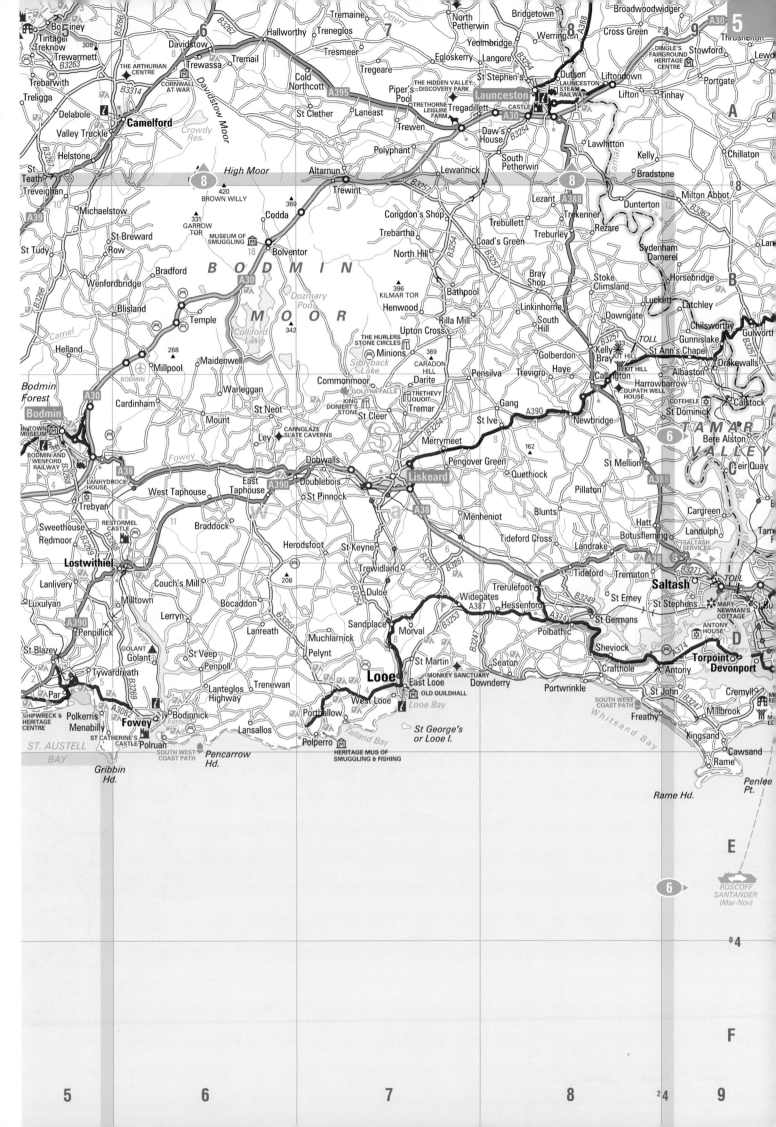

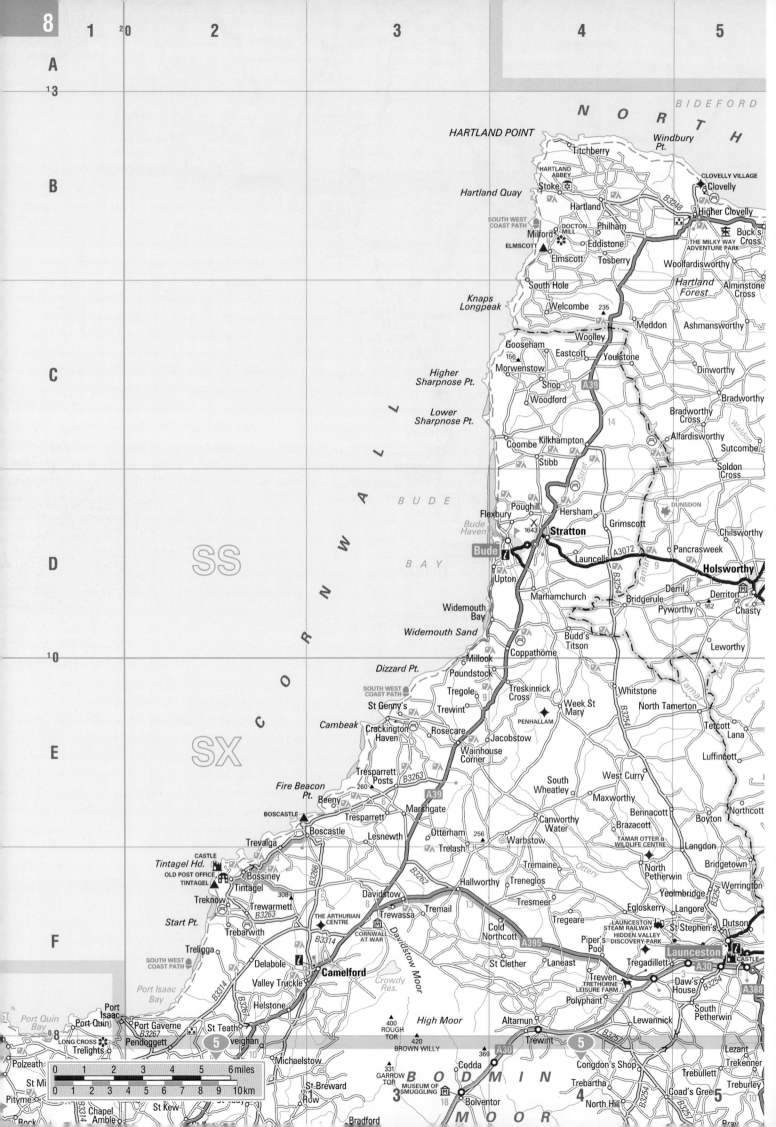

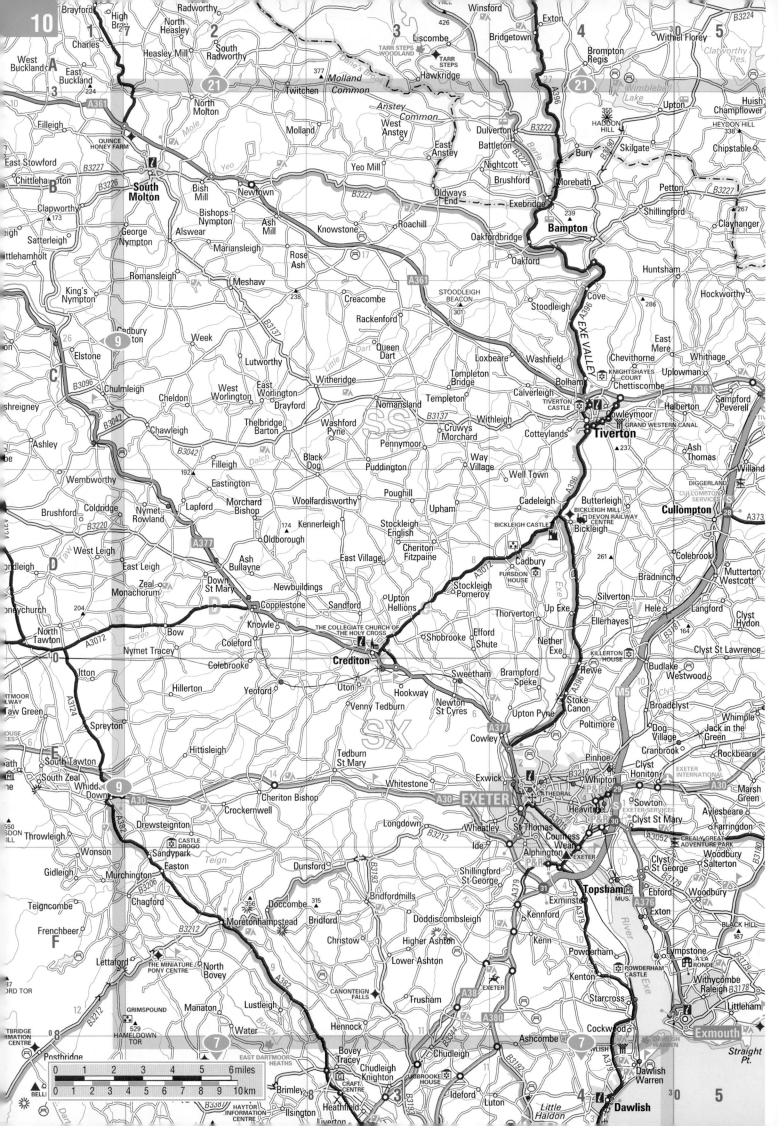

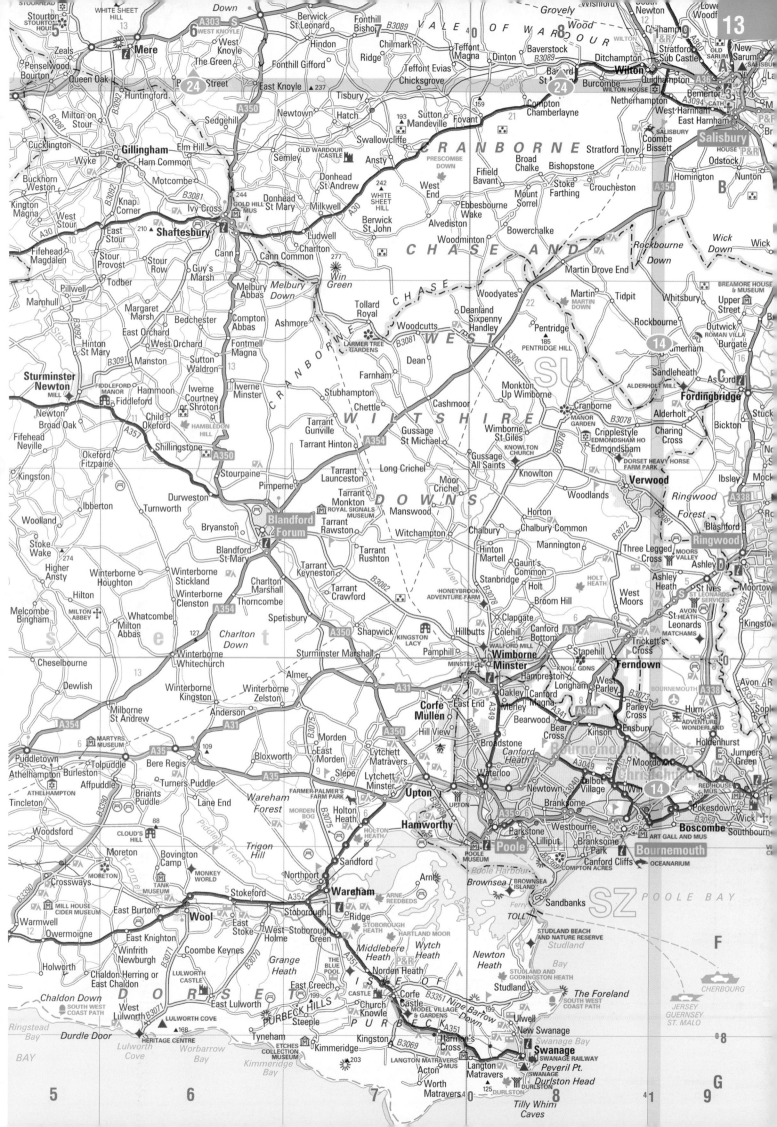

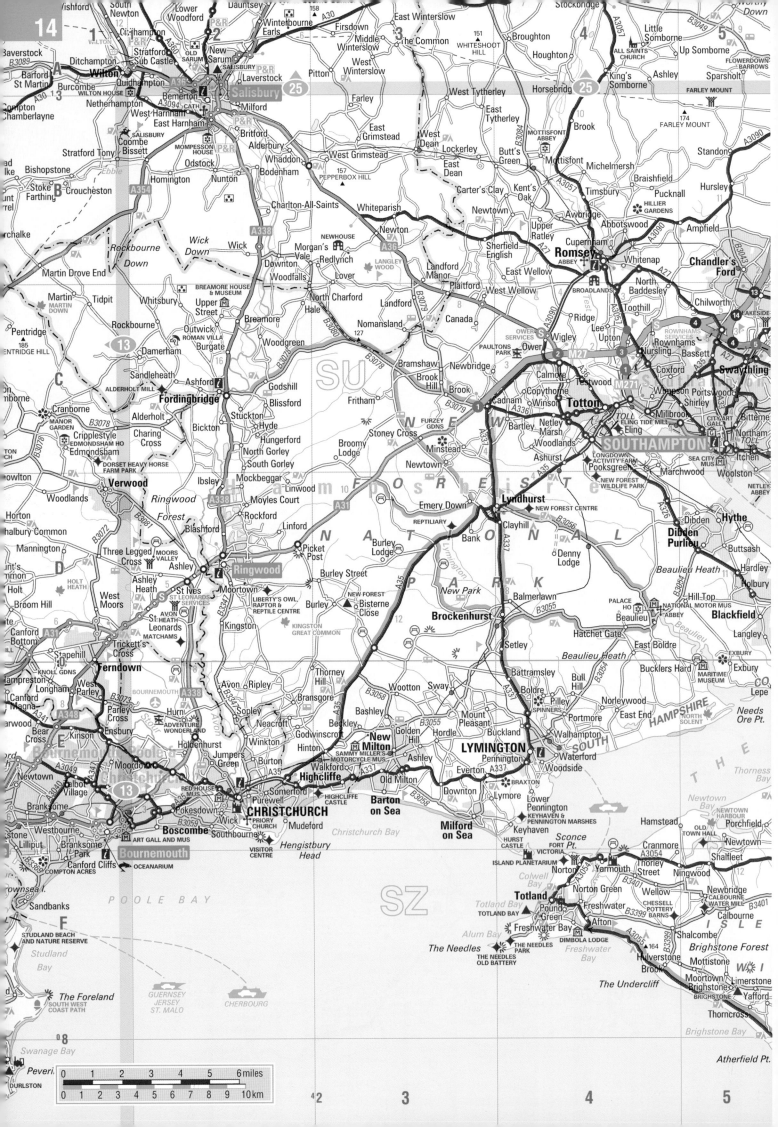

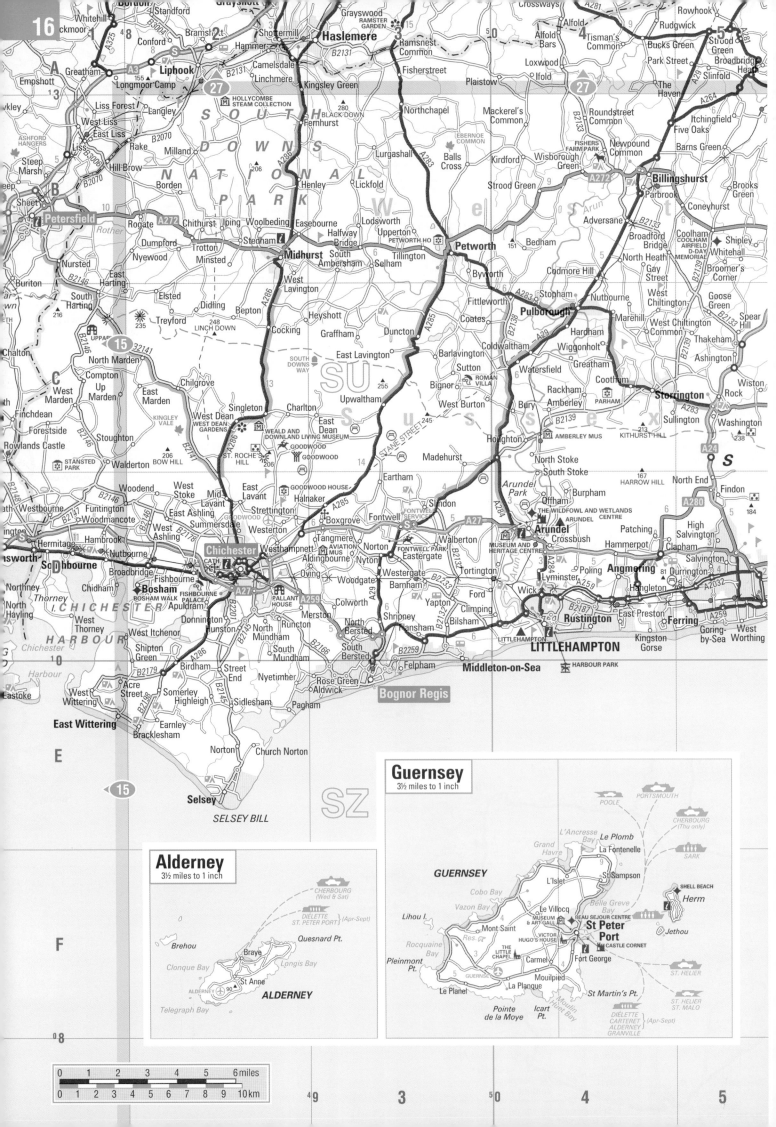

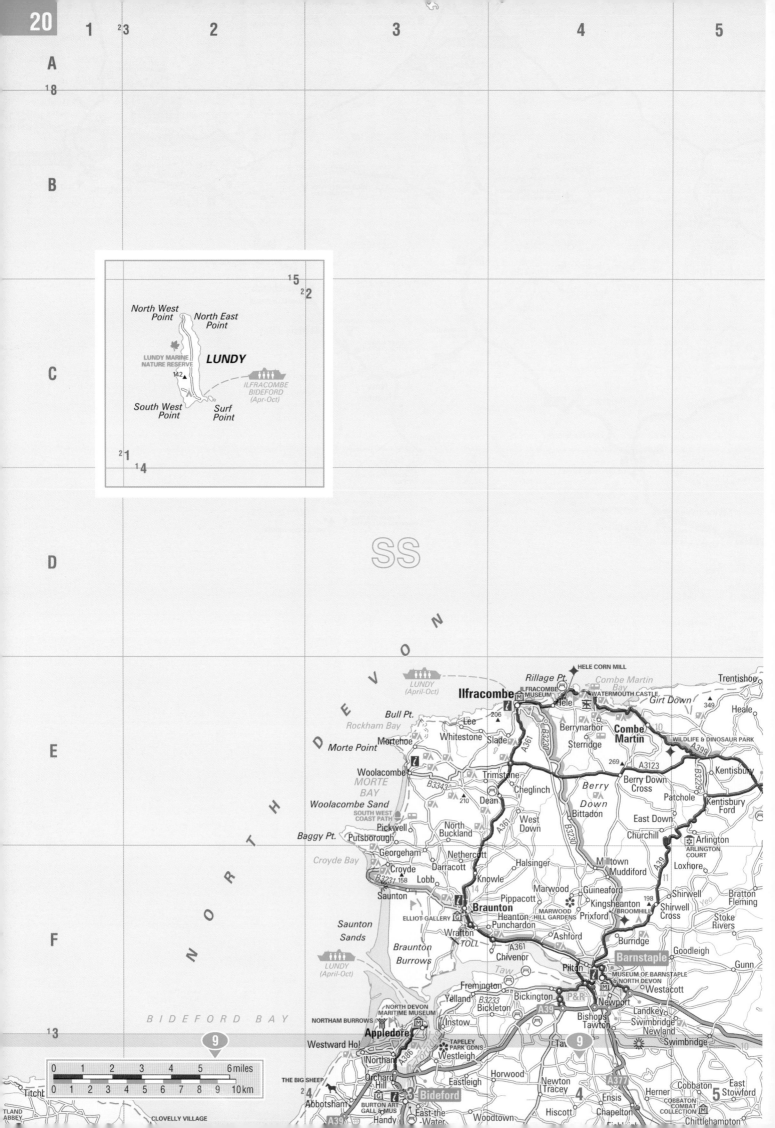

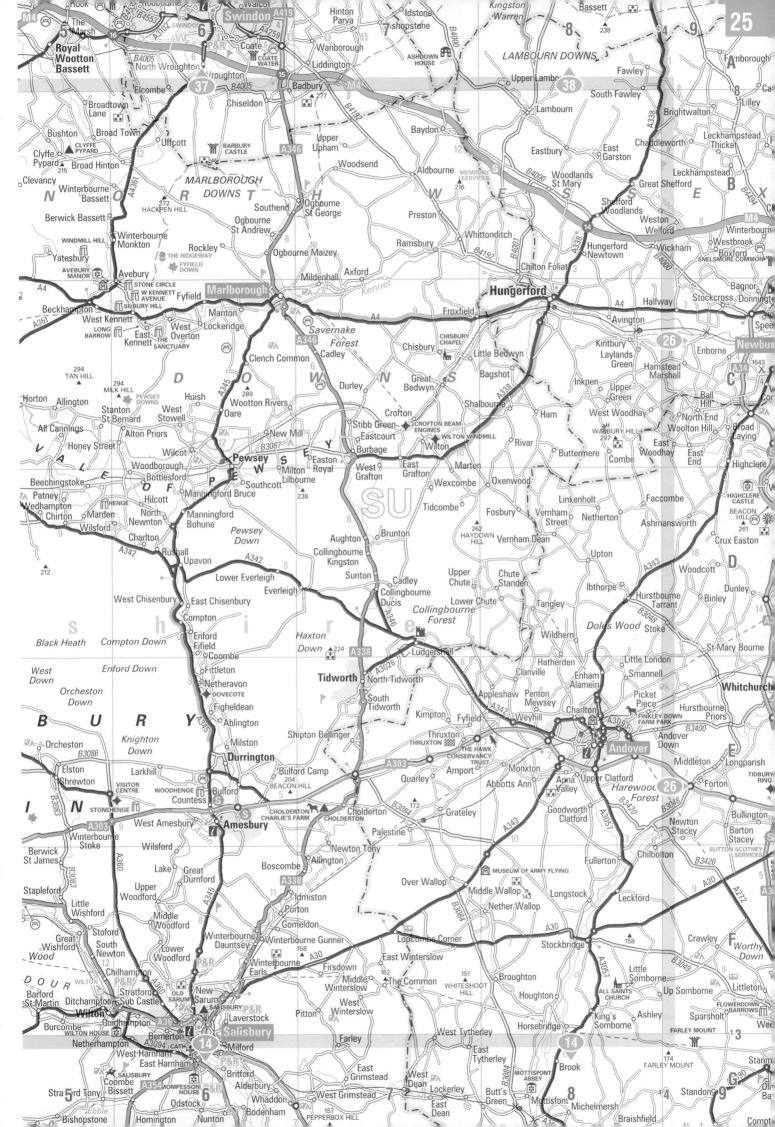

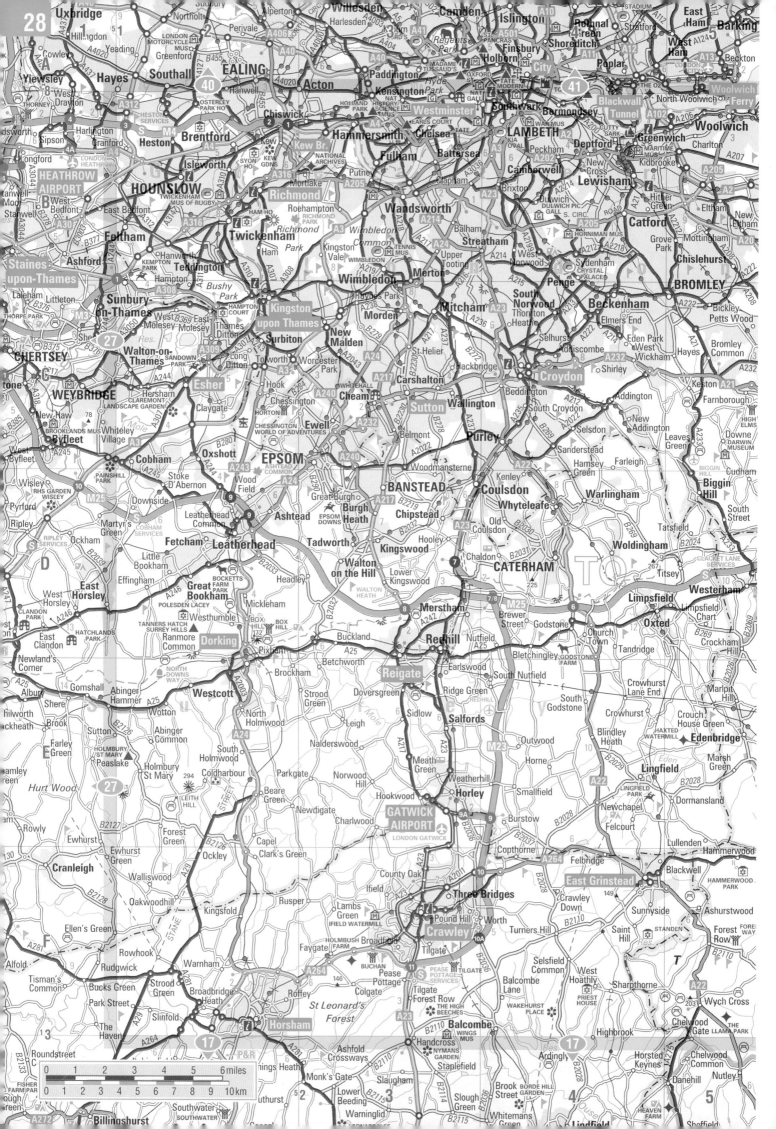

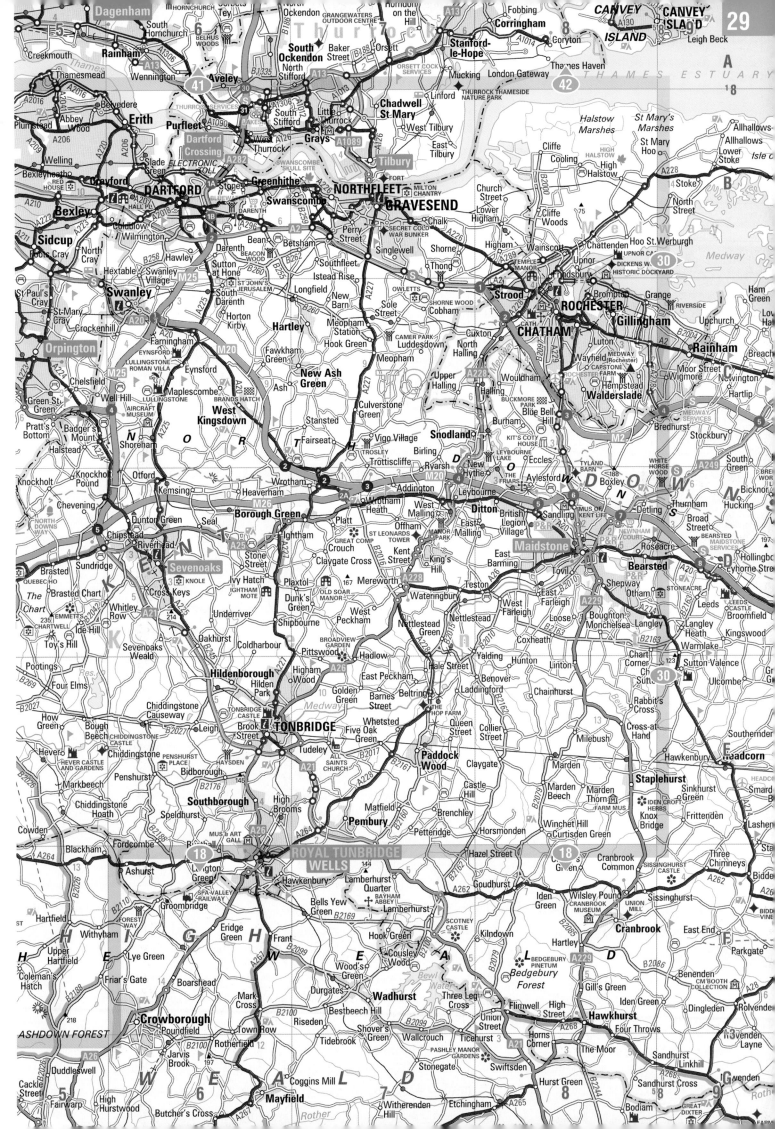

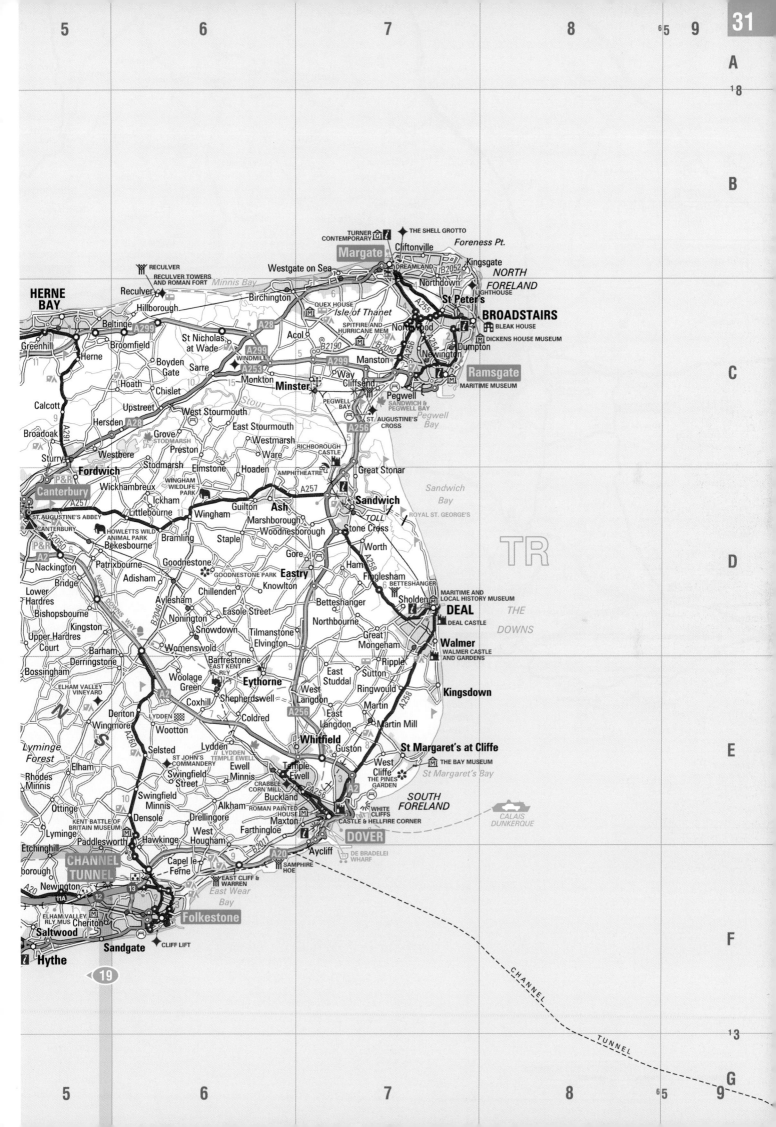

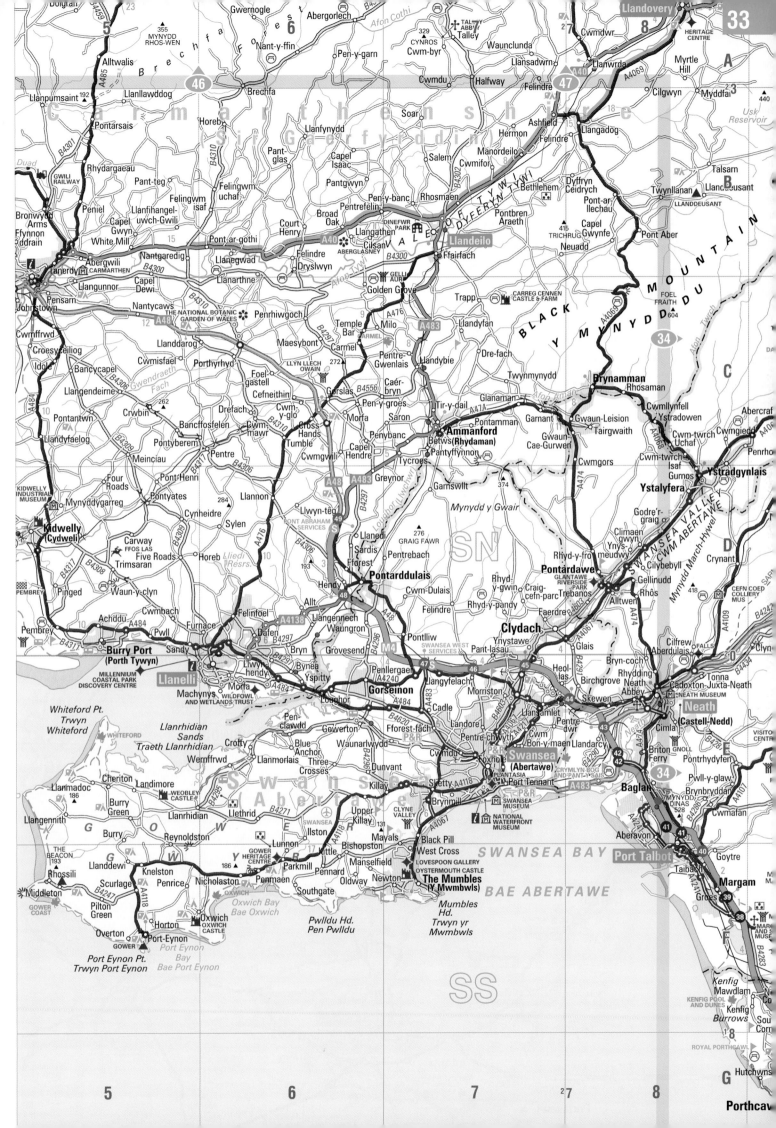

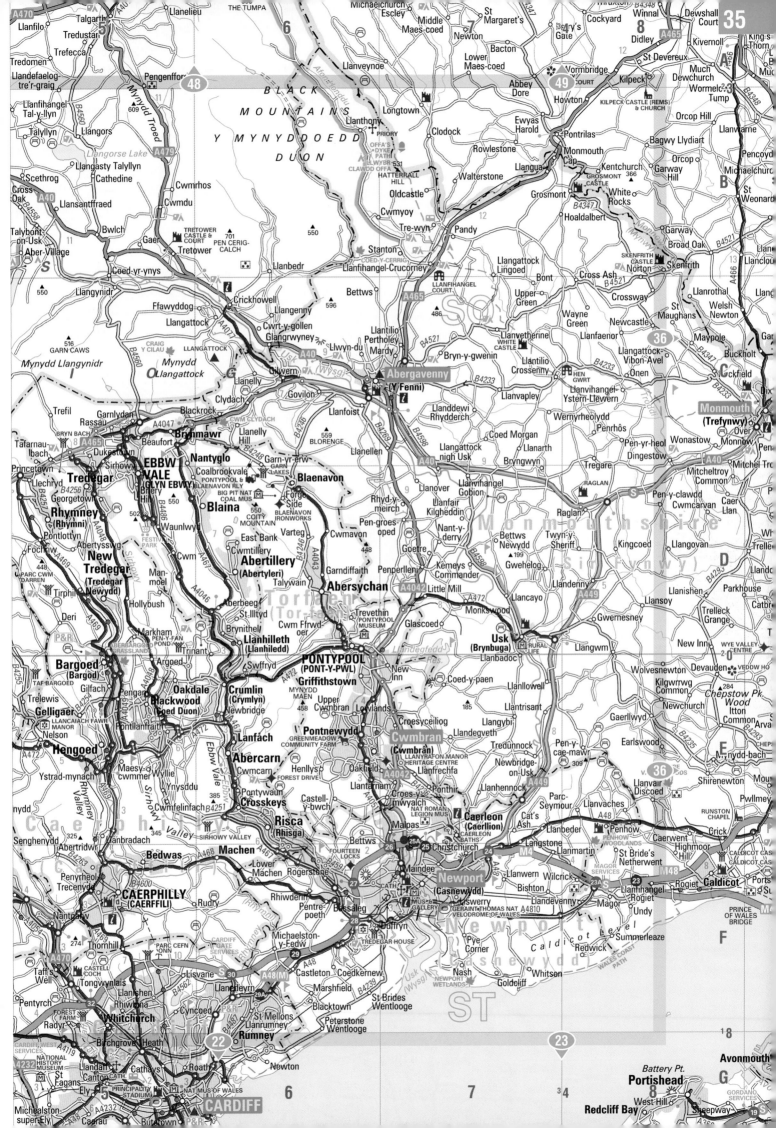

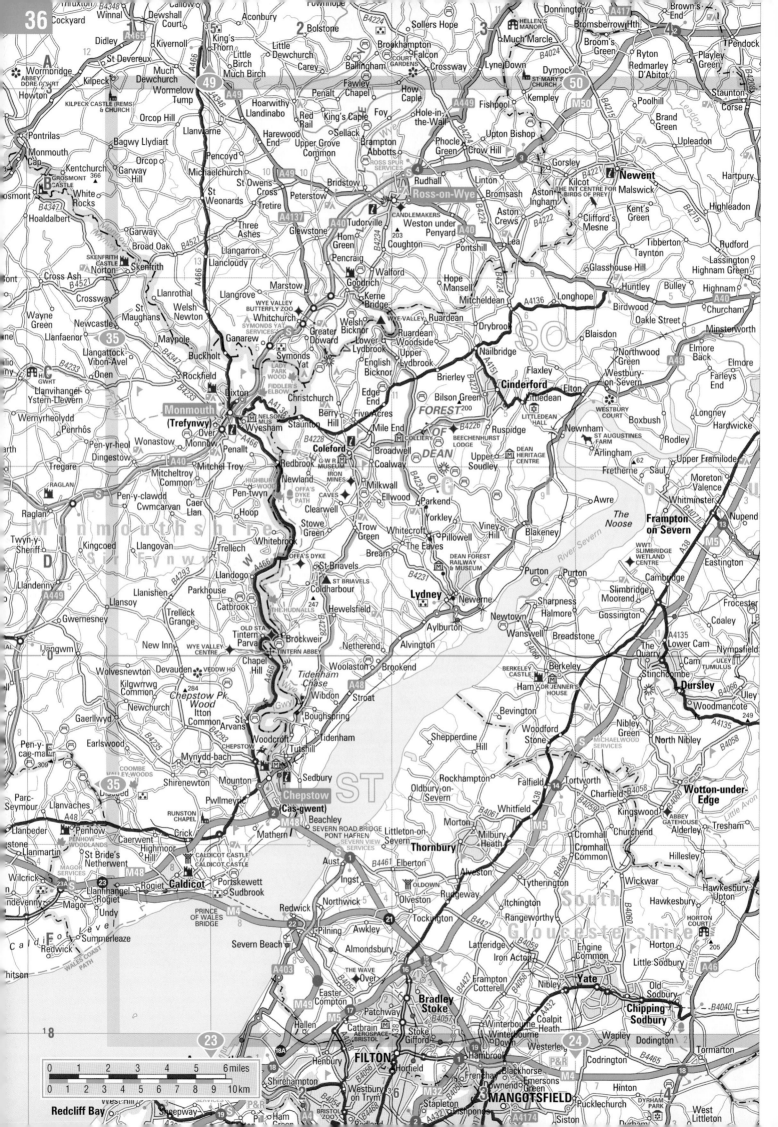

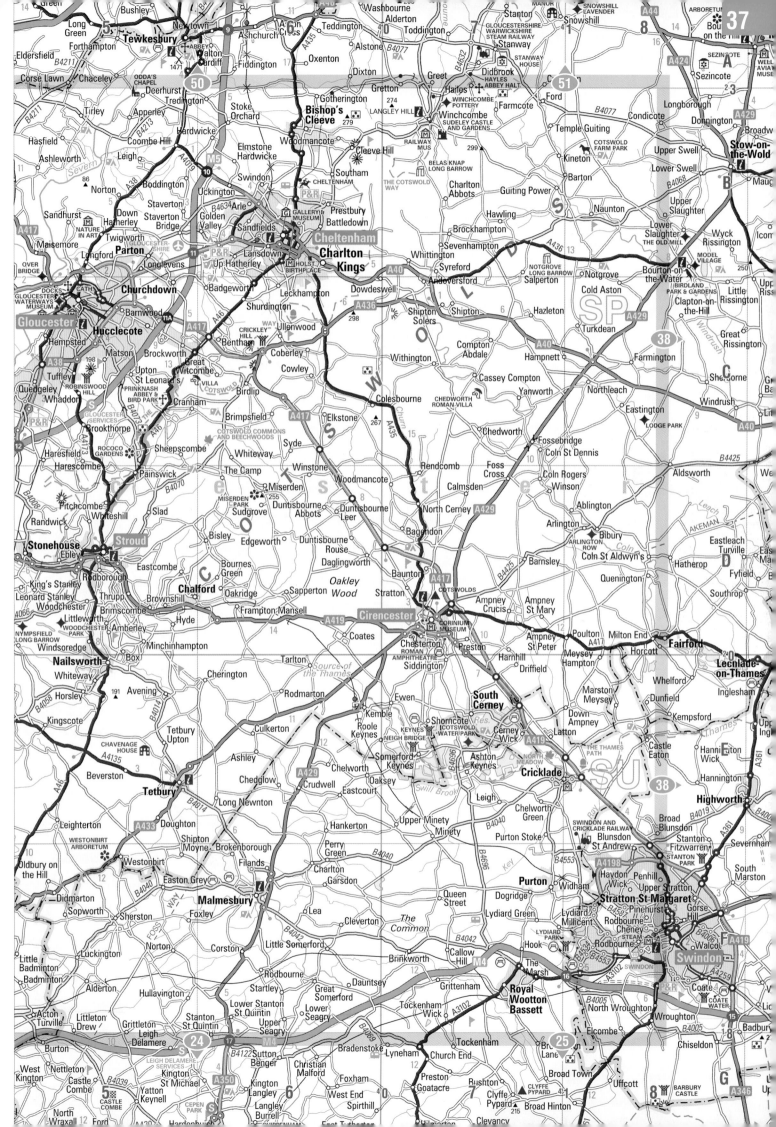

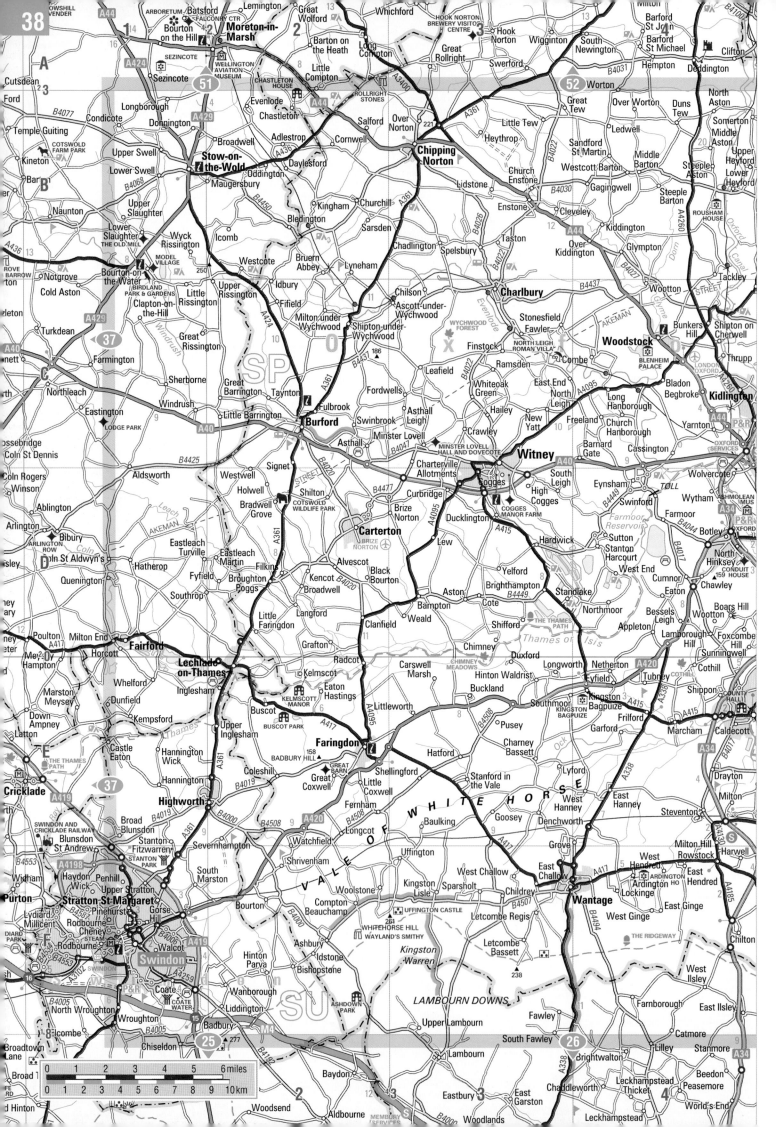

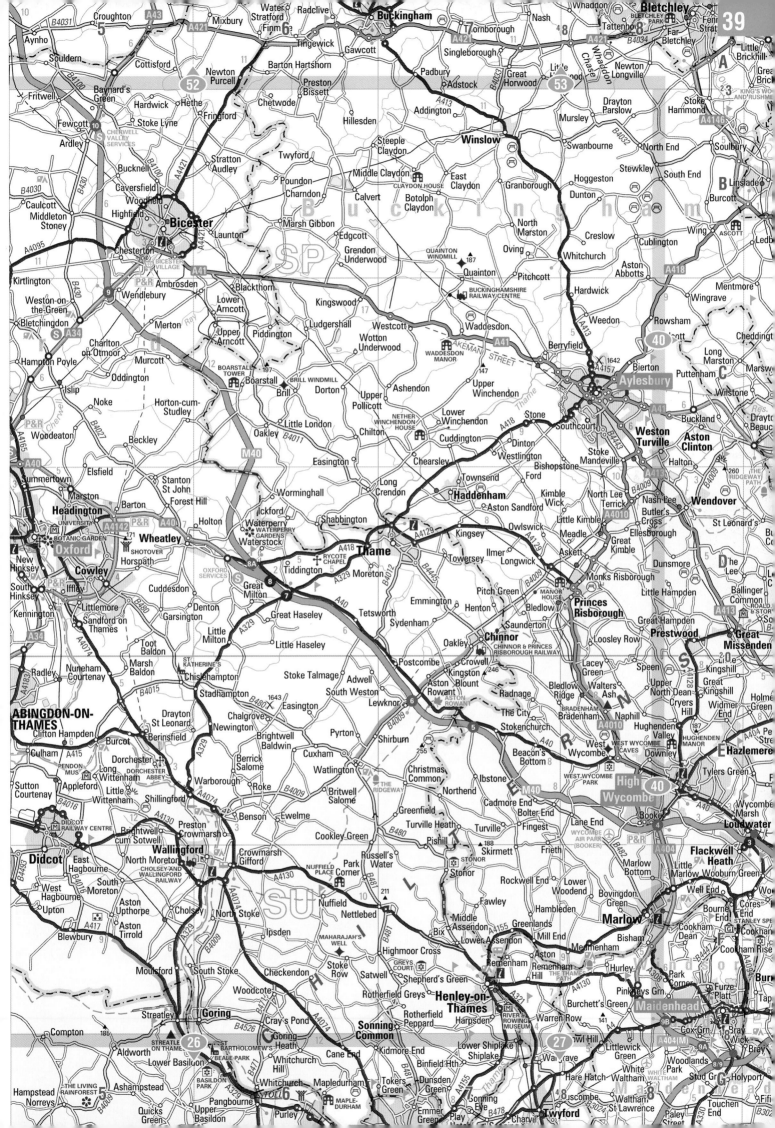

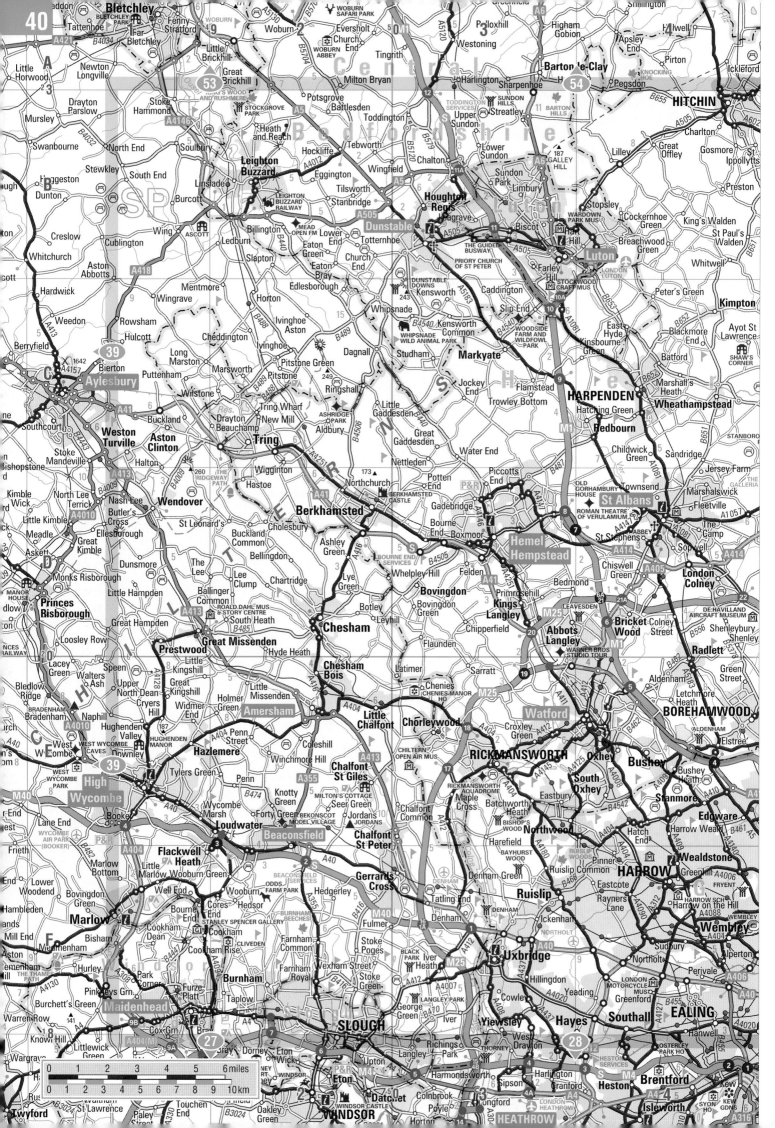

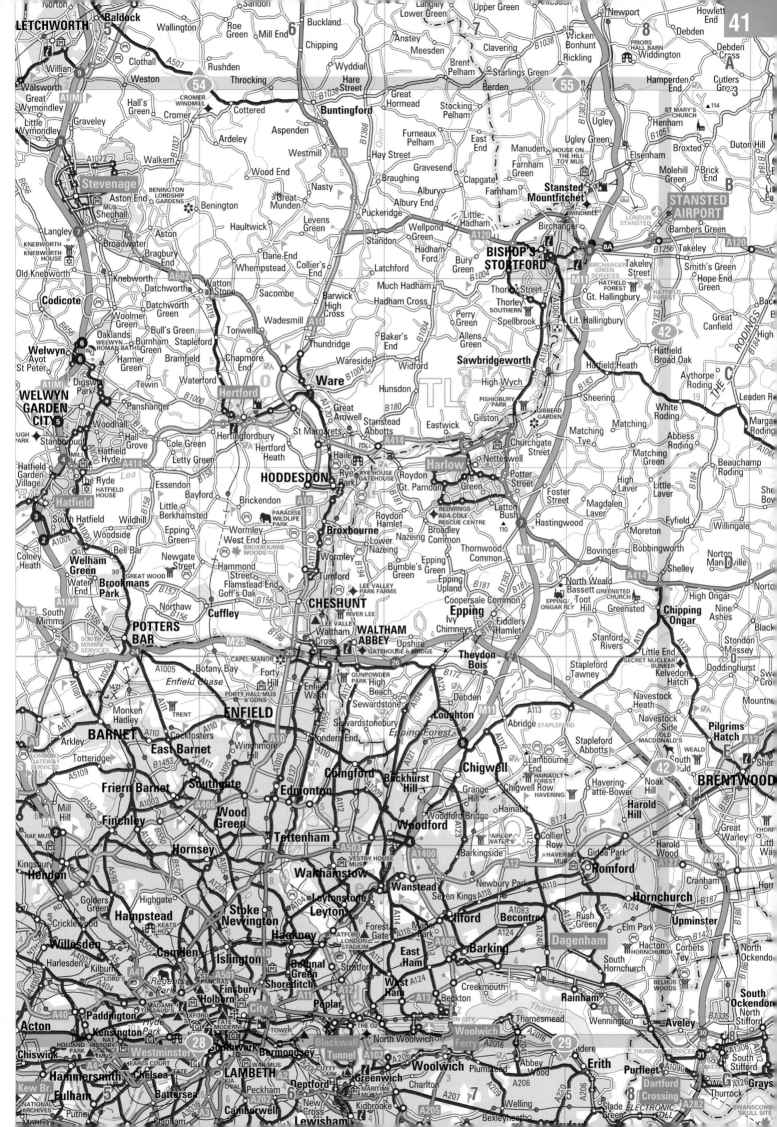

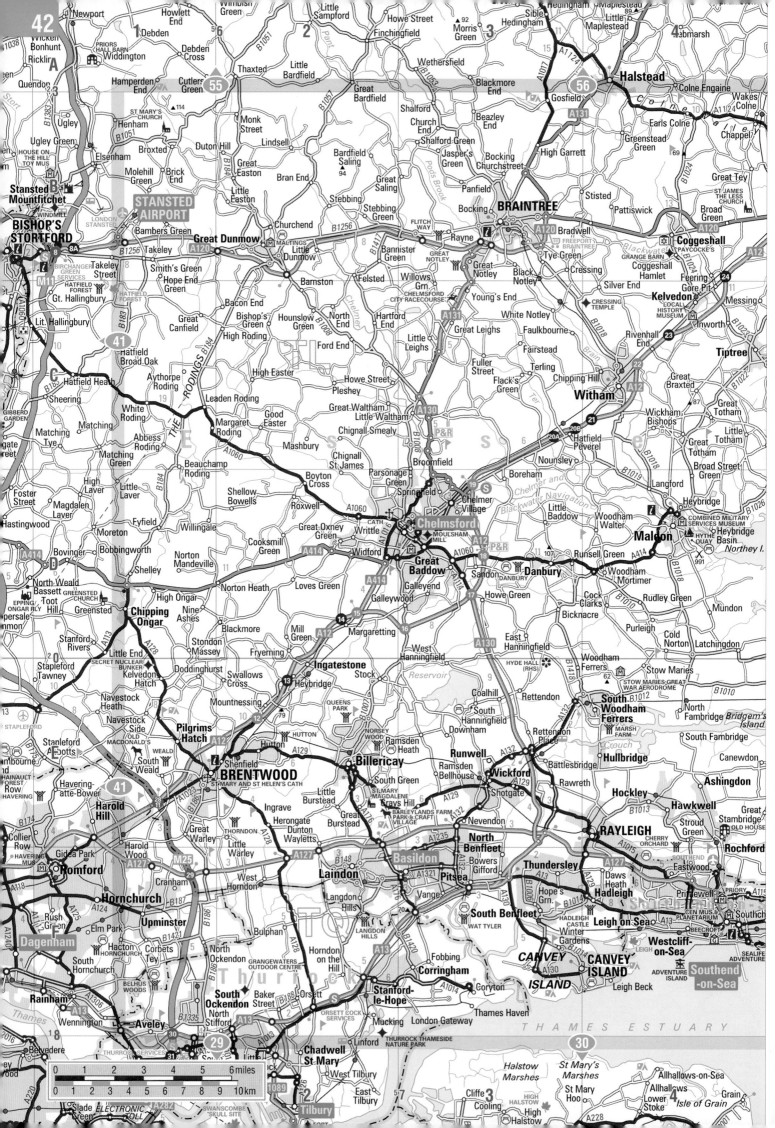

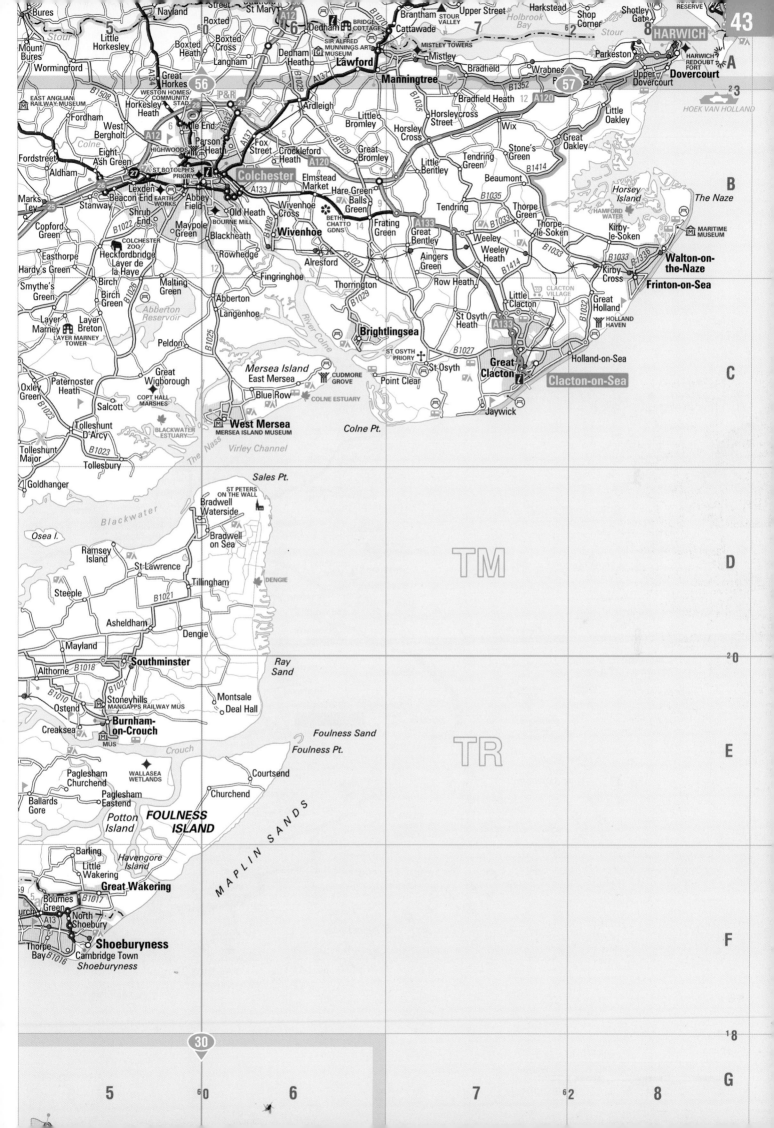

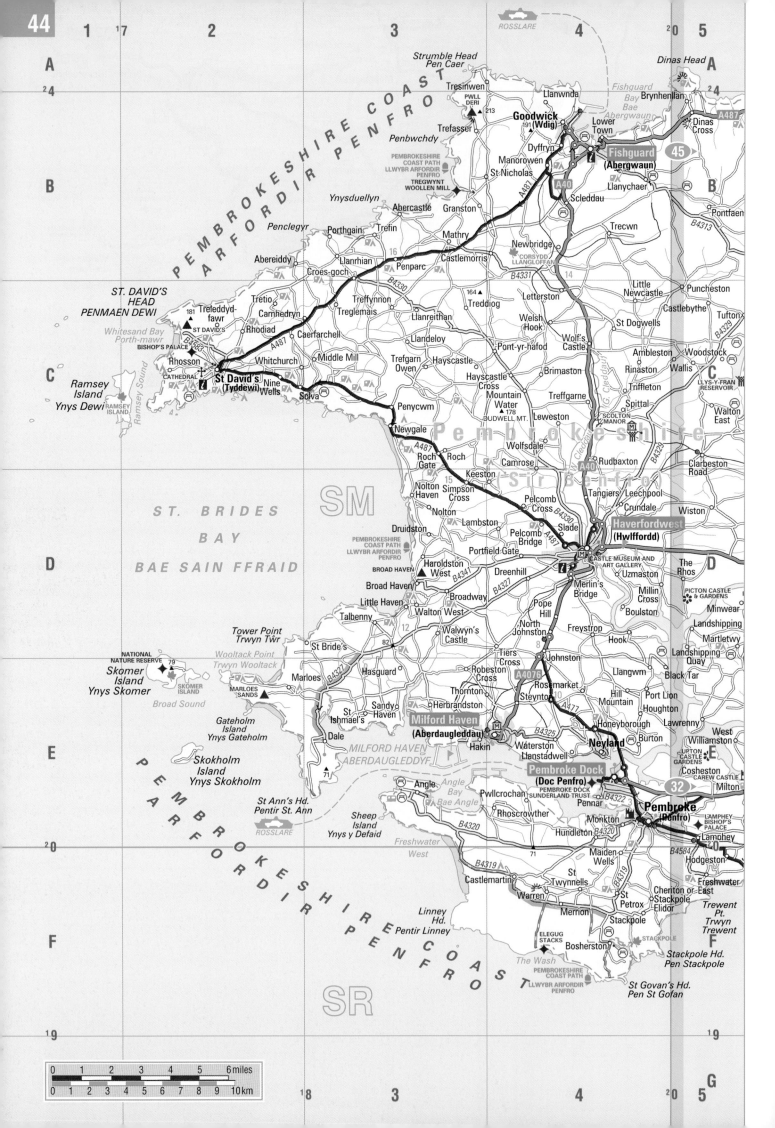

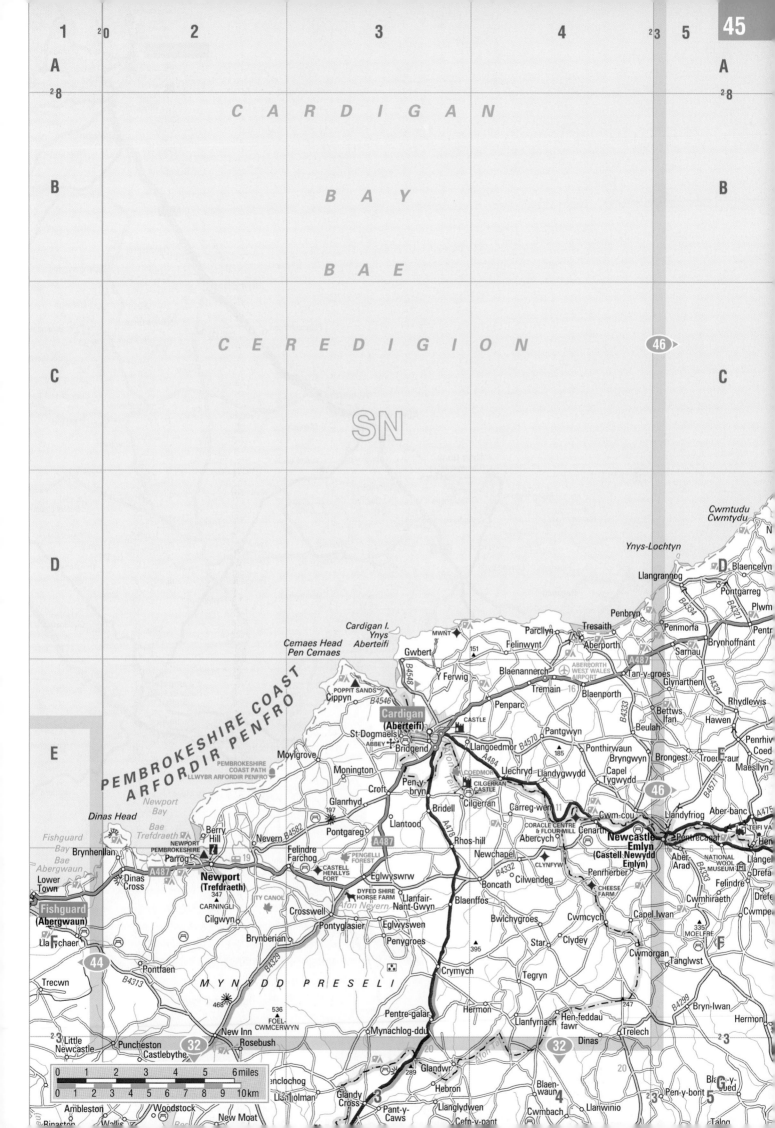

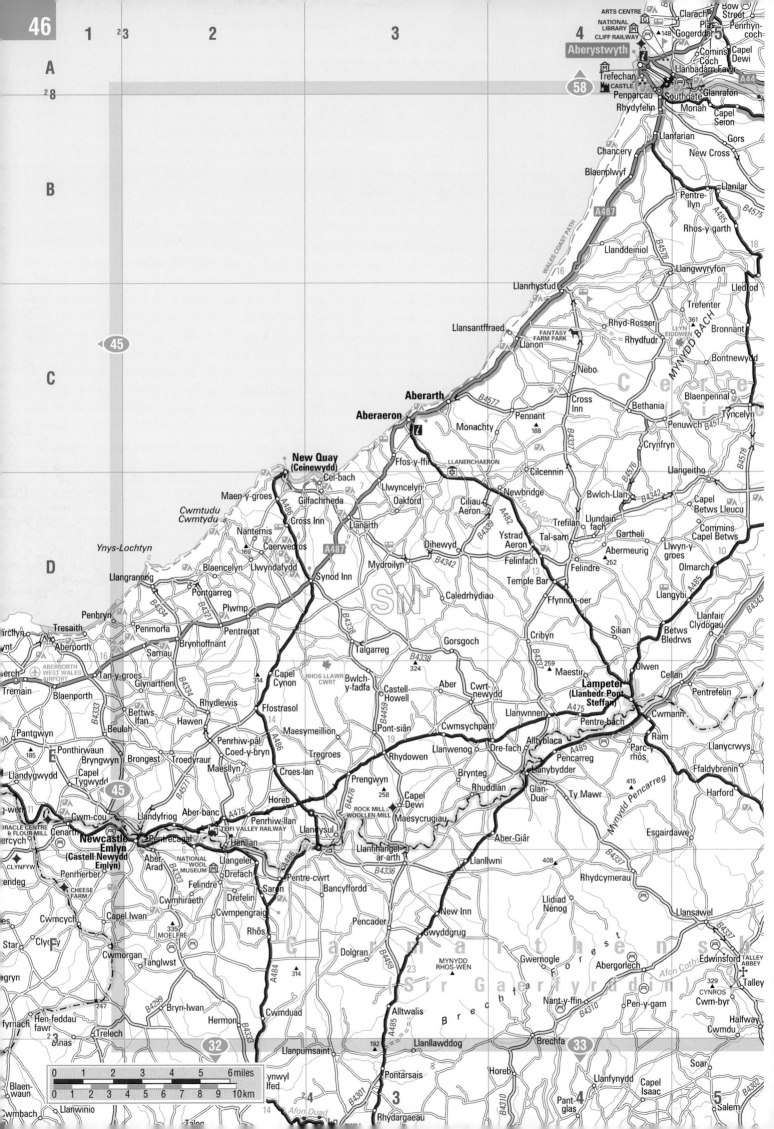

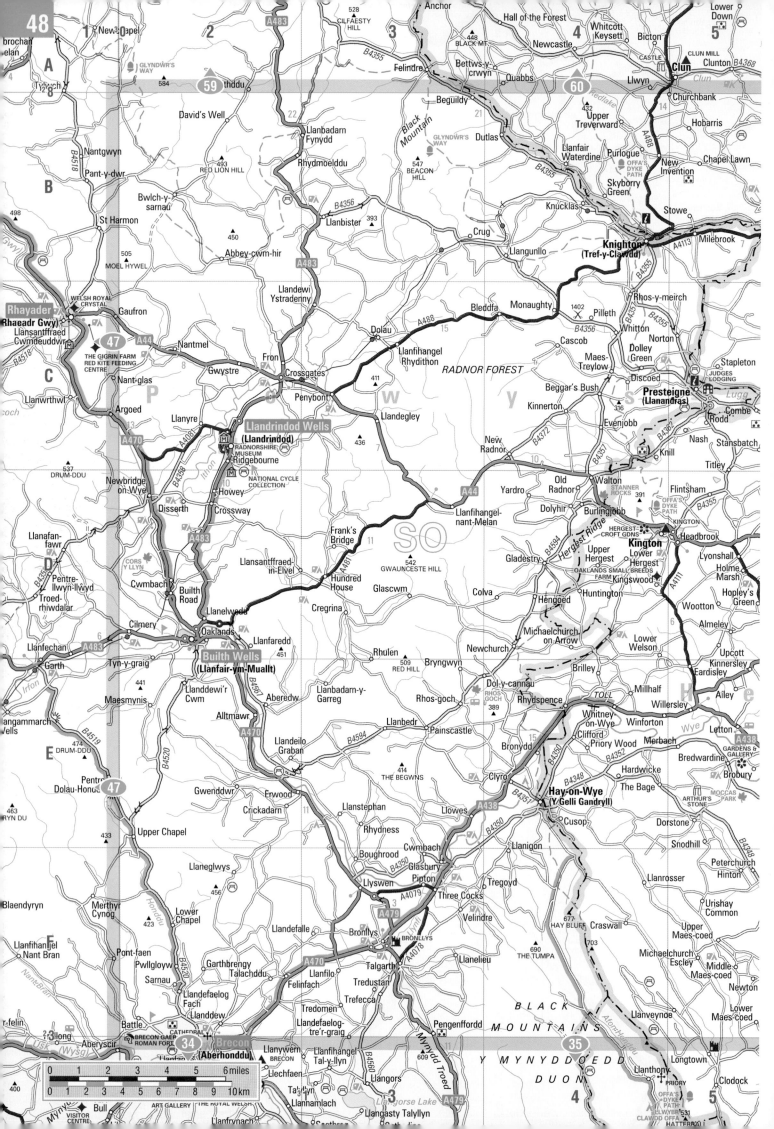

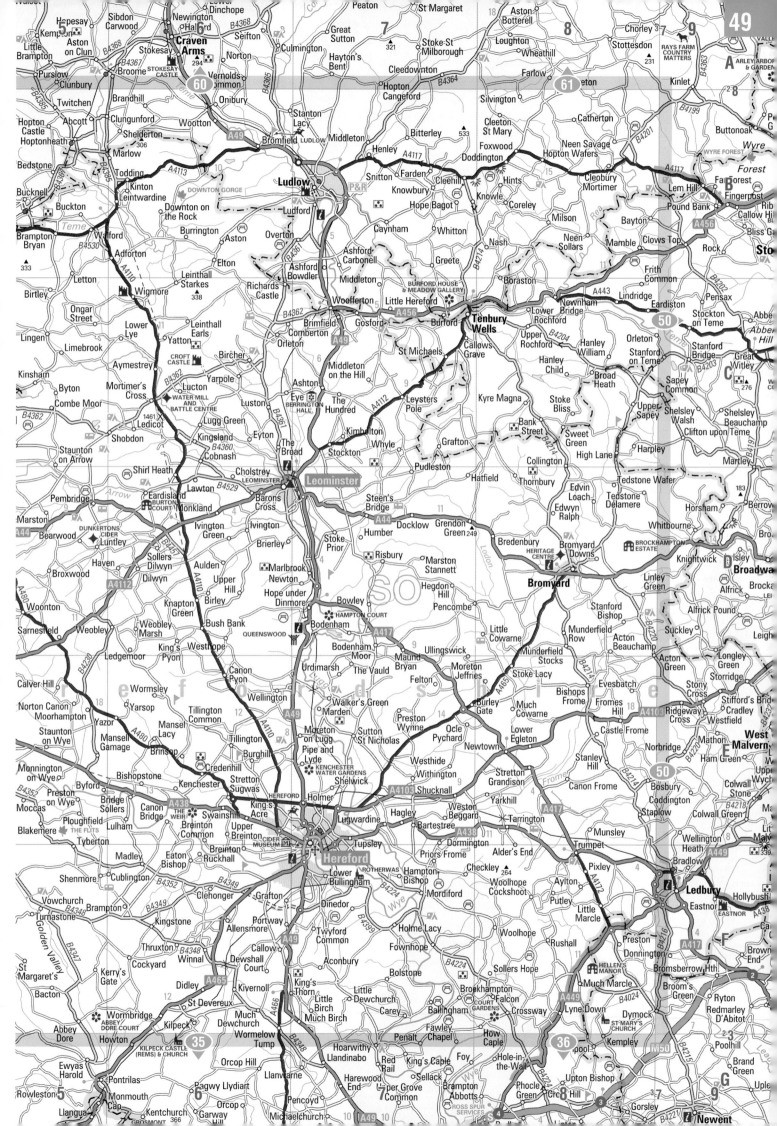

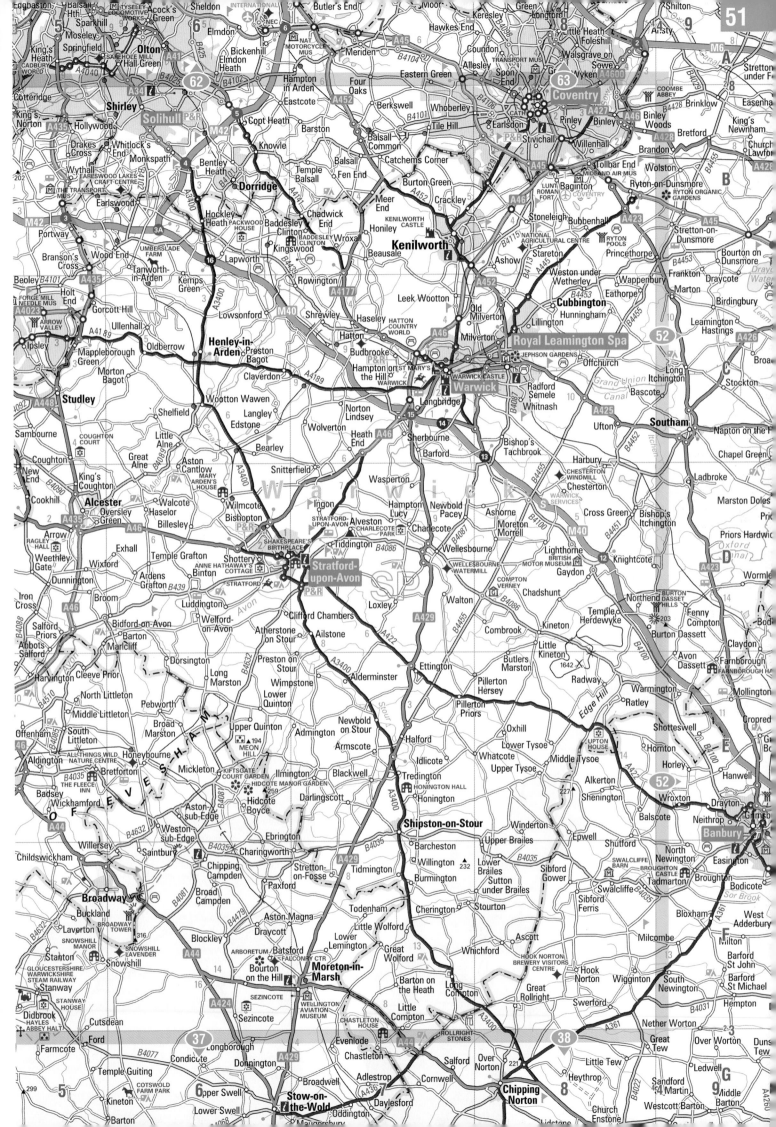

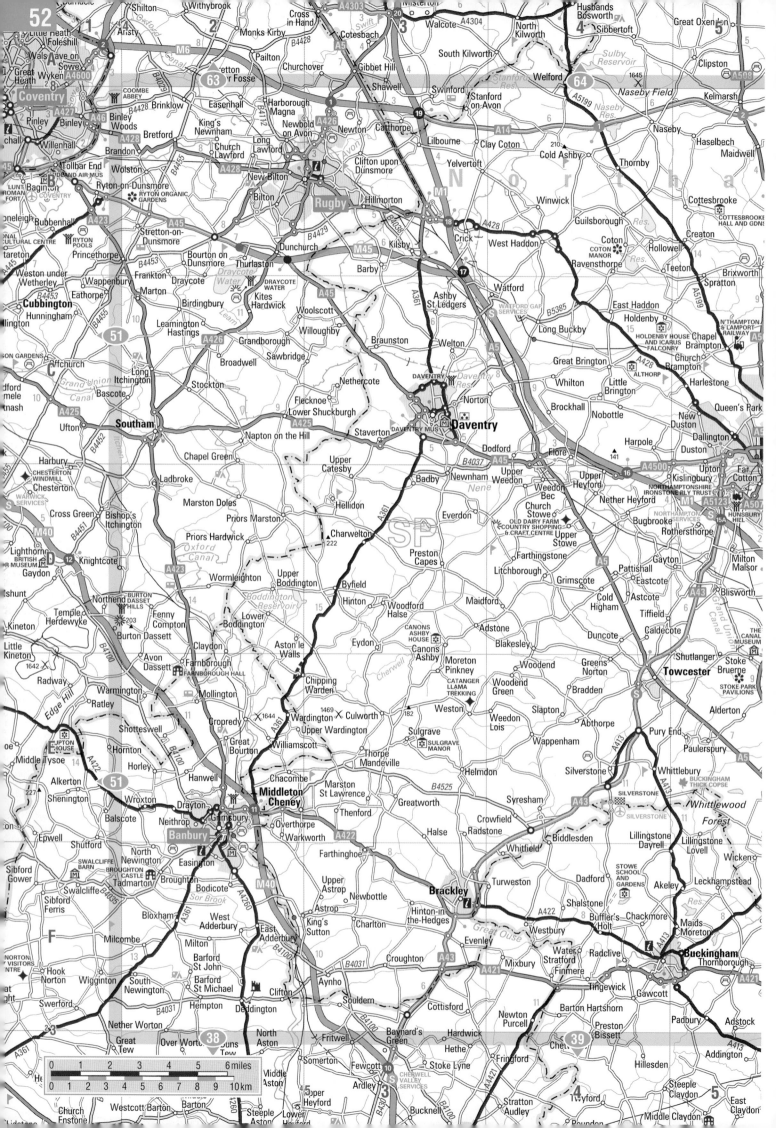

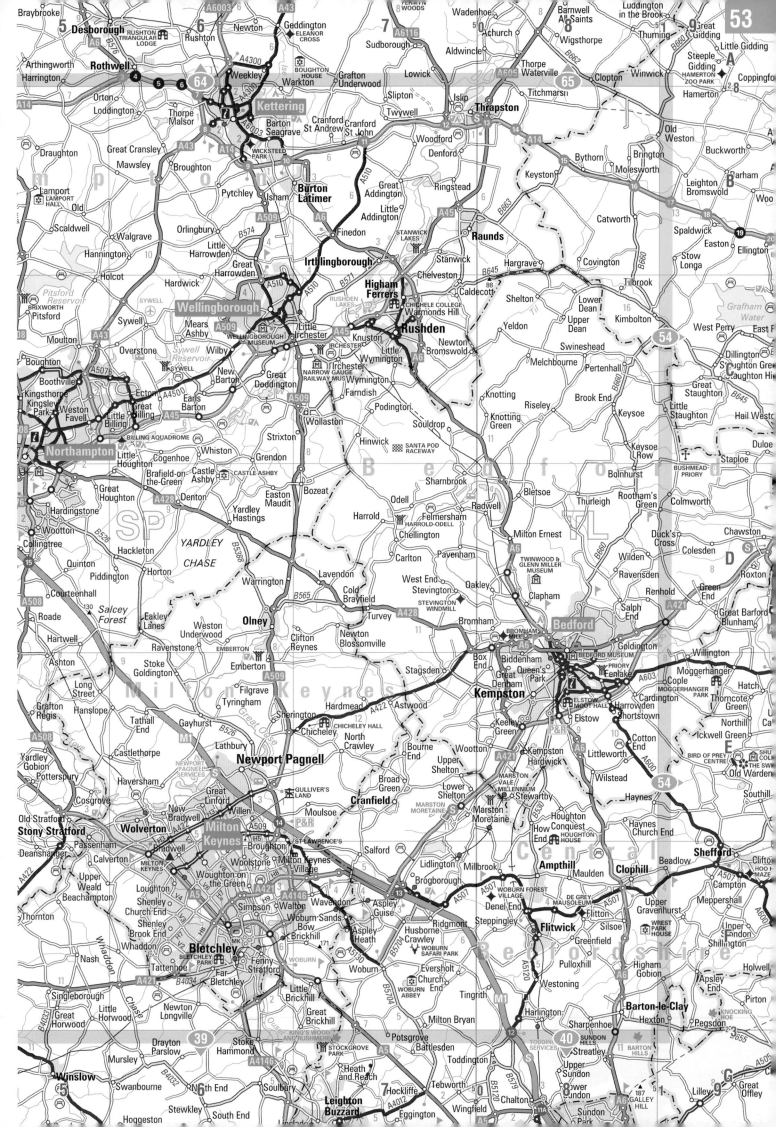

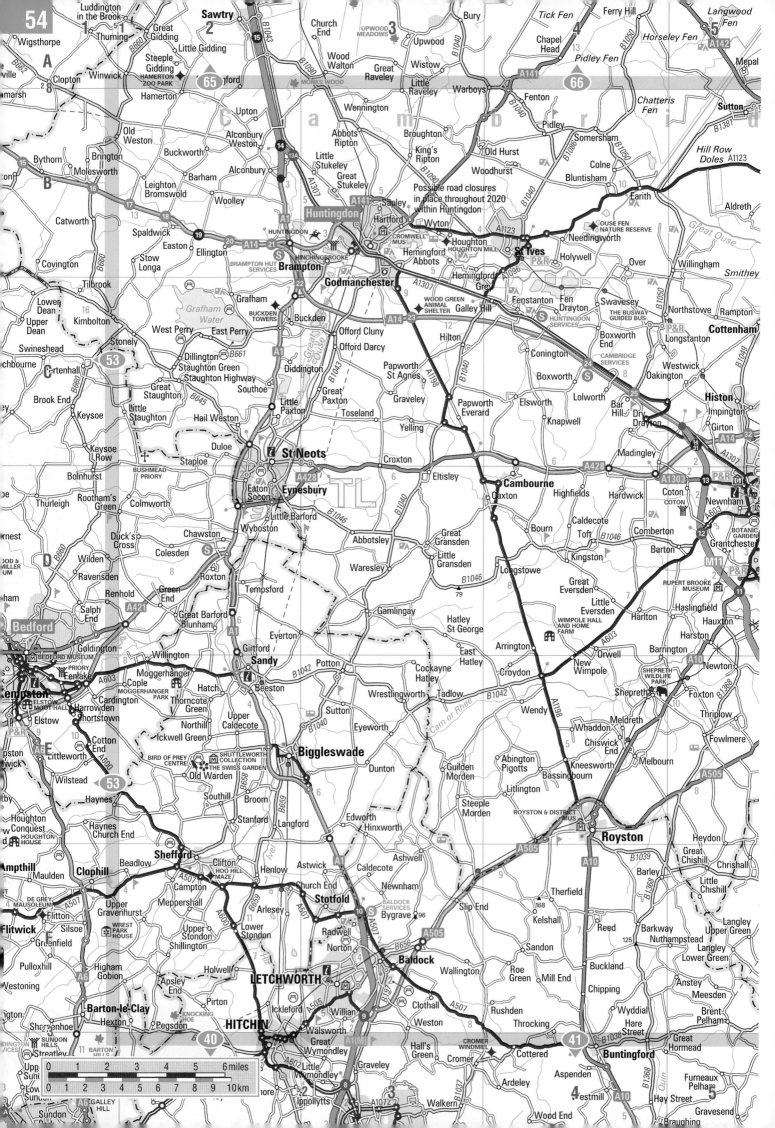

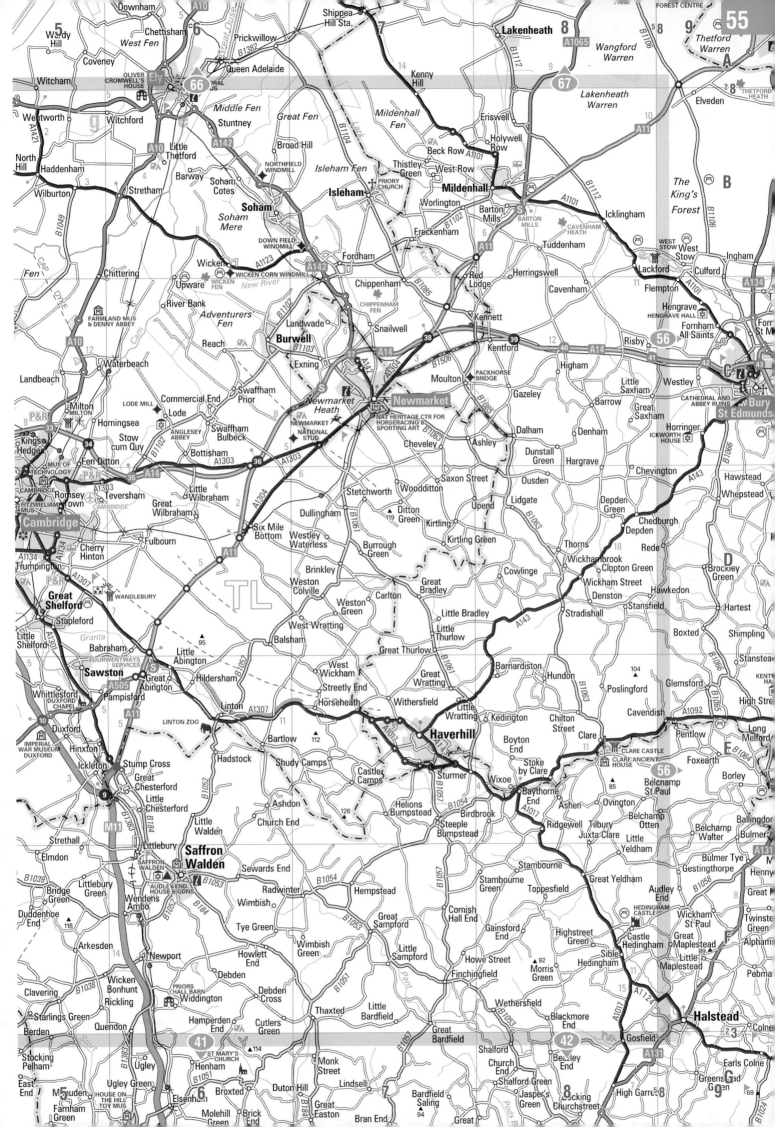

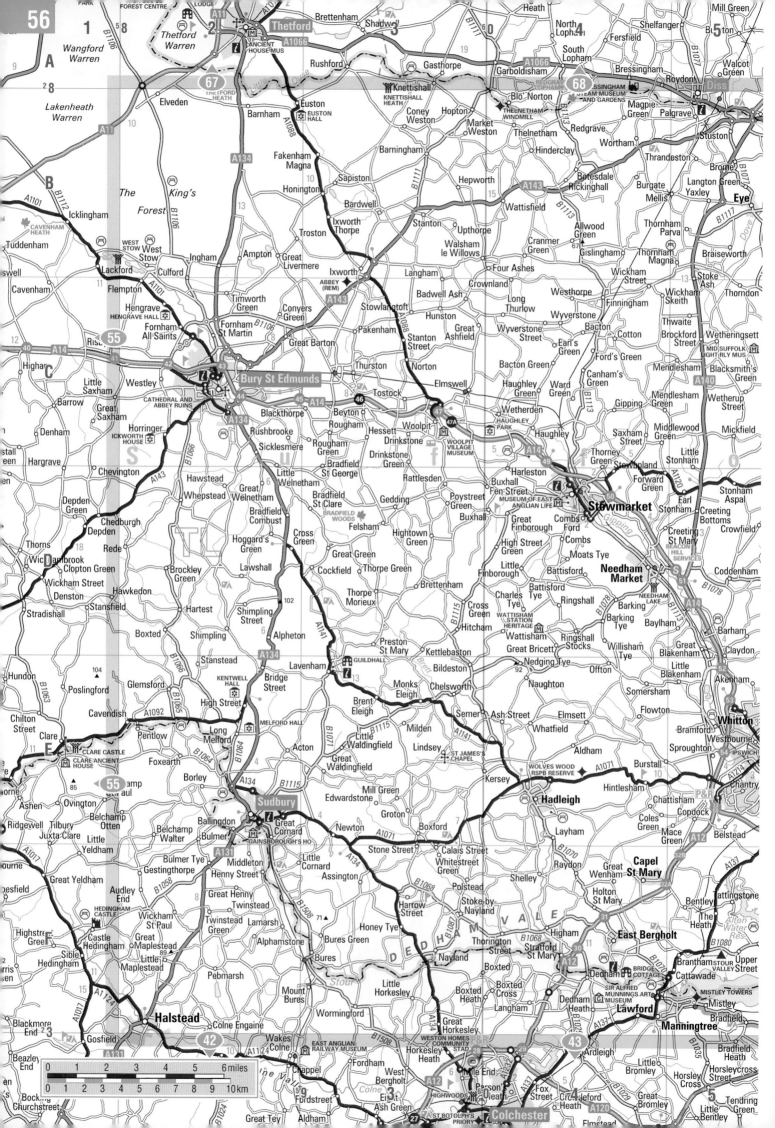

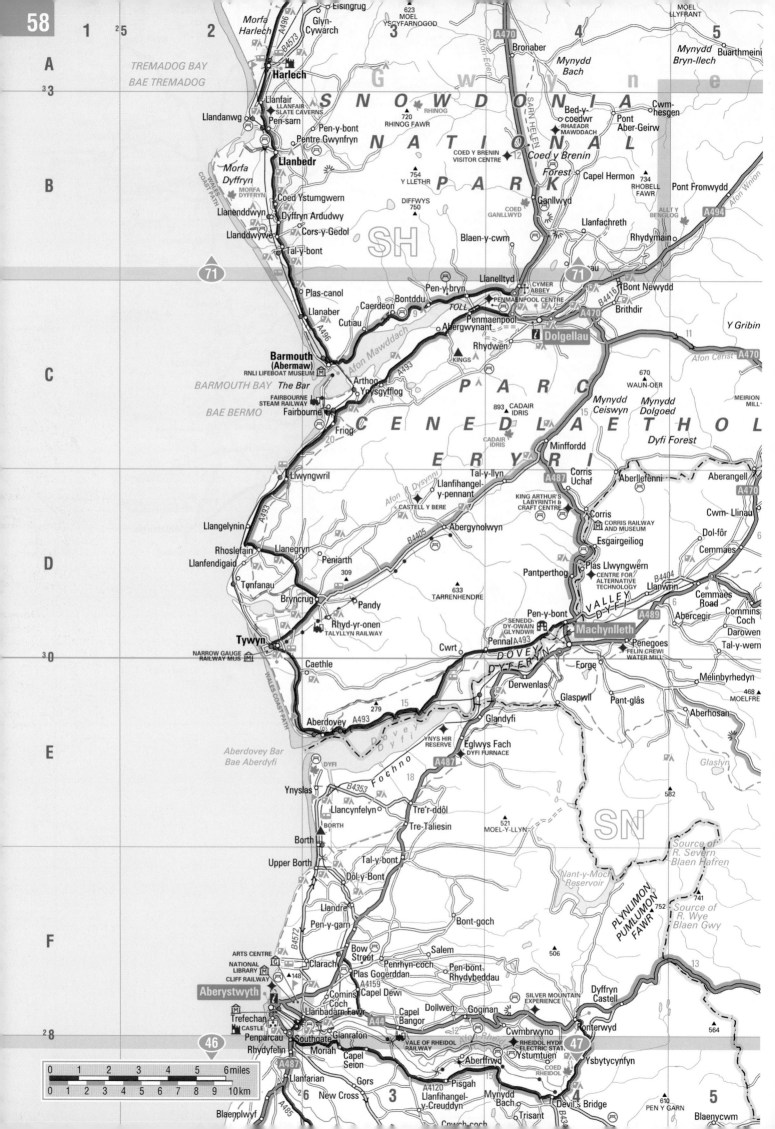

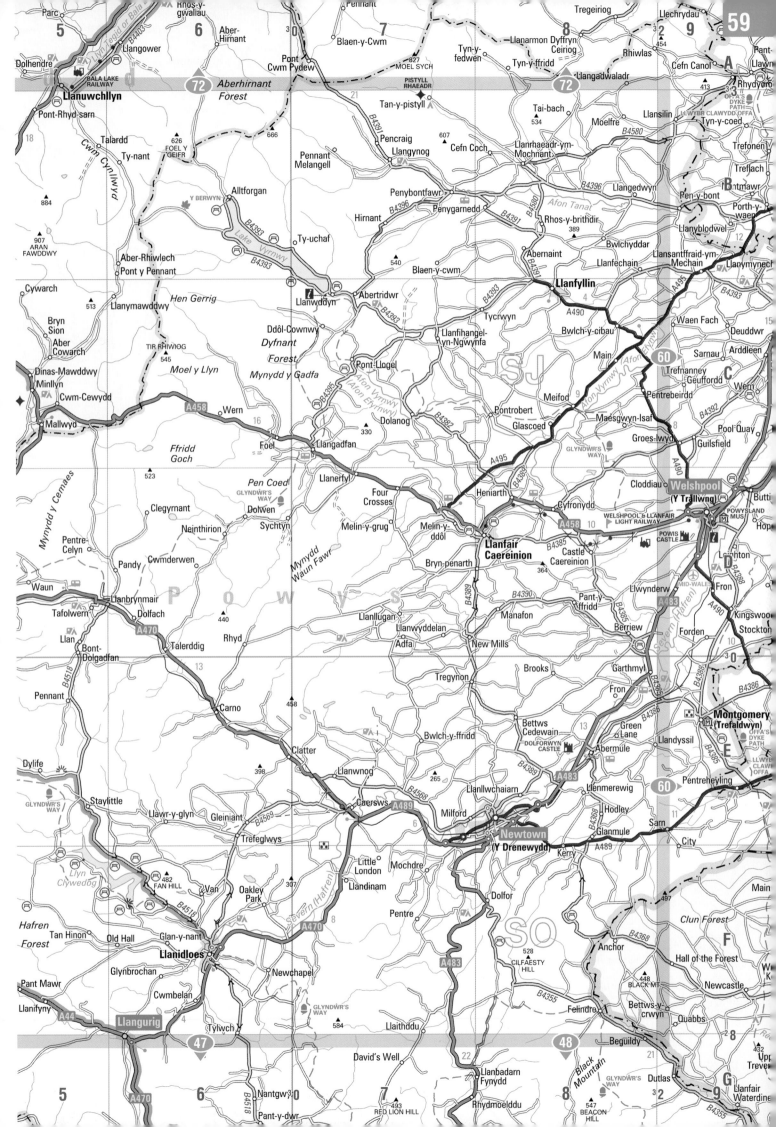

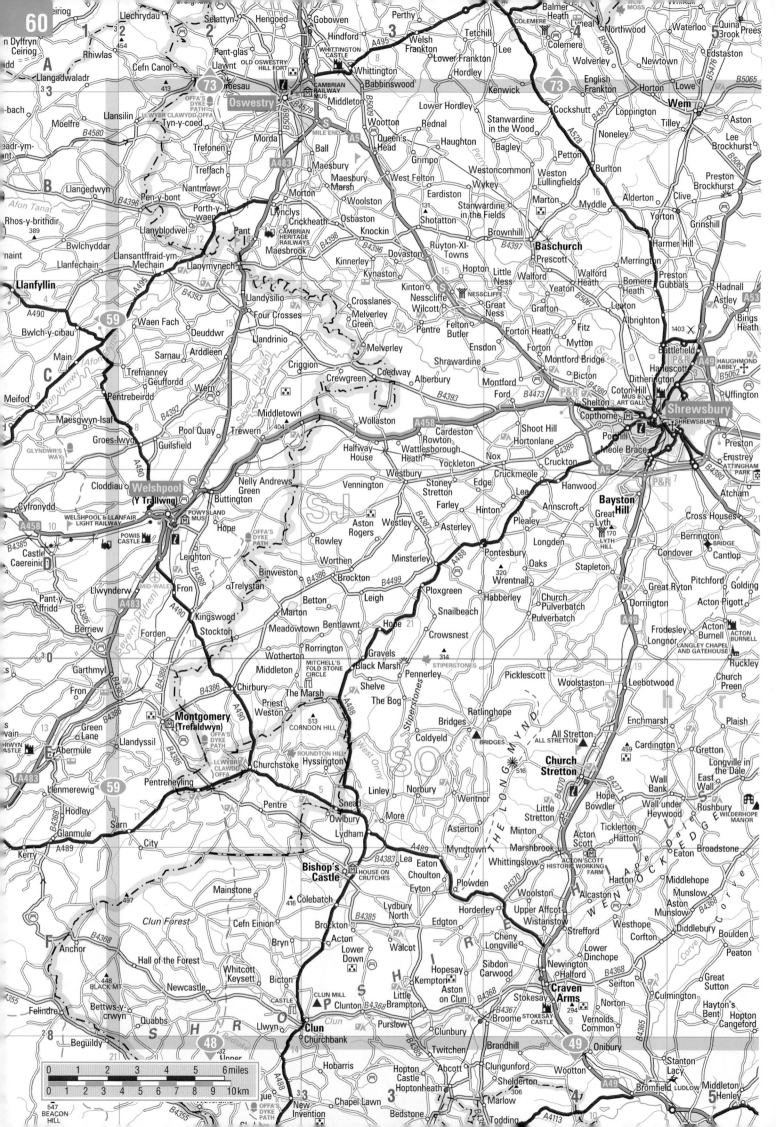

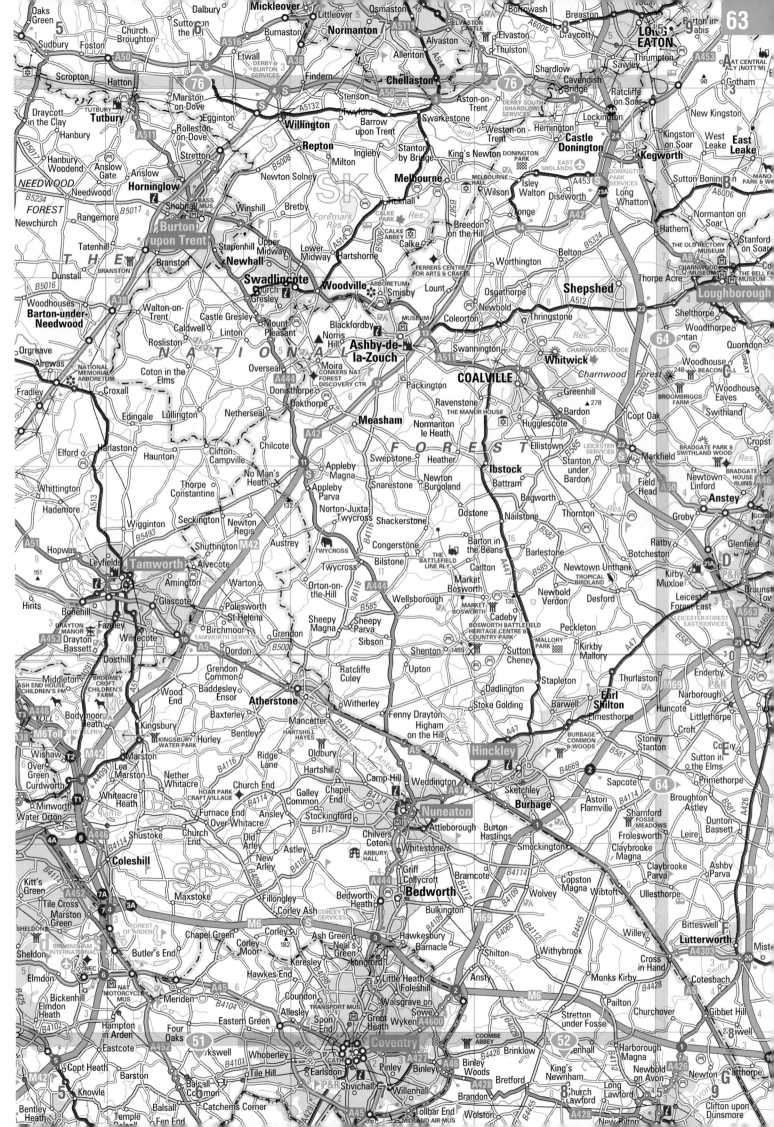

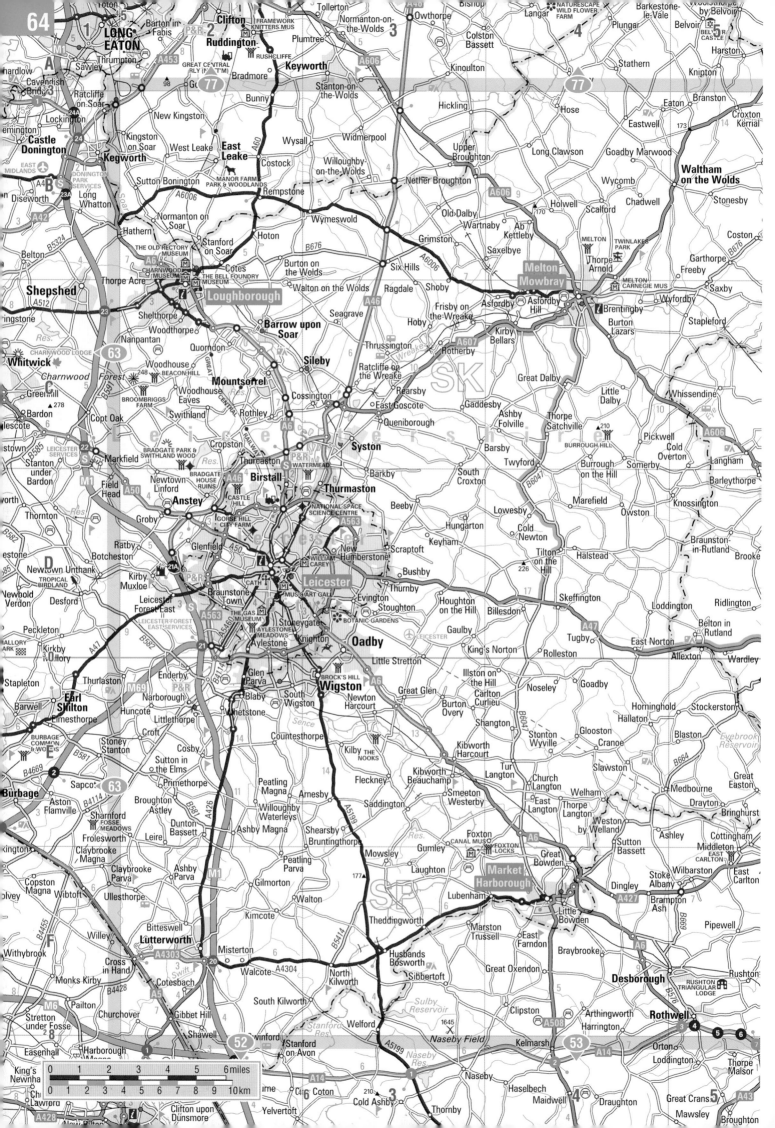

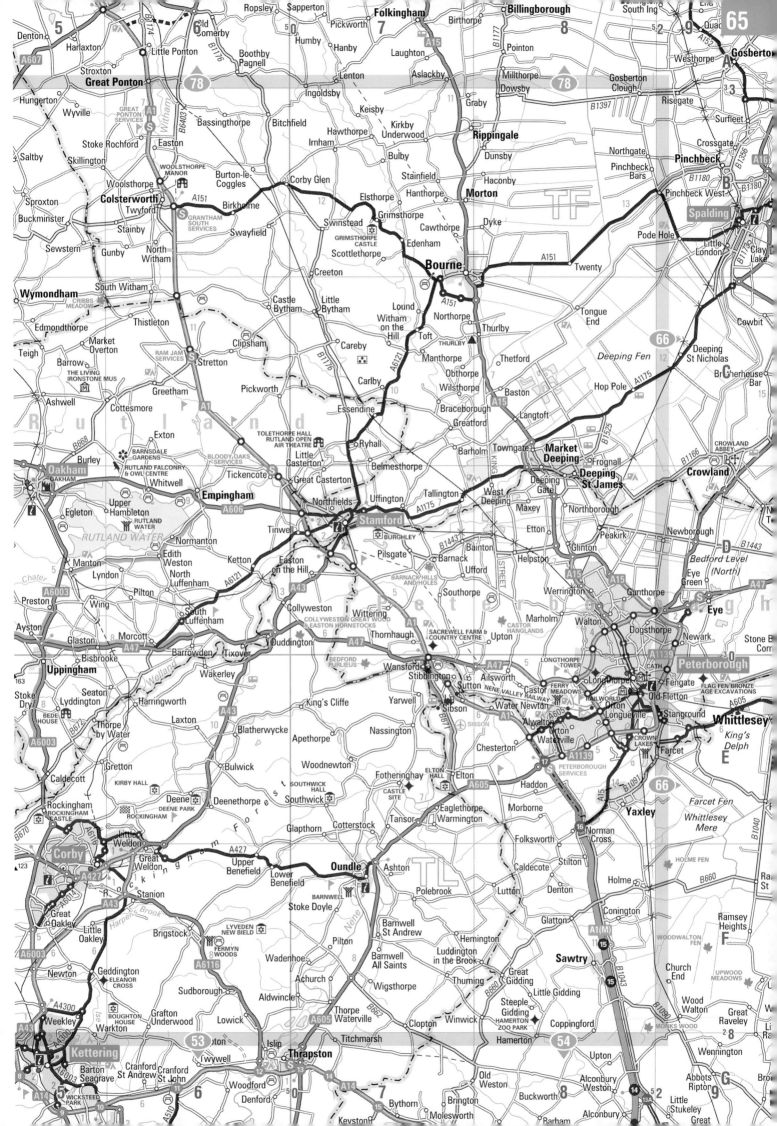

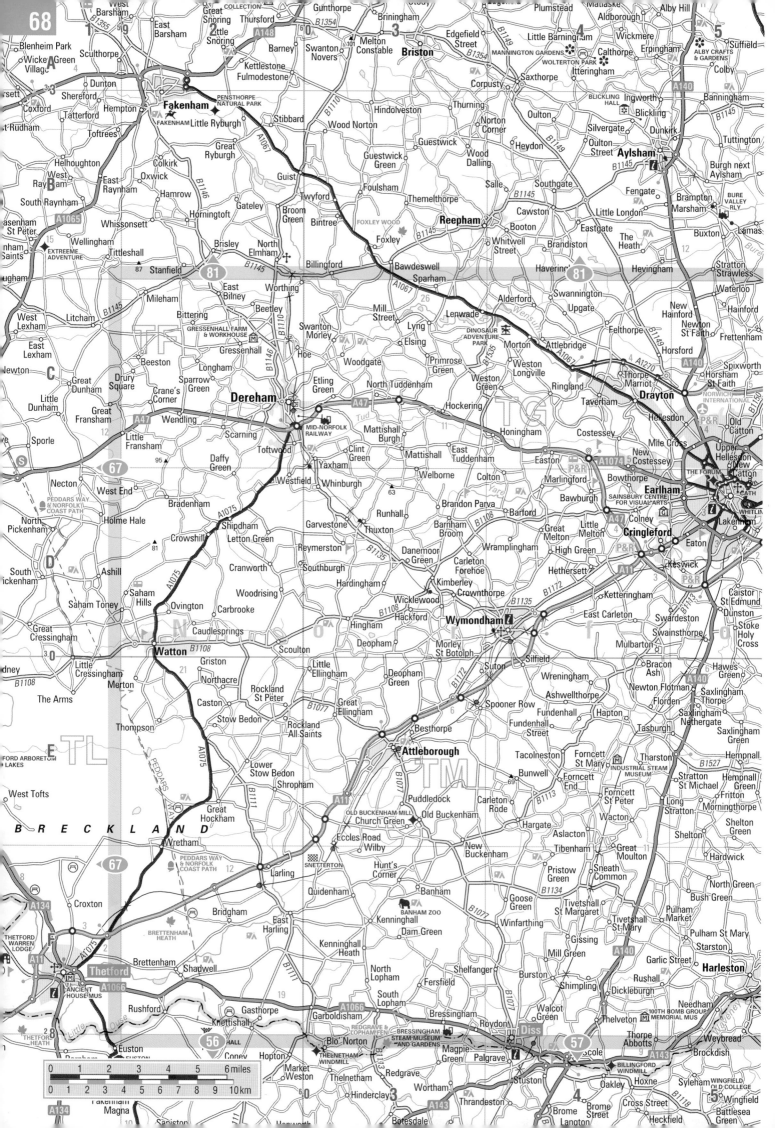

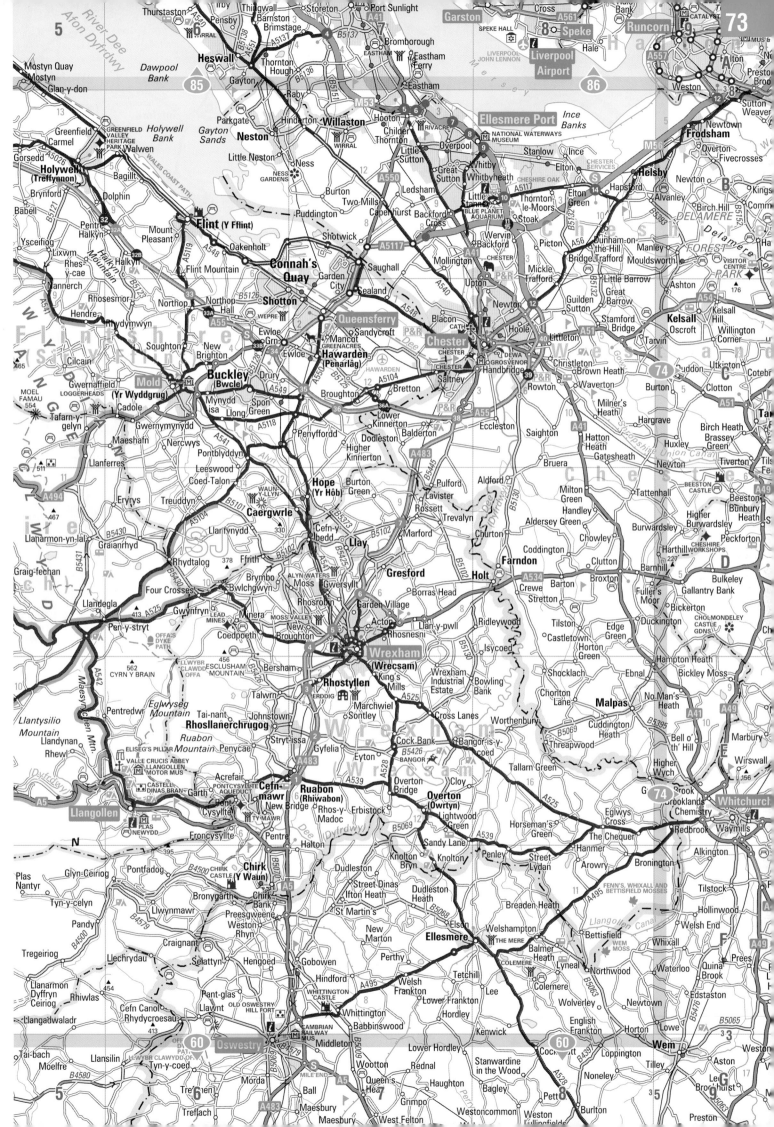

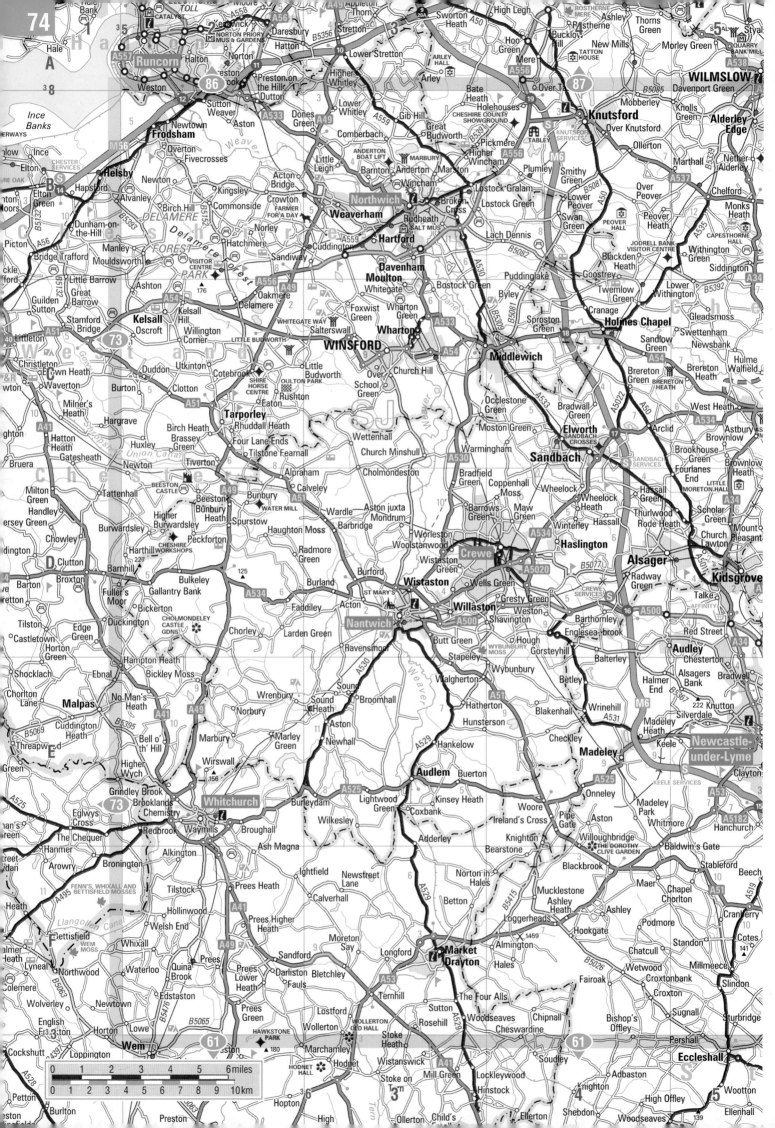

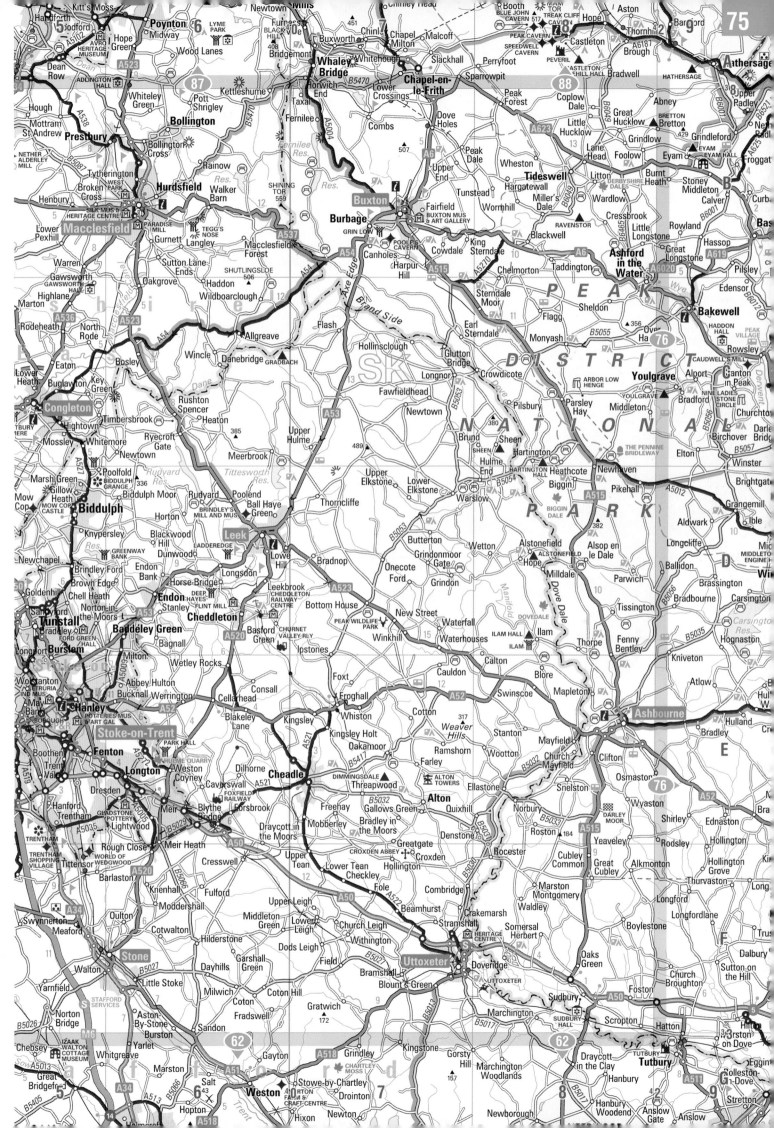

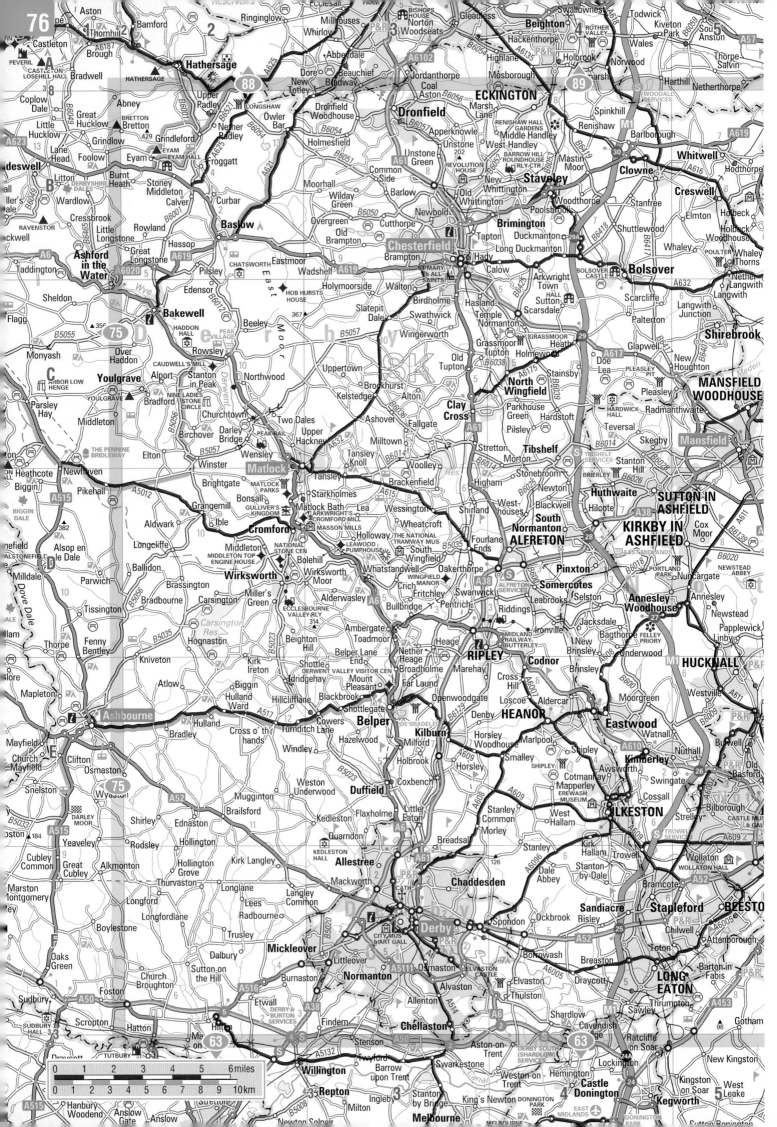

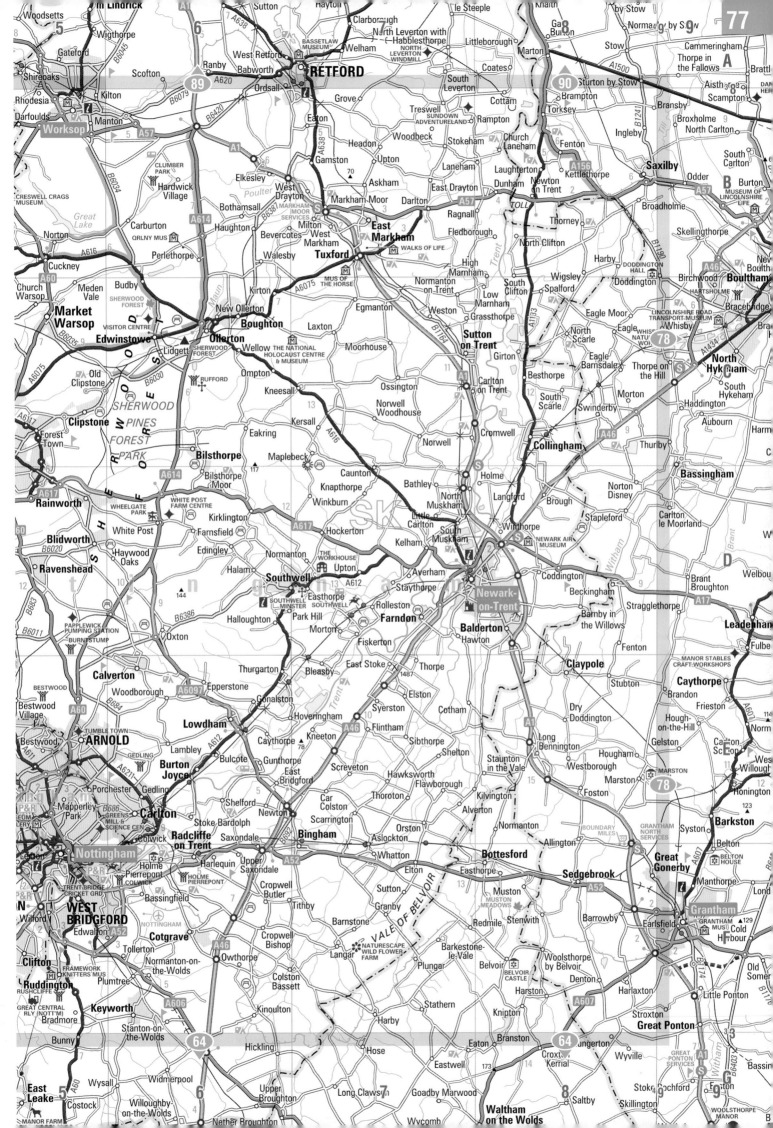

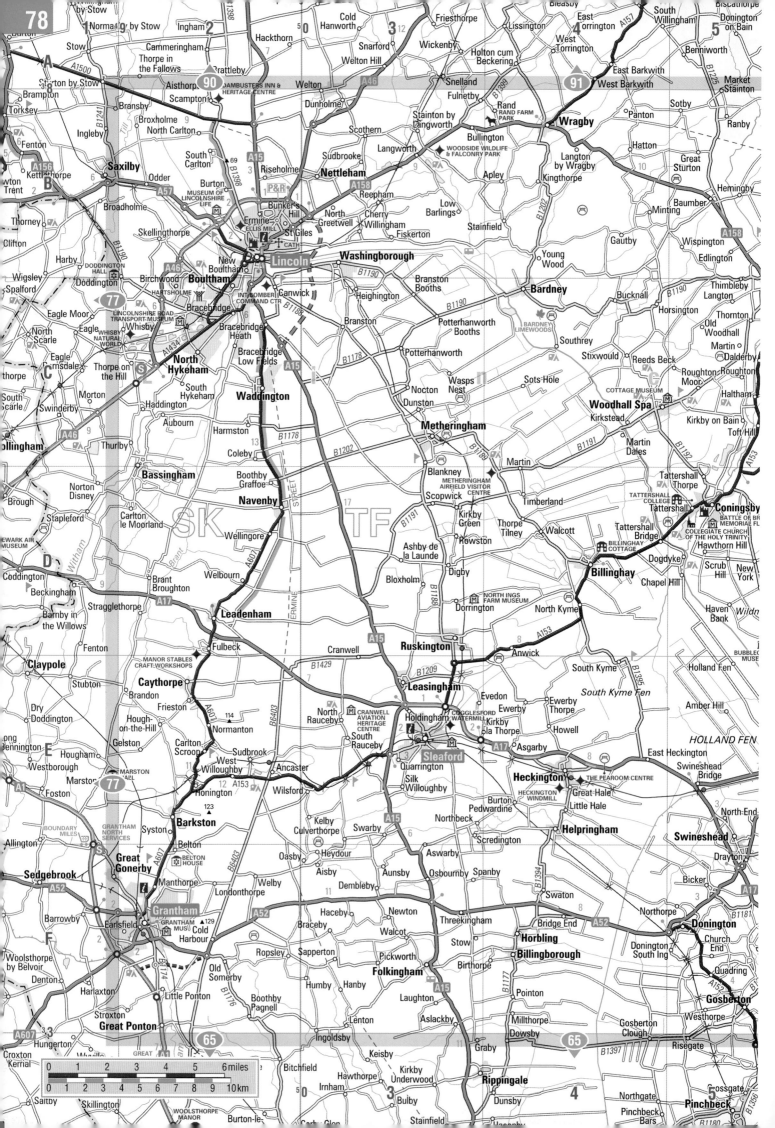

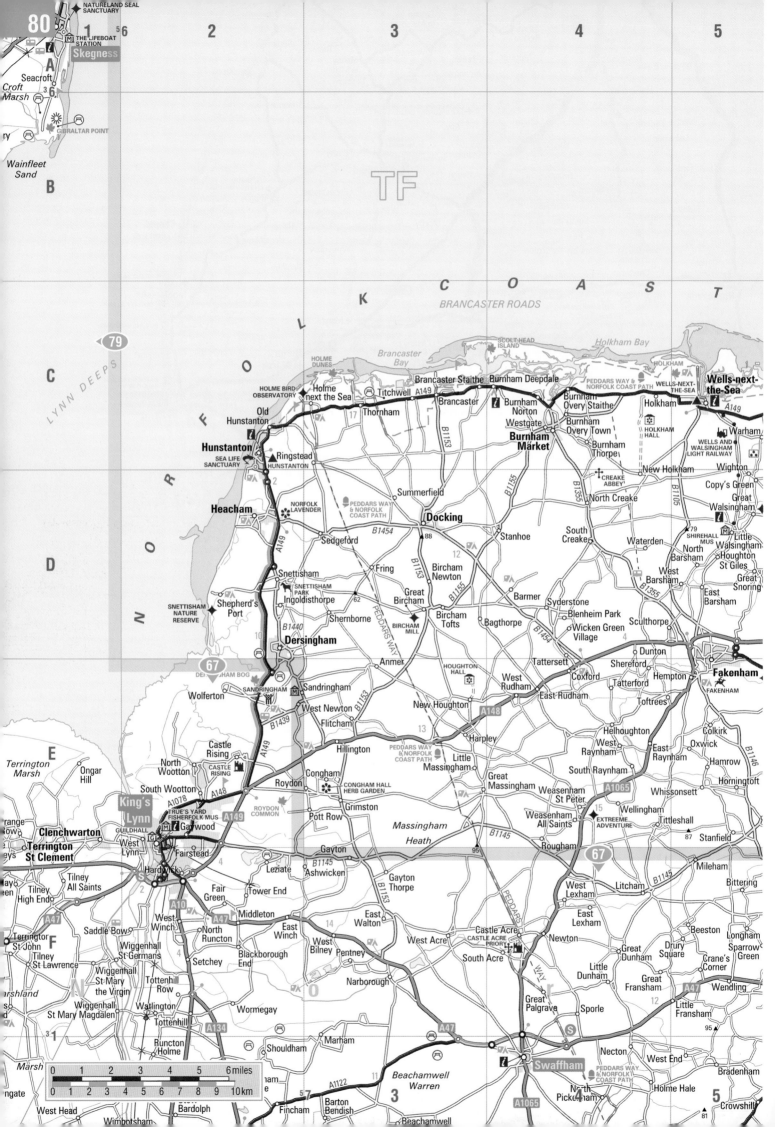

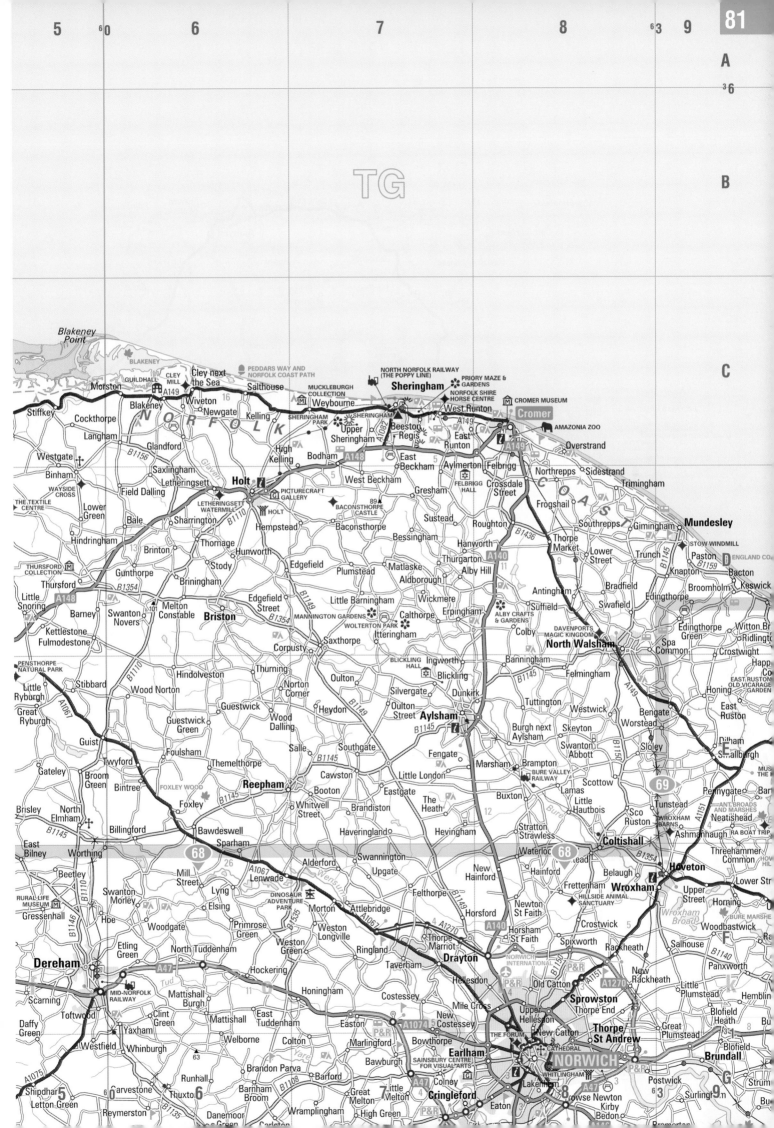

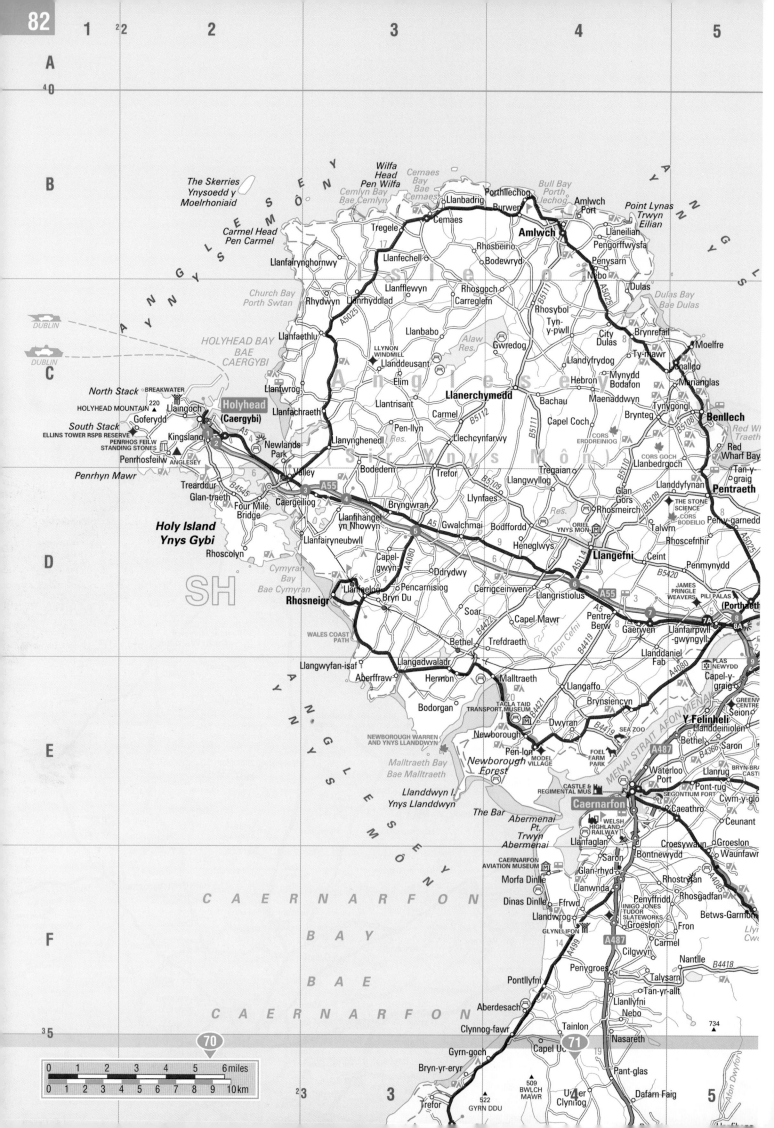

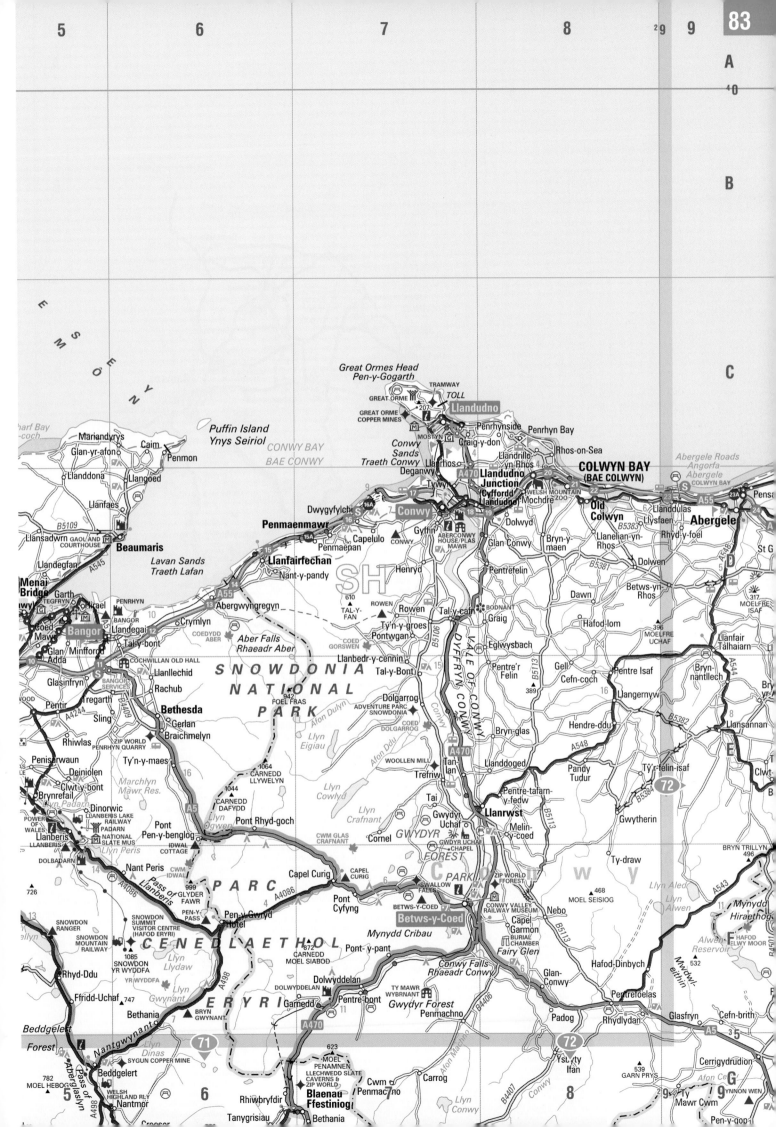

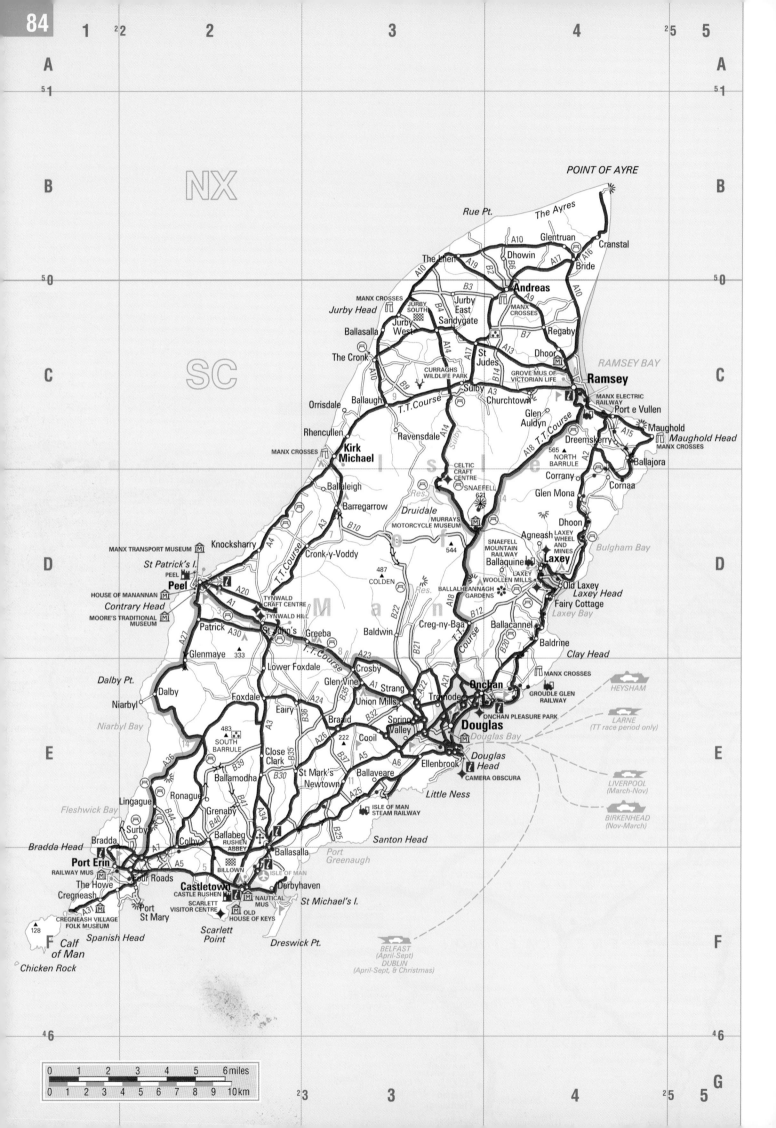

POINT OF AYRE

Rue Pt.

The Ayres

Glentruan
Cranstal
Dhowin
Bride
The Lhen
A10
A19
B2
B6
A17
A16

A10
B3
A9
Andreas
Regaby
MANX CROSSES
Jurby Head
JURBY
SOUTH
Jurby
East
Sandygate
B7
Ballasalla
Jurby
West
B4
A13
Dhoor
A14
St
Judes
B14
A10
The Cronk
A17
CURRAGHS
WILDLIFE PARK
Churchtown
GROVE MUS OF
VICTORIAN LIFE
RAMSEY BAY
Orrisdale
Ballaugh
Sulby
A3
Ramsey
MANX ELECTRIC
RAILWAY
T.T. Course
9
Port e Vullen
Rhencullen
Glen
Auldyn
Maughold
Ravensdale
A14
A18 T.T. Course
Dreemskerry
A15
Maughold Head
**Kirk
Michael**
Isle
565
NORTH
BARRULE
MANX CROSSES
Ballajora
MANX CROSSES
Ballaleigh
CELTIC
CRAFT
CENTRE
Corrany
Cornaa
Barregarrow
SNAEFELL
Glen Mona
9
B10
Druidale
MURRAYS
MOTORCYCLE MUSEUM
621
14
Dhoon
MANX TRANSPORT MUSEUM
Knocksharry
A4
Cronk-y-Voddy
7
544
Agneash
SNAEFELL
MOUNTAIN
RAILWAY
LAXEY
WHEEL
AND
MINES
Bulgham Bay
St Patrick's I.
487
COLDEN
Ballaquine
Laxey
Peel
HOUSE OF MANANNAN
Contrary Head
A20
A3
Res.
LAXEY
WOOLLEN MILLS
Old Laxey
Laxey Head
MOORE'S TRADITIONAL
MUSEUM
A1
Patrick
TYNWALD
CRAFT CENTRE
TYNWALD HILL
St John's
3
Greeba
BALLALHEENNAGH
GARDENS
Fairy Cottage
Laxey Bay
A27
A30
Baldwin
B22
Creg-ny-Baa
B12
Ballacannel
Glenmaye
333
Lower Foxdale
Crosby
A23
B21
Baldrine
Clay Head
Glen Vine
A1
Strang
B20
Dalby Pt.
Foxdale
A24
B35
Union Mills
A22
B32
A21
Creg-ny-Baa
Onchan
GROUDLE GLEN
RAILWAY
HEYSHAM
Dalby
Eairy
B36
Braaid
Tromode
MANX CROSSES
Niarbyl
Spring
Valley
ONCHAN PLEASURE PARK
LARNE
(TT race period only)
Niarbyl Bay
483
SOUTH
BARRULE
222
Cooil
A26
A6
Douglas
Douglas Bay
Close
Clark
B37
A5
Ellenbrook
*Douglas
Head*
LIVERPOOL
(March-Nov)
Lingague
A36
B39
B30
St Mark's
Newtown
11
Ballaveare
CAMERA OBSCURA
Ronague
B41
A25
Little Ness
BIRKENHEAD
(Nov-March)
Ballamodha
Grenaby
A34
ISLE OF MAN
STEAM RAILWAY
Fleshwick Bay
Surby
B44
B40
Ballabeg
RUSHEN ABBEY
Ballasalla
*Port
Greenaugh*
Santon Head
Bradda Head
Bradda
Colby
A7
BILLOWN
*Port
Greenaugh*
Port Erin
RAILWAY MUS
A5
5
ISLE OF MAN
Derbyhaven
St Michael's I.
The Howe
Four Roads
Castletown
CASTLE RUSHEN
SCARLETT
VISITOR CENTRE
NAUTICAL
MUS
OLD
HOUSE OF KEYS
St Michael's I.
Cregneash
Port
St Mary
*Scarlett
Point*
Dreswick Pt.
128
CREGNEASH VILLAGE
FOLK MUSEUM
Spanish Head
*Calf
of Man*
BELFAST
(April-Sept)
DUBLIN
(April-Sept, & Christmas)
Chicken Rock

NX

SC

Isle *of* *Man*

RAMSEY BAY

0   1   2   3   4   5   6 miles
0 1 2 3 4 5 6 7 8 9 10km

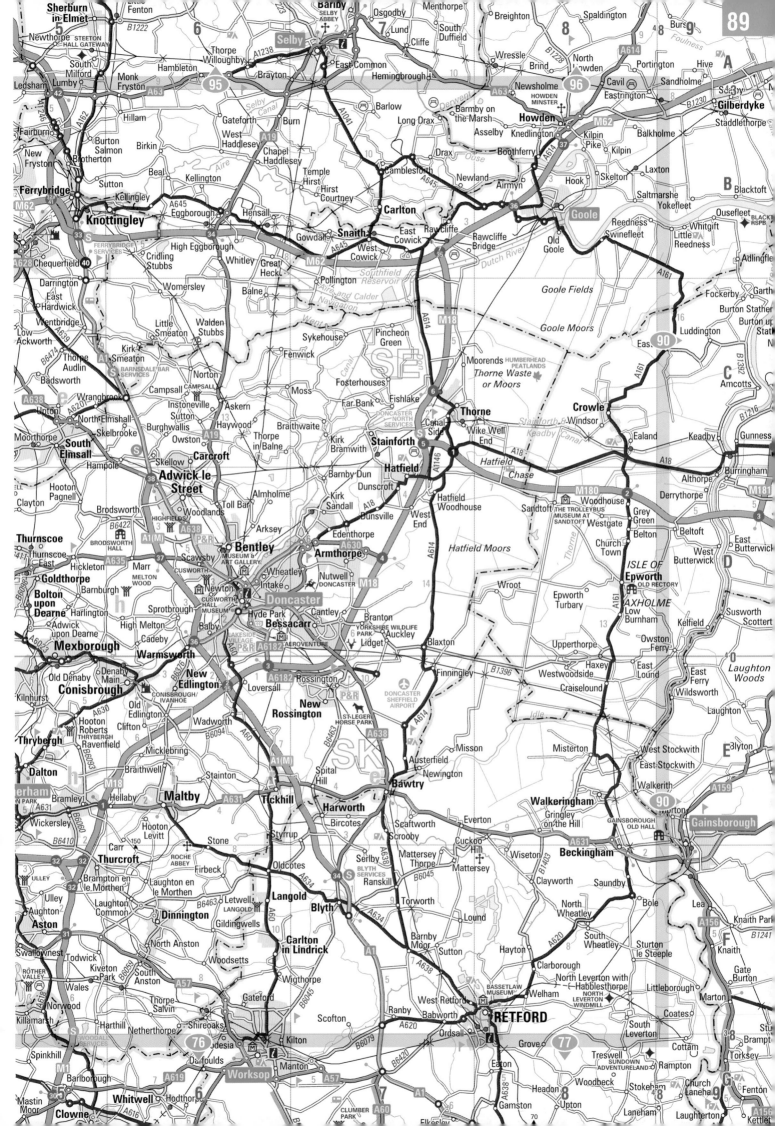

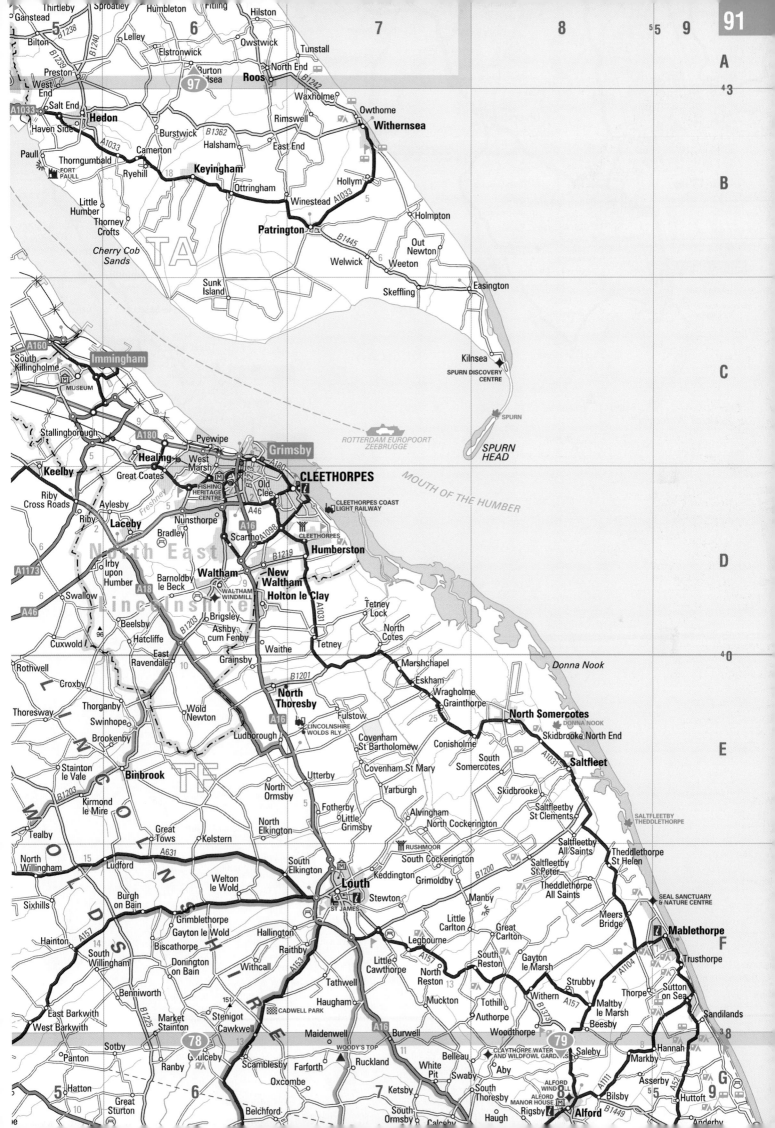

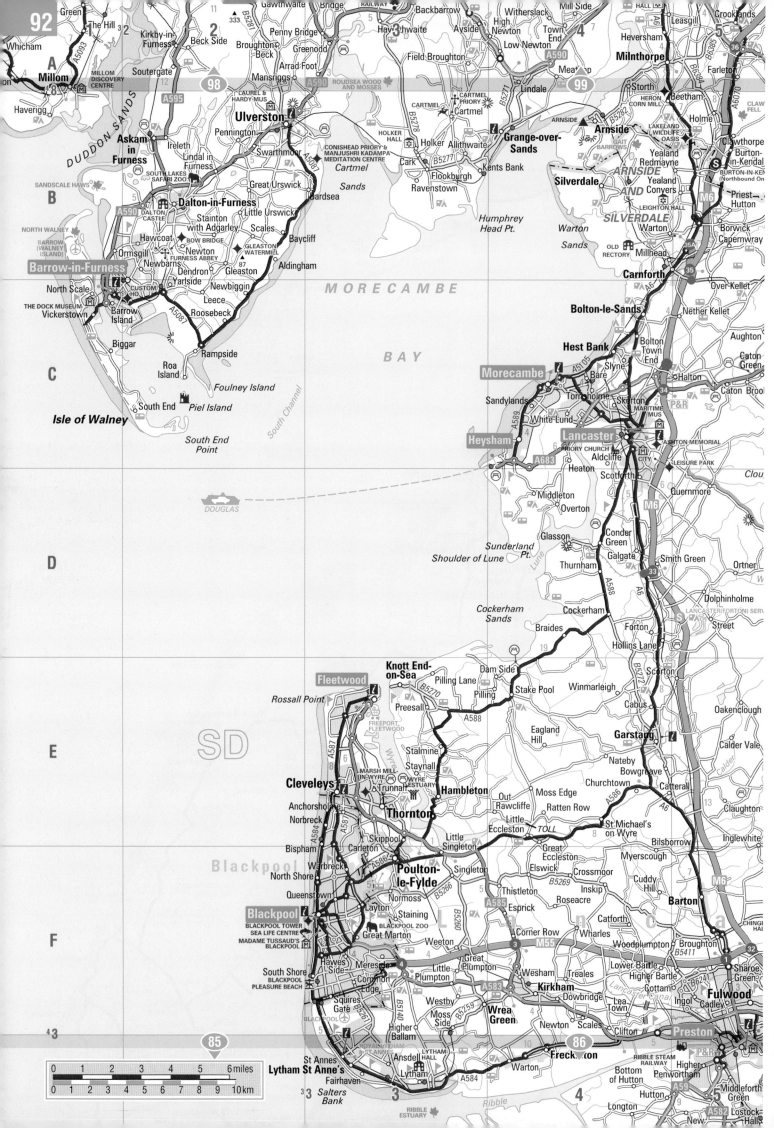

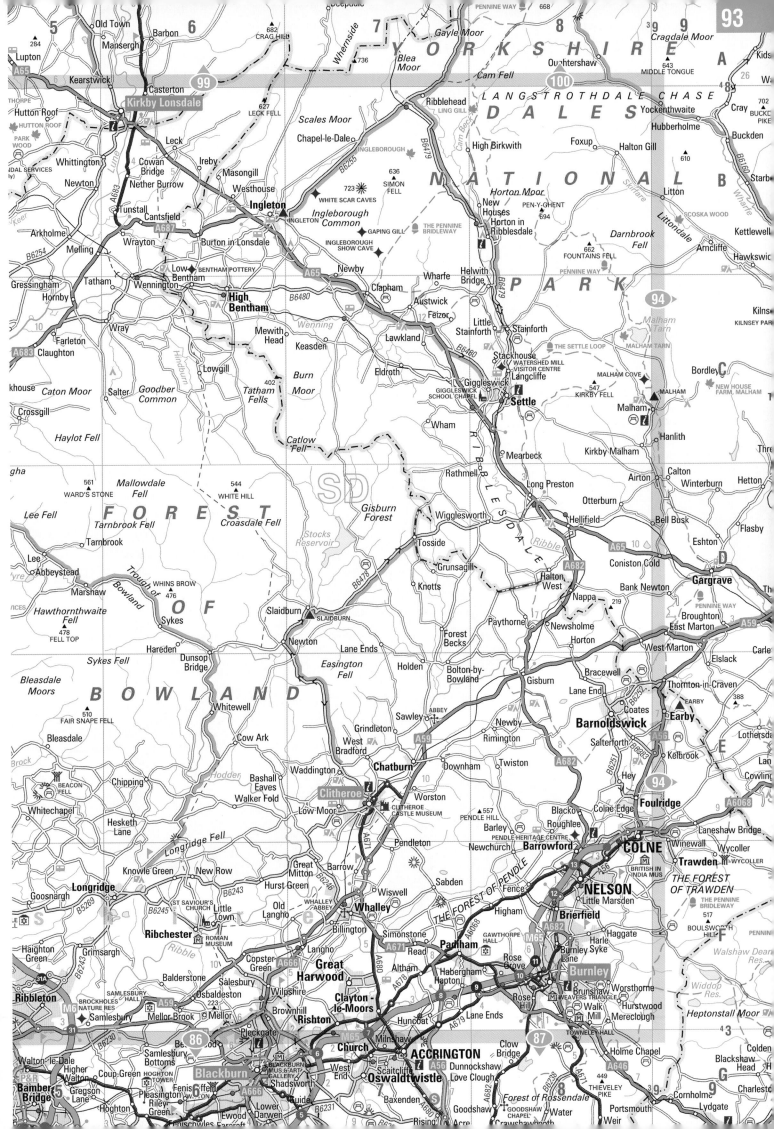

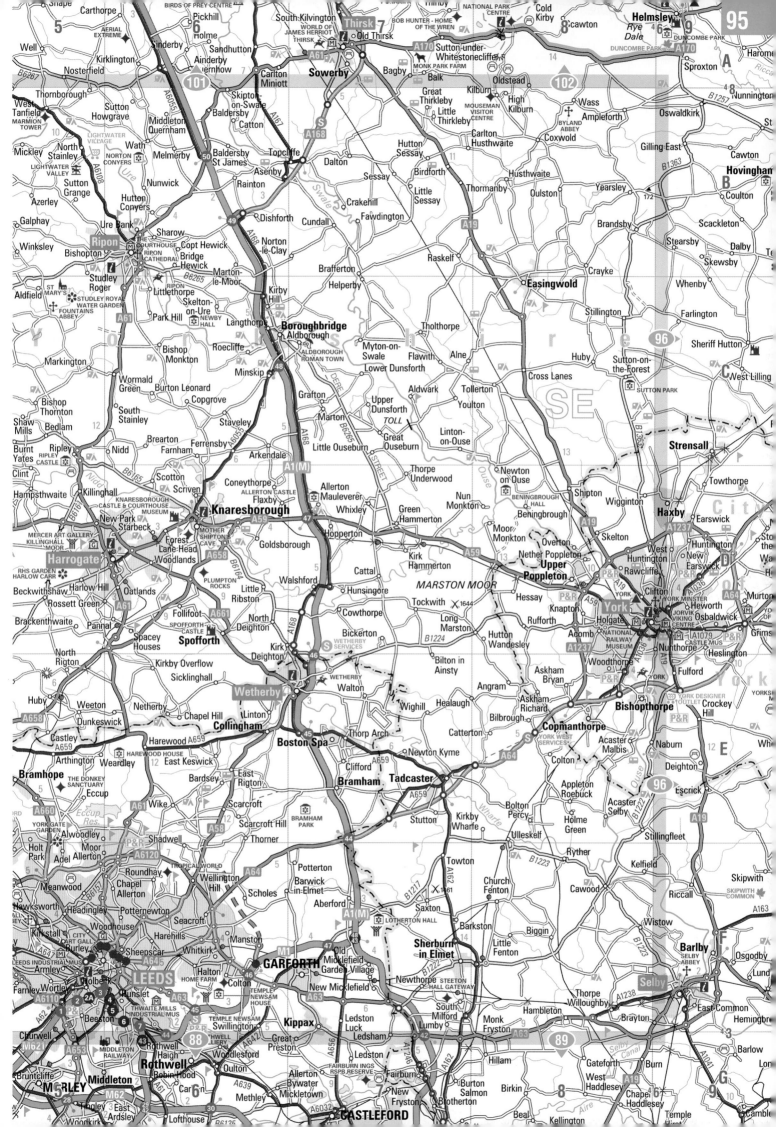

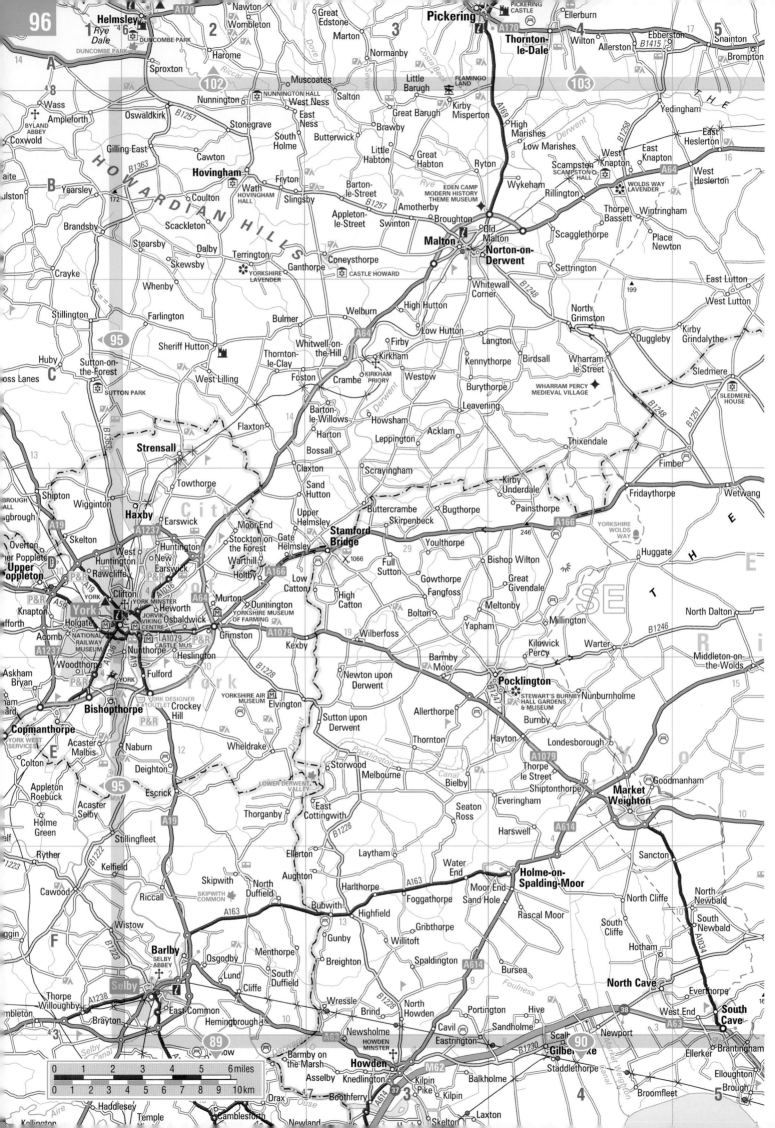

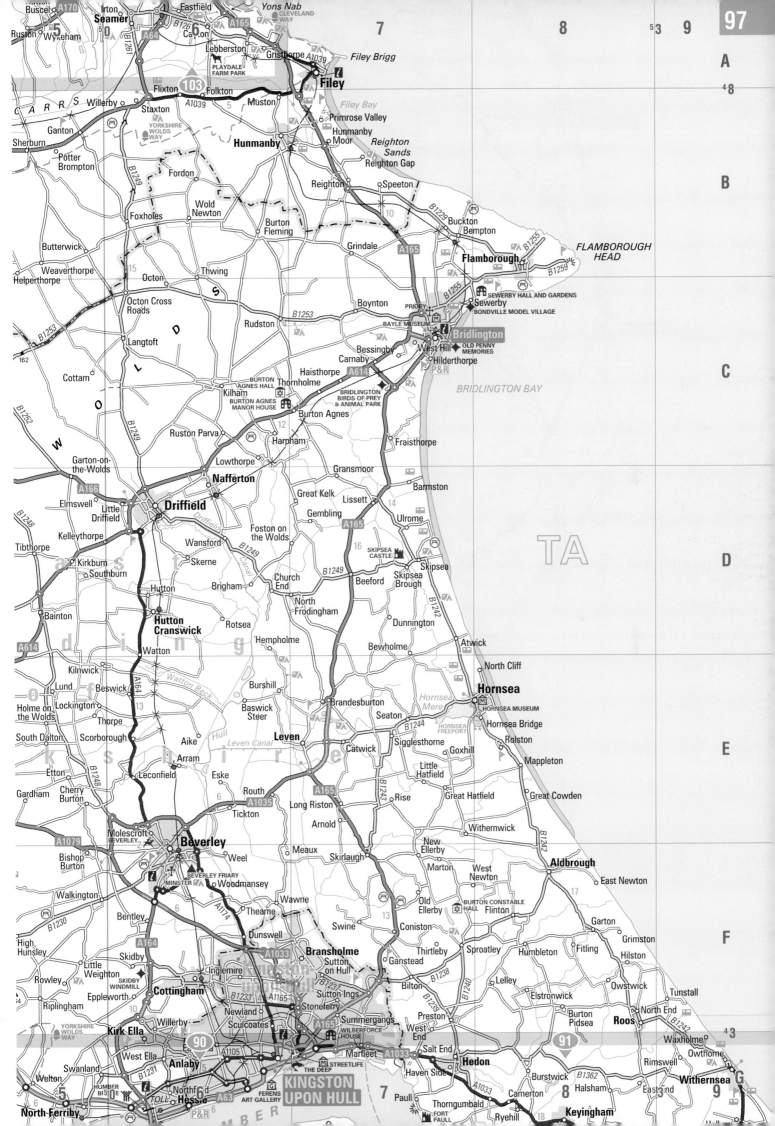

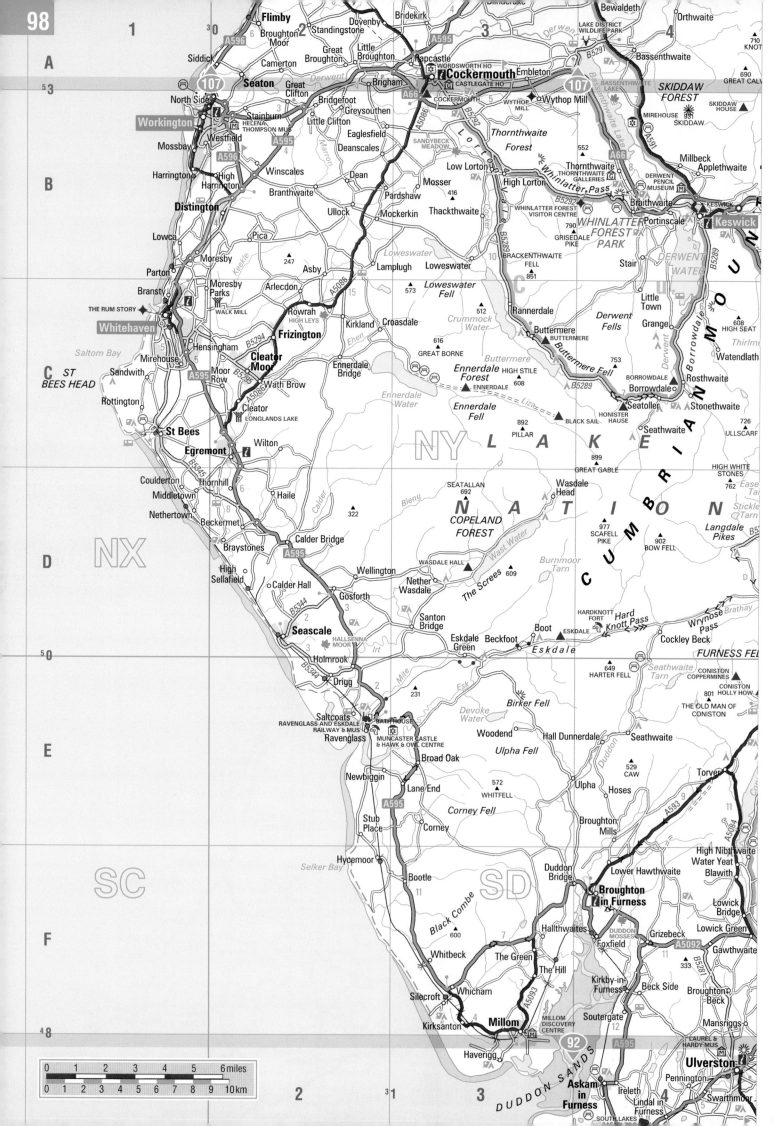

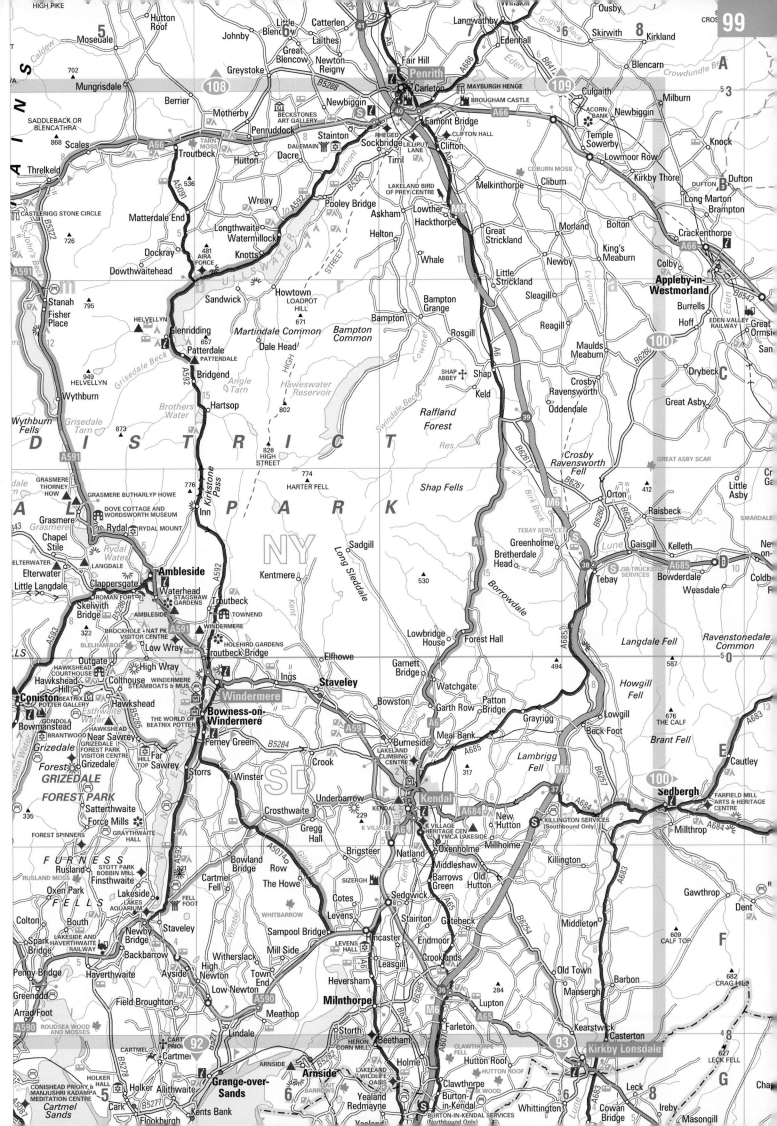

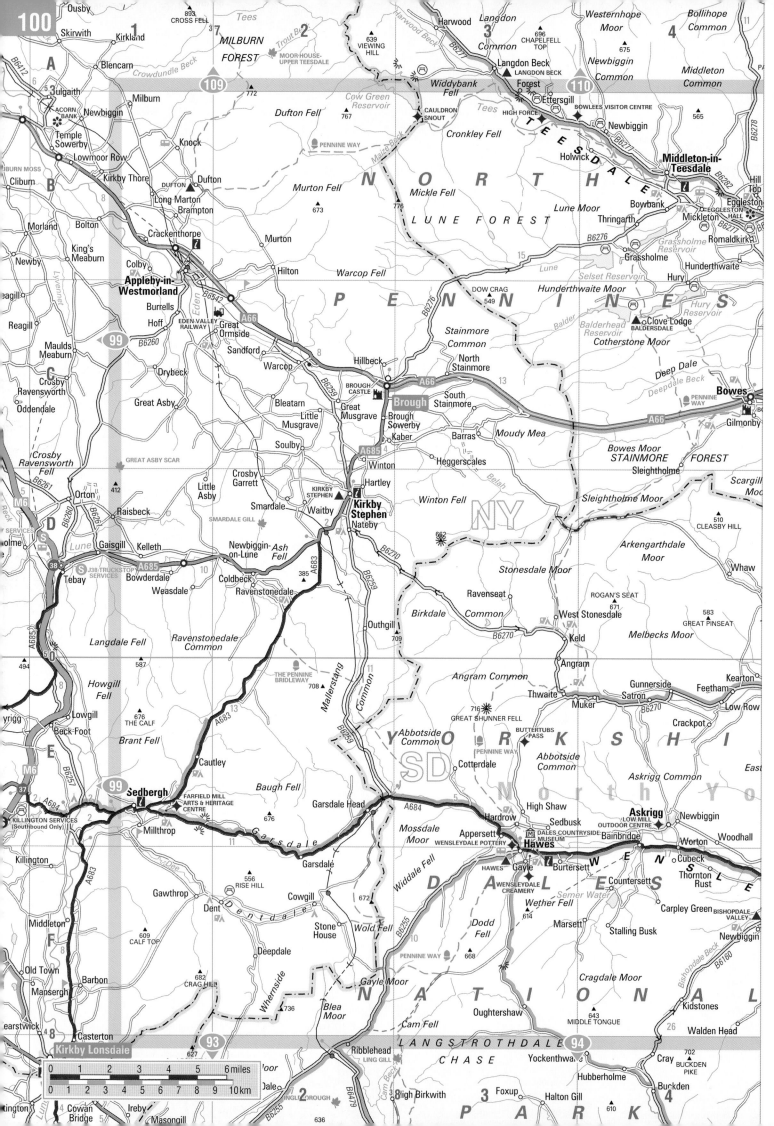

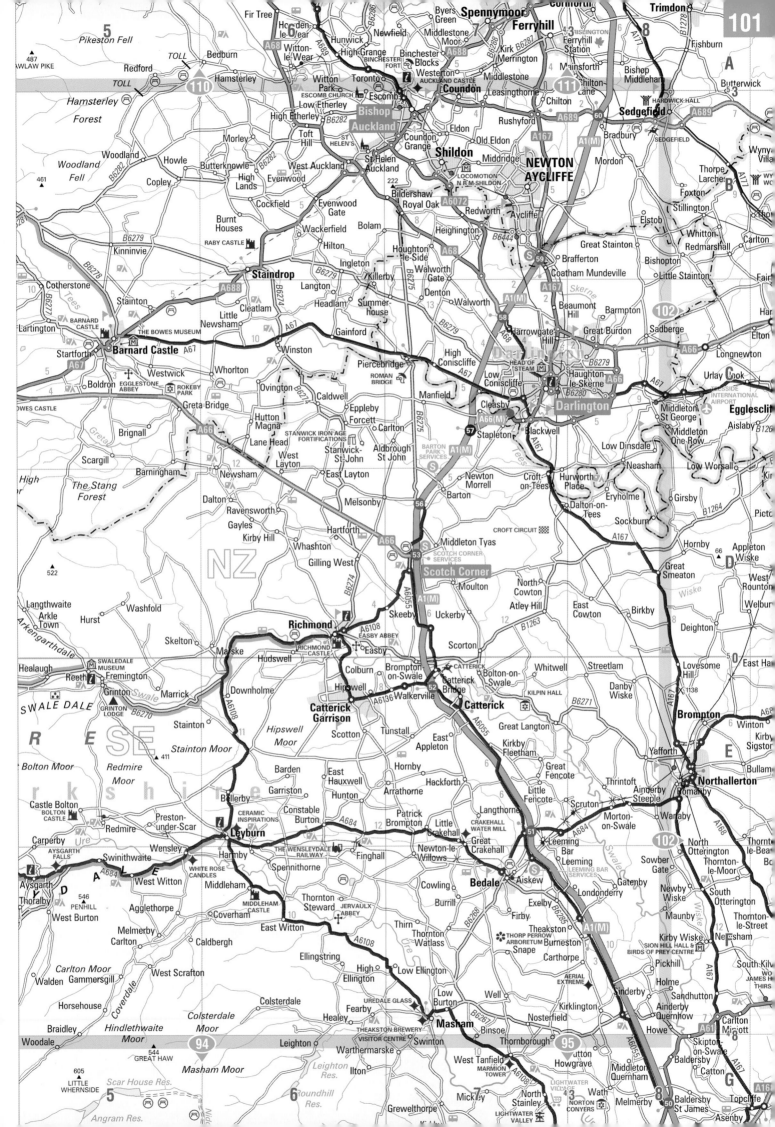

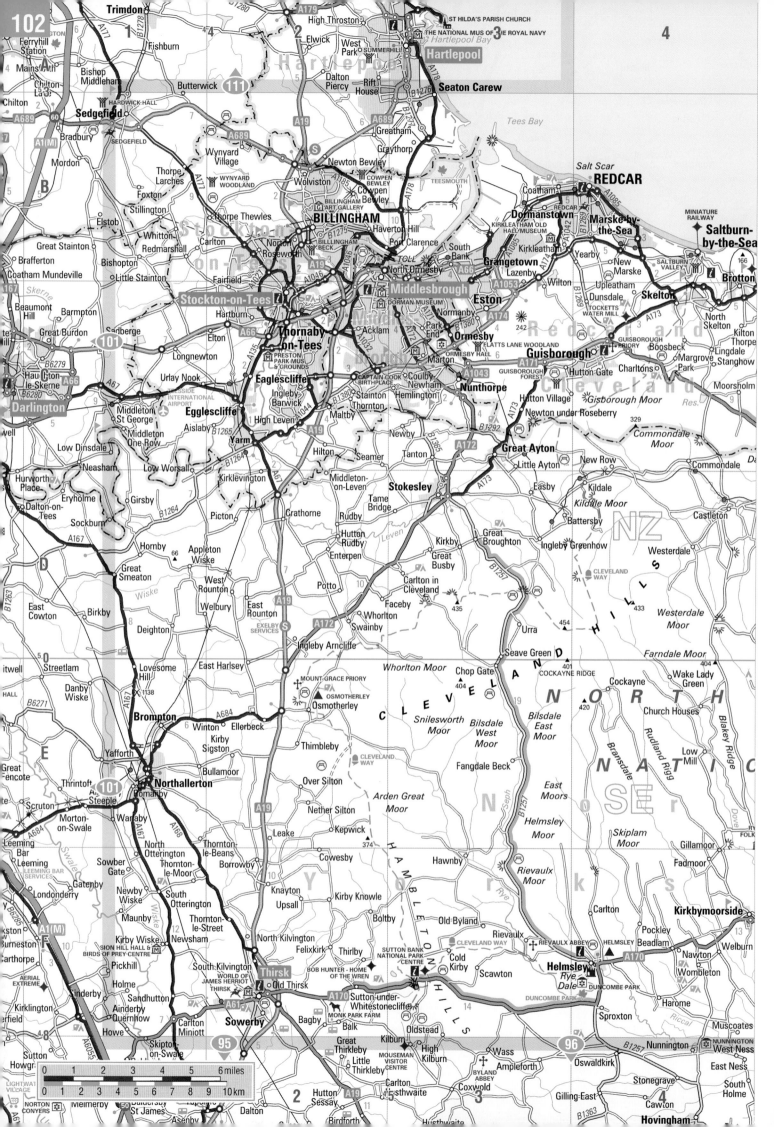

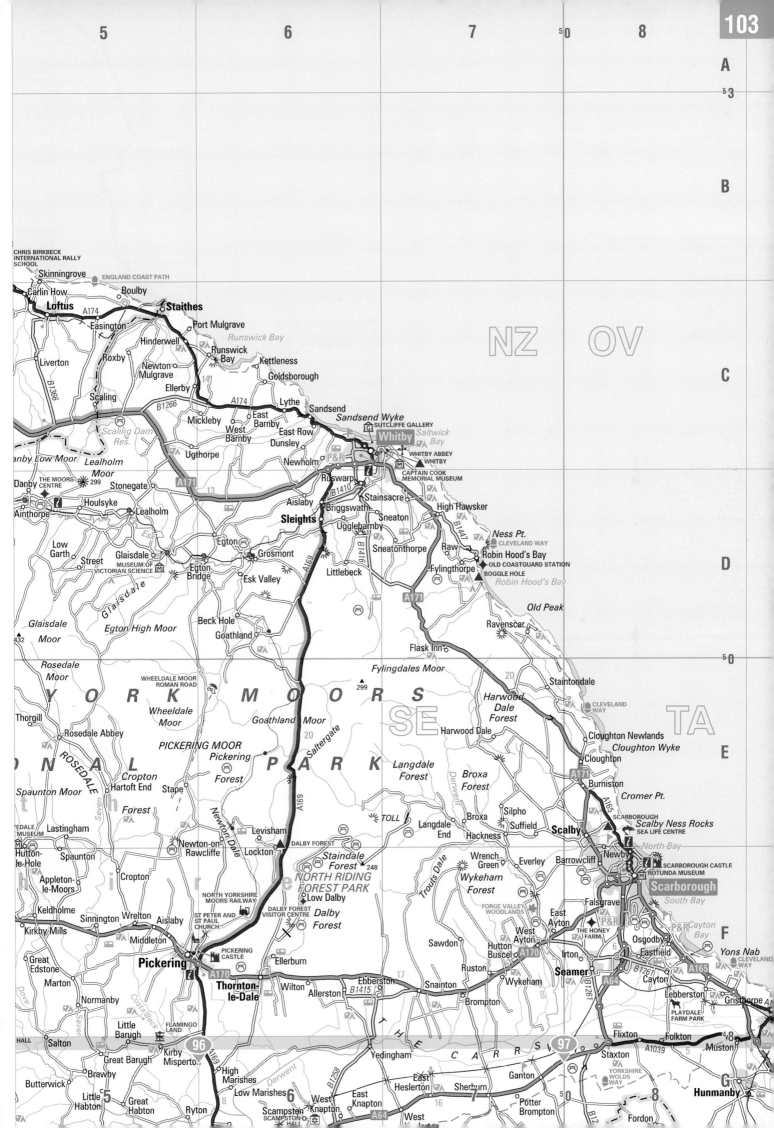

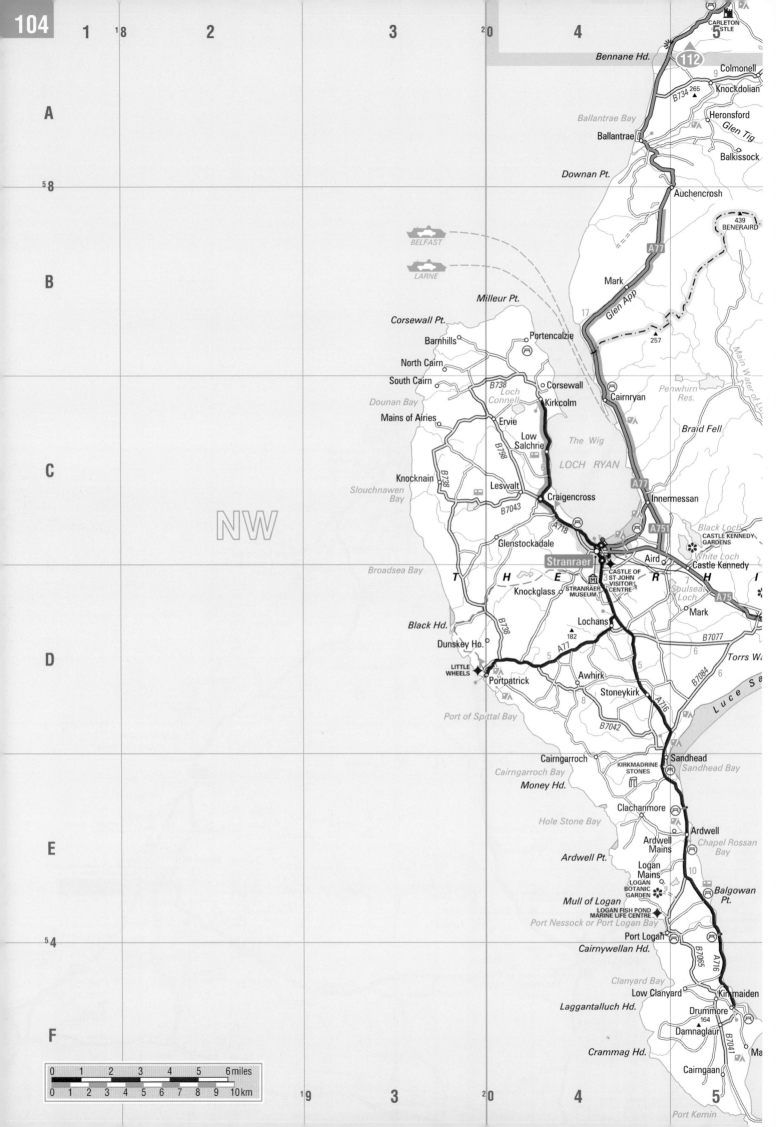

A

B

C

NW

D

E

F

1   8   2   3   0   4   5

Bennane Hd.
112
Colmonell
B734 265
Knockdolian
Heronsford
Glen Tig
Ballantrae Bay
Ballantrae
Balkissock

Downan Pt.
Auchencrosh

439
BENERAIRD

BELFAST

LARNE

Milleur Pt.
Mark
Glen App
17
Corsewall Pt.
Barnhills
Portencalzie
Penwhirn
Res.
North Cairn
257
B738
Corsewall
South Cairn
Loch
Connell
Kirkcolm
Cairnryan
Dounan Bay
Mains of Airies
Ervie
The Wig
Braid Fell
B798
Low
Salchrie
LOCH RYAN
Knocknain
Leswalt
A718
Craigencross
Innermessan
Slouchnawen
Bay
B7043
Black Loch
A77
A751
CASTLE KENNEDY
GARDENS
Glenstockadale
White Loch
Broadsea Bay
Stranraer
CASTLE OF
ST JOHN
VISITOR
CENTRE
Aird
Castle Kennedy
T   H   E   M
E
R
H   I
Knockglass
STRANRAER
MUSEUM
Soulseat
Loch
Mark
A75
Black Hd.
B738
Lochans
182
B7077
Dunskey Ho.
A77
Torrs Wa
LITTLE
WHEELS
Awhirk
5
Portpatrick
Stoneykirk
A716
B7084
6
Port of Spittal Bay
8
B7042

Cairngarroch
Sandhead
KIRKMADRINE
STONES
Sandhead Bay
Cairngarroch Bay
Money Hd.
Clachanmore
Hole Stone Bay
Ardwell
Ardwell
Mains
Chapel Rossan
Bay
Ardwell Pt.
Logan
Mains
10
LOGAN
BOTANIC
GARDEN
Balgowan
Pt.
Mull of Logan
LOGAN FISH POND
MARINE LIFE CENTRE
Port Nessock or Port Logan Bay
Port Logan
Cairnywellan Hd.
B7065
A716
Clanyard Bay
Low Clanyard
Kirkmaiden
Laggantalluch Hd.
Drummore
164
Damnaglaur
B7041
Crammag Hd.
Cairngaan
Port Kemin

0   1   2   3   4   5   6 miles
0   1   2   3   4   5   6   7   8   9   10 km

1   9   3   0   4   5

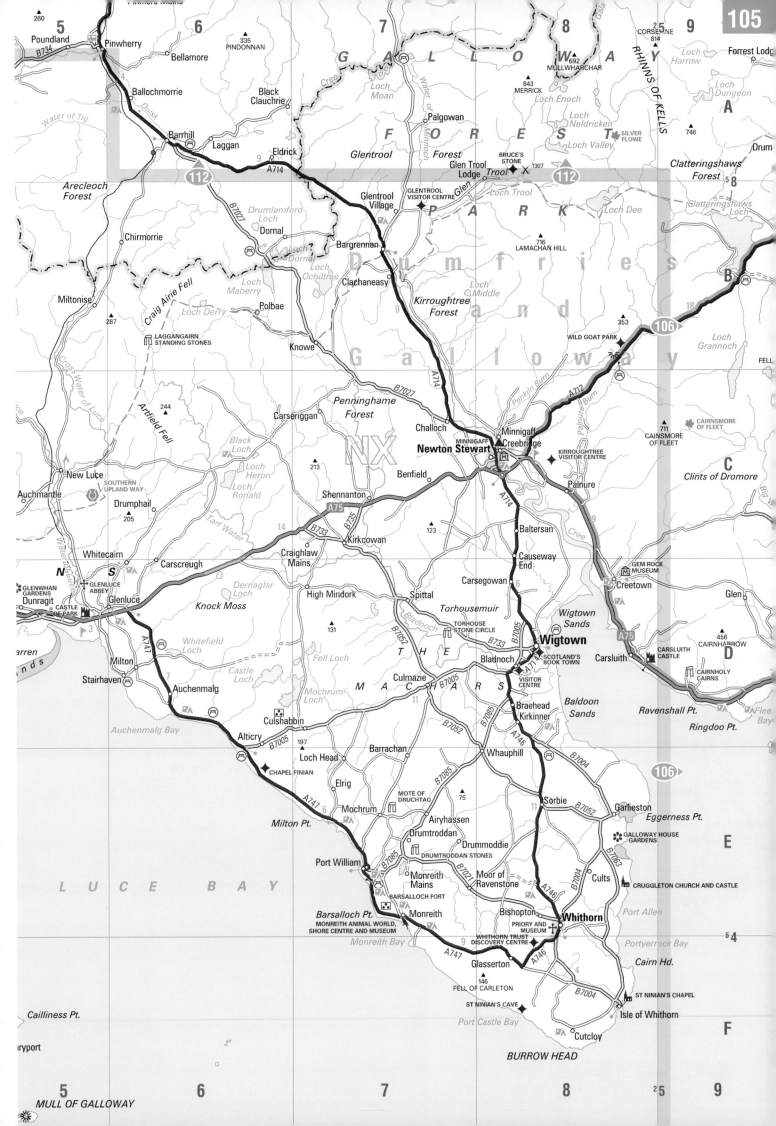

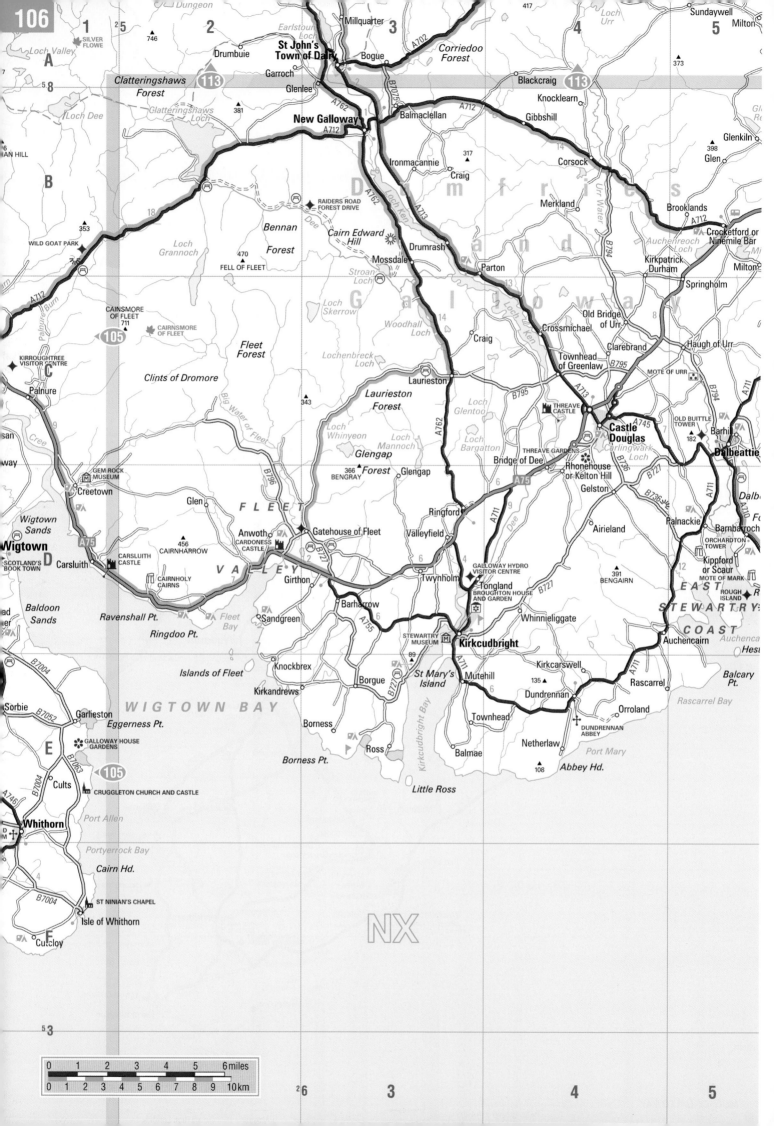

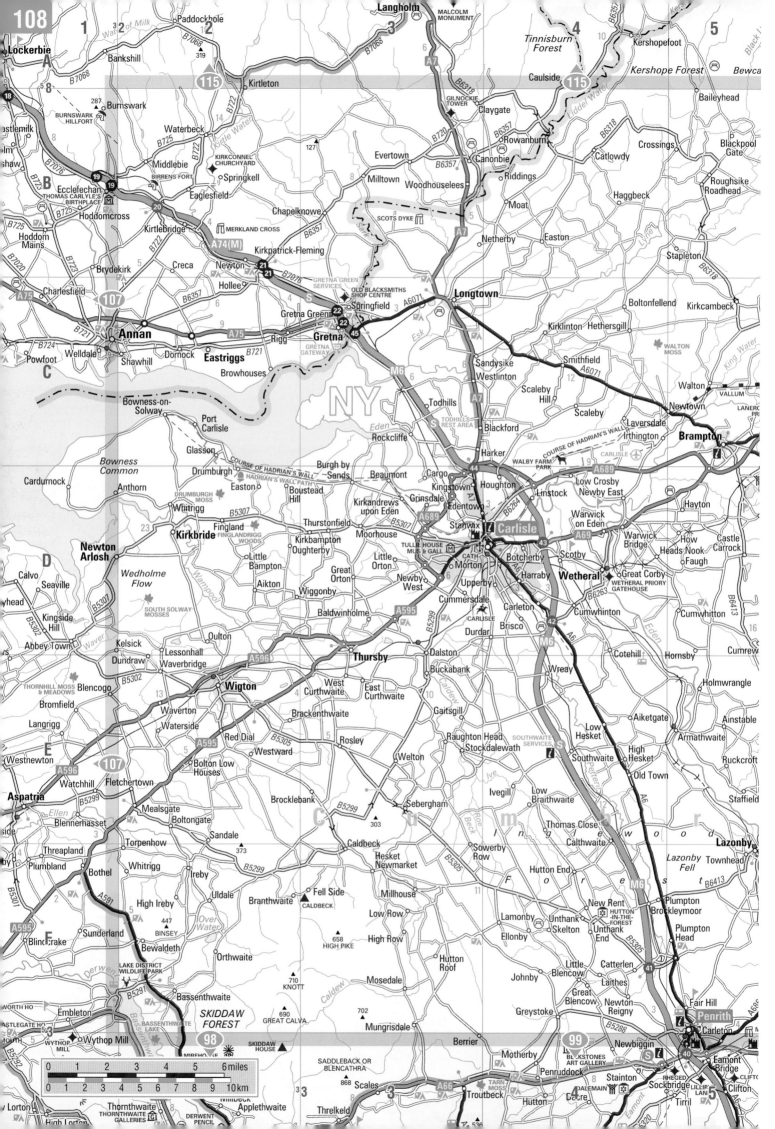

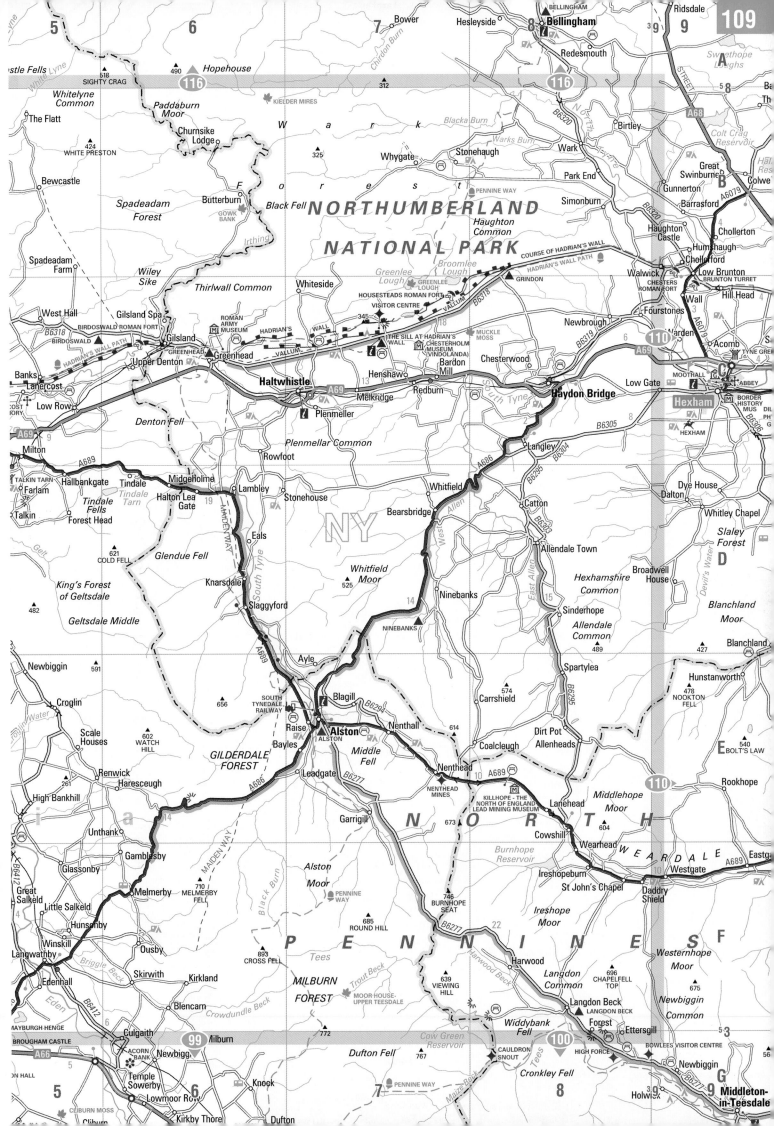

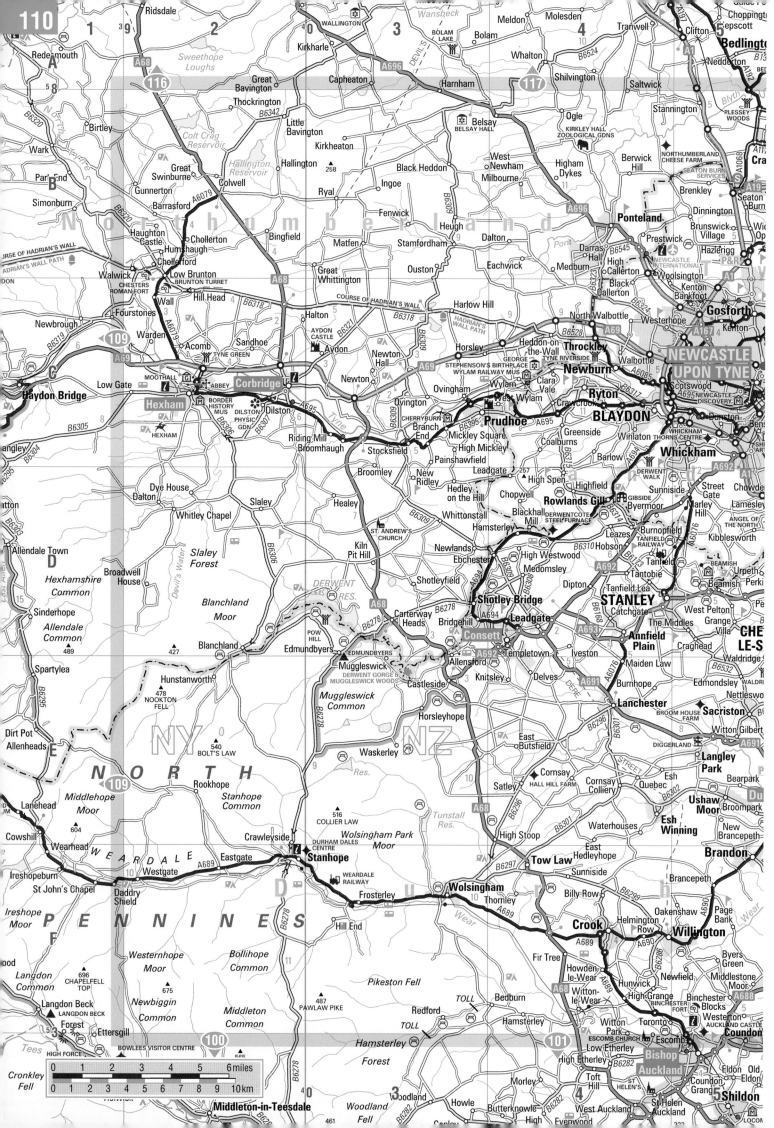

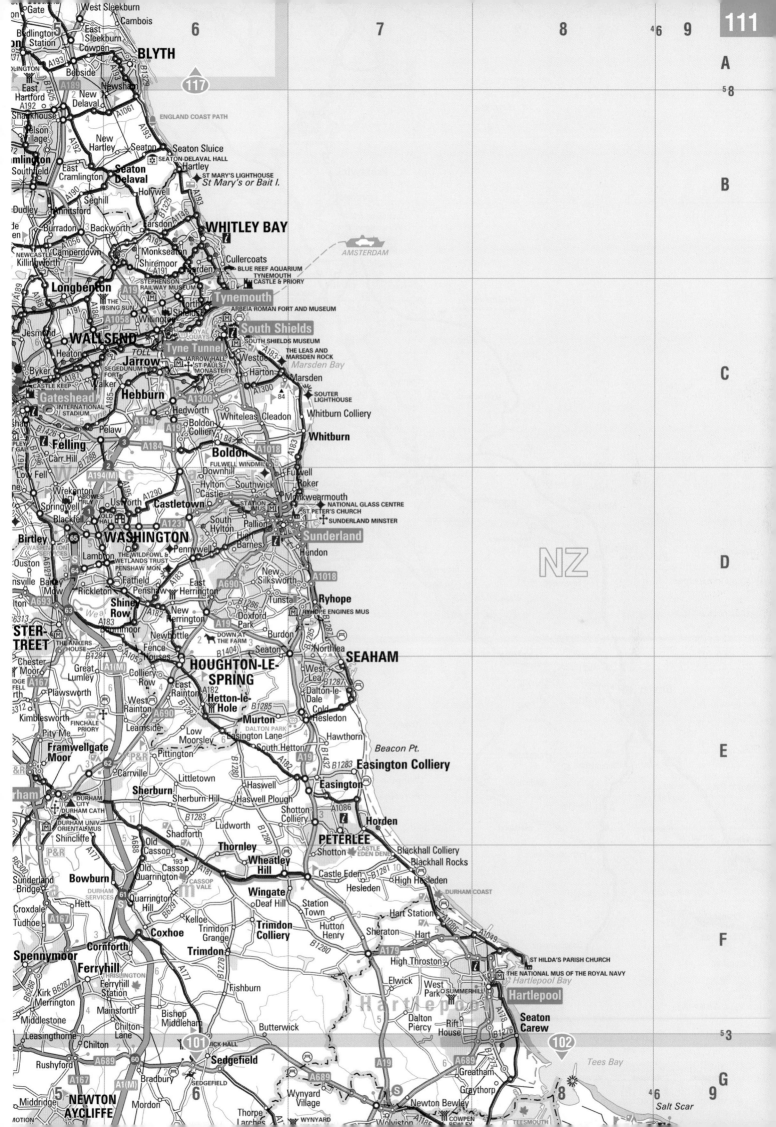

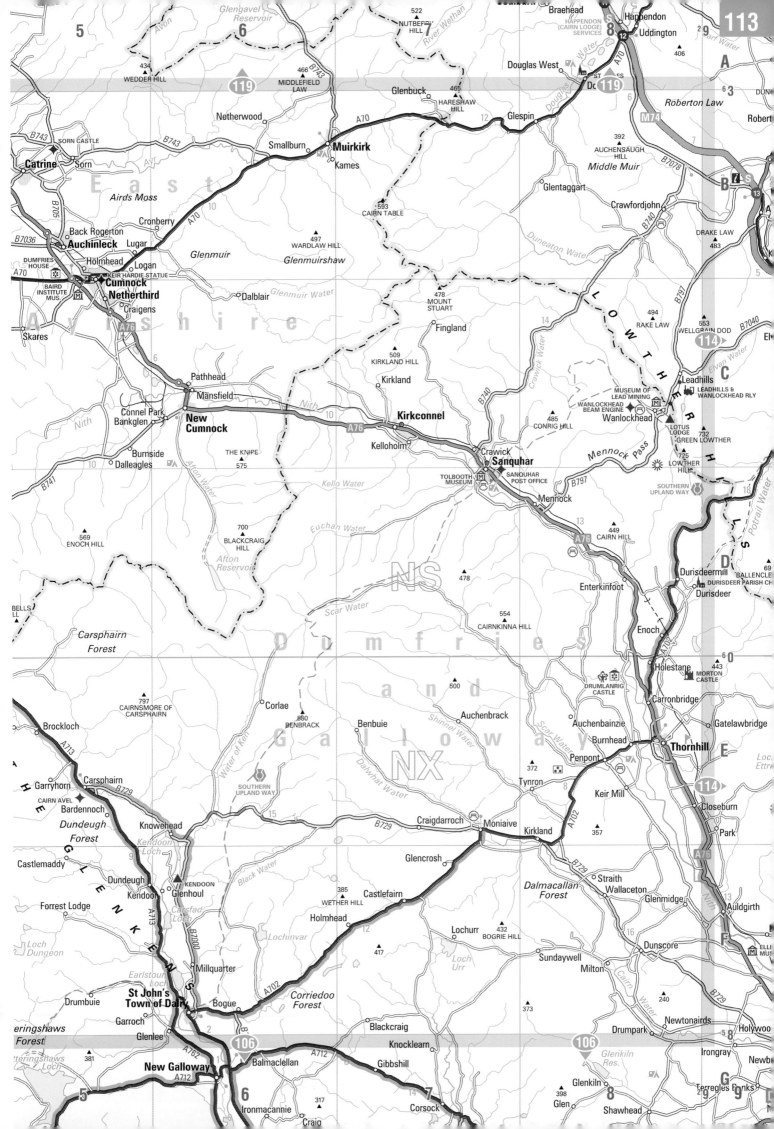

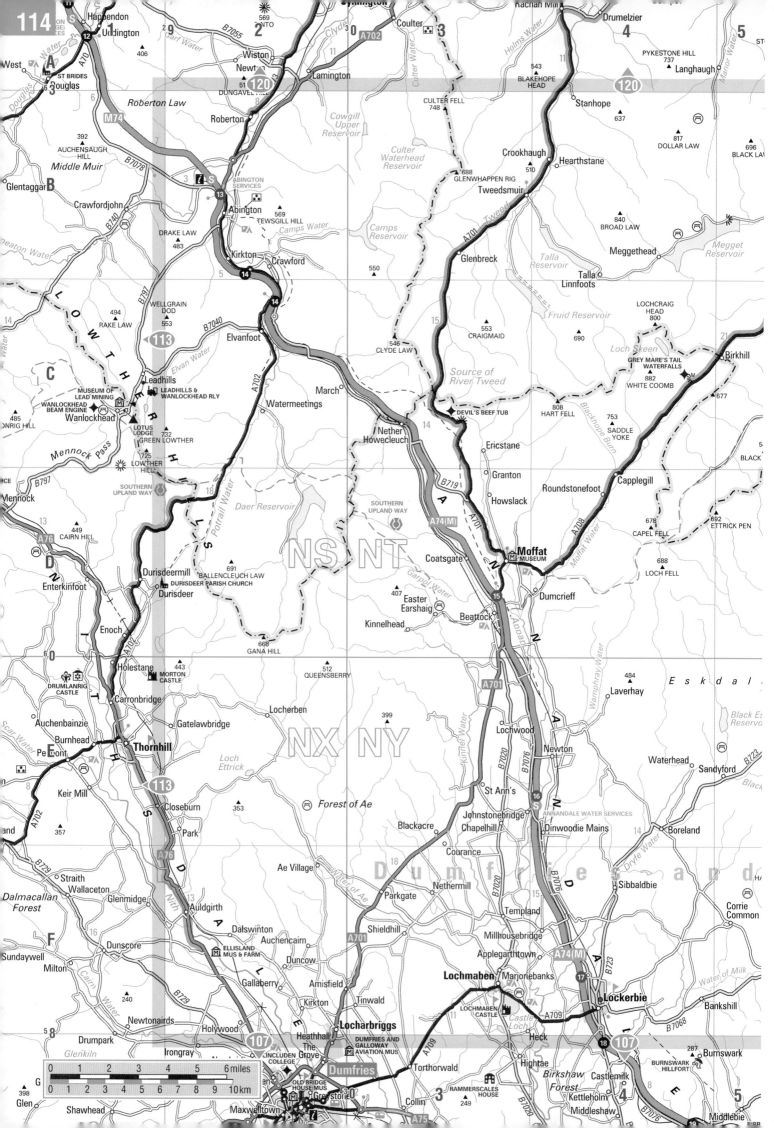

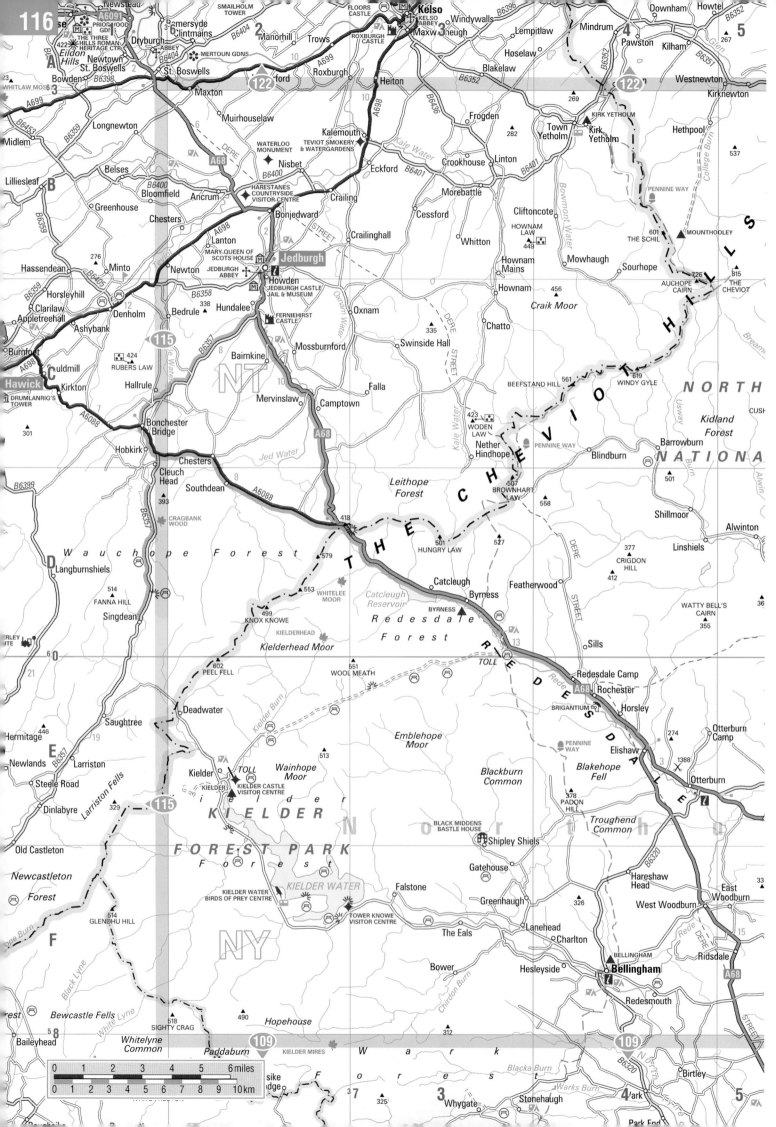

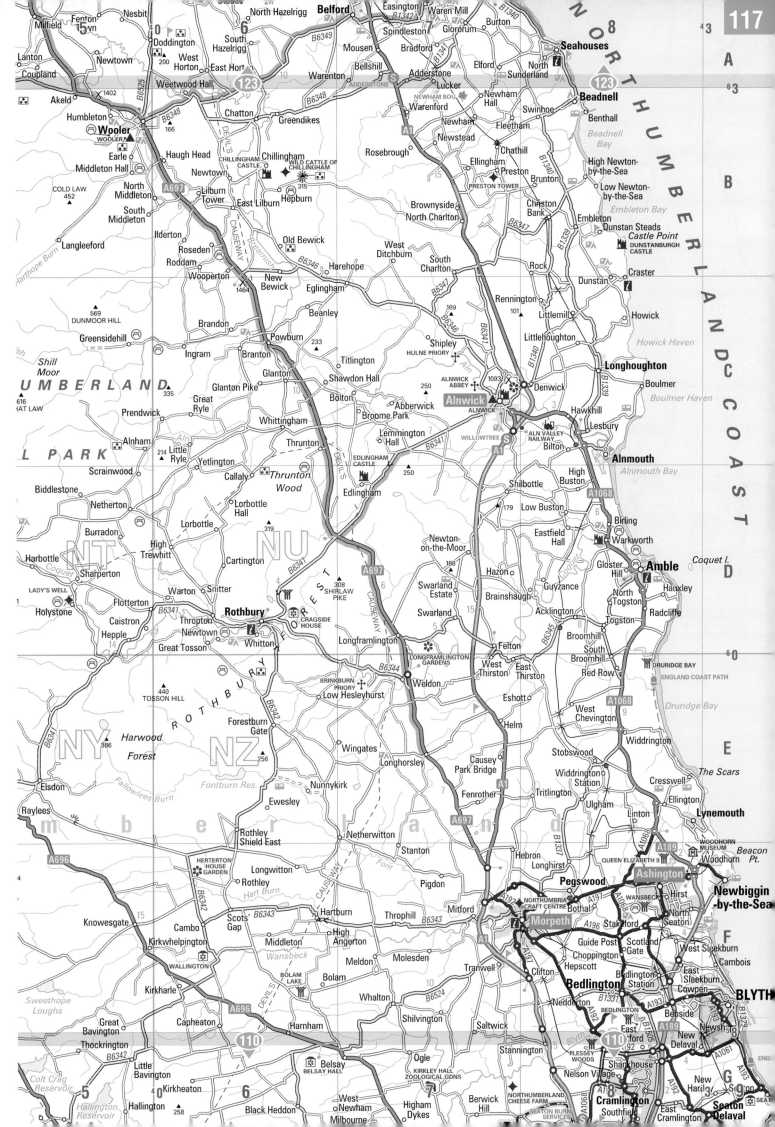

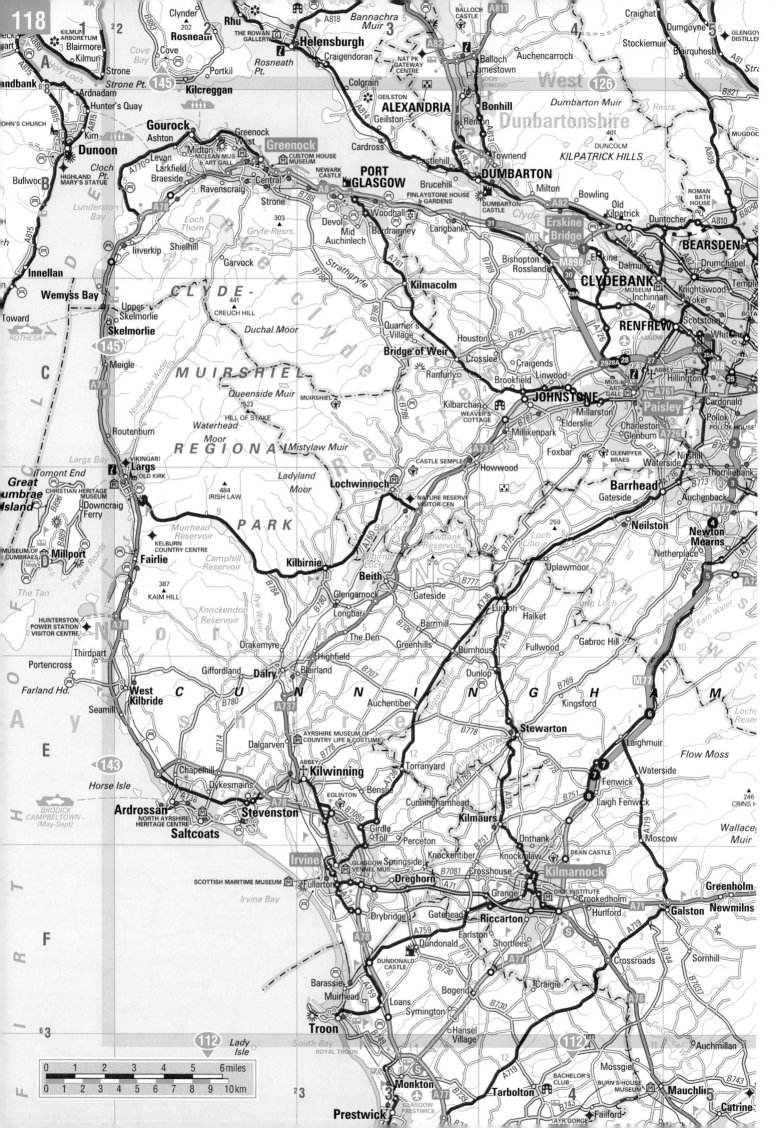

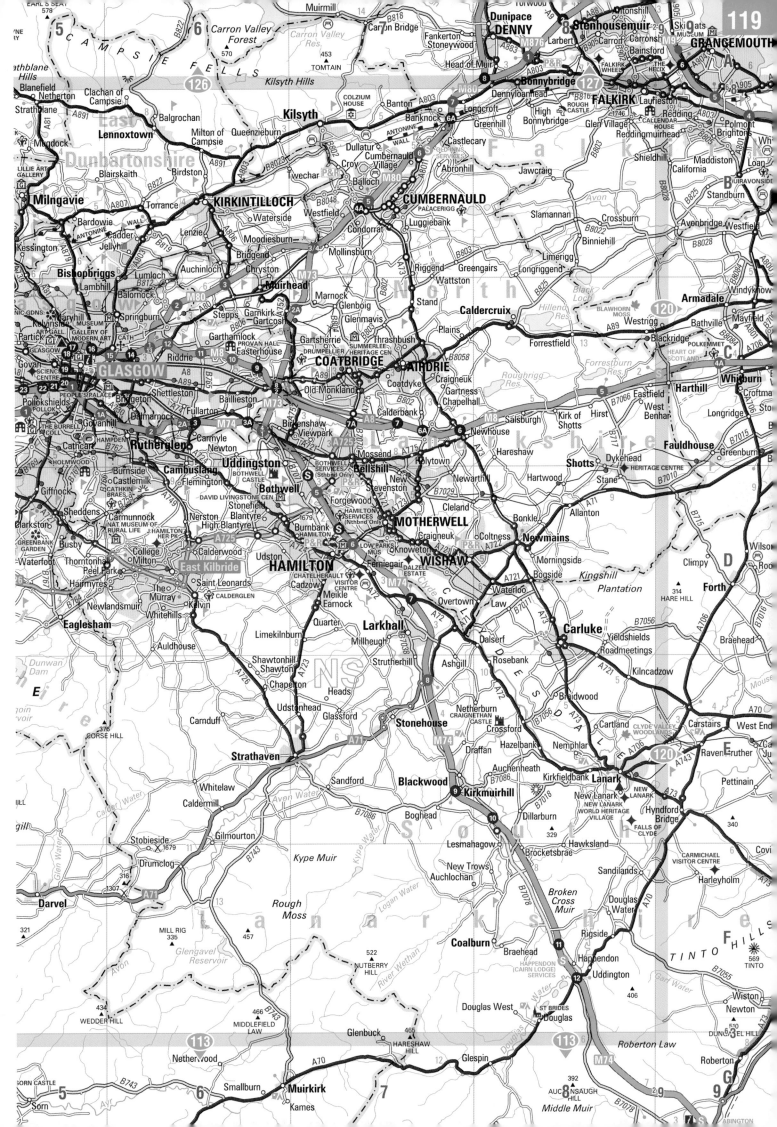

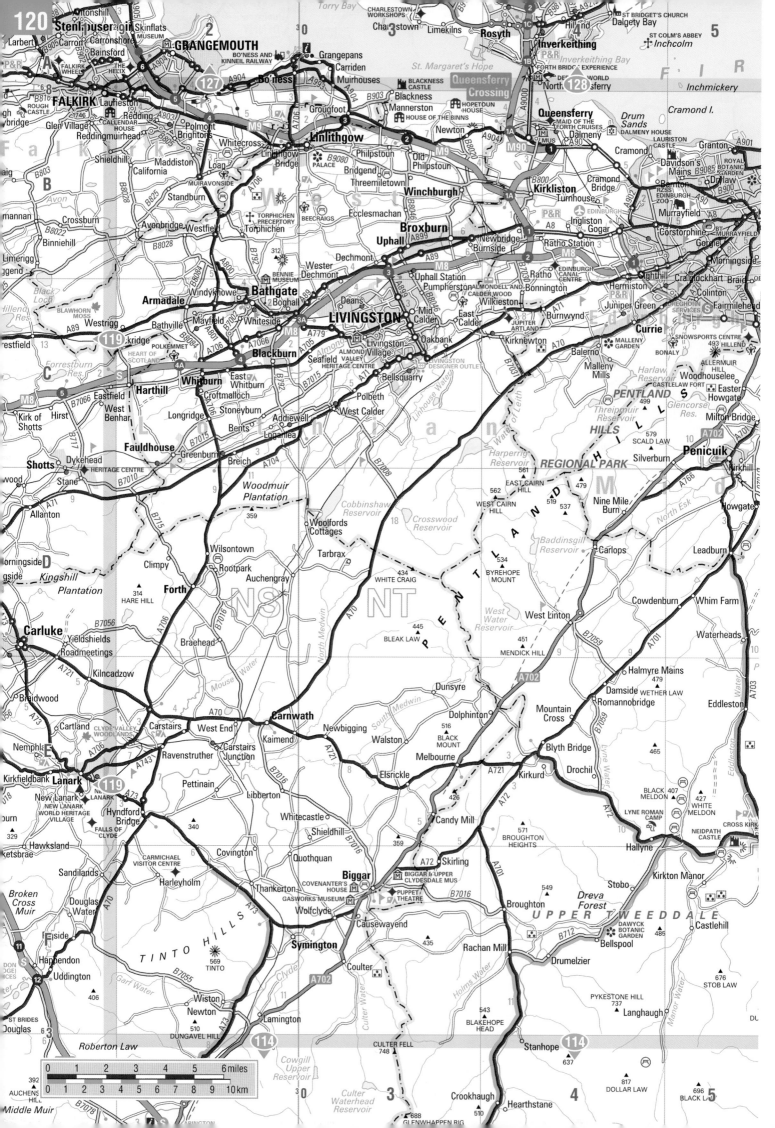

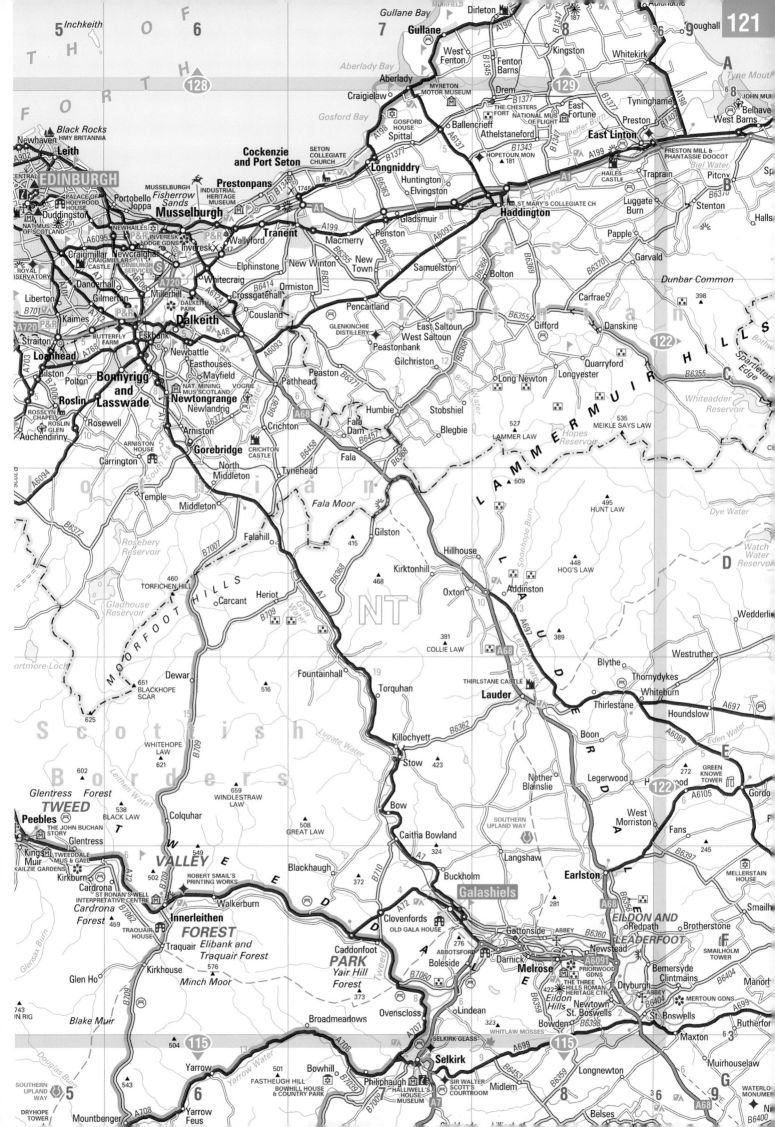

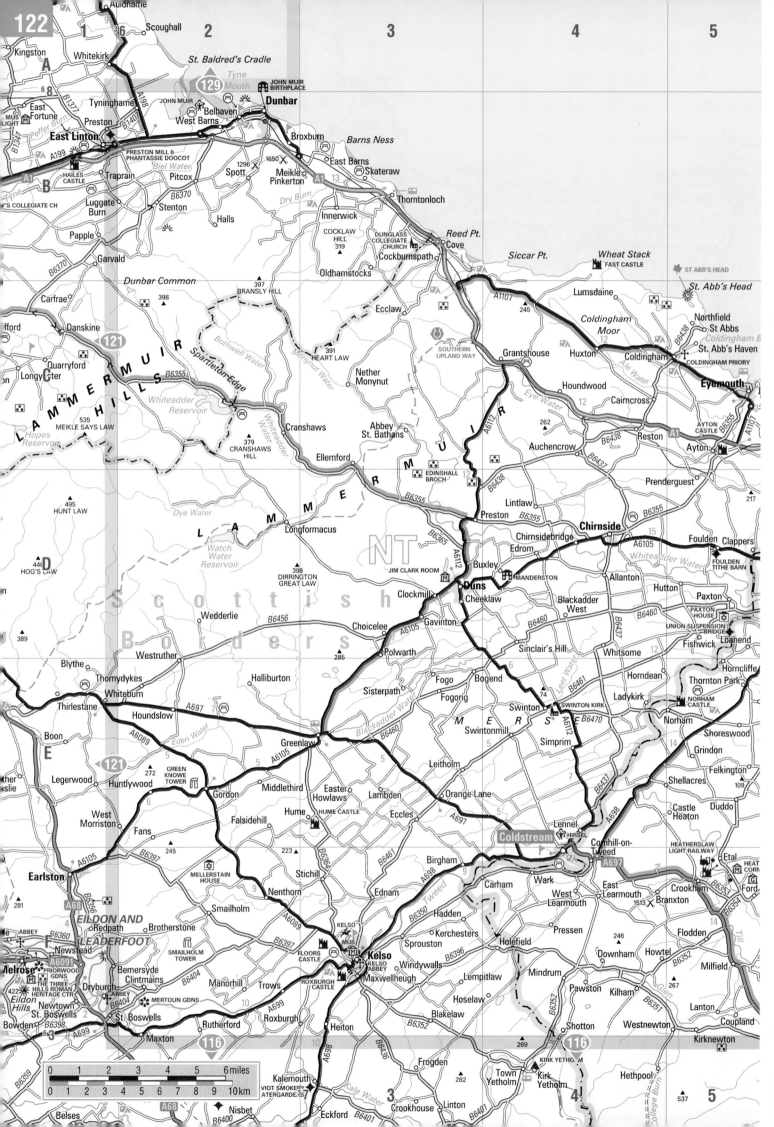

5 ⁴0 6 7 8 ⁴3 9

A

⁶8

B

Bay

C

EYEMOUTH MUSEUM

Burnmouth

Lamberton Beach

Lamberton

NU

D

1333

Highfields

Berwick-upon-Tweed

B6461

BERWICK-UPON-TWEED
BARRACKS & MAIN GUARD

BERWICK

East Ord

Tweedmouth Spittal

Tweed

Prior Park

Redshin Cove

108

Murton

Thornton

Screwerston

West Allerdean

Cheswick

Shoresdean

North Low

Goswick

E

B6354

DEVIL'S CAUSEWAY

Ancroft

Haggerston

Berrington

South Low

LINDISFARNE

Beal

Emmanuel Hd.

**Holy Island
(Lindisfarne)**

A1

82

Bowsden

Causeway
Holy
Island
Sands

Holy
Island

LINDISFARNE CASTLE

Castle Pt.

LINDISFARNE
PRIORY

HERITAGE
CENTRE

12

Barmoor
Lane End

West
Kyloe

Fenwick

Fenham

*Guile
Pt.*

Barmoor
Castle

Lowick

B6353

Farne
Islands

Staple Sound

HERSLAW
MILL

B6353

LADY WATERFORD HALL

*Kyloe
Hills*

East
Kyloe

Buckton

Elwick Ross

*Budle
Bay*

FARNE ISLANDS

Inner Sound

157

Holburn

Detchant

BAMBURGH
CASTLE

Kimmerston

Hetton
Steads

211

Middleton

Budle

Bamburgh

F

Fenton
Town

Nesbit

North Hazelrigg

Belford

Easington

Waren Mill

Burton

B1340

Doddington

200

South
Hazelrigg

B6349

Mousen

Spindlestone

Glororum

B1342

Newtown

West
Horton

East Horton

10

Warenton

Bellshill

Bradford

B1341

Elford

North
Sunderland

Seahouses

Akeld

1402

B6525

Weetwood Hall

ADDERSTONE

Adderstone

Lucker

Newham
Hall

Swinhoe

Bea 117

A697

Humbleton

117

B6348

Chatton

Greendikes

NEWHAM BOG

Warenford

Newham

Benthall

*Beadnell
Bay*

⁶3

Wooler

WOOLER

166

Haugh Head

Chillingham

WILD CATTLE OF
CHILLINGHAM

A1

Rosebrough

Fleetham

B1340

Chathill

5 ⁴0 6 7 8 ⁴3 9 G

Middleton Hall

Earle

Newtown

CHILLINGHAM
CASTLE

15

Ellingham

Preston

High Newton-
by-the-Sea

N O R T H U M B E R L A N D   C O A S T

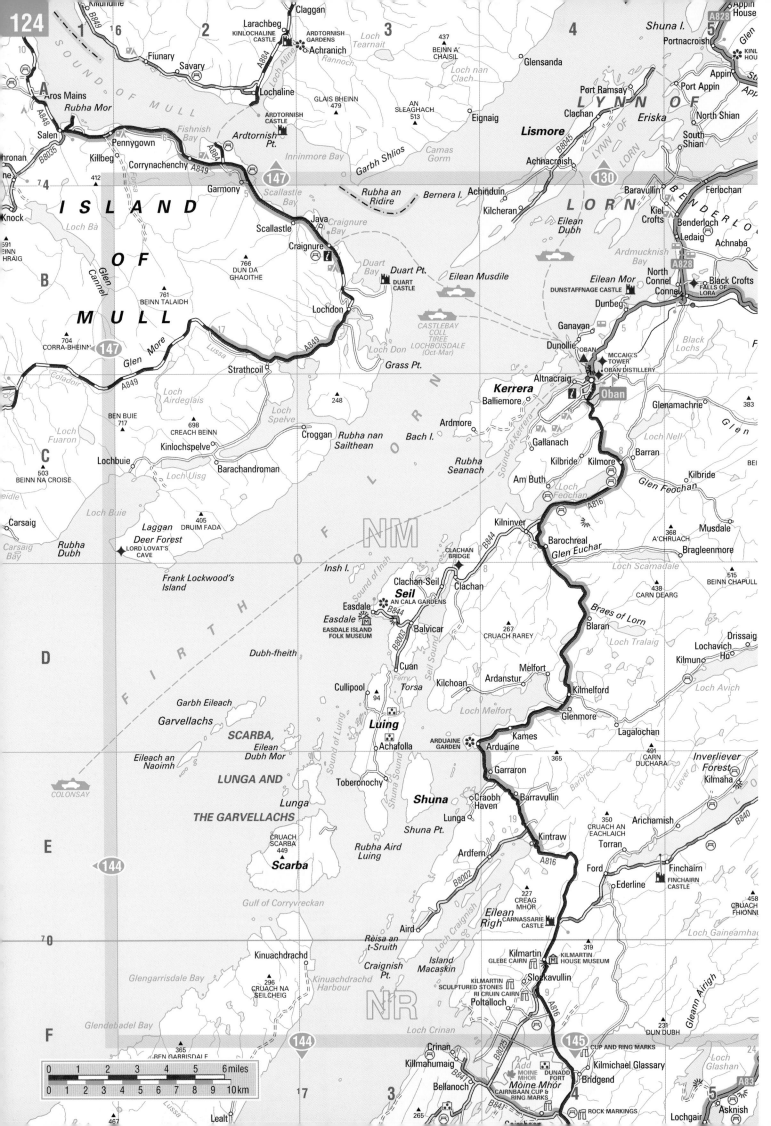

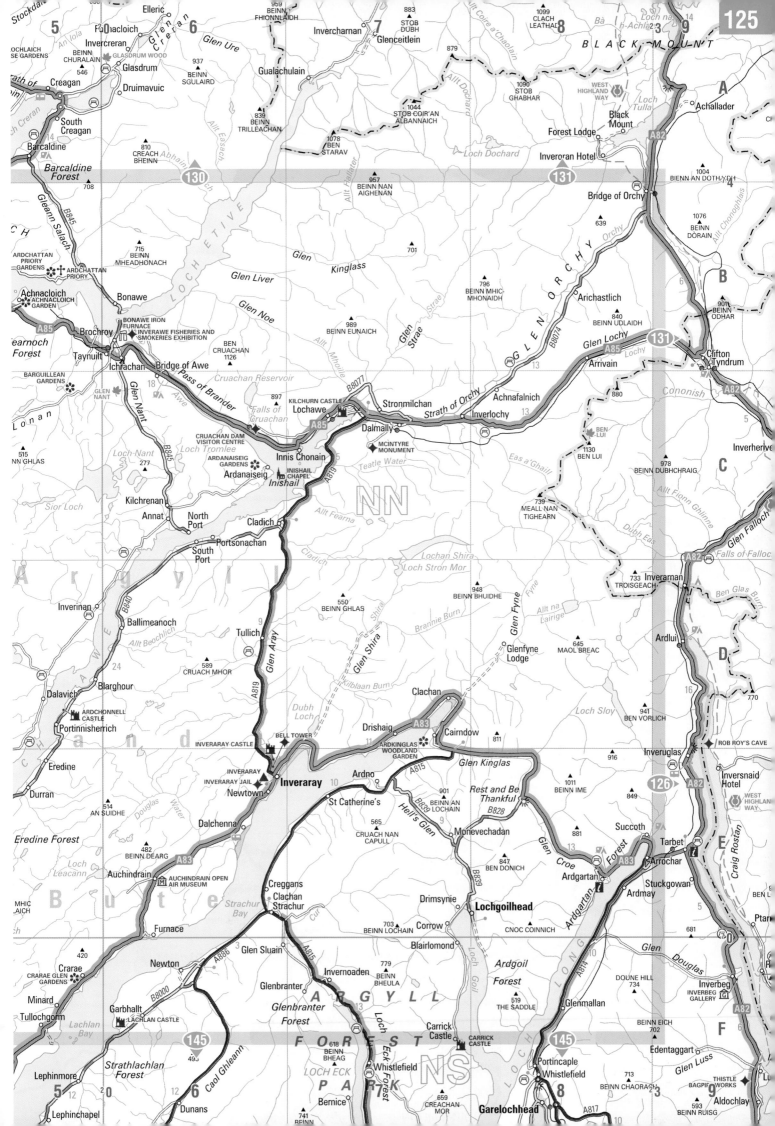

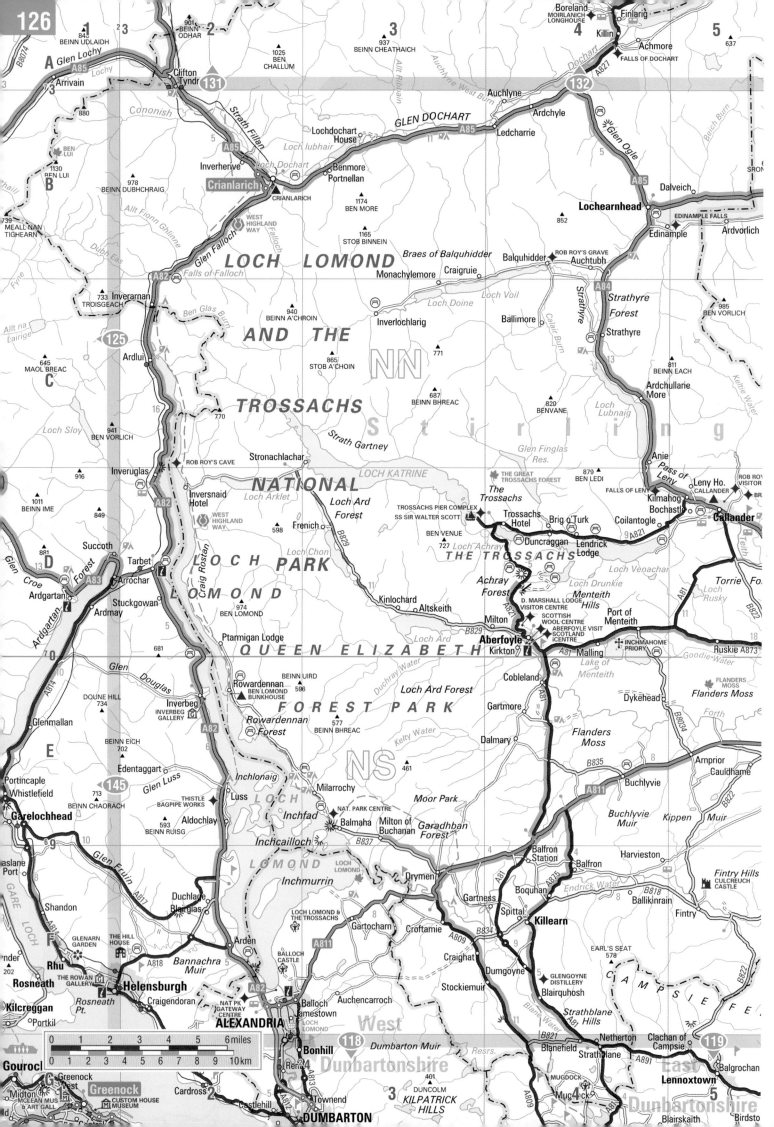

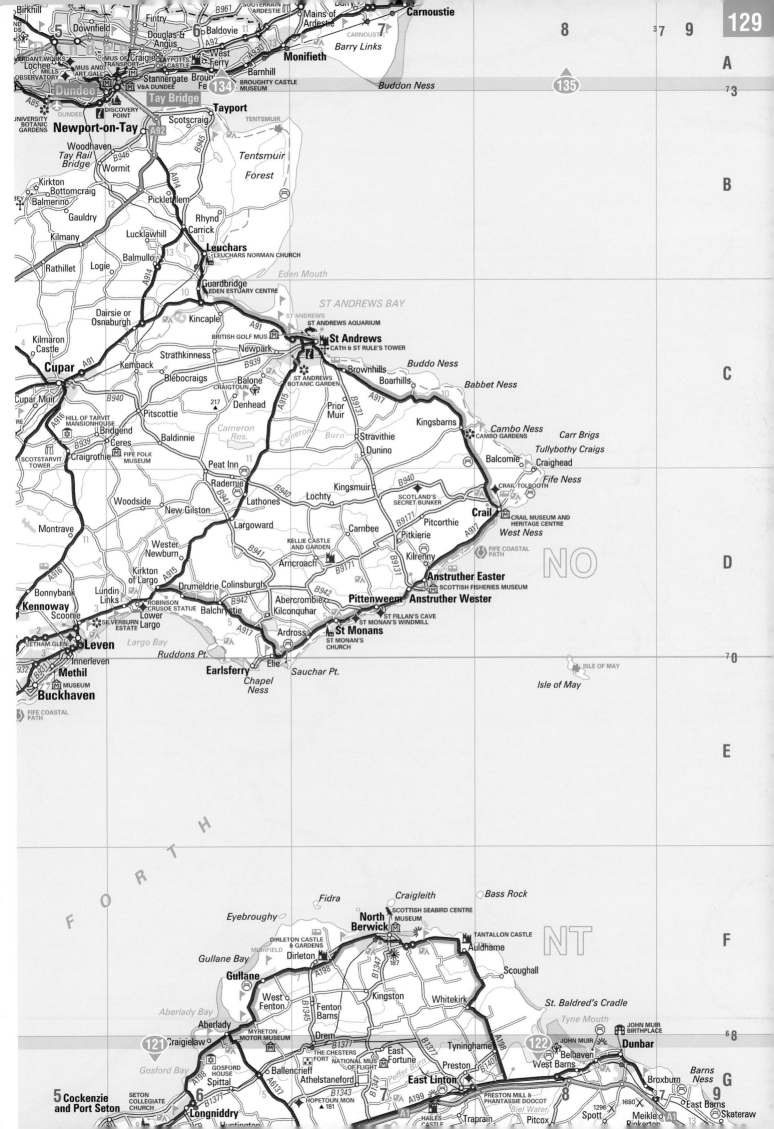

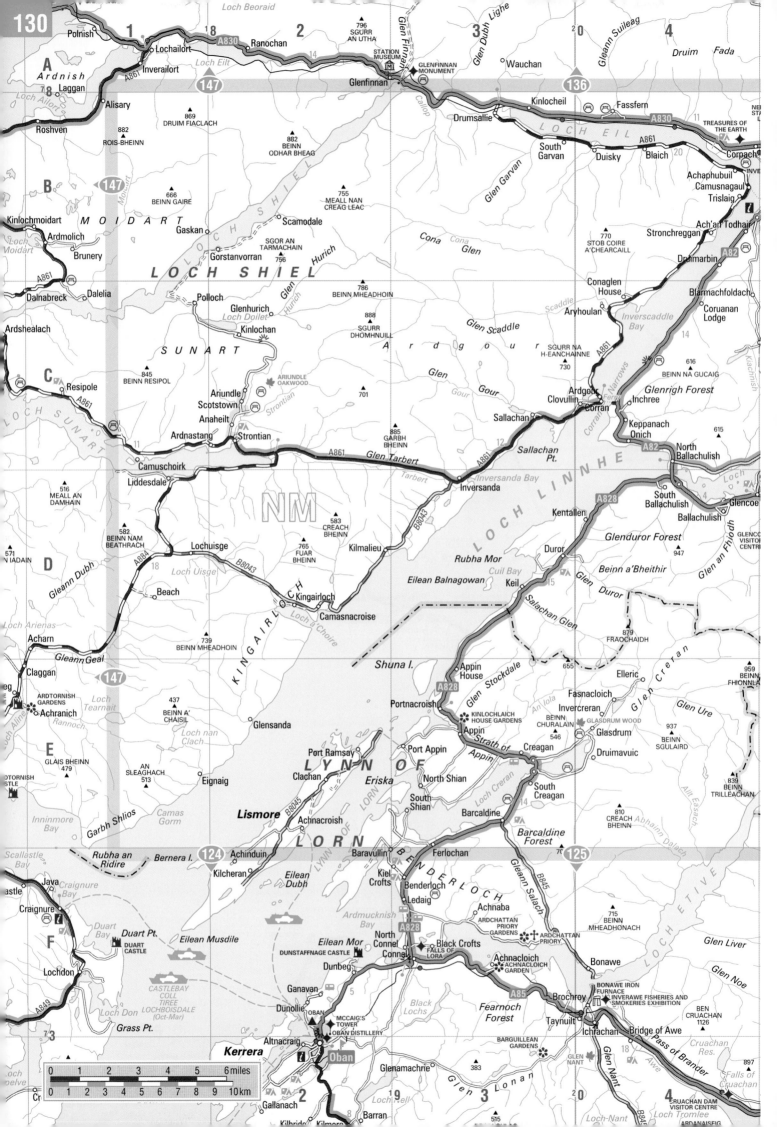

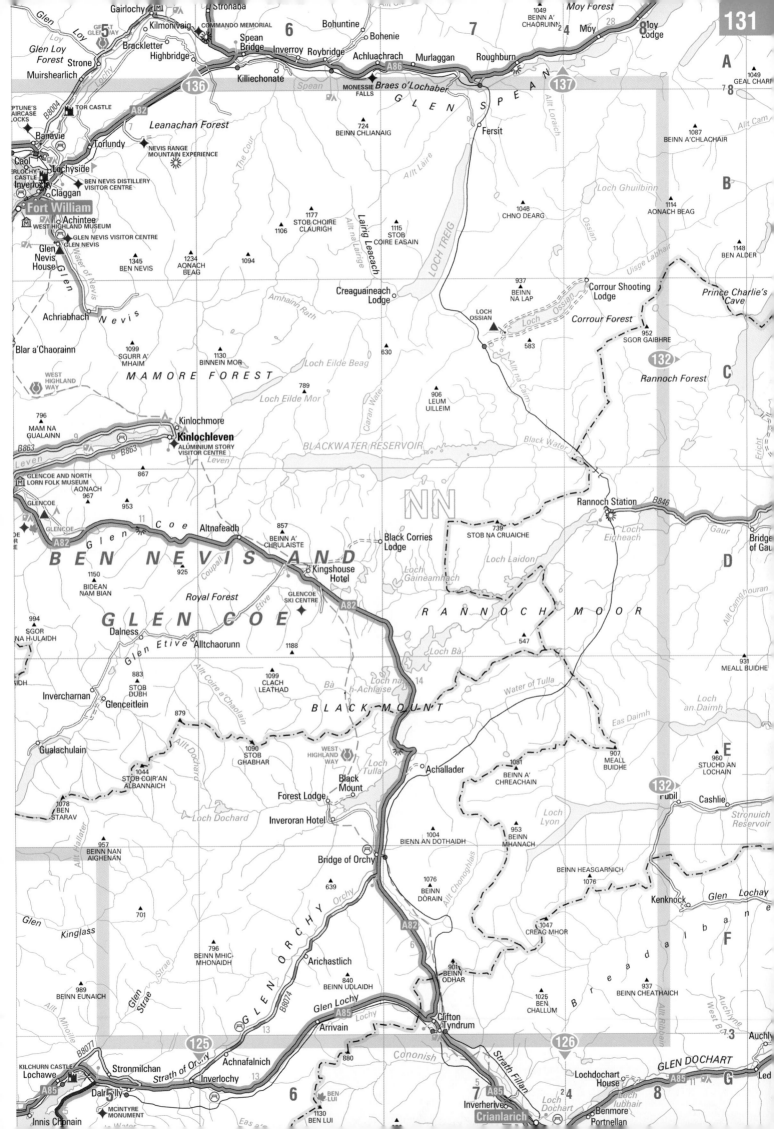

Moy 28 1 Moy Lodge 5 BEINN EILDE 911 2 3 Gaick 4 Forest
Loch Bhrodainn Falt Gharbh Ghaig

Ardverikie Forest 137 1049 GEAL CHARN Loch Pattack A 941 CARN'NA CAIM 138 Loch an Duin

A 7 8 Loch Pattack Ben Alder Lodge 774 CREAGAN MOR Cama Choire Sronphadruig Lodge Dail-na-Mine Forest 816 SRON A'CHLEIRICH

1087 BEINN A'CHLACHAIR 917 936 A'BHUIDHEANACH BHEAG FOREST

Allt Cam Allt a'Chaoil-réidhe 1114 AONACH BEAG 934 803 THE SOW OF ATHOLL Dalnacardoch Forest N Dalnacardoch Lodge

B Loch Ghuilbinn Loch a' Bhealaich Bheithe BEINN UDLAMAIN Dalnaspidal Lodge 17 A9 A Dalnacardoch Lodge T H

1148 BEN ALDER Corrievarkie Lodge Dalnaspidal Forest 775 MEALL NA LEITREACH I Eig
Corrour Shooting Lodge 855 Loch Con P GLEN GARRY A9

Corrour Forest Talla Bheith Forest M Loch Errochty Dalchalloch B847 Trinafour 10 Errochty Water GLEN ERROCHT

952 SGOR GAIBHRE 131 841 BEINN MHOLACH 612 A Tummel Forest 477

Rannoch Forest NN 891 BEINN A'CHUALLAICH B847 Tummel Bridge B8019

G Bridge of Ericht Killichonan B846 Craiganor Lodge Kinloch Rannoch Dunalastair 4 Foss

Rannoch Station B846 LOCH RANNOCH 19 Carie Inverhadden Dunalastair Water Loch Kinardochy

Loch Eigheach Bridge of Gaur Finnart Black Wood of Rannoch TAY FOR

D Camghouran Rannoch 1083 SCHIEHALLION B846

Forest LOCH RANNOCH AND 1042 CARN MAIRG

GLEN LYON Keltneyburn

931 MEALL BUIDHE 745 MEALL A'MHUIC 1029 CARN GORM Invervar St Fillan's Church & Fortingall Yew Taymouth Castle

Loch an Daimh GLEN LYON GALLERY Camusvrachan Lyon Fortingall Kenmore

E 907 MEALL BUIDHE 960 STUCHD AN LOCHAIN Gallin Innerwick Bridge of Balgie 1118 Fearnan Remony Scottish Crann

131 Pubil Cashlie Stronuich Reservoir 780 Lawers Burn Acharn Falls of Acharn

Loch Lyon BEINN HEASGARNICH 1076 Kenknock Glen Lochay 1214 BEN LAWERS Lawers 25 716 BEINN BHREAC Quaich

MEALL NAN TARMACHAN 1043 Loch na Lairige Carie Ardtalnaig 888 Gleann a'Chilleine

F BEINN CHEATHAICH 937 Morenish Milton Morenish Ardeonaig 637 879 CREAG UCHDAG

Falls of Lochay and Fish Lift Boreland MOIRLANICH LONGHOUSE Finlarig Loch Lednock Reservoir 931 BEN CHONZIE

Killin Achmore Falls of Dochart

126 Auchlyne 127

Ardchyle A85 Invergeldie Glen Lednock

0 1 2 3 4 5 6 miles
0 1 2 3 4 5 6 7 8 9 10 km 2 5 Glen Ogle 6 3 672 SRON MHOR 13 4

Benmore Portnellan Dochart

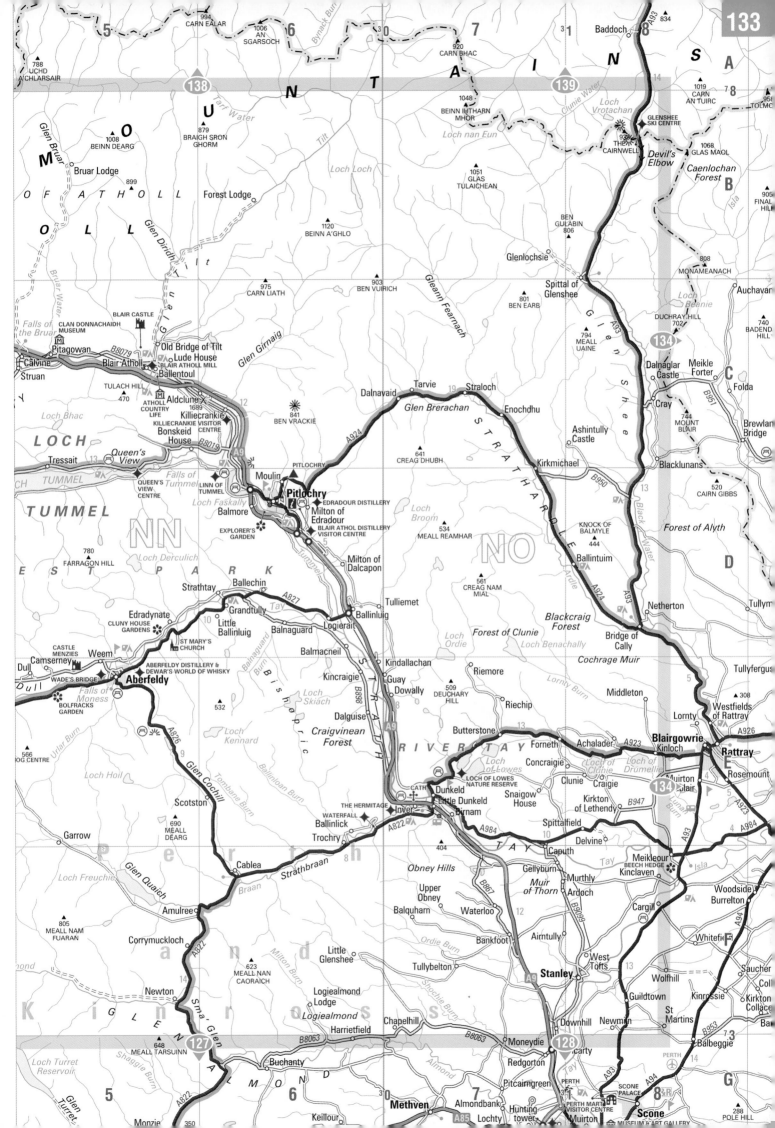

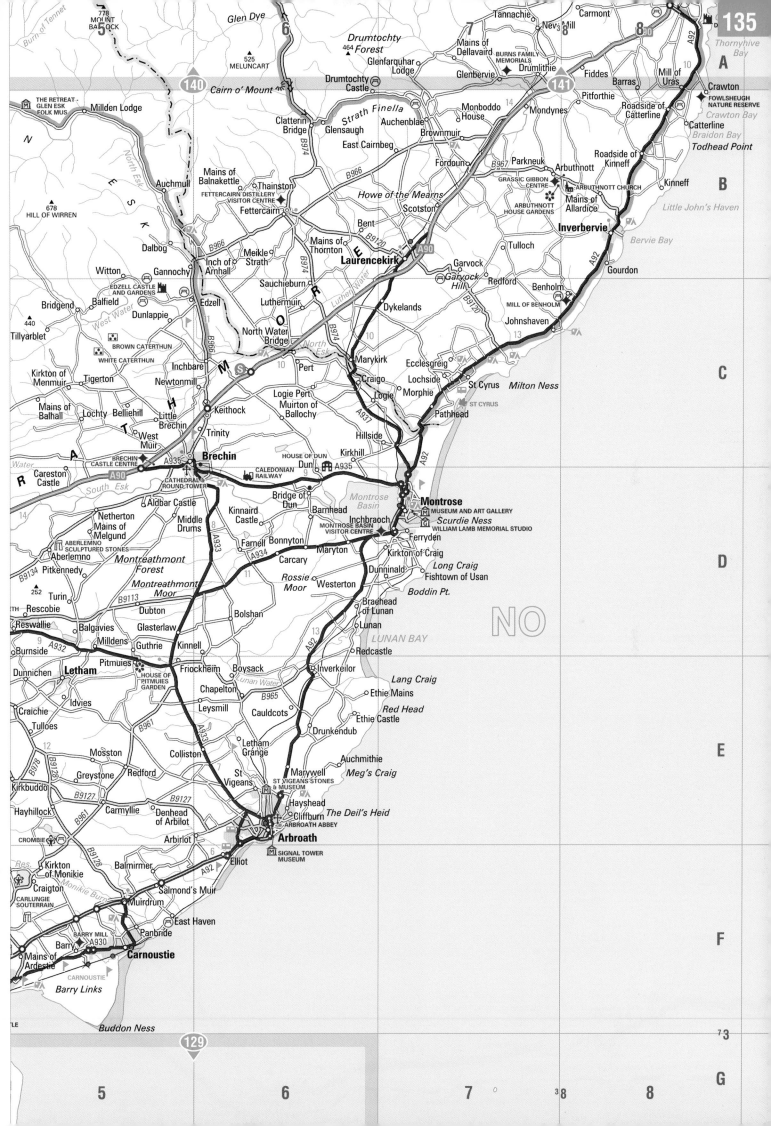

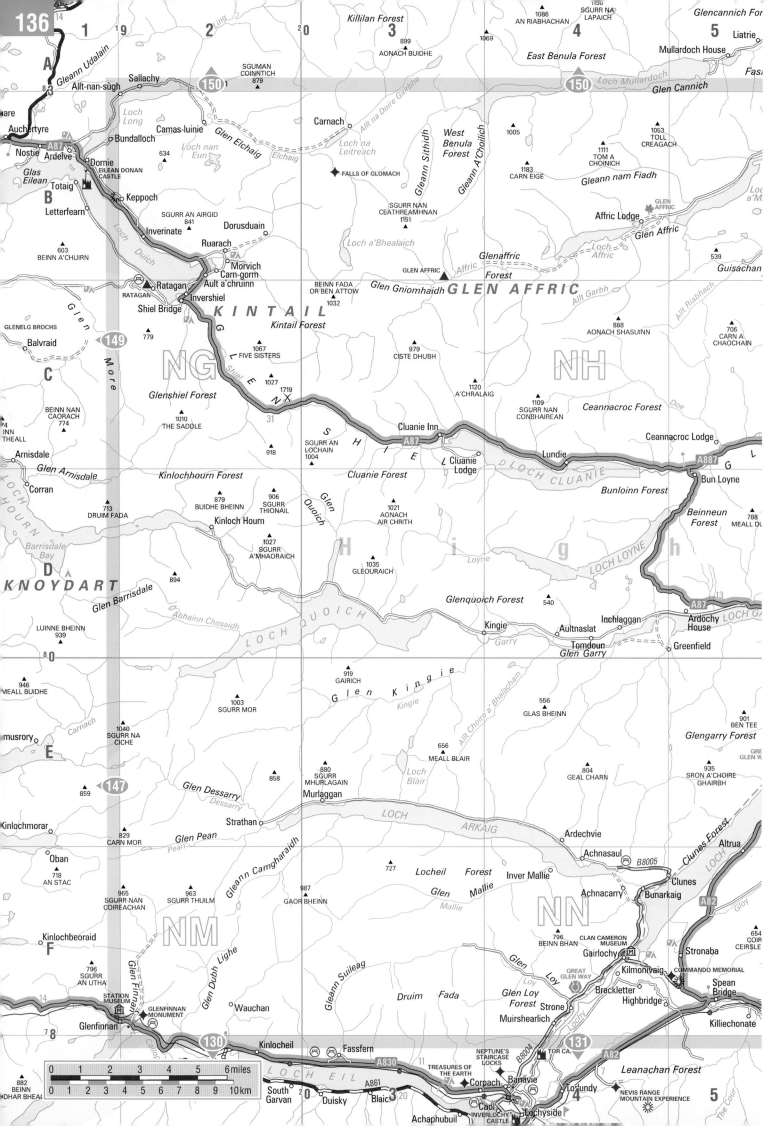

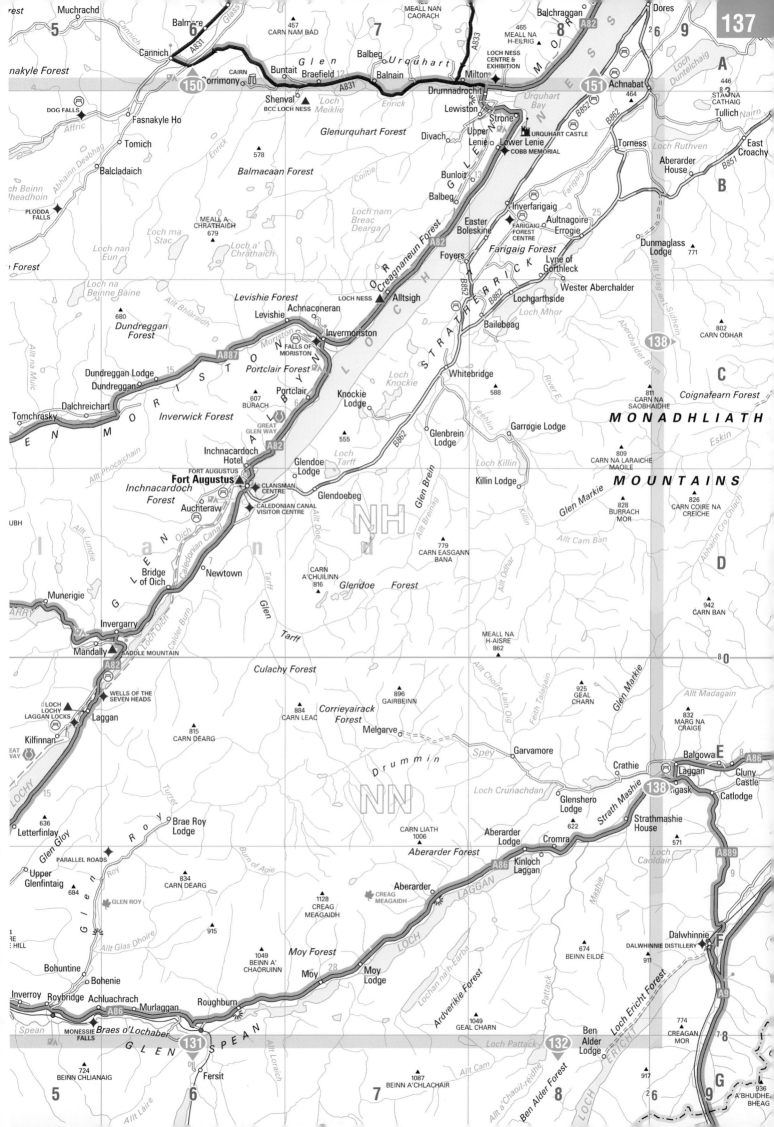

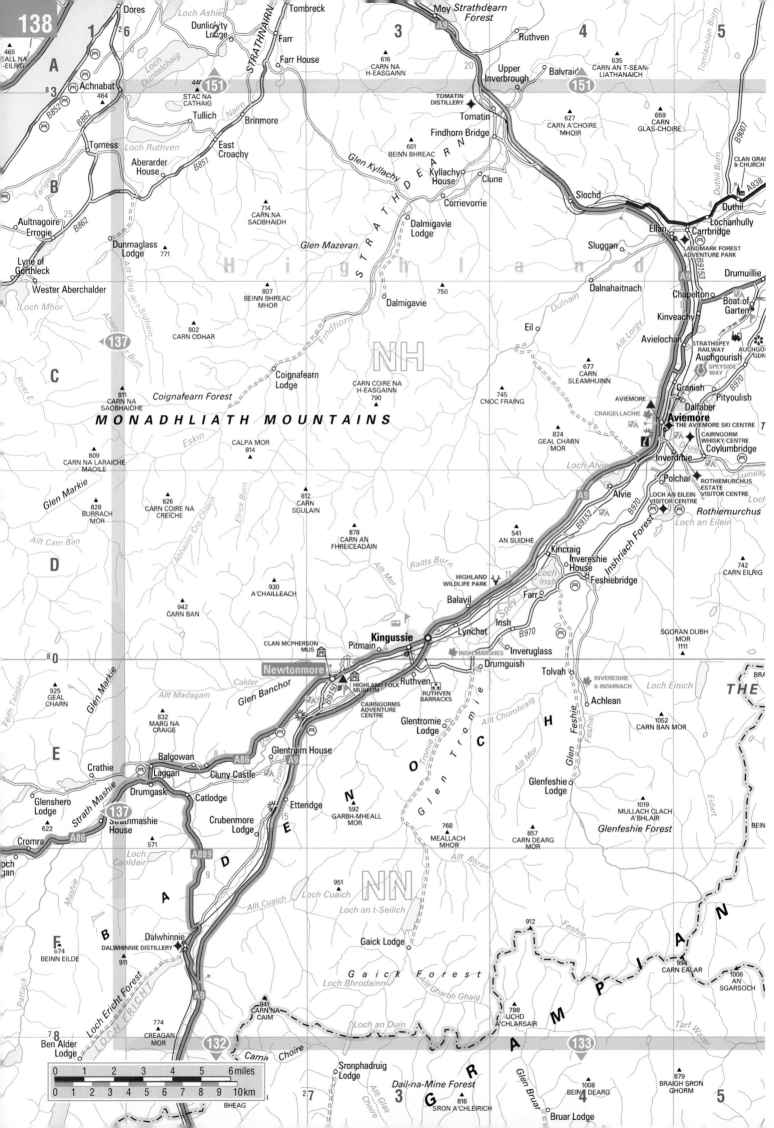

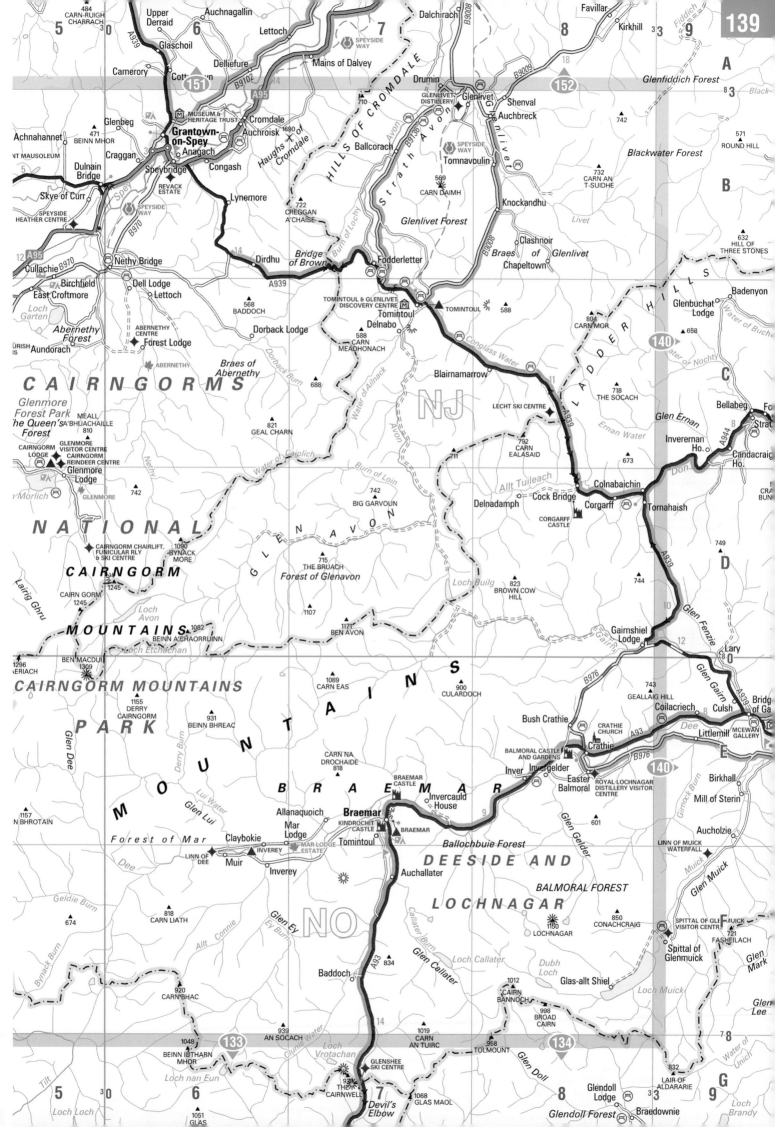

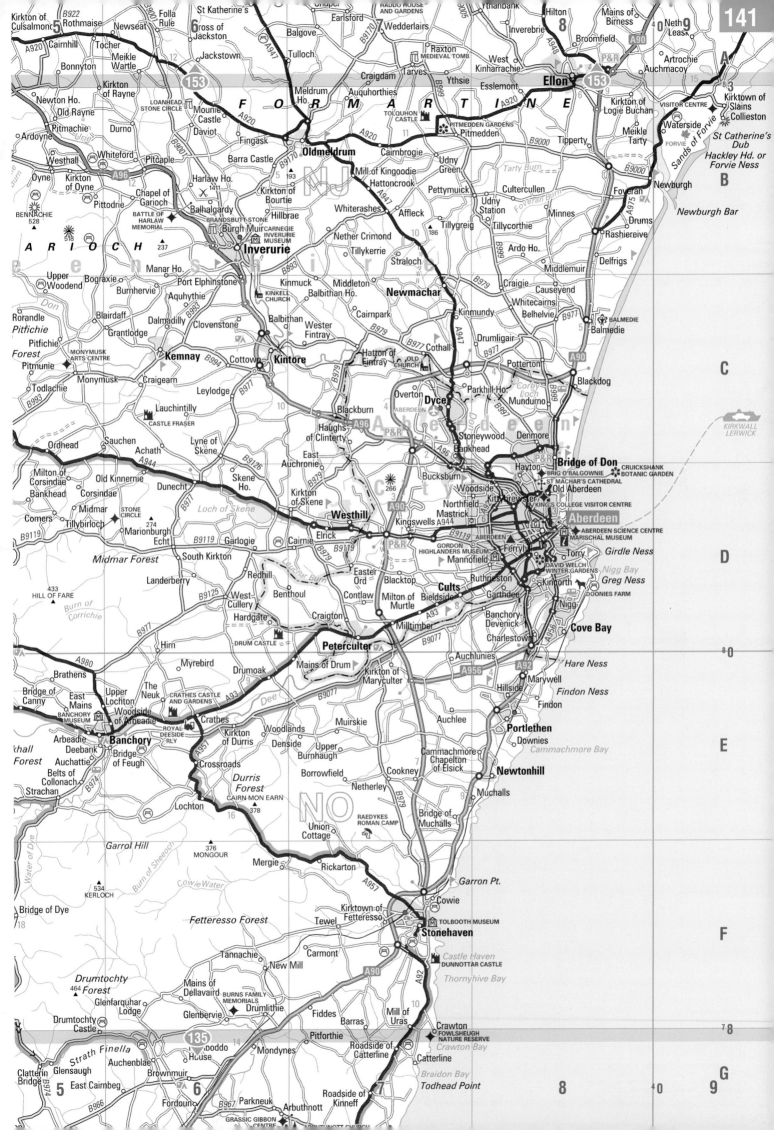

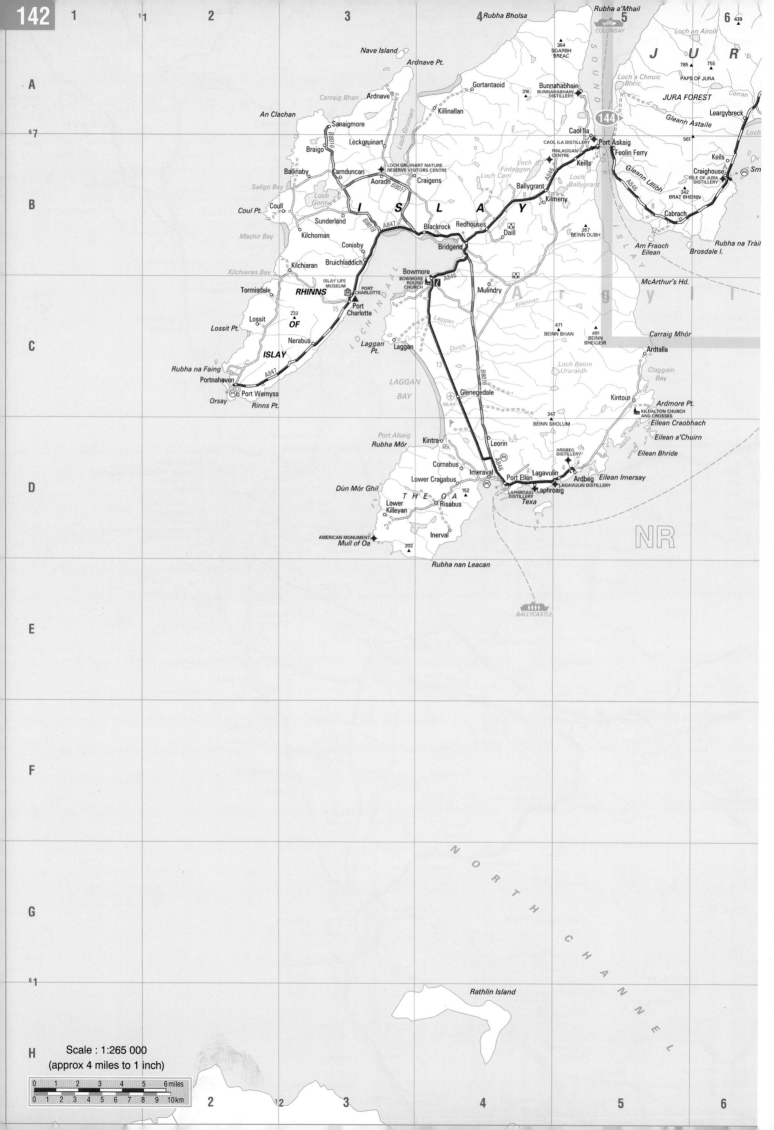

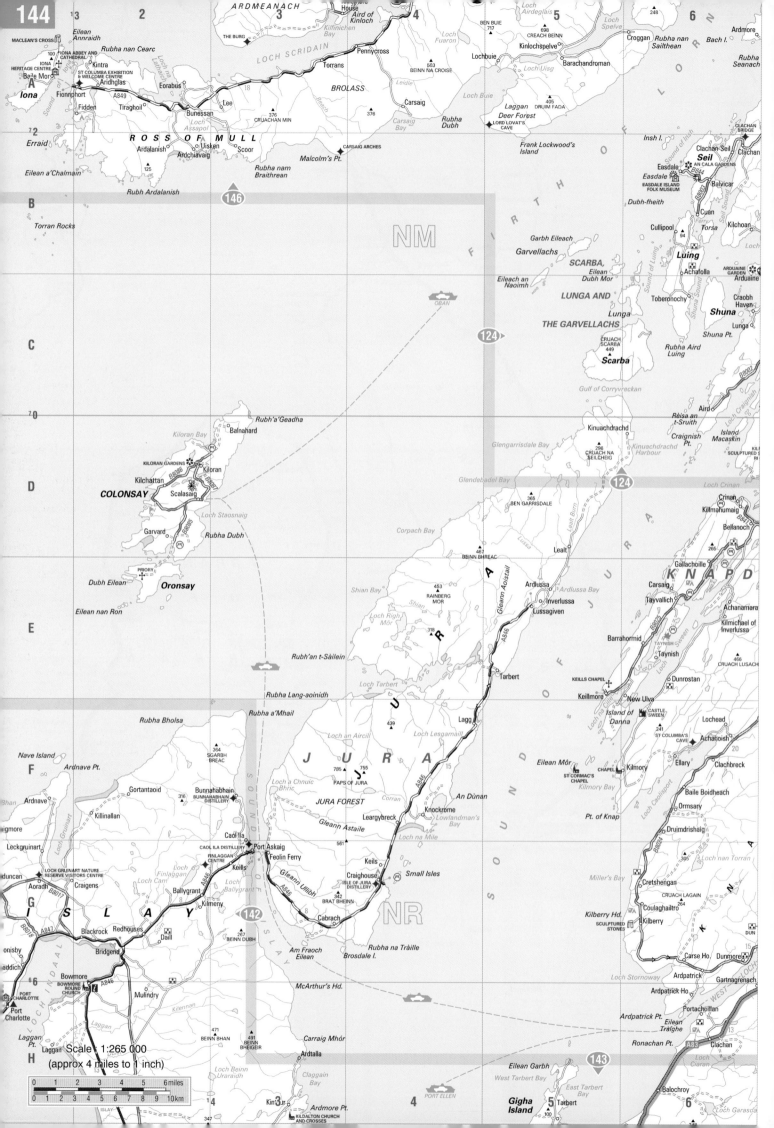

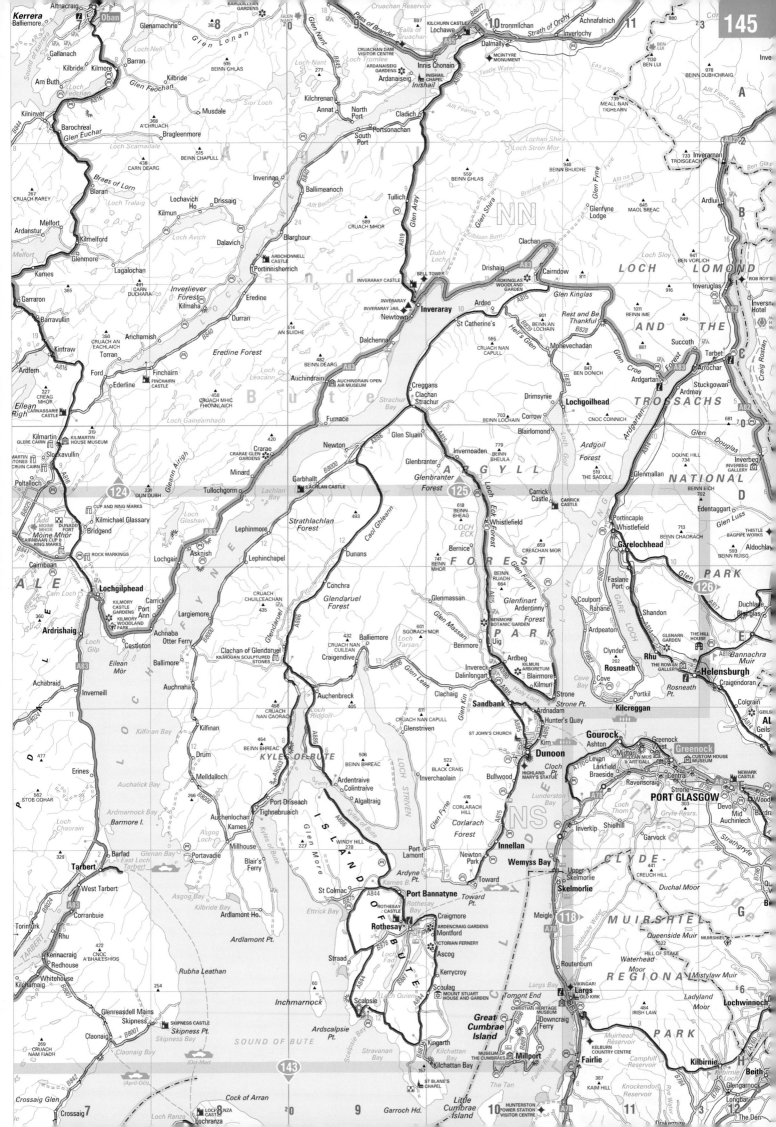

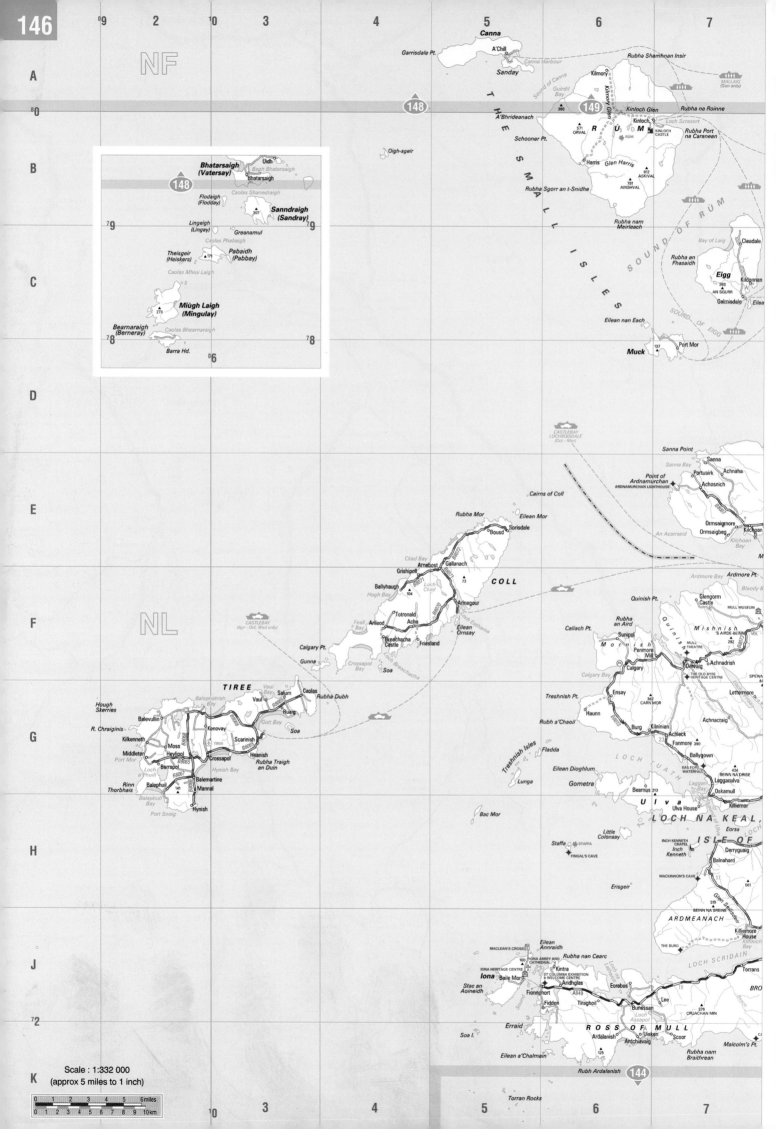

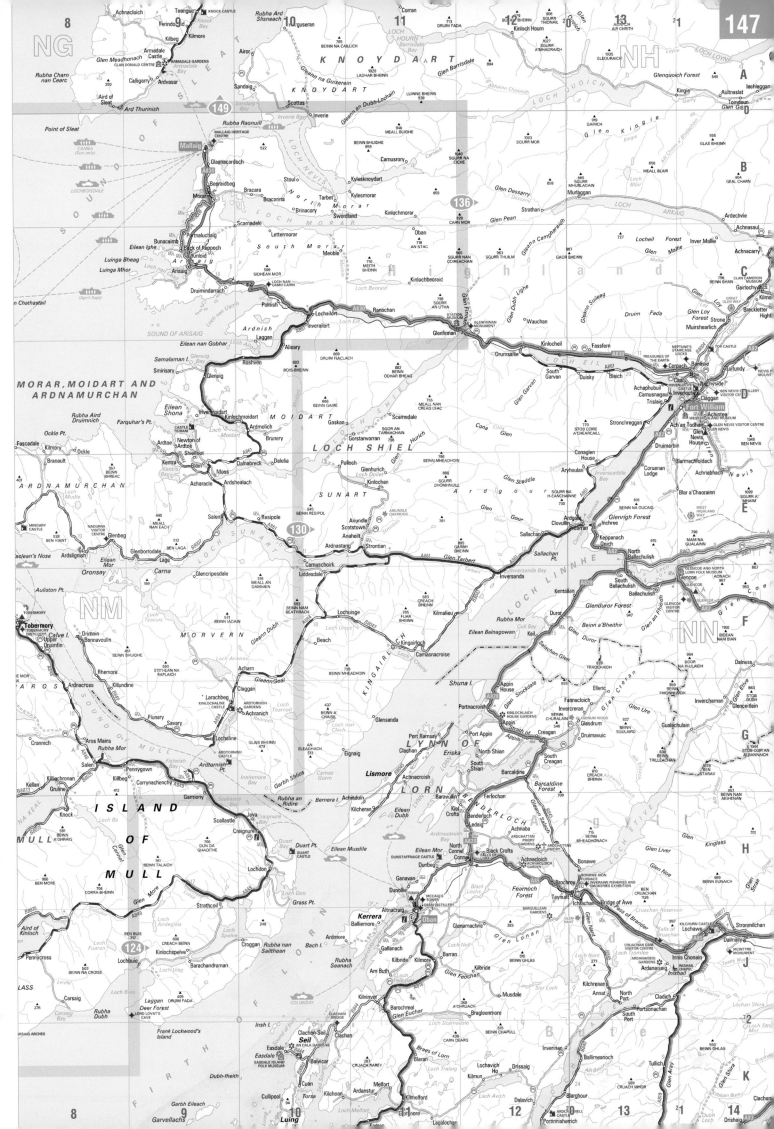

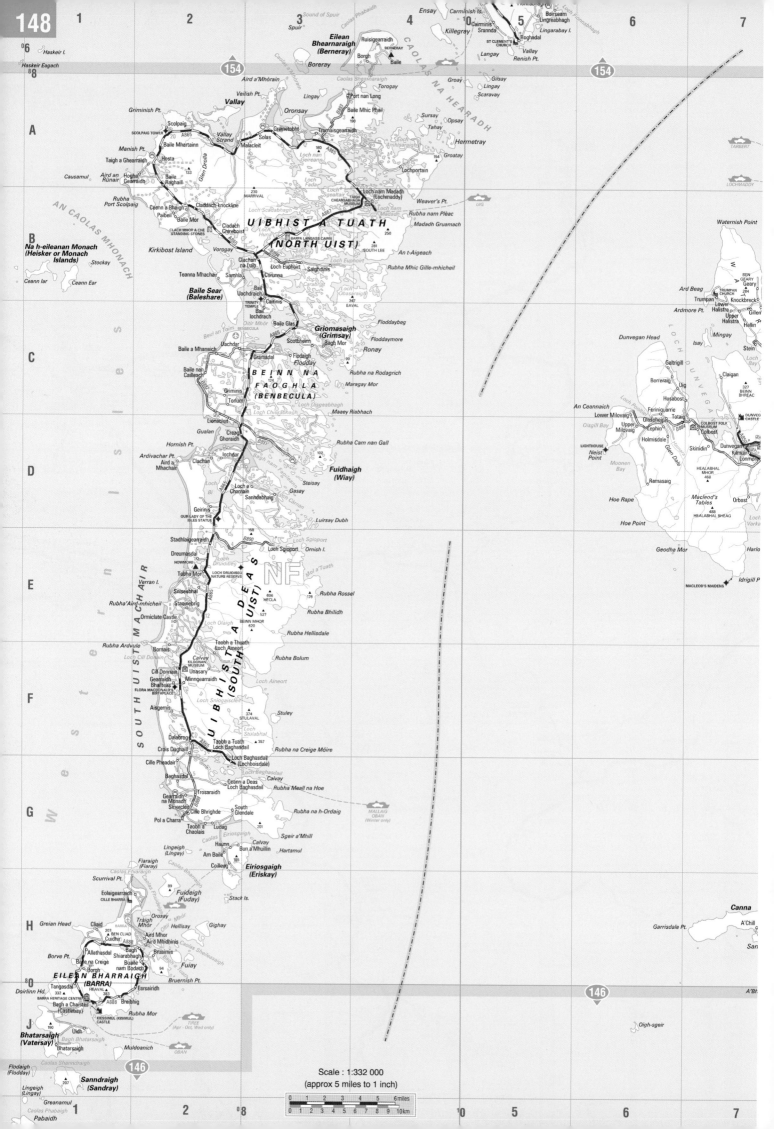

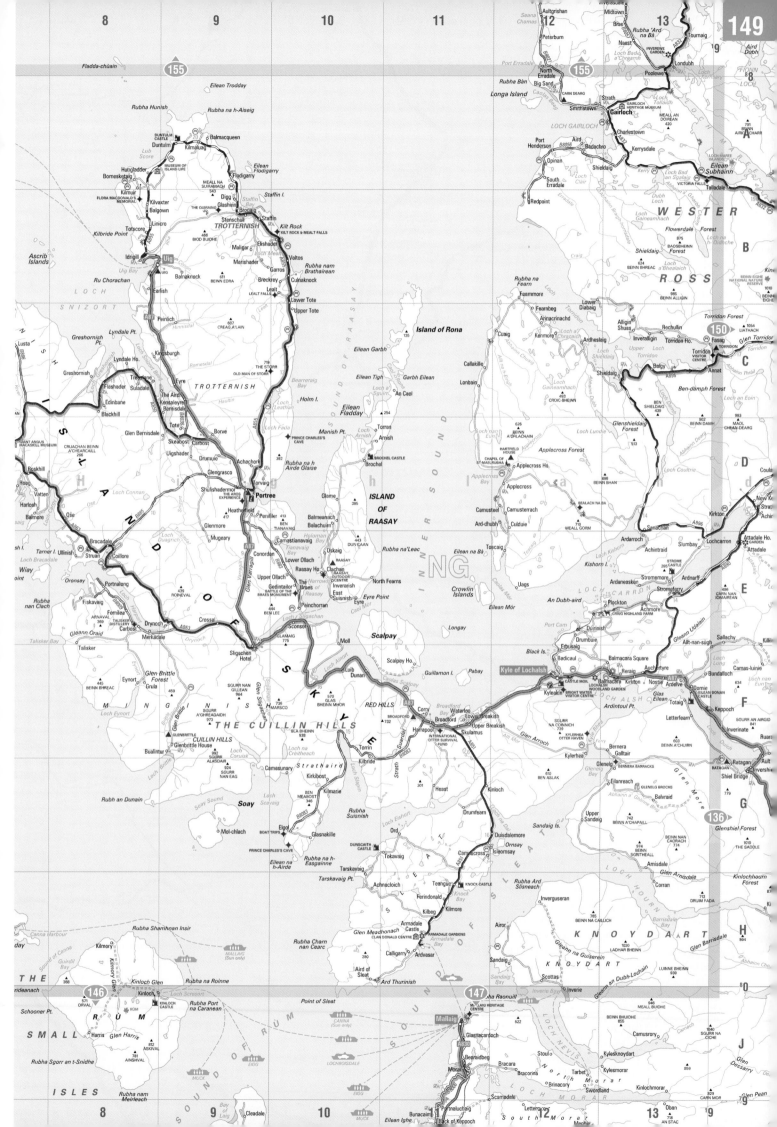

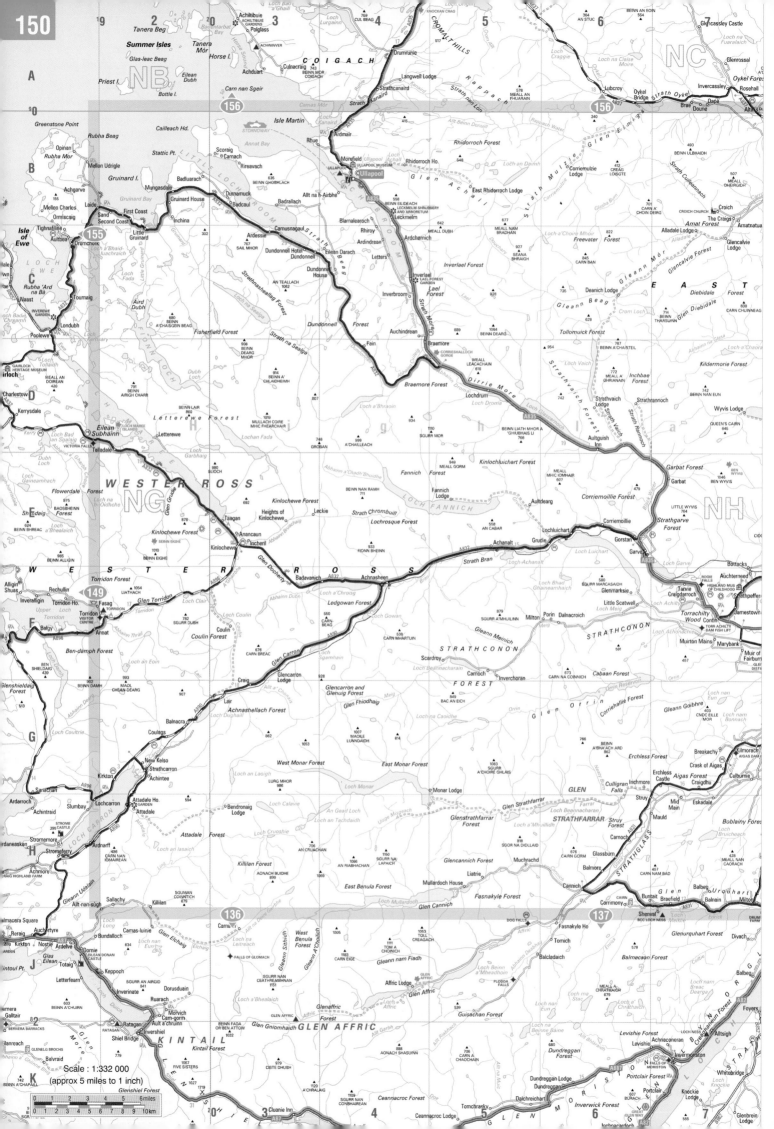

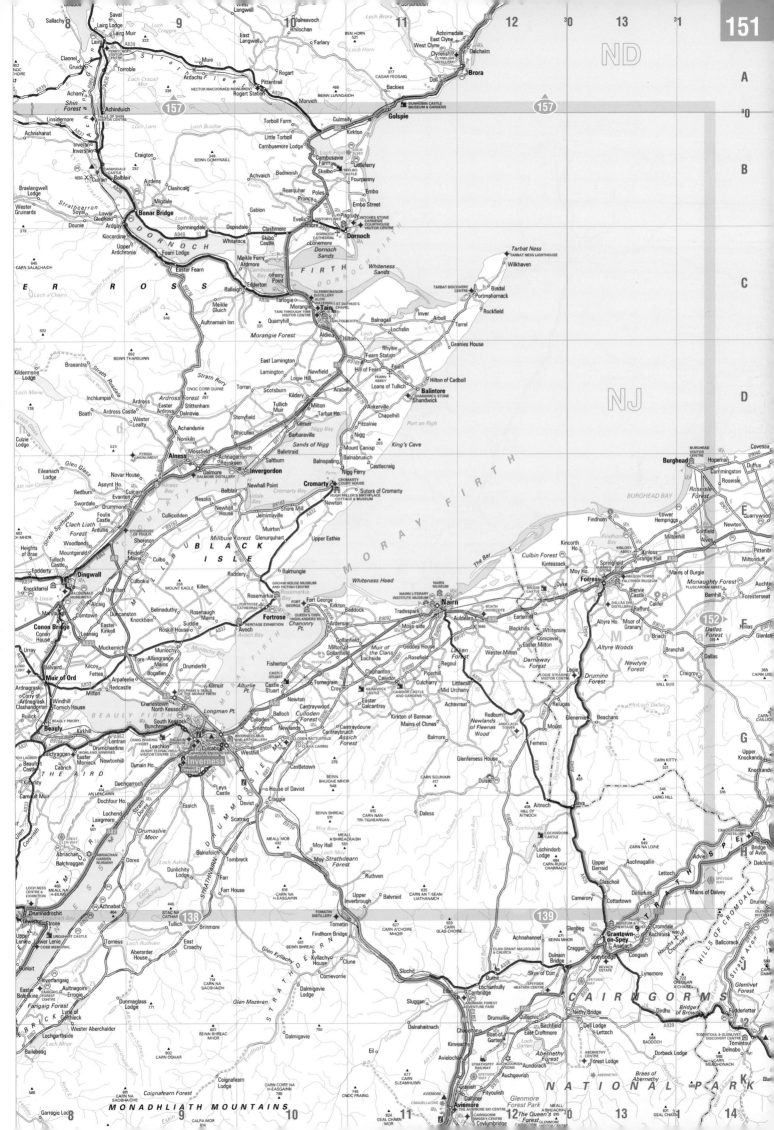

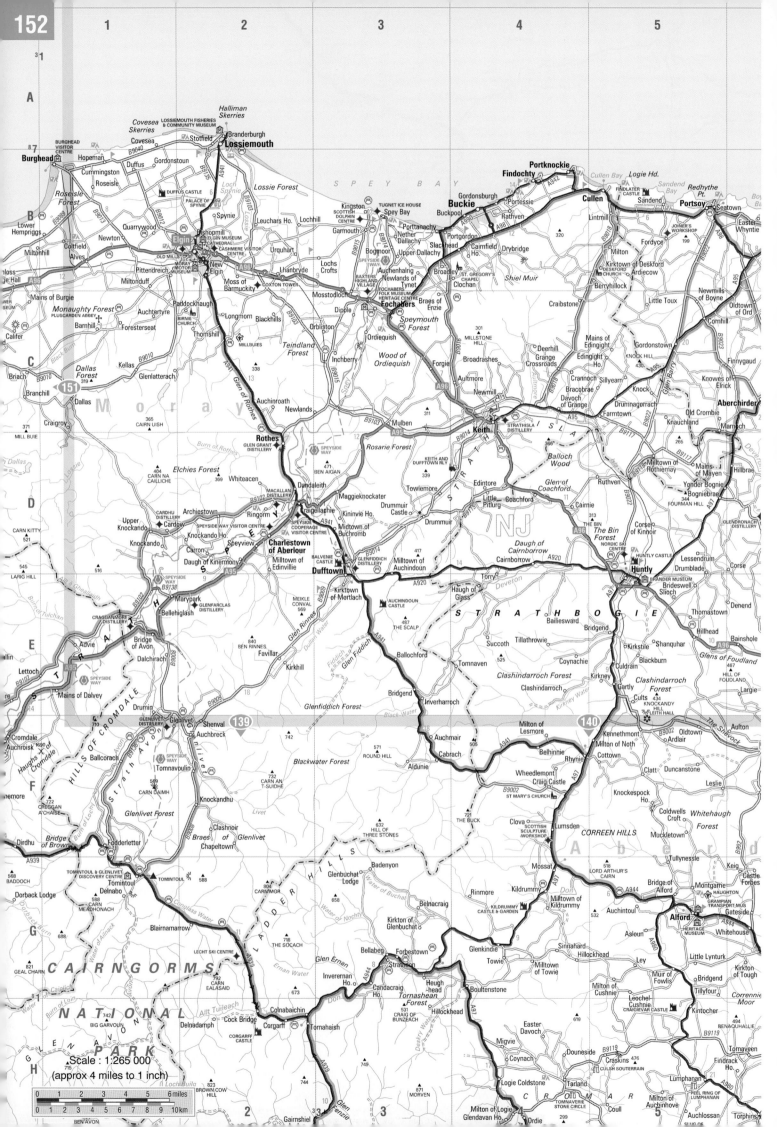

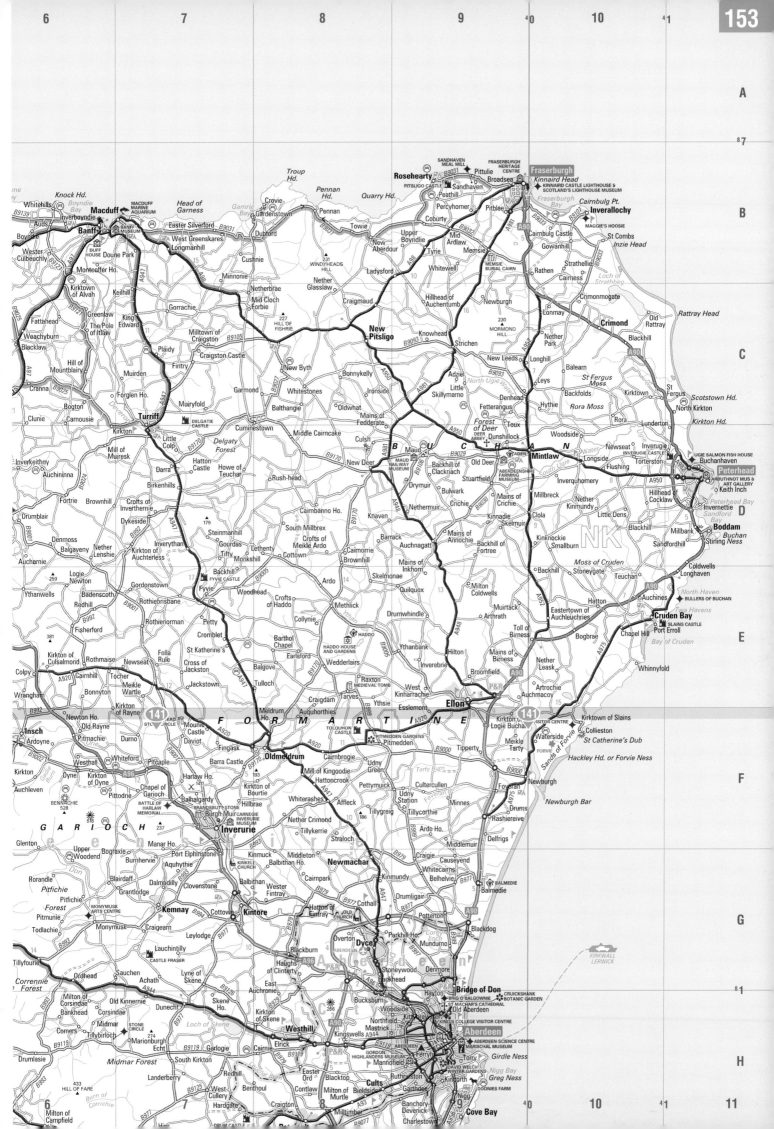

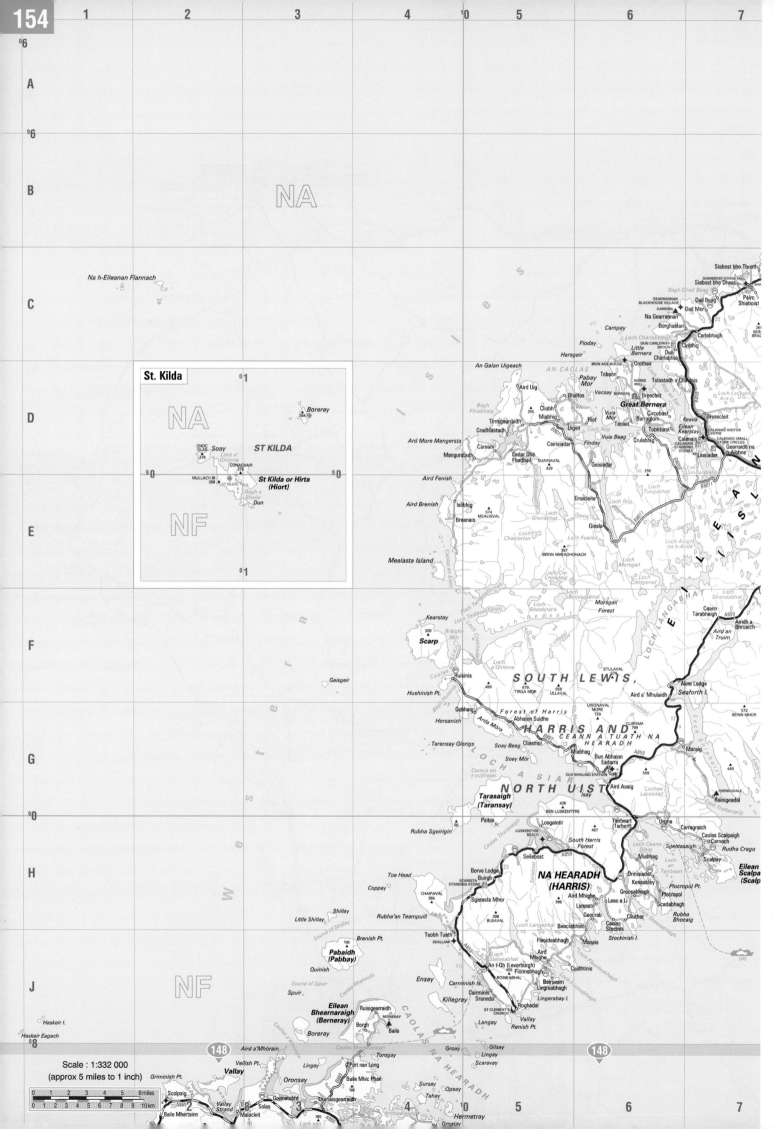

St. Kilda

NA

NF

ST KILDA

Boreray

Soay
CNOC GLAS 376
Loch a' Ghlinne
CONACHAIR 376
MULLACH BI 358
ST KILDA
Bàgh a' Bhaile
Dun
St Kilda or Hirta (Hiort)

Scale : 1:332 000
(approx 5 miles to 1 inch)

0 1 2 3 4 5 6 miles
0 1 2 3 4 5 6 7 8 9 10km

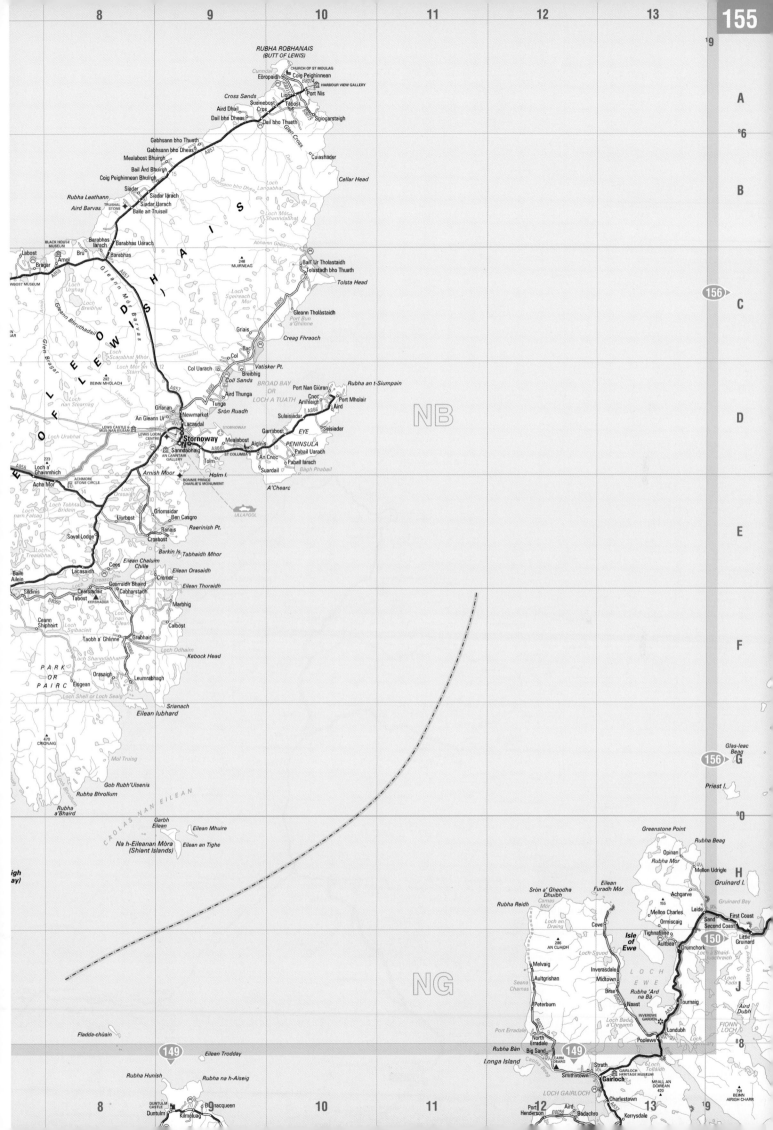

RUBHA ROBHANAIS
(BUTT OF LEWIS)

CHURCH OF ST MOULAG
Eòropaidh Còig Peighinnean
HARBOUR VIEW GALLERY
Lional Port Nis
Cross Sands Tàbost
Suaineabost Sgiogarstaigh
Aird Dhail Cros
Dail bho Dheas
Dail bho Thuath

Gabhsann bho Thuath
Gabhsann bho Dheas
Mealabost Bhuirgh
Bail Àrd Bhuirgh
Coig Peighinnean Bhuirgh
Siadar
Rubha Leathann Siadar Iarach
Aird Barvas Siadar Uarach
TRUSHAL STONE Baile an Truiseil

Cuiashader

Cellar Head

Loch
Langabhat

BLACK HOUSE MUSEUM
Labost Barabhas Iarach
Bragar Arnol Barabhas Uarach
Brù Barabhas
Loch
Urghag   Bail Ur Tholastaidh
Loch Breibhat Tolastadh bho Thuath
Gleann Bhruthadail
WBOST MUSEUM Tolsta Head
248
MUIRNEAG
Abhainn Ghearadha

Loch Mòr
Shanndabhat

Loch
Sgeireach
Mòr Gleann Tholàstaidh
Port Bun
a'Ghlinne

292
BEINN MHOLACH Griais
Loch Mòr an
Stairr Creag Fhraoch
A857
Loch nan Stearnag Col
Lacasdal Col Uarach
Grìanan Breibhig
An Gleann Ùr Coll Sands
Newmarket Aird Thunga
Lacasdal Tunga Vatisker Pt.
LEWS CASTLE & MÙS NAN EILEAN Sròn Ruadh
Port Nan Giùran
Cnoc
Amhlaigh
Aird
Rubha an t-Siumpain
Port Mholair
Sulaisiadar
Seisiadar
Garrabost
EYE
Mealabost PENINSULA
ST COLUMBA'S Aiginis
Sanndabhaig An Cnoc
Tolm Pabail Uarach
Suardail Pabail Iarach
Bàgh Phabail

STORNOWAY
AN LANNTAIR GALLERY
LEWIS LOOM CENTRE
Loch Urabhal
223
Loch a'
Ghainmhich A'Chearc
ACHMORE STONE CIRCLE
Acha Mòr
Arnish Moor
BONNIE PRINCE CHARLIE'S MONUMENT
Holm I.
ULLAPOOL

Loch Tobhta
Brideil Griomsidar Ben Casgro
Liurbost Ranais Raerinish Pt.
Loch nam Falcag Crosbost
Soval Lodge Barkin Is. Tabhaidh Mhor
Ceòs Eilean Chaluim
Baile Ailein Chille
Lacasaidh Eilean Orasaidh
Sildinis Geàrraidh Bhaird Eilean Thoraidh
Cearsiadair Cabharstadh
KERSHADER
Tabost Marbhig
Ceann
Shiphoirt Calbost
Loch
Sgibacleit Grabhair
Taobh a' Ghlinne
Loch Shanndabhat
Loch Odhairn
Kebock Head
PARK
OR
PAIRC Orasaigh Leumrabhagh
Eisgean
Loch Shell or Loch Sealg
470
CRIONAIG
Mol Truisg
Srianach
Eilean Iubhard
Gob Rubh'Uisenis
Rubha Bhrollum
Rubha
a'Bhaird
Garbh
Eilean Eilean Mhuire
Na h-Eileanan Mòra
(Shiant Islands) Eilean an Tighe

igh
ay)

CAOLAS NAN EILEAN

NG

Greenstone Point
Rubha Beag
Opinan
Rubha Mòr Mellon Udrigle
Gruinard I.
Sròn a' Gheodha
Dhuibh Eilean
Furadh Mòr Achgarve
Rubha Reidh Camas
Mòr Mellon Charles Laide
Loch an
Draing Cove Ormiscaig Sand First Coast
296
AN CUAIDH Tighnafiline Second Coast
Isle
of
Ewe Aultbea Little
Gruinard
Melvaig Inverasdale Drumchork
Aultgrishan Midtown
Brae
Seana
Chamas Rubha 'Àrd
na Bà Naast Tournaig
INVEREWE
GARDEN
Peterburn
Port Erradale
Rubha Bàn North
Erradale Londubh
Big Sand Poolewe
149 Loch Badachro
a'Chramaig

LOCH
EWE

Aird
Dubh

FIONN
LOCH

149

8

Longa Island

Fladda-chùain

149

Eilean Troddday

Rubha Hunish Rubha na h-Aiseig

DUNTULM
CASTLE
Duntulm Bornacquee
Kilmaluag

GAIRLOCH
HERITAGE MUSEUM
CARN
DEARG Strath
Smithstown Gairloch
MEALL AN
DOIREAN
420
Charlestown
Port
Henderson Aird
Badachro
B8056
Kerrysdale
791
BEINN
AIRIGH CHARR

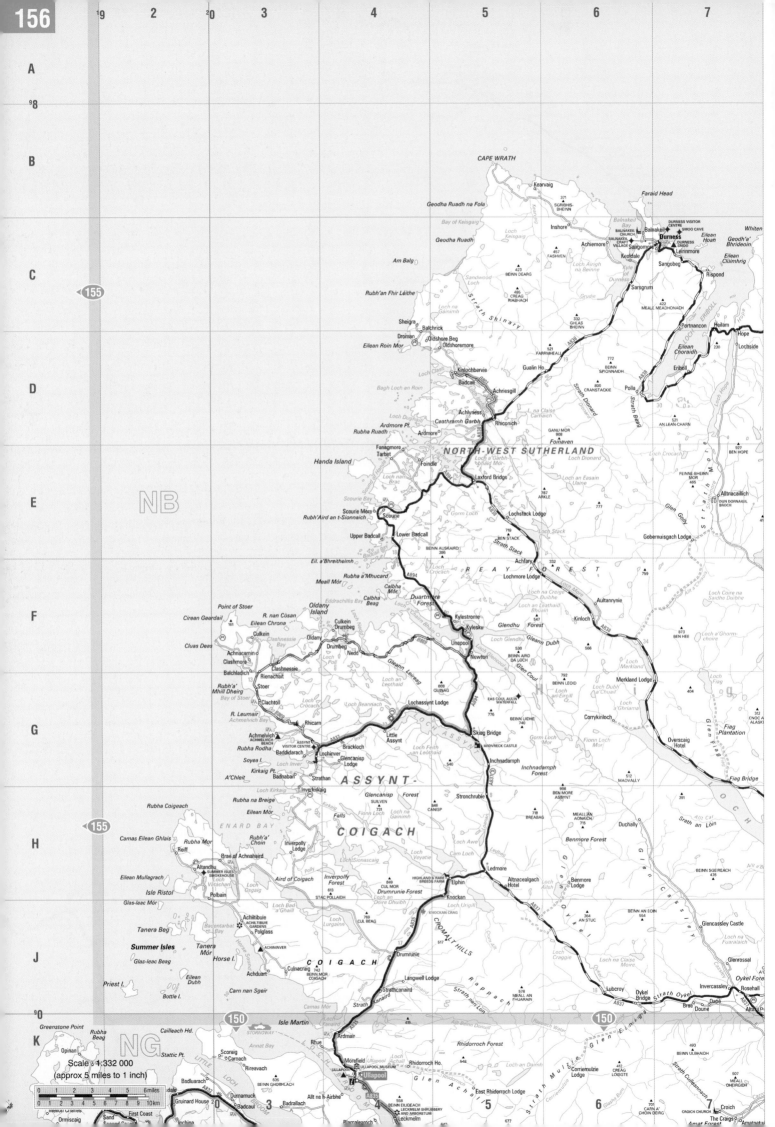

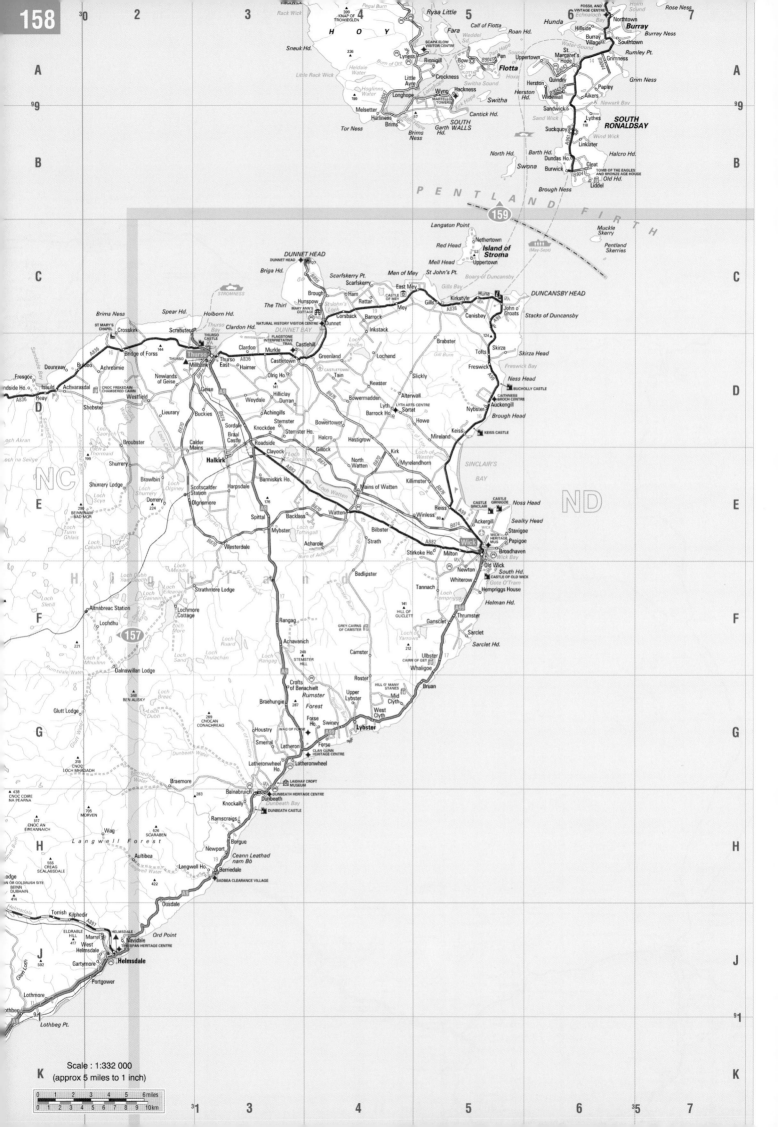

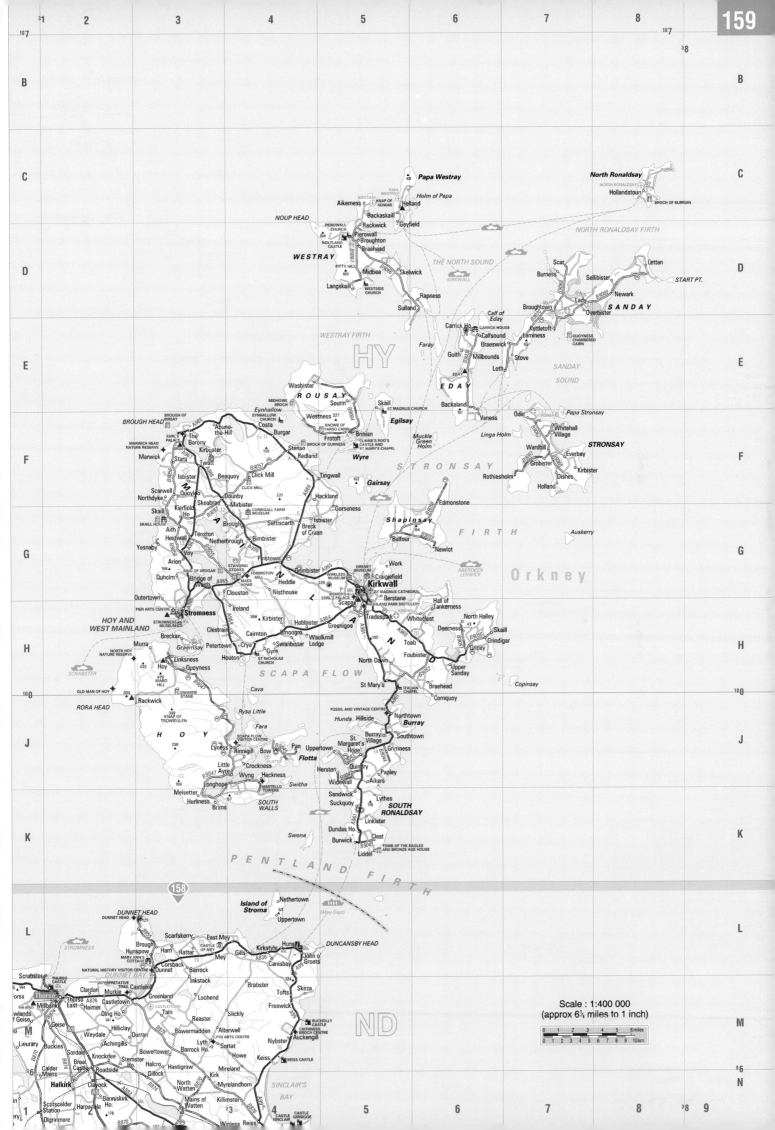

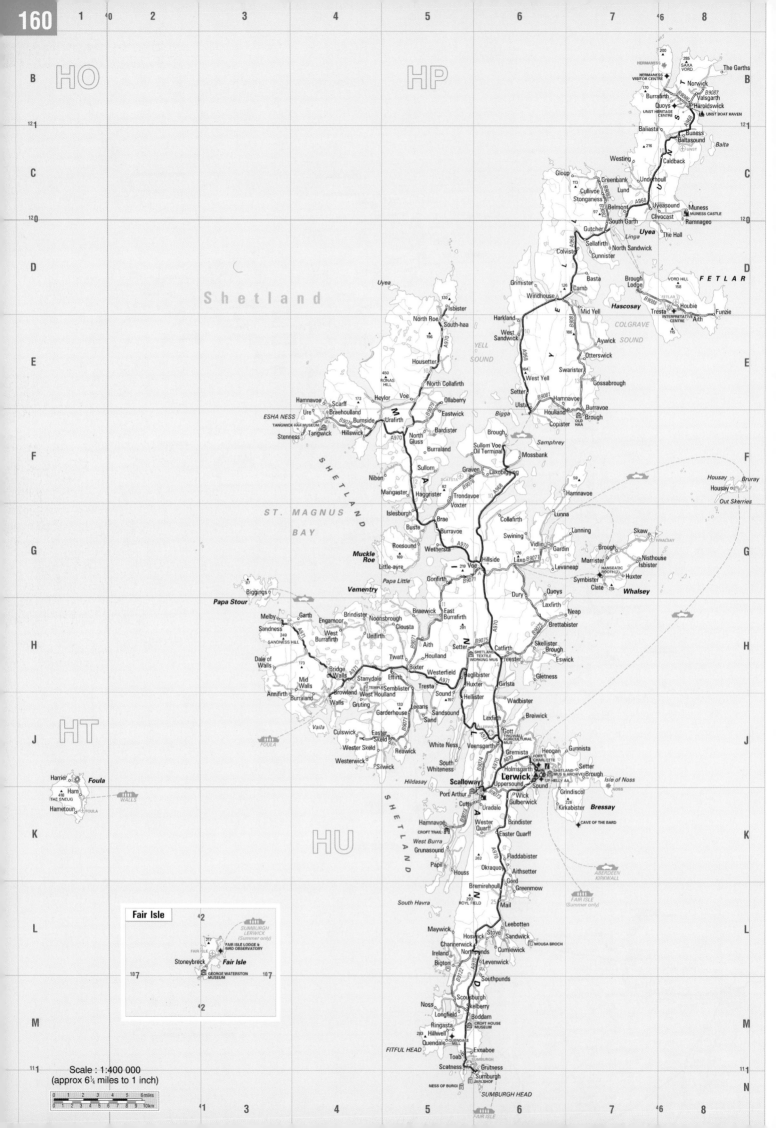

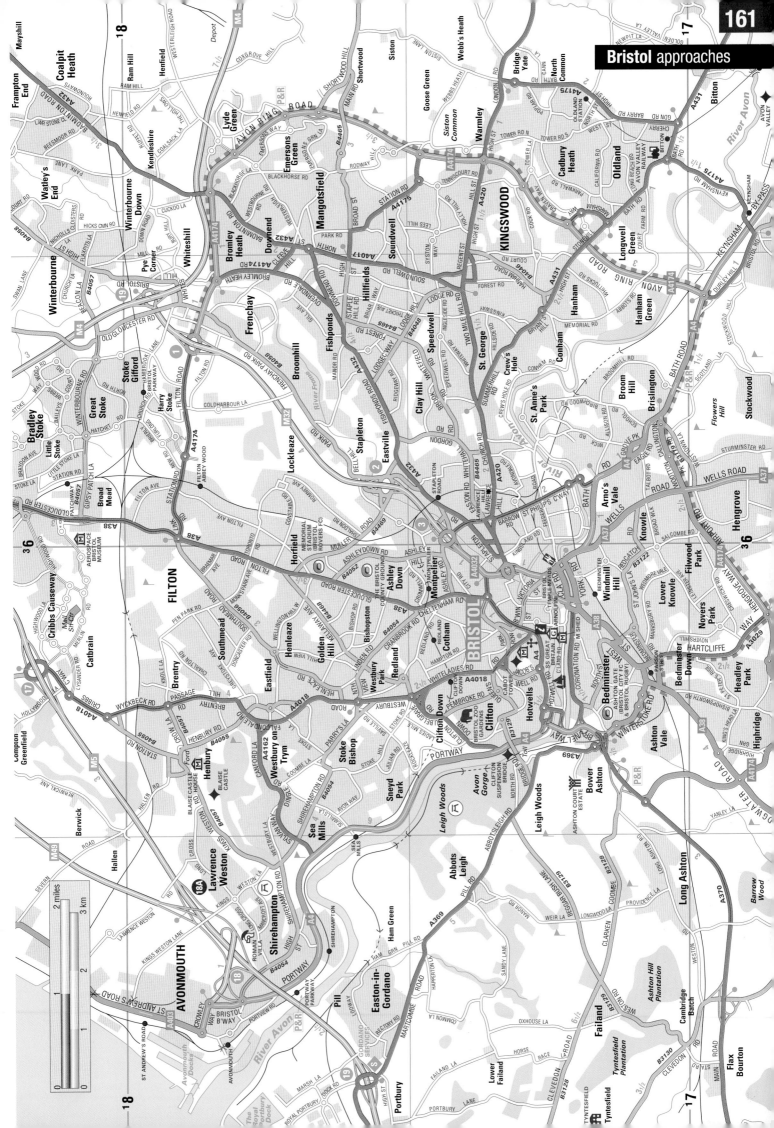

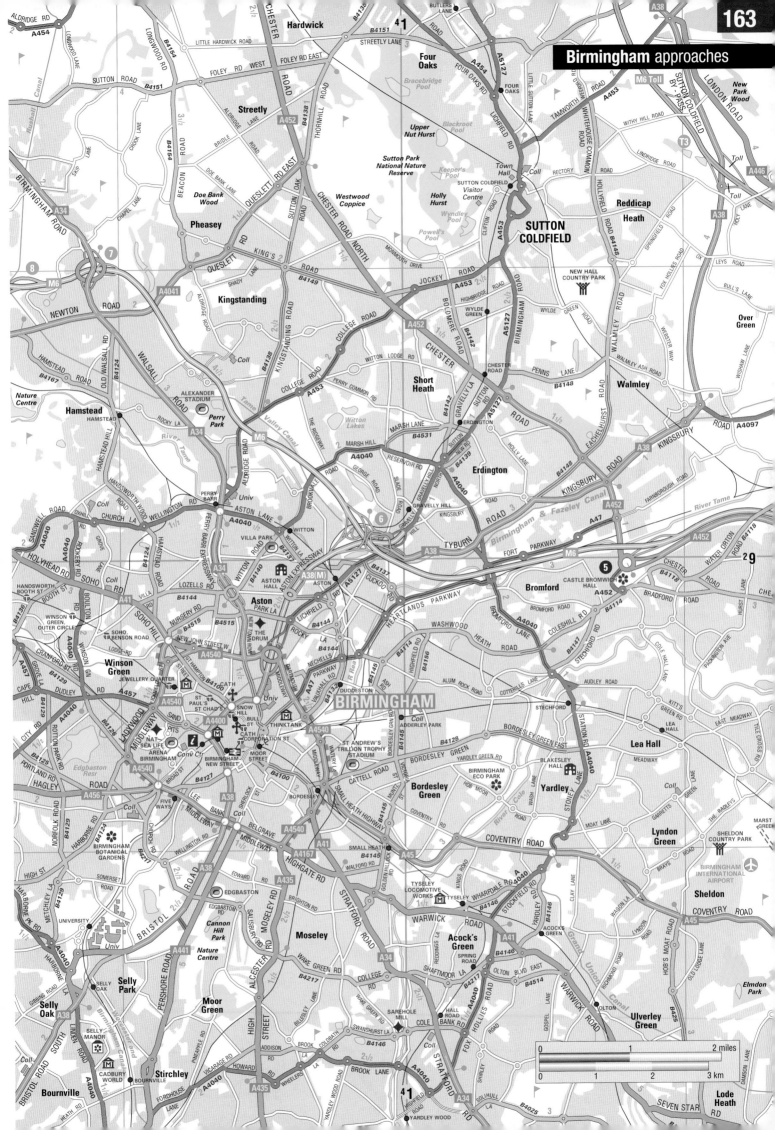

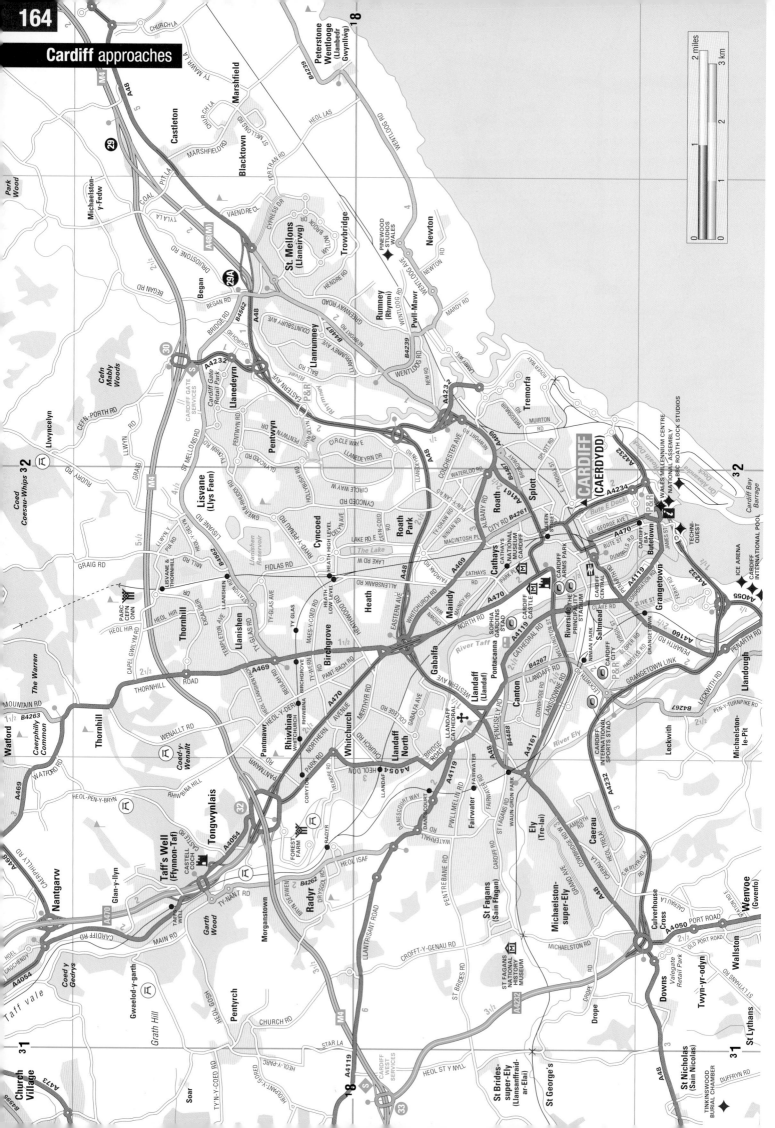

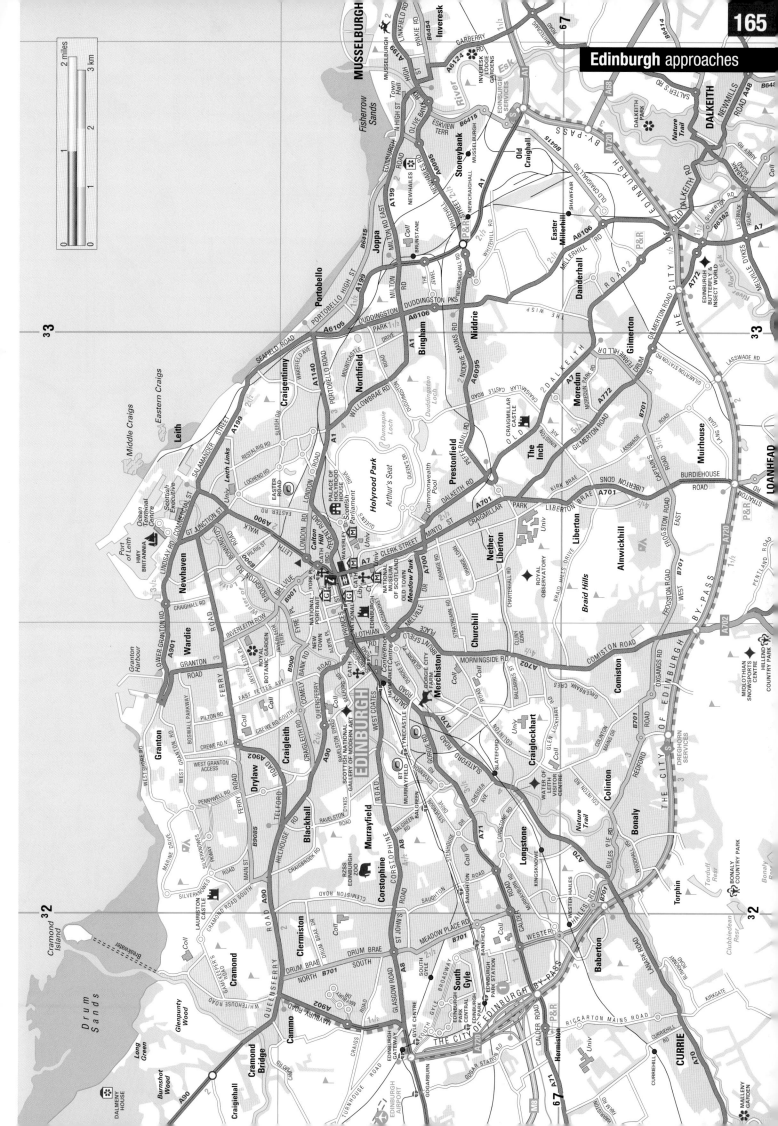

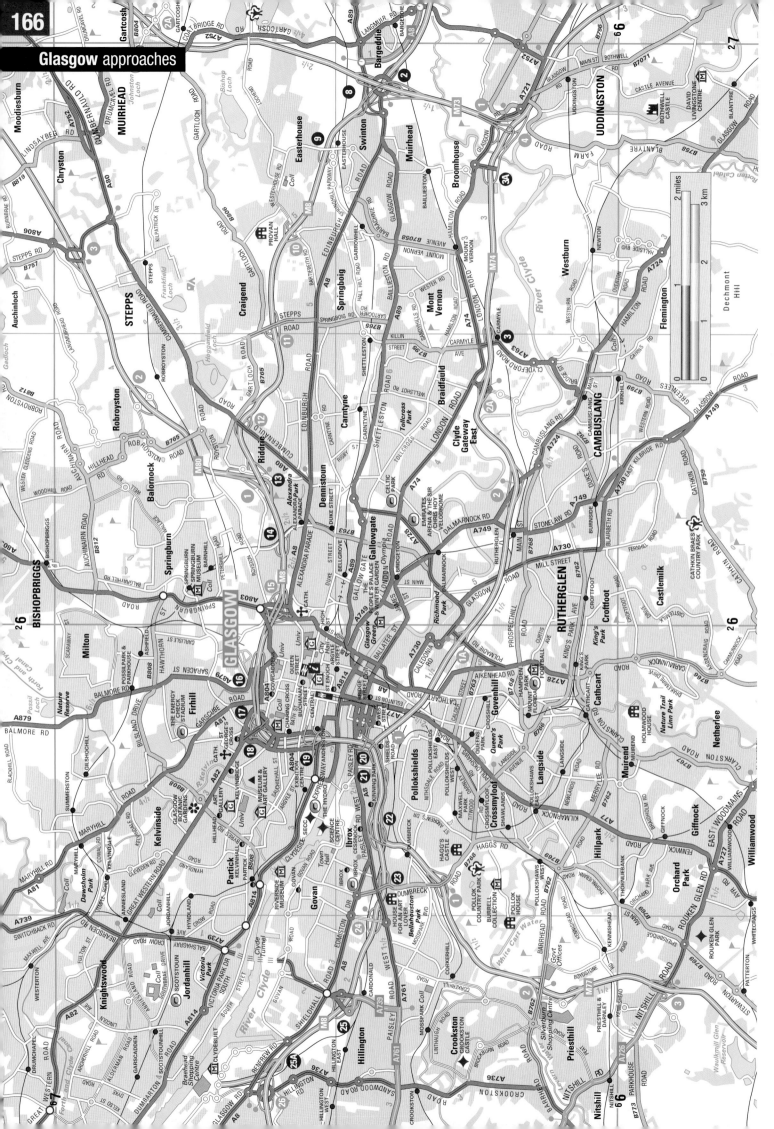

Glasgow approaches

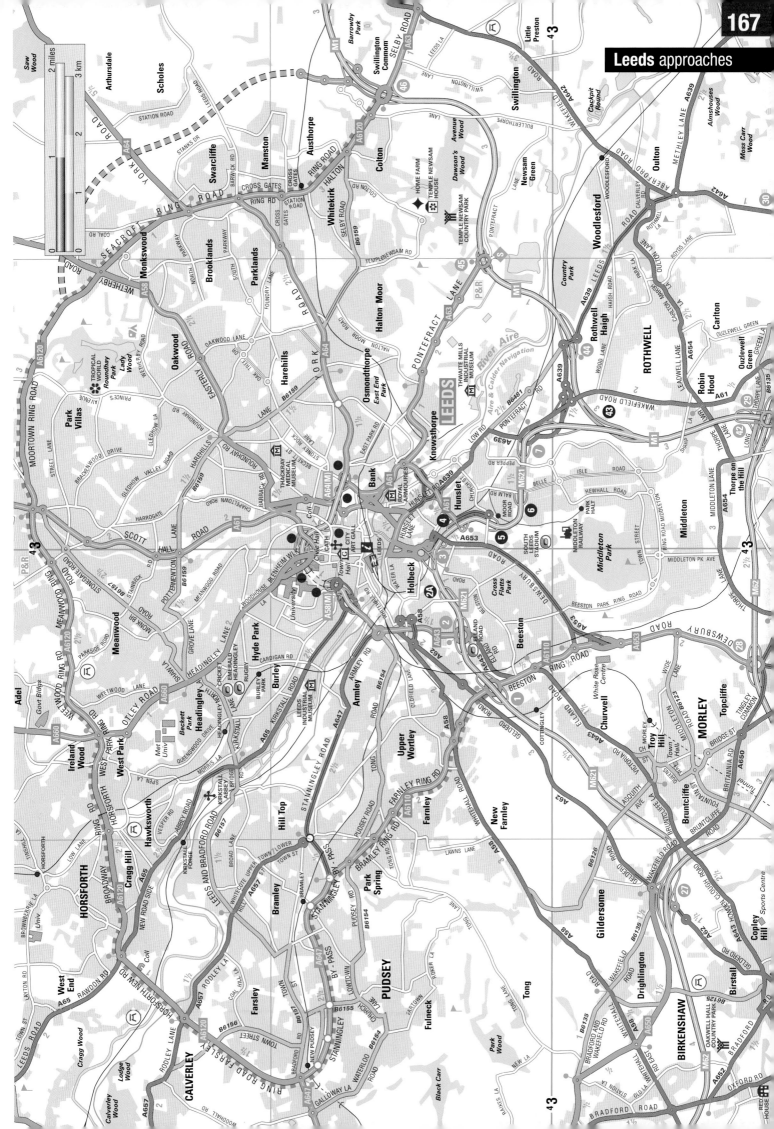

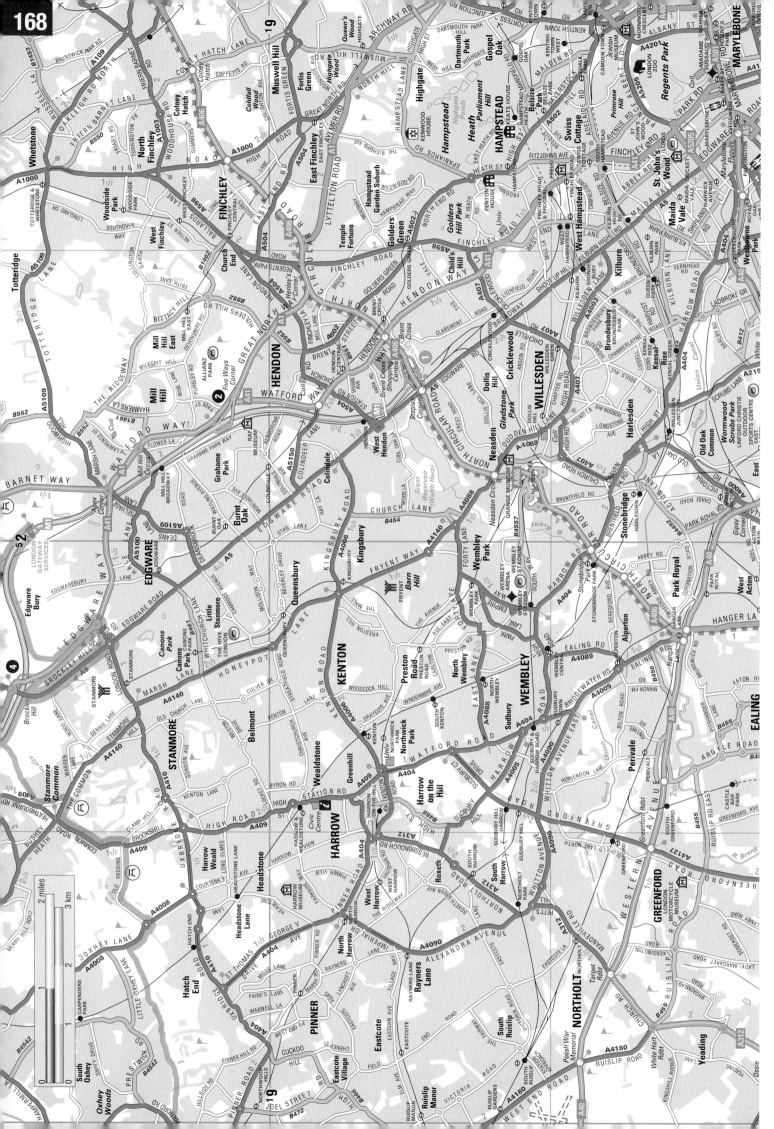

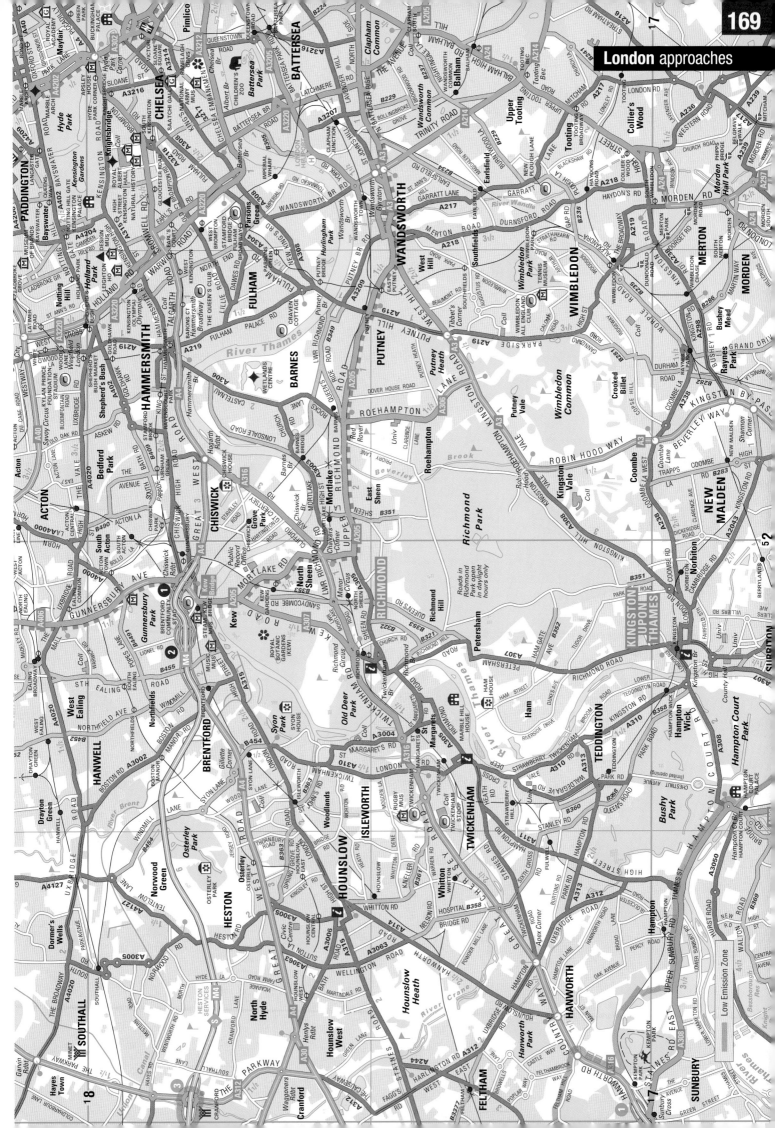

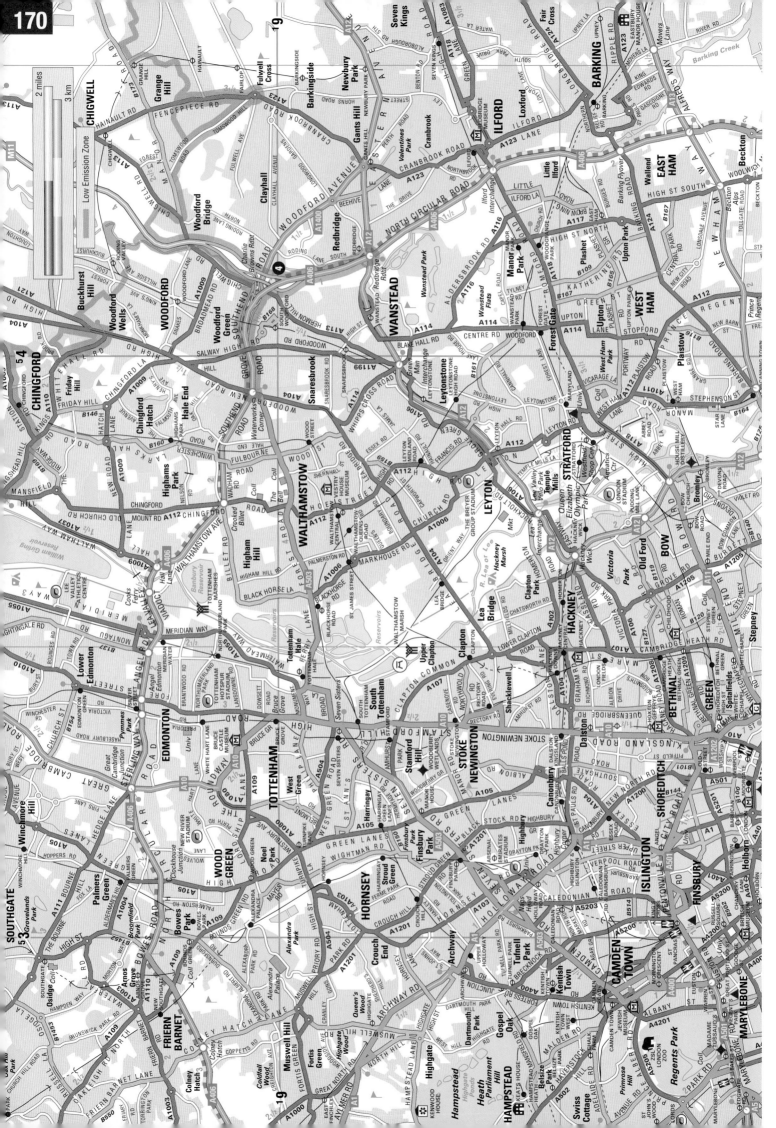

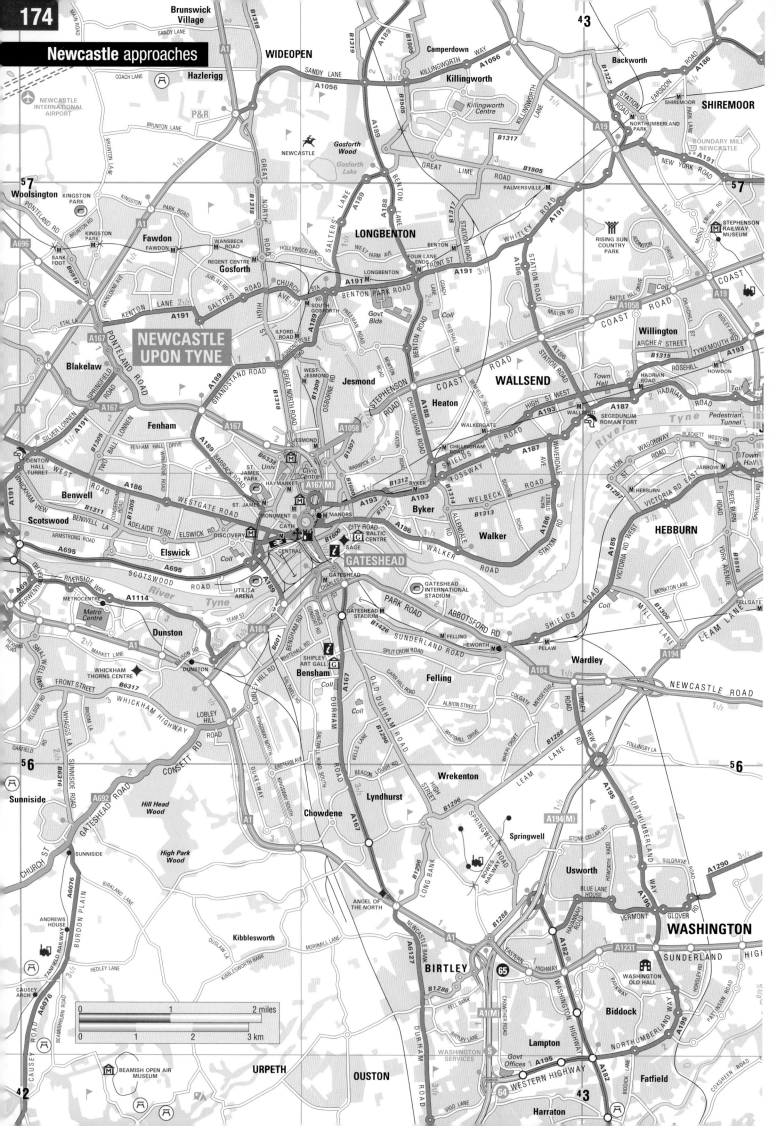

Town plan symbols

Motorway

Primary route – dual, single carriageway

A road – dual, single carriageway

B road – dual, single carriageway

Minor through road

One-way street

Pedestrian roads

Shopping streets

Railway with station

City Hall

Tramway with station

Bank | West St

Underground or
Metro station

H Hospital

P Parking

Police

PO Post Office

Shopmobility

▲ Youth hostel

Bus or railway
station building

Shopping precinct or
retail park

Park

Congestion charge zone

✝ Abbey or cathedral

Ancient monument

Aquarium

Art gallery

Bird collection or aviary

Building of interest

Castle

Church of interest

Cinema

Garden

Historic ship

House

House and garden

Museum

Preserved railway

Roman antiquity

Safari park

Theatre

Tourist information

Zoo

✦ Other place of interest

Aberdeen

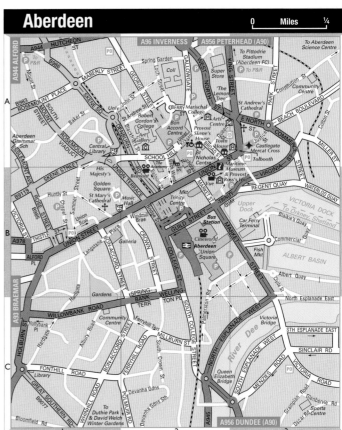

Ayr

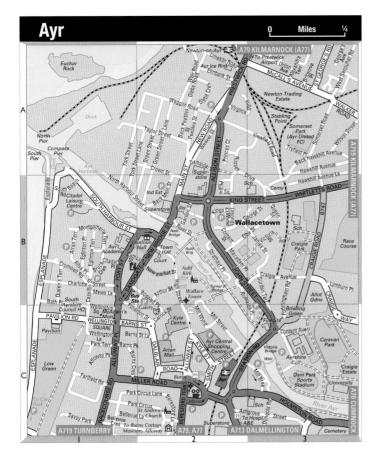

Bath

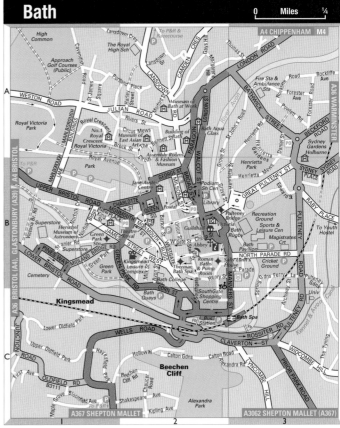

Birmingham

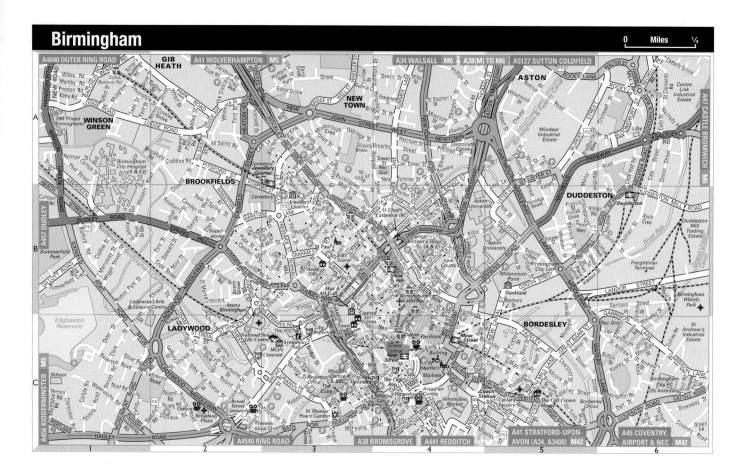

Blackpool

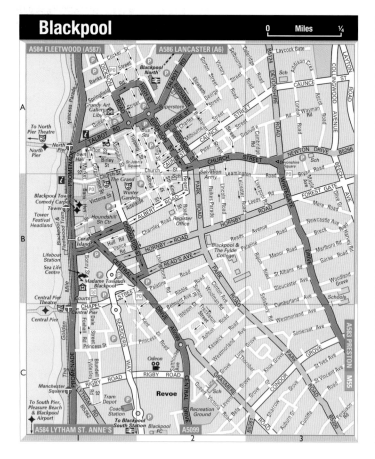

Bournemouth

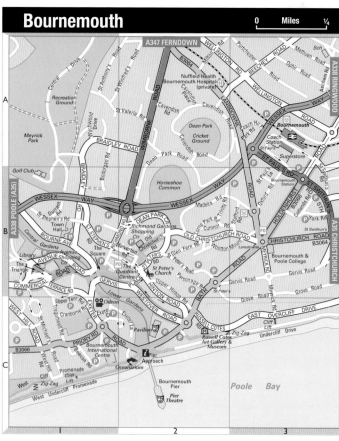

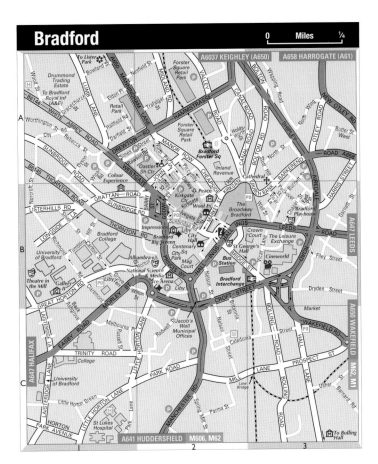

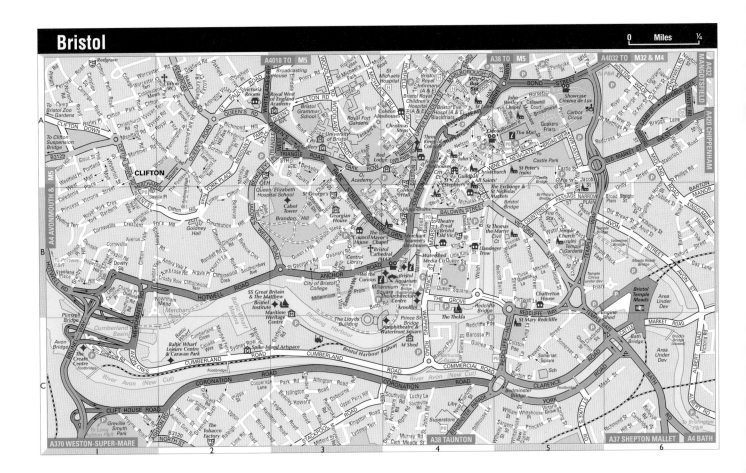

Bury St Edmunds

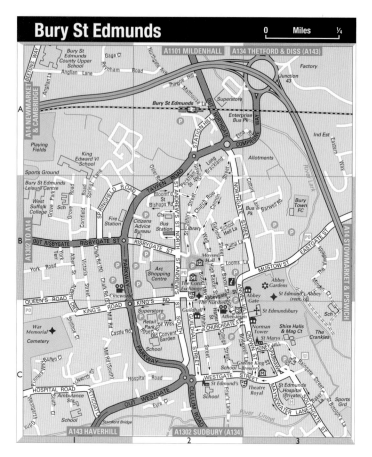

Cambridge

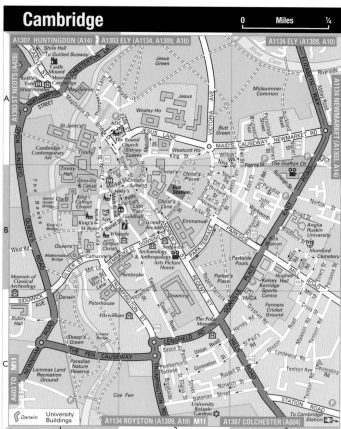

Canterbury

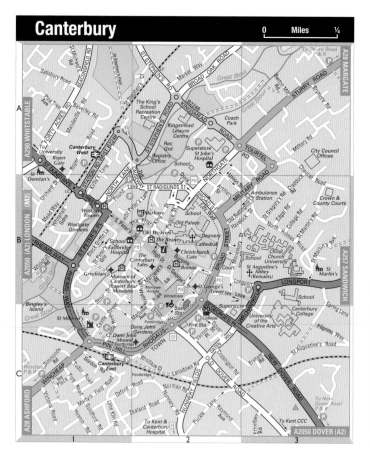

Cardiff / Caerdydd

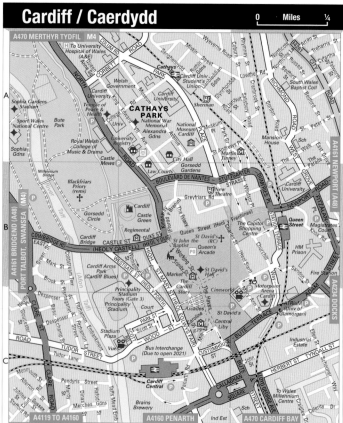

Carlisle

0 Miles ¼

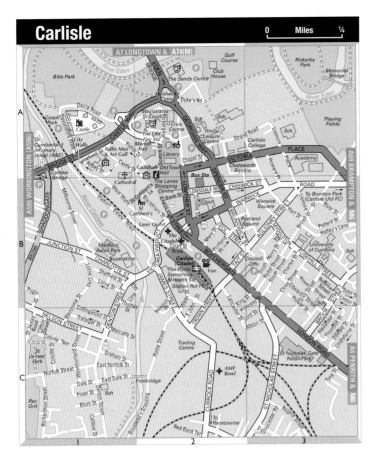

Chelmsford

0 Miles ¼

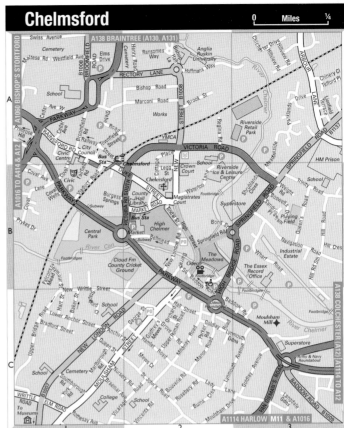

Cheltenham

0 Miles ¼

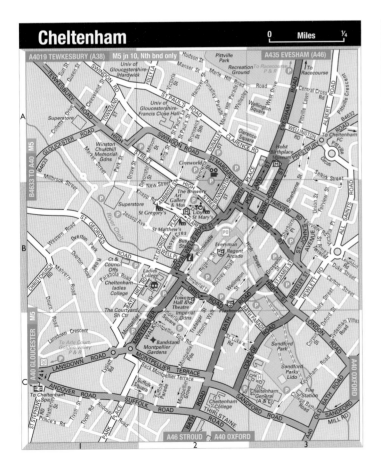

Chester

0 Miles ¼

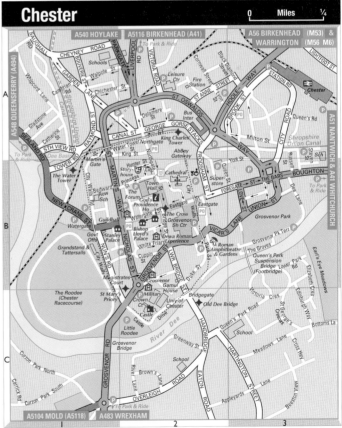

Chichester

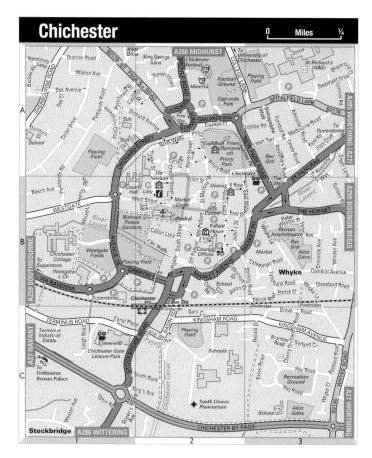

Colchester

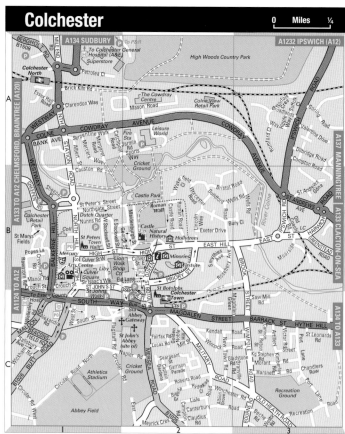

Coventry

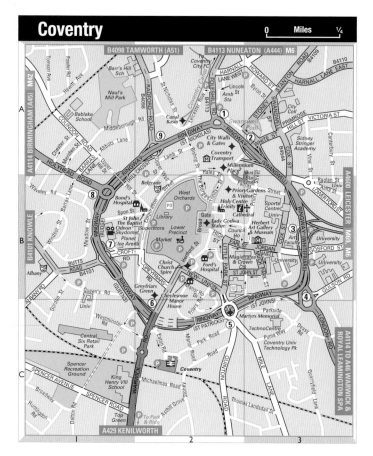

Derby

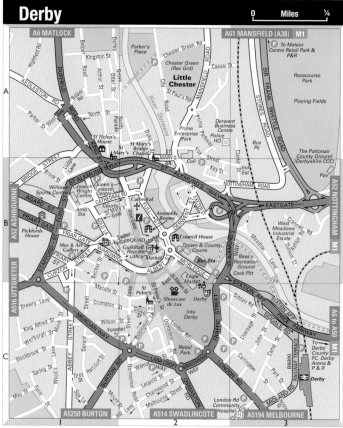

Dorchester

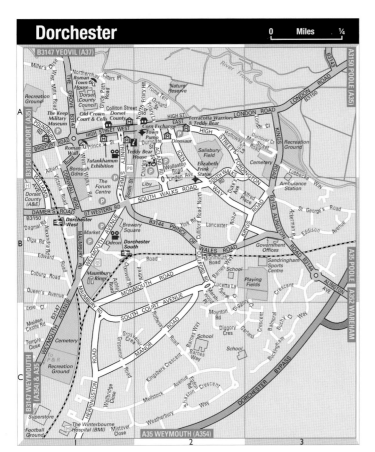

Dumfries

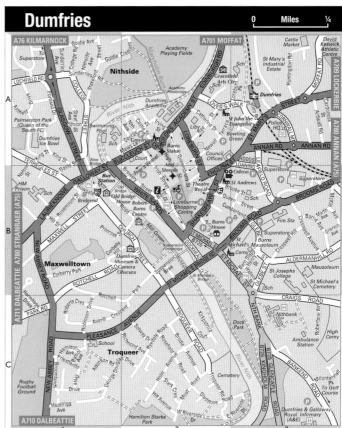

Dundee

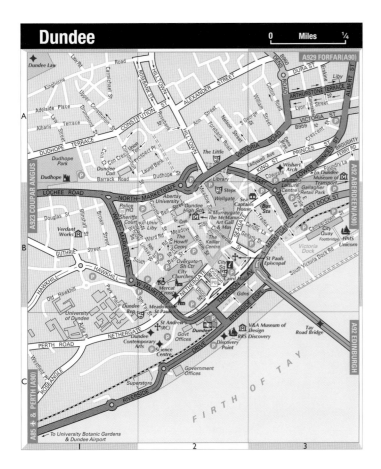

Durham

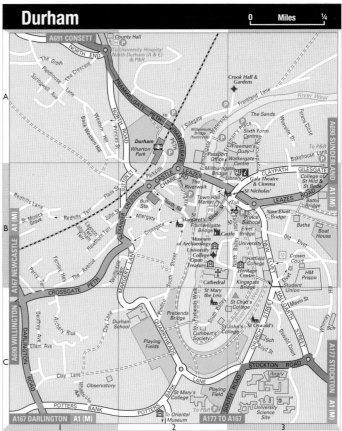

Edinburgh

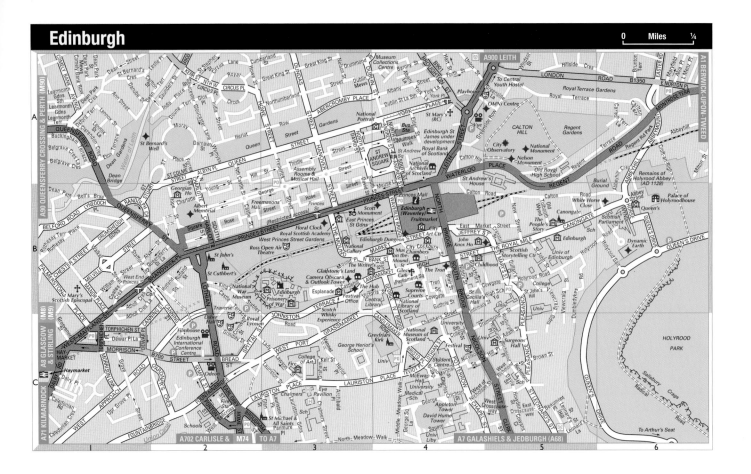

Exeter

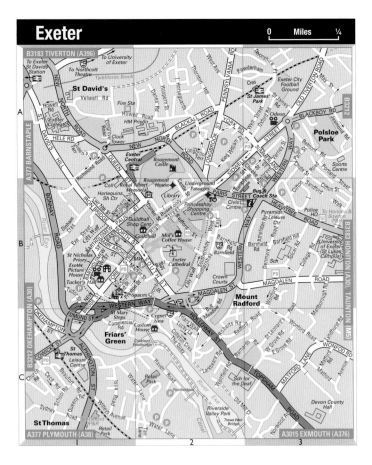

Gloucester

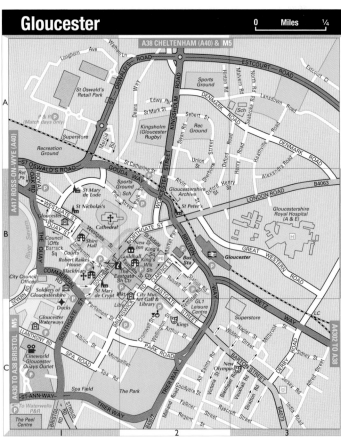

Glasgow

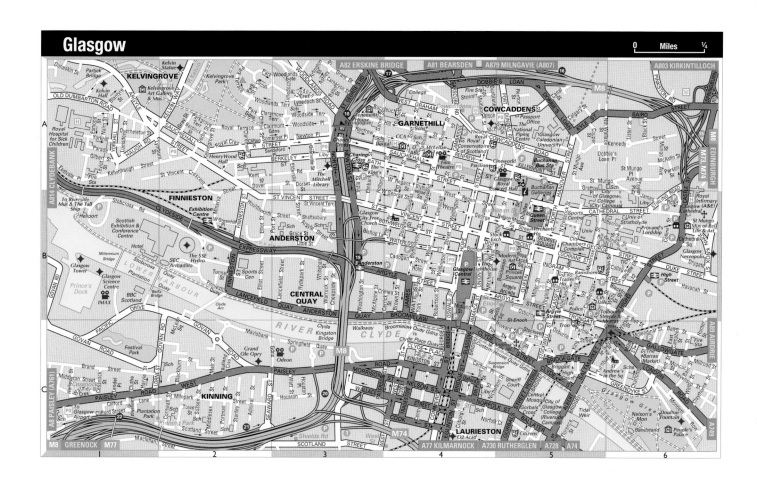

Grimsby

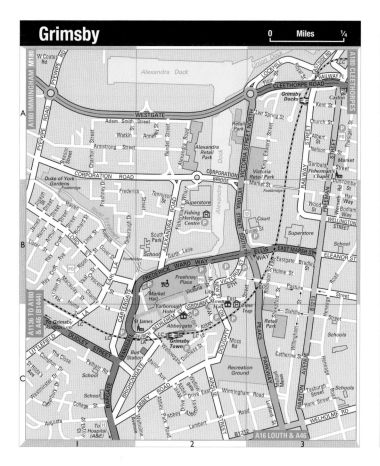

Harrogate

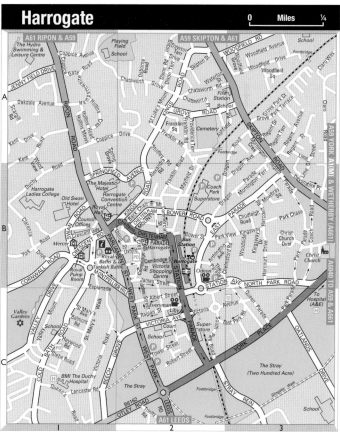

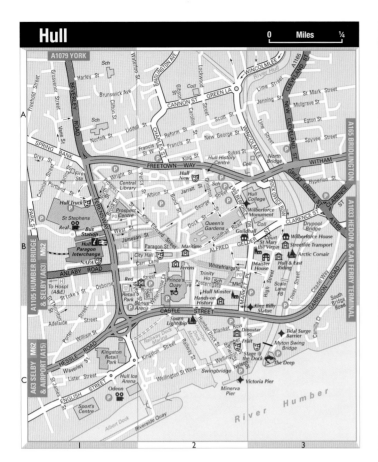

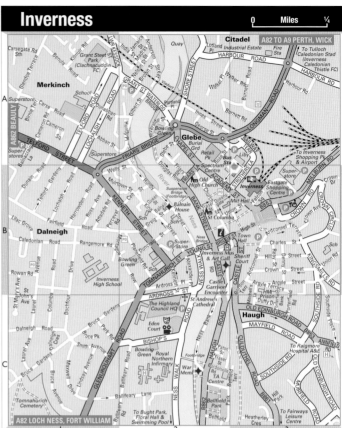

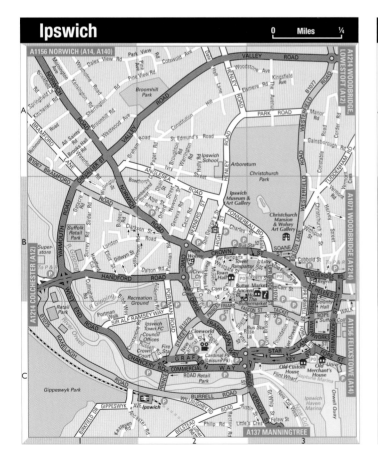

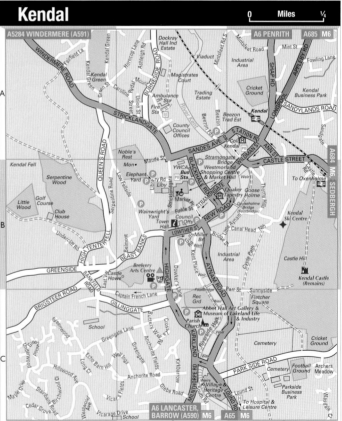

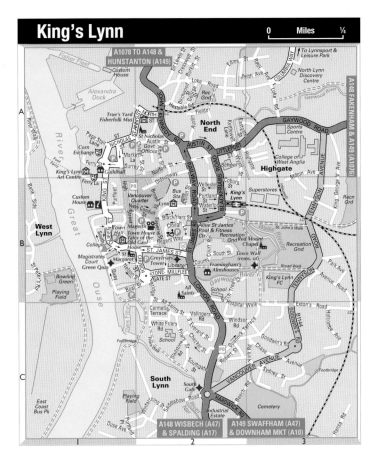

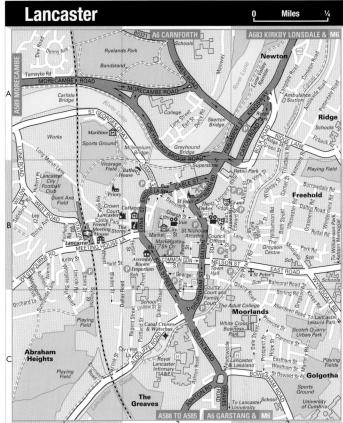

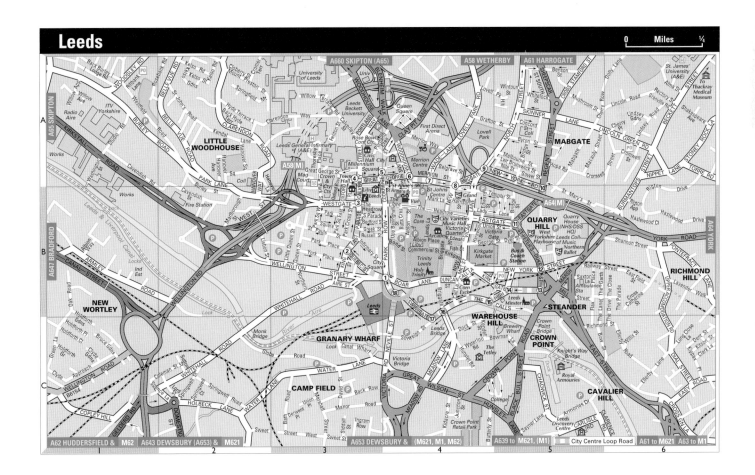

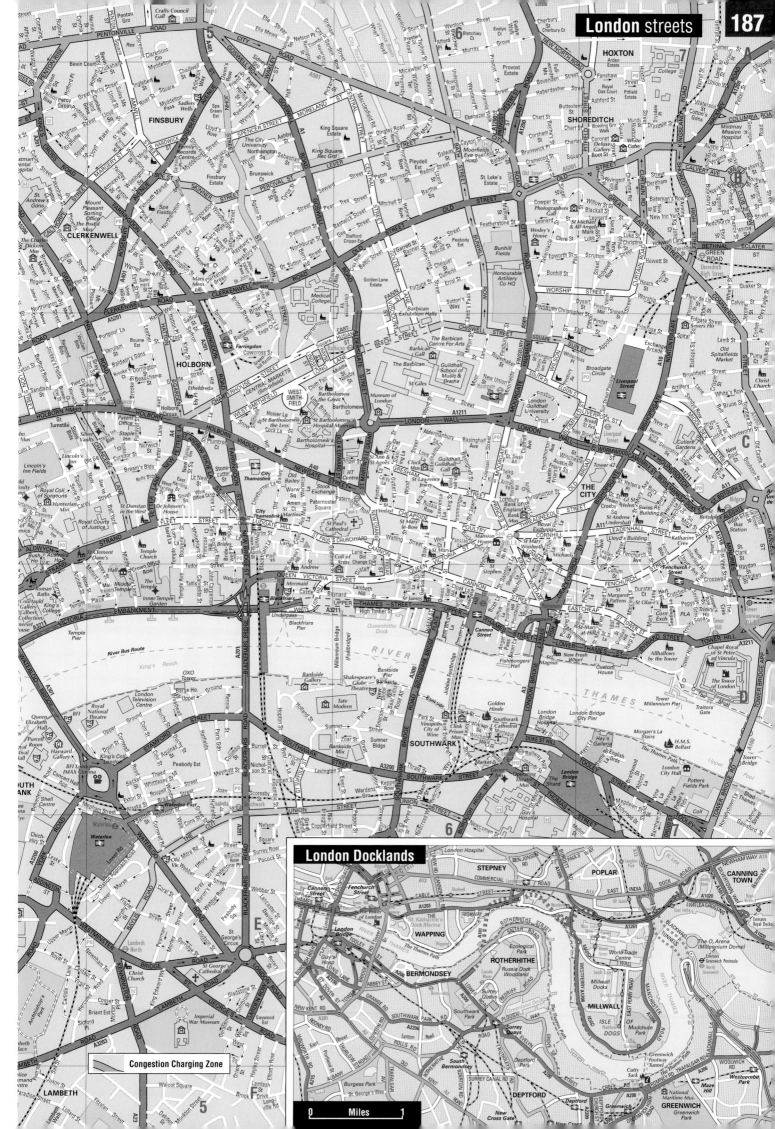

Congestion Charging Zone

London Docklands

0 Miles 1

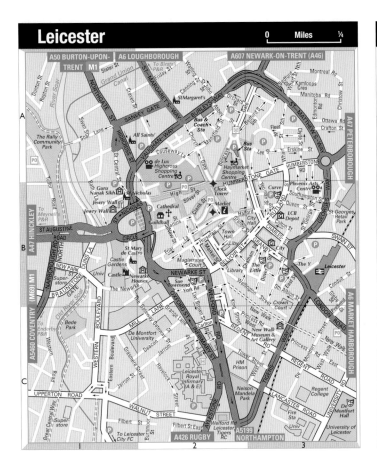

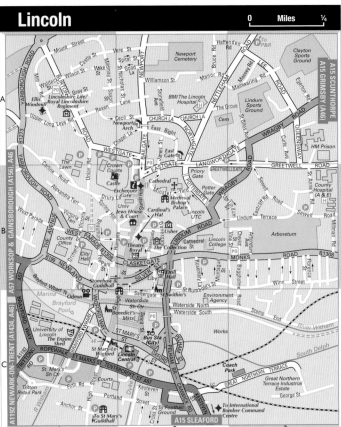

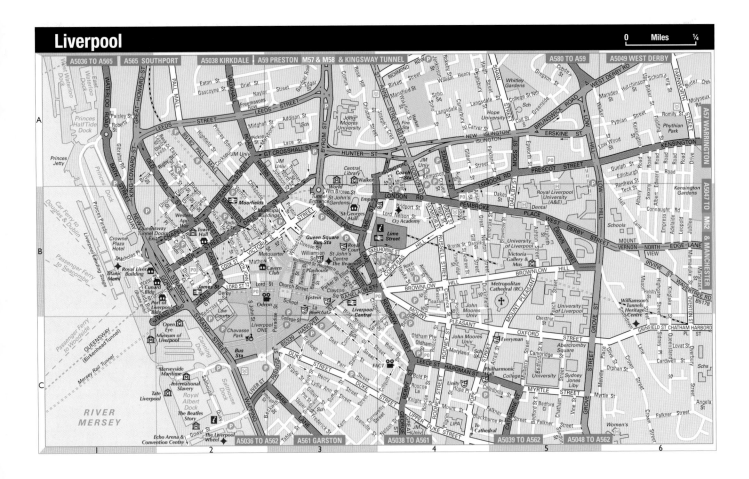

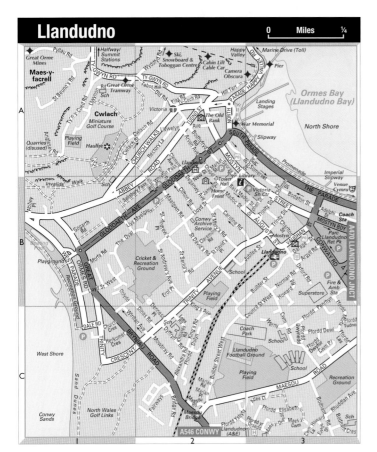

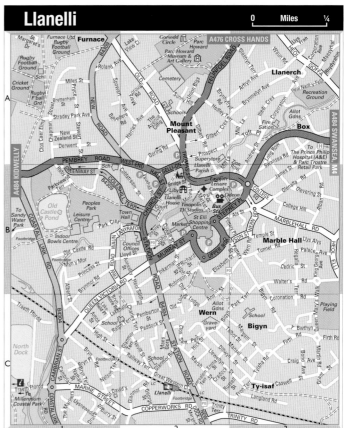

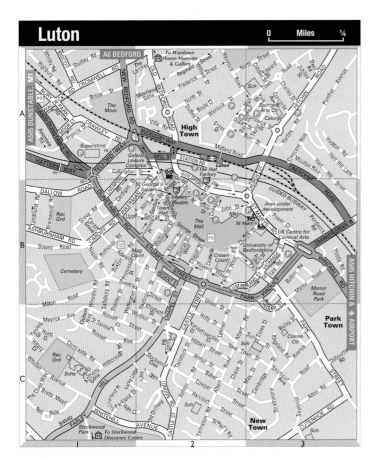

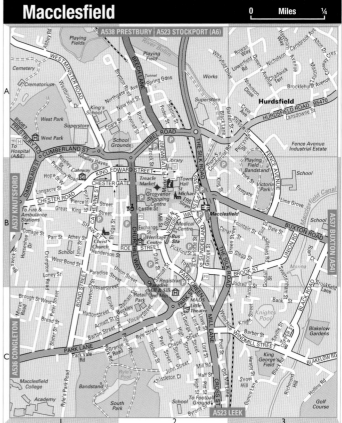

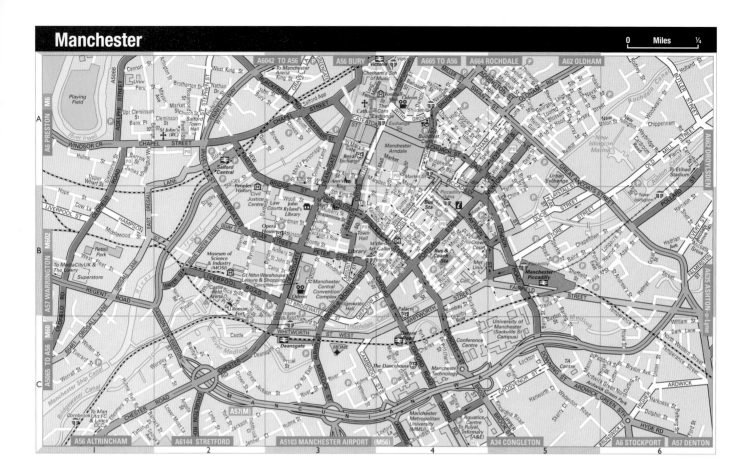

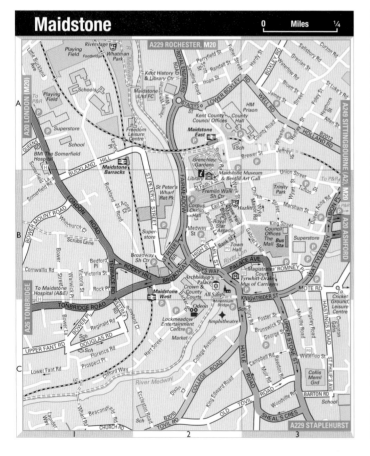

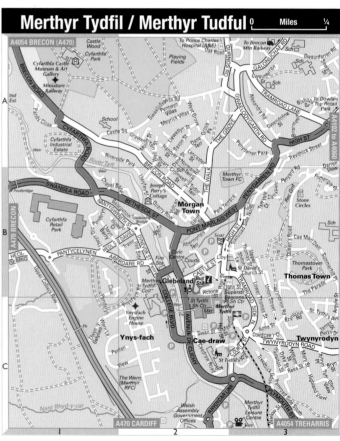

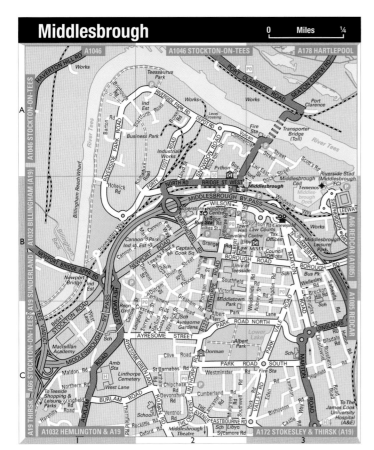

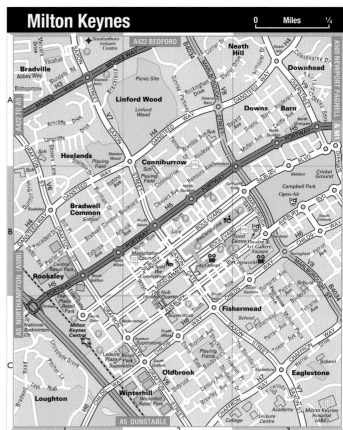

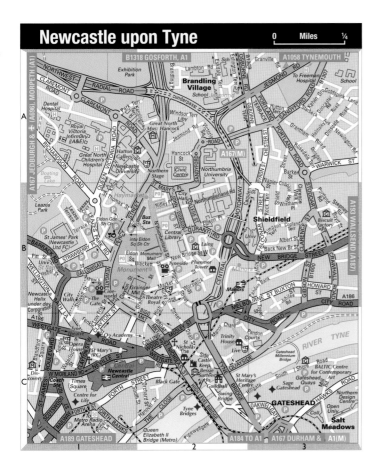

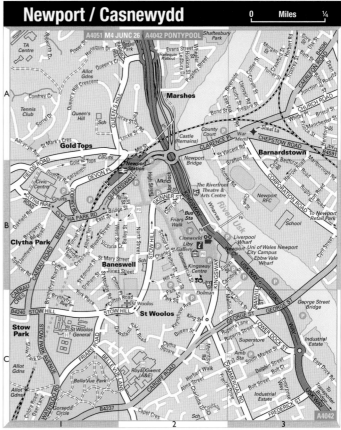

Newquay

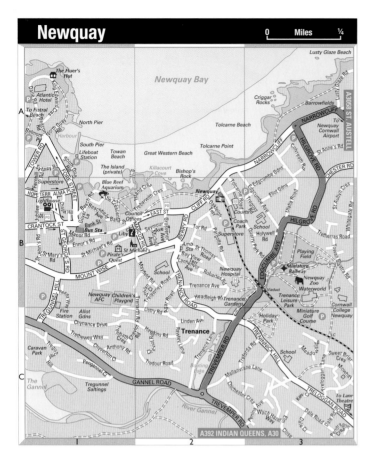

Northampton

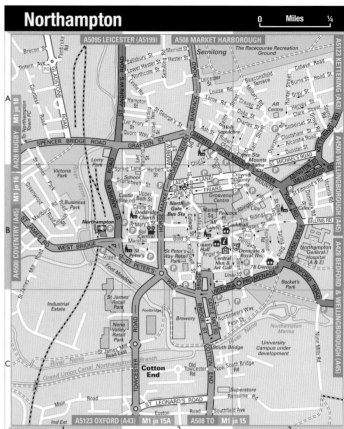

Norwich

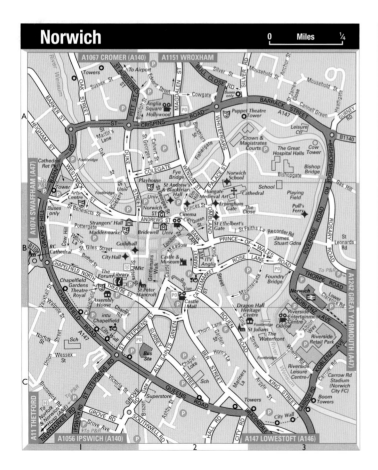

Nottingham

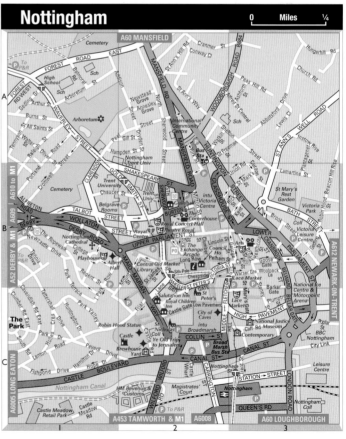

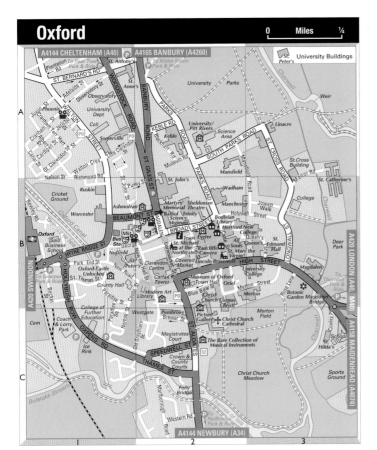

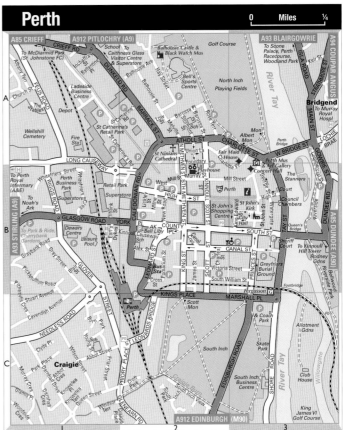

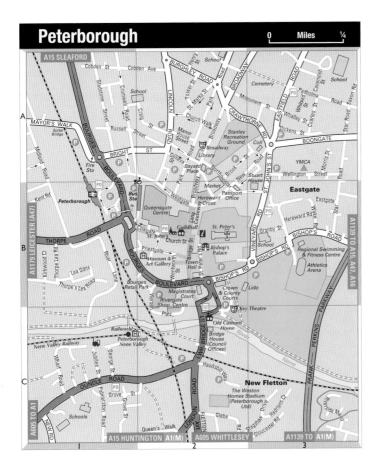

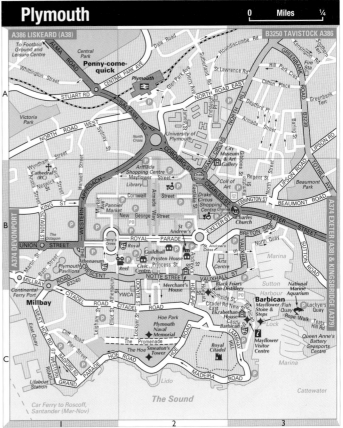

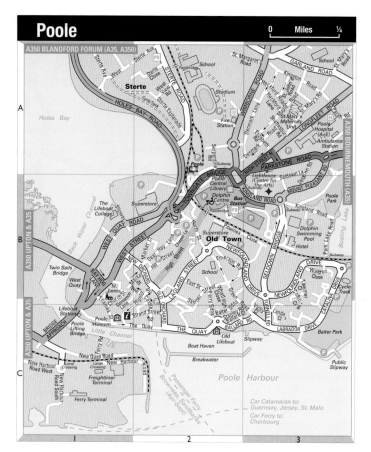

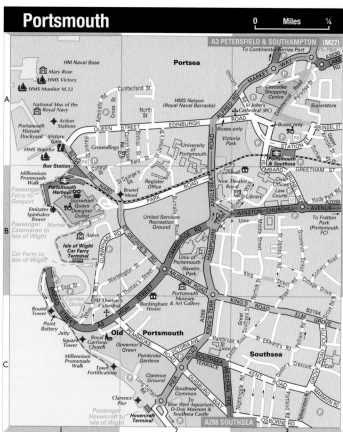

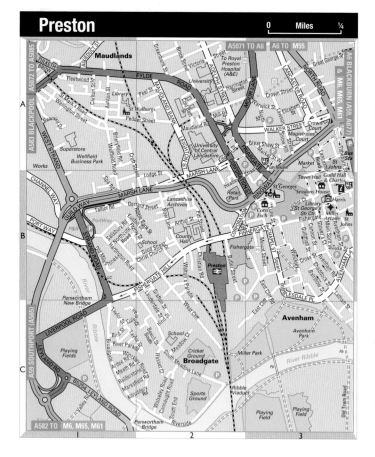

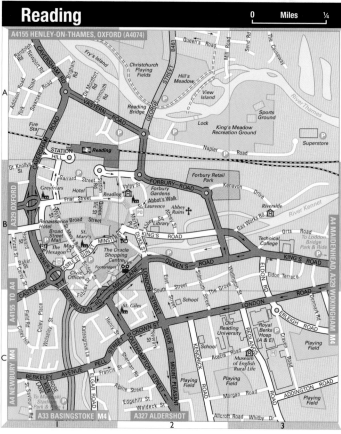

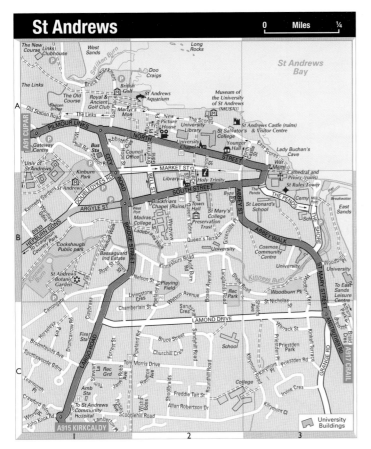

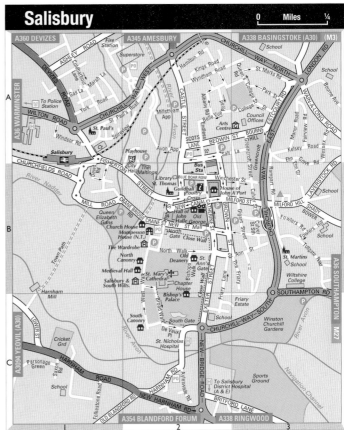

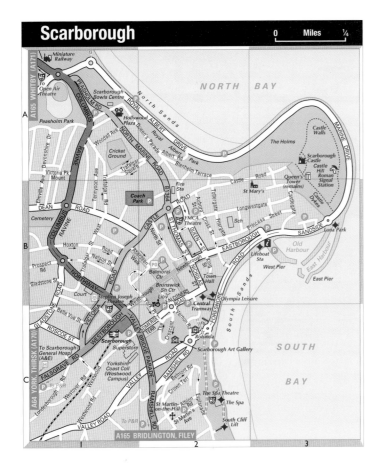

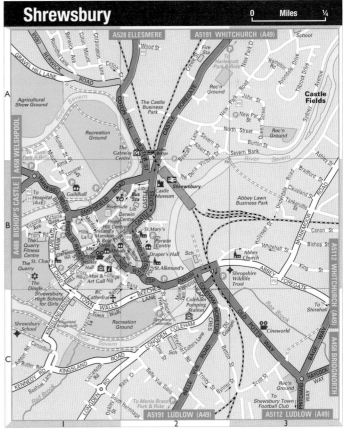

Sheffield

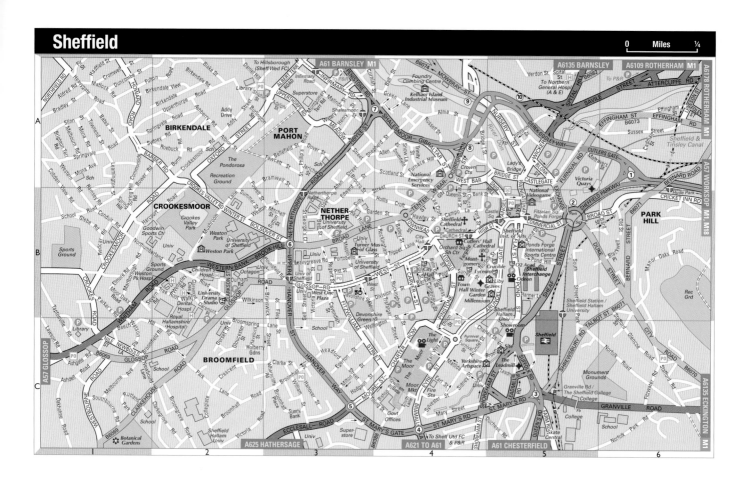

Stoke-on-Trent (Hanley)

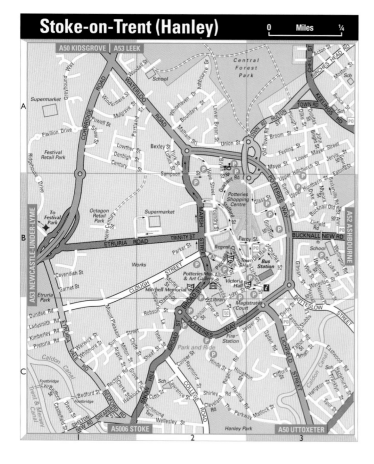

Southampton

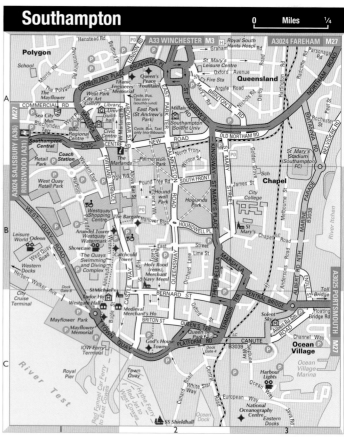

Southend-on-Sea

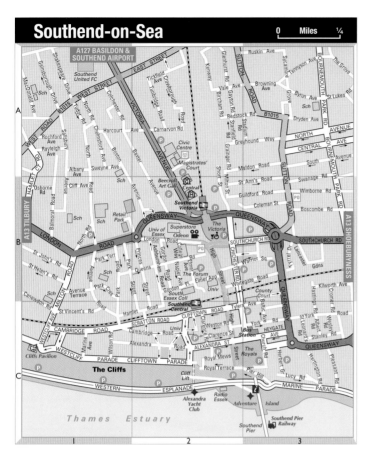

Stirling

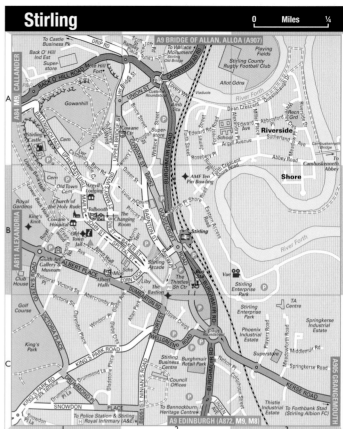

Stratford-upon-Avon

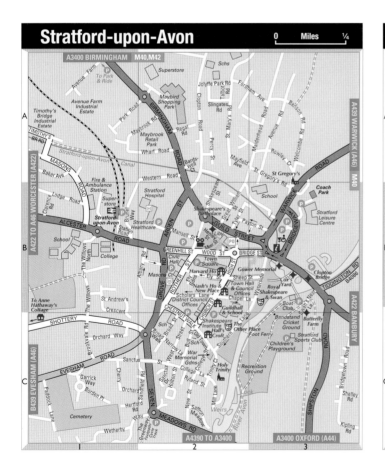

Sunderland

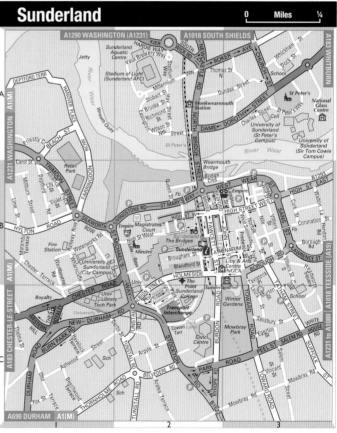

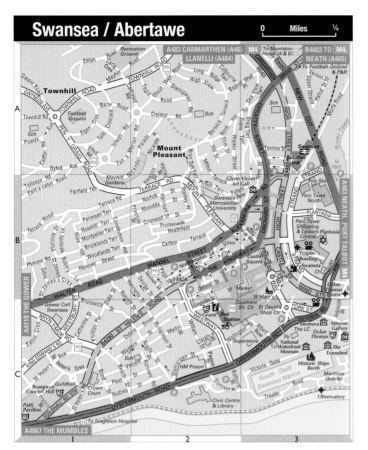

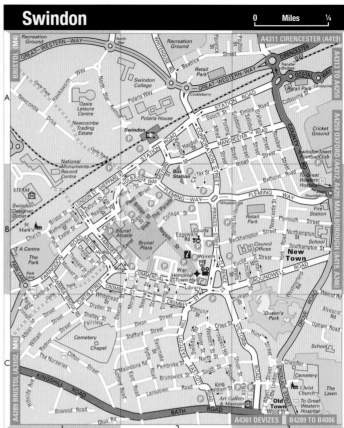

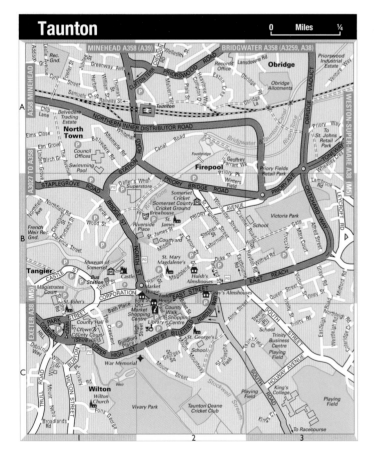

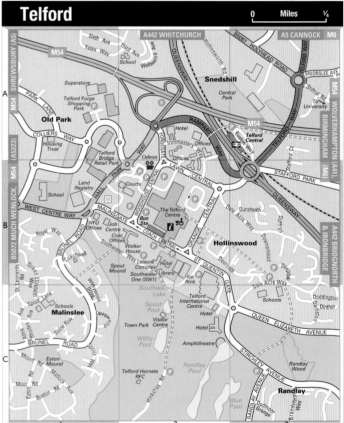

Torquay
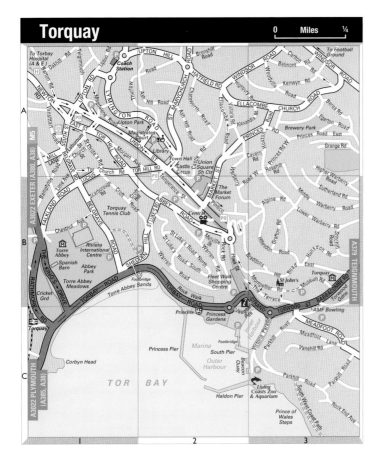

Truro
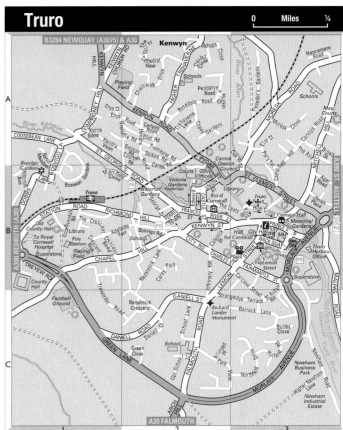

Winchester
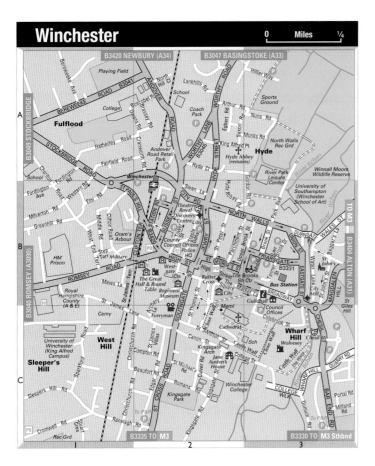

Windsor
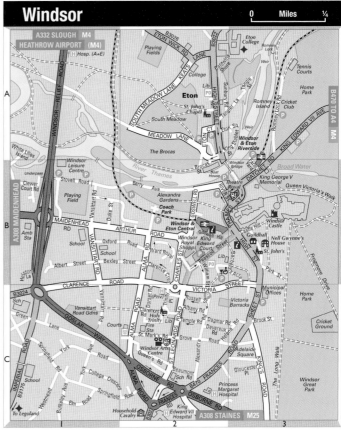

Wolverhampton

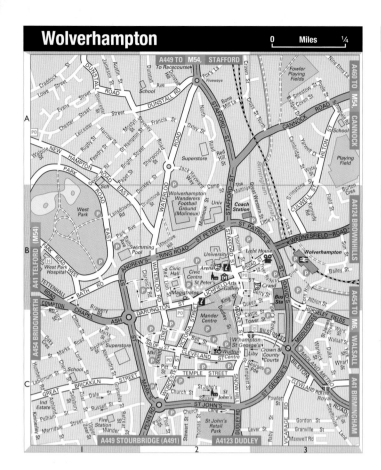

Worcester

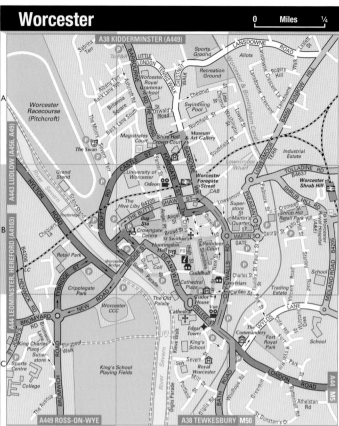

Wrexham / Wrecsam

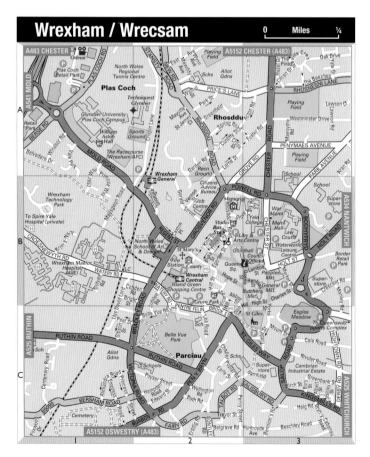

York

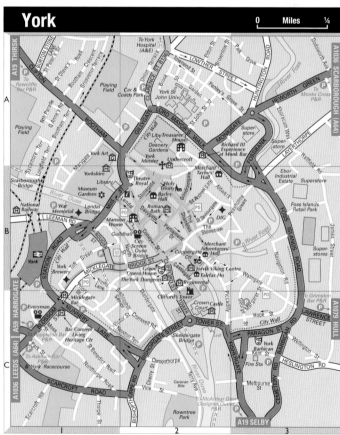

Town plan indexes

Aberdeen 175
Aberdeen.....B2
Aberdeen Grammar School.....A1
Academy,The.....B2
Albert Basin.....B3
Albert Quay.....B3
Albury Rd.....C1
Alford Place.....B1
Art Gallery.....A2
Arts Centre.....A2
Back Wynd.....A2
Baker St.....A1
Beach Blvd.....A3
Belmont.....B2
Belmont St.....B2
Berry St.....A2
Blackfriars St.....A2
Blaikie's Quay.....B3
Bloomfield Rd.....C1
Bon Accord Ctr.....A2
Bon-Accord St.....B1/C1
Bridge St.....B2
Broad St.....A2
Bus Station.....B2
Car FerryTerminal.....B3
Castlegate.....A3
Central Library.....A2
Chapel St.....B1
Cineworld.....B2
Clyde St.....B3
College.....B2
College St.....B2
Commerce St.....A3
Commercial Quay.....B3
Com Centre.....A3/C1
Constitution St.....A3
Cotton St.....A3
Crown St.....B2
Denburn Rd.....A2
Devanha Gdns.....C2
Devanha Gdns South.....C2
East North St.....A3
Esslemont Ave.....A1
Ferryhill Rd.....C2
Ferryhill Terr.....C2
Fish Market.....B3
Fonthill Rd.....C1
Galleria.....B1
Gallowgate.....A2
George St.....A2
Glenbervie Rd.....C3
Golden Sq.....B1
Grampian Rd.....C3
Great Southern Rd.....C1
Guild St.....B2
Hardgate.....B1/C1
His Majesty's Theatre.....A1
Holburn St.....C1
Hollybank Place.....C1
Huntly St.....B1
Hutcheon St.....A1
Information Ctr.....B2
John St.....A2
Justice St.....A3
King St.....B2
Langstane Place.....B1
LemonTree,The.....A3
Library.....C1
Loch St.....A2
Maberly St.....A1
Mariscal Coll.....A2
Maritime Museum & Provost Ross's House.....B2
Market.....B2
Market St.....B2/B3
Menzies Rd.....C3
Mercat Cross.....A3
Millburn St.....C2
Miller St.....A3
Mount St.....A1
Music Hall.....B1
North Esp East.....C3
North Esp West.....C2
Oscar Rd.....C3
Palmerston Rd.....C2
Park St.....A3
Police Station.....A2
Polmuir Rd.....C2
Post Office.....A1/A2/A3/B2/B1
Provost Skene's House.....A2
Queen Elizabeth Br.....C2
Queen St.....A2
Regent Quay.....B3
Regent Road.....B3
Robert Gordon's College.....C1
Rose St.....B1
Rosemount Place.....A1
RosemountViaduct.....A1
St Andrew St.....A2
St Andrew's Cath.....A2
St Mary's Cath.....A1
St Nicholas Centre.....A2
St Nicholas St.....A2
School Hill.....A2
Sinclair Rd.....C3
Skene Sq.....A1
Skene St.....B1
South College St.....C2
South Crown St.....C1
South Esp East.....C3
South Esp West.....C3
South Mount St.....A1
Sports Centre.....C2
Spring Garden.....A2
SpringbankTerr.....C1
Summer St.....B1
Superstore.....B1
Thistle St.....B1
Tolbooth.....A3
Town House.....A3
Trinity Centre.....B2
Union Row.....B1
Union Square.....B2
Union St.....B1/B2
University.....A2
Upper Dock.....B3
Upper Kirkgate.....A2
Victoria Bridge.....C3
Victoria Dock.....B3
Victoria Rd.....C3
Victoria St.....B1
Vue.....B2
Waterloo Quay.....A3
Willowbank Place.....C1
West North St.....A2
Willowbank Rd.....C1
Windmill Brae.....B2

Ayr 175
Ailsa Place.....A1
AlexandraTerr.....A3
Allison St.....B1
Alloway Pk.....C1
Alloway Place.....C1
Alloway St.....C2
Arran Mall.....C2
ArranTerr.....C2
Arthur St.....B2
Ashgrove St.....C2
Auld Brig.....B2
Auld Kirk.....B2
Ayr.....B1
Ayr Academy.....B1
Ayr Central Shopping Centre.....C2
Ayr Harbour.....A1
Ayr Ice Rink.....A2
Ayrshire Coll.....C1
Back Hawkhill Ave.....A3
Back Main St.....B2
Back Peebles St.....B2
Barns Cres.....C1
Barns Pk.....C1
Barns St.....C1
Barns Street La.....C1
Bath Place.....B1
Bellevue Cres.....C1
Bellevue La.....C1
Beresford La.....C2
BeresfordTerr.....C2
Boswell Pk.....B2
Britannia Place.....A3
Bruce Cres.....A1
Burns Statue.....C1
Bus Sta.....B1
Carrick St.....B1
Cassillis St.....A1
Cathcart St.....B1
Charlotte St.....C2
Citadel Leisure Ctr.....B1
Citadel Place.....B1
Compass Pier.....A1
Content Ave.....C3
Content St.....B2
Craigie Ave.....B3
Craigie Rd.....B3
Craigie Way.....B3
Cromwell Rd.....A3
Crown St.....A2
Dalblair Rd.....C2
Dam Park Sports Stadium.....A2
Damside.....A2
Dongola Rd.....C2
Eglinton Place.....B1
EglintonTerr.....B1
Elba St.....B2
Elmbank St.....A3
Esplanade.....B1
Euchar Rock.....A1
Farifield Rd.....C1
Fort St.....B1
Fothringham Rd.....C3
Fullarton St.....B1
Gaiety.....C2
Garden St.....B2
George St.....B2
George's Ave.....A3
Glebe Cres.....A2
Glebe Rd.....A2
GordenTerr.....B3
Green St.....A2
Green Street La.....A2
Hawkhill Ave.....A3
Hawkhill Avenue Lane.....B3
High St.....B2
Holmston Rd.....C3
Information Ctr.....B1
James St.....B3
John St.....B2
King St.....B1
Kings Ct.....B2
Kyle Centre.....C2
Kyle St.....C2
Library.....B2
Limekiln Rd.....A2
Limonds Wynd.....A2
Loudoun Hall.....B2
Lymburn Place.....A3
Macadam Place.....B2
Main St.....B2
Mcadam's Monument.....C1
Mccall's Ave.....C1
Mews La.....B1
Mill Brae.....C2
Mill St.....B2
Mill Wynd.....C2
Miller Rd.....C2
MontgomerieTerr.....B1
New Bridge.....B2
New Bridge St.....B2
New Rd.....A2
Newmarket St.....B2
Newton-on-Ayr Station.....A2
North Harbour St.....B2
North Pier.....A1
Odeon.....C2
Park Circus.....C1
Park Circus La.....C1
ParkTerr.....C1
Pavilion Rd.....A1
Peebles St.....A2
Philip Sq.....C2
Police Station.....B2
Prestwick Rd.....B1
Princes St.....A1
Queen St.....B3
Queen'sTerr.....B1
Racecourse Rd.....C1
River St.....B2
Riverside Place.....B2
Russell Dr.....C1
St Andrews Church.....C2
St George's Rd.....B1
Sandgate.....B1
Savoy Park.....C1
Smith St.....C2
Somerset Park (Ayr United FC).....A1
Somerset Rd.....A3
South Beach Rd.....C1
South Harbour St.....B1
South Pier.....A1
Station Rd.....B2
Strathayr Place.....B2
Superstore.....A2/B2
Taylor St.....A3
Town Hall.....B2
Tryfield Place.....A3
Turner's Bridge.....B2

Bath 175
Alexandra Park.....C2
Alexandra Rd.....C1
Ambulance Sta.....B1
Approach Golf Courses (Public).....A1
Archway St.....C3
Assembly Rooms & Fashion Mus.....B2
Avon St.....B2
Barton St.....B2
Bath Abbey.....B2
Bath Aqua Glass.....B2
Bath College.....B2
Bath Rugby (The Rec).....B3
Bath Spa Station.....C3
Bathwick St.....A3
Beckford Road.....A3
Beechen Cliff Rd.....C2
Bennett St.....A2
Bloomfield Ave.....C1
Broad Quay.....C2
Broad St.....B2
Brock St.....A1
Building of Bath Museum.....A2
Bus Station.....C2
Calton Gdns.....C2
Calton Rd.....C2
Camden Cres.....A2
Cavendish Rd.....A1
Cemetery.....B1
Charlotte St.....B1
Chaucer Rd.....C2
Cheap St.....B2
Circus Mews.....A2
Claverton St.....C2
Corn St.....C2
Cricket Ground.....B3
Daniel St.....A3
Edward St.....B3
Ferry La.....B3
Fire Station.....C1
First Ave.....C1
Forester Ave.....A3
Forester Rd.....A3
Gays Hill.....A2
George St.....B2
Great Pulteney St.....B3
Green Park.....B1
Green Park Rd.....B1
Green Park Station.....B1
Grove St.....B2
Guildhall.....B2
Harley St.....A1
Hayesfield Park.....C1
Henrietta Gdns.....A3
Henrietta Mews.....B3
Henrietta Park.....B3
Henrietta Rd.....A3
Henrietta St.....B3
Henry St.....B2
Herschel Museum of Astronomy.....B1
High Common.....A1
Holburne Mus.....B3
Holloway.....C2
Information Ctr.....B2
James St West.....B1/B2
Jane Austen Ctr.....B2
Julian Rd.....A1
Junction Rd.....C1
Kingsmead Leisure Complex.....B1
Kipling Ave.....C1
Lansdown Cres.....A1
Lansdown Grove.....A2
Lansdown Rd.....A2
Library.....B2
London Rd.....A3
London St.....A2
Lower Bristol Rd.....C1
Lower Oldfield Park.....C1
Lyncombe Hill.....C3
Magistrates' Court.....B2
Manvers St.....C2
Maple Grove.....C3
Margaret's Hill.....A2
Marlborough Bldgs.....A1
Marlborough La.....B1
Midland Bridge Rd.....B1
Milk St.....B2
Milsom St.....B2
Monmouth St.....B2
Morford St.....A2
Museum of Bath at Work.....A2
Museum of East Asian Art.....A2
New King St.....B1
No 1 Royal Cres.....A1
Norfolk Bldgs.....B1
Norfolk Cres.....B1
North Parade Rd.....C3
Oldfield Rd.....C1
Paragon.....A2
Pines Way.....C1
Podium Shopping Centre.....B2
Police Station.....B2
Portland Place.....A2
Post Office.....A3/B2/C2
Postal Museum.....B2
Powlett Rd.....A3
Prior Park Rd.....C3
Pulteney Bridge.....B2
Pulteney Gdns.....B3
Pulteney Rd.....B3/C3
Queen Sq.....B2
Raby Place.....B3
Recreation Ground.....B3
Rivers St.....A2
Rockliffe Ave.....A3
Rockliffe Rd.....A3
Roman Baths & Pump Room.....B2
Rossiter Rd.....C3
Royal Ave.....A1
Royal Cres.....A1
Royal High School,The.....A1
Royal Victoria Park.....B1
St James Sq.....B1
St John's Rd.....A3
Sally Lunn's Ho.....B2
Shakespeare Ave.....C1
Shopmobility.....B2
South Pde.....C2
SouthGate Shopping Centre.....C2
Sports & Leisure Ctr.....B3
Spring Gdns.....C3
Stall St.....B2
Stanier Rd.....B1
Superstore.....C1
Sydney Gdns.....A3
Sydney Place.....B3
Sydney Rd.....B3
Theatre Royal.....B2
Thermae Bath Spa.....B2
Thomas St.....A3
Tyning,The.....A3
Union St.....B2
University.....A1
Upper Bristol Rd.....B1
Upper Oldfield Pk.....C1
Victoria Art Gallery.....B2
Victoria Bridge Rd.....B1
Walcot St.....B2
Wells Rd.....C1
Westgate Buildings.....B2
Westgate St.....B2
Weston Rd.....A1
Widcombe Hill.....C3

Birmingham 176
Abbey St.....A1
Aberdeen St.....A1
Acorn Grove.....B1
Adams St.....A5
Adderley St.....C5
Albert St.....B4
Albion St.....A2
Alcester St.....C4
Aldgate Grove.....A3
All Saint's St.....A2
All Saints Rd.....A2
Allcock St.....C5
Allesley St.....A4
Allison St.....C4
Alma Cres.....B6
Alston Rd.....C6
Arcadian Centre.....C3
Arena Birmingham.....C2
Arthur St.....C6
Assay Office.....A3
Aston Expressway.....A5
Aston St.....B4
Aston University.....B4/B5
Avenue Rd.....A6
Bacchus Rd.....A1
Bagot St.....A4
Banbury St.....B4
Barford Rd.....B1
Barford St.....C4
Barn St.....B5
Barnwell Rd.....C5
Barr St.....A3
Barrack St.....B5
Barwick St.....B3
Bath Row.....C2
Beaufort Rd.....C1
Belmont Row.....B5
Benson Rd.....A1
Berkley St.....C2
Bexhill Grove.....C4
Birchall St.....C5
Birmingham City FC.....C6
Birmingham City Hospital (A&E).....A1
Birmingham City Univ.....A3
Birmingham Wheels Park.....B6
Bishopsgate St.....C2
Blews St.....A4
Bloomsbury St.....A5
Blucher St.....C3
Bordesley St.....C5
Bowyer St.....C5
Bradburne Way.....A5
Bradford St.....C4
Branston St.....A3
Brearley St.....A4
Brewery St.....A4
Bridge St.....C2
Bridge St West.....A3
Brindley Dr.....B2
Broad St.....C2
Broad Street Cineworld.....C2
Broadway Plaza.....C1
Bromley St.....C5
Bromsgrove St.....C4
Brookfield Rd.....A1
Browning St.....C1
Bryant St.....A1
BT Tower.....A3
Buckingham St.....A3
Bull St.....B4
Bullring.....C4
Cambridge St.....B2
Camden Dr.....B2
Camden St.....B1
Cannon St.....B3
Cardigan St.....B5
Carlisle St.....A1
Carlyle Rd.....B1
Caroline St.....A3
Carver St.....B2
Cato St.....B6
Cattell Rd.....C6
Cattells Grove.....A6
Cawdor Cres.....C1
Cecil St.....B4
Cemetery.....A2/B2
Cemetery La.....A2
Ctr Link Ind Est.....A6
Charlotte St.....B2
Cheapside.....C4
Chester St.....A5
Children's Hospital (A&E).....B4
Church St.....B4
Claremont Rd.....A2
Clarendon Rd.....C1
Clark St.....C1
Clement St.....B3
Clissold St.....B2
Cliveland St.....B4
Coach Station.....C5
College St.....B2
Colmore Circus.....B4
Colmore Row.....B4
Commercial St.....C3
Constitution Hill.....B3
Cope St.....C2
Coplow St.....C1
Corporation St.....C4
Council House.....B3
County Court.....B4
Coveley Grove.....A2
Coventry Rd.....C6
Coventry St.....C5
Cox St.....B3
Crabtree Rd.....A2
Cregoe St.....C3
Crescent Ave.....C2
CrescentTheatre.....C3
Crescent,The.....A2
Cromwell St.....A6
Cromwell St.....B5
Cube,The.....C3
Curzon St.....B5
Custard Factory.....C5
Cuthbert Rd.....B1
Dale End.....B4
Dart St.....C6
Dartmouth Circus.....A4
Dartmouth Middleway.....A5
Deritend.....C4
Devon St.....A6
Devonshire St.....A1
Digbeth High St.....C4
Dolman St.....B6
Dover St.....A1
Duchess Rd.....C2
Duddeston.....B6
Duddeston Manor Rd.....B5
Duddeston Mill Rd.....B6
Duddeston Mill Trading Estate.....B6
Dudley Rd.....C1
Edmund St.....B3
Edward St.....B2
Elkington St.....A4
Ellen St.....A3
Ellis St.....C3
Erskine St.....B5
Essex St.....C4
Eyre St.....B1
Farm Croft.....A3
Farm St.....A3
Fazeley St.....B4/C5
Felstead Way.....B6
Finstall Cl.....B5
Five Ways.....C2
Fiveway Shopping Centre.....C2
Fleet St.....B3
Floodgate St.....C5
Ford St.....A2
Fore St.....C4
Forster St.....B5
Francis Rd.....C1
Francis St.....B5
Frankfort St.....A4
Frederick St.....B3
Freeth St.....C1
Freightliner Terminal.....B6
Garrison La.....C6
Garrison St.....B6
Gas St.....C2
Geach St.....A4
George St.....B3
George St West.....B2
Gibb St.....C5
Gilby Rd.....C1
Gillott Rd.....B1
Glover St.....C5
Goode Ave.....A2
Goodrick Way.....A6
Gordon St.....B6
Graham St.....B2
Grand Central.....C4
Granville St.....C2
Gray St.....C5
Great Barr St.....C5
Great Charles St Queensway.....B3
Great Francis St.....B6
Great Hampton Row.....A3
Great Hampton St.....A3
Great King St.....A3
Great Lister St.....A5
GreatTindal St.....C1
Green La.....C6
Green St.....C5
Greenway St.....C6
Grosvenor St West.....C2
Guest Grove.....A3
Guild Cl.....C2
Guildford Dr.....A4
Guthrie Cl.....A3
Hagley Rd.....C1
Hall St.....B3
Hampton St.....A3
Handsworth New Rd.....A1
Hanley St.....B4
Harford St.....A3
Harmer Rd.....A1
Hatchett St.....A4
Heath Mill La.....C5
Heath St.....B1
Heath St South.....B1
Heaton St.....A2
Heneage St.....B5
Henrietta St.....B3
Herbert Rd.....C6
High St.....C4
Hilden Rd.....C6
Hill St.....C3/C4
Hindlow Cl.....C5
Hingeston St.....B2
Hippodrome Theatre.....C4
HM Prison.....A1
Hockley Circus.....A2
Hockley Hill.....A3
Hockley St.....A3
Holliday St.....C2
Holloway Circus.....C4
Holloway Head.....C3
Holt St.....B5
Hooper St.....B1
Horse Fair.....C4
Hospital St.....A4
Howard St.....A3
Howe St.....B5
Hubert St.....A5
Hunters Rd.....A3
Hunters Vale.....A3
Huntly Rd.....C1
Hurst St.....C4
Icknield Port Rd.....B1
Icknield Sq.....B2
Icknield St.....A2/B2
IKON Information Ctr.....C3
Inge St.....C3
Irving St.....C3
James Watt Queensway.....B4
Jennens Rd.....B5
Jewellery Quarter.....A3
Jewellery Quarter Museum.....A3
John Bright St.....C3
Keeley St.....C5
Kellett Rd.....B5
Kent St.....C4
Kenyon St.....A3
Key Hill.....A3
Kilby Ave.....C2
King Edwards Rd.....B2
King Edwards Rd.....B2
Kingston Rd.....C6
Ladywood Arts & Leisure Centre.....B1
Ladywood Middleway.....C2/C3
Lancaster St.....B4
Landor St.....B6
Law Courts.....B4
Lawden Rd.....C6
Lawford Cl.....B5
Lawley Middleway.....B5
Ledsam St.....C1
Lees St.....A1
Legge La.....B2
Lennox St.....A3
Library.....A6/C3
Lighthouse Ave.....A5
Link Rd.....A1
Lionel St.....B3
Lister St.....B5
Little Ann St.....C5
Little Hall Rd.....A6
Liverpool St.....C5
Livery St.....B3/B4
Lodge Rd.....A1
Lord St.....A5
Love La.....A5
Lovely St.....C1
Lower Dartmouth St.....C6
Lower Loveday St.....B4
LowerTower St.....A4
LowerTrinty St.....C5
Ludgate Hill.....B3
Mailbox Ctr & BBC.....C3
Margaret St.....B3
Markby Rd.....A1
Marroway St.....B1
Maxstoke St.....C6
Melvina Rd.....A6
Meriden St.....C4
Metropolitan (RC).....B4
Midland St.....B6
Milk St.....C5
Millennium Point.....B5
Miller St.....A4
Moat La.....C4
Montague Rd.....C6
Montague St.....B5
Monument Rd.....C1
Moor St.....B4
Moor St Queensway.....B4
Moor Street.....C4
Moorsom St.....A4
Morville St.....C1
Mosborough Cres.....A3
Moseley St.....C4
Mott St.....A3
Museum & Art Gallery.....B3
Musgrave Rd.....A1
National Sea Life Centre.....C2
Navigation St.....C3
Nechell's Park Rd.....A6
Nechells Parkway.....B5
Nechells Place.....A6
New Alexandra.....C3
New Bartholomew St.....C4
New Canal St.....C5
New John St West.....A3
New Spring St.....B2
New St.....C3
New Street.....C3
New Summer St.....A4
NewTown Row.....A4
Newhall Hill.....B3
Newhall St.....B3
Newton St.....B4
Noel Rd.....C1
Norman St.....A1
Northbrook St.....C1
Northwood St.....B3
Norton St.....A2
Old Crown Ho.....C4
Old RepTheatre,The.....C3
Old Snow Hill.....B4
Oliver Rd.....C1
Oliver St.....A6
Osler St.....C1
Oxford St.....C4
Palmer St.....C5
Paradise Circus.....B3
Paradise St.....C3
Park Rd.....A3
Park St.....C4
Pavilions.....C4
Paxton Rd.....A2
Peel St.....C4
Pershore St.....C4
Phillips St.....A4
Pickford St.....C5
Pinfold St.....C3
Pitsford St.....A2
Plough & Harrow Rd.....C1
Police Station.....A4/B4/C2/C4
Pope St.....B2
Portland Rd.....C1
Princip St.....B4
Printing House St.....B4
Priory Queensway.....B4
Pritchett St.....A4
Proctor St.....A5
Radnor St.....A3
Rea St.....C4
Regent Place.....B3
Register Office.....C3
Repertory Theatre.....C2
Reservoir Rd.....C1
Richard St.....A5
River St.....C5
Rocky La.....A5/A6
Rodney Cl.....C1
Roseberry St.....B1
Rotton Park St.....B1
Rupert St.....A5
Ruston St.....C1
Ryland St.....C1
St Andrew's Ind Est.....C6
St Andrew's St.....C6
St Bolton St.....C5
St Chads.....B4
St Chads Queensway.....B4
St Clements Rd.....A6
St George's St.....B3
St James Place.....B6
St Marks Cres.....B2
St Martin's.....C4
St Paul's.....B3
St Paul's.....B3
St Paul's Sq.....B3
St Philip's.....B3
St Stephen's St.....A4
StThomas' Peace Garden.....C3
StVincent St.....C1
Saltley Rd.....A5
Sand Pits Pde.....B2
Severn St.....C3
Shadwell St.....B4
Sheepcote St.....C2
Shefford Rd.....A4
Sherborne St.....C2
Shylton's Croft.....C2
Skipton Rd.....C1
Smallbrook Queensway.....C4
Smith St.....A3
Snow Hill.....B4
Snow Hill Queensway.....B4
Soho, Benson Rd.....A1
South Rd.....A2
Spencer St.....B3
Spring Hill.....B1
Staniforth St.....B4
Station St.....C3
Steelhouse La.....B4
Stephenson St.....C3
Steward St.....B1
Stirling Rd.....C1
Stour St.....B1
Suffolk St Queensway.....C3
Summer Hill Rd.....B2
Summer Hill St.....B2
Summer HillTerr.....B2
Summer La.....A4
Summer Row.....B3
Summerfield Cres.....B1
Summerfield Park.....B1
Superstore.....C4
Sutton St.....C3
Swallow St.....C3
Sydney Rd.....C6
Symphony Hall.....C2
Talbot St.....B1
Temple Row.....B4
Temple St.....B3
Templefield St.....C6
Tenby St.....B2
Tenby St North.....B2
Tennant St.....C2
Thimble Mill La.....A6
Thinktank (Science & Discovery).....B5
Thomas St.....A4
Thorpe St.....C3
Tilton Rd.....C6
Tower St.....A4
Town Hall.....B3
Trent St.....C5
Turner's Buildings.....A1
Unett St.....A3
UnionTerr.....B6
UpperTrinity St.....C5
Uxbridge St.....A3
Vauxhall Grove.....B5
Vauxhall Rd.....B5
Vernon Rd.....C1
Vesey St.....B4
Viaduct St.....B5
Victoria Sq.....B3
Villa St.....A3
Vittoria St.....B3
Vyse St.....A3
Walter St.....A6
Wardlow Rd.....A5
Warstone La.....B2
Washington St.....C3
Water St.....B3
Waterworks Rd.....C1
Watery La.....C6
Well St.....A3
Western Rd.....B1
Wharf St.....A3
Wheeler St.....A3
Whitehouse St.....A4
Whitmore St.....A3
Whittall St.....B4
Wholesale Market.....C4
Wiggin St.....C1
Willes Rd.....A1
Windsor Ind Est.....A5
Windsor St.....A5
Winson Green Rd.....A1
Witton St.....C6
Wolseley St.....C6
Woodcock St.....B5

Blackpool 176
Abingdon St.....B1
Addison Cres.....A3
Adelaide St.....B1
Albert Rd.....B2
Alfred St.....B2
Ascot Rd.....A3
Ashton Rd.....C2
Auburn Grove.....C3
Bank Hey St.....B1
Banks St.....A1
Beech Ave.....C3
Bela Grove.....C3
Belmont Ave.....C3
Birley St.....B1
Blackpool & FleetwoodTram.....A1
Blackpool & the Fylde College.....A2
Blackpool FC.....C2
Blackpool North.....A2
BlackpoolTower.....B1
Blundell St.....C1
Bonny St.....B1
Breck Rd.....A3
Bryan Rd.....A3
Buchanan St.....A2
Bus Station.....C1
Cambridge Rd.....A3
Caunce St.....A2/A3
Central Dr.....B1/C2
Central Pier.....C1
Central Pier Theatre.....C1
Chapel St.....C1
Charles St.....A2
Charnley Rd.....B1
Church St.....A1/A2
Clinton Ave.....B2
Coach Station.....A2/C1
Cocker St.....A1
Coleridge Rd.....A3
Collingwood Ave.....A3
Comedy Carpet.....B1
Condor Grove.....C3
Cookson St.....A1
Coronation St.....B1
Corporation St.....B1
Courts.....A2
Cumberland Ave.....A3
Cunliffe Rd.....A3
Dale St.....C1
Devonshire Rd.....A3
Devonshire Sq.....A3
Dickson Rd.....A1
Elizabeth St.....A2
Ferguson Rd.....C3
Forest Gate.....C3
Foxhall Rd.....C1
Freckleton St.....C2
George St.....A2
Gloucester Ave.....A3
Golden Mile,The.....C1
Gorse Rd.....C3
Gorton St.....A2
GrandTheatre,The.....B1
Granville Rd.....A2
Grasmere Rd.....C2
Grosvenor St.....A2
Grundy Art Gallery.....A1
Harvey Rd.....A3
Hornby Rd.....B2
Houndshill Shopping Centre.....B1
Hull Rd.....B1
Ibbison Ct.....C1
Information Ctr.....A1
Kent Rd.....C2
Keswick Rd.....C2
King St.....A2
Knox Grove.....C3
Laycock Gate.....A3
Layton Rd.....A3
Leamington Rd.....B2
Leeds Rd.....B2
Leicester Rd.....B2
Levens Grove.....C3
Library.....A2
Lifeboat Station.....B1
Lincoln Rd.....B2
Liverpool Rd.....B2
Livingstone Rd.....B2
London Rd.....A2
Lune Grove.....C2
Lytham Rd.....C1
Madame Tussaud's Blackpool.....C1
Manchester Sq.....C1
Manor Rd.....A3
Maple Ave.....C3
Market St.....B1
Marlboro Rd.....B2
Mere Rd.....A2
Milbourne St.....A2
Newcastle Ave.....B3
Newton Dr.....A3
North Pier.....B1
North PierTheatre.....B1
North Pier.....B1
Odeon.....C1
Olive Grove.....C3
Palatine Rd.....B2
Park Rd.....B2/C3
Peter St.....B2
Police Station.....B2
Post Office.....A1/B1/B3/C3
Princess Parade.....A1
Promenade.....A1/C1
Queen St.....A1
Queen Victoria Rd.....C2
Raikes Pde.....B2
Reads Ave.....B2
Regent Rd.....B2
Register Office.....B2
Ribble Rd.....B2
Rigby Rd.....C1/C2
Ripon Rd.....B2
St Albans Rd.....B2
St Ives Ave.....C3
St John's Square.....B1
StVincent Ave.....C3
Salisbury Rd.....B2
Salthouse Ave.....C2
Salvation Army Ctr.....C2
Sands Way.....C1
Sea Life Centre.....B1
Seasiders Way.....C1
Selbourne Rd.....A3
Sharrow Grove.....C3
Somerset Ave.....C3
South King St.....B2
Springfield Rd.....A1
Sutton Place.....B2
Talbot Rd.....A1/A2
Thornber Grove.....C2
Topping St.....B1
Tower.....B1
Town Hall.....B1
Tram Depot.....C1
Tyldesley Rd.....C1
Vance Rd.....B1
Victoria St.....B1
Victory Rd.....A2
Wayman Rd.....A3
Westmorland Ave.....C2/C3
Whitegate Dr.....C3
Winter Gardens Theatre.....B1
Woodland Grove.....C3
Woolman Rd.....B2

Bournemouth 176
Ascham Rd.....A3
Avenue Rd.....B1
Ave Shopping Ctr.....B1
Bath Rd.....C2
Beacon Rd.....C1
Beechey Rd.....A3
Bodorgan Rd.....B1
Bourne Ave.....B1
Bournemouth.....A3
Bournemouth & Poole College.....B3
Bournemouth International Ctr.....C1
Bournemouth Pier.....C2
Bournemouth Station.....B3
Braidley Rd.....A1
Cavendish Place.....A1
Cavendish Rd.....A2
Central Drive.....A1
Central Gdns.....A1
Christchurch Rd.....B3
Cliff Lift.....C1/C3
Coach House Place.....A3
Coach Station.....A3
Commercial Rd.....B1
Cotlands Rd.....B3
Cranborne Rd.....C1
Cricket Ground.....A2
Cumnor Rd.....B2
Dean Park.....A2
Dean Park Cres.....B2
Dean Park Rd.....B2
Durrant Rd.....B1
East Overcliff Dr.....C2
Exeter Cres.....C1
Exeter La.....C2
Exeter Rd.....C1
Gervis Place.....B1
Gervis Rd.....C2
Glen Fern Rd.....B2
Golf Club.....A3
Grove Rd.....B3
Hinton Rd.....B2
Holdenhurst Rd.....B3
Horseshoe Comm.....B1
Information Ctr.....B2
Lansdowne.....B2
Lansdowne Rd.....A2
Lorne Park Rd.....B2
Lower Gdns.....B1/C2
Madeira Rd.....A2
Methuen Rd.....A3
Meyrick Park.....A1
Meyrick Rd.....B3
Milton Rd.....A2
Nuffield Health Bournemouth Hosp (private).....A2
Oceanarium.....C2
Odeon Cinema.....B1
Old Christchurch Rd.....B2
Ophir Rd.....A3
Oxford Rd.....B3
Park Rd.....A3
Parsonage Rd.....B2
Pavilion.....C2
Pier Approach.....C2
PierTheatre.....C2
Police Station.....A3/B3
Portchester Rd.....B3
Post Office.....B1/B3
Priory Rd.....C1
Quadrant,The.....B1
Recreation Ground.....A1
Richmond Gardens Shopping Centre.....B2
Richmond Hill Rd.....B1
Russell-Cotes Art Gallery & Mus.....C2
Russell Cotes Rd.....C2
St Anthony's Rd.....A1
St Michael's Rd.....C1
St Paul's La.....B3
St Paul's Rd.....B3
St Peter's.....B2
St Peter's Rd.....B2
St Stephen's Rd.....B1/B2
St Swithun's Rd.....B3
St Swithun's Rd.....B3
StValerie Rd.....A2
StWinifred's Rd.....A1
Square,The.....B1
Stafford Rd.....B2
Terrace Rd.....B1
Town Hall.....A1
Tregonwell Rd.....C1
Triangle,The.....B1
Trinity Rd.....B2
Undercliff Drive.....C3
Upper Hinton Rd.....B2
UpperTerr Rd.....C1
WellingtonRd.....A2/A3
Wessex Way.....A3/B1/B2
West Cliff Prom.....C1
West Hill Rd.....C1
West Undercliff Promenade.....C1
Westover Rd.....B2
Wimborne Rd.....C1
Wootton Mount.....C1
Wychwood Dr.....A1
Yelverton Rd.....B2
York Rd.....B3
Zig-Zag Walks.....C1/C3

Bradford 177
Alhambra.....B1
Back Ashgrove.....B1
Barkerend Rd.....A3
Barnard Rd.....C2
Barry St.....B2
Bolling Rd.....C3
Bolton Rd.....A3
Bowland St.....A1
Bradford Big Screen.....B1
Bradford College.....B1
Bradford Forster Sq.....A2
Bradford Interchange.....B2
Bradford Playhouse.....B2
Bridge St.....B2
Britannia St.....B1
Broadway Bradford,The.....A2
Burnett St.....B3
Bus Station.....B2
Butler St West.....A3
Caledonia St.....C2
Canal Rd.....A2
Carlton St.....B1
Cathedral.....A2
Centenary Sq.....B1
Chapel St.....B2
Cheapside.....A2
Church Bank.....B2
Cineworld.....B1
City Hall.....B2
City Rd.....A1
Claremont.....C1
Colour Experience.....B1
Croft St.....B2
Crown Court.....A1
Darfield St.....A1
Darley St.....A2
Drewton Rd.....A1
Drummond Trading Estate.....A1
Dryden St.....B3
Dyson St.....A1
Easby Rd.....C1
East Parade.....B3
Eldon Place.....A1
Filey St.....B3
Forster Square Retail Park.....A2
Gallery II.....A1
Garnett St.....C3
Godwin St.....B2
Gracechurch St.....A1
Grattan Rd.....B1
Great Horton Rd.....B1/B2
GroveTerr.....B1
Hall Ings.....B2
Hall La.....C3
Hallfield Rd.....A1
Hammstrasse.....A2
Harris St.....B3
Holdsworth St.....A2
Ice Arena.....B2
Impressions.....B2
Information Ctr.....B2
Inland Revenue.....B2
Ivegate.....B2
Jacob's Well.....B2
James St.....A2
John St.....A2
Kirkgate.....B2
Kirkgate Centre.....B2
Laisteridge La.....C1
Leeds Rd.....B3
Leisure Exchange,The.....B3
Library.....B1/B2
Listerhills Rd.....C1
Little Horton Green.....C1
Little Horton La.....C1
Longside La.....A1
Lumb La.....A1
Magistrates Court.....B2
Manchester Rd.....C2
Manningham La.....A1
Manor Row.....A2
Market.....A3
Market St.....B2
Melbourne Place.....C1
Midland Rd.....A2
Mill La.....C2
Morley St.....B1
Municipal Offices.....B2
National Science and Media Museum.....B2
Nelson St.....B2/C2
Nesfield St.....A1
New Otley Rd.....A3
Norcroft St.....B1
North Parade.....A1
North St.....A2
North Wing.....A3
Oastler Shopping Centre.....A2
Otley Rd.....A3
Park Ave.....C1
Park La.....C1
Park Rd.....C2
Parma St.....C2
Peace Museum.....B2
Peckover St.....B3
Piccadilly.....A2
Police Station.....A2
Post Office.....B1/B2/B3/C3
Princes Way.....B2
Prospect St.....C2
Radwell Drive.....C1
Rawson Rd.....A1
Rebecca St.....A1
Richmond Rd.....B1
Russell St.....B1
St George's Hall.....B2
St Lukes Hospital.....C1
Shipley Airedale Rd.....A3/B3
Shopmobility.....A2

Simes St A1
Smith St B1
Spring Mill St C2
Stott Hill B2
Sunbridge
  Rd A1/B1/B2
Theatre in the Mill A1/B1
Thornton Rd A1/B1
Trafalgar St. A1
Trinity Rd B1
Tumbling Hill St A1
Tyrrel St B2
University of
  Bradford B1/C1
Usher St B1
Valley Rd A1
Vicar La. C1
Wakefield Rd A3
Wapping Rd C2
Well St. B2
Westgate A1
White Abbey Rd A1
Wigan St A1
Wilton St B1
Wood St A1
Wool Exchange 🏛 . . . B2
Worthington St A1

Brighton 177

Addison Rd A1
Albert Rd B2
Albion Hill B3
Albion St B3
Ann St A3
Baker St A3
Black Lion St B2
Brighton 🚉 B2
Brighton Centre 🏛 C2
Brighton Fishing
  Museum 🏛 C2
Brighton Pier
  (Palace Pier) ◆ . . . C2
Brighton Wheel ◆ . C2
British Airways i360
  Tower ◆ C1
Broad St C2
Buckingham Place . . A1
Buckingham Rd B2
Cannon Place C1
Carlton Hill B3
Chatham Place A3
Cheapside A3
Church St B2
Churchill Square
  Shopping Centre . . B2
Clifton Hill B1
Clifton Place B1
Clifton Rd B1
Clifton St B2
Clifton Terr B1
Clyde Rd A3
Coach Station A2
Compton Ave A1
Davigdor Rd A1
Denmark Terr A1
Ditchling Rd A3
Dome 🏛 B2
Duke St B2
Duke's La B2
Dyke Rd A1/B2
East St C2
Edward St B3
Elmore Rd B3
Fleet St B1
Frederick St B2
Gardner St B2
Gloucester Place . . . B2
Gloucester Rd B2
Goldsmid Rd A1
Grand Junction Rd . . C2
Grand Parade B3
Grove Hill B3
Guildford Rd B2
Hampton Place B1
Hanover Terrace B3
High St B3
Highdown Rd A1
Information Ctr ✓ . . . B2
John St B3
Jubilee Clock
  Tower B2
Kemp St B2
Kensington Place . . . B2
Kings Rd C1
Lanes, The B2
Law Courts B3
Lewes Rd A3
Library B3
London Rd A3
Madeira Dr C3
Marine Pde C3
Middle St B2
Montpelier Place B1
Montpelier Rd B1
Montpelier St B1
Museum &
  Art Gallery 🏛 B3
New England Rd A2
New England St A2
New Rd B2
Nizells Ave A1
Norfolk Rd B1
Norfolk Terr B1
North Rd B2
North St B2
Odeon 🎬 B1
Old Shoreham Rd . . . A1
Old Steine B3
Osmond Rd A1
Over St B2
Oxford St A3
Park Crescent Terr . . A3
Phoenix Brighton
  🏛 B3
Phoenix Rise A3
Police Station 🏛 . . . B3
Post Office
  🏤 A1/A3/C3
Preston Rd A2
Preston St B1
Prestonville Rd A2
Queen's Rd B2
Queen Sq B2
Regency Sq C1
Regent St B2
Richmomd Place B3
Richmond St B3
Richmond Terr A3
Rose Hill Terr A3
Royal Pavilion 🏛 . . . B2
St Bartholomew's
  🏛 A3
St James's St C3
St Nicholas Rd B2
St Nicholas' 🏛 B2

St Peter's 🏛 A3
Sea Life
  Brighton 🏛 C3
Shaftesbury Rd A3
Ship St C2
Sillwood Rd B1
Sillwood St B1
Southover St A3
Spring Gdns B2
Stanford Rd A1
Stanley Rd B3
Surrey St B2
Sussex St B3
Swimming Pool B3
Sydney St B3
Temple Gdns B1
Terminus Rd B2
Theatre Royal 🎭 . . . B2
Tidy St B2
Town Hall C2
Toy & Model Mus 🏛 A2
Trafalgar St B2
Union Rd A3
Univ of Brighton B3
Upper Lewes Rd A3
Upper North St B1
Viaduct Rd A3
Victoria Gdns B3
Volk's Electric
  Railway 🚉 C3
West Pier (derelict) C1
West St C2
Western Rd B1
Whitecross St B2
YHA ▲ C3
York Ave B1
York Place B3
York Rd B1

Bristol 177

Acramans Rd C4
Albert Rd C6
Alfred Hill A4
All Saint's St A4
All Saints' 🏛 B3
Allington Rd C3
Alpha Rd C5
Ambra Vale B1
Ambra Vale East B1
Ambrose Rd B2
Amphitheatre &
  Waterfront Sq ◆ . . C4
Anchor Rd B3
Anvil St B6
Arcade, The A5
Architecture
  Centre, The ◆ B4
Argyle Place B1
Arlington Villas B1
Arnolfini 🏛 B4
Art Gallery 🏛 A1
Ashton Gate Rd C2
Ashton Rd C1
Avon Bridge C1
Avon Cres C1
Avon St B6
Baldwin St B4
Baltic Wharf C2
Baltic Wharf Leisure
  Centre & Caravan
  Park ◆ C2
Baltic Wharf
  Marina C2
Barossa Place C4
Barton Manor B6
Barton St B6
Barton Vale B6
Bath Rd C6
Bathurst Basin C4
Bathurst Parade C4
Beauley Rd C3
Bedminster Bridge . . C5
Bedminster Parade . . C4
Bellevue B2
Bellevue Cres B2
Bellevue Rd C6
Berkeley Place B2
Berkeley Sq A3
Birch Rd C2
Blackfriars A4
Bond St A5
Braggs La A6
Brandon Hill B3
Brandon Steep B3
Bristol Aquarium
  🐠 B4
Bristol Bridge B5
Bristol Cath (CE) † . . B3
Bristol Eye Hospital
  (A&E) A4
Bristol Grammar
  School A3
Bristol Harbour
  Railway 🚉 C4
Bristol Royal
  Children's Hosp Ⓗ A4
Bristol Royal Infirmary
  (A&E) Ⓗ A4
Bristol Temple Meads
  🚉 Station B6
Broad Plain B6
Broad Quay B4
Broad St A4
Broad Weir A5
Broadcasting Ho . . . A4
Broadmead A5
Brunel Institute ◆ . . B3
Brunel Way C1
Brunswick Sq A5
Burton Cl C5
Bus Station A5
Butts Rd B3
Cabot Circus A5
Cabot Tower ◆ B3
Caledonia Place B1
Callowhill Ct A5
Camden Rd C4
Camp Rd A1
Canada Way C3
Cannon St A4
Canon's Way C3
Cantock's Cl A3
Canynge Rd B1
Canynge Sq B1
Castle Park A5
Castle St A5
Cathedral Walk B3
Catherine Meade St C4
Cattle Market Rd . . . C6
Central Library B3
Charles Place B1
Charlotte St B3
Charlotte St South . . B3
Chatterton Ho 🏛 . . . B5

Chatterton Sq C5
Chatterton St C5
Cheese La B5
Christchurch A4
Christchurch Rd B1
Christmas Steps ◆ . A4
Church La B2/B5
Church St B5
City Museum 🏛 A3
City of Bristol
  College A4
Civil and Family
  Justice Centre . . . A4
Clare St B4
Clarence Rd C5
Cliff Rd C1
Clift House Rd C1
Clifton Cath (RC) † . . A2
Clifton Down A1
Clifton Down Rd A1
Clifton Hill B2
Clifton Park A1/A2
Clifton Park Rd A1
Clifton Rd A2
Cliftonwood Cres . . . B2
Cliftonwood Rd B2
Cliftonwood Terr B2
Cobblestone Mews A1
College Green B3
College Rd A1
College St B3
Colston
  Almshouses 🏛 . . A4
Colston Ave B4
Colston Hall 🏛 A4
Colston Parade C5
Colston St A4
Commercial Rd C4
Constitution Hill B2
Cooperage La C3
Corn St B4
Cornwallis Ave B1
Cornwallis Cres B1
Coronation Rd . . . C2/C4
Council House 🏛 . . B3
Countership B5
Create Ctr, The ◆ . . C1
Crosby Row B5
Crown Court A4
Culver St B3
Cumberland Basin . . C1
Cumberland Cl C2
Cumberland Rd . . . C2/C3
Dean La C4
Deanery Rd B3
Denmark St B4
Dowry Sq B1
Eaton Cres A2
Elmdale Rd A3
Elton Rd A3
Eugene St A4/A6
Exchange and
  St Nicholas' Mkts,
  The 🏛 B4
Fairfax St A4
Fire Station B5
Floating Harbour . . . C3
Fosseway, The A2
Foster
  Almshouses 🏛 . . A4
Frayne Rd C1
Frederick Place B2
Freeland Place B1
Friary B6
Frogmore St B3
Fry's Hill C2
Gas La B6
Gasferry Rd C3
Georgian House 🏛 . . B3
Glendale B1
Glentworth Rd A3
Gloucester St A1
Goldney Hall B2
Goldney Rd B2
Gordon Rd A2
Granby Hill B1
Grange Rd A1
Great Ann St A6
Great George Rd B3
Great George St A6/B3
Green St North B1
Green St South B1
Greenay Bush La . . . C2
Greenbank Rd C2
Greville Smyth Pk . C1
Grove, The B4
Guildhall 🏛 B4
Guinea St C4
Hamilton Rd C3
Hanbury Rd A2
Hanover Place C2
Harley Place B1
Haymarket A5
Hensman's Hill B1
High St B4
Highbury Villas A3
Hill St B3
Hill St C6
Hippodrome 🎭 B4
Hopechapel Hill B1
Horfield Rd A4
Horsefair, The A5
Horton St B6
Host St A4
Hotwell Rd B1/B2
Houlton St A6
Howard Rd C6
IMAX Cinema 🎬 . . . B4
Information Ctr ✓ . . A5
Islington Rd C3
Jacob St A5/A6
Jacob's Wells Rd . . . B2
John Carr's Terr B2
John Wesley's
  Chapel 🏛 A5
Joy Hill B1
Jubilee St B6
Kensington Place . . . B1
Kilkenny St A6
King St B4
Kingsland Rd B6
Kingston Rd C3
Lamb St A6
Lansdown Rd A2
Lawford St A6
Lawfords Gate A6
Leighton Rd C3
Lewins Mead A4
Lime Rd C3
Little Ann St A6
Little Caroline
  Place A4
Little George St A6
Little King St B4
Llandoger Trow 🏛 . . B4

Lloyds' Building,
  The C3
Lodge St A4
Lord Mayor's
  Chapel, The 🏛 . . B4
Lower Castle St A5
Lower Church La A4
Lower Clifton Hill . . . B2
Lower Guinea St C4
Lower Lamb St B3
Lower Maudlin St . . . A4
Lower Park Rd A4
Lower Sidney St C2
Lucky La C4
Lydstep Terr C4
M Shed 🏛 C4
Magistrates' Court . . A5
Mall (Galleries
  Shopping Ctr), The A5
Mall, The B1
Manilla Rd B1
Mardyke Ferry Rd . . . C2
Maritime Heritage
  Centre ◆ C3
Marlborough Hill A4
Marlborough St A4
Marsh St B4
Mead St C5
Merchant Dock C2
Merchant Seamen's
  Almshouses 🏛 . . A5
Merchant St A5
Merchants Rd C1
Merchants Rd B1
Meridian Place A2
Meridian Vale A2
Merrywood Rd C3
Midland Rd A6
Milford St C4
Millennium Prom B3
Millennium Sq B3
Mitchell La B5
Mortimer Rd B1
Murray Rd C4
Myrtle Rd A3
Narrow Plain B5
Narrow Quay B4
Nelson St A4
New Charlotte St . . . C4
New Kingsley Rd B6
New Queen St C5
New St A6
Newgate A5
Newton St A6
North St C2
O2 Academy 🏛 B4
Oakfield Grove A2
Oakfield Place A1
Oakfield Rd A1
Old Bread St B6
Old Market St A6
Old Park Hill A4
Oldfield Rd B1
Orchard Ave B4
Orchard La B4
Orchard St B4
Osbourne Rd C3
Oxford St B6
Park Place A2
Park Rd C4
Park Row A3
Park St A3
Passage St B5
Pembroke Grove A1
Pembroke Rd A2
Pembroke Rd B1
Pembroke St A5
Penn St A5
Pennywell Rd A6
Percival Rd A1
Pero's Bridge B4
Perry Rd A4
Phipps St C2
Pip 'n' Jay 🏛 B5
Plimsoll Bridge C1
Police Sta 🏛 A6
Polygon Rd B1
Portland St A1
Portwall La B5
Post Office 🏤 . . A1/A3/
  . . . . A5/B1/B4/C4/C5
Prewett St C5
Prince St B4
Prince St Bridge C4
Princess St C4
Princess Victoria St . B1
Priory Rd A2
Pump La C5
QEH Theatre 🎭 A2
Quakers Friars A5
Quay St A4
Queen Charlotte St . B4
Queen Elizabeth
  Hospital School . . B2
Queen Sq B4
Queen's Ave A3
Queen's Parade B3
Queen's Rd A2/A3
Raleigh Rd C2
Randall Rd B2
Red Lodge 🏛 A4
Redcliffe Backs B5
Redcliffe Bridge B4
Redcliffe Hill C5
Redcliffe Parade C4
Redcliffe Way B5
Redcross St A6
Redgrave
  Theatre 🎭 A1
Regent St B1
Richmond Hill B1
Richmond Hill Ave . . B1
Richmond La A2
Richmond Park Rd . . A1
Richmond Terr A1
River St A6
Rownham Mead C2
Royal Fort Rd A3
Royal Park A2
Royal West of England
  Academy 🏛 A3
Royal York Cres B1
Royal York Villas B1
Rupert St A4
Russ St B6
St Andrew's Walk . . . B1
St George's Rd B3
St James' 🏛 A5
St James Barton A5
St John's 🏛 B4
St John's Rd C3
St Luke's Rd C5
St Mary Redcliffe 🏛 C5

St Matthias Park . . . A6
St Michael's Hill A3
St Michael's Hospital Ⓗ A4
St Michael's Park . . . A3
St Nicholas St B4
St Paul St A5
St Paul's Rd A2
St Peter's (ruin) 🏛 . . B5
St Philip's Bridge . . . B5
St Philips Rd A6
St Stephen's 🏛 B4
St Stephen's St B4
St Thomas St B5
St Thomas the
  Martyr 🏛 B5
Sandford Rd B1
Sargent St C5
Saville Place B1
Ship La C5
Shopmobility A5
Showcase Cinema
  de Lux 🎬 A5
Silver St A5
Sion Hill B1
Small St A4
Smeaton Rd C1
Somerset Sq C5
Somerset St C5
Southernhay Ave . . . B2
Southville Rd C4
Spike Island
  Artspace 🏛 C2
Spring St C5
SS Great Britain and
  the Matthew ⚓ . . B2
Stackpool Rd C3
Staight St B6
Stillhouse La C5
Sydney Row C3
Tankard's Cl A3
Temple Back B5
Temple Back East . . . B5
Temple Bridge B5
Temple Church 🏛 . . B5
Temple Circus B5
Temple Gate C5
Temple St B5
Temple Way B5
Terrell St A4
Theatre Royal
  (Bristol Old Vic) 🎭 B4
Thekla ⚓ B4
Thomas La B5
Three Kings of
  Cologne 🏛 A4
Three Queens La . . . B5
Tobacco Factory,
  The 🎭 C2
Tower Hill A5
Tower La A4
Trenchard St A4
Triangle South A3
Triangle West A3
Trinity Rd A6
Trinity St B3
Tyndall Ave A3
Union St A5
Union St B6
Unity St A6
Unity St B3
University of Bristol A3
University Rd A3
Upper Byron Place . . A3
Upper Maudlin St . . . A4
Upper Perry Hill C3
Upton Rd C2
Valentine Bridge B6
Victoria Grove C5
Victoria Rd C6
Victoria Rooms 🏛 . . A2
Victoria Sq B1
Victoria St B5
Vyvyan Rd B1
Vyvyan Terr B1
Wade St A6
Walter St C2
Wapping Rd C4
Water La B5
Waterloo Rd A6
Waterloo St A1
Waterloo St B4
Watershed Media
  Centre ◆ B4
We the Curious ◆ . . B4
Welling Terr B1
Welsh Back B4
West Mall B1
West St A6
Westfield Place A1
Wetherell Place A2
Whitehouse Place . . . C5
Whitehouse St C5
Whiteladies Rd A2
Whitson St A4
William St C5
Willway St C5
Windsor Place B1
Wine St B4
Woodland Rd A3
Woodland Rise A3
Worcester Rd B1
Worcester Terr B1
YHA ▲ B4
York Gdns B1
York Place B1
York Rd C5

**Bury
St Edmunds** 178

Abbey Gardens 🏛 . . B3
Abbey Gate 🏛 B3
Abbeygate St B2
Albert Cres B2
Albert St B2
Ambulance Sta A3
Angel Hill B3
Angel La B3
Anglian Lane A1
Arc Shopping Ctr . . . B2
Athenaeum 🏛 B3
Baker's La B3
Barwell Rd A3
Beetons Way A1
Bishops Rd C1
Bloomfield St C3
Bridewell La B2
Bullen Cl C1
Bury
  St Edmunds 🚉 . . A2
Bury St Edmunds
  County Upper
  School A1
Bury St Edmunds
  Leisure Centre . . . B1

Bury Town FC B3
Bus Station B2
Business Park A3
Butter Mkt B2
Cannon St A2
Castle Rd C1
Cemetery C1
Chalk Rd (N) C1
Chalk Rd (S) C1
Church Row B2
Churchgate St C2
Cineworld 🎬 B2
Citizens Advice
  Bureau B2
College St B2
Compiegne Way A3
Corn Exchange,
  The B2
Cornfield Rd B1
Cotton Lane B2
Courts B2
Covent Garden C2
Crown St B3
Cullum Rd C3
Eastern Way A3
Eastgate St B3
Enterprise Bsns Pk . A3
Etna Rd A2
Eyre Cl C1
Fire Station B2
Friar's Lane C2
Gage Cl A1
Garland St B2
Greene King
  Brewery 🏛 C3
Grove Park B1
Grove Rd B1
Guildhall 🏛 C2
Guildhall St B2
Hatter St B2
High Baxter St B2
Honey Hill C3
Hospital Rd C1/C2
Ickworth Dr C1
Industrial Estate . . . A3
Information Ctr ✓ . . B3
Ipswich St A2
King Edward VI
  School A2
King's Rd C1/B2
Library B2
Long Brackland A2
Looms La B2
Lwr Baxter St B2
Malthouse La C2
Maynewater La C3
Mill Rd C1
Mill Rd (South) C1
Minden Close B3
Moyses Hall 🏛 B2
Mustow St B3
Norman Tower 🏛 . . B3
Northgate Ave A3
Northgate St B2
Nutshell, The 🍺 . . . B2
Osier Rd A2
Out Northgate A2
Out Risbygate B1
Out Westgate C2
Parkway B1/C2
Peckham St B2
Petticoat La C2
Phoenix
  Day Hospital Ⓗ . . . C1
Pinners Way C1
Police Station 🏛 . . . C1
Post Office 🏤 . . B2/B3
Pump La C2
Queen's Rd B1
Raingate St C2
Raynham Rd A1
Retail Park A2
Risbygate St B1/B2
Robert Boby Way 🏛 . B2
St Andrew's St
  North B2
St Andrew's St
  South B2
St Botolph's La C2
St Edmund's La B2
St Edmund's Abbey
  (Remains) ◆ B3
St Edmunds Hospital
  (private) Ⓗ B1
St Edmundsbury † . . B3
St John's St B2
St Marys St C2
School Hall La B2
Shire Halls &
  Magistrates Ct . . . C3
South Cl C3
Southgate St C3
Sparhawk St C3
Spring Lane A1
Springfield Rd A1
Station Hill A2
Swan La B2
Tayfen Rd A2
Theatre Royal 🎭 . . . C3
Thingoe Hill A2
Victoria St B1
Vinefields, The B3
War Memorial ◆ . . . B3
Well St B2
West Suffolk Coll . . . A1
Westgarth Gdns C1
Westgate St C2
Whiting St C2
York Rd B1
York Terr B1

Cambridge 178

Abbey Rd A3
ADC 🎭 A2
Anglia Ruskin Univ. . B3
Archaeology &
  Anthropology 🏛 . B2
Arts Picture Ho 🎬 . . B2
Arts Theatre 🎭 B1
Auckland Rd A3
Backs, The B1
Bateman St C2
Benet St B1
Bradmore St B3
Bridge St A1
Broad St B3
Brookside C2
Brunswick Terr A3
Burleigh St B3
Bus Station B2
Butt Green A2
Cambridge
  Contemporary Art
  Gallery 🏛 B1
Castle Mound 🏛 . . . A1

Castle St A1
Chesterton La A1
Christ's (Coll) B2
Christ's Lane B2
Christ's Pieces B2
City Rd B3
Clare (Coll) B1
Clarendon St B2
Coe Fen C1
Coronation St C2
Corpus Christi
  (Coll) B1
Court A2
Cross St C3
Crusoe Bridge C1
Darwin (Coll) B1
Devonshire Rd C3
Downing (Coll) C2
Downing St B2
Earl St B2
East Rd B3
Eden St B3
Elizabeth Way A3
Elm St B2
Emery St B3
Emmanuel (Coll) . . . B2
Emmanuel Rd B2
Emmanuel St B2
Fair St A3
Fen Causeway, The . . C1
Fenner's Cricket Gd . C3
Fitzroy St B3
Fitzwilliam Mus 🏛 . . C2
Fitzwilliam St C2
Garret Hostel
  Bridge B1
Glisson Rd C3
Gonville & Caius
  (Coll) B1
Gonville Place C3
Grafton Centre, The . A3
Grand Arcade B2
Green St B1
Gresham Rd C3
Guest Rd B3
Guildhall 🏛 B2
Harvey Rd C3
Hills Rd C3
Hobson St B2
Hughes Hall (Coll) . . C3
Information Ctr ✓ . . B2
James St B3
Jesus (Coll) A2
Jesus Green A2
Jesus La A2
Jesus Terr B3
John St B3
Kelsey Kerridge
  Sports Centre B3
Kettle's Yard 🏛 A1
King's Bridge B1
King St B2
King's (Coll) B1
King's College
  Chapel 🏛 B1
King's Parade B1
Lammas Land
  Recreation Gd . . . C1
Lensfield Rd C2
Library B3
Lion Yard B2
Little St Mary's La . . B1
Lyndewood Rd C3
Magdalene (Coll) . . . A1
Magdalene St A1
Maid's Causeway . . . A3
Malcolm St B2
Market Hill B2
Market St B2
Mathematical
  Bridge B1
Mawson Rd C3
Midsummer Comm . . A3
Mill La B1
Mill Rd B3
Mill St C3
Mumford 🎭 B3
Museum of
  Cambridge 🏛 . . . A1
Museum of Classical
  Archeology 🏛 . . . A1
Napier St A3
New Square B2
Newmarket Rd A3
Newnham Rd C1
Norfolk St B3
Northampton St A1
Norwich St C2
Orchard St B2
Panton St C2
Paradise Nature
  Reserve C1
Paradise St B3
Park Parade A1
Park St A2
Park Terr B2
Parker St B2
Parker's Piece B2
Parkside B3
Parkside Pools B3
Parsonage St A3
Pemberton Terr C2
Pembroke (Coll) B2
Pembroke St B2
Perowne St B3
Peterhouse (Coll) . . . C1
Petty Cury B2
Polar Mus, The 🏛 . . C2
Police Station 🏛 . . . C3
Post Office 🏤 . . A1/A3/
  . . . B2/B3/C2/C2/C3
Queen's La B1
Queen's Rd B1
Queens' (Coll) B1
Regent St B2
Regent Terr C2
Ridley Hall (Coll) . . . C1
Riverside A3
Round Church,
  The 🏛 A1
Russell St C3
St Andrew's St B2
St Benet's 🏛 B1
St Catharine's
  (Coll) B1
St Eligius St C2
St John's (Coll) A1
St Mary's 🏛 B1
St Paul's Rd C3
Saxon St C2
Sedgwick Mus 🏛 . . . B2
Sheep's Green C1
Shire Hall A1
Sidgwick Ave B1
Sidney St B2

Sidney Sussex
  (Coll) A2
Silver St B1
Station Rd C3
Tenison Ave C3
Tenison Rd C3
Tennis Court Rd B2
Thompson's La A1
Trinity (Coll) A1
Trinity Hall (Coll) . . . B1
Trinity St B1
Trumpington Rd C2
Trumpington St B1
Union Rd C2
University Botanic
  Gardens 🌸 C2
Victoria Ave A2
Victoria St B2
Warkworth St B3
Warkworth Terr B3
Wesley House (Coll) A2
West Rd B1
Westcott Ho (Coll) . . A2
Westminster (Coll) . . A1
Whipple 🏛 B2
Willis Rd B3
Willow Walk A2
YMCA C3

Canterbury 178

Artillery St A2
Barton Mill Rd A3
Beaconsfield Rd A1
Beaney, The 🏛 B2
Beverley Rd A1
Bingley's Island B1
Black Griffin La B1
Broad Oak Rd A2
Broad St B2
Brymore Rd A3
Burgate B2
Bus Station C2
Canterbury College C3
Canterbury East 🚉 . . C1
Canterbury Tales,
  The ◆ B2
Canterbury West 🚉 . A1
Castle 🏛 C1
Castle Row C1
Castle St C1
Cathedral † B2
Causeway, The A2
Chaucer Rd A3
Christ Church Univ. . B3
Christchurch
  Gate ◆ B2
City Council Offices A3
City Wall B3
Coach Park C2
College Rd B3
Cossington Rd C2
Court B2
Craddock Rd A3
Crown & County
  Courts B2
Dane John Gdns . . . C2
Dane John Mound
  ◆ C1
Deanery B2
Dover St C2
Duck La B2
Eastbridge Hosp 🏛 . B1
Edgar Rd B3
Ersham Rd C3
Ethelbert Rd C3
Fire Station C2
Forty Acres Rd A1
Friars, The B2
Gordon Rd C1
Greyfriars 🏛 B2
Guildford Rd C1
Havelock St B2
Heaton Rd C1
High St B2
Information Ctr
  ✓ A2/B2
Ivy La B3
Ivy Place C1
King St B2
King's School B2
King's School Rec Ctr,
  The A2
Kingsmead Leisure
  Centre A2
Kingsmead Rd A2
Kirby's La B1
Lansdown Rd C2
Lime Kiln Rd C1
Longport B3
Lower Chantry La . . . C3
Mandeville Rd A1
Market Way A2
Marlowe Arcade B2
Marlowe Ave C2
Marlowe Theatre 🎭 . B2
Martyrs Field Rd C1
Mead Way A1
Military Rd B2
Monastery St B2
Museum of
  Canterbury (Rupert
  Bear Museum) 🏛 . B1
New Dover Rd C3
Norman Rd C2
North Holmes Rd . . . B3
North La B1
Northgate A2
Nunnery Fields C2
Nunnery Rd C2
Oaten Hill C2
Odeon Cinema 🎬 . . C1
Old Dover Rd C2
Old Palace B2
Old Ruttington La . . . B2
Old Weavers 🏛 B2
Orchard St B1
Oxford Rd C1
Palace St B2
Pilgrims Way C3
Pin Hill C1
Pine Tree Ave A1
Police Station 🏛 . . . A2
Post Office 🏤 B2
Pound La B1
Puckle La C2
Raymond Ave C1
Recreation Ground . . A2
Registry Office B3
Rheims Way B1
Rhodaus Cl C2
Rhodaus Town C2
Roman Museum 🏛 . . B2
Roper Gateway A1
Roper Rd A1
Rose La B2
Shopmobility B2

Sidney Sussex . . .
St Augustine's Abbey
  (remains) † B3
St Augustine's Rd . . . C3
St Dunstan's A1
St Dunstan's St B1
St George's Place . . . C2
St George's
  Tower ◆ B2
St Gregory's Rd B3
St John's Hosp 🏛 . . B2
St Margaret's St B2
St Martin's 🏛 B3
St Martin's Ave B3
St Martin's Rd B3
St Michael's Rd A1
St Mildred's 🏛 C1
St Peter's Grove B1
St Peter's La B1
St Peter's Place B1
St Peter's St B1
St Radigunds St B1
St Stephen's Path . . A1
St Stephen's Rd A1
Salisbury Rd A1
Simmonds Rd C1
Spring La C3
Station Rd West B1
Stour St B1
Sturry Rd A3
Tourtel Rd A3
Tudor Rd C1
Union St B2
University for the
  Creative Arts C2
Vernon Place C2
Victoria Rd C1
Watling St B2
Westgate Gdns B1
Westgate Towers 🏛 . B1
Whitefriars B2
Whitehall Gdns B1
Whitehall Rd B1
Wincheap C1
York Rd C1
Zealand Rd C2

Cardiff
Caerdydd 178

Adam St B3
Alexandra Gdns A2
Allerton St C1
Arran St A3
ATRiuM (Univ of
  Glamorgan) 🏛 . . . C3
Beauchamp St C1
Bedford St A3
Blackfriars Priory
  (rems) † B1
Bvd De Nantes B2
Brains Brewery C2
Brook St C1
Bute Park A1
Bute St C2
Bute Terr C3
Callaghan Sq C2/C3
Capitol Shopping
  Centre, The B3
Cardiff Arms Park
  (Cardiff Blues) . . . B1
Cardiff Bridge B1
Cardiff Castle 🏛 . . . B2
Cardiff Central
  🚉 Station C2
Cardiff Story,
  The B2
Cardiff Univ A1/A2/B3
Cardiff University
  Student's Union . . A2
Caroline St C2
Castle Green B2
Castle Mews A1
Castle St (Heol y
  Castell) B2
Cathays Station 🚉 . . A2
Celerity Drive C3
Central Library C2
Charles St B3
City Hall 🏛 A2
City Rd A3
Clare Rd C1
Clare St C1
Coburn St A3
Coldstream Terr B1
College Rd A1
Colum Rd A1
Court C2
Court Rd C1
Craiglee Drive C3
Cranbrook St A3
Customhouse St . . . C2
Cyfartha St A3
David's 🏛 B2
Despenser Place . . . C1
Despenser St C1
Dinas St C1
Duke St (Heol y
  Dug) B2
Dumfries Place B3
East Grove A3
Ellen St C3
Fire Station B3
Fitzalan Rd B3
Fitzhamon Emb C1
Friary, The B2
g39 🏛 B3
Gloucester St C1
Glynrhondda St A2
Gordon Rd A3
Gorsedd Gdns A2
Green St B1
Greyfriars Rd B2
Hafod St C1
Hayes, The 🛒 B2
Herbert St C3
High St B2
HM Prison B3
Industrial Estate . . . C3
John St C2
Jubilee St C1
King Edward VII
  Ave A2
Kingsway (Ffordd y
  Brenin) B2
Knox Rd B3
Law Courts B2
Llanbleddian Gdns . . A2
Lloyd George Ave . . . C2
Lower Cathedral Rd B1
Lowther Rd A3

Mansion House A3
Mardy St C1
Mark St B1
Market B2
Mary Ann St C3
Merches Gdns C1
Mill La C2
Millennium Bridge . . B1
Miskin St A2
Monmouth St C1
Motorpoint Arena
  Cardiff ◆ C3
Museum Ave A2
Museum Place A2
National Museum
  Cardiff 🏛 A2
National War
  Memorial ◆ A2
Neville Place C1
New Theatre 🎭 B2
Newport Rd B3
Northcote La A3
Northcote St A3
Parade, The A3
Park Grove A2
Park Place A2
Park St C2
Penarth Rd C1
Pendyris St C1
Plantaganet St C1
Post Office 🏤 B2
Principality
  Stadium C2
Principality Stadium
  Tours (Gate 3) ◆ . B2
Quay St B2
Queen's Arcade B2
Queen Anne Sq A1
Queen St (Heol y
  Frenhines) B2
Queen St Station 🚉 . B3
Regimental
  Museums 🏛 B2
Rhymney St A3
Richmond Rd A3
Royal Welsh Coll of
  Music and Drama . A1
Russell St A3
Ruthin Gdns A2
St Andrews Place . . . A2
St David's 🏛 B3
St David's Hall ◆ . . . B2
St John the Baptist
  🏛 B2
St Mary St (Heol
  Eglwys Fair) B2
St Peter's St A3
Salisbury Rd A3
Sandon St B3
Schooner Way C3
Scott Rd C2
Scott St C2
Senghennydd Rd . . . A2
Sherman Theatre 🎭 . A2
Sophia Gardens A1
Sophia Gardens
  Stadium ◆ A1
South Wales Baptist
  College A3
Sport Wales
  National Ctr ◆ . . . A1
Stafford Rd C1
Stadium Plaza C1
Station Terr B3
Stuttgarter Strasse . B2
Sussex St C1
Taffs Mead Emb . . . C1
Talworth St A3
Temple of Peace &
  Health ◆ A1
Treharris St A3
Trinity St B2
Tudor La C1
Tudor St C1
Tyndall St C3
Vue 🎬 C1
Walk, The A3
Welsh Government A1
West Grove A3
Westgate St
  (Heol y Porth) B2
Windsor Place B3
Womanby St B2
Wood St C2
Working St B2
Wyeverne Rd A2

Carlisle 179

Abbey St B1
Aglionby St B3
Albion St C3
Alexander St C3
AMF Bowl ◆ A1
Annetwell St B1
Bank St B2
Bitts Park A1
Blackfriars St B2
Blencome St C1
Blunt St C1
Botchergate C2
Boustead's
  Grassing C2
Bowman St B3
Bridge St B1
Broad St B3
Brook St C3
Brunswick St B2
Bus Station B2
Caldew Bridge A1
Caldew St C1
Carlisle (Citadel)
  🚉 Station B2
Carlisle College B2
Castle 🏛 A1
Castle St A1
Castle Way A1
Cathedral † B1
Cecil St B3
Chapel St B2
Charles St C3
Charlotte St B1
Chatsworth Sq B3
Chiswick St B3
Citadel, The ◆ B2
City Walls B1
Civic Centre A2
Clifton St C1
Close St C3
Collingwood St C1
Colville St C2
Colville Terr C2
Council Offices B1
Court B2
Court St Brow B2
Crosby St B2
Crown St C2

Chelmsford • Cheltenham • Chester • Chichester • Colchester • Coventry • Derby • Dorchester • Dumfries 203

Currock Rd C2
Dacre Rd A1
Dale St C1
Denton St C1
Devonshire Walk A1
Duke's Rd A2
East Dale St C1
East Norfolk St C1
Eden Bridge A2
Edward St B3
Elm St B3
English St B2
Fire Station A2
Fisher St A1
Flower St B3
Freer St C1
Fusehill St B3
Georgian Way A2
Gloucester Rd C3
Golf Course A2
Graham St C1
Grey St B3
Guildhall Mus A2
Halfey's La B3
Hardwicke Circus A2
Hart St B3
Hewson St C2
Howard Place A3
Howe St B3
Information Ctr B2
James St B2
Junction St B1
King St B2
Lancaster St B2
Lanes Shopping Centre, The B2
Laser Quest ✦ B2
Library A2
Lime St B1
Lindisfarne St C3
Linton St B3
Lismore Place A3
Lismore St B3
London Rd C3
Lonsdale Rd B2
Lord St C3
Lorne Cres B1
Lorne St B1
Lowther St B2
Madford Retail Pk B1
Magistrates' Ct A2
Market Hall A2
Mary St B2
Memorial Bridge A3
Metcalfe St C1
Milbourne St B1
Myddleton St B3
Nelson St C1
Norfolk St C1
Old Fire Sta, The A2
Old Town Hall A2
Oswald St C3
Peter St A2
Petteril St B3
Pools B2
Portland Place B2
Portland Sq B2
Post Office A2/B2/C1/C3
Princess St C2
Pugin St B1
Red Bank Terr C2
Regent St C3
Richardson St C1
Rickerby Park A3
Rickergate A2
River St B3
Rome St C2
Rydal St B3
St Cuthbert's B2
St Cuthbert's La B2
St James' Park C1
St James' Rd C1
St Nicholas Gate Retail Park C3
St Nicholas St C3
Sands Centre, The A2
Scotch St A2
Shaddongate B1
Sheffield St B1
Shopmobility A2
South Henry St B3
South John St C2
South St B3
Spencer St B2
Station Retail Park B2
Strand Rd A2
Superstore B1
Sybil St B3
Tait St B2
Thomas St B1
Thomson St C3
Trafalgar St C1
Trinity Leisure Ctr A2
Tullie Museum & Art Gallery A1
Tyne St C3
Univ of Cumbria B3
Viaduct Estate Rd B1
Victoria Place A2
Victoria Viaduct B2
Vue B2
Warwick Rd B2
Warwick Sq B3
Water St B2
West Walls B1
Westmorland St C1

Chelmsford 179
Anchor St C1
Anglia Ruskin Univ A2
Arbour La A3
Baddow Rd B2/C3
Baker St C1
Barrack Sq B2
Bellmead B2
Bishop Hall La A2
Bishop Rd A2
Bond St B2
Boswells Dr B3
Bouverie Rd C2
Bradford St C1
Braemar Ave C1
Brook St A2
Broomfield Rd A1
Burgess Springs B2
Burns Cres C2
Bus Station B1/B2
Cedar Ave A1
Cedar Ave West A1
Cemetery A1
Cemetery C1
Cemetery C1
Central Park B1
Chelmsford ✝ B2
Chelmsford ⇌ A1
Chichester Dr A3
Chinery Cl A3
City Council A1
Civic Centre A1
Civic Theatre B1
Cloud Fm County Cricket Ground B2
College C1
Cottage Place A2
County Hall B2
Coval Ave B1
Coval La B1
Coval Wells B1
Crown Court B2
Duke St B2
Elm Rd C1
Elms Dr B1
Essex Record Office, The B3
Fairfield Rd B1
Falcons Mead B1
George St C2
Glebe Rd A1
Godfrey's Mews C2
Goldlay Ave C3
Goldlay Rd C2
Grove Rd C2
Hall St C2
Hamlet Rd C2
Hart St C1
Henry Rd A2
High Bridge Rd B2
High Chelmer Shopping Centre B2
High St B2
Hill Cres B3
Hill Rd B3
Hill Rd Sth B3
Hillview Rd A3
HM Prison A3
Hoffmans Way A2
Hospital B2
Lady La C2
Langdale Gdns C3
Legg St B2
Library B2
Lionfield Terr A3
Lower Anchor St C1
Lynmouth Ave C2
Lynmouth Gdns C3
Magistrates Court B2
Maltese Rd A1
Manor Rd C2
Marconi Rd A2
Market B2
Market Rd B2
Marlborough Rd C1
Meadows Shopping Centre, The B2
Meadowside A3
Mews Ct C2
Mildmay Rd C2
Moulsham Dr C2
Moulsham Mill ✦ C3
Moulsham St C1/C2
Navigation Rd B3
New London Rd B2/C1
New St A2/B2
New Writtle St C1
Nursery Rd C2
Orchard St C2
Odeon B2
Parker Rd C2
Parklands Dr A3
Parkway A1/B1/B2
Police Station A2
Post Office B2/C2
Primrose Hill A1
Prykes Dr B1
Queen St C1
Queen's Rd B3
Railway St A1
Rainsford Rd A1
Ransomes Way A2
Rectory La A2
Regina Rd A2
Riverside Ice & Leisure Centre B2
Riverside Retail Pk A3
Rosebery Rd C2
Rothesay Ave C1
St John's Rd C2
Sandringham Place B3
Seymour St B1
Shopmobility B2
Shrublands Cl B3
Southborough Rd C1
Springfield Rd A3/B2/B3
Stapleford Cl C1
Superstore B2/C3
Swiss Ave A1
Telford Place A3
Tindal St B2
Townfield St A1
Trinity Rd B3
University B1
Upper Bridge Rd C1
Upper Roman Rd C2
Van Dieman's Rd C3
Viaduct Rd B1
Vicarage Rd C1
Victoria Rd A2
Victoria Rd South B2
Vincents Rd C2
Waterloo La B2
Weight Rd B3
Westfield Ave A1
Wharf Rd B3
Writtle Rd C1
YMCA A2
York Rd C1

Cheltenham 179
Albert Rd A3
Albion St B3
All Saints Rd B3
Ambrose St B2
Andover Rd C1
Art Gallery & Museum B2
Back Montpellier Terrace C2
Bandstand ✦ C2
Bath Pde B2
Bath Rd C2
Bays Hill Rd C1
Bennington St B2
Berkeley St B3
Brewery, The A2
Brunswick St South A2
Bus Station B2
Carlton St B3
Central Cross Road A3
Cheltenham Coll C2
Cheltenham FC A3
Cheltenham General (A&E) C3
Cheltenham Ladies College B2
Christchurch Rd B1
Cineworld A2
Clarence Rd A2
Clarence Sq A2
Clarence St B2
Cleveland St A1
College Baths Rd C3
College Rd C2
Colletts Dr A1
Corpus St C3
Council Office B1
Court B1
Devonshire St A2
Douro Rd B1
Duke St B3
Dunalley Parade A2
Dunalley St A2
Everyman B2
Evesham Rd A3
Fairview Rd B3
Fairview St B3
Fire Station C3
Folly La A2
Gloucester Rd A1
Grosvenor St B3
Grove St A1
Hanover St A2
Hatherley St C1
Henrietta St A2
Hewlett Rd B3
High St B2/B3
Holst Birthplace Museum A3
Hudson St A2
Imperial Gdns C2
Imperial La B2
Imperial Sq C2
Information Ctr B2
Keynsham Rd C3
King St A2
Knapp Rd B2
Ladies College B2
Lansdown Cres C1
Lansdown Rd C1
Leighton Rd B3
Library B2
London Rd C3
Lypiatt Rd C1
Malvern Rd B1
Manser St A2
Market St A1
Marle Hill Parade A2
Marle Hill Rd A2
Millbrook St A1
Milsom St A2
Montpellier Gdns C2
Montpellier Grove C2
Montpellier Pde C2
Montpellier Spa Rd C2
Montpellier St C1
Montpellier Terr C2
Montpellier Walk C2
New St B2
North Place B2
Old Bath Rd C3
Oriel Rd B2
Overton Park Rd B1
Overton Rd B1
Oxford St C3
Parabola Rd B1
Park Place C1
Park St A1
Pittville Circus A3
Pittville Crescent A3
Pittville Lawn A3
Pittville Park A2
Playhouse B2
Police Station C1
Portland St B3
Prestbury Rd A3
Prince's Rd C1
Priory St B3
Promenade B2
Queen St A1
Recreation Ground A2
Regent Arcade B2
Regent St B2
Rodney Rd B2
Royal Cres B2
Royal Wells Rd B2
St George's Place B2
St Georges Rd B1
St Gregory's B2
St James St B3
St John's Ave B3
St Luke's Rd C2
St Margarets Rd A2
St Mary's B2
St Matthew's B2
St Paul's La A2
St Paul's Rd A2
St Paul's St A2
St Stephen's Rd C1
Sandford Parks Lido C3
Sandford Mill Rd C3
Sandford Park C3
Sandford Rd C2
Selkirk St A3
Sherborne Place B3
Sherborne St B3
Shopmobility B2
Suffolk Parade C2
Suffolk Rd C1
Suffolk Sq C1
Sun St A1
Swindon Rd B2
Sydenham Villas Rd C3
Tewkesbury Rd A1
The Courtyard B1
Thirlstaine Rd C2
Tivoli Rd C1
Tivoli St C1
Town Hall & Theatre B2
Townsend St A1
Trafalgar St C2
Union St B3
Univ of Gloucestershire (Francis Close Hall) A2
University of Gloucestershire (Hardwick) A1
Victoria Place B3
Victoria St A2
Vittoria Walk C2
Wel Place B2
Wellesley Rd A2
Wellington Rd A3
Wellington Sq A3
Wellington St B2
West Drive A3
Western Rd B1
Winchcombe St B3
Winston Churchill Meml Gardens A1

Chester 179
Abbey Gateway A2
Appleyards La C3
Bars, The B3
Bedward Row B1
Beeston View C3
Bishop Lloyd's Palace B2
Black Diamond St A2
Bottoms La C3
Boughton B3
Bouverie St A1
Bus Interchange A2
Bridge St B2
Bridgegate C2
Brook St A3
Brown's La C2
Cambrian Rd A1
Canal St A2
Carrick Rd C1
Castle C2
Castle Dr C2
Cathedral ✝ B2
Catherine St A1
Chester ⇌ A3
Cheyney Rd A1
Chichester St A1
City Rd A3
City Walls B1/B2
City Walls Rd B1
Cornwall St A2
Cross Hey C3
Cross, The ✦ B2
Crown Ct C2
Cuppin St B2
Curzon Park North C1
Curzon Park South C1
Dee Basin A1
Dee La B3
Delamere St A2
Dewa Roman Experience B2
Duke St B2
Eastgate B2
Eastgate St B2
Eaton Rd C2
Edinburgh Way C3
Elizabeth Cres B3
Fire Station A2
Foregate St B2
Forum, The B2
Frodsham St B2
Gamul House B2
Garden La A1
George St A2
Gladstone Ave A1
God's Providence House B2
Gorse Stacks A2
Greenway St C2
Grosvenor Bridge C1
Grosvenor Mus B2
Grosvenor Park B3
Grosvenor Park Terrace C1
Grosvenor Shopping Ctr B2
Grosvenor St B2
Groves Rd B3
Groves, The B3
Guildhall Mus B1
Handbridge C2
Hartington St C3
Hoole Way A2
Hunter St B2
Information Ctr B2
King Charles' Tower ✦ A2
King St A2
Leisure Centre A2
Library B2
Lightfoot St A3
Little Roodee C2
Liverpool Rd A2
Love St B3
Lower Bridge St B2
Lower Park Rd B3
Lyon St A2
Magistrates Court B2
Meadows La C3
Meadows, The B3
Military Museum C2
Milton St A3
New Crane St B1
Nicholas St B2
Northgate A2
Northgate St A2
Nun's Rd B1
Old Dee Bridge ✦ C2
Overleigh Rd C2
Park St B2
Police Station B2
Post Office A2/A3/B2
Princess St B2
Queen St B2
Queen's Park Rd C3
Queen's Rd A3
Race Course B1
Raymond St A1
River La C2
Roman Amphitheatre & Gardens B2
Roodee (Chester Racecourse), The B1
Russell St A3
St Anne St A2
St George's Cres C3
St Martin's Gate A1
St Martin's Way B1
St Mary's Priory ✦ B2
St Oswalds Way A2
Saughall Rd A1
Sealand Rd A1
South View Rd A1
Stanley Palace B1
Station Rd A3
Steven St A3
Storyhouse B2
Superstore B2
Tower Rd B1
Town Hall B2
Union St B3
Univ of Chester C2
Vicar's La B2
Victoria Cres C3
Victoria Rd A2
Walpole St A1
Water Tower St A1
Water Tower, The ✦ B1
Watergate B1
Watergate St B2
Whipcord La A1
White Friars B2
York St B3

Chichester 180
Adelaide Rd A3
Alexandra Rd A3
Arts Centre B2
Ave de Chartres B1/B2
Barlow Rd A1
Basin Rd C2
Beech Ave B1
Bishops Palace Gardens B2
Bishopsgate Walk A3
Bramber Rd C3
Broyle Rd A2
Bus Station B2
Caledonian Rd B3
Cambrai Ave B3
Canal Place C1
Canal Wharf C2
Canon La B2
Cathedral ✝ B2
Cavendish St A1
Cawley Rd B2
Cedar Dr A1
Chapel St A2
Cherry Orchard Rd C3
Chichester ⇌ B2
Chichester By-Pass C2/C3
Chichester Coll B1
Chichester Cinema B3
Chichester Festival A2
Chichester Gate Leisure Pk C1
Churchside A2
Cineworld C1
City Walls A2
Cleveland Rd B3
College La A2
Cory Cl C2
Council Offices B2
County Hall B2
District B2
Duncan Rd A1
Durnford Close A1
East Pallant B2
East Row B2
East St B2
East Walls B3
Eastland Rd C3
Ettrick Cl B1
Ettrick Rd B1
Exton Rd C3
Fire Station A2
Football Ground A2
Franklin Place A2
Friary (Rems of) B2
Garland Close C3
Green La A3
Grove Rd C3
Guilden Rd B3
Guildhall A2
Hawthorn Close A1
Hay Rd C3
Henty Gdns B1
Herald Dr C3
Hornet, The B3
Information Ctr B2
John's St B2
Joys Croft A3
Jubilee Pk A3
Jubilee Rd A3
Juxon Cl B1
Kent Rd A3
King George Gdns A2
King's Ave C2
Kingsham Ave C3
Kingsham Rd C2
Laburnum Grove B2
Leigh Rd C1
Lennox Rd A3
Lewis Rd A3
Library B2
Lion St B2
Litten Terr A3
Litten, The A3
Little London B2
Lyndhurst Rd B3
Market B3
Market Ave B2
Market Cross B2
Market Rd B3
Melbourne Rd A3
Minerva A2
Mount La B1
New Park Rd A3
Newlands La A1
North Pallant B2
North St A2
North Walls A2
Northgate A2
Novium, The B2
Oak Ave A1
Oak Cl A1
Oaklands Park A2
Oaklands Way A2
Orchard Ave A1
Orchard St A1
Ormonde Ave B3
Pallant House B2
Parchment St A1
Parklands Rd A1/B1
Peter Weston Place B3
Police Station C2
Post Office A1/B2/C3
Priory La A2
Priory Park A2
Priory Rd A2
Queen's Ave C1
Riverside A3
Roman Amphitheatre B3
St Cyriacs A2
St Martins' St B2
St Pancras A3
St Paul's Rd A2
St Richard's Hospital (A&E) A3
Shamrock Cl A3
Sherbourne Rd A1
Somerstown A2
South Bank C2
South Downs Planetarium ✦ C2
South Pallant B2
South St B2
Southgate B2
Spitalfield La A3
Stirling Rd B3
Stockbridge Rd C1/C2
Swanfield Dr A3
Terminus Ind Est C1
Tower St A2
Tozer Way A3
Turnbull Rd A3
Upton Rd C1
Velyn Ave B3
Via Ravenna B1
Walnut Ave A1
West St B2
Westgate B1
Westgate Fields B1
Westgate Leisure Centre B1
Weston Ave C1
Whyke Cl C3
Whyke La B3
Whyke Rd C3
Winden Ave B3

Colchester 180
Abbey Gateway ✝ C2
Albert St A1
Albion Grove C2
Alexandra Rd C1
Artillery St C3
Arts Centre B1
Balkerne Hill B1
Barrack St C3
Beaconsfield Rd C1
Beche Rd C3
Bergholt Rd A1
Bourne Rd C3
Brick Kiln Rd A1
Brigade Grove C2
Bristol Rd B2
Broadlands Way A3
Brook St B3
Bury Cl B2
Bus Sta C2
Butt Rd C1
Campion Rd C2
Cannon St C3
Canterbury Rd C2
Captain Gardens C2
Castle B2
Castle Park B2
Castle Rd B2
Catchpool Rd A1
Causton Rd B1
Chandlers Row C3
Circular Rd East C2
Circular Rd North C1
Circular Rd West C1
Clarendon Way A1
Claudius Rd C2
Colchester ⇌ A1
Colchester Camp Abbey Field C1
Colchester Retail Park B1
Colchester Town ⇌ C2
Colne Bank Ave A1
Colne View Retail Park A2
Compton Rd A3
Cowdray Ave A1/A2
Cowdray Ctr, The A2
Crouch St B1
Crowhurst Rd B1
Culver Square Shopping Centre B1
Culver St East B2
Culver St West B1
Dilbridge Rd A3
East Hill B2
East St B3
East Stockwell St B1
Eld La B1
Essex Hall Rd A1
Exeter Dr B2
Fairfax Rd C2
Fire Station A2
Firstsite B2
Flagstaff Rd C1
Garrison Parade C2
George St B2
Gladstone Rd C2
Golden Noble Hill C2
Goring Rd A3
Granville Rd C3
Greenstead Rd B3
Guildford Rd B2
Harsnett Rd C3
Harwich Rd B3
Head St B1
High St B1/B2
High Woods Cty Pk A2
Hollytrees B2
Hyderabad Cl C2
Hythe Hill C3
Information Ctr B2
Jarmin Rd A2
Kendall Rd C2
Kimberley Rd C3
King Stephen Rd C3
Leisure World A2
Library B1
Lincoln Way B2
Lion Walk Shopping Centre B1
Lisle Rd C2
Lucas Rd C2
Magdalen Green C3
Magdalen St C2
Maidenburgh St B2
Maldon Rd C1
Manor Rd B1
Margaret Rd A1
Mason Rd A2
Mercers Way A1
Mercury B1
Mersea Rd C2
Meyrick Cres C2
Mile End Rd A1
Military Rd C2
Mill St C2
Minories B2
Moorside B3
Morant Rd C3
Napier Rd C2
Natural History B2
New Town Rd C2
Norfolk Cres A3
North Hill B1
North Station Rd A1
Northgate St B1
Nunns Rd B1
Odeon B1
Old Coach Rd B3
Old Heath Rd C3
Osborne St B2
Petrolea Cl A1
Police Station C1
Popes La B1
Port La C3
Post Office B2/C1
Priory St B2
Queen St B2
Rawstorn Rd B1
Rebon St C3
Recreation Rd C3
Ripple Way A3
Roberts Rd C2
Roman Rd B2
Roman Wall B2
Romford Cl A3
Rosebery Ave B2
St Andrews Ave B3
St Andrews Gdns B3
St Botolph St B2
St Botolphs B2
St John's Abbey (site of) ✝ C2
St John's St B1
St Johns Walk Shopping Centre B1
St Leonards Rd C3
St Marys Fields B1
St Peter's St B1
St Peters B1
Salisbury Ave C1
Saw Mill Rd C3
Sergeant St C2
Serpentine Walk A1
Sheepen Place B1
Sheepen Rd B1
Sir Isaac's Walk B1
Smythies Ave B2
South St C1
South Way C1
Sports Way A2
Suffolk Cl A3
Superstore A1
Town Hall B1
Valentine Dr A3
Victor Rd C3
Wakefield Cl B2
Wellesley Rd C1
Wells Rd B2/B3
West St C1
West Stockwell St B1
Weston Rd C3
Westway A1
Wickham Rd C1
Wimpole Rd C3
Winchester Rd C2
Winnock Rd C2
Worcester Rd B2

Coventry 180
Abbots La A1
Albany B1
Albany Rd B1
Alma St B3
Ambulance Sta A2
Art Faculty B3
Asthill Grove C2
Bablake School A1
Barras La A1/B1
Barr's Hill School A1
Belgrade B2
Bishop St A2
Bond's Hospital B1
Broad Gate B2
Broadway C1
Burges, The B2
Bus Station A3
Butts Radial B1
Byron St A3
Canal Basin ✦ A2
Canterbury St A3
Cathedral ✝ B3
Central Six Retail Park C1
Chester St A1
Cheylesmore Manor House B2
Christ Church Spire ✦ B2
City Coll A3
City Walls & Gates ✦ A2
Corporation St B2
Council House B2
Coundon Rd A1
Coventry Sta ⇌ C2
Coventry Transport Museum A2
Coventry University Technology Park C3
Cox St A3
Croft Rd B1
Dalton Rd C1
Deasy Rd C3
Earl St B2
Eaton Rd C2
Fairfax St B2
Foleshill Rd A2
Ford's Hospital B2
Fowler Rd A1
Friars Rd C2
Gordon St C1
Gosford St B3
Greyfriars Green ✦ B2
Greyfriars Rd B2
Gulson Rd B3
Hales St A2
Harnall Lane East A3
Harnall Lane West A2
Herbert Art Gallery & Museum B3
Hertford St B2
Hewitt Ave A1
High St B2
Hill St B1
Holy Trinity B2
Holyhead Rd A1
Howard St A3
Huntingdon Rd C1
Information Ctr B2
Jordan Well B3
King Henry VIII School C1
Lady Godiva Statue ✦ B2
Lamb St A2
Leicester Row A2
Library B2
Lincoln St A2
Little Park St B2
London Rd C3
Lower Ford St B3
Lower Precinct Shopping Centre B2
Magistrates & Crown Courts B2
Manor House Drive B2
Manor Rd C2
Market B2
Martyrs Meml ✦ C2
Meadow St B1
Meriden St A1
Michaelmas Rd C2
Middleborough Rd A1
Mile La C3
Millennium Place ✦ A2
Much Park St B3
Naul's Mill Park A1
New Union B2
Odeon B1
Park Rd C2
Parkside C3
Planet Ice Arena B1
Post Office B2
Primrose Hill St A3
Priory Gardens & Visitor Centre B2
Priory St B3
Puma Way C3
Quarryfield La C3
Queen's Rd B1
Quinton Rd C2
Radford Rd A2
Raglan St B3
Ringway (Hill Cross) A1
Ringway (Queens) B1
Ringway (Rudge) B1
Ringway (St Johns) B3
Ringway (St Nicholas) A2
Ringway (St Patricks) C2
Ringway (Swanswell) A2
Ringway (Whitefriars) B3
St John St B2
St John the Baptist B2
St Nicholas St A2
Sidney Stringer Academy A3
Skydome B1
Spencer Ave C1
Spencer Rec Gnd C1
Spencer Rd C1
Spon St B1
Sports Centre B3
Stoney Rd C2
Stoney Stanton Rd A3
Superstore B2
Swanswell Pool A3
Technocentre C3
Thomas Landsdail St C2
Tomson Ave A1
Top Green C1
Trinity St B2
University B3
Univ Sports Ctr B3
Upper Hill St A1
Upper Well St A2
Victoria St A3
Vine St A3
Warwick Rd C2
Waveley Rd B1
West Orchards Shopping Ctr B2
Westminster Rd C1
White St A3
Windsor St B1

Derby 180
Abbey St C1
Agard St B1
Albert St B2
Albion St B2
Ambulance Station B1
Arthur St A1
Ashlyn Rd B3
Assembly Rooms B2
Babington La C2
Becket St B1
Belper Rd A1
Bold La B1
Bradshaw Way C2
Bradshaw Way Retail Park C2
Bridge St B1
Brook St B1
Burton Rd C1
Bus Station B2
Business Park A3
Caesar St A2
Canal St C3
Carrington St C3
Cathedral ✝ B2
Cathedral Rd B1
Charnwood St C2
Chester Green Rd A2
City Rd A2
Clarke St A3
Cock Pitt B3
Council House B2
Courts B1
Cranmer Rd B3
Crompton St C1
Crown & County Courts B2
Curzon St B1
Darley Grove A1
Derby ⇌ C3
Derby B2
Derwent Bsns Ctr A2
Derwent St B2
Drewry La C1
Duffield Rd A1
Duke St A2
Dunton Cl B3
Eagle Market C2
East St B2
Eastgate B3
Exeter St B2
Farm St C1
Ford St B1
Forester St C1
Fox St A2
Friar Gate B1
Friary St B1
Full St B2
Gerard St C1
Gower St C2
Green La C2
Grey St C1
Guildhall B2
Harcourt St C1
Highfield Rd A1
Hill La C2
Information Ctr B2
intu Derby C2
Iron Gate B2
John St C3
Joseph Wright Ctr B1
Kedleston Rd A1
Key St B2
King Alfred St C1
King St A1
Kingston St A1
Lara Croft Way C2
Leopold St C2
Library B1
Liversage St C3
Lodge La B1
London Rd C2
London Rd Com Hosp C2
Macklin St C1
Mansfield Rd A2
Market B2
Market Place B2
May St C1
Meadow La B3
Melbourne St C2
Mercian Way C1
Midland Rd C3
Monk St C1
Morledge B2
Mount St C1
Museum & Art Gallery B1
Noble St C3
North Parade A1
North St A1
Nottingham Rd B3
Osmaston Rd C2
Otter St A1
Park St C3
Parker St A1
Pickfords House B1
Police HQ A2
Police Station B2
Post Office A1/A2/B1/C2/C3
Pride Parkway C3
Prime Enterprise Park A2
Prime Parkway A2
QUAD ✦ B2
Queens Leisure Ctr B1
Racecourse Park A3
Railway Terr C3
Register Office B2
Sadler Gate B1
St Alkmund's Way B1/B2
St Helens House ✦ A1
St Mary's A1
St Mary's Bridge A2
St Mary's Bridge Chapel A2
St Mary's Gate B1
St Paul's Rd A2
St Peter's C2
St Peter's St C2
Showcase De Lux C2
Siddals Rd C3
Sir Frank Whittle Rd A3
Spa La C1
Spring St C1
Stafford St B1
Station Approach C3
Stockbrook St C1
Stores Rd A3
The Pattonair County Ground (Derbyshire CCC) B3
Traffic St C2
Wardwick B1
Werburgh St C1
West Ave A1
West Meadows Industrial Estate B3
Wharf Rd A2
Wilmot St C2
Wilson St C1
Wood's La C1

Dorchester 181
Ackerman Rd B3
Acland Rd A2
Albert Rd A1
Alexandra Rd B1
Alfred Place B3
Alfred Rd B2
Alington Ave B3
Alington Rd B3
Ambulance Station B3
Ashley Rd B1
Balmoral Cres C3
Barnes Way B2/C2
Borough Gdns A1
Brewery Sq B1
Bridport Rd A1
Buckingham Way C3
Caters Place A1
Cemetery A3/C1
Charles St A2
Coburg Rd B1
Colliton St A1
Cornwall Rd A1
Cromwell Rd B1
Culliford Rd B2
Culliford Rd North B2
Dagmar Rd B1
Damer's Rd B1
Diggory Cres C2
Dinosaur Mus A2
Dorchester Bypass C2
Dorchester South Station B1
Dorchester West Station B1
Dorset County (A&E) B1
Dorset County Council Offices A1
Dorset County Museum A1
Duchy Close C3
Duke's Ave B2
Durngate St A2
Durnover Court A3
Eddison Ave B3
Edward Rd B1
Egdon Rd C2
Elizabeth Frink Statue ✦ B2
Farfrae Cres B2
Forum Centre, The B1
Friary Hill A2
Friary Lane A2
Frome Terr A2
Garland Cres C3
Glyde Path Rd A1
Government Offices B3
Grosvenor Cres C1
Grosvenor Rd C1
Grove, The A1
Gt Western Rd B1
Herringston Rd C1
High St East A2
High St Fordington A2
High Street West A1
Holloway Rd A2
Icen Way A2
Keep Military Museum, The A1
Kings Rd A3/B3
Kingsbere Cres C2
Lancaster Rd B2
Library B1
Lime Cl C1
Linden Ave B2
London Cl A3
London Rd A2/A3
Lubbecke Way A3
Lucetta La B2
Maiden Castle Rd C1
Manor Rd C2
Market B1
Marshwood Place B2
Maumbury Rd B1
Maumbury Rings B1
Mellstock Ave C2
Mill St A3
Miller's Cl A1
Mistover Cl C1
Monmouth Rd B1/B2
Moynton Rd C2
Nature Reserve A2
North Sq A2
Northernhay A1
Odeon B1
Old Crown Court & Cells A1
Olga Rd B1
Orchard St A2
Police Station B1
Post Office A1
Pound Lane A2
Poundbury Rd A1
Prince of Wales Rd B2
Prince's St A1
Queen's Ave B1
Roman Town Ho A1
Roman Wall A1
Rothesay Rd C2
St George's Rd B3
Salisbury Field A2
Sandringham Sports Centre B3
Shaston Cres C2
Smokey Hole La B3
South Court Ave C1
South St B1
South Walks Rd B2
Superstore C3
Teddy Bear Ho A1
Temple Cl C1
Terracotta Warriors & Teddy Bear Mus A2
Town Hall A2
Town Pump ✦ A2
Trinity St A1
Tutankhamun Exhibition A1
Victoria Rd B1
Weatherbury Way C2
Wellbridge Cl C1
West Mills Rd A1
West Walks Rd A1
Weymouth Ave C1
Williams Ave B1
Winterbourne (BMI) C1
Wollaston Rd A2
York Rd B2

Dumfries 181
Academy St A2
Aldermanhill Rd B3
Ambulance Station C3
Annan Rd A3
Ardwall Rd A3
Ashfield Dr A1
Atkinson Rd C1
Averill Cres C1
Balliol Ave C1
Bank St B2
Bankend Rd C3
Barn Slaps B3
Barrie Ave B3
Beech Ave A1
Bowling Green A3
Brewery St B1
Bridgend Theatre B1
Brodie Ave C2
Brooke St B2
Broomlands Dr C1
Brooms Rd B3
Buccleuch St A2
Burns House B2
Burns Mausoleum B3
Burns St B2
Burns Statue ✦ A2
Bus Station B1
Cardoness St A3
Castle St A2
Catherine St A2
Cattle Market A3
Cemetery B3
Cemetery C2
Church Cres A2
Church St B2
College Rd A1
College St A1
Corbelly Hill B1
Corberry Park B1
Cornwall Mt A3
Council Offices A2
Court A2
Craigs Rd C3
Cresswell Ave B3
Cresswell Hill B3
Cumberland St B3
David Keswick Athletic Centre A3
David St B1
Dock Park C3
Dockhead B2
Dumfries ⇌ A3
Dumfries Academy A2
Dumfries Ice Bowl A1
Dumfries Museum & Camera Obscura B2
Dumfries & Galloway Royal Infirmary (A&E) C3
East Riverside Dr C3
Edinburgh Rd A2
English St B2

204 Dundee • Durham • Edinburgh • Exeter • Glasgow

Fire Station B3
Friar's Vennel A2
Galloway St B1
George Douglas Dr C1
George St A2
Gladstone Rd C2
Glasgow St A1
Glebe St B3
Glencaple Rd C3
Goldie Ave A1
Goldie Cres A1
Golf Course C3
Gracefield Arts Centre A2
Greyfriars A2
Grierson Ave B3
Hamilton Ave C1
Hamilton Starke Pk C2
Hazelrigg Ave C1
Henry St B3
Hermitage Dr C1
High Cemetery C3
High St A2
Hill Ave C2
Hill St B1
HM Prison B1
Holm Ave C2
Hoods Loaning A3
Howgate St B1
Huntingdon Rd A3
Information Ctr B2
Irish St B2
Irving St A2
King St A1
Kingholm Rd C3
Kirkpatrick Ct C2
Laurieknowe B1
Leafield Rd B3
Library A2
Lochfield Rd A1
Loreburn Pk A3
Loreburn St A2
Loreburne Shopping Centre B2
Lover's Walk A2
Martin Ave B3
Mausoleum B3
Maxwell St B1
McKie Ave B3
Mews La A2
Mid Steeple ✦ B2
Mill Green B2
Mill Rd B1
Moat Rd C2
Moffat Rd A3
Mountainhall Pk C3
Nelson St B1
New Abbey Rd B1/C1
New Bridge B1
Newall Terr A2
Nith Ave A2
Nith Bank C3
Nithbank Hosp C3
Nithside Ave A1
Odeon B2
Old Bridge B1
Old Bridge Ho B1
Palmerston Park (Queen of the South FC) A1
Park Rd C1
Pleasance Ave C1
Police HQ A3
Police Sta A2/A3
Portland Dr A1
Post Office B1/B2/B3
Priestlands Dr C1
Primrose St B1
Queen St B3
Queensberry St A2
Rae St A2
Richmond Ave C2
Robert Burns Ctr B2
Roberts Cres C1
Robertson Ave C3
Robinson Dr C1
Rosefield Rd C2
Rosemount St B1
Rotchell Park C1
Rotchell Rd B1
Rugby Football Gd C1
Ryedale Rd C2
St Andrews B2
St John the Evangelist A2
St Josephs College B3
St Mary's Ind Est A3
St Mary's St A3
St Michael St B2
St Michael's B2
St Michael's Bridge B2
St Michael's Bridge Rd B2
St Michael's Cemetery B3
Shakespeare St B2
Solway Dr C2
Stakeford St A1
Stark Cres C2
Station Rd A3
Steel Ave A1
Sunderries Ave A1
Sunderries Rd A1
Superstore B3
Suspension Brae B2
Swimming Pool A1
Terregles St B1
Theatre Royal B2
Troqueer Rd C2
Union St A1
Wallace St B3
Welldale B2
West Riverside Dr C2
White Sands B2

Dundee 181

Abertay University B2
Adelaide Place A1
Airlie Place C1
Albany Terr A1
Albert St A3
Alexander St A2
Ann St A2
Arthurstone Terr A3
Bank St B2
Barrack Rd A1
Barrack St B2
Bell St B2
Blinshall St B1
Broughty Ferry Rd A3
Brown St B1
Bus Station B3
Caird Hall B2
Camperdown St B3
Candle La B3
Carmichael St A1
City Churches B2
City Quay B3
City Sq B2
Commercial St B2
Constable St A3
Constitution Cres A2
Constitution Ct A1
Constitution St A1/B2
Cotton Rd A3
Courthouse Sq B1
Cowgate A3
Crescent St A3
Crichton St B2
Dens Brae A3
Dens Rd A3
Discovery Point ✦ C2
Douglas St B1
Drummond St A1
Dudhope Castle A1
Dudhope St A2
Dudhope Terr A1
Dundee C2
Dundee Contemporary Arts ✦ C2
Dundee High School B2
Dundee Law ✦ A1
Dundee Repertory C2
Dunhope Park A1
Dura St A3
East Dock St B3
East Marketgait B3
East Whale La B3
Erskine St A3
Euclid Cres B2
Forebank Rd A2
Foundry La A3
Gallagher Retail Pk B3
Gellatly St B3
Government Offices C2
Guthrie St B1
Hawkhill B1
Hilltown A2
HMS Unicorn ✦ B3
Howff Cemetery, The B2
Information Ctr B2
Keiller Shopping Centre B2
Keiller Ctr, The B2
King St A3
Kinghorne Rd A1
Ladywell Ave A3
Laurel Bank A2
Law Rd A1
Law St A1
Library A2/A3
Library and Steps Theatre A2
Little Theatre, The A2
Lochee Rd B1
Lower Princes St A3
Lyon St A3
McManus Art Gallery & Museum, The B2
Meadow Side B2
Meadowside St Pauls B2
Mercat Cross ✦ B2
Murraygate B2
Nelson St A2
Nethergate B2/C1
North Lindsay St B2
North Marketgait B2
Old Hawkhill B1
Olympia Leisure Centre B3
Overgate Shopping Centre B2
Park Place B1
Perth Rd C1
Police Station B1
Post Office B2
Princes St A3
Prospect Place A2
Reform St B2
Riverside Dr C2
Riverside Esplanade C2
Roseangle C1
Rosebank St A2
RRS Discovery C2
St Andrew's ✝ C2
St Pauls Episcopal ✝ B3
Science Centre ✦ C2
Seagate B2
Sheriffs Court B1
Shopmobility B2
South George St A2
South Marketgait B3
South Tay St B2
South Victoria Dock Road B3
South Ward Rd B2
Tay Road Bridge ✦ C3
Thomson Ave B2
Trades La B3
Union St B2
Union Terr A1
University Library B2
Univ of Dundee B1
Upper Constitution St A1
Verdant Works ✦ B1
V&A Museum of Design C2
Victoria Dock B3
Victoria Rd A2
Victoria St A3
Ward Rd B1
Wellgate B2
West Bell St B1
West Marketgait B1/B2
Westfield Place C1
William St A3
Wishart Arch ✦ A3

Durham 181

Alexander Cres B2
Allergate B2
Archery Rise C1
Avenue, The B1
Back Western Hill A1
Bakehouse La A3
Baths B3
Baths Bridge B3
Boat House B3
Bowling A2
Boyd St C3
Bus Station B2
Castle B2
Castle Chare B2
Cathedral ✝ B2
Church St C3
Clay La C1
Claypath B3
College of St Hild & St Bede B3
County Hall A1
County Hospital B1
Crescent, The A1
Crook Hall & Gardens ✦ A3
Crossgate B2
Crossgate Peth C1
Crown Court B3
Darlington Rd C1
Durham A2
Durham School C2
Durham University Science Site C3
Ellam Ave C1
Elvet Bridge B3
Elvet Court B3
Farnley Hey B1
Ferens Cl A3
Fieldhouse La A1
Flass St B1
Framwelgate Bridge B2
Framwelgate A2
Framwelgate Peth A2
Framwelgate Waterside A2
Frankland La A3
Freeman's Place A3
Freeman's Quay Leisure Centre A3
Gala Theatre & Cinema B3
Geoffrey Ave C1
Gilesgate B3
Grey College C3
Grove, The A1
Hallgarth St C3
Hatfield College B3
Hawthorn Terr B1
Heritage Centre B3
HM Prison B3
Information Ctr B3
John St B1
Kingsgate Bridge B3
Laburnum Terr B1
Lawson Terr B1
Leazes Rd B2/B3
Library B2
Library C3
Margery La B2
Market B2
Mavin St C3
Millburngate B2
Millburngate Bridge B2
Millennium Bridge (foot/cycle) A2
Mountjoy Research Centre C3
Museum of Archaeology B2
Nevilledale Terr B1
New Elvet B3
New Elvet Bridge B3
North Bailey B3
North End A1
North Rd A1/B2
Observatory C1
Old Elvet B3
Open Treasure B2
Oriental Mus C2
Oswald Court C3
Parkside B2
Passport Office A2
Percy Terr B1
Pimlico C2
Police Station B3
Post Office A1/B2
Potters Bank C1/C2
Prebends Bridge C2
Prebends Walk C2
Prince Bishops Shopping Centre B3
Princes St A1
Providence Row A3
Quarryheads La C2
Redhills La B1
Redhills Terr B1
Riverwalk, The B2
Saddler St B3
St Chad's College C3
St Cuthbert's Society C2
St John's College C2
St Margaret's B2
St Mary the Less C2
St Mary's College C2
St Monica Grove B1
St Nicholas' B3
St Oswald's C3
Sands, The A3
Shopmobility B3
Sidegate A2
Silver St B2
Sixth Form College A3
South Bailey C2
South Rd C3
South St B2
Springwell Ave A1
Stockton Rd C3
Student Union B3
Sutton St B2
Town Hall B2
Univ Arts Block B3
University Coll ✦ B2
Walkergate Centre A3
Wearside Dr A3
Western Hill A1
Wharton Park A2
Whinney Hill C3
Whitehouse Ave C1
YHA C3

Edinburgh 182

Abbey Strand B6
Abbeyhill B6
Abbeyhill Cres B6
Abbeymount A6
Abercromby Place A3
Adam St C5
Albany La A4
Albany St A4
Albert Memorial ✦ B2
Albyn Place A2
Alva Place A6
Alva St B1
Ann St A1
Appleton Tower C4
Archibald Place C3
Assembly Rooms & Musical Hall A3
Atholl Cres B1
Atholl Crescent La C1
Bank St B4
Barony St A4
Beaumont Place C5
Belford Rd B1
Belgrave Cres A1
Belgrave Cres La A1
Bell's Brae B1
Blackfriars St B4
Blair St B4
Bread St C2
Bristo Place C4
Bristo St C4
Brougham St C2
Broughton St A4
Brown St C5
Brunton Terr A6
Buckingham Terr A1
Burial Ground A6
Bus Station A4
Caledonian Cres C1
Caledonian Rd C1
Calton Hill A4
Calton Hill A5
Calton Rd B4
Camera Obscura & Outlook Tower ✦ B3
Candlemaker Row C4
Canning St B2
Canongate B5
Canongate B5
Carlton St A1
Carlton Terr A6
Carlton Terrace La A6
Castle St B2
Castle Terr B2
Castlehill B3
Central Library B4
Chalmers Hosp C3
Chalmers St C3
Chambers St C4
Chapel St C4
Charles St C4
Charlotte Sq B2
Chester St B1
Circus La A2
Circus Place A2
City Art Centre B4
City Chambers B4
City Observatory ✦ A5
Clarendon Crescent A1
Clerk St C5
Coates Cres B1
Cockburn St B4
College of Art C3
Comely Bank Ave A1
Comely Bank Row A1
Cornwall St C2
Cowans Cl C5
Cowgate B4
Cranston St B5
Crichton St C4
Croft-An-Righ A6
Cumberland St A2
Dalry Place C1
Dalry Rd C1
Danube St A1
Darnawy St A2
David Hume Tower C4
Davie St C5
Dean Bridge A1
Dean Gdns A1
Dean Park Cres A1
Dean Park Mews A1
Dean Park St A1
Dean Path B1
Dean St A1
Dean Terr A1
Dewar Place C1
Dewar Place La C1
Doune Terr A2
Drummond Place A3
Drummond St C5
Drumsheugh Gdns B1
Dublin Mews A3
Dublin St A4
Dublin St La South A4
Dumbiedykes Rd B5
Dundas St A3
Dynamic Earth ✦ B6
Earl Grey St C2
East Crosscauseway C5
East Market St B4
East Norton Place A6
East Princes St Gdns B3
Easter Rd A6
Edinburgh (Waverley) B4
Edinburgh Castle B3
Edinburgh Dungeon ✦ B4
Edinburgh Int Conference Ctr C2
Elder St A4
Esplanade B3
Eton Terr A1
Eye Pavilion C3
Festival Office B3
Festival Theatre Edinburgh C4
Filmhouse C2
Fire Station C2
Floral Clock ✦ B3
Forres St A2
Forth St A4
Fountainbridge C2
Frederick St A3
Freemasons' Hall B3
Fruitmarket B4
Gardner's Cres C2
George Heriot's School C3
George IV Bridge B4
George Sq C4
George Sq La C4
George St B3
Georgian House B2
Gladstone's Land B3
Glen St C3
Gloucester La A2
Gloucester Place A2
Gloucester St A2
Graham St C3
Grassmarket C3
Great King St A3
Great Stuart B1
Greenside La A5
Greenside Row A5
Greyfriars Kirk C4
Grindlay St C2
Grosvenor St C1
Grove St C1
Gullan's Cl B5
Guthrie St B4
Hanover St A3
Hart St A4
Haymarket C1
Haymarket Sta C1
Heriot Place C3
Heriot Row A2
High School Yard B5
High St B4
Hill Place C5
Hill St A2
Hillside Cres A5
Holyrood Abbey, remains of (AD 1128) A6
Holyrood Gait B6
Holyrood Park C6
Holyrood Rd B5
Home St C2
Hope St B2
Horse Wynd B6
Howden St C5
Howe St A2
Hub, The ✦ B3
India Place A2
India St A2
Infirmary St B4
Information Ctr B4
Jeffrey St B4
John Knox Ho B4
Johnston Terr C3
Keir St C3
Kerr St A2
King's Stables Rd B2
Lady Lawson St C3
Lauriston Gdns C3
Lauriston Park C3
Lauriston Place C3
Lauriston St C3
Lawnmarket B3
Learmonth Gdns A1
Learmonth Terr A1
Leith St A4
Lennox St A1
Lennox St La A1
Leslie Place A2
London Rd A5
Lothian Rd B2
Lothian St C4
Lower Menz Place A6
Lynedoch Place B1
Manor Place B1
Market St B4
Marshall St C4
Maryfield A6
McEwan Hall C4
Medical School C4
Melville St B1
Meuse La B4
Middle Mdw Walk C4
Milton St A6
Montrose Terr A6
Moray Place A2
Morrison Link C1
Morrison St C1
Mound Place B3
Mound, The B3
Multrees Walk A4
Mus Collections Ctr A4
Museum of Childhood B5
Museum of Edinburgh B5
Museum of Fire C3
Museum on the Mound B4
National Archives of Scotland A4
National Museum of Scotland C4
National Gallery B3
National Library of Scotland B4
National Monument ✦ A5
National Portrait Gallery B4
National War Museum B3
Nelson Monument ✦ A5
Nelson St A3
New St B5
Nicolson Sq C4
Nicolson St C4
Niddry St B4
North Bank St B3
North Bridge B4
North Castle St A2
North Charlotte St A2
North Meadow Walk C3
North St Andrew St A4
North St David St A3
North West Circus Place A2
Northumberland St A3
Odeon C2
Old Royal High School A5
Old Tolbooth Wynd B5
OMNi Centre ✦ A4
Oxford Terr A1
Palace of Holyroodhouse B6
Palmerston Place B1
Panmure Place C3
Parliament Sq B4
People's Story, The B5
Playhouse Theatre A4
Pleasance C5
Police Station C2
Ponton St C2
Post Office A3/B4/B5/C1/C2/C4
Potterrow C4
Princes Mall B4
Princes St B3
Princes St B3
Prisoners of War B3
Queen's Gallery B6
Queen St A2
Queen Street Gdns A3
Queen's Dr B6/C6
Queensferry Rd A1
Queensferry St B1
Queensferry St La B2
Radical Rd C6
Randolph Cres B1
Regent Gdns A5
Regent Rd B5
Regent Rd Park A6
Regent Terr A5
Richmond La C5
Richmond Place C5
Rose St B2
Ross Open Air Theatre B3
Rothesay Place B1
Rothesay Terr B1
Roxburgh Place C5
Roxburgh St C5
Royal Bank of Scotland A4
Royal Circus A2
Royal Lyceum C2
Royal Mile, The B5
Royal Scottish Academy B3
Royal Terr A5
Royal Terrace Gdns A5
Rutland Sq B2
Rutland St B2
St Andrew Sq A4
St Andrew Sq A4
St Andrew's House A4
St Bernard's Cres A1
St Bernard's Well ✦ A1
St Cecilia's Hall B4
St Colme St A2
St Cuthbert's B2
St Giles' ✝ B4
St John St B5
St John's B2
St John's Hill B5
St Leonard's Hill C5
St Leonard's La C5
St Leonard's St C5
St Mary's A4
St Mary's Scottish Episcopal ✝ B1
St Mary's St B5
St Michael & All Saints C3
St Stephen St A2
Salisbury Crags C6
Saunders St A2
Scotch Whisky Experience ✦ B3
Scott Monument ✦ B4
Scottish Parliament B6
Scottish Storytelling Centre ✦ B5
Semple St C2
Shandwick Place B2
South Bridge B4
South Charlotte St B2
South College St C4
South Learmonth Gdns A1
South St Andrew St A4
South St David St A3
Spittal St C2
Stafford St B1
Student Centre C4
Surgeons' Hall C5
Supreme Courts B4
Teviot Place C4
Thistle St A3
Torphichen Place C1
Torphichen St C1
Traverse Theatre B2
Tron Sq B4
Tron, The ✦ B4
Union St A4
University C4
University Library C4
Univ of Edinburgh B5
Upper Grove Place C1
Usher Hall C2
Vennel C3
Victoria St B3
Viewcraig Gdns B5
Viewcraig St B5
Vue A4
Walker St B1
Waterloo Place A4
Waverley Bridge B4
Wemyss Place A2
West Approach Rd C1
West Crosscauseway C5
West End Princess St B1
West Maitland St C1
West of Nicholson St C4
West Port C3
West Princes Street Gardens B3
West Richmond St C5
West Tollcross C2
White Horse Cl ✦ B6
William St B1
Windsor St A5
Writer's Museum, The B4
York La A4
York Place A4
York Place A4
Young St B2

Exeter 182

Alphington St C1
Athelstan Rd B3
Bampfylde St B2
Barnardo Rd C3
Barnfield Hill B3
Barnfield Rd B2/B3
Barnfield Theatre B2
Bartholomew St East B1
Bartholomew St West B1
Bear St B2
Beaufort Rd C1
Bedford St B2
Belgrave Rd A3
Belmont Rd A3
Blackall Rd A2
Blackboy Rd A3
Bonhay Rd B1
Bull Meadow Rd C2
Bus & Coach Sta B3
Castle St B2
Cecil Rd C1
Cheeke St A3
Church Rd C1
Chute St A3
City Wall B1/B2
Civic Centre B2
Clifton Rd B3
Clifton St B3
Clock Tower A1
College Rd B3
Colleton Cres C2
Commercial Rd C1
Coombe St B2
Cowick St C1
Crown Courts B2
Custom House C2
Cygnet New Theatre C2
Danes' Rd A2
Denmark Rd B3
Devon County Hall C3
Devonshire Place A3
Dinham Cres B1
East Grove Rd C3
Edmund St C1
Elmgrove Rd A1
Exe St B1
Exeter Cathedral ✝ B2
Exeter Central Station A1
Exeter City Football Ground A3
Exeter College A1
Exeter Picture House B1
Fire Station A1
Fore St B1
Friars Walk C2
Guildhall B2
Guildhall Shopping Centre B2
Harlequins Shopping Centre B1
Haven Rd C2
Heavitree Rd B3
Hele Rd A1
High St B2
HM Prison A2
Holloway St C2
Hoopern St A2
Horseguards A2
Howell Rd A1
Information Ctr B3
Iron Bridge B1
Isca Rd C1
Jesmond Rd A3
King St B1
King William St A2
Larkbeare Rd C2
Leisure Centre C1
Library B2
Longbrook St A2
Longbrook Terr A2
Lower North St B1
Lucky La C2
Lyndhurst Rd C3
Magdalen Rd B3
Magdalen St B2
Market B2
Market St B2
Marlborough Rd C3
Mary Arches St B1
Matford Ave C3
Matford La C3
Matford Rd C3
May St A3
Mol's Coffee House B2
New Bridge St B1
New North Rd A1/A2
North St B1
Northernhay St B1
Norwood Ave C3
Odeon A3
Okehampton St C1
Old Mill Close C2
Old Tiverton Rd A3
Oxford Rd A3
Paris St B2
Parr St A3
Paul St B1
Pennsylvania Rd A2
Police HQ B3
Portland Street A3
Post Office A3/B2/B3/C1
Powderham Cres A3
Preston St B1
Princesshay Shopping Centre B2
Pyramids Leisure Centre B3
Quay, The C2
Queen St A1
Queen's Terr A1
Queens Rd C1
Radford Rd C2
Richmond Rd A1
Roberts Rd C2
Rougemont Castle A2
Rougemont Ho ✦ B2
Royal Albert Memorial Museum B2
St David's Hill A1
St James' Pk Sta A3
St James' Rd A3
St Leonard's Rd C3
St Mary Steps C1
St Nicholas Priory B1
St Thomas Sta C1
Sandford Walk B3
School for the Deaf C2
School Rd C1
Sidwell St A2
Smythen St B1
South St B2
Southernhay East B2
Southernhay West B2
Spacex Gallery B1
Spicer Rd B3
Sports Centre A3
Summerland St A3
Sydney Rd C1
Tan La C2
Thornton Hill A2
Topsham Rd C3
Tucker's Hall B1
Tudor St B1
Underground Passages ✦ B2
University of Exeter (St Luke's Campus) B3
Velwell Rd A1
Verney St A3
Water La C1/C2
Weirfield Rd C2
Well St A3
West Ave A2
West Grove Rd C3
Western Way A3/B1/B2
Willeys Ave C1
Wonford Rd B3/C3
York Rd A2

Glasgow 183

Admiral St C2
Albert Bridge C5
Albion St B5
Anderston B3
Anderston Quay B3
Argyle Arcade B5
Argyle St A1/A2/B3/B4/B5
Argyle Street B5
Arlington St A3
Arts Centre B3
Ashley St A3
Bain St C6
Baird St A6
Baliol St A3
Ballater St C5
Barras (Mkt), The C6
Bath St A3
BBC Scotland B1
Bell St C6
Bell's Bridge B1
Bentinck St A2
Berkeley St A3
Bishop La B3
Black St A6
Blackburn St C2
Blackfriars St B6
Blantyre St A1
Blythswood Sq A4
Blythswood St B4
Bothwell St B4
Brand St C1
Breadalbane St A2
Bridge St C4
Bridge St C4
Bridgegate C5
Briggait C5
Broomielaw B4
Broomielaw Quay Gdns B3
Brown St B4
Brunswick St B5
Buccleuch St A3
Buchanan Bus Sta A5
Buchanan Galleries A5
Buchanan St B5
Buchanan St B5
Cadogan St B4
Caledonian Univ A5
Calgary St A5
Cambridge St A4
Canal St A5
Candleriggs B5
Carlton Place C4
Carnarvon St A3
Carrick St B4
Castle St B6
Cathedral Sq B6
Cathedral St B5
Central Mosque C5
Ctr for Contemporary Arts A4
Centre St C4
Cessnock C1
Cessnock St C1
Charing Cross A3
Charlotte St C6
Cheapside St B3
Cineworld A5
Citizens' Theatre C5
City Chambers Complex B5
City Halls B5
City of Glasgow Coll (City Campus) B5
City of Glasgow Coll (Riverside Campus) C5
Clairmont Gdns A2
Claremont St A2
Claremont Terr A2
Claythorne St C6
Cleveland St A3
Clifford La C1
Clifford St C1
Clifton Place A2
Clifton St A2
Clutha St C1
Clyde Arc B2
Clyde Place C4
Clyde Place Quay C4
Clyde St C5
Clyde Walkway C3
Clydeside Expressway B2
Coburg St C4
Cochrane St B5
College St B6
Collins St B6
Commerce St C4
Cook St C4
Cornwall St C2
Couper St A5
Cowcaddens A4
Cowcaddens Rd A4
Crimea St B3
Custom House Quay Gardens C4
Dalhousie St A4
Dental Hospital A4
Derby St A2
Dobbie's Loan A4/A5
Dobbie's Loan Place A5
Dorset St A3
Douglas St B4
Doulton Fountain ✦ C6
Dover St A2
Drury St B4
Drygate B6
Duke St B6
Dunaskin St A1
Dunblane St A4
Dundas St B5
Dunlop St C5
East Campbell St C6
Eastvale Place A1
Eglinton St C4
Elderslie St A3
Elliot St B2
Elmbank St A3
Esmond St A1
Exhibition Ctr B2
Festival Park C1
Film Theatre A4
Finnieston Quay B2
Finnieston St B2
Fire Station C6
Florence St C5
Fox St C5
Gallowgate C6
Garnet St A3
Garnethill St A4
Garscube Rd A4
George Sq B5
George St B5
George V Bridge C4
Gilbert St A1
Glasgow Bridge C4
Glasgow Cath ✝ B6
Glasgow Central B4
Glasgow City Free Church B4
Glasgow Green C6
Glasgow Necropolis ✦ B6
Glasgow Royal Concert Hall A5
Glasgow Science Centre ✦ B1
Glasgow Tower ✦ B1
Glassford St B5
Glebe St A6
Gorbals Cross C5
Gorbals St C5
Gordon St B4
Govan Rd B1/C1/C2
Grace St B3
Grafton Place A5
Grand Ole Opry ✦ C2
Grant St A3
Granville St A3
Gray St A2
Greendyke St C6
Grey Eagle St B7
Harley St C1
Harvie St C1
Haugh Rd A1
Havanah St B6
Heliport B1
Henry Wood Hall A2
High Court C5
High St B6
High Street B6
Hill St A3
Holland St A3
Holm St B4
Hope St A5
Houldsworth St B2
Houston Place C3
Houston St C3
Howard St C5
Hunter St C6
Hutcheson St B5
Hydepark St B3
Imax Cinema B1
India St A3
Information Ctr B5
Ingram St B5
Jamaica St B4
James Watt St B4
John Knox St B6
John St B5
Kelvin Hall ✦ A1
Kelvin Statue ✦ A2
Kelvin Way A2
Kelvingrove Art Gallery & Mus A1
Kelvingrove Park A2
Kelvingrove St A2
Kelvinhaugh St A1
Kennedy St A6
Kent Rd A2
Killermont St A5
King St B5
King's, The A3
Kingston Bridge C3
Kingston St C4
Kinning Park C2
Kyle St A5
Lancefield Quay B2
Lancefield St B3
Langshot St C1
Lendel Place C1
Lighthouse, The ✦ B4
Lister St A6
Little St B3
London Rd C6
Lorne St C1
Lower Harbour B1
Lumsden St A1
Lymburn St A1
Lyndoch Cres A3
Lynedoch Place A3
Lynedoch St A3
Maclellan St C1
Mair St C2
Maitland St A4
Mansell St C7
Mavisbank Gdns C2
Mcalpine St B3
Mcaslin St A6
McLean Sq C2
McLellan Gallery A4
McPhater St A4
Merchants' Ho B5
Middlesex St C2
Middleton St C1
Midland St B4
Miller St B5
Millennium Bridge B1
Millroad St C6
Milnpark St C2
Milton St A4
Minerva St B2
Mitchell St West B4
Mitchell Liby, The ✦ A3
Modern Art Gall B5
Moir St C6
Molendinar St C6
Moncur St C6
Montieth Row C6
Montrose St B5
Morrison St C3
Nairn St A1
National Piping Centre, The ✦ A5
Nelson Mandela Sq B5
Nelson St C4
Nelson's Monument C6
Newton Place A3
Newton St A3
Nicholson St C4
Nile St B5
Norfolk Court C4
Norfolk St C4
North Frederick St B5
North Hanover St B5
North Portland St B6
North St A3
North Wallace St A5
O2 ABC A4
O2 Academy ✦ C4
Odeon C3
Old Dumbarton Rd A1
Osborne St B5/C5
Oswald St B4
Overnewton St A1
Oxford St C4
Pacific Dr B1
Paisley Rd C3
Paisley Rd West C1
Park Circus A2
Park Gdns A2
Park St South A2
Park Terr A2
Parkgrove Terr A2
Parnie St C5
Parson St A6
Partick Bridge A1
Passport Office A5
Pavilion Theatre A4
Pembroke St A3
People's Palace C6
Pinkston Rd A6
Pitt St A4/B4
Plantation Park C1
Plantation Quay B1
Police Mus B5
Police Station A4/A6
Port Dundas Rd A5
Port St B2
Portman St C2
Prince's Dock B1
Princes Sq B5
Provand's Lordship B6
Queen St B5
Queen Street B5
Ramshorn B5
Renfrew St A3/A4
Renton St A5
Richmond St B5
Robertson St B4
Rose St A4
Rottenrow B5
Royal Concert Hall A5
Royal Conservatoire of Scotland A4
Royal Cres A2
Royal Exchange Sq B5
Royal Highland Fusiliers Mus A3
West Glasgow Ambulatory Care A1
Royal Infirmary B6
Royal Terr A2
Rutland Cres C2
St Andrew's in the Square C6
St Andrew's (RC) ✝ C5
St Andrew's St C5
St Enoch B5
St Enoch Shopping Centre B5
St Enoch Sq B4
St George's Rd A3
St James Rd B6
St Kent St C6
St Mungo Ave A5/A6
St Mungo Museum of Religious Life & Art B6
St Mungo Place A6
St Vincent Cres A2
St Vincent Place B5
St Vincent St B3/B4
St Vincent Terr B3
Saltmarket C5
Sandyford Place A3
Sauchiehall St A2/A4
SEC Armadillo B2
School of Art A4
Sclater St B7
Scotland St C2
Scott St A4
Scottish Exhibition & Conference Ctr B1
Seaward St C2
Shaftesbury St B3
Sheriff Court C5
Shields Rd C3
Shopmobility A5
Shuttle St B6
Somerset Place A2
South Portland St C4
Springburn Rd A6
Springfield Quay C3
SSE Hydro The ✦ B2
Stanley St C2
Stevenson St C6
Stewart St A4
Stirling Rd B6
Stobcross Quay B1
Stobcross Rd B1
Stock Exchange B5
Stockwell Place C5
Stockwell St B5
Stow College A4
Sussex St C2
Synagogue A3
Taylor Place A6
Tenement House A3
Teviot St A1
Theatre Royal A4
Tolbooth Steeple & Mercat Cross ✦ C6
Tower St C2
Trades House B5
Tradeston St C4
Transport Mus A1
Tron C5
Trongate B5
Tunnel St B2
Turnbull St C5
Union St B4
Univ of Strathclyde B6
Victoria Bridge C5
Virginia St B5
Wallace St C3
Walls St B6
Walmer Cres C1
Warrock St B3
Washington St B3
Waterloo St B4
Watson St B6
Watt St C3
Wellington St B4
West Campbell St B4
West George St B4
West Graham St A4
West Greenhill Place B2
West Regent St A4
West Regent St B4
West St C4
West St C4
Whitehall St B3
Wilkes St C7
Wilson St B5
Woodlands Gate A3
Woodlands Rd A3
Woodlands Terr A2
Woodside Place A3
Woodside Terr A3

York St B4
Yorkhill Pde A1
Yorkhill St A1

Gloucester 182

Albion St C1
Alexandra Rd B3
Alfred St C3
All Saints Rd C2
Alvin St B2
Arthur St C2
Barrack Square B1
Barton St C2
Blackfriars B1
Blenheim Rd C2
Bristol Rd C1
Brunswick Rd C2
Bruton Way B2
Bus Station B2
Cineworld C1
City Council Offices B1
City Mus, Art Gallery & Library B2
Clarence St B2
Commercial Rd B1
Council Offices B1
Courts B1
Cromwell St C2
Deans Way A2
Denmark Rd A3
Derby Rd C3
Docks C1
Eastgate St B2
Eastgate, The B1
Edwy Pde A2
Estcourt Cl A3
Estcourt Rd A3
Falkner St C2
GL1 Leisure Centre C2
Gloucester Cath B1
Gloucester Life B1
Gloucester Quays Outlet C1
Gloucester Sta B2
Gloucester Waterways C1
Gloucestershire Archive B2
Gloucestershire Royal Hospital (A&E) B3
Goodyere St C2
Gouda Way A1
Great Western Rd B3
Guildhall B2
Heathville Rd A3
Henry Rd B3
Henry St B2
Hinton Rd A2
India Rd C3
Information Ctr B1
Jersey Rd C3
King's C2
King's Walk Shopping Centre B2
Kingsholm (Gloucester Rugby) A2
Kingsholm Rd A2
Lansdown Rd A3
Library C2
Llanthony Rd C1
London Rd B3
Longhorn Ave A1
Longsmith St B1
Malvern Rd A3
Market B2
Market Parade B2
Mercia Rd A1
Metz Way C3
Midland Rd C2
Millbrook St C3
Montpellier C1
Napier St C3
Nettleton Rd C2
New Inn B2
New Olympus C3
North Rd A3
Northgate St B2
Oxford Rd A2
Oxford St B2
Park & Ride Gloucester A1
Park Rd C2
Park St B2
Park, The C2
Parliament St C1
Peel Centre, The C1
Pitt St B1
Police Station C3
Post Office B2
Quay St B1
Quay, The B1
Recreation Gd A1/A2
Regent St C2
Robert Raikes Ho B1
Royal Oak Rd B1
Russell St B2
Ryecroft St C2
St Aldate St B2
St Ann Way C1
St Catherine St A2
St Mark St A2
St Mary de Crypt B1
St Mary de Lode B1
St Nicholas's B1
St Oswald's Rd A1
St Oswald's Retail Park A1
St Peter's B2
Seabroke Rd A3
Sebert St A2
Severn Rd C1
Sherborne St B2
Shire Hall B1
Sidney St C3
Soldiers of Gloucestershire B1
Southgate St B1/C1
Spa Field C1
Spa Rd C1
Sports Ground A2/B2
Station Rd B2
Stratton Rd C3
Stroud Rd C1
Superstore A1
Swan Rd A2
Trier Way C1/C2
Union St A2
Vauxhall Rd C3
Victoria St C2
Walham Lane A1
Wellington St C2
Westgate Retail Pk B1
Westgate St B1
Widden St C2
Worcester St B2

Grimsby 183

Abbey Drive East C2
Abbey Drive West C2
Abbey Park Rd C2
Abbey Rd C2
Abbey Walk C2
Abbeygate Shopping Centre C2
Abbotsway C2
Adam Smith St A1/A2
Ainslie St C2
Albert St A3
Alexandra Dock A2/B2
Alexandra Rd A2/B2
Alexandra Retail Pk A2
Annesley St A2
Armstrong St A1
Arthur St B2
Augusta St C1
Bargate C1
Beeson St A1
Bethlehem St C2
Bodiam Way B3
Bradley St B3
Brighowgate C1/C2
Bus Station C2
Canterbury Dr C1
Cartergate B1/C1
Catherine St C3
Caxton A3
Chantry La B1
Charlton St A1
Church La C2
Church St A3
Cleethorpe Rd A3
Close, The C1
College St C1
Compton Dr C1
Corporation Bridge A2
Corporation Rd A1
Court B3
Crescent St B1
Deansgate C1
Doughty Rd C2
Dover St B1
Duchess St C2
Dudley St C1
Duke of York Gardens B1
Duncombe St B3
Earl La B1
East Marsh St B3
East St B2
Eastgate B3
Eastside Rd A3
Eaton Ct C1
Eleanor St B3
Ellis Way B3
Fisherman's Chapel A3
Fisherman's Wharf B2
Fishing Heritage Centre B2
Flour Sq A3
Frederick St B1
Frederick Ward Way B2
Freeman St A3/B3
Freshney Dr B1
Freshney Place B2
Garden St C2
Garibaldi St A3
Garth La B2
Grime St B3
Grimsby Docks Station A3
Grimsby Town Station C2
Hainton Ave C3
Har Way B3
Hare St C3
Harrison St B1
Haven Ave B1
Hay Croft Ave B1
Hay Croft St B1
Heneage Rd B3/C3
Henry St B1
Holme St B3
Hume St C1
James St B1
Joseph St B1
Kent St A3
King Edward St A3
Lambert Rd C2
Library B2
Lime St B1
Lister St B1
Littlefield La C1
Lockhill A3
Lord St B1
Lower Spring St A3
Ludford St C2
Macaulay St B1
Mallard Mews C3
Manor Ave C2
Market A3
Market Hall B2
Market St B3
Moss Rd C2
Nelson St A3
New St B2
Osbourne St B2
Pasture St B3
Peaks Parkway C3
Pelham Rd C1
Police Station B3
Post Office B1/B2
Pyewipe Rd A1
Railway Place A3
Railway St A3
Recreation Ground C2
Rendel St A2
Retail Park A2/B3
Richard St B1
Ripon St B1
Robinson St East B3
Royal St A3
St Hilda's Ave C1
St James C2
Sheepfold St B3/C3
Shopmobility B2
Sixhills St C3
South Park B2
Superstore B3/B2
Tasburgh St C3
Tennyson St B2
Thesiger St A3
Time Trap C2
Town Hall B2
Veal St B1
Victoria Retail Park A3
Victoria St North A2
Victoria St South B2
Victoria St West B2
Watkin St A1
Welholme Ave C2
Welholme Rd C3
Wellington St B3
Wellowgate C2
Werneth Rd B3
West Coates Rd A1
Westgate A2
Westminster Dr C1
Willingham St C3
Wintringham Rd C2
Wood St B3
Yarborough Dr B1
Yarborough Hotel C2

Harrogate 183

Albert St C2
Alexandra Rd B2
Arthington Ave B2
Ashfield Rd A2
Back Cheltenham Mount B2
Beech Grove C1
Belmont Rd C1
Bilton Dr A2
BMI The Duchy Hospital C1
Bower Rd B2
Bower St B2
Bus Station B2
Cambridge Rd B2
Cambridge St B2
Cemetery A2
Chatsworth Grove A2
Chatsworth Place A2
Chatsworth Rd A2
Chelmsford Rd B3
Cheltenham Cres B2
Cheltenham Mt B2
Cheltenham Pde B2
Christ Church B3
Christ Church Oval B3
Chudleigh Rd B3
Clarence Dr B1
Claro Rd A3
Claro Way A3
Coach Park B2
Coach Rd B3
Cold Bath Rd C1
Commercial St B2
Coppice Ave A1
Coppice Dr A1
Coppice Gate A1
Cornwall Rd B1
Council Offices B1
Crescent Gdns B1
Crescent Rd B1
Dawson Terr A2
Devonshire Place B3
Dixon Rd A2
Dixon Terr A2
Dragon Ave B3
Dragon Parade B2
Dragon Rd B2
Duchy Rd B1
East Parade B2
East Park Rd C3
Esplanade B1
Everyman B2
Fire Station A2
Franklin Mount A2
Franklin Rd B2
Franklin Square A2
Glebe Rd C1
Grove Park Ct A3
Grove Park Terr A3
Grove Rd A2
Hampsthwaite Rd A1
Harcourt Dr B3
Harcourt Rd B3
Harrogate B2
Harrogate Convention Ctr B1
Harrogate Justice Ctr (Magistrates' and County Courts) C2
Harrogate Ladies College B1
Harrogate Theatre B2
Heywood Rd C1
Hollins Cres A1
Hollins Mews A1
Hollins Rd A1
Hydro Leisure Centre, The A1
Information Ctr B1
James St B2
Jenny Field Dr A1
John St B2
Kent Dr A1
Kent Rd A1
Kings Rd A2
Kingsway B3
Kingsway Dr B3
Lancaster Rd C1
Leeds Rd C2
Lime Grove B3
Lime St A3
Mayfield Grove B2
Mercer B1
Montpellier Hill B1
Mornington Cres A3
Mornington Terr B3
Mowbray Sq B3
North Park Rd B3
Oakdale Ave A1
Oatlands Dr C3
Odeon B2
Osborne Rd A2
Otley Rd C2
Oxford St B2
Parade, The B2
Park Chase B3
Park Parade B3
Park View B2
Parliament St B1
Police Station C3
Post Office B2/C1
Providence Terr A2
Queen Parade C3
Queen's Rd C1
Raglan St C2
Regent Ave A3
Regent Grove A3
Regent Parade A3
Regent St A3
Regent Terr A3
Ripon Rd A1
Robert St C2
Royal Baths & Turkish Baths B1
Royal Pump Room B1
St Luke's Mount A2
St Mary's Ave C1
St Mary's Walk C1
Scargill Rd A1
Skipton Rd A3
Skipton St A2
Slingsby Walk C3
South Park Rd C2
Spring Grove A1
Springfield Ave B1
Station Ave B2
Station Parade B2
Stray Rein C3
Stray, The C2/C3
Studley Rd A2
Superstore B2/C1
Swan Rd B1
Tower St C2
Trinity Rd C2
Union St B2
Valley Dr C1
Valley Gardens C1
Valley Mount C1
Victoria Ave C2
Victoria Rd C1
Victoria Shopping Centre B2
Waterloo St A2
West Park C2
West Park St C2
Wood View A1
Woodfield Ave A3
Woodfield Dr A3
Woodfield Grove A3
Woodfield Rd A3
Woodfield Square A3
Woodside B3
York Place C3
York Rd B1

Hull 184

Adelaide St C1
Albert Dock C1
Albion St B2
Alfred Gelder St B2
Anlaby Rd B1
Arctic Corsair B3
Beverley Rd A1
Blanket Row C2
Bond St B2
Bonus Arena B2
Bridlington Ave A2
Brook St B1
Brunswick Ave A1
Bus Station B1
Camilla Cl C3
Cannon St A2
Caroline St A2
Carr La B2
Castle St C2
Central Library B1
Charles St A2
Citadel Way B3
City Hall B2
City Hall Theatre B2
Clarence St B3
Cleveland St A3
Clifton St A1
Colonial St B1
Court B2
Deep, The C3
Dinostar C2
Dock Office Row B3
Dock St B2
Drypool Bridge B3
Egton St A3
English St C1
Ferens Gallery B2
Ferensway B1
Fire Sta A1
Francis St A2
Francis St West A2
Freehold St A1
Freetown Way A2
Früit Theatre C2
Garrison Rd B3
George St B2
Gibson St A2
Great Thornton St B1
Great Union St A3
Green La A2
Grey St A1
Grimston St B2
Grosvenor St A1
Guildhall B2
Guildhall Rd B2
Hands-on History B2
Harley St A1
Hessle Rd C1
High St B3
Hull Minster B2
Hull Paragon Interchange Sta B1
Hull & East Riding Museum B3
Hull Ice Arena C1
Hull College B3
Hull History Centre A2
Hull New Theatre A2
Hull Truck Theatre B1
Humber Dock Marina C2
Humber Dock St C2
Humber St C2
Hyperion St A3
Information Ctr B1
Jameson St B1
Jarratt St B2
Jenning St A3
King Billy Statue C2
King Edward St B2
King St A2
Kingston Retail Pk C1
Kingston St C2
Liddell St A1
Lime St A3
Lister St C1
Lockwood St A2
Maister House B3
Maritime Mus B2
Market B2
Market Place B2
Minerva Pier C2
Mulgrave St A3
Myton Swing Bridge C3
Myton St B1
NAPA (Northern Acad of Performing Arts) B1
Nelson St C2
New Cleveland St A3
New George St A2
Norfolk St A1
North Bridge A3
North St B1
Odeon C1
Old Harbour C3
Osborne St B1
Paragon St B2
Park St B1
Percy St A2
Pier St C2
Police Station B1
Porter St C1
Portland St B1
Post Office B1/B2
Posterngate B2
Prince's Quay B2
Prospect Centre B1
Prospect St B1
Queen's Gdns B2
Railway Dock Marina C2
Railway St C2
Real B1
Red Gallery B1
Reform St A2
Retail Park B1
Riverside Quay C2
Roper St B2
St James St C1
St Luke's St B1
St Mark St A3
St Mary the Virgin B3
St Stephens Shopping Centre B1
Scale Lane Footbridge B3
Scott St A2
South Bridge Rd B3
Sport's Centre C1
Spring Bank A1
Spring St B1
Spurn Lightship C2
Spyvee St A3
Stage @ the Dock C3
Streetlife Transport Museum B3
Sykes St A2
Tidal Surge Barrier C3
Tower St B3
Trinity House B2
Vane St A1
Victoria Pier C2
Waterhouse La B2
Waterloo St A1
Waverley St C1
Wellington St C2
Wellington St West C2
West St B1
Whitefriargate B2
Wilberforce Dr B2
Wilberforce Ho B3
Wilberforce Monument B3
William St C1
Wincolmlee A3
Witham A3
Wright St A1

Inverness 184

Abban St A1
Academy St B2
Alexander Place B2
Anderson St A2
Annfield Rd C3
Ardconnel St B3
Ardconnel Terr B3
Ardross Place B2
Ardross St B2
Argyle St B3
Argyle Terr B3
Attadale Rd B1
Ballifeary La C2
Ballifeary Rd C1/C2
Balnacraig La A1
Balnain House B2
Balnain St B2
Bank St B2
Bellfield Park C2
Bellfield Terr C3
Benula Rd A1
Birnie Terr A1
Bishop's Rd C2
Bowling Green B2
Bridge St B2
Brown St A2
Bruce Ave C1
Bruce Gdns C1
Bruce Pk C1
Burial Ground A2
Burnett Rd A3
Bus Station B3
Caledonian Rd B1
Cameron Rd A1
Cameron Sq A1
Carse Rd A1
Carsegate Rd Sth A1
Castle Garrison Encounter B2
Castle Rd B2
Castle St B3
Celt St B2
Chapel St A2
Charles St B3
Church St B2
Columba Rd B1/C1
Crown Ave B3
Crown Circus B3
Crown Dr B3
Crown Rd B3
Crown St B3
Culduthel Rd C3
Dalneigh Cres C1
Dalneigh Rd C1
Denny St B3
Dochfour Dr B1/C1
Douglas Row B2
Duffy Dr C3
Dunabban Rd A1
Dunain Rd B1
Duncraig St B2
Eastgate Shopping Centre B3
Eden Court C2
Fairfield Rd B1
Falcon Sq B3
Fire Station A3
Fraser St B2
Fraser St C2
Friars' Bridge A2
Friars' La B2
Friars' St A2
George St A2
Gilbert St A2
Glebe St A2
Glendoe Terr A1
Glenurquhart Rd C1
Gordon Terr B3
Gordonville Rd C2
Grant St A2
Grant Street Park (Clachnacuddin FC) A1
Greig St B2
Harbour Rd A3
Harrowden Rd B1
Haugh Rd C2
Heatherley Cres C3
High St B3
Highland Council HQ, The C2
Hill Park C3
Hill St B3
HM Prison B3
Huntly Place A2
Huntly St B2
India St A2
Industrial Estate A3
Information Ctr B2
Innes St A2
Inverness B3
Inverness High School B1
Inverness Museum & Art Gallery B2
Jamaica St A2
Kenneth St B2
Kilmuir Rd A1
King St B2
Kingsmills Rd B3
Laurel Ave B1/C1
Library A3
Lilac Grove B1
Lindsay Ave C1
Lochalsh Rd A1/B1
Longman Rd A3
Lotland Place A2
Lower Kessock St A1
Madras St A2
Maxwell Dr C1
Mayfield Rd C3
Millburn Rd B3
Mitchell's La C3
Montague Row B2
Muirfield Rd C3
Muirtown St B1
Nelson St A2
Ness Bank C2
Ness Bridge B2
Ness Walk B2/C2
Old Edinburgh Rd C3
Old High Church B2
Park Rd C1
Paton St C2
Perceval Rd B1
Planefield Rd B2
Police Station A3
Porterfield Bank C3
Porterfield Rd C3
Portland Place A2
Post Office A2/B1/B2
Queen St B2
Queensgate B2
Railway Terr A3
Rangemore Rd B1
Reay St B3
Riverside St A2
Rose St A2
Ross Ave B1
Rowan Rd B1
Royal Northern Infirmary C2
St Andrew's Cathedral C2
St Columba B2
St John's Ave C1
St Mary's Ave C1
Sheriff Court B3
Shore St A2
Smith Ave C1
Southside Place C3
Southside Rd C3
Spectrum Centre B2
Strothers La B3
Superstore A1/B2
TA Centre C2
Telford Gdns B1
Telford Rd A1
Telford St A1
Tomnahurich Cemetery C1
Tomnahurich St B2
Town Hall B3
Union Rd B3
Union St B3
Victorian Market B3
Walker Place A2
Walker Rd A3
War Memorial C2
Waterloo Bridge A2
Wells St B1
Young St B2

Ipswich 184

Alderman Rd B2
All Saints' Rd A1
Alpe St B2
Ancaster Rd C1
Ancient House B3
Anglesea Rd B2
Ann St B2
Arboretum A2
Austin St C2
Avenue, The A3
Belstead Rd C2
Berners St B2
Bibb Way B1
Birkfield Dr C1
Black Horse La B2
Bolton La B3
Bond St C3
Bowthorpe Cl B2
Bramford La A1
Bramford Rd A1
Bridge St C2
Brookfield Rd A1
Brooks Hall Rd A1
Broomhill A2
Broomhill Rd A1
Broughton Rd A2
Bulwer Rd B1
Burrell Rd C2
Bus Station B2
Butter Market B2
Buttermarket Shopping Ctr, The B3
Cardinal Park Leisure Park C2
Carr St B3
Cecil Rd B2
Cecilia St C2
Chancery Rd C2
Charles St B2
Chevallier St A1
Christchurch Mansion & Wolsey Art Gallery B3
Christchurch Park A3
Christchurch St B3
Cineworld C2
Civic Centre B2
Civic Dr B2
Clarkson St B1
Cobbold St B3
Commercial Rd C2
Constable Rd A3
Constantine Rd C1
Constitution Hill A2
Corder Rd A3
Corn Exchange B2
Cotswold Ave A2
Council Offices C2
County Hall B3
Crown Court C2
Crown St B2
Cullingham Rd B1
Cumberland St B2
Curriers La B2
Dale Hall La A2
Dales View Rd A1
Dalton Rd B2
Dillwyn St B1
Elliot St B1
Elm St B2
Elsmere Rd A3
Falcon St C2
Felaw St C3
Fire Station C2
Flint Wharf C3
Fonnereau Rd B2
Fore St C3
Foundation St C3
Franciscan Way C2
Friars St C2
Gainsborough Rd A3
Gatacre Rd B1
Geneva Rd B2
Gippeswyk Ave C1
Gippeswyk Park C1
Grafton Way C2
Graham Rd A1
Great Whip St C3
Grimwade St C3
Handford Cut B1
Handford Rd B1
Henley Rd A2
Hervey St B3
High St B2
Holly Rd A2
Information Ctr B3
Ipswich Haven Marina C3
Ipswich Museum & Art Gallery B2
Ipswich School A2
Ipswich Station C2
Ipswich Town FC (Portman Road) C2
Ivry St A2
Kensington Rd A1
Kesteven Rd C1
Key St C3
Kingsfield Ave A3
Kitchener Rd A1
Little's Cres C2
London Rd B1
Low Brook St C3
Lower Orwell St C3
Luther Rd C2
Magistrates Court B2
Manor Rd A3
Mornington Ave A1
Museum St B2
Neale St B3
New Cardinal St C2
New Cut East C3
New Cut West C3
New Wolsey B2
Newson St B2
Norwich Rd A1/B1
Oban St B2
Old Custom Ho C3
Old Foundry Rd B3
Old Merchant's House C3
Orford St B2
Paget Rd A2
Park Rd A3
Park View Rd A2
Peter's St C2
Philip Rd C2
Pine Ave A2
Pine View Rd A2
Police Station B2
Portman Rd B2
Portman Walk C1
Post Office B2
Princes St C2
Prospect St B1
Queen St B2
Ranelagh Rd C1
Recreation Ground B1
Rectory Rd C2
Regent Theatre B3
Retail Park C1
Retail Park C2
Richmond Rd A1
Rope Walk C3
Rose La C2
Russell Rd C2
St Edmund's Rd A2
St George's St B2
St Helen's St B3
Sherrington Rd A1
Shopmobility B2
Silent St C2
Sir Alf Ramsey Way C1
Sirdar Rd B1
Soane St B3
Springfield La A1
Star La C3
Stevenson Rd B1
Suffolk College C3
Suffolk Retail Park B1
Superstore B1
Surrey Rd B1
Tacket St C3
Tavern St B3
Tower Ramparts B2
Tower Ramparts Shopping Ctr B2
Tower St B3
Town Hall B2
Tuddenham Rd A3
University C3
Upper Brook St B3
Upper Orwell St B3
Valley Rd A2
Vermont Cres B3
Vermont Rd B3
Vernon St C3
Warrington Rd A2
Waterloo Rd A1
Waterworks St C3
Wellington St B1
West End Rd B1
Westerfield Rd A3
Westgate St B2
Westholme Rd A1
Westwood Ave A1
Willoughby Rd C2
Withipoll St B3
Woodbridge Rd B3
Woodstone Ave A3
Yarmouth Rd B1

Kendal 184

Abbot Hall Art Gallery & Mus of Lakeland Life & Industry C2
Ambulance Station A2
Anchorite Fields C2
Anchorite Rd C2
Ann St A3
Appleby Rd A3
Archers Meadow C3
Ashleigh Rd A2
Aynam Rd B2
Bankfield Rd B1
Beast Banks B2
Beezon Fields A2
Beezon Rd A2
Beezon Trad Est A3
Belmont B2
Birchwood Cl C1
Blackhall Rd B2
Brewery Arts Centre B2
Bridge St B2
Brigsteer Rd C1
Burneside Rd A2
Bus Station B2
Buttery Well Rd C2
Canal Head North B3
Captain French La C2
Caroline St A2
Castle Hill B3
Castle Howe B2
Castle Rd B3
Castle St A3/B3
Cedar Grove C1
Council Offices B2
County Council Offices A2
Cricket Ground A3
Cricket Ground C3
Cross La C2
Dockray Hall Industrial Estate A2
Dowker's La B2
East View B1
Echo Barn Hill C1
Elephant Yard B2
Fairfield La A1
Finkle St B2
Fire Station A2
Fletcher Square C3
Football Ground C3
Fowling La A3
Gillinggate C2
Glebe Rd C2
Golf Course B1
Goose Holme B3
Gooseholme Bridge B3
Green St A1
Greengate C2
Greengate La C1/C2
Greenside B1
Greenwood C1
Gulfs Rd B2
High Tenterfell B1
Highgate B2
Hillswood Ave C1
Horncop La A2
Information Ctr B2
Kendal A3
Kendal Bsns Park A3
Kendal Castle (Remains) B3
Kendal Fell B1
Kendal Green A1
Kendal Ski Ctr B3
Kendal Station A3
Kent Place B2
Kirkbarrow C2
Kirkland C2
Library B2
Library Rd B2
Little Aynam B3
Little Wood B3
Long Cl C1
Longpool A3
Lound Rd C3
Lound St C3
Low Fellside B2
Lowther St B2
Magistrates Court A2
Maple Dr C1
Market Place B2
Maude St B2
Miller Bridge B2
Milnthorpe Rd C2
Mint St A3
Mintsfeet Rd A3
Mintsfeet Rd South A2
New Rd B2
Noble's Rest B2
Parish Church C2
Park Side Rd C3
Parkside Bsns Park C3
Parr St B3
Police Station A2
Post Office A3/B2
Quaker Tapestry B2
Queen's Rd B1
Riverside Walk C2
Rydal Mount A2
Sandes Ave A2
Sandgate A3
Sandylands Rd A3
Serpentine Rd B1
Serpentine Wood B1
Shap Rd A3
South Rd C2
Stainbank Rd C1
Station Rd A3
Stramongate B2
Stramongate Bridge B2
Stricklandgate A2/B2
Sunnyside C3
Thorny Hills B3
Town Hall B2
Undercliff Rd B1
Underwood C1
Union St A2
Vicar's Fields C2
Vicarage Dr C1/C2
Wainwright's Yard B2
Wasdale Close C3
Well Ings C2
Westmorland Shopping Centre & Market Hall B2
Westwood Ave C1
Wildman St A3
Windermere Rd A1
YHA B2
YWCA B2

King's Lynn 185

Albert St A2
Albion St B2
Alive St James' Swimming Pool B2
All Saints B2
All Saints St B2
Austin Fields A2
Austin St A2
Avenue Rd B3
Bank Side B1
Beech Rd C2
Birch Tree Cl B2
Birchwood St A2
Blackfriars Rd B2
Blackfriars St B2
Boal St B1
Bridge St B2
Broad St B2
Broad Walk B3
Burkitt St A2
Bus Station A2
Carmelite Terr C2
Chapel St A2
Chase Ave C3
Checker St C2
Church St B2
Clough La B2
Coburg St B2
Coll of West Anglia A3
Columbia Way A3
Corn Exchange A1
County Court Rd B2
Cresswell St A2
Custom House A1
East Coast Bsns Pk C1
Eastgate St A2
Edma St A2
Exton's Rd C3
Ferry La B1
Ferry St A1
Framingham's Almshouses B2
Friars St C2
Friars Walk C2
Gaywood Rd A3
George St A2
Gladstone Rd C2
Goodwin's Rd C3
Green Quay B1
Greyfriars' Tower B2
Guanock Terr C2
Guildhall A1
Hansa Rd C3
Hardwick Rd C2
Hextable Rd A2
High St B1
Holcombe Ave C3
Hospital Walk C2
Information Ctr B1
John Kennedy Rd A2
Kettlewell Lane A2
King George V Ave B3
King St B1
King's Lynn Art Centre A1
King's Lynn FC B3
King's Lynn Sta B2
Library B2
Littleport St A2
Loke Rd A2
London Rd B2
Lynn Museum B2
Magistrates Court B1
Majestic B2
Market La A1
Millfleet B2
Milton Ave A3
Nar Valley Walk C2
Nelson St B1
New Conduit St B2
Norfolk St A2
North Lynn Discovery Centre A3
North St A2
Oldsunway B2
Ouse Ave C1
Page Stair Lane A1
Park Ave B3
Police Station B2
Portland Place C1
Portland St B2
Purfleet B1
Queen St B1
Raby Ave A3
Railway Rd A2
Red Mount Chapel B3
Regent Way B2
River Walk A1
Robert St C2
Saddlebow Rd C2
Shopmobility B2
St Ann's St A1
St James St B2
St James' Rd B2
St John's Walk B3
St Margaret's B1
St Nicholas A2
St Nicholas St A1
St Peter's Rd B1
Sir Lewis St A2
Smith Ave A3
South Everard St C2
South Gate C2
South Quay B1
South St B2
Southgate St C2
Stonegate St B2
Surrey St A1
Sydney St C3
Tennyson Ave B3
Tennyson Rd B3
Tower St B2
Town Hall B1
Town Ho & Tales of the Old Gaol Ho B1
Town Wall (Remains) B3
True's Yard Fisherfolk Museum A2
Valingers Rd C2
Vancouver Ave C2
Vancouver Quarter B2
Waterloo St B2
Wellesley St B2
White Friars Rd C2
Windsor Rd C2
Winfarthing St C2
Wyatt St A2
York Rd C3

Lancaster 185

Aberdeen Rd C3
Adult College, The C3
Aldcliffe Rd C2
Alfred St B3
Ambleside Rd A3
Ambulance Sta A3
Ashfield Ave B1
Ashton Rd C2
Assembly Rooms Emporium B2
Balmoral Rd B3
Bath House B2
Bath Mill La B3
Bath St B3
Blades St B1
Borrowdale Rd B3
Bowerham Rd C3
Brewery La B2
Bridge La B2
Brook St C1
Bulk Rd A3
Bulk St B2
Bus Station B2
Cable St B2
Canal Cruises & Waterbus C2
Carlisle Bridge A1
Carr House La C2
Castle B1
Castle Park B1
Caton Rd A3
China St B2
Church St B2
City Museum B2
Clarence St C3
Common Gdn St B2
Coniston Rd A3
Cottage Museum B2
Council Offices B2
County Court & Family Court B2
Cromwell Rd C1
Crown Court B1
Dale St C3
Dallas Rd B1/C1
Dalton Rd B3
Dalton Sq B2
Damside St B2
De Vitre St B3
Dee Rd A1
Denny Ave A1
Derby Rd A2
Dukes, The B2
Earl St A2
East Rd B3
Eastham St C3
Edward St B3
Fairfield Rd B1
Fenton St B2
Firbank Rd A3
Fire Station B2
Friend's Meeting House B1
Garnet St B3
George St B2
Giant Axe Field B1
Grand B2
Grasmere Rd B3
Greaves Rd C2
Green St A3
Gregson Ctr, The B3
Gregson Rd C3
Greyhound Bridge A2
Greyhound Bridge Rd A2
High St B2
Hill Side B1
Hope St C3
Hubert Place B1
Information Ctr B2
Kelsy St B1
Kentmere Rd B3
King St B2
Kingsway A3
Kirkes Rd C3
Lancaster & Lakeland C3
Lancaster City Football Club B1
Lancaster Sta B1
Langdale Rd A3
Ley Ct B1
Library B2
Lincoln Rd B1
Lindow St C2
Lodge St B2
Long Marsh La B1
Lune Rd A1
Lune St A2
Lune Valley Ramble A3
Mainway A2
Maritime Mus A1
Marketgate Shopping Centre B2
Market St B2
Meadowside C2
Meeting House La B1
Millennium Bridge A2
Moor La B2
Moorgate B3
Morecambe Rd A1/A2
Nelson St B2
North Rd B2
Orchard La C1
Owen Rd A2
Park Rd B3
Parliament St A3
Patterdale Rd A3
Penny St B2
Police Station B2
Portland St C2
Post Office B2
Primrose St C3
Priory B1
Prospect St C3
Quarry Rd B3
Queen St C2
Regent St C2
Ridge La A3
Ridge St A3
Royal Lancaster Infirmary (A&E) C2
Rydal Rd B3
Ryelands Park A1
St Georges Quay A1
St John's B2

St Leonard's Gate . B2
St Martin's Rd . C3
St Nicholas Arcades Shopping Centre . B2
St Oswald St . B3
St Peter's † . B3
St Peter's Rd . B3
Salisbury Rd . A6
Scotch Quarry Urban Park . C3
Sibsey St . B1
Skerton Bridge . A2
South Rd . C2
Station Rd . B1
Stirling Rd . B1
Storey Ave . B1
Sunnyside La . C1
Sylvester St . B1
Tarnsyke Rd . C2
Thurnham St . B2
Town Hall . B2
Troutbeck Rd . B3
Ulleswater Rd . B3
Univ of Cumbria . C3
Vicarage Field . B1
Vue . B1
West Rd . B1
Westbourne Dr . C1
Westbourne Rd . B1
Westham St . C3
Wheatfield St . B1
White Cross Business Park . C2
Williamson Rd . B3
Willow La . B1
Windermere Rd . B3
Wingate-Saul Rd . B1
Wolseley St . B3
Woodville St . B3
Wyresdale Rd . C3

Leeds 185
Aire St . B4
Albion Place . B4
Albion St . B4
Albion Way . A6
Alma St . A6
Ambulance Sta . B5
Arcades . B4
Armley Rd . B1
Armories Dr . C5
Back Burley Lodge Rd . A1
Back Hyde Terr . A2
Back Row . C3
Bath Rd . C3
Beckett St . A6
Bedford St . B3
Belgrave St . A4
Belle Vue Rd . A2
Benson St . A5
Black Bull St . C5
Blenheim Walk . A3
Boar La . B4
Bond St . B4
Bow St . C5
Bowman La . C4
Brewery ✦ . C4
Brewery Wharf . C5
Bridge St . A5/B5
Briggate . B4
Bruce Gdns . C1
Burley Rd . A1
Burley St . B3
Burmantofts St . B6
Bus & Coach Sta . B6
Butterly St . C4
Butts Cres . C4
Byron St . A5
Call La . B4
Calls, The . B5
Calverley St . A3/B3
Canal St . B3
Canal Wharf . C3
Carlisle Rd . C5
Cavendish Rd . A1
Cavendish St . A2
Chadwick St . C5
Cherry Place . A6
Cherry Row . A5
City Museum . A4
City Varieties Music Hall . B4
City Sq . B3
Civic Hall . A3
Clarence Rd . C5
Clarendon Rd . A2
Clarendon Way . A3
Clark La . C6
Clay Pit La . A4
Cloberry St . A2
Close, The . B6
Clyde Approach . C1
Clyde Gdns . C1
Coleman St . C2
Commercial St . B4
Concord St . A5
Cookridge St . A4
Copley Hill . C1
Core, The . B4
Corn Exchange . B4
Cromer Terr . A2
Cromwell St . A5
Cross Catherine St . B6
Cross Green La . C6
Cross Stamford St . A5
Crown & County Courts . A3
Crown Point Bridge . C5
Crown Point Rd . C4
Crown Point Retail Park . C4
David St . C3
Dent St . C6
Derwent Place . C3
Dial St . C6
Dock St . C4
Dolly La . A6
Domestic St . C2
Drive, The . B6
Duke St . B5
Duncan St . B4
Dyer St . B5
East Field St . B6
East Pde . B3
East St . C5
Eastgate . B5
Easy Rd . C6
Edward St . B4
Ellerby La . C6
Ellerby St . C6
Fenton St . A3
Fire Station . B2
First Direct Arena . A4
Fish St . B4
Flax Place . C5

Garth, The . B5
Gelderd Rd . C1
George St . B4
Globe Rd . C2
Gower St . A5
Grafton St . A4
Grand Theatre . B4
Granville Rd . A6
Great George St . A3
Great Wilson St . C4
Greek St . B3
Green La . C1
Hanover Ave . A2
Hanover La . A2
Hanover Sq . A2
Hanover Way . A2
Harewood St . B4
Harrison St . B4
Haslewood Cl . B6
Haslewood Drive . B6
Headrow, The . B3/B4
High Court . B5
Holbeck La . C2
Holdforth Cl . C1
Holdforth Gdns . C1
Holdforth Grove . C1
Holdforth Place . C1
Holy Trinity . B4
Hope Rd . A5
Hunslet La . C4
Hunslet Rd . C4
Hyde Terr . A2
Infirmary St . B4
Information Ctr . B3
Ingram Row . C3
ITV Yorkshire . A1
Junction St . C4
Kelso Gdns . A2
Kelso Rd . A2
Kelso St . A2
Kendal La . A2
Kendell St . C4
Kidacre St . C4
King Edward St . B4
King St . B3
Kippax Place . C6
Kirkgate . B4
Kirkgate Market . B4
Kirkstall Rd . A1
Kitson St . C6
Knight's Way Bridge . C5
Lady La . B4
Lands La . B4
Lane, The . B6
Lavender Walk . B6
Leeds Art Gallery . B3
Leeds Beckett Univ . A3
Leeds Bridge . C4
Leeds Coll of Music . B5
Leeds Discovery Centre . C5
Leeds General Infirmary (A&E) . A3
Leeds Minster . B5
Leeds Station . B3
Library . B3/B4
Light, The . B4
Lincoln Green Rd . A6
Lincoln Rd . A6
Lindsey Gdns . A6
Lindsey Rd . A6
Lisbon St . B3
Little Queen St . B3
Long Close La . C6
Lord St . C2
Lovell Park Hill . A4
Lovell Park Rd . A4
Lower Brunswick St . A5
Mabgate . A5
Macaulay St . A5
Magistrates Court . A3
Manor Rd . C3
Mark La . B4
Marlborough St . B2
Marsh La . B5
Marshall St . C3
Meadow La . C4
Meadow Rd . C3
Melbourne St . A5
Merrion Centre . A4
Merrion St . A4
Merrion Way . A4
Mill St . B5
Millennium Sq . A3
Monk Bridge . C2
Mount Preston St . A2
Mushroom St . A5
Neville St . C4
New Briggate . A4/B4
New Market St . B4
New York Rd . A5
New York St . B5
Nile St . B5
Nippet La . A6
North St . A4
Northern Ballet . B5
Oak Rd . B1
Oxford Place . A3
Oxford Row . A3
Parade, The . B6
Park Cross St . B3
Park La . A2
Park Place . B3
Park Row . B4
Park Sq . B3
Park Sq East . B3
Park Sq West . B3
Police Station . A3
Pontefract La . B6
Portland Cres . A3
Portland Way . A3
Post Office . B4/B5
Quarry House (NHS/DSS HQ) . B5
Quebec St . B3
Queen St . B3
Radio Aire . A1
Railway St . B5
Rectory St . A6
Regent St . A5
Richmond St . C5
Rigton Approach . B6
Rigton Dr . B6
Rillbank La . A1
Rose Bowl Conference Ctr . A3
Royal Armouries . C5
Russell St . B3
St Anne's Cathedral (RC) † . A4
St Anne's St . A4
St James' Hosp . A6

St John's Rd . A2
St Johns Centre . B4
St Mary's St . B5
St Pauls St . B3
Saxton La . B5
Sayner La . C5
Shakespeare Ave . A6
Shannon St . B6
Sheepscar St South . A5
Siddall St . C3
Skinner La . A5
South Pde . B3
Sovereign St . C4
Spence La . C2
Springfield Mount . A2
Springwell Ct . C2
Springwell Rd . C2
Springwell St . C2
Stoney Rock La . A6
Studio Rd . A1
Sutton St . C2
Sweet St . C3
Sweet St West . C3
Swinegate . B4
Templar St . B5
Tetley, The . C4
Thoresby Place . A3
Torre Rd . A6
Town Hall . A3
Trinity Leeds . B4
Union Place . C3
Union St . B5
University of Leeds . A3
Upper Accomodation Rd . B6
Upper Basinghall St . B4
Vicar La . B4
Victoria Bridge . C4
Victoria Gate . B4
Victoria Quarter . B4
Victoria Rd . C4
Vue . B3
Wade La . A4
Washington St . A1
Water La . C3
Waterloo Rd . C4
Wellington Rd . B2/C1
Wellington St . B3
West St . B3
West Yorkshire Playhouse . B5
Westfield Rd . A1
Westgate . B3
Whitehall Rd . B3/C2
Whitelock St . A5
Willis St . C6
Willow Approach . A1
Willow Ave . A1
Willow Terrace Rd . A3
Wintoun St . A5
Woodhouse La . A3/A4
Woodsley Rd . A2
York Place . B3
York Rd . B6

Leicester 188
Abbey St . A2
All Saints' . A2
Aylestone Rd . C2
Bath La . A1
Bede Park . C1
Bedford St . A3
Bedford St South . A3
Belgrave Gate . A2
Belvoir St . B2
Braunstone Gate . B1
Burleys Way . A2
Burnmoor St . C2
Bus & Coach Sta . A3
Canning St . A2
Carlton St . C2
Castle . B1
Castle Gardens . B1
Cathedral † . B2
Causeway La . A2
Charles St . B3
Chatham St . B2
Christow St . A3
Church Gate . A2
City Gallery . B3
City Hall . B3
Clank St . B2
Clock Tower ✦ . B2
Clyde St . A3
Colton St . B3
Conduit St . B3
Crafton St . B3
Craven St . A1
Crown Courts . B3
Curve . B2
De Lux . A2
De Montfort Hall . C3
De Montfort St . C3
De Montfort Univ . C1
Deacon St . C2
Dover St . B3
Duns La . B1
Dunton St . A1
East St . B3
Eastern Boulevard . C1
Edmonton Rd . A3
Erskine St . A3
Filbert St . C1
Filbert St East . C1
Fire Station . C2
Fleet St . A3
Friar La . B2
Friday St . A2
Gateway St . C1
Gateway, The . C1
Glebe St . B3
Granby St . B3
Grange La . C2
Grasmere St . C1
Great Central St . A1
Guildhall . B2
Guru Nanak Sikh Museum . A1
Halford St . B3
Havelock St . C2
Haymarket Shopping Centre . A2
High St . A2
Highcross Shopping Centre . A2
Highcross St . A1
HM Prison . C2
Horsefair St . B2
Humberstone Gate . A3
Humberstone Rd . A3
Infirmary St . C2
Information Ctr . B2
Jarrom St . C1
Jewry Wall . B1
Kamloops Cres . A3
King St . B2

Lancaster Rd . C2
LCB Depot . B3
Lee St . A3
Leicester Royal Infirmary (A&E) . C2
Leicester Sta . B3
Library . B2
London Rd . B3
Lower Brown St . B2
Magistrates' Court . B2
Manitoba Rd . A3
Mansfield St . A2
Market . B2
Market St . B2
Mill La . C2
Montreal Rd . A3
Narborough Rd North . C1
Nelson Mandela Pk . C2
New Park St . B1
New St . B2
New Walk . C3
New Walk Museum & Art Gallery . C3
Newarke Houses . B2
Newarke St . B2
Newarke, The . B1
Northgate St . A1
Orchard St . A3
Ottawa Rd . A3
Oxford St . C2
Phoenix Arts Ctr . B3
Police Station . A3
Post Office . A1/B2/C3
Prebend St . C3
Princess Rd East . C3
Princess Rd West . C3
Queen St . B3
Rally Community Park, The . A2
Regent College . C3
Regent Rd . C2/C3
Repton St . A1
Rutland St . B3
St Augustine Rd . B1
St Georges Retail Park . B3
St Georges Way . B3
St John St . A2
St Margaret's . A2
St Margaret's Way . A2
St Martins . B2
St Mary de Castro . B1
St Matthew's Way . A3
St Nicholas . B1
St Nicholas Circle . B1
Sanvey Gate . A2
Silver St . B2
Slater St . A1
Soar La . A1
South Albion St . B3
Southampton St . B3
Sue Townsend Theatre . B2
Swain St . B3
Swan St . A1
Tigers Way . C3
Tower St . C3
Town Hall . B2
Tudor Rd . B1
Univ of Leicester . C3
University Rd . C3
Upper Brown St . B2
Upperton Rd . C1
Vaughan Way . A2
Walnut St . C1
Watling St . A2
Welford Rd . B2
Welford Rd Leicester Tigers RC . C2
Wellington St . B2
West St . C2
West Walk . C2
Western Boulevard . C1
Western Rd . C1
Wharf St North . A3
Wharf St South . A3
Y Theatre, The . B3
Yeoman St . B3
York Rd . B2

Lincoln 188
Alexandra Terr . B1
Anchor St . C1
Arboretum . B3
Arboretum Ave . B3
Avenue, The . B1
Baggholme Rd . B3
Bailgate . A2
Beaumont Fee . B1
Brayford Way . C1
Brayford Wharf East . C1
Brayford Wharf North . C1
Bruce Rd . A3
Burton Rd . A1
Bus Station (City) . B2
Canwick Rd . C2
Cardinal's Hat ✦ . B2
Carline Rd . B1
Castle . B1
Castle St . B1
Cathedral † . B2
Cathedral St . B2
Cecil St . A2
Chapel La . A2
Cheviot St . B3
Church La . A2
City Hall . A1
Clasketgate . B2
Clayton Sports Gd . A3
Coach Park . C2
Collection, The . B2
County Hospital (A&E) . B3
County Office . B1
Courts . B2
Cross St . B2
Crown Courts . B1
Curle Ave . A3
Danesgate . B2
Drill Hall . B2
Drury La . B1
East Bight . A2
East Gate . A2
Eastcliff Rd . B3
Eastgate . A2
Egerton Rd . A3
Ellis Windmill . A1
Engine Shed, The . C1

Environment Agency . C2
Exchequer Gate ✦ . B2
Firth Rd . C1
Flaxengate . B2
Florence St . B3
George St . C2
Good La . A2
Gray St . A1
Great Northern Terr . C3
Great Northern Terr Ind Est . C3
Greetwell Rd . B3
Greetwellgate . B3
Grove, The . A3
Haffenden Rd . A3
High St . B2/C1
HM Prison . A1
Hungate . B2
James St . A2
Jews House & Ct . B2
Kesteven St . C2
Langworthgate . A2
Lawn, The . B1
Lee Rd . A3
Library . B2
Lincoln Central Station . C2
Lincoln College . B2
Lincolnshire Life/Royal Lincolnshire Regiment Mus . A1
Lincoln University Tech Coll (UTC) . C2
Lindum Rd . B2
Lindum Sports Gd . A3
Lindum Terr . B3
Mainwaring Rd . A3
Manor Rd . A3
Market . C2
Massey Rd . A3
Medieval Bishop's Palace . B2
Mildmay St . B1
Mill Rd . A1
Millman Rd . B3
Minster Yard . B2
Monks Rd . B2
Montague St . B2
Mount St . A1
Nettleham Rd . A2
Newland . B1
Newport . A2
Newport Arch . A2
Newport Cemetery . A2
Northgate . A2
Odeon . C1
Orchard St . B1
Oxford St . C2
Park St . C2
Pelham Bridge . C2
Pelham St . C2
Police Station . B2
Portland St . C2
Post Office . A1/B3/C2
Potter Gate . B2
Priory Gate . B2
Queensway . A3
Rasen La . A1
Ropewalk . C1
Rosemary La . B2
St Anne's Rd . B3
St Benedict's . C1
St Giles Ave . A3
St Mark's Shopping Centre . C1
St Marks St . C1
St Mary-le-Wigford † . C2
St Mary's St . C2
St Nicholas St . A2
St Rumbold's St . B2
St Swithin's . B2
Saltergate . B2
Saxon St . A1
Sewell Rd . B3
Silver St . B2
Sincil St . C2
Spital St . A2
Spring Hill . B1
Stamp End . C3
Steep Hill . B2
Stonebow & Guildhall . C2
Stonefield Ave . A1
Tentercroft St . C1
Theatre Royal . B2
Tritton Rd . C1
Tritton Retail Park . C1
Union Rd . B1
Univ of Lincoln . C1
Upper Lindum St . B3
Upper Long Leys Rd . A1
Usher . B2
Vere St . A3
Victoria St . B1
Victoria Terr . B1
Vine St . B3
Wake St . A1
Waldeck St . A1
Waterside North . C2
Waterside Shopping Centre . C2
Waterside South . C2
West Pde . B1
Westgate . A2
Wigford Way . C1
Williamson St . A2
Wilson St . A3
Winn St . B3
Wragby Rd . B3
Yarborough Rd . A1

Liverpool 188
Abercromby Sq . C6
Addison St . A4
Adelaide St . B4
Ainsworth St . B4
Albany Rd . B6
Albert Edward Rd . C6
Angela St . C6
Anson St . B4
Argyle St . C3
Arrad St . C5
Ashton St . B5
Audley St . A4
Back Leeds St . A2
Basnett St . B3
Bath St . A1
Beacon, The ✦ . B3
Beatles Story, The . C1
Beckwith St . C3
Bedford Close . C6
Bedford St North . C5

Bedford St South . C5
Benson St . B4
Berry St . B4
Birkett St . A4
Bixteth St . B2
Blackburne Place . C5
Bluecoat . B3
Bold Pl . C4
Bold St . C4
Bolton St . B3
Bridport St . B4
Bronte St . B4
Brook St . A1
Brownlow Hill . B4/B5
Brownlow St . B5
Brunswick Rd . A5
Brunswick St . B1
Bus Station . B3
Butler Cres . A6
Byrom St . A3
Caledonia St . C5
Cambridge St . C5
Camden St . A4
Canada Blvd . B1
Canning Dock . C2
Canterbury St . A4
Cardwell St . C6
Carver St . A5
Cases St . B3
Castle St . B2
Cathedral (RC) † . C5
Cavern Club . B3
Central Library . A3
Chapel St . B2
Charlotte St . B3
Chatham Place . C6
Chatham St . C5
Cheapside . A2
Chavasse Park . C2
Chestnut St . C6
Christian St . A3
Church St . B3
Clarence St . B4
Clayton Square Shopping Centre . B3
Coach Station . A5
Cobden St . A5
Cockspur St . A2
College St . C5
College St North . C5
College St South . C5
Colquitt St . C4
Comus St . A3
Concert St . C4
Connaught Rd . B6
Cook St . B2
Copperas Hill . B4
Cornwallis St . C4
Covent Garden . A2
Craven St . A4
Cropper St . B3
Crown St . B5/C6
Cumberland St . B2
Cunard Building . B1
Dale St . B2
Dansie St . B4
Daulby St . B5
Dawson St . B3
Dental Hospital . B5
Derby Sq . B2
Drury La . B2
Duckinfield St . B5
Duke St . C3
Earle St . A2
East St . A2
Eaton St . A2
Echo Arena ✦ . C2
Edgar St . A3
Edge La . B6
Edinburgh Rd . B6
Edmund St . B2
Elizabeth St . B5
Elliot St . B3
Empire Theatre . B4
Empress Rd . B6
Epstein Theatre . B3
Epworth St . A5
Erskine St . A5
Everyman Theatre . C5
Exchange St East . B2
FACT . C4
Falkland St . A5
Falkner St . C5/C6
Farnworth St . A6
Fenwick St . B2
Fielding St . A6
Fire Sta . A4
Fleet St . C4
Fraser St . A4
Freemasons Row . A2
Gardner Row . A3
Gascoyne St . A2
George St . B2
Gibraltar Road . A1
Gilbert St . C3
Gildart St . B5
Gill St . B5
Goree . B1
Gower St . C2
Gradwell St . C3
Great Crosshall St . A3
Great George St . C4
Great Howard St . A1
Great Newton St . B5
Greek St . B4
Green La . B4
Greenside . A5
Greetham St . C3
Gregson St . A5
Grenville St . C3
Grinfield St . C6
Grove St . C5
Guelph St . A6
Hackins Hey . B2
Haigh St . A5
Hall La . A5
Hanover St . B3
Harbord St . C6
Hardman St . C4
Hart St . B4
Hatton Garden . A2
Hawke St . B4
Helsby St . B6
Henry St . C3
Highfield St . A2
Highgate St . B6
Hilbre St . B4
Hope Place . C4
Hope St . C5
Hope University . C6
Houghton St . B3
Hunter St . A4
Hutchinson St . A6
Information Centre . B4/C2

Institute for the Performing Arts . C4
International Slavery Mus . C1
Irvine St . B6
Irwell St . B2
Islington . A4
James St . B2
James St Station . B2
Jenkinson St . A4
John Moores Univ . A2/A3/A4/B4/C4
Johnson St . A3
Jubilee Drive . B6
Kempston St . A4
Kensington . A6
Kensington Gdns . B6
Kensington St . A6
Kent St . C3
King Edward St . A1
Kinglake St . B6
Knight St . C4
Lace St . A3
Langsdale St . A4
Law Courts . C2
Leece St . C4
Leeds St . A2
Leopold Rd . B6
Lime St . B3
Lime St Station . B4
Liver St . C2
Liverpool Central Station . B3
Liverpool Landing Stage . B1
Liverpool Institute for Performing Arts (LIPA) . C4
Liverpool ONE . C2
Liverpool Wheel, The . C1
London Rd . A4/B4
Lord Nelson St . B4
Lord St . B2
Lovat St . C6
Low Hill . A5
Low Wood St . A6
Lydia Ann St . C3
Mansfield St . A4
Marmaduke St . B6
Marsden St . A6
Martensen St . B6
Marybone . A3
Maryland St . C4
Mason St . B6
Mathew St . B3
May St . B4
Melville Place . C6
Merseyside Maritime Museum . C1
Metquarter . B3
Metropolitan Cathedral (RC) † . B5
Midghall St . A2
Molyneux Rd . B6
Moor Place . B4
Moorfields . B2
Moorfields Sta . B2
Moss St . A5
Mount Pleasant . B4/B5
Mount St . C4
Mount Vernon . B6
Mulberry St . C5
Municipal Buildings . B2
Mus of Liverpool . C1
Myrtle St . C5
Naylor St . A3
Nelson St . C4
New Islington . A4
New Quay . B1
Newington St . C3
North John St . B2
North St . A3
North View . B6
Norton St . A4
O2 Academy . B4
Odeon . B3
Old Hall St . A1
Old Leeds St . A2
Oldham Place . C4
Oldham St . C4
Olive St . C6
Open Eye Gallery . C2
Oriel St . A3
Ormond St . B2
Orphan St . C6
Overbury St . B6
Overton St . B6
Oxford St . C5
Paisley St . A1
Pall Mall . A2
Paradise St . C3
Park La . C3
Parker St . B3
Parr St . C4
Peach St . B5
Pembroke Place . B4
Pembroke St . B5
Philharmonic Hall . C5
Phythian Park . A6
Pickop St . A2
Pilgrim St . C4
Pitt St . C3
Playhouse Theatre . B3
Pleasant St . B4
Pomona St . B4
Port of Liverpool Building . B1
Post Office . A2/A4/A5/B2/B3/B4/C4
Pownall St . C2
Prescot St . A5
Preston St . B3
Princes Dock . A1
Princes Gdns . A2
Princes Jetty . A1
Princes Pde . B1
Princes St . B2
Pythian St . A6
Queen Sq Bus Sta . B3
Queensland St . C6
Queensway Tunnel (Docks exit) . A1
Queensway Tunnel (Entrance) . B3
Radio City . B2
Ranelagh St . B3
Redcross St . B2
Renshaw St . B4
Richmond Row . A4
Richmond St . B3

Rigby St . A2
Roberts St . A1
Rock St . A6
Rodney St . C4
Rokeby St . A4
Romily St . A6
Roscoe La . C4
Roscoe St . C4
Rose Hill . A3
Royal Albert Dock . C2
Royal Ct Theatre . B3
Royal Liver Building . B1
Royal Liverpool Hospital (A&E) . B5
Royal Mail St . B4
Rumford Place . B2
Rumford St . B2
Russell St . B4
St Andrew St . B4
St Anne St . A4
St Georges Hall . B3
St John's Centre . B3
St John's Gdns . B3
St John's La . B3
St Joseph's Cres . A4
St Minishull St . B5
St Nicholas Place . B1
St Paul's Sq . A2
Salisbury St . A4
Salthouse Dock . C2
Salthouse Quay . C2
Saxony Rd . B6
Schomberg St . A6
School La . B3
Seel St . C4
Seymour St . B4
Shaw St . A5
Shopmobility . C2
Sidney Place . C6
Sir Thomas St . B2
Skelhorne St . B4
Slater St . C3
Smithdown La . B6
Soho Sq . A5
Soho St . A5
South John St . B2
Springfield . A4
Stafford St . A4
Standish St . A3
Stanley St . B2
Strand St . C1
Strand, The . B2
Suffolk St . C3
Sydney Jones Liby . C5
Tabley St . C3
Tarleton St . B3
Tate Liverpool Gallery . C1
Teck St . B6
Temple St . B2
Titanic Memorial ✦ . B1
Tithebarn St . B2
Town Hall . B2
Trowbridge St . B4
Trueman St . A3
Union St . B2
Unity Theatre . C4
University . B5
Univ of Liverpool . B5
Upper Baker St . A6
Upper Duke St . C4
Upper Frederick St . C3
Vauxhall Rd . A2
Vernon St . B2
Victoria Gallery & Museum . B5
Victoria St . B2
Vine St . C5
Wakefield St . A4
Walker Art Gallery . B3
Walker St . A6
Wapping . C2
Water St . B1/B2
Waterloo Rd . A1
Wavertree Rd . B6
West Derby Rd . A6
West Derby St . B5
Western Approaches War Museum . B2
Whitechapel . B3
Whitley Gdns . A5
William Brown St . B3
William Henry St . A4
Williamson Sq . B3
Williamson St . B3
Williamson's Tunnels Heritage Centre ✦ . C6
Women's Hosp . C6
Wood St . C3
World Museum, Liverpool . B3
York St . C3

Llandudno 189
Abbey Place . B1
Abbey Rd . B1
Adelphi St . B2
Alexandra Rd . C2
Anglesey Rd . A1
Argyll Rd . C2
Arvon Ave . B2
Atlee Cl . C2
Augusta St . B2
Back Madoc St . B2
Bodafon St . B3
Bodhyfryd Rd . B2
Bodnant Cres . C3
Bodnant Rd . C3
Bryniau Rd . C1
Bryn-y-Bia Rd . A3
Builder St . C2
Builder St West . C2
Cabin Lift . A2
Cable Car ✦ . A2
Camera Obscura ✦ . A3
Caroline Rd . B2
Chapel St . B2
Charlton St . B2
Church Cres . C2
Church Walks . B2
Claremont Rd . C2
Clement Ave . C2
Clifton Rd . B2
Clonmel St . B2
Coach Station . B2
Conway Rd . B2
Conwy Archive Service . C2
Council St West . C1
Cricket and Rec Gd . C2
Cwlach Rd . A1
Cwlach St . A1
Cwm Howard La . C3

Cwm Place . C3
Cwm Rd . C3
Dale Rd . C1
Deganwy Ave . B2
Denness Place . C1
Dinas Rd . C2
Dolydd . B1
Erol Place . B1
Ewloe Dr . C1
Fairways . B2
Fforod Dewi . C3
Fforod Dulyn . C3
Fforod Dwyfor . C3
Fforod Elisabeth . C3
Fforod Gwynedd . C3
Fforod La . C3
Fforod Morfa . C3
Fforod Penrhyn . C3
Fforod yr Orsedd . C3
Fforod Ysbyty . C3
Fire & Ambulance Station . B3
Garage St . B2
George St . B2
Gloddaeth Ave . B1
Gloddaeth St . B2
Gogarth Rd . B1
Great Orme Mines ✦ . A1
Great Ormes Rd . B1
Great Orme Tramway ✦ . A2
Happy Valley . A2
Happy Valley Rd . A2
Haulfre Gardens ❀ . A1
Herkomer Cres . C1
Hill Terr . A2
Home Front Mus . B2
Hospice . A1
Howard Rd . B2
Information Ctr . B2
Invalids' Walk . B1
James St . B2
Jubilee St . B3
King's Ave . C2
King's Rd . C2
Knowles Rd . C2
Lees Rd . C2
Library . B2
Llandudno . B2
Llandudno (A&E) . C2
Llandudno Sta . B2
Llandudno Football Ground . C2
Llewelyn Ave . A2
Lloyd St . B2
Lloyd St West . B1
Llwynon Rd . A1
Llys Maelgwn . C3
Madoc St . B2
Maelgwn Rd . C3
Maes-y-Cwm . C3
Maes-y-Orsedd . C3
Maesdu Bridge . C2
Maesdu Rd . C2/C3
Marian Place . C2
Marian Rd . C2
Marine Drive (Toll) . A3
Market St . B2
Miniature Golf Course . A1
Morfa Rd . B1
Mostyn . B2
Mostyn Broadway . B2
Mostyn St . B2
Mowbray Rd . C2
New St . B2
Norman Rd . B3
North Parade . A2
North Wales Golf Links . C1
Old Bank, The . B2
Old Rd . A2
Oval, The . B2
Oxford Rd . B2
Parc Llandudno Retail Park . B3
Pier ✦ . A3
Plas Rd . B2
Police Station . A2/B3
Post Office . A2/B3
Promenade . B2
Pyllau Rd . A1
Rectory La . A1
Rhuddlan Ave . C3
St Andrew's Ave . B2
St Andrew's Place . B2
St Beuno's Rd . A1
St David's Place . B1
St David's Rd . B1
St George's Place . A2
St Mary's Rd . B1
St Seriol's Rd . B1
Salisbury Pass . B1
Salisbury Rd . B2
Somerset St . B2
South Parade . A2
Stephen St . B2
Tabor Hill . A1
Town Hall . B2
Trinity Ave . B2
Trinity Cres . B2
Trinity Sq . B2
Tudno St . A2
Ty-Coch Rd . A2/C2
Ty-Gwyn Rd . A1
Ty'n-y-Coed Rd . A1
Vaughan St . B2
Victoria Shopping Centre . B2
War Memorial ✦ . A2
Werny Wylan . C3
West Parade . A1
Whiston Pass . A1
Winllan Ave . C2
Yorkfryd Rd . C3

Llanelli 189
Alban Rd . C2
Albert St . A2
Als St . A2
Amos St . C1
Andrew St . A2
Ann St . C2
Annesley St . A1
Arfryn Ave . A3
Avenue Cilfig, The . A2
Belvedere Rd . A3
Bigyn La . C3
Bigyn Park Terr . C3
Bigyn Rd . C3
Bond St . B3
Brettenham St . A1

Bridge St . B2
Bryn Place . C1
Bryn Rd . C1
Bryn Terr . C1
Bryn-More Rd . C1
Brynhyfryd Rd . A2
Brynmelyn Ave . A3
Brynmor Rd . B1
Burry St . C1
Bus Station . C2
Caersalem Terr . C2
Cambrian St . C2
Caswell St . C3
Cedric St . B1
Cemetery . A2
Chapman St . A2
Charles Terr . C2
Church St . A1
Clos Caer Elms . A1
Clos Sant Paul . A1
Coastal Link Rd . B1/C1
Coldstream St . B2
Coleshill Terr . B1
College Hill . B2
College Sq . C1
Copperworks Rd . C1
Coronation Rd . C1
Corporation Ave . A3
Council Offices . B2
Court . B2
Cowell St . B2
Cradock St . B2
Craig Ave . C3
Cricket Ground . A1
Derwent St . A1
Dillwyn St . B2
Druce St . C1
Eastgate Leisure Complex ✦ . B2
Elizabeth St . B2
Emma St . C2
Erw Rd . B1
Felinfoel Rd . A1
Fire Station . A2
Firth Rd . C2
Fron Terr . A1
Furnace United Rugby Football Ground . A1
Gelli-On . B2
George St . B2
Gilbert Cres . A3
Gilbert Rd . A3
Glanmor Rd . C2
Glanmor Terr . C2
Glasfryn Terr . A3
Glenalla Rd . C3
Glevering St . B3
Goring Rd . C3
Gorsedd Circle ✦ . B2
Grant St . C3
Graveyard . C2
Great Western Cl . B1
Greenway St . B1
Hall St . B2
Harries Ave . A2
Hedley Terr . A1
Heol Elli . B3
Heol Goffa . A3
Heol Nant-y-Felin . A3
Heol Siloh . B2
Hick St . C2
High St . C1
Indoor Bowls Ctr . B1
Inkerman St . B2
Island Place . A2
James St . B3
John St . B2
King George Ave . B1
Lake View Cl . C1
Lakefield Place . C1
Lakefield Rd . C1
Langland Rd . C1
Leisure Centre . B1
Library . B1
Llanelli House . B1
Llanelli Parish Church . B2
Llanelli Station . B2
Llewellyn St . C2
Lliedi Cres . A3
Lloyd St . B2
Llys Alys . B3
Llys Fran . A3
Llysnewedd . C1
Long Row . A1
Maes Gors . C1
Maesyrhaf . A3
Mansel St . B2
Marblehall Rd . A3
Marborough Rd . A3
Margam St . C1
Marged St . C1
Marine St . C1
Mariners, The . C1
Market . B2
Market St . B2
Marsh St . C2
Martin Rd . B2
Miles St . C1
Mill La . A3/B2
Mincing La . B2
Murray St . B2
Myn y Mor . B1
Nathan St . C1
Nelson Terr . C1
Nevill St . C1
New Dock Rd . C2
New Rd . A1
New Zealand St . A1
Odeon . B2
Old Lodge . C2
Old Rd . A2
Paddock St . C2
Palace Ave . B3
Parc Howard . A2
Parc Howard Museum & Art Gallery . A2
Park Cres . B1
Park St . B2
Parkview Terr . A1
Pemberton St . C2
Pembrey Rd . A1
Peoples Park . B1
Police Station . B1
Post Office . B2/C2
Pottery Place . C2
Pottery St . C2
Princess St . B2
Prospect Place . A1
Pryce St . A2
Queen Mary's Walk . C3
Queen Victoria Rd . C3
Raby St . C1
Railway Terr . C2
Ralph St . C2
Ralph Terr . C2
Regalia Terr . B3

London • Luton • Macclesfield • Maidstone 207

Rhydyrafon A3
Richard St B2
Robinson St B2
Roland Ave A1
Russell St C3
St David's Cl C1
St Elli Shopping Ctr B2
St Margaret's Dr A1
Spowart Ave A1
Station Rd B2/C2
Stepney Place B2
Stepney St B2
Stewart St A1
Stradey Park Ave A1
Sunny Hill A2
Superstore A2
Swansea Rd A3
Talbot St C3
Temple St B3
Thomas St A2
Tinopolos TV Studios ✦ B2
Toft Place A3
Town Hall B2
Traeth Ffordd C1
Trinity Rd C3
Trinity Terr C2
Tunnel Rd B3
Tyisha Rd C3
Union Blgs A2
Upper Robinson St B2
Vauxhall Rd B2
Walter's Rd B3
Waun Lanyrafon B2
Waun Rd A3
Wern Rd B3
West End A2
Y Bwthyn C3
Zion Row B3

London 186

Abbey Orchard St E3
Abchurch La D6
Abingdon St E4
Achilles Way D2
Acton St B4
Addington St E4
Air St D3
Albany St B2
Albemarle St D3
Albert Embankment F4
Aldenham St A3
Aldersgate St C6
Alford St D2
Aldgate ⊖ C7
Aldgate High St C7
Aldwych C4
Allsop Place B1
Amwell St B5
Andrew Borde St C3
Angel ⊖ A5
Appold St C7
Argyle Sq B4
Argyle St B4
Argyll St C3
Arnold Circus B7
Artillery La C7
Artillery Row E3
Association of Photographers Gallery 🏛 B6
Baker St ⊖ B1
Baker St B1
Baldwin's Gdns C5
Baltic St B6
Bank ⊖ C6
Bank Museum 🏛 C6
Bank of England C6
Bankside D6
Bankside Gallery 🏛 D5
Banner St B6
Barbican ⇌⊖ C6
Barbican Centre for Arts, The C6
Barbican Gallery 🏛 C6
Basil St E1
Bastwick St B6
Bateman's Row B7
Bath St B6
Bayley St C3
Baylis Rd E5
Beak St D3
Bedford Row C4
Bedford Sq C3
Bedford St D4
Bedford Way B3
Beech St C6
Belgrave Place E2
Belgrave Sq E2
Bell La C7
Belvedere Rd E4
Berkeley Sq D2
Berkeley St D2
Bernard St B4
Berners Place C3
Berners St C3
Berwick St C3
Bethnal Green Rd B7
Bevenden St B6
Bevis Marks C7
BFI (British Film Institute) 🎬 D4
BFI London IMAX Cinema 🎬 D5
Bidborough St B4
Binney St C2
Birdcage Walk E3
Bishopsgate C7
Blackfriars ⇌⊖ D5
Blackfriars Bridge D5
Blackfriars Rd E5
Blandford St C1
Blomfield St C6
Bloomsbury St C3
Bloomsbury Way C4
Bolton St D2
Bond St ⊖ C2
Borough High St E6
Boswell St C4
Bow St C4
Bowling Green La B5
Brad St D5
Bressenden Place E3
Brewer St D3
Brick St D2
Bridge St E4
Britannia Walk B6
British Film Institute (BFI) 🎬 D4
British Library 🏛 B3
British Museum 🏛 C4
Britton St B5
Broad Sanctuary E3
Broadway E3
Brook Dr F5
Brook St D2
Brunswick Place B6
Brunswick Shopping Centre, The B4
Brunswick Sq B4
Brushfield St C7
Bruton St D2
Bryanston St C1
BT Centre C6
Buckingham Gate E3
Buckingham Pal 🏛 E3
Buckingham Pal Rd F2
Bunhill Row B6
Byward St D7
Cabinet War Rooms & Churchill Mus 🏛 E3
Cadogan La E2
Cadogan Place E1
Cadogan Sq F1
Caledonian Rd A4
Calshot St A4
Calthorpe St B4
Calvert Ave B7
Cambridge Circus C3
Camomile St C7
Cannon St D6
Cannon St ⇌⊖ D6
Carey St C4
Carlisle La E4
Carlisle Place E3
Carlton House Terr D3
Carmelite St D5
Carnaby St C3
Carter La C5
Carthusian St C6
Cartwright Gdns B4
Castle Baynard St D5
Cavendish Place C2
Cavendish Sq C2
Caxton Hall E3
Caxton St E3
Central St B6
Chalton St B3
Chancery Lane ⊖ C5
Chapel St E2
Charing Cross ⇌⊖ D4
Charing Cross Rd C3
Charles II St D3
Charles Dickens Museum 🏛 B4
Charles Sq B6
Charles St D2
Charlotte Rd B7
Charlotte St C3
Chart St B6
Charterhouse Sq C5
Charterhouse St C5
Cheapside C6
Chenies St C3
Chesham St E2
Chester Sq F2
Chesterfield Hill D2
Chiltern St C2
Chiswell St C6
City Garden Row A5
City Rd B6
City Thameslink ⇌ C5
City University, The B5
Claremont Sq A5
Clarges St D2
Clerkenwell Cl B5
Clerkenwell Green B5
Clerkenwell Rd B5
Cleveland St C3
Clifford St D3
Clink Prison Mus 🏛 D6
Clock Museum 🏛 C6
Club Row B7
Cockspur St D3
Coleman St C6
Columbia Rd B7
Commercial St C7
Compton St B5
Conduit St D2
Constitution Hill E2
Copperfield St E5
Coptic St C4
Cornhill C6
Cornwall Rd D5
Coronet St B7
Courtauld Gallery 🏛 D4
Covent Garden ⊖ D4
Covent Garden ✦ D4
Cowcross St C5
Cowper St B6
Cranbourn St D3
Craven St D4
Crawford St C1
Creechurch La C7
Cremer St A7
Cromer St B4
Cumberland Gate D1
Cumberland Terr A2
Curtain Rd B7
Curzon St D2
Cut, The E5
D'arblay St C3
Davies St C2
Dean St C3
Deluxe Gallery 🏛 B7
Denmark St C3
Dering St C2
Devonshire St C2
Diana, Princess of Wales Meml Wlk E3
Dingley Rd B6
Dorset St C1
Doughty St B4
Dover St D2
Downing St E4
Druid St E7
Drummond St B3
Drury La C4
Drysdale St B7
Duchess St C2
Dufferin St B6
Duke of Wellington Place E2
Duke St C2
Duke St D3
Duke St Hill D6
Duke's Place C7
Duncannon St D4
East Rd B6
Eastcastle St C3
Eastcheap D7
Eastman Dental Hospital [H] B4
Eaton Place E2
Eaton Sq E2
Eccleston St E2
Edgware Rd C1
Eldon St C6
Embankment ⊖ D4
Endell St C4
Endsleigh Place B3
Euston ⇌⊖ B3
Euston Rd B3
Euston Square ⊖ B3
Evelina Children's Hospital E4
Eversholt St A3
Exmouth Market B5
Fann St B6
Farringdon ⇌⊖ C5
Farringdon Rd C5
Farringdon St C5
Featherstone St B6
Fenchurch St D7
Fenchurch St ⇌ D7
Fetter La C5
Finsbury Circus C6
Finsbury Pavement C6
Finsbury Sq B6
Fitzalan St F5
Fitzmaurice Place D2
Fleet St C5
Floral St D4
Florence Nightingale Museum 🏛 E4
Folgate St C7
Foot Hospital [H] B3
Fore St C6
Foster La C6
Francis St F3
Frazier St E5
Freemason's Hall C4
Friday St C6
Gainsford St E7
Garden Row E5
Gee St B6
George St C1
Gerrard St D3
Giltspur St C5
Glasshouse St D3
Gloucester Place C1
Golden Hinde ⛵ D6
Golden La B6
Golden Sq D3
Goodge St ⊖ C3
Goodge St C3
Gordon Sq B3
Goswell Rd B5
Gough St B4
Goulston St C7
Gower St B3
Gracechurch St D6
Grafton Way B3
Gray's Inn Rd B4
Great College St E4
Great Cumberland Place C1
Great Eastern St B7
Great Guildford St D6
Great Marlborough St C3
Great Ormond St B4
Great Ormond St Children's Hosp [H] B4
Great Percy St B4
Great Peter St E3
Great Portland St ⊖ B2
Great Portland St C2
Great Queen St C4
Great Russell St C3
Great Scotland Yd D4
Great Smith St E3
Great Suffolk St D5
Great Titchfield St C3
Great Tower St D7
Great Windmill St D3
Greek St C3
Green Park ⊖ D3
Green St D2
Greencoat Place F3
Gresham St C6
Greville St B4/C5
Greycoat Hosp Sch E3
Greycoat Place E3
Grosvenor Cres E2
Grosvenor Gdns E2
Grosvenor Place E2
Grosvenor Sq D2
Grosvenor St D2
Guards Museum and Chapel 🏛 E3
Guildhall Art Gallery 🏛 C6
Guilford St B4
Guy's Hospital [H] D6
Haberdasher St B6
Hackney Rd B7
Half Moon St D2
Halkin St E2
Hall St B5
Hallam St C2
Hampstead Rd B3
Hanover Sq C2
Hans Cres E1
Hanway St C3
Hardwick St B5
Harley St C2
Harrison St B4
Hastings St B4
Hatfields D5
Hay's Galleria D7
Hay's Mews D2
Hayles St F5
Haymarket D3
Hayne St C5
Hayward Gallery 🏛 D4
Helmet Row B6
Herbrand St B4
Hercules Rd E4
Hertford St D2
High Holborn C4
Hill St D2
HMS Belfast ⛵ D7
Hobart Place E2
Holborn ⊖ C4
Holborn C5
Holborn Viaduct C5
Holland St D5
Holmes Mus 🏛 B1
Holywell La B7
Horse Guards' Rd D3
Houndsditch C7
Houses of Parliament 🏛 E4
Howland St C3
Hoxton Sq B7
Hoxton St B7
Hunter St B4
Hunterian Mus 🏛 C4
Hyde Park D1
Hyde Park Cnr ⊖ E2
Imperial War Museum 🏛 E5
Inner Circle B2
Inst of Archaeology (London Univ) B2
Ironmonger Row B6
James St C2
James St D4
Jermyn St D3
Jockey's Fields C4
John Carpenter St D5
John St B4
Judd St B4
Kennington Rd E5
King Charles St E4
King St D3
King St D4
King William St C6
King's Coll London D5
King's Cross ⇌ A4
King's Cross Rd B4
King's Cross St Pancras ⊖ A4
King's Rd E2
Kingley St C3
Kingsland Rd B7
Kingsway C4
Kinnerton St E2
Knightsbridge ⊖ E1
Lamb St C7
Lamb's Conduit St C4
Lambeth Bridge F4
Lambeth High St F4
Lambeth North ⊖ E5
Lambeth Palace 🏛 E4
Lambeth Palace Rd E4
Lambeth Rd E5
Lambeth Walk F4
Lancaster Place D4
Langham Place C2
Leadenhall St C7
Leake St E4
Leather La C5
Leicester Sq ⊖ D3
Leicester St D3
Leonard St B6
Lever St B6
Lexington St D3
Lidlington Place A3
Lime St D7
Lincoln's Inn Fields C4
Lindsey St C5
Lisle St D3
Liverpool St C7
Liverpool St ⇌⊖ C7
Lloyd Baker St B5
Lloyd Sq B5
Lombard St C6
London Aquarium 🐟 E4
London Bridge ⇌⊖ D6
London Bridge Hospital [H] D6
London City Hall 🏛 D7
London Dungeon, The 🏛 E4
London Film Mus ✦ E4
London Guildhall University C6
London Rd E5
London Transport Museum 🏛 D4
London Wall C6
London Eye ✦ E4
Long Acre D4
Long La C5
Longford St B2
Lower Belgrave St E2
Lower Grosvenor Place E2
Lower Marsh E5
Lower Thames St D6
Lowndes St E2
Ludgate Circus C5
Ludgate Hill C5
Luxborough St C2
Lyall St E2
Macclesfield Rd B6
Madame Tussaud's ✦ B2
Maddox St D2
Malet St C3
Mall, The E3
Manchester Sq C2
Manchester St C2
Mandeville Place C2
Mansell St D7
Mansion House 🏛 C6
Mansion House ⊖ D6
Maple St C3
Marble Arch ⊖ C1
Marble Arch D1
Marchmont St B4
Margaret St C3
Margery St B5
Mark La D7
Marlborough Rd D3
Marshall St C3
Marsham St E3
Marylebone High St C2
Marylebone La C2
Marylebone Rd B2
Marylebone St C2
Mecklenburgh Sq B4
Middle Temple La C5
Middlesex St (Petticoat La) C7
Midland Rd A3
Migration Mus 🏛 F5
Minories C7
Monck St E3
Monmouth St C4
Montagu Place C1
Montagu Sq C1
Montagu St C4
Montague Place C3
Monument ⊖ D6
Monument St D6
Monument, The ✦ D6
Moor La C6
Moorfields C6
Moorfields Eye Hospital [H] B6
Moorgate C6
Moorgate ⇌⊖ C6
Moreland St B5
Morley St E5
Mortimer St C3
Mount Pleasant B5
Mount St D2
Murray Grove A6
Museum of Garden History 🏛 E4
Mus of London 🏛 C6
Museum St C4
Myddelton Sq B5
Myddelton St B5
National Gallery 🏛 D3
National Hospital [H] B4
National Portrait Gallery 🏛 D3
Neal St C4
Nelson's Column ✦ D4
New Bond St C2/D2
New Bridge St C5
New Cavendish St C2
New Change C6
New Fetter La C5
New Inn Yard B7
New North Rd A6
New Oxford St C3
New Scotland Yard E3
New Sq C4
Newgate St C5
Newton St C4
Nile St B6
Noble St C6
Noel St C3
North Audley St D2
North Cres C3
North Row D2
Northampton Sq B5
Northington St B4
Northumberland Ave D4
Norton Folgate C7
Nottingham Place C2
Obstetric Hosp [H] B3
Old Bailey C5
Old Broad St C6
Old Compton St C3
Old County Hall E4
Old Gloucester St C4
Old King Edward St C6
Old Nichol St B7
Old Paradise St F4
Old Spitalfields Mkt C7
Old St B6
Old St ⇌⊖ B6
Old Vic 🎭 E5
Open Air Theatre 🎭 B2
Operating Theatre Museum 🏛 D6
Orange St D3
Orchard St C2
Ossulston St A3
Outer Circle B1
Oxford Circus ⊖ C3
Oxford St C2/C3
Paddington St C2
Palace St E3
Pall Mall D3
Pall Mall East D3
Pancras Rd A4
Panton St D3
Paris Gdn D5
Park Cres B2
Park La D2
Park Rd B1
Park St D2
Park St D6
Parker St C4
Parliament Sq E4
Parliament St E4
Paternoster Sq C5
Paul St B6
Pear Tree St B5
Penton Rise B4
Penton St A5
Pentonville Rd A4/A5
Percival St B5
Petticoat La (Middlesex St) C7
Petty France E3
Phoenix Place B4
Phoenix Rd A3
Photo Gallery 🏛 D3
Piccadilly D2
Piccadilly Circus ⊖ D3
Pitfield St B7
Pollock's Toy Museum 🏛 C3
Polygon Rd A3
Pont St E1
Portland Place C2
Portman Mews C2
Portman Sq C2
Portman St C1
Portugal St C4
Postal Museum, The 🏛 B4
Poultry C6
Primrose St C7
Princes St C6
Procter St C4
Provost St B6
Quaker St B7
Queen Anne St C2
Queen Elizabeth Hall 🎭 D4
Queen Sq B4
Queen St D6
Queen Street Place D6
Queen Victoria St D5
Queens Gallery 🏛 E3
Radnor St B6
Rathbone Place C3
Rawstorne St B5
Red Lion Sq C4
Red Lion St C4
Redchurch St B7
Redcross Way D6
Regency St F3
Regent Sq B4
Regent St C3
Regent's Park B2
Richmond Terr E4
Ridgmount St C3
Rivington St B7
Robert St B2
Rochester Row F3
Ropemaker St C6
Rosebery Ave B5
Roupell St D5
Royal Academy of Arts 🏛 D3
Royal Academy of Dramatic Art B3
Royal Acad of Music B2
Royal Artillery Memorial ✦ E2
Royal College of Nursing C2
Royal College of Surgeons C4
Royal Festival Hall 🎭 D4
Royal London Hospital for Integrated Medicine C4
Royal National Theatre 🎭 D5
Royal National Throat, Nose and Ear Hospital [H] B4
Royal Opera Ho 🎭 D4
Russell Sq B3
Russell Square ⊖ B4
Sackville St D3
Sadlers Wells 🎭 B5
Saffron Hill C5
St Alban's St D3
St Andrew St C5
St Bartholomew's Hospital [H] C5
St Botolph St C7
St Bride St C5
St George's Circus E5
St George's Rd E5
St Giles High St C3
St James's Pal 🏛 D3
St James's Park ⊖ E3
St James's St D3
St John St B5
St Margaret St E4
St Mark's Hosp [H] B5
St Martin's La D4
St Martin's Le Grand C6
St Mary Axe C7
St Pancras Int ⇌ A4
St Paul's ⊖ C6
St Paul's Cath ✝ C6
St Paul's Churchyard C5
St Peter's Hosp [H] D4
St Thomas St D6
St Thomas' Hosp [H] E4
Savile Row D3
Savoy Place D4
Savoy St D4
School of Hygiene & Tropical Medicine C3
Scrutton St B7
Sekforde St B5
Serpentine Rd D1
Seven Dials C4
Seward St B5
Seymour St C1
Shad Thames D7
Shaftesbury Ave D3
Shakespeare's Globe Theatre 🎭 D6
Shepherd Market D2
Sherwood St D3
Shoe La C5
Shoreditch High St B7
Shoreditch High St ⊖ B7
Shorts Gdns C4
Sidmouth St B4
Silk St C6
Sir John Soane's Museum 🏛 C4
Skinner St B5
Sloane St E1
Snow Hill C5
Soho Sq C3
Somerset House 🏛 D4
South Audley St D2
South Carriage Dr E1
South Molton St C2
South Place C6
South St D2
Southampton Row C4
Southampton St D4
Southwark ⊖ D5
Southwark Bridge D6
Southwark Bridge Rd D6
Southwark Cath ✝ D6
Southwark St D6
Speakers' Corner D1
Spencer St B5
Spital Sq C7
Stamford St D5
Stanhope St B3
Stephenson Way B3
Stock Exchange C5
Stoney St D6
Strand C5
Stratton St D2
Sumner St D5
Sutton's Way B6
Swanfield St B7
Swinton St B4
Tabernacle St B6
Tate Modern 🏛 D6
Tavistock Place B4
Tavistock Sq B3
Tea & Coffee Museum 🏛 D6
Temple ⊖ D5
Temple Ave D5
Temple Place D4
Terminus Place E2
Thayer St C2
Theobald's Rd C4
Thorney St F4
Threadneedle St C6
Throgmorton St C6
Tonbridge St B4
Tooley St D7
Torrington Place B3
Tothill St E3
Tottenham Ct Rd B3
Tottenham Ct Rd ⊖ C3
Tottenham St C3
Tower Bridge ✦ D7
Tower Bridge App D7
Tower Bridge Rd E7
Tower Hill D7
Tower Hill ⊖ D7
Tower of London, The 🏛 D7
Toynbee St C7
Trafalgar Square D3
Trinity Sq D7
Trocadero Centre D3
Tudor St D5
Turnmill St C5
Ufford St E5
Union St D5
Univ Coll Hosp [H] B3
Univ of London C3
University of Westminster C2
University St B3
Upper Belgrave St E2
Upper Berkeley St C1
Upper Brook St D2
Upper Grosvenor St D2
Upper Ground D5
Upper Montague St C1
Upper St Martin's La D4
Upper Thames St D6
Upper Wimpole St C2
Upper Woburn Place B3
Vere St C2
Vernon Place C4
Vestry St B6
Victoria ⇌⊖ E2
Victoria Emb D4
Victoria Place Shopping Centre F2
Victoria St E3
Villiers St D4
Vincent Sq F3
Vinopolis City of Wine 🏛 D6
Virginia Rd B7
Wakley St B5
Walbrook C6
Wallace Collection 🏛 C2
Wardour St C3/D3
Warner St B5
Warren St ⊖ B3
Warren St B3
Waterloo ⇌⊖ E5
Waterloo Bridge D4
Waterloo East ⇌ D5
Waterloo Rd E5
Watling St C6
Webber St E5
Welbeck St C2
Wellington Arch ✦ E2
Wellington Mus 🏛 E2
Wells St C3
Wenlock St A6
Wentworth St C7
West Smithfield C5
West Sq E5
Westminster ⊖ E4
Westminster Abbey ✝ E4
Westminster Bridge E4
Westminster Bridge Rd E5
Westminster Cathedral (RC) ✝ E3
Westminster City Hall E3
Westminster Hall 🏛 E4
Weymouth St C2
Wharf Rd A6
Wharton St B4
Whitcomb St D3
White Cube 🏛 B7
White Lion Hill D5
White Lion St A5
Whitecross St B6
Whitefriars St C5
Whitehall D4
Whitehall Place D4
Wigmore Hall C2
Wigmore St C2
William IV St D4
Wilmington Sq B5
Wilson St C6
Wilton Cres E2
Wimpole St C2
Windmill Walk D5
Woburn Place B4
Woburn Sq B3
Women's Hosp [H] C3
Wood St C6
Woodbridge St B5
Wootton St D5
Wormwood St C7
Worship St B6
Wren St B4
Wynyatt St B5
York Rd E4
York St C1
York Terrace East B2
York Terrace West B2
York Way A4

Luton 189

Adelaide St B1
Albert Rd C2
Alma St B2
Alton Rd C3
Anthony Gdns C3
Arthur St C2
Ashburnham Rd B1
Ashton Rd C2
Avondale Rd A1
Back St A2
Bailey St C3
Baker St C2
Biscot Rd A1
Bolton Rd B3
Boyle Cl A2
Brantwood Rd B1
Bretts Mead C1
Bridge St B2
Brook St A1
Brunswick St A3
Burr St A3
Bury Park Rd A1
Bute St B2
Buxton Rd B2
Cambridge St C3
Cardiff Grove B1
Cardiff Rd B1
Cardigan St A2
Castle St B2/C2
Chapel St C2
Charles St A3
Chase St C2
Cheapside B2
Chequer St C3
Chiltern Rise C1
Church St B2/B3
Cinema 🎬 A2
Cobden St A3
College A3
Collingdon St A1
Community Centre C3
Concorde Ave A3
Corncastle Rd C1
Cowper St C2
Crawley Green Rd B3
Crawley Rd A1
Crescent Rd A3
Crescent Rise A3
Cromwell Rd A1
Cross St A2
Cross Way, The C1
Crown Court B2
Cumberland St B2
Cutenhoe Rd C3
Dallow Rd B1
Downs Rd B1
Dudley St A2
Duke St A2
Dumfries St B1
Dunstable Place B2
Dunstable Rd A1/B1
Edward St A3
Elizabeth St C2
Essex Cl C3
Farley Hill C1
Farley Lodge C1
Flowers Way B2
Francis St A1
Frederick St A2
Galaxy Leisure Complex A2
George St B2
George St West B2
Gordon St B2
Grove Rd B1
Guildford St A2
Haddon Rd A3
Harcourt St C2
Hart Hill Drive A3
Hart Hill Lane A3
Hartley Rd A3
Hastings St B2
Hat Factory, The 🎭 B2
Hatters Way A1
Havelock Rd A2
Hibbert St C2
High Town Rd A3
Highbury Rd A1
Hightown Community Sports & Arts Ctr A3
Hillary Cres C1
Hillborough Rd C1
Hitchin Rd A3
Holly St C2
Holm C1
Hucklesby Way A2
Hunts Cl C1
Inkerman St A2
John St B2
Jubilee St A3
Kelvin Cl C2
King St B2
Kingsland Rd C3
Larches, The A2
Latimer Rd C2
Lawn Gdns C2
Lea Rd B3
Library B2
Library Rd B2
Library Theatre 🎭 B2
Liverpool Rd B1
London Rd C2
Luton Station ⇌ A2
Lyndhurst Rd B1
Magistrates Court B2
Mall, The B2
Manchester St B2
Manor Rd B3
Manor Road Park B3
May St C3
Meyrick Ave C1
Midland Rd A2
Mill St A2
Milton Rd B1
Moor St A1
Moor, The A1
Moorland Gdns A2
Moulton Rise A3
Napier Rd B1
New Bedford Rd A1
New Town St C2
North St A3
Old Bedford Rd A2
Old Orchard C2
Osbourne Rd C3
Oxen Rd A3
Park Sq B2
Park St B3/C3
Park St West B2
Park Viaduct B3
Parkland Drive C1
Police Station [Pol] B1
Pomfret Ave A3
Pondwicks Rd B3
Post Office [PO] A1/B2
Power Court B3
Princess St B1
Red Rails C1
Regent St B2
Reginald St A2
Rothesay Rd B1
Russell Rise C1
Russell St C1
St Ann's Rd B3
St George's Square B2
St Mary's ⛪ B3
St Marys Rd B3
St Paul's Rd C2
St Saviour's Cres C1
Salisbury Rd B1
Seymour Ave C3
Seymour Rd C3
Silver St B2
South Rd C2
Stanley St B1
Station Rd A2
Stockwood Cres C2
Stockwood Park C1
Strathmore Ave C2
Stuart St B2
Studley Rd A1
Surrey St C3
Sutherland Place C1
Tavistock St C2
Taylor St A3
Telford Way A1
Tennyson Rd C2
Tenzing Grove C1
Thistle Rd B3
Town Hall B2
Townsley Cl C2
UK Centre for Carnival Arts ✦ B3
Union St B2
University of Bedfordshire B3
Upper George St B2
Vicarage St B3
Villa Rd A2
Waldeck Rd A1
Wardown House Mus & Gallery 🏛🏛 A2
Wellington St B1/B2
Wenlock St A2
Whitby Rd A1
Whitehill Ave C1
William St A2
Wilsden Ave C1
Windmill Rd B3
Windsor St C2
Winsdon Rd B1
York St A3

Macclesfield 189

108 Steps B2
Abbey Rd A1
Alton Dr A3
Armett St C1
Athey St B1
Bank St C3
Barber St C3
Barton St C1
Beech La A2
Beswick St B1
Black La A2
Black Rd C3
Blakelow Gardens C3
Blakelow Rd C3
Bond St B1/C1
Bread St C1
Bridge St B1
Brock St A2
Brocklehurst Ave A3
Brook St B3
Brookfield La B3
Brough St West C1
Brown St C1
Brynton Rd A2
Buckley St C2
Bus Station B2
Buxton Rd B3
Byrons St C2
Canal St B3
Carlsbrook Ave A3
Castle St B2
Catherine St B1
Cemetery A1
Chadwick Terr A3
Chapel St C2
Charlotte St B2
Chester Rd B1
Chestergate B1
Christ Church ⛪ B1
Churchill Way B2
Coare St A1
Commercial Rd B2
Conway Cres A3
Copper St C3
Cottage St B1
Crematorium A1
Crew Ave A3
Crompton Rd B1/C1
Cross St C2
Crossall St C1
Cumberland St A1/B1
Dale St B3
Duke St B2
Eastgate B3
Exchange St B2
Fence Ave B3
Fence Ave Ind Est A3
Flint St B3
Foden St A2
Fountain St B3
Garden St A3
Gas Rd B2
Gateway Gallery ✦ B1
George St B2
Glegg St B3
Golf Course C3
Goodall St B3
Grange Rd C1
Great King St B1
Green St B3
Grosvenor Shopping Centre B2
Gunco La C3
Half St C1
Hallefield Rd B3
Hatton St C1
Hawthorn Way A3
Heapy St C3
Henderson St B1
Heritage Centre 🏛 B2
Hibel Rd A2
High St C2
Hobson St C2
Hollins Rd C3
Hope St West C1
Horseshoe Dr B1
Hurdsfield Rd A3
Information Ctr [i] B2
James St C2
Jodrell St B3
John St C2
Jordangate A2
King Edward St B2
King George's Field C3
King St B2
King's School A1
Knight Pool C3
Knight St C3
Lansdowne St A3
Library B2
Lime Grove B3
Loney St B1
Longacre St B1
Lord St C2
Lowe St C2
Lowerfield Rd A3
Lyon St B1
Macclesfield Coll C1
Macclesfield Sta ⇌ B2
MADS Little Theatre 🎭 C2
Marina B3
Market B2
Market Place B2
Masons La A3
Mill La C2
Mill Rd C2
Mill St B2
Moran Rd C1
New Hall St A2
Newton St C1
Nicholson Ave A3
Nicholson Cl A3
Northgate Ave A2
Old Mill La C2
Paradise Mill 🏛 C2
Paradise St B1
Park Green B2
Park La C1
Park Rd C1
Park St C2
Park Vale Rd C1
Parr St B1
Peel St C3
Percyvale St A3
Peter St C1
Pickford St B2
Pierce St B1
Pinfold St B1
Pitt St C2
Police Station [Pol] B2
Pool St C2
Poplar Rd C2
Post Office [PO] B2
Pownall St A2
Prestbury Rd A1/B1
Queen Victoria St B2
Queen's Ave A3
Registrar B2
Retail Park C2
Richmond Hill C3
Riseley St B1
Roan Ct B3
Roe St B2
Rowan Way A3
Ryle St C2
Ryle's Park Rd C1
St George's St C2
St Michael's ⛪ B2
Samuel St B2
Saville St C3
Shaw St B1
Silk Rd, The A2/B2
Slater St C1
Snow Hill C3
South Park C1
Spring Gdns A2
Statham St C2
Station St A2
Steeple St A3
Sunderland St B2
Superstore A1/A2/C2
Swettenham St B3
Thistleton Cl C2
Thorp St B2
Town Hall B2
Townley St B2
Treacle Market ✦ B2
Turnock St C3
Union Rd B3
Union St B2
Victoria Park B3
Vincent St C2
Waters Green B2
Waterside C2
West Bond St B1
West Park A1
West Park Mus 🏛 A1
Westbrook Dr A1
Westminster Rd A1
Whalley Hayes B1
Windmill St C3
Withyfold Dr A2
York St B3

Maidstone 190

Albion Place B3
All Saints ⛪ B2
Allen St A3
Amphitheatre ✦ C2
Archbishop's Palace 🏛 B2
Bank St B2
Barker Rd C2
Barton Rd C3
Beaconsfield Rd C1
Bedford Place B1
Bishops Way B2
Bluett St A3
BMI The Somerfield Hospital [H] A1
Bower La C1
Bower Mount Rd B1
Bower Place C1
Bower St B1
Boxley Rd A3
Brenchley Gardens A2
Brewer St A3
Broadway B2
Broadway Shopping Centre B2
Brunswick St C3
Buckland Hill A1
Buckland Rd B1
Bus Station B3
Campbell Rd C3
Church Rd C1
Church St B3
Cinema 🎬 C2
Clifford Way C1/C2
College Ave C2
College Rd C2
Collis Meml Gdn C3
Cornwallis Rd B1
Corpus Christi Hall B2
Council Offices B3
County Hall A2
County Rd A3
Crompton Gdns C3
Crown & County Courts B2
Curzon Rd A3
Dixon Cl C2
Douglas Rd C1
Earl St B2
Eccleston Rd C2
Fairmeadow B2
Fisher St A2
Florence Rd C1
Foley St A3
Foster St C3
Freedom Leisure Centre A1/A2
Fremlin Walk Shopping Centre B2
Gabriel's Hill B3
George St C3
Grecian St A3
Hardy St A3
Hart St C2
Hastings Rd C3
Hayle Rd C3
Hazlitt 🎭 B2
Heathorn St A3
Hedley St A3
High St B2
HM Prison A3
Holland Rd A3
Hope St A2
Information Ctr [i] B2
James St A3
James Whatman Way A2
Jeffrey St A3
Kent County Council Offices A2
Kent History & Library Centre A2
King Edward Rd C2
King St B3
Kingsley Rd C3
Knightrider St B3
Launder Way C1
Lesley Place A1
Library B2
Little Buckland Ave A1
Lockmeadow Leisure Complex C2
London Rd B1
Lower Boxley Rd A2
Lower Fant Rd C1
Magistrates Court B3
Maidstone Barracks Station ⇌ A1
Maidstone East Station ⇌ A2
Maidstone Museum & Bentlif Art Gall 🏛 B2
Maidstone Utd FC A2
Maidstone West Station ⇌ B2
Mall, The B3
Market C2
Market Buildings B2

208 Manchester • Merthyr Tydfil • Middlesbrough • Milton Keynes • Newcastle • Newport • Newquay

Marsham St B3
Medway St B2
Melville Rd C3
Mill St B2
Millennium Bridge. C2
Mote Rd B3
Muir Rd. C3
Old Tovil Rd. C2
Palace Ave B3
Perryfield St. A2
Police Station . . . B3
Post Office . . B2/C3
Priory Rd. C3
Prospect Place. . . . C1
Pudding La B2
Queen Anne Rd . . . B3
Queens Rd A1
Randall St. A2
Rawdon Rd C3
Reginald Rd C1
Riverstage A1
Rock Place B1
Rocky Hill B1
Romney Place B3
Rose Yard B2
Rowland Cl C1
Royal Engineers' Rd A2
Royal Star Arcade . B2
St Annes Ct B1
St Faith's St B2
St Luke's Rd A3
St Peter St. B2
St Peter's Bridge . . B2
St Peter's Wharf Retail Park B2
St Philip's Ave C3
Salisbury Rd A3
Sandling Rd A2
Scott St. A2
Scrubs La B1
Sheal's Cres C3
Somerfield La. B1
Somerfield Rd B1
Staceys St. A2
Station Rd. A2
Superstore . A1/B2/B3
Terrace Rd B1
Tonbridge Rd C1
Tovil Rd. C2
Town Hall B2
Trinity Park. B3
Tufton St. B3
Tyrwhitt-Drake Mus of Carriages B2
Union St B3
Upper Fant Rd C1
Upper Stone St. . . . C3
Victoria St. B1
Warwick Place. . . . B1
Wat Tyler Way B3
Waterloo St C3
Waterlow Rd. A3
Week St. B2
Well Rd A3
Westree Rd. C1
Wharf Rd. C1
Whatman Park. . . . A1
Wheeler St A3
Whitchurch Close . B1
Woodville Rd C3
Wyatt St B3
Wyke Manor Rd . . . B3

Manchester 190

Adair St. B6
Addington St A5
Adelphi St. A1
Albert Sq. B3
Albion St. C3
Ancoats Grove B6
Ancoats Grove North. B6
Angela St C2
Aquatics Centre . . . C4
Ardwick Green North. C5
Ardwick Green Pk . C5
Ardwick Green South. C5
Arlington St A2
Artillery St B3
Arundel St. C2
Atherton St. B2
Atkinson St. B3
Aytoun St B4
Back Piccadilly. . . . A4
Baird St. B5
Balloon St. A4
Bank Place A1
Baring St. B5
Barrack St. C1
Barrow St A1
Bendix St A5
Bengal St A5
Berry St. C5
Blackfriars Rd A3
Blackfriars St A3
Blantyre St C2
Bloom St. B4
Blossom St A5
Boad St B5
Bombay St B4
Booth St A3
Booth St B4
Bootle St. B3
Brazennose St B3
Brewer St A5
Bridge St. A3
Bridgewater Hall . . B3
Bridgewater Place. A4
Bridgewater St. . . . B2
Brook St C4
Brotherton Dr. A2
Brown St. A3
Brown St. B4
Brunswick St C6
Brydon Ave C6
Buddhist Centre. . . A4
Bury St A2
Bus & Coach Sta. . . B4
Bus Station B4
Butler St A6
Buxton St C5
Byrom St. B3
Cable St A5
Cambridge St. . C3/C4
Camp St B3
Canal St B4
Cannon St. A1
Cardroom Rd A6
Carruthers St A6
Castle St C2
Castlefield Arena. . B2
Cateaton St. A3
Cathedral A3
Cathedral St A3
Cavendish St C4
Chapel St A1/A3
Chapeltown St. . . . B5
Charles St C4
Charlotte St. B4
Chatham St. B4
Chepstow St B3
Chester Rd C1/C2
Chester St. C4
Chetham's Sch of Music. A3
China La B5
Chippenham Rd . . . A6
Chorlton Rd C2
Chorlton St. B4
Church St A2
Church St A4
City Park A4
City Rd East. C3
Civil Justice Ctr . . . B2
Cleminson St A2
Clowes St A3
College Land A3
Collier St. B2
Commercial St C3
Conference Centre C4
Cooper St B4
Copperas St A4
Corn Exchange, The A4
Cornbrook C1
Cornell St A5
Corporation St A4
Cotter St C6
Cotton St. A5
Cow La B1
Cross St. B3
Crown Court. B4
Crown St. C2
Dalberg St. C6
Dale St A4/B5
Dancehouse, The . C4
Dantzic St A4
Dark La C6
Dawson St. C2
Dean St. A5
Deansgate . A3/B3/C2
Deansgate Castlefield C3
Deansgate Sta . . . C3
Dolphin St. C6
Downing St. C5
Ducie St B5
Duke Place B2
Duke St B2
Durling St C6
East Ordsall La . A2/B1
Edge St A4
Egerton St. C2
Ellesmere St. C1
Everard St. C1
Every St. B6
Exchange Sq A4
Fairfield St B5
Faulkner St. B4
Fennel St A3
Ford St A2
Ford St C6
Fountain St. B4
Frederick St A2
Gartside St B2
Gaythorne St A1
George Leigh St . . . A5
George St B4
Gore St A2
Goulden St A5
Granby Row B4
Gravel La. A3
Great St. B6
Great Ancoats St . . A5
Great Bridgewater St B3
Great George St . . . A1
Great Jackson St . . C2
Great Marlborough St C4
Great Northern Warehouse Leisure & Shopping Complex B3
Greengate A3
Grosvenor St C5
Gun St A5
Hadrian Ave B6
Hall St B3
Hampson St B1
Hanover St A4
Hanworth Cl C5
Hardman St B3
Harkness St C6
Harrison St. B6
Hart St. B4
Helmet St B6
Henry St A5
Heyrod St B6
High St A4
Higher Ardwick C6
Hilton St. A4/A5
Holland St. A6
HOME C3
Hood St. A5
Hope St. B1
Hope St. B4
Houldsworth St . . . A5
Hoyle St. C6
Hulme Hall Rd C1
Hulme St. A1
Hulme St. C3
Hyde Rd C6
Islington Way A1
Information Ctr . . . B4
Irwell St A2
Jackson Cres C2
Jackson's Row B3
James St A1
Jenner Cl C2
Jersey St A5
John Dalton St B3
John Ryland's Library B3
John St A2
Kennedy St B3
Kincardine Rd C5
King St A3
King St West A3
Law Courts B3
Laystall St B5
Lever St A5
Library B3
Linby St. C2
Little Lever St A4
Liverpool Rd B2
Liverpool St B1
Lloyd St B3
Lockton Cl C5
London Rd B5
Long Millgate A3
Longacre St B6
Loom St A5
Lower Byrom St . . . B2
Lower Mosley St . . . B3
Lower Moss La C2
Lower Ormond St. . . C4
Loxford La. C4
Luna St A5
Major St B4
Manchester Arndale A4
Manchester Art Gallery B4
Manchester Central Convention Complex B3
Manchester Metropolitan Univ (MMU). B4/C4
Manchester Piccadilly Station B5
Manchester Technology Ctr . . . C4
Mancunian Way C5
Manor St C5
Marble St A4
Market St A2
Market St A4
Market St A4
Marsden St A3
Marshall St A5
Mayan Ave A2
Medlock St C3
Middlewood St. B1
Miller St A4
Minshull St B4
Mosley St A4
Mount St B3
Mulberry St B3
Murray St A5
Museum of Science & Industry (MOSI) . B2
Nathan Dr A2
National Football Museum A4
Naval St A5
New Bailey St A2
New Elm Rd B2
New Islington A6
New Islington Sta B6
New Quay St B2
New Union St A6
Newgate St A4
Newton St. A5
Nicholas St B4
North Western St . . C6
Oak St A4
Odeon A4/B3
Old Mill St. A6
Oldfield Rd A1/C1
Oldham Rd A5
Oldham St. A4
Opera House B3
Ordsall La C1
Oxford Rd C4
Oxford Rd C4
Oxford St. B4
Paddock St C6
Palace Theatre B4
Pall Mall A3
Palmerston St B6
Parker St. B4
Peak St B5
Penfield Cl C5
Peoples' History Museum B2
Peru St A1
Peter St. B3
Piccadilly A4
Piccadilly B5
Piccadilly Gdns . . . B4
Piercy St A6
Poland St A5
Police Sta B3/B5
Pollard St B6
Port St. A5
Portland St B4
Portugal St East . . . B5
Post Office . . . A1/A2/ A4/A5/B3/B4
Potato Wharf B2
Princess St B3/C4
Pritchard St C4
Quay St A2
Quay St B2
Queen St B3
Radium St. A5
Redhill St A5
Regent Rd. B1
Retail Park A5
Rice St. B2
Richmond St. B4
River St C3
Roby St B5
Rodney St A6
Roman Fort B2
Rosamond St A2
Royal Exchange . . . A3
Sackville St. B4
St Andrew's St B6
St Ann St. A3
St Ann's A3
St George's Ave . . . C1
St James St. B4
St John St. B3
St John's Cathedral (RC) A2
St Mary's B3
St Mary's Gate A3
St Mary's Parsonage. A3
St Peter's Sq B3
St Stephen St A2
Salford Approach. . A3
Salford Central . . . A2
Sheffield St. B5
Sherratt St A5
Shopmobility A4
Shudehill A4
Shudehill A4
Sidney St C4
Silk St A5
Silver St B4
Skerry Cl C5
Snell St B6
South King St B3
Sparkle St B5
Spear St A4
Spring Gardens A4
Stanley St A2/B2
Store St B5
Superstore B1
Swan St A4
Tariff St B5
Tatton St. C1
Temperance St. B6/C6
Thirsk St C6
Thomas St. A4
Thompson St A5
Tib La B3
Tib St. A4
Town Hall (Manchester) B3
Town Hall (Salford) A2
Trafford St C3
Travis St B5
Trinity Way A2
Turner St. A4
Union St C6
Univ of Manchester (Sackville St Campus) C5
Univ of Salford A1
Upper Brook St. . . . C5
Upper Cleminson St A1
Upper Wharf St . . . A1
Urban Exchange. . . A5
Vesta St. B6
Victoria A4
Victoria Station . . A4
Wadesdon Rd. C5
Water St B2
Watson St B3
West Fleet St B1
West King St A2
West Mosley St B4
Weybridge Rd. A6
Whitworth St B4
Whitworth St West. C3
William St. A2
William St. C6
Wilmott St C3
Windmill St. B3
Windsor Cres A1
Withy Grove A4
Woden St C1
Wood St B3
Woodward St A6
Worrall St C1
Worsley St C2
York St B4
York St C2
York St C4

Merthyr Tydfil
Merthyr Tudful 190

Aberdare Rd B2
Abermorlais Terr . . B2
Alexandra Rd A3
Alma St. C3
Arfryn Place C3
Argyle St C3
Avenue De Clichy . . C2
Beacons Place Shopping Centre . . C2
Bethesda St B2
Bishops Grove A3
Brecon Rd A1/B2
Briarmead A3
Bryn St C3
Bryntirion Rd . . . B3/C3
Bus Station. B2
Cae Mari Dwn. B3
Caedraw Rd C2
Castle Sq. A1
Castle St B2
Chapel. C2
Chapel Bank. B1
Church St B3
Civic Centre B2
Clos Penderyn B1
Coedcae'r Ct C3
College Blvd. C2
County and Crown Courts B2
Court St. C3
Cromwell St B2
Cyfarthfa Castle, Mus and Art Gallery . . A1
Cyfarthfa Ind Est . . A1
Cyfarthfa Park A1
Cyfarthfa Retail Pk. B1
Cyfarthfa Rd A1
Dane St A2
Dane Terr A2
Danyparc B3
Darren View A3
Dixon St B2
Dyke St C3
Dynevor St B2
Elwyn Dr C3
Fire Station. B2
Fothergill St B3
Galonuchaf Rd A3
Garth St. B2
Georgetown B2
Grawen Terr A2
Grove Pk A2
Grove, The. A2
Gurnos Rd. A2
Gwaelodygarth Rd A2/A3
Gwaunfarren Grove. A3
Gwaunfarren Rd. . . A3
Gwendoline St A3
Hampton St C3
Hanover St A2
Heol S O Davies . . . B1
Heol-Gerrig B1
High St . . A3/B2/B3/C2
Highland View C3
Howell Cl B1
Information Ctr . . . B2
Jackson's Bridge. . . B2
James St. C3
John St B3
Joseph Parry's Cottage B2
Lancaster St A2
Library B2
Llewellyn St A2
Llwyfen St. B2
Llwyn Berry B1
Llwyn Dic Penderyn B1
Llwyn-y-Gelynen. . C1
Lower Thomas St . . B3
Market C2
Mary St C3
Masonic St C2
Merthyr Tydfil Coll . B2
Merthyr Town FC . . B3
Merthyr Tydfil Leisure Centre C3
Merthyr Tydfil Station C3
Meyrick Villas A2
Miniature Railway A1
Mount St. A2
Nantygwenith St . . B1
Norman Terr. B2
Oak Rd. A2
Old Cemetery B3
Pandy Cl A1
Pantycelynen B1
Parade, The. B3
Park Terr B2
Penlan View C2
Penry St B2
Pentwyn Villas A2
Penyard Rd B3
Penydarren Park . . . A3
Penydarren Rd B3
Plymouth St C3
Police Station C2
Pont Marlais West . B2
Post Office B2
Quarry Row. B2
Queen's Rd B3
Rees St C3
Rhydycar Link. C2
Riverside Park A1
St David's B3
St Tydfil's C2
St Tydfil's Ave C3
St Tydfil's Square Shopping Centre . C2
Saxon St A2
School of Nursing . A2
Seward St A3
Shiloh La. B3
Stone Circles B3
Stuart St A2
Summerhill Place . . B3
Superstore B3
Swan St. C2
Swansea Rd B1
Taff Glen View. C3
Taff Vale Ct B3
Theatre Soar B2
Thomastown Park . . B3
Tramroad La A3
Tramroad Side B2
Tramroad Side North. B3
Tramroad Side South. C3
Trevithick Gdns . . . C3
Trevithick St A3
Tudor Terr B2
Twynyrodyn Rd. . . . C3
Union St B3
Upper Colliers Row B1
Upper Thomas St . . B3
Victoria St. B2
Vue C3
Vulcan Rd B2
Walk, The B2
Warlow St C3
Well St. A2
Welsh Assembly Government Offices. C2
Wern La. C1
Wern, The (Merthyr RFC). . . . C2
West Grove A2
William St. C3
Yew St C3
Ynysfach Engine House C2
Ynysfach Rd C2

Middlesbrough 191

Abingdon Rd C3
Acklam Rd C1
Albert Park C2
Albert Rd B2
Albert Terr. C2
Ambulance Station C1
Aubrey St C3
Avenue, The C2
Ayresome Gdns . . . C2
Ayresome Green La C1
Ayresome St C2
Barton Rd A1
Bilsdale Rd C3
Bishopton Rd C3
Borough Rd B2/B3
Bowes Rd A2
Breckon Hill Rd . . . B3
Bridge St West B2
Brighouse Rd A1
Burlam Rd. C1
Bus Station. B2
Cannon Park. B1
Cannon Park Way. . B2
Cannon St. B1
Captain Cook Sq. . . B2
Carlow St C1
Castle Way C3
Chipchase Rd C2
Cineworld B3
Cleveland Centre. . B2
Clive Rd. C2
Commercial St A2
Corporation Rd B2
Costa St. C2
Council Offices. . . . B3
Crescent Rd C2
Crescent, The C2
Cumberland Rd C2
Depot Rd A2
Derwent St. B2
Devonshire Rd C2
Diamond Rd B2
Dock St B3
Dorman Mus C2
Douglas St B3
Eastbourne Rd C2
Eden Rd. C3
Fire Sta A3
Forty Foot Rd A2
Gilkes St B2
Gosford St. A2
Grange Rd. B2
Gresham Rd B2
Harehills Rd C1
Harford St. C2
Hartington Rd B2
Haverton Hill Rd. . . A1
Hey Wood St B1
Highfield Rd C3
Hillstreet Centre . . B2
Holwick Rd B1
Hutton Rd C3
Ironmasters Way . . B1
Lambton Rd C3
Lancaster Rd C2
Lansdowne Rd C3
Latham Rd. C2
Law Courts B2/B3
Lees Rd B2
Leeway B3
Library B2/C2
Linthorpe Cemetery C1
Linthorpe Rd B2
Lloyd St. B2
Longford St. C2
Longlands Rd C3
Lower East St A3
Lower Lake. C3
Macmillan Acad . . . C1
Maldon Rd C1
Manor St. B2
Marsh St B2
Marton Rd. B3
Middlesbrough By-Pass. B2/C1
Middlesbrough Coll B3
Middlesbrough Dock B3
Middlesbrough Leisure Park B3
Middlesbrough Station B2
Middletown Park . . C2
MIMA B3
Mulgrave Rd. C2
Newport Bridge . . . B1
Newport Bridge Approach Rd. B1
Newport Rd B2
North Ormesby Rd . B3
North Rd B2
Northern Rd C1
Outram St B2
Oxford Rd C2
Park La C2
Park Rd North. C2
Park Rd South C2
Park Vale Rd C3
Parliament Rd B1
Police Station A2
Port Clarence Rd . . A3
Portman St B2
Post Office B3/C1/C2
Princes Rd B2
Python A2
Riverside Park Rd . A1
Riverside Stadium (Middlesbrough FC). B3
Rockliffe Rd C2
Romaldkirk Rd B1
Roman Rd. C2
Roseberry Rd C3
St Barnabas' Rd . . . C2
St Paul's Rd B2
Saltwells Rd B3
Scott's Rd A3
Seaton Carew Rd . . A3
Shepherdson Way . B3
Shopmobility B2
Snowdon Rd. A2
South West Ironmasters Park . B1
Southfield Rd B2
Southwell Rd C2
Springfield Rd C1
Startforth Rd A2
Stockton Rd C1
Stockton St. A2
Superstore B2
Surrey St. C2
Sycamore Rd C2
Tax Offices B3
Tees Viaduct C1
Teessaurus Park . . . A2
Teesside Tertiary College C3
Temenos B3
Thornfield Rd C1
Town Hall B2
Transporter Bridge (Toll) A3
Union St B2
Univ of Teesside . . . B2
Upper Lake C2
Valley Rd C3
Ventnor Rd C2
Victoria Rd B2
Vulcan St. A2
Warwick St C2
Wellesley Rd. B3
West La C1
West Lane Hosp . . . C1
Westminster Rd . . . C2
Wilson St B2
Windward Way B3
Woodlands Rd B2
York Rd C3

Milton Keynes 191

Abbey Way A1
Arbrook Ave B1
Armourer Dr. A3
Arncliffe Dr. A1
Avebury C2
Avebury Blvd C2
Bankfield B3
Bayard Ave A2
Belvedere A2
Bishopstone A1
Blundells Rd A1
Boundary, The. C3
Boycott Ave. C2
Bradwell Common Blvd B1
Bradwell Rd C1
Bramble Ave A2
Brearley Ave C2
Breckland A1
Brill Place B1
Burnham Dr B1
Campbell Park B3
Cantle Ave. A3
Central Retail Park C1
Century Ave C2
Chaffron Way C3
Childs Way C1
Christ the Cornerstone B2
Cineworld B2
Civic Offices B2
Cleavers Ave. B2
Colesbourne Dr . . . A3
Conniburrow Blvd . B2
Currier Dr A2
Dansteed Way A2/A3/B1
Deltic Ave B1
Downs Barn A2
Downs Barn Blvd . . A3
Eaglestone C3
Eelbrook Ave B1
Elder Gate. B1
Evans Gate C2
Fairford Cres A3
Falcon Ave B3
Fennel Dr A2
Fishermead Blvd . . C3
Food Centre B3
Fulwoods Dr. C3
Glazier Dr A2
Glovers La. A1
Grafton Gate. C1
Grafton St A1/C2
Gurnards Ave B3
Harrier Dr. C3
The Hub Leisure Quarter B2/C2
Ibstone Ave. B1
intu Milton Keynes. B2
Langcliffe Dr A1
Leisure Centre C3
Leisure Plaza C1
Leys Rd C1
Library B2
Linceslade Grove . . C1
Linford Wood A2
Magistrates Court . B2
Marlborough Gate . B3
Marlborough St A2/B3
Mercers Dr A1
Midsummer C2
Midsummer Blvd . . B2
Milton Keynes Central C1
Milton Keynes Hospital (A&E) . . C3
Monks Way. A1
Mullen Ave A3
Mullion Place. C3
Neath Hill A3
North Elder C1
North Grafton B1
North Overgate . . . A3
North Row B2
North Saxon B2
North Secklow B2
North Skeldon A3
North Witan B1
Oakley Gdns A3
Odeon B2
Oldbrook Blvd C2
Open-Air Theatre . B3
Overgate. A3
Overstreet A3
Patriot Dr B1
Pencarrow Place . . . B3
Penryn Ave B3
Perran Ave C3
Pitcher La C1
Place Retail Pk, The C1
Police Station B2
Portway B2
Post Office A2/B2/B3
Precedent Dr B1
Quinton Dr B1
Ramsons Ave B2
Retail Park C2
Rockingham Dr . . . A2
Rooksley B1
Saxon Gate B2
Saxon St A1/C3
Secklow Gate B2
Shackleton Place. . . C2
Shopmobility B2
Silbury Blvd B2
Skeldon A3
South Enmore B3
South Grafton C2
South Row C2
South Saxon C2
South Secklow B3
South Witan C2
Springfield B3
Stainton Dr. A1/B1
Stanton Wood A1
Stantonbury A1
Stantonbury Leisure Centre A1
Strudwick Dr C2
Sunrise Parkway . . . A2
Superstore C1/C2
Theatre & Art Gallery B3
theCentre:mk. B2
Tolcarne Ave. C3
Towan Ave. C3
Trueman Place. C2
Vauxhall A1
Winterhill Retail Pk C2
Witan Gate B2
Xscape B3

Newcastle upon Tyne 191

Albert St B3
Argyle St B3
Back New Bridge St B3
BALTIC Centre for Contemporary Art C3
Barker St. A3
Barrack Rd B1
Bath La B1
Bessie Surtees House C2
Bigg Market C2
Biscuit Factory . . . B3
Black Gate C2
Blackett St B2
Blandford Sq C1
Boating Lake A1
Boyd St B3
Brandling Park A2
Bus Station. B2
Buxton St B3
Byron St A3
Camden St B2
Castle Keep C2
Central C1
Central Library. . . . B2
Central Motorway . B2
Chester St. A3
Cineworld B1
City Hall B2
City Rd. B3/C3
City Walls C1
Civic Centre A2
Claremont Rd. A1
Clarence St. B3
Clarence Walk B3
Clayton St C1/B1
Clayton St West . . . C1
Close, The C2
Coach Station. C1
College St. B2
Collingwood St C2
Copland Terr. B3
Coppice Way B3
Corporation St B1
Courts C3
Crawhall Rd B3
Dean St C2
Dental Hospital . . . A1
Dinsdale Place. A3
Dinsdale Rd A3
Discovery C1
Doncaster Rd A3
Durant Rd B2
Eldon Sq. B1
Ellison Place. B2
Eskdale Terr A2
Eslington Terr. A2
Exhibition Park . . . A1
Falconar St. B3
Fenkle St. C1
Forth Banks C1
Forth St C1
Gallowgate. B1
Gate, The B1
Gateshead Millennium Bridge C3
Gateshead Quays . . C3
Gibson St B3
Goldspink La A3
Grainger Market . . . B2
Grainger St. B2
Grantham Rd A3
Granville Rd A3
Great North Children's Hospital. A1
Great North Mus: Hancock A2
Grey St B2
Groat Market C2
Guildhall C2
Hancock St. A2
Hanover St C2
Hatton Gallery . . . A1
Hawks Rd C3
Haymarket B2
Heber St B1
Helmsley Rd A3
High Bridge B2
High Level Bridge . C2
Hillgate. C3
Howard St B3
Hutton Terr A3
intu Eldon Sq Shopping Centre . B2
Jesmond A2
Jesmond Rd . . . A2/A3
John Dobson St . . . B2
Jubilee Rd B3
Kelvin Grove. A3
Kensington Terr . . . A2
Laing Gallery B2
Lambton Rd A2
Leazes Cres B1
Leazes La B1
Leazes Park B1
Leazes Park Rd. . . . B1
Leazes Terr B1
Library A2
Live C2
Low Friar St C1
Manor Chare C2
Manors B2
Manors Station . . . B2
Market St B2
Melbourne St B2
Mill Rd. C3
Monument B2
Monument Mall Shopping Centre . B2
Morpeth St A2
Mosley St C2
Napier St A3
New Bridge St West. B2/B3
Newcastle Central Station C1
Newcastle Univ . . . A1
Newgate St B1
Newington Rd A3
Northern Design Centre C3
Northern Stage Theatre A2
Northumberland Rd B2
Northumberland St B2
Northumbria Univ . A2
Northwest Radial Rd A1
O2 Academy C1
Oakwellgate. C3
Open Univ. C3
Orchard St C1
Osborne Rd. A2
Osborne Terr. A3
Pandon C3
Pandon Bank B3
Park Terr A1
Percy St B1
Pilgrim St B2
Pipewellgate C2
Pitt St B1
Plummer Tower . . . A2
Police Station C1
Portland Rd A3/B3
Portland Terr A3
Post Office B1/B2
Pottery La C1
Prudhoe Place B1
Prudhoe St. B1
Quayside. C2
Queen Elizabeth II Bridge. C2
Queen Victoria Rd . A1
Richardson Rd A1
Ridley Place B2
Rock Terr B3
Rosedale Terr A3
Royal Victoria Infirmary A1
Sage Gateshead . . C3
St Andrew's St B1
St James B1
St James' Blvd C1
St James' Park (Newcastle Utd FC). B1
St Mary's Heritage Centre C3
St Mary's (RC) . . . C1
St Mary's Place B2
St Nicholas C2
St Nicholas St. C2
St Thomas' St B1
Sandyford Rd . . A2/A3
Shield St B3
Shieldfield B3
Shopmobility B1
Side, The. C2
Simpson Terrace . . B3
South Shore Rd . . . C3
South St C1
Starbeck Ave A3
Stepney Rd B3
Stoddart St B3
Stowell St B1
Strawberry Place. . . B1
Swing Bridge C2
Temple St C1
Terrace Place B1
Theatre Royal B2
Times Sq. C1
Tower St B3
Trinity House C2
Tyne Bridge C2
Tyne Bridges C2
Tyne Theatre & Opera House C1
Tyneside B2
Victoria Sq A2
Warwick St A3
Waterloo St C1
Wellington St B1
Westgate Rd. . . . C1/C2
Windsor Terr. A2
Worswick St B2
Wretham Place B3

Newport
Casnewydd 191

Albert Terr. B1
Allt-yr-Yn Ave A1
Alma St. C2
Ambulance Sta. . . . C3
Bailey St B2
Barrack Hill A2
Bath St A3
Bedford Rd B3
Belle Vue La C1
Belle Vue Park C1
Bishop St A3
Blewitt St B1
Bolt Cl. C3
Bolt St C3
Bond St. A2
Bosworth Dr. A1
Bridge St. B1
Bristol St. A3
Bryngwyn Rd B1
Brynhyfryd Ave. . . . C1
Brynhyfryd Rd C1
Bus Station. B2
Caerau Cres C1
Caerau Rd. B1
Caerleon Rd A3
Capel Cres C2
Cardiff Rd C2
Caroline St B3
Castle (Remains). . . A2
Cedar Rd. B3
Charles St. B2
Charlotte Dr C2
Chepstow Rd A3
Church Rd. A3
Cineworld B2
Civic Centre B1
Clarence Place. A2
Clifton Place. B1
Clifton Rd C1
Clyffard Cres B1
Clytha Park Rd B1
Clytha Sq. C2
Coldra Rd C1
Collier St A3
Colne St B3
Comfrey Cl A1
Commercial Rd C3
Commercial St B2
Corelli St. A3
Corn St B2
Corporation Rd B3
Coulson Cl C2
County Court A2
Courts A1
Courts B1
Crawford St A3
Cyril St B3
Dean St A3
Devon Place. B1
Dewsland Park Rd . C2
Dolman B2
Dolphin St. C3
East Dock Rd C3
East St. B1
East Usk Rd A3
Ebbw Vale Wharf . . A3
Emlyn St B2
Enterprise Way. . . . C3
Eton Rd B3
Evans St A2
Factory Rd A2
Fields Rd. B1
Francis Dr. C2
Frederick St C3
Friars Rd C1
Friars Walk. B2
Gaer La C1
George St C3
George St Bridge. . . C3
Godfrey Rd B1
Gold Tops B1
Gore St A3
Gorsedd Circle. C1
Grafton Rd A3
Graham St. B1
Granville St C3
Harlequin Dr. A1
Harrow Rd B3
Herbert Rd A3
Herbert Walk C2
Hereford St. A3
High St B2
Hill St B2
Hoskins St. A2
Information Ctr . . . B2
Ivor St B2
Jones St B1
Junction Rd A3
Keynshaw Ave C2
King St C2
Kingsway B2
Kingsway Centre . . B2
Ledbury Dr A2
Library A3
Library, Museum & Art Gallery B2
Liverpool Wharf. . . B3
Llanthewy Rd B1
Llanvair Rd A3
Locke St A2
Lower Dock St C3
Lucas St A2
Manchester St A3
Market B2
Marlborough Rd. . . B3
Mellon St C3
Mill St A2
Morgan St. A3
Mountjoy Rd. C2
Newport Bridge . . . A2
Newport Ctr B2
Newport RFC B3
Newport Sta B2
North St B2
Oakfield Rd. B1
Park Sq C2
Police Sta A3/C2
Post Office B2/C3
Power St A1
Prince St. A3
Pugsley St. A2
Queen St C2
Queen's Cl A1
Queen's Hill A1
Queen's Hill Cres . . A1
Queensway. B2
Railway St. B2
Riverfront Theatre & Arts Centre, The B2
Riverside A3
Rodney Rd B2
Royal Gwent (A&E) C2
Rudry St A3
Rugby Rd B3
Ruperra La C3
Ruperra St C3
St Edmund St B1
St Mark's Cres A1
St Mary St B1
St Vincent Rd A3
St Woolos C2
St Woolos General (no A&E) C1
St Woolos Rd B1
School La B2
Serpentine Rd B1
Shaftesbury Park . . A2
Sheaf La A3
Skinner St. B2
Sorrel Dr. A1
South Market St . . . C3
Spencer Rd B1
Stow Hill . . . B2/C1/C2
Stow Park Ave C1
Stow Park Dr C1
TA Centre A1
Talbot St B2
Tennis Club. A1
Tregare St A3
Trostrey St A3
Tunnel Terr B1
Turner St. A3
Univ of Wales Newport City Campus. B3
Upper Dock St B2
Usk St A3
Usk Way B3/C3
Victoria Cres. B1
War Memorial A3
Waterloo Rd C1
West St B1
Wharves B2
Wheeler St A2
Whitby Place A3
Windsor Terr. B1
York Place C1

Newquay 192

Agar Rd. B2
Alma Place B1
Ambulance Station B2
Anthony Rd. C1
Atlantic Hotel. A1
Bank St B1
Barrowfields. A3
Bay View Terr B2
Beach Rd. B1
Beachfield Ave B1
Beacon Rd A1
Belmont Place A1
Berry Rd B2
Blue Reef Aquarium B1
Boating Lake C2
Bus Station B2
Chapel Hill B1
Chester Rd A3
Cheviot Rd C1/C2
Chichester Cres . . . C2
Chynance Dr. C1
Chyverton Cl. C1
Cliff Rd B2
Coach Park. B2
Colvreath Rd. A3
Cornwall College Newquay. B3
Council Ofices B3
Crantock St. B1
Crescent, The B1
Criggar Rocks A3
Dale Cl C3
Dale Rd C3
Dane Rd A1
East St. B2
Edgcumbe Ave B3
Edgcumbe Gdns. . . B3
Eliot Gdns. B3
Elm Cl C3
Ennor's Rd B1
Fernhill Rd B1
Fire Station. B1
Fore St B1
Gannel Rd C2
Golf Driving Range B3
Gover La B1
Great Western Beach A2
Grosvenor Ave B2
Harbour A1
Hawkins Rd. C2
Headleigh Rd B2
Hilgrove Rd. . . . A3/B3
Holywell Rd B3
Hope Terr B1
Huer's Hut, The . . . A1
Information Ctr . . . B1
Island Cres B2
Jubilee St B1
Kew Close C3
Killacourt Cove A2
King Edward Cres . . A1
Lanhenvor Ave B2
Library B1
Lifeboat Station . . . A1
Lighthouse B1
Linden Ave C2
Listry Rd C2
Lusty Glaze Beach . A3
Lusty Glaze Rd A3
Manor Rd B1
Marcus Hill B2
Mayfield Rd B2
Meadowside. C3
Mellanvrane La C2

(Newquay, continued)

Michell Ave. B2
Miniature Golf Course C3
Miniature Railway B3
Mount Wise B1
Mowhay Rd C3
Narrowcliff A3
Newquay B2
Newquay Hosp [H] B2
Newquay Town Football Ground B1
Newquay Zoo B2
North Pier A1
North Quay Hill A1
Oakleigh Terr B2
Pargolla Rd B2
Pendragon Cres C1
Pengannel Cl C1
Penina Ave C3
Pirate's Quest B1
Police Station & Courts B2
Post Office A1/B3
Quarry Park Rd B3
Rawley La C2
Reeds Way B3
Robartes Rd A3
St Anne's Rd A3
St Aubyn Cres B1
St George's Rd B1
St John's Rd B1
St Mary's Rd B1
St Michael's B2
St Michael's Rd B1
St Thomas' Rd B2
Seymour Ave A3
South Pier A1
South Quay Hill A1
Superstore C3
Sweet Briar Cres C3
Sydney Rd A2
Tolcarne Beach A2
Tolcarne Point A2
Tolcarne Rd A2
Tor Rd B2
Towan Beach A1
Towan Blystra Rd B3
Tower Rd A1
Trebarwith Cres B2
Tredour Rd C2
Treforda Rd B2
Tregoss Rd B3
Tregunnel Hill B1/C1
Tregunnel Saltings C1
Trelawney Rd B2
Treloggan La C3
Treloggan Rd C3
Trembath Cres C1
Trenance Ave B2
Trenance Gardens B2
Trenance La C3
Trenance Leisure Park B3
Trenance Rd B3
Trenarth Rd B2
Treninnick Hill C3
Tretherras Rd C2
Trethewey Way C1
Trevemper Rd C2
Ulalia Rd B3
Vivian Cl B2
Waterworld B3
Whitegate Rd B3
Wych Hazel Way C3

Northampton 192

78 Derngate B3
Abington Sq B3
Abington St B3
Alcombe St A3
All Saints' B2
Ambush St B1
Angel St B2
AR Centre A2
Arundel St A2
Ash St A3
Auctioneers Way C2
Bailiff St B3
Barrack Rd A2
Beaconsfield Terr A3
Becket's Park C3
Bedford Rd B3
Billing Rd B3
Brecon St A1
Brewery Bridge St B2
Broad St B2
Burns St A3
Bus Station B2
Campbell St B2
Castle (Site of) B2
Castle St B2
Cattle Market Rd C2
Central Museum & Art Gallery B2
Charles St A3
Cheyne Walk B3
Church La A2
Clare St A3
Cloutsham St A3
College St B2
Colwyn Rd A3
Cotton End C2
Countess Rd A1
County Hall A3
Court A3
Craven St A3
Crown & County Courts B3
Denmark Rd B3
Derngate B3
Derngate & Royal Theatres B3
Doddridge Church B2
Drapery,The B2
Duke St A3
Dunster St A3
Earl St A3
Euston Rd A3
Fire Station A3
Foot Meadow B2
Gladstone Rd A1
Gold St B2
Grafton St B1
Gray St A1
Green St B2
Greenwood Rd B1
Greyfriars B2
Grosvenor Centre B2
Grove Rd A3
Guildhall B3
Hampton St B3
Harding St A1
Hazelwood Rd B3
Herbert St B1
Hervey St A3
Hester St A3
Holy Sepulchre A2
Hood St A3
Horse Market B2
Hunter St A3
Information Ctr [i] B2
Kettering Rd A3
Kingswell St B2
Lady's La B2
Leicester St A2
Leslie Rd A2
Library B3
Lorne Rd A2
Lorry Park A1
Louise Rd A1
Lower Harding St A2
Lower Hester St A2
Lower Mounts B3
Lower Priory St B2
Main Rd C1
Marefair B2
Market Sq B2
Marlboro Rd B1
Marriott St A2
Military Rd A3
Mounts Baths Leisure Centre A3
Nene Valley Retail Park C1
New South Bridge Rd C2
Northampton General Hospital (A&E) [H] C3
Northampton Marina C3
Northampton Sta [≷] B1
Northcote St A2
Nunn Mills Rd C3
Old Towcester Rd C2
Overstone Rd A3
Peacock Place B2
Pembroke Rd A1
Penn Court C2
Police Station B2
Post Office A1/B3
Quorn Way A2
Ransome Rd C3
Regent Sq A2
Ridings,The B3
Robert St A1
St Andrew's Rd A1
St Andrew's St A2
St Edmund's Rd B3
St George's St A2
St Giles B3
St Giles St B3
St Giles' Terr B3
St James Park Rd A1
St James Rd A1
St James Retail Pk C1
St James' Mill Rd C1
St James' Mill Rd East C1
St Leonard's Rd C2
St Mary's St B2
St Michael's Rd A3
St Peter's Shopping Precinct B2
St Peter's Way B2
Salisbury St A2
Scarletwell St B2
Semilong Rd A1
Sheep St B2
Sol Central (Leisure Centre) B2
Somerset St A3
South Bridge C2
Southfield Ave C2
Spencer Bridge Rd A1
Spencer Rd A1
Spring Gdns B3
Spring La A2
Superstore B3
Swan St B3
Tintern Ave A1
Towcester Rd C2
Upper Bath St B2
Upper Mounts B3
Victoria Prom A1
Victoria Rd B3
Victoria St B3
Wellingborough Rd B3
West Bridge B2
York Rd B3

Norwich 192

Albion Way C3
All Saints Green C2
Anchor St C3
Anglia Sq A2
Argyle St C3
Arts Centre B1
Ashby St C2
Assembly House B1
Bank Plain B2
Barker St A1
Barn Rd B1
Barrack St A3
Ber St C2
Bethel St B1
Bishop Bridge A3
Bishopbridge Rd A3
Bishopgate B2
Blackfriars St A2
Botolph St A2
Bracondale C3
Brazen Gate C2
Bridewell B2
Brunswick Rd C1
Bull Close Rd A2
Bus Station C1
Calvert St A2
Cannell Green A3
Carrow Rd C3
Castle & Mus B2
Castle Mall B2
Castle Meadow B2
Cathedral [†] B2
Cath Retail Park A1
Cattlemarket St B2
Chantry Rd C1
Chapel Loke C2
Chapelfield East B1
Chapelfield Gdns C1
Chapelfield North B1
Cinema City B2
City Hall B1
City Rd C2
City Wall C1/C3
Close,The B2/B3
Colegate A2
Coslany St B1
Cow Hill B1
Cow Tower A3
Cowgate A2
Crown & Magistrates' Courts C1
Dragon Hall Heritage Centre C3
Duke St B1
Edward St A2
Elm Hill B2
Erpingham Gate B2
Fishergate A2
Forum,The B1
Foundry Bridge B3
Fye Bridge A2
Garden St C2
Gas Hill B3
Gentlemans Walk B1
Grapes Hill B1
Great Hospital Halls, The A3
Grove Ave C1
Grove Rd C1
Guildhall B1
Gurney Rd A3
Hall Rd C2
Heathgate A3
Heigham St A1
Hollywood B1
Horn's La C2
Hungate Medieval Art B2
Information Ctr [i] B1
intu Chapelfield B1
Ipswich Rd C1
ITV Anglia B3
James Stuart Gdns A3
King St B2
King St C3
Koblenz Ave C3
Leisure Centre C1
Library B1
London St B2
Lower Clarence Rd B3
Maddermarket B1
Magdalen St A2
Mariners La C2
Market B1
Market Ave B2
Mountergate B2
Mousehold St A3
Newmarket Rd C1
Norfolk St C1
Norwich City FC C3
Norwich Gallery B2
Norwich School B2
Norwich Station [≷] B3
Oak St A1
Odeon B1
Palace St B2
Pitt St A2
Playhouse B2
Police Station B1
Post Office A2/B2/B3/C1
Pottergate B1
Prince of Wales Rd B2
Princes St B2
Pull's Ferry B3
Puppet Theatre A2
Queen St B2
Queens Rd C2
RC Cathedral [†] B1
Recorder Rd B3
Riverside Entertainment Ctr C3
Riverside Leisure Centre A3
Riverside Rd A3
Riverside Retail Pk C3
Rosary Rd B3
Rose La B2
Rouen Rd B2
St Andrews St B2
St Augustines St A1
St Benedicts St B1
St Ethelbert's Gate B2
St Faiths La B2
St Georges St A2
St Giles St B1
St James Cl A3
St Julians La C1
St Leonards Rd B3
St Martin's La A1
St Peter Mancroft B1
St Peters St B1
St Stephens Rd C1
St Stephens St C1
Shopmobility C1
Silver Rd A2
Silver St A2
Southwell Rd C2
St. Andrew's & Blackfriars' Hall B2
Strangers' Hall B1
Superstore C2
Surrey St C2
Sussex St A1
Theatre Royal B1
Theatre St B1
Thorn La C2
Thorpe Rd B3
Tombland B2
Union St C1
Vauxhall St B1
Victoria St C1
Vue B2
Walpole St B1
Waterfront,The C3
Wensum St B2
Wessex St C2
Westwick St B1
Wherry Rd C3
Whitefriars A2
Willow La B1

Nottingham 192

Abbotsford Dr A3
Addison St A1
Albert Hall B1
Alfred St Central A3
Alfreton Rd A1
All Saints St A1
Annesley Grove A2
Arboretum A1
Arboretum St A1
Arthur St A1
Arts Theatre B3
Ashforth St A3
Balmoral Rd A1
Barker Gate B3
Bath St B3
BBC Nottingham C3
Beacon Hill Rise B3
Belgrave Rooms B1
Bellar Gate B3
Belward St B3
Brewhouse Yard C1
Broad Marsh Bus Station C2
Broad St B3
Brook St A3
Burns St A1
Burton St B2
Bus Station C2
Canal St C2
Carlton St B3
Carrington St C2
Castle C1
Castle Blvd C1
Castle Gate C2
Castle Meadow Rd C1
Castle Meadow Retail Park C1
Castle Wharf C2
Cavendish Rd East C1
Cemetery A1/B1
Chaucer St B1
Cheapside B2
Church Rd A3
City Link C3
City of Caves C2
Clarendon St A1
Cliff Rd C3
Clumber Rd East C1
Clumber St B2
College St B1
Collin St C2
Contemporary C2
Conway Cl A2
Cornerhouse, The B2
Council House B2
Cranbrook St B3
Cranmer St A2
Cromwell St B1
Curzon St A3
Derby Rd B1
Dryden St A2
Exchange Ctr,The B2
Fishpond Dr C1
Fletcher Gate B2
Forest Rd East A1
Forest Rd West A1
Friar La C2
Gedling Grove A1
Gedling St B3
George St B3
Gill St A2
Glasshouse St B2
Goldsmith St B2
Goose Gate B3
Great Freeman St A2
Guildhall B2
Hamilton Dr C1
Hampden St A1
Heathcote St B3
High Pavement C3
High School [≷] A1
HM Revenue & Customs C2
Holles Cres C1
Hope Dr C1
Hungerhill Rd A3
Huntingdon Dr C1
Huntingdon St A2
Information Ctr [i] B2
Instow Rise A3
Ison Ct A2
Kent St B3
Lace Market B3
Lace Mkt Theatre C3
Lamartine St B3
Lenton Rd C1
Lewis Cl A3
Lincoln St B2
London Rd C3
Long Row B2
Low Pavement C2
Lower Parliament St A2/B2
Magistrates' Court C2
Maid Marian Way A2/B2
Mansfield Rd A2/B2
Middle Hill C2
Milton St B2
Mount St B1
National Ice Centre & Motorpoint Arena C3
National Justice Museum B2
Newcastle Dr B1
Newstead Grove A1
North Sherwood St A2
Nottingham Arena C3
Nottingham Cath [†] B1
Nottingham Coll C2
Nottingham Station [≷] C3
Nottingham Trent University A2/B2
Old Mkt Square B2
Oliver St A1
Park Dr C1
Park Row B1
Park Terr C1
Park Valley C1
Park,The C1
Peas Hill Rd A3
Peel St A1
Peveril Dr C1
Plantagenet St A3
Playhouse Theatre B1
Plumptre St C3
Police Sta B1/B2
Poplar St C3
Portland Rd B1
Queen's Rd C2
Raleigh St A1
Regent St B1
Rick St B3
Robin Hood Statue C2
Robin Hood St B3
Ropewalk,The B1
Royal Centre B1
Royal Children Inn B2
Royal Concert Hall B1
St Ann's Hill Rd A1
St Ann's Way A2
St Ann's Well Rd A3
St James' St B2
St Mark's St A3
St Mary's Rest Gdn B3
St Mary's Gate B3
St Nicholas C2
St Peter's B2
St Peter's Gate B2
Salutation Inn C2
Shakespeare St B1
Shelton St A2
Shopmobility A2
South Parade B2
South Rd C1
South Sherwood St B2
Station Street [≷] C3
Stoney St B3
Talbot St B1
Tattershall Dr C1
Tennis Dr B1
Tennyson St A1
Theatre Royal B2
Trent St C2
Trent University [≷] B2
Union Rd B3
Upper Parliament St B2
Victoria Leisure Centre B3
Victoria Park B3
Victoria St B2
Walter St A1
Warser Gate B3
Watkin St A2
Waverley St A1
Wheeler Gate B2
Wilford Rd C2
Wilford St C2
Wollaton St B1
Woodborough Rd A2
Woolpack La B3
Ye Old Trip to Jerusalem C2
York St A2

Oxford 193

Adelaide St A1
Albert St A1
All Souls (Coll) B2
Ashmolean Mus B2
Balliol (Coll) B2
Banbury Rd A2
Bate Collection of Musical Instruments C2
Beaumont St B1
Becket St B1
Blackhall Rd A2
Blue Boar St B2
Bodleian Library B2
Botanic Garden B3
Brasenose (Coll) B2
Brewer St C2
Broad St B2
Burton-Taylor Theatre B2
Bus Station B1
Canal St A1
Cardigan St A1
Carfax Tower B2
Castle St B1
Catte St B2
Cemetery A1
Christ Church (Coll) B2
Christ Church Cathedral [†] C2
Christ Church Meadow C2
Clarendon Centre B2
Coach & Lorry Park C1
College B1
Coll of Further Ed C1
Cornmarket St B2
Corpus Christi (Coll) B2
County Hall B1
Covered Market B2
Cowley Place C3
Cranham St A1
Cranham Terr A1
Cricket Ground B1
Crown & County Courts C2
Deer Park B2
Exeter (Coll) B2
Folly Bridge C2
George St B1
Great Clarendon St A1
Hart St A1
Hertford (Coll) B2
High St B3
Hollybush Row B1
Holywell St B2
Hythe Bridge St B1
Ice Rink B1
Information Ctr [i] B2
Jericho St A1
Jesus (Coll) B2
Jowett Walk B3
Juxon St A1
Keble (Coll) A2
Keble Rd A2
Library C3
Linacre (Coll) A3
Lincoln (Coll) B2
Little Clarendon St A1
Longwall St B3
Magdalen (Coll) B3
Magdalen Bridge B3
Magdalen St B2
Magistrate's Court C1
Manchester (Coll) B2
Manor Rd B3
Mansfield (Coll) A3
Mansfield Rd B3
Market B2
Marlborough Rd C2
Merton (Coll) C2
Merton Field C2
Merton St C2
Museum of Modern Art B2
Mus of Oxford B2
Museum Rd A2
New College (Coll) B3
New Inn Hall St B2
New Rd B1
New Theatre B2
Norfolk St C1
Nuffield (Coll) B1
Observatory A1
Observatory St A1
Odeon B1/B2
Old Fire Station B1
Old Greyfriars St C2
Oriel (Coll) C2
Oxford Station [≷] B1
Oxford University Research Centres A1
Oxpens Rd C1
Paradise Sq C1
Paradise St B1
Park End St B1
Parks Rd A2/B2
Pembroke (Coll) C2
Phoenix A1
Picture Gallery A1
Plantation Rd A1
Playhouse B2
Police Station C2
Post Office A1/B2
Pusey St B2
Queen's (Coll) B3
Queen's La B3
Radcliffe Camera B2
Rewley Rd B1
Richmond Rd B1
Rose La C3
Ruskin (Coll) B1
Said Bsns School C1
St Aldates C2
St Antony's (Coll) A1
St Bernard's Rd A1
St Catherine's (Coll) B3
St Cross Building B3
St Cross Rd B3
St Edmund Hall (Coll) B3
St Giles St A2
St Hilda's (Coll) C3
St John St B2
St John's (Coll) B2
St Mary the Virgin B2
St Michael at the Northgate B2
St Peter's (Coll) B1
St Thomas St B1
Science Area A2
Science Museum B2
Sheldonian Theatre B2
Somerville (Coll) A1
South Parks Rd A2
Speedwell St C2
Sports Ground C3
Thames St C1
Town Hall B2
Trinity (Coll) B2
Turl St B2
Univ Coll (Coll) B2
Univ Mus & Pitt Rivers Mus A2
University Parks A2
Wadham (Coll) B2
Walton Cres A1
Walton St A1
Western Rd C2
Westgate C2
Woodstock Rd A1
Worcester (Coll) B1

Perth 193

AK Bell Library B2
Abbot Cres C1
Abbot St C1
Albany Terr A1
Albert Monument A3
Alexandra St B2
Atholl St A2
Balhousie Ave A2
Balhousie Castle & Black Watch Museum A2
Balhousie St A2
Ballantine Place A1
Barossa Place A2
Barossa St A2
Barrack St A2
Bell's Sports Ctr A2
Bellwood B3
Blair St B1
Burn Park C1
Bus Station B2
Caledonian Rd B1
Canal Cres C2
Canal St B2
Cavendish Ave C1
Charles St A2
Charlotte Place A2
Charlotte St A2
Church St A1
City Hall B2
Club House C3
Clyde Place C1
Coach Park B1
Commercial St A2
Concert Hall B2
Council Chambers B2
County Place B2
Court B2
Craigie Place C1
Crieff Rd A1
Croft Park C1
Cross St B2
Darnhall Cres C1
Darnhall Dr C1
Dewars Centre A1
Dundee Rd B3
Earl's Dykes B1
Edinburgh Rd C1
Elibank St C1
Fair Maid's Ho B2
Feus Rd A1
Fire Station B1
Foundary La A2
Friar St C1
George St B3
Glamis Place A1
Glasgow Rd B1
Glenearn Rd C2
Glover St B1/C1
Golf Course A3
Gowrie St A3
Gray St B1
Graybank Rd B1
Greyfriars Burial Grnd B3
Hay St A2
High St B2/B3
Inchaffray St A1
Ind/Retail Park C2
Information Ctr [i] B2
Isla Rd A3
James St B3
Keir St A1
King Edward St B2
King James VI Golf Course C3
King St B2
Kings Place C1
Kinnoull Causeway B1
Kinnoull St B2
Knowelea Place C1
Knowelea Terr C1
Ladeside Bsns Ctr A1
Leisure Pool A3
Leonard St B1
Lickley St A3
Lochie Brae A3
Long Causeway A1
Low St A2
Main St A3
Marshall Place C3
Melville St A2
Mill St A2
Milne St B2
Murray Cres C1
Murray St B1
Needless Rd C1
New Rd B1
North Inch A3
North Methven St A2
Park Place C2
Perth A3
Perth Bridge A3
Perth Business Pk B1
Perth Museum & Art Gallery B3
Perth Station [≷] B2
Pickletullum Rd C1
Pitheavlis Cres C1
Playhouse B2
Police Station A2
Pomarium St B1
Post Office B2/C2
Priestgate B2
Queen's Bridge B3
Queensgate Ctr C2
Railworld B1
Regional Swimming & Fitness Centre B3
River La A2
Rivergate Shopping Centre B2
Riverside Mead C3
Russell St A1
St John's A3
St Marks St A2
St Peter's [†] B2
Saxon Rd C1
Spital Bridge A3
Stagshaw Dr C1
Star Rd B3
The Weston Homes Stadium (Peterborough United) C2
Thorpe Lea Rd B1
Thorpe Rd B1
Thorpe's Lea Rd B1
Tower St A2
Town Hall B2
Viersen Platz A2
Vineyard Rd A3
Wake Rd A3
Wellington St A3
Wentworth St B2
Westgate A2
Whalley St A3
Wharf Rd A2
Whitsed St A3
YMCA A3

Peterborough 193

Athletics Arena A2
Bishop's Palace B2
Bishop's Rd B2/B3
Boongate A3
Bourges Boulevard A1
Bourges Retail Park B1/B2
Bridge House (Council Offices) C2
Bridge St B2
Bright St A1
Broadway A2
Broadway B2
Brook St A2
Burghley Rd A2
Bus Station B2
Cavendish St A3
Charles St A2
Church St B2
Church Walk B2
Cobden Ave A1
Cobden St A1
Cowgate B2
Craig St A1
Crawthorne Rd A2
Cromwell Rd A1
Dickens St A2
Eastfield Rd A3
Eastgate B3
Fire Station A2
Fitzwilliam St A2
Frank Perkins Parkway C3
Geneva St A2
George St C1
Gladstone St B1
Glebe Rd C2
Gloucester Rd C2
Granby St A3
Grove St C1
Guildhall B2
Hadrians Ct C2
Hawksbill Way C1
Henry St A1
Hereward Cross (shopping) B2
Hereward Rd B3
Information Ctr [i] B2
Jubilee St C1
Kent Rd A3
Key Theatre C2
Kirkwood Cl A1
Lea Gdns B1
Library A2
Lincoln Rd A2
London Rd C2
Long Causeway B2
Lower Bridge St C2
Magistrates Court C2
Manor House St A1
Mayor's Walk A1
Midland Rd A1
Monument St A1
Morris St A3
Museum & Art Gallery B2
Nene Valley Railway [≷] C1
New Rd B2
Northminster B2
Old Customs Ho C2
Oundle Rd C1
Padholme Rd A3
Palmerston Rd C1
Park Rd A2
Passport Office A2
Peterborough Nene Valley [≷] C1
Peterborough Station [≷] B1
Police Station B2
Post Office A3/B1/B2/B3/C1
Priestgate B2
Queen's Walk C2
Queensgate Ctr B2
Railworld B1
Regional Swimming & Fitness Centre B3
River La A2
Rivergate Shopping Centre B2
Riverside Mead C3
Russell St A1
St John's B2
St Marks St A1
St Peter's [†] B2
Saxon Rd C1
Spital Bridge A1
Stagshaw Dr C1
Star Rd B3

Plymouth 193

Alma Rd A2/A3
Anstis St A1
Armada Shopping Ctr B2
Armada St A3
Armada Way B2
Arts Centre A2
Athenaeum B1
Athenaeum St B1
Barbican C3
Barbican [▨] C3
Baring St A3
Bath St B1
Beaumont Park A3
Beaumont Rd A3
Black Friars Gin Distillery C3
Breton Side B3
Castle St C3
Cathedral (RC) [†] B1
Cecil St A1
Central Park A1
Central Park Ave A1
Charles Church [†] B3
Charles Cross B3
Charles St B2
Citadel Rd C1
Citadel Rd East C2
City Museum & Art Gallery A2
Civic Centre B2
Cliff Rd C1
Clifton Place A2
Cobourg St A2
College of Art A2
Continental Ferry Port A1
Cornwall St B2
Crescent,The B1
Dale Rd A1
Deptford Place A3
Derry Ave A2
Derry's Cross B1
Drake Circus B2
Drake Circus Shopping Centre B2
Eastlake St B2
Ebrington St B3
Elizabethan Ho C3
Elliot St C1
Endsleigh Place A2
Exeter St B3
Fire Station B2
Fish Quay C3
Gibbons St A3
Glen Park Ave A2
Grand Parade C1
Great Western Rd C1
Greenbank Rd A3
Greenbank Terr A3
Guildhall B2
Hampton St B3
Harwell St A1
Hastings St A1
Hill Park Cres A3
Hoe Approach C2
Hoe Rd C2
Hoe,The C2
Hoegate St C2
Houndiscombe Rd A2
Information Ctr [i] B3
James St A2
Kensington Rd A3
King St B1
Lambhay Hill C3
Lipson Rd A3/B3
Lockyer St C2
Lockyers Quay C3
Looe St B3
Madeira Rd C2
Marina C3
Market Ave B1
Martin St B1
Mayflower St B2
Mayflower Stone & Steps C2
Mayflower Visitor Centre C2
Merchant's Ho B2
Millbay Rd C1
National Marine Aquarium C3
Neswick St B1
New George St B2
New St C3
North Cross A2
North Hill A3
North Quay B1
North Rd East A2
North Rd West A1
North St A3
Notte St C2
Octagon,The B1
Octagon St B1
Pannier Market B1
Pennycomequick A2
Pier St C1
Plymouth Naval Memorial C1
Plymouth Pavilions B1
Plymouth Sta [≷] A2
Police Station A2
Post Office B2/C2
Princess St C2
Promenade,The C1
Prysten House C2
Queen Anne's Battery Seasports Centre C3
Radford Rd C1
Reel B2
Regent St B3
Rope Walk C3
Royal Citadel C2
Royal Pde B2
Royal Theatre B2
St Andrew's B2
St Andrew's Cross B2
St Andrew's St B2
St Lawrence Rd A2
Saltash Rd A1
Shopmobility B2
Smeaton's Tower C2
Southern Terr A3
Southside St C3
Stuart Rd A1
Sutherland Rd A2
Sutton Rd B3
Sydney St A1
Teats Hill Rd C3
Tothill Ave A3
Union St B1
Univ of Plymouth A2
Vauxhall St B2/3
Victoria Park A1
West Hoe Rd C1
Western Approach B1
Whittington St A1
Wyndham St A1
YMCA B2
YWCA A2

Poole 194

Ambulance Station A3
Baiater Gdns C2
Baiter Park C3
Ballard Cl C2
Ballard Rd C2
Bay Hog La B1
Bridge Approach B1
Bus Station B1
Castle St B2
Catalina Dr A3
Chapel La B2
Church St B1
Cinnamon La B1
Colborne Cl B3
Dear Hay La B2
Denmark La A3
Denmark Rd A3
Dolphin Ctr B2
East St B2
Elizabeth Rd A3
Emerson Rd B2
Ferry Rd C1
Ferry Terminal C1
Fire Station B3
Freightliner Terminal A1/B3
Furnell Rd B2
Garland Rd A3
Green Rd B2
Heckford La A3
Heckford Rd A3
High St B2
High St North A3
Hill St B2
Holes Bay Rd A1
Hospital (A&E) [H] A3
Information Ctr [i] C2
Kingland Rd B3
Kingston Rd A3
Labrador Dr C3
Lagland St B3
Lander Cl B3
Lifeboat Coll,The C1
Lighthouse, Poole Ctr for the Arts B2
Longfleet Rd A3
Maple Rd A3
Market Cl B2
Market St B2
Mount Pleasant Rd B3
New Harbour Rd South C1
New Harbour Rd West C1
New Orchard B2
New Quay Rd C2
New St B2
Newfoundland Dr B1
Old Lifeboat C1
Old Orchard B2
Parish Rd A3
Park Lake Rd B3
Parkstone Rd A3
Perry Gdns B2

Portsmouth 194

Action Stations C1
Admiralty Rd A1
Alfred Rd A2
Anglesea Rd B2
Arundel St B3
Aspex C2
Bishop St A2
Broad St C1
Buckingham Ho C2
Burnaby Rd B2
Bus Station B1
Camber Dock C1
Cambridge Rd B2
Car Ferry to Isle of Wight B1
Cascades Shopping Centre A3
Castle Rd C2
Civic Offices B3
Clarence Pier C2
College St B1
Commercial Rd A3
Cottage Grove C3
Cross St B1
Cumberland St A1
Duisburg Way C2
Durham St A3
East St B1
Edinburgh Rd A2
Elm Grove C3
Emirates Spinnaker Tower B1
Governor's Grn C1
Great Southsea St C3
Green Rd C3
Greetham St B3
Grosvenor St C3
Groundlings A2
Grove Rd North C3
Grove Rd South C3
Guildhall B3
Guildhall Walk B3
Gunwharf Quays Designer Outlet B1
Gunwharf Rd B1
Hambrook St C2
Hampshire Terrace B2
Hanover St A1
Hard,The B1
High St C1
HM Naval Base A1
HMS Nelson (Royal Naval Barracks) A2
HMS Monitor M.33 B1
HMS Victory A1
HMS Warrior A1
Hovercraft Terminal C2
Hyde Park Rd B3
Information Ctr [i] A1/B3
Isambard Brunel Rd B3
Isle of Wight Car Ferry Terminal B1
Kent Rd C2
Kent St A2
King St B2
King's Rd C2
King's Terr C2
Lake Rd A3
Law Courts B3
Library B3
Long Curtain Rd C1
Marina B1
Market Way A3
Marmion Rd C3
Mary Rose B1
Middle St B3
Millennium Prom Walk B1/C1
Museum Rd B2
National Museum of the Royal Navy A1
Naval Rec Gd C2
Nightingale Rd C3
Norfolk St B3
North St C2
Osborne Rd C3
Paradise St A3
Park Rd B2
Passenger Catamaran to Isle of Wight B1
Passenger Ferry to Gosport A1
Pelham Rd C3
Pembroke Gdns C2
Pier Rd C2
Point Battery C1
Police Station B3
Portsmouth & Southsea Sta [≷] A3

Portsmouth Harbour Station B1
Portsmouth Historic Dockyard A1
Portsmouth Museum & Art Gallery B2
Post Office A1/A3/B3
Queen St A1
Queen's Cres C3
Ravelin Park B2
Register Office B2
Round Tower C1
Royal Garrison Church C1
St Edward's Rd C3
St George's Rd B2
St George's Sq B1
St George's Way B2
St James's Rd B3
St James's St A2
St John's Cathedral (RC) A3
St Thomas's Cath C1
St Thomas's St B2
Shopmobility A3/B1
Somers Rd B3
Southsea Common C2
Southsea Terr C2
Square Tower C1
Station St A3
Town Fortifications C1
Unicorn Rd A2
United Services Recreation Ground B2
University of Portsmouth A2/B2
Univ of Portsmouth B3
Upper Arundel St A3
Victoria Ave C2
Victoria Park A2
Victory Gate A1
Vue B1
Warblington St B1
Western Pde C2
White Hart Rd C1
Winston Churchill Ave B3

Preston 194

Adelphi St A2
Anchor Ct B3
Aqueduct St A1
Ardee Rd C1
Arthur St B2
Ashton St A1
Avenham La B3
Avenham Park C3
Avenham Rd B3
Avenham St B3
Bairstow St B3
Balderstone Rd C1
Beamont Dr A1
Beech St South C2
Bird St C1
Bow La B2
Brieryfield Rd A1
Broadgate C1
Brook St A2
Bus Station A3
Butler St B2
Cannon St B3
Carlton St A1
Chaddock St B3
Channel Way B1
Chapel St B3
Christ Church St B2
Christian Rd B2
Cold Bath St A2
Coleman Ct C1
Connaught Rd C2
Corn Exchange B3
Corporation St A2/B2
County Hall B2
Cricket Ground C2
Croft St A1
Cross St B3
Crown Court A3
Crown St A3
East Cliff C3
East Cliff Rd B3
Edward St A2
Elizabeth St A3
Euston St B1
Fishergate B2/B3
Fishergate Hill B2
Fishergate Shopping Centre B2
Fitzroy St B1
Fleetwood St A1
Friargate A3
Fylde Rd A1/A2
Gerrard St B2
Glover's Ct B3
Good St B2
Grafton St B2
Great George St A3
Great Shaw St A3
Greenbank St A2
Guild Way B1
Guild Hall & Charter B3
Guildhall St B3
Harrington St A2
Harris Museum B3
Hartington Rd B1
Hasset Cl C2
Heatley St B2
Hind St C2
Information Ctr B3
Kilruddery Rd C1
Lancashire Archives B2
Lancaster Rd A3/B3
Latham St B3
Lauderdale St C2
Lawson St A3
Leighton St A2
Leyland Rd C1
Library A1
Library B3
Liverpool Rd C1
Lodge St B2
Lune St B3
Magistrate's Court A3
Main Sprit West B3
Maresfield Rd C1
Market St West A3
Marsh La B1/B2
Maudland Bank A2
Maudland Rd A2
Meadow Ct C2
Meath Rd C1
Mill Hill A2
Miller Arcade B3
Miller Park C3
Moor La A3
Mount St B3
North Rd A3
North St A3
Northcote Rd B1
Old Milestones B1
Old Tram Rd C3
Pedder St A1/A2
Peel St A2
Penwortham Bridge C2
Penwortham New Bridge C1
Pitt St B2
Playhouse A3
Police Station A3
Port Way B1
Post Office B3
Preston Station B2
Retail Park B2
Ribble Bank St B2
Ribble Viaduct C2
Ribblesdale Place B3
Ringway B3
River Parade C1
Riverside C2
St George's Shopping Centre B3
St Georges B3
St Johns B3
St Johns Shopping Centre A3
St Mark's Rd A1
St Walburges A1
Salisbury Rd B1
Sessions House B3
Snow Hill A3
South End C2
South Meadow La C2
Spa Rd B1
Sports Ground C2
Strand Rd B1
Syke St B3
Talbot Rd B1
Taylor St C1
Tithebarn St A3
Town Hall B3
Tulketh Brow A1
University of Central Lancashire A2
Valley Rd C1
Victoria St A2
Walker St A3
Walton's Parade B2
Warwick St A3
Wellfield Bsns Park A1
Wellfield Rd A1
Wellington St A1
West Cliff C2
West Strand A1
Winckley Rd C1
Winckley Square B3
Wolseley Rd C2

Reading 194

Abbey Ruins B2
Abbey Sq B2
Abbey St B2
Abbot's Walk B2
Acacia Rd C2
Addington Rd C3
Addison Rd A1
Allcroft Rd C3
Alpine St C2
Baker St B1
Berkeley Ave C1
Bridge St B1
Brigham Rd A1
Broad St B1
Broad Street Mall B1
Carey St B1
Castle Hill C1
Castle St B1
Causeway, The A3
Caversham Rd A1
Christchurch Playing Fields A2
Civic Offices B1
Coley Hill C1
Coley Place C1
Craven Rd C3
Crown St C2
De Montfort Rd A1
Denmark Rd C3
Duke St B2
East St B2
Edgehill St C2
Eldon Rd B3
Eldon Terr B3
Elgar Rd C1
Erleigh Rd C3
Field Rd C1
Fire Station A1
Fobney St B1
Forbury Gdns B2
Forbury Rd B2
Forbury Retail Park B2
Francis St C1
Friar St B1
Garrard St B1
Gas Works Rd B3
George St A2
Great Knollys St B1
Greyfriars B1
Grove, The B2
Gun St B1
Henry St C1
Hexagon Theatre, The B1
Hill's Meadow A2
Howard St B1
Inner Distribution Rd B1
Katesgrove La C1
Kenavon Dr B2
Kendrick Rd C2
King's Meadow Recreation Gd A2
King's Rd B2
Library B2
London Rd C3
London St B2
Lynmouth Rd A1
Magistrate's Court B1
Market Place B2
Mill La B2
Mill Rd A2
Minster St B1
Morgan Rd C3
Mount Pleasant C2
Museum of English Rural Life C3
Napier Rd A2
Newark St C2
Newport Rd A1
Old Reading Univ C3
Oracle Shopping Centre, The B1
Orts Rd B3
Pell St C1
Police Station B1
Post Office B2
Queen Victoria St B1
Queen's Rd A2
Queen's Rd B2
Randolph Rd A1
Reading Bridge A2
Reading Station A1
Redlands Rd C3
Renaissance Hotel B1
Riverside Mus B3
Rose Kiln La C1
Royal Berks Hospital (A&E) C3
St Giles C2
St Laurence B2
St Mary's B1
St Mary's Butts B1
St Saviour's Rd C1
Send Rd A3
Sherman Rd C2
Sidmouth St B2
Silver St C2
South St B2
Southampton St C2
Station Hill A1
Station Rd B1
Superstore A3
Swansea Rd A1
Technical College B3
Valpy St B2
Vastern Rd A1
Vue B2
Waldeck St C2
Watlington St B3
West St B1
Whitby Dr C3
Wolseley St C1
York Rd A1
Zinzan St B1

St Andrews 195

Abbey St B2
Abbey Walk B3
Abbotsford Cres A1
Albany Pk C3
Allan Robertson Dr C2
Ambulance Station C1
Anstruther Rd C3
Argyle St B1
Auld Burn Rd B2
Bassaguard Ind Est B1
Bell St B2
Blackfriars Chapel (Ruins) B2
Boase Ave B2
Braid Cres C3
Brewster Place C3
Bridge St B1
British Golf Mus A1
Broomfaulds Ave C1
Bruce Embankment A1
Bruce St C2
Bus Station A1
Byre Theatre B2
Canongate C1
Cathedral and Priory (Ruins) B3
Cemetery B3
Chamberlain St C1
Church St B2
Churchill Cres C2
City Rd A1
Claybraes C1
Cockshaugh Public Park B1
Cosmos Com Ctr B3
Council Office A2
Crawford Gdns C1
Doubledykes Rd B1
Drumcarrow Rd C1
East Sands B3
East Scores A3
Fire Station C1
Forrest St C1
Fraser Ave C1
Freddie Tait St C2
Gateway Centre A1
Glebe Rd B2
Golf Place A1
Grange Rd C3
Greenside Place B2
Greyfriars Gdns A2
Hamilton Ave C2
Hepburn Gdns B1
Holy Trinity B2
Horseleys Park C1
Information Ctr B2
Irvine Cres C3
James Robb Ave C1
James St B1
John Knox Rd C1
Kennedy Gdns B1
Kilrymont Close C3
Kilrymont Place C3
Kilrymont Rd C3
Kinburn Park B1
Kinkell Terr C3
Kinnesburn Rd B2
Ladebraes Walk B2
Lady Buchan's Cave A3
Lamberton Place C1
Lamond Dr C2
Langlands Rd B2
Largo Rd C1
Learmonth Place C1
Library B2
Links Clubhouse A1
Links, The A1
Livingstone Cres B2
Long Rocks A2
Madras College B2
Market St A2
Martyr's Monument A1
Murray Pk A2
Murray Place A2
Mus of the Univ of St Andrews (MUSA) A2
Nelson St B2
New Course, The A1
New Picture Ho A2
North Castle St A3
North St A2
Old Course, The A1
Old Station Rd A1
Pends, The B3
Pilmour Links A1
Pipeland Rd B2/C2
Police Sta A2/C1
Post Office B2
Preservation Trust B2
Priestden Pk C3
Priestden Place C3
Priestden Rd C3
Queen's Gdns B2
Queen's Terr B2
Roundhill Rd C2
Royal & Ancient Golf Club A1
St Andrews B1
St Andrews Aquarium A2
St Andrews Botanic Garden B1
St Andrews Castle (Ruins) & Visitor Centre A2
St Leonard's Sch B3
St Mary St B3
St Mary's College B2
St Nicholas St C3
St Rules Tower B3
St Salvator's Coll A2
Sandyhill Cres C2
Sandyhill Rd C2
Scooniehill Rd C2
Scores, The A2
Shields Ave C3
Shoolbraids C2
Shore, The B3
Sloan St B1
South St B2
Spottiswoode Gdns C1
Station Rd A1
Swilcen Bridge A1
Tom Morris Dr C2
Tom Stewart La C1
Town Hall B2
Union St A2
Univ Chapel A2
University Library A2
Univ of St Andrews A1
Viaduct Walk B1
War Memorial A3
Wardlaw Gdns B1
Warrack St C3
Watson Ave B2
West Port B2
West Sands A1
Westview B2
Windmill Rd A1
Winram Place C1
Wishart Gdns C2
Woodburn Pk B3
Woodburn Place B3
Woodburn Terr B3
Younger Hall A2

Salisbury 195

Albany Rd A2
Arts Centre A3
Ashley Rd A1
Avon Approach A2
Ayleswade Rd C2
Bedwin St A2
Belle Vue A2
Bishop's Palace C2
Bishops Walk B2
Blue Boar Row B2
Bourne Ave A3
Bourne Hill A3
Britford La C2
Broad Walk C2
Brown St B2
Bus Station B2
Castle St A2
Catherine St B2
Chapter House B2
Church House B2
Churchfields Rd B1
Churchill Way East B3
Churchill Way North A3
Churchill Way South C2
Churchill Way West A1
City Hall B2
Close Wall B2
Coldharbour La A1
College St A3
Council Offices A3
Court A1
Crane Bridge Rd B2
Crane St B2
Cricket Ground C1
Culver St South B3
De Vaux Place C2
Devizes Rd A1
Dews Rd B1
Elm Grove B3
Elm Grove Rd A3
Endless St A2
Estcourt Rd A3
Exeter St C2
Fairview Rd A3
Fire Station A1
Fisherton St A1
Folkestone Rd C1
Fowlers Hill B3
Fowlers Rd B3
Friary Estate C3
Friary La B2
Friary, The B3
Gas La A1
Gigant St B3
Greencroft B3
Greencroft St A3
Guildhall B2
Hall of John Halle B2
Hamilton Rd A2
Harnham Mill B1
Harnham Rd C1/C2
High St B2
Hospital A1
House of John A'Port B2
Information Ctr B2
Kelsey Rd A3
King's Rd A2
Laverstock Rd B3
Library B2
London Rd A3
Lower St C1
Maltings, The B2
Manor Rd A3
Marsh La A1
Medieval Hall B2
Milford Hill B3
Milford St B3
Mill Rd B1
Millstream Approach A2
Mompesson House (NT) B2
New Bridge Rd C2
New Canal B2
New Harnham Rd C2
New St B2
North Canonry B2
North Gate B2
North Walk B2
Old Blandford Rd C1
Old Deanery B2
Old George Hall B2
Park St A3
Parsonage Green C1
Playhouse Theatre A2
Post Office A2/B2/C2
Poultry Cross B2
Queen Elizabeth Gardens B1
Queen's Rd A3
Rampart Rd B3
St Ann St B2
St Ann's Gate B2
St Marks Rd A3
St Martins B3
St Mary's Cath B2
St Nicholas Hosp C2
St Paul's A1
St Paul's Rd A1
St Thomas B2
Salisbury & South Wiltshire Mus B2
Salisbury Station A1
Salt La A3
Saxon Rd C1
Scots La A2
Shady Bower B3
South Canonry C2
South Gate C2
Southampton Rd B2
Spire View A1
Sports Ground C3
Tollgate Rd B3
Town Path B1
Wain-a-Long Rd A3
Wardrobe, The B2
Wessex Rd A3
West Walk C2
Wilton Rd A1
Wiltshire College B3
Winchester St B3
Windsor Rd A1
Winston Churchill Gdns C3
Wyndham Rd A2
YHA B3
York Rd A1

Scarborough 195

Aberdeen Walk B2
Albert Rd A2
Albion Rd C2
Auborough St B2
Balmoral Ctr B2
Belle Vue St C1
Belmont Rd C2
Blenheim Terrace A2
Brunswick Shopping Centre B2
Castle Dykes B3
Castle Hill A3
Castle Rd B2
Castle Walls A3
Castlegate B3
Cemetery B1
Central Tramway B2
Coach Park B1
Columbus Ravine A1
Court B1
Crescent, The C2
Cricket Ground A1
Cross St B2
Crown Terrace C2
Dean Rd B1
Devonshire Dr A1
East Harbour B3
East Pier B3
Eastborough B2
Elmville Ave B1
Esplanade C2
Falconers Rd B2
Falsgrave Rd C1
Fire Station B2
Foreshore Rd B2
Friargate B2
Gladstone Rd B1
Gladstone St B1
Hollywood Plaza A1
Holms, The A3
Hoxton Rd B1
King St B2
Library B2
Lifeboat Station B3
Londesborough Rd C1
Longwestgate B3
Marine Dr A3
Luna Park B3
Miniature Railway A1
Nelson St B1
Newborough B2
Nicolas St B2
North Marine Rd A1
North St B2
Northway B1
Old Harbour B3
Olympia Leisure B2
Peasholm Park A1
Peasholm Rd A1
Police Station B1
Post Office B2
Princess St B3
Prospect Rd B1
Queen St B2
Queen's Parade A2
Queen's Tower (Remains) A3
Ramshill Rd C2
Roman Signal Station A3
Roscoe St C1
Rotunda Mus C2
Royal Albert Dr A2
Royal Albert Park A2
St Martin-on-the-Hill C2
St Martin's Ave C2
St Mary's B3
St Thomas St B2
Sandside B3
Scarborough C1
Scarborough Art Gallery C2
Scarborough Bowls Centre A1
Scarborough Castle A3
Shopmobility C2
Somerset Terr C2
South Cliff Lift C2
Spa Theatre, The C2
Spa, The C2
Stephen Joseph Theatre C1
Tennyson Ave B1
Tollergate B2
Town Hall B2
Trafalgar Rd B1
Trafalgar Square A1
Trafalgar St West B1
Valley Bridge Par C2
Valley Rd C1
Vernon Rd C2
Victoria Park Mount A1
Victoria Rd B1
West Pier B3
Westborough C1
Westover Rd C1
Westwood C1
Woodall Ave A1
YMCA Theatre B2
York Place B2
Yorkshire Coast College (Westwood Campus) C1

Sheffield 196

Addy Dr A2
Addy St A2
Adelphi St A3
Albert Terrace Rd A3
Albion St A2
Aldred Rd A1
Allen St A4
Alma St A4
Angel St B5
Arundel Gate B5
Arundel St C4
Ashberry Rd A2
Ashdell Rd C1
Ashgate Rd C1
Athletics Centre B2
Attercliffe Rd A6
Bailey St B4
Ball St A4
Balm Green B4
Bank St B4
Barber Rd A2
Bard St B5
Barker's Pool B4
Bates St A1
Beech Hill Rd C1
Beet St B3
Bellefield St A3
Bernard Rd A6
Bernard St B6
Birkendale A2
Birkendale Rd A2
Birkendale View A1
Bishop St C4
Blackwell Place B6
Blake St A2
Blonk St A5
Bolsover St B2
Botanical Gdns C1
Bower Rd A1
Bradley St A1
Bramall La C4
Bramwell St A3
Bridge St A4/A5
Brighton Terr Rd A1
Broad La B3
Broad St B6
Brocco St A3
Brook Hill B3
Broomfield Rd C1
Broomgrove Rd C2
Broomhall Place C3
Broomhall Rd C2
Broomhall St C3
Broomspring La C2
Brown St C5
Brunswick St B3
Burgess St B4
Burlington St A2
Burns Rd A2
Cadman St A6
Cambridge St B4
Campo La B4
Carver St B4
Castle Square B5
Castlegate A5
Cathedral B4
Cathedral (RC) B4
Cavendish St B3
Charles St C4
Charter Row C4
Children's Hosp B2
Church St B4
City Hall B4
City Hall B4
City Rd C6
Claremont Cres B2
Claremont Place B2
Clarke St C3
Clarkegrove Rd C2
Clarkehouse Rd C1
Clarkson St B2
Cobden View Rd A1
Collegiate Cres C2
Commercial St B5
Commonside A1
Conduit Rd B1
Cornish St A3
Corporation St A4
Cricket Inn Rd B6
Cromwell St A1
Crookes Rd B1
Crookes Valley Park B2
Crookes Valley Rd B2
Crookesmoor Rd A2
Crown Court A4
Crucible Theatre B5
Cutlers' Hall B4
Cutlers Gate A6
Daniel Hill A2
Dental Hospital B2
Derek Dooley Way A5
Devonshire Green B3
Devonshire St B3
Division St B4
Dorset St C2
Dover St A3
Duchess Rd C5
Duke St B5
Duncombe St A1
Durham Rd B2
Earl St C4
Earl Way C4
Ecclesall Rd C3
Edward St B3
Effingham Rd A6
Effingham St A6
Egerton St C3
Eldon St B3
Elmore Rd B1
Exchange St B5
Eyre St C4
Fargate B4
Farm Rd C5
Fawcett St A3
Filey St B3
Fir St A1
Fire Station C4
Fitzalan Sq/Ponds Forge B5
Fitzwater Rd C6
Fitzwilliam Gate C4
Fitzwilliam St B3
Flat St B5
Foley St A6
Foundry Climbing Centre A4
Fulton Rd A1
Furnace Hill A4
Furnival Rd A5
Furnival Sq C4
Furnival St C4
Garden St B3
Gell St B3
Gibraltar St A4
Glebe Rd B1
Glencoe Rd C6
Glossop Rd B2/B3/C1
Gloucester St C2
Government Offices C4
Granville Rd C6
Granville Rd / The Sheffield Coll C5
Graves Gallery B5
Green La A4
Hadfield St A1
Hanover St C3
Hanover Way C3
Harcourt Rd B1
Harmer La B5
Havelock St C2
Hawley St B4
Haymarket B5
Headford St C3
Heavygate Rd A1
Henry St A3
High St B4
Hodgson St C3
Holberry Gdns C2
Hollis Croft B4
Holly St B4
Hounsfield Rd B3
Howard Rd A1
Hoyle St A3
Hyde Park A6
Infirmary Rd A3
Infirmary Rd A3
Jericho St A3
Johnson St A5
Kelham Island Industrial Mus A4
Lawson Rd C1
Leadmill Rd C5
Leadmill St C5
Leadmill, The C5
Leamington St A1
Leavygreave Rd B3
Lee Croft B4
Leopold St B4
Leveson St A6
Library A2/B5/C1
Light, The C4
Lyceum Theatre B5
Malinda St A3
Maltravers St A5
Manor Oaks Rd B6
Mappin St B3
Marlborough Rd B1
Mary St C4
Matilda St C4
Matlock Rd A1
Meadow St A3
Melbourn Rd A1
Melbourne Ave C1
Millennium Galleries B5
Milton St C3
Mitchell St B3
Mona Ave A1
Mona Rd A1
Montgomery Terrace Rd A3
Montgomery Theatre B4
Monument Grounds C6
Moor Oaks Rd B1
Moor, The C4
Moor, The C4
Moor Market C4
Moore St C3
Mowbray St A4
Mushroom La B2
National Emergency Service A4
National Videogame B5
Netherthorpe Rd B3
Netherthorpe Rd B3
Newbould La C1
Nile St C1
Norfolk Park Rd C6
Norfolk Rd C6
Norfolk St B4
North Church St B4
Northfield Rd A1
Northumberland Rd B1
Nursery St A5
O2 Academy B5
Oakholme Rd C1
Octagon B2
Odeon B5
Old St B6
Orchard Square B4
Orchard Square Shopping Ctr B4
Oxford St A2
Paradise St B4
Park La C2
Park Sq B5
Parker's Rd B1
Pearson Building (Univ) C2
Penistone Rd A3
Pinstone St B4
Pitt St B3
Police Station B5
Pond Hill B5
Pondorosa, The A2
Pond St B5
Ponds Forge Int Sports Ctr B5
Portobello St B3
Post Office A2/B3/B5/C1/C3/C4/C6
Powell St A2
Queen St B4
Queen's Rd C5
Ramsey Rd B1
Red Hill B3
Redcar Rd B1
Regent St B3
Rockingham St B4
Roebuck Rd A2
Royal Hallamshire Hospital C2
Russell St A4
Rutland Park C1
St George's Cl B3
St Mary's Gate C3
St Mary's Rd C4/C5
St Philip's Rd A3
Savile St A5
School Rd B1
Scotland St A4
Severn Rd B1
Shalesmoor A4
Shalesmoor A3
Sheaf St B5
Sheffield Cath B4
Sheffield Hallam University B5
Sheffield Ice Sports Centre – Skate Central C5
Sheffield Institute of Arts B5
Sheffield Interchange B5
Sheffield Parkway A6
Sheffield Station C5
Sheffield Station/ Sheffield Hallam University B5
Sheffield University B2
Shepherd St A3
Shipton St A2
Shopmobility B3
Shoreham St C4
Showroom C5
Shrewsbury Rd C5
Sidney St C4
Site Gallery C5
Slinn St A1
Smithfield A4
Snig Hill A5
Snow La A4
Solly St B3
South La C4
South Street Park B5
Southbourne Rd C1
Spital Hill A5
Spital St A5
Spring Hill B1
Spring Hill Rd B1
Springvale Rd A1
Stafford Rd C6
Stafford St B6
Suffolk Rd C5
Summer St B2
Sunny Bank C3
Superstore A3/C3
Surrey St B4
Sussex St A6
Sutton St B3
Sydney Rd A2
Sylvester St C4
Talbot St B5
Taptonville Rd B1
Tenter St B4
Town Hall B4
Townend St A1
Townhead St B4
Trafalgar St B4
Tree Root Walk B2
Trinity St A4
Trippet La B4
Turner Museum of Glass B3
Union St B4
University Drama Studio B2
Univ of Sheffield B3
Upper Allen St A3
Upper Hanover St B3
Upperthorpe Rd A2/A3
Verdon St A5
Victoria Rd C2
Victoria St B3
Waingate B5
Watery St A3
Watson Rd C1
Wellesley Rd B2
Wellington St C3
West Bar A4
West Bar Green A4
West One Plaza B3
West St B3
West St B3
Westbourne Rd C1
Western Bank B2
Western Rd A1
Weston Park B2
Weston Park Hospital B2
Weston Park Museum B2
Weston St B2
Wharncliffe Rd C3
Whitham Rd B1
Wicker A5
Wilkinson St B2
William St C3
Winter Garden B4
Winter St B2
York St B4
Yorkshire Artspace C5
Young St C4

Shrewsbury 195

Abbey Church B3
Abbey Foregate B3
Abbey Lawn Business Park B3
Abbots House B2
Agricultural Show Ground A1
Albert St A2
Alma St B1
Ashley St A3
Ashton Rd C1
Avondale Dr A3
Bage Way C3
Barker St B1
Beacall's La A2
Beeches La C2
Beehive La C1
Belle Vue Gdns C2
Belle Vue Rd C2
Belmont Bank C1
Berwick Ave A1
Berwick Rd A1
Betton St C2
Bishop St B3
Bradford St B3
Bridge St B1
Burton St A3
Bus Station B2
Butcher Row B2
Butler Rd C1
Bynner St C2
Canon St B3
Canonbury C1
Castle Business Park, The A2
Castle Foregate A2
Castle Gates B2
Castle Museum B2
Castle St B2
Cathedral (RC) C1
Chester St A2
Cineworld C3
Claremont Bank B1
Claremont Hill B1
Cleveland St B3
Coleham Head B2
Coleham Pumping Station C2
College Hill B1
Corporation La A1
Coton Cres A1
Coton Hill A2
Coton Mount A1
Crescent La C1
Crewe St A2
Cross Hill B1
Dana, The B2
Darwin Centre B2
Dingle, The B1
Dogpole B2
Draper's Hall B2
English Bridge B2
Fish St B2
Frankwell B1
Gateway Centre, The A2
Gravel Hill La A1
Greyfriars Rd C2
Guildhall B1
Hampton Rd A3
Haycock Way C3
High St B1
Hills La B1
Holywell St B3
Hunter St A1
Information Ctr B1
Ireland's Mansion & Bear Steps B1
John St A3
Kennedy Rd C1
King St B3
Kingsland Bridge C1
Kingsland Bridge (toll) C1
Kingsland Rd C1
Library B2
Lime St C2
Longden Coleham C2
Longden Rd C1
Longner St B1
Luciefelde Rd C1
Mardol B1
Marine Terr C2
Market B1
Monkmoor Rd B3
Moreton Cres C2
Mount St A1
New Park Cl A3
New Park Rd A2
New Park St A3
North St A2
Oakley St C1
Old Coleham C2
Old Market Hall B1
Old Potts Way C3
Parade Centre B2
Police Station B1
Post Office A2/B1/B2/B3
Pride Hill B1
Pride Hill Centre B1
Priory Rd B1
Pritchard Way C3
Quarry, The B1
Queen St A3
Raby Cres C2
Rad Brook C1
Rea Brook C3
Riverside B1
Roundhill La A1
St Alkmund's B2
St Chad's B1
St Chad's Terr B1
St John's Hill B1
St Julians Friars C2
St Mary's B2
St Mary's St B2
Salters La C2
Scott St C3
Severn Bank A3
Severn St A2
Shrewsbury B2
Shrewsbury High School for Girls C1
Shrewsbury Mus & Art Gallery B1
Shrewsbury School C1
Shropshire Wildlife Trust B3
Smithfield Rd B1
South Hermitage C1
Square, The B1
Swan Hill B1
Sydney Ave A3
Tankerville St B3
Tilbrook Dr A3
Town Walls C1
Trinity St C2
Underdale Rd B3
Victoria Ave B1
Victoria Quay B1
Victoria St B2
Welsh Bridge B1
Whitehall St B3
Wood St A2
Wyle Cop B2

Southampton 196

Above Bar St A2
Albert Rd North B3
Albert Rd South C3
Andersons Rd B3
Argyle Rd A2
Arundel Tower B1
Bargate, The B2
BBC Regional Ctr A1
Bedford Place A1
Belvidere Rd A3
Bernard St C2
Blechynden Terr A1
Brinton's Rd A2
Britannia Rd A3
Briton St C2
Brunswick Place A2
Bugle St C1
Canute Rd C3
Castle Way C2
Catchcold Tower B1
Central Bridge C3
Central Rd C2
Channel Way C3
Chapel Rd B3
City Art Gallery A1
City College B3
City Cruise Terminal C1
Civic Centre A1
Civic Centre Rd A1
Coach Station B1
Commercial Rd A1
Cumberland Place A1
Cunard Rd C2
Derby Rd A3
Devonshire Rd A1
Dock Gate 4 C2
Dock Gate 8 B1
East Park (Andrew's Park) A2
East Park Terr A2
East St B2
Endle St B3
European Way C2
Fire Station A2
Floating Bridge Rd C3
God's Ho Tower C2
Golden Grove A3
Graham Rd A2
Guildhall A1
Hanover Buildings B2
Harbour Lights C3
Harbour Pde B1
Hartington Rd A3
Havelock Rd A1
Henstead Rd A1
Herbert Walker Ave B1
High St B2
Hoglands Park B2
Holy Rood (Rems), Merchant Navy Memorial B2
Houndwell Park B2
Houndwell Place B2
Hythe Ferry C2
Information Ctr A1
Isle of Wight Ferry Terminal C1
James St B3
Kingsway A2
Leisure World B1
Library A1
Lime St B2
London Rd A2
Marine Pde B3
Marlands Shopping Centre, The A1
Marsh La B2
Mayflower Meml C1
Mayflower Park C1
Mayflower Theatre, The A1
Medieval Merchant's House C1
Melbourne St B3
Millais A2
Morris Rd A1
National Oceanography Centre C3
Neptune Way C3
New Rd A2
Nichols Rd A3
North Front A2
Northam Rd A3
Ocean Dock C2
Ocean Village Marina C3
Ocean Way C3
Odeon B1
Ogle Rd B1
Old Northam Rd A2
Orchard La B2
Oxford Ave A2
Oxford St C2
Palmerston Park A2
Palmerston Rd A2
Parsonage Rd A3
Peel St A3
Platform Rd C2
Polygon, The A1
Portland Terr B1
Post Office A2/A3/B2
Pound Tree Rd B2
Quays Swimming & Diving Complex, The B1
Queen's Park C2
Queen's Peace Fountain A2
Queen's Terr C2
Queensway B2
Radcliffe Rd A3
Rochester St A3
Royal Pier C1
Royal South Hants Hospital A2
St Andrew's Rd A2
St Mary's B3
St Mary St A2
St Mary's Leisure Centre A2
St Mary's Place B2
St Mary's Rd A2
St Mary's Stadium (Southampton FC) A3
St Michael's C1
Sea City Mus A1
Showcase Cinema de Lux B1
Solent Sky C3
South Front B2
Southampton Central Station A1

Southend • Stirling • Stoke-on-Trent (Hanley) • Stratford-upon-Avon • Sunderland • Swansea • Swindon • Taunton • Telford 211

Southampton Solent University A2
SS Shieldhall C2
Terminus Terr C2
Threefield La B2
Titanic Engineers' Memorial ✦ A2
Town Quay C1
Town Walls B2
Tudor House C1
Vincent's Walk B2
Westgate Hall C1
West Marlands Rd A1
West Park A1
West Park Rd A1
West Quay Rd B1
West Quay Retail Pk B1
Western Esplanade B1
Westquay Shopping Centre B1
Westquay Watermark B1
White Star Way C2
Winton St A2

Southend-on-Sea 197

Adventure Island ✦ C3
Albany Ave A1
Albert Rd C3
Alexandra Rd C2
Alexandra St C2
Alexandra Yacht Club ✦ C2
Ashburnham Rd B2
Ave Rd B1
Avenue Terr B1
Balmoral Rd B1
Baltic Ave B3
Baxter Ave A2/B2
Beecroft Art Gallery B2
Bircham Rd A2
Boscombe Rd B3
Boston Ave A1/B2
Bournemouth Park Rd A3
Browning Ave A3
Bus Station C3
Byron Ave A3
Cambridge Rd C1/C2
Canewdon Rd B1
Carnarvon Rd A2
Central Ave A3
Central Museum B2
Chelmsford Ave A1
Chichester Rd B2
Church Rd C3
Civic Centre A2
Clarence Rd C2
Clarence St C2
Cliff Ave B1
Cliffs Pavilion C1
Clifftown Parade C2
Clifftown Rd C2
Colchester Rd A1
Coleman St B3
College Way B2
County Court B3
Cromer Rd B3
Crowborough Rd A2
Dryden Ave A3
East St A2
Elmer App B2
Elmer Ave B2
Forum, The B2
Gainsborough Dr A1
Gayton Rd A2
Glenhurst Rd A2
Gordon Place B2
Gordon Rd B2
Grainger Rd A2
Greyhound Way A3
Grove, The A3
Guildford Rd B3
Hamlet Ct Rd B1
Hamlet Rd C1
Harcourt Ave A1
Hartington Rd C3
Hastings Rd B3
Herbert Grove C3
Heygate Ave C3
High St B2/C2
Information Ctr C3
Kenway A2
Kilworth Ave B3
Lancaster Gdns B3
London Rd B1
Lucy Rd C3
MacDonald Ave A1
Magistrates' Court A2
Maldon Rd A2
Marine Ave C1
Marine Parade C3
Marine Rd C1
Milton Rd B1
Milton St B2
Napier Ave B2
North Ave A3
North Rd A1/B1
Odeon B2
Osborne Rd B1
Park Cres B1
Park Rd B1
Park St B1
Park Terr B1
Pier Hill C3
Pleasant Rd C3
Police Station A2
Post Office B2/B3
Princes St B2
Queens Rd B2
Queensway B2/B3/C3
Radio Essex C2
Rayleigh Ave A1
Redstock Rd A2
Rochford Ave A1
Royal Mews C2
Royal Terr C2
Royals Shopping Centre, The C3
Ruskin Ave A3
St Ann's Rd B3
St Helen's Rd B1
St John's Rd B1
St Leonard's Rd C3
St Lukes Rd A3
St Vincent's Rd C1
Salisbury Ave A1/B1
Scratton Rd C2
Shakespeare Dr A1
Shopmobility B2
Short St A2
South Ave A3
Southchurch Rd B3
Southend Central B2
Southend Pier Railway C3
Southend United FC A1
Southend Victoria B2
Stanfield Rd A2
Stanley Rd C3
Sutton Rd A3/B3
Swanage Rd B3
Sweyne Ave A1
Sycamore Grove A3
Tennyson Ave A3
Tickfield Ave A2
Tudor Rd A1
Tunbridge Rd A2
Tylers Ave B3
Tyrrel Dr B3
Univ of Essex B2/C2
Vale Ave A2
Victoria Ave A2
Victoria Shopping Centre, The B2
Warrior Sq B3
Wesley Rd C3
West Rd A1
West St A1
Westcliff Ave C1
Westcliff Parade C1
Western Esplanade C1
Weston Rd C2
Whitegate Rd B3
Wilson Rd C1
Wimborne Rd B3
York Rd C3

Stirling 197

Abbey Rd A3
Abbotsford Place A3
Abercromby Place C1
Albert Halls B1
Albert Place B1
Alexandra Place A3
Allan Park C2
Ambulance Station A2
AMF Ten Pin Bowling ✦ B2
Argyll Ave A3
Argyll's Lodging ✦ B1
Back O' Hill Ind Est A1
Back O' Hill Rd A1
Baker St B2
Ballengeich Pass A1
Balmoral Place B1
Barn Rd B1
Barnton St B2
Bastion, The ✦ C2
Bow St B2
Bruce St A2
Burghmuir Retail Park C2
Burghmuir Rd A2/B2/C2
Bus Station B2
Cambuskenneth Bridge A3
Castle Ct B1
Causewayhead Rd A2
Cemetery A1
Changing Room, The B1
Church of the Holy Rude B1
Clarendon Place C1
Club House B1
Colquhoun St C3
Corn Exchange B2
Council Offices C2
Court B2
Cowane Ctr A2
Cowane St A2
Cowane's Hosp B1
Crofthead Rd A1
Dean Cres A3
Douglas St A2
Drip Rd A1
Drummond La C1
Drummond Place C1
Drummond Pl La C1
Dumbarton Rd C2
Eastern Access Rd B2
Edward Ave A3
Edward Rd A2
Forrest Rd A2
Fort A1
Forth Cres B2
Forth St A2
Gladstone Place C1
Glebe Ave C1
Glebe Cres C1
Golf Course C1
Goosecroft Rd B2
Gowanhill A1
Greenwood Ave B1
Harvey Wynd A1
Information Ctr B1
Irvine Place B2
James St A2
John St B1
Kerse Rd C3
King's Knot ✦ B1
King's Park C1
King's Park Rd C1
Laurencecroft Rd A2
Leisure Pool B2
Library B2
Linden Ave C2
Lovers Wk A2
Lower Back Walk B1
Lower Bridge St A2
Lower Castlehill A1
Mar Place B1
Meadow Place A3
Meadowforth Rd C3
Middlemuir Rd C3
Millar Place A3
Morris Terr B2
Mote Hill A1
Murray Place B2
Nelson Place C2
Old Town Cemetery B1
Old Town Jail ✦ B1
Park Terr C1
Phoenix Ind Est C3
Players Rd C3
Port St C2
Post Office B2
Princes St B2
Queen St B2
Queen's Rd B1
Queenshaugh Dr A3
Ramsay Place A2
Riverside Dr A3
Ronald Place A1
Rosebery Place A2
Royal Gardens B1
Royal Gdns B1
St Mary's Wynd B1
St Ninian's Rd C2
Scott St A2
Seaforth Place B2
Shore Rd B2
Smith Art Gallery & Museum B1
Snowdon Place C1
Snowdon Place La C1
Spittal St B2
Springkerse Ind Est C3
Springkerse Rd C3
Stirling Arcade B2
Stirling Bsns Centre C2
Stirling Castle A1
Stirling County Rugby Football Club A3
Stirling Enterprise Park B3
Stirling Old Bridge A2
Stirling Station B2
Superstore A1/A2
Sutherland Ave A3
TA Centre C3
Tannery La A2
Thistle Ind Est C3
Thistles Shopping Centre, The B2
Tolbooth ✦ B1
Town Wall B1
Union St A2
Upper Back Walk B1
Upper Bridge St A1
Upper Castlehill B1
Upper Craigs C2
Victoria Place C1
Victoria Rd B1
Victoria Sq B1/C1
Vue B2
Wallace St A2
Waverley Cres A3
Wellgreen Rd C2
Windsor Place C1
YHA B1

Stoke-on-Trent (Hanley) 196

Acton St A3
Albion St B2
Argyle St C1
Ashbourne Grove A2
Avoca St A3
Baskerville Rd B3
Bedford Rd C1
Bedford St C1
Bethesda St B2
Bexley St A2
Birches Head Rd A3
Botteslow St C3
Boundary St A2
Broad St C2
Broom St A3
Bryan St A2
Bucknall New Rd B3
Bucknall Old Rd B3
Bus Station B3
Cannon St C2
Castlefield St C1
Cavendish St B1
Central Forest Pk A2
Charles St B3
Cheapside B2
Chell St A3
Clarke St C1
Cleveland Rd C2
Clifford St C3
Clough St B2
Clyde St C1
College Rd C2
Cooper St C2
Corbridge Rd A1
Cutts St C2
Davis St C1
Denbigh St A1
Derby St C3
Dilke St A3
Dundas St A3
Dundee Rd C1
Dyke St B3
Eastwood Rd C3
Eaton St A3
Etruria Park B1
Etruria Rd B1
Etruria Vale Rd C1
Festing St A3
Festival Retail Park A1
Fire Station C2
Foundry St B2
Franklyn St C3
Garnet St B1
Garth St B3
George St A3
Gilman St B3
Glass St B3
Goodson St B3
Greyhound Way A1
Grove Place C1
Hampton St C3
Hanley Park C2
Hanley Park C2
Harding Rd C2
Hassall St B3
Havelock Place C1
Hazlehurst St C3
Hinde St C2
Hope St B2
Houghton St C2
Hulton St A3
Information Ctr B3
Jasper St C2
Jervis St A3
John Bright St A3
John St B2
Keelings Rd A3
Kimberley Rd C1
Ladysmith Rd C1
Lawrence St C2
Leek Rd C3
Library C2
Lichfield St C3
Linfield Rd B3
Loftus St A2
Lower Bedford St C1
Lower Bryan St A2
Lower Mayer St A3
Lowther St A1
Magistrates Court C2
Malham St A2
Marsh St B2
Matlock St C3
Mayer St A3
Milton St C1
Mitchell Memorial Theatre B2
Morley St B2
Moston St A3
Mount Pleasant C1
Mulgrave St A1
Mynors St B3
Nelson Place B3
New Century St B1
Octagon Retail Park B1
Ogden Rd C3
Old Hall St B3
Old Town Rd A3
Pall Mall B2
Palmerston St C3
Park and Ride C2
Parker St B2
Parkway, The C2
Pavilion Dr A1
Pelham St C3
Percy St B2
Piccadilly B2
Picton St B3
Plough St A3
Police Station C2
Portland St A1
Post Office A3/B3/C3
Potteries Museum & Art Gallery B2
Potteries Shopping Centre B2
Potteries Way C2
Powell St A1
Pretoria Rd C1
Quadrant Rd B2
Ranelagh St C2
Raymond St C2
Rectory Rd C1
Regent Rd C2
Regent Theatre B2
Richmond Terr C2
Ridgehouse Dr A1
Robson St C2
St Ann St B3
St Luke St B3
Sampson St B2
Shaw St A1
Sheaf St C2
Shearer St C1
Shelton New Rd C1
Shirley Rd C2
Slippery La B2
Snow Hill C2
Spur St C3
Stafford St B2
Statham St B2
Stubbs La C3
Sun St C1
Supermarket A1/B2
Talbot St C3
Town Hall B2
Town Rd B3
Trinity St B2
Union St A2
Upper Hillchurch St A3
Upper Huntbach St B3
Victoria Hall Theatre B3
Warner St C2
Warwick St C1
Waterloo Rd A1
Waterloo St B3
Well St B3
Wellesley St C2
Wellington Rd B3
Wellington St B3
Whitehaven Dr A2
Whitmore St C1
Windermere St A1
Woodall St A1
Yates St C2
York St A2

Stratford-upon-Avon 197

Albany Rd B1
Alcester Rd B1
Ambulance Station B1
Arden St B2
Avenue Farm A1
Ave Farm Ind Est A1
Avenue Rd A3
Baker Ave A1
Bandstand C3
Benson Rd A3
Birmingham Rd A2
Boat Club B3
Borden Place C1
Bridge St B2
Bridgetown Rd C3
Bridgeway B3
Broad St C2
Broad Walk C2
Brookvale Rd C1
Brunel Way B1
Bull St C2
Butterfly Farm ✦ C3
Cemetery C1
Chapel La B2
Cherry Orchard C1
Chestnut Walk B2
Children's Playground C3
Church St C2
Civic Hall B2
Clarence Rd B1
Clopton Bridge ✦ B3
Clopton Rd A2
College B1
College La C2
College St C2
Com Sports Centre B1
Council Offices (District) B2
Courtyard, The C2
Cox's Yard ✦ B3
Cricket Ground C3
Ely Gdns B2
Ely St B2
Evesham Rd C1
Fire Station B1
Foot Ferry C3
Fordham Ave A2
Garrick Way C1
Gower Memorial ✦ B3
Great William St B2
Greenhill St B2
Greenway, The C2
Grove Rd B2
Guild St B2
Guildhall & School B2
Hall's Croft C2
Harvard House B2
Henley St B2
Hertford Rd C1
High St B2
Holton St C2
Holy Trinity C2
Information Ctr B3
Jolyffe Park Rd A2
Kipling Rd C3
Library B2
Lodge Rd B1
Maidenhead Rd A3
Mansell St B2
Masons Court B2
Masons Rd A1
Maybird Shopping Park A2
Maybrook Retail Park A2
Maybrook Rd A1
Mayfield Ave A2
Meer St B2
Mill La C2
Moat House Hotel B3
Narrow La C2
Nash's House & New Place B2
New St C2
Old Town C2
Orchard Way C1
Other Place, The C2
Paddock La C1
Park Rd A1
Payton St B2
Percy St A2
Police Station B2
Post Office B2
Recreation Ground C2
Regal Road A2
Rother St B2
Rowley Cres A3
Royal Shakespeare Theatre B3
Ryland St C2
Saffron Meadow C2
St Andrew's Cres B1
St Gregory's A3
St Gregory's Rd A3
St Mary's Rd A2
Sanctus Dr C2
Sanctus St C1
Sandfield Rd C2
Scholars La B2
Seven Meadows Rd C2
Shakespeare Inst C2
Shakespeare St B2
Shakespeare's Birthplace ✦ B2
Sheep St B2
Shelley Rd C3
Shipston Rd C3
Shottery Rd C1
Slingates Rd A2
Southern La C2
Station Rd B1
Stratford Healthcare B2
Stratford Hosp B2
Stratford Leisure Centre B3
Stratford Sports Club B1
Stratford-upon-Avon Station B1
Swan Theatre B3
Swan's Nest La B3
Talbot Rd A2
Tiddington Rd B3
Timothy's Bridge Industrial Estate A1
Timothy's Bridge Rd A1
Town Hall & Council Offices B2
Town Sq B2
Trinity Cl C2
Tyler St B2
War Memorial Gdns B3
Warwick Rd B3
Waterside B3
Welcombe Rd A3
West St C2
Western Rd A2
Wharf Rd A2
Willows North, The B1
Willows, The B1
Wood St B2

Sunderland 197

Albion Place C2
Alliance Place B1
Argyle St C2
Ashwood St C1
Athenaeum St B2
Azalea Terr C2
Beach St A1
Bedford St B2
Beechwood Terr C1
Belvedere Rd C2
Blandford St B2
Borough Rd B3
Bridge Cres B2
Bridge St B2
Bridges, The B2
Brooke St A2
Brougham St B2
Burdon Rd C2
Burn Park C1
Burn Park Rd C1
Burn Park Tech Park C1
Carol St B1
Charles St A3
Chester Rd C1
Chester Terr B1
Church St A3
Civic Centre C2
Cork St B3
Coronation St B3
Cowan Terr C2
Dame Dorothy St A2
Deptford Rd B1
Deptford Terr A1
Derby St C2
Derwent St C2
Dock St A3
Dundas St A2
Durham Rd C1
Easington St A2
Egerton St C3
Empire B3
Empire Theatre B2
Farringdon Row B1
Fawcett St B2
Fire Station B1
Fox St C1
Foyle St B3
Frederick St B3
Hanover Place A1
Havelock Terr C1
Hay St A2
Headworth Sq B3
Hendon Rd B3
High St East B3
High St West B2/B3
Holmeside B2
Hylton Rd B1
Information Ctr B2
John St B3
Kier Hardie Way A2
Lambton St B3
Laura St C3
Lawrence St B3
Library & Arts Ctr B3
Lily St B1
Lime St B1
Livingstone Rd B2
Low Row B2
Magistrates' Court B2
Matamba Terr B1
Millburn St B1
Millennium Way A2
Minster B2
Monkwearmouth Sta Mus A2
Mowbray Park C3
Mowbray Rd C3
Murton St C3
National Glass Centre ✦ A3
New Durham Rd C1
Newcastle Rd A2
Nile St B3
Norfolk St B3
North Bridge St A2
Northern Gallery for Contemporary Art B3
Otto Terr C1
Park La C2
Park Lane C2
Park Rd C2
Paul's Rd B3
Peel St C3
Point, The ✦ B2
Police Station B2
Priestly Cres A1
Queen St B2
Railway Row B1
Retail Park B1
Richmond St A2
Roker Ave A2
Royalty Theatre C1
Royalty, The C1
Ryhope Rd C2
St Mary's Way B2
St Michael's Way B2
St Peter's A3
St Peter's A2
St Peter's Way A3
St Vincent St C3
Salem Rd C3
Salem St C3
Salisbury St C3
Sans St B3
Shopmobility B1
Silkworth Row B1
Southwick Rd A2
Stadium of Light (Sunderland AFC) A2
Stadium Way A2
Stobart St A2
Stockton Rd C2
Suffolk St C3
Sunderland B2
Sunderland Aquatic Centre A2
Sunderland College C2
Sunderland Mus B3
Sunderland St B3
Sunderland Sta B2
Tatham St C3
Tavistock Place B3
Thelma St C1
Thomas St North A2
Thornholme Rd C1
Toward Rd C3
Transport Interchange C2
Trimdon St Way B1
Tunstall Rd C2
University C1
University Library C1
Univ of Sunderland (City Campus) B1
Univ of Sunderland (St Peter's Campus) A3
University of Sunderland (Sir Tom Cowie Campus) A3
Vaux Brewery Way A2
Villiers St B3
Villiers St South B3
Vine Place C2
Violet St B1
Walton La B3
Waterworks Rd B1
Wearmouth Bridge B2
West Sunniside B3
West Wear St B3
Westbourne Rd B1
Western Hill C1
Wharncliffe B1
Whickham St A3
White House Rd C3
Wilson St North A2
Winter Gdns C3
Wreath Quay A1

Swansea Abertawe 198

Adelaide St C3
Albert Row C3
Alexandra Rd B3
Argyle St C1
Baptist Well Place A2
Beach St C1
Belle Vue Way B3
Berw Rd A1
Berwick Terr A2
Bond St C1
Brangwyn Concert Hall C1
Bridge St A3
Brookands Terr B1
Brunswick St C1
Bryn-Syfi Terr A2
Bryn-y-Mor Rd C1
Bullins La B1
Burrows Rd C1
Bus Station C2
Bus/Rail link A3
Cadfan Rd A1
Cadrawd Rd A1
Caer St B3
Carig Cres A1
Carlton Terr B2
Carmarthen Rd A3
Castle Square B3
Castle St B3
Catherine St C1
Cinema C3
Civic Ctr & Library C2
Clarence St C2
Colbourne Terr A2
Constitution Hill B1
Court B3
Creidiol Rd A2
Cromwell St B2
Crown Courts C1
Duke St B1
Dunvant Place C2
Dyfatty Park A3
Dyfatty St A3
Dyfed Ave A1
Dylan Thomas Ctr ✦ B3
Dylan Thomas Theatre C3
Eaton Cres C1
Eigen Cres A1
Elfed Rd A1
Emlyn Rd A1
Evans Terr A3
Fairfield Terr B1
Ffynone Dr B1
Ffynone Rd B1
Fire Station B3
Firm St A2
Fleet St C1
Francis St C1
Fullers Row B2
George St B2
Glamorgan St C2
Glynn Vivian Art Gallery B3
Gower Coll Swansea C1
Graig Terr A3
Grand Theatre C2
Granogwen Rd A2
Guildhall C1
Guildhall Rd South C1
Gwent Rd A1
Gwynedd Ave A1
Hafod St A3
Hanover St B1
Harcourt St B2
Harries St A2
Heathfield B2
Henrietta St B1
Hewson St B2
High St A3/B3
High View A2
Hill St A2
Historic Ships Berth C3
HM Prison C2
Information Ctr C2
Islwyn Rd A1
King Edward's Rd C1
Kingsway, The B2
LC, The C3
Long Ridge A2
Madoc St C2
Mansel St B2
Maritime Quarter C3
Market B3
Mayhill Gdns B1
Mayhill Rd A1
Milton Terr A2
Mission Gallery C3
Montpelier Terr B1
Morfa Rd A3
Mount Pleasant B2
National Waterfront Museum C3
New Cut Rd A3
New St A3
Nicander Parade A2
Nicander Place A2
Nicholl St B2
Norfolk St B2
North Hill Rd A2
Northampton La B2
Observatory ✦ C3
Orchard St B3
Oxford St B2
Oystermouth Rd C1
Page St B2
Pant-y-Celyn Rd B1
Parc Tawe North B3
Parc Tawe Shopping & Leisure Centre B3
Patti Pavilion C1
Paxton St C2
Pen-y-Graig Rd A1
Penmaen Terr B1
Phillips Parade C1
Picton Terr B2
Plantasia B3
Plantasia B3
Police Station B2
Post Office A1/A2/C1/C2
Powys Ave A1
Primrose St B2
Princess Way B3
Promenade B2
Pryder Gdns A1
Quadrant Shopping Centre C2
Quay Park B3
Rhianfa La B1
Rhondda St B2
Richardson St C2
Rodney St C1
Rose Hill B1
Rosehill Terr B1
Russell St B1
St David's Shopping Centre C3
St Helen's Ave C1
St Helen's Cres C1
St Helen's Rd C1
St James Gdns B1
St James's Cres B1
St Mary's B3
Sea View Terr A3
Singleton St C2
South Dock C3
Stanley Place B2
Strand B3
Swansea Castle B3
Swansea Metropolitan University B2
Swansea Mus C3
Swansea Station A3
Taliesyn Rd B1
Tan y Marian Rd A1
Tegid Rd A2
Teilo Cres A1
Tenpin Bowling ✦ B3
Terrace Rd B1/B2
Tontine St A3
Townhill Rd A1
Tramshed, The C3
Trawler Rd C3
Union St B2
Upper Strand A3
Vernon St A3
Victoria Quay C3
Victoria Rd B3
Vincent St C1
Walter Rd B1
Watkin St A2
Waun-Wen Rd A2
Wellington St C2
Westbury St C1
Western St C1
Westway C2
William St C2
Wind St B3
Woodlands Terrace B1
YMCA B2
York St C3

Swindon 198

Albert St C3
Albion St C1
Alfred St A2
Alvescot Rd C3
Art Gallery & Museum C3
Ashford Rd C1
Aylesbury St A2
Bath Rd C2
Bathampton St B1
Bathurst Rd B3
Beatrice St A2
Beckhampton St B3
Bowood Rd C1
Bristol St B1
Broad St A3
Brunel Arcade B2
Brunel Plaza B2
Brunswick St C2
Bus Station B2
Cambria Bridge Rd B1
Cambria Place B1
Canal Walk B2
Carfax St B2
Carr St B1
Cemetery C1/C3
Chandler Cl C3
Chapel C1
Chester St B1
Christ Church C3
Church Place B1
Cirencester Way A3
Clarence St B2
Clifton St C1
Cockleberry A2
Colbourne A3
Colbourne St A3
College St B2
Commercial Rd B2
Corporation St A2
Council Offices B3
County Rd A3
Courts B2
Cricket Ground A3
Cricklade Street C3
Crombey St B1/C2
Cross St C2
Curtis St B1
Deacon St C1
Designer Outlet (Great Western) B1
Dixon St C2
Dover St C2
Dowling St C2
Drove Rd C3
Dryden St C1
Durham St C3
East St B1
Eastcott Hill C2
Eastcott Rd C2
Edgeware Rd B2
Edmund St C2
Elmina Rd A3
Emlyn Square B1
Euclid St B3
Exeter St B1
Fairview C1
Faringdon Rd B1
Farnsby St B1
Fire Station B3
Fleet St B2
Fleming Way B2/B3
Florence St A2
Gladstone St A3
Gooch St A2
Graham St A3
Great Western Way A1/A2
Groundwell Rd B3
Hawksworth Way A1
Haydon St A2
Henry St B2
Hillside Ave C1
Holbrook Way B2
Hunt St C3
Hydro B1
Hythe Rd C2
Information Ctr B2
Joseph St C1
Kent Rd C2
King William St C2
Kingshill Rd C1
Lansdown Rd C2
Lawn, The C3
Leicester St B3
Library B2
Lincoln St B3
Little London C3
London St B1
Magic B3
Maidstone Rd C2
Manchester Rd A3
Maxwell St B1
Milford St B2
Milton Rd B1
Morse St C2
National Monuments Record Centre B1
Newcastle St B3
Newcombe Drive A1
Newcombe Trading Estate A1
Newhall St C2
North St C2
North Star A1
North Star Ave A1
Northampton St B3
Nurseries, The C1
Oasis Leisure Ctr A1
Ocotal Way A3
Okus Rd C1
Old Town C3
Oxford St B1
Parade, The B2
Park Lane B1
Park Lane B1
Park, The B1
Pembroke St C2
Plymouth St B3
Polaris House A2
Polaris Way A2
Police Station B2
Ponting St A2
Post Office B1/B2/C1/C3
Poulton St A3
Princes St B2
Prospect Hill C2
Prospect Place C2
Queen St B2
Queen's Park C3
Radnor St C1
Read St C1
Reading St B1
Regent St B2
Retail Park A2/A3/B3
Rosebery St A3
St Mark's B1
Salisbury St A3
Savernake St C2
Shelley St C1
Sheppard St B1
South St C2
Southampton St B3
Spring Gardens B3
Stafford Street C2
Stanier St C2
Station Road A2
STEAM B1
Swindon College A2
Swindon Rd C2
Swindon Station A2
Swindon Town Football Club A3
T A Centre B1
Tennyson St B1
Theobald St B1
Town Hall B2
Transfer Bridges A3
Union St C2
Upham Rd C3
Victoria Rd C3
Walcot Rd B3
War Memorial ✦ B2
Wells St B3
Western St C2
Westmorland Rd B3
Whalebridge B2
Whitehead St C1
Whitehouse Rd A2
William St C1
Wood St C3
Wyvern Theatre & Arts Centre B2
York Rd B3

Taunton 198

Addison Grove A1
Albemarle Rd A1
Alfred St B3
Alma St C2
Avenue, The A1
Bath Place C1
Belvedere Rd A1
Billet St B2
Billetfield C2
Birch Grove A1
Brewhouse Theatre B2
Bridge St B1
Bridgwater & Taunton Canal A2
Broadlands Rd C1
Burton Place C1
Bus Station B1
Canal Rd A2
Cann St C1
Canon St B2
Castle B1
Castle St B1
Cheddon Rd A2
Chip Lane A1
Clarence St B1
Cleveland St B1
Clifton Terr A2
Coleridge Cres C3
Compass Hill C1
Compton Cl A2
Corporation St B1
Council Offices A1
County Walk Shopping Centre C2
Courtyard B2
Cranmer Rd B2
Crescent, The C1
Critchard Way B3
Cyril St A1
Deller's Wharf B1
Duke St B2
East Reach B3
East St B3
Eastbourne Rd B2
Eastleigh Rd C3
Eaton Cres A2
Elm Grove A1
Elms Cl A1
Fons George C1
Fore St B2
Fowler St A1
French Weir Recreation Grd B1
Geoffrey Farrant Walk A2
Gray's Almshouses B2
Grays Rd B3
Greenway Ave A1
Guildford Place C1
Hammet St B2
Haydon Rd B3
Heavitree Way A2
Herbert St A1
High St C2
Holway Ave C3
Hugo St B3
Huish's Almshouses B2
Hurdle Way C2
Information Ctr C2
Jubilee St A1
King's College C3
Kings Cl C3
Laburnum St B2
Lambrook Rd B3
Lansdowne Rd A3
Leslie Ave A1
Leycroft Rd B3
Library C2
Linden Grove A1
Magdalene St B2
Magistrates Court B1
Malvern Terr A2
Market House B2
Mary St C2
Middle St B2
Midford Rd B3
Mitre Court B3
Mount Nebo C1
Mount St C2
Mount, The C2
Mountway C2
Mus of Somerset B1
North St B2
Northern Inner Distributor Rd A1
Northfield Ave B1
Northfield Rd B1
Northleigh Rd C3
Obridge Allotments A3
Obridge Lane A3
Obridge Rd A3
Obridge Viaduct A3
Old Market Shopping Centre C2
Osborne Way C1
Park St C1
Paul St C2
Plais St A2
Playing Field C3
Police Station C1
Portland St B1
Post Office B1/B2/C1
Priorswood Ind Est A3
Priorswood Rd A2
Priory Ave B2
Priory Bridge Rd B2
Priory Fields Retail Park A3
Priory Park A2
Priory Way A3
Queen St B3
Railway St A1
Records Office A2
Recreation Grd A1
Riverside Place B2
St Augustine St B2
St George's C2
St Georges Sq C2
St James B2
St James St B2
St John's C1
St John's Rd B1
St Josephs Field C2
St Mary Magdalene's B2
Samuels Ct A1
Shire Hall & Law Courts C1
Somerset County Cricket Ground B2
Somerset County Hall C1
Somerset Cricket B2
South Rd C3
South St C3
Staplegrove Rd B1
Station Rd A1
Stephen St B2
Swimming Pool A1
Tancred St B2
Tauntfield Cl C3
Taunton Dean Cricket Club C2
Taunton Station A2
Thomas St A1
Toneway A3
Tower St B1
Trevor Smith Place C3
Trinity Bsns Centre C3
Trinity Rd C3
Trinity St B3
Trull Rd C1
Tudor House B2
Upper High St C1
Venture Way A3
Victoria Gate B3
Victoria Park B3
Victoria St B3
Viney St B3
Vivary Park C2
Vivary Rd C1
War Memorial ✦ C1
Wellesley St A2
Wheatley Cres A3
Whitehall A1
Wilfred Rd B3
William St A1
Wilton Church C1
Wilton Cl C1
Wilton Grove C1
Wilton St C1
Winchester St B2
Winters Field B2
Wood St B1
Yarde Place B1

Telford 198

Alma Ave C1
Amphitheatre C2
Bowling Alley B2
Brandsfarm Way C3
Brunel Rd B1
Bus Station B2
Buxton Rd C1
Central Park A2
Civic Offices B2
Coach Central B2
Coachwell Cl B1
Colliers Way A1
Courts B2
Dale Acre Way B3
Darliston C3
Deepdale B3
Deercote B2
Dinthill C3
Doddington C3
Dodmoor Grange C3
Downemead B3
Duffryn B3
Dunsheath B3
Euston Way A3
Eyton Mound C1
Eyton Rd C1
Forgegate A2
Grange Central B2
Hall Park Way B1
Hinkshay Rd C2
Hollinsworth Rd A2

212 Torquay • Truro • Winchester • Windsor • Wolverhampton • Worcester • Wrexham • York

Holyhead Rd A3
Housing Trust A1
Ice Rink B2
Information Ctr B2
Ironmasters Way A2
Job Centre B1
Land Registry B1
Lawn Central B2
Lawnswood C1
Library B2
Malinsgate B1
Matlock Ave C1
Moor Rd C1
Mount Rd C1
NFU Offices B1
Odeon B2
Park Lane A1
Police Station B1
Priorslee Ave A3
Queen Elizabeth Ave C3
Queen Elizabeth Way B1
Queensway A2/B3
Rampart Way A2
Randlay Ave C3
Randlay Wood C3
Rhodes Ave C1
Royal Way B1
St Leonards Rd B1
St Quentin Gate B2
Shifnal Rd A3
Sixth Ave A1
Southwater One (SW1) B2
Southwater Way B1
Spout Lane C1
Spout Mound B1
Spout Way C1
Stafford Court B3
Stafford Park B3
Stirchley Ave C3
Stone Row C1
Telford Bridge Retail Park A1
Telford Central Station A3
Telford Centre, The B2
Telford Forge Shopping Park A1
Telford Hornets RFC C2
Telford Int Ctr C2
Telford Way A3
Third Ave A2
Town Park C2
Town Pk Visitor Ctr B2
Walker House B2
Wellswood Ave A2
West Centre Way B1
Withywood Drive C1
Woodhouse Central B2
Yates Way A1

Torquay 199
Abbey Rd B2
Alexandra Rd A2
Alpine Rd B3
AMF Bowling C3
Ash Hill Rd A2
Babbacombe Rd B3
Bampfylde Rd B1
Barton Rd A1
Beacon Quay C2
Belgrave Rd A1/B1
Belmont Rd A3
Berea Rd A3
Braddons Hill Rd East B3
Brewery Park A3
Bronshill Rd A2
Carlton Rd A3
Castle Circus A2
Castle Rd A2
Cavern Rd A3
Central B2
Chatsworth Rd A2
Chestnut Ave B1
Church St A1
Coach Station A1
Corbyn Head C1
Croft Hill B1
Croft Rd B1
East St A1
Egerton Rd A3
Ellacombe Church Rd A3
Ellacombe Rd A2
Falkland Rd B1
Fleet St B2
Fleet Walk Shopping Centre B2
Grafton Rd B3
Grange Rd A3
Haldon Pier C2
Hatfield Rd A2
Highbury Rd A2
Higher Warberry Rd A3
Hillesdon Rd B3
Hoxton Rd A3
Hunsdon Rd B3
Information Ctr B2
Inner Harbour C3
Kenwyn Rd A3
King's Drive, The B1
Laburnum St A1
Law Courts A2
Library A2
Lime Ave B1
Living Coasts C3
Lower Warberry Rd B3
Lucius St B1
Lymington Rd A1
Magdalene Rd A1
Marina C2
Market Forum, The B2
Market St B2
Meadfoot Lane C3
Meadfoot Rd C3
Melville St B2
Middle Warberry Rd B3
Mill Lane A1
Montpellier Rd B3
Morgan Ave A1
Museum Rd B3
Newton Rd A1
Oakhill Rd A1
Outer Harbour C2
Parkhill Rd C3
Pimlico B2
Police Station A1
Post Office A1/B2
Prince of Wales Steps C3
Princes Rd A3
Princes Rd East A3
Princes Rd West A3
Princess Gdns C2
Princess Pier C2
Princess Theatre C2
Rathmore Rd B1
Recreation Grd B1
Riviera Int Ctr B1
Rock End Ave C3
Rock Rd B2
Rock Walk B2
Rosehill Rd A3
South West Coast Path C3
St Efride's Rd A1
St John's B3
St Luke's Rd B2
St Luke's Rd North B2
St Luke's Rd South B2
St Marychurch Rd A2
Scarborough Rd B1
Shedden Hill B2
South Pier C2
South St A1
Spanish Barn B1
Stitchill Rd B3
Strand B3
Sutherland Rd B3
Teignmouth Rd A1
Temperance St B2
Terrace, The B3
Thurlow Rd A1
Tor Bay B1
Tor Church Rd A1
Tor Hill Rd A1
Torbay Rd B2
Torquay Mus B3
Torquay Station C1
Torquay Tennis Club B1
Torre Abbey B1
Torre Abbey Meadows B1
Torre Abbey Sands B1
Torwood Gdns B3
Torwood St C3
Town Hall A2
Union Square Shopping Centre A2
Union St A1
Upton Hill A2
Upton Park A1
Upton Rd A1
Vanehill Rd C3
Vansittart Rd A1
Vaughan Parade C3
Victoria Parade C3
Victoria Rd A2
Warberry Rd West B2
Warren Rd B2
Windsor Rd A2/A3
Woodville Rd A3

Truro 199
Adelaide Ter B1
Agar Rd B3
Arch Hill C2
Arundell Place C2
Avenue, The A3
Avondale Rd B1
Back Quay B3
Barrack La C3
Barton Meadow A1
Benson Rd A2
Bishops Cl A2
Bosvean Gardens B1
Bosvigo Gardens B1
Bosvigo La A1
Bosvigo Rd B2
Broad St A3
Burley Cl C3
Bus Station B3
Calenick St B2
Campfield Hill B3
Carclew St B3
Carew Rd A2
Carey Park B2
Carlyon Rd A2
Carvoza Rd A3
Castle St B2
Cathedral View A2
Chainwalk Dr A2
Chapel Hill B1
Charles St B2
City Hall B3
City Rd B2
Coinage Hall B3
Comprigney Hill A1
Coosebean La A1
Copes Gdns A2
County Hall B1
Courtney Rd A2
Crescent Rd B1
Crescent Rise B1
Crescent, The B1
Daniell Court C2
Daniell Rd C2
Daniell St C2
Daubuz Close A2
Dobbs La B1
Edward St B2
Eliot Rd A2
Elm Court A3
Enys Cl A1
Enys Rd A1
Fairmantle St B3
Falmouth Rd C2
Ferris Town B2
Fire Station B1
Frances St B2
George St B2
Green Close C2
Green La C1
Grenville Rd A2
Hall For Cornwall B3
Hendra Rd A2
Hendra Vean A1
High Cross B3
Higher Newham La C3
Higher Trehaverne A2
Hillcrest Ave B1
Hospital B2
Hunkin Cl A2
Hurland Rd C3
Infirmary Hill B2
James Place B3
Kenwyn Church Rd A1
Kenwyn Hill A1
Kenwyn Rd A2
Kenwyn St B2
Kerris Gdns A1
King St B3
Leats, The B2
Lemon Quay B3
Lemon St Gallery B3
Library B1/B3
Malpas Rd B3
Magistrates Court A3
Market B3
Memorial Gdns B3
Merrifield Close B1
Mitchell Hill A3
Moresk Cl A3
Moresk Rd A3
Morlaix Ave C3
Nancemere Rd A3
Newham Bsns Park C3
Newham Ind Est C3
Newham Rd C3
Northfield Dr C3
Oak Way A3
Pal's Terr A3
Park View C2
Pendarves Rd A2
Plaza Cinema B3
Police Station B3
Post Office B2/B3
Prince's St B3
Pydar St A2
Quay St B3
Redannick Cres C2
Redannick La B2
Richard Lander Monument C2
Richmond Hill B1
River St B2
Rosedale Rd A2
Royal Cornwall Museum B2
St Aubyn Rd C3
St Clement St B3
St George's Rd A1
School La C2
Spires, The A2
Station Rd B1
Stokes Rd A2
Strangways Terr C3
Tabernacle St B3
Trehaverne La A2
Tremayne Rd A2
Treseder's Gdns A3
Treworder Rd B1
Treyew Rd B1
Truro Cathedral B3
Truro Harbour Office B3
Truro Station B3
Union St B3
Upper School La C2
Victoria Gdns B2
Waterfall Gdns B2

Winchester 199
Andover Rd A2
Andover Road Retail Park A2
Archery La C2
Arthur Rd A2
Bar End Rd C3
Beaufort Rd C2
Beggar's La B3
Bereweeke Ave A1
Bereweeke Rd A1
Boscobel Rd A2
Brassey Rd A2
Broadway B3
Brooks Shopping Centre, The B3
Bus Station B3
Butter Cross B2
Canon St C2
Castle Wall C2/C3
Cathedral C2
Cheriton Rd A1
Chesil St C3
Chesil Theatre C3
Christchurch Rd C1
City Mill B3
City Museum B2
City Rd B2
Clifton Rd B1
Clifton Terr B2
Close Wall C2/C3
Coach Park A2
Colebrook St C3
College St C2
College Walk C3
Compton Rd C2
Council Offices C3
County Council Offices B2
Cranworth Rd A2
Cromwell Rd C1
Culver Rd C2
Domum Rd C3
Durngate Place B3
Eastgate St B3
East Hill C3
Edgar Rd C2
Egbert Rd A2
Elm Rd B1
Everyman B2
Fairfield Rd A1
Fire Station B3
Fordington Ave B1
Fordington Rd A1
Friarsgate B3
Gordon Rd B3
Great Hall & Round Table, The B2
Greenhill Rd B1
Guildhall B3
Hatherley Rd A1
High St B2
Hillier Way A3
HM Prison B1
Hyde Abbey (Remains) A2
Hyde Abbey Rd B2
Hyde Cl A2
Hyde St A2
Information Ctr B3
Jane Austen's House C2
Jewry St B2
King Alfred Place A2
Kingsgate Arch C2
Kingsgate Park C2
Kingsgate Rd C2
Kingsgate St C2
Lankhills Rd A2
Law Courts B2
Library B2
Lower Brook St B3
Magdalen Hill B3
Market La B2
Mews La B1
Middle Brook St B3
Middle Rd B1
Military Museums B2
Milland Rd C3
Milverton Rd B1
Monks Rd A3
North Hill Cl A2
North Walls B2
North Walls Rec Ground A3
Nuns Rd A3
Oram's Arbour B1
Owens Rd A2
Parchment St B2
Park & Ride C3
Park Ave B3
Playing Field A1
Police HQ B1
Portal Rd C3
Post Office B2/C1
Ranelagh Rd C1
Regiment Mus B2
River Pk Leisure Ctr B3
Romans' Rd C2
Romsey Rd B1
Royal Hampshire County Hospital (A&E) B1
St Cross Rd C2
St George's St B2
St Giles Hill C3
St James Villas C2
St James' La B1
St James' Terr B1
St John's B3
St John's St B3
St Michael's Rd C2
St Paul's Hill B1
St Peter St B2
St Swithun St C2
St Thomas St C2
Saxon Rd A2
School of Art B3
Sleepers Hill Rd C1
Southgate St B2
Sparkford Rd C1
Square, The B2
Staple Gdns B2
Station Rd B2
Step Terr B1
Stockbridge Rd A1
Stuart Cres C1
Sussex St B2
Swan Lane B2
Tanner St B3
Theatre Royal B2
Tower St B2
Union St B3
Univ of Southampton (Winchester School of Art) B3
University of Winchester (King Alfred Campus) C1
Upper Brook St B2
Wales St B3
Water Lane B3
Weirs, The C3
West End Terr B1
Western Rd B1
Westgate B2
Wharf Hill C3
Winchester Sta A2
Winnall Moors Wildlife Reserve A3
Wolvesey Castle C3
Worthy Lane A2
Worthy Rd A2

Windsor 199
Adelaide Sq C3
Albany Rd C2
Albert St B1
Alexandra Gdns B2
Alexandra Rd C2
Alma Rd B2
Ambulance Station B1
Arthur Rd B2
Bachelors Acre B3
Barry Ave B2
Beaumont Rd C2
Bexley St B1
Boat House B2
Brocas St B2
Brocas, The A2
Brook St C3
Bulkeley Ave C1
Castle Hill B3
Charles St B2
Claremont Rd C2
Clarence Cres B2
Clarence Rd B1
Clewer Court Rd B1
Coach Park B2
College Cres C1
Courts C2
Cricket Club A3
Cricket Ground C3
Dagmar Rd C2
Datchet Rd B3
Devereux Rd C2
Dorset Rd C2
Duke St B1
Elm Rd C1
Eton College A3
Eton Court A2
Eton Sq A2
Eton Wick Rd A2
Farm Yard B3
Fire Station C2
Frances Rd C2
Frogmore Dr B3
Gloucester Place C3
Goslar Way C1
Goswell Hill B2
Goswell Rd B2
Green La C1
Grove Rd C2
Guildhall B3
Helena Rd C2
Helston La B1
High St A2/B3
Holy Trinity C2
Home Park, The A3/C3
Hosp (Private) C2
Household Cavalry C2
Imperial Rd C1
Information Ctr B2/B3
Keats La A2
King Edward Ct B2
King Edward VII Ave A3
King Edward VII Hospital C2
King George V Memorial B3
King Stable St A2
King's Rd C3
Library C2
Long Walk, The C3
Maidenhead Rd B1
Meadow La A2
Municipal Offices C3
Nell Gwynne's House B3
Osborne Rd C2
Oxford Rd B1
Park St B3
Peascod St B2
Police Station C2
Post Office A2
Princess Margaret Hospital C2
Queen Victoria's Walk B3
Queen's Rd C2
River St B2
Romney Island A3
Romney Lock A3
Romney Lock Rd A3
Russell St C2
St John's B3
St John's Chapel A2
St Leonards Rd C2
St Mark's Rd C2
Sheet St C3
South Meadow A2
South Meadow La A2
Springfield Rd C1
Stovell Rd B1
Sunbury Rd A3
Tangier La A2
Tangier St A3
Temple Rd C2
Thames St B3
Theatre Royal B3
Trinity Place C2
Vansittart Rd B1/C1
Vansittart Rd Gdns C1
Victoria Barracks C2
Victoria St C2
Ward Royal B2
Westmead C1
White Lilies Island A1
William St B2
Windsor & Eton Central B2
Windsor & Eton Riverside A3
Windsor Arts Centre C2
Windsor Bridge B3
Windsor Castle B3
Windsor Great Park C3
Windsor Leisure Ctr B1
Windsor Relief Rd A1
Windsor Royal Shopping B2
York Ave C1
York Rd C1

Wolverhampton 200
Albion St B3
Alexandra St C1
Arena B2
Arts Gallery B2
Ashland St C1
Austin St A1
Badger Dr A3
Bailey St B3
Bath Ave B1
Bath Rd B1
Bell St C2
Berry St B3
Bilston Rd C3
Bilston St C3
Birmingham Canal A3
Bone Mill La A2
Brewery Rd B1
Bright St A1
Burton Cres B3
Bus Station B3
Cambridge St A3
Camp St B2
Cannock Rd A3
Castle St C2
Chapel Ash C1
Cherry St C1
Chester St A1
Church La C2
Church St C2
Civic Centre B2
Civic Hall B2
Clarence Rd B2
Cleveland St C2
Clifton St C1
Coach Station B2
Compton Rd B1
Corn Hill B3
Coven St A3
Craddock St A1
Cross St North A2
Crown & County Courts C3
Crown St A2
Culwell St B3
Dale St C1
Darlington St C1
Devon Rd A1
Drummond St B2
Dudley Rd C2
Dudley St B2
Duke St C3
Dunkley St B1
Dunstall Ave A2
Dunstall Hill A2
Dunstall Rd A1/A2
Evans St A1
Fawdry St A1
Field St B3
Fire Station C1
Fiveways A2
Fowler Playing Fields A3
Fox's La A2
Francis St A2
Fryer St B3
Gloucester St A1
Gordon St C3
Graiseley St C1
Grand B3
Granville St C3
Great Brickkiln St C1
Great Hampton St A1
Great Western St A2
Grimstone St B3
Harrow St A1
Hilton St A3
Hive Liby The B2
Horseley Fields C3
Humber Rd C1
Jack Hayward Way A2
Jameson St A1
Jenner St C3
Kennedy Rd B3
Kimberley St C1
King St B2
Laburnum St C1
Lansdowne Rd B1
Leicester St A1
Lever St C3
Library C3
Lichfield St B2
Light House B3
Little's La B3
Lock St B3
Lord St C1
Lowe St A1
Maltings, The B2
Mander Centre C2
Mander St C1
Market C2
Market St B2
Maxwell Rd C3
Merridale St C1
Middlecross C3
Molineux St B2
Mostyn St A1
New Hampton Rd East A1
Nine Elms La A3
North Rd A2
Oaks Cres C1
Oxley St A2
Paget St A1
Park Ave B1
Park Road East A1
Park Road West B1
Paul St C2
Pelham St C1
Penn Rd C2
Piper's Row B3
Pitt St C2
Police Station C3
Pool St C2
Poole St A3
Post Office A1/B2/B2/C2
Powlett St C3
Queen St B2
Raby St C3
Railway Dr B3
Red Hill St A2
Red Lion St B2
Retreat St C1
Ring Rd B2
Royal, The C3
Rugby St A1
Russell St C1
St Andrew's B1
St David's B3
St George's C3
St George's Parade C2
St James St C3
St John's C2
St John's C2
St John's Retail Pk C2
St John's Square C2
St Mark's C1
St Marks Rd C1
St Marks St C1
St Patrick's B2
St Peter's B2
St Peter's B2
Salisbury St C1
Salop St C2
School St C2
Sherwood St A2
Smestow St A3
Snow Hill C2
Springfield Rd A3
Stafford St A2/B2
Staveley Rd A1
Steelhouse La C3
Stephenson St C1
Stewart St C2
Sun St B3
Tempest St C2
Temple St C2
Tettenhall Rd B1
Thomas St C2
Thornley St B2
Tower St C2
University B2
Upper Zoar St C1
Vicarage Rd C3
Victoria St C2
Walpole St A1
Walsall St C3
Ward St C3
Warwick St C3
Water St A3
Waterloo Rd B2
Wednesfield Rd B3
West Park (not A&E) B1
West Park Swimming Pool B1
Wharf St C3
Whitmore Hill B2
Wolverhampton B3
Wolverhampton St George's C2
Wolverhampton Wanderers Football Gnd (Molineux) B2
Worcester St C2
Wulfrun Centre C2
Yarwell Cl A3
York St C3
Zoar St C1

Worcester 200
Albany Terr A1
Angel Place B2
Angel St B2
Ashcroft Rd A2
Athelstan Rd C3
Avenue, The C1
Back Lane North A1
Back Lane South A1
Barbourne Rd A2
Bath Rd C2
Battenhall Rd C3
Bridge St B2
Britannia Sq A1
Broad St B2
Bromwich La C1
Bromwich Rd C1
Bromyard Rd C1
Bus Station B2
Butts, The B2
Carden St B3
Castle St A2
Cathedral C2
Cathedral Plaza B2
Charles St B3
Chequers La B1
Chestnut St A2
Chestnut Walk A2
Citizens' Advice Bureau B2
City Walls Rd B2
Cole Hill C3
College St C2
Commandery, The C3
Cripplegate Park B1
Croft Rd B1
Cromwell St B3
Cross, The B2
Crowngate Ctr B2
Deansway B2
Diglis Pde C2
Diglis Rd C2
Edgar Tower C2
Farrier St A2
Foregate St B2
Fort Royal Hill C3
Fort Royal Park C3
Foundry St B3
Friar St C2
George St B3
Grand Stand Rd B1
Greenhill C3
Greyfriars B2
Guildhall B2
Henwick Rd B1
High St B2
Hill St B3
Hive, The B2
Huntingdon Hall B2
Hylton Rd B1
Information Ctr B2
King Charles Place Shopping Centre C1
King's School C2
King's School Playing Field C2
Kleve Walk C2
Lansdowne Cres A3
Lansdowne Rd A3
Lansdowne Walk A3
Laslett St A3
Little Chestnut St A2
Little London A2
London Rd C3
Lowell St A3
Lowesmoor B2
Lowesmoor Terr A3
Lowesmoor Wharf A3
Magistrates Court A2
Midland Rd B3
Mill St C2
Moors Severn Terr, The A1
Museum & Art Gallery A2
Museum of Royal Worcester C2
New Rd C1
New St B2
Northfield St A2
Odeon B2
Old Palace The C2
Padmore St B3
Park St C3
Pheasant St B3
Pitchcroft Racecourse A1
Police Station A2
Portland St C2
Post Office B2
Quay St B2
Queen St B2
Rainbow Hill A3
Recreation Ground A2
Reindeer Court B2
Rogers Hill A3
Sabrina Terr A1
St Dunstan's Cres C3
St John's C1
St Martin's Gate B3
St Martin's Quarter B3
St Oswald's Rd A2
St Paul's St B3
St Swithin's Church B2
St Wulstans Cres C3
Sansome Walk A2
Severn St C2
Shambles, The B2
Shaw St B2
Shire Hall Crown Ct A2
Shrub Hill Rd B3
Shrub Hill Retail Pk B3
Slingpool Walk C1
South Parade B2
Southfield St A2
Sports Centre A3
Stanley Rd B3
Swan, The A1
Swimming Pool A2
Tallow Hill B3
Tennis Walk A2
Tolladine Rd B3
Tudor House B2
Tybridge St B1
Tything, The A2
Univ of Worcester B2
Vincent Rd B3
Vue C2
Washington St A3
Woolhope Rd C3
Worcester Bridge B2
Worcester County Cricket Club C1
Worcester Foregate Street B2
Worcester Shrub Hill B3
Worcester Royal Grammar School A2
Wylds La C3

Wrexham
Wrecsam 200
Abbot St B2
Acton Rd A3
Albert St C3
Alexandra Rd C1
Aran Rd A3
Barnfield C3
Bath Rd C2
Beeches, The A3
Beechley Rd C3
Belgrave Rd C2
Belle Vue Park C2
Belle Vue Rd C2
Belvedere Dr A1
Bennion's Rd C3
Berse Rd A1
Bersham Rd C1
Birch St C3
Bodhyfryd B3
Border Retail Park B3
Bradley Rd C2
Bright St B1
Bron-y-Nant B1
Brook St C2
Bryn-y-Cabanau Rd C3
Bury St C3
Bus Station B2
Butchers Market B3
Caia Rd C3
Cambrian Ind Est C3
Caxton Place B2
Cemetery C1
Centenary Rd C1
Chapel St C2
Charles St B3
Chester Rd A3
Chester St B3
Cilcen Grove A3
Citizens Advice Bureau B2
Cobden Rd B1
Council Offices B3
County B2
Crescent Rd B3
Crispin La A2
Croesnewyth Rd B1
Cross St A2
Cunliffe St A2
Derby Rd C3
Dolydd Rd B1
Duke St B2
Eagles Meadow C3
Earle St C2
East Ave A2
Edward St C2
Egerton St B2
Empress Rd C1
Erddig Rd C2
Fairy Rd C2
Fire Station B2
Foster Rd A3
Foxwood Dr C1
Garden Rd A2
General Market B3
Gerald St B2
Gibson St C1
Glyndŵr University Plas Coch Campus A1
Greenbank St C3
Greenfield A2
Grosvenor Rd B2
Grove Park B2
Grove Park Rd B3
Grove Rd A3
Guildhall B2
Haig Rd C3
Hampden Rd C2
Hazel Grove A3
Henblas St B3
High St B3
Hightown Rd C3
Hill St B2
Holt Rd B3
Holt St B3
Hope St B2
Huntroyde Ave C3
Information Ctr B3
Island Green Shopping Centre B2
Job Centre B2
Jubilee Rd B2
King St B2
Kingsmills Rd C3
Lambpit St B3
Law Courts B3
Lawson Cl A3
Lawson Rd A3
Lea Rd C2
Library & Arts Ctr B2
Lilac Way B1
Llys David Lord B1
Lorne St A2
Maesgwyn Rd B1
Maesydre Rd A3
Manley Rd B3
Market St B3
Mawddy Ave A2
Mayville Ave A2
Meml Gallery B2
Memorial Hall B3
Mold Rd A1
Mount St C3
Neville Cres A3
New Rd A2
North Wales Regional Tennis Centre A1
North Wales School of Art & Design B2
Oak Dr A3
Park Ave A3
Park St A2
Peel St C1
Pen y Bryn C2
Pentre Felin C2
Penymaes Ave A3
Peoples Market B3
Percy St C2
Pines, The A3
Plas Coch Rd A1
Plas Coch Retail Pk A1
Police Station B3
Poplar Rd C2
Post Office A2/B2/C2/C3
Powell Rd B3
Poyser St C2
Price's La A2
Primose Way B1
Princess St C1
Queen St B3
Queens Sq B2
Regent St B2
Rhosddu Rd A2/B2
Rhosnesni La A3
Rivulet Rd C3
Ruabon Rd C2
Ruthin Rd C1/C2
St Giles C3
St Giles Way C3
St James Ct A2
St Mary's B2
Salisbury Rd C3
Salop Rd C3
Sontley Rd C2
Spring Rd A2
Stanley St C3
Stansty Rd A2
Station Approach B2
Studio B2
Talbot Rd C2
Techniquest Glyndŵr A2
Town Hill C2
Trevor St C2
Trinity St B2
Tuttle St C3
Vale Park A1
Vernon St B2
Vicarage Hill B2
Victoria Rd B2
Walnut St A2
War Memorial B3
Waterworld Leisure Centre B3
Watery Rd B1/B2
Wellington Rd C2
Westminster Dr A3
William Aston Hall A1
Windsor Rd A1
Wrecsam
Wrexham AFC A1
Wrexham Central B2
Wrexham General B2
Wrexham Maelor Hospital (A&E) B1
Wrexham Technology Park B1
Wynn Ave A2
Yale College B3
Yale Grove A3
Yorke St C3

York 200
Aldwark B2
Barbican Rd C3
Bar Convent Living Heritage Ctr C1
Barley Hall B2
Bishopgate St C2
Bishophill Senior C2
Bishopthorpe Rd C2
Blossom St C1
Bootham A1
Bootham Cres A1
Bootham Terr A1
Bridge St B2
Brook St A2
Brownlow St A2
Burton Stone La A1
Castle Museum C2
Castlegate B2
Cemetery Rd C3
Cherry St C2
City Screen B2
City Wall A2/B1/C3
Clarence St A2
Clementhorpe C2
Clifford St B2
Clifford's Tower B2
Clifton A1
Coach park A2
Coney St B2
Coppergate Ctr B2
Cromwell Rd C2
Crown Court C2
Davygate B2
Deanery Gdns A2
DIG B2
Dodsworth Ave A3
Eboracum Way A3
Ebor Industrial Est B3
Eldon St A2
Everyman C1
Fairfax House B2
Fire Station C3
Fishergate C3
Foss Islands Rd B3
Foss Islands Retail Park B3
Fossbank A3
Garden St A2
George St C3
Gillygate A2
Goodramgate B2
Grand Opera Ho B2
Grosvenor Terr A1
Guildhall B2
Hallfield Rd A3
Heslington Rd C3
Heworth Green A3
Holy Trinity B2
Hope St C3
Huntington Rd A3
Information Ctr B2
James St B3
Jorvik Viking Ctr B2
Kent St C3
Lawrence St C3
Layerthorpe A3
Leeman Rd B1
Lendal B2
Lendal Bridge B1
Library A2/B1
Longfield Terrace A1
Lord Mayor's Walk A2
Lowther St A2
Mansion House B2
Margaret St C3
Marygate A1
Melbourne St C3
Merchant Adventurers' Hall B2
Merchant Taylors' Hall B2
Micklegate B1
Micklegate Bar C1
Monkgate A2
Moss St C1
Museum Gdns B1
Museum St B1
National Railway Museum B1
Navigation Rd B3
Newton Terr C2
North Pde A1
North St B2
Nunnery La C1
Nunthorpe Rd C1
Ouse Bridge B2
Paragon St C3
Park Grove A3
Park St C1
Parliament St B2
Peasholme Green B3
Penley's Grove St A2
Piccadilly B2
Police Station B2
Post Office B1/B2/C3
Priory St B1
Queen Anne's Rd A1
Regimental Mus B2
Richard III Experience at Monk Bar A2
Roman Bath B2
Rowntree Park C2
St Andrewgate B2
St Benedict Rd C1
St John St A2
St Olave's Rd A1
St Peter's Grove A1
St Saviourgate B2
Scarcroft Hill C1
Scarcroft Rd C1
Shambles, The B2
Shopmobility B2
Skeldergate C2
Skeldergate Bridge C2
Station Rd B1
Stonebow, The B2
Stonegate B2
Superstore A3
Sycamore Terr A1
Terry Ave C2
Theatre Royal B2
Thorpe St C1
Toft Green B1
Tower St C2
Townend St A2
Treasurer's Ho A2
Trinity La B1
Undercroft Mus A2
Union Terr A2
Victor St C2
Vine St C2
Walmgate B3
War Memorial B1
Wellington St C3
York Art Gallery A1
York Barbican C3
York Brewery B1
York Dungeon, The B2
York Minster A2
York St John Uni A2
York Station B1

Index

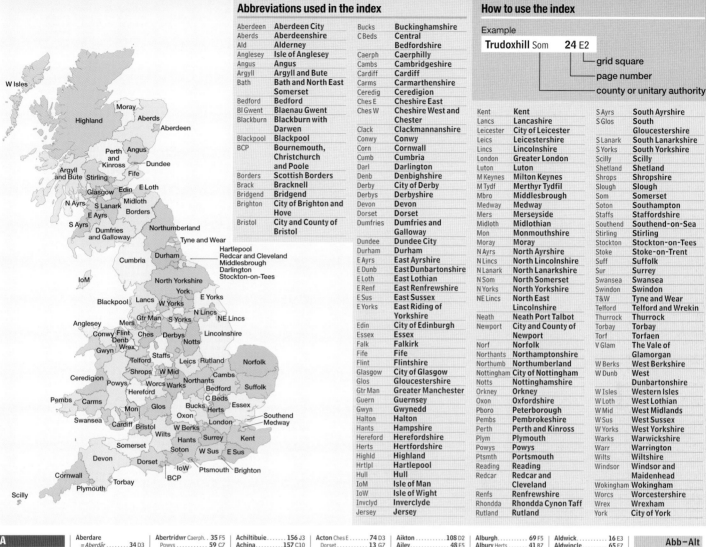

Abbreviations used in the index

Aberdeen	Aberdeen City	Bucks	Buckinghamshire
Aberds	Aberdeenshire	C Beds	Central Bedfordshire
Ald	Alderney	Caerph	Caerphilly
Anglesey	Isle of Anglesey	Cambs	Cambridgeshire
Angus	Angus	Cardiff	Cardiff
Argyll	Argyll and Bute	Carms	Carmarthenshire
Bath	Bath and North East Somerset	Ceredig	Ceredigion
Bedford	Bedford	Ches E	Cheshire East
Bl Gwent	Blaenau Gwent	Ches W	Cheshire West and Chester
Blackburn	Blackburn with Darwen	Clack	Clackmannanshire
Blackpool	Blackpool	Conwy	Conwy
BCP	Bournemouth, Christchurch and Poole	Corn	Cornwall
		Cumb	Cumbria
Borders	Scottish Borders	Darl	Darlington
Brack	Bracknell	Denb	Denbighshire
Bridgend	Bridgend	Derby	City of Derby
Brighton	City of Brighton and Hove	Derbys	Derbyshire
Bristol	City and County of Bristol	Devon	Devon
		Dorset	Dorset
		Dumfries	Dumfries and Galloway
		Dundee	Dundee City
		Durham	Durham
		E Ayrs	East Ayrshire
		E Dunb	East Dunbartonshire
		E Loth	East Lothian
		E Renf	East Renfrewshire
		E Sus	East Sussex
		E Yorks	East Riding of Yorkshire
		Edin	City of Edinburgh
		Essex	Essex
		Falk	Falkirk
		Fife	Fife
		Flint	Flintshire
		Glasgow	City of Glasgow
		Glos	Gloucestershire
		Gtr Man	Greater Manchester
		Guern	Guernsey
		Gwyn	Gwynedd
		Halton	Halton
		Hants	Hampshire
		Hereford	Herefordshire
		Herts	Hertfordshire
		Highld	Highland
		Hrtlpl	Hartlepool
		Hull	Hull
		IoM	Isle of Man
		IoW	Isle of Wight
		Invclyd	Inverclyde
		Jersey	Jersey

How to use the index

Example

Trudoxhill Som **24** E2

— grid square
— page number
— county or unitary authority

Kent	Kent	S Ayrs	South Ayrshire
Lancs	Lancashire	S Glos	South Gloucestershire
Leicester	City of Leicester	S Lanark	South Lanarkshire
Leics	Leicestershire	S Yorks	South Yorkshire
Lincs	Lincolnshire	Scilly	Scilly
London	Greater London	Shetland	Shetland
Luton	Luton	Shrops	Shropshire
M Keynes	Milton Keynes	Slough	Slough
M Tydf	Merthyr Tydfil	Som	Somerset
Mbro	Middlesbrough	Soton	Southampton
Medway	Medway	Staffs	Staffordshire
Mers	Merseyside	Southend	Southend-on-Sea
Midloth	Midlothian	Stirling	Stirling
Mon	Monmouthshire	Stockton	Stockton-on-Tees
Moray	Moray	Stoke	Stoke-on-Trent
N Ayrs	North Ayrshire	Suff	Suffolk
N Lincs	North Lincolnshire	Sur	Surrey
N Lanark	North Lanarkshire	Swansea	Swansea
N Som	North Somerset	Swindon	Swindon
N Yorks	North Yorkshire	T&W	Tyne and Wear
NE Lincs	North East Lincolnshire	Telford	Telford and Wrekin
Neath	Neath Port Talbot	Thurrock	Thurrock
Newport	City and County of Newport	Torbay	Torbay
Norf	Norfolk	Torf	Torfaen
Northants	Northamptonshire	V Glam	The Vale of Glamorgan
Northumb	Northumberland	W Berks	West Berkshire
Nottingham	City of Nottingham	W Dunb	West Dunbartonshire
Notts	Nottinghamshire	W Isles	Western Isles
Orkney	Orkney	W Loth	West Lothian
Oxon	Oxfordshire	W Mid	West Midlands
Pboro	Peterborough	W Sus	West Sussex
Pembs	Pembrokeshire	W Yorks	West Yorkshire
Perth	Perth and Kinross	Warks	Warwickshire
Plym	Plymouth	Warr	Warrington
Powys	Powys	Wilts	Wiltshire
Ptsmth	Portsmouth	Windsor	Windsor and Maidenhead
Reading	Reading	Wokingham	Wokingham
Redcar	Redcar and Cleveland	Worcs	Worcestershire
Renfs	Renfrewshire	Wrex	Wrexham
Rhondda	Rhondda Cynon Taff	York	City of York
Rutland	Rutland		

A

Abbas Combe 12 B5
Abberley. 50 C2
Abberton Essex . . 43 C6
  Worcs 50 D4
Abberwick 117 C7
Abbess Roding . . 42 C1
Abbey 11 C6
Abbey-cwm-hir . . 48 B2
Abbeydale 88 F4
Abbey Dore 49 F5
Abbey Field 43 B5
Abbey Hulton 75 E6
Abbey St Bathans . 122 C3
Abbeystead 93 D5
Abbey Town 107 D8
Abbey Village. . . . 86 B4
Abbey Wood 29 B5
Abbots Bickington . 9 C5
Abbots Bromley . . 62 B4
Abbotsbury 12 F3
Abbotsham 9 B6
Abbotskerswell . . 7 C6
Abbots Langley . . 40 D3
Abbots Leigh 23 B7
Abbotsley 54 D3
Abbots Morton . . 50 D5
Abbots Ripton . . . 54 B3
Abbots Salford . . 51 D5
Abbotswood 14 B4
Abbotts Ann. 25 E8
Abcott 49 B5
Abdon 61 F5
Aber 46 E3
Aberaeron 46 C3
Aberaman 34 D4
Aberangell 58 C5
Aber-Arad 46 F2
Aberarder 137 F7
Aberarder House . 138 B2
Aberargie 128 C3
Aberarth 46 C3
Aberavon 33 E8
Aber-banc 46 E2
Aberbeeg 35 D6
Abercanaid 34 D4
Abercarn 35 E6
Abercastle 44 B3
Abercegir 58 D5
Aberchirder 152 C6
Aber Cowarth . . . 59 C5
Abercraf 34 C2
Abercrombie . . . 129 D7
Abercych 45 E4
Abercynafon 34 C4
Abercynon 34 E4
Aberdalgie 128 B2
Aberdâr
  = Aberdare 34 D3

Aberdare
  = Aberdâr 34 D3
Aberdaron 70 E2
Aberdaugleddau
  = Milford Haven . . 44 E4
Aberdeen 141 D8
Aberdesach 82 F4
Aberdour 128 F3
Aberdovey 58 E3
Aberdulais 34 D1
Aberedw 48 E2
Abereiddy 44 B2
Abererch 70 D4
Aberfan 34 D4
Aberfeldy 133 E5
Aberffraw 82 E3
Aberffrwd 47 B5
Aberford 95 F7
Aberfoyle 126 D4
Abergavenny
  = Y Fenni 35 C6
Abergele. 72 B3
Aber-Giâr 46 E4
Abergorlech 46 F4
Abergwaun
  = Fishguard 44 B4
Abergwesyn 47 D7
Abergwili 33 B5
Abergwyngregyn . 83 D6
Abergwynfi 34 E2
Abergynolwyn . . . 58 D3
Aber-Hirnant 72 F3
Aberhonddu
  = Brecon 34 B4
Aberhosan 58 E5
Aberkenfig 34 F2
Aberlady 129 F6
Aberlemno 135 D5
Aberllefenni 58 D4
Aber-miwl
  = Abermule 59 E8
Abermagwr 47 B5
Abermaw
  = Barmouth 58 C3
Abermeurig 46 D4
Abermule 59 E8
Abernaint 59 B8
Abernant 32 B4
Aber-nant 34 D4
Abernethy 128 C3
Abernyte 134 F2
Aberpennar
  = Mountain Ash . . 34 E4
Aberporth 45 D4
Aber-Rhiwlech. . . 59 B6
Abersoch 70 E4
Abersychan 35 D6
Abertawe
  = Swansea 33 E7
Aberteifi
  = Cardigan 45 E3
Aberthin 22 B2
Abertillery
  = Abertyleri 35 D6

Abertridwr Caerph. . 35 F5
  Powys 59 C7
Abertyleri
  = Abertillery 35 D6
Abertysswg 35 D5
Aberuthven 127 C8
Aber-Village 35 B5
Aberyscir 34 B3
Aberystwyth 58 F2
Abhainn Suidhe . 154 G5
Abingdon-on-
  Thames 38 E4
Abinger Common . 28 E2
Abinger Hammer . 27 E8
Abington 114 B2
Abington Pigotts . 54 E4
Ab Kettleby 64 B4
Ab Lench 50 D5
Ablington Glos . . . 37 D8
  Wilts 25 E6
Abney 75 B8
Aboyne 140 E4
Abram 86 D4
Abriachan 151 H8
Abridge. 41 E7
Abronhill 119 B7
Abson 24 B2
Abthorpe 52 E4
Abune-the-Hill . . 159 F3
Aby 79 B7
Acaster Malbis . . 95 E8
Acaster Selby . . . 95 E8
Accrington. 87 B5
Acha 146 F4
Achabraid 145 E7
Achachork 149 D9
Achafolla 124 D3
Achagary 157 D10
Achahoish 144 F6
Achalader 133 E8
Achallader 131 E7
Acha Mor 155 E8
Achanalt 150 E5
Achanamara . . . 144 E6
Achandunie 151 D9
Ach'an Todhair . . 130 B4
Achany 157 J8
Achaphubuil 130 B4
Acharacle 147 E9
Acharn Highld . . 147 F10
  Perth 132 E4
Acharole 158 E4
Achath 141 C6
Achavanich 158 F3
Achavraat 151 G12
Achddu 33 D5
Achduart 156 J3
Achentoul 157 F11
Achfary 156 F5
Achgarve 155 H13
Achiemore Highld 156 C6
  Highld 157 D11
A'Chill 148 H7

Achiltibuie. 156 J3
Achina. 157 C10
Achinduich 157 J8
Achindown. 124 B4
Achingills 158 D3
Achintee Highld . . 131 B5
  Highld 150 G2
Achintraid 149 E13
Achlean 138 E4
Achleck 146 G7
Achluachrach . . . 137 F5
Achlyness 156 D5
Achmelvich 156 G3
Achmore Highld . 149 E13
  Stirling 132 F2
Achnaba Argyll . . 124 B5
  Argyll 145 E8
Achnabat 151 H8
Achnacarnin . . . 156 F3
Achnacarry 136 F4
Achnacloich Argyll 125 B5
  Highld 149 H10
Achnaconeran . . . 137 C7
Achnacraig 146 G7
Achnacroish 130 E2
Achnadrish 146 F7
Achnafalnich. . . . 125 C8
Achnagarron . . . 151 E9
Achnaha 146 E7
Achnahanat 151 B8
Achnahannet . . . 139 B5
Achnairn. 157 H8
Achnasheen 150 F4
Achosnich 146 E7
Achranich 147 G10
Achreamie 157 C13
Achriabhach 131 C5
Achriesgill 156 D5
Achrimsdale 157 J12
Achtoty 157 C9
Achurch 65 F7
Achuvoldrach. . . 157 D8
Achvaich. 151 B10
Achvarasdal. . . . 157 C12
Ackergill 158 E5
Acklam Mbro. . . . 102 C2
  N Yorks. 96 C3
Ackleton 61 E7
Acklington 117 D8
Ackton. 88 B5
Ackworth Moor
  Top. 88 C5
Acle 69 C7
Acock's Green. . . . 62 F5
Acol 31 C7
Acomb Northumb . 110 C2
  York 95 D8
Aconbury 49 F7
Acre 87 B5
Acrefair 73 E6
Acre Street. 15 E8

Acton Ches E 74 D3
  Dorset 13 G7
  London 41 F5
  Shrops. 60 F3
  Suff 56 E2
  Wrex 73 D7
Acton Beauchamp. 49 D8
Acton Bridge. . . . 74 B2
Acton Burnell . . . 60 D5
Acton Green 49 D8
Acton Pigott 60 D5
Acton Round 61 E6
Acton Scott 60 F4
Acton Trussell . . . 62 C3
Acton Turville . . . 37 F5
Adbaston 61 B7
Adber. 12 B3
Adderley 74 E3
Adderstone 123 F7
Addiewell 120 C2
Addingham 94 E3
Addington Bucks . . 39 B7
  Kent. 29 D7
  London 28 C4
Addinston 121 D8
Addiscombe 28 C4
Addlestone 27 C8
Addlethorpe 79 C8
Adel 95 F5
Adeney 61 C7
Adfa 59 D7
Adforton 49 B6
Adisham 31 D6
Adlestrop 38 B2
Adlingfleet 90 B2
Adlington 86 C4
Admaston Staffs . . 62 B4
  Telford. 61 C6
Admington 51 E7
Adstock. 52 F5
Adstone 52 D3
Adversane 16 B4
Advie 152 E1
Adwalton 88 B3
Adwell 39 E6
Adwick le Street. . 89 D6
Adwick upon
  Dearne 89 D5
Adziel 153 C9
Ae Village 114 F2
Affleck 141 B7
Affpuddle 13 E6
Affric Lodge 136 B4
Afon-wen 72 B5
Afton 14 F4
Agglethorpe . . . 101 F5
Agneash 84 D4
Aigburth 85 F4
Aiginis 155 D9
Aike 97 E6
Aikerness 159 C5
Aikers 159 J5
Aiketgate 108 E4

Aikton 108 D2
Ailey. 48 E5
Ailstone 51 D7
Ailsworth 65 E8
Ainderby
  Quernhow 102 F1
Ainderby Steeple. 101 E8
Aingers Green. . . 43 B7
Ainsdale 85 C4
Ainsdale-on-Sea . 85 C4
Ainstable 108 E5
Ainsworth 87 C5
Ainthorpe 103 D5
Aintree 85 E4
Aird Argyll 124 E3
  Dumfries 104 C4
  Highld 149 A12
  W Isles 155 D10
Aird a Mhachair . 148 D2
Aird a'Mhulaidh . 154 F6
Aird Asaig 154 G6
Aird Dhail 155 A9
Airdens. 151 B9
Aird Mhidhinis . . 148 H2
Aird Mhige
  W Isles 154 H6
  W Isles 154 J5
Aird Mhor. 148 H2
Aird of Sleat. . . . 149 H10
Airdrie. 119 C7
Aird Thunga 155 D9
Airdtorrisdale. . . 157 C9
Aird Uig. 154 D5
Airidh a Bhruaich. 154 F7
Airieland. 106 D4
Airmyn. 89 B8
Airntully 133 F7
Aira. 99 B8
Aire . . . . 99 B8 (?)
Airor. 149 H12
Airth. 127 F7
Airton 94 D2
Airyhassen 105 E7
Aisby Lincs. 78 F3
  Lincs. 90 E2
Aisgernis 148 F2
Aiskew. 101 F7
Aislaby N Yorks . . 103 D6
  N Yorks. 103 F5
  Stockton 102 C2
Aisthorpe 78 A2
Aith Orkney 159 G3
  Shetland 160 D8
  Shetland 160 H5
Aithsetter 160 K6
Aitkenhead 112 D3
Aitnoch 151 H12
Akeld. 117 B5
Akeley. 52 F5
Akenham 56 E5
Akeld. 117 B5
Albaston 6 B2
Alberbury 60 C3
Albourne 17 C6
Albrighton Shrops. 60 C4
  Shrops 62 D2

Alburgh. 69 F5
Albury Herts 41 B7
  Sur. 27 E8
Albury End 41 B7
Alby Hill 81 D7
Alcaig 151 F8
Alcaston 60 F4
Alcester 51 D5
Alciston 18 E2
Alcombe Som . . . 21 E8
  Wilts 24 C3
Alconbury. 54 B2
Alconbury Weston. 54 B2
Aldborough Norf . 81 D7
  N Yorks. 95 C7
Aldbourne 25 B7
Aldbrough 97 F8
Aldbrough
  St John. 101 C7
Aldbury. 40 C2
Aldcliffe 92 C4
Aldclune 133 C6
Aldeburgh 57 D8
Aldeby 69 E7
Aldenham. 40 E4
Alderbury 14 B2
Aldercar 76 E4
Alderford 68 C4
Alderholt 14 C2
Alderley 36 E4
Alderley Edge . . . 74 B5
Aldermaston 26 C3
Aldermaston
  Wharf 26 C4
Alderminster 51 E7
Alder's End 49 E8
Aldersey Green. . . 73 D8
Aldershot 27 D6
Alderton Glos . . . 50 F5
  Northants 52 E5
  Shrops. 60 B4
  Suff 57 E7
  Wilts 37 F5
Alderwasley 76 D3
Aldfield 95 C5
Aldford 73 D8
Aldham Essex . . . 43 B5
  Suff 56 E4
Aldie 151 C10
Aldingbourne . . . 16 D3
Aldingham 92 B2
Aldington Kent . . 19 B7
  Worcs 51 E5
Aldington Frith. . . 19 B7
Aldochlay 126 E2
Aldreth 54 B5
Aldridge 62 D4
Aldringham. 57 C8
Aldsworth 38 C1
Aldunie 140 B2
Aldwark Derbys . . 76 D2
Aldwark N Yorks . . 95 C7

Aldwick. 16 E3
Aldwincle. 65 F7
Aldworth 26 B3
Alexandria 118 B3
Alfardisworthy . . . 8 C4
Alfington 11 E6
Alfold. 27 F8
Alfold Bars 27 F8
Alfold Crossways . 27 F8
Alford Aberds . . . 140 C4
  Lincs 79 B7
  Som 23 F8
Alfreton 76 D4
Alfrick 50 D2
Alfrick Pound . . . 50 D2
Alfriston 18 E2
Algaltraig 145 F9
Algarkirk 79 F5
Alhampton 23 F8
Aline Lodge 154 F6
Alisary 147 D10
Alkborough 90 B2
Alkerton 51 E8
Alkham 31 E6
Alkington 74 F2
Alkmonton 75 F8
Alladale Lodge . . 150 C7
Allaleigh 7 D6
Allanaquoich . . . 139 E7
Allangrange
  Mains 151 F9
Allanton Borders . 122 D4
  N Lanark 119 D8
Allathasdal. 148 H1
All Cannings 25 C5
Allendale Town . . 109 D8
Allenheads 109 E8
Allensford 110 D3
Allens Green 41 C7
Allensmore 49 F6
Allenton 76 F3
Aller 12 B2
Allerby 107 F7
Allerford 21 E8
Allerston 103 F6
Allerthorpe 96 E3
Allerton Mers . . . 86 F2
  W Yorks 94 F4
Allerton Bywater . 88 B5
Allerton
  Mauleverer 95 D7
Allesley 63 F7
Allestree 76 F3
Allet 3 B6
Allexton 64 D5
Allgreave 75 C6
Allhallows 30 B2
Allhallows-on-Sea 30 B2
Alligin Shuas . . . 149 C13
Allimore Green . . 62 C2
Allington Lincs . . . 77 E8
  Wilts 25 C5
  Wilts 25 F7

Abb-Alt

Allithwaite 92 B3
Alloa 127 E7
Allonby 107 E7
Alloway 112 C3
All Saints South
  Elmham 69 F6
All Stretton 60 E4
Allt 33 D6
Alltchaorunn. . . . 131 D5
Alltforgan. 59 B6
Alltmawr. 48 E2
Alltnacaillich. . . 156 E7
Allt na h-Airbhe . 150 B4
Allt-nan-sùgh . . 136 B2
Alltsigh 137 C7
Alltwalis 46 F3
Alltwen 33 D8
Alltyblaca. 46 E4
Allwood Green . . 56 B4
Almeley. 48 D5
Almer. 13 E7
Almholme 89 D6
Almington 74 F4
Alminstone Cross . .8 B5
Almondbank . . . 128 B2
Almondbury 88 C2
Almondsbury . . . 36 F3
Alne 95 C7
Alness 151 E9
Alnham 117 C5
Alnmouth 117 C8
Alnwick 117 C7
Alperton 40 F4
Alphamstone 56 F2
Alpheton. 56 D2
Alphington 10 E4
Alport 76 C2
Alpraham 74 D2
Alresford 43 B6
Alrewas 63 C5
Alsager 74 D4
Alsagers Bank. . . 74 E5
Alsop en le Dale . 75 D8
Alston Cumb . . . 109 E7
  Devon 11 D8
Alstone 50 F4
Alstonefield. 75 D8
Alswear. 10 B2
Altandhu. 156 H2
Altanduin 157 G11
Altarnun 8 F4
Altass. 156 J7
Alterwall. 158 D4
Altham. 93 F7
Althorne 43 E5
Althorpe 90 D2
Alticry 105 D6
Altnabreac
  Station 157 E13

Altnacealgach Hotel...156 H5
Altnacraig...124 C4
Altnafeadh...131 D6
Altnaharra...157 F8
Altofts...88 B4
Alton Derbys...76 C3
Hants...26 F5
Staffs...75 E7
Alton Pancras...12 D5
Alton Priors...25 C6
Altrincham...87 F5
Altrua...136 F5
Altskeith...126 D3
Altyre House...151 F13
Alva...127 E7
Alvanley...73 B8
Alvaston...76 F3
Alvechurch...50 B5
Alvecote...63 D6
Alvediston...13 B7
Alveley...61 F7
Alverdiscott...9 B7
Alverstoke...15 E7
Alverstone...15 F6
Alverton...77 E7
Alves...152 B1
Alvescot...38 D2
Alveston S Glos...36 F3
Warks...51 D7
Alvie...138 D4
Alvingham...91 E7
Alvington...36 D3
Alwalton...65 E8
Alweston...12 C4
Alwinton...116 D5
Alwoodley...95 E5
Alyth...134 E2
Amatnatua...150 B7
Am Baile...148 G2
Ambergate...76 D3
Amber Hill...78 E5
Amberley Glos...37 D5
W Sus...16 C4
Amble...117 D8
Amblecote...62 F2
Ambler Thorn...87 B8
Ambleside...99 D5
Ambleston...44 C5
Ambrosden...39 C6
Am Buth...124 C4
Amcotts...90 C2
Amersham...40 E2
Amesbury...25 E6
Amington...63 D6
Amisfield...114 F2
Amlwch...82 B4
Amlwch Port...82 B4
Ammanford =Rhydaman...33 C7
Amod...143 E8
Amotherby...96 B3
Ampfield...14 B5
Ampleforth...95 B8
Ampney Crucis...37 D7
Ampney St Mary...37 D7
Ampney St Peter...37 D7
Amport...25 E7
Ampthill...53 F8
Ampton...56 B2
Amroth...32 D2
Amulree...133 F5
Anagach...139 B6
Anaheilt...130 C2
Anancaun...150 E3
An Caol...149 C11
Ancaster...78 E2
Anchor...59 F8
Anchorsholme...92 E3
An Cnoc...155 D9
Ancroft...123 E5
Ancrum...116 B2
Anderby...79 B8
Anderson...13 E6
Anderton...74 B3
Andover...25 E8
Andover Down...25 E8
Andoversford...37 C7
Andreas...84 C4
Anfield...85 E4
Angersleigh...11 C6
Angle...44 E3
An Gleann Ur...155 D9
Angmering...16 D4
Angram N Yorks...95 E8
N Yorks...100 E3
Anie...126 C4
Ankerville...151 D11
Anlaby...90 B4
Anmer...80 E3
Annan...107 C8
Annat Argyll...125 C6
Highld...149 C13
Anna Valley...25 E8
Annbank...112 B4
Annesley...76 D5
Annesley Woodhouse...76 D4
Annfield Plain...110 D4
Annifirth...160 J3
Annitsford...111 B5
Annscroft...60 D4
Ansdell...85 B4
Ansford...23 F8
Ansley...63 E6
Anslow...63 B6
Anslow Gate...63 B6
Anstey Herts...54 F5
Leics...64 D2
Anstruther Easter...129 D7
Anstruther Wester...129 D7
Ansty Hants...26 E5
Warks...63 F7
Wilts...13 B7
W Sus...17 B6
Anthill Common...15 C7
Anthorn...107 D8
Antingham...81 D8
An t-Ob =Leverburgh...154 J5
Anton's Gowt...79 E5
Antonshill...127 F7
Antony...5 D8
Anwick...78 D4

Anwoth...106 D2
Aoradh...142 B3
Apes Hall...67 E5
Apethorpe...65 E7
Apeton...62 C2
Apley...78 B4
Apperknowle...76 B3
Apperley...37 B5
Apperley Bridge...94 F4
Appersett...100 E3
Appin...130 E3
Appin House...130 E3
Appleby...90 C3
Appleby-in-Westmorland...100 B1
Appleby Magna...63 D7
Appleby Parva...63 D7
Applecross...149 D12
Applecross House...149 D12
Appledore Devon...11 C5
Devon...20 F3
Kent...19 C6
Appledore Heath...19 B6
Appleford...39 E5
Applegarthtown...114 F4
Appleshaw...25 E8
Applethwaite...98 B4
Appleton Halton...86 F3
Oxon...38 D4
Appleton-le-Moors...103 F5
Appleton-le-Street...96 B3
Appleton Roebuck...95 E8
Appleton Thorn...86 F4
Appleton Wiske...102 D1
Appletreehall...115 C8
Appletreewick...94 C3
Appley...11 B5
Appley Bridge...86 D3
Apse Heath...15 F6
Apsley End...54 F2
Apuldram...16 D2
Aquhythie...141 C6
Arabella...151 D11
Arbeadie...141 E5
Arberth =Narberth...32 C2
Arbirlot...135 E6
Arboll...151 C11
Arborfield...27 C5
Arborfield Cross...27 C5
Arborfield Garrison...27 C5
Arbourthorne...88 F4
Arbroath...135 E6
Arbuthnott...135 B7
Archiestown...152 D2
Arclid...74 C4
Ardachu...157 J9
Ardalanish...146 K6
Ardanaiseig...125 C6
Ardaneaskan...149 E13
Ardanstur...124 D4
Ardargie House Hotel...128 C2
Ardarroch...149 E13
Ardbeg Argyll...142 D5
Argyll...145 E10
Ardcharnich...150 C4
Ardchiavaig...146 K6
Ardchullarie More...126 C4
Ardchyle...126 B4
Ard-dhubh...149 D12
Arddleen...60 C2
Ardechvie...136 E4
Ardeley...41 B6
Ardelve...149 F13
Arden...126 F2
Ardens Grafton...51 D6
Ardentinny...145 E10
Ardeonaig...132 F3
Ardersier...151 F10
Ardessie...150 C3
Ardfern...124 E4
Ardgartan...125 E8
Ardgay...150 B4
Ardglass...149 E11
Ardgour...130 C2
Ardheslaig...149 C12
Ardiecow...152 B5
Ardindrean...150 C4
Ardingly...17 B7
Ardington...38 F4
Ardlair...140 B4
Ardlamont House...145 G8
Ardleigh...43 B6
Ardler...134 E2
Ardley...39 B5
Ardlui...126 C2
Ardlussa...144 E5
Ardmair...150 B4
Ardmay...125 E8
Ardminish...143 D7
Ardmolich...147 D10
Ardmore Argyll...124 C3
Highld...151 C10
Highld...156 D5
Ardnacross...147 G8
Ardnadam...145 F10
Ardnagrask...151 G8
Ardnarff...149 E13
Ardnastang...130 C2
Ardnave...142 A3
Ardno...125 E7
Ardo...153 E8
Ardoch...133 F7
Ardochy House...136 D5
Ardo House...141 B8
Ardoyne...141 B5
Ardpatrick...144 G6
Ardpatrick House...144 H6
Ardpeaton...145 E11
Ardrishaig...145 E7
Ardross Fife...129 D7
Highld...151 D9
Ardrossan...118 E2
Ardross Castle...151 D9
Ardshealach...147 E9
Ardsley...88 D4
Ardslignish...147 E8
Ardtalla...142 C5
Ardtalnaig...132 F4
Ardtoe...147 D9
Ardtrostan...127 B5
Arduaine...124 D3
Ardullie...151 E8

Ardvasar...149 H11
Ardvorlich...126 B5
Ardwell...104 E5
Ardwell Mains...104 E5
Ardwick...87 E6
Areley Kings...50 B3
Arford...27 F6
Argoed Caerph...35 E5
Powys...47 C8
Arichamish...124 E4
Arichastlich...125 B8
Aridhglas...146 J6
Arileod...149 C11
Arinacrinachd...149 C12
Arinagour...146 F5
Arion...159 G3
Arisaig...147 C9
Ariundle...130 C2
Arkendale...95 C6
Arkesden...55 F5
Arkholme...93 B5
Arkle Town...101 D5
Arkley...41 E5
Arksey...89 D6
Arkwright Town...76 B4
Arle...37 B6
Arlecdon...98 C2
Arlesey...54 F2
Arleston...61 C6
Arley...86 F4
Arlingham...36 C4
Arlington Devon...20 E5
E Sus...18 E2
Glos...37 D8
Armadale Highld...157 C10
W Loth...120 C2
Armadale Castle...149 H11
Armathwaite...108 E5
Arminghall...69 D5
Armitage...62 C4
Armley...95 F5
Armscote...51 E7
Armthorpe...89 D7
Arnabost...146 F5
Arncliffe...94 B2
Arncroach...129 D7
Arne...13 F7
Arnesby...64 E3
Arngask...128 C3
Arnisdale...149 G13
Arnish...149 D10
Arniston Engine...121 C6
Arnol...159 C8
Arnold E Yorks...97 E7
Notts...77 E5
Arnprior...126 E5
Arnside...92 B4
Aros Mains...147 G8
Arowry...73 F8
Arpafeelie...151 F9
Arrad Foot...99 F5
Arram...97 E6
Arrathorne...101 E7
Arreton...15 F6
Arrington...54 D4
Arrivain...125 B8
Arrochar...125 E8
Arrow...51 D5
Arthington...95 E5
Arthingworth...64 F4
Arthog...58 C3
Arthrath...153 E9
Arthurstone...134 E2
Artrochie...153 E10
Arscaig...156 H7
Asby...98 B2
Ascog...145 G10
Ascot...27 C7
Ascott...51 F8
Ascott-under-Wychwood...38 C3
Asenby...95 B6
Asfordby...64 C4
Asfordby Hill...64 C4
Asgarby Lincs...78 E4
Lincs...79 C6

Ashill continued
Norf...67 D8
Som...11 C8
Ashingdon...42 E4
Ashington Northumb...117 F8
Som...12 B3
W Sus...16 C5
Ashintully Castle...133 C8
Ashkirk...115 B7
Ashlett...15 D5
Ashleworth...37 B5
Ashley Cambs...55 C7
Ches E...87 F5
Devon...9 C8
Dorset...14 D2
Glos...37 E6
Hants...14 E3
Hants...25 F8
Northants...64 E4
Staffs...74 F4
Ashley Green...40 D2
Ashley Heath Dorset...14 D2
Staffs...74 F4
Ash Magna...74 F2
Ashmanhaugh...69 B6
Ashmansworth...26 D2
Ashmansworthy...8 C5
Ash Mill...10 B2
Ashmore...13 C7
Ashorne...51 D8
Ashover...76 C3
Ashow...51 B8
Ashprington...7 D6
Ash Priors...11 B6
Ashreigney...9 C8
Ash Street...56 E4
Ashtead...28 D2
Ash Thomas...11 C5
Ashton Ches W...74 C2
Corn...2 D5
Hants...15 C6
Hereford...49 C7
Invclyd...118 B2
Northants...53 E5
Northants...65 F7
Ashton Common...24 D3
Ashton-in-Makerfield...86 E3
Ashton Keynes...37 E7
Ashton under Hill...50 F4
Ashton-under-Lyne...87 E7
Ashton upon Mersey...87 E5
Ashurst Hants...14 C4
Kent...18 B2
W Sus...17 C5
Ashurstwood...28 F5
Ash Vale...27 D6
Ashwater...9 E5
Ashwell Herts...54 F3
Rutland...65 C5
Som...11 C8
Ashwellthorpe...68 E4
Ashwick...23 E8
Ashwicken...67 C7
Ashybank...115 C8
Askam in Furness...92 B2
Askern...89 C6
Askerswell...12 E3
Askett...39 D8
Askham Cumb...99 B7
Notts...77 B7
Askham Bryan...95 E8
Askham Richard...95 E8
Asknish...145 D8
Askrigg...100 E4
Askwith...94 E4
Aslackby...78 F3
Aslacton...68 E4
Aslockton...77 F7
Asloun...140 C4
Aspatria...107 E8
Aspenden...41 B6
Asperton...79 F5
Aspley Guise...53 F7
Aspley Heath...53 F7
Aspull...86 D4
Asselby...89 B8
Asserby...79 B7
Assington...56 F3
Assynt House...151 E8
Astbury...74 C5
Astcote...52 D4
Asterley...60 D3
Asterton...60 E3
Asthall...38 C2
Asthall Leigh...38 C3
Astley Shrops...60 C5
Warks...63 F7
Worcs...50 C2
Astley Abbotts...61 E7
Astley Bridge...86 C5
Astley Cross...50 C3
Astley Green...86 E5
Aston Ches E...74 E3
Ches W...74 B2
Derbys...88 F2
Hereford...49 B6
Herts...41 B5
Oxon...38 D3
Shrops...60 B5
Staffs...74 E4
S Yorks...89 F5
Telford...61 D6
W Mid...62 F4
Wokingham...39 F7
Aston Abbotts...39 B8
Aston Botterell...61 F6
Aston-by-Stone...75 F6
Aston Cantlow...51 D6
Aston Clinton...40 C1
Aston Crews...36 B3
Aston Cross...50 F4
Aston End...41 B5
Aston Eyre...61 E6
Aston Fields...50 C4
Aston Flamville...63 E8
Aston Ingham...36 B3
Aston juxta Mondrum...74 D3
Aston le Walls...52 D2
Aston Magna...51 F6
Aston Munslow...60 F5
Aston on Clun...60 F3
Aston-on-Trent...63 B8
Aston Rogers...60 D3

Aston Rowant...39 E7
Aston Sandford...39 D7
Aston Somerville...50 F5
Aston Subedge...51 E6
Aston Tirrold...39 F5
Aston Upthorpe...39 F5
Astrop...52 F3
Astwick...54 F3
Astwood M Keynes...53 E7
Worcs...50 D3
Astwood Bank...50 C5
Aswarby...78 F3
Aswardby...79 B6
Atcham...60 D5
Atch Lench...50 D5
Athelhampton...13 E5
Athelington...57 B6
Athelney...11 B8
Athelstaneford...121 B8
Atherington...9 B7
Atherstone...63 E7
Atherstone on Stour...51 D7
Atherton...86 D4
Atley Hill...101 D7
Atlow...76 E2
Attadale...150 H2
Attadale House...150 H2
Attenborough...76 F5
Atterby...90 E3
Attercliffe...88 F4
Attleborough Norf...68 E3
Warks...63 E7
Attlebridge...68 C4
Atwick...97 D7
Atworth...24 C3
Aubourn...78 C2
Auchagallon...143 E9
Auchallater...139 F7
Auchenback...118 D5
Auchenbainzie...113 E8
Auchenblae...135 B7
Auchenbrack...113 E7
Auchenbreck...145 E9
Auchencairn Dumfries...106 D4
Dumfries...114 F2
N Ayrs...143 F11
Auchencrosh...104 B5
Auchencrow...122 C4
Auchendinny...121 C5
Auchengray...120 D2
Auchenhalrig...152 B3
Auchenheath...119 E8
Auchenlochan...145 F8
Auchenmalg...105 D6
Auchensoul...112 E2
Auchentiber...118 E3
Auchertyre...149 F13
Auchgourish...138 C5
Auchincarroch...126 F3
Auchindrain...125 E6
Auchindrean...150 C4
Auchininna...153 D6
Auchinleck...113 B5
Auchinloch...119 B6
Auchinroath...152 C2
Auchintoul...140 C4
Auchiries...153 E10
Auchlee...141 E7
Auchleven...140 B5
Auchlochan...119 F8
Auchlossan...140 D4
Auchlunies...141 E7
Auchlyne...126 B4
Auchmacoy...153 E9
Auchmair...140 B2
Auchmantle...105 C5
Auchmillan...112 B5
Auchmithie...135 E6
Auchmuirbridge...128 D3
Auchmull...135 B5
Auchnacree...134 C4
Auchnagallin...151 H13
Auchnagatt...153 D9
Auchnaha...145 E8
Auchnashelloch...127 C6
Aucholzie...140 E2
Auchrannie...134 D2
Auchroisk...139 B6
Auchronie...140 F3
Auchterarder...127 C8
Auchteraw...137 D6
Auchterderran...128 E4
Auchterhouse...134 F3
Auchtermuchty...128 C4
Auchterneed...150 F7
Auchtertool...128 E4
Auchtertyre...152 C1
Auchtubh...126 B4
Auckengill...158 D5
Auckley...89 D7
Audenshaw...87 E7
Audlem...74 E3
Audley...74 D4
Audley End...56 F6
Auds...153 B6
Aughertree...108 F2
Aughton E Yorks...96 F3
Lancs...85 D4
Lancs...93 C5
S Yorks...89 F5
Wilts...25 D7
Aughton Park...86 D2
Auldearn...151 F12
Aulden...49 D6
Auldgirth...114 F2
Auldhame...129 F7
Auldhouse...119 D6
Ault a'chruinn...136 B2
Aultanrynie...156 F6
Aultbea...155 J13
Aultdearg...150 E5
Aultgrishan...155 J12
Aultguish Inn...150 D6
Aultibea...157 G13
Aultiphurst...157 C11
Aultmore...152 C4
Aultnagoire...137 B8
Aultnamain Inn...151 C9
Aultnaslat...136 D4
Aulton...140 B5
Aundorach...139 C5
Aunsby...78 F3
Auquhorthies...141 B7
Aust...36 F2

Austendike...66 B2
Austerfield...89 E7
Austrey...63 D6
Austwick...93 C7
Authorpe...91 F8
Authorpe Row...79 B8
Avebury...25 C6
Aveley...42 F1
Avening...37 E5
Averham...77 D7
Aveton Gifford...6 E4
Avielochan...138 C5
Aviemore...138 C4
Avington Hants...26 F3
W Berks...25 C8
Avoch...151 F10
Avon...14 E2
Avonbridge...120 B2
Avon Dassett...52 E2
Avonmouth...23 B7
Avonwick...6 D5
Awbridge...14 B4
Awhirk...104 D4
Awkley...36 F2
Awliscombe...11 D6
Awre...36 D4
Awsworth...76 E4
Axbridge...23 D6
Axford Hants...26 E4
Wilts...25 B7
Axminster...11 E7
Axmouth...11 E7
Axton...85 F2
Aycliff...31 E7
Aycliffe...101 B7
Aydon...110 C3
Aylburton...36 D3
Ayle...109 E7
Aylesbeare...10 E5
Aylesbury...39 C8
Aylesby...91 D6
Aylesford...29 D8
Aylesham...31 D6
Aylestone...64 D2
Aylmerton...81 D7
Aylsham...81 E7
Aylton...49 F8
Aymestrey...49 C6
Aynho...52 F3
Ayot St Lawrence...40 C4
Ayot St Peter...41 C5
Ayr...112 B3
Aysgarth...101 F5
Ayside...99 F5
Ayston...65 D5
Aythorpe Roding...42 C1
Ayton...122 C5
Aywick...160 E7
Azerley...95 B5

B

Babbacombe...7 C7
Babbinswood...73 F7
Babcary...12 B3
Babel...47 F7
Babell...73 B5
Babraham...55 D6
Babworth...89 F7
Bac...155 C9
Bachau...82 C4
Backaland...159 E6
Backaskaill...159 C5
Backbarrow...99 F5
Backe...32 C3
Backfolds...153 C10
Backford...73 B8
Backford Cross...73 B7
Backhill Aberds...153 E7
Aberds...153 E10
Backhill of Clackriach...153 D9
Backhill of Fortree...153 D9
Backhill of Trustach...140 E5
Backies...157 J11
Backlass...158 E4
Back of Keppoch...147 C9
Back Rogerton...113 B5
Backwell...23 C6
Backworth...111 B6
Bacon End...42 C2
Baconsthorpe...81 D7
Bacton Hereford...49 F5
Norf...81 D9
Suff...56 C4
Bacton Green...56 C4
Bacup...87 B6
Badachro...149 A12
Badanloch Lodge...157 F10
Badavanich...150 F4
Badbury...38 F1
Badby...52 D3
Badcall...156 D5
Badcall...156 D5
Badcaul...150 B3
Baddeley Green...75 D6
Baddesley Clinton...51 B7
Baddesley Ensor...63 E6
Baddidarroch...156 G3
Baddoch...139 F7
Baddock...151 F10
Badenscoth...153 E7
Badenyon...140 C2
Badger...61 E7
Badger's Mount...29 C5
Badgeworth...37 C6
Badgworth...23 D5
Badicaul...149 F12
Badingham...57 C7
Badlesmere...30 D4
Badlipster...158 F4
Badluarach...150 B2
Badminton...37 F5
Badnaban...156 G3
Badnagie...158 G3
Badninish...151 B10
Badrallach...150 B3
Badsey...51 E5
Badshot Lea...27 E6
Badsworth...89 C5
Badwell Ash...56 C3

Bagh a Chaisteil =Castlebay...148 J1
Baghasdal...148 G2
Bagh Mor...148 C3
Bagh Shiarabhagh...148 H2
Bagillt...73 B6
Baginton...51 B8
Baglan...33 E8
Bagnall...75 D6
Bagnor...26 C2
Bagshot Sur...27 C7
Wilts...25 C8
Bagthorpe Norf...80 D3
Notts...76 D4
Bagworth...63 D8
Bagwy Llydiart...35 B8
Baildon...94 F4
Baile...154 J4
Baile Ailein...155 E7
Baile a Mhanaich...148 C2
Baile an Truiseil...155 B8
Bailebeag...137 C8
Baile Boidheach...144 F6
Baile Glas...148 C3
Baile Mhartainn...148 A2
Baile Mhic Phail...148 A3
Baile Mor Argyll...146 J5
W Isles...148 B2
Baile nan Cailleach...148 C2
Baile Raghaill...148 A2
Baileyhead...108 B5
Bailiesward...152 E4
Baillieston...119 C6
Bail'lochdrach...148 C3
Bail Uachdraich...148 B3
Bail'Ur Tholastaidh...155 C10
Bainbridge...100 E4
Bainsford...127 F7
Bainshole...152 E6
Bainton E Yorks...97 D5
Pboro...65 D7
Bairnkine...116 C2
Baker's End...41 C6
Baker Street...42 F2
Bakewell...76 C2
Bala =Y Bala...72 F3
Balachuirn...149 D10
Balavil...138 D3
Balbeg Highld...137 B7
Highld...151 E10
Balbeggie...128 B3
Balbithan...141 C6
Balbithan House...141 C7
Balblair Highld...151 B8
Highld...151 E10
Balby...89 D6
Balchladich...156 F3
Balchraggan Highld...151 G8
Highld...151 H8
Balchrick...156 D4
Balchrystie...129 D6
Balcombe...28 F4
Balcombe Lane...28 F4
Balcomie...129 C8
Balcurvie...128 D5
Baldersby...95 B6
Baldersby St James...95 B6
Balderstone...93 F6
Balderton Ches W...73 C7
Notts...77 D8
Baldhu...3 B6
Baldinnie...129 C6
Baldock...54 F3
Baldovie...134 F4
Baldrine...84 D4
Baldslow...18 D4
Baldwin...84 D3
Baldwinholme...108 D3
Baldwin's Gate...74 E4
Bale...81 D6
Balearn...153 C10
Balemartine...146 G2
Balephuil...146 G2
Balerno...120 C4
Balevullin...146 G2
Balfield...135 C5
Balfour...159 G5
Balfron...126 F4
Balfron Station...126 F4
Balgaveny...153 D6
Balgavies...135 D5
Balgonar...128 E2
Balgove...153 E8
Balgowan...138 E2
Balgown...149 B8
Balgrochan...119 B6
Balgy...149 C13
Balhaldie...127 D7
Balhalgardy...141 B6
Balham...28 B3
Balhary...134 E2
Baliasta...160 C8
Baligill...157 C11
Balintore Angus...134 D2
Highld...151 D11
Balintraid...151 D10
Balk...102 F2
Balkeerie...134 E3
Balkemback...134 F3
Balkholme...89 B8
Balkissock...104 A5
Ball...60 B3
Ballabeg...84 E2
Ballacannell...84 D4
Ballachulish...130 C4
Ballajora...84 C4
Ballaleigh...84 D3
Ballamodha...84 E2
Ballantrae...104 A4
Ballaquine...84 D4
Ballards Gore...43 E5
Ballasalla IoM...84 C3
IoM...84 E2
Ballater...140 E2
Ballaugh...84 C3
Ballaveare...84 E3
Ballcorach...139 B7
Ballechin...133 D6
Balleigh...151 C10
Ballencrieff...121 B7

Ballentoul...133 C5
Ball Haye Green...75 D6
Ball Hill...26 C2
Ballidon...76 D2
Balliemore Argyll...124 C4
Argyll...145 E9
Ballikinrain...126 F4
Ballimeanoch...125 D6
Ballimore Argyll...145 E8
Stirling...126 C4
Ballinaby...142 B3
Ballindean...128 B4
Ballingdon...56 E2
Ballinger Common...40 D2
Ballingham...49 F7
Ballingry...128 E3
Ballinlick...133 E6
Ballinluig...133 D6
Ballintuim...133 D8
Balloch Angus...134 D3
Highld...151 G10
N Lanark...119 B7
W Dunb...126 F2
Ballochford...152 E3
Ballochmorrie...112 F2
Ballochmyle...112 B5
Ballochroy...143 D7
Balls Cross...16 B3
Balls Green...43 B6
Ballygown...146 G7
Ballygrant...142 B4
Ballyhaugh...146 F4
Balmacara...149 F13
Balmacara Square...149 F13
Balmaclellan...106 B3
Balmacneil...133 D6
Balmacqueen...149 A9
Balmae...106 E3
Balmaha...126 E3
Balmalcolm...128 D5
Balmeanach...149 D10
Balmedie...141 C8
Balmer Heath...73 F8
Balmerino...129 B5
Balmerlawn...14 D4
Balmichael...143 E10
Balmirmer...135 F5
Balmore Highld...149 D7
Highld...150 H6
Highld...151 G11
Perth...133 D6
Balmule...128 F4
Balmullo...129 B6
Balmungie...151 F10
Balnaboth...134 C3
Balnabruaich...151 E10
Balnabruich...158 H3
Balnacoil...157 H11
Balnacra...150 G2
Balnafoich...151 H9
Balnagall...151 C11
Balnaguard...133 D6
Balnahard Argyll...144 D3
Argyll...146 H7
Balnain...150 H7
Balnakeil...156 C6
Balnaknock...149 B9
Balnapaling...151 E10
Balnespick...138 D4
Balquharn...133 F7
Balquhidder...126 B4
Balsall...51 B7
Balsall Common...51 B7
Balsall Heath...62 F4
Balscott...51 E8
Balsham...55 D6
Baltasound...160 C8
Balterley...74 D4
Baltersan...105 C8
Balthangie...153 C8
Baltonsborough...23 F7
Balvaird...151 F8
Balvicar...124 D3
Balvraid Highld...149 G13
Highld...151 H11
Bamber Bridge...86 B3
Bambers Green...42 B1
Bamburgh...123 F7
Bamff...134 D2
Bamford Derbys...88 F3
Gtr Man...87 C6
Bampton Cumb...99 C7
Devon...10 B4
Oxon...38 D3
Bampton Grange...99 C7
Banavie...131 B5
Banbury...52 E2
Bancffosfelen...33 C5
Banchory...141 E5
Banchory-Devenick...141 D8
Bancycapel...33 C5
Bancyfelin...32 C4
Bancyffordd...46 F3
Bandirran...134 F2
Banff...153 B6
Bangor...83 D6
Bangor-is-y-coed =Bangor-on-Dee...73 E7
Bangor-on-Dee =Bangor-is-y-coed...73 E7
Banham...68 F3
Bank...14 D3
Bankend...107 C7
Bankfoot...133 F7
Bankglen...113 C6
Bankhead Aberden...141 C7
Aberds...141 D5
Bank Newton...94 D2
Banknock...119 B7
Banks Cumb...109 C5
Lancs...85 B4
Bankshill...114 F4
Bank Street...49 C8
Banningham...81 E8
Banniskirk House...158 E3
Bannister Green...42 B2
Bannockburn...127 E7
Banstead...28 D3
Bantham...6 E4
Banton...119 B7
Banwell...23 D5
Banyard's Green...57 B6

Bapchild...30 C3
Barabhas...155 C8
Barabhas Iarach...155 C8
Barabhas Uarach...155 B8
Barachandroman...124 C2
Barassie...118 F3
Baravullin...124 E4
Barbaraville...151 D10
Barber Booth...88 F2
Barbieston...112 C4
Barbon...99 F8
Barbridge...74 D3
Barbrook...21 E6
Barby...52 B3
Barcaldine...130 E3
Barcheston...51 F7
Barcombe...17 C8
Barcombe Cross...17 C8
Barden...101 E6
Barden Scale...94 D3
Bardfield Saling...42 B2
Bardister...160 F5
Bardney...78 C4
Bardon...63 C8
Bardon Mill...109 C7
Bardowie...119 B5
Bardrainney...118 B3
Bardsea...92 B3
Bardsey...95 E6
Bardwell...56 B3
Bare...92 C4
Barfad...145 G7
Barford Norf...68 D4
Warks...51 C7
Barford St John...52 F2
Barford St Martin...25 F5
Barford St Michael...52 F2
Barfrestone...31 D6
Bargod =Bargoed...35 E5
Bargoed =Bargod...35 E5
Bargrennan...105 B7
Barham Cambs...54 B2
Kent...31 D6
Suff...56 D5
Barharrow...106 D3
Barhill...106 C5
Bar Hill...54 C4
Barholm...65 C7
Barkby...64 D3
Barkestone-le-Vale...77 F7
Barkham...27 C5
Barking London...41 F7
Suff...56 D4
Barkingside...41 F7
Barking Tye...56 D4
Barkisland...87 C8
Barkston Lincs...78 E2
N Yorks...95 F7
Barkway...54 F4
Barlaston...75 F5
Barlavington...16 C3
Barlborough...76 B4
Barlby...96 F2
Barlestone...63 D8
Barley Herts...54 F4
Lancs...93 E8
Barley Mow...111 D5
Barleythorpe...64 D5
Barling...43 F5
Barlow Derbys...76 B3
N Yorks...89 B7
T&W...110 C4
Barmby Moor...96 E3
Barmby on the Marsh...89 B7
Barmer...80 D4
Barmoor Castle...123 F5
Barmoor Lane End...123 F6
Barmouth =Abermaw...58 C3
Barmpton...101 C8
Barmston...97 D7
Barnack...65 D7
Barnacle...63 F7
Barnard Castle...101 C5
Barnard Gate...38 C4
Barnardiston...55 E8
Barnbarroch...106 D5
Barnburgh...89 D5
Barnby...69 F7
Barnby Dun...89 D7
Barnby in the Willows...77 D8
Barnby Moor...89 F7
Barnes Street...29 E7
Barnet...41 E5
Barnetby le Wold...90 D4
Barney...81 D5
Barnham Suff...56 B2
W Sus...16 D3
Barnham Broom...68 D3
Barnhead...135 D6
Barnhill Ches W...73 D8
Dundee...134 F4
Moray...152 C1
Barnhills...104 B3
Barningham Durham...101 C5
Suff...56 B3
Barnoldby le Beck...91 D6
Barnoldswick...93 E8
Barns Green...16 B5
Barnsley Glos...37 D7
S Yorks...88 D4
Barnstaple...20 F4
Barnston Essex...42 C2
Mers...85 F3
Barnstone...77 F7
Barnt Green...50 B5
Barnton Ches W...74 B3
Barnwell All Saints...65 F7
Barnwell St Andrew...65 F7
Barnwood...37 C5
Barochreal...124 C4
Barons Cross...49 D6
Barr...112 E2
Barra Castle...141 B6
Barrachan...105 E7
Barrack...153 D8
Barraglom...154 D6
Barrahormid...144 E6
Barran...124 C4
Barrapol...146 G2
Barras Aberds...141 F7

Barras continued
Cumb 100 C3
Barrasford 110 B2
Barravullin 124 E4
Barregarrow 84 D3
Barrhead 118 D4
Barrhill 112 F2
Barrington Cambs 54 E4
  Som 11 C8
Barripper 2 C5
Barrmill 118 D3
Barrock 158 C4
Barrock House 158 B4
Barrow Lancs 93 F7
  Rutland 65 C5
  Suff 55 C8
Barroway Drove 67 D5
Barrowburn 116 C4
Barrowby 77 F8
Barrowcliff 103 F8
Barrowden 65 D6
Barrowford 93 F8
Barrow Green 30 C3
Barrow Gurney 23 C7
Barrow Haven 90 B4
Barrow-in-Furness 92 C2
Barrow Island 92 C1
Barrow Nook 86 D2
Barrows Green
  Ches E 74 D3
  Cumb 99 F7
Barrow's Green 86 F3
Barrow Street 24 F3
Barrow upon Humber 90 B4
Barrow upon Soar 64 C2
Barrow upon Trent 63 B7
Barry 135 F5
Barry = Y Barri 22 C3
Barry Island 22 C3
Barsby 64 C3
Barsham 69 F6
Barston 51 B7
Bartestree 49 E7
Barthol Chapel 153 E8
Barthomley 74 D4
Bartley 14 C4
Bartley Green 62 F4
Bartlow 55 E6
Barton Cambs 54 D5
  Ches W 73 D8
  Glos 37 B8
  Lancs 85 D4
  Lancs 92 F5
  N Yorks 101 D7
  Oxon 39 D5
  Torbay 7 C7
  Warks 51 D6
Barton Bendish 67 D7
Barton Hartshorn 52 F4
Barton in Fabis 76 F5
Barton in the Beans 63 D7
Barton-le-Clay 53 F8
Barton-le-Street 96 B3
Barton-le-Willows 96 C3
Barton Mills 55 B8
Barton on Sea 14 E3
Barton on the Heath 51 F7
Barton St David 23 F7
Barton Seagrave 53 B6
Barton Stacey 26 E2
Barton Turf 69 B6
Barton-under-Needwood 63 C5
Barton-upon-Humber 90 B4
Barton Waterside 90 B4
Barugh 88 D4
Barway 55 B6
Barwell 63 E8
Barwick Herts 41 C6
  Som 12 C3
Barwick in Elmet 95 F6
Baschurch 60 B4
Bascote 52 C2
Basford Green 75 D6
Bashall Eaves 93 E6
Bashley 14 E3
Basildon 42 F3
Basingstoke 26 D4
Baslow 76 B2
Bason Bridge 22 E5
Bassaleg 35 F6
Bassenthwaite 108 F2
Bassett 14 C5
Bassingbourn 54 E4
Bassingfield 77 F6
Bassingham 78 C2
Bassingthorpe 65 B6
Basta 160 D7
Baston 65 C8
Bastwick 69 C7
Baswick Steer 97 E6
Batchworth Heath 40 E3
Batcombe Dorset 12 D4
  Som 23 F8
Bate Heath 74 B3
Batford 40 C4
Bath 24 C2
Bathampton 24 C2
Bathealton 11 B5
Batheaston 24 C2
Bathford 24 C2
Bathgate 120 C2
Bathley 77 D7
Bathpool Corn 5 B7
  Som 11 B7
Bathville 120 C2
Batley 88 B3
Batsford 51 F6
Battersby 102 D3
Battersea 28 B3
Battisborough Cross 6 E3
Battisford 56 D4
Battisford Tye 56 D4
Battle E Sus 18 D4
  Powys 48 F2
Battledown 37 B6
Battlefield 60 C5
Battlesbridge 42 E3
Battlesden 40 B2
Battlesea Green 57 B6
Battleton 10 B4
Battram 63 D8
Battramsley 14 E4

Baughton 50 E3
Baughurst 26 D3
Baulking 38 E3
Baumber 78 B5
Baunton 37 D7
Baverstock 24 F5
Bawburgh 68 D4
Bawdeswell 81 E6
Bawdrip 22 F5
Bawdsey 57 E7
Bawtry 89 E7
Baxenden 87 B5
Baxterley 63 E6
Baybridge 15 B6
Baycliff 92 B2
Baydon 25 B7
Bayford Herts 41 D6
  Som 12 B5
Bayles 109 E7
Baylham 56 D5
Baynard's Green 39 B5
Bayston Hill 60 D4
Baythorn End 55 E8
Bayton 49 B8
Beach 130 D1
Beachampton 53 F5
Beachamwell 67 D7
Beachans 151 G13
Beacharr 143 D7
Beachborough 19 B8
Beachley 36 E2
Beacon 11 D6
Beacon End 43 B5
Beacon Hill 27 F6
Beacon's Bottom 39 E7
Beacrabhaic 154 H6
Beadlam 102 F4
Beadlow 54 F2
Beadnell 117 B8
Beaford 9 C7
Beal Northumb 123 E6
  N Yorks 89 B6
Beamhurst 75 F7
Beaminster 12 D2
Beamish 110 D5
Beamsley 94 D3
Bean 29 B6
Beanacre 24 C4
Beanley 117 C6
Beaquoy 159 F4
Bear Cross 13 E8
Beardwood 86 B4
Beare Green 28 E2
Bearley 51 C6
Bearnus 146 G6
Bearpark 110 E5
Bearsbridge 109 D7
Bearsden 118 B5
Bearsted 29 D8
Bearstone 74 F4
Bearwood BCP 13 E8
  Hereford 49 D5
  W Mid 62 F4
Beattock 114 D3
Beauchamp Roding 42 C1
Beauchief 88 F4
Beaufort 35 C5
Beaufort Castle 151 G8
Beaulieu 14 D4
Beauly 151 G8
Beaumaris 83 D6
Beaumont Cumb 108 D3
  Essex 43 B7
Beaumont Hill 101 C7
Beausale 51 B7
Beauworth 15 B6
Beazley End 42 B3
Bebington 85 F4
Bebside 117 F8
Beccles 69 F7
Becconsall 86 B2
Beckbury 61 D7
Beckenham 28 C4
Beckermet 98 D2
Beckfoot Cumb 98 D3
  Cumb 107 E7
Beck Foot 99 E8
Beckford 50 F4
Beckhampton 25 C5
Beck Hole 103 D6
Beckingham Lincs 77 D8
  Notts 89 F8
Beckington 24 D3
Beckley E Sus 19 C5
  Hants 14 E3
  Oxon 39 C5
Beck Row 55 B7
Beck Side 98 F4
Beckton 41 F7
Beckwithshaw 95 D5
Becontree 41 F7
Bedale 101 F7
Bedburn 110 F4
Bedchester 13 C6
Beddau 34 F4
Beddgelert 71 C6
Beddingham 17 D8
Beddington 28 C4
Bedfield 57 C6
Bedford 53 D8
Bedham 16 B4
Bedhampton 15 D8
Bedingfield 57 C5
Bedlam 95 C5
Bedlington 117 F8
Bedlington Station 117 F8
Bedling 34 D4
Bedminster 23 B7
Bedmond 40 D3
Bednall 62 C3
Bedrule 116 C2
Bedstone 49 B5
Bedwas 35 F5
Bedworth 63 F7
Bedworth Heath 63 F7
Bed-y-coedwr 71 E8
Beeby 64 D3
Beech Hants 26 F4
  Staffs 75 F5
Beech Hill Gtr Man 86 D3
  W Berks 26 C4
Beechingstoke 25 D5
Beedon 26 B2
Beeford 97 D7
Beeley 76 C2

Beelsby 91 D6
Beenham 26 C3
Beeny 8 E3
Beer 11 F7
Beercrocombe 11 B8
Beer Hackett 12 C3
Beesands 7 E6
Beesby 91 F8
Beeson 7 E6
Beeston C Beds 54 E2
  Ches W 74 D2
  Norf 68 C2
  Notts 76 F5
  W Yorks 95 F5
Beeston Regis 81 C7
Beeswing 107 C5
Beetham 92 B4
Beetley 68 C2
Begbroke 38 C4
Begelly 32 D2
Beggar's Bush 48 C4
Beguildy 48 B3
Beighton Norf 69 D6
  S Yorks 88 F5
Beighton Hill 76 D2
Beith 118 D3
Bekesbourne 31 D5
Belaugh 69 C5
Belbroughton 50 B4
Belchamp Otten 56 E2
Belchamp St Paul 55 E8
Belchamp Walter 56 E2
Belchford 79 B5
Belford 123 F7
Belhaven 122 B2
Belhelvie 141 C8
Belhinnie 140 B3
Bellabeg 140 C2
Bellamore 112 F2
Bellanoch 144 D6
Bellaty 134 D2
Belleau 79 B7
Bellehiglash 152 E1
Bell End 50 B4
Bellerby 101 E6
Bellever 6 B4
Belliehill 135 C5
Bellingdon 40 D2
Bellingham 116 F4
Belloch 143 E7
Bellochantuy 143 E7
Bell o'th'Hill 74 E2
Bellsbank 112 D4
Bellshill N Lanark 119 C7
  Northumb 123 F7
Bellspool 120 F4
Bellsquarry 120 C3
Bells Yew Green 18 B3
Belmaduthy 151 F9
Belmesthorpe 65 C7
Belmont Blackburn 86 C4
  London 28 C3
  S Ayrs 112 B3
  Shetland 160 C7
Belnacraig 140 C2
Belowda 4 C4
Belper 76 E3
Belper Lane End 76 E3
Belsay 110 B4
Belses 115 B8
Belsford 7 D5
Belstead 56 E5
Belston 112 B3
Belstone 9 E8
Belthorn 86 B5
Beltinge 31 C5
Beltoft 90 D2
Belton Leics 63 B8
  Lincs 78 F2
  N Lincs 89 D8
  Norf 69 D7
Belton in Rutland 64 D5
Beltring 29 E7
Belts of Collonach 141 E5
Belvedere 29 B5
Belvoir 77 F8
Bembridge 15 F7
Bemersyde 121 F8
Bemerton 25 F6
Bempton 97 B7
Benacre 69 F8
Ben Alder Lodge 132 B2
Ben Armine Lodge 157 H10
Benbuie 113 E7
Ben Casgro 155 E9
Benderloch 124 B5
Bendronaig Lodge 150 H3
Benenden 18 B5
Benfield 105 C7
Bengate 69 B6
Bengeworth 50 E5
Benhall Green 57 C7
Benhall Street 57 C7
Benholm 135 C8
Beningbrough 95 D8
Benington Herts 41 B5
  Lincs 79 E6
Benllech 82 C5
Benmore Argyll 145 E10
  Stirling 126 B3
Benmore Lodge 156 H6
Bennacott 8 E4
Bennan 143 F10
Benniworth 91 F6
Benover 29 E8
Bensham 110 C5
Benslie 118 E3
Benson 39 E6
Bent 135 B6
Bent Gate 87 B5
Benthall Northumb 117 B8
  Shrops 61 D6
Bentham 37 C6
Benthoul 141 D7
Bentlawnt 60 D3
Bentley E Yorks 97 F6
  Hants 27 E5
  S Yorks 89 D6
  Suff 56 F5
  Warks 63 E6
  Worcs 50 C4
Bentley Heath 51 B6
Benton 21 F5
Bentpath 115 E6

Bents 120 C2
Bentworth 26 E4
Benvie 134 F3
Benwick 66 E3
Beoley 51 C5
Beoraidbeg 147 B9
Bepton 16 C2
Berden 41 B7
Bere Alston 6 C2
Bere Ferrers 6 C2
Berepper 3 D5
Bere Regis 13 E6
Bergh Apton 69 D6
Berinsfield 39 E5
Berkeley 36 E3
Berkhamsted 40 D2
Berkley 24 E3
Berkswell 51 B7
Bermondsey 28 B4
Bernera 149 F13
Bernice 145 D10
Bernisdale 149 C9
Berrick Salome 39 E6
Berriedale 158 H3
Berrier 99 B5
Berriew 59 D8
Berrington Northumb 123 E6
  Shrops 60 D5
Berrow 22 D5
Berrow Green 50 D2
Berry Down Cross 20 E4
Berry Hill Glos 36 C2
  Pembs 45 E2
Berryhillock 152 B5
Berrynarbor 20 E4
Berry Pomeroy 7 C6
Bersham 73 E7
Berstane 159 G5
Berwick 18 E2
Berwick Bassett 25 B6
Berwick Hill 110 B4
Berwick St James 25 F5
Berwick St John 13 B7
Berwick St Leonard 24 F4
Berwick-upon-Tweed 123 D5
Bescar 85 C4
Besford 50 E4
Bessacarr 89 D7
Bessels Leigh 38 D4
Bessingby 97 C7
Bessingham 81 D7
Bestbeech Hill 18 B3
Besthorpe Norf 68 E3
  Notts 77 C8
Bestwood 77 E5
Bestwood Village 77 E5
Beswick 97 E6
Betchworth 28 E3
Bethania Ceredig 47 C5
  Gwyn 71 C8
  Gwyn 83 F6
Bethel Anglesey 82 D3
  Gwyn 72 F3
  Gwyn 59 B7
Bethersden 30 E3
Bethesda Gwyn 83 E6
  Pembs 32 C1
Bethlehem 33 B7
Bethnal Green 41 F6
Betley 74 E4
Betsham 29 B7
Betteshanger 31 D7
Bettiscombe 11 E8
Bettisfield 73 F8
Betton Shrops 60 D3
  Shrops 74 F3
Bettws Bridgend 34 F3
  Mon 35 C6
  Newport 35 E6
Bettws Cedewain 59 E8
Bettws Gwerfil Goch 72 E4
Bettws Ifan 46 E2
Bettws Newydd 35 D7
Bettws-y-crwyn 60 F2
Bettws-yn-Rhos 72 B3
Beulah Ceredig 45 E4
  Powys 47 D8
Bevendean 17 D7
Bevercotes 77 B6
Beverley 97 F6
Beverston 37 E5
Bevington 36 E3
Bewaldeth 108 F2
Bewcastle 109 B5
Bewdley 50 B2
Bewerley 94 C4
Bewholme 97 D7
Bexhill 18 E4
Bexley 29 B5
Bexleyheath 29 B5
Bexwell 67 D6
Beyton 56 C3
Bhaltos 154 D5
Bhatarsaigh 148 J1
Bibury 37 D8
Bicester 39 B5
Bickenhall 11 C7
Bickenhill 63 F5
Bicker 78 F5
Bickershaw 86 D4
Bickerstaffe 86 D2
Bickerton Ches E 74 D2
  N Yorks 95 D7
Bickington Devon 7 B5
  Devon 20 F4
Bickleigh Devon 10 D4
  Devon 6 C3
Bickleton 20 F4
Bickley 28 C5
Bickley Moss 74 E2
Bicknacre 42 D3
Bicknoller 22 F3
Bicknor 30 D2
Bickton 14 C2
Bicton Shrops 60 C4
  Shrops 60 F2
Bidborough 29 E6
Biddenden 19 B5
Biddenham 53 E8

Biddestone 24 B3
Biddisham 23 D5
Biddlesden 52 E4
Biddlestone 117 D5
Biddulph 75 D5
Biddulph Moor 75 D6
Bideford 9 B6
Bidford-on-Avon 51 D6
Bidston 85 E3
Bielby 96 E3
Bieldside 141 D7
Bierley IoW 15 G6
  W Yorks 94 F4
Bierton 39 C8
Big Sand 149 A12
Bigbury 6 E4
Bigbury on Sea 6 E4
Bigby 90 D4
Biggar Cumb 92 C1
  S Lanark 120 F3
Biggin Derbys 75 D8
  Derbys 76 E2
  N Yorks 95 F8
Biggings 160 G3
Biggin Hill 28 D5
Biggleswade 54 E2
Bighouse 157 C11
Bighton 26 F4
Bignor 16 C3
Bigton 160 L5
Bilberry 4 C5
Bilborough 76 E5
Bilbrook 22 E2
Bilbrough 95 E8
Bilbster 158 E4
Bildershaw 101 B7
Bildeston 56 E3
Billericay 42 E2
Billesdon 64 D4
Billesley 51 D6
Billingborough 78 F4
Billinge 86 D3
Billingford 81 E6
Billingham 102 B2
Billinghay 78 D4
Billingley 88 D5
Billingshurst 16 B4
Billingsley 61 F7
Billington C Beds 40 B2
  Lancs 93 F7
Billockby 69 C7
Billy Row 110 F4
Bilsborrow 92 F5
Bilsby 79 B7
Bilsham 16 D3
Bilsington 19 B7
Bilson Green 36 C3
Bilsthorpe 77 C6
Bilsthorpe Moor 77 D6
Bilston Midloth 121 C5
  W Mid 62 E3
Bilstone 63 D7
Bilting 30 E4
Bilton E Yorks 97 F7
  Northumb 117 C8
  Warks 52 B2
Bilton in Ainsty 95 E7
Bimbister 159 G4
Binbrook 91 E6
Binchester Blocks 110 F5
Bincombe 12 F4
Bindal 151 C12
Binegar 23 E8
Binfield 27 B6
Binfield Heath 26 B5
Bingfield 110 B3
Bingham 77 F7
Bingley 94 F4
Bings Heath 60 C5
Binham 81 D5
Binley Hants 26 D2
  W Mid 51 B8
Binley Woods 51 B8
Binniehill 119 B8
Binsoe 94 B5
Binstead 15 E6
Binsted 27 E5
Binton 51 D6
Bintree 81 E6
Binweston 60 D3
Birch Essex 43 C5
  Gtr Man 87 D6
Bircham Newton 80 D3
Bircham Tofts 80 D3
Birchanger 41 B8
Birchencliffe 88 C2
Bircher 49 C6
Birch Green 43 C5
Birchgrove Cardiff 22 B3
  Swansea 33 E8
Birch Heath 74 C2
Birch Hill 74 B2
Birchington 31 C6
Birchmoor 63 D6
Birchover 76 C2
Birch Vale 87 F8
Birchwood Lincs 78 C2
  Warr 86 E4
Bircotes 89 E7
Birdbrook 55 E8
Birdforth 95 B7
Birdham 16 E2
Birdholme 76 C3
Birdingbury 52 C2
Birdlip 37 C6
Birds Edge 88 D3
Birdsall 96 C4
Birdsgreen 61 F7
Birdsmoor Gate 11 D8
Birdston 119 B6
Birdwell 88 D4
Birdwood 36 C4
Birgham 122 F3
Birkby 101 D8
Birkdale 85 C4
Birkenhead 85 F4
Birkenhills 153 D7
Birkenshaw N Lanark 119 C6
  W Yorks 88 B3
Birkhall 140 E2
Birkhill Angus 134 F3
  Borders 114 C5
Birkholme 65 B6
Birkin 89 B6
Birley 49 D6
Birling Kent 29 C7
  Northumb 117 D8

Birling Gap 18 F2
Birlingham 50 E4
Birmingham 62 F4
Birnam 133 E7
Birse 140 E4
Birsemore 140 E4
Birstall Leics 64 D2
  W Yorks 88 B3
Birstwith 94 D5
Birthorpe 78 F4
Birtley Hereford 49 C5
  Northumb 109 B8
  T&W 111 D5
Birts Street 50 F2
Bisbrooke 65 E5
Biscathorpe 91 F6
Biscot 40 B3
Bish Mill 10 B2
Bishop Auckland 101 B7
Bishopbridge 90 E4
Bishopbriggs 119 C6
Bishop Burton 97 F5
Bishop Middleham 111 F6
Bishopmill 152 B2
Bishop Monkton 95 C6
Bishop Norton 90 E3
Bishopsbourne 31 D5
Bishops Cannings 24 C5
Bishop's Castle 60 F3
Bishop's Caundle 12 C4
Bishop's Cleeve 37 B6
Bishops Frome 49 E8
Bishop's Green 42 C2
Bishop's Hull 11 B7
Bishop's Itchington 51 D8
Bishops Lydeard 11 B6
Bishops Nympton 10 B2
Bishop's Offley 61 B7
Bishop's Stortford 41 B7
Bishop's Sutton 26 F4
Bishop's Tachbrook 51 C8
Bishops Tawton 20 F4
Bishopsteignton 7 B7
Bishopstoke 15 C5
Bishopston 33 F6
Bishopstone Bucks 39 C8
  E Sus 17 D8
  Hereford 49 E6
  Swindon 38 F2
  Wilts 13 B8
Bishopstrow 24 E3
Bishop Sutton 23 D7
Bishop's Waltham 15 C6
Bishopswood 11 C7
Bishop's Wood 62 D2
Bishopsworth 23 C7
Bishop Thornton 95 C5
Bishopthorpe 95 E8
Bishopton Darl 102 B1
  Dumfries 105 E8
  N Yorks 95 B6
  Renfs 118 B4
  Warks 51 D6
Bishop Wilton 96 D3
Bishton 35 F7
Bisley Glos 37 D6
  Sur 27 D7
Bispham 92 E3
Bispham Green 86 C2
Bissoe 3 B6
Bisterne Close 14 D3
Bitchfield 65 B6
Bittadon 20 E4
Bittaford 6 D4
Bittering 68 C2
Bitterley 49 B7
Bitterne 15 C5
Bitteswell 64 F2
Bitton 23 C8
Bix 39 F7
Bixter 160 H5
Blaby 64 E2
Blackacre 114 E3
Blackadder West 122 D4
Blackawton 7 D6
Blackborough 11 D5
Blackborough End 67 C6
Black Bourton 38 D2
Blackboys 18 C2
Blackbrook Derbys 76 E3
  Mers 86 E3
  Staffs 74 F4
Blackburn Aberds 141 C7
  Aberds 152 E5
  Blackburn 86 B4
  W Loth 120 C2
Black Callerton 110 C4
Black Clauchrie 112 F2
Black Corries Lodge 131 D6
Blackcraig 113 F7
Black Crofts 124 B5
Blackden Heath 74 B4
Blackdog 141 C8
Black Dog 10 D3
Blackfell 111 D5
Blackfield 14 D5
Blackford Cumb 108 C3
  Perth 127 D7
  Som 12 B4
  Som 23 E6
Blackfordby 63 C7
Blackgang 15 G5
Blackhall Colliery 111 F7
Blackhall Mill 110 D4
Blackhall Rocks 111 F7
Blackham 29 F5
Blackheath Essex 43 B6
  Suff 57 B8
  Sur 27 E8
  W Mid 62 F3

Black Marsh 60 E3
Blackmill 34 F3
Blackmoor 27 F5
Blackmoor Gate 21 E5
Blackmore 42 D2
Blackmore End Essex 55 F8
  Herts 40 C4
Black Mount 131 E6
Blackness 120 B3
Blacknest 27 E5
Black Notley 42 B3
Blacko 93 E8
Black Pill 33 E7
Blackpool Blackpool 92 F3
  Devon 7 E6
Blackpool Gate 108 B5
Blackridge 119 C8
Blackrock Argyll 142 B4
  Mon 35 C6
Blackrod 86 C4
Blackshaw 107 C7
Blackshaw Head 87 B7
Blacksmith's Green 56 C5
Blackstone 17 C6
Black Tar 44 E4
Blackthorn 39 C6
Blackthorpe 56 C3
Blacktoft 90 B2
Blacktop 141 D7
Black Torrington 9 D6
Blacktown 35 F6
Blackwall Tunnel 41 F6
Blackwater Corn 3 B6
  Hants 27 D6
  IoW 15 F6
Blackwaterfoot 143 F9
Blackwell Darl 101 C7
  Derbys 75 B8
  Derbys 76 C4
  Warks 51 E7
  Worcs 50 B4
  W Sus 28 F4
Blackwood = Coed Duon 35 E5
Blackwood 119 E7
Blackwood Hill 75 D6
Blacon 73 C7
Bladnoch 105 D8
Bladon 38 C4
Blaenannerch 45 E4
Blaenau Ffestiniog 71 C8
Blaenavon 35 D6
Blaencelyn 46 D2
Blaendyryn 47 F8
Blaenffos 45 F3
Blaengarw 34 E3
Blaengwrach 34 D2
Blaen-gwynfi 34 E2
Blaenpennal 46 C5
Blaenplwyf 46 B4
Blaenporth 45 E4
Blaenrhondda 34 D3
Blaen-waun 32 B3
Blaen-y-coed 32 B4
Blaenycwm 47 B7
Blaen-y-Cwm Denb 72 F4
  Gwyn 71 E8
  Powys 59 B7
Blagdon N Som 23 D7
  Torbay 7 C6
Blagdon Hill 11 C7
Blagill 109 E7
Blaguegate 86 D2
Blaich 130 B4
Blain 147 E9
Blaina 35 D6
Blair Atholl 133 C5
Blairbeg 143 E11
Blairdaff 141 C5
Blair Drummond 127 E6
Blairglas 126 F2
Blairgowrie 134 E1
Blairhall 128 F2
Blairingone 127 E8
Blairland 118 E3
Blairlogie 127 E7
Blairlomond 125 F7
Blairmore 145 E10
Blairnamarrow 139 C8
Blairquhosh 126 F4
Blair's Ferry 145 G8
Blairskaith 119 B5
Blaisdon 36 C4
Blakebrook 50 B3
Blakedown 50 B3
Blakelaw 122 F3
Blakeley 62 E2
Blakeley Lane 75 E6
Blakemere 49 E5
Blakeney Glos 36 D3
  Norf 81 C6
Blakenhall Ches E 74 E4
  W Mid 62 E3
Blakeshall 50 B3
Blakesley 52 D4
Blanchland 110 D2
Blandford Forum 13 D6
Blandford St Mary 13 D6
Bland Hill 94 D5
Blanefield 119 B5
Blankney 78 C3
Blantyre 119 D6
Blar a'Chaorainn 131 C4
Blaran 124 D4
Blarghour 125 D5
Blarmachfoldach 130 C4
Blarnalearoch 150 B4
Blashford 14 D2
Blaston 64 E5
Blatherwycke 65 E6
Blawith 98 F4
Blaxhall 57 D7
Blaxton 89 D7
Blaydon 110 C4
Bleadon 22 D5
Bleak Hey Nook 87 D8
Blean 30 C5
Bleasby Lincs 90 F5
  Notts 77 E7
Bleasdale 93 E5
Bleatarn 100 C2
Blebocraigs 129 C6
Bleddfa 48 C4
Bledington 38 B2
Bledlow 39 D7
Bledlow Ridge 39 E7

Blegbie 121 C7
Blencarn 109 F6
Blencogo 107 E8
Blendworth 15 C8
Blenheim Park 80 D4
Blennerhasset 107 E8
Blervie Castle 151 F13
Bletchingdon 39 C5
Bletchingley 28 D4
Bletchley M Keynes 53 F6
  Shrops 74 F3
Bletherston 32 B1
Bletsoe 53 D8
Blewbury 39 F5
Blickling 81 E7
Blidworth 77 D5
Blindburn 116 C4
Blindcrake 107 F8
Blindley Heath 28 E4
Blisland 5 B6
Blissford 14 C2
Bliss Gate 50 B2
Blisworth 52 D5
Blithbury 62 B4
Blitterlees 107 D8
Blockley 51 F6
Blofield 69 D6
Blofield Heath 69 C6
Blo' Norton 56 B4
Bloomfield 115 B8
Blore 75 E8
Blount's Green 75 F7
Blowick 85 C4
Bloxham 52 F2
Bloxholm 78 D3
Bloxwich 62 D3
Bloxworth 13 E6
Blubberhouses 94 D4
Blue Anchor Som 22 E2
  Swansea 33 E6
Blue Row 43 C6
Blundeston 69 E8
Blunham 54 D2
Blunsdon St Andrew 37 F8
Bluntington 50 B3
Bluntisham 54 B4
Blunts 5 C8
Blyborough 90 E3
Blyford 57 B8
Blymhill 62 C2
Blyth Northumb 117 F9
  Notts 89 F7
Blyth Bridge 120 E4
Blythburgh 57 B8
Blythe Bridge 75 E6
Blyton 90 E2
Boarhills 129 C7
Boarhunt 15 D7
Boars Head 86 D3
Boars Hill 38 D4
Boarstall 39 C6
Boasley Cross 9 E6
Boath 151 D8
Boat of Garten 138 C5
Bobbing 30 C2
Bobbington 62 E2
Bobbingworth 41 D8
Bocaddon 5 D6
Bochastle 126 D5
Bocking 42 B3
Bocking Churchstreet 42 B3
Boddam Aberds 153 D11
  Shetland 160 M5
Boddington 37 B5
Bodedern 82 C3
Bodelwyddan 72 B4
Bodenham Hereford 49 D7
  Wilts 14 B2
Bodenham Moor 49 D7
Bodermid 70 E2
Bodewryd 82 B3
Bodfari 72 B4
Bodham 81 C7
Bodiam 18 C4
Bodicote 52 F2
Bodieve 4 B4
Bodinnick 5 D6
Bodle Street Green 18 D3
Bodmin 5 C5
Bodney 67 E8
Bodorgan 82 D3
Bodsham 30 E5
Boduan 70 D4
Bodymoor Heath 63 E5
Bogallan 151 F9
Bogbrae 153 E10
Bogend Borders 122 E3
  S Ayrs 118 F3
Boghall 120 C2
Boghead 119 E7
Bogmoor 152 B3
Bogniebrae 152 D5
Bognor Regis 16 E3
Bograxie 141 C6
Bogside 119 D8
Bogton 153 C6
Bogue 113 F6
Bohenie 137 F5
Bohortha 3 C7
Bohuntine 137 F5
Boirseam 154 J5
Bojewyan 2 C2
Bolam Durham 101 B6
  Northumb 117 F6
Bolberry 6 F4
Bold Heath 86 E3
Boldon 111 C6
Boldon Colliery 111 C6
Boldre 14 E4
Boldron 101 C5
Bole 89 F8
Bolehill 76 D2
Boleside 121 F7
Bolham 10 C4
Bolham Water 11 C6
Bolingey 4 D2
Bollington 75 B6
Bollington Cross 75 B6
Bolney 17 B6
Bolnhurst 53 D8
Bolshan 135 D6
Bolsover 76 B4

Bolsterstone 88 E3
Bolstone 49 F7
Boltby 102 F2
Bolter End 39 E7
Bolton Cumb 99 B8
  E Loth 121 B8
  Gtr Man 86 D5
  Northumb 117 C7
Bolton Abbey 94 D3
Bolton Bridge 94 D3
Bolton-by-Bowland 93 E7
Boltonfellend 108 C4
Boltongate 108 E2
Bolton-le-Sands 92 C4
Bolton Low Houses 108 E2
Bolton-on-Swale 101 E7
Bolton Percy 95 E8
Bolton Town End 92 C4
Bolton upon Dearne 89 D5
Bolventor 5 B6
Bomere Heath 60 C4
Bonawe 125 B6
Bonby 90 C4
Boncath 45 F4
Bonchester Bridge 115 C8
Bonchurch 15 G6
Bondleigh 9 D8
Bonehill Devon 6 B5
  Staffs 63 D5
Bo'ness 127 F8
Bonhill 118 B3
Boningale 62 D2
Bonjedward 116 B2
Bonkle 119 D8
Bonnavoulin 147 F8
Bonnington Edin 120 C4
  Kent 19 B7
Bonnybank 129 D5
Bonnybridge 127 F7
Bonnykelly 153 C8
Bonnyrigg and Lasswade 121 C6
Bonnyton Aberds 153 E6
  Angus 134 F3
  Angus 135 D6
Bonsall 76 D2
Bonskeid House 133 C5
Bont 35 C7
Bontddu 58 C3
Bont-Dolgadfan 59 D5
Bont-goch 58 F3
Bontnewydd Ceredig 46 C5
  Gwyn 82 F4
Bont-newydd 72 B4
Bont Newydd Gwyn 71 C8
  Gwyn 71 E8
Bontuchel 72 D4
Bonvilston 22 B2
Bon-y-maen 33 E7
Booker 39 E8
Boon 121 E8
Boosbeck 102 C4
Boot 98 D3
Booth 87 B8
Boothby Graffoe 78 D2
Boothby Pagnell 78 F2
Boothen 75 E5
Boothferry 89 B8
Boothville 53 C5
Booth Wood 87 C8
Bootle Cumb 98 F3
  Mers 85 E4
Booton 81 E7
Boquhan 126 F4
Boraston 49 B8
Borden Kent 30 C2
  W Sus 16 B2
Bordley 94 C2
Bordon 27 F6
Boreham Essex 42 D3
  Wilts 24 E3
Boreham Street 18 D3
Borehamwood 40 E4
Boreland Dumfries 114 E4
  Stirling 132 F2
Borgh W Isles 148 H1
  W Isles 16 J4
Borghastan 154 C7
Borgie 157 D9
Borgue Dumfries 106 E3
  Highld 158 H3
Borley 56 E2
Bornais 148 F2
Bornesketaig 149 A8
Borness 106 E3
Boroughbridge 95 C6
Borough Green 29 D7
Borras Head 73 D7
Borreraig 148 C6
Borrobol Lodge 157 G11
Borrowash 76 F4
Borrowby 102 F2
Borrowdale 98 C4
Borrowfield 141 E7
Borth 58 E3
Borthwickbrae 115 C7
Borthwickshields 115 C7
Borth-y-Gest 71 D6
Borve 149 D9
Borve Lodge 154 H5
Borwick 92 B5
Bosavern 2 C2
Bosbury 49 E8
Boscastle 8 E3
Boscombe BCP 14 E2
  Wilts 25 F7
Bosham 16 D2
Bosherston 44 F4
Boskenna 2 D3
Bosley 75 C6
Bossall 96 C3
Bossiney 8 F2
Bossingham 31 E5
Bossington 21 E7
Bostock Green 74 C3

Boston 79 E6
Boston Long Hedges 79 E6
Boston Spa 95 E7
Boston West 79 E5
Boswinger 3 B8
Botallack 2 C2
Botany Bay 41 E5
Botcherby 108 D4
Botcheston 63 D8
Botesdale 56 B4
Bothal 117 F8
Bothamsall 77 B6
Bothel 107 F8
Bothenhampton 12 E2
Bothwell 119 D7
Botley Bucks 40 D2
Hants 15 C6
Oxon 38 D4
Botolph Claydon 39 B7
Botolphs 17 D5
Bottacks 150 E7
Bottesford Leics 77 F8
N Lincs 90 D2
Bottisham 55 C6
Bottlesford 25 D6
Bottom Boat 88 B4
Bottomcraig 129 B5
Bottom House 75 D7
Bottom of Hutton 86 B2
Bottom o'th'Moor 86 C4
Botusfleming 6 C2
Botwnnog 70 D3
Bough Beech 29 E5
Boughrood 48 F3
Boughspring 36 E2
Boughton Norf 67 D6
Northants 53 C5
Notts 77 C6
Boughton Aluph 30 E4
Boughton Lees 30 E4
Boughton Malherbe 30 E2
Boughton Monchelsea 29 D8
Boughton Street 30 D4
Boulby 103 C5
Boulden 60 F5
Boulmer 117 C8
Boulston 44 D4
Boultenstone 140 C3
Boultham 78 C2
Bourn 54 D4
Bourne 65 B7
Bourne End Bucks 40 F1
C Beds 53 E7
Herts 40 D3
Bournemouth 13 E8
Bournes Green
Glos 37 D6
Southend 43 F5
Bournheath 50 B4
Bournmoor 111 D6
Bournville 62 F4
Bourton Dorset 24 F2
N Som 23 C5
Oxon 38 F2
Shrops 61 E5
Bourton on Dunsmore 52 B2
Bourton on the Hill 51 F6
Bourton-on-the-Water 38 B1
Bousd 146 E5
Boustead Hill 108 D2
Bouth 99 F5
Bouthwaite 94 B4
Boveney 27 B7
Boverton 21 C8
Bovey Tracey 7 B6
Bovingdon 40 D3
Bovingdon Green
Bucks 39 F8
Herts 40 D3
Bovinger 41 D8
Bovington Camp 13 F6
Bow Borders 121 E7
Devon 10 D2
Orkney 159 J4
Bowbank 100 B4
Bow Brickhill 53 F7
Bowburn 111 F6
Bowcombe 15 F5
Bowd 11 E6
Bowden Borders 121 F8
Devon 7 E6
Bowden Hill 24 C4
Bowderdale 100 D1
Bowdon 87 F5
Bower 116 F3
Bowerchalke 13 B8
Bowerhill 24 C4
Bower Hinton 12 C2
Bowermadden 158 D4
Bowers Gifford 42 F3
Bowershall 128 E2
Bowertower 158 D4
Bowes 100 C4
Bowgreave 92 E4
Bowgreen 87 F5
Bowhill 115 B7
Bowhouse 107 C7
Bowland Bridge 99 F6
Bowley 49 D7
Bowlhead Green 27 F7
Bowling W Dunb 118 B4
W Yorks 94 F4
Bowling Bank 73 E7
Bowling Green 50 D3
Bowmanstead 99 E5
Bowmore 142 C4
Bowness-on-Solway 108 C2
Bowness-on-Windermere 99 E6
Bow of Fife 128 C5
Bowsden 123 E5
Bowside Lodge 157 C11
Bowston 99 E6
Bow Street 58 F3
Bowthorpe 68 D4
Box Glos 37 D5
Wilts 24 C3
Boxbush 36 C4
Box End 53 E8
Boxford Suff 56 E3
W Berks 26 B2
Boxgrove 16 D3
Boxley 29 D8
Boxmoor 40 D3
Boxted Essex 56 F4
Suff 56 D2
Boxted Cross 56 F4
Boxted Heath 56 F4
Boxworth 54 C4
Boxworth End 54 C4
Boyden Gate 31 C6
Boylestone 75 F8
Boyndie 153 B6
Boynton 97 C7
Boysack 135 E6
Boyton Corn 8 E5
Suff 57 E7
Wilts 24 F4
Boyton Cross 42 D2
Boyton End 55 E8
Bozeat 53 D7
Braaid 84 E3
Braal Castle 158 D3
Brabling Green 57 C6
Brabourne 30 E4
Brabourne Lees 30 E4
Brabster 158 D5
Bracadale 149 E8
Bracara 147 B10
Braceborough 65 C7
Bracebridge 78 C2
Bracebridge Heath 78 C2
Bracebridge Low Fields 78 C2
Braceby 78 F3
Bracewell 93 E8
Brackenfield 76 D3
Brackenthwaite
Cumb 108 E2
N Yorks 95 D5
Bracklesham 16 E2
Brackletter 136 F4
Brackley Argyll 143 D8
Northants 52 F3
Brackloch 156 G4
Bracknell 27 C6
Braco 127 D7
Bracobrae 152 C5
Bracon Ash 68 E4
Bracorina 147 B10
Bradbourne 76 D2
Bradbury 101 B8
Bradda 84 F1
Bradden 52 E4
Braddock 5 C6
Bradeley 75 D5
Bradenham Bucks 39 E8
Norf 68 D2
Bradenstoke 24 B5
Bradfield Essex 56 F5
Norf 81 D8
W Berks 26 B4
Bradfield Combust 56 D2
Bradfield Green 74 D3
Bradfield Heath 43 B7
Bradfield St Clare 56 D3
Bradfield St George 56 C3
Bradford Corn 5 B6
Derbys 76 C2
Devon 9 D6
Northumb 123 F7
W Yorks 94 F4
Bradford Abbas 12 C3
Bradford Leigh 24 C3
Bradford-on-Avon 24 C3
Bradford-on-Tone 11 B6
Bradford Peverell 12 E4
Brading 15 F7
Bradley Derbys 76 E2
Hants 26 E4
NE Lincs 91 D6
Staffs 62 C2
W Mid 62 E3
W Yorks 88 B2
Bradley Green 50 C4
Bradley in the Moors 75 E7
Bradley Stoke 36 F3
Bradlow 50 F2
Bradmore Notts 77 F5
W Mid 62 E2
Bradninch 10 D5
Bradnop 75 D7
Bradpole 12 E2
Bradshaw Gtr Man 86 C5
W Yorks 87 C8
Bradstone 9 F5
Bradwall Green 74 C4
Bradway 88 F4
Bradwell Derbys 88 F2
Essex 42 B4
M Keynes 53 F6
Norf 69 D8
Staffs 74 E5
Bradwell Grove 38 D2
Bradwell on Sea 43 D6
Bradwell Waterside 43 D5
Bradworthy 8 C5
Bradworthy Cross 8 C5
Brae Dumfries 107 B5
Highld 155 J13
Highld 156 J7
Shetland 160 G5
Braeantra 151 D8
Braedownie 134 B2
Braefield 150 H7
Braegrum 128 B2
Braehead
Dumfries 105 D8
Orkney 159 D5
Orkney 159 H6
S Lanark 119 F8
S Lanark 120 D2
Braehead of Lunan 135 D6
Braehoulland 160 F4
Braehungie 158 G3
Braelangwell Lodge 151 B8
Braemar 139 E7
Braemore Highld 150 D4
Highld 158 G2
Brae of Achnahaird 156 H3
Brae Roy Lodge 137 E6
Braeside 118 B2
Braes of Enzie 152 C3
Braeswick 159 E7
Braewick 160 H5
Brafferton Darl 101 B7
N Yorks 95 B7
Brafield-on-the-Green 53 D6
Bragar 155 C7
Bragbury End 41 B5
Bragleenmore 124 C5
Braichmelyn 83 E6
Braid 120 C5
Braides 92 D4
Braidley 101 F5
Braidwood 119 E8
Braigo 142 B3
Brailsford 76 E2
Brainshaugh 117 D8
Braintree 42 B3
Braiseworth 56 B5
Braishfield 14 B4
Braithwaite Cumb 98 B4
S Yorks 89 C7
W Yorks 94 E3
Braithwell 89 E6
Bramber 17 C5
Bramcote Notts 76 F5
Warks 63 F8
Bramdean 15 B7
Bramerton 69 D5
Bramfield Herts 41 C5
Suff 57 B7
Bramford 56 E5
Bramhall 87 F6
Bramham 95 E7
Bramhope 95 E5
Bramley Hants 26 D4
Sur 27 E8
S Yorks 89 E5
W Yorks 94 F5
Bramling 31 D6
Brampford Speke 10 E4
Brampton Cambs 54 B3
Cumb 100 B1
Cumb 108 C5
Derbys 76 B3
Hereford 49 F6
Lincs 77 B8
Norf 81 E8
Suff 69 F7
S Yorks 88 D5
Brampton Abbotts 36 B3
Brampton Ash 64 F4
Brampton Bryan 49 B5
Brampton en le Morthen 89 F5
Bramshall 75 F7
Bramshaw 14 C3
Bramshill 26 C5
Bramshott 27 F6
Branault 147 E8
Brancaster 80 C3
Brancaster Staithe 80 C3
Brancepeth 110 F5
Branch End 110 C3
Branchill 151 F13
Branderburgh 152 A2
Brandesburton 97 E7
Brandeston 57 C6
Brand Green 36 B4
Brandhill 49 B6
Brandis Corner 9 D6
Brandiston 81 E7
Brandon Durham 110 F5
Lincs 78 E2
Northumb 117 C6
Suff 67 F7
Warks 52 B2
Brandon Bank 67 F6
Brandon Creek 67 E6
Brandon Parva 68 D3
Brandsby 95 B8
Brandy Wharf 90 E4
Brane 2 D3
Bran End 42 B2
Branksome 13 E8
Branksome Park 13 E8
Bransby 77 B8
Branscombe 11 F6
Bransford 50 D2
Bransgore 14 E2
Branshill 127 E7
Bransholme 97 F7
Branson's Cross 51 B5
Branston Leics 64 B5
Lincs 78 C3
Staffs 63 B6
Branston Booths 78 C3
Branstone 15 F6
Bransty 98 C1
Brant Broughton 78 D2
Brantham 56 F5
Branthwaite Cumb 98 B2
Cumb 108 F2
Brantingham 90 B3
Branton Northumb 117 C6
S Yorks 89 D7
Branxholme 115 C7
Branxholm Park 115 C7
Branxton 122 F4
Brassey Green 74 C2
Brassington 76 D2
Brasted 29 D5
Brasted Chart 29 D5
Brathens 141 E5
Bratoft 79 C7
Brattleby 90 F3
Bratton Telford 61 C6
Wilts 24 D4
Bratton Clovelly 9 E6
Bratton Fleming 20 F5
Bratton Seymour 12 B4
Braughing 41 B6
Braunston 52 C3
Braunstone Town 64 D2
Braunston-in-Rutland 64 D5
Braunton 20 F3
Brawby 96 B3
Brawl 157 C11
Brawlbin 158 E2
Bray 27 B7
Braybrooke 64 F4
Braye Ald 16
Brayford 21 F5
Bray Shop 5 B8
Braystones 98 D2
Braythorn 94 E5
Brayton 95 F9
Bray Wick 27 B6
Brazacott 8 E4
Breach 30 C2
Breachacha Castle 146 F4
Breachwood Green 40 B4
Breacleit 154 D6
Breaden Heath 73 F8
Breadsall 76 F3
Breadstone 36 D4
Breage 2 D5
Breakachy 150 G7
Bream 36 D3
Breamore 14 C2
Brean 22 D4
Breanais 154 E4
Brearton 95 C6
Breascleit 154 D7
Breaston 76 F4
Brechfa 46 F4
Brechin 135 C5
Breckan 159 H3
Breck of Cruan 159 G4
Breckrey 149 B10
Brecon = Aberhonddu 34 B4
Bredbury 87 E7
Brede 18 D5
Bredenbury 49 D8
Bredfield 57 D6
Bredgar 30 C2
Bredhurst 29 C8
Bredicot 50 D4
Bredon 50 F4
Bredon's Norton 50 F4
Bredwardine 48 E5
Breedon on the Hill 63 B8
Breibhig W Isles 148 J1
W Isles 155 D9
Breich 120 C2
Breightmet 86 D5
Breighton 96 F3
Breinton 49 F6
Breinton Common 49 E6
Breiwick 160 J6
Bremhill 24 B4
Bremirehoull 160 L6
Brenchley 29 E7
Brendon 21 E6
Brenkley 110 B5
Brent Eleigh 56 E3
Brentford 28 B2
Brentingby 64 C4
Brent Knoll 22 D5
Brent Pelham 54 F5
Brentwood 42 E1
Brenzett 19 C7
Brereton 62 C4
Brereton Green 74 C4
Brereton Heath 74 C5
Bressingham 68 F3
Bretby 63 B6
Bretford 52 B2
Bretforton 51 E5
Bretherdale Head 99 D7
Bretherton 86 B2
Brettabister 160 H6
Brettenham Norf 68 F2
Suff 56 D3
Bretton Derbys 76 B2
Flint 73 C7
Brewer Street 28 D4
Brewlands Bridge 134 C1
Brewood 62 D2
Briach 151 F13
Briants Puddle 13 E6
Brick End 42 B1
Brickendon 41 D6
Bricket Wood 40 D4
Bricklehampton 50 E4
Bride 84 B4
Bridekirk 107 F8
Bridell 45 E3
Bridestowe 9 F7
Brideswell 152 E5
Bridford 10 F3
Bridfordmills 10 F3
Bridge 31 D5
Bridge End 78 F4
Bridgefoot Angus 134 F3
Cumb 98 B2
Bridge Green 55 F5
Bridgehampton 12 B3
Bridge Hewick 95 B6
Bridgehill 110 D3
Bridgemary 15 D6
Bridgemont 87 F8
Bridgend Aberds 140 C4
Aberds 152 E5
Angus 135 C5
Argyll 142 B4
Argyll 143 E8
Argyll 145 D7
Cumb 99 C5
Fife 129 C5
Moray 152 E3
N Lanark 119 B6
Pembs 45 E3
W Loth 120 B3
Bridgend = Pen-y-Bont Ar Ogwr 21 B8
Bridgend of Lintrathen 134 D2
Bridge of Alford 140 C4
Bridge of Allan 127 E6
Bridge of Avon 152 E1
Bridge of Awe 125 C6
Bridge of Balgie 132 E2
Bridge of Cally 133 D8
Bridge of Canny 141 E5
Bridge of Craigisla 134 D2
Bridge of Dee 106 D4
Bridge of Don 141 C8
Bridge of Dun 135 D6
Bridge of Dye 141 F5
Bridge of Earn 128 C3
Bridge of Ericht 132 D2
Bridge of Feugh 141 E6
Bridge of Forss 157 C13
Bridge of Gairn 140 E2
Bridge of Gaur 132 D2
Bridge of Muchalls 141 E7
Bridge of Oich 137 D6
Bridge of Orchy 125 B8
Bridge of Waith 159 G3
Bridge of Walls 160 H4
Bridge of Weir 118 C3
Bridgerule 8 D4
Bridges 60 E3
Bridge Sollers 49 E6
Bridge Street 56 E2
Bridgeton 119 C6
Bridgetown Corn 8 F5
Som 21 F8
Bridge Trafford 73 B8
Bridge Yate 23 B8
Bridgham 68 F2
Bridgnorth 61 E7
Bridgtown 62 D3
Bridgwater 22 F5
Bridlington 97 C7
Bridport 12 E2
Bridstow 36 B2
Brierfield 93 F8
Brierley Glos 36 C3
Hereford 49 D6
S Yorks 88 C5
Brierley Hill 62 F3
Briery Hill 35 D5
Brigg 90 D4
Briggswath 103 D6
Brigham Cumb 107 F7
E Yorks 97 D6
Brighouse 88 B2
Brighstone 14 F5
Brightgate 76 D2
Brighthampton 38 D3
Brightling 18 C3
Brightlingsea 43 C6
Brighton Brighton 17 D7
Corn 4 D4
Brighton Hill 26 E4
Brightons 120 B2
Brightwalton 26 B2
Brightwell 57 E6
Brightwell Baldwin 39 E6
Brightwell cum Sotwell 39 E5
Brignall 101 C5
Brig o'Turk 126 D4
Brigsley 91 D6
Brigsteer 99 F6
Brigstock 65 F6
Brill 39 C6
Brilley 48 E4
Brimaston 44 C4
Brimfield 49 C7
Brimington 76 B4
Brimley 7 B5
Brimpsfield 37 C6
Brimpton 26 C3
Brims 159 K3
Brimscombe 37 D5
Brimstage 85 F4
Brinacory 147 B10
Brind 96 F3
Brindister
Shetland 160 H4
Shetland 160 K6
Brindle 86 B4
Brindley Ford 75 D5
Brineton 62 C2
Bringhurst 64 E5
Brington 53 B8
Brinian 159 F5
Briningham 81 D6
Brinkhill 79 B6
Brinkley 55 D7
Brinklow 52 B2
Brinkworth 37 F7
Brinmore 138 B2
Brinscall 86 B4
Brinsea 23 C6
Brinsley 76 E4
Brinsop 49 E6
Brinsworth 88 F5
Brinton 81 D6
Brisco 108 D4
Brisley 81 E5
Brislington 23 B8
Bristol 23 B7
Briston 81 D6
Britannia 87 B6
Britford 14 B2
Brithdir 58 C4
British Legion Village 29 D8
Briton Ferry 33 E8
Britwell Salome 39 E6
Brixham 7 D7
Brixton Devon 6 D3
London 28 B4
Brixton Deverill 24 F3
Brixworth 52 B5
Brize Norton 38 D3
Broad Blunsdon 38 E1
Broadbottom 87 E7
Broadbridge 16 D2
Broadbridge Heath 28 F2
Broad Campden 51 F6
Broad Chalke 13 B8
Broadclyst 10 E4
Broadfield Gtr Man 87 C6
Lancs 86 B3
Pembs 32 D2
W Sus 28 F3
Broadford 149 F11
Broadford Bridge 16 B4
Broad Green
C Beds 53 E7
Essex 42 B4
Worcs 50 D2
Broadhaugh 115 D7
Broadhaven 158 E5
Broad Haven 44 D3
Broadheath 87 F5
Broad Heath 49 C8
Broadhembury 11 D6
Broadhempston 7 C6
Broad Hill 55 B6
Broad Hinton 25 B6
Broadholme Derbys 76 E3
Lincs 77 B8
Broadland Row 18 D5
Broadlay 32 D4
Broad Laying 26 C2
Broadley Lancs 87 C6
Moray 152 B3
Broadley Common 41 D7
Broad Marston 51 E6
Broadmayne 12 F5
Broadmeadows 121 F7
Broadmere 26 E4
Broadmoor 32 D1
Broadoak 31 C5
Broad Oak Carms 33 B6
Cumb 98 E3
Dorset 12 E2
Dorset 13 C5
E Sus 18 C3
E Sus 18 D5
Hereford 36 B1
Mers 86 E3
Broadrashes 152 C4
Broadsea 153 B9
Broadstairs 31 C7
Broadstone BCP 13 E8
Shrops 60 F5
Broad Street 30 D2
Broad Street Green 42 D4
Broad Town 25 B5
Broadtown Lane 25 B5
Broadwas 50 D2
Broadwater Herts 41 B5
W Sus 17 D5
Broadway Carms 32 D3
Pembs 44 D3
Som 11 C8
Suff 57 B7
Worcs 51 F5
Broadwell Glos 36 C2
Glos 38 B2
Oxon 38 D2
Warks 52 C2
Broadwell House 110 D2
Broadwey 12 F4
Broadwindsor 12 D2
Broadwood Kelly 9 D8
Broadwoodwidger 9 F6
Brobury 48 E5
Brochel 149 D10
Brochloch 113 E5
Brochroy 125 B6
Brockamin 50 D2
Brockbridge 15 C7
Brockdam 117 B7
Brockdish 57 B6
Brockenhurst 14 D4
Brocketsbrae 119 F8
Brockford Street 56 C5
Brockhall 52 C4
Brockham 28 E2
Brockhampton
Glos 37 B7
Hereford 49 F7
Brockholes 88 C2
Brockhurst Derbys 76 C3
Hants 15 D7
Brocklebank 108 E3
Brocklesby 90 C5
Brockley 23 C6
Brockley Green 56 D2
Brockleymoor 108 F4
Brockton Shrops 60 D3
Shrops 60 F3
Shrops 61 D7
Shrops 61 E5
Telford 61 C7
Brockweir 36 D2
Brockwood 15 B7
Brockworth 37 C5
Brocton 62 C3
Brodick 143 E11
Brodsworth 89 D6
Brogaig 149 B9
Brogborough 53 F7
Brokenborough 37 F6
Broken Cross
Ches E 75 B5
Ches W 74 B3
Bromborough 85 F4
Brome 56 B5
Brome Street 57 B5
Bromeswell 57 D7
Bromfield Cumb 107 E8
Shrops 49 B6
Bromham Bedford 53 D8
Wilts 24 C4
Bromley London 28 C5
W Mid 62 F3
Bromley Common 28 C5
Bromley Green 19 B6
Brompton Medway 29 C8
N Yorks 102 E1
N Yorks 103 F7
Brompton-on-Swale 101 E7
Brompton Ralph 22 F2
Brompton Regis 21 F8
Bromsash 36 B3
Bromsberrow Heath 50 F2
Bromsgrove 50 B4
Bromyard 49 D8
Bromyard Downs 49 D8
Bronaber 71 D8
Brongest 46 E2
Bronington 73 F8
Bronllys 48 F3
Bronnant 46 C5
Bronwydd Arms 33 B5
Bronydd 48 E4
Bronygarth 73 F6
Brook Carms 32 D3
Hants 14 B4
Hants 14 C3
IoW 14 F4
Kent 30 E4
Sur 27 E8
Sur 27 F7
Brooke Norf 69 E5
Rutland 64 D5
Brookenby 91 E6
Brookend 36 E2
Brook End 53 C8
Brookfield 118 C4
Brook Hill 14 C3
Brookhouse 92 C5
Brookhouse Green 74 C5
Brookland 19 C6
Brooklands
Dumfries 106 B5
Gtr Man 87 E5
Shrops 74 E2
Brookmans Park 41 D5
Brooks 59 E8
Brooks Green 16 B5
Brook Street Kent 19 B6
Kent 29 E6
W Sus 17 B7
Brookthorpe 37 C5
Brookville 67 E7
Brookwood 27 D7
Broom C Beds 54 E2
S Yorks 88 E5
Warks 51 D5
Worcs 50 B4
Broome Norf 69 E6
Shrops 60 F4
Broomedge 86 F5
Broome Park 117 C7
Broomer's Corner 16 B5
Broomfield Aberds 153 E9
Essex 42 C3
Kent 30 D2
Kent 31 C5
Som 22 F4
Broomfleet 90 B2
Broom Green 81 E5
Broomhall Ches E 74 E3
Windsor 27 C7
Broomhaugh 110 C3
Broomhill Norf 67 D6
Northumb 117 D8
S Yorks 88 D5
Broom Hill 13 D8
Broomholm 81 D9
Broomley 110 C3
Broompark 110 E5
Broom's Green 50 F2
Broomy Lodge 14 C3
Brora 157 J12
Broseley 61 D6
Brotherhouse Bar 66 C2
Brotherstone 122 F2
Brothertoft 79 E5
Brotherton 89 B5
Brotton 102 C4
Broubster 157 C13
Brough Cumb 100 C2
Derbys 88 F2
E Yorks 90 B3
Highld 158 C4
Notts 77 D8
Orkney 159 G4
Shetland 160 F6
Shetland 160 F7
Shetland 160 G7
Shetland 160 H6
Shetland 160 J7
Broughall 74 E2
Brough Lodge 160 D7
Brough Sowerby 100 C2
Broughton
Borders 120 F4
Cambs 54 B3
Flint 73 C7
Hants 25 F8
Lancs 92 F5
M Keynes 53 E6
N Lincs 90 D3
Northants 53 B6
N Yorks 94 D2
N Yorks 96 B3
Orkney 159 D5
Oxon 52 F2
V Glam 21 B8
Broughton Astley 64 E2
Broughton Beck 98 F4
Broughton Common 24 C3
Broughton Gifford 24 C3
Broughton Hackett 50 D4
Broughton in Furness 98 F4
Broughton Mills 98 E4
Broughton Moor 107 F7
Broughton Park 87 D6
Broughton Poggs 38 D2
Broughtown 159 D7
Broughty Ferry 134 F4
Browhouses 108 C2
Browland 160 H4
Brown Candover 26 F3
Brown Edge Lancs 85 C4
Staffs 75 D6
Brown Heath 73 C8
Brownhill Aberds 153 D6
Aberds 153 D8
Blackburn 93 F6
Shrops 60 B4
Brownhills Fife 129 C7
W Mid 62 D4
Brownlow 74 C5
Brownlow Heath 74 C5
Brownmuir 135 B7
Brown's End 50 F2
Brownshill 37 D5
Brownston 6 D4
Brownyside 117 B7
Broxa 103 E7
Broxbourne 41 D6
Broxburn E Loth 122 B2
W Loth 120 B3
Broxholme 78 B2
Broxted 42 B1
Broxton 73 D8
Broxwood 49 D5
Broyle Side 17 C8
Brù 155 C8
Bruairnis 148 H2
Bruan 158 G5
Bruar Lodge 133 B5
Brucehill 118 B3
Bruera 73 C8
Bruern Abbey 38 B2
Bruichladdich 142 B3
Bruisyard 57 C7
Brumby 90 D2
Brund 75 C8
Brundall 69 D6
Brundish 57 C6
Brundish Street 57 B6
Brunery 147 D10
Brunshaw 93 F8
Brunswick Village 110 B5
Bruntcliffe 88 B3
Bruntingthorpe 64 E3
Brunton Fife 128 B5
Northumb 117 B8
Wilts 25 D7
Brushford Devon 9 D8
Som 10 B4
Bruton 23 F8
Bryanston 13 D6
Brydekirk 107 B8
Bryher 2 E3
Brymbo 73 D6
Brympton 12 C3
Bryn Carms 33 D6
Gtr Man 86 D3
Neath 34 E2
Shrops 60 F2
Brynamman 33 C8
Brynberian 45 F3
Brynbryddan 34 E1
Brynbuga = Usk 35 D7
Bryncae 34 F3
Bryncethin 34 F3
Bryncir 71 C5
Bryn-coch 33 E8
Bryncroes 70 D3
Bryncrug 58 D3
Bryn Du 82 D3
Bryneglwys 72 E5
Brynford 73 B5
Bryn Gates 86 D3
Bryn-glas 83 E8
Bryn Golau 34 F3
Bryngwran 82 D3
Bryngwyn Ceredig 45 E4
Mon 35 D7
Powys 48 E3
Brynhenllan 45 F2
Brynhoffnant 46 D2
Brynithel 35 D6
Bryn-Iwan 46 F2
Brynmawr 35 C5
Bryn-mawr 70 D3
Brynmenyn 34 F3
Brynmill 33 E7
Brynna 34 F3
Bryn-nantllech 72 C3
Bryn-penarth 59 D8
Brynrefail Anglesey 82 C4
Gwyn 83 E5
Bryn Rhyd-yr-Arian 72 C3
Brynsadler 34 F4
Bryn Saith Marchog 72 D4
Brynsiencyn 82 E4
Bryn Sion 59 C5
Brynteg Anglesey 82 C4
Ceredig 46 E3
Bryn-y-gwenin 35 C7
Bryn-y-maen 83 D8
Bryn-yr-eryr 70 C4
Buaile nam Bodach 148 H2
Bualintur 149 F9
Buarthmeini 72 F2
Bubbenhall 51 B8
Bubwith 96 F3
Buccleuch 115 C6
Buchanhaven 153 D11
Buchanty 127 B8
Buchlyvie 126 E4
Buckabank 108 E3
Buckden Cambs 54 C2
N Yorks 94 B2
Buckenham 69 D6
Buckerell 11 D6
Buckfast 6 C5
Buckfastleigh 6 C5
Buckhaven 129 E5
Buckholm 121 F7
Buckholt 36 C2
Buckhorn Weston 13 B5
Buckhurst Hill 41 E7
Buckie 152 B4
Buckies 158 D3
Buckingham 52 F4
Buckland Bucks 40 C1
Devon 6 E4
Glos 51 F5
Hants 14 E4
Herts 54 F4
Kent 31 E7
Oxon 38 E3
Sur 28 D3
Buckland Brewer 9 B6
Buckland Common 40 D2
Buckland Dinham 24 D2
Buckland Filleigh 9 D6
Buckland in the Moor 6 B5
Buckland Monachorum 6 C2
Buckland Newton 12 D4
Buckland St Mary 11 C7
Bucklebury 26 B3
Bucklegate 79 F6
Bucklerheads 134 F4
Bucklers Hard 14 E5
Bucklesham 57 E6
Buckley = Bwcle 73 C6
Bucklow Hill 86 F5
Buckminster 65 B5
Bucknall Lincs 78 C4
Stoke 75 E6
Bucknell Oxon 39 B5
Shrops 49 B5
Buckpool 152 B4
Bucksburn 141 D7
Buck's Cross 8 B5
Bucks Green 27 F8
Buckshaw Village 86 B3
Bucks Horn Oak 27 E6
Buckskin 26 D4
Buck's Mills 9 B5
Buckton E Yorks 97 B7
Hereford 49 B5
Northumb 123 F6
Buckworth 54 B2
Budbrooke 51 C7
Budby 77 C6
Budd's Titson 8 D4
Bude 8 D4
Budlake 10 E4
Budle 123 F7
Budleigh Salterton 11 F5
Budock Water 3 C6
Buerton 74 E3
Buffler's Holt 52 F4
Bugbrooke 52 D4
Buglawton 75 C5
Bugle 4 D5
Bugley 24 E3
Bugthorpe 96 D3
Buildwas 61 D6
Builth Road 48 D2
Builth Wells = Llanfair-ym-Muallt 48 D2
Buirgh 154 H5
Bulby 65 B7
Bulcote 77 E6
Buldoo 157 C12
Bulford 25 E6
Bulford Camp 25 E6
Bulkeley 74 D2
Bulkington Warks 63 F7
Wilts 24 D4
Bulkworthy 9 C5
Bullamoor 102 E1
Bullbridge 76 D3
Bullbrook 27 C6
Bulley 36 C4
Bullgill 107 F7
Bull Hill 14 E4
Bullington Hants 26 E2
Lincs 78 B3
Bull's Green 41 C5
Bullwood 145 F10
Bulmer Essex 56 E2
N Yorks 96 C2
Bulmer Tye 56 F2
Bulphan 42 F2
Bulverhythe 18 E4
Bulwark 153 D9
Bulwell 76 E5
Bulwick 65 E6
Bumble's Green 41 D7
Bun Abhainn Eadarra 154 G6
Bunacaimb 147 C9
Bun a'Mhuillin 148 G2
Bunarkaig 136 F4
Bunbury 74 D2
Bunbury Heath 74 D2
Bunchrew 151 G9
Bundalloch 149 F13
Buness 160 C8
Bunessan 146 J6
Bungay 69 F6
Bunkers Hill 38 C4
Bunker's Hill Lincs 78 B2
Lincs 79 D5
Bunloit 137 B8
Bun Loyne 136 D5
Bunnahabhain 142 A5
Bunny 64 B2
Buntait 150 H6
Buntingford 41 B6
Bunwell 68 E4
Burbage Derbys 75 B7
Leics 63 E8
Wilts 25 C7
Burchett's Green 39 F8
Burcombe 25 F5
Burcot 39 E5
Burcott 40 B1
Burdon 111 D6
Bures 56 F3
Bures Green 56 F3
Burford Ches E 74 D3
Oxon 38 C2
Shrops 49 C7
Burg 146 G6
Burgar 159 F4
Burgate Hants 14 C2
Suff 56 B4
Burgess Hill 17 C7
Burgh 57 D6
Burgh by Sands 108 D3
Burgh Castle 69 D7
Burghclere 26 C2
Burghead 151 E14
Burghfield 26 C4
Burghfield Common 26 C4
Burghfield Hill 26 C4
Burgh Heath 28 D3
Burghill 49 E6
Burgh le Marsh 79 C8
Burgh Muir 141 B6
Burgh next Aylsham 81 E8
Burgh on Bain 91 F6
Burgh St Margaret 69 C7
Burgh St Peter 69 E7
Burghwallis 89 C6
Burham 29 C8
Buriton 15 B8
Burland 74 D3
Burlawn 4 B4
Burleigh 27 C6
Burlescombe 11 C5
Burleston 13 E5
Burley Hants 14 D3
Rutland 65 C5
W Yorks 95 F5
Burleydam 74 E3
Burley Gate 49 E7
Burley in Wharfedale 94 E4
Burley Lodge 14 D3
Burley Street 14 D3
Burlingjobb 48 D4
Burlow 18 D2
Burlton 60 B4
Burmarsh 19 B7
Burmington 51 F7
Burn 89 B6
Burnaston 76 F2
Burnbank 119 D7
Burnby 96 E4
Burncross 88 E4
Burneside 99 E7
Burness 159 D7
Burneston 101 F8
Burnett 23 C8
Burnfoot Borders 115 C7
Borders 115 C8
E Ayrs 112 D4
Perth 127 D8
Burnham Bucks 40 F2
N Lincs 90 C4
Burnham Deepdale 80 C4
Burnham Green 41 C5
Burnham Market 80 C4
Burnham Norton 80 C4
Burnham-on-Crouch 43 E5
Burnham-on-Sea 22 E5
Burnham Overy Staithe 80 C4
Burnham Overy Town 80 C4
Burnham Thorpe 80 C4
Burnhead Dumfries 113 E8
S Ayrs 112 D2

Burnhervie 141 C6
Burnhill Green 61 D7
Burnhope 110 E4
Burniston 103 E8
Burnlee 88 D2
Burnley 93 F8
Burnley Lane 93 F8
Burnmouth 123 C5
Burn of Cambus . . 127 D6
Burnopfield 110 D4
Burnsall 94 C3
Burnside *Angus* . 135 D5
E Ayrs. 113 C5
Fife 128 D3
Shetland 160 F4
S Lanark. 119 C6
W Loth 120 B3
Burnside of
Duntrune 134 F4
Burnswark 107 B8
Burntcommon 27 D8
Burnt Heath 76 B2
Burnthouse 3 C6
Burnt Houses 101 B6
Burntisland 128 F4
Burnton 112 D4
Burntwood 62 D4
Burnt Yates 95 C5
Burnwynd 120 C4
Burpham *Sur* 27 D8
W Sus 16 D4
Burradon
Northumb 117 D5
T&W 111 B5
Burrafirth *Shetland* 160 F5
Shetland 160 J4
Burras 3 C5
Burravoe *Shetland* 160 F7
Shetland 160 G5
Burray Village . . . 159 J5
Burrells 100 C1
Burrelton 134 F2
Burridge *Devon* . . 20 F4
Hants. 15 C6
Burrill 101 F7
Burringham 90 D2
Burrington *Devon* . . 9 B8
Hereford 49 B6
N Som 23 D7
Burrough Green . . . 55 D7
Burrough on the
Hill 64 C4
Burrow-bridge 11 B8
Burrowhill 27 C7
Burry 33 E5
Burry Green 33 E5
Burry Port
= *Porth Tywyn* . . 33 D5
Burscough 86 C2
Burscough Bridge . . 86 C2
Bursea 96 F4
Burshill 97 E6
Bursledon 15 D5
Burslem 75 E5
Burstall 56 E4
Burstock 12 D2
Burston *Norf.* 68 F4
Staffs. 75 F6
Burstow 28 E4
Burswick 91 B6
Burtersett 100 F3
Burtle 23 E5
Burton *BCP* 14 E2
Ches W. 73 B7
Ches W. 74 C2
Lincs 78 B2
Northumb 123 F7
Pembs 44 E4
Som 22 E3
Wilts 24 B3
Burton Agnes 97 C7
Burton Bradstock . . 12 F2
Burton Dassett . . . 51 D8
Burton Fleming . . . 97 B6
Burton Green
W Mid 51 B7
Wrex 73 D7
Burton Hastings . . . 63 E8
Burton-in-Kendal . . 92 B5
Burton in Lonsdale . 93 B6
Burton Joyce 77 E6
Burton Latimer 53 B7
Burton Lazars 64 C4
Burton-le-Coggles . 65 B6
Burton Leonard . . . 95 C6
Burton on the
Wolds 64 E3
Burton Overy 64 E3
Burton
Pedwardine 78 E4
Burton Pidsea 97 F8
Burton Salmon 89 B5
Burton Stather 90 C2
Burton upon
Stather 90 C2
Burton upon Trent . 63 B6
Burtonwood 86 E3
Burwardsley 74 D2
Burwarton 61 F6
Burwash 18 C3
Burwash Common . 18 C3
Burwash Weald . . . 18 C3
Burwell *Cambs* . . . 55 C6
Lincs 79 B6
Burwen 82 B4
Burwick 159 K5
Bury *Cambs* 66 F2
Gtr Man 87 C6
Som 10 B4
W Sus 16 C4
Bury Green 41 B7
Bury St Edmunds . . 56 C2
Burythorpe 96 C3
Busby 119 D5
Buscot 38 E2
Bush Bank 49 D6
Bushbury 62 D3
Bushby 64 D3
Bush Crathie 139 E8
Bushey 40 E4
Bushey Heath 40 E4
Bush Green 68 F5
Bushley 50 F3
Bushton 25 B5
Buslingthorpe 90 F4
Busta 160 G5
Butcher's Cross . . . 18 C2

Butcombe 23 C7
Butetown 22 B3
Butleigh 23 F7
Butleigh Wootton . . 23 F7
Butler's Cross 39 D8
Butler's End 63 F6
Butlers Marston . . . 51 E8
Butley 57 D7
Butley High
Corner 57 E7
Butterburn 109 B6
Buttercrambe 96 D3
Butterknowle 101 B6
Butterleigh 10 D4
Buttermere *Cumb* . 98 C3
Wilts 25 C8
Butterstone 133 E7
Butterton 75 D7
Butterwick
Durham 102 B1
Lincs 79 E6
N Yorks. 96 B3
N Yorks. 97 B5
Butt Green 74 D3
Buttington 60 D2
Buttonoak 50 B2
Buttsash 14 D5
Butt's Green 14 B4
Buxhall 56 D4
Buxhall Fen Street . 56 D4
Buxley 122 D4
Buxted 17 B8
Buxton *Derbys* . . . 75 B7
Norf. 81 E8
Buxworth 87 F8
Bwcle = *Buckley* . . 73 C6
Bwlch 35 B5
Bwlchgwyn 73 D6
Bwlch-Llan 46 D4
Bwlchnewydd 32 B4
Bwlchtocyn 70 E4
Bwlch-y-cibau 59 C8
Bwlchyddar 59 B8
Bwlch-y-fadfa 46 E3
Bwlch-y-ffridd 59 E7
Bwlchygroes 45 F4
Bwlch-y-sarnau . . . 48 B2
Byermoor 110 D4
Byers Green 110 F5
Byfield 52 D3
Byfleet 27 C8
Byford 49 E5
Bygrave 54 F3
Byker 111 C5
Bylchau 72 C3
Byley 74 C4
Bynea 33 E6
Byrness 116 D3
Bythorn 53 B8
Byton 49 C5
Byworth 16 B3

C

Cabharstadh 155 E8
Cablea 133 F6
Cabourne 90 D5
Cabrach *Argyll* . . 144 G3
Moray 140 B2
Cabrich 151 G8
Cabus 92 E4
Cackle Street 17 B8
Cadbury 10 D4
Cadbury Barton 9 C8
Cadder 119 B6
Caddington 40 C3
Caddonfoot 121 F7
Cadeby *Leics* 63 D8
S Yorks. 89 D6
Cadeleigh 10 D4
Cade Street 18 C3
Cadgwith 3 E6
Cadham 128 D4
Cadishead 86 E5
Cadle 33 E7
Cadley *Lancs* 92 F5
Wilts 25 C7
Wilts 25 D7
Cadmore End 39 E7
Cadnam 14 C3
Cadney 90 D4
Cadole 73 C6
Cadoxton 22 C3
Cadoxton-Juxta-
Neath 34 E1
Cadshaw 86 C5
Cadzow 119 D7
Caeathro 82 E4
Caehopkin 34 C2
Caenby 90 F4
Caenby Corner 90 F4
Caerau *Bridgend* . . 34 E2
Cardiff 22 B3
Caér-bryn 33 C6
Caerdeon 58 C3
Caerdydd = *Cardiff* . 22 B3
Caerfarchell 44 C2
Caerffili
= *Caerphilly* 35 F5
Caerfyrddin
= *Carmarthen* . . . 33 B5
Caergeiliog 82 D3
Caergwrle 73 D7
Caergybi
= *Holyhead* 82 C2
Caerleon
= *Caerllion* 35 E7
Caer Llan 36 D1
Caerllion
= *Caerleon* 35 E7
Caernarfon 82 E4
Caerphilly
= *Caerffili* 35 F5
Caersws 59 E7
Caerwedros 46 D2
Caerwent 36 E1
Caerwych 71 D7
Caerwys 72 B5
Caethle 58 E3
Caim 83 C6
Caio 47 F5
Cairinis 148 B3
Cairisiadar 154 D5
Cairminis 154 J5
Cairnbaan 145 D7
Cairnbanno
House 153 D8

Cairnborrow 152 D4
Cairnbrogie 141 B7
Cairnbulg Castle . . 153 B10
Cairncross *Angus.* . 134 B4
Borders 122 C4
Cairndow 125 D7
Cairness 153 B10
Cairneyhill 128 F2
Cairnfield House . . 152 B4
Cairngaan 104 F5
Cairngarroch 104 E4
Cairnhill 153 E6
Cairnie *Aberds* . . 141 D7
Aberds 152 D4
Cairnorrie 153 D8
Cairnpark 141 C7
Cairnryan 104 C4
Cairnton 159 H4
Caister-on-Sea . . . 69 C8
Caistor 90 D5
Caistor St Edmund . 68 D5
Caistron 117 D5
Caitha Bowland . . 121 E7
Calais Street 56 F3
Calanais 154 D7
Calbost 155 F9
Calbourne 14 F5
Calceby 79 B6
Calcot Row. 26 B4
Calcott 31 C5
Caldback 160 C8
Caldbeck 108 F3
Caldbergh 101 F5
Caldecote *Cambs* . 54 D4
Cambs 65 F8
Herts. 54 F3
Northants 52 D4
Caldecott *Northants* 53 C7
Oxon 38 E4
Rutland 65 E5
Calder Bridge 98 D2
Calderbank 119 C7
Calderbrook 87 C7
Caldercruix 119 C8
Calder Hall 98 D2
Calder Mains 158 E2
Caldermill 119 E6
Calder Vale 92 E5
Calderwood 119 D6
Caldhame 134 E4
Caldicot 36 F1
Caldwell *Derbys* . . 63 C6
N Yorks. 101 C6
Caldy 85 F3
Caledrhydiau 46 D3
Calfsound 159 E6
Calgary 146 F6
Califer 151 F13
California *Falk* . . . 120 B2
Norf. 69 C8
Calke 63 B7
Callakille 149 C11
Callaly 117 D6
Callander 126 D5
Callaughton 61 E6
Callestick 4 D2
Calligarry 149 H11
Callington 5 C8
Callow 49 F6
Callow End 50 E3
Callow Hill *Wilts* . . 37 F7
Worcs 50 B2
Callows Grave 49 C7
Calmore 14 C4
Calmsden 37 D7
Calne 24 B5
Calow 76 B4
Calshot 15 D5
Calstock 6 C2
Calstone
Wellington 24 C5
Calthorpe 81 D7
Calthwaite 108 E4
Calton *N Yorks* . . . 94 D2
Staffs. 75 D8
Calveley 74 D2
Calver 76 B2
Calverhall 74 F3
Calver Hill 49 E5
Calverleigh 10 C4
Calverley 94 F5
Calvert 39 B6
Calverton *M Keynes* 53 F5
Notts 77 E6
Calvine 133 C5
Calvo 107 D8
Cam 36 E4
Camas-luinie 136 B2
Camasnacroise. . . 130 D2
Camastianavaig . . 149 E10
Camasunary 149 G10
Camault Muir 151 G8
Camb 160 D7
Camber 19 D6
Camberley 27 C6
Camberwell 28 B4
Camblesforth 89 B7
Cambo 117 F6
Cambois 117 F9
Camborne 3 B5
Cambourne 54 D4
Cambridge *Cambs* . 54 D5
Glos 36 D4
Cambridge Town . . 43 F5
Cambus 127 E7
Cambusavie
Farm 151 B10
Cambusbarron . . . 127 E6
Cambuskenneth . . 127 E7
Cambuslang 119 C6
Cambusmore
Lodge 151 B10
Camden 41 F5
Camelford 8 F3
Camelsdale 27 F6
Camer's Green . . . 50 F2
Camerton *Bath* . . 23 D8
Cumb 107 F7
E Yorks. 91 B6
Camghouran 132 D2
Cammachmore . . . 141 E8
Cammeringham . . . 90 F3
Camore 151 B10
Campbeltown . . . 143 F8
Camperdown 111 B5
Camp Hill 63 E7
Campmuir 134 F2
Campsall 89 C6

Campsey Ash 57 D7
Campton 54 F2
Camptown 116 C2
Camrose 44 C4
Camserney 133 E5
Camster 158 F4
Camuschoirk 130 C1
Camuscross. 149 G11
Camusnagaul
Highld 130 B4
Highld 150 C3
Camusrory 147 B11
Camusteel 149 D12
Camusterrach . . . 149 D12
Camusvrachan . . . 132 E3
Canada 14 C3
Canadia 18 D4
Canal Side 89 C7
Candacraig
House 140 C2
Candlesby 79 C7
Candy Mill 120 E3
Cane End 26 B4
Canewdon 42 E4
Canford Bottom . . 13 D8
Canford Cliffs 13 F8
Canford Magna . . . 13 E8
Canham's Green . . 56 C4
Canholes 75 B7
Canisbay 158 C5
Cann 13 B6
Cann Common . . . 13 B6
Cannard's Grave . . 23 E8
Cannich 150 H6
Cannington 22 F4
Cannock 62 D3
Cannock Wood . . . 62 C4
Canon Bridge 49 E6
Canon Frome 49 E8
Canon Pyon 49 E6
Canons Ashby 52 D3
Canonstown 2 C4
Canterbury. 30 D5
Cantley *Norf.* 69 D6
S Yorks. 89 D7
Cantlop 60 D5
Canton 22 B3
Cantraybruich. . . 151 G10
Cantraydoune . . . 151 G10
Cantraywood. . . . 151 G10
Cantsfield 93 B6
Canvey Island 42 F3
Canwick 78 C2
Canworthy Water. . 8 E4
Caol 131 B5
Caolas 146 G3
Caolas Scalpaigh . 154 H7
Caolas Stocinis . . 154 H6
Caol Ila 142 A5
Capel 28 E2
Capel Bangor 58 F3
Capel Betws
Lleucu 46 D5
Capel Carmel 70 E2
Capel Coch 82 C4
Capel Curig 83 F7
Capel Cynon 46 E2
Capel Dewi *Carms* . 33 B5
Ceredig 46 E3
Ceredig 58 F3
Capel Garmon . . . 83 F8
Capel-gwyn. 82 D3
Capel Gwyn 33 B5
Capel Gwynfe 33 B8
Capel Hendre 33 C6
Capel Hermon . . . 71 E8
Capel Isaac 33 B6
Capel Iwan 45 F4
Capel le Ferne . . . 31 F6
Capel Llanilltern . . 34 F4
Capel Mawr 82 D4
Capel St Andrew . . 57 E7
Capel St Mary . . . 56 F4
Capel Seion 46 B5
Capel Tygwydd . . . 45 E4
Capel Uchaf. 70 C5
Capel-y-graig 82 E5
Capelulo 83 D7
Capel-y-ffin 48 F4
Capenhurst 73 B7
Capernwray 92 B5
Capheaton 117 F6
Cappercleuch . . . 115 B5
Capplegill 114 D4
Capton 7 D6
Caputh 133 F7
Carbis Bay 2 C4
Carbost *Highld* . . 149 D9
Highld 149 E8
Carbrook 88 F4
Carbrooke 68 D2
Carburton 77 B6
Carcant 121 D6
Carcary 135 D6
Carclaze 4 D5
Car Colston 77 E7
Carcroft 89 C6
Cardenden 128 E4
Cardeston 60 C3
Cardiff = *Caerdydd* . 22 B3
Cardigan = *Aberteifi* 45 E3
Cardington *Bedford* . 53 E8
Shrops 60 E5
Cardinham 5 C6
Cardonald 118 C5
Cardow 152 D1
Cardrona 121 F6
Cardross 118 B3
Cardurnock 107 D8
Careby 65 C7
Careston Castle . . 135 D5
Carew 32 D1
Carew Cheriton . . 32 D1
Carew Newton . . . 32 D1
Carey 49 F7
Carfrae 121 C8
Cargenbridge . . . 107 B6
Cargill 134 F1
Cargo 108 D3
Cargreen 6 C2
Carham 122 F4
Carhampton 22 E2
Carharrack 3 B6
Carie *Perth* 132 D3
Perth 132 F3
Carines 4 D2
Carisbrooke 15 F5
Cark 92 B3
Carlabhagh 154 C7

Carland Cross 4 D3
Carlby 65 C7
Carlecotes 88 D2
Carlesmoor 94 B4
Carleton *Cumb* . . . 99 B7
Cumb. 108 D4
Lancs. 92 F3
N Yorks. 94 E2
Carleton Forehoe . . 68 D4
Carleton Rode. . . . 68 E4
Carlingcott 23 D8
Carlin How 103 C5
Carlisle 108 D4
Carlops 120 D4
Carlton *Bedford* . . 53 D7
Cambs 55 D7
Leics 63 D7
Notts 77 E6
N Yorks. 89 B7
N Yorks. 101 C6
N Yorks. 101 F5
N Yorks. 102 A4
Stockton 102 B1
Suff. 57 C7
S Yorks. 88 C4
W Yorks. 88 B4
Carlton Colville . . . 69 F8
Carlton Curlieu. . . . 64 E3
Carlton
Husthwaite 95 B7
Carlton in
Cleveland 102 D3
Carlton in Lindrick . 89 F6
Carlton le
Moorland 78 D2
Carlton Miniott. . . 102 F1
Carlton on Trent . . 77 C7
Carlton Scroop . . . 78 E2
Carluke 119 D8
Carmarthen
= *Caerfyrddin* . . . 33 B5
Carmel *Anglesey* . . 82 C3
Carms 33 C6
Flint 73 B5
Guern 16
Gwyn 82 F4
Carmont 141 F7
Carmunnock 119 D6
Carmyle 119 C6
Carmyllie 135 E5
Carnaby 97 C7
Carnach *Highld* . 136 B3
Highld 150 B3
W Isles 154 H7
Carnachy 157 D10
Càrnais 154 D5
Carnbee 129 D7
Carnbo 128 D2
Carnbrea 3 B5
Carnduff 119 E6
Carnduncan 142 B3
Carne 3 C8
Carnforth 92 B4
Carn-gorm 136 B2
Carnhedryn 44 C3
Carnhell Green . . . 2 C5
Carnkie *Corn.* . . . 3 C5
Corn. 3 C6
Carno 59 E6
Carnoch *Highld.* . 150 F5
Highld 150 H6
Carnock 128 F2
Carnon Downs 3 C6
Carnousie 153 C6
Carnoustie 135 F5
Carnwath 120 E2
Carnyorth 2 C2
Carperby 101 F5
Carpley Green . . . 100 F4
Carr 89 E6
Carradale 143 E9
Carragrich. 154 H6
Carrbridge 138 B5
Carrefour
Selous *Jersey* . . . 17
Carreglefn 82 C3
Carreg-wen 45 E4
Carr Hill 111 C5
Carrick *Argyll* . . . 145 E8
Fife 129 B6
Carrick Castle . . . 145 D10
Carrick House . . . 159 E6
Carriden 128 F2
Carrington *Gtr Man* . 86 E5
Lincs 79 D6
Midloth 121 C6
Carrog *Conwy* . . . 71 C8
Denb 72 E5
Carron *Falk* 127 F7
Moray 152 D2
Carronbridge 113 E8
Carron Bridge . . . 127 F6
Carronshore 127 F7
Carrshield 109 E8
Carrutherstown . . 107 B8
Carrville 111 E6
Carsaig *Argyll* . . . 144 E6
Argyll 147 J8
Carscreugh 105 D6
Carse Gray 134 D4
Carse House 144 G6
Carseriggan 105 C6
Carsethorn 107 D6
Carshalton 28 C3
Carsington 76 D2
Carskiey 143 H7
Carsluith 105 D8
Carsphairn 113 E5
Carstairs 120 E2
Carstairs
Junction 120 E2
Carswell Marsh . . . 38 E3
Carter's Clay 14 B4
Carterton 38 D2
Carterway Heads . 110 D3
Carthew 4 D5
Carthorpe 101 F8
Cartington 117 D6
Cartland 119 E8
Cartmel 92 B3
Cartmel Fell 99 F6
Carway 33 D5
Cary Fitzpaine . . . 12 B3
Cascob 48 C4
Cas-gwent
= *Chepstow* 36 E2
Cashlie 132 E1
Cashmoor 13 C7

Casnewydd
= *Newport* 35 F7
Cassey Compton . . 37 C7
Cassington 38 C4
Cassop 111 F6
Castell 72 C5
Castellau 34 F4
Castell-Howell 46 E3
Castell-Nedd
= *Neath* 33 E8
Castell Newydd Emlyn
= *Newcastle
Emlyn.* 46 E2
Castell-y-bwch . . . 35 E6
Casterton 93 B6
Castle Acre 67 C8
Castle Ashby 53 D6
Castlebay =
Bagh a Chaisteil . 148 J1
Castle Bolton . . . 101 E5
Castle Bromwich . . 62 F5
Castle Bytham . . . 65 C6
Castlebythe 32 B1
Castle Caereinion . 59 D8
Castle Camps 55 E7
Castle Carrock . . . 108 D5
Castlecary 119 B7
Castle Cary 23 F8
Castle Combe 24 B3
Castlecraig 151 E11
Castle Donington . . 63 B8
Castle Douglas . . . 106 C4
Castle Eaton 37 E8
Castle Eden 111 F7
Castlefairn 113 F7
Castle Forbes . . . 140 C5
Castleford 88 B5
Castle Green 27 C7
Castle Gresley 63 C6
Castle Heaton . . . 122 E5
Castle Hedingham . 55 F8
Castlehill *Borders* . 120 F5
Highld 158 D3
W Dunb 118 B3
Castle Hill 29 E7
Castle Huntly . . . 128 B5
Castle Kennedy . . 104 D5
Castlemaddy 113 F5
Castlemartin 44 F4
Castlemilk
Dumfries 107 B8
Glasgow 119 D6
Castlemorris 44 B4
Castlemorton 50 F2
Castle O'er 115 E5
Castle
Pulverbatch 60 D4
Castle Rising 67 B6
Castleside 110 E3
Castle Stuart 151 G10
Castlethorpe 53 E6
Castleton *Angus* . . 134 E3
Argyll 145 E7
Derbys. 88 F2
Gtr Man 87 C6
Newport 35 F6
N Yorks. 102 D4
Castletown *Ches W* . 73 D8
Highld 151 G10
Highld 158 D3
IoM 84 F2
T&W 111 D6
Castleweary 115 D7
Castley 95 E5
Caston 68 E2
Castor 65 E8
Caswell 33 F6
Catacol 143 D10
Catbrain 36 F2
Catbrook 36 D2
Catchall 2 D3
Catchems Corner . . 51 B7
Catchgate 110 D4
Catcleugh 116 D3
Catcliffe 88 F5
Catcott 23 F5
Caterham 28 D4
Catfield 69 B6
Catford 28 B4
Catforth 92 F4
Cathays 22 B3
Cathcart 119 C5
Cathedine 35 B5
Catherington 15 C7
Catherton 49 B8
Catlodge 138 E2
Catlowdy 108 B4
Catmore 38 F4
Caton 92 C5
Caton Green 92 C5
Catrine 113 B5
Cat's Ash 35 E7
Catsfield 18 D4
Catshill 50 B4
Cattal 95 D7
Cattawade 56 F5
Catterall 92 E4
Catterick 101 E7
Catterick Bridge . . 101 E7
Catterick
Garrison 101 E6
Catterlen 108 F4
Catterline 135 B8
Catterton 95 E8
Catthorpe 52 B3
Cattistock 12 E3
Catton *Northumb* . 109 D8
N Yorks. 95 B6
Catwick 97 E7
Catworth 53 B8
Caudlesprings 68 D2
Caulcott 39 B5
Cauldcots 135 E6
Cauldhame 126 E5
Cauldmill 115 C8
Cauldon 75 E7
Caulkerbush 107 D6
Caulside 115 F7
Caunsall 62 F2
Caunton 77 D7
Causeway End . . . 105 C8
Causewayhead
Cumb 107 D8
Stirling 127 E6
Causeyend 141 C8

Causey Park
Bridge 117 E7
Cautley 100 E1
Cavendish 56 E2
Cavendish Bridge . 63 B8
Cavenham 55 C8
Caversfield 39 B5
Caversham 26 B5
Caverswall 75 E6
Cavil 96 F3
Cawdor 151 F11
Cawkwell 79 B5
Cawood 95 F8
Cawsand 6 D2
Cawston 81 E7
Cawthorne 88 D3
Cawthorpe 65 B7
Cawton 96 B2
Caxton 54 D4
Caynham 49 B7
Caythorpe *Lincs* . . 78 E2
Notts 77 E6
Cayton 103 F8
Ceann a Bhaigh . . 148 B2
Ceannacroc
Lodge 136 C5
Ceann a Deas Loch
Baghasdail 148 G2
Ceann Shiphoirt . . 155 F7
Ceann
Tarabhaigh 154 F7
Cearsiadair 155 E8
Cefn Berain 72 C3
Cefn-brith 72 D3
Cefn Canol 73 F6
Cefn-coch 83 E8
Cefn Coch 59 B8
Cefn-coed-y-
cymmer 34 D4
Cefn Cribwr 34 F2
Cefn Cross 34 F2
Cefn-ddwysarn . . . 72 F3
Cefn Einion 60 F2
Cefneithin 33 C6
Cefn-gorwydd . . . 47 E8
Cefn-mawr 73 E6
Cefn-y-bedd 73 D7
Cefn-y-pant 32 B2
Cei-bach 46 D3
Ceinewydd
= *New Quay* 46 D2
Ceint 82 D4
Cellan 46 E5
Cellarhead 75 E6
Cemaes 82 B3
Cemmaes 58 D5
Cemmaes Road . . 58 D5
Cenarth 45 E4
Cenin 71 C5
Central 118 B2
Ceos 155 E8
Ceres 129 C6
Cerne Abbas 12 D4
Cerney Wick 37 E7
Cerrigceinwen . . . 82 D4
Cerrigydrudion . . . 72 E3
Cessford 116 B3
Ceunant 82 E5
Chaceley 50 F3
Chacewater 3 B6
Chackmore 52 F4
Chacombe 52 E2
Chadderton 87 D7
Chadderton Fold . . 87 D6
Chaddesden 76 F3
Chaddesley
Corbett 50 B3
Chaddleworth 26 B2
Chadlington 38 B3
Chadshunt 51 D8
Chad Valley 62 F4
Chadwell 64 B4
Chadwell St Mary . 29 B7
Chadwick End . . . 51 B7
Chadwick Green . . 86 E3
Chaffcombe 11 C8
Chagford 10 F2
Chailey 17 C7
Chainbridge 66 D4
Chain Bridge 79 E6
Chainhurst 29 E8
Chalbury 13 D8
Chalbury Common . 13 D8
Chaldon 28 D4
Chaldon Herring . . 13 F5
Chale 15 G5
Chale Green 15 G5
Chalfont Common . 40 E3
Chalfont St Giles . . 40 E2
Chalfont St Peter . . 40 E3
Chalford 37 D5
Chalgrove 39 E6
Chalk 29 B7
Challaborough . . . 6 E4
Challacombe 21 E5
Challoch 105 C7
Challock 30 D4
Chalton *C Beds* . . 40 B3
Hants. 15 C8
Chalvington 18 E2
Chancery 46 B4
Chandler's Ford . . 14 B5
Channel Tunnel . . . 19 B8
Channerwick 160 L6
Chantry *Som* 24 E2
Suff. 56 E5
Chapel 128 E4
Chapel Allerton
Som 23 D6
W Yorks. 95 F6
Chapel Amble 4 B4
Chapel Brampton . 52 C5
Chapel Chorlton . . 74 F5
Chapel End 63 E7
Chapel-en-le-
Frith 87 F8
Chapelgate 66 B4
Chapel Green
Warks 51 B8
Warks 63 F6
Chapel Haddlesey . 89 B6
Chapelhall 119 C7
Chapel Head 66 F3
Chapelhill
Dumfries 114 E3
Highld 151 D11
N Ayrs 118 E2
Perth 128 B4
Perth 133 F7

Chapel Hill
Aberds 153 E10
Lincs 78 D5
Mon 36 E2
N Yorks. 95 E6
Chapelknowe 108 B3
Chapel-le-Dale . . . 93 B7
Chapel Milton 87 F8
Chapel of
Garioch 141 B6
Chapel Row 26 C3
Chapel St
Leonards 79 B8
Chapel Stile 99 D5
Chapelton *Angus* . 135 E6
Devon 9 B7
Highld 138 C5
S Lanark. 119 E6
Chapeltown
Blackburn 86 C5
Moray 139 B8
S Yorks. 88 E4
Chapmanslade . . . 24 E3
Chapmans Well 9 E5
Chapmore End . . . 41 C6
Chappel 42 B4
Chard 11 D8
Chardstock 11 D8
Charfield 36 E4
Charford 50 C4
Charing 30 E3
Charing Cross . . . 14 C2
Charing Heath . . . 30 E3
Charingworth 51 F7
Charlbury 38 C3
Charlcombe 24 C2
Charlecote 51 D7
Charles 21 F5
Charlesfield 107 C8
Charleston *Angus* . 134 E3
Renfs. 118 C4
Charlestown
Aberdeen 141 D8
Corn. 4 D5
Derbys. 87 E8
Dorset 12 G4
Fife 128 F2
Gtr Man 87 D6
Highld 149 A13
Highld 151 G9
W Yorks. 87 B7
Charlestown of
Aberlour 152 D2
Charles Tye 56 D4
Charlesworth 87 E8
Charleton 7 E5
Charlton *Hants* . . 25 E8
Herts. 40 B4
London 28 B5
Northants. 52 F3
Northumb 116 F4
Som 23 D8
Telford 61 C5
Wilts 13 B7
Wilts 25 D6
Wilts 37 F6
W Sus 16 C2
Worcs 50 E5
Worcs 50 E5
Charlton Abbots . . 37 B7
Charlton Adam . . . 12 B3
Charlton-All-
Saints 14 B2
Charlton Down . . . 12 E4
Charlton
Horethorne 12 B4
Charlton Kings . . . 37 B6
Charlton
Mackerell 12 B3
Charlton Marshall . 13 D6
Charlton
Musgrove 12 B5
Charlton on
Otmoor 39 C5
Charltons 102 C4
Charlwood 28 E3
Charlynch 22 F4
Charminster 12 E4
Charmouth 11 E8
Charndon 39 B6
Charney Bassett . . 38 E3
Charnock Richard . 86 C3
Charsfield 57 D6
Chart Corner 29 D8
Charter Alley 26 D3
Charterhouse 23 D6
Charterville
Allotments 38 C3
Chartham 30 D5
Chartham Hatch . . 30 D5
Chartridge 40 D2
Chart Sutton 30 E2
Charvil 27 B5
Charwelton 52 D3
Chasetown 62 D4
Chastleton 38 B2
Chasty 8 D5
Chatburn 93 E7
Chatcull 74 F4
Chatham 29 C8
Chathill 117 B7
Chattenden 29 B8
Chatteris 66 F3
Chattisham 56 E4
Chatto 116 C3
Chatton 117 B6
Chawleigh 10 C2
Chawley 38 D4
Chawston 54 D2
Chawton 26 F5
Cheadle *Gtr Man* . 87 F6
Staffs. 75 E7
Cheadle Heath . . . 87 F6
Cheadle Hulme . . . 87 F6
Cheam 28 C3
Cheapside 27 C7
Chearsley 39 C7
Chebsey 62 B2
Checkendon 39 F6
Checkley *Ches E* . . 74 E4
Hereford 49 F7
Staffs. 75 F7
Chedburgh 55 D8
Cheddar 23 D6
Cheddington 40 C2
Cheddleton 75 D6
Cheddon Fitzpaine . 11 B7
Chedglow 37 E6
Chedgrave 69 E6

Bur–Chi **217**

Chedington 12 D2
Chediston 57 B7
Chedworth 37 C7
Chedzoy 22 F5
Cheeklaw 122 D3
Cheeseman's
Green 19 B7
Cheglinch 20 E4
Cheldon 10 C2
Chelford 74 B5
Chellaston 76 F3
Chell Heath 75 D5
Chellington 53 D7
Chelmarsh 61 F7
Chelmer Village . . 42 D3
Chelmondiston . . . 57 F6
Chelmorton 75 C8
Chelmsford 42 D3
Chelsea 28 B3
Chelsfield 29 C5
Chelsworth 56 E3
Cheltenham 37 B6
Chelveston 53 C7
Chelvey 23 C6
Chelwood 23 C8
Chelwood
Common 17 B8
Chelwood Gate . . . 17 B8
Chelworth 37 E6
Chelworth Green . . 37 E7
Chemistry 74 E2
Chenies 40 E3
Cheny Longville . . 60 F4
Chepstow
= *Cas-gwent* 36 E2
Chequerfield 89 B5
Cherhill 24 B5
Cherington *Glos* . . 37 E6
Warks 51 F7
Cheriton *Devon* . . 21 E6
Hants. 15 B6
Kent 19 B8
Swansea 33 E5
Cheriton Bishop . . 10 E2
Cheriton Fitzpaine . 10 D3
Cheriton or Stackpole
Elidor 44 F4
Cherrington 61 B6
Cherrybank 128 B3
Cherry Burton . . . 97 E5
Cherry Hinton 55 D5
Cherry Orchard . . . 50 D3
Cherry Willingham . 78 B3
Chertsey 27 C8
Cheselbourne 13 E5
Chesham 40 D2
Chesham Bois 40 E2
Cheshunt 41 D6
Cheslyn Hay 62 D3
Chessington 28 C2
Chester 73 C8
Chesterblade 23 E8
Chesterfield 76 B3
Chester-le-
Street 111 D5
Chester Moor . . . 111 E5
Chesters *Borders* . 116 B2
Borders 116 C2
Chesterton *Cambs* . 55 C5
Cambs 65 E8
Glos 37 D7
Oxon 39 B5
Shrops 61 E7
Staffs. 74 E5
Warks 51 D8
Chesterwood 109 C8
Chestfield 30 C5
Cheston 6 D4
Cheswardine 61 B7
Cheswick 123 E6
Chetnole 12 D4
Chettiscombe 10 C4
Chettisham 66 F5
Chettle 13 C7
Chetton 61 E6
Chetwode 39 B6
Chetwynd Aston . . 61 C7
Cheveley 55 C7
Chevening 29 D5
Chevington 55 D8
Chevithorne 10 C4
Chew Magna 23 C7
Chew Stoke 23 C7
Chewton
Keynsham 23 C8
Chewton Mendip . . 23 D7
Chicheley 53 E7
Chichester 16 D2
Chickerell 12 F4
Chicklade 24 F4
Chidden 15 C7
Chiddingfold 27 F7
Chiddingly 18 D2
Chiddingstone . . . 29 E5
Chiddingstone
Causeway 29 E6
Chiddingstone
Hoath 29 E5
Chideock 12 E2
Chidham 15 D8
Chidswell 88 B3
Chieveley 26 B2
Chignall St James . 42 D2
Chignall Smealy . . 42 C2
Chigwell 41 E7
Chigwell Row 41 E7
Chilbolton 25 F8
Chilcombe 12 E3
Chilcompton 23 D8
Chilcote 63 C6
Childer Thornton . . 73 B7
Child Okeford 13 C6
Childrey 38 F3
Child's Ercall 61 B6
Childswickham . . . 51 F5
Childwall 86 F2
Childwick Green . . 40 C4
Chilfrome 12 E3
Chilgrove 16 C2
Chilham 30 D4
Chilhampton 25 F5
Chilla 9 D6
Chillaton 9 F6
Chillenden 31 D6

Chillerton 15 F5
Chillesford 57 D7
Chillingham . . . 117 B6
Chillington Devon . . 7 E5
  Som 11 C8
Chilmark 24 F4
Chilson 38 C3
Chilsworthy Corn. . . 6 B2
  Devon 8 D5
Chilthorne Domer . 12 C3
Chiltington 17 C7
Chilton Bucks . . . 39 C6
  Durham 101 B7
  Oxon 38 F4
Chilton Cantelo . . 12 B3
Chilton Foliat . . . 25 B8
Chilton Lane . . . 111 F6
Chilton Polden . . . 23 F5
Chilton Street . . . 55 E8
Chilton Trinity . . . 22 F4
Chilvers Coton . . . 63 E7
Chilwell 76 F5
Chilworth Hants . . 14 C5
  Sur. 27 E8
Chimney 38 D3
Chineham 26 D4
Chingford 41 E6
Chinley 87 F8
Chinley Head . . . 87 F8
Chinnor 39 D7
Chipnall 74 F4
Chippenhall Green 57 B6
Chippenham Cambs 55 C7
  Wilts 24 B4
Chipperfield 40 D3
Chipping Herts . . . 54 F4
  Lancs 93 E6
Chipping Campden 51 F6
Chipping Hill . . . 42 C4
Chipping Norton . 38 B3
Chipping Ongar . 42 D1
Chipping Sodbury . 36 F4
Chipping Warden . 52 E2
Chipstable 10 B5
Chipstead Kent. . . 29 D5
  Sur. 28 D3
Chirbury 60 E2
Chirk = Y Waun . . 73 F6
Chirk Bank 73 F6
Chirmorrie 105 B6
Chirnside 122 D4
Chirnsidebridge . . 122 D4
Chirton 25 D5
Chisbury 25 C7
Chiselborough . . 12 C2
Chiseldon 25 B6
Chiserley 87 B8
Chislehampton . . 39 E5
Chislehurst 28 B5
Chislet 31 C6
Chiswell Green . . 40 D4
Chiswick 28 B3
Chiswick End . . . 54 E4
Chisworth 87 E7
Chithurst 16 B2
Chittering 55 B5
Chitterne 24 E4
Chittlehamholt . . . 9 B8
Chittlehampton . . 9 B8
Chittoe 24 C4
Chivenor 20 F4
Chobham 27 C7
Choicelee 122 D3
Cholderton 25 E7
Cholesbury 40 D2
Chollerford 110 B2
Chollerton 110 B2
Cholmondeston . . 74 C3
Cholsey 39 F5
Cholstrey 49 D6
Chop Gate 102 E3
Choppington . . . 117 F8
Chopwell 110 D4
Chorley Ches E . . 74 D2
  Lancs 86 C3
  Shrops 61 F6
  Staffs 62 C4
Chorleywood . . . 40 E3
Chorlton cum
  Hardy 87 E6
Chorlton Lane . . . 73 E8
Choulton 60 F3
Chowdene 111 D5
Chowley 73 D8
Chrishall 54 F5
Christchurch BCP . 14 E2
  Cambs 66 E4
  Glos 36 C2
  Newport 35 F7
Christian Malford . 24 B4
Christleton 73 C8
Christmas
  Common 39 E7
Christon 23 D5
Christon Bank . . 117 B8
Christow 10 F3
Chryston 119 B6
Chudleigh 7 B6
Chudleigh Knighton . 7 B6
Chulmleigh 9 C8
Chunal 87 E8
Church 86 B5
Churcham 36 C4
Church Aston . . . 61 C7
Churchbank 48 B4
Church Brampton . 52 C5
Churchbridge . . . 62 D3
Church Broughton . 76 F2
Church Crookham . 27 D6
Churchdown . . . 37 C5
Church Eaton . . 62 C2
Churchend Essex . . 42 B2
  Essex 43 E6
  S Glos. 36 E4
Church End Cambs . 66 D3
  Cambs 66 F2
  C Beds 40 B2
  C Beds 53 F7
  C Beds 54 F2
  Essex 42 B3
  Essex 55 E6
  E Yorks 97 D6
  Hants 26 D4
  Lincs 78 F5
  Warks 63 E6
  Warks 63 E6

Church End continued
  Wilts 24 B3
Church Enstone . . 38 B3
Church Fenton . . 95 F8
Churchfield 62 E4
Churchgate Street . 41 C7
Church Green
  Devon 11 E6
  Norf 68 E3
Church Gresley . . 63 C6
Church
  Hanborough . . 38 C4
Church Hill 74 C3
Church Houses . . 102 E4
Churchill Devon . . 11 D8
  Devon 20 E4
  N Som 23 D6
  Oxon 38 B2
  Worcs 50 B3
  Worcs 50 D4
Churchinford . . 11 C7
Church Knowle . . 13 F7
Church Laneham . . 77 B8
Church Langton . . 64 E4
Church Lawford . 52 B2
Church Lawton . . 74 D5
Church Leigh . . 75 F7
Church Lench . . 50 D5
Church Mayfield . . 75 E8
Church Minshull . . 74 C3
Church Norton . . 16 E2
Churchover 64 F2
Church Preen . . 60 E5
Church
  Pulverbatch . . 60 D4
Churchstanton . . 11 C6
Church Stoke . . 60 E2
Churchstow 6 E5
Church Stowe . . 52 D4
Church Street . . 29 B8
Church Stretton . . 60 E4
Churchtown Derbys 76 C2
  IoM 84 C4
  Lancs 92 E4
  Mers 85 C4
Church Town
  N Lincs 89 D8
  Sur. 28 D4
Church Village . . 34 F4
Church Warsop . . 77 C5
Churnsike Lodge . 109 B6
Churston Ferrers . . 7 D7
Churt 27 F6
Churwell 88 B3
Chwilog 70 D5
Chyandour 2 C3
Cilan Uchaf . . . 70 E3
Cilcain 73 C5
Cilcennin 46 C4
Cilfor 71 D7
Cilfrew 34 D1
Cilfynydd 34 E4
Cilgerran 45 E3
Cilgwyn Carms . . 33 B8
  Gwyn 82 F4
  Pembs 45 F2
Ciliau Aeron . . 46 D3
Cill Donnain . . 148 F2
Cille Bhrighde . . 148 G2
Cille Pheadair . . 148 G2
Cilmery 48 D2
Cilsan 33 B6
Ciltalgarth 72 E2
Cilwendeg 45 F4
Cilybebyll 33 D8
Cilycwm 47 F6
Cimla 34 E1
Cinderford 36 C3
Cippyn 45 E3
Circebost 154 D6
Cirencester 37 D7
Ciribhig 154 C6
City London . . . 41 F6
  Powys 60 F2
City Dulas 82 C4
Clachaig Argyll . . 145 E10
  Argyll 124 D3
  Argyll 125 D7
  Argyll 130 E2
  Argyll 144 H6
  Highld 149 E10
  W Isles 148 D2
Clachan Argyll . . 145 E11
  Argyll 124 D3
  Argyll 125 D7
  Highld 149 E10
  W Isles 148 D2
Clachan na Luib . 148 B3
Clachan of
  Campsie 119 B6
Clachan of
  Glendaruel . . 145 E8
Clachan-Seil . . 124 D3
Clachan Strachur . 125 E6
Clachbreck 144 F6
Clachnabrain . . 134 C3
Clachtoll 156 G3
Clackmannan . . 127 E8
Clacton-on-Sea . . 43 C7
Cladach
  Chireboist . . 148 B2
Claddach-
  knockline . . 148 B2
Cladich 125 C6
Claggan Highld . . 131 B5
  Highld 147 G9
Claigan 148 C7
Claines 50 D3
Clandown 23 D8
Clanfield Hants . . 15 C7
  Oxon 38 D2
Clanville 25 E8
Claonaig 145 H7
Claonel 157 J8
Clapgate Dorset . . 13 D8
  Herts 41 B7
Clapham Bedford . 53 D8
  London 28 B3
  N Yorks 93 C7
  W Sus 16 D4
Clap Hill 19 B7
Clappers 122 D5
Clappersgate . . . 99 D5
Clapton 12 D2
Clapton-in-
  Gordano . . . 23 B6
Clapton-on-the-
  Hill 38 C1
Clapworthy 9 B8
Clarach 58 F3

Clara Vale 110 C4
Clarbeston 32 B1
Clarbeston Road . . 32 B1
Clarborough . . . 89 F8
Clardon 158 D3
Clare 55 E8
Clarebrand 106 C4
Clarencefield . . 107 C7
Clarilaw 115 C8
Clark's Green . . . 28 F2
Clarkston 119 D5
Clashandorran . . 151 G8
Clashcoig 151 C9
Clashindarroch . . 152 E4
Clashmore
  Highld 151 C10
  Highld 156 F3
Clashnessie 156 F3
Clashnoir 139 B8
Clate 160 G7
Clathy 127 C8
Clatt 140 B4
Clatter 59 E6
Clatterford 15 F5
Clatterin Bridge . 135 B6
Clatworthy 22 F2
Claughton Lancs . . 92 E5
  Lancs 93 C5
  Mers 85 F4
Claverdon 51 C6
Claverham 23 C6
Clavering 55 F5
Claverley 61 E7
Claverton 24 C2
Clawdd-newydd . 72 D4
Clawthorpe 92 B5
Clawton 9 E5
Claxby Lincs . . . 79 B7
  Lincs 90 E5
Claxton Norf . . . 69 D6
  N Yorks 96 C2
Claybokie 139 E6
Claybrooke Magna 63 F8
Claybrooke Parva . 63 F8
Clay Common . . 69 F7
Clay Coton 52 B3
Clay Cross 76 C3
Claydon Oxon . . 52 D2
  Suff 56 D5
Claygate Dumfries 108 B3
  Kent 29 E8
  Sur. 28 C2
Claygate Cross . 29 D7
Clayhanger Devon . 10 B5
  W Mid 62 D4
Clayhidon 11 C6
Clayhill E Sus. . . . 19 C5
  Hants 14 D4
Clay Hill 26 B3
Clay Lake 66 B2
Clayock 158 E3
Claypole 77 E8
Clayton Staffs . . . 75 E5
  S Yorks 89 D5
  W Sus 17 C6
  W Yorks 94 F4
Clayton Green . . 86 B3
Clayton-le-Moors . 93 F7
Clayton-le-Woods 86 B3
Clayton West . . 88 C3
Clayworth 89 F8
Cleadale 146 C7
Cleadon 111 C6
Clearbrook 6 C3
Clearwell 36 D2
Cleasby 101 C7
Cleat 159 K5
Cleatlam 101 C6
Cleator 98 C2
Cleator Moor . . 98 C2
Clebrig 157 F8
Cleckheaton . . . 88 B2
Cleedownton . . 61 F5
Cleehill 49 B7
Clee St Margaret . 61 F5
Cleethorpes . . . 91 D7
Cleeton St Mary . 49 B8
Cleeve 23 C6
Cleeve Hill 37 B6
Cleeve Prior . . 51 E5
Clegyrnant 59 D6
Clehonger 49 F6
Cleish 128 E2
Cleland 119 D8
Clench Common . . 25 C6
Clenchwarton . . 67 B5
Clent 50 B4
Cleobury
  Mortimer . . . 49 B8
Cleobury North . . 61 F6
Cleongart 143 E7
Clephanton 151 F11
Clerklands 115 B8
Clestrain 159 H4
Cleuch Head . . 115 C8
Cleughbrae 107 B7
Clevancy 25 B5
Clevedon 23 B6
Cleveley 38 B3
Cleveleys 92 E3
Cleverton 37 F6
Clevis 21 B7
Clewer 23 D6
Cley next the Sea . 81 C6
Cliaid 148 H1
Cliasmol 154 G5
Cliburn 99 B7
Click Mill 159 F4
Cliddesden 26 E4
Cliff End 19 D5
Cliffe Medway . . 29 B8
  N Yorks 95 F6
Cliff End 19 D5
Cliffe Woods . . . 29 B8
Clifford Hereford . . 48 E4
  W Yorks 95 E7
Clifford Chambers 51 D6
Clifford's Mesne . 36 B4
Cliffsend 31 C7
Clifton Bristol . . . 23 B7
  C Beds 54 F2
  Cumb 99 B7
  Derbys 75 E8
  Lancs 92 F4
  Northumb . . . 117 F8
  Nottingham . . . 77 F5
  N Yorks 94 E4
  Oxon 52 F2
  Stirling 131 F7

Clifton continued
  S Yorks 89 E6
  Worcs 50 D3
  York 95 D8
Clifton Campville . 63 C6
Cliftoncote 116 B4
Clifton Green . . 87 D5
Clifton Hampden . 39 E5
Clifton Reynes . . 53 D7
Clifton upon
  Dunsmore . . 52 B3
Clifton upon Teme . 50 C2
Cliftonville 31 B7
Climaen gwyn . . 33 D8
Climping 16 D4
Climpy 120 D2
Clink 24 E2
Clint 95 D5
Clint Green 68 C3
Clintmains 122 F2
Cliobh 154 D5
Clippesby 69 C7
Clipsham 65 C6
Clipston Northants . 64 F4
  Notts 77 F6
Clipstone 77 C5
Clitheroe 93 E7
Cliuthar 154 H6
Clive 60 B5
Clivocast 160 C8
Clixby 90 D5
Clocaenog 72 D4
Clochan 152 B4
Clock Face 86 E3
Clockmill 122 D3
Cloddiau 60 D2
Clodock 35 B7
Clola 153 D10
Clophill 53 F8
Clopton Northants . 65 F7
  Suff 57 D6
Clopton Corner . . 57 D6
Clopton Green . . 55 D8
Closeburn 113 E8
Close Clark 84 E2
Closworth 12 C3
Clothall 54 F3
Clotton 74 C2
Clough Foot . . . 87 B7
Cloughton 103 E8
Cloughton
  Newlands . . 103 E8
Clousta 160 H5
Clouston 159 G3
Clova Aberds . . 140 B3
  Angus 134 B3
Clovelly 8 B5
Clove Lodge . . . 100 C4
Clovenfords 121 F7
Clovenstone . . 141 C6
Clovullin 130 C4
Clow Bridge . . 87 B6
Clowne 76 B4
Clows Top 50 B2
Cloy 73 E7
Cluanie Inn . . . 136 C3
Cluanie Lodge . . 136 C3
Clun 60 F3
Clunbury 60 F3
Clunderwen . . . 32 C2
Clune 138 B3
Clunes 136 F5
Clungunford . . . 49 B5
Clunie Aberds . . 153 C6
  Perth 133 E8
Clunton 60 F3
Cluny 128 E4
Cluny Castle . . 138 E2
Clutton Bath . . . 23 D8
  Ches W 73 D8
Clwt-grugoer . . 72 C3
Clwt-y-bont . . . 83 E5
Clydach Mon . . . 35 C6
  Swansea 33 D7
Clydach Vale . . 34 E3
Clydebank 118 B4
Clydey 45 F4
Clyffe Pypard . . 25 B5
Clynder 145 E11
Clyne 34 D2
Clynelish 157 J11
Clynnog-fawr . . 82 F4
Clyro 48 E4
Clyst Honiton . . 10 E4
Clyst Hydon . . . 10 D5
Clyst St George . . 10 F4
Clyst St Lawrence . 10 D5
Clyst St Mary . . 10 E4
Cnoc Amhlaigh . 155 D10
Cnwch-coch . . 47 B5
Coachford 152 D4
Coad's Green . . . 5 B7
Coal Aston 76 B3
Coalbrookdale . . 61 D6
Coalbrookvale . . 35 D5
Coalburn 119 F8
Coalburns 110 C4
Coalcleugh 109 E8
Coaley 36 D4
Coalhall 112 C4
Coalhill 42 E3
Coalpit Heath . . 36 F3
Coalport 61 D6
Coalsnaughton . . 127 E8
Coaltown of
  Balgonie . . . 128 E4
Coaltown of
  Wemyss . . . 128 E5
Coalville 63 C8
Coalway 36 C2
Coat 12 B2
Coatbridge 119 C7
Coatdyke 119 C7
Coate Swindon . . 38 F1
  Wilts 24 C5
Coates Cambs . . . 66 E3
  Glos 37 D6
  Lancs 93 E8
  Notts 90 F2
  W Sus 16 C3
Coatham 102 B3
Coatham
  Mundeville . . 101 B7
Coatsgate 114 D3
Cobbaton 9 B8
Cobbler's Green . 69 E5
Coberley 37 C6
Cobham Kent . . . 29 C7
  Sur. 28 C2
Cobholm Island . 69 D8

Cobleland 126 E4
Cobnash 49 C6
Coburty 153 B9
Cockayne 102 E4
Cockayne Hatley . 54 E3
Cock Bank 73 E7
Cock Bridge . . . 139 D8
Cockburnspath . . 122 B3
Cock Clarks . . . 42 D4
Cockenzie and Port
  Seton 121 B7
Cockerham 92 D4
Cockermouth . . 107 F8
Cockernhoe Green 40 B4
Cockfield Durham . 101 B6
  Suff 56 D3
Cockfosters 41 E5
Cocking 16 C2
Cockington 7 C6
Cocklake 23 E6
Cockley Beck . . 98 D4
Cockley Cley . . 67 D7
Cockshutt 60 B4
Cockthorpe 81 C5
Cockwood 10 F4
Cockyard 49 F6
Codda 5 B6
Coddenham . . . 56 D5
Coddington
  Ches W 73 D8
  Hereford 50 E2
  Notts 77 D8
Codford St Mary . 24 F4
Codford St Peter . 24 F4
Codicote 41 C5
Codmore Hill . . 16 B4
Codnor 76 E4
Codrington 24 B2
Codsall 62 D2
Codsall Wood . . 62 D2
Coed Duon
  = Blackwood . . 35 E5
Coedely 34 F4
Coedkernew . . 35 F6
Coed Mawr . . 83 D5
Coed Morgan . . 35 C7
Coedpoeth 73 D6
Coed-Talon . . 73 D6
Coedway 60 C3
Coed-y-bryn . . 46 E2
Coed-y-paen . . 35 E7
Coed-yr-ynys . . 35 B5
Coed Ystumgwern 71 E6
Coelbren 34 C2
Coffinswell 7 C6
Cofton Hackett . . 50 B5
Cogan 22 B3
Cogenhoe 53 C6
Cogges 38 D3
Coggeshall 42 B4
Coggeshall Hamlet 42 B4
Coggins Mill . . 18 C2
Coignafearn
  Lodge 138 C2
Coig
  Peighinnean . 155 A10
Coig Peighinnean
  Bhuirgh . . 155 B9
Coilacriech . . 140 E2
Coilantogle . . 126 D4
Coilleag 148 G2
Coillore 149 E8
Coity 34 F3
Col 155 C9
Colaboll 157 H8
Colan 4 C3
Colaton Raleigh . 11 F5
Colbost 148 D7
Colburn 101 E6
Colby Cumb . . . 100 B1
  IoM 84 E2
  Norf 81 D8
Colchester 43 B6
Colcot 22 C3
Cold Ash 26 C3
Cold Ashby 52 B4
Cold Ashton . . 24 B2
Cold Aston . . 37 C8
Coldbackie . . 157 D9
Coldbeck 100 D2
Cold Blow 32 C2
Cold Brayfield . . 53 D7
Coldean 17 D7
Coldeast 7 B6
Colden 87 B7
Colden Common . 15 B5
Coldfair Green . . 57 C8
Coldham 66 D4
Cold Hanworth . 90 F4
Coldharbour Glos . 36 D2
  Kent 29 D6
  Sur. 28 E2
  Suff 56 D4
Cold Harbour . . 78 F2
Cold Hatton . . 61 B6
Cold Hesledon . 111 E7
Cold Higham . . 52 D4
Cold Kirby . . 102 F3
Coldingham . . 122 C5
Cold Newton . . 64 D4
Cold Northcott . . 8 F4
Cold Norton . . 42 D4
Cold Overton . . 64 C5
Coldrain 128 D2
Coldred 31 E6
Coldridge 9 D8
Coldstream Angus 134 F3
  Borders 122 F4
Coldwaltham . . 16 C4
Coldwells 153 D11
Coldwells Croft . 140 B4
Coldyeld 60 E3
Cole 23 F8
Colebatch 60 F3
Colebrook 10 D5
Colebrooke . . 10 E2
Coleby Lincs . . . 78 C2
  N Lincs 90 C2
Coleford Devon . . 10 D2
  Glos 36 C2
  Som 23 E8
Cole Green 41 C5
Cole Henley . . 26 D2
Colehill 13 D8
Coleman's Hatch . 29 F5
Colemere 73 F8
Colemore 26 F5
Coleorton 63 C8
Colerne 24 B3

Colesbourne . . 37 C6
Colesden 54 D2
Coles Green . . 56 E4
Cole's Green . . 57 C6
Coleshill Bucks . . 40 E2
  Oxon 38 E2
  Warks 63 F6
Colestocks 11 D5
Colgate 28 F3
Colgrain 126 F2
Colinsburgh . . 129 D6
Colinton 120 C5
Colintraive . . 145 F9
Colkirk 80 E5
Collace 134 F2
Collafirth 160 G6
Collaton St Mary . 7 D6
College Milton . . 119 D6
Collessie 128 C4
Collier Row . . 41 E8
Collier's End . . 41 B6
Collier's Green . . 18 B4
Collier Street . . 29 E8
Colliery Row . . 111 E6
Colliston 135 E6
Collycroft 63 F7
Collynie 153 E8
Collyweston . . 65 D6
Colmonell 104 A5
Colmworth 54 D2
Colnabaichin . . 139 D8
Colnbrook 27 B8
Colne Cambs . . 54 B4
  Lancs 93 E8
Colne Edge . . 93 E8
Colne Engaine . . 56 F2
Colney 68 D4
Colney Heath . . 41 D5
Colney Street . . 40 D4
Coln Rogers . . 37 D7
Coln St Aldwyn's . 37 D8
Coln St Dennis . . 37 C7
Colpy 153 E6
Colquhar 121 E6
Colsterdale 101 F6
Colsterworth . . 65 B6
Colston Bassett . 77 F6
Coltfield 151 E14
Colthouse 99 E5
Coltishall 69 C5
Coltness 119 D8
Colton Cumb . . . 99 F5
  Norf 68 D4
  N Yorks 95 E8
  Staffs 62 B4
  W Yorks 95 F6
Colva 48 D4
Colvend 107 D5
Colvister 160 D7
Colwall Green . . 50 E2
Colwall Stone . . 50 E2
Colwell 110 B2
Colwich 62 B4
Colwick 77 E6
Colwinston . . 21 B8
Colworth 16 D3
Colwyn Bay
  = Bae Colwyn . 83 D8
Colyford 11 E7
Colyton 11 E7
Combe Hereford . . 48 C5
  Oxon 38 C4
  W Berks 25 C8
Combe Common . 27 F7
Combe Down . . 24 C2
Combe Florey . . 22 F3
Combe Hay . . 24 D2
Combeinteignhead . 7 B7
Combe Martin . . 20 E4
Combe Moor . . 49 C5
Combe Raleigh . 11 D6
Comberbach . . 74 B3
Comberton Cambs . 54 D4
  Hereford 49 C6
Combe
  St Nicholas . . 11 C8
Combpyne 11 E7
Combridge 75 F7
Combrook 51 D8
Combs Derbys . . 75 B7
  Suff 56 D4
Combs Ford . . 56 D4
Combwich 22 E4
Comers 141 D5
Comins Coch . . 58 F3
Commercial End . 55 C6
Commins Capel
  Betws 46 D5
Commins Coch . 58 D5
Commondale . . 102 C4
Commonmoor . . 5 C7
Commonside . . 74 B2
Common Edge . . 92 F3
Common Side . . 76 B3
Compstall 87 E7
Compton Devon . . 7 C6
  Hants 15 B5
  Sur. 27 E6
  Sur. 27 E7
  W Berks 26 B3
  Wilts 25 D6
Compton Abbas . 13 C6
Compton Abdale . 37 C7
Compton Bassett . 24 B5
Compton
  Beauchamp . . 38 F2
Compton Bishop . 23 D5
Compton
  Chamberlayne . 13 B8
Compton Dando . 23 C8
Compton Dundon . 23 F6
Compton Martin . 23 D7
Compton
  Pauncefoot . . 12 B4
Compton Valence . 12 E3
Comrie Fife . . . 128 F2
  Perth 127 B6

Comrie continued
  Perth 127 B6
Conaglen House . 130 C4
Conchra 145 E11
Concraigie 133 E8
Conder Green . . 92 D4
Conderton 50 F4
Condicote 38 B1
Condorrat 119 B7
Condover 60 D4
Coney Hill 37 C5
Coneyhurst 16 B5
Coneysthorpe . . 96 B3
Coneythorpe . . 95 D6
Coney Weston . . 56 B3
Conford 27 F6
Congash 139 B6
Congdon's Shop . . 5 B7
Congerstone . . 63 D7
Congham 80 E3
Congl-y-wal . . 71 C8
Congresbury . . 23 C6
Congreve 62 C3
Conicavel 151 F12
Coningsby 78 D5
Conington Cambs . 54 C4
  Cambs 65 F8
Conisbrough . . 89 E6
Conisby 142 B3
Conisholme . . 91 E8
Coniston Cumb . . 99 E5
  E Yorks 97 F7
Coniston Cold . . 94 D2
Conistone 94 C2
Connah's Quay . . 73 C6
Connel 124 B5
Connel Park . . 113 C6
Connor Downs . . 2 C4
Conon Bridge . . 151 F8
Conon House . . 151 F8
Cononley 94 E2
Conordan 149 E10
Consall 75 E6
Consett 110 D4
Constable Burton 101 E6
Constantine 3 D6
Constantine Bay . . 4 B3
Contin 150 F7
Contlaw 141 D7
Conwy 83 D7
Conyer 30 C3
Conyers Green . . 56 C2
Cooden 18 E4
Cooil 84 E3
Cookbury 9 D6
Cookham 40 F1
Cookham Dean . . 40 F1
Cookham Rise . . 40 F1
Cookhill 51 D5
Cookley Suff . . . 57 B7
  Worcs 62 F2
Cookley Green . . 39 E6
Cooksbridge . . 17 C8
Cooksmill Green . 42 D2
Coolham 16 B5
Cooling 29 B8
Coombe Corn . . 4 D4
  Corn. 8 C4
  Hants 15 B7
  Wilts 25 D6
Coombe Bissett . 14 B2
Coombe Hill . . 37 B5
Coombe Keynes . 13 F6
Coombes 17 D5
Coopersale
  Common . . . 41 D7
Cootham 16 C4
Copdock 56 E5
Copford Green . . 43 B5
Copgrove 95 C6
Copister 160 F6
Cople 54 E2
Copley 101 B5
Coplow Dale . . 75 B8
Copmanthorpe . . 95 E8
Coppathorne . . 8 D4
Coppenhall . . 62 C3
Coppenhall Moss . 74 D4
Copperhouse . . 2 C4
Coppingford . . 65 F8
Copplestone . . 10 D2
Coppull 86 C3
Coppull Moor . . 86 C3
Copsale 17 B5
Copster Green . . 93 F6
Copston Magna . 63 F8
Copt Heath . . 51 B6
Copt Hewick . . 95 B6
Copthorne Shrops . 60 C4
  Sur. 28 F4
Copt Oak 63 C8
Copy's Green . . 80 D5
Copythorne . . 14 C4
Corbets Tey . . 42 F1
Corbridge 110 C2
Corby 65 F5
Corby Glen . . 65 B6
Cordon 143 E11
Coreley 49 B8
Cores End . . 40 F2
Corfe 11 C7
Corfe Castle . . 13 F7
Corfe Mullen . . 13 E7
Corfton 60 F4
Corgarff 139 D8
Corhampton . . 15 B7
Corlae 113 E6
Corley 63 F7
Corley Ash . . 63 F6
Corley Moor . . 63 F6
Cornaa 84 D4
Cornabus 142 D4
Cornel 83 E7
Corner Row . . 92 F4
Corney 98 E3
Cornforth 111 F6
Cornhill 152 C5
Cornhill-on-
  Tweed 122 F4
Cornholme . . 87 B7
Cornish Hall End . 55 F7
Cornquoy 159 J6
Cornsay 110 E4
Cornsay Colliery . 110 E4
Corntown Highld . 151 F8
  V Glam 21 B8
Cornwell 38 B2

Cornwood 6 D4
Cornworthy 7 D6
Corpach 130 B4
Corpusty 81 D7
Corran Highld . . 130 C4
  Highld 149 H13
Corranbuie . . 145 G7
Corrany 84 D4
Corrie 143 D11
Corrie Common . 114 F5
Corriecravie . . 143 F10
Corriemoillie . . 150 E6
Corriemulzie
  Lodge 150 B6
Corrievarkie
  Lodge 132 B2
Corrievorrie . . 138 B3
Corrimony 150 H6
Corringham Lincs . 90 E2
  Thurrock . . . 42 F3
Corris 58 D4
Corris Uchaf . . 58 D4
Corrour Shooting
  Lodge 131 C8
Corrow 125 E7
Corry 149 F11
Corry of
  Ardnagrask . . 151 G8
Corsback 158 C4
Corscombe . . 12 D3
Corse Aberds . . 152 D6
  Glos 36 B4
Corse Lawn . . 50 F3
Corse of Kinnoir . 152 D5
Corsewall 104 C4
Corsham 24 B3
Corsindae 141 D5
Corsley 24 E3
Corsley Heath . . 24 E3
Corsock 106 B4
Corston Bath. . . . 23 C8
  Wilts 37 F6
Corstorphine . . 120 B4
Cors-y-Gedol . . 71 E6
Cortachy 134 D3
Corton Suff . . . 69 E8
  Wilts 24 E4
Corton Denham . 12 B4
Coruanan Lodge . 130 C4
Corunna 148 B3
Corwen 72 E4
Coryton Devon . . 9 F6
  Thurrock . . . 42 F3
Cosby 64 E2
Coseley 62 E3
Cosgrove 53 E5
Cosham 15 D7
Cosheston 32 D1
Cossall 76 E4
Cossington Leics . 64 C3
  Som 23 E5
Costa 159 F4
Costessey 68 C4
Costock 64 B2
Coston 64 D5
Cote 38 D3
Cotebrook 74 C2
Cotehill 108 D4
Cotes Cumb . . . 99 F6
  Leics 64 B2
  Staffs 74 F5
Cotesbach 64 F2
Cotgrave 77 F6
Cothall 141 C7
Cotham 77 E7
Cothelstone . . 22 F3
Cotherstone . . 101 C5
Cothill 38 E4
Cotleigh 11 D7
Cotmanhay . . 76 E4
Cotmaton 11 F6
Coton Cambs . . 54 D5
  Northants . . . 52 B4
  Staffs 62 B2
  Staffs 75 F6
Coton Clanford . 62 B2
Coton Hill Shrops . 60 C4
  Staffs 75 F6
Coton in the Elms . 63 C6
Cott 7 C5
Cottam E Yorks . . 97 C5
  Notts 77 B8
Cottartown . . 151 H13
Cottenham . . 54 C5
Cotterdale 100 E3
Cottered 41 B6
Cotteridge . . 50 B5
Cotterstock . . 65 E7
Cottesbrooke . . 52 B5
Cottesmore . . 65 C6
Cottingham
  E Yorks 97 F6
  Northants . . . 64 E5
Cottingley 94 F4
Cottisford 52 F3
Cotton Staffs . . . 75 E7
  Suff 56 C4
Cotton End . . 53 E8
Cottown Aberds . 140 B4
  Aberds 141 C6
  Aberds 153 D8
Cotwalton 75 F6
Couch's Mill . . 5 D6
Coughton Hereford . 36 B2
  Warks 51 C5
Coulaghailtro . . 144 G6
Coulags 150 G2
Coulby Newham . 102 C3
Coulderton . . 98 D1
Couldoran . . 149 D13
Coulin 150 F3
Coull Aberds . . 140 D4
  Argyll 142 B3
Coulport 145 E11
Coulsdon 28 D3
Coulston 24 D4
Coulter 120 F3
Coulton 96 B2
Cound 61 D5
Coundon Durham . 101 B7
  W Mid 63 F7
Coundon Grange . 101 B7
Countersett . . 100 F4
Countess 25 E6
Countess Wear . 10 F4

Countesthorpe . . 64 E2
Countisbury . . . 21 E6
Coupar Angus . . 134 E2
Coup Green . . 86 B3
Coupland 122 F5
Cour 143 D9
Courance 114 E3
Court-at-Street . 19 B7
Courteenhall . . 53 D5
Court Henry . . 33 B6
Courtsend 43 E6
Courtway 22 F4
Cousland 121 C6
Cousley Wood . . 18 B3
Coustonn 145 F9
Cove Argyll . . . 145 E11
  Borders 122 B3
  Devon 10 C4
  Hants 27 D6
  Highld 155 H13
Cove Bay 141 D8
Cove Bottom . . 57 B8
Covehithe 69 F8
Coven 62 D3
Coveney 66 F4
Covenham
  St Bartholomew . 91 E7
Covenham St Mary 91 E7
Coventry 51 B8
Coverack 3 E6
Coverham 101 F6
Covesea 152 A1
Covington Cambs . 53 B8
  S Lanark 120 F2
Cowan Bridge . . 93 B6
Cow Ark 93 E6
Cowbeech 18 D3
Cowbit 66 C2
Cowbridge Lincs . 79 E6
  Som 21 E8
Cowbridge
  = Y Bont-Faen . 21 B8
Cowdale 75 B7
Cowden 29 E5
Cowdenbeath . . 128 E3
Cowdenburn . . 120 D5
Cowers Lane . . 76 E3
Cowes 15 E5
Cowesby 102 F2
Cowfold 17 B6
Cowgill 100 F2
Cowie Aberds . . 141 F7
  Stirling 127 F7
Cowley Devon . . 10 E4
  Glos 37 C6
  London 40 F3
  Oxon 39 D5
Cowleymoor . . 10 C4
Cowling Lancs . . 86 C3
  N Yorks 94 E2
  N Yorks 101 F7
Cowlinge 55 D8
Cowpe 87 B6
Cowpen 117 F8
Cowpen Bewley . 102 B2
Cowplain 15 C7
Cowshill 109 E8
Cowslip Green . . 23 C6
Cowstrandburn . 128 E2
Cowthorpe . . 95 D7
Coxbank 74 E3
Coxbench 76 E3
Cox Common . . 69 F6
Coxford Norf . . 80 E4
  Soton 14 C4
Cox Green . . 27 B6
Coxheath 29 D8
Coxhill 31 E6
Coxhoe 111 F6
Cox Moor . . 76 D5
Coxwold 95 B8
Coychurch . . 21 B8
Coylton 112 C4
Coylumbridge . . 138 C5
Coynach 140 D3
Coynachie . . 152 E4
Coytrahen . . 34 F2
Crabadon 7 D5
Crabbs Cross . . 50 C5
Crabtree 17 B6
Crackenthorpe . 100 B1
Crackington Haven . 8 E3
Crackley 51 B7
Crackleybank . . 61 C7
Crackpot 100 E4
Cracoe 94 C2
Craddock 11 C5
Cradhlastadh . . 154 D5
Cradley 50 E2
Cradley Heath . . 62 F3
Crafthole 5 D8
Craggan Highld . . 151 H10
  Highld 157 H11
Craggie Highld . . 151 H10
  Highld 157 H11
Cragg Vale . . 87 B8
Craghead 110 D5
Crai 34 B2
Craibstone . . 152 C4
Craichie 135 E5
Craig Dumfries . . 106 B3
  Dumfries 106 B3
  Highld 150 G3
Craiganour Lodge 132 D3
Craig Castle . . 140 B3
Craig-cefn-parc . 33 D7
Craigdam 153 E8
Craigdarroch
  Dumfries 113 E7
  Highld 150 F7
Craigdhu 150 G7
Craigearn . . 141 C6
Craigellachie . . 152 D2
Craigencross . . 104 C4
Craigend Perth . . 128 B3
  Stirling 127 F6
Craigendive . . 145 E9
Craigendoran . . 126 F2
Craigends 118 C4
Craigens Argyll . 142 B3
  E Ayrs. 113 C5
Craighat 126 F3
Craighead . . 129 D8
Craighlaw Mains 105 C7
Craighouse . . 144 G4
Craigie Aberds . . 141 C8
  Dundee 134 F4
  Perth 128 B3
  Perth 133 E8

Craigie continued
  Perth 133 E8
  S Ayrs 118 F4
Craigiefield 159 G5
Craigielaw 121 B7
Craiglockhart . . 120 B5
Craigmalloch . . 112 E4
Craigmaud 153 C8
Craigmillar 121 B5
Craigmore 145 G10
Craignant 73 F6
Craigneuk
  N Lanark 119 C7
  N Lanark 119 D7
Craignure 124 B3
Craigo 135 C6
Craigow 128 D2
Craigrothie 129 C5
Craigroy 151 F14
Craigruie 126 B3
Craigston Castle . 153 C7
Craigton Aberdeen 141 D7
  Angus 134 D3
  Angus 135 F5
  Highld 151 B9
Craigtown 157 D11
Craig-y-don . . 83 C7
Craig-y-nos . . 34 C2
Craik 115 D6
Crail 129 D8
Crailing 116 B2
Crailinghall . . 116 B2
Craiselound . . 89 E8
Crakehill 95 B7
Crakemarsh . . 75 F7
Crambe 96 C3
Cramlington . . 111 B5
Cramond 120 B4
Cramond Bridge . 120 B4
Cranage 74 C4
Cranberry 74 F5
Cranborne 13 C8
Cranbourne . . 27 B7
Cranbrook Devon . 10 E5
  Kent 18 B4
Cranbrook
  Common . . . 18 B4
Crane Moor . . 88 D4
Crane's Corner . . 68 C2
Cranfield 53 E7
Cranford 28 B2
Cranford St
  Andrew 53 B7
Cranford St John . 53 B7
Cranham Glos . . 37 C5
  London 42 F1
Crank 86 E3
Crankwood . . 86 D4
Cranleigh 27 F8
Cranley 57 B5
Cranmer Green . 56 B4
Cranmore 14 F4
Cranna 153 C6
Crannich 147 G8
Crannoch 152 C4
Cranoe 64 E4
Cransford 57 C7
Cranshaws . . 122 C2
Cranstal 84 B4
Crantock 4 C2
Cranwell 78 E3
Cranwich 67 E7
Cranworth . . 68 D2
Craobh Haven . 124 E3
Crarae 125 F5
Crask Inn 157 G8
Crask of Aigas . 150 G7
Craster 117 C8
Craswall 48 F4
Cratfield 57 B7
Crathes 141 E6
Crathie Aberds . . 139 E8
  Highld 137 E8
Crathorne 102 D2
Craven Arms . . 60 F4
Crawcrook 110 C4
Crawford Lancs . . 86 D3
  S Lanark 114 B2
Crawfordjohn . . 113 B8
Crawick 113 C7
Crawley Hants . . 26 F2
  Oxon 38 C3
  W Sus 28 F3
Crawley Down . . 28 F4
Crawleyside . . 110 E2
Crawshawbooth . 87 B6
Crawton 135 B8
Cray N Yorks . . 94 B2
  Perth 133 C8
Crayford 29 B6
Crayke 95 B8
Crays Hill 42 E3
Cray's Pond . . 39 F6
Creacombe 10 C3
Creag Ghoraidh . 148 D2
Creagan 130 E3
Creag Aoil . . . 131 B5
Creaguaineach
  Lodge 131 C7
Creaksea 43 E5
Creaton 52 B5
Creca 108 B2
Credenhill 49 E6
Crediton 10 D3
Creebridge 105 C8
Creech Heathfield 11 B7
Creech St Michael 11 B7
Creed 3 B8
Creekmouth . . 41 F7
Creeting Bottoms 56 D5
Creeting St Mary . 56 D4
Creeton 65 B7
Creetown 105 D8

Craigie continued
S Ayrs. 118 F4
Craigiefield 159 G5
Craigielaw 121 B7
Craiglockhart 120 B5
Craigmalloch 112 E4
Craigmillar 121 B5
Craigmore 145 G10
Craignant 73 F6
Craigneuk
N Lanark 119 C7
N Lanark 119 D7
Craigo 135 C6
Craigow 128 D2
Craig Penllyn 21 B8
Craigrothie 129 C5
Craigroy 151 F14
Craigruie 126 B3
Craigton Aberdeen ..141 D7
Angus 134 D3
Angus 135 F5
Highld 151 B9
Craigtown 157 D11
Craig-y-don 83 C7
Craig-y-nos 34 C2
Craik 115 D6
Crail 129 D8
Crailing 116 B2
Crailinghall 116 B2
Craiselound 89 E8
Crakehill 95 B7
Crakemarsh 75 F7
Crambe 96 C3
Cramlington 111 B5
Cramond 120 B4
Cramond Bridge .120 B4
Cranage 74 C4
Cranberry 74 F5
Cranborne 13 C8
Cranbourne 27 B7
Cranbrook Devon...10 E5
Kent.....18 B4
Cranbrook
Common 18 B4
Crane Moor 88 D4
Crane's Corner ..68 C2
Cranfield 53 E7
Cranford 28 B2
Cranford
St Andrew 53 B7
Cranford St John .. 53 B7
Cranham Glos. 37 C5
London.....42 F1
Crank 86 E3
Crank Wood 86 D4
Cranleigh 27 F8
Cranley 57 B5
Cranmer Green 56 B4
Cranmore 14 F4
Cranna 153 C6
Crannich 147 G8
Crannoch 152 C4
Cranoe 64 E4
Cransford 57 C7
Cranshaws 122 C2
Cranstal 84 B4
Crantock 4 C2
Cranwell 78 E3
Cranwich 67 E7
Cranworth 68 D2
Craobh Haven ..124 E3
Crapstone 6 C3
Crarae 125 F5
Crask Inn 157 G8
Craskins 140 D4
Crask of Aigas ..150 G7
Craster 117 C8
Craswall 48 F4
Cratfield 57 B7
Crathes 141 E6
Crathie Aberds ..139 E8
Highld 137 E8
Crathorne 102 D2
Craven Arms 60 F4
Crawcrook 110 C4
Crawford Lancs ..86 D2
S Lanark. 114 B2
Crawfordjohn ..113 B8
Crawick 113 C7
Crawley Hants .. 26 F2
Oxon 38 C3
W Sus 28 F3
Crawley Down ..28 F3
Crawleyside 110 E2
Crawshawbooth ..87 B6
Crawton 135 B8
Cray N Yorks 94 B2
Perth 133 C8
Crayford 29 B6
Crayke 95 B8
Crays Hill 42 E3
Cray's Pond 39 F6
Creacombe 10 C3
Creagan 130 E3
Creag Ghoraidh ..148 D2
Creaguaineach
Lodge 131 C7
Creaksea 43 E5
Creaton 52 B5
Creca 108 B2
Credenhill 49 E6
Crediton 10 D3
Creebridge 105 C8
Creech Heathfield ..11 B7
Creech St Michael. 11 B7
Creed 3 B8
Creekmouth 41 F7
Creeting Bottoms ..56 D5
Creeting St Mary .. 56 D4
Creeton 65 B7
Creetown 105 D8
Creggans 125 E6
Cregneash 84 F1
Creg-ny-Baa 84 D3
Cregrina 48 D3
Creich 128 B5
Creigiau 34 F4
Cremyll 6 D2
Creslow 39 B8
Cressage 61 D5
Cressbrook 75 B8
Cresselly 32 D1
Cressing 42 B3
Cresswell
Northumb 117 E8
Staffs.....75 F6

Cresswell Quay.... 32 D1
Creswell 76 B5
Cretingham 57 C6
Cretshengan 144 G6
Crewe Ches E. 74 D4
Ches W. 73 D8
Crewgreen 60 C3
Crewkerne 12 D2
Crianlarich 126 B2
Cribyn 46 D4
Criccieth 71 D5
Crich 76 D3
Crichie 153 D9
Crichton 121 C6
Crick Mon 36 E1
Northants.....52 B3
Crickadarn 48 E2
Cricket Malherbie .. 11 C8
Cricket St Thomas .. 11 D8
Crickheath 60 B2
Crickhowell 35 C6
Cricklade 37 E8
Cricklewood 41 F5
Cridling Stubbs .. 89 B6
Crieff 127 B7
Criggion 60 C2
Crigglestone 88 C4
Crimond 153 C10
Crimonmogate ..153 C10
Crimplesham 67 D6
Crinan 144 D6
Cringleford 68 D4
Cringles 94 E3
Crinow 32 C2
Cripplesease 2 C4
Cripplestyle 13 C8
Cripp's Corner ..18 C4
Croasdale 98 C2
Crockenhill 29 C6
Crockernwell 10 E2
Crockerton 24 E3
Crocketford or
Ninemile Bar .. 106 B5
Crockey Hill 96 E2
Crockham Hill ..28 D5
Crockleford Heath. 43 B6
Crockness 159 J4
Crock Street 11 C8
Croeserw 34 E2
Croes-goch 44 B3
Croes-lan 46 E2
Croesor 71 C7
Croesyceiliog
Carms 33 C5
Torf 35 E7
Croes-y-mwyalch .35 E7
Croesywaun 82 F5
Croft Leics 64 E2
Lincs 79 C8
Pembs.....45 E3
Warr 86 E4
Croftamie 126 F3
Croftmalloch 120 C2
Crofton Wilts 25 C7
W Yorks 88 C4
Croft-on-Tees ..101 D7
Crofts of
Benachielt ..158 G3
Crofts of Haddo .. 153 E8
Crofts of
Inverthernie ..153 D7
Crofts of Meikle
Ardo 153 D8
Crofty. 33 E6
Croggan 124 C3
Croglin 109 E5
Croich 150 B7
Crois Dughaill.. 148 F2
Cromarty 151 E10
Cromblet 153 E7
Cromdale 139 B6
Cromer Herts ..41 B5
Norf.....81 C8
Cromford 76 D2
Cromhall 36 E3
Cromhall Common 36 E3
Cromor 155 E9
Cromra 137 E8
Cromwell 77 C7
Cronberry 113 B6
Crondall 27 E5
Cronk-y-Voddy .. 84 D3
Cronton 86 F2
Crook Cumb. 99 E6
Durham 110 F4
Crookedholm ..118 F4
Crookes 88 F4
Crookham
Northumb 122 F5
W Berks. 26 C3
Crookham Village .27 D5
Crookhaugh. ..114 B4
Crookhouse. ..116 B3
Crooklands 99 F7
Crook of Devon. 128 D2
Cropredy 52 E2
Cropston 64 C2
Cropthorne 50 E4
Cropton 103 F5
Cropwell Bishop. 77 F6
Cropwell Butler .. 77 F6
Cros 155 A10
Crosbost 155 E8
Crosby Cumb. 107 F7
IoM 84 E3
N Lincs. 90 C2
Crosby Garrett ..100 D2
Crosby
Ravensworth .. 99 C8
Crosby Villa ..107 F7
Croscombe 23 E7
Cross 23 D6
Crossaig 143 C9
Crossal 149 E9
Crossapol 146 G2
Cross Ash 35 C8
Cross-at-Hand ..29 E8
Crossburn 119 B8
Crossbush 16 D4
Crosscanonby ..107 F7
Crossdale Street .. 81 D8
Crossens 85 C4
Crossflatts 94 E4
Crossford Fife. ..128 F2
S Lanark. 119 E8
Crossgate 66 B2
Crossgatehall ..121 C6
Crossgates Fife .. 128 F3
Powys 48 C2

Crossgill 93 C5
Cross Green Devon...9 F5
Suff 56 D2
Suff 56 D3
Warks 51 D8
Cross-hands 32 B2
Cross Hands Carms. 33 C6
Pembs.....32 C1
Crosshill E Ayrs. ..112 B4
Fife 128 E3
S Ayrs. 112 D3
Cross Hill 76 E4
Crosshouse 118 F3
Cross Houses ..60 D5
Crossings 108 B5
Cross in Hand
E Sus 18 C2
Leics 64 F2
Cross Inn Ceredig... 46 C4
Ceredig 46 D2
Rhondda 34 F4
Crosskeys 35 E6
Cross Keys 29 D6
Cross Lane Head .. 61 E7
Cross Lanes 60 C3
Cross Lanes Corn... 3 D5
N Yorks. 95 C8
Wrex 73 E7
Crossle 118 C4
Crosslee 115 C6
Crossmichael ..106 C4
Crossmoor 92 F4
Cross Oak 35 B5
Cross of
Jackston 153 E7
Cross o'th'hands .. 76 E2
Crossroads Aberds 141 E6
E Ayrs. 118 F4
Cross Street. 57 B5
Crossway Hereford .. 49 F8
Mon 35 C8
Powys 48 D2
Crossway Green ..50 C3
Crossways 13 F5
Crosswell 45 F3
Crosswood 47 B5
Crosthwaite 99 E6
Croston 86 C2
Crostwick 69 C5
Crostwight 69 B6
Crothair 154 D6
Crouch 29 D7
Croucheston 13 B8
Crouch Hill 12 C5
Crouch House
Green 28 E5
Croughton 52 F3
Crovie 153 B8
Crowan 2 C5
Crowborough ..18 B2
Crowcombe 22 F3
Crowdecote 75 C8
Crowden 87 E8
Crow Edge 88 D2
Crowell 39 E7
Crowfield Northants 52 E4
Suff 56 D5
Crow Hill. 36 B3
Crowhurst E Sus. ..18 D4
Sur.....28 E4
Crowhurst Lane
End 28 E4
Crowland 66 C2
Crowlas 2 C4
Crowle N Lincs. ..89 C8
Worcs 50 D4
Crowmarsh
Gifford 39 F6
Crown Corner ..57 B6
Crownhill 6 D2
Crownland 56 C4
Crownthorpe ..68 D3
Crowntown 2 C5
Crows-an-wra .. 2 D2
Crowshill 68 D2
Crowsnest 60 D3
Crowthorne 27 C6
Crowton 74 B2
Croxall 63 C5
Croxby 91 E5
Croxdale 111 F5
Croxden 75 F7
Croxley Green ..40 E3
Croxton Cambs ..54 C3
N Lincs. 90 C4
Norf.....67 F8
Staffs.....74 F4
Croxton Kerrial .. 64 B5
Croxtonbank ..74 F4
Croy Highld .. 151 G10
N Lanark 119 B7
Croydon Cambs .. 54 E4
London..... 28 C4
Crubenmore
Lodge 138 E2
Cruckmeole 60 D4
Cruckton 60 C4
Cruden Bay ..153 E10
Crudgington ..61 C6
Crudwell 37 E6
Crug 48 B3
Crugmeer 4 B4
Crugybar 47 F5
Crulabhig ..154 D6
Crumlin = Crymlyn .35 E6
Crumpsall. 87 D6
Crundale Kent .. 30 E4
Pembs.....44 D4
Cruwys Morchard .10 C3
Crux Easton ..26 D2
Crwbin 33 C5
Cryers Hill 40 E1
Crymlyn 83 D6
Crymlyn = Crumlin. 35 E6
Crymych 45 F3
Crynant 34 D1
Crynfryn 46 C5
Cuaig 149 C12
Cuan 124 D3
Cubbington ..51 C8
Cubeck 100 F4
Cubert 4 D2
Cubley 88 D3
Cubley Common .. 75 F8
Cublington Bucks .. 39 B8
Hereford.....49 F6

Cuckfield 17 B7
Cucklington 13 B5
Cuckney 77 B5
Cuckoo Hill 89 E8
Cuddesdon 39 D6
Cuddington Bucks. 39 C7
Ches W. 74 B3
Cuddington Heath. 73 E8
Cuddy Hill 92 F4
Cudham 28 C5
Cudliptown 6 B3
Cudworth Som ..11 C8
S Yorks. 88 D4
Cuffley 41 D6
Cuiashader 155 B10
Cuidhir 148 H1
Cuidhtinis 154 J5
Culbo 151 E9
Culbokie 151 E9
Culburnie 150 G7
Culcabock 151 G9
Culcairn 151 E9
Culcharry 151 F11
Culcheth 86 E4
Culdrain 152 E5
Culduie 149 D12
Culford 56 B2
Culgaith 99 B8
Culham 39 E5
Culkein 156 F3
Culkein Drumbeg 156 F4
Culkerton 37 E6
Cullachie 139 B5
Cullen 152 B5
Cullercoats 111 B6
Cullicudden 151 E9
Cullingworth ..94 F3
Cullipool 124 D3
Cullivoe 160 C7
Culloch 127 C6
Culloden 151 G10
Cullompton 10 D5
Culmaily 151 B11
Culmazie 105 D7
Culmington ..60 F4
Culmstock 11 C6
Culnacraig 156 J3
Culnaknock ..149 B10
Culpho. 57 E6
Culrain 151 B8
Culross 127 F8
Culroy 112 C3
Culsh E Ayrs. ..140 E2
Aberds. 153 D8
Culshabbin ..105 D7
Culswick 160 J4
Cultercullen ..141 B8
Cults Aberdeen ..141 D7
Aberds. 152 E5
Dumfries 105 E8
Culverstone Green 29 C7
Culverthorpe ..78 E3
Culworth. 52 E3
Culzie Lodge ..151 D8
Cumberland ..119 B7
Cumbernauld
Village 119 B7
Cumberworth ..79 B8
Cuminestown ..153 C8
Cumlewick 160 L6
Cummersdale ..108 D3
Cummertrees ..107 C8
Cumminstown ..152 B1
Cumnock 113 B5
Cumnor 38 D4
Cumrew 108 D5
Cumwhinton ..108 D4
Cumwhitton ..108 D5
Cundall 95 B7
Cunninghamhead 118 E3
Cunnister 160 D7
Cupar. 129 C5
Cupar Muir. 129 C5
Cupernham ..14 B4
Curbar 76 B2
Curbridge Hants .. 15 C6
Oxon 38 D3
Curdridge 15 C6
Curdworth 63 E5
Curland 11 C7
Curlew Green ..57 C7
Currarie 112 E1
Curridge 26 B2
Currie 120 C4
Curry Mallet ..11 B8
Curry Rivel 11 B8
Curtisden Green. 29 E8
Curtisknowle.. 6 D5
Cury 3 D5
Cushnie 153 B7
Cushuish. 22 F3
Cusop 48 E4
Cutcloy 105 F8
Cutcombe 21 F8
Cutgate 87 C6
Cutiau 58 C3
Cutlers Green .. 55 F6
Cutnall Green ..50 C3
Cutsdean 51 F5
Cutthorpe 76 B3
Cutts 160 K6
Cuxham 39 E6
Cuxton 29 C8
Cuxwold 91 D5
Cwm BI Gwent ..35 D5
Denb 72 B4
Swansea 33 E7
Cwmafan 34 E1
Cwmaman 34 E4
Cwmann 46 E4
Cwmavon 35 D6
Cwmbach Carms ..32 B3
Carms 33 D5
Powys 48 E3
Powys 48 F3

Cwmderwen 59 D6
Cwmdu Carms 46 F5
Powys 35 B5
Swansea 33 E7
Cwmduad 46 F2
Cwm-Dulais 33 D7
Cwmdwr 47 F6
Cwmfelin Bridgend .34 F2
M Tydf 34 D4
Cwmfelin Boeth .. 32 C2
Cwm-felin-fach... 35 E5
Cwmfelin Mynach. 32 B3
Cwmffrwd 33 C5
Cwmgiedd 34 C1
Cwmgors 33 C8
Cwmgwili 33 C6
Cwmgwrach ..34 D2
Cwm-hesgen ..71 E8
Cwmhiraeth ..46 F2
Cwm-hwnt 34 D3
Cwmifor 33 B7
Cwm Irfon 47 E8
Cwm Isaf 33 C5
Cwm-Llinau ..58 D5
Cwmllynfell 33 C8
Cwm-mawr ..33 C6
Cwm-morgan ..45 F4
Cwm-parc 34 E3
Cwmpengraig ..46 F2
Cwm Penmachno 71 C8
Cwmrhos 35 B5
Cwmsychpant.. 46 E3
Cwmtillery 35 D6
Cwm-twrch Isaf .. 34 C1
Cwm-twrch Uchaf. 34 C1
Cwmwysg 34 B2
Cwm-y-glo Carms. .82 E5
Gwyn 82 E5
Cwmyoy 35 B6
Cwmystwyth ..47 B6
Cwrt 58 D3
Cwrt-newydd ..46 E3
Cwrt-y-cadno ..47 E5
Cwrt-y-gollen ..35 C6
Cydweli
= Kidwelly 33 D5
Cyffordd Llandudno
= Llandudno
Junction 83 D7
Cyffylliog 72 D4
Cyfronydd 59 D8
Cymer 34 E2
Cyncoed 35 F5
Cynghordy ..47 E7
Cynheidre 33 D5
Cynwyd 72 E4
Cynwyl Elfed ..32 B4
Cywarch 59 C5

D
Dacre Cumb. 99 B6
N Yorks. 94 C4
Dacre Banks ..94 C4
Daddry Shield ..109 F8
Dadford 52 F4
Dadlington 63 E8
Dafarn Faig ..71 C5
Dafen 33 D6
Daffy Green ..68 D2
Dagenham 41 F7
Daglingworth ..37 D6
Dagnall 40 C2
Dail Beag ..154 C7
Dail bho Dheas .155 A9
Dail bho Thuath .155 A9
Daill 142 B4
Dailly 112 D2
Dail Mor 154 C7
Dairsie or
Osnaburgh ..129 C6
Daisy Hill 86 D4
Dalabrog 148 F2
Dalavich 125 D5
Dalbeattie 106 C5
Dalblair 113 C6
Dalbog 135 B5
Dalbury 76 F2
Dalby IoM 84 E2
N Yorks. 96 B2
Dalchalloch ..132 C4
Dalchalm 157 J12
Dalchenna ..125 E6
Dalchirach ..152 E1
Dalchork 157 H8
Dalchreichart ..137 C5
Dalchruin 127 C6
Dalderby 78 C5
Dale 44 E3
Dale Abbey ..76 F4
Dale Head 99 C6
Dalelia 147 E10
Dale of Walls ..160 H3
Daless 151 H11
Dalfaber 138 C5
Dalgarven 118 E2
Dalgety Bay ..128 F3
Dalginross 127 B6
Dalguise 133 E6
Dalhalvaig ..157 D11
Dalham 55 C8
Dalinlongart ..145 E10
Dalkeith 121 C6
Dallam. 86 E3
Dallas 151 F14
Dalleagles 113 C5
Dallinghoo 57 D6
Dallington E Sus...18 D3
Northants 52 C5
Dallow 94 B4
Dalmadilly 141 C6
Dalmally 125 C7
Dalmarnock ..119 C6
Dalmary 126 E4
Dalmellington ..112 D4
Dalmeny 120 B4
Dalmigavie ..138 C3
Dalmigavie
Lodge 138 D3
Dalmore 151 E9
Dalmuir 118 B4
Dalnabreck ..147 E9
Dalnacardoch
Lodge 132 B4
Dalnacroich ..150 F6
Dalnaglar Castle .133 C8
Dalnahaitnach ..138 B4

Dalnaspidal
Lodge 132 B3
Dalnavaid 133 C7
Dalnavie 151 D9
Dalnawillan
Lodge 157 E13
Dalness 131 D5
Dalnessie 157 H9
Dalqueich 128 D2
Dalreavoch 157 J10
Dalry 118 E2
Dalrymple 112 C3
Dalserf 119 D8
Dalston 108 D3
Dalswinton 114 F2
Dalton Dumfries ..107 B8
Lancs. 86 D2
Northumb 110 B4
Northumb 110 D2
N Yorks. 95 B7
N Yorks. 101 D6
S Yorks. 89 E5
Dalton-in-Furness 92 B2
Dalton-le-Dale ..111 E7
Dalton-on-Tees .101 D7
Dalton Piercy ..111 F7
Dalveich 126 B5
Dalvina Lodge ..157 E9
Dalwhinnie ..138 F2
Dalwood 11 D7
Dalwyne 112 E3
Damerham 14 C2
Damgate 69 D7
Dam Green. 68 F3
Damnaglaur ..104 F5
Damside 120 E4
Dam Side 92 E4
Danbury 42 D3
Danby 103 D5
Danby Wiske ..101 E8
Dandaleith 152 D2
Danderhall ..121 C6
Danebridge ..75 C6
Dane End 41 B6
Danehill 17 B8
Danemoor Green .. 68 D3
Danesford 61 E7
Daneshill 26 D4
Dangerous Corner. 86 C3
Danskine 121 C8
Darcy Lever ..86 D5
Darenth 29 B6
Daresbury 86 F3
Darfield 88 D5
Darfoulds 77 B5
Dargate 30 C4
Darite 5 C7
Darlaston 62 E3
Darley 94 D5
Darley Bridge ..76 C2
Darley Head ..94 D4
Darlingscott ..51 E7
Darlington 101 C7
Darliston 74 F2
Darlton 77 B7
Darnall 88 F4
Darnick 121 F8
Darowen 58 D5
Darra 153 D7
Darracott 20 F3
Darras Hall ..110 B4
Darrington ..89 B5
Darsham 57 C8
Dartford 29 B6
Dartford Crossing . 29 B6
Dartington 7 C5
Dartmeet 6 B4
Dartmouth 7 D6
Darton 88 D4
Darvel 119 F5
Darwell Hole ..18 D3
Darwen 86 B4
Datchet 27 B7
Datchworth ..41 C5
Datchworth Green. 41 C5
Daubhill 86 D5
Daugh of
Kinermony ..152 D2
Dauntsey 37 F6
Davenham 74 B3
Davenport Green .. 74 B5
Daventry 52 C3
Davidson's Mains 120 B5
Davidstow 8 F3
David's Well ..48 B2
Davington 115 D5
Daviot Aberds ..141 B6
Highld 151 H10
Davoch of
Grange 152 C4
Davyhulme ..87 E5
Dawley 61 D6
Dawlish 7 B7
Dawlish Warren ..7 B7
Dawn 83 D8
Daws Heath ..42 F4
Daw's House Corn...8 F5
Corn. 8 F5
Dawsmere 79 F7
Dayhills 75 F6
Daylesford ..38 B2
Ddôl-Cownwy ..59 C7
Ddrydwy 82 D3
Deadwater ..116 E2
Deaf Hill 111 F6
Deal 31 D7
Deal Hall 43 E6
Dean Cumb ..98 B2
Devon 6 C5
Dorset 13 C7
Hants. 15 C6
Som 23 E8
Dean Prior 6 C5
Dean Row 87 F6
Deans 120 C3
Deanscales ..98 B2
Deanshanger ..53 E6
Deanston 127 D6
Debach 57 D6
Debden Essex ..41 E7
Essex. 55 F6

Debden Cross 55 F6
Debenham 57 C5
Dechmont 120 B3
Deddington 52 F2
Dedham 56 F4
Dedham Heath ..56 F4
Deebank 141 E5
Deene 65 E6
Deenethorpe ..65 E6
Deepcar 88 E3
Deepdale 100 F2
Deeping Gate ..65 D8
Deeping St James .65 D8
Deeping
St Nicholas ..66 C2
Deerhill 152 C4
Deerhurst 37 B5
Deerness 159 H6
Defford 50 E4
Defynnog 34 B3
Deganwy 83 D7
Deighton N Yorks ..102 D1
York 96 E2
Deiniolen 83 E5
Delabole 8 F2
Delamere 74 C2
Delfrigs. 141 B8
Dell Lodge ..139 C6
Delliefure ..151 H13
Delnabo 139 C7
Delnadamph ..139 D8
Delph. 87 D7
Delves 110 E4
Delvine 133 E8
Dembleby 78 F3
Denaby Main ..89 E5
Denbigh
= Dinbych ..72 C4
Denbury 7 C6
Denby 76 E3
Denby Dale ..88 D3
Denchworth ..38 E3
Dendron 92 B2
Denel End. 53 F8
Denend 152 E6
Denford 53 B7
Dengie 43 D5
Denham Bucks ..40 F3
Suff 55 C8
Suff 57 B5
Denham Street ..57 B5
Denhead Aberds ..153 C9
Denhead of Gray .134 F3
Denholm 115 C8
Denholme 94 F3
Denholme Clough . 94 F3
Denio 70 D4
Denmead 15 C7
Denmore 141 C8
Denmoss 153 D6
Dennington ..57 C6
Denny 127 F7
Dennyloanhead ..127 F7
Denny Lodge ..14 D4
Denshaw 87 C7
Denside 141 E7
Densole. 31 E6
Denstone 75 E8
Denstroude 30 C5
Dent 100 F2
Denton Cambs ..65 F8
Darl 101 C7
E Sus 17 D8
Gtr Man 87 E7
Kent 31 E6
Lincs 77 F8
Norf. 69 F5
Northants 53 D6
N Yorks. 94 E4
Oxon 39 D5
Denton's Green ..86 E2
Denver 67 D6
Denwick 117 C8
Deopham 68 D3
Deopham Green. 68 E3
Deptford London ..28 B4
Wilts. 24 F5
Derby 76 F3
Derbyhaven ..84 F2
Dereham 68 C2
Deri 35 D5
Derril 8 D5
Derringstone ..31 E6
Derrington ..62 B2
Derriton 8 D5
Derryguaig.. ..146 H7
Derrythorpe ..90 D2
Dersingham ..80 D2
Dervaig 146 F7
Derwen 72 D4
Derwenlas ..58 E4
Desborough ..64 F5
Desford 63 D8
Detchant 123 F6
Detling 29 D8
Deuddwr 60 C2
Devauden 36 E1
Devil's Bridge ..47 B6
Devizes 24 C5
Devol 118 B3
Devonport 6 D2
Devonside 127 E8
Devoran 3 C6
Dewar 121 E6
Dewlish 13 E5
Dewsbury 88 B3
Dewsbury Moor .. 88 B3
Dewshall Court .. 49 F6
Dhoon 84 D4
Dhoor 84 C4
Dhowin 84 B4
Dial Post 17 C5
Dibden 14 D5
Dibden Purlieu ..14 D5
Dickleburgh ..68 F4
Didbrook 51 F5
Didcot 39 F5
Diddington ..54 C2
Diddlebury ..60 F5
Didley 49 F6
Didling 16 C2

Didmarton 37 F5
Didsbury 87 E6
Didworthy 6 C4
Digby 78 D3
Digg 149 B9
Diggle 87 D8
Digmoor 86 D2
Digswell Park ..41 C5
Dihewyd 46 D3
Dilham 69 B6
Dilhorne 75 E6
Dillarburn 119 E8
Dillington 54 C2
Dilston 110 C2
Dilton Marsh ..24 E3
Dilwyn 49 D6
Dinas Carms 45 F4
Gwyn 70 D3
Dinas Cross 45 F2
Dinas Dinlle 82 F4
Dinas-Mawddwy .. 59 C5
Dinas Powys 22 B3
Dinder 23 E7
Dinedor 49 F7
Dingestow 36 C1
Dingle 85 F4
Dingleden 18 B5
Dingley 64 F4
Dingwall 151 F8
Dinlabyre 115 E8
Dinmael 72 E4
Dinnet 140 E3
Dinnington Som .. 12 C2
S Yorks. 89 F6
T&W 110 B5
Dinorwic. 83 E5
Dinton Bucks. ..39 C7
Wilts 24 F5
Dinwoodie Mains 114 E4
Dinworthy 8 C5
Dippen 143 F11
Dippenhall 27 E6
Dipple Moray ..152 C3
S Ayrs. 112 D2
Diptford 6 D5
Dipton 110 D4
Dirdhu 139 B6
Dirleton 129 F7
Dirt Pot 109 E8
Discoed 48 C4
Diseworth ..63 B8
Dishes 159 F7
Dishforth ..95 B6
Disley 87 F7
Diss 56 B5
Disserth 48 D2
Distington ..98 B2
Ditchampton ..25 F5
Ditcheat 23 F8
Ditchingham ..69 E6
Ditchling 17 C7
Ditherington ..60 C5
Dittisham 7 D6
Ditton Halton ..86 F2
Kent. 29 D8
Ditton Green ..55 D7
Ditton Priors ..61 F6
Divach 137 B7
Divlyn 47 F6
Dixton Glos 50 F4
Mon 36 C2
Dobcross 87 D7
Dobwalls 5 C7
Doccombe 10 F2
Dochfour House. .151 H9
Dochgarroch ..151 G9
Docking 80 D3
Docklow 49 D7
Dockray 99 B5
Dockroyd ..94 F3
Doc Penfro
= Pembroke Dock. 44 E4
Dodburn 115 D7
Doddinghurst ..42 E1
Doddington
Cambs. 66 E3
Kent 30 D3
Lincs 78 B2
Northumb 123 F5
Shrops. 49 B8
Doddiscombsleigh 10 F3
Dodford Northants. 52 C4
Worcs 50 B4
Dodington ..24 A2
Dodleston 73 C7
Dods Leigh ..75 F7
Dodworth 88 D4
Doe Green ..86 F3
Doe Lea 76 C4
Dogdyke ..78 D5
Dogmersfield ..27 D5
Dogridge 37 F7
Dogsthorpe ..65 D8
Dog Village ..10 E4
Dolanog 59 C7
Dolau Powys ..48 C3
Rhondda 34 F3
Dolbenmaen ..71 C6
Dolfach 59 F8
Dolfor 59 F8
Dôl-fôr 58 D5
Dol-y-cannau ..48 E4
Dolhyr 48 E4
Doll 157 J11
Dollar 127 E8
Dolley Green ..48 C4
Dollwen 58 F3
Dolphin 73 B5
Dolphinholme ..92 D5
Dolphinton ..120 E4
Dolton 9 C7
Dolwen Conwy ..83 D8
Powys 59 D6
Dolwyd 83 D7
Dolwyddelan ..83 F7
Dôl-y-Bont ..58 F3
Dol-y-cannau ..48 E4
Dolyhir 48 D4
Doncaster 89 D6
Dones Green ..74 B3
Donhead
St Andrew ..13 B7
St Mary 13 B7

Donibristle 128 F3
Donington 78 F5
Donington on Bain 91 F6
Donington South
Ing 78 F5
Donisthorpe ..63 C7
Donkey Town ..27 C7
Donnington Glos...38 B1
Hereford.....50 F2
Shrops. 61 D5
Telford.....61 C7
W Berks. 26 C2
W Sus 16 D2
Donnington Wood 61 C7
Donyatt 11 C8
Doonfoot 112 C3
Dorback Lodge ..139 C6
Dorchester Dorset.. 12 E4
Oxon 39 E5
Dordon 63 D6
Dore 88 F4
Dores 151 H8
Dorking 28 E2
Dormansland ..28 E5
Dormanstown ..102 B3
Dormington ..49 E7
Dormston 50 D4
Dornal 105 B6
Dorney 27 B7
Dornie 149 F13
Dornoch 151 C10
Dornock 108 C2
Dorrery 158 E2
Dorridge 51 B6
Dorrington Lincs ..78 D3
Shrops. 60 D4
Dorsington 51 E6
Dorstone 48 E5
Dorton 39 C6
Dorusduain ..136 B2
Dosthill 63 E6
Dottery 12 E2
Doublebois 5 C6
Dougarie 143 E9
Doughton 37 E5
Douglas IoM 84 E3
S Lanark. 119 F8
Douglas & Angus .134 F4
Douglastown ..134 E4
Douglas Water ..119 F8
Douglas West ..119 F8
Doulting 23 E8
Dounby 159 F3
Doune Highld ..156 J7
Stirling. 127 D6
Doune Park ..153 B7
Douneside ..140 D3
Dounie 151 B8
Dounreay ..157 C12
Dousland 6 C3
Dovaston 60 B3
Dove Holes. 75 B7
Dovenby 107 F7
Dover. 31 E7
Dovercourt 57 F6
Doverdale. 50 C3
Doveridge 75 F8
Doversgreen ..28 E3
Dowally. 133 E7
Dowbridge ..92 F4
Dowdeswell. ..37 C6
Dowlais 34 D4
Dowland 9 C7
Dowlish Wake ..11 C8
Down Ampney. ..37 E8
Downcraig
Ferry 145 H10
Downderry 5 D8
Downe. 28 C5
Downend IoW ..15 F6
S Glos. 23 B8
W Berks. 26 B2
Downfield 134 F3
Downgate. 5 B8
Downham Essex ..42 E3
Lancs. 93 E7
Northumb 122 F4
Downham Market .67 D6
Down Hatherley ..37 B5
Downhead 23 E8
Downhill Perth ..133 F7
T&W 111 D6
Downholland
Cross 85 D4
Downholme ..101 E6
Downies 141 E8
Downley 39 E8
Down St Mary ..10 D2
Downside Som ..23 E8
Sur. 28 D2
Down Thomas ..6 D3
Downton Hants ..14 E3
Wilts. 14 B2
Downton on the
Rock 49 B6
Dowsby 65 B8
Dowsdale 66 C2
Dowthwaitehead .99 B5
Doxey 62 B3
Doxford 117 B7
Doynton 24 B2
Draffan 119 E7
Dragonby 90 C4
Drakeland Corner . 6 D3
Drake's Broughton 50 E4
Drakes Cross ..51 B5
Drakewalls.....6 B2

Draughton
Northants. 53 B5
N Yorks. 94 D3
Drax 89 B7
Draycote 52 B2
Draycott Derbys ..76 F4
Glos. 51 F6
Som 23 D6
Draycott in the
Clay 63 B5
Draycott in the
Moors 75 E6
Drayford 10 C2
Drayton Leics ..64 E5
Lincs 78 F5
Norf 68 C4
Oxon.....38 E4

Drayton continued
Oxon 52 E2
Ptsmth 15 D7
Som 12 B2
Worcs 50 B4
Drayton Bassett . . 63 D5
Drayton
Beauchamp . . . 40 C2
Drayton Parslow . . 39 B8
Drayton
St Leonard 39 E5
Drebley 94 D3
Dreemskerry . . . 84 C4
Dreenhill 44 D4
Drefach Carms . . 33 C6
Carms 46 F2
Dre-fach Carms . . 33 C7
Ceredig 46 E4
Drefelin 46 F2
Dreghorn 118 F3
Drellingore 31 E6
Drem 121 B8
Dresden 75 E6
Dreumasdal . . . 148 E2
Drewsteignton . . 10 E2
Driby 79 B6
Driffield E Yorks . . 97 D6
Glos 37 E7
Drigg 98 E2
Drighlington . . . 88 B3
Drimnin 147 F8
Drimpton 12 D2
Drimsynie 125 E7
Drinisiadar 154 H6
Drinkstone 56 C3
Drinkstone Green . 56 C3
Drishaig 125 D7
Drissaig 124 D5
Drochil 120 E4
Droitwich Spa . . 50 C3
Droman 156 D4
Dron 128 C3
Dronfield 76 B3
Dronfield
Woodhouse . . . 76 B3
Drongan 112 C4
Dronley 134 F3
Droxford 15 C7
Droylsden 87 E7
Druid 72 E4
Druidston 44 D3
Druimarbin . . . 130 B4
Druimavuic . . . 130 E4
Druimdrishaig . . 144 F6
Druimindarroch . 147 C9
Druimyeon More . 143 C7
Drum Argyll . . . 145 F8
Perth 128 D2
Drumbeg 156 F4
Drumblade . . . 152 D5
Drumblair 153 D6
Drumbuie
Dumfries 113 F5
Highld 149 E12
Drumburgh . . . 108 D2
Drumburn 107 C6
Drumchapel . . . 118 B5
Drumchardine . . 151 G8
Drumchork . . . 155 J13
Drumclog 119 F6
Drumderfit 151 F9
Drumeldrie . . . 129 D6
Drumelzier 120 F4
Drumfearn 149 G11
Drumgask 138 E2
Drumgley 134 D4
Drumguish 138 E3
Drumin 152 E1
Drumlasie 140 D5
Drumlemble . . . 143 G7
Drumligair 141 C8
Drumlithie 141 F6
Drummoddie . . . 105 E7
Drummond 151 E9
Drummore 104 F5
Drummuir 152 D3
Drummuir Castle 152 D3
Drumnadrochit . . 137 B8
Drumnagorrach . 152 C5
Drumoak 141 E6
Drumpark 107 A5
Drumphail 105 C6
Drumrash 106 B3
Drumrunie 156 J4
Drums 141 B8
Drumsallie 130 B3
Drumstinchall . . 107 D5
Drumsturdy . . . 134 F4
Drumtochty
Castle 135 B6
Drumtroddan . . . 105 E7
Drumuie 149 D9
Drumuillie 138 B5
Drumvaich 127 D5
Drumwhindle . . . 153 E9
Drunkendub . . . 135 E6
Drury 73 C6
Drury Square . . . 68 C2
Drybeck 100 C1
Drybridge Moray . 152 B4
N Ayrs 118 F3
Drybrook 36 C3
Dryburgh 121 F8
Dry Doddington . 77 E8
Dry Drayton . . . 54 C4
Dryhope 115 B5
Drylaw 120 B5
Drym 2 C5
Drymen 126 F3
Drymuir 153 D9
Drynoch 149 E9
Dryslwyn 33 B6
Dryton 61 D5
Dubford 153 B8
Dubton 135 D5
Duchally 156 H6
Duchlage 126 F2
Duck Corner . . . 57 E7
Duckington 73 D8
Ducklington . . . 38 D3
Duckmanton . . . 76 B4
Duck's Cross . . . 54 D2
Duddenhoe End . 55 F5
Duddingston . . . 121 B5
Duddington 65 D6

Duddleswell 17 B8
Duddo 122 E5
Duddon 74 C2
Duddon Bridge . . 98 F4
Dudleston 73 F7
Dudleston Heath . 73 F7
Dudley T&W . . . 111 B5
W Mid 62 E3
Dudley Port . . . 62 E3
Duffield 76 E3
Duffryn Neath . . 34 E2
Newport 35 F6
Dufftown 152 E3
Duffus 152 B1
Dufton 100 B1
Duggleby 96 C4
Duirinish 149 E12
Duisdalemore . . 149 G12
Duisky 130 B4
Dukestown 35 C5
Dukinfield 87 E7
Dulas 82 C4
Dulcote 23 E7
Dulford 11 D5
Dull 133 E5
Dullatur 119 B7
Dullingham . . . 55 D7
Dulnain Bridge . . 139 B5
Duloe Bedford . . 54 C2
Corn 5 D7
Dulsie 151 G12
Dulverton 10 B4
Dulwich 28 B4
Dumbarton . . . 118 B3
Dumbleton 50 F5
Dumcrieff 114 D4
Dumfries 107 B6
Dumgoyne 126 F4
Dummer 26 E3
Dumpford 16 B2
Dumpton 31 C7
Dun 135 D6
Dunach 124 C4
Dunalastair . . . 132 D4
Dunan 149 F10
Dunans 145 D9
Dunball 22 E5
Dunbar 122 B2
Dunbeath 158 H3
Dunbeg 124 B4
Dunblane 127 D6
Dunbog 128 C4
Duncanston . . . 151 F8
Duncanstone . . . 140 B4
Dun
Charlabhaigh . . 154 C6
Dunchurch 52 B2
Duncote 52 D4
Duncow 114 F2
Duncraggan . . . 126 D4
Duncrievie 128 D3
Duncton 16 C3
Dundas House . . 159 K5
Dundee 134 F4
Dundeugh 113 F5
Dundon 23 F6
Dundonald 118 F3
Dundonnell . . . 150 C3
Dundonnell Hotel 150 C3
Dundonnell
House 150 C4
Dundraw 108 E2
Dundreggan . . . 137 C6
Dundreggan
Lodge 137 C6
Dundrennan . . . 106 E4
Dundry 23 C7
Dunecht 141 D6
Dunfermline . . . 128 F2
Dunfield 37 E8
Dunford Bridge . . 88 D2
Dungworth 88 F3
Dunham 77 B8
Dunham-on-the-
Hill 73 B8
Dunhampton . . . 50 C3
Dunham Town . . 86 F5
Dunholme 78 B3
Dunino 129 C7
Dunipace 127 F7
Dunira 127 B6
Dunkeld 133 E7
Dunkerton 24 D2
Dunkeswell 11 D6
Dunkeswick . . . 95 E6
Dunkirk Kent . . . 30 D4
Norf 81 E8
Dunk's Green . . . 29 D7
Dunlappie 135 C5
Dunley Hants . . . 26 D2
Worcs 50 C2
Dunlichity Lodge 151 H9
Dunlop 118 E4
Dunmaglass
Lodge 137 B8
Dunmore Argyll . 144 G6
Falk 127 F7
Dunnet 158 C4
Dunnichen 135 E5
Dunninald 135 D7
Dunning 128 C2
Dunnington
E Yorks 97 D7
Warks 51 D5
York 96 D2
Dunnockshaw . . 87 B6
Dunollie 124 B4
Dunoon 145 F10
Dunragit 105 D5
Dunrostan 144 E6
Duns 122 D3
Dunsby 65 B8
Dunscore 113 F8
Dunscroft 89 D7
Dunsdale 102 C4
Dunsden Green . 26 B5
Dunsfold 27 F8
Dunsford 10 E3
Dunshalt 128 C4
Dunshillock . . . 153 D9
Dunskey House . 104 D3
Dunsley 103 C6
Dunsmore 40 D1
Dunsop Bridge . . 93 D6
Dunstable 40 B3
Dunstall 63 B5
Dunstall Common 50 E3
Dunstall Green . . 55 C8
Dunstan 117 C8

Dunstan Steads . 117 B8
Dunster 21 E8
Duns Tew 38 B4
Dunston Lincs . . 78 C3
Norf 68 D5
Staffs 62 C3
T&W 110 C5
Dunsville 89 D7
Dunswell 97 F6
Dunsyre 120 E3
Dunterton 9 F5
Duntisbourne
Abbots 37 D6
Duntisbourne Leer 37 D6
Duntisbourne
Rouse 37 D6
Duntish 12 D4
Duntocher 118 B4
Dunton Bucks . . 54 E3
C Beds 54 E3
Norf 80 D4
Dunton Bassett . 64 E2
Dunton Green . . 29 D6
Dunton Wayletts . 42 E2
Duntulm 149 A9
Dunure 112 C2
Dunvant 33 E6
Dunvegan 148 D7
Dunwich 57 B8
Dunwood 75 D6
Dupplin Castle . . 128 C2
Durdar 108 D4
Durgates 18 B3
Durham 111 E5
Durisdeer 113 D8
Durisdeermill . . . 113 D8
Durkar 88 C4
Durleigh 22 F4
Durley Hants . . . 15 C6
Wilts 25 C7
Durley Street . . . 15 C6
Durnamuck . . . 150 B3
Durness 156 C7
Durno 141 B6
Duror 130 D3
Durran Argyll . . . 125 E5
Highld 158 C3
Durrington Wilts . 25 E6
W Sus 16 D5
Dursley 36 E4
Durston 11 B7
Durweston 13 D6
Dury 160 G6
Duston 52 C5
Duthil 138 B5
Dutlas 48 B4
Duton Hill 42 B2
Dutson 8 F5
Dutton 74 B2
Duxford Cambs . 55 E5
Oxon 38 E3
Dwygyfylchi . . . 83 D7
Dwyran 82 E4
Dyce 141 C7
Dye House 110 D2
Dyffryn Bridgend . 34 E2
Carms 32 B4
Pembs 44 B4
Dyffryn Ardudwy 71 E6
Dyffryn Castell . . 58 F4
Dyffryn Ceidrych 33 B8
Dyffryn Cellwen . 34 D2
Dyke Lincs 65 B8
Moray 151 F12
Dykehead Angus 134 C3
N Lanark 119 D8
Stirling 126 E4
Dykelands 135 C7
Dykends 134 D2
Dykeside 153 D7
Dykesmains . . . 118 E2
Dylife 59 E5
Dymchurch . . . 19 C7
Dymock 50 F2
Dyrham 24 B2
Dysart 128 E5
Dyserth 72 B4

E

Eadar Dha
Fhadhail 154 D5
Eagland Hill . . . 92 E4
Eagle 77 C8
Eagle Barnsdale . 77 C8
Eagle Moor . . . 77 C8
Eaglescliffe 102 C2
Eaglesfield Cumb . 98 B2
Dumfries 108 B2
Eaglesham 119 D5
Eaglethorpe . . . 65 E7
Eairy 84 E2
Eakley Lanes . . . 53 D6
Eakring 77 C6
Ealand 89 C8
Ealing 40 F4
Eals 109 D6
Eamont Bridge . . 99 B7
Earby 94 E2
Earcroft 86 B4
Eardington 61 E7
Eardisland 49 D6
Eardisley 48 E5
Eardiston Shrops . 60 B3
Worcs 49 C8
Earith 54 B4
Earle 117 B5
Earley 27 B5
Earlham 68 D5
Earlish 149 B8
Earls Barton . . . 53 C6
Earls Colne 42 B4
Earl's Croome . . 50 E3
Earlsdon 51 B8
Earlsferry 129 E6
Earlsfield 153 E8
Earl's Green . . . 56 C4
Earlsheaton . . . 88 B3
Earl Shilton 63 E8
Earlsmill 151 F12
Earl Soham 57 C6
Earl Sterndale . . 75 C7
Earlston Borders 121 F8
E Ayrs 118 F4
Earl Stonham . . 56 D5
Earlswood Mon . 36 E1
Sur 28 E3
Warks 51 B6

Earnley 16 E2
Earsairidh 148 J2
Earsdon 111 B6
Earsham 69 F6
Earswick 96 D2
Eartham 16 D3
Easby N Yorks . . 101 D6
N Yorks 102 D3
Easdale 124 D3
Easebourne . . . 16 B2
Easenhall 52 B2
Eashing 27 E7
Easington Bucks . 39 C6
Durham 111 E7
E Yorks 91 C7
Northumb . . . 123 F7
Oxon 39 E6
Oxon 52 F2
Redcar 103 C5
Easington
Colliery 111 E7
Easington Lane . 111 E6
Easingwold . . . 95 C8
Easole Street . . . 31 D6
Eassie 134 E3
East Aberthaw . . 22 C2
East Adderbury . 52 F2
East Allington . . 7 E5
East Anstey . . . 10 B3
East Appleton . . 101 E7
East Ardsley . . . 88 B4
East Ashling . . . 16 D2
East Auchronie . . 141 D7
East Ayton 103 F7
East Bank 35 D6
East Barkwith . . 91 F5
East Barming . . 29 D8
East Barnby . . . 103 C6
East Barnet . . . 41 E5
East Barns 122 B3
East Barsham . . 80 D5
East Beckham . . 81 D7
East Bedfont . . . 27 B8
East Bergholt . . 56 F4
East Bilney 68 C2
East Blatchington 17 D8
East Boldre . . . 14 D4
Eastbourne . . . 18 F3
East Brent 22 D5
Eastbridge 57 C8
East Bridgford . . 77 E6
East Buckland . . 21 F5
East Budleigh . . 11 F5
Eastburn 94 E3
East Burrafirth . . 160 H5
East Burton . . . 13 F6
Eastbury London . 40 E3
W Berks 25 B8
East Butsfield . . 110 E4
East Butterwick . 90 D2
Eastby 94 D3
East Cairnbeg . . 135 B7
East Calder . . . 120 C3
East Carleton . . 68 D4
East Carlton
Northants . . . 64 F5
W Yorks 94 E5
East Chaldon . . 13 F5
East Challow . . . 38 F3
East Chiltington . 17 C7
East Chinnock . . 12 C2
East Chisenbury . 25 D6
Eastchurch . . . 30 B3
East Clandon . . 27 D8
East Claydon . . 39 B7
East Clyne 157 J12
East Coker 12 C3
Eastcombe 37 D5
East Combe . . . 22 F3
East Common . . 96 F2
East Compton . . 23 E8
Eastcote London . 40 F4
Northants . . . 52 D4
W Mid 51 B6
Eastcott Corn . . 8 C4
Wilts 24 D5
East Cottingwith . 96 E3
Eastcourt Wilts . . 25 C7
Wilts 37 E6
East Cowes . . . 15 E6
East Cowick . . . 89 B7
East Cowton . . . 101 D8
East Cramlington 111 B5
East Cranmore . 23 E8
East Creech . . . 13 F7
East Croachy . . 138 B2
East Croftmore . 139 C5
East Curthwaite . 108 E3
East Dean E Sus . 18 F2
Hants 14 B3
W Sus 16 C3
East Down 20 E5
East Drayton . . . 77 B7
East Ella 90 B4
East End Dorset . 13 E7
E Yorks 91 B6
Hants 14 E4
Hants 15 B7
Herts 41 B7
Kent 18 B5
N Som 23 B6
Oxon 38 C3
Easter Ardross . . 151 D9
Easter Balmoral . 139 E8
Easter Boleskine . 137 B8
Easter Compton . 36 F2
Easter Cringate . 127 F6
Easter Davoch . . 140 D3
Easter Earshaig . 114 D3
Easter Fearn . . . 151 C9
Easter
Galcantray . . . 151 G11
Eastergate 16 D3
Easterhouse . . . 119 C6
Easter Howgate . 120 C5
Easter Howlaws . 122 E3
Easter Kinkell . . 151 F8
Easter Lednathie 134 C3
Easter Milton . . 151 F12
Easter Moniack . 151 G8
Eastern Green . . 63 F7
Easter Ord 141 D7
Easter Quarff . . 160 K6
Easter Rhynd . . 128 C3
Easter Row . . . 127 E6
Easter Silverford 153 B7
Easter Skeld . . . 160 J5
Easterton 24 D5

Eastertown 22 D5
Eastertown of
Auchleuchries . 153 E10
Easter Whyntie . 152 B6
East Farleigh . . . 29 D8
East Farndon . . 64 F4
East Ferry 90 E2
Eastfield N Lanark 119 C8
N Yorks 103 F8
Eastfield Hall . . . 117 D8
East Fortune . . . 121 B8
East Garston . . . 25 B8
Eastgate Durham 110 F2
Norf 81 E7
East Ginge 38 F4
East Goscote . . 64 C3
East Grafton . . . 25 C7
East Grimstead . 14 B3
East Grinstead . 28 F4
East Guldeford . . 19 C6
East Haddon . . . 52 C4
East Hagbourne . 39 F5
East Halton . . . 90 C5
East Hanney . . . 38 E4
East Hanningfield 42 D3
East Hardwick . . 89 C5
East Harling . . . 68 F2
East Harlsey . . . 102 E2
East Harnham . . 14 B2
East Harptree . . 23 D7
East Hartford . . 111 B5
East Harting . . . 15 C8
East Hatley 54 D3
East Hauxwell . . 101 E6
East Haven 135 F5
East Heckington . 78 E4
East Hedleyhope 110 E4
East Hendred . . 38 F4
East Herrington . 111 D6
East Heslerton . . 96 B5
East Hoathly . . . 18 D2
East Horndon . . 42 E2
Easthope 61 E5
Easthorpe Essex . 43 B5
Leics 77 F8
Notts 77 D7
East Horrington . 23 E7
East Horsley . . . 27 D8
East Horton . . . 123 F6
Easthouses . . . 121 C6
East Huntspill . . 22 E5
East Hyde 40 C4
East Ilkerton . . . 21 E6
East Ilsley 38 F4
East Keal 79 C6
East Kennett . . . 25 C6
East Keswick . . . 95 E6
East Kilbride . . . 119 D6
East Kirkby 79 C6
East Knapton . . 96 B4
East Knighton . . 13 F6
East Knoyle . . . 24 F3
East Kyloe 123 F6
East Lambrook . . 12 C2
East Lamington . 151 D10
East Langdon . . 31 E7
East Langton . . 64 E4
East Langwell . . 157 J10
East Lavant . . . 16 D2
East Lavington . . 16 C3
East Layton . . . 101 D6
Eastleach Martin 38 D2
Eastleach Turville 38 D1
East Leake 64 B2
East Learmouth . 122 F4
Eastleigh Devon . 9 B6
Hants 14 C5
East Leigh 9 D8
East Lexham . . . 67 C8
East Lilburn . . . 117 B6
Eastling 30 D3
East Linton . . . 121 B8
East Liss 15 B8
East Looe 5 D7
East Lound 89 E8
East Lulworth . . 13 F6
East Lutton . . . 96 C5
East Lydford . . . 23 F7
East Mains 141 E5
East Malling . . . 29 D8
East March 134 F4
East Marden . . . 16 C2
East Markham . . 77 B7
East Marton . . . 94 D2
East Meon 15 B7
East Mere 10 C4
East Mersea . . . 43 C6
East Mey 158 C5
East Molesey . . 28 C2
Eastmoor Derbys 76 B3
Norf 67 D7
East Morden . . . 13 E7
East Morton . . . 94 E3
East Ness 96 B2
East Newton . . . 97 F8
Eastney 15 E7
Eastnor 50 F2
East Norton . . . 64 D4
East Nynehead . 11 B6
East Oakley . . . 26 D3
Eastoft 90 C2
East Ogwell . . . 7 B6
Easton Cambs . . 54 B2
Cumb 108 B4
Cumb 108 D2
Devon 10 F2
Dorset 12 G4
Hants 26 F3
Lincs 65 B6
Norf 68 C4
Som 23 E7
Suff 57 D6
Wilts 24 B3
Easton Grey . . . 37 F5
Easton-in-
Gordano 23 B7
Easton Maudit . . 53 D6
Easton on the Hill 65 D7
Easton Royal . . . 25 C7
East Orchard . . 13 C6
East Ord 123 D5

East Panson . . . 9 E5
Eastpark 107 C7
East Peckham . . 29 E7
East Pennard . . 23 F7
East Perry 54 C2
East Portlemouth . 6 F5
East Prawle . . . 7 F5
East Preston . . . 16 D4
East Putford . . . 9 C5
East Quantoxhead 22 E3
East Rainton . . . 111 E6
East Ravendale . 91 E6
East Raynham . . 80 E4
Eastrea 66 E2
East Rhidorroch
Lodge 150 B5
Eastriggs 108 C2
East Rigton . . . 95 E6
Eastrington . . . 89 B8
East Rounton . . 102 D2
East Row 103 C6
East Rudham . . 80 E4
East Runton . . . 81 C7
East Ruston . . . 69 B6
Eastry 31 D7
East Saltoun . . . 121 C7
East Sleekburn . 117 F8
East Somerton . 69 C7
East Stockwith . 89 E8
East Stoke Dorset 13 F6
Notts 77 E7
East Stour 13 B6
East Stourmouth 31 C6
East Stowford . . 9 B8
East Stratton . . 26 F3
East Studdal . . . 31 E7
East Suisnish . . 149 E10
East Taphouse . . 5 C6
East-the-Water . 9 B6
East Thirston . . 117 E7
East Tilbury . . . 29 B7
East Tisted 26 F5
East Torrington . 90 F5
East Tuddenham . 68 C3
East Tytherley . . 14 B3
East Tytherton . . 24 B4
East Village . . . 10 D3
Eastville Bristol . 23 B8
Lincs 79 D7
East Wall 60 E5
East Walton . . . 67 C7
East Water 54 E3
East Wellow . . . 14 B4
East Wemyss . . 128 E5
East Whitburn . . 120 C2
Eastwick Herts . . 41 C7
Shetland 160 F5
East Williamston . 32 D1
East Winch 67 C6
East Winterslow . 25 F7
East Wittering . . 15 E8
East Witton . . . 101 F6
Eastwood Notts . 76 E4
Southend . . . 42 F4
W Yorks 87 B7
East Woodburn . 116 F5
East Woodhay . . 26 C2
East Worldham . 26 F5
East Worlington . 10 C2
East Worthing . . 17 D5
Eathorpe 51 C8
Eaton Ches E . . 75 C5
Ches W 73 B8
Leics 64 B4
Norf 68 D5
Notts 77 B7
Oxon 38 D4
Shrops 60 E5
Shrops 60 F5
Eaton Bishop . . 49 F6
Eaton Bray . . . 40 B2
Eaton Constantine 61 D5
Eaton Green . . . 40 B2
Eaton Hastings . 38 E2
Eaton on Tern . . 61 B6
Eaton Socon . . 54 D2
Eavestone 94 C5
Ebberston 103 F6
Ebbesbourne
Wake 13 B7
Ebbw Vale
= Glyn Ebwy . . 35 D5
Ebchester 110 D4
Ebford 10 F4
Ebley 37 D5
Ebnal 73 E8
Ebrington 51 E6
Ecchinswell . . . 26 D2
Ecclaw 122 C3
Ecclefechan . . . 107 B8
Eccles Borders . . 122 E3
Gtr Man 87 E5
Kent 29 C8
Ecclesall 88 F4
Ecclesfield 88 E4
Ecclesgreig . . . 135 C7
Eccleshall 62 B2
Eccleshill 94 F4
Ecclesmachan . . 120 B3
Eccles on Sea . . 69 B7
Eccles Road . . . 68 E3
Eccleston Ches W 73 C8
Lancs 86 C3
Mers 86 E2
Eccleston Park . . 86 E2
Eccup 95 E5
Echt 141 D6
Eckford 116 B3
Eckington Derbys 76 B4
Worcs 50 E4
Ecton 53 C6
Edale 88 F2
Edburton 17 C6
Edderside 107 E7
Edderton 151 C10
Eddistone 8 B4
Eddleston 120 E5
Edenbridge . . . 28 E5
Edenfield 87 C5
Edenhall 109 F5
Edenham 65 B7
Eden Park 28 C4
Edensor 76 C2
Edentaggart . . . 126 E2
Edenthorpe . . . 89 D7
Edern 70 D3
Ederline 124 E4
Edgarley 23 F7

Edgbaston 62 F4
Edgcott Bucks . . 39 B6
Som 21 F7
Edge 60 D3
Edgebolton . . . 61 B5
Edge End 36 C2
Edgefield 81 D6
Edgefield Street . 81 D6
Edge Green . . . 73 D8
Edge Hill 85 F4
Edgeside 87 B6
Edgeworth 37 D6
Edgmond 61 C7
Edgmond Marsh . 61 B7
Edgton 60 F3
Edgware 40 E4
Edgworth 86 C5
Edinample 126 B4
Edinbane 149 C8
Edinburgh 121 B5
Edingale 63 C6
Edingight House 152 C5
Edingley 77 D6
Edingthorpe . . . 69 A6
Edingthorpe
Green 69 A6
Edington Som . . 23 F5
Wilts 24 D4
Edintore 152 D4
Edithmead 22 E5
Edith Weston . . 65 D6
Edlesborough . . 40 C2
Edlingham 117 D7
Edlington 78 B5
Edmondsham . . 13 C8
Edmondsley . . . 110 E5
Edmondthorpe . 65 C5
Edmonstone . . 159 F6
Edmonton 41 E6
Edmundbyers . . 110 D3
Ednam 122 F3
Ednaston 76 E2
Edradynate . . . 133 D5
Edrom 122 D4
Edstaston 74 F2
Edstone 51 C6
Edvin Loach . . . 49 D8
Edwalton 77 F5
Edwardstone . . 56 E3
Edwinsford . . . 46 F5
Edwinstowe . . . 77 C6
Edworth 54 E3
Edwyn Ralph . . 49 D8
Edzell 135 C5
Efail Isaf 34 F4
Efailnewydd . . . 70 D4
Efailwen 32 B2
Efenechtyd . . . 72 D5
Effingham 28 D2
Effirth 160 H5
Efford 10 D3
Egdon 50 D4
Egerton Gtr Man 86 C5
Kent 30 E3
Egerton Forstal . 30 E2
Eggborough . . . 89 B6
Eggbuckland . . . 6 D3
Eggington 40 B2
Egginton 63 B6
Egglescliffe . . . 102 C2
Eggleston 100 B4
Egham 27 B8
Egleton 65 D5
Eglingham 117 C7
Egloshayle 4 B5
Egloskerry 8 F4
Eglwys-Brewis . . 22 C2
Eglwys Cross . . 73 E8
Eglwys Fach . . . 58 E3
Eglwyswen 45 F3
Eglwyswrw . . . 45 F3
Egmanton 77 C7
Egremont Cumb . 98 C2
Mers 85 E4
Egton 103 D6
Egton Bridge . . 103 D6
Eight Ash Green . 43 B5
Eignaig 130 E1
Eil 138 C4
Eilanreach 149 G13
Eileanach Lodge 151 E8
Eilean Darach . . 150 C4
Einacleite 154 E6
Eisgean 155 F8
Eisingrug 71 D7
Elan Village . . . 47 C8
Elberton 36 F3
Elburton 6 D3
Elcho 128 B3
Elcombe 37 F8
Eldernell 66 E3
Eldersfield 50 F3
Eldersli 118 C4
Eldon 101 B7
Eldroth 93 C7
Eldwick 94 E4
Elfhowe 99 E6
Elford Northumb 123 F7
Staffs 63 C5
Elgin 152 B2
Elgol 149 G10
Elham 31 E5
Elie 129 D6
Elim 82 C3
Eling 14 C4
Elishader 149 B10
Elishaw 116 E4
Elkesley 77 B6
Elkstone 37 C6
Ellan 138 B4
Elland 88 B2
Ellary 144 F6
Ellastone 75 E8
Ellemford 122 C3
Ellenbrook . . . 86 D5
Ellenhall 62 B2
Ellen's Green . . 27 F8
Ellerbeck 102 E2
Ellerburn 103 F6
Ellerby 103 C6
Ellerdine Heath . 61 B6
Elleric 130 E4
Ellerker 90 B3
Ellerton E Yorks . 96 F3
Shrops 61 B7

Ellesborough . . . 39 D8
Ellesmere 73 F8
Ellesmere Port . . 73 B8
Ellingham Norf . . 69 E6
Northumb . . . 117 B7
Ellingstring . . . 101 F6
Ellington Cambs . 54 B2
Northumb . . . 117 E8
Elliot 135 F6
Ellisfield 26 E4
Ellistown 63 C8
Ellon 153 E9
Ellonby 108 F4
Ellough 69 F7
Elloughton 90 B3
Ellwood 36 D2
Elm 66 D4
Elmbridge 50 C4
Elmdon Essex . . 55 F5
W Mid 63 F5
Elmdon Heath . . 63 F5
Elmers End . . . 28 C4
Elmesthorpe . . . 63 E8
Elmfield 15 E7
Elm Hill 13 B6
Elmhurst 62 C5
Elmley Castle . . 50 E4
Elmley Lovett . . 50 C3
Elmore 36 C4
Elmore Back . . . 36 C4
Elm Park 41 F8
Elmscott 8 B4
Elmsett 56 E4
Elmstead Market 43 B6
Elmsted 30 E5
Elmstone 31 C6
Elmstone
Hardwicke . . . 37 B6
Elmswell E Yorks . 97 D5
Suff 56 C3
Elmton 76 B5
Elphin 156 H5
Elphinstone . . . 121 B6
Elrick 141 D7
Elrig 105 E7
Elsdon 117 E5
Elsecar 88 E4
Elsenham 41 B8
Elsfield 39 C5
Elsham 90 C4
Elsing 68 C3
Elslack 94 E2
Elson 73 F7
Elsrickle 120 E3
Elstead 27 E7
Elsted 16 C2
Elsthorpe 65 B7
Elstob 101 B8
Elston Notts . . . 77 E7
Wilts 25 E5
Elstone 9 C8
Elstow 53 E8
Elstree 40 E4
Elstronwick . . . 97 F8
Elswick 92 F4
Elsworth 54 C4
Elterwater 99 D5
Eltham 28 B5
Eltisley 54 D3
Elton Cambs . . . 65 E7
Ches W 73 B8
Derbys 76 C2
Glos 36 C4
Hereford 49 B6
Notts 77 F7
Stockton 102 C2
Elton Green . . . 73 B8
Elvanfoot 114 C2
Elvaston 76 F4
Elveden 56 B2
Elvingston 121 B7
Elvington Kent . . 31 D6
York 96 E2
Elwick Hrtlpl . . . 111 F7
Northumb . . . 123 F7
Elworth 74 C4
Elworthy 22 F2
Ely Cambs 66 F5
Cardiff 22 B3
Emberton 53 E6
Embleton Cumb . 107 F8
Northumb . . . 117 B8
Embo 151 B11
Emborough . . . 23 D8
Embo Street . . . 151 B11
Embsay 94 D3
Emersons Green . 23 B8
Emery Down . . . 14 D3
Emley 88 C3
Emmbrook 27 C5
Emmer Green . . 26 B5
Emmington . . . 39 D7
Emneth 66 D4
Emneth Hungate 66 D5
Empingham . . . 65 D6
Empshott 27 F5
Emstrey 60 C5
Emsworth 15 D8
Enborne 26 C2
Enchmarsh . . . 60 E5
Enderby 64 E2
Endmoor 99 F7
Endon 75 D6
Endon Bank . . . 75 D6
Enfield 41 E6
Enfield Wash . . 41 E6
Enford 25 D6
Engamoor 160 H4
Engine Common . 36 F3
Englefield 26 B4
Englefield Green . 27 B7
Englesea-brook . 74 D4
English Bicknor . 36 C2
English Frankton 60 B4
Enham Alamein . 25 E8
Enmore 22 F4
Ennerdale Bridge 98 C2
Enoch 113 D8
Enochdhu 133 C7
Ensay 146 G6
Ensbury 13 E8
Ensdon 60 C4
Ensis 9 B7
Enstone 38 B3
Enterkinfoot . . . 113 D8
Enterpen 102 D2
Enville 62 F2
Eolaigearraidh . 148 H2

Eorabus 146 J6
Eòropaidh 155 A10
Epperstone . . . 77 E6
Epping 41 D7
Epping Green
Essex 41 D7
Herts 41 D5
Epping Upland . . 41 D7
Eppleby 101 C6
Eppleworth . . . 97 F6
Epsom 28 C3
Epwell 51 E8
Epworth 89 D8
Epworth Turbary 89 D8
Erbistock 73 E7
Erbusaig 149 F12
Erchless Castle . 150 G7
Erdington 62 E5
Eredine 125 E5
Eriboll 156 D7
Ericstane 114 C3
Eridge Green . . 18 B2
Erines 145 F7
Eriswell 55 B8
Erith 29 B6
Erlestoke 24 D4
Ermine 78 B2
Ermington 6 D4
Erpingham 81 D7
Errogie 137 B8
Errol 128 B4
Erskine 118 B4
Erskine Bridg . . 118 B4
Ervie 104 C4
Erwarton 57 F6
Erwood 48 E2
Eryholme 101 D8
Eryrys 73 D6
Escomb 101 B6
Escrick 96 E2
Esgairdawe . . . 46 E5
Esgairgeiliog . . 58 D4
Esh 110 E4
Esher 28 C2
Esholt 94 E4
Eshott 117 E8
Eshton 94 D2
Esh Winning . . . 110 E4
Eskadale 150 H7
Eskbank 121 C6
Eskdale Green . . 98 D3
Eskdalemuir . . . 115 E5
Eske 97 E6
Eskham 91 E7
Esk Valley 103 D6
Esprick 92 F4
Essendine 65 C7
Essendon 41 D5
Essich 151 H9
Essington 62 D3
Esslemont 141 B8
Eston 102 C3
Eswick 160 H6
Etal 122 F5
Etchilhampton . . 24 C5
Etchingham . . . 18 C4
Etchinghill Kent . 19 B8
Staffs 62 C4
Ethie Castle . . . 135 E6
Ethie Mains . . . 135 E6
Etling Green . . . 68 C3
Eton 27 B7
Eton Wick 27 B7
Etteridge 138 E2
Ettersgill 100 B3
Ettington 51 E7
Etton E Yorks . . 97 E5
Pboro 65 D8
Ettrick 115 C5
Ettrickbridge . . 115 B6
Ettrickhill 115 C5
Etwall 76 F2
Euston 56 B2
Euximoor Drove 66 E4
Euxton 86 C3
Evanstown 34 F3
Evanton 151 E9
Evedon 78 E3
Evelix 151 B10
Evenjobb 48 C4
Evenley 52 F3
Evenlode 38 B2
Evenwood 101 B6
Evenwood Gate . 101 B6
Everbay 159 F7
Evercreech . . . 23 F8
Everdon 52 D3
Everingham . . . 96 E4
Everleigh 25 D7
Everley 103 F7
Eversholt 53 F7
Evershot 12 D3
Eversley 27 C5
Eversley Cross . . 27 C5
Everthorpe . . . 96 F5
Everton C Beds . 54 D3
Hants 14 E3
Mers 85 E4
Notts 89 E7
Evertown 108 B3
Evesbatch 49 E8
Evesham 50 E5
Evington 64 D3
Ewden Village . . 88 E3
Ewell 28 C3
Ewell Minnis . . 31 E6
Ewelme 39 E6
Ewen 37 E7
Ewenny 21 B8
Ewerby 78 E4
Ewerby Thorpe . 78 E4
Ewes 115 E6
Ewesley 117 E6
Ewhurst 27 E8
Ewhurst Green
E Sus 18 C4
Sur 27 F8
Ewloe 73 C7
Ewloe Green . . . 73 C6
Ewood 86 B4
Eworthy 9 E6
Ewshot 27 E6
Ewyas Harold . . 35 B7
Exbourne 9 D8
Exbury 14 E5
Exebridge 10 B4
Exelby 101 F7
Exeter 10 E4

Exford 21 F7
Exhall. 51 D6
Exley Head 94 F3
Exminster 10 F4
Exmouth 10 F5
Exnaboe 160 M5
Exning 55 C7
Exton Devon 10 F4
  Hants. 15 B7
  Rutland 65 C6
  Som 21 F8
Exwick 10 E4
Eyam 76 B2
Eydon. 52 D3
Eye Hereford 49 C6
  Pboro. 66 D2
  Suff 56 B5
Eye Green. 66 D2
Eyemouth. 122 C5
Eyeworth 54 E3
Eyhorne Street . . . 30 D2
Eyke 57 D7
Eynesbury 54 D2
Eynort 149 F8
Eynsford 29 C6
Eynsham 38 D4
Eype. 12 E2
Eyre Highld. 149 C9
  Highld 149 E10
Eythorne. 31 E6
Eyton Hereford . . . 49 C6
  Shrops. 60 F3
  Wrex. 73 E7
Eyton upon the Weald
  Moors 61 C6

F

Faceby. 102 D2
Facit 87 C6
Faddiley 74 D2
Fadmoor 102 F4
Faerdre 33 D7
Failand 23 B7
Failford 112 B4
Failsworth 87 D6
Fain 150 D4
Fairbourne. 58 C3
Fairburn 89 B5
Fairfield Derbys . . .75 B7
  Stockton 102 C2
  Worcs 50 B5
  Worcs. 50 E5
Fairford. 38 D1
Fair Green 67 C6
Fairhaven. 85 B4
Fair Hill 108 F5
Fairlie 118 D2
Fairlight 19 D5
Fairlight Cove . . . 19 D5
Fairmile 11 E5
Fairmilehead 120 C5
Fair Oak 15 C5
Fair Oak Green . . 26 C4
Fairseat. 29 C7
Fairstead Essex . . 42 C3
  Norf. 67 C6
Fairwarp 17 B8
Fairy Cottage 84 D4
Fairy Cross. 9 B6
Fakenham 80 E5
Fakenham Magna . 56 B3
Fala 121 C7
Fala Dam 121 C7
Falahill 121 D6
Falcon 49 F8
Faldingworth 90 F4
Falfield 36 E3
Falkenham 57 F6
Falkirk 119 B8
Falkland 128 D4
Falla 116 C3
Fallgate 76 C3
Fallin 127 E7
Fallowfield 87 E6
Fallsidehill 122 E2
Falmer 17 D7
Falmouth 3 C7
Falsgrave 103 F8
Falstone 116 F3
Fanagmore 156 E4
Fangdale Beck . . .102 E3
Fangfoss 96 D3
Fankerton 127 F6
Fanmore 146 G7
Fannich Lodge . . .150 E5
Fans 122 E2
Far Bank. 89 C7
Far Bletchley 53 F6
Farcet 66 E2
Far Cotton 52 D5
Farden 49 B7
Fareham 15 D6
Farewell 62 C4
Far Forest 50 B2
Farforth 79 B6
Faringdon 38 E2
Farington 86 B3
Farlam. 109 D5
Farlary. 157 J10
Far Laund 76 E3
Farleigh N Som . . .23 C6
  Sur. 28 C4
Farleigh
  Hungerford. . . . 24 D3
Farleigh Wallop . . 26 E4
Farlesthorpe 79 B7
Farleton Cumb . . .99 F7
  Lancs. 93 C5
Farley Shrops 60 D3
  Staffs. 75 E7
  Wilts 14 B3
Farley Green 27 E8
Farley Hill Luton . 40 B3
  Wokingham 26 C5
Farleys End 36 C4
Farlington 96 C2
Farlow 61 F6
Farmborough . . . 23 C8
Farmcote Glos . . .37 B7
  Shrops. 61 F7
Farmington 37 C8
Farmoor 38 D4
Farmtown 152 C5
Farnborough Hants 27 D6
  London. 28 C5
  Warks 52 E2

Farnborough continued
  W Berks. 38 F4
Farnborough
  Green 27 D6
Farncombe 27 E7
Farndish 53 C7
Farndon Ches W . . 73 D8
  Notts 77 D7
Farnell. 135 D6
Farnham Dorset . . 13 C7
  Essex 41 B7
  N Yorks 95 C6
  Suff 57 C7
  Sur. 27 E6
Farnham Common 40 F2
Farnham Green . . 41 B7
Farnham Royal . . 40 F2
Farnhill 94 E3
Farningham 29 C6
Farnley N Yorks . . .94 E5
  W Yorks 95 F5
Farnley Tyas 88 C2
Farnsfield. 77 D6
Farnworth Gtr Man .86 D5
  Halton 86 F3
Farr Highld. 138 D4
  Highld 151 H9
  Highld 157 C10
Farr House 151 H9
Farringdon 10 E5
Farrington Gurney. 23 D8
Far Sawrey 99 E5
Farsley 94 F5
Farthing 52 F3
Farthinghoe 31 E6
Farthingstone . . . 52 D4
Fartown 88 C2
Farway 11 E6
Fasag 149 C13
Fascadale. 147 D8
Faslane Port 145 E11
Fasnacloich 130 E4
Fasnakyle Ho. . . .137 B6
Fassfern 130 B4
Fatfield 111 D6
Fattahead 153 C6
Faugh 108 D5
Fauldhouse 120 C2
Faulkbourne 42 C3
Faulkland 24 D2
Fauls 74 F2
Faversham 30 C4
Favillar 152 E2
Fawdington 95 B7
Fawfieldhead . . . 75 C7
Fawkham Green . 29 C6
Fawler 38 C3
Fawley Bucks 39 F7
  Hants. 15 D5
  W Berks. 38 F3
Fawley Chapel . . 36 B2
Faxfleet 90 B2
Faygate 28 F3
Fazakerley 85 E4
Fazeley 63 D6
Fearby 101 F6
Fearn 151 D11
Fearnan 132 E4
Fearnbeg 149 C12
Fearn Lodge 151 C9
Fearnmore 149 B12
Fearn Station . . .151 D11
Featherstone Staffs 62 D3
  W Yorks 88 B5
Featherwood. . . .116 D4
Feckenham 50 C5
Feering 42 B4
Feetham 100 E4
Feizor 93 C7
Felbridge 28 F4
Felbrigg 81 D8
Felcourt 28 E4
Felden 40 D3
Felin-Crai 34 B2
Felindre Carms. . . 33 B8
  Carms 33 B8
  Carms 46 F2
  Carms 47 F5
  Ceredig. 46 D4
  Powys 59 D8
  Powys 48 F2
  Swansea 33 D7
Felindre Farchog . 45 F3
Felinfach Ceredig. 46 D4
  Powys 48 F2
Felinfoel 33 D6
Felingwmisaf . . . 33 B6
Felingwmuchaf . . 33 B6
Felinwynt 45 D4
Felixkirk 102 F2
Felixstowe 57 F6
Felixstowe Ferry . 57 F7
Felkington 122 E5
Felkirk. 88 C4
Felling 111 C5
Fell Side 108 F3
Felmersham 53 D7
Felmingham 81 E8
Felpham 16 E3
Felsham 56 D3
Felsted 42 B2
Feltham 28 B2
Felthorpe 68 C4
Felton Hereford . . 49 E7
  Northumb 117 D7
  N Som 23 C7
Felton Butler 60 C3
Feltwell 67 E7
Fenay Bridge . . . 88 C2
Fence 93 F8
Fence Houses . . .111 D6
Fen Ditton 55 C5
Fen Drayton 54 C4
Fen End. 51 B7
Fengate Norf 81 E7
  Pboro. 66 E2
Fenham 123 E6
Fenhouses 79 E5
Feniscliffe 86 B4
Feniscowles 86 B4
Feniton 11 E6
Fenlake 53 E8
Fenny Bentley . . . 75 D8
Fenny Bridges . . . 11 E6
Fenny Compton . . 52 D2
Fenny Drayton . . 63 E7
Fenny Stratford . . 53 F6
Fenrother 117 E7
Fen Side 79 D6

Fenstanton 54 C4
Fenton Cambs . . . 54 B4
  Lincs 77 B8
  Lincs 77 D8
  Stoke 75 E5
Fenton Barns . . .129 F7
Fenton Town . . . 123 F5
Fenwick E Ayrs . .118 E4
  Northumb 110 B3
  Northumb 123 E6
  S Yorks 89 C6
Feochaig 143 G8
Feock. 3 C7
Feolin Ferry 144 G3
Ferindonald. 149 H11
Feriniquarrie 148 C6
Ferlochan 130 E3
Fern 134 C4
Ferndale. 34 E4
Ferndown 13 D8
Ferness 151 G12
Ferney Green . . . 99 E6
Fernham 38 E2
Fernhill Heath . . . 50 D3
Fernhurst 16 B2
Fernie 128 C5
Ferniegair 119 D7
Fernilea 149 E8
Fernilee 75 B7
Fernsby 95 C6
Ferrensby 95 C6
Ferrybridge 89 B5
Ferryden 135 D7
Ferryhill Aberdeen 141 D8
  Durham 111 F5
Ferry Hill Station .111 F6
Ferry Point. 151 C10
Ferryside 32 C4
Fersfield 68 F3
Fersit 131 B7
Ferwig 45 E3
Feshiebridge . . . 138 D4
Fetcham 28 D2
Fetterangus 153 C9
Fettercairn 135 B6
Fettes 151 F11
Fewcott 39 B5
Fewston 94 D4
F Faccombe 25 D8
Ffairfach. 33 B7
Ffair-Rhos 47 C6
Ffaldybrenin 46 E5
Ffarmers 47 E5
Ffawyddog 35 C6
Fforest 33 D6
Fforest-fâch 33 E7
Ffostrasol 46 E2
Ffos-y-ffin 46 C3
Ffrith 73 D6
Ffrwd 82 F4
Ffynnon ddrain. . . 33 B5
Ffynnongroyw. . . 85 F2
Ffynnon-oer 46 D4
Fidden 146 J6
Fiddes 141 F7
Fiddington Glos . . 50 F4
  Som 22 E4
Fiddleford 13 C6
Fiddlers Hamlet . 41 D7
Field. 75 F7
Field Broughton . 99 F5
Field Dalling . . . 81 D6
Field Head 63 D8
Fifehead
  Magdalen 13 B5
Fifehead Neville . .13 C5
Fifield Oxon 38 C2
  Wilts 25 D6
  Windsor. 27 B7
Fifield Bavant . . . 13 B8
Figheldean. 25 E6
Filands 37 F6
Filby 69 C7
Filey 97 A7
Filgrave 53 E6
Filkins 38 D2
Filleigh Devon 9 B8
  Devon 10 C2
Fillingham 90 F3
Fillongley 63 F6
Filton 23 B8
Fimber. 96 C4
Finavon 134 D4
Finchairn 124 E5
Fincham 67 D6
Finchampstead . . 27 C5
Finchdean 15 C8
Finchingfield. . . . 55 F7
Finchley 41 E5
Findern 76 F3
Findhorn 151 E13
Findhorn Bridge . 138 B4
Findochty 152 B4
Findo Gask. 128 B2
Findon Aberds . . 141 E8
  W Sus 16 D5
Findon Mains . . .151 E9
Findrack House . .140 D5
Finedon. 53 B7
Fingal Street . . . 57 C6
Fingask 141 B6
Fingerpost 50 B2
Fingest 39 E7
Finghall. 101 F6
Fingland Cumb . . 108 D2
  Dumfries 113 C7
Finglesham 31 D7
Fingringhoe 43 B6
Finlarig 132 F2
Finmere 52 F4
Finnart 132 D2
Finningham 56 C4
Finningley 89 E7
Finnygaud 152 C5
Finsbury 41 F6
Finstall. 50 C4
Finsthwaite 99 F5
Finstock 38 C3
Finstown 159 G4
Fintry Aberds 153 C7
  Dundee 134 F4
  Stirling. 126 F5
Finzean 140 E5
Fionnphort. 146 J6
Fionnsbhagh. . . .154 J5
Firbeck 89 F6
Firby N Yorks 96 C3

Firby continued
  N Yorks. 101 F7
Firgrove 87 C7
Firsby. 79 C7
Firsdown 25 F7
First Coast 150 B2
Fir Tree 110 F4
Fishbourne IoW . . 15 E6
  W Sus 16 D2
Fishburn 111 F6
Fishcross 127 E7
Fisherford 153 E6
Fisher Place 99 C5
Fisher's Pond . . . 15 B5
Fisherstreet 27 F7
Fisherton Highld .151 F10
  S Ayrs. 112 C2
Fishguard
  = Abergwaun . . 44 B4
Fishlake 89 C7
Fishleigh Barton . .9 B7
Fishpond 36 B3
Fishponds 23 B8
Fishpool 36 B2
Fishtoft 79 E6
Fishtoft Drove . . 79 E6
Fishwick 122 D5
Fiskavaig 149 E8
Fiskerton Lincs . . .78 B3
  Notts 77 D7
Fitling 97 F8
Fittleton 25 E6
Fittleworth 16 C4
Fitton End 66 C4
Fitz. 60 C4
Fitzhead 11 B6
Fitzwilliam 88 C5
Fiunary 147 G9
Five Acres 36 C2
Five Ashes 18 C2
Fivecrosses 74 B2
Fivehead. 11 B8
Five Oak Green . 29 E7
Five Oaks Jersey . . .17
  W Sus 16 B4
Five Roads 33 D5
Flack's Green . . . 42 C3
Flackwell Heath . 40 F1
Fladbury 50 E4
Fladdabister . . . 160 K6
Flagg 75 C8
Flamborough . . . 97 B8
Flamstead 40 C3
Flamstead End . . 41 D6
Flansham 16 D3
Flanshaw 88 B4
Flasby 94 D2
Flash 75 C7
Flashader 149 C8
Flask Inn 103 D7
Flaunden 40 D3
Flawborough . . . 77 E7
Flawith 95 C7
Flax Bourton . . . 23 C7
Flaxby 95 D6
Flaxholme 76 E3
Flaxley 36 C3
Flaxpool 22 F3
Flaxton 96 C2
Fleckney 64 E3
Flecknoe. 52 C3
Fledborough 77 B8
Fleet Hants 15 D8
  Hants 27 D6
  Lincs 66 B3
Fleetham 117 B7
Fleet Hargate . . . 66 B3
Fleetlands 15 D6
Fleetville 40 D4
Fleetwood 92 E3
Flemingston 22 B2
Flemington 119 D6
Flempton 56 C2
Fleoideabhagh . . 154 J5
Fletchertown . . .108 E2
Fletching 17 B8
Flexbury 8 D4
Flexford 27 E7
Flimby 107 F7
Flimwell 18 B4
Flint = Y Fflint. . .73 B6
Flint Mountain . . 73 B6
Flinton. 97 F8
Flintsham 48 D5
Flitcham 80 E3
Flitton 53 F8
Flitwick 53 F8
Flixborough 90 C2
Flixborough
  Stather 90 C2
Flixton Gtr Man . . .86 E5
  N Yorks. 97 B6
  Suff 69 F6
Flockton 88 C3
Flodaigh 148 C3
Flodden 122 F5
Flodigarry 149 A9
Flood's Ferry . . . 66 E3
Flookburgh 92 B3
Florden 68 E4
Flore 52 C4
Flotterton 117 D5
Flowton. 56 E4
Flush House 88 D2
Flushing Aberds . 153 D10
  Corn. 3 C7
Flyford Flavell . . . 50 D4
Foals Green 57 B6
Fobbing 42 F3
Fochabers 152 C3
Fochriw. 35 D5
Fockerby. 90 C2
Foddersoe . . . . . . —
Fodderletter . . . 139 B7
Foel 59 C6
Foel-gastell. 33 C6
Foffarty. 134 E4
Foggathorpe . . . 96 F3
Fogo 122 E3
Fogorig 122 E3
Foindle 156 E4
Fole 75 F7
Foleshill 63 F7
Folke. 12 C4
Folkestone 31 F6
Folkingham 78 F3
Folkington 18 E2

Folksworth. 65 F8
Folkton 97 B6
Folla Rule. 153 E7
Follifoot 95 D6
Folly Gate 9 E7
Fonthill Bishop . . 24 F4
Fonthill Gifford. . 24 F4
Fontmell Magna . 13 C6
Fontwell 16 D3
Foolow 75 B8
Foots Cray 29 B5
Forbestown 140 C2
Force Mills. 99 E5
Forcett 101 C6
Ford Argyll 124 E4
  Bucks. 39 D7
  Devon 9 E7
  Glos 37 B7
  Northumb 122 F5
  Shrops. 60 C4
  Staffs. 75 D7
  Wilts 24 B3
  W Sus 16 D3
Fordcombe 29 E6
Fordell 128 F3
Forden 60 D2
Ford End 42 C2
Forder Green 7 C5
Fordham Cambs . .55 B7
  Essex 43 B5
  Norf. 67 E6
Fordhouses 62 D3
Fordingbridge . . 14 C2
Fordon 97 B6
Fordoun 135 B7
Ford's Green . . . 56 C4
Fordstreet 43 B5
Ford Street 11 C6
Fordwells 38 C3
Fordwich 31 D5
Fordyce 152 B5
Forebridge 62 B3
Forest 109 F8
Forest Becks . . . 93 D7
Forestburn Gate . 117 E6
Foresterseat 152 C2
Forest Gate 41 F7
Forest Green . . . 28 E2
Forest Hall 99 D7
Forest Head 109 D5
Forest Hill 39 D5
Forest Lane Head . 95 D6
Forest Lodge
  Argyll 131 E6
  Highld 139 C6
  Perth 133 B6
Forest Mill 127 E8
Forest Row 28 F5
Forestside 15 C8
Forest Town 77 C5
Forfar 134 D4
Forgandenny . . .128 C2
Forge 58 E4
Forge Side 35 D6
Forgewood 119 D7
Forgie 152 C3
Forglen House . .153 C6
Formby 85 D4
Forncett End . . . 68 E4
Forncett St Mary . 68 E4
Forncett St Peter . 68 E4
Forneth 133 E7
Fornham All
  Saints 56 C2
Fornham
  St Martin 56 C2
Forres 151 F13
Forrestfield 119 C8
Forrest Lodge . . .113 F5
Forsbrook 75 E6
Forse 158 G4
Forse House 158 G4
Forsinain 157 E12
Forsinard 157 E11
Forsinard
  Station 157 E11
Forston 12 E4
Fort Augustus . .137 D6
Forteviot. 128 C2
Fort George Guern . 17
  Highld 151 F10
Forth 120 D2
Forthampton . . . 50 F3
Forth Road
  Bridge. 120 B4
Fortingall 132 E4
Forton Hants. . . . 26 E2
  Lancs 92 D4
  Shrops. 60 C4
  Som 11 D8
  Staffs. 61 B7
Forton Heath . . . 60 C4
Fortrie. 153 D6
Fortrose 151 F10
Fortuneswell. . . . 12 G4
Fort William 131 B5
Forty Green 40 E2
Forty Hill 41 E6
Forward Green . . 56 D4
Fosbury 25 D8
Fosdyke 79 F6
Foss 132 D4
Foss Cross 37 D7
Fossebridge 37 C7
Fosterhouses . . . 89 C7
Foster Street . . . 41 D7
Foston Derbys . . .75 F8
  Lincs 77 E8
  N Yorks. 96 C2
Foston on the
  Wolds 97 D7
Fotherby 91 E7
Fotheringhay . . . 65 E7
Foubister 159 H6
Foul Anchor 66 C4
Foulden Borders . 122 D5
  Norf. 67 E7
Foulis Castle . . . 151 E8
Foul Mile 18 D3
Foulridge 93 E8
Foulsham 81 E6
Fountainhall 121 E7
Four Ashes Staffs . 62 F2
  Suff 56 B4
Four Crosses
  Powys 59 D7
  Powys 60 C2
  Wrex. 73 D6
Four Elms 29 E5

Four Forks 22 F4
Four Gotes 66 C4
Fourlane Ends . . 76 D3
Four Lane Ends . . 74 C2
Four Lanes 3 C5
Fourlanes End . . 74 C5
Four Marks 26 F4
Four Mile Bridge . 82 D2
Four Oaks E Sus . .19 C5
  W Mid 62 E5
  W Mid 63 F6
Fourpenny 151 B11
Four Roads Carms. 33 D5
  IoM 84 F2
Fourstones 109 C8
Four Throws 18 C4
Fovant 13 B8
Foveran 141 B8
Fowey 5 D6
Fowley Common . 86 E4
Fowlis 134 F3
Fowlis Wester . . 127 B8
Fowlmere 54 E5
Fownhope 49 F7
Foxbar 118 C4
Foxcombe Hill. . . 38 D4
Foxdale 84 E2
Foxearth 56 E2
Foxfield 98 F4
Foxham 24 B4
Foxhole Corn 4 D4
  Swansea 33 E7
Foxholes 97 B6
Foxhunt Green . . 18 D2
Fox Lane 27 D6
Foxley Norf 81 E6
  Wilts 37 F5
Fox Street. 43 B6
Foxt 75 E7
Foxton Cambs . . 54 E5
  Durham 102 B1
  Leics 64 F4
Foxup 93 B8
Foxwist Green . . 74 C3
Foxwood. 49 B8
Foy 36 B2
Foyers 137 B7
Fraddam 2 C4
Fraddon 4 D4
Fradley 63 C5
Fradswell 75 F6
Fraisthorpe 97 C7
Framfield 17 B8
Framingham Earl. . 69 D5
Framingham Pigot 69 D5
Framlingham . . . 57 C6
Frampton Dorset . 12 E4
  Lincs 79 F6
Frampton
  Cotterell 36 F3
Frampton Mansell . 37 D6
Frampton on
  Severn 36 D4
Frampton West
  End 79 E5
Framsden. 57 D5
Framwellgate
  Moor 111 E5
Franche 50 B3
Frankby. 85 F3
Frankley 62 F3
Frank's Bridge . . 48 D3
Frankton 52 B2
Frant 18 B2
Fraserburgh 153 B9
Frating Green . . . 43 B6
Fratton 15 E7
Freathy 5 D8
Freckenham 55 B7
Freckleton 86 B2
Freeby 64 B5
Freehay 75 E7
Freeland 38 C4
Freester 160 H6
Freethorpe. 69 D7
Freiston 79 E6
Fremington Devon . 20 F4
  N Yorks. 101 E5
Frenchbeer 9 F8
Frenich 126 D3
Frensham 27 E6
Fresgoe. 157 C12
Freshfield 85 D3
Freshford 24 C2
Freshwater 14 F4
Freshwater Bay . 14 F4
Freshwater East . 32 E1
Fressingfield . . . 57 B6
Freston 57 F5
Freswick 158 D5
Fretherne 36 C4
Frettenham 68 C5
Freuchie 128 D4
Freuchies 134 C2
Freystrop 44 D4
Friar's Gate 29 F5
Friarton 128 B3
Friday Bridge . . . 66 D4
Friday Street . . . 18 E3
Fridaythorpe . . . 96 D4
Friern Barnet . . . 41 E5
Friesland 146 F4
Friesthorpe 90 F4
Frieston 78 E2
Frieth 39 E7
Frilford 38 E4
Frilsham 26 B3
Frimley 27 D6
Frimley Green . . 27 D6
Frindsbury 29 B8
Fring 80 D3
Fringford 39 B6
Frinsted 30 D2
Frinton-on-Sea . . 43 B8
Friockheim 135 E5
Friog 58 C3
Frisby on the
  Wreake 64 C3
Friskney 79 D7
Friskney Eaudike . 79 D7
Friskney Tofts . . 79 D7
Friston E Sus 18 F2
  Suff 57 C8
Fritchley 76 D3
Fritham 14 C3
Frith Bank 79 E6
Frith Common . . 49 C8

Frithelstock 9 C6
Frithelstock Stone. 9 C6
Frithville 79 D6
Frittenden 30 E2
Frittiscombe 7 E6
Fritton Norf. 68 E5
  Norf. 69 D7
Fritwell 39 B5
Frizinghall 94 F4
Frizington 98 C2
Frocester 36 D4
Frodesley 60 D5
Frodingham 90 C2
Frodsham 74 B2
Frogden 116 B3
Froggatt 76 B2
Froghall 75 E7
Frogmore Devon . . 7 E5
  Hants. 27 D6
Frognall. 65 C8
Frogshail 81 D8
Frolesworth 64 E2
Frome 24 E2
Frome St Quintin . 12 D3
Fromes Hill 49 E8
Fron Denb 72 C4
  Gwyn 70 D4
  Gwyn 82 F5
  Powys 48 C2
  Powys 59 D8
  Powys 60 D2
Froncysyllte 73 E6
Frongoch 72 F3
Frostenden 69 F7
Frosterley 110 F3
Frotoft. 159 F5
Froxfield 25 C7
Froxfield Green . . 15 B8
Froyle 27 E5
Fryerning 42 D2
Fryton 96 B2
Fulbeck 78 D2
Fulbourn 55 D6
Fulbrook 38 C2
Fulford Som 11 B7
  York. 96 E2
Fulham 28 B3
Fulking 17 C6
Fullarton Glasgow . 119 C6
  N Ayrs 118 F3
Fuller's Moor . . . 73 D8
Fuller Street 42 C3
Fullerton 25 F8
Fulletby 79 B5
Full Sutton 96 D3
Fullwood 118 D4
Fulmer 40 F2
Fulmodestone . . 81 D5
Fulnetby 78 B3
Fulstow 91 E7
Fulwell 111 D6
Fulwood Lancs . . .92 F5
  S Yorks. 88 F4
Fundenhall 68 E4
Fundenhall Street . 68 E4
Funtington 15 D8
Funtley 15 D6
Funtullich 127 B6
Funzie 160 D8
Furley 11 D7
Furnace Argyll . . 125 E6
  Carms 33 D6
Furnace End 63 E6
Furneaux Pelham . 41 B7
Furness Vale . . . 87 F8
Furzehill 21 E6
Furze Platt 40 F1
Fyfett 11 C7
Fyfield Essex 42 D1
  Glos 38 D2
  Hants 25 E7
  Oxon 38 E4
  Wilts 25 C6
Fylingthorpe . . .103 D7
Fyvie 153 E7

G

Gabhsann bho
  Dheas 155 B9
Gabhsann bho
  Thuath 155 B9
Gablon. 151 B10
Gabroc Hill 118 D4
Gaddesby 64 C3
Gadebridge 40 D3
Gaer 35 B5
Gaerllwyd 35 E8
Gaerwen. 82 D4
Gagingwell 38 B4
Gaick Lodge . . . 138 F3
Gailey 62 C3
Gainford 101 C6
Gainsborough Lincs 90 E2
  Suff 57 E5
Gainsford End . . 55 F8
Gairloch 149 A13
Gairlochy 136 F4
Gairney Bank. . .128 E3
Gairnshiel Lodge .139 D8
Gaisgill 99 D8
Gaitsgill 108 E3
Galashiels 121 F7
Galgate 92 D4
Galhampton 12 B4
Gallaberry 114 F2
Gallachoille 144 E6
Gallanach Argyll. .124 C4
  Argyll 146 E5
Gallantry Bank . . 74 D2
Gallatown 128 E4
Galley Common . 63 E7
Galleyend 42 D3
Galleywood 42 D3
Gallin 132 E2
Gallowfauld 134 E4
Gallows Green . . 75 E7
Galltair 149 F13
Galmisdale. 146 C7
Galmpton Devon . .6 E4
  Torbay. 7 D6
Galphay. 95 B5
Galston 118 F5
Galtrigill 148 C6
Gamblesby 109 F6
Gamblesmore . . 87 D8
Gamelsley 87 E8
Gamlingay 54 D3
Gammersgill 101 F5
Gamston 77 B7
Ganarew 36 C2
Ganavan 124 B4
Gang 5 C8
Ganllwyd 71 E8
Gannochy Angus .135 B5
  Perth 128 B3
Ganstead 97 F7
Ganthorpe 96 B2
Ganton 97 B5
Garbat 150 E7
Garbhallt 125 F6
Garboldisham . . . 68 F3
Garden City 73 C7
Gardenstown . . .153 B7
Garden Village
  Wrex 73 D7
  W Yorks 95 F7
Garderhouse . . .160 J5
Gardham. 97 E5
Gardin 160 G6
Gare Hill 24 E2
Garelochhead . . 145 D11
Garford 38 E4
Garforth 95 F7
Gargrave 94 D2
Gargunnock 127 E6
Garlic Street . . . 68 F5
Garlieston 105 E8
Garlinge Green . . 30 D5
Garlogie 141 D6
Garmond 153 C8
Garmony 147 G9
Garmouth 152 B3
Garn-Dolbenmaen . 71 C5
Garnant. 33 C7
Garndiffaith. . . . 35 D6
Garndolbenmaen . 71 C5
Garnedd 83 F7
Garnett Bridge . . 99 E7
Garnfadryn 70 D3
Garnkirk 119 C6
Garnlydan 35 C5
Garnswllt 33 D7
Garn-yr-erw 35 C6
Garrabost 155 D10
Garraron 124 E4
Garras 3 D6
Garreg 71 C7
Garrick 127 C7
Garrigill 109 E7
Garriston 101 E6
Garroch. 113 F8
Garrogie Lodge . 137 C8
Garros 149 B9
Garrow 133 E5
Garryhorn 113 E5
Garsdale 100 F2
Garsdale Head . . 100 E2
Garsdon 37 F6
Garshall Green . . 75 F6
Garsington 39 D5
Garstang 92 E4
Garston 86 F2
Garswood 86 E3
Gartcosh 119 C6
Garth Bridgend . . 34 E2
  Gwyn 83 D5
  Powys 47 E8
  Shetland 160 H4
  Wrex. 73 E6
Garthamlock . . .119 C6
Garthbrengy . . . 48 F2
Garthdee 141 D8
Gartheli. 46 D4
Garthmyl 59 E8
Garthorpe Leics . .64 B5
  N Lincs 90 C2
Garth Row 99 E7
Gartly 152 E5
Gartmore 126 E4
Gartnagrenach . .144 H6
Gartness N Lanark .119 C7
  Stirling. 126 F4
Gartocharn 126 F3
Garton 97 F8
Garton-on-the-
  Wolds 97 D5
Gartsherrie 119 C6
Gartymore 157 H13
Garvald 121 B8
Garvamore 137 E8
Garvard 144 D2
Garvault Hotel . . 157 F10
Garve 150 E6
Garvestone 68 D3
Garvock Aberds . .135 B7
  Inclyd. 118 B2
Garway 36 B1
Garway Hill 35 B8
Gaskan 130 B1
Gastard 24 C3
Gasthorpe 68 F2
Gatcombe 15 F5
Gateacre 86 F2
Gatebeck 99 F7
Gate Burton 90 F2
Gateford 89 F6
Gateforth 95 F6
Gatehead 118 F3
Gate Helmsley . . 96 D2
Gatehouse 116 F3
Gatehouse of
  Fleet 106 D3
Gatelawbridge . .114 E2
Gateley 81 E5
Gatenby 101 F8
Gateshead 111 C5
Gatesheath 73 C8
Gateside Aberds . .153 A9
  Angus 134 E4
  E Renf 118 D4
  Fife 128 D3
  N Ayrs 118 D3
Gathurst 86 D3
Gatley 87 F6
Gattonside 121 F8
Gatwick Airport . 28 E3
Gaufron 47 C8
Gaulby 64 D3
Gauldry 129 B5
Gaunt's Common . 13 D8
Gautby 78 B4
Gavinton 122 D3
Gawber 88 D4
Gawcott 52 F4
Gawsworth 75 C5

Gawthorpe. 88 B3
Gawthrop 100 F1
Gawthwaite 98 F4
Gaydon 51 D8
Gayfield 159 C5
Gayhurst 53 E6
Gayle 100 F3
Gayles 101 D6
Gayton Mers 85 F3
  Norf. 67 C7
  Northants 52 D5
  Staffs. 62 B3
Gayton le Marsh. .91 F8
Gayton le Wold . . 91 F6
Gayton Thorpe . . 67 C7
Gaywood 67 B6
Gazeley 55 C8
Geanies House . .151 D11
Gearraidh
  Bhailteas 148 F2
Gearraidh Bhaird. 155 E8
Gearraidh na h-
  Aibhne 154 D7
Gearraidh na
  Monadh 148 G2
Geary 148 B7
Geddes House . .151 F11
Gedding 56 D3
Geddington 65 F5
Gedintailor 149 E10
Gedling 77 E6
Gedney 66 B4
Gedney Broadgate. 66 B4
Gedney Drove End. 66 B4
Gedney Dyke . . . 66 B4
Gedney Hill 66 C3
Gee Cross 87 E7
Geilston 118 B3
Geirinis 148 D2
Geise 158 D3
Geisiadar 154 D6
Geldeston 69 E6
Gell. 83 E8
Gelli Pembs 32 C1
  Rhondda 34 E3
Gellideg 34 D4
Gellifor 72 C5
Gelligaer. 35 E5
Gellilydan 71 D7
Gellinudd 33 D8
Gellyburn 133 F7
Gellywen. 32 B3
Gelston Dumfries .106 D4
  Lincs 78 E2
Gembling 97 D7
Gentleshaw 62 C4
Geocrab 154 H6
Georgefield 115 E5
George Green . . . 40 F3
Georgeham 20 F3
George Nympton . 10 B2
Georgetown . . . 35 D5
Gerlan 83 E6
Germansweek 9 E6
Germoe 2 D4
Gerrans 3 C7
Gerrards Cross . . 40 F3
Gestingthorpe . . 56 F2
Geuffordd. 60 C2
Gibbet Hill 64 F2
Gibbshill 106 B4
Gib Hill 74 B3
Gidea Park 41 F8
Gidleigh 9 F8
Giffnock 119 D5
Gifford 121 C8
Giffordland 118 E2
Giffordtown 128 C4
Giggleswick 93 C8
Gilberdyke 90 B2
Gilchriston 121 C7
Gilcrux 107 F8
Gildersome 88 B3
Gildingwells 89 F6
Gileston 22 C2
Gilfach. 35 E5
Gilfach Goch . . . 34 F3
Gilfachrheda . . . 46 D3
Gilamoor 102 F4
Gillar's Green . . . 86 E2
Gillen 148 C7
Gilling East 96 B2
Gillingham Dorset . 13 B6
  Medway 29 C8
  Norf. 69 E7
Gilling West . . . 101 D6
Gillock 158 E4
Gillow Heath . . . 75 D5
Gills 158 C5
Gill's Green 18 B4
Gilmanscleuch . .115 B6
Gilmerton Edin . .121 C5
  Perth 127 B7
Gilmonby 100 C4
Gilmorton. 64 F2
Gilmourton 119 E6
Gilsland 109 C6
Gilsland Spa . . . 109 C6
Gilston Borders . .121 D7
  Herts 41 C7
Gilwern 35 C6
Gimingham 81 D8
Giosla 154 E6
Gipping 56 C4
Gipsey Bridge . . 79 E5
Girdle Toll 118 E3
Girlsta 160 H6
Girsby 102 D1
Girtford 54 D2
Girthon 106 D3
Girton Cambs . . 54 C5
  Notts 77 C8
Gisburn 93 E8
Gisleham 69 F8
Gislingham 56 B4
Gissing 68 F4
Gittisham 11 E6
Gladestry 48 D4
Gladsmuir 121 B7
Glais 33 D8
Glaisdale 103 D5
Glame 149 D10
Glamis 134 E3
Glan Adda. 83 D5

Glanaman....33 C7
Glan Conwy Conwy .83 D8
Conwy....83 F8
Glandford....81 C6
Glan-Duar....46 E4
Glandwr....32 B2
Glan-Dwyfach....71 C5
Glandy Cross....32 B2
Glandyfi....58 E3
Glan Gors....82 D4
Glangrwyney....35 C6
Glanmule....59 E8
Glanrafon....58 F3
Glanrhyd Gwyn..70 D3
Pembs....45 E3
Glan-rhyd,....117 C6
Glanton Pike....117 C6
Glan-traeth....82 D2
Glanvilles Wootton 12 D4
Glan-y-don....73 B5
Glan-y-nant....59 F6
Glan-yr-afon
Anglesey....83 C6
Gwyn....72 E3
Gwyn....72 E4
Glan-y-wern....71 D7
Glapthorn....65 E7
Glapwell....76 C4
Glas-allt Shiel..139 F8
Glasbury....48 F3
Glaschoil....151 H13
Glascoed Denb....35 D7
Mon....35 D7
Powys....59 C8
Glascorrie....140 E2
Glascote....63 D6
Glascwm....48 D3
Glasdrum....130 E4
Glasfryn....72 D3
Glasgow....119 C5
Glashvin....149 B9
Glasinfryn....83 E5
Glasnacardoch..147 B9
Glasnakille....149 G10
Glasphein....148 D6
Glaspwll....58 E4
Glassburn....150 H6
Glasserton....105 F8
Glassford....119 E7
Glasshouse Hill...36 B4
Glasshouses....94 C4
Glasslie....128 D4
Glasson Cumb...108 C2
Lancs....92 D4
Glassonby....109 F5
Glasterlaw....135 D5
Glaston....65 D5
Glastonbury....23 F7
Glatton....65 F8
Glazebrook....86 E4
Glazebury....86 E4
Glazeley....61 F7
Gleadless....88 F4
Gleadsmoss....74 C5
Gleann
Tholàstaidh...155 C10
Gleaston....92 B2
Gleiniant....59 E6
Glemsford....56 E2
Glen Dumfries....106 D2
Dumfries....106 D2
Glenamachrie...124 C5
Glen Auldyn....84 C4
Glenbarr....143 E7
Glenbeg Highld...139 B6
Highld....147 E8
Glen Bernisdale 149 D9
Glenbervie....141 F6
Glenboig....119 C7
Glenborrodale...147 E9
Glenbranter....125 F7
Glenbreck....114 B3
Glenbrein Lodge .137 C2
Glenbrittle House 149 F9
Glenbuchat
Lodge....140 C2
Glenbuck....113 B7
Glenburn....118 C4
Glencalvie Lodge .150 C7
Glencanisp
Lodge....156 G4
Glencaple....107 C6
Glencarron
Lodge....150 F3
Glencarse....128 B3
Glencassley
Castle....156 J7
Glenceitlein....131 E5
Glencoe....130 D4
Glencraig....128 E3
Glencripesdale...147 F9
Glencrosh....113 F7
Glendavan House 140 D3
Glendevon....127 D8
Glendoebeg....137 D7
Glendoe Lodge....137 D7
Glendoick....128 B4
Glendoll Lodge...134 B2
Glendoune....112 E1
Glenduckie....128 C4
Glendye Lodge...140 F5
Gleneagles Hotel .127 C8
Gleneagles
House....127 C8
Glenegedale....142 C4
Glenelg....149 G13
Glenernie....151 G13
Glenfarg....128 C3
Glenfarquhar
Lodge....141 F6
Glenferness
House....151 G12
Glenfield....64 D2
Glenfinnan....147 C11
Glenfoot....128 C3
Glenfyne Lodge ..125 D8
Glengap....106 D3
Glengarnock....118 D3
Glengorm Castle .146 F7
Glengrasco....149 D9
Glenhead Farm..134 C2
Glen Ho....121 F5
Glenhoul....113 F6
Glenhurich....130 C2

Glenkerry....115 C5
Glenkiln....106 B5
Glenkindie....140 C3
Glenlatterach....152 C1
Glenlee....113 F6
Glenlichorn....127 C6
Glenlivet....139 B7
Glenlochsie....133 B7
Glenloig....143 E10
Glenluce....105 D6
Glenmallan....125 F8
Glenmarksie....150 F6
Glenmassan....145 E10
Glenmavis....119 C7
Glenmaye....84 E2
Glenmidge....113 F8
Glen Mona....84 D4
Glenmore Argyll..124 D4
Highld....149 D9
Glenmore Lodge .139 D5
Glenmoy....134 C4
Glen Nevis House 131 B5
Glenogil....134 C4
Glenprosen
Lodge....134 C2
Glenprosen
Village....134 C3
Glenquiech....134 C4
Glenreasdell
Mains....145 H7
Glenree....143 F10
Glenridding....99 C5
Glenrossal....156 J7
Glenrothes....128 D4
Glensanda....130 E2
Glensaugh....135 B6
Glenshero Lodge .137 E8
Glen Sluain....125 F6
Glenstockadale..104 C4
Glenstriven....145 F9
Glentaggart....113 B8
Glen Tanar
House....140 E3
Glentham....90 E4
Glentirranmuir..127 E5
Glenton....140 B5
Glentress....121 F5
Glentromie
Lodge....138 E3
Glen Trool Lodge .112 F4
Glentrool Village .105 B7
Glentruan....84 B4
Glentruim House .138 E2
Glentworth....90 F3
Glenuig....147 D9
Glenurquhart....151 E10
Glen Village....119 B8
Glen Vine....84 E3
Glespin....113 B8
Gletness....160 H6
Glewstone....36 B2
Glinton....65 D8
Glooston....64 E4
Glororum....123 F7
Glossop....87 E8
Gloster Hill....117 D8
Gloucester....37 C5
Gloup....160 C7
Glusburn....94 E3
Glutt Lodge....157 F12
Glutton Bridge....75 C7
Glympton....38 B4
Glynarthen....46 E2
Glynbrochan....59 F6
Glyn-Ceiriog....73 F6
Glyncoch....34 E4
Glyncorrwg....34 E2
Glyn-cywarch....71 D7
Glynde....17 C8
Glyndebourne....17 C8
Glyndyfrdwy....72 E5
Glyn Ebwy
= Ebbw Vale....35 D5
Glynedd
= Glynneath....34 D2
Glyn-neath
= Glynedd....34 D2
Glynogwr....34 F3
Glyntaff....34 F4
Glyntawe....34 C2
Gnosall....62 B2
Gnosall Heath....62 B2
Goadby....64 E4
Goadby Marwood .64 B4
Goatacre....24 B5
Goathill....12 C4
Goathland....103 D6
Goathurst....22 F4
Goat Lees....30 E4
Gobernuisgach
Lodge....156 E7
Gobhaig....154 G5
Gobowen....73 F7
Godalming....27 E7
Godley....87 E7
Godmanchester...54 B4
Godmanstone....12 E4
Godmersham....30 D4
Godney....23 E6
Godolphin Cross....2 C5
Godre'r-graig....34 D1
Godshill Hants....14 C2
IoW....15 F6
Godstone....28 D4
Godwinscroft....14 E2
Goetre....35 D7
Goferydd....82 C2
Goff's Oak....41 D6
Gogar....120 B4
Goginan....58 F3
Golan....71 C6
Golant....5 D6
Golberdon....5 B8
Golborne....86 E4
Golcar....88 C2
Golden Cross....18 D2
Golden Green....29 E7
Golden Grove....33 C6
Goldenhill....75 D5
Golden Hill....14 L3
Golden Pot....26 E5
Golden Valley....37 B8
Golders Green....41 F5
Goldhanger....43 D5
Gold Hill....65 E5
Golding....60 D5
Goldington....53 D8
Goldsborough
N Yorks....95 D6
N Yorks....103 C6
Goldsithney....2 C4
Goldsworthy....9 B5
Goldthorpe....89 D5
Gollanfield....151 F11
Golspie....157 J11
Golval....157 C11
Gomeldon....25 F6
Gomersal....88 B3
Gomshall....27 E8
Gonalston....77 E6
Gonfirth....160 G5
Good Easter....42 C2
Gooderstone....67 D7
Goodleigh....20 F5
Goodmanham....96 E4
Goodnestone Kent..31 D6
Kent....31 D6
Goodrich....36 C2
Goodrington....7 D6
Goodshaw....87 B6
Goodwick = Wdig..44 B4
Goodworth
Clatford....25 E8
Goole....89 B8
Goonbell....3 B6
Goonhavern....4 D2
Goose Eye....94 E3
Goose Green
Gtr Man....86 D3
Norf....68 F4
W Sus....16 C5
Gooseham....8 C4
Goosey....38 E3
Goosnargh....93 F5
Goostrey....74 B4
Gorcott Hill....51 C5
Gord....160 L6
Gordon....122 E2
Gordonbush....157 J11
Gordonsburgh...152 B4
Gordonstoun....152 B1
Gordonstown
Aberds....152 C5
Aberds....153 E7
Gore....31 D7
Gorebridge....121 C6
Gore Cross....24 D5
Gorefield....66 C4
Gore Pit....42 C4
Gorey Jersey....17
Gorgie....120 B5
Goring....29 B7
Goring-by-Sea....16 D5
Goring Heath....26 B4
Gorleston-on-Sea 69 D8
Gornalwood....62 E3
Gorrachie....153 C7
Gorran Churchtown..3 B8
Gorran Haven....3 B9
Gorrenberry....115 E7
Gors....46 B5
Gorsedd....73 B5
Gorse Hill....38 F1
Gorseinon....33 E6
Gorseness....159 G5
Gorsgoch....46 D3
Gorslas....33 C6
Gorsley....36 B3
Gorstan....150 E6
Gorstanvorran...130 B2
Gorsteyhill....74 D4
Gorsty Hill....62 B5
Gortantaoid....142 A4
Gorton....87 E6
Gosberton....78 F5
Gosberton Clough..65 B8
Gosfield....42 B3
Gosford....49 C7
Gosforth Cumb....98 D2
T&W....110 C5
Gosmore....40 B4
Gosport....15 E7
Gossabrough....160 E7
Gossington....36 D4
Goswick....123 E6
Gotham....76 F5
Gotherington....37 B6
Gott....160 J6
Goudhurst....18 B4
Goulceby....79 B5
Gourdas....153 D7
Gourdon....135 B8
Gourock....118 B2
Govan....119 C5
Govanhill....119 C5
Goveton....7 E5
Govilon....35 C6
Gowanhill....153 B10
Gowdall....89 B7
Gowerton....33 E6
Gowkhall....128 F2
Gowthorpe....96 D3
Goxhill E Yorks....97 F7
N Lincs....90 B5
Goxhill Haven....90 B5
Goytre....34 F1
Grabhair....155 F8
Graby....65 B7
Grade....3 E6
Graffham....16 C3
Grafham Cambs....54 C2
Sur....27 E8
Grafton Hereford....49 F6
N Yorks....95 C7
Oxon....38 D2
Shrops....60 C4
Worcs....49 C7
Grafton Flyford....50 D4
Grafton Regis....53 E5
Grafton
Underwood....65 F6
Grafty Green....30 E2
Graianrhyd....73 D6
Graig Conwy....83 D8
Denb....72 B4
Graig-fechan....72 D5
Grain....30 B2
Grainsby....91 E6
Grainthorpe....91 E7
Grampound....4 D4
Grampound Road....4 D4
Gramsdal....148 C3
Granborough....39 B7
Granby....77 F7
Grandborough....52 C2

Grandtully....133 D6
Grange Cumb....98 C4
E Ayrs....118 F4
Medway....29 C8
Mers....85 F3
Perth....128 B4
Grange
Crossroads....152 C4
Grange Hall....151 E13
Grange Hill....41 E7
Grangemill....76 D2
Grange Moor....88 C3
Grangemouth....127 F8
Grange of
Lindores....128 C4
Grange-over-
Sands....92 B4
Grangepans....128 F2
Grangetown Cardiff 22 B3
Redcar....102 B3
Grange Villa....110 D5
Granish....138 C5
Gransmoor....97 D7
Granston....44 B3
Grantchester....54 D5
Grantham....78 F2
Grantley....94 C5
Grantlodge....141 C6
Granton Dumfries..114 D3
Edin....120 B5
Grantown-on-
Spey....139 B6
Grantshouse....122 C4
Grappenhall....86 F4
Grasby....90 D4
Grasmere....99 D5
Grasscroft....87 D7
Grassendale....85 F4
Grassholme....100 B4
Grassington....94 C3
Grassmoor....76 C4
Grassthorpe....77 C7
Grateley....25 E7
Gratwich....75 F7
Graveley Cambs....54 C3
Herts....41 B5
Gravelly Hill....62 E5
Gravels....60 D3
Graven....160 F6
Graveney....30 C4
Gravesend Herts....41 B7
Kent....29 B7
Grayingham....90 E3
Grayrigg....99 E7
Grays....29 B7
Grayshott....27 F6
Grayswood....27 F7
Graythorp....102 B3
Grazeley....26 C4
Greasbrough....88 E5
Greasby....85 F3
Great Abington....55 E6
Great Addington....53 B7
Great Alne....51 D6
Great Altcar....85 D4
Great Amwell....41 C6
Great Asby....100 C1
Great Ashfield....56 C3
Great Ayton....102 C3
Great Baddow....42 D3
Great Bardfield....55 F7
Great Barford....54 D2
Great Barr....62 E4
Great Barrington..38 C2
Great Barrow....73 C8
Great Barton....56 C2
Great Barugh....96 B3
Great Bavington..117 F5
Great Bealings....57 E6
Great Bedwyn....25 C7
Great Bentley....43 B7
Great Billing....53 C6
Great Bircham....80 D3
Great Blakenham..56 D5
Great Blencow....108 F4
Great Bolas....61 B6
Great Bookham....28 D2
Great Bourton....52 E2
Great Bowden....64 F4
Great Bradley....55 D7
Great Braxted....42 C4
Great Bricett....56 D4
Great Brickhill....53 F7
Great Bridge....62 E3
Great Bridgeford..62 B2
Great Brington....52 C4
Great Bromley....43 B6
Great Broughton
Cumb....107 F7
N Yorks....102 D3
Great Budworth...74 B3
Great Burdon....101 C8
Great Burgh....28 D3
Great Burstead....42 E2
Great Busby....102 D3
Great Canfield....42 C1
Great Carlton....91 F8
Great Casterton...65 D7
Great Chart....30 E3
Great Chatwell....61 C7
Great Chesterford 55 E6
Great Cheverell...24 D4
Great Chishill....54 F5
Great Clacton....43 C7
Great Cliff....88 C4
Great Clifton....98 B2
Great Coates....91 D6
Great Comberton..50 E4
Great Corby....108 D4
Great Cornard....56 E2
Great Cowden....97 E8
Great Coxwell....38 E2
Great Crakehall..101 E7
Great Cransley....53 B6
Great
Cressingham....67 D8
Great Crosby....85 E4
Great Cubley....75 F8
Great Dalby....64 C4
Great Denham....53 E8
Great Doddington 53 C6
Great Dunham....67 C8
Great Dunmow....42 B2
Great Durnford...25 F6
Great Easton Essex 42 B2
Leics....64 E5
Great Eccleston...92 E4
Great Edstone....103 F5
Great Ellingham..68 E3

Great Elm....24 E2
Greater Doward...36 C2
Great Eversden....54 D4
Great Fencote....101 E7
Great Finborough 56 D4
Greatford....65 C7
Great Fransham....67 C8
Great Gaddesden..40 C3
Greatgate....75 E7
Great Gidding....65 F8
Great Givendale...96 D4
Great Glemham....57 C7
Great Glen....64 E3
Great Gonerby....77 F8
Great Green Norf...69 F5
Suff....56 D3
Great Habton....96 B3
Great Hale....78 E4
Great Hallingbury 41 C8
Greatham Hants....15 B8
Hrtlpl....102 B2
W Sus....16 C4
Great Hampden...39 D8
Great Harrowden...53 B6
Great Harwood...93 F7
Great Haseley....39 D6
Great Hatfield....97 E7
Great Haywood....62 B4
Great Heath....63 F7
Great Heck....89 B6
Great Henny....56 F2
Great Hinton....24 D4
Great Hockham....68 E2
Great Holland....43 C8
Great Horkesley...56 F3
Great Hormead....41 B6
Great Horton....94 F4
Great Horwood...53 F5
Great Houghton
Northants....53 D5
S Yorks....88 D5
Great Hucklow....75 B8
Great Kelk....97 D7
Great Kimble....39 D8
Great Kingshill...40 E1
Great Langton....101 E7
Great Leighs....42 C3
Great Lever....86 D5
Great Limber....90 D5
Great Linford....53 E6
Great Livermere...56 B2
Great Longstone...76 B2
Great Lumley....111 E5
Great Lyth....60 D4
Great Malvern....50 E2
Great Maplestead 56 F2
Great Marton....92 F3
Great Massingham 80 E3
Great Melton....68 D4
Great Milton....39 D6
Great Missenden...40 D1
Great Mitton....93 F7
Great Mongeham..31 D7
Great Moulton....68 E4
Great Munden....41 B6
Great Musgrave..100 C2
Great Ness....60 C3
Great Notley....42 B3
Great Oakley Essex 43 B7
Northants....65 F5
Great Offley....40 B4
Great Ormside...100 C2
Great Orton....108 D3
Great Ouseburn...95 C7
Great Oxendon...64 F4
Great Oxney
Green....42 D2
Great Palgrave....67 C8
Great Parndon....41 D7
Great Paxton....54 C3
Great Plumpton...92 F3
Great Plumstead..69 C6
Great Ponton....78 F2
Great Preston....88 B5
Great Raveley....66 F2
Great Rissington...38 C1
Great Rollright....51 F8
Great Ryburgh....81 E5
Great Ryle....117 C6
Great Ryton....60 D4
Great Saling....42 B3
Great Salkeld....109 F5
Great Sampford...55 F7
Great Sankey....86 F3
Great Saxham....55 C8
Great Shefford....25 B8
Great Shelford....55 D5
Great Smeaton...101 D8
Great Snoring....80 D5
Great Somerford..37 F6
Great Stainton...101 B8
Great Stambridge 42 E4
Great Staughton...54 C2
Great Steeping....79 C7
Great Stonar....31 D7
Greatstone on Sea 19 C7
Great Strickland...99 B7
Great Stukeley....54 B3
Great Sturton....78 B5
Great Sutton
Ches W....73 B7
Shrops....60 F5
Great Swinburne 110 B2
Great Tew....38 B3
Great Tey....42 B4
Great Thurlow....55 D7
Great Torrington....9 C6
Great Tosson....117 D6
Great Totham
Essex....42 C4
Essex....42 C4
Great Tows....91 E6
Great Urswick....92 B2
Great Wakering....43 E5
Great Waldingfield 56 E3
Great Walsingham 80 D5
Great Waltham....42 C2
Great Warley....42 E1
Great Washbourne 50 F4
Great Weldon....65 F6
Great Welnetham..56 D2
Great Wenham....56 F4
Great
Whittington....110 B3
Great Wigborough 43 C5
Great Wilbraham 55 D6
Great Wishford....25 F5

Great Witcombe...37 C6
Great Witley....50 C2
Great Wolford....51 F7
Greatworth....52 E3
Great Wratting....55 E7
Great Wymondley 41 B5
Great Wyrley....62 D3
Great Wytheford..61 C5
Great Yarmouth...69 D8
Great Yeldham....55 F8
Greave....87 B6
Greeba....84 D3
Green....72 C4
Greenbank....160 C7
Greenburn....120 C2
Greendikes....117 B6
Green End....54 D2
Greenfield C Beds..53 F8
Flint....73 B5
Gtr Man....87 D7
Highld....136 D5
Oxon....39 E7
Greenford....40 F4
Greengairs....119 B7
Greenham....26 C2
Green Hammerton 95 D7
Greenhaugh....116 F3
Greenhead....109 C6
Greenhill Falk....119 B8
Kent....31 C5
Leics....63 C8
London....40 F4
Greenhills....118 D3
Greenhithe....29 B6
Greenholm....118 F5
Greenholme....99 D7
Greenhouse....115 B8
Greenhow Hill....94 C4
Greenigoe....159 H5
Greenland....158 D4
Greenlands....39 F7
Green Lane....59 E8
Greenlaw Aberds..153 C6
Borders....122 E3
Greenlea....107 B7
Greenloaning....127 D7
Greenmount....87 C5
Greenmow....160 L6
Greenock....118 B2
Greenock West...118 B2
Greenodd....99 F5
Green Ore....23 D7
Greenow....107 D8
Green St Green...29 C5
Greenside....110 C4
Greensidehill....117 C5
Greens Norton....52 E4
Greenstead Green 42 B4
Greensted....41 D8
Green Street....40 E4
Greenwich....28 B4
Greet....50 F5
Greete....49 B7
Greetham Lincs....79 B6
Rutland....65 C6
Greetland....87 B8
Gregg Hall....99 E6
Gregson Lane....86 B3
Greinetobht....148 A3
Greinton....23 F6
Gremista....160 J6
Grenaby....84 E2
Grendon Northants 53 C6
Warks....63 D6
Grendon Common 63 E6
Grendon Green...49 D7
Grendon
Underwood....39 B6
Grenofen....6 B2
Grenoside....88 E4
Greosabhagh....154 H6
Gresford....73 D7
Gresham....81 D7
Greshornish....149 C8
Gressenhall....68 C2
Gressingham....93 C5
Gresty Green....74 D4
Greta Bridge....101 C5
Gretna....108 C3
Gretna Green....108 C3
Gretton Glos....50 F5
Northants....65 E5
Shrops....60 E5
Grewelthorpe....94 B5
Greygarth....94 B4
Grey Green....89 D8
Greynor....33 D6
Greysouthen....98 B2
Greystoke....108 F4
Greystone Angus..135 E5
Dumfries....107 B6
Greywell....26 D5
Griais....155 C9
Grianan....155 D9
Gribothorpe....96 F4
Gridley Corner....9 E5
Griff....63 F7
Griffithstown....35 E6
Grimbister....159 G4
Grimblethorpe....91 F6
Grimeford Village..86 C4
Grimethorpe....88 D5
Griminis....148 C2
Grimister....160 D6
Grimley....50 C3
Grimness....159 J5
Grimoldby....91 F7
Grimpo....60 B3
Grimsargh....93 F5
Grimsbury....52 E2
Grimsby....91 C6
Grimscote....52 D4
Grimscott....8 D4
Grimshader....155 E9
Grimsthorpe....65 B7
Grimston E Yorks..97 F8
Leics....64 B3
Norf....80 E3
York....96 D2
Grimstone....12 E4
Grinacombe Moor..9 E7
Grindale....97 B7
Grindigar....159 H6
Grindiscol....160 K6
Grindle....61 D7
Grindleford....76 B2
Grindleton....93 E7
Grindley....62 B4
Grindley Brook....74 E2
Grindlow....75 B8

Grindon Northumb 122 E5
Staffs....75 D7
Grindonmoor Gate 75 D7
Gringley on the
Hill....89 E8
Grinsdale....108 D3
Grinshill....60 B5
Grinton....101 E5
Griomsidar....155 E8
Grishipoll....146 F4
Grisling Common..17 B8
Gristhorpe....103 F8
Griston....68 E2
Gritley....159 H6
Grittenham....37 F7
Grittleton....37 F5
Grizebeck....98 F4
Grizedale....99 E5
Grobister....159 F7
Groby....64 D2
Groes Conwy....72 C4
Neath....34 F1
Groes-faen....34 F4
Groesffordd Marli 72 B4
Groeslon Gwyn....82 E5
Gwyn....82 F4
Groes-lwyd....60 C2
Groombridge....18 B2
Grosmont Mon....35 B8
N Yorks....103 D6
Groton....56 E3
Grougfoot....120 B3
Grove Dorset....12 G5
Kent....31 C6
Notts....77 B7
Oxon....38 E4
Grove Park....28 B5
Grovesend....33 D6
Grove Vale....62 E4
Grudie....150 E6
Gruids....157 J8
Gruinard House....150 B2
Grula....149 F8
Gruline....147 G8
Grunasound....160 K5
Grundisburgh....57 D6
Grunsagill....93 D7
Gruting....160 J4
Grutness....160 N6
Gualachulain....131 E5
Gualin House....156 D6
Guardbridge....129 C6
Guarlford....50 E3
Guay....133 E7
Gubbergill....98 E1
Gubblecote....40 C2
Guestling Green....19 D5
Guestling Thorn...18 D5
Guestwick....81 E6
Guestwick Green..81 E6
Guide....86 B5
Guide Post....117 F8
Guilden Morden...54 E3
Guilden Sutton....73 C8
Guildford....27 E7
Guildtown....133 F8
Guilsborough....52 B4
Guilsfield....60 C2
Guilton....31 D6
Guineaford....20 F4
Guisborough....102 C4
Guiseley....94 E4
Guist....81 E5
Guith....159 E6
Guiting Power....37 B7
Gulberwick....160 K6
Gullane....129 F6
Gulval....2 C3
Gulworthy....6 B2
Gumfreston....32 D2
Gumley....64 E3
Gummow's Shop....4 D3
Gunby E Yorks....96 F3
Lincs....65 B6
Gundleton....26 F4
Gun Hill....18 D2
Gunn....20 F5
Gunnerside....100 E4
Gunnerton....110 B2
Gunness....90 C2
Gunnislake....6 B2
Gunnista....160 J7
Gunthorpe Norf....81 D6
Notts....77 E6
Pboro....65 D8
Gunville....15 F5
Gunwalloe....3 D5
Gurnard....15 E5
Gurnett....75 B6
Gurney Slade....23 E8
Gurnos....33 D8
Gussage All Saints 13 C8
Gussage
St Michael....13 C7
Guston....31 E7
Gutcher....160 D7
Guthrie....135 D5
Guyhirn....66 D3
Guyhirn Gull....66 D3
Guy's Head....66 B4
Guy's Marsh....13 B6
Guyzance....117 D8
Gwaenysgor....72 A4
Gwalchmai....82 D3
Gwaun-Cae-
Gurwen....33 C8
Gwaun-Leision....33 C8
Gwbert....45 E3
Gweek....3 D6
Gwehelog....35 D7
Gwenddwr....48 E2
Gwennap....3 C6
Gwenter....3 E6
Gwernaffield....73 C6
Gwernesney....35 D8
Gwernogle....46 F4
Gwernymynydd....73 C6
Gwersyllt....73 D7
Gwespyr....85 F2
Gwinear....2 C4
Gwithian....2 B4
Gwredog....82 C4
Gwyddelwern....72 E4
Gwyddgrug....46 F3
Gwydyr Uchaf....83 E7
Gwynfryn....73 D6
Gwystre....48 C2
Gwytherin....83 E8

Gyfelia....73 E7
Gyffin....83 D7
Gyre....159 H4
Gyrn-goch....70 C5

H

Habberley....60 D3
Habergham....93 F8
Habrough....90 C5
Haceby....78 F3
Hacheston....57 D7
Hackbridge....28 C3
Hackenthorpe....88 F5
Hackford....68 D3
Hackforth....101 E7
Hackland....159 F4
Hackleton....53 D6
Hackness N Yorks..103 E7
Orkney....159 J4
Hackney....41 F6
Hackthorn....90 F3
Hackthorpe....99 B7
Haconby....65 B8
Hacton....41 F8
Hadden....122 F3
Haddenham Bucks..39 D7
Cambs....55 B5
Haddington
E Loth....121 B8
Lincs....78 C2
Haddiscoe....69 E7
Haddon Cambs....65 E8
Ches E....75 C6
Hade Edge....88 D2
Hademore....63 D5
Hadfield....87 E8
Hadham Cross....41 C7
Hadham Ford....41 B7
Hadleigh Essex....42 F4
Suff....56 E4
Hadley....61 C6
Hadley End....62 B5
Hadlow....29 E7
Hadlow Down....18 C2
Hadnall....60 C5
Hadstock....55 E6
Hady....76 B3
Hadzor....50 C4
Haffenden Quarter 30 E2
Hafod-Dinbych...83 F8
Hafod-lom....83 D8
Haggate....93 F8
Haggbeck....108 B4
Haggerston....123 E6
Haggs....119 B7
Hagley Hereford....49 E7
Worcs....62 F3
Hagworthingham 79 C6
Haigh Gtr Man....86 D4
S Yorks....88 C3
Haigh Moor....88 B3
Haighton Green...93 F5
Haile....98 D2
Hailes....50 F5
Hailey Herts....41 C6
Oxon....38 C3
Hailsham....18 E2
Hail Weston....54 C2
Haimer....158 D3
Hainault....41 E7
Hainford....68 C5
Hainton....91 F5
Hairmyres....119 D6
Haisthorpe....97 C7
Hakin....44 E3
Halam....77 D6
Halbeath....128 F3
Halberton....10 C5
Halcro....158 D4
Hale Gtr Man....87 F5
Halton....86 F3
Hants....14 C2
Hale Bank....86 F2
Halebarns....87 F5
Hales Norf....69 E6
Staffs....74 F4
Hales Place....30 D5
Hale Street....29 E7
Halesworth....57 B7
Halewood....86 F2
Halford Shrops....60 F4
Warks....51 E7
Halfpenny Furze...32 C3
Halfpenny Green...62 E2
Halfway Carms....46 F5
Carms....47 F7
W Berks....26 C2
Halfway Bridge....16 B3
Halfway House....60 C3
Halfway Houses...30 B3
Halifax....87 B8
Halket....118 D4
Halkirk....158 D3
Halkyn....73 B6
Halland....18 D2
Hallaton....64 E4
Hallatrow....23 D8
Hallbankgate....109 D5
Hall Dunnerdale...98 E4
Hallen....36 F2
Hall Green W Mid...62 F5
W Yorks....88 C4
Hall Grove....41 C5
Halliburton....122 E2
Hallin....148 C7
Halling....29 C8
Hallington Lincs....91 F7
Northumb....110 B2
Halloughton....77 D6
Hallow....50 D3
Hallrule....115 C8
Halls....122 B2
Hall's Green....41 B5
Hallthwaites....98 F3
Hallworthy....8 F3
Hallyburton
House....134 F2
Hallyne....120 E4

Halmore....36 D3
Halmyre Mains....120 D4
Halnaker....16 D3
Halsall....85 C4
Halse Northants....52 E3
Som....11 B6
Halsetown....2 C4
Halsham....91 B6
Halsinger....20 F4
Halstead Essex....56 F2
Kent....29 C5
Leics....64 D4
Halstock....12 D3
Haltham....78 C5
Haltoft End....79 E6
Halton Bucks....40 C1
Halton....86 F3
Lancs....92 C5
Northumb....110 C2
Wrex....73 F7
W Yorks....95 F6
Halton East....94 D3
Halton Gill....93 B8
Halton Holegate...79 C7
Halton Lea Gate..109 D6
Halton West....93 D8
Haltwhistle....109 C7
Halvergate....69 D7
Halwell....7 D5
Halwill....9 E6
Halwill Junction....9 D6
Ham Devon....11 D7
Glos....36 E3
Highld....158 C4
Kent....31 D7
London....28 B2
Shetland....160 K1
Wilts....25 C8
Hambleden....39 F7
Hambledon Hants..15 C7
Sur....27 F7
Hamble-le-Rice....15 D5
Hambleton Lancs...92 E3
N Yorks....95 F8
Hambridge....11 B8
Hambrook S Glos...23 B8
W Sus....15 D8
Ham Common....13 B6
Hameringham....79 C6
Hamerton....54 B2
Hametoun....160 K1
Ham Green
Hereford....50 E2
Kent....19 C5
Kent....30 C2
N Som....23 B7
Worcs....50 C5
Hamilton....119 D7
Hammer....27 F6
Hammerpot....16 D4
Hammersmith....28 B3
Hammerwich....62 D4
Hammerwood....28 F5
Hammond Street..41 D6
Hammoon....13 C6
Hamnavoe
Shetland....160 E4
Shetland....160 E6
Shetland....160 F6
Shetland....160 K5
Hampden Park....18 E3
Hamperden End....55 F6
Hampnett....37 C7
Hampole....89 C6
Hampreston....13 E8
Hampstead....41 F5
Hampstead
Norreys....26 B3
Hampsthwaite....95 D5
Hampton London...28 C2
Shrops....61 F7
Worcs....50 E5
Hampton Bishop...49 F7
Hampton Heath....73 E8
Hampton in Arden 63 F6
Hampton Loade....61 F7
Hampton Lovett...50 C3
Hampton Lucy....51 D7
Hampton on the
Hill....51 C7
Hampton Poyle....39 C5
Hamrow....80 E5
Hamsey....17 C8
Hamsey Green....28 D4
Hamstall Ridware 62 C5
Hamstead IoW....14 E5
W Mid....62 E4
Hamstead
Marshall....26 C2
Hamsterley
Durham....110 D4
Durham....110 F4
Hamstreet....19 B7
Ham Street....23 F7
Hamworthy....13 E7
Hanbury Staffs....63 B5
Worcs....50 C4
Hanbury Woodend 63 B5
Hanby....78 F3
Hanchurch....74 E5
Handbridge....73 C8
Handcross....17 B6
Handforth....87 F6
Handley....73 D8
Handsacre....62 C4
Handsworth
S Yorks....88 F5
W Mid....62 E4
Handy Cross....9 B6
Hanford....75 E5
Hanging Langford 24 F5
Hangleton....16 D4
Hanham....23 B8
Hankelow....74 E3
Hankerton....37 E6
Hankham....18 E3
Hanley....75 E5
Hanley Castle....50 E3
Hanley Child....49 C8
Hanley Swan....50 E3
Hanley William....49 C8
Hanlith....94 C2
Hanmer....73 F8
Hannah....79 B8
Hannington Hants..26 D3
Northants....53 B6
Swindon....38 E1
Hannington Wick..38 E1
Hansel Village....118 F3

Hanslope 53 E6
Hanthorpe 65 B7
Hanwell London 40 F4
Oxon 52 E2
Hanwood 60 D4
Hanworth London 28 B2
Norf 81 D7
Happendon 119 F8
Happisburgh 69 A6
Happisburgh Common 69 B6
Hapsford 73 B8
Hapton Lancs 93 F7
Norf 68 E4
Harberton 7 D5
Harbertonford 7 D5
Harbledown 30 D5
Harborne 62 F4
Harborough Magna 52 B2
Harbottle 117 D5
Harbury 51 D8
Harby Leics 77 F7
Notts 77 B8
Harcombe 11 E6
Harden W Mid 62 D4
W Yorks 94 F3
Hardenhuish 24 B4
Hardgate 141 D6
Hardham 16 C4
Hardingham 68 D3
Hardingstone 53 D5
Hardington 24 D2
Hardington Mandeville 12 C3
Hardington Marsh 12 D3
Hardley 14 D5
Hardley Street 69 D6
Hardmead 53 E7
Hardrow 100 E3
Hardstoft 76 C4
Hardway Hants 15 D7
Som 24 F2
Hardwick Bucks 39 C8
Cambs 54 D4
Norf 67 C6
Norf 68 F5
Northants 53 C6
Notts 77 B6
Oxon 38 D3
Oxon 39 B5
W Mid 62 E4
Hardwicke Glos 36 C4
Glos 37 B6
Hereford 48 E4
Hardy's Green 43 B5
Hareby 79 C6
Hareden 93 D6
Harefield 40 E3
Hare Green 43 B6
Hare Hatch 27 B6
Harehills 95 F6
Harehope 117 B6
Haresceugh 109 E6
Harescombe 37 C5
Haresfield 37 C5
Hareshaw 119 C8
Hareshaw Head 116 F4
Hare Street 41 B6
Harewood 95 E6
Harewood End 36 B2
Harford Carms 46 E5
Devon 6 D4
Hargate 68 E4
Hargatewall 75 B8
Hargrave Ches W 73 C8
Northants 53 B8
Suff 55 D8
Harker 108 C3
Harkland 160 E6
Harkstead 57 F5
Harlaston 63 C6
Harlaw House 141 B6
Harlaxton 77 F8
Harlech 71 D6
Harlequin 77 F6
Harlescott 60 C5
Harlesden 41 F5
Harleston Devon 7 E5
Norf 68 F5
Suff 56 D4
Harlestone 52 C5
Harle Syke 93 F8
Harley Shrops 61 D5
S Yorks 88 E4
Harleyholm 120 F2
Harlington C Beds 53 F8
London 27 B8
S Yorks 89 D5
Harlosh 149 D7
Harlow 41 C7
Harlow Hill Northumb 110 C3
N Yorks 95 D5
Harlthorpe 96 F3
Harlton 54 D4
Harman's Cross 13 F7
Harmby 101 F6
Harmer Green 41 C5
Harmer Hill 60 B4
Harmondsworth 27 B8
Harmston 78 C2
Harnham 110 B3
Harnhill 37 D7
Harold Hill 41 E8
Haroldston West 44 D3
Haroldswick 160 B8
Harold Wood 41 E8
Harome 102 F4
Harpenden 40 C4
Harpford 11 E5
Harpham 97 C6
Harpley Norf 80 E3
Worcs 49 C8
Harpole 52 C4
Harpsdale 158 E3
Harpsden 39 F7
Harpswell 90 F3
Harpurhey 87 D6
Harpur Hill 75 B7
Harraby 108 D4
Harrapool 149 F11
Harrier 160 J1
Harrietfield 127 B8
Harrietsham 30 D2
Harrington Cumb 98 B1
Lincs 79 B6
Northants 64 F4
Harringworth 65 E6
Harris 146 B6
Harrogate 95 D6
Harrold 53 D7
Harrow 40 F4
Harrowbarrow 5 C8
Harrowden 53 E8
Harrowgate Hill 101 C7
Harrow on the Hill 40 F4
Harrow Street 56 F3
Harrow Weald 40 E4
Harston Cambs 54 D5
Leics 77 F8
Harswell 96 E4
Hart 111 F7
Hartburn Northumb 117 F6
Stockton 102 C2
Hart Common 86 D4
Hartest 56 D2
Hartfield 29 F5
Hartford Cambs 54 B3
Ches W 74 B3
Hartfordbridge 27 D5
Hartford End 42 C2
Hartforth 101 D6
Harthill Ches W 74 D2
N Lanark 120 C2
S Yorks 89 F5
Hart Hill 40 B4
Hartington 75 C8
Hartland 8 B4
Hartlebury 50 B3
Hartlepool 111 F8
Hartley Cumb 100 D2
Kent 18 B4
Kent 29 C7
Northumb 111 B6
Hartley Westpall 26 D4
Hartley Wintney 27 D5
Hartlip 30 C2
Hartoft End 103 E5
Harton N Yorks 96 C3
Shrops 60 F4
T&W 111 C6
Hartpury 36 B4
Hartshead 88 B2
Hartshill 63 E7
Hartshorne 63 B7
Hartsop 99 C6
Hart Station 111 F7
Hartwell 53 D5
Hartwood 119 D8
Harvieston 126 F4
Harvington 51 E5
Harvington Cross 51 E5
Harwell 38 F4
Harwich 57 F6
Harwood Durham 109 F8
Gtr Man 86 C5
Harwood Dale 103 E7
Harworth 89 E7
Hasbury 62 F3
Hascombe 27 E7
Haselbech 52 B5
Haselbury Plucknett 12 C2
Haseley 51 C7
Haselor 51 D6
Hasfield 37 B5
Hasguard 44 E3
Haskayne 85 D4
Hasketon 57 D6
Hasland 76 C3
Haslemere 27 F7
Haslingden 87 B5
Haslingfield 54 D5
Haslington 74 D4
Hassall 74 D4
Hassall Green 74 D4
Hassell Street 30 E4
Hassendean 115 B8
Hassingham 69 D6
Hassocks 17 C6
Hassop 76 B2
Hastigrow 158 D4
Hastingleigh 30 E4
Hastings 18 E5
Hastingwood 41 D7
Hastoe 40 D2
Haswell 111 E6
Haswell Plough 111 E6
Hatch C Beds 54 E2
Hants 26 D4
Wilts 13 B7
Hatch Beauchamp 11 B8
Hatch End 40 E4
Hatchet Gate 14 D4
Hatch Green 11 C8
Hatching Green 40 C4
Hatchmere 74 B2
Hatcliffe 91 D6
Hatfield Hereford 49 D7
Herts 41 D5
S Yorks 89 D7
Worcs 50 D3
Hatfield Broad Oak 41 C8
Hatfield Garden Village 41 D5
Hatfield Heath 41 C8
Hatfield Hyde 41 C5
Hatfield Peverel 42 C3
Hatfield Woodhouse 89 D7
Hatford 38 E3
Hatherden 25 D8
Hatherleigh 9 D7
Hathern 63 B8
Hatherop 38 D1
Hathersage 88 F3
Hathershaw 87 D7
Hatherton Ches E 74 E3
Staffs 62 C3
Hatley St George 54 D3
Hatt 5 C8
Hattingley 26 F4
Hatton Aberds 153 E10
Derbys 63 B6
Lincs 78 B4
Shrops 60 E4
Warks 51 C7
Warr 86 F3
Hatton Castle 153 D7
Hattoncrook 141 B7
Hatton Heath 73 C8
Hatton of Fintray 141 C7
Haugh E Ayrs 112 B4
Gtr Man 87 C7
Lincs 79 B7
Haugham 91 F7
Haugh Head 117 B6
Haughley 56 C4
Haughley Green 56 C4
Haugh of Glass 152 E4
Haugh of Urr 106 C5
Haughs of Clinterty 141 C7
Haughton Notts 77 B6
Shrops 60 B3
Shrops 61 C5
Shrops 61 D7
Shrops 61 E6
Staffs 62 B2
Haughton Castle 110 B2
Haughton Green 87 E7
Haughton Moss 74 D2
Haultwick 41 B6
Haunn Argyll 146 G6
W Isles 148 G2
Haunton 63 C6
Hauxley 117 D8
Hauxton 54 D5
Havant 15 D8
Haven 49 D6
Haven Bank 78 D5
Haven Side 91 B5
Havenstreet 15 E6
Havercroft 88 C4
Haverfordwest = Hwlffordd 44 D4
Haverhill 55 E7
Haverigg 92 B1
Havering-atte-Bower 41 E8
Haveringland 81 E7
Haversham 53 E6
Haverthwaite 99 F5
Haverton Hill 102 B2
Hawarden = Penarlâg 73 C7
Hawcoat 92 B2
Hawen 46 E2
Hawes 100 F3
Hawes' Green 68 E5
Hawes Side 92 F3
Hawford 50 C3
Hawick 115 C8
Hawkchurch 11 D8
Hawkedon 55 D8
Hawkenbury Kent 18 B2
Kent 30 E2
Hawkeridge 24 D3
Hawkerland 11 F5
Hawkesbury S Glos 36 F4
Warks 63 F7
Hawkesbury Upton 36 F4
Hawkes End 63 F7
Hawk Green 87 F7
Hawkhill 117 C8
Hawkhurst 18 B4
Hawkinge 31 F6
Hawkley 15 B8
Hawkridge 21 F7
Hawkshead 99 E5
Hawkshead Hill 99 E5
Hawksland 119 F8
Hawkswick 94 B2
Hawksworth Notts 77 E7
W Yorks 94 E4
W Yorks 95 F5
Hawkwell 42 E4
Hawley Hants 27 D6
Kent 29 B6
Hawling 37 B7
Hawnby 102 F3
Haworth 94 F3
Hawstead 56 D2
Hawthorn Durham 111 E7
Rhondda 35 F5
Wilts 24 C3
Hawthorn Hill Brack 27 B6
Lincs 78 D5
Hawthorpe 65 B7
Hawton 77 D7
Haxby 96 D2
Haxey 89 D8
Haydock 86 E3
Haydon 12 C4
Haydon Bridge 109 C8
Haydon Wick 37 F8
Haye 5 C8
Hayes London 28 C5
London 40 F4
Hayfield Derbys 87 F8
Fife 128 E4
Hay Green 66 C5
Hayhill 112 C4
Hayhillock 135 E5
Hayle 2 C4
Haynes 53 E8
Haynes Church End 53 E8
Hay-on-Wye = Y Gelli Gandryll 48 E4
Hayscastle 44 C3
Hayscastle Cross 44 C4
Hayshead 135 E6
Hay Street 41 B6
Hayton Aberdeen 141 D8
Cumb 107 E8
Cumb 108 D5
E Yorks 96 E4
Notts 89 F8
Hayton's Bent 60 F5
Haytor Vale 7 B5
Haywards Heath 17 B7
Haywood 89 C6
Haywood Oaks 77 D6
Hazelbank 119 E8
Hazelbury Bryan 12 D5
Hazeley 26 D5
Hazel Grove 87 F7
Hazelhurst 87 D7
Hazelslade 62 C4
Hazel Street 18 B3
Hazelton 37 C7
Hazelton Walls 128 B5
Hazelwood 76 E3
Hazlemere 40 E1
Hazlerigg 110 B5
Hazlewood 94 D3
Hazon 117 D7
Heacham 80 D2
Headbourne Worthy 26 F2
Headbrook 48 D5
Headcorn 30 E2
Headingley 95 F5
Headington 39 D5
Headlam 101 C6
Headless Cross 50 C5
Headley Hants 26 C3
Hants 27 F6
Sur 28 D3
Head of Muir 127 F7
Headon 77 B7
Heads 119 E7
Heads Nook 108 D4
Heage 76 D3
Healaugh N Yorks 95 E7
N Yorks 101 E5
Heald Green 87 F6
Heale Devon 20 E5
Som 23 E8
Healey Gtr Man 87 C6
Northumb 110 D3
N Yorks 101 F6
Healing 91 C6
Heamoor 2 C3
Heanish 146 G3
Heanor 76 E4
Heanton Punchardon 20 F4
Heapham 90 F2
Hearthstane 114 B4
Heasley Mill 21 F6
Heast 149 G11
Heath Cardiff 22 B3
Derbys 76 C4
Heath and Reach 40 B2
Heathcote 75 C8
Heath End Hants 26 C3
Sur 27 E6
Warks 51 C7
Heather 63 C7
Heatherfield 149 D9
Heathfield Devon 7 B6
E Sus 18 C2
Som 11 B6
Heathhall 107 B6
Heath Hayes 62 C4
Heath Hill 61 C7
Heath House 23 E6
Heathrow Airport 27 B8
Heathstock 11 D7
Heathton 62 E2
Heath Town 62 E3
Heatley 86 F5
Heaton Lancs 92 C4
Staffs 75 C6
T&W 111 C5
W Yorks 94 F4
Heaton Moor 87 E6
Heaverham 29 D6
Heaviley 87 F7
Heavitree 10 E4
Hebburn 111 C6
Hebden 94 C3
Hebden Bridge 87 B7
Hebron Anglesey 82 C4
Carms 32 B2
Northumb 117 F7
Heck 114 F3
Heckfield 26 C5
Heckfield Green 57 B5
Heckfordbridge 43 B5
Heckington 78 E4
Heckmondwike 88 B3
Heddington 24 C4
Heddle 159 G4
Heddon-on-the-Wall 110 C4
Hedenham 69 E6
Hedge End 15 C5
Hedgerley 40 F2
Hedging 11 B8
Hedley on the Hill 110 D3
Hednesford 62 C4
Hedon 91 B5
Hedsor 40 F2
Hedworth 111 C6
Hegdon Hill 49 D7
Heggerscales 100 C3
Heglibister 160 H5
Heighington Darl 101 B7
Lincs 78 C3
Heights of Brae 151 E8
Heights of Kinlochewe 150 E3
Heilam 156 C7
Heiton 122 F3
Hele Devon 10 D4
Devon 20 E4
Helensburgh 145 E11
Helford 3 D6
Helford Passage 3 D6
Helhoughton 80 E4
Helions Bumpstead 55 E7
Hellaby 89 E6
Helland 5 B5
Hellesdon 68 C5
Hellidon 52 D3
Hellifield 93 D8
Hellingly 18 D2
Hellington 69 D6
Hellister 160 J5
Helm 117 E7
Helmdon 52 E3
Helmingham 57 D5
Helmington Row 110 F4
Helmsdale 157 H13
Helmshore 87 B5
Helmsley 102 F4
Helperby 95 C7
Helperthorpe 97 B5
Helpringham 78 E4
Helpston 65 D8
Helsby 73 B8
Helsey 79 B8
Helston 3 D5
Helstone 8 F2
Helton 99 B7
Helwith Bridge 93 C8
Hemblington 69 C6
Hemel Hempstead 40 D3
Hemingbrough 96 F2
Hemingby 78 B5
Hemingford Abbots 54 B3
Hemingford Grey 54 B3
Hemingstone 57 D5
Hemington Leics 63 B8
Northants 65 F7
Som 24 D2
Hemley 57 E6
Hemlington 102 C3
Hemp Green 57 C7
Hempholme 97 D6
Hempnall 68 E5
Hempnall Green 68 E5
Hempriggs House 158 F5
Hempstead Essex 55 F7
Medway 29 C8
Norf 69 B7
Norf 81 D7
Hempsted 37 C5
Hempton Norf 80 E5
Oxon 52 F2
Hemsby 69 C7
Hemswell 90 E3
Hemswell Cliff 90 F3
Hemsworth 88 C5
Hemyock 11 C6
Henbury Bristol 23 B7
Ches E 75 B5
Hendon London 41 F5
T&W 111 D7
Hendre 73 C5
Hendre-ddu 83 E8
Hendreforgan 34 F3
Hendy 33 D6
Heneglwys 82 D4
Hen-feddau fawr 45 F4
Henfield 17 C6
Henford 9 E5
Henghurst 19 B6
Hengoed Caerph 35 E5
Powys 48 D4
Shrops 73 F6
Hengrave 56 C2
Henham 41 B8
Heniarth 59 D8
Henlade 11 B7
Henley Shrops 49 B7
Som 23 F6
Suff 57 D5
W Sus 16 B2
Henley-in-Arden 51 C6
Henley-on-Thames 39 F7
Henley's Down 18 D4
Henllan Ceredig 46 E2
Denb 72 C4
Henllan Amgoed 32 B2
Henllys 35 E6
Henlow 54 F2
Hennock 10 F3
Henny Street 56 F2
Henryd 83 D7
Henry's Moat 32 B1
Hensall 89 B6
Henshaw 109 C7
Hensingham 98 C1
Henstead 69 F7
Henstridge 12 C5
Henstridge Ash 12 B5
Henstridge Marsh 12 B5
Henton Oxon 39 D7
Som 23 E6
Henwood 5 B7
Heogan 160 J6
Heol-las 33 E7
Heol Senni 34 B3
Heol-y-Cyw 34 F3
Hepburn 117 B6
Hepple 117 D5
Hepscott 117 F8
Heptonstall 87 B7
Hepworth Suff 56 B3
W Yorks 88 D2
Herbrandston 44 E3
Hereford 49 E7
Heriot 121 D6
Hermiston 120 B4
Hermitage Borders 115 E8
Dorset 12 D4
W Berks 26 B3
W Sus 15 D8
Hermon Anglesey 82 E3
Carms 33 B7
Carms 46 F2
Pembs 45 F4
Herne 31 C5
Herne Bay 31 C5
Herner 9 B7
Hernhill 30 C4
Herodsfoot 5 C7
Herongate 42 E2
Heronsford 104 A5
Herriard 26 E4
Herringfleet 69 E7
Herringswell 55 B8
Hersden 31 C6
Hersham Corn 8 D4
Sur 28 C2
Herstmonceux 18 D3
Herston 159 J5
Hertford 41 C6
Hertford Heath 41 C6
Hertingfordbury 41 C6
Hesketh Bank 86 B2
Hesketh Lane 93 E6
Hesket Newmarket 108 F3
Heskin Green 86 C3
Hesleden 111 F7
Hesleyside 116 F4
Heslington 96 D2
Hessay 95 D8
Hessenford 5 D8
Hessett 56 C3
Hessle 90 B4
Hest Bank 92 C4
Heston 28 B2
Hestwall 159 G3
Heswall 85 F3
Hethe 39 B5
Hethersett 68 D4
Hethersgill 108 C4
Hethpool 116 B4
Hett 111 F5
Hetton 94 D2
Hetton-le-Hole 111 E6
Hetton Steads 123 F6
Heugh 110 B3
Heugh-head 140 C2
Heveningham 57 B7
Hever 29 E5
Heversham 99 F6
Hevingham 81 E7
Hewas Water 3 B8
Hewelsfield 36 D2
Hewish N Som 23 C6
Som 12 D2
Heworth 96 D2
Hexham 110 C2
Hextable 29 B6
Hexton 54 F2
Hexworthy 6 B4
Hey 93 E8
Heybridge Essex 42 D4
Essex 42 E2
Heybridge Basin 42 D4
Heybrook Bay 6 E3
Heydon Cambs 54 E5
Norf 81 E7
Heydour 78 F3
Heylipol 146 G2
Heylor 160 E4
Heysham 92 C4
Heyshott 16 C2
Heyside 87 D7
Heytesbury 24 E4
Heythrop 38 B3
Heywood Gtr Man 87 C6
Wilts 24 D3
Hibaldstow 90 D3
Hickleton 89 D5
Hickling Norf 69 B7
Notts 64 B3
Hickling Green 69 B7
Hickling Heath 69 B7
Hickstead 17 B6
Hidcote Boyce 51 E6
High Ackworth 88 C5
Higham Derbys 76 D3
Kent 29 B8
Lancs 93 F8
Suff 55 C8
Suff 56 F4
Higham Dykes 110 B4
Higham Ferrers 53 C7
Higham Gobion 54 F2
Higham on the Hill 63 E7
Highampton 9 D6
Higham Wood 29 E6
High Angerton 117 F6
High Bankhill 109 E5
High Barnes 111 D6
High Beach 41 E7
High Bentham 93 C6
High Bickington 9 B8
High Birkwith 93 B7
High Blantyre 119 D6
High Bonnybridge 119 B8
High Bradfield 88 E3
High Bray 21 F5
Highbridge Highld 136 F4
Som 22 E5
Highbrook 28 F4
High Brooms 29 E6
High Bullen 9 B7
Highburton 88 C2
Highbury 23 E8
High Buston 117 D8
High Callerton 110 B4
High Catton 96 D3
Highclere 26 C2
Highcliffe 14 E3
High Cogges 38 D3
High Coniscliffe 101 C7
High Cross Hants 15 B8
Herts 41 C6
High Easter 42 C2
High Eggborough 89 B6
High Ellington 101 F6
Higher Ansty 13 D5
Higher Ashton 10 F3
Higher Ballam 92 F3
Higher Bartle 92 F5
Higher Boscaswell 2 C2
Higher Burwardsley 74 D2
Higher Ercall 61 C5
Higher Clovelly 8 B5
Higher End 86 D3
Higher Kinnerton 73 C7
Higher Penwortham 86 B3
Higher Town 2 E4
Higher Walreddon 6 B2
Higher Walton Lancs 86 B3
Warr 86 F3
Higher Wheelton 86 B4
Higher Whitley 86 F4
Higher Wincham 74 B3
Higher Wych 73 E8
High Etherley 101 B6
Highfield E Yorks 96 F3
Gtr Man 86 D5
N Ayrs 118 D3
Oxon 39 B5
S Yorks 88 F4
T&W 110 D4
Highfields Cambs 54 D4
Northumb 123 D5
High Garrett 42 B3
Highgate 41 F5
High Grange 110 F4
High Green Norf 68 D4
S Yorks 88 E4
Worcs 50 E3
High Halden 19 B5
High Halstow 29 B8
High Ham 23 F6
High Harrington 98 B2
High Hatton 61 B6
High Hawsker 103 D7
High Hesket 108 E4
High Hesleden 111 F7
High Hoyland 88 C3
High Hunsley 97 F5
High Hurstwood 17 B8
High Hutton 96 C3
High Ireby 108 F2
High Kelling 81 C7
High Kilburn 95 B8
High Lands 101 B6
Highlane Ches E 75 C5
Derbys 88 F5
High Lane Gtr Man 87 F7
Worcs 49 C8
High Laver 41 D8
Highlaws 107 E8
Highleadon 36 B4
High Legh 86 F5
Highleigh 16 E2
High Leven 102 C2
Highley 61 F7
High Littleton 23 D8
High Lorton 98 B3
High Marishes 96 B4
High Marnham 77 B8
High Melton 89 D6
High Mickley 110 C3
High Mindork 105 D7
Highmoor Cross 39 F7
Highmoor Hill 36 F1
Highnam 36 C4
Highnam Green 36 B4
High Newton 99 F6
High Newton-by-the-Sea 117 B8
High Nibthwaite 98 F4
High Offley 61 B7
High Ongar 42 D1
High Onn 62 C2
High Roding 42 C2
High Row 108 F3
High Salvington 16 D5
High Sellafield 98 D2
High Shaw 100 E3
High Spen 110 D4
Highsted 30 C3
High Stoop 110 E4
High Street Corn 4 D4
Kent 18 B4
Suff 56 E2
Suff 57 B8
Suff 57 D8
Highstreet Green 55 F8
High Street Green 56 D4
Hightae 107 B7
High Throston 111 F7
Hightown Ches E 75 C5
Mers 85 D4
Hightown Green 56 D3
High Toynton 79 C5
High Trewhitt 117 D6
High Valleyfield 128 F2
Highway 24 B5
Highweek 7 B6
High Westwood 110 D4
Highworth 38 E2
High Wray 99 E5
High Wych 41 C7
High Wycombe 40 E1
Hilborough 67 D8
Hilcote 76 D4
Hilcott 25 D6
Hildenborough 29 E6
Hilden Park 29 E6
Hildersham 55 E6
Hilderstone 75 F6
Hilderthorpe 97 C7
Hilfield 12 D4
Hilgay 67 E6
Hill Pembs 32 D2
S Glos 36 E3
W Mid 62 E5
Hillam 89 B6
Hillbeck 100 C2
Hillborough 31 C6
Hillbrae Aberds 141 B6
Aberds 152 D6
Aberds 153 E8
Hill Brow 15 B8
Hillbutts 13 D7
Hillclifflane 76 E2
Hillcommon 11 B6
Hill Dale 86 C2
Hill Dyke 79 E6
Hillend 128 F3
Hill End Durham 110 F3
Fife 128 E2
N Yorks 94 D3
Hillerton 10 E2
Hillesden 39 B6
Hillesley 36 F4
Hillfarance 11 B6
Hillhead Aberds 152 E5
Devon 7 D7
S Ayrs 112 C4
Hill Head Hants 15 D6
Northumb 110 C2
Hillhead of Auchentumb 153 C9
Hillhead of Cocklaw 153 D10
Hillhouse 121 D8
Hilliclay 158 D3
Hillingdon 40 F3
Hillington Glasgow 118 C5
Norf 80 E3
Hillmorton 52 B3
Hill Mountain 44 E4
Hillockhead Aberds 140 C3
Aberds 140 D2
Hill of Beath 128 E3
Hill of Fearn 151 D11
Hill of Mountblairy 153 C6
Hill Ridware 62 C4
Hillside Aberds 141 E8
Angus 135 C7
Mers 85 C4
Orkney 159 J5
Shetland 160 G6
Hillswick 160 F4
Hill Top Durham 100 B4
Hants 14 D5
W Mid 62 E3
W Yorks 88 C4
Hill View 13 E7
Hillway 15 F7
Hillwell 160 M5
Hilmarton 24 B5
Hilperton 24 D3
Hilsea 15 D7
Hilston 97 F8
Hilton Aberds 153 E9
Cambs 54 C3
Cumb 100 B2
Derbys 76 F2
Dorset 13 D5
Durham 101 B6
Highld 151 C10
Shrops 61 E7
Stockton 102 C2
Hilton of Cadboll 151 D11
Himbleton 50 D4
Himley 62 E2
Hincaster 99 F7
Hinckley 63 E8
Hinderclay 56 B4
Hinderton 73 B7
Hinderwell 103 C5
Hindford 73 F7
Hindhead 27 F6
Hindley 86 D4
Hindley Green 86 D4
Hindlip 50 D3
Hindolveston 81 E6
Hindon 24 F4
Hindringham 81 D5
Hingham 68 D3
Hinstock 61 B6
Hintlesham 56 E4
Hinton Hants 14 E3
Hereford 48 F5
Northants 52 D3
S Glos 24 B2
Shrops 60 D4
Hinton Ampner 15 B6
Hinton Blewett 23 D7
Hinton Charterhouse 24 D2
Hinton-in-the-Hedges 52 F3
Hinton Martell 13 D8
Hinton on the Green 50 E5
Hinton Parva 38 F2
Hinton St George 12 C2
Hinton St Mary 13 C5
Hinton Waldrist 38 E3
Hints Shrops 49 B8
Staffs 63 D5
Hinwick 53 C7
Hinxhill 30 E4
Hinxton 55 E5
Hinxworth 54 E3
Hipperholme 88 B2
Hipswell 101 E6
Hirael 83 D5
Hiraeth 32 B2
Hirn 141 D6
Hirnant 59 B7
Hirst N Lanark 119 C8
Northumb 117 F8
Hirst Courtney 89 B7
Hirwaen 72 C5
Hirwaun 34 D3
Hiscott 9 B7
Histon 54 C5
Hitcham 56 D3
Hitchin 40 B4
Hither Green 28 B4
Hittisleigh 10 E2
Hive 96 F4
Hixon 62 B4
Hoaden 31 D6
Hoaldalbert 35 B7
Hoar Cross 62 B5
Hoarwithy 36 B2
Hoath 31 C6
Hobarris 48 B5
Hobbister 159 H4
Hobkirk 115 C8
Hobson 110 D4
Hoby 64 C3
Hockering 68 C3
Hockerton 77 D7
Hockley 42 E4
Hockley Heath 51 B6
Hockliffe 40 B2
Hockwold cum Wilton 67 F7
Hockworthy 10 C5
Hoddesdon 41 D6
Hoddlesden 86 B5
Hoddomcross 107 B8
Hoddom Mains 107 B8
Hodgeston 32 E1
Hodley 59 E8
Hodnet 61 B6
Hodthorpe 76 B5
Hoe Hants 15 C6
Norf 68 C2
Hoe Gate 15 C7
Hoff 100 C1
Hoggard's Green 56 D2
Hoggeston 39 B8
Hogha Gearraidh 148 A2
Hoghton 86 B4
Hognaston 76 D2
Hog Patch 27 E6
Hogsthorpe 79 B8
Holbeach 66 B3
Holbeach Bank 66 B3
Holbeach Clough 66 B3
Holbeach Drove 66 C3
Holbeach Hurn 66 B3
Holbeach St Johns 66 C3
Holbeach St Marks 79 F6
Holbeach St Matthew 79 F7
Holbeck Notts 76 B5
W Yorks 95 F5
Holbeck Woodhouse 76 B5
Holberrow Green 50 D5
Holbeton 6 D4
Holborn 41 F6
Holbrook Derbys 76 E3
Suff 57 F5
S Yorks 88 F5
Holburn 123 F6
Holbury 14 D5
Holcombe Devon 7 B7
Som 23 E8
Holcombe Rogus 11 C5
Holcot 53 C5
Holden 93 E7
Holdenby 52 C4
Holdenhurst 14 E2
Holdgate 61 F5
Holdingham 78 E3
Holditch 11 D8
Holefield 122 F4
Holehouses 74 B4
Hole-in-the-Wall 36 B3
Holemoor 9 D6
Holestane 113 E8
Holford 22 E3
Holgate 95 D8
Holker 92 B3
Holkham 80 C4
Hollacombe 9 D5
Holland Orkney 159 C5
Orkney 159 F7
Holland Fen 78 E5
Holland-on-Sea 43 C8
Hollandstoun 159 C8
Hollee 108 C2
Hollesley 57 E7
Hollicombe 7 C6
Hollingbourne 30 D2
Hollington Derbys 76 F2
E Sus 18 D4
Staffs 75 F7
Hollington Grove 76 F2
Hollingworth 87 E8
Hollins 87 D6
Hollinsclough 75 C7
Hollins Green 86 E4
Hollins Lane 92 D4
Hollinwood Gtr Man 87 D7
Shrops 74 F2
Hollocombe 9 C8
Holloway 76 D3
Hollowell 52 B4
Hollow Meadows 88 F3
Hollybush Caerph 35 D5
E Ayrs 112 C3
Worcs 50 F2
Holly End 66 D4
Holly Green 50 E3
Hollym 91 B7
Hollywood 51 B5
Holmbridge 88 D2
Holmbury St Mary 28 E2
Holmbush 4 D5
Holmcroft 62 B3
Holme Cambs 65 F8
Cumb 92 B5
Notts 77 D8
N Yorks 102 F1
W Yorks 88 D2
Holme Chapel 87 B6
Holme Green 95 E8
Holme Hale 67 D8
Holme Lacy 49 F7
Holme Marsh 48 D5
Holme next the Sea 80 C3
Holme-on-Spalding-Moor 96 F4
Holme on the Wolds 97 E5
Holme Pierrepont 77 F6
Holmer 49 E7
Holmer Green 40 E2
Holme St Cuthbert 107 E8
Holmes Chapel 74 C4
Holmesfield 76 B3
Holmeswood 86 C2
Holmewood 76 C4
Holme Wood 94 F4
Holmfirth 88 D2
Holmhead Dumfries 113 F7
E Ayrs 113 B5
Holmisdale 148 D6
Holmpton 91 B7
Holmrook 98 E2
Holmsgarth 160 J6
Holmwrangle 108 E5
Holne 6 C5
Holnest 12 D4
Holsworthy 8 D5
Holsworthy Beacon 9 D5
Holt Dorset 13 D8
Norf 81 D6
Wilts 24 C3
Worcs 50 C3
Wrex 73 D8
Holtby 96 D2
Holt End Hants 26 F4
Worcs 51 C5
Holt Fleet 50 C3
Holt Heath 50 C3
Holton Oxon 39 D6
Som 12 B4
Suff 57 B7
Holton cum Beckering 90 F5
Holton Heath 13 E7
Holton le Clay 91 D6
Holton le Moor 90 E4
Holton St Mary 56 F4
Holt Park 95 E5
Holwell Dorset 12 C5
Herts 54 F2
Leics 64 B4
Oxon 38 D2
Holwick 100 B4
Holworth 13 F5
Holybourne 26 E5
Holy Cross 50 B4
Holyhead = Caergybi 82 C2
Holy Island 123 E7
Holymoorside 76 C3
Holyport 27 B6
Holystone 117 D5
Holytown 119 C7
Holywell Cambs 54 B4
Corn 4 D2
Dorset 12 D3
E Sus 18 F2
Northumb 111 B6
Holywell = Treffynnon 73 B5
Holywell Green 87 C8
Holywell Lake 11 B6
Holywell Row 55 B8
Holywood 114 F2
Homer 61 D6
Homersfield 69 F5
Hom Green 36 B2
Homington 14 B2
Honeyborough 44 E4
Honeybourne 51 E6
Honeychurch 9 D8
Honey Hill 30 C5
Honey Street 25 C6
Honey Tye 56 F3
Honiley 51 B7
Honing 69 B6
Honingham 68 C4
Honington Lincs 78 E2
Suff 56 B3
Warks 51 E7
Honiton 11 D6
Honley 88 C2
Hood Green 88 D4
Hooe E Sus 18 E3
Plym 6 D3

Hooe Common 18 D3
Hoo Green 86 F5
Hook E Yorks ...89 B8
  Hants 26 D5
  London 28 C2
  Pembs 44 D4
  Wilts 37 F7
Hooke 12 E3
Hookgate 74 F4
Hook Green Kent ..18 B3
  Kent 29 C7
Hook Norton 51 F8
Hookway 10 E3
Hookwood 28 E3
Hoole 73 C8
Hooley 28 D3
Hoop 36 D2
Hoo St Werburgh ..29 B8
Hooton 73 B7
Hooton Levitt ...89 E6
Hooton Pagnell ..89 D5
Hooton Roberts ..89 E5
Hope Derbys 88 F2
  Devon 6 F4
  Highld 156 M7
  Powys 60 D2
  Shrops 60 D3
  Staffs 75 D8
Hope = Yr Hôb ..73 D7
Hope Bagot 49 B7
Hope Bowdler ...60 E4
Hope End Green ..42 B1
Hope Green 87 F7
Hopeman 152 B1
Hope Mansell ...36 C3
Hopesay 60 F3
Hope's Green ...42 F3
Hope under
  Dinmore 49 D7
Hopley's Green ..48 D5
Hopperton 95 D7
Hop Pole 65 C8
Hopton Shrops ...60 B3
  Shrops 61 B5
  Staffs 62 B3
  Suff 56 B3
Hopton Cangeford .60 F5
Hopton Castle ...49 B5
Hoptonheath ...49 B5
Hopton on Sea ...69 D8
Hopton Wafers ..49 B8
Hopwas 63 D5
Hopwood Gtr Man ..87 D6
  Worcs 50 B5
Horam 18 D2
Horbling 78 F4
Horbury 88 C3
Horcott 38 D1
Horden 111 E7
Horderley 60 F4
Hordle 14 E3
Hordley 73 F7
Horeb Carms 33 B6
  Carms 33 D5
  Ceredig 46 E2
Horfield 23 B8
Horham 57 B6
Horkesley Heath ..43 B5
Horkstow 90 C3
Horley Oxon 52 E2
  Sur 28 E3
Hornblotton Green 23 F7
Hornby Lancs 93 C5
  N Yorks 101 E7
  N Yorks 102 D1
Horncastle 79 C5
Hornchurch 41 F8
Horncliffe ...122 E6
Horndean Borders .122 E4
  Hants 15 C8
Horndon 6 B3
Horndon on the
  Hill 42 F2
Horne 28 E4
Horniehaugh ...134 C4
Horning 69 C6
Horninghold ...64 E5
Horninglow 63 B6
Horningsea 55 C5
Horningtoft 80 E5
Hornsby 108 D5
Horns Corner ...18 C4
Horns Cross Devon ..9 B5
  E Sus 18 C5
Hornsea 97 E8
Hornsea Bridge ..97 E8
Hornsey 41 F6
Hornton 51 E8
Horrabridge 6 C3
Horringer 56 C2
Horringford 15 F6
Horse and Jockey 75 F5
Horsebridge Devon ..6 B2
  Hants 25 F8
Horse Bridge ...75 D6
Horsebrook 62 C2
Horsehay 61 D6
Horseheath 55 E7
Horsehouse ...101 F5
Horsell 27 D7
Horseman's Green 73 E8
Horseway 66 F4
Horsey 69 B7
Horsford 68 C4
Horsforth 94 F5
Horsham Worcs ...50 D2
  W Sus 28 F2
Horsham St Faith ..68 C5
Horsington Lincs ..78 C5
  Som 12 B5
Horsley Derbys ..76 E3
  Glos 37 E5
  Northumb 110 C3
  Northumb 116 E4
Horsley Cross ...43 B7
Horsleycross
  Street 43 B7
Horsleyhill ...115 C8
Horsleyhope ...110 E3
Horsley
  Woodhouse 76 E3
Horsmonden 29 E7
Horspath 39 D5
Horstead 69 C5
Horsted Keynes ..17 B7

Horton Bucks 40 C2
  Dorset 13 D8
  Lancs 93 D8
  Northants 53 D6
  S Glos 36 F4
  Shrops 60 B4
  Som 11 C8
  Staffs 75 D6
  Swansea 33 F5
  Wilts 25 C5
  Windsor 27 B8
Horton-cum-
  Studley 39 C5
Horton Green ...73 E8
Horton Heath ...15 C5
Horton in
  Ribblesdale ...93 B8
Horton Kirby ...29 C6
Hortonlane 60 C4
Horwich 86 C4
Horwich End 87 F8
Horwood 9 B7
Hose 64 B4
Hoselaw 122 F4
Hoses 98 E4
Hosh 127 B7
Hosta 148 A2
Hoswick 160 L6
Hotham 96 F4
Hothfield 30 E3
Hoton 64 B2
Houbie 160 D8
Houdston 112 E1
Hough Ches E 74 D4
  Ches E 75 B5
Hougham 77 E8
Hough Green 86 F2
Hough-on-the-
  Hill 78 E2
Hougharry 148 A2
Houghton Cambs ...54 B3
  Cumb 108 D4
  Hants 25 F8
  Pembs 44 E4
  W Sus 16 C4
Houghton
  Conquest 53 E8
Houghton Green
  E Sus 19 C6
  Warr 86 E4
Houghton-le-
  Side 101 B7
Houghton-le-
  Spring 111 E6
Houghton on the
  Hill 64 D3
Houghton Regis ..40 B3
Houghton St Giles .80 D5
Houlland Shetland .160 F7
  Shetland 160 H5
Houlsyke 103 D5
Hound 15 D5
Hound Green 26 D5
Houndslow 122 E2
Houndwood 122 C4
Hounslow 28 B2
Hounslow Green ..42 C2
Housay 160 F8
House of Daviot .151 G10
House of
  Glenmuick ...140 E2
Housetter 160 E5
Houss 160 K5
Houston 118 C4
Houstry 158 G3
Houton 159 H4
Hove 17 D6
Hoveringham 77 E6
Hoveton 69 C6
Hovingham 96 B2
How 108 D5
Howbrook 88 E4
How Caple 49 F8
Howden Borders ..116 B2
  E Yorks 89 B8
Howden-le-Wear .110 F4
Howe Highld ...158 D5
  Norf 69 D5
  N Yorks 101 F8
How Bridge 86 D4
Howe Green 42 D3
Howell 78 E4
How End 53 E8
Howe of Teuchar .153 D7
Howe Street Essex .42 C2
  Essex 55 F7
Howey 48 D2
Howgate 120 D5
How Green 29 E5
Howick 117 C8
Howle Durham ..101 B5
  Telford 61 B6
Howlett End 55 F6
Howley 11 D7
Hownam 116 C3
Hownam Mains ..116 B3
Howpasley 115 D6
Howsham N Lincs ..90 D4
  N Yorks 96 C3
Howslack 114 D3
Howtel 122 F4
Howton 35 B8
Howton 99 C6
Howwood 118 C3
Hoxne 57 B5
Hoy 159 H3
Hoylake 85 F3
Hoyland 88 D4
Hoylandswaine ..88 D3
Hubberholme 94 B2
Hubbert's Bridge .79 E5
Huby N Yorks 95 C8
  N Yorks 95 E5
Hucclecote 37 C5
Hucking 30 D2
Hucknall 76 E5
Huddersfield ...88 C2
Huddington ...50 D4
Hudswell 101 D6
Huggate 96 D4
Hugglescote 63 C8
Hughenden Valley .40 E1
Hughley 61 E5
Hugh Town 2 E4
Huish Devon 9 C7
  Wilts 25 C6
Huish
  Champflower ..11 B5
Huish Episcopi ..12 B2
Huisinis 154 F4

Hulcott 40 C1
Hulland 76 E2
Hulland Ward ...76 E2
Hullavington ...37 F5
Hullbridge 42 E4
Hulme 87 E6
Hulme End 75 D8
Hulme Walfield ..74 C5
Hulverstone 14 F4
Hulver Street ...69 F7
Humber 49 D7
Humber Bridge ..90 B4
Humberston 91 D7
Humbie 121 C7
Humbleton E Yorks .97 F8
  Northumb 117 B5
Humby 78 F3
Hume 122 E3
Humshaugh 110 B2
Huna 158 C5
Huncoat 93 F7
Huncote 64 E2
Hundalee 116 C2
Hunderthwaite .100 B4
Hundleby 79 C6
Hundle Houses ..79 D5
Hundleton 44 E4
Hundon 55 E8
Hundred Acres ..15 C6
Hundred End ...85 B4
Hundred House ..48 D3
Hungarton 64 D3
Hungerford Hants ..14 C2
  W Berks 25 C8
Hungerford
  Newtown 25 B8
Hungerton 65 B5
Hunglader 149 A8
Hunmanby 97 B6
Hunmanby Moor ..97 B7
Hunningham 51 C8
Hunny Hill 15 F5
Hunsdon 41 C7
Hunsingore 95 D7
Hunslet 95 F6
Hunsonby 109 F5
Hunspow 158 C4
Hunstanton 80 C2
Hunstanworth ..110 E2
Hunsterson 74 E3
Hunston Suff 56 C3
  W Sus 16 D2
Hunstrete 23 C8
Hunt End 50 C5
Hunter's Quay .145 F10
Hunthill Lodge .134 B4
Huntingdon 54 B3
Huntingfield ...57 B7
Huntingford 24 F3
Huntington E Loth .121 B7
  Hereford 48 D4
  Staffs 62 C3
  York 96 D2
Huntingtower ..128 B2
Huntley 36 C4
Huntly 152 E5
Huntlywood ...122 E2
Hunton Kent 29 E8
  N Yorks 101 E6
Hunt's Corner ..68 F3
Hunt's Cross ...86 F2
Huntsham 10 B5
Huntspill 22 E5
Huntworth 22 F5
Hunwick 110 F4
Hunworth 81 D6
Hurdsfield 75 B6
Hurley Warks 63 E6
  Windsor 39 F8
Hurlford 118 F4
Hurliness 159 K3
Hurn 14 E2
Hurn's End 79 E7
Hursley 14 B5
Hurst N Yorks ...101 D5
  Som 12 C2
  Wokingham 27 B5
Hurstbourne
  Priors 26 E2
Hurstbourne
  Tarrant 25 D8
Hurst Green E Sus .18 C4
  Lancs 93 F6
Hurstpierpoint ..17 C6
Hurst Wickham ...17 C6
Hurstwood 93 F8
Hurtmore 27 E7
Hurworth Place .101 D7
Hury 100 C4
Husabost 148 C7
Husbands
  Bosworth 64 F3
Husborne Crawley .53 F7
Husthwaite 95 B8
Hutchwns 21 B7
Huthwaite 76 D4
Huttoft 79 B8
Hutton Borders .122 D5
  Cumb 99 B6
  Essex 42 E2
  E Yorks 97 D6
  Lancs 86 B2
  N Som 22 D5
Hutton Buscel ..103 F7
Hutton Conyers ..95 B6
Hutton Cranswick ..97 D6
Hutton End 108 F4
Hutton Gate ...102 C3
Hutton Henry ..111 F7
Hutton-le-Hole ..103 E5
Hutton Magna ..101 C6
Hutton Roof Cumb ..93 B5
  Cumb 108 F3
Hutton Rudby ..102 D2
Hutton Sessay ..95 B8
Hutton Village .102 C3
Hutton Wandesley ..95 D8
Huxley 74 C2
Huxter Shetland .160 H5
  Shetland 160 H5
Huxton 86 E2
Hwlffordd
  = Haverfordwest ..44 D4
Hycemoor 98 F2
Hyde Glos 37 D5
  Gtr Man 87 E7
  Hants 14 C2
Hyde Heath 40 D2

Hyde Park 89 D6
Hydestile 27 E7
Hylton Castle .111 D6
Hyndford Bridge .120 E2
Hynish 146 H2
Hyssington 60 E3
Hythe Hants 14 D5
  Kent 19 B8
Hythe End 27 B8
Hythie 153 C10

I

Ibberton 13 D5
Ible 76 D2
Ibsley 14 D2
Ibstock 63 C8
Ibstone 39 E7
Ibthorpe 25 D8
Ibworth 26 D3
Ichrachan 125 B6
Ickburgh 67 E8
Ickenham 40 F3
Ickford 39 D6
Ickham 31 D6
Ickleford 54 F2
Icklesham 19 D5
Ickleton 55 E5
Icklingham 55 B8
Ickwell Green ..54 E2
Icomb 38 B2
Idbury 38 C2
Iddesleigh 9 D7
Ide 10 E3
Ideford 7 B6
Ide Hill 29 D5
Iden 19 C6
Iden Green Kent ..18 B4
  Kent 18 B5
Idle 94 F4
Idlicote 51 E7
Idmiston 25 F6
Idole 33 C5
Idridgehay 76 E2
Idrigill 149 B8
Idstone 38 F2
Idvies 135 E5
Iffley 39 D5
Ifield 28 F3
Ifold 27 F8
Iford 17 D8
Ifton Heath ...73 F7
Ightfield 74 F2
Ightham 29 D6
Iken 57 D8
Ilam 75 D8
Ilchester 12 B3
Ilderton 117 B6
Ilford 41 F7
Ilfracombe 20 E4
Ilkeston 76 E4
Ilketshall
  St Andrew 69 F6
Ilketshall
  St Lawrence ...69 F6
Ilketshall
  St Margaret ...69 F6
Ilkley 94 E4
Illey 62 F3
Illingworth ...87 B8
Illogan 3 B5
Illston on the Hill .64 E4
Ilmer 39 D7
Ilmington 51 E7
Ilminster 11 C8
Ilsington 7 B5
Ilston 33 E6
Ilton N Yorks ...94 B4
  Som 11 C8
Imachar 143 D9
Imeraval 142 D4
Immingham 91 C5
Impington 54 C5
Ince 73 B8
Ince Blundell ..85 D4
Ince in Makerfield .86 D3
Inchbare 135 C6
Inchberry 152 C3
Inchbraoch ...135 D7
Incheril 150 E3
Inchgrundle ..134 B4
Inchina 150 B2
Inchinnan 118 C4
Inchkinloch ..157 E8
Inchlaggan ...136 D4
Inchlumpie ...151 D8
Inchmore 150 G6
Inchnacardoch
  Hotel 137 C6
Inchnadamph ..156 G5
Inch of Arnhall .135 B6
Inchree 130 C4
Inchture 128 B4
Inchyra 128 B3
Indian Queens ...4 D4
Inerval 142 D4
Ingatestone ...42 E2
Ingbirchworth ..88 D3
Ingestre 62 B3
Ingham Lincs ...90 F3
  Norf 69 B6
  Suff 56 B2
Ingham Corner ..69 B6
Ingleborough ...66 C4
Ingleby Derbys ..63 B7
  Lincs 77 B8
Ingleby
  Greenhow 102 D3
Inglemire 97 F6
Inglesbatch 24 C2
Inglesham 38 E2
Ingleton Durham .101 B6
  N Yorks 93 B6
Inglewhite 92 E5
Ingliston 120 B4
Ingoe 110 B3
Ingol 92 F5
Ingoldisthorpe ..80 D2
Ingoldmells 79 C8
Ingoldsby 78 F3
Ingon 51 D7
Ingram 117 C6
Ingrow 94 F3
Ings 99 E6
Ingst 36 F2
Ingworth 81 E7

Inham's End 66 E2
Inkberrow 50 D5
Inkpen 25 C8
Inkstack 158 C4
Inn 99 D6
Innellan 145 F10
Innerleithen ..121 F6
Innerleven ...129 D5
Innermessan ...104 C4
Innerwick E Loth .122 B3
  Perth 132 E2
Innis Chonain .125 C7
Insch 140 B5
Insh 138 D4
Inshore 156 C6
Inskip 92 F4
Instoneville ...89 C6
Instow 20 F3
Intake 89 D6
Inver Aberds ..139 E8
  Highld 151 C11
  Perth 133 E7
Inverailort ..147 C10
Inveraldie 134 F4
Inverallochy ..153 B10
Inveran 151 B8
Inveraray 125 E6
Inverarish ...149 E10
Inverarity 134 E4
Inverarnan ...126 C2
Inverasdale ..155 J13
Inverbeg 126 E2
Inverbervie ..135 B8
Inverboyndie .153 B6
Inverbroom ...150 B4
Invercassley ..156 J7
Invercauld House .139 E7
Inverchaolain .145 F9
Invercharnan .131 E5
Inverchoran ..150 F5
Invercreran ..130 E4
Inverdruie ...138 D5
Inverebrie ...153 E9
Invereck 145 E10
Invereshie House .138 D4
Inveresk 121 B6
Inverey 139 F6
Inverfarigaig .137 B8
Invergarry ...137 D6
Invergelder ..139 E8
Invergeldie ..127 B6
Invergordon ..151 E10
Invergowrie ..134 F3
Inverguseran .149 H12
Inverhadden ..132 D3
Inverharroch ..152 E3
Inverherive ..126 C2
Inverie 147 B10
Inverinan 125 D5
Inverinate ...136 B2
Inverkeilor ..135 E6
Inverkeithing .128 F3
Inverkeithny .153 D6
Inverkip 118 B2
Inverkirkaig .156 H3
Inverlael 150 C4
Inverliever
  House 124 E4
Inverliver ...125 B6
Inverlochlarig .126 C3
Inverlochy Argyll .125 C7
Invermark Lodge .140 F3
Invermoidart ..147 D9
Invermoriston .137 C7
Invernaver ...157 C10
Inverneill ...145 E7
Inverness 151 G9
Invernettie ..153 D11
Invernoaden ..125 F7
Inveroran Hotel .131 E6
Inverpolly Lodge .156 H3
Inverquharity .134 D4
Inverquhomery .153 D10
Inverroy 137 F5
Inversanda ...130 D3
Invershiel ...136 C2
Invershin 157 J8
Inversnaid Hotel .126 D2
Inveruglas ...126 D2
Inveruglass ..138 D4
Inverurie 141 B6
Invervar 132 E3
Inverythan ...153 D7
Inwardleigh 9 E7
Inworth 42 C4
Iochdar 148 D2
Iping 16 B2
Ipplepen 7 C6
Ipsden 39 F6
Ipsley 51 C5
Ipstones 75 D7
Ipswich 57 E5
Irby 85 F3
Irby in the Marsh .79 C7
Irby upon Humber .91 D5
Irchester 53 C7
Ireby Cumb 108 F2
  Lancs 93 B6
Ireland Orkney .159 H4
  Shetland 160 L5
Ireland's Cross ..74 E4
Ireleth 98 B2
Ireshopeburn .109 F8
Irlam 86 E5
Irnham 65 B7
Iron Acton 36 F3
Ironbridge 61 D6
Iron Cross 51 D5
Irongray 107 B6
Ironmacannie .106 B3
Ironside 153 C8
Ironville 76 D4
Irstead 69 B6
Irthington ...108 C4
Irthlingborough .53 B7
Irton 103 F8
Irvine 118 F3
Isauld 157 C12
Isbister Orkney .159 F3
  Orkney 159 G4
  Shetland 160 D5
  Shetland 160 G7
Isfield 17 C8
Isham 53 B6
Isle Abbotts ...11 B8

Isle Brewers 11 B8
Isleham 55 B7
Isle of Whithorn .105 F8
Isleornsay ...149 G12
Islesburgh ...160 G5
Islesteps 107 B6
Isleworth 28 B2
Isley Walton ..63 B8
Islibhig 154 E4
Islington 41 F6
Islip Northants .53 B7
  Oxon 39 C5
Istead Rise ...29 C7
Isycoed 73 D8
Itchen 14 C5
Itchen Abbas ...26 F3
Itchen Stoke ...26 F3
Itchingfield ...16 B5
Itchington 36 F3
Itteringham ...81 D7
Itton 9 E8
Itton Common ...36 E1
Ivegill 108 E4
Iver 40 F3
Iver Heath 40 F3
Iveston 110 D4
Ivinghoe 40 C2
Ivinghoe Aston ..40 C2
Ivington 49 D6
Ivington Green ..49 D6
Ivybridge 6 D4
Ivy Chimneys ...41 D7
Ivy Cross 13 B6
Ivychurch 19 C7
Ivy Hatch 29 D6
Iwade 30 C2
Iwerne Courtney or
  Shroton 13 C6
Iwerne Minster ..13 C6
Ixworth 56 B3
Ixworth Thorpe ..56 B3

J

Jack Hill 94 D5
Jack in the Green .10 E5
Jacksdale 76 D4
Jackstown 153 E7
Jacobstow 8 E3
Jacobstowe 9 D7
Jameston 32 E1
Jamestown
  Dumfries 115 E6
  Highld 150 F7
  W Dunb 126 F2
Jarrow 111 C6
Jarvis Brook ...18 C2
Jasper's Green ..42 B3
Java 124 B3
Jawcraig 119 B8
Jaywick 43 C7
Jealott's Hill ..27 B6
Jedburgh 116 B2
Jeffreyston ...32 D1
Jellyhill 119 B6
Jemimaville ..151 E10
Jersey Farm ...40 D4
Jesmond 111 C5
Jevington 18 E2
Jockey End 40 C3
Johnby 108 F4
John o'Groats .158 C5
John's Cross ...18 C4
Johnshaven ...135 C7
Johnston E Renfs .118 C4
  Pembs 44 D4
Johnstonebridge .114 E3
Johnstown Carms .33 C5
  Wrex 73 E7
Joppa Edin 121 B6
  S Ayrs 112 C4
Jordans 40 E2
Jordanthorpe ..88 F4
Jump 88 D4
Jumpers Green ..14 E2
Juniper Green .121 C5
Jurby East 84 C3
Jurby West 84 C3

K

Kaber 100 C2
Kaimend 120 E2
Kaimes 121 C5
Kalemouth ...116 B3
Kames Argyll ..124 D4
  Argyll 145 F8
  E Ayrs 113 B6
Kea 3 B7
Keadby 90 C2
Keal Cotes 79 C6
Kearsley 87 D5
Kearstwick 99 F8
Kearton 101 E5
Kearvaig 156 B5
Keasden 93 C7
Keckwick 86 F3
Keddington 91 F7
Kedington 55 E8
Kedleston 76 E3
Keelby 91 C5
Keele 74 E5
Keeley Green ..53 E8
Keeston 44 D4
Keevil 24 D4
Kegworth 63 B8
Kehelland 2 B5
Keig 140 C5
Keighley 94 E3
Keil 130 D3
Keilarsbrae ..127 E7
Keilhill 153 C7
Keillmore 144 E5
Keillor 134 E2
Keillour 127 B8
Keills 142 B5
Keils 144 G4
Keinton
  Mandeville ...12 B3
Keir Mill 113 E8
Keisby 65 B7
Keiss 158 D5
Keith 152 C4
Keith Inch ...153 D11
Keithock 135 C6
Kelbrook 94 E2
Kelby 78 E2

Keld Cumb 99 C7
  N Yorks 100 D3
Keldholme 103 F5
Kelfield N Lincs .90 D2
  N Yorks 95 F8
Kelham 77 D7
Kellan 147 G8
Kellas Angus ...134 F4
  Moray 152 C1
Kellaton 7 F6
Kelleth 100 D1
Kelleythorpe ..97 D5
Kelling 81 C6
Kellingley 89 B6
Kellington 89 B6
Kelloe 111 F6
Kelloholm 113 C7
Kelly Bray 5 B8
Kelmarsh 52 B5
Kelmscot 38 E2
Kelsale 57 C7
Kelsall 74 C2
Kelsall Hill ...74 C2
Kelshall 54 F4
Kelsick 107 D8
Kelso 122 F3
Kelstedge 76 C3
Kelstern 91 E6
Kelston 24 C2
Kelton 107 B6
Kelty 128 E3
Kelvedon 42 C4
Kelvedon Hatch ..42 E1
Kelvin 119 D6
Kelvinside ...119 C5
Kelynack 2 C2
Kemback 129 C6
Kemberton 61 D7
Kemble 37 E6
Kemerton 50 F4
Kemeys
  Commander ...35 E7
Kemnay 141 C6
Kempley 36 B3
Kempsey 50 E3
Kempsford 38 E1
Kemps Green ...51 B6
Kempshott 26 D4
Kempston 53 E8
Kempston
  Hardwick 53 E8
Kempton 60 F3
Kemp Town 17 D7
Kemsing 29 D6
Kemsley 30 C3
Kenardington ..19 B6
Kenchester 49 E6
Kencot 38 D2
Kendal 99 E7
Kendoon 113 F6
Kenfig 34 F2
Kenfig Hill ...34 F2
Kenilworth 51 B7
Kenknock 132 F1
Kenley London ..28 D4
  Shrops 61 D5
Kenmore Highld .149 C12
  Perth 132 E4
Kenn Devon 10 F4
  N Som 23 C6
Kennacley 154 H6
Kennacraig ...145 G7
Kennerleigh ...10 D3
Kennet 127 E8
Kennethmont ..140 B4
Kennett 55 C7
Kennford 10 F4
Kenninghall ...68 F3
Kenninghall Heath .68 F3
Kennington Kent .30 E4
  Oxon 39 D5
Kennoway 129 D5
Kenny Hill 55 B7
Kennythorpe ...96 C3
Kenovay 146 G2
Kensaleyre ...149 C9
Kensington 28 B3
Kensworth
  Common 40 C3
Kentallen 130 D4
Kentchurch 35 B8
Kentford 55 C8
Kentisbeare ...11 D5
Kentisbury 20 E5
Kentisbury Ford ..20 E5
Kentmere 99 D6
Kenton Devon ...10 F4
  Suff 57 C5
  T&W 110 C5
Kenton Bankfoot .110 C5
Kentra 147 E9
Kents Bank 92 B3
Kent's Green ...36 B4
Kent's Oak 14 B4
Kent Street E Sus .18 D4
  Kent 29 D7
  W Sus 17 B6
Kenwick 73 F8
Kenwyn 3 B7
Kenyon 86 E4
Keoldale 156 C6
Keppanach 130 C4
Keppoch 136 B2
Keprigan 143 G7
Kepwick 102 E2
Kerchesters ..122 F3
Keresley 63 F7
Kernborough ...7 E5
Kerne Bridge ...36 C2
Kerris 2 D3
Kerry 59 E8
Kerrycroy ...145 G10
Kerry's Gate ...49 F5
Kersall 77 C7
Kersey 56 E4
Kershopefoot .115 F7
Kersoe 50 F4
Kerswell 11 D5
Kerswell Green ..50 E3
Kesgrave 57 E6
Kessingland ...69 F8
Kessingland Beach 69 F8
Kestle 3 B8
Kestle Mill 4 D3

Keston 28 C5
Keswick Cumb ...98 B4
  Norf 68 D5
  Norf 81 D9
Ketley 61 C6
Ketley Bank ...61 C6
Ketsby 79 B6
Kettering 53 B6
Ketteringham ..68 D4
Kettins 134 F2
Kettlebaston ..56 D3
Kettlebridge .128 D5
Kettleburgh ...57 C6
Kettlehill ...128 D5
Kettleholm ...107 B8
Kettleness ...103 C6
Kettleshume ..75 B6
Kettlesing 94 D5
Kettlesing Bottom .94 D5
Kettlesing Head ..94 D5
Kettlestone ...81 D5
Kettlethorpe ..77 B8
Kettletoft ...159 E7
Kettlewell 94 B2
Ketton 65 D6
Kew 28 B2
Kewstoke 22 C5
Kexbrough 88 D4
Kexby Lincs 90 F2
  York 96 D3
Key Green 75 C5
Keyhaven 14 E4
Keyingham 91 B6
Keymer 17 C7
Keynsham 23 C8
Keysoe 53 C8
Keysoe Row 53 C8
Keyston 53 B8
Keyworth 77 F6
Kibblesworth .110 D5
Kibworth
  Beauchamp ...64 E3
Kibworth Harcourt 64 E3
Kidbrooke 28 B5
Kiddemore Green .62 D2
Kidderminster ..50 B3
Kiddington 38 B4
Kidlington 38 C4
Kidmore End ...26 B4
Kidsgrove 74 D5
Kidstones 100 F4
Kidwelly
  = Cydweli 33 D5
Kiel Crofts ..124 B5
Kielder 116 E2
Kierfiold Ho ..159 G3
Kilbagie 127 F8
Kilbarchan ...118 C4
Kilbeg 149 H11
Kilberry 144 G6
Kilbirnie 118 D3
Kilbride Argyll .124 C4
  Argyll 124 C5
  Highld 149 F10
Kilburn Angus ..134 C3
  Derbys 76 E3
  London 41 F5
  N Yorks 95 B8
Kilby 64 E3
Kilchamaig ...145 G2
Kilchattan ...145 H10
Kilchattan Bay .145 H10
Kilchenzie ...143 F7
Kilcheran 124 B4
Kilchiaran ...142 B3
Kilchoan Argyll .124 D3
  Highld 146 E7
Kilchoman 142 B3
Kilchrenan ...125 C6
Kilconquhar ..129 D6
Kilcot 36 B3
Kilcoy 151 F8
Kilcreggan ...145 E11
Kildale 102 D4
Kildalloig ...143 G8
Kildary 151 D10
Kildermorie
  Lodge 151 D8
Kildonan 143 F11
Kildonan Lodge .157 G12
Kildonnan 146 C7
Kildrummy 140 C3
Kildwick 94 E3
Kilfinan 145 F8
Kilfinnan 137 E5
Kilgetty 32 D2
Kilgwrrwg
  Common 36 E1
Kilham E Yorks ..97 C6
  Northumb 122 F4
Kilkenneth ...146 G2
Kilkerran 143 G8
Kilkhampton 9 E6
Killamarsh 89 F5
Killay 33 E7
Killbeg 147 G9
Killean 143 D7
Killearn 126 F4
Killen 151 F9
Killerby 101 C6
Killichonan ..132 D2
Killiechonate .136 F5
Killiecrankie .133 C6
Killiemor 146 H7
Killilan 150 H2
Killimster ...158 E5
Killin 132 F2
Killinallan ..142 A4
Killinghall ...95 D5
Killington 99 F8
Killingworth .111 B5
Killin Lodge .137 D8
Killmahumaig .144 D6
Killochyett ..121 E7
Killocraw 143 E7
Killundine ...147 G8
Kilmacolm 118 C3
Kilmaha 124 E5
Kilmahog 126 D5
Kilmalieu 130 D2
Kilmaluag ...149 A9
Kilmany 129 B5
Kilmarie 149 G10
Kilmarnock ...118 F4
Kilmaron Castle .129 C5
Kilmartin 124 F4
Kilmaurs 118 E4

Kilmelford ...124 D4
Kilmeny 142 B4
Kilmersdon 23 D8
Kilmeston 15 B6
Kilmichael ...143 F7
Kilmichael
  Glassary 145 D7
Kilmichael of
  Inverlussa ...144 E6
Kilmington Devon .11 E7
  Wilts 24 F2
Kilmonivaig ..136 F4
Kilmorack 150 G7
Kilmore Argyll .124 C4
  Highld 149 H11
Kilmory Argyll .144 F6
  Highld 147 D8
  Highld 149 H8
  N Ayrs 143 F10
Kilmuir Highld .148 D7
  Highld 149 A8
  Highld 151 D10
  Highld 151 G9
Kilmun Argyll ..124 D5
  Argyll 145 E10
Kilncadzow ...119 E8
Kilndown 18 B4
Kilnhurst 89 E5
Kilninian 146 G6
Kilninver 124 C4
Kiln Pit Hill .110 D3
Kilnsea 91 C8
Kilnsey 94 C2
Kilnwick 97 E5
Kilnwick Percy ..96 D4
Kiloran 144 D2
Kilpatrick ...143 F10
Kilpeck 49 F6
Kilphedir ...157 H12
Kilpin 89 B8
Kilpin Pike ...89 B8
Kilrenny 129 D7
Kilsby 52 B3
Kilspindie ...128 B4
Kilsyth 119 B7
Kiltarlity ...151 G8
Kilton Notts ...77 B5
  Som 22 E3
Kilton Thorpe .102 C4
Kilvaxter 149 B8
Kilve 22 E3
Kilvington 77 E7
Kilwinning ...118 E3
Kimberley Norf ..68 D3
  Notts 76 E5
Kimberworth ...88 E5
Kimble Wick ...39 D8
Kimbolton Cambs .53 C8
  Hereford 49 C7
Kimcote 64 F2
Kimmeridge 13 G7
Kimmerston ...123 F5
Kimpton Hants ..25 E7
  Herts 40 C4
Kinbrace 157 F11
Kinbuck 127 D6
Kincaple 129 C6
Kincardine Fife .127 F8
  Highld 151 C9
Kincardine
  Bridge 127 F8
Kincardine O'Neil .140 E4
Kinclaven 134 F1
Kincorth 119 A8
Kincorth House .151 E13
Kincraig 138 D4
Kincraigie ...133 E6
Kindallachan .133 E6
Kineton Glos ...37 B7
  Warks 51 D8
Kinfauns 128 B3
Kingairloch ..130 D2
Kingarth 145 H9
Kingcoed 35 D8
King Edward ..153 C7
Kingerby 90 E4
Kingham 38 B2
Kingholm Quay .107 B6
Kingie 136 D4
Kinglassie ...128 E4
Kingoodie 128 B5
King's Acre ...49 E6
Kingsand 6 D2
Kingsbarns ...129 C7
Kingsbridge Devon .6 E5
  Som 21 F8
King's Bromley .62 C5
Kingsburgh ...149 C8
Kingsbury London .41 F5
  Warks 63 E6
Kingsbury
  Episcopi 12 B2
King's Caple ...36 B2
Kingsclere 26 D3
King's Cliffe ..65 E7
Kingscote 37 E5
Kingscott 9 C7
King's Coughton .51 D5
Kingscross ...143 F11
Kingsdon 12 B3
Kingsdown 31 E7
Kingseat 128 E3
Kingsey 39 D7
King's Heath ..62 F4
Kings Hedges ...55 C5
King's Hill 29 D7
Kingskerswell ..7 C6
Kingskettle ..128 D5
Kingsland Anglesey .82 C2
  Hereford 49 C6
Kings Langley ..40 D3
Kingsley Ches W ..74 B2
  Hants 27 F5
  Staffs 75 E7
Kingsley Green ..27 F6
Kingsley Holt ...75 E7
Kingsley Park ..53 C5

King's Lynn 67 B6
King's Meaburn . . 99 B8
King's Mills . . . 73 E7
Kingsmuir Angus . . 129 D7
Kings Muir . . . 121 F5
King's Newnham . . 52 B2
King's Newton . . 63 B7
Kingsnorth . . . 19 B7
King's Norton Leics 64 D3
 W Mid . . . 51 B5
King's Nympton . . 9 C8
King's Pyon . . . 49 D6
King's Ripton . . . 54 B3
King's Somborne . . 25 F8
King's Stag . . . 12 C5
King's Stanley . . 37 D5
King's Sutton . . . 52 F2
Kingstanding . . . 62 E4
Kingsteignton . . 7 B6
King Sterndale . . 75 B7
King's Thorn . . . 49 F7
Kingsthorpe . . . 53 C5
Kingston Cambs . . 54 D4
 Devon . . . 6 E4
 Dorset . . . 13 D5
 Dorset . . . 13 G7
 E Loth . . . 129 F7
 Hants . . . 14 D2
 IoW . . . 15 F5
 Kent . . . 31 D5
 Moray . . . 152 B3
Kingston Bagpuize 38 E4
Kingston Blount . . 39 E7
Kingston by Sea . . 17 D6
Kingston Deverill . 24 F3
Kingstone Hereford . 49 F6
 Som . . . 11 C8
 Staffs . . . 62 B4
Kingston Gorse . . 16 D4
Kingston Lisle . . 38 F3
Kingston Maurward . 12 E5
Kingston near Lewes . . . 17 D7
Kingston on Soar . 64 B2
Kingston Russell . 12 E3
Kingston St Mary . 11 B7
Kingston Seymour 23 C6
Kingston upon Hull . . . 90 B4
Kingston upon Thames . . 28 C2
Kingstown . . . 108 D3
King's Walden . . 40 B4
Kingswear . . . 7 E6
Kingswells . . . 141 D7
Kingswinford . . 62 F2
Kingswood Bucks . 39 C6
 Glos . . . 36 E4
 Hereford . . 48 D4
 Kent . . . 30 D2
 Powys . . . 60 D2
 S Glos . . . 23 B8
 Sur . . . 28 D3
 Warks . . . 51 B6
Kings Worthy . . 26 F2
Kingthorpe . . . 78 B4
Kington Hereford . 48 D4
 Worcs . . . 50 D4
Kington Langley . 24 B4
Kington Magna . . 13 B5
Kington St Michael . . 24 B4
Kingussie . . . 138 D3
Kingweston . . . 23 F7
Kininvie House . . 152 D3
Kinkell Bridge . . 127 C8
Kinknockie . . . 153 D10
Kinlet . . . 61 F7
Kinloch Fife . . 128 C4
 Highld . . . 146 B6
 Highld . . . 149 G11
 Highld . . . 156 F6
 Perth . . . 133 B8
 Perth . . . 134 E2
Kinlochan . . . 130 C2
Kinlochard . . . 126 D3
Kinlochbeoraid . 147 C11
Kinlochbervie . . 156 D5
Kinlocheil . . . 130 B3
Kinlochewe . . . 150 E3
Kinloch Hourn . . 136 D2
Kinloch Laggan . 137 F8
Kinlochleven . . 137 C5
Kinloch Lodge . . 157 D8
Kinlochmoidart . 147 D10
Kinlochmorar . . 147 B11
Kinlochmore . . 131 C5
Kinloch Rannoch . 132 D3
Kinlochspelve . . 124 C2
Kinloid . . . 147 C9
Kinloss . . . 151 E13
Kinmel Bay . . . 72 A3
Kinmuck . . . 141 C7
Kinmundy . . . 141 C7
Kinnadie . . . 153 D9
Kinnaird . . . 128 B4
Kinnaird Castle . 135 D6
Kinneff . . . 135 B8
Kinnelhead . . . 114 D3
Kinnell . . . 135 D6
Kinnerley . . . 60 B3
Kinnersley Hereford 48 E5
 Worcs . . . 50 E3
Kinnerton . . . 48 C4
Kinnesswood . . 128 D3
Kininvie . . . 101 B5
Kinnordy . . . 134 D3
Kinoulton . . . 77 F6
Kinross . . . 128 D3
Kinrossie . . . 134 F1
Kinsbourne Green . 40 C4
Kinsey Heath . . 74 E3
Kinsham Hereford . 49 C5
 Worcs . . . 50 F4
Kinsley . . . 88 C5
Kinson . . . 13 E8
Kintbury . . . 25 C8
Kintessack . . 151 E12
Kintillo . . . 128 C3
Kintocher . . . 140 D4
Kinton Hereford . 49 B6
 Shrops . . . 60 C3
Kintore . . . 141 C6
Kintour . . . 142 C5
Kintra Argyll . . 142 D4
 Argyll . . . 146 J6

Kintraw . . . 124 E4
Kinuachdrachd . . 124 F3
Kinveachy . . . 138 C5
Kinver . . . 62 F2
Kippax . . . 95 F7
Kippen . . . 127 E5
Kippford or Scaur . . . 106 D5
Kirbister Orkney . 159 F7
 Orkney . . . 159 H4
Kirby Bedon . . 69 D5
Kirby Bellars . . 64 C4
Kirby Cane . . . 69 E6
Kirby Cross . . . 43 B8
Kirby Grindalythe . 96 C5
Kirby Hill N Yorks . 95 C6
 N Yorks . . 101 D6
Kirby Knowle . . 102 F2
Kirby-le-Soken . . 43 B8
Kirby Misperton . 96 B3
Kirby Muxloe . . 64 D2
Kirby Row . . . 69 E6
Kirby Sigston . . 102 E2
Kirby Underdale . 96 C4
Kirby Wiske . . . 102 F1
Kirdford . . . 16 B4
Kirk . . . 158 E4
Kirkabister . . . 160 K6
Kirkandrews . . 106 E3
Kirkandrews upon Eden . . . 108 D3
Kirkbampton . . 108 D3
Kirkbean . . . 107 D6
Kirk Bramwith . . 89 C7
Kirkbride . . . 108 D2
Kirkbuddo . . . 135 E5
Kirkburn Borders . 121 F5
 E Yorks . . 97 D5
Kirkburton . . . 88 C2
Kirkby Lincs . . 90 E4
 Mers . . . 86 E2
 N Yorks . . 102 D3
Kirkby Fleetham . 101 E7
Kirkby Green . . 78 D3
Kirkby-in-Ashfield 76 D5
Kirkby-in-Furness 98 F4
Kirkby la Thorpe . 78 E3
Kirkby Lonsdale . 93 B6
Kirkby Malham . . 93 C8
Kirkby Mallory . . 63 D8
Kirkby Malzeard . 94 B5
Kirkby Mills . . 103 F5
Kirkbymoorside . 102 F4
Kirkby on Bain . 78 C5
Kirkby Overblow . 95 E6
Kirkby Stephen . 100 D2
Kirkby Thore . . 99 B8
Kirkby Underwood 65 B7
Kirkby Wharfe . . 95 E8
Kirkcaldy . . . 128 E4
Kirkcambeck . . 108 C5
Kirkcarswell . . 106 E4
Kirkcolm . . . 104 C4
Kirkconnel . . . 113 C7
Kirkconnell . . 107 C6
Kirkcowan . . . 105 C7
Kirkcudbright . . 106 D3
Kirkdale . . . 85 E4
Kirk Deighton . . 95 D6
Kirk Ella . . . 90 B4
Kirkfieldbank . . 119 E8
Kirkgunzeon . . 107 C5
Kirk Hallam . . . 76 E4
Kirkham Lancs . . 92 F4
 N Yorks . . 96 C3
Kirkhamgate . . 88 B3
Kirk Hammerton . 95 D7
Kirkharle . . . 117 F6
Kirkheaton Northumb . . 110 B3
 W Yorks . . 88 C2
Kirkhill Angus . . 135 C6
 Highld . . . 151 G8
 Midloth . . 120 C5
 Moray . . . 152 E2
Kirkhope . . . 115 B6
Kirkhouse . . . 121 F6
Kirkiboll . . . 157 D8
Kirkibost . . . 149 G10
Kirkinch . . . 134 E3
Kirkinner . . . 105 D8
Kirkintilloch . . 119 B6
Kirk Ireton . . . 76 D2
Kirkland Cumb . . 98 C2
 Cumb . . . 109 F6
 Dumfries . . 113 C7
 Dumfries . . 113 E8
Kirk Langley . . 76 F2
Kirkleatham . . 102 B3
Kirklevington . . 102 D2
Kirkley . . . 69 E8
Kirklington Notts . 77 D6
 N Yorks . . 101 F8
Kirklinton . . . 108 C4
Kirkliston . . . 120 B4
Kirkmaiden . . 104 F5
Kirk Merrington . 111 F5
Kirkmichael Perth 133 D7
 S Ayrs . . . 112 D3
Kirk Michael . . 84 C3
Kirkmuirhill . . 119 E7
Kirknewton Northumb . . 122 F5
 W Loth . . . 120 C4
Kirkney . . . 152 E5
Kirk of Shotts . . 119 C8
Kirkoswald Cumb . 109 E5
 S Ayrs . . . 112 D2
Kirkpatrick Durham . . 106 B4
Kirkpatrick-Fleming . . . 108 B2
Kirk Sandall . . 89 D7
Kirksanton . . . 98 F3
Kirk Smeaton . . 89 C6
Kirkstall . . . 95 F5
Kirkstead . . . 78 C4
Kirkstile . . . 152 E5
Kirkstyle . . . 158 C5
Kirkton Aberds . . 140 B5
 Aberds . . . 153 D6
 Angus . . . 134 E4
 Angus . . . 134 F4
 Borders . . 115 C8
 Dumfries . . 114 D3
 Fife . . . 129 B5
 Highld . . . 149 F13
 Highld . . . 150 H7

Kirkton continued
 Highld . . . 151 B10
 Highld . . . 151 F10
 Perth . . . 127 C8
 S Lanark . . 114 B2
 Stirling . . 126 D4
Kirktonhill . . . 121 D7
Kirkton Manor . . 120 F5
Kirkton of Airlie . 134 D3
Kirkton of Auchterhouse . 134 F3
Kirkton of Auchterless . 153 D7
Kirkton of Barevan . . . 151 G11
Kirkton of Bourtie . . . 141 B7
Kirkton of Collace . . . 134 F1
Kirkton of Craig . 135 D7
Kirkton of Culsalmond . 153 E6
Kirkton of Durris . 141 E6
Kirkton of Glenbuchat . . 140 C2
Kirkton of Glenisla . . . 134 C2
Kirkton of Kingoldrum . . 134 D3
Kirkton of Largo . 129 D6
Kirkton of Lethendy . . . 133 E8
Kirkton of Logie Buchan . . . 141 B8
Kirkton of Maryculter . . 141 E7
Kirkton of Menmuir . . . 135 C5
Kirkton of Monikie . . . 135 F5
Kirkton of Oyne . 141 B5
Kirkton of Rayne . 153 F6
Kirkton of Skene . 141 D7
Kirkton of Tough . 140 C5
Kirktown . . . 153 C10
Kirktown of Alvah . . . 153 B6
Kirktown of Deskford . . 152 B5
Kirktown of Fetteresso . . 141 F7
Kirktown of Mortlach . . 152 E3
Kirktown of Slains . . . 141 B9
Kirkurd . . . 120 E4
Kirkwall . . . 159 G5
Kirkwhelpington 117 F5
Kirk Yetholm . . 116 B4
Kirmington . . . 90 C5
Kirmond le Mire . 91 E5
Kirn . . . 145 F10
Kirriemuir . . . 134 D3
Kirstead Green . 69 E5
Kirtlebridge . . 108 B2
Kirtleton . . . 115 F5
Kirtling . . . 55 D7
Kirtling Green . . 55 D7
Kirtlington . . . 38 C4
Kirtomy . . . 157 C10
Kirton Lincs . . 79 F6
 Notts . . . 77 C6
 Suff . . . 57 F6
Kirton End . . . 79 E5
Kirton Holme . . 79 E5
Kirton in Lindsey . 90 E3
Kislingbury . . 52 D4
Kites Hardwick . 52 C2
Kittisford . . . 11 B5
Kittle . . . 33 F6
Kitt's Green . . 63 F5
Kitt's Moss . . . 87 F6
Kittybrewster . . 141 D8
Kitwood . . . 26 F4
Kivernoll . . . 49 F6
Kiveton Park . . 89 F5
Knaith . . . 90 F2
Knaith Park . . 90 F2
Knap Corner . . 13 B6
Knaphill . . . 27 D7
Knapp Perth . . 134 F2
 Som . . . 11 B8
Knapthorpe . . 77 D7
Knapton Norf . . 81 D9
 York . . . 95 D8
Knapton Green . 49 D6
Knapwell . . . 54 C4
Knaresborough . 95 D6
Knarsdale . . . 109 D6
Knauchland . . 152 C5
Knaven . . . 153 D8
Knayton . . . 102 F2
Knebworth . . . 41 B5
Knedlington . . 89 B8
Kneesall . . . 77 C7
Kneesworth . . 54 E4
Kneeton . . . 77 E7
Knelston . . . 33 F5
Knenhall . . . 75 F6
Knettishall . . . 68 F2
Knightacott . . . 21 F5
Knightcote . . . 51 D8
Knightley Dale . . 62 B2
Knighton Devon . . 6 E3
 Leicester . . 64 D2
 Staffs . . . 61 B7
 Staffs . . . 74 E4
Knighton = Tref-y-Clawdd . . 48 B4
Knightswood . . 118 C5
Knightwick . . 50 D2
Knill . . . 48 C4
Knipton . . . 77 F8
Knitsley . . . 110 E4
Kniveton . . . 76 D2
Knock Argyll . . 147 H8
 Cumb . . . 100 B1
 Moray . . . 152 C5
Knockally . . . 158 H3
Knockan . . . 156 H5
Knockandhu . . 139 B8
Knockando . . 152 D1
Knockando House . . . 152 D2
Knockbain . . . 151 F9
Knockbreck . . 148 B7
Knockbrex . . . 106 E2
Knockdee . . . 158 D3
Knockdolian . . 104 A5

Knockenkelly . . 143 F11
Knockentiber . . 118 F3
Knockespock House . . . 140 B4
Knockfarrel . . 151 F8
Knockglass . . . 104 D4
Knockholt . . . 29 D5
Knockholt Pound . 29 D5
Knockin . . . 60 B3
Knockinlaw . . . 118 F4
Knocklearn . . . 106 B4
Knocknaha . . . 143 G7
Knocknain . . . 104 C3
Knockrome . . . 144 F4
Knocksharry . . 84 D2
Knodishall . . . 57 C8
Knolls Green . . 74 B5
Knolton . . . 73 F7
Knolton Bryn . . 73 F7
Knook . . . 24 E4
Knossington . . 64 D5
Knott End-on-Sea 92 E3
Knotting . . . 53 C8
Knotting Green . 53 C8
Knottingley . . 89 B6
Knotts Cumb . . 99 B7
 Lancs . . . 93 D7
Knotty Ash . . . 86 E2
Knotty Green . . 40 E2
Knowbury . . . 49 B7
Knowe . . . 105 B7
Knowehead . . 113 E6
Knowesgate . . 117 F5
Knowes of Elrick 152 C6
Knoweton . . . 119 D7
Knowhead . . . 153 C9
Knowle Bristol . . 23 B8
 Devon . . . 10 D2
 Devon . . . 11 F5
 Devon . . . 20 F3
 Shrops . . . 49 B7
 W Mid . . . 51 B6
Knowle Green . . 93 F6
Knowle Park . . 94 E3
Knowl Hill . . . 27 B6
Knowlton Dorset . 13 C8
 Kent . . . 31 D6
Knowsley . . . 86 E2
Knowstone . . . 10 B3
Knox Bridge . . 29 E8
Knucklas . . . 48 B4
Knuston . . . 53 C7
Knutsford . . . 74 B4
Knutton . . . 74 E5
Knypersley . . 75 D5
Kuggar . . . 3 E6
Kyleakin . . . 149 F12
Kyle of Lochalsh 149 F12
Kylerhea . . . 149 F12
Kylesknoydart . 147 B11
Kylesku . . . 156 F5
Kylesmorar . . 147 B11
Kylestrome . . 156 F5
Kyllachy House . 138 B3
Kynaston . . . 60 B3
Kynnersley . . . 61 C6
Kyre Magna . . 49 C8

L

Labost . . . 155 C7
Lacasaidh . . . 155 D7
Lacasdal . . . 155 D9
Laceby . . . 91 D6
Lacey Green . . 39 E8
Lach Dennis . . 74 B4
Lackford . . . 55 B8
Lacock . . . 24 C4
Ladbroke . . . 52 D2
Laddingford . . 29 E7
Lade Bank . . . 79 D6
Ladock . . . 4 D3
Lady . . . 159 D7
Ladybank . . . 128 C5
Ladykirk . . . 122 E4
Ladywood . . . 50 C3
Laga . . . 147 E9
Lagalochan . . 124 D4
Lagavulin . . . 142 D5
Lagg Argyll . . 144 F4
 N Ayrs . . . 143 F10
Laggan Argyll . . 142 C3
 Highld . . . 137 E5
 Highld . . . 138 E2
 Highld . . . 147 D10
 S Ayrs . . . 112 F2
Lagganulva . . 146 G7
Laide . . . 155 H13
Laigh Fenwick . 118 F4
Laigh Glengall . 112 C3
Laighmuir . . . 118 F4
Laindon . . . 42 F2
Lair . . . 150 G3
Lairg . . . 157 J8
Lairg Lodge . . 157 J8
Lairgmore . . 151 H8
Lairg Muir . . . 157 J8
Laisterdyke . . 94 F4
Laithes . . . 108 F4
Lake IoW . . . 15 F6
 Wilts . . . 25 F6
Lakenham . . . 68 D5
Lakenheath . . 67 F7
Lakesend . . . 66 E5
Lakeside . . . 99 F5
Laleham . . . 27 C8
Laleston . . . 21 B7
Lamarsh . . . 56 F2
Lamas . . . 81 E8
Lambden . . . 122 E3
Lamberhurst Quarter . . . 18 B3
Lamberton . . 123 D5
Lamberton . . 28 D4
Lambhill . . . 119 C5
Lambley Northumb . 109 D6
 Notts . . . 77 E6
Lamborough Hill . 38 D4
Lambourn . . . 25 B8
Lambourne End . 41 E7
Lambs Green . . 28 F3
Lambston . . . 44 D4
Lambton . . . 111 D5
Lamerton . . . 6 B2
Lamesley . . . 111 D5

Laminess . . . 159 E7
Lamington Highld . . . 151 D10
 S Lanark . . 120 F2
Lamlash . . . 143 E11
Lamloch . . . 112 E5
Lamonby . . . 108 F4
Lamorna . . . 2 D3
Lamorran . . . 3 B7
Lampardbrook . . 57 C6
Lampeter = Llanbedr Pont Steffan . . 46 E4
Lampeter Velfrey . 32 C2
Lamphey . . . 32 D1
Lamplugh . . . 98 B2
Lamport . . . 53 B5
Lamyatt . . . 23 F8
Lana . . . 8 E5
Lanark . . . 119 E8
Lancaster . . . 92 C4
Lanchester . . 110 E4
Lancing . . . 17 D5
Landbeach . . 55 C5
Landcross . . 9 B6
Landerberry . . 141 D6
Landford . . . 14 C3
Landford Manor . 14 B3
Landimore . . . 33 E5
Landkey . . . 20 F4
Landore . . . 33 E7
Landrake . . . 5 C8
Landscove . . . 7 C5
Landshipping . . 32 C1
Landshipping Quay . . . 32 C1
Landulph . . . 6 C2
Landwade . . . 55 C7
Lane . . . 4 C3
Laneast . . . 8 F4
Lane End Bucks . 39 E8
 Cumb . . . 98 E3
 Dorset . . . 13 E6
 Hants . . . 15 B6
 IoW . . . 15 F7
 Lancs . . . 93 E8
Lane Ends Lancs . 93 D7
 Lancs . . . 93 F7
 N Yorks . . 94 E2
Laneham . . . 77 B8
Lanehead Durham . 109 E8
 Northumb . . 116 F3
Lane Head Derbys . 75 B8
 Durham . . 101 C6
 Gtr Man . . 86 E4
 W Yorks . . 88 D2
Lanercost . . . 109 C5
Laneshaw Bridge . 94 E2
Lanfach . . . 35 E6
Langar . . . 77 F7
Langbank . . . 118 B3
Langbar . . . 94 D3
Langburnshields . 115 D8
Langcliffe . . . 93 C8
Langdale . . . 156 F5
Langdale End . . 103 E7
Langdon . . . 8 F5
Langdon Beck . . 109 F8
Langdon Hills . . 42 F2
Langdyke . . . 128 D5
Langenhoe . . 43 C6
Langford C Beds . 54 E2
 Devon . . . 10 D5
 Essex . . . 42 D4
 Notts . . . 77 D8
 Oxon . . . 38 D2
Langford Budville . 11 B6
Langham Essex . . 56 F4
 Norf . . . 81 C6
 Rutland . . 64 C5
 Suff . . . 56 C3
Langhaugh . . 120 F5
Langho . . . 93 F7
Langholm . . . 115 F6
Langleeford . . 117 B5
Langley Ches E . . 75 B6
 Hants . . . 14 D5
 Herts . . . 41 B5
 Kent . . . 30 D2
 Northumb . . 109 D8
 Slough . . . 27 B8
 Warks . . . 51 C6
 W Sus . . . 16 B2
Langley Burrell . 24 B4
Langley Common . 76 F2
Langley Heath . . 30 D2
Langley Lower Green . . . 54 F5
Langley Marsh . . 11 B5
Langley Park . . 110 E5
Langley Street . . 69 D6
Langley Upper Green . . . 54 F5
Langney . . . 18 E3
Langold . . . 89 F6
Langore . . . 8 F5
Langport . . . 12 B2
Langrick . . . 79 E5
Langridge . . . 24 C2
Langridge Ford . . 9 B7
Langrigg . . . 107 E8
Langrish . . . 15 B8
Langsett . . . 88 D3
Langshaw . . . 121 F8
Langside . . . 127 C6
Langskaill . . . 159 D5
Langstone Hants . 15 D8
 Newport . . 35 E7
Langthorne . . 101 E7
Langthorpe . . 95 C6
Langthwaite . . 101 D5
Langtoft E Yorks . 97 C6
 Lincs . . . 65 C8
Langton Durham . 101 C6
 Lincs . . . 78 C5
 N Yorks . . 96 C3
Langton by Wragby . . . 78 B4
Langton Green Kent . . . 18 B2
 Suff . . . 56 B5
Langton Herring . 12 F4
Langton Matravers . . 13 G8
Langtree . . . 9 C6
Langwathby . . 109 F5
Langwell House . 158 H3
Langwell Lodge . 156 J4

Langwith . . . 76 C5
Langwith Junction 76 C5
Langworth . . . 78 B3
Lanivet . . . 4 C5
Lanlivery . . . 5 D5
Lanner . . . 3 C6
Lanreath . . . 5 D6
Lansallos . . . 5 D6
Lansdown . . . 37 B6
Lanteglos Highway . 5 D6
Lanton Borders . . 116 B2
 Northumb . . 122 F5
Lapford . . . 10 D2
Laphroaig . . . 142 D4
Lapley . . . 62 C2
Lapworth . . . 51 B6
Larachbeg . . . 147 G9
Larbert . . . 127 F7
Larden Green . . 74 D2
Largie . . . 152 E6
Largiemore . . 145 E8
Largoward . . 129 D6
Largs . . . 118 D2
Largybeg . . . 143 F11
Largymore . . 143 F11
Larkfield . . . 118 B2
Larkhall . . . 119 D7
Larkhill . . . 25 E6
Larling . . . 68 F2
Larriston . . . 115 E8
Lartington . . . 101 C5
Lary . . . 140 D2
Lasham . . . 26 E4
Lashenden . . 30 E2
Lassington . . . 36 B4
Lassodie . . . 128 E3
Lastingham . . 103 E5
Latcham . . . 23 E6
Latchford Herts . . 41 B6
 Warr . . . 86 F4
Latchingdon . . 42 D4
Latchley . . . 6 B2
Lately Common . 86 E4
Lathbury . . . 53 E6
Latheron . . . 158 G3
Latheronwheel . 158 G3
Latheronwheel House . . . 158 G3
Lathones . . . 129 D6
Latimer . . . 40 E3
Latteridge . . . 36 F3
Lattiford . . . 12 B4
Latton . . . 37 E7
Latton Bush . . 41 D7
Lauchintilly . . 141 C6
Lauder . . . 121 E8
Laugharne . . 32 C4
Laughterton . . 77 B8
Laughton E Sus . . 18 D2
 Leics . . . 64 F3
 Lincs . . . 78 F3
 Lincs . . . 90 E2
Laughton Common 89 F6
Laughton en le Morthen . . . 89 F6
Launcells . . . 8 D4
Launceston . . 8 F5
Launton . . . 39 B6
Laurencekirk . . 135 B7
Laurieston Dumfries . . 106 C3
 Falk . . . 120 B2
Lavendon . . . 53 D7
Lavenham . . 56 E3
Laverhay . . . 114 E4
Laversdale . . 108 C4
Laverstock . . 25 F6
Laverstoke . . 26 E2
Laverton Glos . . 51 F5
 N Yorks . . 94 B5
 Som . . . 24 D2
Lavister . . . 73 D7
Law . . . 119 D8
Lawers Perth . . 127 B6
 Perth . . . 132 F3
Lawford . . . 56 F4
Lawhitton . . . 9 F5
Lawkland . . . 93 C7
Lawley . . . 61 D6
Lawnhead . . . 62 B2
Lawrenny . . . 32 D1
Lawshall . . . 56 D2
Lawton . . . 49 D6
Laxey . . . 84 D4
Laxfield . . . 57 B6
Laxfirth Shetland . 160 H6
 Shetland . . 160 J6
Laxford Bridge . 156 E5
Laxo . . . 160 G6
Laxobigging . . 160 F6
Laxton E Yorks . . 89 B8
 Northants . . 65 E6
 Notts . . . 77 C7
Laycock . . . 94 E3
Layer Breton . . 43 C5
Layer de la Haye . 43 C5
Layer Marney . . 43 C5
Layham . . . 56 E4
Laylands Green . 25 C8
Laytham . . . 96 F3
Layton . . . 92 F3
Lazenby . . . 102 B3
Lazonby . . . 108 F5
Lea Derbys . . 76 D3
 Hereford . . 36 B3
 Lincs . . . 90 F2
 Shrops . . . 60 D4
 Shrops . . . 60 F4
 Wilts . . . 37 F6
Leabrooks . . 76 D4
Leac a Li . . . 154 H6
Leachkin . . . 151 G9
Leadburn . . . 120 D5
Leaden Roding . 42 C1
Leadgate Cumb . 109 E7
 Durham . . 110 D4
 T&W . . . 110 D4
Leadhills . . . 113 C8
Leafield . . . 38 C3
Leagrave . . . 40 B3
Leake . . . 102 E2
Leake Commonside . . 79 D6
Lealholm . . . 103 D5
Lealt Argyll . . 144 D5
 Highld . . . 149 B10
Lea Marston . . 63 E6

Leamington Hastings . . . 52 C2
Leamonsley . . 62 D5
Leanaig . . . 151 F8
Leargybreck . . 144 F4
Leasingham . . 78 E3
Leasingthorne . 101 B7
Leasowe . . . 85 E3
Leatherhead . . 28 D2
Leatherhead Common . . . 28 D2
Leathley . . . 94 E5
Leaton . . . 60 C4
Lea Town . . . 92 F4
Leaveland . . 30 D4
Leavening . . 96 C3
Leaves Green . . 28 C5
Leazes . . . 110 D4
Lebberston . . 103 F8
Lechlade-on-Thames . . 38 E2
Leck . . . 93 B6
Leckford . . . 25 F8
Leckfurin . . . 157 D10
Leckgruinart . . 142 B3
Leckhampstead Bucks . . . 52 F5
 W Berks . . 26 B2
Leckhampstead Thicket . . . 26 B2
Leckhampton . 37 C6
Leckie . . . 150 E3
Leckmelm . . 150 B4
Leckwith . . . 22 B3
Leconfield . . 97 E6
Ledaig . . . 124 B5
Ledburn . . . 40 B2
Ledbury . . . 50 F2
Ledcharrie . . 126 B4
Leddington . . 50 F2
Ledgemoor . . 49 D6
Ledicot . . . 49 C6
Ledmore . . . 156 H5
Lednagullin . . 157 C10
Ledsham Ches W . 73 B7
 W Yorks . . 89 B5
Ledston . . . 88 B5
Ledston Luck . . 95 F7
Ledwell . . . 38 B4
Lee Argyll . . 146 K2
 Devon . . . 20 E3
 Hants . . . 14 C4
 Lancs . . . 93 D5
 Shrops . . . 73 F8
Leeans . . . 160 J5
Leebotten . . 160 L6
Leebotwood . . 60 E4
Lee Brockhurst . 60 B5
Leece . . . 92 C2
Leechpool . . 44 D4
Lee Clump . . 40 D2
Leeds Kent . . 30 D2
 W Yorks . . 95 F5
Leedstown . . 2 C5
Leek . . . 75 D6
Leek Wootton . 51 C7
Lee Mill . . . 6 D4
Leeming . . . 101 F7
Leeming Bar . . 101 E7
Lee Moor . . . 6 C3
Lee-on-the-Solent . . 15 D6
Lees Derbys . . 76 F2
 Gtr Man . . 87 D7
 W Yorks . . 94 F3
Leeswood . . 73 C6
Legbourne . . 91 F7
Legerwood . . 121 E8
Legsby . . . 90 F5
Leicester . . . 64 D2
Leicester Forest East . . . 64 D2
Leigh Dorset . . 12 D4
 Glos . . . 37 B5
 Gtr Man . . 86 D4
 Kent . . . 29 E6
 Shrops . . . 60 D3
 Sur . . . 28 E3
 Wilts . . . 37 E7
 Worcs . . . 50 D2
Leigh Beck . . 42 F4
Leigh Common . 12 B5
Leigh Delamere . 24 B3
Leigh Green . . 19 B6
Leigh on Sea . . 42 F4
Leigh Park . . 15 D8
Leigh Sinton . . 50 D2
Leighswood . . 62 D4
Leighterton . . 37 E5
Leigh upon Mendip . . . 23 E8
Leigh Woods . . 23 B7
Leinthall Earls . 49 C6
Leinthall Starkes . 49 B6
Leintwardine . . 49 B6
Leire . . . 64 E2
Leirinmore . . 156 C7
Leiston . . . 57 C8
Leitfie . . . 134 E2
Leith . . . 121 B5
Leitholm . . . 122 E3
Lelant . . . 2 C4
Lelley . . . 97 F8
Lem Hill . . . 50 B2
Lemington Hall 117 C7
Lempitlaw . . 122 F3
Lenchwick . . 50 E5
Lendalfoot . . 112 F1
Lendrick Lodge . 126 D4
Lenham . . . 30 D2
Lenham Heath . 30 E3
Lennel . . . 122 E4
Lennoxtown . . 119 B6
Lenton Lincs . . 78 F3
 Nottingham . . 77 F5
Lentran . . . 151 G8
Lenwade . . 68 C3
Leny House . . 126 D5
Lenzie . . . 119 B6
Leoch . . . 134 F3

Leochel-Cushnie 140 C4
Leominster . . 49 D6
Leonard Stanley . 37 D5
Leorin . . . 142 D4
Lepe . . . 15 E5
Lephin . . . 148 D6
Lephinchapel . 145 D8
Lephinmore . . 145 D8
Le Planel Guern . 16
Leppington . . 96 C3
Lepton . . . 88 C3
Lerryn . . . 5 D6
Lerwick . . . 160 J6
Lesbury . . . 117 C8
Le Skerne Haughton . . 101 C8
Leslie Aberds . . 140 B4
 Fife . . . 128 D4
Lesmahagow . 119 F8
Lesnewth . . 8 E3
Lessendrum . . 152 D5
Lessingham . . 69 B6
Lessonhall . . 108 D2
Leswalt . . . 104 C4
Letchmore Heath 40 E4
Letchworth . . 54 F3
Letcombe Bassett 38 F3
Letcombe Regis . 38 F3
Letham Angus . . 135 E5
 Falk . . . 127 F7
 Fife . . . 128 C5
 Perth . . . 128 B2
Letham Grange . 135 E6
Lethenty . . . 153 D8
Letheringham . 57 D6
Letheringsett . . 81 D6
Lettaford . . . 10 F2
Lettan . . . 159 D8
Letterewe . . 150 D2
Letterfearn . . 149 F13
Letterfinlay . . 137 E5
Lettermorar . . 147 C10
Lettermore . . 146 G7
Letters . . . 150 C4
Letterston . . 44 C4
Lettoch Highld . 139 C6
 Highld . . . 151 H13
Letton Hereford . 48 E5
 Hereford . . 49 B5
Letton Green . . 68 D2
Letty Green . . 41 C5
Letwell . . . 89 F6
Leuchars . . . 129 B6
Leuchars House . 152 B2
Leumrabhagh . . 155 F8
Levan . . . 118 B2
Levaneap . . 160 G6
Levedale . . . 62 C2
Leven E Yorks . . 97 E7
 Fife . . . 129 D5
Levencorroch . 143 F11
Levens . . . 99 F6
Levens Green . . 41 B6
Levenshulme . . 87 E6
Levenwick . . 160 L6
Leverburgh = An t-Ob . . 154 J5
Leverington . . 66 C4
Leverton . . . 79 E7
Leverton Highgate 79 E7
Leverton Lucasgate . . . 79 E7
Leverton Outgate . 79 E7
Levington . . . 57 F6
Levisham . . 103 E6
Levishie . . . 137 C7
Lew . . . 38 D3
Lewannick . . 8 F4
Lewdown . . . 9 F6
Lewes . . . 17 C8
Leweston . . 44 C4
Lewisham . . 28 B4
Lewiston . . . 137 B8
Lewistown . . 34 F3
Lewknor . . . 39 E7
Leworthy Devon . 8 D5
 Devon . . . 21 F5
Lewtrenchard . . 9 F6
Lexden . . . 43 B5
Ley Aberds . . 140 C4
 Corn . . . 5 C6
Leybourne . . 29 D7
Leyburn . . . 101 E6
Leyfields . . . 63 D6
Leyhill . . . 40 D2
Leyland . . . 86 B3
Leylodge . . . 141 C6
Leymoor . . . 88 C2
Leys Aberds . . 153 C10
 Perth . . . 134 F2
Leys Castle . . 151 G9
Leys of Cossans . 134 E3
Leysmill . . . 135 E6
Leysters Pole . . 49 C7
Leyton . . . 41 F6
Leytonstone . . 41 F6
Lezant . . . 5 B8
Leziate . . . 67 C6
Lhanbryde . . 152 B2
Liatrie . . . 150 H5
Libanus . . . 34 B3
Libberton . . 120 E2
Liberton . . . 121 C5
Liceasto . . . 154 H6
Lichfield . . . 62 D5
Lickey . . . 50 B4
Lickey End . . 50 B4
Lickfold . . . 16 B3
Liddel . . . 159 K5
Liddesdale . . 130 D1
Liddington . . 38 F2
Lidgate . . . 55 D8
Lidget . . . 89 D7
Lidget Green . . 77 C6
Lidgett . . . 77 C6
Lidlington . . . 53 F7
Lidstone . . . 38 B3
Lieurary . . . 158 D2
Liff . . . 134 F3
Lifton . . . 9 F5
Liftondown . . 9 F5
Lighthorne . . 51 D8
Lightwater . . 27 C7
Lightwood . . 75 E6
Lightwood Green Ches E . . 74 E3
 Wrex . . . 73 E7

Lilbourne . . . 52 B3
Lilburn Tower . . 117 B6
Lilleshall . . . 61 C7
Lilley Herts . . 40 B4
 W Berks . . 26 B2
Lilliesleaf . . . 115 B8
Lillingstone Dayrell . . . 52 F5
Lillingstone Lovell 52 E5
Lillington Dorset . 12 C4
 Warks . . . 51 C8
Lilliput . . . 13 E8
Lilstock . . . 22 E3
Lilyhurst . . . 61 C7
Limbury . . . 40 B3
Limebrook . . 49 C5
Limefield . . . 87 C6
Limekilns . . . 128 F2
Limerigg . . . 119 B8
Limerstone . . 14 F5
Limington . . 12 B3
Limpenhoe . . 69 D6
Limpley Stoke . 24 C2
Limpsfield . . 28 D5
Limpsfield Chart 28 D5
Linby . . . 76 D5
Linchmere . . 27 F6
Lincluden . . . 107 B6
Lincoln . . . 78 B2
Lincomb . . . 50 C3
Lincombe . . . 6 D5
Lindale . . . 99 F6
Lindal in Furness 92 B2
Lindean . . . 121 F7
Lindfield . . . 17 B7
Lindford . . . 27 F6
Lindifferon . . 128 C5
Lindley . . . 88 C2
Lindley Green . . 94 E5
Lindores . . . 128 C4
Lindridge . . . 49 C8
Lindsell . . . 42 B2
Lindsey . . . 56 E3
Linford Hants . . 14 D2
 Thurrock . . 29 B7
Lingague . . . 84 E2
Lingards Wood . 87 C8
Lingbob . . . 94 F3
Lingdale . . . 102 C4
Lingen . . . 49 C5
Lingfield . . . 28 E4
Lingreabhagh . . 154 J5
Lingwood . . 69 D6
Linicro . . . 149 B8
Linkenholt . . 25 D8
Linkhill . . . 18 C5
Linkinhorne . . 5 B8
Linklater . . . 159 K5
Linksness . . 159 H3
Linktown . . 128 E4
Linley . . . 60 E3
Linley Green . . 49 D8
Linlithgow Bridge . . . 120 B2
Linshiels . . . 116 D4
Linsidemore . . 151 B8
Linslade . . . 40 B2
Linstead Parva . 57 B7
Linstock . . . 108 D4
Linthwaite . . 88 C2
Lintlaw . . . 122 D4
Lintmill . . . 152 B5
Linton Borders . . 116 B3
 Cambs . . . 55 E6
 Derbys . . . 63 C6
 Hereford . . 36 B3
 Kent . . . 29 E8
 Northumb . . 117 E8
 N Yorks . . 94 C2
Linton-on-Ouse . 95 C7
Linwood Hants . . 14 D2
 Lincs . . . 90 F5
 Renfs . . . 118 C4
Lionacleit . . . 148 D2
Lional . . . 155 A10
Liphook . . . 27 F6
Liscard . . . 85 E4
Liscombe . . 21 F7
L'Islet Guern . . 16
Liss . . . 15 B8
Lissett . . . 97 D7
Liss Forest . . 15 B8
Lissington . . 90 F5
Lisvane . . . 35 F5
Liswerry . . . 35 F7
Litcham . . . 67 C8
Litchborough . . 52 D4
Litchfield . . . 26 D2
Litherland . . 85 E4
Litlington Cambs . 54 E4
 E Sus . . . 18 E2
Little Abington . 55 E6
Little Addington . 53 B7
Little Alne . . . 51 C6
Little Altcar . . 85 D4
Little Asby . . 100 D1
Little Assynt . . 156 G4
Little Aston . . 62 D4
Little Atherfield . 15 F5
Little Ayre . . 159 J4
Little-ayre . . 160 G5
Little Ayton . . 102 C3
Little Baddow . . 42 D3
Little Badminton 37 F5
Little Ballinluig . 133 D6
Little Bampton . 108 D2
Little Bardfield . 55 F7
Little Barford . . 54 D2
Little Barningham 81 D7
Little Barrington 38 C2
Little Barrow . . 73 B8
Little Barugh . . 96 B3
Little Bavington 110 B2
Little Bealings . 57 E6
Little Bedwyn . 25 C7
Little Bentley . . 43 B7
Little Berkhamsted . 41 D5
Little Billing . . 53 C6
Little Birch . . 49 F7

Little Blakenham . . 56 E5
Little Blencow . . . 108 F4
Little Bollington . . 86 F5
Little Bookham . . 28 D2
Littleborough
  Gtr Man 87 C7
  Notts 90 F2
Littlebourne 31 D6
Little Bowden . . . 64 F4
Little Bradley . . . 55 D7
Little Brampton . . 60 F3
Little Brechin . . 135 C5
Littlebredy 12 C5
Little Brickhill . . . 53 F7
Little Brington . . . 52 C4
Little Bromley . . . 43 B6
Little Broughton . 107 F7
Little Budworth . . 74 C2
Little Burstead . . 42 E2
Littlebury 55 F6
Littlebury Green . . 55 F5
Little Bytham . . . 65 C7
Little Carlton Lincs . 91 F7
  Notts 77 D7
Little Casterton . . 65 D7
Little Cawthorpe . . 91 F7
Little Chalfont . . . 40 E2
Little Chart 30 E3
Little Chesterford . 55 E6
Little Cheverell . . 24 D4
Little Chishill . . . 54 F5
Little Clacton . . . 43 C7
Little Clifton . . . 98 B2
Little Colp 153 D7
Little Comberton . . 50 E4
Little Common . . 18 E4
Little Compton . . 51 F7
Little Cornard . . . 56 F2
Little Cowarne . . . 49 D8
Little Coxwell . . . 38 E2
Little Crakehall . . 101 E7
Little Cressingham 67 D8
Little Crosby . . . 85 D4
Little Dalby 64 C4
Little Dawley . . . 61 D6
Littledean 36 C3
Little Dens 153 D10
Little Dewchurch . 49 F7
Little Downham . . 66 F5
Little Driffield . . . 97 D6
Little Dunham . . . 67 C8
Little Dunkeld . . 133 E7
Little Dunmow . . . 42 B2
Little Easton . . . 42 B2
Little Eaton 76 E3
Little Eccleston . . 92 E4
Little Ellingham . . 68 E3
Little End 41 D8
Little Eversden . . 54 D4
Little Faringdon . . 38 D2
Little Fencote . . 101 E7
Little Fenton . . . 95 F8
Littleferry 151 B11
Little Finborough . . 56 D4
Little Fransham . . 68 C2
Little Gaddesden . . 40 C2
Little Gidding . . . 65 F8
Little Glemham . . 57 D7
Little Glenshee . . 133 F6
Little Gransden . . 54 D3
Little Green 24 E2
Little Grimsby . . . 91 E7
Little Gruinard . . 150 C2
Little Habton . . . 96 B3
Little Hadham . . . 41 B7
Little Hale 78 E4
Little Hallingbury . 41 C7
Littleham Devon . . .9 B6
  Devon 10 F5
Little Hampden . . 40 D1
Littlehampton . . . 16 D4
Little Harrowden . . 53 B6
Little Haseley . . . 39 D6
Little Hatfield . . . 97 E7
Little Hautbois . . 81 E8
Little Haven 44 D3
Little Hay 62 D5
Little Hayfield . . . 87 F8
Little Haywood . . 62 B4
Little Heath 63 F7
Littlehempston . . . 7 C6
Little Hereford . . 49 C7
Little Horkesley . . 56 F3
Little Horsted . . . 17 C8
Little Horton . . . 94 F4
Little Horwood . . 53 F5
Littlehoughton . . 117 C8
Little Houghton
  Northants 53 D6
  S Yorks 88 D5
Little Hucklow . . . 75 B8
Little Hulton . . . 86 D5
Little Humber . . . 91 B5
Little Hungerford . 26 B3
Little Irchester . . 53 C7
Little Kimble . . . 39 D8
Little Kineton . . . 51 D8
Little Kingshill . . 40 E1
Little Langdale . . 99 D5
Little Langford . . 25 F5
Little Laver 41 D8
Little Leigh 74 B3
Little Leighs . . . 42 C3
Little Lever 86 D5
Little London Bucks 39 C6
  E Sus 18 D2
  Hants 25 E8
  Hants 26 D4
  Lincs 66 B2
  Lincs 66 B4
  Norf 81 E7
  Powys 59 F7
Little Longstone . . 75 B8
Little Lynturk . . . 140 C4
Little Malvern . . . 50 E2
Little Maplestead . 56 F2
Little Marcle . . . 49 F8
Little Marlow . . . 40 F1
Little Marsden . . . 93 F8
Littlemill Aberds . . 140 E2
  E Ayrs 112 C4
  Highld 151 F12
  Northumb 117 C8
Little Mill 35 D7

Little Milton 39 D6
Little Missenden . . 40 E2
Littlemoor 12 F4
Littlemore 39 D5
Little Musgrave . . 100 C2
Little Ness 60 C4
Little Neston . . . 73 B6
Little Newcastle . . 44 C4
Little Newsham . . 101 C6
Little Oakley Essex . 43 B8
  Northants 65 F5
Little Orton . . . 108 D3
Little Ouseburn . . 95 C7
Littleover 76 F3
Little Paxton . . . 54 C2
Little Petherick . . .4 B4
Little Pitlurg . . . 152 D4
Little Plumpton . . 92 F3
Little Plumstead . . 69 C6
Little Ponton . . . 78 F2
Littleport 67 F5
Little Raveley . . . 54 B3
Little Reedness . . 90 B2
Little Ribston . . . 95 D6
Little Rissington . . 38 C1
Little Ryburgh . . . 81 E5
Little Ryle 117 C6
Little Salkeld . . . 109 F5
Little Sampford . . 55 F7
Little Sandhurst . . 27 C6
Little Saxham . . . 55 C8
Little Scatwell . . 150 F6
Little Sessay . . . 95 B7
Little Shelford . . 54 D5
Little Singleton . . 92 F3
Little
  Skillymarno . . 153 C9
Little Smeaton . . 89 C6
Little Snoring . . . 81 D5
Little Sodbury . . . 36 F4
Little Somborne . . 25 F8
Little Somerford . . 37 F6
Little Stainforth . . 93 C8
Little Stainton . . 101 B8
Little Stanney . . 73 B8
Little Staughton . . 54 C2
Little Steeping . . 79 C7
Little Stoke 75 F6
Littlestone on Sea . 19 C7
Little Stonham . . 56 C5
Little Stretton Leics 64 D3
  Shrops 60 E4
Little Strickland . . 99 C7
Little Stukeley . . 54 B3
Little Sutton . . . 73 B7
Little Tew 38 B3
Little Thetford . . 55 B6
Little Thirkleby . . 95 B7
Littlethorpe Leics . 64 E2
  N Yorks 95 C6
Little Thurlow . . . 55 D7
Little Thurrock . . 29 B7
Littleton Ches W . . 73 C8
  Hants 26 F2
  Perth 134 F2
  Som 23 F6
  Sur 27 C8
  Sur 27 E7
Littleton Drew . . 37 F5
Littleton-on-
  Severn 36 F2
Littleton Pannell . 24 D5
Little Torboll . . 151 B10
Little Torrington . . 9 C6
Little Totham . . . 42 C4
Little Toux . . . 152 C5
Littletown 111 E6
Little Town Cumb . 98 C4
  Lancs 93 F6
Little Urswick . . . 92 B2
Little Wakering . . 43 F5
Little Walden . . . 55 E6
Little Waldingfield . 56 E3
Little Walsingham . 80 D5
Little Waltham . . 42 C3
Little Warley . . . 42 E2
Little Weighton . . 97 F5
Little Welnetham . 56 C2
Little Wenlock . . 61 D6
Little Whittingham
  Green 57 B6
Littlewick Green . . 27 B6
Little Wilbraham . . 55 D6
Little Wishford . . 25 F5
Little Witley . . . 50 C2
Little Wittenham . 39 E5
Little Wolford . . . 51 F7
Littleworth Bedford. 53 E8
  Glos 37 D5
  Oxon 38 E3
  Staffs 62 C4
  Worcs 50 D3

Llanarthne 33 B6
Llanasa 85 F2
Llanbabo 82 C3
Llanbadarn Fawr . . 58 F3
Llanbadarn Fynydd 48 B3
Llanbadarn-y-
  Garreg 48 E3
Llanbadoc 35 E7
Llanbadrig 82 B3
Llanbeder 35 E7
Llanbedr Gwyn . . 71 E6
  Powys 35 B6
  Powys 48 E3
Llanbedr-Dyffryn-
  Clwyd 72 D5
Llanbedrgoch . . . 82 C5
Llanbedrog 70 D4
Llanbedr Pont Steffan
  =Lampeter . . . 46 E4
Llanbedr-y-cennin 83 E7
Llanberis 83 E5
Llanbethery 22 C2
Llanbister 48 B3
Llanblethian . . . 21 B8
Llanboidy 32 B3
Llanbradach 35 E5
Llanbrynmair . . . 59 D5
Llancarfan 22 B2
Llancayo 35 D7
Llancloudy 36 B1
Llancynfelyn . . . 58 E3
Llandaff 22 B3
Llandanwg 71 E6
Llandarcy 33 E8
Llandawke 32 C3
Llanddaniel Fab . . 82 D4
Llanddarog 33 C6
Llanddeiniol . . . 46 B4
Llanddeiniolen . . 82 E5
Llandderfel . . . 72 F3
Llanddeusant
  Anglesey 82 C3
  Carms 34 B1
Llanddew 48 F2
Llanddewi 33 F5
Llanddewi-Brefi . . 47 D5
Llanddewi'r Cwm . 48 E2
Llanddewi
  Rhydderch . . . 35 C7
Llanddewi Velfrey 32 C2
Llanddoged . . . 83 E8
Llanddona 83 D5
Llanddowror . . . 32 C3
Llanddulas 72 B3
Llanddwywe . . . 71 E6
Llanddyfnan . . . 82 D5
Llandefaelog Fach 48 F2
Llandefaelog-
  tre'r-graig . . . 35 B5
Llandefalle 48 F3
Llandegai 83 D5
Llandegfan 83 D5
Llandegla 73 D5
Llandegley 48 C3
Llandegveth . . . 35 E7
Llandegwning . . 70 D3
Llandeilo 33 B7
Llandeilo Graban . 48 E2
Llandeilo'r Fan . . 47 F7
Llandeloy 44 C3
Llandenny 35 D8
Llandevenny . . . 35 F8
Llandewednock . . .3 E6
Llandewi
  Ystradenny . . . 48 C3
Llandinabo 36 B2
Llandinam 59 F7
Llandissilio 32 B2
Llandogo 36 D2
Llandough V Glam . 21 B8
  V Glam 22 B3
Llandovery
  =Llanymddyfri . 47 F6
Llandow 21 B8
Llandre
  Carms 47 E5
  Ceredig 58 F3
Llandrillo 72 F4
Llandrillo-yn-
  Rhos 83 C8
Llandrindod
  =Llandrindod Wells .48 C2
Llandrindod Wells
  =Llandrindod . . 48 C2
Llandrinio 60 C2
Llandudno 83 C7
Llandudno Junction
  =Cyffordd
  Llandudno . . . 83 D7
Llandwrog 82 F4
Llandybie 33 C7
Llandyfaelog . . . 33 C5
Llandyfan 33 C7
Llandyfriog 46 E2
Llandyfrydog . . . 82 C4
Llandygwydd . . . 45 E4
Llandynan 73 E5
Llandyrnog 72 C5
Llandysilio 60 C2
Llandyssil 59 E8
Llandysul 46 E3
Llanedeyrn 35 F6
Llanedi 33 D6
Llaneglwys 48 F2
Llanegryn 58 D2
Llanegwad 33 B6
Llaneilian 82 B4
Llaneilian-yn-Rhos 83 D8
Llanelian 72 C5
Llanelidan 72 D5
Llanelieu 48 F3
Llanellen 35 C7
Llanelli 33 E6
Llanelltyd 58 C4
Llanelly 35 C6
Llanelly Hill . . . 35 C6
Llanelwedd . . . 48 D2
Llanelwy
  =St Asaph . . . 72 B4
Llanenddwyn . . . 71 E6
Llanengan 70 E3
Llanerchymedd . . 82 C4
Llanerfyl 59 D7
Llanfachraeth . . . 82 C3
Llanfachreth . . . 71 E8
Llanfaelog 82 D3
Llanfaelrhys . . . 70 E3
Llanfaenor 35 C8
Llanfaes Anglesey . 83 D6
  Powys 35 B5
Llanfaethlu 82 C3

Llanfaethlu 82 C3
Llanfaglan 82 E4
Llanfair 71 E6
Llanfair
  Caereinion . . . 59 D8
Llanfair Clydogau . 46 D5
Llanfair-Dyffryn-
  Clwyd 72 D5
Llanfairfechan . . 83 D6
Llanfair
  Kilgheddin . . . 35 D7
Llanfair-Nant-
  Gwyn 45 F3
Llanfairpwllgwyngyll
  . . . . 82 D5
Llanfair Talhaiarn . 72 B3
Llanfair Waterdine 48 B4
Llanfair-ym-Muallt
  =Builth Wells . . 48 D2
Llanfairyneubwll . 82 D3
Llanfairynghornwy 82 B3
Llanfallteg 32 C2
Llanfaredd 48 D2
Llanfarian 46 B4
Llanfechain 59 B8
Llanfechan 47 D8
Llanfechell 82 B3
Llanfendigaid . . . 58 D2
Llanferres 73 C5
Llan Ffestiniog . . 71 C8
Llanfflewyn 82 C3
Llanfihangel-
  ararth 46 F3
Llanfihangel-
  Crucorney . . . 35 B7
Llanfihangel Glyn
  Myfyr 72 E3
Llanfihangel Nant
  Bran 47 F8
Llanfihangel-nant-
  Melan 48 D3
Llanfihangel
  Rhydithon . . . 48 C3
Llanfihangel
  Rogiet 35 F8
Llanfihangel Tal-y-
  llyn 35 B5
Llanfihangel-uwch-
  Gwili 33 B5
Llanfihangel-y-
  Creuddyn . . . 47 B5
Llanfihangel-yn-
  Ngwynfa 59 C7
Llanfihangel yn
  Nhowyn 82 D3
Llanfihangel-
  ypennant
  Gwyn 58 D3
  Gwyn 71 C6
Llanfihangel-
  ytraethau . . . 71 D6
Llanfilo 48 F3
Llanfoist 35 C6
Llanfor 72 F3
Llanfrechfa 35 E7
Llanfrothen 71 C7
Llanfrynach 34 B4
Llanfwrog Anglesey 82 C3
  Denb 72 D5
Llanfyllin 59 C8
Llanfynydd Carms . 33 B6
  Flint 73 D6
Llanfyrnach 45 F4
Llangadfan 59 C7
Llangadog 33 B8
Llangadwaladr
  Anglesey 82 E3
  Powys 73 F5
Llangaffo 82 E4
Llangain 32 C4
Llangammarch
  Wells 47 E8
Llangan 21 B8
Llangarron 36 B2
Llangasty Talyllyn . 35 B5
Llangathen 33 B6
Llangattock . . . 35 C6
Llangattock Lingoed 35 B7
Llangattock nigh
  Usk 35 D7
Llangattock-Vibon-
  Avel 36 C1
Llangedwyn . . . 59 B8
Llangefni 82 D4
Llangeinor 34 F3
Llangeitho 46 D5
Llangeler 46 F2
Llangelynin 58 D2
Llangendeirne . . 33 C5
Llangennech . . . 33 D6
Llangennith . . . 33 E5
Llangenny 35 C6
Llangernyw 83 E8
Llangian 70 E3
Llanglydwen . . . 32 B2
Llangoed 83 D6
Llangoedmor . . . 45 E3
Llangollen 73 E6
Llangolman 32 B2
Llangors 35 B5
Llangovan 36 D1
Llangower 72 F3
Llangrannog . . . 46 D2
Llangristiolus . . . 82 D4
Llangrove 36 C2
Llangua 35 B7
Llangunllo 48 B4
Llangunnor 33 C5
Llangurig 47 B8
Llangwm Conwy . 72 E3
  Mon 35 D8
  Pembs 44 E4
Llangwnnadl . . . 70 D3
Llangwyfan 72 C5
Llangwyfan-isaf . . 82 E3
Llangwyllog . . . 82 D4
Llangwyryfon . . . 46 B4
Llangybi Ceredig . 46 D5
  Gwyn 70 C5
  Mon 35 E7
Llangyfelach . . . 33 E7
Llangynhafal . . . 72 C5
Llangynidr 35 C5
Llangynin 32 C3
Llangynog Carms . 32 C4
  Powys 59 B7
Llangynwyd . . . 34 F2

Llanhamlach . . . 34 B4
Llanharan 34 F4
Llanharry 34 F4
Llanhennock . . . 35 E7
Llanhiledd
  =Llanhilleth . . 35 D6
Llanhilleth
  =Llanhiledd . . 35 D6
Llanidloes 59 F6
Llaniestyn 70 D3
Llanifyny 59 F5
Llanigon 48 F4
Llanilar 46 B5
Llanilid 34 F3
Llanilltud Fawr
  =Llantwit Major. 21 C8
Llanishen Cardiff . 35 F5
  Mon 36 D1
Llanllawddog . . . 33 B5
Llanllechid 83 E6
Llanllowell 35 E7
Llanllugan 59 D7
Llanllwch 32 C4
Llanllwchaiarn . . 59 E8
Llanllwni 46 F3
Llanllyfni 82 F4
Llanmadoc 33 E5
Llanmaes 21 C8
Llanmartin 35 F7
Llanmihangel . . . 21 B8
Llanmorlais 33 E6
Llannefydd 72 B3
Llannon 33 D6
Llannor 70 D4
Llanover 35 D7
Llanpumsaint . . . 33 B5
Llanreithan 44 C3
Llanrhaeadr . . . 72 C4
Llanrhaeadr-ym-
  Mochnant . . . 59 B8
Llanrhian 44 B3
Llanrhidian 33 E5
Llanrhos 83 C7
Llanrhyddlad . . . 82 C3
Llanrhystud . . . 46 C4
Llanrosser 48 F4
Llanrothal 36 C1
Llanrug 82 E5
Llanrumney . . . 35 F6
Llanrwst 83 E8
Llansadurnen . . . 32 C3
Llansadwrn
  Anglesey 83 D5
  Carms 33 B7
Llansaint 32 D4
Llansamlet 33 E7
Llansanffraid-ym-
  Mechain 60 B2
Llansannan 72 C3
Llansannor 21 B8
Llansantffraed
  Ceredig 46 C4
  Powys 35 B5
Llansantffraed
  Cwmdeuddwr . 47 C8
Llansantffraed-in-
  Elvel 48 D2
Llansawel 46 F5
Llansilin 60 B2
Llansoy 35 D8
Llanspyddid . . . 34 B4
Llanstadwell . . . 44 E4
Llansteffan 32 C4
Llanstephan . . . 48 E3
Llantarnam 35 E7
Llanteg 32 C2
Llanthony 35 B6
Llantilio
  Crossenny . . . 35 C7
Llantilio Pertholey 35 C7
Llantood 45 E3
Llantrisant
  Anglesey 82 C3
  Mon 35 E7
  Rhondda 34 F4
Llantrithyd 22 B2
Llantwit Fardre . . 34 F4
Llantwit Major
  =Llanilltud Fawr . 21 C8
Llanuwchllyn . . . 72 F2
Llanvaches 35 E8
Llanvair Discoed . 35 E8
Llanvapley 35 C7
Llanvetherine . . . 35 C7
Llanveynoe 48 F5
Llanvihangel
  Gobion 35 D7
Llanvihangel-Ystern-
  Llewern 35 C8
Llanwarne 36 B2
Llanwddyn 59 C7
Llanwenog 46 E3
Llanwern 35 F7
Llanwinio 32 B3
Llanwnda Gwyn . 82 F4
  Pembs 44 B4
Llanwnnen 46 E4
Llanwnog 59 E7
Llanwrda 47 F6
Llanwrin 58 D4
Llanwrthwl 47 C8
Llanwrtud
  =Llanwrtyd Wells. 47 E7
Llanwrtyd 47 E7
Llanwrtyd Wells
  =Llanwrtud . . 47 E7
Llanwyddelan . . . 59 D7
Llanyblodwel . . . 60 B2
Llanybri 32 C4
Llanybydder . . . 46 E4
Llanycefn 32 B1
Llanychaer 44 B4
Llanycil 72 F3
Llanycrwys 46 E5
Llanymawddwy . . 59 C6
Llanymddyfri
  =Llandovery . . 47 F6
Llanymynech . . . 60 B2
Llanynghenedl . . 82 C3
Llanynys 72 C5
Llan-y-pwll 73 D7
Llanyre 48 C2
Llanystumdwy . . 71 D5
Llanywern 35 B5
Llawhaden 32 C1
Llawndy 85 F2
Llawnt 73 F6
Llawr Dref 70 E3
Llawryglyn 59 E6

Llay 73 D7
Llechcynfarwy . . 82 C3
Llecheiddior . . . 71 C5
Llechfaen 34 B4
Llechryd Caerph . 35 D5
  Ceredig 45 E4
Llechrydau 73 F6
Lledrod 46 B5
Llenmerewig . . . 59 E8
Llethrid 33 E6
Llidiad Nenog . . 46 F4
Llidiardau 72 F2
Llidiart-y-parc . . 72 E5
Llithfaen 70 C4
Llong 73 C6
Llowes 48 E3
Llundain-fach . . . 46 D4
Llwydcoed 34 D3
Llwyn 60 F2
Llwyncelyn 46 D3
Llwyndafydd . . . 46 D2
Llwynderw 60 D2
Llwyn-du 35 C6
Llwyndyrys 70 C4
Llwyngwril 58 D2
Llwyn-hendy . . . 33 E6
Llwynmawr 73 F6
Llwyn-têg 33 D6
Llwyn-y-brain . . 32 C2
Llwyn-y-groes . . 46 D4
Llwynypia 34 E3
Llynclys 60 B2
Llynfaes 82 D4
Llysfaen 83 D8
Llyswen 48 F3
Llysworney 21 B8
Llysyfran 32 B1
Llys-y-frân 32 B1
Llywel 47 F7
Loan 120 B2
Loanend 122 D5
Loanhead 121 C5
Loans 118 F3
Loans of Tullich . 151 D11
Lobb 20 F3
Loch a Charnain . 148 D3
Loch a'
  Ghainmhich . . 155 E7
Lochailort 147 C10
Lochaline 147 G9
Lochanhully . . . 138 B5
Lochans 104 D4
Locharbriggs . . . 114 F2
Lochassynt
  Lodge 156 G4
Lochavich House . 124 D5
Lochawe 125 C7
Loch Baghasdail
  =Lochboisdale. . 148 G2
Lochboisdale
  =Loch Baghasdail .148 G2
Lochbuie 124 C2
Lochcarron . . . 149 E13
Loch Choire
  Lodge 157 H11
Lochdhu 157 E13
Lochdochart
  House 126 B3
Lochdon 124 B3
Lochdrum 150 D5
Lochead 144 F6
Lochearnhead . . 126 B4
Lochee 134 F3
Lochend Highld . . 151 H8
  Highld 158 D4
Locherben 114 E2
Loch Euphoirt . . 148 B3
Lochfoot 107 B5
Lochgair 145 D8
Lochgarthside . . 137 C8
Lochgelly 128 E3
Lochgilphead . . . 145 E7
Lochgoilhead . . 125 E8
Loch Head . . . 105 E7
Lochhill 152 B2
Lochindorb
  Lodge 151 H12
Lochinver 156 G3
Lochlane 127 B7
Loch Loyal Lodge 157 E9
Lochluichart . . . 150 E6
Lochmaben . . . 114 F3
Lochmaddy =Loch
  nam Madadh . . 148 B4
Lochmore
  Cottage . . . 158 E2
Lochmore Lodge . 156 F5
Loch nam Madadh
  =Lochmaddy . . 148 B4
Lochore 128 E3
Lochportain . . . 148 A4
Lochranza . . . 143 C10
Lochs Crofts . . . 152 B3
Loch Sgioport . . 148 E3
Lochside Aberds . 135 C7
  Highld 151 F11
  Highld 156 D7
  Highld 157 C11
Lochslin 151 D11
Lochstack Lodge . 156 F5
Lochton 141 E6
Lochty Angus . . 135 C5
  Fife 129 D7
  Perth 128 B2
Lochuisge 130 D1
Lochurr 113 F7
Lochwinnoch . . 118 D3
Lochwood 114 E3
Lochyside 131 B5
Lockengate 4 C5
Lockerbie 114 F4
Lockeridge . . . 25 C6
Lockerley 14 B3
Locking 23 D5
Lockinge 38 F4
Lockington E Yorks 97 E5
  Leics 63 B8
Lockleywood . . . 61 B6
Locks Heath . . . 15 D6
Lockton 103 E6
Lockwood 88 C2
Loddington Leics . 64 D4
  Northants . . . 53 B6
Loddiswell 6 E5
Loddon 69 E6
Lode 55 C6
Loders 12 E2
Lodsworth 16 B3
Lofthouse N Yorks 94 B4
  W Yorks 88 B4

Loftus 103 C5
Logan 113 B5
Loganlea 120 C2
Logan Mains . . 104 E4
Loggerheads . . 74 F4
Logie Angus . . . 135 C6
  Fife 129 B6
Logie Coldstone . 140 D3
Logie Hill . . . 151 D10
Logie Newton . . 153 E6
Logie Pert . . . 135 C6
Logierait 133 D6
Login 32 B2
Lolworth 54 C4
Lonbain 149 C11
Londesborough . . 96 E4
London Colney . . 40 D4
Londonderry . . . 101 F8
Londonthorpe . . 78 F2
Londubh 155 J13
Lonemore . . . 151 C10
Long Ashton . . . 23 B7
Longbar 118 D3
Long Bennington . 77 E8
Longbenton . . . 111 C5
Longborough . . 38 B1
Long Bredy . . . 12 E3
Longbridge Warks. 51 C7
  W Mid 50 B5
Longbridge
  Deverill 24 E3
Long Buckby . . 52 C4
Longburton . . . 12 C4
Long Clawson . . 64 B4
Longcliffe 76 D2
Long Common . . 15 C6
Long Compton
  Staffs 62 B2
  Warks 51 F7
Longcot 38 E2
Long Crendon . . 39 D6
Long Crichel . . . 13 C7
Longcroft 119 B7
Longden 60 D4
Long Ditton . . . 28 C2
Longdon Staffs . . 62 C4
  Worcs 50 F3
Longdon Green . . 62 C4
Longdon on Tern . 61 C6
Longdown 10 E3
Longdowns 3 C6
Long Drax 89 B7
Long Duckmanton 76 B4
Long Eaton . . . 76 F4
Longfield Kent . . 29 C7
  Shetland . . . 160 M5
Longford Derbys . 76 F3
  Glos 37 B5
  London 27 B8
  Shrops 74 F3
  Telford 61 C7
  W Mid 63 F7
Longfordlane . . . 76 F2
Longforgan . . . 128 B5
Longformacus . . 122 D2
Longframlington . 117 D7
Long Green . . . 50 F3
Longham Dorset . 13 E8
  Norf 68 C2
Long Hanborough 38 C4
Longhaven . . . 153 E11
Longhill 153 C9
Longhirst 117 F8
Longhope Glos . . 36 C3
  Orkney 159 J4
Longhorsley . . . 117 E7
Longhoughton . . 117 C8
Long Itchington . 52 C2
Longlane Derbys . 76 F2
  W Berks 26 B2
Long Lawford . . 52 B2
Longlevens . . . 37 B5
Longley 88 D2
Longley Green . . 50 D2
Long Load 12 B2
Longmanhill . . . 153 B7
Long Marston
  Herts 40 C1
  N Yorks 95 D8
  Warks 51 E6
Long Marton . . 100 B1
Long Melford . . 56 E2
Longmoor Camp . 27 F5
Longmorn . . . 152 C2
Long Newnton . . 37 E6
Long Newton
  Borders . . . 115 B8
  Stockton . . . 102 C1
Long Newton . . 121 C1
Longney 36 C4
Longniddry . . . 121 B7
Longnor Shrops . 60 D4
  Staffs 75 C7
Longparish . . . 26 E2
Longport 75 E5
Long Preston . . 93 D8
Longridge Lancs . 93 F6
  Staffs 62 C3
  W Loth 120 C2
Longriggend . . . 119 B8
Long Riston . . . 97 E7
Longsdon 75 D6
Longshaw 86 D3
Longside 153 D10
Long Sight 87 D7
Longstanton . . . 54 C4
Longstock 25 F8
Longstone 32 D2
Longstowe . . . 54 D4
Long Stratton . . 68 E4
Long Street . . . 53 E5
Long Sutton Hants 26 E5
  Lincs 66 B4
  Som 12 B2
Longthorpe . . . 65 E8
Long Thurlow . . 56 C4
Longthwaite . . . 99 B6
Longton Lancs . . 86 B2
  Stoke 75 E6
Longtown Cumb . 108 C3
  Hereford . . . 35 B7
Longview 86 E2
Longville in the
  Dale 60 E5
Long Whatton . . 63 B8
Longwick 39 D7

Long Wittenham . 39 E5
Longwitton . . . 117 F6
Longwood 61 D6
Longworth . . . 38 E3
Longyester . . . 121 C8
Lonmay 153 C10
Lonmore 148 D7
Loose 29 D8
Loosley Row . . 39 D8
Lopcombe Corner 25 F7
Lopen 12 C2
Loppington . . . 60 B4
Lopwell 6 C2
Lorbottle . . . 117 D6
Lorbottle Hall . . 117 D6
Lornty 134 E1
Loscoe 76 E4
Losgaintir . . . 154 H5
Lossiemouth . . 152 A2
Lossit 142 C2
Lostford 74 F3
Lostock Gralam . 74 B3
Lostock Green . . 74 B3
Lostock Hall . . 86 B3
Lostock Junction . 86 D4
Lostwithiel 5 D1
Loth 159 E7
Lothbeg . . . 157 H12
Lothersdale . . . 94 E2
Lothmore . . . 157 H12
Loughborough . . 64 C2
Loughor 33 E6
Loughton Essex . 41 E7
  M Keynes . . . 53 F6
  Shrops 61 F6
Lound Lincs . . . 65 C7
  Notts 89 F7
  Suff 69 E8
Lount 63 C7
Louth 91 F7
Love Clough . . 87 B6
Lovedean 15 C7
Lover 14 B3
Loversall 89 E6
Loves Green . . . 42 D2
Lovesome Hill . . 102 E1
Loveston 32 D1
Lovington 23 F7
Low Ackworth . . 89 C5
Low Barlings . . 78 B3
Low Bentham . . 93 C6
Low Bradfield . . 88 E3
Low Bradley . . . 94 E3
Low Braithwaite . 108 E4
Lowbridge House . 99 D7
Low Brunton . . 110 B2
Low Burnham . . 89 D8
Low Burton . . . 101 F7
Low Buston . . . 117 D8
Low Catton . . . 96 D3
Low Clanfield . . 104 F5
Low Coniscliffe . 101 C7
Low Crosby . . . 108 D4
Low Dalby . . . 103 F6
Lowdham 77 E6
Low Dinsdale . . 101 C8
Lowdwell 23 B6
Low Ellington . . 101 F7
Lower Aisholt . . 22 F4
Lower Arncott . . 39 C6
Lower Ashton . . 10 F3
Lower Assendon . 39 F7
Lower Badcall . . 156 E4
Lower Bartle . . . 92 F4
Lower Basildon . . 26 B4
Lower Beeding . . 17 B6
Lower Benefield . 65 F6
Lower Boddington 52 D2
Lower Brailes . . 51 F8
Lower Breakish . 149 F11
Lower Broadheath 50 D3
Lower Bullingham 49 F7
Lower Cam . . . 36 D4
Lower Chapel . . 48 F2
Lower Chute . . . 25 D8
Lower Cragabus . 142 D4
Lower Crossings . 87 F8
Lower
  Cumberworth . 88 D3
Lower Darwen . . 86 B4
Lower Dean . . . 53 C8
Lower Diabaig . 149 B12
Lower Dicker . . 18 D2
Lower Dinchope . 60 F4
Lower Down . . . 60 F3
Lower Drift 2 D3
Lower Dunsforth . 95 C7
Lower Egleton . . 49 E8
Lower Elkstone . . 75 D7
Lower End 40 B2
Lower Everleigh . 25 D6
Lower Farringdon 26 F5
Lower Foxdale . . 84 E2
Lower Frankton . 73 F7
Lower Froyle . . 27 E5
Lower Gledfield . 151 B8
Lower Green . . . 81 D5
Lower Hacheston 57 D7
Lower Halistra . . 148 C7
Lower Halstow . . 30 C2
Lower Hardres . . 31 D5
Lower Hawthwaite 98 F4
Lower Heath . . . 75 C5
Lower
  Hempriggs . . 151 E14
Lower Hergest . . 48 D4
Lower Heyford . . 38 B4
Lower Higham . . 29 B8
Lower Holbrook . 57 F5
Lower Hordley . . 60 B3
Lower
  Horsebridge . . 18 D2
Lower Killeyan . 142 D3
Lower Kingswood 28 D3
Lower Kinnerton . 73 C7
Lower Langford . 23 C6
Lower Largo . . 129 D6
Lower Leigh . . . 75 F7
Lower Lemington 51 F7
Lower Lenie . . 137 B8
Lower Lydbrook . 36 C2
Lower Lye . . . 49 C6
Lower Machen . . 35 F6
Lower Maes-coed 48 F5
Lower Mayland . 43 D5

Lower Midway . . 63 B7
Lower Milovaig . 148 C6
Lower Moor . . . 50 E4
Lower Nazeing . . 41 D6
Lower Netchwood 61 E6
Lower Ollach . . 149 E10
Lower Penarth . . 22 B3
Lower Penn . . . 62 E2
Lower Pennington 14 E4
Lower Peover . . 74 B4
Lower Pexhill . . 75 B5
Lower Place . . . 87 C7
Lower Quinton . . 51 E6
Lower Rochford . 49 C8
Lower Seagry . . 37 F6
Lower Shelton . . 53 E7
Lower Shiplake . . 27 B5
Lower
  Shuckburgh . . 52 C2
Lower Slaughter . 38 B1
Lower Stanton
  St Quintin . . . 37 F6
Lower Stoke . . . 30 B2
Lower Stondon . . 54 F2
Lower Stow Bedon 68 E2
Lower Street Norf . 69 C6
  Norf 81 D8
Lower Strensham . 50 E4
Lower Stretton . . 86 F4
Lower Sundon . . 40 B3
Lower Swanwick . 15 D5
Lower Swell . . . 38 B1
Lower Tean . . . 75 F7
Lower Thurlton . 69 E7
Lower Tote . . . 149 B10
Lower Town . . . 44 B4
Lower Tysoe . . . 51 E8
Lower Upham . . 15 C6
Lower Vexford . . 22 F3
Lower Weare . . . 23 D6
Lower Welson . . 48 D4
Lower Whitley . . 74 B3
Lower Wield . . . 26 E4
Lower
  Winchendon . . 39 C7
Lower Withington 74 C5
Lower Woodend . 39 F8
Lower Woodford . 25 F6
Lower Wyche . . 50 E2
Lowesby 64 D4
Lowestoft 69 E8
Loweswater . . . 98 B3
Low Etherley . . 101 B6
Low Fell 111 D5
Lowford 15 C5
Low Fulney . . . 66 B2
Low Garth . . . 103 D5
Low Gate . . . 110 C2
Lowgill Cumb . . 99 E8
  Lancs 93 C6
Low Grantley . . 94 B5
Low Habberley . . 50 B3
Low Ham 12 B2
Low Hesket . . . 108 E4
Low Hesleyhurst 117 E6
Low Hutton . . . 96 C3
Lowick Northants . 65 F6
  Northumb . . . 123 F6
Lowick Bridge . . 98 F4
Lowick Green . . 98 F4
Low Laithe . . . 94 C4
Lowlands 35 E6
Low Leighton . . 87 F8
Low Lorton . . . 98 B3
Low Marishes . . 96 B4
Low Marnham . . 77 C8
Low Mill 102 E4
Low Moor Lancs . 93 E7
  W Yorks 88 B2
Lowmoor Row . . 99 B8
Low Moorsley . . 111 E6
Low Newton . . . 99 F6
Low Newton-by-the-
  Sea 117 B8
Lownie Moor . . 134 E4
Low Row Cumb . 108 C5
  Cumb 109 C5
  N Yorks 100 E4
Low Salchrie . . 104 C4
Low Smerby . . . 143 F8
Lowsonford . . . 51 C6
Lowther 99 B7
Lowthorpe . . . 97 C6
Lowton 86 E4
Lowton Common . 86 E4
Low Torry . . . 128 F2
Low Worsall . . . 102 D1
Low Wray . . . 99 D5
Loxbeare 10 C4
Loxhill 27 F8
Loxhore 20 F5
Loxley 51 D7
Loxton 23 D5
Loxwood 27 F8
Lubcroy 156 J6
Lubenham 64 F4
Luccombe 21 E8
Luccombe Village . 15 G6
Lucker 123 F7
Luckett 5 B8
Luckington . . . 37 F5
Lucklawhill . . . 129 B6
Luckwell Bridge . 21 F8
Lucton 49 C6
Ludag 148 G2
Ludborough . . . 91 E6
Ludchurch . . . 32 C2
Luddenden . . . 87 B8
Luddenden Foot . 87 B8
Luddesdown . . 29 C7
Luddington N Lincs 90 C2
  Warks 51 D6
Luddington in the
  Brook 65 F8
Lude House . . . 133 C5
Ludford Lincs . . 91 F6
  Shrops 49 B7
Ludgershall Bucks. 39 C6
  Wilts 25 D7
Ludgvan 2 C4
Ludham 69 C6
Ludlow 49 B7
Ludwell 13 B7
Ludworth . . . 111 E6
Luffincott 8 E5
Lugar 113 B5
Luggate Burn . . 122 B2
Lugg Green . . . 49 C6
Luggiebank . . . 119 B7

Lugton 118 D4
Lugwardine 49 E7
Luib 149 F10
Lulham 49 E6
Lullenden 28 E5
Lullington Derbys 63 C6
  Som 24 D2
Lulsgate Bottom 23 C7
Lulsley 50 D2
Lumb 87 B8
Lumby 95 F7
Lumloch 119 C6
Lumphanan 140 D4
Lumphinnans 128 E3
Lumsdaine 122 C4
Lumsden 140 B3
Lunan 135 D6
Lunanhead 134 D4
Luncarty 128 B2
Lund E Yorks 97 E5
  N Yorks 96 F2
  Shetland 160 C7
Lunderton 153 D11
Lundie Angus 134 F2
  Highld 136 C4
Lundin Links 129 D6
Lunga 124 E3
Lunna 160 G6
Lunning 160 G7
Lunnon 33 F6
Lunsford's Cross 18 D4
Lunt 85 D4
Luntley 49 D5
Luppitt 11 D6
Lupset 88 C4
Lupton 99 F7
Lurgashall 16 B3
Lusby 79 C6
Luson 6 E4
Luss 126 E2
Lussagiven 144 E5
Lusta 149 C7
Lustleigh 10 F2
Luston 49 C6
Luthermuir 135 C6
Luthrie 128 C5
Luton Devon 7 B7
  Luton 40 B3
  Medway 29 C8
Lutterworth 64 F2
Lutton Devon 6 D3
  Lincs 66 B4
  Northants 65 F8
Lutworthy 10 C2
Luxborough 21 F8
Luxulyan 5 D5
Lybster 158 G4
Lydbury North 60 F3
Lydcott 21 F5
Lydd 19 C7
Lydden 31 E6
Lyddington 65 E5
Lydd on Sea 19 C7
Lydeard
  St Lawrence 22 F3
Lyde Green 26 D5
Lydford 9 F7
Lydford-on-Fosse 23 F7
Lydgate 87 B7
Lydham 60 E3
Lydiard Green 37 F7
Lydiard Millicent 37 F7
Lydiate 85 D4
Lydlinch 12 C5
Lydney 36 D3
Lydstep 32 E1
Lye 62 F3
Lye Green Bucks 40 D2
  E Sus 18 B2
Lyford 38 E3
Lymbridge Green 30 E5
Lyme Regis 11 E8
Lymington 14 E4
Lyminster 16 D4
Lymm 86 F4
Lymore 14 E3
Lympne 19 B8
Lympsham 22 D5
Lympstone 10 F4
Lynchat 138 D3
Lyndale House 149 C8
Lyndhurst 14 D4
Lyndon 65 D6
Lyne 27 C8
Lyneal 73 F8
Lyne Down 49 F8
Lyneham Oxon 38 B2
  Wilts 24 B5
Lynemore 139 B6
Lynemouth 117 E8
Lyne of
  Gorthleck 137 B8
Lyne of Skene 141 C6
Lyness 159 J4
Lyng Norf 68 C3
  Som 11 B8
Lynmouth 21 E6
Lynsted 30 C3
Lynton 21 E6
Lyon's Gate 12 D4
Lyonshall 48 D5
Lytchett Matravers 13 E7
Lytchett Minster 13 E7
Lyth 158 D4
Lytham 85 B4
Lytham St Anne's 85 B4
Lythe 103 C6
Lythes 159 K5

M
Mabe Burnthouse 3 C6
Mabie 107 B6
Mablethorpe 91 F9
Macclesfield 75 B6
Macclesfield
  Forest 75 B6
Macduff 153 B7
Mace Green 56 E5
Macharioch 143 H8
Machynlleth 58 D4
Machynys 33 E6
Mackerel's
  Common 16 B4
Mackworth 76 F3

Macmerry 121 B7
Madderty 127 B8
Maddiston 120 B2
Madehurst 16 C3
Madeley Staffs 74 E4
  Telford 61 D6
Madeley Heath 74 E4
Madeley Park 74 E4
Madingley 54 C4
Madley 49 F6
Madresfield 50 E3
Madron 2 C3
Maenaddwyn 82 C4
Maenclochog 32 B1
Maendy 22 B2
Maentwrog 71 C7
Maen-y-groes 46 D2
Maer 74 F4
Maerdy Conwy 72 E4
  Rhondda 34 E3
Maesbrook 60 B3
Maesbury 60 B3
Maesbury Marsh 60 B3
Maesgwyn-Isaf 59 C8
Maesgwynne 32 B3
Maeshafn 73 C6
Maesllyn 46 E2
Maesmynis 48 E2
Maesteg 34 E2
Maestir 46 E4
Maes-Treylow 48 C4
Maesybont 33 C6
Maesycrugiau 46 E3
Maesy cwmmer 35 E5
Maesymeillion 46 E3
Magdalen Laver 41 D8
Maggieknockater 152 D3
Magham Down 18 D3
Maghull 85 D4
Magor 35 F8
Magpie Green 56 B4
Maiden Bradley 24 F3
Maiden Cross 40 E3
Maidenhall 7 C7
Maidenhead 40 F1
Maiden Law 110 E4
Maiden Newton 12 E3
Maidens 112 D2
Maidensgrave 57 E6
Maiden's Green 27 B6
Maidenwell Corn 4 D2
  Lincs 79 B6
Maiden Wells 44 F4
Maidford 52 D4
Maids Moreton 52 F5
Maidstone 29 D8
Maidwell 52 B5
Mail 160 L6
Main 59 C8
Maindee 35 F7
Mainsforth 111 F6
Mains of Airies 104 C3
Mains of
  Allardice 135 B8
Mains of
  Annochie 153 D9
Mains of Ardestie 135 F5
Mains of Balhall 135 C5
Mains of
  Ballindarg 134 D4
Mains of
  Balnakettle 135 B6
Mains of Birness 153 E9
Mains of Burgie 151 F13
Mains of Clunas 151 G11
Mains of Crichie 153 D9
Mains of Dalvey 151 H14
Mains of
  Dellavaird 141 F6
Mains of Drum 141 E7
Mains of
  Edingight 152 C5
Mains of
  Fedderate 153 D9
Mains of Inkhorn 153 E9
Mains of Mayen 152 D5
Mains of
  Melgund 135 D5
Mains of
  Thornton 135 B6
Mains of Watten 158 E4
Mainsriddle 107 D6
Mainstone 60 F2
Maisemore 37 B5
Malacleit 148 A2
Malborough 6 F5
Malcoff 87 F8
Maldon 42 D4
Malham 94 C2
Maligar 149 B9
Mallaig 149 B9
Malleny Mills 120 C4
Malling 126 D4
Malltraeth 82 E4
Mallwyd 59 C5
Malmesbury 37 F6
Malmsmead 21 E6
Malpas Ches W 73 E8
  Corn 3 B7
  Newport 35 E7
Malswick 36 B4
Maltby Stockton 102 C2
  S Yorks 89 E6
Maltby le Marsh 91 F8
Malting Green 43 B5
Maltman's Hill 30 E3
Malton 96 B3
Malvern Link 50 E2
Malvern Wells 50 E2
Mamble 49 B8
Manaccan 3 D6
Manafon 59 D8
Manais 154 J6
Manar House 141 B6
Manaton 10 F2
Mancetter 63 E7
Manchester 87 E6
Manchester
  Airport 87 F6
Mancot 73 C7
Mandally 137 D5
Manea 66 F4
Manfield 101 C6
Mangaster 160 F5
Mangotsfield 23 B8
Mangurstadh 154 D5
Mankinholes 87 B7
Manley 74 B2

Manmoel 35 D5
Mannal 146 G2
Mannerston 120 B3
Manningford
  Bohune 25 D6
Manningford
  Bruce 25 D6
Manningham 94 F4
Mannings Heath 17 B6
Mannington 13 D8
Manningtree 56 F4
Mannofield 141 D8
Manor 41 F7
Manorbier 32 E1
Manordeilo 33 B7
Manor Estate 88 F4
Manorhill 122 F2
Manorowen 44 B4
Manselfield 33 F6
Mansel Lacy 49 E6
Mansell Gamage 49 E5
Mansergh 99 F8
Mansfield E Ayrs 113 C6
  Notts 76 C5
Mansfield
  Woodhouse 76 C5
Mansriggs 98 F4
Manston Dorset 13 C6
  Kent 31 C7
  W Yorks 95 F6
Manswood 13 D7
Manthorpe Lincs 65 C7
  Lincs 78 F2
Manton N Lincs 90 D3
  Notts 77 B5
  Rutland 65 D5
  Wilts 25 C6
Manuden 41 B7
Maperton 12 B4
Maplebeck 77 C7
Maple Cross 40 E3
Mapledurham 26 B4
Mapledurwell 26 D4
Maplehurst 17 B5
Maplescombe 29 C6
Mapleton 75 E8
Mapperley 76 E4
Mapperley Park 77 E5
Mapperton 12 E3
Mappleborough
  Green 51 C5
Mappleton 97 E8
Mappowder 12 D5
Maraig 154 G6
Marazanvose 4 D3
Marazion 2 C4
Marbhig 155 F9
Marbury 74 E2
March Cambs 66 E4
  S Lanark 114 C2
Marcham 38 E4
Marchamley 61 B5
Marchington 75 F8
Marchington
  Woodlands 62 B5
Marchroes 70 E4
Marchwiel 73 E7
Marchwood 14 C4
Marcross 21 C8
Marden Hereford 49 E7
  Kent 29 E8
  T&W 111 B6
  Wilts 25 D5
Marden Beech 29 E8
Marden Thorn 29 E8
Mardy 35 C7
Marefield 64 D4
Mareham le Fen 79 C5
Mareham on the
  Hill 79 C5
Marehay 76 E3
Marehill 16 C4
Maresfield 17 B8
Marfleet 90 B5
Marford 73 D7
Margam 34 F1
Margaret Marsh 13 C6
Margaret Roding 42 C1
Margaretting 42 D2
Margate 31 B7
Margnaheglish 143 E11
Margrove Park 102 C4
Marham 67 C7
Marhamchurch 8 D4
Marholm 65 D8
Mariandyrys 83 C6
Mariansleigh 10 B2
Marionburgh 141 D6
Marishader 149 B9
Marjoriebanks 114 F3
Mark Dumfries 104 C5
  S Ayrs 104 B4
  Som 23 E5
Markbeech 29 E5
Markby 79 B7
Mark Causeway 23 E5
Mark Cross E Sus 17 C8
  E Sus 18 B2
Market Bosworth 63 D8
Market Deeping 65 D8
Market Drayton 74 F3
Market
  Harborough 64 F4
Markethill 134 F2
Market Lavington 24 D5
Market Overton 65 C5
Market Rasen 90 F5
Market Stainton 78 B5
Market Warsop 77 C5
Market Weighton 96 E4
Market Weston 56 B3
Markfield 63 C8
Markham 77 B7
Markham Moor 77 B7
Markinch 128 D4
Markington 95 C5
Marksbury 23 C8
Marks Tey 43 B5
Markyate 40 C3
Marland 87 C6
Marlborough 25 C6
Marlbrook Hereford 49 D7
  Worcs 50 B4
Marlcliff 51 D5
Marldon 7 C6
Marlesford 57 D7
Marley Green 74 E2
Marley Hill 110 D5

Marley Mount 14 E3
Marlingford 68 D4
Mar Lodge 139 E6
Marloes 44 E2
Marlow Bucks 39 F8
  Hereford 49 B6
Marlow Bottom 40 F1
Marlpit Hill 28 E5
Marlpool 76 E4
Marnhull 13 C5
Marnoch 152 C5
Marnock 119 C7
Marple 87 F7
Marple Bridge 87 F7
Marr 89 D6
Marrel 157 H13
Marrick 101 E5
Marrister 160 G7
Marros 32 D3
Marsden T&W 111 C6
  W Yorks 94 F3
Marshall's Heath 40 C4
Marshalsea 11 D8
Marshalswick 40 D4
Marsham 81 E7
Marshaw 93 D5
Marsh Baldon 39 E5
Marshborough 31 D7
Marshbrook 60 F4
Marshchapel 91 E7
Marshfield Newport 35 F6
  S Glos 24 B2
Marshgate 8 E3
Marsh Gibbon 39 B6
Marsh Green Devon 10 E5
  Kent 28 E5
  Staffs 75 D5
Marshland
  St James 66 D5
Marsh Lane 76 B4
Marshside 85 C4
Marsh Street 21 E8
Marshwood 11 E8
Marske 101 D6
Marske-by-the-
  Sea 102 B4
Marston Ches W 74 B3
  Hereford 49 D5
  Lincs 77 E8
  Oxon 39 D5
  Staffs 62 B3
  Staffs 62 C2
  Warks 63 E6
  Wilts 24 D4
Marston Doles 52 D2
Marston Green 63 F5
Marston Magna 12 B3
Marston Meysey 37 E8
Marston
  Montgomery 75 F8
Marston
  Moretaine 53 E7
Marston on Dove 63 B6
Marston
  St Lawrence 52 E3
Marston Stannett 49 D7
Marston Trussell 64 F3
Marstow 36 C2
Marsworth 40 C2
Marten 25 D7
Marthall 74 B5
Martham 69 C7
Martin Hants 13 C8
  Kent 31 E7
  Lincs 78 C5
  Lincs 78 C5
Martin Dales 78 C4
Martin Drove End 13 B8
Martinhoe 21 E5
Martinhoe Cross 21 E5
Martin
  Hussingtree 50 C3
Martin Mill 31 E7
Martinscroft 86 F4
Martinstown 12 F4
Martlesham 57 E6
Martlesham Heath 57 E6
Martletwy 32 C1
Martley 50 D2
Martock 12 C2
Marton Ches E 75 C5
  E Yorks 97 F7
  Lincs 90 F2
  Mbro 102 C3
  N Yorks 95 C7
  N Yorks 103 F5
  Shrops 60 D4
  Warks 52 C2
Marton-le-Moor 95 B6
Martyr's Green 27 D8
Martyr Worthy 26 F3
Marwick 159 F3
Marwood 20 F4
Marybank 150 F7
Maryburgh 151 F8
Maryhill 119 C5
Marykirk 135 C6
Marylebone 86 D3
Marypark 152 E1
Maryport Cumb 107 F7
  Dumfries 104 F5
Mary Tavy 6 B3
Maryton 135 D6
Marywell Aberds 140 E4
  Aberds 141 E8
  Angus 135 E6
Masham 101 F7
Mashbury 42 C2
Masongill 93 B6
Masonhill 112 B3
Mastin Moor 76 B4
Mastrick 141 D7
Matching 41 C8
Matching Green 41 C8
Matching Tye 41 C8
Matfen 110 B3
Matfield 29 E7
Mathern 36 E2
Mathon 50 E2
Mathry 44 B3
Matlaske 81 D7
Matlock 76 C2
Matlock Bath 76 C2
Matson 37 C5
Matterdale End 99 B5

Mattersey 89 F7
Mattersey Thorpe 89 F7
Mattingley 26 D5
Mattishall 68 C3
Mattishall Burgh 68 C3
Mauchline 112 B4
Maud 153 D9
Maugersbury 38 B2
Maughold 84 C4
Mauld 150 H7
Maulden 53 F8
Maulds Meaburn 99 C8
Maunby 102 F1
Maund Bryan 49 D7
Maundown 11 B5
Mautby 69 C7
Mavis Enderby 79 C6
Mawbray 107 E7
Mawdesley 86 C2
Mawdlam 34 F2
Mawgan 3 D6
Maw Green 74 D4
Mawla 3 B6
Mawnan 3 D6
Mawnan Smith 3 D6
Mawsley 53 B6
Maxey 65 D8
Maxstoke 63 F6
Maxton Borders 122 F2
  Kent 31 E7
Maxwellheugh 122 F3
Maxwelltown 107 B6
Maxworthy 8 E4
Mayals 33 E7
May Bank 75 E5
Maybole 112 D3
Mayfield E Sus 18 C2
  Midloth 121 C6
  Staffs 75 E8
  W Loth 120 C2
Mayford 27 D7
Mayland 43 D5
Maynard's Green 18 D2
Maypole Mon 36 C1
  Scilly 2 E4
Maypole Green
  Essex 43 B5
  Norf 69 E7
  Suff 57 C6
Maywick 160 L5
Meadle 39 D8
Meadowtown 60 D3
Meaford 75 F5
Mealabost 155 D9
Mealabost
  Bhuirgh 155 B9
Meal Bank 99 E7
Mealsgate 108 E2
Meanwood 95 F5
Mearbeck 93 C8
Meare 23 E6
Meare Green 11 B8
Mears Ashby 53 C6
Measham 63 C7
Meath Green 28 E3
Meathop 99 F6
Meaux 97 F6
Meavy 6 C3
Medbourne 64 E4
Medburn 110 B4
Meddon 8 C4
Meden Vale 77 C5
Medlam 79 D6
Medmenham 39 F8
Medomsley 110 D4
Medstead 26 F4
Meerbrook 75 C6
Meer End 51 B7
Meers Bridge 91 F8
Meesden 54 F5
Meeth 9 D7
Meggethead 114 B4
Meidrim 32 B3
Meifod Denb 72 D4
  Powys 59 C8
Meigle N Ayrs 118 C1
  Perth 134 E2
Meikle Earnock 119 D7
Meikle Ferry 151 C10
Meikle Forter 134 C1
Meikle Gluich 151 C9
Meikleour 134 F1
Meikle Pinkerton 122 B3
Meikle Strath 135 B6
Meikle Tarty 141 B8
Meikle Wartle 153 E7
Meinciau 33 C5
Meir 75 E6
Meir Heath 75 E6
Melbourn 54 E4
Melbourne Derbys 63 B7
  E Yorks 96 E3
Melbury Abbas 13 B6
Melbury Bubb 12 D3
Melbury Osmond 12 D3
Melbury Sampford 12 D3
Melby 160 H3
Melchbourne 53 C8
Melcombe
  Bingham 13 D5
Melcombe Regis 12 F4
Meldon Devon 9 E7
  Northumb 117 F7
Meldreth 54 E4
Meldrum House 141 B7
Melfort 124 D4
Melgarve 137 E7
Meliden 72 A4
Melin-byrhedyn 58 E5
Melincourt 34 D2
Melin-y-coed 83 E8
Melin-y-ddôl 59 D7
Melin-y-grug 59 D7
Melin-y-Wig 72 E4
Melkinthorpe 99 B7
Melkridge 109 C7
Melksham 24 C4
Melldalloch 145 F8
Melling Lancs 93 B5
  Mers 85 D4
Mellis 56 B5
Mellon Charles 155 H13
Mellon Udrigle 155 H13
Mellor Gtr Man 87 F7
  Lancs 93 F6
Mellor Brook 93 F6
Mells 24 E2

Melmerby Cumb 109 F6
  N Yorks 95 B6
  N Yorks 101 F5
Melplash 12 E2
Melrose 121 F8
Melsetter 159 K3
Melsonby 101 D6
Meltham 88 C2
Melton 57 D6
Meltonby 96 D3
Melton Constable 81 D6
Melton Mowbray 64 C4
Melton Ross 90 C4
Melvaig 155 H12
Melverley 60 C3
Melverley Green 60 C3
Melvich 157 C11
Membury 11 D7
Memsie 153 B9
Memus 134 D4
Menabilly 5 D5
Menai Bridge
  =Porthaethwy 83 D5
Mendham 69 F5
Mendlesham 56 C5
Mendlesham
  Green 56 C4
Menheniot 5 C7
Mennock 113 D8
Menston 94 E4
Menstrie 127 E7
Menthorpe 96 F2
Mentmore 40 C2
Meoble 147 C10
Meole Brace 60 C4
Meols 85 E3
Meonstoke 15 C7
Meopham 29 C7
Meopham Station 29 C7
Mepal 66 F4
Meppershall 54 F2
Merbach 49 E5
Mere Ches E 86 F5
  Wilts 24 F3
Mere Brow 86 C2
Mereclough 93 F8
Mere Green 62 E5
Mereside 92 F3
Mereworth 29 D7
Mergie 141 F6
Meriden 63 F6
Merkadale 149 E8
Merkland Dumfries 106 B4
  S Ayrs 112 E2
Merkland Lodge 156 G7
Merley 13 E8
Merlin's Bridge 44 D4
Merrington 60 B4
Merrion 44 F4
Merriott 12 C2
Merrivale 6 B3
Merrow 27 D8
Merrymeet 5 C7
Mersham 19 B7
Merstham 28 D3
Merston 16 D2
Merstone 15 F6
Merther 3 B7
Merthyr 32 B4
Merthyr Cynog 47 F8
Merthyr-Dyfan 22 C3
Merthyr Mawr 21 B7
Merthyr Tudful
  =Merthyr Tydfil 34 D4
Merthyr Tydfil
  =Merthyr Tudful 34 D4
Merthyr Vale 34 E4
Merton Devon 9 C7
  London 28 B3
  Norf 68 E2
  Oxon 39 C5
Mervinslaw 116 C2
Meshaw 10 C2
Messing 42 C4
Messingham 90 D2
Metfield 69 F5
Metheringham 78 C3
Methil 129 E5
Methlem 70 D2
Methley 88 B4
Methlick 153 E8
Methven 127 B8
Methwold 67 E7
Methwold Hythe 67 E7
Mettingham 69 F6
Mevagissey 3 B9
Mewith Head 93 C7
Mexborough 89 D5
Mey 158 C4
Meysey Hampton 37 E8
Miabhag W Isles 154 G5
  W Isles 154 H6
Miabhig 154 D5
Michaelchurch 36 B2
Michaelchurch
  Escley 48 F5
Michaelchurch on
  Arrow 48 D4
Michaelston-le-
  Pit 22 B3
Michaelston-y-
  Fedw 35 F6
Michaelstow 5 B5
Michealston-super-
  Ely 22 B3
Micheldever 26 F3
Michelmersh 14 B4
Mickfield 56 C5
Mickleby 103 C6
Micklefield 95 F7
Mickleham 28 D2
Mickleover 76 F3
Micklethwaite 94 E4
Mickleton Durham 100 B4
  Glos 51 E6
Mickletown 88 B4
Mickle Trafford 73 C8
Mickley 95 B5
Mickley Square 110 C3
Mid Ardlaw 153 B9
Mid Auchinleck 118 B3
Mid Beltie 140 D5
Mid Calder 120 C3
Mid Cloch Forbie 153 C7
Mid Clyth 158 G4
Mid Main 150 H7
Middle Aston 38 B4

Middle Barton 38 B4
Middlebie 108 B2
Middle
  Cairncake 153 D8
Middle Claydon 39 B7
Middle Drums 135 D5
Middleforth Green 86 B3
Middleham 101 F6
Middle Handley 76 B4
Middle Littleton 51 E5
Middle Maes-coed 48 F5
Middlemarsh 12 D4
Middle Mill 44 C3
Middlemuir 141 B8
Middle Rasen 90 F4
Middle Rigg 128 D2
Middlesbrough 102 B3
Middleshaw Cumb 99 F7
  Dumfries 107 B8
Middlesmoor 94 B3
Middlestone 111 F5
Middlestone
  Moor 110 F5
Middlestown 88 C3
Middlethird 122 E2
Middleton Aberds 141 C7
  Argyll 146 G2
  Cumb 99 F8
  Derbys 75 C8
  Derbys 76 D2
  Essex 56 F2
  Gtr Man 87 D6
  Hants 26 E2
  Hereford 49 C7
  Lancs 92 D4
  Midloth 121 D6
  Norf 67 C6
  Northants 64 F5
  Northumb 117 F6
  N Yorks 94 E4
  N Yorks 103 F5
  Perth 128 D3
  Perth 133 E8
  Shrops 49 B7
  Shrops 60 B3
  Shrops 60 E2
  Suff 57 C8
  Swansea 33 F5
  Warks 63 E5
  W Yorks 88 B3
Middleton Cheney 52 E2
Middleton Green 75 F6
Middleton Hall 117 B5
Middleton-in-
  Teesdale 100 B4
Middleton Moor 57 C8
Middleton One
  Row 102 C1
Middleton-on-
  Leven 102 D2
Middleton-on-Sea 16 D3
Middleton on the
  Hill 49 C7
Middleton-on-the-
  Wolds 97 E5
Middleton Priors 61 E6
Middleton
  Quernham 95 B6
Middleton
  St George 101 C8
Middleton Scriven 61 F6
Middleton Stoney 39 B5
Middleton Tyas 101 D7
Middletown Cumb 98 D1
  Powys 60 C3
Middle Tysoe 51 E8
Middle Wallop 25 F7
Middlewich 74 C3
Middle Winterslow 25 F7
Middle Woodford 25 F6
Middlewood
  Green 56 C4
Middlezoy 23 F5
Middridge 101 B7
Midfield 157 C8
Midge Hall 86 B3
Midgeholme 109 D6
Midgham 26 C3
Midgley W Yorks 87 B8
  W Yorks 88 C3
Midhopestones 88 E3
Midhurst 16 B2
Mid Lavant 16 D2
Midlem 115 B8
Mid Main 150 H7
Midmar 141 D5
Midsomer Norton 23 D8
Midton 118 B2
Midtown Highld 155 H13
  Highld 157 C8
Midtown of
  Buchromb 152 D3
Mid Urchany 151 G11
Midville 79 D6
Mid Walls 160 H4
Mid Yell 160 D7
Migdale 151 B9
Migvie 140 D3
Milarrochy 126 E3
Milborne Port 12 C4
Milborne
  St Andrew 13 E6
Milborne Wick 12 B4
Milbourne 110 B4
Milburn 100 B1
Milbury Heath 36 E3
Milcombe 52 F2
Milden 56 E3
Mildenhall Suff 55 B8
  Wilts 25 C7
Mile Cross 68 C5
Mile Elm 24 C4
Mile End Essex 43 B5
  Glos 36 C2
Mileham 68 C2
Mile Oak 17 D6
Milesmark 128 F2
Milfield 122 F5
Milford Derbys 76 E3
  Devon 8 B4

Milford Haven
  =Aberdaugleddau 44 E4
Milford on Sea 14 E4
Milkwall 36 D2
Milkwell 13 B7
Milland 16 B2
Millarston 118 C4
Millbank 153 D11
  Highld 158 D3
Mill Bank 87 B8
Millbeck 98 B4
Millbounds 159 E6
Millbreck 153 D10
Millbridge 27 E6
Millbrook C Beds 53 F8
  Corn 6 D2
  Soton 14 C4
Millcombe 7 E6
Mill Common 69 F7
Millcorner 18 C5
Milldale 75 D8
Mill End Bucks 39 F7
  Herts 54 F4
Millerhill 121 C6
Miller's Dale 75 B8
Miller's Green 76 D2
Millgreen 61 B6
Mill Green Essex 42 D2
  Norf 68 F4
  Suff 56 E3
Millhalf 48 E4
Millhayes 11 D7
Millhead 92 B4
Millheugh 119 D7
Mill Hill 41 E5
Millholme 99 E7
Millhouse Argyll 145 F8
  Cumb 108 F3
Millhousebridge 114 F4
Millhouse Green 88 D3
Millhouses 88 F4
Millikenpark 118 C4
Millin Cross 44 D4
Millington 96 D4
Mill Lane 27 D5
Millmeece 74 F5
Mill of Kingoodie 141 B7
Mill of Muiresk 153 D6
Mill of Sterin 140 E2
Mill of Uras 141 F7
Millom 98 F3
Millook 8 E3
Mill Place 90 D3
Millpool 5 B6
Millport 145 H10
Mill Side 99 F6
Mill Street 68 C3
Millthorpe 78 F4
Millthrop 100 E1
Milltimber 141 D7
Milltown Corn 5 D6
  Derbys 76 C3
  Devon 20 F4
  Dumfries 108 B3
Milltown of
  Aberdalgie 128 B2
Milltown of
  Auchindoun 152 D3
Milltown of
  Craigston 153 C7
Milltown of
  Edinvillie 152 D2
Milltown of
  Kildrummy 140 C3
Milltown of
  Rothiemay 152 D5
Milltown of
  Towie 140 C3
Milnathort 128 D3
Milner's Heath 73 C8
Milngavie 119 B5
Milnrow 87 C7
Milnshaw 87 B5
Milnthorpe 99 F6
Milo 33 C6
Milson 49 B8
Milstead 30 D3
Milston 25 E6
Milton Angus 134 E3
  Cambs 55 C5
  Cumb 109 C5
  Derbys 63 B7
  Dumfries 105 D6
  Dumfries 106 B5
  Dumfries 113 F8
  Highld 150 H7
  Highld 151 D10
  Highld 151 G8
  Highld 151 G9
  Moray 152 B5
  Notts 77 B7
  N Som 22 C5
  Oxon 38 E4
  Oxon 52 F2
  Pembs 32 D1
  Perth 127 C8
  Ptsmth 15 E7
  Stirling 126 E4
  Stoke 75 D6
  W Dunb 118 B4
Milton Abbas 13 D6
Milton Abbot 6 B2
Milton Bridge 120 C5
Milton Bryan 53 F7
Milton Clevedon 23 F8
Milton Coldwells 153 E9
Milton Combe 6 C2
Milton Damerel 9 C5
Milton End 37 D8
Milton Ernest 53 D8
Milton Green 73 D8
Miltonhill 151 E13
Milton Hill 38 E4
Miltonise 105 B5
Milton Keynes 53 F6
Milton Keynes
  Village 53 F6
Milton Lilbourne 25 C6
Milton Malsor 52 D5
Milton Morenish 132 F3
Milton of
  Auchinhove 140 D4

Milton of
  Balgonie 128 D5
Milton of
  Buchanan 126 E3
Milton of
  Campfield 140 D5
Milton of
  Campsie 119 B6
Milton of
  Corsindae 141 D5
Milton of
  Cushnie 140 C4
Milton of
  Dalcapon 133 D6
Milton of
  Edradour 133 D6
Milton of
  Gollanfield 151 F10
Milton of
  Lesmore 140 B3
Milton of Logie 140 D3
Milton of Murtle 141 D7
Milton of Noth 140 B4
Milton of Tullich 140 E2
Milton on Stour 13 B5
Milton Regis 30 C3
Milton under
  Wychwood 38 C2
Milverton Som 11 B6
  Warks 51 C8
Milwich 75 F6
Minard 125 F5
Minchinhampton 37 D5
Mindrum 122 F4
Minehead 21 E8
Minera 73 D6
Minety 37 E7
Minffordd Gwyn 58 C4
  Gwyn 71 D6
  Gwyn 83 D5
Miningsby 79 C6
Minions 5 B7
Minishant 112 C3
Minllyn 59 C5
Minnes 141 B8
Minngearraidh 148 F2
Minnigaff 105 C8
Minnonie 153 B7
Minskip 95 C6
Minstead 14 C3
Minsted 16 B2
Minster Kent 30 B3
  Kent 31 C7
Minsterley 60 D3
Minster Lovell 38 C3
Minsterworth 36 C4
Minterne Magna 12 D4
Minting 78 B4
Mintlaw 153 D9
Minto 115 B8
Minton 60 E4
Minwear 32 C1
Minworth 63 E5
Mirbister 159 F4
Mirehouse 98 C1
Mireland 158 D5
Mirfield 88 C3
Miserden 37 D6
Miskin 34 F4
Misson 89 E7
Misterton Leics 64 F2
  Notts 89 E8
  Som 12 D2
Mistley 56 F5
Mitcham 28 C3
Mitcheldean 36 C3
Mitchell 4 D3
Mitchel Troy 36 C1
Mitcheltroy
  Common 36 D1
Mitford 117 F7
Mithian 4 D2
Mitton 62 C2
Mixbury 52 F4
Moat 108 B4
Moats Tye 56 D4
Mobberley Ches E 74 B4
  Staffs 75 E7
Moccas 49 E5
Mochdre Conwy 83 D8
  Powys 59 F7
Mochrum 105 E7
Mockbeggar 14 D2
Mockerkin 98 B2
Modbury 6 D4
Moddershall 75 F6
Moelfre Anglesey 82 C5
  Powys 59 B8
Moffat 114 D3
Moggerhanger 54 E2
Moira 63 C7
Molash 30 D4
Mol-chlach 149 G9
Mold
  =Yr Wyddgrug 73 C6
Moldgreen 88 C2
Molehill Green 42 B1
Molescroft 97 E6
Molesden 117 F7
Molesworth 53 B8
Moll 149 E10
Molland 10 B3
Mollington Ches W 73 B7
  Oxon 52 E2
Mollinsburn 119 B7
Monachty 46 C4
Monachylemore 126 C3
Monar Lodge 150 G5
Monaughty 48 C4
Monboddo House 135 B7
Mondynes 135 B7
Monevechadan 125 E7
Monewden 57 D6
Moneydie 128 B2
Moniaive 113 E7
Monifieth 134 F4
Monikie 135 F4
Monimail 128 C4
Monington 45 E3
Monk Bretton 88 D4
Monken Hadley 41 E5
Monk Fryston 89 B6
Monkhopton 61 E6
Monkland 49 D6
Monkleigh 9 B6
Monknash 21 B8

Monkokehampton 9 D7
Monkseaton 111 B6
Monks Eleigh 56 E3
Monk's Gate 17 B6
Monks Heath 74 B5
Monk Sherborne 26 D4
Monkshill 153 D7
Monksilver 22 F2
Monks Kirby 63 F8
Monk Soham 57 C6
Monkspath 51 B6
Monks Risborough 39 D8
Monk Street 42 B2
Monkswood 35 D7
Monkton Devon 11 D6
Kent 31 C6
Pembs 44 E4
S Ayrs 112 B3
Monkton Combe 24 C2
Monkton Deverill 24 F3
Monkton Farleigh 24 C3
Monkton Heathfield 11 B7
Monkton Up Wimborne 13 C8
Monkwearmouth 111 D6
Monkwood 26 F4
Monmouth = Trefynwy 36 C2
Monmouth Cap 35 B7
Monnington on Wye 49 E5
Monreith 105 E7
Monreith Mains 105 E7
Montacute 12 C2
Montcoffer House 153 B6
Montford Argyll 145 G10
Shrops 60 C4
Montford Bridge 60 C4
Montgarrie 140 C4
Montgomery = Trefaldwyn 60 E2
Montrave 129 D5
Montrose 135 D7
Mont Saint Guern 16
Montsale 43 E6
Monxton 25 E8
Monyash 75 C8
Monymusk 141 C5
Monzie 127 B7
Monzie Castle 127 B7
Moodiesburn 119 B6
Moonzie 128 C5
Moor Allerton 95 F5
Moorby 79 C5
Moor Crichel 13 D7
Moordown 13 E8
Moore 86 F3
Moorend 36 D4
Moor End E Yorks 96 F4
York 96 D2
Moorends 89 C7
Moorgate 88 E5
Moorgreen 76 E4
Moorhall 76 B3
Moorhampton 49 E5
Moorhead 94 F4
Moorhouse Cumb 108 D3
Notts 77 C7
Moorlinch 23 F5
Moor Monkton 95 D8
Moor of Granary 151 F13
Moor of Ravenstone 105 E7
Moor Row 98 C2
Moorsholm 102 C4
Moorside 87 D7
Moor Street 30 C2
Moorthorpe 89 C5
Moortown Hants 14 D2
IoW 14 F5
Lincs 90 E4
Morangie 151 C10
Morar 147 B9
Morborne 65 E8
Morchard Bishop 10 D2
Morcombelake 12 E2
Morcott 65 D6
Morda 60 B2
Morden Dorset 13 E7
London 28 C3
Mordiford 49 F7
Mordon 101 B8
More 60 E3
Morebath 10 B4
Morebattle 116 B3
Morecambe 92 C4
Morefield 150 B4
Moreleigh 7 D5
Morenish 132 F2
Moresby 98 B1
Moresby Parks 98 C1
Morestead 15 B6
Moreton Dorset 13 F6
Essex 41 D8
Mers 85 E3
Oxon 39 D6
Staffs 61 C7
Moreton Corbet 61 B5
Moretonhampstead 10 F2
Moreton-in-Marsh 51 F7
Moreton Jeffries 49 E8
Moreton Morrell 51 D8
Moreton on Lugg 49 E7
Moreton Pinkney 52 E3
Moreton Say 74 F3
Moreton Valence 36 D4
Morfa Carms 33 C6
Carms 33 E6
Morfa Bach 32 C4
Morfa Bychan 71 D6
Morfa Dinlle 82 F4
Morfa Glas 34 D2
Morfa Nefyn 70 C3
Morfydd 72 E5
Morgan's Vale 14 B2
Moriah 46 B5
Morland 99 B7
Morley Derbys 76 E3
Durham 101 B6
W Yorks 88 B3
Morley Green 87 F6
Morley St Botolph 68 E3
Morningside Edin 120 B5
Morningside *continued*
N Lanark 119 D8
Morningthorpe 68 E5
Morpeth 117 F8
Morphie 135 C7
Morrey 62 C5
Morris Green 55 F8
Morriston 33 E7
Morston 81 C6
Mortehoe 20 E3
Mortimer 26 C4
Mortimer's Cross 49 C6
Mortimer West End 26 C4
Mortlake 28 B3
Morton Cumb 108 D3
Derbys 76 C4
Lincs 65 B7
Lincs 77 C8
Lincs 90 E2
Norf 68 C4
Notts 77 D7
S Glos 36 E3
Shrops 60 B2
Morton Bagot 51 C6
Morton-on-Swale 101 E8
Morvah 2 C3
Morval 5 D7
Morvich Highld 136 B2
Highld 157 J10
Morville 61 E6
Morville Heath 61 E6
Morwenstow 8 C4
Mosborough 88 F5
Moscow 118 E4
Mosedale 108 F3
Moseley W Mid 62 E3
W Mid 62 F4
Worcs 50 D3
Moss Argyll 146 G2
Highld 147 E9
S Yorks 89 C6
Wrex 73 D7
Mossat 140 C3
Mossbank 160 F6
Moss Bank 86 E3
Mossbay 98 B1
Mossblown 112 B4
Mossbrow 86 F5
Mossburnford 116 C2
Mossdale 106 B3
Moss Edge 92 E4
Mossend 119 C7
Moss End 27 B6
Mosser 98 B3
Mossfield 151 D9
Mossgiel 112 B4
Mosside 134 D4
Mossley Ches E 75 C5
Gtr Man 87 D7
Mossley Hill 85 F4
Moss of Barmuckity 152 B2
Moss Pit 62 B3
Moss-side 151 F11
Moss Side 92 F3
Mosstodloch 152 B3
Mosston 135 E5
Mossy Lea 86 C3
Mosterton 12 D2
Moston Gtr Man 87 D6
Shrops 61 B5
Moston Green 74 C4
Mostyn 85 F2
Mostyn Quay 85 F2
Motcombe 13 B6
Mothecombe 6 E4
Motherby 99 B6
Motherwell 119 D7
Mottingham 28 B5
Mottisfont 14 B4
Mottistone 14 F5
Mottram in Longdendale 87 E7
Mottram St Andrew 75 B5
Mouilpied Guern 16
Mouldsworth 74 B2
Moulin 133 D6
Moulsecoomb 17 D7
Moulsford 39 F5
Moulsoe 53 E7
Moulton Ches W 74 C3
Lincs 66 B3
Northants 53 C5
N Yorks 101 D7
Suff 55 C7
V Glam 22 B2
Moulton Chapel 66 C2
Moulton Eaugate 66 C3
Moulton St Mary 69 D6
Moulton Seas End 66 B3
Mounie Castle 141 B6
Mount Corn 4 D2
Corn 5 C6
Highld 151 G12
Mountain 94 F3
Mountain Ash = Aberpennar 34 E4
Mountain Cross 120 E4
Mountain Water 44 C4
Mountbenger 115 B6
Mount Bures 56 F3
Mount Canisp 151 D10
Mountfield 18 C4
Mountgerald 151 E8
Mount Hawke 3 B6
Mountjoy 4 C3
Mountnessing 42 E2
Mounton 36 E2
Mount Pleasant Ches E 74 D5
Derbys 63 C6
Derbys 76 E3
Flint 73 B6
Hants 14 E3
W Yorks 88 B3
Mountsorrel 64 C2
Mount Sorrel 13 B8
Mount Tabor 87 B8
Mousehole 2 D3
Mousen 123 F7
Mouswald 107 B7
Mow Cop 75 D5
Mowhaugh 116 B4
Mowsley 64 F3
Moxley 62 E3
Moy Highld 137 F7
Moy *continued*
Highld 151 H10
Moy Hall 151 H10
Moy House 151 E13
Moyles Court 14 D2
Moylgrove 45 E3
Moy Lodge 137 F7
Muasdale 143 D7
Muchalls 141 E8
Much Birch 49 F7
Much Cowarne 49 E8
Much Dewchurch 49 F6
Muchelney 12 B2
Much Hadham 41 C7
Much Hoole 86 B2
Muchlarnick 5 D7
Much Marcle 49 F8
Muchrachd 150 H5
Much Wenlock 61 D6
Muckernich 151 F8
Mucking 42 F2
Muckleford 12 E4
Mucklestone 74 F4
Muckleton 61 B5
Muckletown 140 B4
Muckley Corner 62 D4
Muckton 91 F7
Mudale 157 F8
Muddiford 20 F4
Mudeford 14 E2
Mudford 12 C3
Mudgley 23 E6
Mugdock 119 B5
Mugeary 149 E9
Mugginton 76 E2
Muggleswick 110 E3
Muie 157 J9
Muir 139 F6
Muirden 153 C7
Muirdrum 135 F5
Muirhead Angus 134 F3
Fife 128 D4
N Lanark 119 C6
S Ayrs 118 F3
Muirhouselaw 116 B2
Muirhouses 128 F2
Muirkirk 113 B6
Muirmill 127 F6
Muir of Fairburn 150 F7
Muir of Fowlis 140 C4
Muir of Ord 151 F8
Muir of Pert 134 F4
Muirshearlich 136 F4
Muirskie 141 E7
Muirtack 153 E9
Muirton Highld 151 E10
Perth 127 C8
Perth 128 B3
Muirton Mains 150 F7
Muirton of Ardblair 134 E1
Muirton of Ballochy 135 C6
Muiryfold 153 C7
Muker 100 E4
Mulbarton 68 D4
Mulben 152 C3
Mulindry 142 C4
Mullardoch House 150 H5
Mullion 3 E5
Mullion Cove 3 E5
Mumby 79 B8
Munderfield Row 49 D8
Munderfield Stocks 49 D8
Mundesley 81 D9
Mundford 67 E8
Mundham 69 E6
Mundon 42 D4
Mundurno 141 C8
Munerigie 137 D5
Muness 160 C8
Mungasdale 150 B2
Mungrisdale 108 F3
Munlochy 151 F9
Munsley 49 E8
Munslow 60 F5
Murchington 9 F8
Murcott 39 C5
Murkle 158 D3
Murlaggan Highld 136 E3
Highld 137 F6
Murra 159 H3
Murrayfield 120 B5
Murrow 66 D3
Mursley 39 B8
Murthill 134 D4
Murthly 133 F7
Murton Cumb 100 B2
Durham 111 E6
Northumb 123 E5
York 96 D2
Musbury 11 E7
Muscoates 102 F4
Musdale 124 C5
Musselburgh 121 B6
Muston Leics 77 F8
N Yorks 97 B6
Mustow Green 50 B3
Mutehill 106 E3
Mutford 69 F7
Muthill 127 C7
Mutterton 10 D5
Muxton 61 C7
Mybster 158 E3
Myddfai 34 B1
Myddle 60 B4
Mydroilyn 46 D3
Myerscough 92 F4
Mylor Bridge 3 C7
Mynachlog-ddu 45 F3
Myndtown 60 F3
Mynydd Bach 47 B6
Mynydd-bach 36 E1
Mynydd Bodafon 82 C4
Mynydd Isa 73 C6
Mynyddygarreg 33 D5
Mynytho 70 D4
Myrebird 141 E6
Myrelandhorn 158 E4
Myreside 128 B4
Myrtle Hill 47 F6
Mytchett 27 D6
Mytholm 87 B7
Mytholmroyd 87 B8
Myton-on-Swale 95 C7
Mytton 60 C4

N

Naast 155 J13
Naburn 95 E8
Nackington 31 D5
Nacton 57 E6
Nafferton 97 D6
Na Gearrannan 154 C6
Nailbridge 36 C3
Nailsbourne 11 B7
Nailsea 23 B6
Nailstone 63 D8
Nailsworth 37 E5
Nairn 151 F11
Nalderswood 28 E3
Nancegollan 2 C5
Nancledra 2 C3
Nanhoron 70 D3
Nannau 71 E8
Nannerch 73 C5
Nanpantan 64 C2
Nanpean 4 D4
Nanstallon 4 C5
Nant-ddu 34 C4
Nanternis 46 D2
Nantgaredig 33 B5
Nantgarw 35 F5
Nant-glas 47 C8
Nantglyn 72 C4
Nantgwyn 47 B8
Nantlle 82 F5
Nantmawr 60 B2
Nantmel 48 C2
Nantmor 71 C7
Nant Peris 83 F6
Nant Uchaf 72 D4
Nantwich 74 D3
Nant-y-Bai 47 E6
Nant-y-cafn 34 D2
Nantycaws 33 C5
Nant-y-derry 35 D7
Nant-y-ffi 46 F4
Nantyffyllon 34 E2
Nantyglo 35 C5
Nant-y-moel 34 E3
Nant-y-pandy 83 D6
Naphill 39 E8
Nappa 93 D8
Napton on the Hill 52 C2
Narberth = Arberth 32 C2
Narborough Leics 64 E2
Norf 67 C7
Nasareth 82 F4
Naseby 52 B4
Nash Bucks 53 F5
Hereford 48 C5
Newport 35 F7
Shrops 49 B8
Nash Lee 39 D8
Nassington 65 E7
Nasty 41 B6
Nateby Cumb 100 D2
Lancs 92 E4
Natland 99 F7
Naughton 56 E4
Naunton Glos 37 B8
Worcs 50 F3
Naunton Beauchamp 50 D4
Navenby 78 D2
Navestock Heath 41 E8
Navestock Side 42 E1
Navidale 157 H13
Nawton 102 F4
Nayland 56 F3
Nazeing 41 D7
Neacroft 14 E2
Neal's Green 63 F7
Neap 160 H7
Near Sawrey 99 E5
Neasham 101 C8
Neath = Castell-Nedd 33 E8
Neath Abbey 33 E8
Neatishead 69 B6
Nebo Anglesey 82 B4
Ceredig 46 C4
Conwy 83 F8
Gwyn 82 F4
Necton 67 D8
Nedd 156 F4
Nedderton 117 F8
Nedging Tye 56 E4
Needham 68 F5
Needham Market 56 D4
Needingworth 54 B4
Needwood 63 B5
Neen Savage 49 B8
Neen Sollars 49 B8
Neenton 61 F6
Nefyn 70 C4
Neilston 118 D4
Neinthirion 59 D6
Neithrop 52 E2
Nelly Andrews Green 60 D2
Nelson Caerph 35 E5
Lancs 93 F8
Nelson Village 111 B5
Nemphlar 119 E8
Nempnett Thrubwell 23 C7
Nene Terrace 66 D2
Nenthall 109 E7
Nenthead 109 E7
Nenthorn 122 F2
Nerabus 142 C3
Nercwys 73 C6
Nerston 119 D6
Nesbit 123 F5
Ness 73 B7
Nesscliffe 60 C3
Neston Ches W 73 B6
Wilts 24 C3
Nether Alderley 74 B5
Netheravon 25 E6
Nether Blainslie 121 E8
Nether Booth 88 F2
Netherbrae 153 C7
Netherbrough 159 G4
Nether Broughton 64 B3
Netherburn 119 E8
Nether Burrow 93 B6
Netherbury 12 E2
Netherby Cumb 108 B3
N Yorks 95 E6
Nether Cerne 12 E4
Nether Compton 12 C3
Nethercote 52 C3
Nethercott 20 F3
Nether Crimond 141 B7
Nether Dalgliesh 115 D5
Nether Dallachy 152 B3
Netherend 36 D2
Nether Exe 10 D4
Netherfield 18 D4
Nether Glasslaw 153 C8
Netherhampton 14 B2
Nether Handwick 134 E3
Nether Haugh 88 E5
Nether Heage 76 D3
Nether Heyford 52 D4
Nether Hindhope 116 C3
Nether Howecleuch 114 C3
Nether Kellet 92 C5
Nether Kinmundy 153 D10
Nether Langwith 76 B5
Netherlaw 106 E4
Nether Leask 153 E10
Nether Lenshie 153 D6
Netherley Aberds 141 E7
Mers 86 F2
Nethermill 114 F3
Nether Monynut 122 C3
Nethermuir 153 D9
Nether Padley 76 B2
Nether Park 153 C10
Netherplace 118 D5
Nether Poppleton 95 D8
Netherseal 63 C6
Nether Silton 102 E2
Nether Stowey 22 F3
Netherthird 113 C5
Netherthong 88 D2
Netherthorpe 89 F6
Netherton Angus 135 D5
Devon 7 B6
Hants 25 D8
Mers 85 D4
Northumb 117 D5
Oxon 38 E4
Perth 133 D8
Stirling 119 B5
W Mid 62 F3
Worcs 50 E4
W Yorks 88 C2
W Yorks 88 C3
Nethertown Cumb 98 D1
Highld 158 C5
Nether Urquhart 128 D3
Nether Wallop 25 F8
Nether Wasdale 98 D3
Nether Whitacre 63 E6
Netherwitton 117 E7
Netherwood 113 B6
Nether Worton 52 F2
Nethy Bridge 139 B6
Netley 15 D5
Netley Marsh 14 C4
Netteswell 41 C7
Nettlebed 39 F7
Nettlebridge 23 E8
Nettlecombe 12 E3
Nettleden 40 C3
Nettleham 78 B3
Nettlestead 29 D7
Nettlestead Green 29 D7
Nettlestone 15 E7
Nettlesworth 111 E5
Nettleton Lincs 90 D5
Wilts 24 B3
Neuadd 33 B7
Nevendon 42 E3
Nevern 45 E2
New Abbey 107 C6
New Aberdour 153 B8
New Addington 28 C4
Newall 94 E4
New Alresford 26 F3
New Alyth 134 E2
Newark Orkney 159 D8
Pboro 66 D2
Newark-on-Trent 77 D7
New Arley 63 F6
Newarthill 119 D7
New Ash Green 29 C7
New Barn 29 C7
New Barnetby 90 C4
Newbarns 92 B2
New Barton 53 C6
Newbattle 121 C6
New Bewick 117 B6
Newbiggin Cumb 92 C2
Cumb 98 E2
Cumb 99 B6
Cumb 99 B8
Cumb 109 E5
Durham 100 B4
N Yorks 100 E4
N Yorks 100 F4
Newbiggin-by-the-Sea 117 F9
Newbigging Angus 134 E2
Angus 134 F4
Angus 134 F4
S Lanark 120 E3
Newbiggin-on-Lune 100 D2
New Bilton 52 B2
Newbold Derbys 76 B3
Leics 63 C8
Newbold on Avon 52 B2
Newbold on Stour 51 E7
Newbold Pacey 51 D7
Newbold Verdon 63 D8
New Bolingbroke 79 D6
Newborough Anglesey 82 E4
Pboro 66 D2
Staffs 62 B5
Newbottle Northants 52 F3
T&W 111 D6
New Boultham 78 B2
Newbourne 57 E6
New Bradwell 53 E6
New Brancepeth 110 E5
Newbridge Caerph 35 E6
Ceredig 46 D4
Corn 2 C3
Corn 5 C8
Dumfries 107 B6
Edin 120 B4
Hants 14 C3
Newbridge *continued*
IoW 14 F5
Pembs 44 B4
New Bridge 73 E6
Newbridge Green 50 F3
Newbridge-on-Usk 35 E7
Newbridge on Wye 48 D2
New Brighton Flint 73 C6
Mers 85 E4
New Brinsley 76 D4
Newbrough 109 C8
New Broughton 73 D7
New Buckenham 68 E3
Newbuildings 10 D2
Newburgh Aberds 141 B8
Aberds 153 C9
Borders 115 C6
Fife 128 C4
Lancs 86 C2
Newburn 110 C4
Newbury 26 C2
Newbury Park 41 F7
Newby Cumb 99 B7
Lancs 93 E8
N Yorks 93 B7
N Yorks 102 C3
N Yorks 103 E8
Newby Bridge 99 F5
Newby East 108 D4
New Byth 153 C8
Newby West 108 D3
Newby Wiske 102 F1
Newcastle Mon 35 C8
Shrops 60 F2
Newcastle Emlyn = Castell Newydd Emlyn 46 E2
Newcastleton or Copshaw Holm 115 F7
Newcastle-under-Lyme 74 E5
Newcastle upon Tyne 110 C5
New Catton 68 C5
Newchapel Pembs 45 F4
Powys 59 F6
Staffs 75 D5
Sur 28 E4
New Cheriton 15 B6
Newchurch Carms 32 B4
IoW 15 F6
Kent 19 B7
Lancs 93 F8
Mon 36 E1
Powys 48 D4
Staffs 62 B5
New Costessey 68 C4
Newcott 11 D7
New Cowper 107 E8
Newcraighall 121 B6
New Cross Ceredig 46 B5
London 28 B4
New Cumnock 113 C6
New Deer 153 D8
New Delaval 111 B5
Newdigate 28 E2
New Duston 52 C5
New Earswick 96 D2
New Edlington 89 E6
New Elgin 152 B2
New Ellerby 97 F7
Newell Green 27 B6
New Eltham 28 B5
New End 51 D5
Newenden 18 C5
Newent 36 B4
Newerne 36 D3
New Farnley 94 F5
New Ferry 85 F4
Newfield Durham 110 F5
Highld 151 D10
Newford 2 E4
Newfound 26 D3
New Fryston 89 B5
Newgale 44 C3
New Galloway 106 B3
Newgate 81 C6
Newgate Street 41 D6
New Gilston 129 D6
New Grimsby 2 E3
New Hainford 68 C5
Newhall Ches E 74 E3
Derbys 63 B6
Newhall House 151 E9
Newhall Point 151 E10
Newham 117 B7
Newham Hall 117 B7
New Hartley 111 B6
Newhaven Derbys 75 D8
Edin 121 B5
E Sus 17 D8
New Haw 27 C8
New Hedges 32 D2
New Herrington 111 D6
Newhey 87 C7
New Hinksey 39 D5
New Holkham 80 D4
New Holland 90 B4
Newholm 103 C6
New Houghton Derbys 76 C4
Norf 80 E3
Newhouse 119 C7
New Houses 93 B8
New Humberstone 64 D3
New Hutton 99 E7
New Hythe 29 D8
Newick 17 B8
Newingreen 19 B8
Newington Kent 19 B8
Kent 30 C2
Kent 31 C7
Notts 89 E7
Oxon 39 E6
Shrops 60 F4
New Inn Carms 46 F3
Mon 36 D1
Pembs 45 F2
Torf 35 E7
New Invention Shrops 48 B4
W Mid 62 D3
New Kelso 150 G2
New Kingston 64 B2
New Lanark 119 E8
Newland Glos 36 D2
Hull 97 F6
Newland *continued*
N Yorks 89 B7
Worcs 50 E2
Newlandrig 121 C6
Newlands Borders 115 E8
Highld 151 G10
Moray 152 C3
Northumb 110 D3
Newland's Corner 27 E8
Newlandsmuir 119 D6
Newlands of Geise 158 D2
Newlands of Tynet 152 B3
Newlands Park 82 C2
New Lane 86 C2
New Lane End 86 E4
New Leake 79 D7
New Leeds 153 C9
New Longton 86 B3
Newlot 159 G6
New Luce 105 C5
Newlyn 2 D3
Newmachar 141 C7
Newmains 119 D8
New Malden 28 C3
Newmarket Suff 55 C7
W Isles 155 D9
New Marske 102 B4
New Marton 73 F7
New Micklefield 95 F7
Newmill Borders 115 C7
Corn 2 C3
Moray 152 C4
New Mill Aberds 141 F6
Herts 40 C2
Wilts 25 C6
W Yorks 88 D2
Newmill of Inshewan 134 C4
New Mills Ches E 87 F5
Corn 4 D3
Derbys 87 F7
Powys 59 D7
Newmills of Boyne 152 C5
Newmiln 133 F8
Newmilns 118 F5
New Milton 14 E3
New Moat 32 B1
Newnham Cambs 54 D5
Glos 36 C3
Hants 26 D5
Herts 54 F3
Kent 30 D3
Northants 52 D3
Newnham Bridge 49 C8
New Ollerton 77 C6
New Oscott 62 E4
Newpark 129 C6
New Park 95 D5
New Pitsligo 153 C8
New Polzeath 4 B4
Newport Devon 20 F4
Essex 55 F6
E Yorks 96 F4
Highld 158 H3
IoW 15 F6
Norf 69 C8
Telford 61 C7
Newport = Casnewydd 35 F7
Newport = Trefdraeth 45 F2
Newport-on-Tay 129 B6
Newport Pagnell 53 E6
Newpound Common 16 B4
Newquay 4 C3
New Quay = Ceinewydd 46 D2
New Rackheath 69 C5
New Radnor 48 C4
New Rent 108 F4
New Ridley 110 D3
New Road Side 94 E2
New Romney 19 C7
New Rossington 89 E7
New Row Ceredig 47 B6
Lancs 93 F6
N Yorks 102 C4
New Sarum 25 F6
Newsbank 74 C5
Newseat Aberds 153 D10
Aberds 153 E7
Newsham Northumb 111 B6
N Yorks 101 C6
N Yorks 102 F1
Newsholme E Yorks 89 B8
Lancs 93 D8
New Silksworth 111 D6
Newsome 88 C2
Newstead Borders 121 F8
Northumb 117 B7
Notts 76 D5
New Stevenston 119 D7
New Street 75 D7
New Street Lane 74 F3
New Swanage 13 F8
Newthorpe 95 F7
Newton Argyll 125 F6
Borders 116 B2
Bridgend 21 B7
Cambs 54 E5
Cambs 66 C4
Cardiff 22 B4
Ches W 73 C8
Ches W 74 B2
Ches W 74 D2
Cumb 92 B2
Derbys 76 D4
Dorset 13 C5
Dumfries 108 B2
Dumfries 114 E4
Gtr Man 87 E7
Hereford 48 F5
Hereford 49 D7
Highld 151 E10
Highld 151 G10
Highld 156 F5
Highld 158 F5
Lancs 92 F4
Lancs 93 B5
Lancs 93 D6
Lincs 78 F3
Moray 152 B1
Norf 67 C8
Newton *continued*
Northants 65 F5
Northumb 110 C3
Notts 77 E6
Perth 133 F5
S Lanark 119 C6
S Lanark 120 F2
Staffs 62 B4
Suff 56 E3
Swansea 33 F7
S Yorks 89 D6
Warks 52 B3
Wilts 14 B3
W Loth 120 B3
Newton Abbot 7 B6
Newtonairds 113 F8
Newton Arlosh 107 D8
Newton Aycliffe 101 B7
Newton Bewley 102 B2
Newton Blossomville 53 D7
Newton Bromswold 53 C7
Newton Burgoland 63 D7
Newton by Toft 90 F4
Newton Ferrers 6 E3
Newton Flotman 68 E5
Newtongrange 121 C6
Newton Hall 110 C3
Newton Harcourt 64 E3
Newton Heath 87 D6
Newtonhill Aberds 141 E8
Highld 151 G8
Newton House 141 B5
Newton Kyme 95 E7
Newton-le-Willows Mers 86 E3
N Yorks 101 F7
Newton Longville 53 F6
Newton Mearns 118 D5
Newtonmill 135 C6
Newtonmore 138 E3
Newton Morrell 101 D7
Newton Mulgrave 103 C5
Newton of Ardtoe 147 D9
Newton of Balcanquhal 128 C3
Newton of Falkland 128 D4
Newton on Ayr 112 B3
Newton on Ouse 95 D8
Newton-on-Rawcliffe 103 E6
Newton-on-the-Moor 117 D7
Newton on Trent 77 B8
Newton Park 145 G10
Newton Poppleford 11 F5
Newton Purcell 52 F4
Newton Regis 63 D6
Newton Reigny 108 F4
Newton St Cyres 10 E3
Newton St Faith 68 C5
Newton St Loe 24 C2
Newton St Petrock 9 C6
Newton Solney 63 B6
Newton Stacey 26 E2
Newton Stewart 105 C8
Newton Tony 25 E7
Newton Tracey 9 B7
Newton under Roseberry 102 C3
Newton upon Derwent 96 E3
Newton Valence 26 F5
New Totley 76 B3
Newtown Argyll 125 E6
BCP 13 E8
Ches W 74 B2
Corn 3 D6
Cumb 107 E7
Cumb 108 C5
Derbys 87 F7
Devon 10 B2
Glos 36 D3
Glos 50 F4
Hants 14 B4
Hants 14 C3
Hants 15 C6
Hants 15 C7
Hants 15 D5
Hants 26 C2
Hereford 49 E8
Highld 137 D6
IoM 84 E3
IoW 14 E5
Northumb 117 B6
Northumb 117 D6
Northumb 123 F5
Shrops 73 F8
Staffs 75 C6
Staffs 75 C7
Wilts 13 B7
New Town 121 B7
Newtown = Y Drenewydd 59 E8
Newtown Linford 64 D2
Newtown St Boswells 121 F8
Newtown Unthank 63 D8
New Tredegar = Tredegar Newydd 35 D5
New Trows 119 F8
Newtyle 134 E2
New Ulva 144 E6
New Walsoken 66 D4
New Waltham 91 D6
New Whittington 76 B3
New Wimpole 54 E4
New Winton 121 B7
New Yatt 38 C3
New York Lincs 78 D5
N Yorks 94 C4
Neyland 44 E4
Niarbyl 84 E2
Nibley 36 F3
Nibley Green 36 E4
Nibon 160 F5
Nicholashayne 11 C6
Nicholaston 33 F6
Nidd 95 C6
Nigg Aberdeen 141 D8
Highld 151 D11
Nigg Ferry 151 E10
Nightcott 10 B3
Nilig 72 D4
Nine Ashes 42 D1
Ninebanks 109 D7
Nine Mile Burn 120 D4
Nine Wells 44 C2
Ninfield 18 D4
Ningwood 14 F4
Nisbet 116 B2
Nisthouse Orkney 159 G4
Shetland 160 G7
Niton 15 G6
Nitshill 118 C5
Noak Hill 41 E8
Noblethorpe 88 D3
Nobottle 52 C4
Nocton 78 C3
Noke 39 C5
Nolton 44 D3
Nolton Haven 44 D3
No Man's Heath Ches W 74 E2
Warks 63 D6
Nomansland Devon 10 C3
Wilts 14 C3
Noneley 60 B4
Nonikiln 151 D9
Nonington 31 D6
Noonsbrough 160 H4
Norbreck 92 E3
Norbridge 50 E2
Norbury Ches E 74 E2
Derbys 75 E8
Shrops 60 E3
Staffs 61 B7
Nordelph 67 D5
Norden 87 C6
Norden Heath 13 F7
Nordley 61 E6
Norham 122 E5
Norley 74 B2
Norleywood 14 E4
Normanby N Lincs 90 C2
N Yorks 103 F5
Redcar 102 C3
Normanby-by-Spital 90 F4
Normanby by Stow 90 F2
Normanby le Wold 90 E5
Norman Cross 65 E8
Normandy 27 D7
Norman's Bay 18 E3
Norman's Green 11 D5
Normanstone 69 E8
Normanton Derby 76 F3
Leics 77 E8
Lincs 78 E2
Notts 77 D7
Rutland 65 D6
W Yorks 88 B4
Normanton le Heath 63 C7
Normanton on Soar 64 B2
Normanton-on-the-Wolds 77 F6
Normanton on Trent 77 C7
Normoss 92 F3
Norney 27 E7
Norrington Common 24 C3
Norris Green 85 E4
Norris Hill 63 C7
Northacre 68 E2
Northallerton 102 E1
Northam Devon 9 B6
Soton 14 C5
Northampton 53 C5
North Anston 89 F6
North Aston 38 B4
Northaw 41 D5
North Baddesley 14 C4
North Ballachulish 130 C4
North Barrow 12 B4
North Barsham 80 D5
Northbeck 78 E3
North Benfleet 42 F3
North Bersted 16 D3
North Berwick 129 F7
North Boarhunt 15 C7
Northborough 65 D8
Northbourne 31 D7
North Bovey 10 F2
North Bradley 24 D3
North Brentor 9 F6
North Brewham 24 F2
Northbridge Street 18 C4
North Buckland 20 E3
North Burlingham 69 C6
North Cadbury 12 B4
North Cairn 104 B3
North Carlton 78 B2
North Carrine 143 H7
North Cave 96 F4
North Cerney 37 D7
Northchapel 16 B3
North Charford 14 C2
North Charlton 117 B7
North Cheriton 12 B4
Northchurch 40 D2
North Cliff 97 E8
North Cliffe 96 F4
North Clifton 77 B8
North Cockerington 91 E7
North Coker 12 C3
North Collafirth 160 E5
North Common 17 B7
North Connel 124 B5
North Cornelly 34 F2
North Cotes 91 D7
Northcott 8 E5
North Cove 69 F7
North Cowton 101 D7
North Crawley 53 E7
North Cray 29 B5
North Creake 80 D4
North Curry 11 B8
North Dalton 96 D5
North Dawn 159 H5
North Deighton 95 D6
Northdown 31 B7
North Duffield 96 F2
Northdyke 159 F3
North Elkington 91 E6
North Elmham 81 E5
North Elmshall 89 C5

Northend Bath 24 C2
Bucks. 39 E7
Warks 51 D8
North End Bucks . . 39 B8
Essex 42 C2
E Yorks 97 F8
Hants. 26 C2
Lincs 78 E5
N Som 23 H5
Ptsmth. 15 D7
Som 11 B7
W Sus 16 D5
Northenden 87 E6
North Erradale . . 155 J12
North Fambridge . 42 E4
North Fearns . . . 149 E10
North
Featherstone . . . 88 B5
North Ferriby . . . 90 B3
Northfield
Aberdeen 141 D6
Borders 122 C5
E Yorks. 90 B4
W Mid 34 G6
Northfields 65 D7
Northfleet 29 B7
North Frodingham 97 D7
Northgate 60 F4
North Gluss 160 F5
North Gorley 14 C2
North Green Norf. 68 F5
Suff 57 C7
North Greetwell . . 78 B3
North Grimston . 96 C4
North Halley . . . 159 H6
North Halling . . . 29 C8
North Hayling . . . 15 D8
North Hazelrigg . 123 F6
North Heasley . . . 21 F6
North Heath 16 B4
North Hill Cambs . 55 B5
Corn. 5 B7
North Hinksey . . . 38 C4
North Holmwood . 28 E2
Northhouse 115 D7
North Howden . . . 96 F3
North Huish 6 D5
North Hykeham . . 78 C2
Northiam 18 C5
Northill 54 E2
Northington 26 F3
North Johnston . . 44 D4
North Kelsey 90 D4
North Kelsey Moor 90 D4
North Kessock . . 151 G9
North
Killingholme. . . 90 C5
North Kilvington . 102 F2
North Kilworth . . 64 F3
North Kirkton . . 153 C11
North Kiscadale . 143 F11
North Kyme 78 D4
North Lancing . . . 17 D5
Northlands 79 D6
Northlea 111 D7
Northleach 37 C8
North Lee 39 D8
Northleigh 11 E6
North Leigh 38 C3
North Leverton with
Habblesthorpe . 89 F8
Northlew 9 E7
North Littleton . . 51 E5
North Lopham . . . 68 F3
North Luffenham . 65 D6
North Marden . . . 16 C2
North Marston . . 39 B7
North Middleton
Midloth 121 D6
Northumb 117 B6
North Molton . . . 10 B2
Northmoor 38 D4
Northmoor Green or
Moorland 22 F5
North Moreton . . 39 F5
Northmuir 134 D3
North Mundham . 16 D2
North Muskham . 77 D7
North Newbald . . 96 F5
North Newington . 52 F2
North Newnton . . 25 D6
North Newton . . . 22 F4
Northney 15 D8
North Nibley 36 E4
North Oakley . . . 26 D3
North Ockendon . 42 F1
Northolt 40 F4
Northop 73 C6
Northop Hall 73 C6
North Ormesby . 102 B3
North Ormsby . . . 91 E6
Northorpe Lincs . 65 C7
Lincs 78 F5
Lincs 90 E2
North
Otterington . . . 102 F2
Northover Som . . 12 B3
Som 23 F6
North Owersby . . 90 E4
Northowram 88 B2
North Perrott . . . 12 D2
North Petherton . 22 F4
North Petherwin . . 8 F4
North Pickenham . 67 D8
North Piddle 50 D4
North Poorton . . . 12 E3
Northport 13 F7
North Port 125 C6
Northpunds 160 L6
North
Queensferry . . . 128 F3
North Radworthy . 21 F6
North Rauceby . . 78 E3
Northrepps 81 D8
North Reston . . . 91 F7
North Rigton 95 E5
North Rode 75 C5
North Roe 160 E5
North Runcton . . 67 C6
North Sandwick . 160 D7
North Scale 92 C1
North Scarle 77 C8
North Seaton . . . 117 F8
North Shian 130 E3
North Shields . . 111 C6
North Shoebury . 43 F5
North Shore 92 F3
North Side Cumb . 98 B2
Pboro. 66 E2

North Skelton . . 102 C4
North Somercotes . 91 E6
North Stainley . . . 95 B5
North Stainmore . 100 C3
North Stifford . . . 42 F2
North Stoke Bath . 24 C2
Oxon 39 F6
W Sus 16 C4
Northstowe 54 C5
North Street Hants. 26 F4
Kent. 30 D4
Medway 30 B2
W Berks. 26 B4
North
Sunderland . . . 123 F8
North Tamerton . . 8 E5
North Tawton 9 D8
North Thoresby . . 91 E6
North Tidworth . . 25 E7
North Togston . . . 117 D8
Northtown 29 E5
North Tuddenham . 68 C3
North Walbottle . 110 C4
North Walsham . . 81 D8
North Waltham . . 26 E3
North
Warnborough . . 26 D5
North Water
Bridge. 135 C6
North Watten . . . 158 E4
Northway 50 F4
North Weald
Bassett 41 D7
North Wheatley . . 89 F8
North Whilborough 7 C6
Northwich 74 B3
Northwick 36 F2
North Wick 23 C7
North Willingham . 91 F5
North Wingfield . . 76 C4
North Witham . . . 65 B6
Northwold 67 E7
Northwood Derbys 76 C2
IoW. 15 E5
Kent. 31 C7
London. 40 E3
Shrops. 73 F8
Northwood Green . 36 C4
North Woolwich . . 28 B5
North Wootton
Dorset 12 C4
Norf 67 B6
Som 23 E7
North Wraxall . . . 24 B3
North Wroughton . 38 F1
Norton E Sus . . . 17 D8
Glos 37 B5
Halton 86 F3
Herts 54 F3
IoW 14 F4
Oxon 39 D7
Suff 57 B5
Northants 52 C4
Notts 77 B5
Powys 48 C5
Shrops. 61 D5
Shrops. 61 D7
Stockton 102 B2
Suff 56 C3
S Yorks 89 C6
Wilts 37 F5
Worcs 50 E5
Worcs 50 D5
W Sus 16 E2
Norton Bavant . . . 24 E4
Norton Bridge . . . 75 F5
Norton Canes . . . 62 D4
Norton Canon . . . 49 E5
Norton Corner . . . 81 E6
Norton Disney . . . 77 D8
Norton East 62 D4
Norton Ferris 24 F2
Norton Fitzwarren 11 B6
Norton Green . . . 14 F4
Norton Hawkfield . 23 C7
Norton Heath . . . 42 D2
Norton in Hales . . 74 F4
Norton-in-the-
Moors. 75 D5
Norton-Juxta-
Twycross 63 D7
Norton-le-Clay . . 95 B7
Norton Lindsey . . 51 C7
Norton Malreward 23 C8
Norton Mandeville 42 D1
Norton-on-
Derwent. 96 B3
Norton St Philip . 24 D2
Norton sub
Hamdon 12 C2
Norton Woodseats 88 F4
Norwell 77 C7
Norwell
Woodhouse. . . . 77 C7
Norwich 68 D5
Norwick 160 B8
Norwood 89 F5
Norwood Hill 28 E3
Norwoodside 66 E4
Noseley 64 E4
Noss 160 M5
Noss Mayo 6 E3
Nosterfield. 101 F7
Nostie 149 F13
Notgrove 37 B8
Nottage 21 B7
Nottingham 77 F5
Nottington 12 F4
Notton Wilts 24 C4
W Yorks. 88 C4
Nounsley 42 C3
Noutard's Green . . 50 C2
Novar House . . . 151 E9
Nox 60 C4
Nuffield 39 F6
Nunburnholme . . 96 E4
Nuncargate 76 D5
Nuneaton 63 E7
Nuneham
Courtenay 39 E5
Nun Hills 87 B6
Nun Monkton . . . 95 D8
Nunney 24 E2
Nunnington 96 B2
Nunnykirk 117 E6
Nunsthorpe 91 D6
Nunthorpe Mbro . 102 C3
York 96 D2

Nunton 14 B2
Nunwick 95 B6
Nupend 36 D4
Nursling 14 C4
Nursted 15 B8
Nutbourne W Sus . 15 D8
W Sus 16 C4
Nutfield 28 D4
Nuthall 76 E5
Nuthampstead . . . 54 F5
Nuthurst 17 B5
Nutley E Sus 17 B8
Hants. 26 E4
Nutwell 89 D7
Nybster 158 D5
Nyetimber 16 E2
Nyewood 16 B2
Nymet Rowland . . 10 D2
Nymet Tracey . . . 10 D2
Nympsfield 37 D5
Nynehead 11 B6
Nyton 16 D3

O

Oadby 64 D3
Oad Street 30 C2
Oakamoor 75 E7
Oakbank. 120 C3
Oak Cross 9 E7
Oakdale 35 E5
Oake 11 B6
Oaken 62 D2
Oakenclough 92 E5
Oakengates 61 C7
Oakenholt 73 B6
Oakenshaw
Durham 110 F5
W Yorks 88 B2
Oakerthorpe 76 D3
Oakes 88 C2
Oakfield 35 E7
Oakford Ceredig . 46 D3
Devon 10 B4
Oakfordbridge . . . 10 B4
Oakgrove 75 C6
Oakham 65 D5
Oakhanger 27 F5
Oakhill. 23 E8
Oakhurst 29 D6
Oakington 54 C5
Oaklands Herts . . 41 C5
Powys 48 D2
Oakle Street 36 C4
Oakley BCP 13 E8
Bedford 53 D8
Bucks. 39 C6
Fife 128 F2
Hants. 26 D3
Oxon 39 D7
Suff 57 B5
Oakley Green . . . 27 B7
Oakley Park 59 F6
Oakmere. 74 C2
Oakridge Glos . . . 37 D6
Hants. 26 D4
Oaks. 60 D4
Oaksey 37 E6
Oaks Green 75 F8
Oakthorpe 63 C7
Oakwoodhill 28 F2
Oakworth 94 F3
Oape 156 J7
Oare Kent. 30 C4
Som 21 E7
W Berks. 26 B3
Wilts 25 C6
Oasby 78 F3
Oathlaw 134 D4
Oatlands 95 D6
Oban Argyll 124 C4
Highld 147 C11
Oborne 12 C4
Obthorpe 65 C7
Occlestone Green . 74 C3
Occold 57 B5
Ochiltree 112 B5
Ochtermuthill . . . 127 C7
Ochtertyre 127 B7
Ockbrook 76 F4
Ockham 27 D8
Ockle 147 D8
Ockley 28 F2
Ocle Pychard. . . . 49 E7
Octon 97 C6
Octon Cross
Roads 97 C6
Odcombe 12 C3
Odd Down 24 C2
Oddendale 99 C7
Odder 78 B2
Oddingley 50 D4
Oddington Glos . . 38 B2
Oxon 39 C5
Odell 53 D7
Odie 159 F7
Odiham 26 D5
Odstock 14 B2
Odstone 63 D7
Offchurch 51 C8
Offenham 51 E5
Offham E Sus. . . . 17 C7
Kent. 29 D7
W Sus 16 D4
Offord Cluny 54 C3
Offord Darcy 54 C3
Offton 56 E4
Offwell 11 E6
Ogbourne Maizey . 25 B6
Ogbourne
St Andrew 25 B6
Ogbourne
St George. 25 B7
Ogil 134 C4
Ogle 110 B4
Ogmore 21 B7
Ogmore-by-Sea . . 21 B7
Ogmore Vale 34 E3
Okeford Fitzpaine . 13 C6
Okehampton 9 E7
Okehampton Camp . 9 E7
Okraquoy 160 K6
Old 53 B5
Old Aberdeen . . 141 D8
Old Alresford . . . 26 F3
Oldany 156 F4
Old Arley 63 E6
Old Basford 76 E5

Old Basing 26 D4
Oldberrow 51 C6
Old Bewick 117 B6
Old Bolingbroke . 79 C6
Oldborough 10 D2
Old Bramhope . . . 94 E5
Old Brampton . . . 76 B3
Old Bridge of Tilt 133 C5
Old Bridge of Urr 106 C4
Old Buckenham . . 68 E3
Old Burghclere . . 26 D2
Oldbury Shrops. . . 61 E7
Warks 63 E7
W Mid 62 F3
Oldbury-on-
Severn 36 E3
Oldbury on the Hill 37 F5
Old Byland 102 F3
Old Cassop. 111 F6
Oldcastle Bridgend. 21 B8
Mon 35 B7
Old Castleton . . 115 E8
Old Catton 68 C5
Old Clee 91 D6
Old Cleeve 22 E2
Old Clipstone . . . 77 C6
Old Colwyn 83 D8
Oldcotes 89 F6
Old Coulsdon . . . 28 D4
Old Crombie . . . 152 C5
Old Dailly 112 E2
Old Dalby 64 B3
Old Deer 153 D9
Old Denaby 89 E5
Old Edlington . . . 89 E6
Old Eldon 101 B7
Old Ellerby 97 F7
Oldfallow 62 C3
Old Felixstowe . . 57 F7
Oldfield 50 C3
Old Fletton 65 E8
Oldford 24 D2
Old Glossop 87 E8
Old Goole 89 B8
Old Hall 59 F6
Oldham 87 D7
Oldhamstocks . . 122 B3
Old Heath 43 B6
Old Heathfield . . . 18 C2
Old Hill 62 F3
Old Hunstanton . . 80 C2
Old Hurst 54 B3
Old Hutton 99 F7
Old Kea 3 B7
Old Kilpatrick . . 118 B4
Old Kinnernie . . 141 D6
Old Knebworth . . 41 B5
Oldland 23 B8
Old Langho 93 F7
Old Laxey 84 D4
Old Leake 79 D7
Old Malton 96 B3
Oldmeldrum . . . 141 B7
Old Micklefield . . 95 F7
Old Milton 14 E3
Old Milverton . . . 51 C7
Old Monkland . . 119 C7
Old Netley 15 D5
Old Philpstoun . . 120 B3
Old Quarrington . 111 F6
Old Radnor 48 D4
Old Rattray 153 C10
Old Rayne 141 B5
Old Romney 19 C7
Oldshore Beg . . 156 D4
Oldshoremore . . 156 D5
Old Sodbury 36 F4
Old Somerby 78 F2
Oldstead 102 F3
Old Stratford . . . 53 E5
Old Thirsk 102 F2
Oldtown 140 B4
Old Town Cumb. . 99 F7
Cumb. 108 E4
Northumb 116 B4
Scilly 2 C3
Oldtown of Ord . 152 C6
Old Trafford 87 E6
Old Tupton 76 C3
Old Warden 54 E2
Oldway 33 F6
Oldways End 10 B3
Old Weston 53 B8
Oldwhat 153 C8
Old Whittington . 76 B3
Old Wick 158 E5
Old Windsor. 27 B7
Old Wives Lees . . 30 D4
Old Woking 27 D8
Old Woodhall . . . 78 C5
Olgrinmore 158 E2
Oliver's Battery . . 15 B5
Ollaberry 160 E5
Ollerton Ches E . . 74 B4
Notts 77 C6
Shrops. 61 B6
Olmarch 46 D5
Olney 53 D6
Olrig House 158 D3
Olton 62 F5
Olveston 36 F3
Olwen 46 E4
Ombersley 50 C3
Ompton 77 C6
Onecote 75 D7
Onen 35 C8
Ongar Hill 67 B5
Ongar Street 49 C5
Onibury 49 B6
Onich 130 C4
Onllwyn 34 C2
Onneley 74 E4
Onslow Village . . 27 D7
Onthank 118 E4
Openwoodgate . . 76 E3
Opinan Highld . . 149 A12
Highld 155 H13
Orange Lane . . . 122 E3
Orange Row. 66 B5
Orasaigh. 155 F8
Orbliston 152 C3
Orbost 148 D7
Orby 79 C7
Orchard Hill 9 B6
Orchard Portman. 11 B7
Orcheston 25 E5
Orcop 36 B1
Orcop Hill 36 B1

Ord 149 G11
Ordhead 141 C5
Ordie 140 D3
Ordiequish 152 C3
Ordsall 89 F7
Ore 18 D5
Oreton 61 F6
Orford Suff 57 E8
Warr 86 E4
Orgreave 63 C5
Orlestone 19 B6
Orleton Hereford . 49 C6
Worcs 49 C8
Orlingbury 53 B6
Ormesby 102 C3
Ormesby
St Margaret . . . 69 C7
Ormesby
St Michael 69 C7
Ormiclate Castle . 148 E2
Ormiscaig 155 H13
Ormiston 121 C7
Ormsaigbeg 146 E7
Ormsaigmore . . . 146 E7
Ormsary 144 F6
Ormsgill 92 B1
Ormskirk 86 D2
Orpington 29 C5
Orrell Gtr Man . . . 86 D3
Mers 85 E4
Orrisdale 84 C3
Orroland 106 E4
Orsett 42 F2
Orslow 62 C2
Orston 77 E7
Orthwaite 108 F2
Ortner 92 D5
Orton Cumb 99 D8
Northants 53 B6
Orton Longueville . 65 E8
Orton-on-the-Hill 63 D7
Orton Waterville . 65 E8
Orwell 54 D4
Osbaldeston 93 F6
Osbaldwick 96 D2
Osbaston 60 B3
Osbournby 78 F3
Oscroft 74 C2
Ose 149 D8
Osgathorpe 63 C8
Osgodby Lincs . . 90 E4
N Yorks 96 F3
N Yorks 103 F8
Oskaig 149 E10
Oskamull 146 G7
Osmaston Derby . 76 F3
Derbys. 76 E2
Osmington 12 F5
Osmington Mills . 12 F5
Osmotherley . . . 102 E2
Ospisdale 151 C10
Ospringe 30 C4
Ossett 88 B3
Ossington 77 C7
Ostend 43 E5
Oswaldkirk 96 B2
Oswaldtwistle. . . 86 B5
Oswestry 60 B2
Otford 29 D6
Otham 29 D8
Othery 23 F5
Otley Suff 57 D6
W Yorks 94 E5
Otterbourne 15 B5
Otterburn
Northumb 116 E4
N Yorks. 93 D8
Otterburn Camp . 116 E4
Otter Ferry 145 E8
Otterham 8 E3
Otterhampton . . . 22 E4
Ottershaw 27 C8
Otterswick 160 E7
Otterton 11 F5
Ottery St Mary. . . 11 E6
Ottinge 31 E5
Ottringham 91 B6
Oughterby 108 D2
Oughtershaw . . . 100 F3
Oughterside 107 E8
Oughtibridge . . . 88 E4
Oughtrington . . . 86 F4
Oulston 95 B8
Oulton Cumb . . . 108 D2
Norf 81 E7
Staffs. 75 F6
Suff 69 E8
W Yorks. 88 B4
Oulton Broad . . . 69 E8
Oulton Street . . . 81 E7
Ousby 109 F6
Ousdale 158 H2
Ousden 55 D8
Ousefleet 90 B2
Ouston Durham . 111 D5
Northumb 110 B3
Outertown 159 G3
Outgate 99 E5
Outhgill 100 D2
Outlane 87 C8
Out Newton 91 B7
Out Rawcliffe . . . 92 E4
Outwell 66 D5
Outwick 14 C2
Outwood Sur . . . 28 E4
W Yorks. 88 B4
Outwoods 61 C7
Ovenden 87 B8
Ovenscloss. 121 F7
Over Cambs 54 B4
Ches W. 74 C3
S Glos. 36 F2
Overbister 159 D7
Overbury 50 F4
Overcombe 12 F4
Overgreen 76 B3
Over Green 63 E5
Over Haddon 76 C2
Over Hulton 86 D4
Over Kellet 92 B5
Over Kiddington . 38 B4
Over Knutsford . . 74 B4
Overleigh 23 F6
Overley Green . . . 51 D5
Over Monnow . . . 36 C2
Over Norton 38 B3
Over Peover 74 B4

Overpool 73 B7
Overscaig Hotel . 156 G7
Overseal 63 C6
Over Silton 102 E2
Oversland 30 D4
Overstone 53 C6
Over Stowey 22 F3
Overstrand 81 C8
Over Stratton . . . 12 C2
Over Tabley. 86 F5
Overthorpe 52 E2
Overton Aberdeen 141 C7
Ches W. 74 B2
Dumfries 107 C6
Hants. 26 E3
Lancs 92 D4
N Yorks. 95 D8
Shrops. 49 B7
Swansea 33 F5
W Yorks 88 C3
Overton = Owrtyn 73 E7
Overton Bridge . . 73 E7
Overtown 119 D8
Over Wallop 25 F7
Over Whitacre . . . 63 E6
Over Worton 38 B4
Oving Bucks. 39 B7
W Sus 16 D3
Ovingdean 17 D7
Ovingham 110 C3
Ovington Durham . 101 C6
Essex 55 E8
Hants. 26 F3
Norf 68 D2
Northumb 110 C3
Ower 14 C4
Owermoigne 13 F5
Owlbury 60 E3
Owler Bar 76 B2
Owlerton 88 F4
Owl's Green 57 C6
Owlswick 39 D7
Owmby 90 D4
Owmby-by-Spital . 90 F4
Owrtyn = Overton 73 E7
Owslebury 15 B6
Owston Leics. . . . 64 D4
S Yorks. 89 C6
Owston Ferry . . . 90 D2
Owstwick. 97 F8
Owthorne 91 B7
Owthorpe 77 F6
Oxborough 67 D7
Oxcombe 79 B6
Oxenholme 99 F7
Oxenhope 94 F3
Oxen Park 99 F5
Oxenton 50 F4
Oxenwood 25 D8
Oxford 39 D5
Oxhey 40 E4
Oxhill 51 E8
Oxley 62 D3
Oxley Green 43 C5
Oxley's Green . . . 18 C3
Oxnam 116 C2
Oxshott 28 C2
Oxspring 88 D3
Oxted 28 D4
Oxton Borders . . 121 D7
Notts 77 D6
Oxwich 33 F5
Oxwick 80 E5
Oykel Bridge . . . 156 J6
Oyne. 141 B5

P

Pabail Iarach . . . 155 D10
Pabail Uarach . . 155 D10
Pace Gate. 94 D4
Packington 63 C7
Padanaram 134 D4
Padbury 52 F5
Paddington 41 F5
Paddlesworth . . . 19 B8
Paddockhaugh . . 152 C2
Paddockhole. . . . 115 F5
Paddock Wood . . 29 E7
Padfield 87 E8
Padiham 93 F7
Padog 83 F8
Padside 94 D4
Padstow 4 B4
Padworth 26 C4
Page Bank 110 F5
Pagham 16 E2
Paglesham
Churchend 43 E5
Paibeil 148 B2
Paible 154 H5
Paignton 7 D6
Pailton 63 F8
Painscastle 48 E3
Painshawfield . . 110 C3
Painsthorpe 96 D4
Painswick 37 D5
Pairc Shiaboist . 154 C7
Paisley 118 C4
Pakefield 69 E8
Pakenham 56 C3
Pale 72 F3
Palestine 25 E7
Paley Street 27 B6
Palfrey 62 E4
Palgowan 112 F3
Palgrave 56 B5
Pallion 111 D6
Palmarsh 19 B8
Palnackie 106 D5
Palnure 105 C8
Palterton 76 C4
Pamber End 26 D4
Pamber Green . . . 26 D4
Pamber Heath. . . 26 C4
Pamphill 13 D7
Pampisford 55 E5
Pan 159 J4
Panbride 135 F5
Pancrasweek 8 D4
Pandy Gwyn. . . . 58 D3
Mon 35 B7
Powys 59 D6
Wrex 73 F5
Pandy Tudur 83 E8
Panfield 42 B3

Pangbourne 26 B4
Pannal 95 D6
Panshanger 41 C5
Pant 60 B2
Pant-glas Carms . 33 B6
Gwyn 71 C5
Pant-glâs 58 E4
Pant-glas 73 F6
Pantgwyn Carms . 33 B6
Ceredig 45 E4
Pant-lasau 33 E7
Pant Mawr 59 F5
Panton 78 B4
Pantperthog 58 D4
Pant-teg. 33 B5
Pant-y-Caws. . . . 32 B2
Pant-y-dwr 47 B8
Pant-y-ffridd . . . 59 D8
Pantyffynnon . . . 33 C7
Pantymwyn 73 C5
Pant-yr-awel . . . 34 F3
Pant-y-Wacco . . . 72 B5
Panxworth 69 C6
Papcastle 107 F8
Papigoe 158 E5
Papil 160 K5
Papley 159 J5
Papple 121 B8
Papplewick 76 D5
Papworth Everard 54 C3
Papworth
St Agnes 54 C3
Par 5 D5
Parbold. 86 C2
Parbrook Som . . . 23 F7
W Sus 16 B4
Parc 72 F2
Parcllyn. 45 D4
Parc-Seymour . . 35 E8
Parc-y-rhôs 46 E4
Pardshaw 98 B2
Parham 57 C7
Park 114 E2
Park Corner Oxon . 39 F6
Windsor. 40 F1
Parkend 36 D3
Park End Mbro . . 102 C3
Northumb 109 B8
Parkeston 57 F6
Parkgate Ches W . 73 B6
Dumfries 114 F3
Kent. 19 B5
Sur 28 E3
Park Gate 15 D6
Parkham 9 B5
Parkham Ash. . . . 9 B5
Park Hill Notts . . 77 D6
N Yorks. 95 C6
Parkhill House . . 141 C7
Parkhouse 36 D1
Parkhouse Green . 76 C4
Parkhurst 15 E5
Parkmill 33 F6
Parkneuk 135 B7
Parkstone 13 E8
Park Street 28 F2
Parley Cross 13 E8
Parracombe 21 E5
Parrog 45 F2
Parsley Hay 75 C8
Parsonage Green . 42 D3
Parsonby 107 F8
Parson Cross . . . 88 E4
Parson Drove . . . 66 D3
Parson's Heath. . 43 B6
Partick 119 C5
Partington 86 E5
Partney 79 C7
Parton Cumb 98 B1
Dumfries 106 B3
Glos 37 B5
Partridge Green . 17 C5
Parwich 75 D8
Passenham 53 F5
Paston 81 D9
Patchacott. 9 E6
Patcham 17 D7
Patching 16 D4
Patchole 20 E5
Pateley Bridge . . 94 C4
Paternoster Heath. 43 C5
Pathe 23 F5
Pathhead Aberds . 135 C7
E Ayrs 113 C6
Fife 128 E4
Midloth 121 C6
Path of Condie . . 128 C2
Pathstruie 128 C2
Patna 112 C4
Patney 25 D5
Patrick 84 D2
Patrick
Brompton 101 E7
Patrington 91 B7
Patrixbourne. . . . 31 D5
Patterdale 99 C5
Pattingham 62 E2
Pattishall 52 D4
Pattiswick Green . 42 B4
Patton Bridge . . . 99 E7
Paul 2 D3
Paulerspury 52 E5
Paull 91 B5
Paulton 23 D8
Pavenham 53 D7
Pawlett 22 E5
Pawston 122 F4
Paxford 51 F6
Paxton 122 D5
Payhembury 11 D5
Paythorne 93 D8
Peacehaven 17 D8
Peak Dale 75 B7
Peak Forest 75 B8
Peakirk 65 D8
Pearsie 134 D3
Peasedown
St John 24 D2
Peasemore 26 B2
Peasenhall 57 C7
Pease Pottage . . 28 F3
Peaslake. 27 E8
Peasley Cross . . . 86 E3
Peasmarsh 19 C5
Peaston 121 C7
Peastonbank. . . . 121 C7
Peathill 153 B9
Peat Inn 129 D6
Peatling Magna . 64 E2

Peatling Parva . . 64 F2
Peaton. 60 F5
Peats Corner . . . 57 C5
Pebmarsh 56 F2
Pebworth 51 E6
Pecket Well 87 B7
Peckforton 74 D2
Peckham 28 B4
Peckleton 63 D8
Pedlinge 19 B8
Pedmore 62 F3
Pedwell. 23 F6
Peebles 121 E5
Peel 84 D2
Peel Common . . . 15 D6
Peel Park 119 D6
Peening Quarter . 19 C5
Pegsdon 54 F2
Pegswood 117 F8
Pegwell. 31 C7
Peinchorran . . . 149 E10
Peinlich 149 C9
Pelaw. 111 C5
Pelcomb Bridge . 44 D4
Pelcomb Cross . . 44 D4
Peldon 43 C5
Pellon 87 B8
Pelsall 62 D4
Pelton 111 D5
Peluthe 107 E8
Pelynt 5 D7
Pemberton. 86 D3
Pembrey 33 D5
Pembridge 49 D5
Pembroke
= Penfro 44 E4
Pembroke Dock =
Doc Penfro. . . . 44 E4
Pembury. 29 E7
Pen-allt 36 C2
Penally 32 E2
Penalt 36 B2
Penare 3 B8
Penarlâg
= Hawarden . . 73 C7
Penarth 22 B3
Pen-bont
Rhydybeddau . 58 F3
Penbryn 45 D4
Pencader 46 F3
Pencaenewydd . 70 C5
Pencaitland . . . 121 C7
Pencarnisiog. . . . 82 D3
Pencarreg 46 E4
Pencelli 34 B4
Pen-clawdd 33 E6
Pencoed 34 F3
Pencombe 49 D7
Pencoyd 36 B2
Pencraig Hereford . 36 B2
Powys 59 B7
Pendeen 2 C2
Penderyn 34 D3
Pendine 32 D3
Pendlebury 87 D5
Pendleton 93 F7
Pendock 50 F2
Pendoggett 4 B5
Pendomer 12 C3
Pendoylan 22 B2
Pendre 34 F3
Penegoes 58 D4
Pen-ffordd. 32 B1
Pengam 35 E5
Penge 28 B4
Pengenffordd . . . 48 F3
Pengorffwysfa . . 82 B4
Pengover Green . . 5 C7
Pen-groes-oped . 35 D7
Penhale Corn . . . 3 E5
Corn. 4 D4
Penhalvaen 3 C6
Penhill 38 F1
Penhow. 35 E8
Penhurst 18 D3
Peniarth 58 D3
Penicuik 120 C5
Peniel Carms. . . 33 B5
Denb 72 C4
Penifiler 149 D9
Peninver 143 F8
Penisarwaun. . . . 83 E5
Penistone 88 D3
Penjerrick 3 C6
Penketh 86 F3
Penkill 112 E2
Penkridge 62 C3
Penley 73 F8
Penllergaer 33 E7
Penllyn 21 B8
Pen-llyn 82 C3
Pen-lon 82 E4
Penmachno 83 F7
Penmaen 33 F6
Penmaenan 83 D7
Penmaenmawr . . 83 D7
Penmaenpool . . . 58 C3
Penmark 22 C2
Penmarth 3 C6
Penmon 83 C6
Penmore Mill . . . 146 F7
Penmorfa Ceredig . 46 D2
Gwyn 71 C6
Penmynydd 82 D5
Penn Bucks 40 E2
W Mid 62 E2
Pennal 58 D4
Pennan 153 B8
Pennant Ceredig. . 46 C4
Denb 72 D4
Denb 72 F4
Powys 59 E6
Pennant Melangell 59 B7
Pennar 33 F6
Pennerley 60 E3
Pennington Cumb . 92 B2
Gtr Man 86 E4
Hants. 14 E4
Penny Bridge . . . 99 F5
Pennycross 147 J8
Pennygate 69 B6
Pennygown 147 G8
Pennymoor 10 C3
Pennywell 111 D6
Penparc Ceredig. . 45 E4

Penparc continued
Pembs. 44 B3
Penparcau 58 F2
Penperlleni 35 D7
Penpillick. 5 D5
Penpol 3 C7
Penpoll 5 D7
Penpont Dumfries 113 E8
Powys 34 B3
Penrherber 45 F4
Penrhiwceiber . . 34 E4
Penrhiw goch . . . 33 C6
Penrhiw-llan . . . 46 E2
Penrhiw-pâl 46 E2
Penrhos 70 D4
Penrhôs 35 C8
Penrhos 34 C1
Penrhosfeilw. . . . 82 C2
Penrhyn Bay . . . 83 C8
Penrhyn-coch . . . 58 F3
Penrhyndeudraeth 71 D7
Penrhynside 83 C8
Penrice 33 F5
Penrith 108 F5
Penrose 4 B3
Penruddock 99 B6
Penryn. 3 C6
Pensarn Carms . . 33 C5
Conwy 72 B3
Pensax 50 C2
Pensby 85 F3
Penselwood. . . . 24 F2
Pensford 23 C8
Penshaw. 111 D6
Penshurst 29 E6
Pensilva 5 C7
Penston 121 B7
Pentewan 3 B9
Pentir 83 E5
Pentire 4 C2
Pentlow 56 E2
Pentney 67 C7
Penton Mewsey . . 25 E8
Pentraeth 82 D5
Pentre Carms . . . 33 C6
Powys 59 F7
Powys 60 E2
Rhondda 34 E3
Shrops. 60 C3
Wrex 72 F5
Wrex 73 E6
Pentrebach M Tydf . 34 D4
Swansea 33 D7
Pentre-bach 46 E4
Pentre bach 47 F8
Pentrebeirdd . . . 59 C8
Pentre Berw 82 D4
Pentre-bont 83 F7
Pentrecagal 46 E2
Pentre-celyn Denb 72 D5
Powys 59 D5
Pentre-chwyth . . 33 E7
Pentre-cwrt 46 F2
Pentre Dolau-
Honddu 47 E8
Pentredwr 73 E5
Pentre-dwr 33 E7
Pentrefelin Carms . 33 B6
Ceredig. 46 E5
Conwy 83 D8
Gwyn 71 D6
Pentrefoelas . . . 83 F8
Pentre-galar . . . 45 F3
Pentregat 46 D2
Pentre-Gwenlais . 33 C7
Pentre-Gwynfryn . 71 E6
Pentre Halkyn . . 73 B6
Corn. 4 D4
Pentre-Isaf 83 E8
Pentre
Llanrhaeadr . . 72 C4
Pentre-llwyn-
ll yd 47 D8
Pentre-llyn 46 B5
Pentre-llyn
cymmer 72 D3
Pentre Meyrick . . 21 B8
Pentre-poeth . . . 35 F6
Pentre'r Felin . . 83 E8
Pentre'r-felin . . . 47 F8
Pentre-rhew . . . 47 D5
Pentre-tafarn-y-
fedw 83 E8
Pentre-ty-gwyn . 47 F7
Pentrich 76 D3
Pentridge 13 C8
Pen-twyn 36 D2
Pentyrch 35 F5
Penuchadre 21 B7
Penuwch 46 C4
Penwithick 4 D5
Penwyllt 34 C2
Penybanc 33 C7
Pen-y-banc. 33 C7
Pen-y-bont Carms 32 B3
Gwyn 58 D4
Powys 48 C3
Pen-y-bont Carms 33 C6
Gwyn 58 D4
Pen-y-Bont Ar Ogwr
= Bridgend . . . 21 B8
Penybontfawr . . . 59 B7
Pen-y-bryn Gwyn . 58 C3
Pembs. 45 E3
Penycae 73 E6
Pen-y-cae 34 C2
Pen-y-cae-mawr . 35 E8
Pen-y-cefn 72 B5
Pen-y-clawdd . . . 36 D1
Pen-y-coedcae . . 34 F4
Penycwm 44 C3
Pen-y-fai 34 F2
Penyffordd 73 D7
Penyffridd 82 E5
Pen-y-garn Carms . 46 F4
Ceredig 58 F3
Penygarnedd . . . 59 B8
Pen-y-garnedd. . 82 D5
Penygraig 34 E3
Pen-y-graig 70 D2
Penygroes Gwyn . 82 F4
Pembs. 45 F3
Pen-y-groes 33 C6

Pen-y-groeslon...70 D3
Pen-y-Gwryd
Hotel...83 F6
Penyrheol...35 F5
Pen-yr-heol...35 C8
Pen-yr-
Heolgerrig...34 D4
Penysarn...82 B4
Pen-y-stryt...73 D5
Penywaun...34 D3
Penzance...2 C3
Peopleton...50 D4
Peover Heath...74 B4
Peper Harow...27 E7
Perceton...118 E3
Percie...140 E4
Percyhorner...153 B9
Periton...21 E8
Perivale...40 F4
Perkinsville...111 D5
Perlethorpe...77 B6
Perranarworthal...3 C6
Perranporth...4 D2
Perranuthnoe...2 D4
Perranzabuloe...4 D2
Perry Barr...62 E4
Perryfoot...88 F2
Perry Green Herts..41 C7
Wilts...37 F6
Perry Street...29 B7
Pershall...74 F5
Pershore...50 E4
Pert...135 C6
Pertenhall...53 C8
Perth...128 B3
Perthy...73 F7
Perton...62 E2
Pertwood...24 F3
Peterborough...65 E8
Peterburn...155 J12
Peterchurch...48 F5
Peterculter...141 D7
Peterhead...153 D11
Peterlee...111 E7
Petersfield...15 B8
Peter's Green...40 C4
Peters Marland...9 C6
Peterstone
Wentlooge...35 F6
Peterston-super-
Ely...22 B2
Peterstow...36 B2
Peter Tavy...6 B3
Petertown...159 H4
Petham...30 D5
Petrockstow...9 D7
Pett...19 D5
Pettaugh...57 D5
Petteridge...29 E7
Pettinain...120 E2
Pettistree...57 D6
Petton Devon...7 D6
Shrops...60 B4
Petts Wood...28 C5
Petty...153 E7
Pettycur...128 F4
Pettymuick...141 B8
Petworth...16 B3
Pevensey...18 E3
Pevensey Bay...18 E3
Pewsey...25 C6
Philham...8 B4
Philiphaugh...115 B7
Phillack...2 C4
Philleigh...3 C7
Philpstoun...120 B3
Phocle Green...36 B3
Phoenix Green...27 D5
Pica...98 B2
Piccotts End...40 D3
Pickering...103 F5
Picket Piece...25 E8
Picket Post...14 D2
Pickhill...101 F8
Picklescott...60 E4
Pickletillem...129 B6
Pickmere...74 B3
Pickney...11 B6
Pickstock...61 B7
Pickwell Devon...20 E3
Leics...64 C4
Pickworth Lincs..78 F3
Rutland...65 C6
Picton Ches W..73 B8
Flint...85 F2
N Yorks...102 D2
Piddinghoe...17 D8
Piddington
Northants...53 D6
Oxon...39 C6
Piddlehinton...12 E5
Piddletrenthide...12 E5
Pidley...54 B4
Piercebridge...101 C7
Pierowall...159 D5
Pigdon...117 F7
Pikehall...75 D8
Pilgrims Hatch...42 E1
Pilham...90 E2
Pill...23 B7
Pillaton...5 C8
Pillerton Hersey...51 E7
Pillerton Priors...51 E7
Pilleth...48 C4
Pilley Hants...14 E4
S Yorks...88 D4
Pilling...92 E4
Pilling Lane...92 E4
Pillowell...36 D3
Pillwell...13 C5
Pilning...36 F2
Pilsbury...75 C8
Pilsdon...12 E2
Pilsgate...65 D7
Pilsley Derbys..76 C3
Derbys...76 C4
Pilton Devon..20 F4
Northants...65 F7
Rutland...65 D6
Som...23 E7

Pinehurst...38 F1
Pinfold...85 C4
Pinged...33 D5
Pinhoe...10 E4
Pinkneys Green...40 F1
Pinley...51 B8
Pin Mill...57 F6
Pinminnoch...112 E1
Pinmore...112 E2
Pinmore Mains...112 E2
Pinner...40 F4
Pinvin...50 E4
Pinwherry...112 F1
Pinxton...76 D4
Pipe and Lyde...49 E7
Pipe Gate...74 E4
Piperhill...151 F11
Piper's Pool...8 F4
Pipewell...64 F5
Pippacott...20 F4
Pipton...48 F3
Pirbright...27 D7
Pirnmill...143 D9
Pirton Herts...54 F2
Worcs...49 E8
Pisgah Ceredig..47 B5
Stirling...127 D6
Pishill...39 F7
Pistyll...70 C4
Pitagowan...133 C5
Pitblae...153 B9
Pitcairngreen...128 B2
Pitcalnie...151 D11
Pitcaple...141 B6
Pitchcombe...37 D5
Pitchcott...39 B7
Pitchford...60 D5
Pitch Green...39 D7
Pitch Place...27 D7
Pitcombe...23 F8
Pitcorthie...129 D7
Pitcox...122 B2
Pitcur...134 F2
Pitfichie...141 C5
Pitforthie...135 B8
Pitgrudy...151 B10
Pitkennedy...135 D5
Pitkevy...128 D4
Pitkierie...129 D7
Pitlessie...128 D5
Pitlochry...133 D6
Pitmachie...141 B5
Pitmain...138 D3
Pitmedden...141 B7
Pitminster...11 C7
Pitmuies...135 E5
Pitmunie...141 C5
Pitney...12 B2
Pitscottie...129 C6
Pitsea...42 F3
Pitsford...53 C5
Pitstone...40 C2
Pitstone Green...40 C2
Pittendreich...152 B1
Pittentrail...157 J10
Pittenweem...129 D7
Pittington...111 E6
Pittodrie...141 B5
Pitton...25 F7
Pittswood...29 E7
Pittulie...153 B9
Pityme...45 E4
Pity Me...111 E5
Pityoulish...138 C5
Pixey Green...57 B6
Pixham...28 D2
Pixley...49 F8
Place Newton...96 B4
Plaidy...153 C7
Plains...119 C7
Plaish...60 E5
Plaistow...27 F8
Plaitford...14 C3
Plank Lane...86 E4
Plas-canol...58 C2
Plas Gogerddan...58 F3
Plas Llwyngwern...58 D4
Plas Nantyr...73 F5
Plastow Green...26 C3
Plas-yn-Cefn...72 B4
Platt...29 D7
Platt Bridge...86 D4
Platts Common...88 D4
Plawsworth...111 E5
Plaxtol...29 D7
Playden...19 C6
Playford...57 E6
Play Hatch...26 B5
Playing Place...3 B7
Playley Green...50 F2
Plealey...60 D4
Plean...127 F7
Pleasington...86 B4
Pleasley...76 C5
Pleckgate...93 F6
Plenmeller...109 C7
Pleshey...42 C2
Plockton...149 E13
Plocrapol...154 H6
Ploughfield...49 E5
Plowden...60 F3
Ploxgreen...60 D3
Pluckley...30 E3
Pluckley Thorne...30 E3
Plumbland...107 F8
Plumley...74 B4
Plumpton Cumb..108 F4
E Sus...17 C7
Plumpton Green...17 C7
Plumpton Head...108 F5
Plumstead London..29 B5
Norf...81 D7
Plumtree...77 F6
Plungar...77 F7
Plush...12 D5
Plwmp...46 D2
Plymouth...6 D3
Plympton...6 D3
Plymstock...6 D3
Plymtree...11 D5
Pockley...102 F4
Pocklington...96 E4
Pode Hole...66 B2
Podimore...12 B3
Podington...53 C7
Podmore...74 F4
Point Clear...43 C6
Pointon...78 F4
Pokesdown...14 E2

Pol a Charra...148 G2
Polbae...105 B6
Polbain...156 H2
Polbathic...5 D8
Polbeth...120 C3
Polchar...138 D4
Polebrook...65 F7
Pole Elm...50 E3
Polegate...18 E2
Poles...151 B10
Polesworth...63 D6
Polgigga...2 D2
Polglass...156 J3
Polgooth...4 D4
Poling...16 D4
Polkerris...5 D5
Polla...156 D6
Pollard...89 C7
Polloch...130 C1
Pollok...118 C5
Pollokshields...119 C5
Polmassick...3 B8
Polmont...120 B2
Polnessan...112 C4
Polnish...147 C10
Polperro...5 D7
Polruan...5 D6
Polsham...23 E7
Polstead...56 F3
Poltalloch...124 F4
Poltimore...10 E4
Polton...121 C5
Polwarth...122 D3
Polyphant...8 F4
Polzeath...4 B4
Pondersbridge...66 E2
Ponders End...41 E6
Pondtail...27 D6
Ponsanooth...3 C6
Ponsonby...98 D2
Ponsworthy...6 B5
Pont Aber...33 C7
Pont Aber-Geirw..71 E8
Pontamman...33 C7
Pontantwn...33 C5
Pontardawe...33 D8
Pontarddulais...33 D6
Pont-ar-gothi...33 B6
Pont-ar-Hydfer...34 B2
Pont-ar-llechau...33 B8
Pontarsais...33 B5
Pontblyddyn...73 C6
Pontbren Araeth..33 B7
Pontbren Llwyd..34 D3
Pont Cwm Pydew..72 F4
Pont Cyfyng...83 F7
Pont Cysyllte...73 E6
Pont Dolydd
Prysor...71 D8
Pontefract...89 B5
Ponteland...110 B4
Ponterwyd...58 F4
Pontesbury...60 D3
Pontfadog...73 F6
Pontfaen...45 F2
Pont-faen...47 F8
Pont Fronwydd..58 B5
Pont-gareg...45 E3
Pontgarreg...46 D2
Pont-Henri...33 D5
Ponthirwaun...45 E4
Pontllanfraith...35 E5
Pontlliw...33 D7
Pont-Llogel...59 C7
Pontllyfni...82 F4
Pontlottyn...35 D5
Pontneddfechan..34 D3
Pontnewydd...35 E6
Pont Pen-y-
benglog...83 E6
Pontrhydfendigaid 47 C6
Pont Rhyd-goch..83 E6
Pont-Rhyd-sarn..59 B5
Pont Rhyd-y-cyff..34 F2
Pontrhydyfen...34 E1
Pont-rhyd-y-
groes...47 B6
Pontrilas...35 B7
Pontrobert...59 C8
Pont-rug...82 E5
Pont Senni
=Sennybridge...34 B3
Ponts Green...18 D3
Pontshill...36 B3
Pont-siân...46 E3
Pontsticill...34 C4
Pontwgan...83 D7
Pontyates...33 D5
Pontyberem...33 C6
Pontyclun...34 F4
Pontycymer...34 E3
Pont-y-gwaith...34 E4
Pont-y-pant...83 F7
Pont y Pennant..59 B6
Pontypool
=Pont-y-pŵl...35 D6
Pontypridd...34 F4
Pont-y-pŵl
=Pontypool...35 D6
Pont yr Afon-Gam 71 C8
Pont-yr-hafod...44 C4
Pontywaun...35 E6
Pooksgreen...14 C4
Pool Corn...3 B5
W Yorks...94 E5
Poole...13 E8
Poole Keynes...37 E6
Poolend...75 D6
Poolewe...155 J13
Pooley Bridge...99 B6
Poolfold...75 D5
Poolhill...36 B4
Pool o'Muckhart..128 D2
Pool Quay...60 C2
Poolsbrook...76 B4
Pootings...29 E5
Pope Hill...44 D4
Popeswood...27 C6
Popham...26 E3
Poplar...41 F6
Popley...26 D4
Porchester...77 E5
Porchfield...14 E5
Porin...150 F6
Poringland...69 D5
Porkellis...3 C5
Porlock...21 E7

Porlock Weir...21 E7
Portachoillan...144 H6
Port Ann...145 E8
Port Appin...130 E3
Port Arthur...160 K5
Port Askaig...142 B5
Portavadie...145 G8
Port Bannatyne..145 G9
Portbury...23 B7
Port Carlisle...108 C2
Port Charlotte...142 C3
Portchester...15 D7
Port Clarence...102 B2
Port Driseach...145 F8
Port Ellen...142 D4
Port Elphinstone 141 C6
Portencalzie...104 B4
Portencross...118 E1
Portesham...12 F4
Port Erroll...153 E10
Portessie...152 B4
Port e Vullen...84 C4
Port-Eynon...33 F5
Portfield Gate...44 D4
Portgate...9 F6
Port Gaverne...8 F2
Port Glasgow...118 B3
Portgordon...152 B3
Portgower...157 H13
Porth Corn...4 C3
Rhondda...34 E4
Porthaethwy
=Menai Bridge..83 D5
Porthallow Corn...3 D6
Corn...5 D7
Porthcawl...21 B7
Porthcothan...4 B3
Porthcurno...2 D2
Port Henderson 149 A12
Porthgain...44 B3
Porthill...60 C4
Porthkerry...22 C2
Porthleven...2 D5
Porthllechog...82 B4
Porthmadog...71 D6
Porthmeor...2 C3
Porth Navas...3 D6
Portholland...3 B8
Porthoustock...3 D7
Porthpean...4 D5
Porthtowan...3 B5
Porth Tywyn
=Burry Port...33 D5
Porthyrhyd Carms..33 C6
Carms...47 F6
Porth-y-waen...60 B2
Portincaple...145 D11
Portington...96 F3
Portinnisherrich 125 D5
Portinscale...98 B4
Port Isaac...4 A4
Portishead...23 B6
Portkil...145 E11
Portknockie...152 B4
Port Lamont...145 F9
Portlethen...141 E8
Portling...107 D5
Port Lion...44 E4
Portloe...3 C8
Port Logan...104 E4
Portmahomack .151 C12
Portmeirion...71 D6
Portmellon...3 B9
Port Mholair...155 D10
Port Mor...146 D7
Portmore...14 E4
Port Mulgrave...103 C5
Portnacroish...130 E3
Portnahaven...142 C2
Portnalong...149 E8
Portnaluchaig...147 C9
Portnancon...156 C7
Port Nan
Giùran...155 D10
Port nan Long...148 A3
Portnellan...126 B3
Port Nis...155 A10
Portobello...121 B6
Port of Menteith .126 D4
Porton...25 F6
Portpatrick...104 D4
Port Quin...4 A4
Port Ramsay...130 E2
Portreath...3 B5
Portree...149 D9
Port St Mary...84 F2
Portscatho...3 C7
Portsea...15 D7
Portskerra...157 C11
Portskewett...36 F2
Portslade...17 D6
Portslade-by-Sea..17 D6
Portsmouth Ptsmth..15 D7
W Yorks...87 B7
Portsonachan...125 C6
Portsoy...152 B5
Port Sunlight...85 F4
Portswood...14 C5
Port Talbot...34 E1
Portuairk...146 E7
Portway Hereford...49 F7
Worcs...51 B5
Port Wemyss...142 C2
Port William...105 E7
Portwrinkle...5 D8
Poslingford...55 E8
Postbridge...6 B4
Postcombe...39 E7
Postling...19 B8
Postwick...69 D5
Potarch...141 E5
Potsgrove...40 B2
Potten End...40 D3
Potter Brompton..97 B5
Potterhanworth...78 C3
Potterhanworth
Booths...78 C3
Potter Heigham...69 C7
Potterne...24 D4
Potterne Wick...24 D5
Potternewton...95 F6
Potters Bar...41 D5
Potter's Cross...62 F2
Potterspury...53 E5
Potter Street...41 D7

Potterton Aberds..141 C8
W Yorks...95 F7
Potto...102 D2
Potton...54 E3
Pott Row...80 E3
Pott Shrigley...75 B6
Poughill Corn...8 D4
Devon...10 D3
Poulshot...24 D4
Poulton Glos...37 D8
Mers...85 E4
Poulton-le-Fylde..92 F3
Pound Bank...50 B2
Poundbury...12 E4
Poundfield...18 B2
Pound Green
E Sus...18 C2
IoW...14 F4
Worcs...50 B2
Pound Hill...28 F3
Poundland...112 F1
Poundon...39 B6
Poundsgate...6 B5
Poundstock...8 E4
Powburn...117 C6
Powderham...10 F4
Powerstock...12 E3
Powfoot...107 C8
Powick...50 D3
Powmill...128 E2
Poxwell...12 F5
Poyle...27 B8
Poynings...17 C6
Poyntington...12 C4
Poynton...87 F7
Poynton Green...61 C5
Poystreet Green..56 D3
Praa Sands...2 D4
Pratt's Bottom...29 C5
Praze...2 C4
Praze-an-Beeble...2 C5
Predannack Wollas..3 E5
Prees...74 F2
Preesall...92 E3
Prees Green...74 F2
Preesgweene...73 F6
Prees Heath...74 F2
Prees Higher
Heath...74 F2
Prees Lower Heath 74 F2
Prenderguest...122 D5
Prendwick...117 C6
Prengwyn...46 E3
Prenteg...71 C6
Prenton...85 F4
Prescot...86 E2
Prescott...60 B4
Pressen...122 F4
Prestatyn...72 A4
Prestbury Ches E..75 B6
Glos...37 B6
Presteigne
=Llanandras...48 C5
Presthope...61 E5
Prestleigh...23 E8
Preston Borders .122 D3
Brighton...17 D7
Devon...7 B6
Dorset...12 F5
E Loth...121 B8
E Yorks...97 F7
Glos...37 D7
Glos...49 F8
Herts...40 B4
Kent...30 C4
Kent...31 C6
Lancs...86 B3
Northumb...117 B7
Rutland...65 D5
Shrops...60 C5
Wilts...24 B5
Wilts...25 B7
Preston Bagot...51 C6
Preston Bissett...39 B6
Preston Bowyer...11 B6
Preston
Brockhurst...60 B5
Preston Brook...86 F3
Preston Candover..26 E4
Preston Capes...52 D3
Preston
Crowmarsh...39 E6
Preston Gubbals...60 C4
Prestonmill...107 D6
Preston on Stour..51 E7
Preston on the Hill 86 F3
Preston on Wye...49 E5
Prestonpans...121 B6
Preston Plucknett 12 C3
Preston St Mary...56 D3
Preston-under-
Scar...101 E5
Preston upon the
Weald Moors...61 C6
Preston Wynne...49 E7
Prestwich...87 D6
Prestwick
Northumb...110 B4
S Ayrs...112 B3
Prestwood...40 D1
Price Town...34 E3
Prickwillow...67 F5
Priddy...23 D7
Priesthaugh...115 D7
Priest Hutton...92 B5
Priest Weston...60 E2
Primethorpe...64 E2
Primrose Green...68 C3
Primrosehill...40 D3
Primrose Valley...97 B7
Princes Gate...32 C2
Princes
Risborough...39 D8
Princethorpe...52 B2
Princetown Caerph..35 C5
Devon...6 B3
Prion...72 C4
Prior Muir...129 C7
Prior Park...123 D5
Priors Frome...49 F7
Priors Hardwick...52 D2
Priorslee...61 C7
Priors Marston...52 D2
Priory Wood...48 E4
Priston...23 C8
Pristow Green...68 F4
Prittlewell...42 F4
Prixford...20 F4

Probus...3 B7
Proncy...151 B10
Prospect...107 E8
Prudhoe...110 C3
Ptarmigan Lodge 126 D2
Pubil...132 E1
Puckeridge...41 B6
Puckington...11 C8
Pucklechurch...23 B8
Pucknall...14 B4
Puckrup...50 F3
Puddinglake...74 C4
Puddington
Ches W...73 B7
Devon...10 C3
Puddledock...68 E3
Puddletown...13 E5
Pudleston...49 D7
Pudsey...94 F5
Pulborough...16 C4
Puleston...61 B7
Pulford...73 D7
Pulham...12 D5
Pulham Market...68 F4
Pulham St Mary...68 F5
Pulloxhill...53 F8
Pumpherston...120 C3
Pumsaint...47 E5
Puncheston...32 B1
Puncknowle...12 F3
Punnett's Town...18 C3
Purbrook...15 D7
Purewell...14 E2
Purfleet...29 B6
Puriton...22 E5
Purleigh...42 D4
Purley London...28 C4
W Berks...26 B4
Purlogue...48 B4
Purls Bridge...66 F4
Purse Caundle...12 C4
Purslow...60 F3
Purston Jaglin...88 C5
Purton Glos...36 D3
Glos...36 D3
Wilts...37 F7
Purton Stoke...37 E7
Pury End...52 E5
Pusey...38 E3
Putley...49 F8
Putney...28 B3
Puttenham Herts...40 C1
Sur...27 E7
Puxton...23 C6
Pwll...33 D5
Pwllcrochan...44 E4
Pwll-glas...72 D5
Pwllgloyw...48 F2
Pwllheli...70 D4
Pwllmeyric...36 E2
Pwll-trap...32 C3
Pwll-y-glaw...34 E1
Pyecombe...17 C6
Pye Corner...35 F7
Pye Green...62 C3
Pyewipe...91 C6
Pyle...15 G5
Pyle = Y Pîl...34 F2
Pylle...23 F8
Pymoor...66 F4
Pyrford...27 D8
Pyrton...39 E6
Pytchley...53 B6
Pyworthy...8 D5

Q

Quabbs...60 F2
Quadring...78 F5
Quainton...39 C7
Quarley...25 E7
Quarndon...76 E3
Quarrier's
Homes...118 C3
Quarrington...78 E3
Quarrington Hill 111 F6
Quarry Bank...62 F3
Quarryford...121 C8
Quarryhill...151 C10
Quarrywood...152 B1
Quarter...119 D7
Quatford...61 E7
Quatt...61 F7
Quebec...110 E4
Quedgeley...37 C5
Queen Adelaide...67 F5
Queenborough...30 B3
Queen Camel...12 B3
Queen Charlton...23 C8
Queen Dart...10 C3
Queenhill...50 F3
Queen Oak...24 F2
Queensbury...94 F4
Queensferry
Edin...120 B4
Flint...73 C7
Queensferry
Crossing...120 B4
Queenstown...92 F3
Queen Street Kent..29 E7
Wilts...37 F7
Queenzieburn...119 B6
Quemerford...24 C5
Quendale...160 M5
Quendon...55 F6
Queniborough...64 C3
Quenington...37 D8
Quernmore...92 D5
Quethiock...5 C8
Quholm...159 G3
Quicks Green...26 B3
Quidenham...68 F3
Quidhampton
Hants...26 D3
Wilts...25 F6
Quilquox...153 E9
Quina Brook...74 F2
Quindry...159 J5
Quinton Northants...53 D5
W Mid...62 F3
Quintrell Downs...4 C3
Quixhill...75 E8
Quoditch...9 E6
Quoig...127 B7
Quoisley...74 E2

Quorndon...64 C2
Quothquan...120 F2
Quoyloo...159 F3
Quoyness...159 H3
Quoys Shetland...160 B8
Shetland...160 G6

R

Raasay House...149 E10
Rabbit's Cross...29 E8
Raby...73 B7
Rachan Mill...120 F4
Rachub...83 E6
Rackenford...10 C3
Rackham...16 C4
Rackheath...69 C5
Racks...107 B7
Rackwick Orkney..159 D5
Orkney...159 J3
Radbourne...76 F2
Radcliffe Gtr Man...87 D5
Northumb...117 D8
Radcliffe on Trent..77 F6
Radclive...52 F4
Radcot...38 E2
Raddery...151 F10
Radernie...129 D6
Radford Semele...51 C8
Radipole...12 F4
Radlett...40 E4
Radley...39 E5
Radmanthwaite...76 C5
Radmoor...61 B6
Radmore Green...74 D2
Radnage...39 E7
Radstock...23 D8
Radstone...52 E3
Radway...51 E8
Radway Green...74 D4
Radwell Bedford...53 D8
Herts...54 F3
Radwinter...55 F7
Radyr...35 F5
Rafford...151 F13
Ragdale...64 C3
Raglan...35 D8
Ragnall...77 B8
Rahane...145 E11
Rainford...86 D2
Rainford Junction 86 D2
Rainham London...41 F8
Medway...30 C2
Rainhill...86 E2
Rainhill Stoops...86 E3
Rainow...75 B6
Rainton...95 B6
Rainworth...77 D5
Raisbeck...99 D8
Raise...109 E7
Rait...128 B4
Raithby Lincs...79 C6
Lincs...91 F7
Rake...16 B2
Rakewood...87 C7
Ram...46 E4
Ramasaig...148 D6
Rame Corn...3 C6
Corn...6 E2
Rameldry Mill
Bank...128 D5
Ram Lane...30 E3
Ramnageo...160 C8
Rampisham...12 D3
Rampside...92 C2
Rampton Cambs...54 C5
Notts...77 B7
Ramsbottom...87 C5
Ramsbury...25 B7
Ramscraigs...158 H3
Ramsdean...15 B8
Ramsdell...26 D3
Ramsden...38 C3
Ramsden
Bellhouse...42 E3
Ramsden Heath...42 E3
Ramsey Cambs...66 F2
Essex...57 F6
IoM...84 C4
Ramsey Forty Foot 66 F3
Ramsey Heights...66 F2
Ramsey Island...43 D5
Ramsey Mereside..66 F2
Ramsey St Mary's..66 F2
Ramsgate...31 C7
Ramsgill...94 B4
Ramshorn...75 E7
Ramsnest
Common...27 F7
Ranais...155 E9
Ranby Lincs...78 B5
Notts...89 F7
Rancliffe...94 F4
Randwick...37 D5
Ranfurly...118 C3
Rangag...158 F3
Rangemore...63 B5
Rangeworthy...36 F3
Rankinston...112 C4
Ranmoor...88 F4
Ranmore Common 28 D2
Rannerdale...98 C3
Rannoch Station .131 D8
Ranochan...147 C11
Ranskill...89 F7
Ranton...62 B2
Ranworth...69 C6
Raploch...127 E6
Rapness...159 D6
Rascal Moor...96 F4
Rascarrel...106 E4
Rashiereive...141 B8
Raskelf...95 B7
Rassau...35 C5
Ratagan...136 C2
Ratby...64 D2
Ratcliffe Culey...63 E7
Ratcliffe on Soar..63 B8
Ratcliffe on the
Wreake...64 C3
Rathen...153 B10
Rathillet...129 B5
Rathmell...93 D8
Ratho...120 B4
Ratho Station...120 B4
Rathven...152 B4

Ratley...51 E8
Ratlinghope...60 E4
Rattar...158 C4
Ratten Row...92 E4
Rattery...6 C5
Rattlesden...56 D3
Rattray...134 E1
Raughton Head...108 E3
Raunds...53 B7
Ravenfield...89 E5
Ravenglass...98 E2
Raveningham...69 E6
Ravenscar...103 D7
Ravenscraig...118 B2
Ravensdale...84 C3
Ravensden...53 D8
Ravenseat...100 D3
Ravenshead...77 D5
Ravensmoor...74 D3
Ravensthorpe
Northants...52 B4
W Yorks...88 B3
Ravenstone Leics...63 C8
M Keynes...53 D6
Ravenstonedale..100 D2
Ravenstown...92 B3
Ravenstruther...120 E2
Ravensworth...101 D6
Raw...103 D7
Rawcliffe E Yorks...89 B7
York...95 D8
Rawcliffe Bridge...89 B7
Rawdon...94 F5
Rawmarsh...88 E5
Rawreth...42 E3
Rawridge...11 D7
Rawtenstall...87 B6
Raydon...56 F4
Raylees...117 E5
Rayleigh...42 E4
Rayne...42 B3
Rayners Lane...40 F4
Raynes Park...28 C3
Reach...55 C6
Read...93 F7
Reading...26 B5
Reading Street...19 B6
Reagill...99 C8
Rearquhar...151 B10
Rearsby...64 C3
Reaster...158 D4
Reawick...160 J5
Reay...157 C12
Rechullin...149 C13
Reculver...31 C6
Redberth...32 D1
Redbourn...40 C4
Redbourne...90 E3
Redbrook Mon...36 C2
Wrex...74 E2
Redburn Highld...151 E8
Highld...151 G12
Northumb...109 C7
Redcar...102 B4
Redcastle Angus..135 D6
Highld...151 G8
Redcliff Bay...23 B6
Red Dial...108 E2
Redding...120 B2
Reddingmuirhead
...120 B2
Reddish...87 E6
Redditch...50 C5
Rede...56 D2
Redenhall...69 F5
Redesdale Camp 116 E4
Redesmouth...116 F4
Redford Aberds...135 B7
Angus...135 E5
Durham...110 F3
Redfordgreen...115 C6
Redgorton...128 B2
Redgrave...56 B4
Redhill Aberds...141 D6
Aberds...153 E6
N Som...23 C7
Sur...28 D3
Red Hill...50 D3
Redhouse...145 G7
Redhouses...142 B4
Red Houses Jersey...17
Redisham...69 F7
Redland Bristol...23 B7
Orkney...159 F4
Redlingfield...57 B5
Red Lodge...55 B8
Redlynch Som...23 F9
Wilts...14 B3
Redmarley
D'Abitot...50 F2
Redmarshall...102 B1
Redmile...77 F7
Redmire...101 E5
Redmoor...5 C5
Rednal...60 B3
Redpath...121 F8
Redpoint...149 B12
Red Rail...36 B2
Red Rock...86 D3
Red Roses...32 C3
Red Row...117 E8
Redruth...3 B5
Red Street...74 D5
Redvales...87 D6
Red Wharf Bay...83 C5
Redwick Newport...35 F8
S Glos...36 F2
Redworth...101 B7
Reed...54 F4
Reedham...69 D7
Reedness...89 B8
Reeds Beck...78 C5
Reepham Lincs...78 B3
Norf...81 E6
Reeth...101 E5
Regaby...84 C4
Regoul...151 F11
Reiff...156 H2
Reigate...28 D3
Reighton...97 B7
Reighton Gap...97 B7
Reinigeadal...154 G7
Reiss...158 E5
Rejerrah...4 D2
Releath...3 C5
Relubbus...2 C4
Relugas...151 G12
Remenham...39 F7

Remenham Hill...39 F7
Remony...132 E4
Rempstone...64 B2
Rendcomb...37 D7
Rendham...57 C7
Rendlesham...57 D7
Renfrew...118 C5
Renhold...53 D8
Renishaw...76 B4
Rennington...117 C8
Renton...118 B3
Renwick...109 E5
Repps...69 C7
Repton...63 B7
Rescobie...135 D5
Resipole...147 E10
Resolis...151 E9
Resolven...34 D2
Reston...122 C4
Reswallie...135 D5
Retew...4 D4
Retford...89 F8
Rettendon...42 E3
Rettendon Place...42 E3
Revesby...79 C5
Revesby Bridge...79 C6
Rewe...10 E4
Rew Street...15 E5
Reydon...57 B8
Reydon Smear...57 B8
Reymerston...68 D3
Reynalton...32 D1
Reynoldston...33 E5
Rezare...5 B8
Rhaeadr Gwy
=Rhayader...47 C8
Rhandirmwyn...47 E6
Rhayader
=Rhaeadr Gwy..47 C8
Rhedyn...70 D3
Rhemore...147 F8
Rhencullen...84 C3
Rhes-y-cae...73 B5
Rhewl Denb...72 C5
Denb...73 E5
Rhian...157 H8
Rhicarn...156 G3
Rhiconich...156 D5
Rhicullen...151 D9
Rhidorroch
House...150 B4
Rhifail...157 E10
Rhigos...34 D3
Rhilochan...157 J10
Rhiroy...150 C4
Rhisga = Risca...35 E6
Rhiw...70 E3
Rhiwabon
=Ruabon...73 E7
Rhiwbina...35 F5
Rhiwbryfdir...71 C7
Rhiwderin...35 F6
Rhiwlas Gwyn...72 F3
Gwyn...83 E5
Powys...73 F5
Rhodes...87 D6
Rhodesia...77 B5
Rhodes Minnis...31 E5
Rhodiad...44 C2
Rhondda...34 E3
Rhonehouse or Kelton
Hill...106 D4
Rhoose = Y Rhws..22 C2
Rhôs Carms...46 F2
Neath...33 D8
Rhosaman...33 C8
Rhosbeirio...82 B3
Rhoscefnhir...82 D5
Rhoscolyn...82 D2
Rhoscrowther...44 E4
Rhosesmor...73 C6
Rhos-fawr...70 D4
Rhosgadfan...82 F5
Rhosgoch...82 C4
Rhos-goch...48 E3
Rhos-hill...45 E3
Rhoshirwaun...70 E2
Rhoslan...71 C5
Rhoslefain...58 D2
Rhosllanerchrugog
...73 E6
Rhosmaen...33 B7
Rhosmeirch...82 D4
Rhosneigr...82 D3
Rhosnesni...73 D7
Rhos-on-Sea...83 C8
Rhosrobin...73 D7
Rhossili...33 F5
Rhosson...44 C2
Rhostryfan...82 F4
Rhostyllen...73 E7
Rhosybol...82 C4
Rhos-y-brithdir...59 B8
Rhos-y-garth...46 B5
Rhos-y-gwaliau...72 F3
Rhos-y-llan...70 D3
Rhos-y-Madoc...73 E7
Rhos-y-meirch...48 C4
Rhu Argyll...145 E11
Argyll...145 G7
Rhuallt...72 B4
Rhuddall Heath...74 C2
Rhuddlan Ceredig...46 E3
Denb...72 B4
Rhue...150 B3
Rhulen...48 E3
Rhunahaorine...143 D8
Rhuthun = Ruthin..72 D5
Rhyd Gwyn...71 C7
Powys...59 D6
Rhydaman
=Ammanford...33 C7
Rhydargaeau...33 B5
Rhydcymerau...46 F4
Rhydd...50 E3
Rhyd-Ddu...83 F5
Rhydfudr...46 C4
Rhydlewis...46 E2
Rhydlios...70 D2
Rhydlydan...83 F8
Rhyd-moel-ddu...48 B2
Rhydness...48 E3
Rhydowen...46 E3
Rhyd-Rosser...46 C4
Rhydspence...48 E4
Rhydtalog...73 D6
Rhyd-uchaf...72 F3

Rhyd-wen 58 C4
Rhydwyn 82 C3
Rhyd-y-clafdy 70 D4
Rhydycroesau 73 F6
Rhydyfelin Ceredig . 46 B4
 Rhondda 34 F4
Rhyd-y-foel 72 B3
Rhyd-y-fro 33 D8
Rhyd-y-gwin 33 D7
Rhydymain 58 B5
Rhyd-y-meirch 35 D7
Rhyd-y-meudwy . 72 D5
Rhydymwyn 73 C6
Rhyd-y-pandy 33 D7
Rhyd-yr-onen 58 D3
Rhyd-y-sarn 71 C7
Rhyl = Y Rhyl 72 A4
Rhymney
 = Rhymni 35 D5
Rhymni
 = Rhymney 35 D5
Rhynd Fife 129 B6
 Perth 128 B3
Rhynie Aberds . 140 B3
 Highld 151 D11
Ribbesford 50 B2
Ribblehead 93 B7
Ribbleton 93 F5
Ribchester 93 F6
Ribigill 157 D8
Riby 91 D5
Riby Cross Roads . 91 D5
Riccall 96 F2
Riccarton 118 F4
Richards Castle . 49 C6
Richings Park . . . 27 B8
Richmond London . 28 B2
 N Yorks 101 D6
Rickarton 141 F7
Rickinghall 56 B4
Rickleton 111 D5
Rickling 55 F5
Rickmansworth . 40 E3
Riddings Cumb . . 108 B4
 Derbys 76 D4
Riddlecombe 9 C8
Riddlesden 94 E3
Riddrie 119 C6
Ridge Dorset 13 F7
 Hants 14 C4
 Wilts 24 F4
Ridgebourne 48 C2
Ridge Green 28 E4
Ridgehill 23 C7
Ridge Lane 63 E6
Ridgeway Cross . 50 E2
Ridgewell 55 E8
Ridgewood 17 C8
Ridgmont 53 F7
Riding Mill 110 C3
Ridleywood 73 D8
Ridlington Norf . . 69 A6
 Rutland 64 D5
Ridsdale 116 F5
Riechip 133 E7
Riemore 133 E7
Rienachait 156 F3
Rievaulx 102 F3
Rift House 111 F7
Rigg 108 C2
Riggend 119 B7
Rigsby 79 B7
Rigside 119 F8
Riley Green 86 B4
Rileyhill 62 C5
Rilla Mill 5 B7
Rillington 96 B4
Rimington 93 E8
Rimpton 12 B4
Rimswell 91 B7
Rinaston 44 C4
Ringasta 160 M5
Ringford 106 D3
Ringinglow 88 F3
Ringland 68 C4
Ringles Cross . . . 17 B8
Ringmer 17 C8
Ringmore 6 E4
Ringorm 152 D2
Ring's End 66 D3
Ringsfield 69 F7
Ringsfield Corner . 69 F7
Ringshall Herts . . 40 C2
 Suff 56 D4
Ringshall Stocks . 56 D4
Ringstead Norf . . 80 C3
 Northants 53 B7
Ringwood 14 D2
Ringwould 31 E7
Rinmore 140 C3
Rinnigill 159 J4
Rinsey 2 D4
Riof 154 D6
Ripe 18 D2
Ripley Derbys . . . 76 D3
 Hants 14 E2
 N Yorks 95 C5
 Sur 27 D8
Riplingham 97 F5
Ripon 95 B6
Rippingale 65 B7
Ripple Kent 31 E7
 Worcs 50 F3
Ripponden 87 C8
Rireavach 150 B3
Risabus 142 D4
Risbury 49 D7
Risby 57 C8
Risca = Rhisga . 35 E6
Rise 97 E7
Riseden 18 B3
Risegate 66 B2
Riseholme 78 B2
Riseley Bedford. . 53 C8
 Wokingham 26 C5
Rishangles 57 C5
Rishton 93 F7
Rishworth 87 C8
Rising Bridge 87 B5
Risley Derbys . 76 F4
 Warr 86 E4
Risplith 94 C5
Rispond 156 C7
Rivar 25 C8
Rivenhall End . . . 42 C4
River Bank 55 C6
Riverhead 29 D6
Rivington 86 C4
Roachill 10 B3

Roade 53 D5
Road Green 69 E5
Roadhead 108 B5
Roadmeetings . . . 119 D8
Roadside 158 D3
Roadside of
 Catterline 135 B8
Roadside of
 Kinneff 135 B8
Roadwater 22 F2
Roag 149 D7
Roa Island 92 C2
Roath 22 B3
Roberton Borders . 115 C7
 S Lanark. . 114 B2
Robertsbridge . . . 18 C4
Roberttown 88 B2
Robeston Cross . 44 E3
Robeston Wathen . 32 C1
Robin Hood 88 B4
Robin Hood's
 Bay 103 D7
Roborough Devon . 6 C3
 Devon 9 C7
Roby 86 E2
Roby Mill 86 D3
Rocester 75 F8
Roch 44 C3
Rochdale 87 C6
Roche 4 C4
Rochester Medway . 29 C8
 Northumb 116 E4
Rochford 42 E4
Roch Gate 44 C3
Rock Corn 4 B4
 Northumb 117 B8
 Worcs 50 B2
 W Sus 16 C5
Rockbeare 10 E5
Rockbourne 14 C2
Rockcliffe Cumb. . 108 C3
 Dumfries 107 D5
Rockfield Highld . 151 C12
 Mon 36 C1
Rockford 14 D2
Rockhampton . . . 36 E3
Rockingham 65 E5
Rockland All
 Saints 68 E2
Rockland St Mary . 69 D6
Rockland St Peter . 68 E2
Rockley 25 B6
Rockwell End 39 F7
Rockwell Green . 11 B6
Rodborough 37 D5
Rodbourne Swindon 37 F8
 Wilts 37 F6
Rodbourne Cheney 37 F8
Rodd 48 C5
Roddam 117 B6
Rodden 12 F4
Rode 24 D3
Rodeheath 75 C5
Rode Heath 74 D5
Roden 61 C5
Rodhuish 22 F2
Rodington 61 C5
Rodley Glos 36 C4
 W Yorks 94 F5
Rodmarton 37 E6
Rodmell 17 D8
Rodmersham 30 C3
Rodney Stoke . . . 23 D6
Rodsley 76 E2
Rodway 22 F4
Rodwell 12 G4
Roe Cross 87 E7
Roe Green 54 F4
Roehampton 28 B3
Roesound 160 G5
Roffey 28 F2
Rogart 157 J10
Rogart Station . 157 J10
Rogate 16 B2
Rogerstone 35 F6
Roghadal 154 J5
Rogiet 36 F1
Rogue's Alley 66 D3
Roke 39 E6
Roker 111 D7
Rollesby 69 C7
Rolleston Leics. . 64 D4
 Notts 77 D7
Rolleston-on-
 Dove 63 B6
Rolston 97 E8
Rolvenden 18 B5
Rolvenden Layne . 19 B5
Romaldkirk 100 B4
Romanby 102 E1
Romannbridge . 120 E4
Romansleigh 10 B2
Romford 41 F8
Romiley 87 E7
Romsey 14 B4
Romsey Town . . . 55 D5
Romsley Shrops . 61 F7
 Worcs 50 B4
Ronague 84 E2
Rookhope 110 E2
Rookley 15 F6
Rooks Bridge . . . 23 D5
Roos 97 F8
Roosebeck 92 C2
Rootham's Green . 54 D2
Rootpark 120 D2
Ropley 26 F4
Ropley Dean 26 F4
Ropsley 78 F2
Rora 153 C10
Rorandle 141 C5
Rorrington 60 D3
Roscroggan 3 B5
Rose 4 D2
Roseacre Kent . 29 D8
 Lancs 92 F4
Rose Ash 10 B2
Rosebank 119 E8
Rosebrough 117 B7
Rosebush 32 B1
Rosecare 8 E3
Rosedale Abbey . 103 E5
Roseden 117 B6
Rosefield 151 F11
Rose Green 16 E3
Rose Grove 93 F8
Rosehall 156 J7

Rosehearty 153 B9
Rosehill E Sus . 17 C8
 Lancs 93 F8
 Suff 57 C5
Roseisle 152 B1
Roselands 18 E3
Rosemarket 44 E4
Rosemarkie 151 F10
Rosemary Lane . 11 C6
Rosemount 134 E1
Rosenannon 4 C4
Rosewell 121 C5
Roseworth 102 B2
Roseworthy 2 C5
Rosgill 99 C7
Roshven 147 D10
Roskhill 149 D7
Roskill House . . . 151 F9
Rosley 108 E3
Roslin 121 C5
Rosliston 63 C6
Rosneath 145 E11
Ross Dumfries . 106 E3
 Northumb 123 F7
 Perth 127 B6
Rossett 73 D7
Rossett Green . . . 95 D6
Rossie Ochill . 128 C2
Rossie Priory . 134 F2
Rossington 89 E7
Rosskeen 151 E9
Rossland 118 B4
Ross-on-Wye . . . 36 B3
Roster 158 G4
Rostherne 86 F5
Rosthwaite 98 C4
Roston 75 E8
Rosyth 128 F3
Rothbury 117 D6
Rotherby 64 C3
Rotherfield 18 C2
Rotherfield Greys . 39 F7
Rotherfield
 Peppard 39 F7
Rotherham 88 E5
Rothersthorpe . 52 D5
Rotherwick 26 D5
Rothes 152 D2
Rothesay 145 G9
Rothiebrisbane . 153 E7
Rothienorman . 153 E7
Rothiesholm 159 F7
Rothley Leics . 64 C2
 Northumb 117 F6
Rothley Shield
 East 117 E6
Rothmaise 153 E6
Rothwell Lincs . 91 E5
 Northants 64 F5
 W Yorks 88 B4
Rothwell Haigh. . 88 B4
Rotsea 97 D6
Rottal 134 C3
Rotten End 57 C7
Rottingdean 17 D7
Rottington 98 C1
Roud 15 F6
Rougham Norf . 80 E4
 Suff 56 C3
Rougham Green . 56 C3
Roughburn 137 F6
Rough Close 75 F6
Rough Common . 30 D5
Roughlee 93 E8
Roughley 62 E5
Roughsike 108 B5
Roughton Lincs . 78 C5
 Norf 81 D8
 Shrops 61 E7
Roughton Moor . 78 C5
Roundhay 95 F6
Roundstonefoot . 114 D4
Roundstreet
 Common 16 B4
Roundway 24 C5
Rousdon 11 E7
Rous Lench 50 D5
Routenburn 118 C1
Routh 97 E6
Row Corn 5 B5
 Cumb 99 F6
Rowanburn 108 B4
Rowardennan . 126 E2
Rowde 24 C4
Rowen 83 D7
Rowfoot 109 C6
Row Heath 43 C7
Rowhedge 43 B6
Rowhook 28 F2
Rowington 51 C7
Rowland 76 B2
Rowlands Castle . 15 C8
Rowlands Gill . 110 D4
Rowledge 27 E6
Rowlestone 35 B7
Rowley E Yorks . 97 F5
 Shrops 60 D3
Rowley Hill 88 C2
Rowley Regis . 62 F3
Rowly 27 E8
Rowney Green . 50 B5
Rownhams 14 C4
Rowrah 98 C2
Rowsham 39 C8
Rowsley 76 C2
Rowstock 38 F4
Rowston 78 D3
Rowton Ches W. . 73 C8
 Shrops 60 C3
 Telford 61 C6
Roxburgh 122 F3
Roxby N Lincs . 90 C3
 N Yorks 103 C5
Roxton 54 D2
Roxwell 42 D2
Royal Leamington
 Spa 51 C8
Royal Oak Darl . 101 B7
 Lancs 86 D2
Royal Tunbridge
 Wells 18 B2
Royal Wootton
 Bassett 37 F7
Roybridge 137 F5
Roydhouse 88 C3
Roydon Essex . 41 D7
 Norf 68 F3
 Norf 80 D3

Roydon Hamlet. . 41 D7
Royston Herts . 54 E4
 S Yorks 88 C4
Royton 87 D7
Rozel Jersey 17
Ruabon
 = Rhiwabon . 73 E7
Ruaig 146 G3
Ruan Lanihorne . 3 B7
Ruan Minor 3 E6
Ruarach 136 B2
Ruardean 36 C3
Ruardean
 Woodside 36 C3
Rubery 50 B4
Ruckcroft 108 E5
Ruckinge 19 B7
Ruckland 79 B6
Ruckley 60 D5
Rudbaxton 44 C4
Rudby 102 D2
Ruddington 77 F5
Rudford 36 B4
Rudge Shrops . 62 E2
 Som 24 D3
Rudgeway 36 F3
Rudgwick 27 F8
Rudhall 36 B3
Rudheath 74 B3
Rudley Green . 42 D4
Rudry 35 F5
Rudston 97 C6
Rudyard 75 D6
Rufford 86 C2
Rufforth 95 D8
Rugby 52 B3
Rugeley 62 C4
Ruglen 112 D2
Ruilick 151 G8
Ruishton 11 B7
Ruisigearraidh . 154 J4
Ruislip 40 F3
Ruislip Common . 40 F3
Rumbling Bridge . 128 E2
Rumburgh 69 F6
Rumford 4 B3
Rumney 22 B4
Runcorn 86 F3
Runcton 16 D2
Runcton Holme . 67 D6
Rundlestone 6 B3
Runfold 27 E6
Runhall 68 D3
Runham Norf . 69 C7
 Norf 69 D8
Runnington 11 B6
Runsell Green . 42 D3
Runswick Bay . 103 C6
Runwell 42 E3
Ruscombe 27 B5
Rushall Hereford . 49 F8
 Norf 68 F4
 Wilts 25 D6
 W Mid 62 D4
Rushbrooke 56 C2
Rushbury 60 E5
Rushden Herts . 54 F4
 Northants 53 C7
Rushenden 30 B3
Rushford 68 F2
Rush Green 41 F8
Rush-head 153 D8
Rushlake Green . 18 D3
Rushmere 69 F7
Rushmere
 St Andrew 57 E6
Rushmoor 27 E6
Rushock 50 B3
Rusholme 87 E6
Rushton Ches W . 74 C2
 Northants 64 F5
 Shrops 61 D6
Rushton Spencer . 75 C6
Rushwick 50 D3
Rushyford 101 B7
Ruskie 126 D5
Ruskington 78 D3
Rusland 99 F5
Rusper 28 F3
Ruspidge 36 C3
Russell's Water . 39 F7
Russel's Green . 57 B6
Rusthall 18 B2
Rustington 16 D4
Ruston 103 F7
Ruston Parva . 97 C6
Ruswarp 103 D6
Rutherford 122 F2
Rutherglen 119 C6
Ruthernbridge . 4 C5
Ruthin = Rhuthun . 72 D5
Ruthrieston 141 D8
Ruthven Aberds . 152 D5
 Angus 134 E2
 Highld 138 E3
 Highld 151 H11
Ruthven House . 134 E3
Ruthvoes 4 C4
Ruthwell 107 C7
Ruyton-XI-Towns . 110 B3
Ryal 110 B3
Ryal Fold 86 B4
Ryall 12 E2
Ryarsh 29 D7
Rydal 99 D5
Ryde 15 E6
Rye 19 C6
Ryecroft Gate . 75 C6
Rye Foreign 19 C5
Rye Harbour 19 D6
Ryehill 91 B6
Rye Park 41 C6
Rye Street 50 F2
Ryhall 65 C7
Ryhill 88 C4
Ryhope 111 D7
Rylstone 94 D2
Ryme Intrinseca . 12 C3
Ryther 95 F8
Ryton Glos 50 F2
 N Yorks 96 B3
 Shrops 61 D7
 T&W 110 C4
Ryton-on-
 Dunsmore 51 B8

S

Sabden 93 F7
Sacombe 41 C6
Sacriston 110 E5
Sadberge 101 C8
Saddell 143 E8
Saddington 64 E3
Saddle Bow 67 C6
Saddlescombe . 17 C6
Sadgill 99 D6
Saffron Walden . 55 F6
Sageston 32 D1
Saham Hills 68 D2
Saham Toney . . . 68 D2
Saighdinis 148 B3
Saighton 73 C8
St Abbs 122 C5
St Abb's Haven . 122 C5
St Agnes Corn . 4 D2
 Scilly 2 F3
St Albans 40 D4
St Allen 4 D3
St Andrews 129 C7
St Andrew's Major . 22 B3
St Anne Ald 17
St Annes 85 B4
St Ann's 114 E3
St Ann's Chapel
 Corn 6 B2
 Devon 6 E4
St Anthony-in-
 Meneage 3 D6
St Anthony's Hill . 18 E3
St Arvans 36 E2
St Asaph
 = Llanelwy . . . 72 B4
St Athan 22 C2
St Aubin Jersey . . 17
St Austell 4 D5
St Bees 98 C1
St Blazey 5 D5
St Boswells 121 F8
St Brelade Jersey . 17
St Breock 4 B4
St Breward 5 B5
St Briavels 36 D2
St Bride's 44 D3
St Brides Major. . 21 B7
St Bride's
 Netherwent. . 35 F8
St Brides-super-
 Ely 22 B2
St Brides
 Wentlooge... 35 F6
St Budeaux 6 D2
Saintbury 51 F6
St Buryan 2 D3
St Catherine 24 B2
St Catherine's . 125 E7
St Clears
 = Sanclêr... 32 C3
St Cleer 5 C7
St Clement 3 B8
St Clements Jersey . 17
St Clether 8 F4
St Colmac 145 G9
St Columb Major . 4 C4
St Columb Minor . 4 C3
St Columb Road . 4 D4
St Combs 153 B10
St Cross South
 Elmham 69 F5
St Cyrus 135 C7
St David's 127 B8
St David's
 = Tyddewi . . . 44 C2
St Day 3 B6
St Dennis 4 D4
St Devereux 49 F6
St Dogmaels 45 E3
St Dogwells 44 C4
St Dominick 6 C2
St Donat's 21 C8
St Edith's 24 C4
St Endellion 4 B4
St Enoder 4 D3
St Erme 4 D3
St Erney 5 D8
St Erth 2 C4
St Ervan 4 C3
St Eval 4 C3
St Ewe 3 B8
St Fagans 22 B3
St Fergus 153 C10
St Fillans 127 B5
St Florence 32 D1
St Genny's 8 E3
St George 72 B3
St George's 22 B2
St Germans 5 D8
St Giles 78 B2
St Giles in the
 Wood 9 C7
St Giles on the
 Heath 9 E5
St Harmon 47 B8
St Helena 63 D6
St Helen
 Auckland 101 B6
St Helens IoW . 15 F7
 Mers 86 E3
St Helen's 18 D5
St Helier Jersey . . 17
 London 28 C3
St Hilary Corn . 2 C4
 V Glam 22 B2
Saint Hill 28 F4
St Illtyd 35 D6
St Ippollitts 40 B4
St Ishmael's 44 E3
St Issey 4 B4
St Ive 5 C8
St Ives Cambs . 54 B4
 Corn 2 B4
 Dorset 14 D2
St James South
 Elmham 69 F6
St Jidgey 4 C4
St John 6 D2
St John's IoM . 84 D2
 Jersey 17
 Sur 27 D7
 Worcs 50 D3
St John's Chapel . 109 F8
St John's Fen End . 66 C5
St John's Highway. 66 C5

St John's Town of
 Dalry 113 F6
St Judes 84 C3
St Just 2 C1
St Just in Roseland . 3 C7
St Katherine's . 153 E7
St Keverne 3 D6
St Kew 4 B5
St Kew Highway . 4 B5
St Keyne 5 C7
St Lawrence Corn . 4 C5
 Essex 43 D5
 IoW 15 G6
St Leonards Dorset . 14 D2
 E Sus 18 E4
 S Lanark... 119 D6
St Leonard's 40 D2
St Levan 2 D1
St Lythans 22 B3
St Mabyn 4 B5
St Madoes 128 B3
St Margarets 41 C6
St Margaret's . 49 F5
St Margaret's at
 Cliffe 31 E7
St Margaret's
 Hope 159 J5
St Margaret South
 Elmham 69 F6
St Mark's 84 E2
St Martin 5 D7
St Martins Corn . 3 D6
 Perth 134 F1
St Martin's Jersey . 17
 Shrops 73 F7
St Mary Bourne . 26 D2
St Mary Church. . 22 B2
St Mary Cray . . . 29 C5
St Mary Hill 21 B8
St Mary Hoo 30 B2
St Mary in the
 Marsh 19 C7
St Mary's Jersey . 17
 Orkney 159 H5
St Mary's Bay . 19 C7
St Maughans . . . 36 C1
St Mawes 3 C7
St Mawgan 4 C3
St Mellion 5 C8
St Mellons 35 F6
St Merryn 4 B3
St Mewan 4 D4
St Michael
 Caerhays 3 B8
St Michael Penkevil . 3 B7
St Michaels 49 C7
St Michael's 19 B5
St Michael's on
 Wyre 92 E4
St Michael South
 Elmham 69 F6
St Minver 4 B4
St Monans 129 D7
St Neot 5 C6
St Neots 54 C2
St Newlyn East . 4 D3
St Nicholas Pembs. . 44 B3
 V Glam 22 B2
St Nicholas at
 Wade 31 C6
St Ninians 127 E6
St Osyth 43 C7
St Osyth Heath . 43 C7
St Ouens Jersey . 17
St Owens Cross . 36 B2
St Paul's Cray . 29 C5
St Paul's Walden . 40 B4
St Peter Port Guern. . 16
St Peter's Jersey . 17
 Kent 31 C7
St Petrox 44 F4
St Pinnock 5 C7
St Quivox 112 B3
St Ruan 3 E6
St Sampson Guern. . 16
St Stephen 4 D4
St Stephens Corn . 6 D2
 Herts 40 D4
St Stephen's 8 F5
St Teath 8 F2
St Thomas 10 E4
St Tudy 5 B5
St Twynnells 44 F4
St Veep 5 D6
St Vigeans 135 E6
St Wenn 4 C4
St Weonards 36 B1
Salcombe 6 F5
Salcombe Regis . 11 F6
Salcott 43 C5
Sale 87 E5
Saleby 79 B7
Sale Green 50 D4
Salehurst 18 C4
Salem Carms . . . 33 B7
 Ceredig 58 F3
Salen Argyll 147 G8
 Highld 147 E9
Salesbury 93 F6
Salford C Beds . 53 F7
 Gtr Man 87 E6
 Oxon 38 B2
Salford Priors . 51 D5
Salfords 28 E3
Salhouse 69 C6
Saline 128 E2
Salisbury 14 B2
Sallachan 130 C3
Sallachy Highld. . 150 H2
 Highld 157 J8
Salle 81 E7
Salmonby 79 B6
Salmond's Muir . 135 F5
Salperton 37 B7
Salph End 53 D8
Salsburgh 119 C8
Salt 62 B3
Saltaire 94 F4
Saltash 6 D2
Saltburn 151 E10
Saltburn-by-the-
 Sea 102 B4
Saltby 65 B5
Saltcoats Cumb . 98 E2
 N Ayrs 118 E2
Salt End 91 B5
Salter 93 C6
Salterforth 93 E8

Salterswall 74 C3
Saltfleet 91 E8
Saltfleetby All
 Saints 91 E8
Saltfleetby
 St Clements . . . 91 E8
Saltfleetby
 St Peter 91 F8
Saltford 23 C8
Salthouse 81 C6
Saltmarshe 89 B8
Saltney 73 C7
Salton 96 B3
Saltwick 110 B4
Saltwood 19 B8
Salum 146 G3
Salvington 16 D5
Salwarpe 50 C3
Salwayash 12 E2
Sambourne 51 C5
Sambrook 61 B7
Samhla 148 B2
Samlesbury 93 F5
Samlesbury
 Bottoms 86 B4
Sampford Arundel . 11 C6
Sampford Brett. . 22 E2
Sampford
 Courtenay 9 D8
Sampford Peverell . 10 C5
Sampford Spiney . 6 B3
Sampool Bridge . 99 F6
Samuelston 121 B7
Sanachan 149 D13
Sanaigmore 142 A3
Sanclêr
 = St Clears . . . 32 C3
Sancreed 2 D3
Sancton 96 F5
Sand Highld 150 B2
 Shetland 160 J5
Sandaig 149 H12
Sandale 108 E2
Sandal Magna . . . 88 C4
Sandbach 74 C4
Sandbank 145 E10
Sandbanks 13 F8
Sandend 152 B5
Sanderstead 28 C4
Sandfields 37 B6
Sandford Cumb. . 100 C2
 Devon 10 D3
 Dorset 13 F7
 IoW 15 F6
 N Som 23 D6
 Shrops 74 F2
 S Lanark... 119 E7
Sandfordhill 153 D11
Sandford on
 Thames 39 D5
Sandford Orcas . 12 B4
Sandford
 St Martin 38 B4
Sandgate 19 B8
Sandgreen 106 D2
Sandhaven 153 B9
Sandhead 104 E4
Sandhills 27 F7
Sandhoe 110 C2
Sand Hole 96 F4
Sandholme E Yorks . 96 F4
 Lincs 79 F6
Sandhurst Brack . 27 C6
 Glos 37 B5
 Kent 18 C4
Sandhurst Cross . 18 C4
Sandhutton 102 F1
Sand Hutton 96 D2
Sandiacre 76 F4
Sandilands Lincs . 91 F9
 S Lanark... 119 F8
Sandiway 74 B3
Sandleheath 14 C2
Sandling 29 D8
Sandlow Green . 74 C4
Sandness 160 H3
Sandon Essex . 42 D3
 Herts 54 F4
 Staffs 75 F6
Sandown 15 F6
Sandplace 5 D7
Sandridge Herts . 40 C4
 Wilts 24 C4
Sandringham . 67 B6
Sandsend 103 C6
Sandside House . 157 C12
Sandsound 160 J5
Sandtoft 89 D8
Sandway 30 D2
Sandwell 62 F4
Sandwich 31 D7
Sandwick Cumb . 99 C6
 Orkney 159 K5
 Shetland 160 L6
Sandwith 98 C1
Sandy Carms . . . 33 D5
 C Beds 54 E2
Sandy Bank 79 D5
Sandycroft 73 C7
Sandyford
 Dumfries 114 E5
 Stoke 75 D5
Sandygate 84 C3
Sandy Haven . . . 44 E3
Sandyhills 107 D5
Sandylands 92 C4
Sandy Lane Wilts . 24 C4
 Wrex 73 E7
Sandypark 10 F2
Sandysike 108 C3
Sangobeg 156 C7
Sangomore 156 C7
Sanna 146 E7
Sanndabhaig
 W Isles 148 D3
 W Isles 155 D9
Sannox 143 D11
Sanquhar 113 D7
Santon 90 C3
Santon Bridge . 98 D3
Santon Downham . 67 F8
Sapcote 63 E8
Sapey Common . 50 C2
Sapiston 56 B3
Sapley 54 B3
Sapperton Glos . 37 D6
 Lincs 78 F3
Saracen's Head . 66 B3
Sarclet 158 F5

Sardis 33 D6
Sarn Bridgend . 34 F3
 Powys 60 E2
Sarnau Carms . 32 C4
 Ceredig 46 D2
 Gwyn 72 F3
 Powys 48 F2
 Powys 60 C2
Sarn Bach 70 E4
Sarnesfield 49 D5
Sarn Meyllteyrn . 70 D3
Saron Carms . . . 33 C7
 Carms 46 F2
 Denb 72 C4
 Gwyn 82 E5
 Gwyn 82 F4
Sarratt 40 E3
Sarre 31 C6
Sarsden 38 B2
Sarsgrum 156 C6
Satley 110 E4
Satron 100 E4
Satterleigh 9 B8
Satterthwaite . . . 99 E5
Satwell 39 F7
Sauchen 141 C5
Saucher 134 F1
Sauchie 127 E7
Sauchieburn 135 C6
Saughall 73 B7
Saughtree 115 E8
Saul 36 D4
Saundby 89 F8
Saundersfoot . . . 32 D2
Saunderton 39 D7
Saunton 20 F3
Sausthorpe 79 C6
Saval 157 J8
Savary 147 G9
Savile Park 87 B8
Sawbridge 52 C3
Sawbridgeworth . 41 C7
Sawdon 103 F7
Sawley Derbys . 76 F4
 Lancs 93 E7
 N Yorks 94 C5
Sawston 55 E5
Sawtry 65 F8
Saxby Leics 64 C5
 Lincs 90 F4
Saxby All Saints . 90 C3
Saxelbye 64 B4
Saxham Street . 56 C4
Saxilby 77 B8
Saxlingham 81 D6
Saxlingham Green. 68 E5
Saxlingham
 Nethergate . . . 68 E5
Saxlingham
 Thorpe 68 E5
Saxmundham . 57 C7
Saxondale 77 F6
Saxon Street . . . 55 D7
Saxtead 57 C6
Saxtead Green . 57 C6
Saxthorpe 81 D7
Saxton 95 F7
Sayers Common . 17 C6
Scackleton 96 B2
Scadabhagh 154 H6
Scaftworth 89 E7
Scagglethorpe . 96 B4
Scaitcliffe 87 B5
Scalasaig 144 D2
Scalby E Yorks . 90 B2
 N Yorks 103 E8
Scaldwell 53 B5
Scale Houses . . . 109 E5
Scales Cumb . . . 92 B2
 Cumb 99 B5
 Lancs 92 F4
Scalford 64 B4
Scaling 103 C5
Scallastle 124 B2
Scalloway 160 K6
Scalpay 154 H7
Scalpay House . 149 F11
Scalpsie 145 H9
Scamadale 147 B10
Scamblesby 79 B5
Scamodale 130 B2
Scampston 96 B4
Scampton 78 B2
Scapa 159 H5
Scapegoat Hill . 87 C8
Scar 159 D7
Scarborough . . . 103 F8
Scarcliffe 76 C4
Scarcroft 95 E6
Scarcroft Hill . . . 95 E6
Scardroy 150 F5
Scarff 160 E4
Scarfskerry 158 C4
Scargill 101 C5
Scarinish 146 G3
Scarisbrick 85 C4
Scarning 68 C2
Scarrington 77 E7
Scartho 91 D6
Scarwell 159 F3
Scatness 160 M5
Scatraig 151 H10
Scawby 90 D3
Scawsby 89 D6
Scawton 102 F3
Scayne's Hill . 17 B7
Scethrog 35 B5
Scholar Green . 74 D5
Scholes W Yorks . 88 B2
 W Yorks 88 B3
 W Yorks 95 F6
School Green . 74 C3
Scleddau 44 B4
Scofton 89 F7
Scole 56 B5
Scolpaig 148 A2
Scone 128 B3
Sconser 149 E10
Scoonie 129 D5
Scoor 146 K7
Scopwick 78 D3
Scoraig 150 B3
Scorborough . . . 97 E6
Scorrier 3 B6
Scorton Lancs . 92 E5
 N Yorks 101 D7
Sco Ruston 81 E8

Scotbheinn 148 C3
Scotby 108 D4
Scotch Corner . . . 101 D7
Scotforth 92 D4
Scothern 78 B3
Scotland Gate . 117 F8
Scotlandwell . . . 128 D3
Scotsburn 151 D10
Scotscalder
 Station 158 E2
Scotscraig 129 B6
Scot's Gap 117 F6
Scotston Aberds. . 135 B7
 Perth 133 E6
Scotstoun 118 C5
Scotstown 130 C2
Scotswood 110 C4
Scottas 149 H12
Scotter 90 D2
Scotterthorpe . 90 D2
Scottlethorpe . . . 65 B7
Scotton Lincs . . . 90 E2
 N Yorks 95 D6
 N Yorks 101 E6
Scottow 81 E8
Scoughall 129 F8
Scoulag 145 H10
Scoulton 68 D2
Scourie 156 E4
Scourie More . . . 156 E4
Scousburgh 160 M5
Scrabster 158 C2
Scrafield 79 C6
Scrainwood 117 D5
Scrane End 79 E6
Scraptoft 64 D3
Scratby 69 C8
Scrayingham . . . 96 C3
Scredington 78 E3
Scremby 79 C7
Scremerston . . . 123 E6
Screveton 77 E7
Scrivelsby 79 C5
Scriven 95 D6
Scrooby 89 E7
Scropton 75 F8
Scrub Hill 78 D5
Scruton 101 E7
Sculcoates 97 F6
Sculthorpe 80 D4
Scunthorpe 90 C2
Scurlage 33 F5
Seaborough 12 D2
Seacombe 85 E4
Seacroft Lincs . . . 79 C8
 W Yorks 95 F6
Seadyke 79 F6
Seafield S Ayrs . 112 B3
 W Loth 120 C3
Seaford 17 E8
Seaforth 85 E4
Seagrave 64 C3
Seaham 111 E7
Seahouses 123 F8
Seal 29 D6
Sealand 73 C7
Seale 27 E6
Seamer N Yorks . 102 C2
 N Yorks 103 F8
Seamill 118 E2
Sea Palling 69 B7
Searby 90 D4
Seasalter 30 C4
Seascale 98 D2
Seathorne 79 C8
Seathwaite Cumb . 98 C4
 Cumb 98 E4
Seatoller 98 C4
Seaton Corn 5 D8
 Cumb 107 F7
 Devon 11 F7
 Durham 111 D6
 E Yorks 97 E7
 Northumb 111 B6
 Rutland 65 E6
Seaton Burn 110 B5
Seaton Carew . 102 B3
Seaton Delaval . 111 B6
Seaton Ross 96 E3
Seaton Sluice . 111 B6
Seatown Aberds. . 152 B5
 Dorset 12 E2
Seave Green . . . 102 D3
Seaview 15 E7
Seaville 107 D8
Seavington
 St Mary 12 C2
Seavington
 St Michael . . . 12 C2
Sebergham 108 E3
Seckington 63 D6
Second Coast . 150 B2
Sedbergh 100 E1
Sedbury 36 E2
Sedbusk 100 E3
Seddington 54 E2
Sedgeberrow . . . 50 F5
Sedgebrook 77 F8
Sedgefield 102 B1
Sedgeford 80 D3
Sedgehill 13 B6
Sedgley 62 E3
Sedgwick 99 F7
Sedlescombe . 18 D4
Sedlescombe
 Street 18 D4
Seend 24 C4
Seend Cleeve . 24 C4
Seer Green 40 E2
Seething 69 E6
Sefton 85 D4
Seghill 111 B5
Seifton 60 F4
Seighford 62 B2
Seilebost 154 H5
Seion 82 E5
Seisdon 62 E2
Seisiadar 155 D10
Selattyn 73 F6
Selborne 26 F5
Selby 96 F2
Selham 16 B3
Selhurst 28 C4
Selkirk 115 B7
Sellack 36 B2
Sellafirth 160 D7
Sellibister 159 D8

Sellindge 19 B7
Sellindge Lees 19 B8
Selling 30 D4
Sells Green 24 C4
Selly Oak 62 F4
Selmeston 18 E2
Selsdon 28 C4
Selsey 16 E2
Selsfield Common . 28 F4
Selsted 31 E6
Selston 76 D4
Selworthy 21 E8
Semblister 160 H5
Semer 56 E3
Semington 24 C3
Semley 13 B6
Send 27 D8
Send Marsh 27 D8
Senghenydd 35 E5
Sennen 2 D2
Sennen Cove 2 D2
Sennybridge
= Pont Senni 34 B3
Serlby 89 F7
Sessay 95 B7
Setchey 67 C6
Setley 14 D4
Setter Shetland . . 160 E6
Shetland 160 H5
Shetland 160 J7
Settiscarth 159 G4
Settle 93 C8
Settrington 96 B4
Sevenhampton 37 B7
Seven Kings 41 F7
Sevenoaks 29 D6
Sevenoaks Weald . 29 E6
Seven Sisters 34 D2
Severn Beach 36 F2
Severnhampton 38 E2
Severn Stoke 50 E3
Sevington 30 E4
Sewards End 55 F6
Sewardstone 41 E6
Sewardstonebury . 41 E6
Sewerby 97 C7
Seworgan 3 C6
Sewstern 65 B5
Sezincote 51 F6
Sgarasta Mhor . . 154 H5
Sgiogarstaigh . . . 155 A10
Shabbington 39 D6
Shackerstone 63 D7
Shackleford 27 E7
Shade 87 B7
Shadforth 111 E6
Shadingfield 69 F7
Shadoxhurst 19 B6
Shadsworth 86 B5
Shadwell Norf 68 F2
W Yorks 95 F6
Shaftesbury 13 B6
Shafton 88 C4
Shalbourne 25 C8
Shalcombe 14 F4
Shalden 26 E4
Shaldon 7 B7
Shalfleet 14 F4
Shalford Essex . . . 42 B3
Sur 27 E8
Shalford Green . . . 42 B3
Shallowford 21 E6
Shalmsford Street . 30 D4
Shalstone 52 F4
Shamley Green . . . 27 E8
Shandon 145 E11
Shandwick 151 D11
Shangton 64 E4
Shankhouse 111 B5
Shanklin 15 F6
Shanquhar 152 E5
Shanzie 134 D2
Shap 99 C7
Shapwick Dorset . 13 D7
Som 23 F6
Shardlow 76 F4
Shareshill 62 D3
Sharlston 88 C4
Sharlston
Common 88 C4
Sharnbrook 53 D7
Sharnford 63 E8
Sharoe Green 92 F5
Sharow 95 B6
Sharpenhoe 53 F8
Sharperton 117 D5
Sharpness 36 D3
Sharp Street 69 B6
Sharpthorne 28 F4
Sharrington 81 D6
Shatterford 61 F7
Shaugh Prior 6 C3
Shavington 74 D4
Shaw Gtr Man 87 D7
W Berks 26 C2
Wilts 24 C3
Shawbury 61 B5
Shawdon Hall 117 C6
Shawell 64 F2
Shawford 15 B5
Shawforth 87 B6
Shaw Green 86 C3
Shawhead 107 B5
Shawhill 108 C2
Shaw Mills 95 C5
Shawton 119 E6
Shawtonhill 119 E6
Shear Cross 24 E3
Shearington 107 C7
Shearsby 64 E3
Shebbear 9 D6
Shebdon 61 B7
Shebster 157 C13
Sheddens 119 D5
Shedfield 15 C6
Sheen 75 C8
Sheepscar 95 F6
Sheepscombe 37 C5
Sheepstor 6 C3
Sheepwash 9 D6
Sheepway 23 F6
Sheepy Magna 63 D7
Sheepy Parva 63 D7
Sheering 41 C8
Sheerness 30 B3
Sheet 15 B8

Sheffield 88 F4
Sheffield Bottom . 26 C4
Sheffield Green . . . 17 B8
Shefford 54 F2
Shefford
Woodlands 25 B8
Sheigra 156 C4
Sheinton 61 D6
Shelderton 49 B6
Sheldon Derbys . . . 75 C8
Devon 11 D6
W Mid 63 F5
Sheldwich 30 D4
Shelf 88 B2
Shelfanger 68 F4
Shelfield Warks . . . 51 C6
W Mid 62 D4
Shelford 77 E6
Shellacres 122 E4
Shelley Essex 42 D1
Suff 56 F4
W Yorks 88 C3
Shellingford 38 E3
Shellow Bowells . 42 D2
Shelsley
Beauchamp 50 C2
Shelsley Walsh . . . 50 C2
Shelthorpe 64 C2
Shelton Bedford . 53 C8
Norf 68 E5
Notts 77 E7
Shrops 60 C4
Shelton Green 68 E5
Shelve 60 E3
Shelwick 49 E7
Shenfield 42 E2
Shenington 51 E8
Shenley 40 D4
Shenley Brook End 53 F6
Shenleybury 40 D4
Shenley Church
End 53 F6
Shenmore 49 F5
Shennanton 105 C7
Shenstone Staffs . . 62 D5
Worcs 50 B3
Shenton 63 D7
Shenval Highld . . 137 B7
Moray 139 B8
Shepeau Stow 66 C3
Shephall 41 B5
Shepherd's Green . 35 F7
Shepherd's Port . 80 D2
Shepherdswell 31 E6
Shepley 88 D2
Shepperdine 36 E3
Shepperton 27 C8
Shepreth 54 E4
Shepshed 63 C8
Shepton
Beauchamp 12 C2
Shepton Mallet . . . 23 E8
Shepton Montague 23 F8
Shepway 29 D8
Sheraton 111 F7
Sherborne Dorset . 12 C4
Glos 38 C1
Sherborne
St John 26 D4
Sherbourne 51 C7
Sherburn Durham . 111 E6
N Yorks 97 B5
Sherburn Hill 111 E6
Sherburn in Elmet . 95 F7
Shere 27 E8
Shereford 80 E4
Sherfield English . 14 B3
Sherfield on
Loddon 26 D4
Sherford 7 E5
Sheriffhales 61 C7
Sheriff Hutton 96 C2
Sheringham 81 C7
Sherington 53 E6
Shernal Green 50 C4
Shernborne 80 D3
Sherrington 24 F4
Sherston 37 F5
Sherwood Green . . 9 B7
Shettleston 119 C6
Shevington 86 D3
Shevington Moor . 86 C3
Shevington Vale . 86 D3
Sheviock 5 D8
Shide 15 F5
Shiel Bridge 136 C2
Shieldaig Highld . 149 A13
Highld 149 C13
Shieldhill Dumfries 114 F3
Falk 119 B8
S Lanark 120 E3
Shielfoot 147 E9
Shielhill Angus . . 134 D4
Involyd 118 B2
Shifford 38 D3
Shifnal 61 D7
Shilbottle 117 D7
Shildon 101 B7
Shillingford Devon . 10 C4
Oxon 39 E5
Shillingford
St George 10 F4
Shillingstone 13 C6
Shillington 54 F2
Shillmoor 116 D4
Shilton Oxon 38 D2
Warks 63 F8
Shilvinghoe 117 F7
Shimpling Norf . . . 68 F4
Suff 56 D2
Shimpling Street . 56 D2
Shincliffe 111 E5
Shiney Row 111 D6
Shinfield 26 C5
Shingham 67 D7
Shingle Street 57 E7
Shinner's Bridge . 7 C5
Shinness 157 H8
Shipbourne 29 D6
Shipdham 68 D2
Shipham 23 D6
Shiphay 7 C6
Shiplake 27 B5
Shipley Derbys . . . 76 E4
Northumb 117 C7
Shrops 62 E2
W Sus 16 B5
W Yorks 94 F4
Shipley Shiels . . . 116 E3

Shipmeadow 69 F6
Shippea Hill
Station 67 F6
Shippon 38 E4
Shipston-on-
Stour 51 E7
Shipton Glos 37 C7
N Yorks 95 D8
Shrops 61 E5
Shipton Bellinger . 25 E7
Shipton Gorge 12 E2
Shipton Green . . . 16 D2
Shipton Moyne . . . 37 F5
Shipton on
Cherwell 38 C4
Shipton Solers . . . 37 C7
Shiptonthorpe . . . 96 E4
Shipton-under-
Wychwood 38 C2
Shirburn 39 E6
Shirdley Hill 85 C4
Shire 109 F8
Shiregreen 88 E4
Shirehampton 23 B7
Shiremoor 111 B6
Shirenewton 36 E1
Shireoaks 89 F6
Shirkoak 19 B6
Shirl Heath 49 D6
Shirland 76 D3
Shirley Derbys . . . 76 E2
London 28 C4
Soton 14 C5
W Mid 51 B6
Shirl Heath 49 D6
Shirrell Heath . . . 15 C6
Shirwell 20 F4
Shirwell Cross . . . 20 F4
Shiskine 143 F10
Shobdon 49 C6
Shobnall 63 B6
Shobrooke 10 D3
Shoby 64 C3
Shocklach 73 E8
Shoeburyness 43 F5
Sholden 31 D7
Sholing 14 C5
Shoot Hill 60 C4
Shop Corn 4 B3
Corn 8 C4
Shop Corner 57 F6
Shoreditch 41 F6
Shoreham 29 C6
Shoreham-by-Sea 17 D6
Shore Mill 151 E10
Shoresdean 123 E5
Shoreswood 122 E5
Shoreton 151 E9
Shorncote 37 E7
Shorne 29 B7
Shortacombe 9 F7
Shortgate 17 C8
Short Heath 62 D3
Shortlanesend 3 B7
Shortlees 118 F4
Shortstown 53 E8
Shorwell 15 F5
Shoscombe 24 D2
Shotatton 60 B3
Shotesham 69 E5
Shotgate 42 E3
Shotley 57 F6
Shotley Bridge . . . 110 D3
Shotleyfield 110 D3
Shotley Gate 57 F6
Shottenden 30 D4
Shottermill 27 F6
Shottery 51 D6
Shotteswell 52 E2
Shottisham 57 E7
Shottle 76 E3
Shottlegate 76 E3
Shotton Durham . 111 F7
Flint 73 C7
Northumb 122 F4
Shotton Colliery . 111 E6
Shotts 119 C8
Shotwick 73 B7
Shouldham 67 D6
Shouldham
Thorpe 67 D6
Shoulton 50 D3
Shover's Green . . . 18 B3
Shrawardine 60 C4
Shrawley 50 C3
Shrewley Common 51 C7
Shrewsbury 60 C4
Shrewton 25 E5
Shripney 16 D3
Shrivenham 38 F2
Shropham 68 E2
Shrub End 43 B5
Shucknall 49 E7
Shudy Camps 55 E7
Shulishadermor . 149 D9
Shurdington 37 C6
Shurlock Row 27 B6
Shurrery 157 D13
Shurrery Lodge . 157 D13
Shurton 22 E4
Shustoke 63 E6
Shute Devon 10 D3
Devon 11 E7
Shutford 51 E8
Shuthonger 50 F3
Shutlanger 52 D5
Shuttington 63 D6
Shuttlewood 76 B4
Siabost bho
Dheas 154 C7
Siabost bho
Thuath 154 C7
Siadar 155 B8
Siadar Iarach 155 B8
Siadar Uarach . . . 155 B8
Sibbaldbie 114 F4
Sibbertoft 64 F3
Sibdon Carwood . 60 F4
Sibford Ferris 51 F8
Sibford Gower . . . 51 F8
Sible Hedingham . 55 F8
Sibsey 79 D6
Sibson Cambs 65 E7
Leics 63 D7
Sibthorpe 77 E7
Sibton 57 C7
Sibton Green 57 B7
Sicklesmere 56 C2
Sicklinghall 95 E6
Sid 11 F6

Sidbury Devon . . . 11 E6
Shrops 61 F6
Sidcot 23 D6
Sidcup 29 B5
Siddick 107 F7
Siddington Ches E . 74 B5
Glos 37 E7
Sidemoor 50 B4
Sidestrand 81 D8
Sidford 11 E6
Sidlesham 16 E2
Sidley 18 E4
Sidlow 28 E3
Sidmouth 11 F6
Sigford 7 B5
Sigglesthorne 97 E7
Sighthill 120 B4
Sigingstone 21 B8
Signet 38 C2
Silchester 26 C4
Sildinis 155 F7
Sileby 64 C2
Silecroft 98 F3
Silfield 68 E4
Silian 46 D4
Silk Willoughby . 78 E3
Silkstone 88 D3
Silkstone
Common 88 D3
Silloth 107 D8
Sills 116 D4
Sillyearn 152 C5
Siloh 47 F6
Silpho 103 E7
Silsden 94 E3
Silsoe 53 F8
Silver End 42 C4
Silvergate 81 E7
Silverhill 18 D4
Silverley's Green . 57 B6
Silverstone 52 E4
Silverton 10 D4
Silvington 49 B8
Silwick 160 J4
Simmondley 87 E8
Simonburn 109 B8
Simonsbath 21 F6
Simonstone 93 F7
Simprim 122 E4
Simpson 53 F6
Simpson Cross . . . 44 D3
Sinclair's Hill 122 D4
Sinclairston 112 C4
Sinderby 101 F8
Sinderhope 109 D8
Sindlesham 27 C5
Singdean 115 D8
Singleborough . . . 53 F5
Singleton Lancs . . . 92 F3
W Sus 16 C2
Singlewell 29 B7
Sinkhurst Green . 30 E2
Sinnahard 140 C3
Sinnington 103 F5
Sinton Green 50 C3
Sipson 27 B8
Sirhowy 35 C5
Sisland 69 E6
Sissinghurst 18 B4
Sisterpath 122 E3
Siston 23 B8
Sithney 2 D5
Sittingbourne 30 C2
Six Ashes 61 F7
Sixhills 91 F5
Six Hills 64 C3
Six Mile Bottom . 55 D6
Sixpenny Handley 13 C7
Sizewell 57 C8
Skail 157 E10
Skaill Orkney 159 E5
Orkney 159 H6
Skares 113 C5
Skateraw 122 B3
Skaw 160 G7
Skeabost 149 D9
Skeabrae 159 F3
Skeeby 101 D7
Skeffington 64 D4
Skeffling 91 C7
Skegby 76 C4
Skegness 79 C8
Skelberry 160 M5
Skelbo 151 B10
Skelbrooke 89 C6
Skeldyke 79 F6
Skellingthorpe . . . 78 B2
Skellister 160 H6
Skellow 89 C6
Skelmanthorpe . . . 88 C3
Skelmersdale 86 D2
Skelmonae 153 E8
Skelmorlie 118 C1
Skelmuir 153 D9
Skelpick 157 D10
Skelton Cumb 108 F4
E Yorks 89 B8
N Yorks 101 D5
Redcar 102 C4
York 95 D8
Skelton-on-Ure . 95 C6
Skelwick 159 D5
Skelwith Bridge . 99 D5
Skendleby 79 C7
Skene House 141 D6
Skenfrith 36 B1
Skerne 97 D6
Skeroblingarry . 143 F8
Skerray 157 C9
Skerton 92 C4
Sketchley 63 E8
Sketty 33 E7
Skewen 33 E8
Skewsby 96 B2
Skeyton 81 E8
Skiag Bridge 156 G5
Skibo Castle 151 C10
Skidbrooke 91 E8
Skidbrooke North
End 91 E8
Skidby 97 F6
Skilgate 10 B4
Skillington 65 B5
Skinburness 107 D8
Skinflats 127 F8

Skinidin 148 D7
Skinnet 157 C16
Skinningrove 103 B5
Skipness 145 H7
Skippool 92 E3
Skipsea 97 D7
Skipsea Brough . 97 D7
Skipton 96 F2
Skipton-on-Swale 95 B6
Skipwith 96 F2
Skirbeck 79 E6
Skirbeck Quarter . 79 E6
Skirlaugh 97 F7
Skirling 120 F3
Skirmett 39 F7
Skirpenbeck 96 D3
Skirwith 109 F6
Skirza 158 D5
Skulamus 149 F11
Skullomie 157 C9
Skyborry Green . 48 B4
Skye of Curr 139 B5
Skyreholme 94 C3
Slackhall 87 F8
Slackhead 152 B4
Slad 37 D5
Slade Devon 20 E4
Pembs 44 D4
Slade Green 29 B6
Slaggyford 109 D6
Slaidburn 93 D7
Slaithwaite 87 C8
Slaley 110 D2
Slamannan 119 B8
Slapton Bucks . . . 40 B2
Devon 7 E6
Northants 52 E4
Slatepit Dale 76 C3
Slattocks 87 D6
Slaugham 17 B6
Slaughterford . . . 24 B3
Slawston 64 E4
Sleaford Hants . . . 27 F6
Lincs 78 E3
Sleagill 99 C7
Sleapford 61 C6
Sledge Green 50 F3
Sledmere 96 C5
Sleightholme 100 C4
Sleights 103 D6
Slepe 13 E7
Slickly 158 D4
Sliddery 143 F10
Sligachan Hotel . 149 F9
Slimbridge 36 D4
Slindon Staffs . . . 74 F5
W Sus 16 D3
Slinfold 28 F2
Sling 83 E6
Slingsby 96 B2
Slioch 152 E5
Slip End C Beds . . 40 C3
Herts 54 F3
Slipton 53 B7
Slitting Mill 62 C4
Slochd 138 B4
Slockavullin 124 F4
Sloley 81 E8
Sloothby 79 B7
Slough 27 B7
Slough Green 17 B6
Sluggan 138 B4
Slumbay 149 E13
Slyfield 27 D7
Slyne 92 C4
Smailholm 122 F2
Smallburgh 69 B6
Smallburn
Aberds 153 D10
E Ayrs 113 B6
Small Dole 17 C6
Smalley 76 E4
Smallfield 28 E4
Small Hythe 19 B5
Smallridge 11 D8
Smannell 25 E8
Smardale 100 D2
Smarden 30 E2
Smarden Bell 30 E2
Smeatharpe 11 C6
Smeeth 19 B7
Smeeton Westerby 64 E3
Smercleit 148 G2
Smerral 158 G3
Smethwick 62 F4
Smirisary 147 D9
Smisby 63 C7
Smith End Green . 50 D2
Smithfield 108 C4
Smith Green 92 D4
Smithincott 11 C5
Smith's Green . . . 42 B1
Smithstown 149 A12
Smithton 151 G10
Smithy Green 74 B4
Smockington 63 F8
Smoogro 159 H4
Smythe's Green . 43 C5
Snaigow House . 133 E7
Snailbeach 60 D3
Snailwell 55 C7
Snainton 103 F7
Snaith 89 B7
Snape N Yorks . . . 101 F7
Suff 57 D7
Snape Green 85 C4
Snarestone 63 D7
Snarford 90 F4
Snargate 19 C6
Snave 19 C7
Snead 60 E3
Sneath Common . 68 F4
Sneaton 103 D6
Sneatonthorpe . 103 D7
Snelland 90 F4
Snelston 75 E8
Snettisham 80 D2
Sniseabhal 148 E2
Snitter 117 D6
Snitterby 90 E3
Snitterfield 51 D7
Snitton 49 B7
Snodhill 48 E5
Snodland 29 C7
Snowden Hill 88 D3
Snowdown 31 D6
Snowshill 51 F5
Snydale 88 C5
Soar Anglesey . . . 82 D3

Soar continued
Carms 33 B7
Devon 6 F5
Soar-y-Mynydd . 47 D6
Soberton 15 C7
Soberton Heath . 15 C7
Sockbridge 99 B7
Sockburn 101 D8
Soham 55 B6
Soham Cotes 55 B6
Solas 148 A3
Soldon Cross 8 C5
Soldridge 26 F4
Sole Street Kent . . 29 C7
Kent 30 E4
Solihull 51 B6
Sollers Dilwyn . . . 49 D6
Sollers Hope 49 F8
Sollom 86 C2
Solva 44 C2
Somerby Leics . . . 64 C4
Lincs 90 D4
Somercotes 76 D4
Somerford 14 E2
Somerford Keynes 37 E7
Somerley 16 E2
Somerleyton 69 E7
Somersal Herbert 75 F8
Somersby 79 B6
Somersham Cambs 54 B4
Suff 56 E4
Somerton Oxon . 38 B4
Som 12 B2
Sompting 17 D5
Sonning 27 B5
Sonning Common . 39 F7
Sonning Eye 27 B5
Sontley 73 E7
Sopley 14 E2
Sopwell 40 D4
Sopworth 37 F5
Sorbie 105 E8
Sordale 158 D3
Sorisdale 146 E5
Sorn 113 B5
Sornhill 118 F5
Sortat 158 D4
Sotby 78 B5
Sots Hole 78 C4
Sotterley 69 F7
Soudley 61 B7
Soughton 73 C6
Soulbury 40 B1
Soulby 100 C2
Souldern 52 F3
Souldrop 53 C7
Sound Ches E 74 E3
Shetland 160 H5
Shetland 160 J6
Sound Heath 74 E3
Soundwell 23 B8
Sourhope 116 B4
Sourin 159 E5
Sourton 9 E7
Soutergate 98 F4
South Acre 67 C8
Southall 40 F4
South Allington . 7 F5
South Alloa 127 E7
Southam Glos 37 B6
Warks 52 C2
South Ambersham 16 B3
Southampton 14 C5
South Anston 89 F6
South Ascot 27 C7
South
Ballachulish . . . 130 D4
South Balloch . . . 112 E3
South Bank 102 B3
South Barrow 12 B4
South Beach 70 D4
South Benfleet . . . 42 F3
South Bersted 16 D3
Southborough . . . 29 E6
Southbourne BCP . 14 E2
W Sus 15 D8
South Brent 6 C4
South Brewham . . 24 F2
South Broomhill . 117 E8
Southburgh 69 D6
South Burlingham 69 D6
Southburn 97 D5
South Cadbury . . . 12 B4
South Cairn 104 C3
South Carlton 78 B2
South Cave 96 F5
South Cerney 37 E7
South Chard 11 D8
South Charlton . . . 117 B7
South Cheriton . . . 12 B4
Southchurch 43 F5
South Cliffe 96 F4
South Clifton 77 B8
South
Cockerington . . . 91 F7
South Cornelly . . . 34 F2
Southcott 25 D6
Southcourt 39 C8
South Cove 69 F7
South Creagan . 130 E3
South Creake 80 D4
South Crosby 63 C3
South Croydon . . . 28 C4
South Dalton 97 E5
South Darenth . . . 29 C6
Southdean 116 D2
South Duffield . . . 96 F2
Southease 17 D8
South Elkington . 91 F6
South Elmsall 89 C5
Southend Argyll . 143 H7
W Berks 26 B3
Wilts 25 B6
South End Bucks . 40 B1
Cumb 92 C2
N Lincs 90 B5
Southend-on-Sea . 42 F4
Southernden 30 E2
Southerndown . . . 21 B7
Southerness 107 D6
South Erradale . 149 A12
Southery 67 E6
South Fambridge . 42 E4
South Fawley 38 F3
South Ferriby 90 B3
Southfield 111 B5
Southfleet 29 B7

South Garvan 130 B3
Southgate Ceredig 46 B4
London 41 E5
Norf 81 E7
Swansea 33 F6
South Glendale . 148 G2
South Gorley 14 C2
South Green Essex 42 E2
Kent 30 C2
South
Hanningfield . . . 42 E3
South Harting . . . 15 C8
South Hatfield . . . 41 D5
South Hayling . . . 15 E8
South Hazelrigg . 123 F6
South Heath 40 D2
South Heighton . 17 D8
South Hetton 111 E6
South Hiendley . 88 C4
South Hill 5 B8
South Hinksey . . . 39 D5
South Hole 8 B4
South Holme 96 B2
South Holmwood . 28 E2
South Hornchurch 41 F8
South Hykeham . 78 C2
South Hylton 111 D6
Southill 54 E2
South Kelsey 90 E4
South Kessock . . . 151 G9
South
Killingholme . . . 91 C5
South Kilvington . 102 F1
South Kilworth . . . 64 F3
South Kirkby 88 C5
South Kirkton . . . 141 D6
South Kiscadale 143 F11
South Kyme 78 E4
South Lancing . . . 17 D5
South Leigh 38 D3
South Leverton . . . 89 F8
South Littleton . . . 51 E5
South Lopham . . . 68 F3
South Luffenham . 65 D6
South Malling . . . 17 C8
South Marston . . . 38 F1
South Middleton 117 B5
South Milford . . . 95 F7
South Millbrex . 153 D8
South Milton 6 E5
South Mimms 41 D5
Southminster 43 E5
South Molton 10 B2
South Moreton . . . 39 F5
South Mundham . 16 D2
South Muskham . 77 D7
South Newbald . 96 F5
South Newington . 52 F2
South Newton . . . 25 F5
South Normanton 76 D4
South Norwood . 28 C4
South Nutfield . . . 28 E4
South Ockendon . 42 F1
Southoe 54 C2
Southolt 57 C5
Southorpe 65 D7
South Ormsby . . . 79 B6
Southowram 88 B2
Southport 85 C4
South Port 74 F4
Southpunds 160 L6
South Radworthy . 21 F6
South Rauceby . . . 78 E3
South Raynham . 80 E4
Southrepps 81 D8
South Reston 91 F8
Southrey 78 C4
Southrop 38 D1
Southrope 26 E4
South Runcton . . . 67 D6
South Scarle 77 C8
Southsea 15 E7
South Shian 130 E3
South Shields 111 C6
South Somercotes 91 E8
South Stainley . . . 95 C6
South Stainmore . 100 C3
South Stifford . . . 29 B6
Southstoke 24 C2
South Stoke Oxon 39 F5
W Sus 16 D4
South Street E Sus 17 C7
Kent 30 C5
Kent 30 D5
London 28 D5
South Tawton 9 E8
South Thoresby . 79 B7
South Tidworth . 25 E7
Southtown Norf . 69 D8
Orkney 159 J5
South Town 26 F4
Southview 108 E4
South Walsham . 69 C6
Southwark 28 B4
South
Warnborough . 26 E5
Southwater 17 B5
Southwater Street 17 B5
Southway 23 E7
Southwell Dorset . 12 G4
Notts 77 D6
South Weston . . . 39 E7
South Wheatley
Corn 8 E4
Notts 89 F8
South Whiteness 160 J5
Southwick Hants . 15 D7
Northants 65 E7
T&W 111 D6
Wilts 24 D3
W Sus 17 D6
South Wigston . . . 64 E2
South Willingham 91 F5
South Wingfield . 76 D3
South Witham . . . 65 B7
Southwold 57 B9
South Wonston . 26 F2
Southwood Norf . 69 D6
Som 23 F7
South Woodham
Ferrers 42 E4
South Wootton . 67 B6
South Wraxall . . . 24 C3
South Zeal 9 E8
Soval Lodge 155 E8
Sowber Gate 102 F1
Sowerby N Yorks . 102 F2
W Yorks 87 B8
Sowerby Bridge . 87 B8
Sowerby Row 87 C8
Sowood 87 C8
Sowton 10 E4
Soyal 151 B8
Spacey Houses . . . 95 D6
Spa Common 81 D8
Spadeadam Farm 109 B5
Spalding 66 B2
Spaldington 96 F3
Spaldwick 54 B2
Spalford 77 C8
Spanby 78 F3
Sparham 68 C3
Spark Bridge 99 F5
Sparkford 12 B4
Sparkhill 62 F4
Sparkwell 6 D3
Sparrow Green . . . 68 C2
Sparrowpit 87 F8
Sparsholt Hants . . 26 F2
Oxon 38 F3
Spartylea 109 E8
Spaunton 103 F5
Spaxton 22 F4
Spean Bridge 136 F5
Spear Hill 16 C5
Speen Bucks 39 E8
W Berks 26 C2
Speeton 97 B7
Speke 86 F2
Speldhurst 29 E6
Spellbrook 41 C7
Spelsbury 38 B3
Spelter 34 E2
Spencers Wood . . 26 C5
Spennithorne 101 F6
Spennymoor 111 F5
Spetchley 50 D3
Spetisbury 13 D7
Spexhall 69 F6
Spey Bay 152 B3
Speybridge 139 B6
Speyview 152 D2
Spilsby 79 C7
Spindlestone 123 F7
Spinkhill 76 B4
Spinningdale 151 C9
Spirthill 24 B4
Spital Hill 89 E7
Spital in the Street 90 F3
Spithurst 17 C8
Spittal Dumfries . 105 D7
E Loth 121 B7
Highld 158 E3
Northumb 123 D6
Pembs 44 C4
Stirling 126 F4
Spittalfield 133 E8
Spittal of
Glenmuick 140 F2
Spittal of
Glenshee 133 B8
Spixworth 68 C5
Splayne's Green . 17 B8
Spofforth 95 D6
Spondon 76 F4
Spon End 51 B8
Spon Green 73 C6
Spooner Row 68 E3
Sporle 67 C8
Spott 122 B2
Spratton 52 B5
Spreakley 27 E6
Spreyton 9 E8
Spridlington 90 F4
Springburn 119 C6
Springfield
Dumfries 108 C3
Essex 42 D3
Fife 128 C5
Moray 151 F13
W Mid 62 F4
Springhill 62 D3
Springholm 106 C5
Springkell 108 B2
Springside 118 F3
Springthorpe 90 F2
Spring Vale 88 D3
Spring Valley 84 E3
Springwell 111 D5
Sproatley 97 F7
Sproston Green . . . 74 C4
Sprotbrough 89 D6
Sproughton 56 E5
Sprouston 122 F3
Sprowston 68 C5
Sproxton Leics . . . 64 B5
N Yorks 102 F4
Spurstow 74 D2
Spynie 152 B2
Squires Gate 92 F3
Srannda 154 J5
Sronphadruig
Lodge 132 B4
Stableford Shrops . 61 E7
Staffs 74 F5
Stacey Bank 88 E3
Stackhouse 93 C8
Stackpole 44 F4
Staddiscombe 6 D3
Staddlethorpe . . . 90 B2
Stadhampton 39 E6
Stadhlaigearraidh . 148 E2
Staffield 108 E5
Stafford 62 B3
Stagsden 53 E7
Stainburn Cumb . 98 B2
N Yorks 95 E5
Stainby 65 B6

Staincross 88 C4
Staindrop 101 B6
Staines-upon-
Thames 27 B8
Stainfield Lincs . . 65 B7
Lincs 78 B4
Stainforth N Yorks 93 C8
S Yorks 89 C7
Staining 92 F3
Stainland 87 C8
Stainsacre 103 D7
Stainsby 76 C4
Stainton Cumb . . . 99 B6
Cumb 99 F7
Durham 101 C5
Mbro 102 C2
N Yorks 101 E6
S Yorks 89 E6
Stainton by
Langworth 78 B3
Staintondale 103 E7
Stainton le Vale . 91 E5
Stainton with
Adgarley 92 B2
Stair Cumb 98 B4
E Ayrs 112 B4
Stairhaven 105 D6
Staithes 103 C5
Stakeford 117 E8
Stake Pool 92 E4
Stalbridge 12 C5
Stalbridge Weston 12 C5
Stalham 69 B6
Stalham Green . . . 69 B6
Stalisfield Green . 30 D3
Stallingborough . 71 C6
Stalling Busk 100 F4
Stalmine 92 E3
Stalybridge 87 E7
Stambourne 55 F8
Stambourne Green 55 F8
Stamford 65 D7
Stamford Bridge
Ches W 73 C8
E Yorks 96 D3
Stamfordham . . . 110 B3
Stanah 99 C5
Stanborough 41 C5
Stanbridge C Beds 40 B2
Dorset 13 D8
Stanbrook 50 E3
Stanbury 94 F3
Stand Gtr Man . . . 87 D5
N Lanark 119 C7
Standburn 120 B2
Standeford 62 D3
Standen 30 E2
Standford 27 F6
Standingstone . . . 107 F7
Standish 86 C3
Standlake 38 D3
Standon Hants . . . 14 B5
Herts 41 B6
Staffs 74 F5
Stane 119 D8
Stanfield 80 E5
Stanford C Beds . 54 E2
Kent 19 B8
Stanford Bridge . 50 C2
Stanford Dingley . 26 B3
Stanford in the
Vale 38 E3
Stanford-le-Hope 42 F2
Stanford on Avon . 52 B3
Stanford on Soar . 64 B2
Stanford on Teme . 50 C2
Stanford Rivers . 41 D8
Stanfree 76 B4
Stanghow 102 C4
Stanground 66 E2
Stanhoe 80 D4
Stanhope Borders 114 B4
Durham 110 F2
Stanion 65 F6
Stanley Derbys . . . 76 E4
Durham 110 D4
Lancs 86 D2
Perth 133 F7
Staffs 75 D6
W Yorks 88 B4
Stanley Common . 76 E4
Stanley Gate 86 D2
Stanley Hill 49 E8
Stanlow 73 B8
Stanmer 17 D7
Stanmore Hants . 15 B5
London 40 E4
W Berks 26 B2
Stannergate 134 F4
Stanningley 94 F5
Stannington
Northumb 110 B5
S Yorks 88 F4
Stansbatch 48 C5
Stansfield 55 D8
Stanstead 56 E2
Stanstead Abbotts 41 C6
Stansted 29 C7
Stansted
Mountfitchet . . . 41 B8
Stanton Glos 51 F5
Mon 35 B7
Northumb 117 F7
Staffs 75 E8
Suff 56 B3
Stanton by Bridge 63 B7
Stanton-by-Dale . 76 F4
Stanton Drew 23 C7
Stanton
Fitzwarren 38 E1
Stanton Harcourt . 38 D4
Stanton Hill 76 C4
Stanton in Peak . 76 C2
Stanton Lacy 49 B6
Stanton Long 61 E5
Stanton-on-the-
Wolds 77 F6
Stanton Prior 23 C8
Stanton
St John 39 D5
Stanton St Quintin 24 B4
Stanton Street . . . 56 C3
Stanton under
Bardon 63 C8
Stanton upon Hine
Heath 61 B5

Stanton Wick 23 C8
Stanwardine in the
Fields 60 B4
Stanwardine in the
Wood 60 B4
Stanway Essex 43 B5
Glos 51 F5
Stanway Green . . . 57 B6
Stanwell 27 B8
Stanwell Moor . . . 27 B8
Stanwick 53 B7
Stanwick-St-
John 101 C6
Stanwix 108 D4
Stanydale 160 H4
Stape 103 E5
Stapehill 13 D8
Stapeley 74 E3
Stapenhill 63 B6
Staple Kent 31 D6
Som 22 E3
Staple Cross 18 C4
Staplefield 17 B6
Staple Fitzpaine . . 11 C7
Stapleford Cambs . . 54 D5
Herts 41 C6
Leics 64 C5
Lincs 77 D8
Notts 76 F4
Wilts 25 F5
Stapleford Abbotts 41 E8
Stapleford Tawney . 41 E8
Staplegrove 11 B7
Staplehay 11 B7
Staplehurst 29 E8
Staplers 15 F6
Stapleton Bristol . . 23 B8
Cumb 108 B5
Hereford 48 C5
Leics 63 E8
N Yorks 101 C7
Shrops 60 D4
Som 12 B2
Stapley 11 C6
Staploe 54 C2
Staplow 49 E8
Star Fife 128 D5
Pembs 45 F4
Som 23 D6
Stara 159 F3
Starbeck 95 D6
Starbotton 94 B2
Starcross 10 F4
Stareton 51 B8
Starkholmes 76 D3
Starlings Green . . . 55 F5
Starston 68 F5
Startforth 101 C5
Startley 37 F6
Stathe 11 B8
Stathern 77 F7
Station Town 111 F7
Staughton Green . . 54 C2
Staughton
Highway 54 C2
Staunton Glos 36 B4
Glos 36 C2
Staunton in the
Vale 77 E8
Staunton on
Arrow 49 C5
Staunton on Wye . . 49 E5
Staveley Cumb . . . 99 E6
Cumb 99 F5
Derbys 76 B4
N Yorks 95 C6
Staverton Devon . . . 7 C5
Glos 37 B5
Northants 52 C3
Wilts 24 C3
Staverton Bridge . . 37 B5
Stawell 23 F5
Staxigoe 158 E5
Staxton 97 B6
Staylittle 59 E5
Staynall 92 E3
Staythorpe 77 D7
Stean 94 B3
Stearsby 96 B2
Steart 22 E4
Stebbing 42 B2
Stebbing Green . . . 42 B2
Stedham 16 B2
Steele Road 115 E8
Steen's Bridge 49 D7
Steep 15 B8
Steeple Dorset . . . 13 F7
Essex 43 D5
Steeple Ashton . . . 24 D4
Steeple Aston 38 B4
Steeple Barton . . . 38 B4
Steeple
Bumpstead 55 E7
Steeple Claydon . . 39 B6
Steeple Gidding . . 65 F8
Steeple Langford . . 24 F5
Steeple Morden . . 54 E3
Steep Marsh 15 B8
Steeton 94 E3
Stein 148 C7
Steinmanhill 153 D7
Stelling Minnis . . . 30 E5
Stemster 158 D3
Stemster House . . 158 D3
Stenalees 4 D5
Stenhousemuir . . . 127 F7
Stenigot 91 F6
Stenness 160 F4
Stenscholl 149 B9
Stenso 159 F4
Stenson 63 B7
Stenton E Loth . . . 122 B2
Fife 128 E4
Stenwith 77 F8
Stepaside 32 D2
Stepping Hill 87 F7
Steppingley 53 F8
Stepps 119 C6
Sterndale Moor . . . 75 C8
Sternfield 57 C7
Sterridge 20 E4
Stert 24 D5
Stetchworth 55 D7
Stevenage 41 B5
Stevenston 118 E2
Steventon Hants . . 26 E3
Oxon 38 E4
Stevington 53 D7

Stewartby 53 E8
Stewarton Argyll . 143 G7
E Ayrs 118 E4
Stewkley 40 B1
Stewton 91 F7
Steyne Cross 15 F7
Steyning 17 C5
Steynton 44 E4
Stibb 8 C4
Stibbard 81 E5
Stibb Cross 9 C6
Stibb Green 25 C7
Stibbington 65 E7
Stichill 122 F3
Sticker 4 D4
Stickford 79 D6
Sticklepath 9 E8
Stickney 79 D6
Stiffkey 81 C5
Stifford's Bridge . . 50 E2
Stillingfleet 95 E8
Stillington N Yorks . 95 C8
Stockton 102 B1
Stilton 65 F8
Stinchcombe 36 E4
Stinsford 12 E5
Stirchley 61 D7
Stirkoke House . . 158 E5
Stirling Aberds . . 153 D11
Stirling 127 E6
Stisted 42 B3
Stithians 3 C6
Stittenham 151 D9
Stivichall 51 B8
Stixwould 78 C4
Stoak 73 B8
Stobieside 119 F6
Stobo 120 F4
Stoborough 13 F7
Stoborough Green . 13 F7
Stobshiel 121 C7
Stobswood 117 E8
Stock 42 E2
Stockbridge 25 F8
Stockbury 30 C2
Stockcross 26 C2
Stockdalewath . . 108 E3
Stockerston 64 E5
Stock Green 50 D4
Stockheath 15 D8
Stockiemuir 126 F4
Stockingford 63 E7
Stocking Pelham . . 41 B7
Stockland 11 D7
Stockland Bristol . . 22 E4
Stockleigh English 10 D3
Stockleigh
Pomeroy 10 D3
Stockley 24 C5
Stocklinch 11 C8
Stockport 87 E6
Stocksbridge 88 E3
Stocksfield 110 C3
Stockton Hereford . . 49 C7
Norf 69 E6
Shrops 60 D2
Shrops 61 E7
Warks 52 C2
Wilts 24 F4
Stockton Heath . . . 86 F4
Stockton-on-
Tees 102 C2
Stockton on Teme . 50 C2
Stockton on the
Forest 96 D2
Stock Wood 50 D5
Stodmarsh 31 C6
Stody 81 D6
Stoer 156 G3
Stoford Som 12 C3
Wilts 25 F5
Stogumber 22 F2
Stogursey 22 E4
Stoke Devon 8 B4
Hants 15 D8
Hants 26 D2
Medway 30 B2
Suff 57 E5
Stoke Abbott 12 D2
Stoulton 50 E4
Stoke Albany 64 F5
Stoke Ash 56 B5
Stoke Bardolph . . . 77 E6
Stoke Bliss 49 C8
Stoke Bruerne 52 E5
Stoke by Clare 55 E8
Stoke-by-Nayland . 56 F3
Stoke Canon 10 E4
Stoke Charity 26 F2
Stoke Climsland . . . 5 B8
Stoke D'Abernon . . 28 D2
Stoke Doyle 65 F7
Stoke Dry 65 E5
Stoke Farthing . . . 13 B8
Stoke Ferry 67 E7
Stoke Fleming 7 E6
Stoke Gabriel 7 D6
Stoke Gifford 23 B8
Stoke Golding 63 E7
Stoke Goldington . 53 E6
Stoke Green 40 F2
Stokeham 77 B7
Stoke Hammond . . 40 B1
Stoke Heath 61 B6
Stoke Holy Cross . . 68 D5
Stokeinteignhead . . 7 B7
Stoke Lacy 49 E8
Stoke Lyne 39 B5
Stoke Mandeville . 39 C8
Stokenchurch 39 E7
Stoke Newington . 41 F6
Stokenham 7 E6
Stoke on Tern 61 B6
Stoke-on-Trent . . . 75 E5
Stoke Orchard 37 B6
Stoke Poges 40 F2
Stoke Prior
Hereford 49 D7
Worcs 50 C4
Stoke Rivers 20 F5
Stoke Rochford . . . 65 B6
Stoke Row 39 F6
Stoke St Gregory . . 11 B8
Stoke St Mary 11 B7
Stoke
St Michael 23 E8
Stoke
St Milborough . . 61 F5
Stokesay 60 F4
Stokesby 69 C7

Stokesley 102 D3
Stoke sub
Hamdon 12 C2
Stoke Talmage . . . 39 E6
Stoke Trister 12 B5
Stoke Wake 13 D5
Stolford 22 E4
Stondon Massey . . 42 D1
Stone Bucks 39 C7
Glos 36 E3
Kent 19 C6
Kent 29 B6
Staffs 75 F6
S Yorks 89 F6
Worcs 50 B3
Stone Allerton . . . 23 D6
Ston Easton 23 D8
Stone Bridge
Corner 66 D2
Stonebroom 76 D4
Stone Chair 88 B2
Stone Cross E Sus . 18 E3
Kent 31 D7
Stone-edge Batch . 23 B6
Stoneferry 97 F7
Stonefield 119 D6
Stonegate E Sus . . . 18 C3
N Yorks 103 D5
Stonegrave 96 B2
Stonehaugh 109 B7
Stonehaven 141 F7
Stonehouse Glos . . 37 D5
Northumb 109 D6
S Lanark 119 E7
Stone House 100 F2
Stoneleigh 51 B8
Stonely 54 C2
Stoner Hill 15 B8
Stonesby 64 B5
Stonesfield 38 C3
Stone's Green 43 B7
Stone Street Kent . 29 D6
Suff 56 F3
Suff 69 F6
Stonethwaite 98 C4
Stoneybreck 160 N8
Stoneyburn 120 C2
Stoney Cross 14 C3
Stoneygate
Aberds 153 E10
Leicester 64 D3
Stoneyhills 43 E5
Stoneykirk 104 D4
Stoney Middleton . 76 B2
Stoney Stanton . . . 63 E8
Stoney Stoke 24 F2
Stoney Stratton . . . 23 F8
Stoney Stretton . . . 60 D3
Stoneywood
Aberdeen 141 C7
Falk 127 F6
Stonganess 160 C7
Stonham Aspal . . . 56 D5
Stonnall 62 D4
Stonor 39 F7
Stonton Wyville . . 64 E4
Stony Cross 50 E2
Stonyfield 151 D9
Stony Stratford . . . 53 E5
Stoodleigh 10 C4
Stopes 88 F3
Stopham 16 C4
Stopsley 40 B4
Stores Corner 57 E7
Storeton 85 F4
Stornoway 155 D9
Storridge 50 E2
Storrington 16 C4
Storrs 99 E5
Storth 99 F6
Storwood 96 E3
Stotfield 152 A2
Stotfold 54 F3
Stottesdon 61 F6
Stoughton Leics . . 64 D3
Sur 27 D7
W Sus 16 C2
Stoul 147 B10
Stoulton 50 E4
Stourbridge 62 F3
Stourpaine 13 D6
Stourport on
Severn 50 B3
Stour Provost 13 B5
Stour Row 13 B6
Stourton Staffs . . . 62 F2
Warks 51 F7
Wilts 24 F2
Stourton Caundle . . 12 C5
Stove Orkney 159 E7
Shetland 160 L6
Stoven 69 F7
Stow Borders 121 E7
Lincs 78 F3
Lincs 90 F2
Stow Bardolph . . . 67 D6
Stow Bedon 68 E2
Stowbridge 67 D6
Stow cum Quy 55 C6
Stowe 48 B5
Stowe-by-
Chartley 62 B4
Stowe Green 36 D2
Stowell 12 B4
Stowford 9 F6
Stowlangtoft 56 C3
Stow Longa 54 B2
Stow Maries 42 E4
Stowmarket 56 D4
Stow-on-the-
Wold 38 B1
Stowting 30 E5
Stowupland 56 D4
Straad 145 G9
Strachan 141 E5
Stradbroke 57 B6
Stradishall 55 D8
Stradsett 67 D6
Stragglethorpe . . . 78 D2
Straid 112 E1
Straith 113 F8
Straiton Edin 121 C5
S Ayrs 112 D3
Straloch Aberds . . 141 B7
Perth 133 C7
Stramshall 75 F7
Strang 84 E3
Stranraer 104 C4

Stratfield
Mortimer 26 C4
Stratfield Saye . . . 26 C4
Stratfield Turgis . . 26 D4
Stratford 41 F6
Stratford
St Andrew 57 C7
Stratford St Mary . 56 F4
Stratford Sub
Castle 25 F6
Stratford Tony . . . 13 B8
Stratford-upon-
Avon 51 D6
Strath Highld . . . 149 A12
Highld 158 E4
Strathan Highld . . 136 E2
Highld 156 G3
Highld 157 C8
Strathaven 119 E7
Strathblane 119 B5
Strathcanaird . . . 156 J4
Strathcarron 150 G2
Strathcoil 124 B2
Strathdon 140 C2
Strathellie 153 B10
Strathkinness . . . 129 C6
Strathmashie
House 137 E8
Strathmiglo 128 C4
Strathmore
Lodge 158 F3
Strathpeffer 150 F7
Strathrannoch . . . 150 D6
Strathtay 133 D6
Strathvaich
Lodge 150 D6
Strathwhillan . . . 143 E11
Strathy 157 C11
Strathyre 126 C4
Stratton Corn 8 D4
Dorset 12 E4
Glos 37 D7
Stratton Audley . . 39 B6
Stratton on the
Fosse 23 D8
Stratton
St Margaret 38 F1
Stratton
St Michael 68 E5
Stratton Strawless 81 E8
Stravithie 129 C7
Streat 17 C7
Streatham 28 B4
Streatley C Beds . . 40 B3
W Berks 39 F5
Street Lancs 92 D5
N Yorks 103 D5
Som 23 F6
Street Dinas 73 F7
Street End Kent . . . 30 D5
W Sus 16 E2
Street Gate 110 D5
Streethay 62 C5
Streetlam 101 E8
Streetly 62 E4
Street Lydan 73 F8
Streetly End 55 E7
Strefford 60 F4
Strelley 76 E5
Strensall 96 C2
Stretcholt 22 E4
Strete 7 E6
Stretford 87 E6
Strethall 55 F5
Stretham 55 B6
Strettington 16 D2
Stretton Ches W . . 73 D8
Derbys 76 C3
Rutland 65 C6
Staffs 62 C2
Staffs 63 B6
Warr 86 F4
Stretton
Grandison 49 E8
Stretton-on-
Dunsmore 52 B2
Stretton-on-Fosse 51 F7
Stretton Sugwas . . 49 E6
Stretton under
Fosse 63 F8
Stretton
Westwood 61 E5
Strichen 153 C9
Strines 87 F7
Stringston 22 E3
Strixton 53 C7
Stroat 36 E2
Stromeferry 149 E13
Stromemore 149 E13
Stromness 159 H3
Stronaba 136 F5
Stronachlachar . . 126 C3
Stronchreggan . . . 130 C4
Stronchrubie 156 H5
Strone Argyll 145 E10
Highld 136 F4
Highld 137 B8
Invclyd 118 B2
Stronmilchan . . . 125 C7
Strontian 130 C2
Strood 29 C8
Strood Green Sur . 28 E3
W Sus 16 B4
W Sus 28 F2
Stroud Glos 37 D5
Hants 15 B8
Stroud Green 42 E4
Stroxton 78 F2
Struan Highld . . . 149 E8
Perth 133 C5
Strubby 91 F8
Strumpshaw 69 D6
Strutherhill 119 E7
Struy 150 H6
Stryd-issa 73 E6
Stryt-issa 73 E6
Stuartfield 153 D9
Stubbington 15 D6
Stubbins 87 C5
Stubbs Cross 19 B6
Stubbs Green 69 E6
Stubb's Green 69 E6
Stubhampton 13 C7
Stub Place 98 E2
Stubton 77 E8
Stuckgowan 126 C2
Studdal 31 E7
Studham 40 C3
Studland 13 F8

Studley Warks . . . 51 C5
Wilts 24 B4
Studley Roger 95 B5
Stump Cross 55 E6
Stuntney 55 B6
Sturbridge 74 F5
Sturmer 55 E7
Sturminster
Marshall 13 D7
Sturminster
Newton 13 C5
Sturry 31 C5
Sturton 90 D3
Sturton by Stow . . 90 F2
Sturton le Steeple . 89 F8
Stuston 56 B5
Stutton N Yorks . . . 95 E7
Suff 57 F5
Styal 87 F6
Styrrup 89 E7
Suainebost 155 A10
Suardail 155 D9
Succoth Aberds . . 152 E4
Argyll 125 E8
Suckley 50 D2
Suckquoy 159 K5
Sudborough 65 F6
Sudbourne 57 D8
Sudbrook Lincs . . . 78 E2
Mon 36 F2
Sudbrooke 78 B3
Sudbury Derbys . . 75 F8
London 40 F4
Suff 56 E2
Suddie 151 F9
Sudgrove 37 D6
Suffield Norf 81 D8
N Yorks 103 E7
Sugnall 74 F4
Sugwas Pool 49 E6
Suladale 149 C8
Sulaisiadar 155 D10
Sulby 84 C3
Sulgrave 52 E3
Sulham 26 B4
Sulhamstead 26 C4
Sulland 159 D6
Sullington 16 C4
Sullom 160 F5
Sullom Voe Oil
Terminal 160 F5
Sully 22 C3
Sumburgh 160 N6
Summer Bridge . . 94 C5
Summercourt 4 D3
Summerfield 80 D3
Summergangs . . . 97 F7
Summer-house . . 101 C7
Summerleaze 35 F8
Summersdale 16 D2
Summerseat 87 C5
Summertown 39 D5
Summit 87 D7
Sunbury-on-
Thames 28 C2
Sundaywell 113 F8
Sunderland Argyll 142 B3
Cumb 107 F8
T&W 111 D6
Sunderland
Bridge 111 F5
Sundhope 115 B6
Sundon Park 40 B3
Sundridge 29 D5
Sunipol 146 F6
Sunk Island 91 C6
Sunningdale 27 C7
Sunninghill 27 C7
Sunningwell 38 D4
Sunniside Durham 110 F4
T&W 110 D5
Sunnyhurst 86 B4
Sunnylaw 127 E6
Sunnyside 28 F4
Sunton 25 D7
Surbiton 28 C2
Surby 84 E2
Surfleet 66 B2
Surfleet Seas End . 66 B2
Surlingham 69 D6
Sustead 81 D7
Susworth 90 D2
Sutcombe 8 C5
Suton 68 E3
Sutors of
Cromarty 151 E11
Sutterby 79 B6
Sutterton 79 F5
Sutton Cambs 54 B5
C Beds 54 E3
Kent 31 E7
London 28 C3
Mers 86 E3
Norf 69 B6
Notts 77 F7
Notts 89 F7
N Yorks 89 B5
Oxon 38 D4
Pboro 65 E7
Shrops 61 F7
Shrops 74 F3
Som 23 F8
Staffs 61 B7
Suff 57 E7
Sur 27 E8
S Yorks 89 C6
W Sus 16 C3
Sutton at Hone . . . 29 B6
Sutton Bassett . . . 64 E4
Sutton Benger . . . 24 B4
Sutton Bonington . 64 B2
Sutton Bridge 66 B4
Sutton Cheney . . . 63 D8
Sutton Coldfield . . 62 E5
Sutton Courtenay . 39 E5
Sutton Crosses . . . 66 B4
Sutton Grange . . . 95 B5
Sutton Green 27 D8
Sutton Howgrave . 95 B6
Sutton in Ashfield . 76 D4
Sutton-in-Craven . 94 E3
Sutton in the
Elms 64 E2
Sutton Ings 97 F7
Sutton Lane Ends . 75 B6
Sutton Leach 86 E3
Sutton Maddock . . 61 D7
Sutton Mallet 23 F5
Sutton Mandeville 13 B7
Sutton Manor 86 E3
Sutton Montis 12 B4

Sutton on Hull . . . 97 F7
Sutton on Sea 91 F9
Sutton-on-the-
Forest 95 C8
Sutton on the Hill . 76 F2
Sutton on Trent . . . 77 C7
Sutton St Edmund . 66 C3
Sutton St James . . 66 C3
Sutton St Nicholas . 49 E7
Sutton Scarsdale . . 76 C4
Sutton Scotney . . . 26 F2
Sutton under
Brailes 51 F8
Sutton-under-
Whitestonecliffe
. . . . 102 F2
Sutton upon
Derwent 96 E3
Sutton Valence . . . 30 E2
Sutton Veny 24 E3
Sutton Waldron . . 13 C6
Sutton Weaver . . . 74 B2
Sutton Wick 23 D7
Swaby 79 B6
Swadlincote 63 C7
Swaffham 67 D8
Swaffham Bulbeck 55 C6
Swaffham Prior . . . 55 C6
Swafield 81 D8
Swainby 102 D2
Swainshill 49 E6
Swainsthorpe 68 D5
Swainswick 24 C2
Swalcliffe 51 F8
Swalecliffe 30 C5
Swallow 90 D5
Swallowcliffe 13 B7
Swallowfield 26 C5
Swallownest 89 F5
Swallows Cross . . . 42 E2
Swanage 13 G8
Swanbister 159 H4
Swanbourne 39 B8
Swan Green
Ches W 74 B4
Suff 57 B6
Swanland 90 B3
Swanley 29 C6
Swanley Village . . 29 C6
Swanmore 15 C6
Swannington Leics 63 C8
Norf 68 C4
Swanscombe 29 B7
Swansea
= Abertawe 33 E7
Swanton Abbott . . 81 E8
Swanton Morley . . 68 C3
Swanton Novers . . 81 D6
Swanton Street . . . 30 D2
Swanwick Derbys . 76 D4
Hants 15 D6
Swarby 78 E3
Swardeston 68 D5
Swarister 160 E7
Swarkestone 63 B7
Swarland 117 D7
Swarland Estate . . 117 D7
Swarthmoor 92 B2
Swathwick 76 C3
Swaton 78 F4
Swavesey 54 C4
Sway 14 E3
Swayfield 65 B6
Swaythling 14 C5
Sweet Green 49 C8
Sweetham 10 E3
Sweethouse 5 C5
Sweffling 57 C7
Swepstone 63 C7
Swerford 51 F8
Swettenham 74 C5
Swetton 94 B4
Swffryd 35 E6
Swiftsden 18 C4
Swilland 57 D5
Swillington 95 F6
Swimbridge 9 B8
Swimbridge
Newland 20 F5
Swinbrook 38 C2
Swinderby 77 C8
Swindon Glos 37 B6
Staffs 62 E2
Swindon 38 F1
Swine 97 F7
Swinefleet 89 B8
Swineshead
Bedford 53 C8
Lincs 78 E5
Swineshead
Bridge 78 E5
Swiney 158 G4
Swinford Leics . . . 52 B3
Oxon 38 D4
Swingate 76 E5
Swingfield Minnis . 31 E6
Swingfield Street . 31 E6
Swinhoe 117 B8
Swinhope 91 E6
Swining 160 G6
Swinithwaite 101 F5
Swinnow Moor . . . 94 F5
Swinscoe 75 E8
Swinside Hall 116 C3
Swinstead 65 B7
Swinton Borders . 122 E4
Gtr Man 87 D5
N Yorks 94 B5
N Yorks 96 B3
S Yorks 88 E5
Swintonmill 122 E4
Swithland 64 C2
Swordale 151 E8
Swordland 147 B10
Swordly 157 C10
Sworton Heath . . . 86 F4
Swyddffynnon . . . 47 C5
Swyre 12 F3
Sychtyn 59 D6
Syde 37 C6
Sydenham London . 28 B4
Oxon 39 D7
Sydenham Damerel 6 B2
Syderstone 80 D4
Sydling
St Nicholas 12 E4
Sydmonton 26 D2
Syerston 77 E7

Syke 87 C6
Sykehouse 89 C7
Sykes 93 D6
Sylen 33 D6
Symbister 160 G7
Symington S Ayrs . 118 F3
S Lanark 120 F2
Symondsbury 12 E2
Symonds Yat 36 C2
Synod Inn 46 D3
Syre 157 E9
Syreford 37 B7
Syresham 52 E4
Syston Leics 64 C3
Lincs 78 E2
Sytchampton 50 C3
Sywell 53 C6

T

Taagan 150 E3
Tàbost 155 A10
Tabost 155 F8
Tackley 38 B4
Tacleit 154 D6
Tacolneston 68 E4
Tadcaster 95 E7
Taddington 75 B8
Taddiport 9 C6
Tadley 26 C4
Tadlow 54 E3
Tadmarton 51 F8
Tadworth 28 D3
Tafarnau-bach . . . 35 C5
Tafarn-y-gelyn . . . 73 C5
Taff's Well 35 F5
Tafolwern 59 D5
Tai 83 E7
Taibach 34 F1
Tai-bach 59 B8
Taigh a
Ghearraidh 148 A2
Tai-mawr 72 E3
Tain Highld 151 C10
Highld 158 D4
Tainant 73 E6
Tainlon 82 F4
Tairbeart
= Tarbert 154 G6
Tai'r-Bull 34 B3
Tairgwaith 33 C8
Tai-Ucha 72 D4
Takeley 42 B1
Takeley Street . . . 41 B8
Talachddu 48 F2
Talacre 85 F2
Talardd 59 B5
Talaton 11 E5
Talbenny 44 D3
Talbot Green 34 F4
Talbot Village 13 E8
Tale 11 D5
Talerddig 59 D6
Talgarreg 46 D3
Talgarth 48 F3
Talisker 149 E8
Talke 74 D5
Talkin 109 D5
Talladale 150 D2
Talla Linnfoots . . . 114 B4
Tallarn Green 73 E8
Tallentire 107 F8
Talley 46 F5
Tallington 65 D7
Talmine 157 C8
Talog 32 B4
Talsarn 34 B1
Tal-sarn 46 D4
Talsarnau 71 D7
Talskiddy 4 C4
Talwrn Anglesey . . 82 D4
Wrex 73 D6
Tal-y-bont Ceredig . 58 F3
Conwy 83 E7
Gwyn 71 E6
Gwyn 83 D7
Talybont-on-Usk . . 35 B5
Tal-y-cafn 83 D7
Talygarn 34 F4
Talyllyn 35 B5
Tal-y-llyn 58 D4
Talysarn 82 F4
Talywain 35 D6
Tal-y-wern 58 D5
Tame Bridge 102 D3
Tamerton Foliot . . . 6 C2
Tamworth 63 D6
Tandem 88 C2
Tanden 19 B6
Tandridge 28 D4
Tanerdy 33 B5
Tanfield 110 D4
Tanfield Lea 110 D4
Tangiers 44 D4
Tangley 25 D8
Tanglwst 46 F2
Tangmere 16 D3
Tan Hinon 59 F5
Tankersley 88 D4
Tankerton 30 C5
Tan-lan Conwy . . . 83 E7
Gwyn 71 C7
Tannach 158 F5
Tannachie 141 F6
Tannadice 134 D4
Tannington 57 C6
Tansley 76 D3
Tansley Knoll 76 C3
Tansor 65 E7
Tantobie 110 D4
Tanton 102 C3
Tanworth-in-
Arden 51 B6
Tan-y-bwlch 71 C7
Tan-y-fron 72 C3
Tan-y-graig
Anglesey 82 D5
Gwyn 70 D4
Tanygrisiau 71 C7
Tan-y-groes 45 E4
Tan-y-pistyll 59 B7
Tan-yr-allt 82 F4
Tanyrhydiau 47 C6
Taobh a Chaolais 148 G2
Taobh a' Ghlinne . 155 F8

Taobh a Thuath Loch
Aineort 148 F2
Taobh a Tuath Loch
Baghasdail 148 F2
Taobh Tuath 154 J4
Tapeley 9 B6
Taplow 40 F2
Tapton 76 B3
Tarbat House . . . 151 D10
Tarbert Argyll . . . 143 C7
Argyll 144 E5
Argyll 145 G7
Tarbert
= Tairbeart . . . 154 G6
Tarbet Argyll 126 D2
Highld 147 B10
Highld 156 E4
Tarbock Green . . . 86 F2
Tarbolton 112 B4
Tarbrax 120 D3
Tardebigge 50 C5
Tarfside 134 B4
Tarland 140 D3
Tarleton 86 B2
Tarlogie 151 C10
Tarlscough 86 C2
Tarlton 37 E6
Tarnbrook 93 D5
Tarporley 74 C2
Tarr 22 F3
Tarrant Crawford . 13 D7
Tarrant Gunville . . 13 C7
Tarrant Hinton . . . 13 C7
Tarrant Keyneston 13 D7
Tarrant
Launceston 13 D7
Tarrant Monkton . 13 D7
Tarrant Rawston . . 13 D7
Tarrant Rushton . . 13 D7
Tarrel 151 C11
Tarring Neville . . . 17 D8
Tarrington 49 E8
Tarsappie 128 B3
Tarskavaig 149 H10
Tarves 153 E8
Tarvie Highld 150 F7
Perth 133 C7
Tarvin 73 C8
Tasburgh 68 E5
Tasley 61 E6
Taston 38 B3
Tatenhill 63 B6
Tathall End 53 E6
Tatham 93 C6
Tathwell 91 F7
Tatling End 40 F3
Tatsfield 28 D5
Tattenhall 73 D8
Tattenhoe 53 F6
Tatterford 80 E4
Tattersett 80 D4
Tattershall 78 D5
Tattershall Bridge 78 D4
Tattershall Thorpe 78 D5
Tattingstone 56 F5
Tatworth 11 D8
Taunton 11 B7
Taverham 68 C4
Tavernspite 32 C2
Tavistock 6 B2
Taw Green 9 E8
Tawstock 9 B7
Taxal 75 B7
Tay Bridge 129 B6
Tayinloan 143 D7
Taymouth Castle . 132 E4
Taynish 144 E6
Taynton Glos 36 C4
Oxon 38 C2
Taynuilt 125 B6
Tayport 129 B6
Tayvallich 144 E6
Tealby 91 E5
Tealing 134 F4
Teangue 149 H11
Teanna Mhachair . 148 B2
Tebay 99 D8
Tebworth 40 B2
Tedburn St Mary . . 10 E3
Teddington Glos . . 50 F4
London 28 B2
Tedstone
Delamere 49 D8
Tedstone Wafre . . 49 D8
Teeton 52 B4
Teffont Evias 24 F4
Teffont Magna . . . 24 F4
Tegryn 45 F4
Teigh 65 C5
Teigncombe 9 F8
Teigngrace 7 B6
Teignmouth 7 B7
Telford 61 D6
Telham 18 D4
Tellisford 24 D3
Telscombe 17 D7
Telscombe Cliffs . . 17 D7
Templand 114 F3
Temple Corn 5 B6
Glasgow 118 C5
Midloth 121 D6
Temple Balsall . . . 51 B7
Temple Bar Carms . 33 C6
Ceredig 46 D4
Temple Cloud 23 D8
Temple Combe . . . 12 B5
Temple Ewell 31 E6
Temple Grafton . . 51 D6
Temple Guiting . . 37 B7
Templehall 128 E3
Temple
Herdewyke 51 D8
Temple Hirst 89 B7
Temple
Normanton 76 C4
Temple Sowerby . . 99 B8
Templeton Devon . 10 C3
Pembs 32 C2
Templeton Bridge . 10 C3
Templetown 110 D4
Tempsford 54 D2
Tenbury Wells . . . 49 C7
Tenby
= Dinbych-y-Pysgod 32 D2
Tendring 43 B7
Tendring Green . . 43 B7
Ten Mile Bank . . . 67 E6
Tenston 159 G3
Tenterden 19 B5

Ternhill 74 F3
Terregles Banks . . 107 B6
Terrick 39 D8
Terrington 96 B2
Terrington
St Clement 66 C5
Terrington
St John 66 C5
Teston 29 D8
Testwood 14 C4
Tetbury 37 E5
Tetbury Upton . . . 37 E5
Tetchill 73 F7
Tetcott 8 E5
Tetford 79 B6
Tetney 91 D7
Tetney Lock 91 D7
Tetsworth 39 D6
Tettenhall 62 E2
Teuchan 153 E10
Teversal 76 C4
Teversham 55 D5
Teviothead 115 D7
Tewel 141 F7
Tewin 41 C5
Tewkesbury 50 F3
Teynham 30 C3
Thackthwaite 98 C3
Thainston 135 B6
Thakeham 16 C5
Thame 39 D7
Thames Ditton . . . 28 C2
Thames Haven . . . 42 F3
Thamesmead 41 F7
Thanington 30 D5
Thankerton 120 F2
Tharston 68 E4
Thatcham 26 C3
Thatto Heath 86 E3
Thaxted 55 F7
The Aird 149 C9
Theakston 101 F8
Thealby 90 C2
Theale Som 23 E6
W Berks 26 B4
The Arms 67 E8
Thearne 97 F6
The Bage 48 E4
The Balloch 127 C7
The Barony 159 F3
Theberton 57 C8
The Bog 60 E3
The Bourne 27 E6
The Braes 149 E10
The Broad 49 C6
The Butts 24 E2
The Camp Glos . . . 37 D6
Herts 40 D4
The Chequer 73 E8
The City 39 E7
The Common 25 F7
The Craigs 150 B7
The Cronk 84 C3
Theddingworth . . 64 F3
Theddlethorpe All
Saints 91 F8
Theddlethorpe
St Helen 69 E7
The Dell 69 E7
The Den 118 D3
The Eals 116 F3
The Eaves 36 D3
The Flatt 109 B5
The Four Alls 74 F3
The Garths 160 B8
The Green Cumb . . 98 F3
Wilts 24 F3
The Grove 107 B6
The Hall 160 D8
The Haven 27 F8
The Heath Norf . . 81 D7
Suff 56 F5
The Hill 98 F3
The Howe Cumb . . 99 F6
IoM 84 F1
The Hundred 49 C7
Thelbridge Barton 10 C2
The Lee 40 D2
The Lhen 84 B3
Thelnetham 56 B4
Thelveton 68 F4
Thelwall 86 F4
The Marsh Powys . 60 E3
Wilts 37 F7
Themelthorpe . . . 81 E6
The Middles 110 D5
The Moor 18 C4
The Mumbles
= Y Mwmbwls . . 33 F7
The Murray 119 D6
The Neuk 141 E6
Thenford 52 E3
The Oval 24 C2
The Pole of Itlaw 153 C6
The Quarry 36 E4
Therfield 54 F4
The Rhos 32 C1
The Rock 61 D6
The Ryde 41 D5
The Sands 27 E6
The Stocks 19 C5
Thetford Lincs . . . 65 C8
Norf 67 F8
The Throat 27 C6
The Vauld 49 E7
The Wyke 61 D7
Theydon Bois . . . 41 E7
Thickwood 24 B3
Thimbleby Lincs . . 78 C5
N Yorks 102 E2
Thingwall 85 F3
Thirdpart 118 E1
Thirlby 102 F2
Thirlestane 121 E8
Thirn 101 F7
Thirsk 102 F2
Thirtleby 97 F7
Thistleton Lancs . . 92 F4
Rutland 65 C6
Thistley Green . . . 55 B7
Thixendale 96 C4
Thockrington . . . 110 B2
Tholomas Drove . . 66 D3
Tholthorpe 95 C7
Thomas Chapel . . 32 D2
Thomas Close . . . 108 E4

Thomastown.....152 E5
Thompson.....68 E2
Thomshill.....152 C2
Thong.....29 B7
Thongsbridge.....88 D2
Thoralby.....101 F5
Thoresway.....91 E5
Thorganby Lincs.....91 E6
 N Yorks.....96 E2
Thorgill.....103 E5
Thorington.....57 B8
Thorington Street.....56 F4
Thorlby.....94 D2
Thorley.....41 C7
Thorley Street
 Herts.....41 C7
 IoW.....14 F4
Thormanby.....95 B7
Thornaby-on-
 Tees.....102 C2
Thornage.....81 D6
Thornborough
 Bucks.....52 F5
 N Yorks.....95 B5
Thornbury Devon.....9 D6
 Hereford.....49 D8
 S Glos.....36 E3
 W Yorks.....94 F4
Thornby.....52 B4
Thorncliffe.....75 D7
Thorncombe
 Dorset.....11 D8
 Dorset.....13 D6
Thorncombe
 Street.....27 E8
Thorncote Green.....54 E2
Thorncross.....14 F5
Thorndon.....56 C5
Thorndon Cross.....9 E7
Thorne.....89 C7
Thorner.....95 E6
Thorne
 St Margaret.....11 B5
Thorney Notts.....77 B8
 Pboro.....66 D2
Thorney Crofts.....91 B6
Thorney Green.....56 C4
Thorney Hill.....14 E2
Thorney Toll.....66 D3
Thornfalcon.....11 B7
Thornford.....12 C4
Thorngumbald.....91 B6
Thornham.....80 C3
Thornham Magna.....56 B5
Thornham Parva.....56 B5
Thornhaugh.....65 D7
Thornhill Cardiff.....35 F5
 Cumb.....98 D2
 Derbys.....88 F2
 Dumfries.....113 E8
 Soton.....15 C5
 Stirling.....127 E5
 W Yorks.....88 C3
Thornhill Edge.....88 C3
Thornhill Lees.....88 C3
Thornholme.....97 C7
Thornley Durham.....110 F4
 Durham.....111 F6
Thornliebank.....118 D5
Thorns.....55 D8
Thornsett.....87 F8
Thorns Green.....87 F5
Thornthwaite Cumb 98 B4
 N Yorks.....94 D4
Thornton Angus..134 E3
 Bucks.....53 F5
 E Yorks.....96 E3
 Fife.....128 E4
 Lancs.....92 E3
 Leics.....63 D8
 Lincs.....78 C5
 Mbro.....102 C2
 Mers.....85 D4
 Northumb.....123 E5
 Pembs.....44 E4
 W Yorks.....94 F4
Thornton Curtis..90 C4
Thorntonhall.....119 D5
Thornton Heath.....28 C4
Thornton Hough.....85 F4
Thornton in
 Craven.....94 E2
Thornton-le-
 Beans.....102 E1
Thornton-le-Clay.96 C2
Thornton-le-
 Dale.....103 F6
Thornton le Moor.90 E4
Thornton-le-
 Moor.....102 F1
Thornton-le-
 Moors.....73 B8
Thornton-le-
 Street.....102 F2
Thorntonloch.....122 B3
Thorntonpark.....122 E5
Thornton Rust.....100 F4
Thornton
 Steward.....101 F6
Thornton Watlass 101 F7
Thornwood
 Common.....41 D7
Thornydykes.....122 E2
Thoroton.....77 E7
Thorp Arch.....95 E7
Thorpe Derbys.....75 D8
 E Yorks.....97 E5
 Lincs.....91 F8
 Norf.....69 E7
 Notts.....77 E7
 N Yorks.....94 C3
 Sur.....27 C8
Thorpe Abbotts.....57 B5
Thorpe Acre.....64 B2
Thorpe Arnold.....64 B4
Thorpe Audlin.....89 C5
Thorpe Bassett.....96 B4
Thorpe Bay.....43 F5
Thorpe by Water..65 E5
Thorpe Common.57 F6
Thorpe
 Constantine.....63 D6
Thorpe Culvert.....79 C7
Thorpe End.....69 C5
Thorpe Fendykes..79 C7

Thorpe Green
 Essex.....43 B7
 Suff.....56 D3
Thorpe Hesley.....88 E4
Thorpe in Balne..89 C6
Thorpe in the
 Fallows.....90 F3
Thorpe Langton....64 E4
Thorpe Larches..102 B1
Thorpe-le-Soken.43 B7
Thorpe le Street..96 E4
Thorpe Malsor.....53 B6
Thorpe Mandeville 52 E3
Thorpe Market.....81 D8
Thorpe Marriott...68 C4
Thorpe Morieux...56 D3
Thorpeness.....57 D8
Thorpe on the Hill.78 C2
Thorpe St Andrew.69 D5
Thorpe St Peter...79 C7
Thorpe Salvin.....89 F6
Thorpe Satchville.64 C4
Thorpe Thewles..102 B2
Thorpe Tilney.....78 D4
Thorpe
 Underwood.....95 D7
Thorpe Waterville.65 F7
Thorpe Willoughby 95 F8
Thorrington.....43 C6
Thorverton.....10 D4
Thrandeston.....56 B5
Thrapston.....53 B7
Thrashbush.....119 C7
Threapland Cumb 107 F8
 N Yorks.....94 C2
Threapwood
 Ches W.....73 E8
 Staffs.....75 E7
Three Ashes.....36 B2
Three Bridges.....28 F3
Three Burrows.....3 B6
Three Chimneys..18 B5
Three Cocks.....48 F3
Three Crosses.....33 E6
Three Cups
 Corner.....18 C3
Threehammer
 Common.....69 C6
Three Holes.....66 D5
Threekingham.....78 F3
Three Leg Cross..18 B3
Three Legged
 Cross.....13 D8
Threemile Cross..26 C5
Threemilestone.....3 B6
Threemiletown..120 B3
Three Oaks.....18 D5
Threlkeld.....99 B5
Threshfield.....94 C2
Thrigby.....69 C7
Thringarth.....100 B4
Thringstone.....63 C8
Thrintoft.....101 E8
Thriplow.....54 E5
Throckenholt.....66 D3
Throcking.....54 F4
Throckley.....110 C4
Throckmorton.....50 E4
Throphill.....117 F7
Thropton.....117 D6
Throsk.....127 E7
Throwleigh.....9 E8
Throwley.....30 D3
Thrumpton.....76 F5
Thrumster.....158 F5
Thrunton.....117 C6
Thrupp Glos.....37 D5
 Oxon.....38 C4
Thrushelton.....9 F6
Thrussington.....64 C3
Thruxton Hants..25 E7
 Hereford.....49 F6
Thrybergh.....89 E5
Thulston.....76 F4
Thundergay.....143 D9
Thundersley.....42 F3
Thundridge.....41 C6
Thurcaston.....64 C2
Thurcroft.....89 F5
Thurgarton Norf..81 D7
 Notts.....77 E6
Thurgoland.....88 D3
Thurlaston Leics.64 E2
 Warks.....52 B2
Thurlbear.....11 B7
Thurlby Lincs.....65 C8
 Lincs.....78 C2
Thurleigh.....53 D8
Thurlestone.....6 E4
Thurloxton.....22 F4
Thurlstone.....88 D3
Thurlton.....69 E7
Thurlwood.....74 D5
Thurmaston.....64 D3
Thurnby.....64 D3
Thurne.....69 C7
Thurnham Kent..30 D2
 Lancs.....92 D4
Thurning Norf.....81 E6
 Northants.....65 F7
Thurnscoe.....89 D5
Thurnscoe East..89 D5
Thursby.....108 D3
Thursford.....81 D5
Thursley.....27 F7
Thurso.....158 D3
Thurso East.....158 D3
Thurstaston.....85 F3
Thurston.....56 C3
Thurstonfield..108 D3
Thurstonland.....88 C2
Thurton.....69 D6
Thurvaston.....76 F2
Thuxton.....68 D3
Thwaite N Yorks.100 E3
 Suff.....56 C5
Thwaites.....94 E3
Thwaite St Mary.69 E6
Thwaites Brow..94 E3
Thwing.....97 B6
Tibbermore.....128 B2
Tibberton Glos.....36 B4
 Telford.....61 B6
 Worcs.....50 D4
Tibenham.....68 F4
Tibshelf.....76 C4
Tibthorpe.....97 D5
Ticehurst.....18 B3
Tichborne.....26 F3

Tickencote.....65 D6
Tickenham.....23 B6
Tickhill.....89 E6
Ticklerton.....60 E4
Ticknall.....63 B7
Tickton.....97 E6
Tidcombe.....25 D7
Tiddington Oxon.39 D6
 Warks.....51 D7
Tidebrook.....18 C3
Tideford.....5 D8
Tideford Cross.....5 C8
Tidenham.....36 E2
Tideswell.....75 B8
Tidmarsh.....26 B4
Tidmington.....51 F7
Tidpit.....13 C8
Tidworth.....25 E7
Tiers Cross.....44 D4
Tiffield.....52 D4
Tifty.....153 D7
Tigerton.....135 C5
Tigh-na-Blair..127 C6
Tighnabruaich..145 F8
Tighnafiline.....155 J13
Tigley.....7 C5
Tilbrook.....53 C8
Tilbury.....29 B7
Tilbury Juxta Clare 55 F8
Tile Cross.....63 F5
Tile Hill.....51 B7
Tilehurst.....26 B4
Tilford.....27 E6
Tilgate.....28 F3
Tilgate Forest Row 28 F3
Tillathrowie.....152 E4
Tilley.....60 B5
Tillicoultry.....127 E8
Tillingham.....43 D5
Tillington Hereford.49 E6
 W Sus.....16 B3
Tillington
 Common.....49 E6
Tillyarblet.....135 C5
Tillybirloch.....141 D5
Tillycorthie.....141 B8
Tillydrine.....140 E5
Tillyfour.....140 C4
Tillyfourie.....140 C5
Tillygarmond.....140 E5
Tillygreig.....141 B7
Tillykerrie.....141 B7
Tilmanstone.....31 D7
Tilney All Saints..67 C5
Tilney High End...67 C5
Tilney
 St Lawrence.....66 C5
Tilshead.....24 E5
Tilstock.....74 F2
Tilston.....73 D8
Tilstone Fearnall.74 C2
Tilsworth.....40 B2
Tilton on the Hill.64 D4
Timberland.....78 D4
Timbersbrook.....75 C5
Timberscombe.....21 E8
Timble.....94 D4
Timperley.....87 F5
Timsbury Bath..23 D8
 Hants.....14 B4
Timsgearraidh..154 D5
Timworth Green..56 C2
Tincleton.....13 E5
Tindale.....109 D6
Tingewick.....52 F4
Tingley.....88 B3
Tingrith.....53 F8
Tingwall.....159 F4
Tinhay.....9 F5
Tinshill.....95 F5
Tinsley.....88 E5
Tintagel.....8 F2
Tintern Parva.....36 D2
Tintinhull.....12 C3
Tintwistle.....87 E8
Tinwald.....114 F3
Tinwell.....65 D7
Tipperty.....141 B8
Tipsend.....66 E5
Tipton.....62 E3
Tipton St John...11 E5
Tiptree.....42 C4
Tirabad.....47 E7
Tiraghoil.....146 J6
Tirley.....37 B5
Tirphil.....35 D5
Tir-y-dail.....33 C7
Tisbury.....13 B7
Tisman's Common 27 F8
Tissington.....75 D8
Titchberry.....8 B4
Titchfield.....15 D6
Titchmarsh.....53 B8
Titchwell.....80 C3
Titley.....48 C5
Titlington.....117 C7
Titsey.....28 D5
Tittensor.....75 F5
Tittleshall.....80 E4
Tiverton Ches W.74 C2
 Devon.....10 C4
Tivetshall
 St Margaret.....68 F4
Tivetshall St Mary.68 F4
Tividale.....62 E3
Tivy Dale.....88 D3
Tixall.....62 B3
Tixover.....65 D6
Toab Orkney.....159 H6
 Shetland.....160 M5
Toadmoor.....76 D3
Tobermory.....147 F8
Toberonochy.....124 E3
Tobha Mor.....148 E2
Tobhtarol.....154 D6
Tobson.....154 D6
Tocher.....153 E6
Tockenham.....24 B5
Tockenham Wick.37 F7
Tockholes.....86 B4
Tockington.....36 F3
Tockwith.....95 D7
Todber.....13 B6
Todding.....49 B6
Toddington C Beds 40 B3
 Glos.....50 F5
Todenham.....51 F7

Todhills.....108 C3
Todlachie.....141 C5
Todmorden.....87 B7
Todrig.....115 C7
Todwick.....89 F5
Toft Cambs.....54 D4
 Lincs.....65 C7
Toft Hill Durham.101 B6
Toft Monks.....69 E7
Toft next Newton.90 F4
Toftrees.....80 E4
Tofts.....158 D5
Toftwood.....68 C2
Togston.....117 D8
Tokavaig.....149 G11
Tokers Green.....26 B5
Tolastadh a
 Chaolais.....154 D6
Tolastadh bho
 Thuath.....155 C10
Toll Bar.....89 D6
Tollard Royal.....13 C7
Tollbar End.....51 B8
Toll End.....62 E3
Toller Fratrum..12 E3
Toller Porcorum.12 E3
Tollerton Notts.....77 F6
 N Yorks.....95 C8
Tollesbury.....43 C5
Tolleshunt D'Arcy.43 C5
Tolleshunt Major.43 C5
Toll of Birness..153 E10
Tolm.....155 D9
Tolpuddle.....13 E5
Tolvah.....138 E4
Tolworth.....28 C2
Tomatin.....138 B4
Tombreck.....151 H9
Tomchrasky.....137 C5
Tomdoun.....136 D4
Tomich Highld.....137 B6
 Highld.....151 D9
Tomich House.....151 G8
Tomintoul Aberds.139 E7
 Moray.....139 C7
Tomnaven.....152 E4
Tomnavoulin.....139 B8
Tonbridge.....29 E6
Tondu.....34 F2
Tonfanau.....58 D2
Tong Shrops.....61 D7
 W Yorks.....94 F5
Tonge.....63 B8
Tongham.....27 E6
Tongland.....106 D3
Tong Norton.....61 D7
Tongue.....157 D8
Tongue End.....65 C8
Tongwynlais.....35 F5
Tonna.....34 E1
Ton-Pentre.....34 E3
Tonwell.....41 C6
Tonypandy.....34 E3
Tonyrefail.....34 F4
Toot Baldon.....39 D5
Toothill.....14 C4
Toot Hill.....41 D8
Topcliffe.....95 B7
Topcroft.....69 E5
Topcroft Street..69 E5
Top of Hebers..87 D6
Toppesfield.....55 F8
Toppings.....86 C5
Topsham.....10 F4
Torbay.....7 D7
Torbeg.....143 F10
Torboll Farm.....151 B10
Torbrex.....127 E6
Torbryan.....7 C6
Torcross.....7 E6
Tore.....151 F9
Torinturk.....145 G7
Torksey.....77 B8
Torlum.....148 C2
Torlundy.....131 B5
Tormarton.....24 B2
Tormisdale.....142 C2
Tormitchell.....112 E2
Tormore.....143 E9
Tornagrain.....151 G10
Tornahaish.....139 D8
Tornaveen.....140 D5
Torness.....137 B8
Toronto.....110 F4
Torpenhow.....108 F2
Torphichen.....120 B2
Torphins.....140 D5
Torpoint.....6 D2
Torquay.....7 C7
Torquhan.....121 E7
Torran Argyll.....124 E4
 Highld.....149 D10
 Highld.....151 D10
Torrance.....119 B6
Torrans.....146 J7
Torranyard.....118 E3
Torre.....7 C7
Torridon.....150 F2
Torridon House.149 C13
Torrin.....149 F10
Torrisdale.....157 C9
Torrisholme.....92 C4
Torroble.....157 J8
Torry Aberdeen..141 D8
 Aberds.....152 E4
Torryburn.....128 F2
Torterston.....153 D10
Torthorwald.....107 B7
Tortington.....16 D4
Tortworth.....36 E4
Torver.....98 E4
Torwood.....127 F7
Torworth.....89 F7
Tosberry.....8 B4
Toscaig.....149 E12
Toseland.....54 C3
Tosside.....93 D7
Tostock.....56 C3
Totaig Highld.....148 C7
 Highld.....149 F13
Tote.....149 D9
Totegan.....157 C11
Tothill.....91 F8

Totland.....14 F4
Totnes.....7 C6
Toton.....76 F5
Totronald.....146 F4
Totscore.....149 B8
Tottenham.....41 E6
Tottenhill.....67 C6
Tottenhill Row..67 C6
Totteridge.....41 E5
Totternhoe.....40 B2
Tottington.....87 C5
Totton.....14 C4
Touchen End.....27 B6
Tournaig.....155 J13
Toux.....153 C9
Tovil.....29 D8
Toward.....145 G10
Towcester.....52 E4
Towednack.....2 C3
Tower End.....67 C6
Towersey.....39 D7
Towie Aberds.....140 C3
 Aberds.....153 B8
Towiemore.....152 D3
Tow Law.....110 F4
Townend.....118 B4
Town End Cambs.66 E4
 Cumb.....99 F6
Towngate.....65 C8
Townhead Cumb.108 F5
 Dumfries.....106 E3
 S Ayrs.....112 D2
 S Yorks.....88 D2
Townhead of
 Greenlaw.....106 C4
Townhill.....128 F3
Town Row.....18 B2
Townsend Bucks.39 D7
 Herts.....40 D4
Townshend.....2 C4
Town Yetholm..116 B4
Towthorpe.....96 D2
Towton.....95 F7
Towyn.....72 B3
Toxteth.....85 F4
Toynton All Saints.79 C6
Toynton Fen Side.79 C6
Toynton St Peter.79 C7
Toy's Hill.....29 D5
Trabboch.....112 B4
Traboe.....3 D6
Tradespark
 Highld.....151 F11
 Orkney.....159 H5
Trafford Park.....87 E5
Trallong.....34 B3
Tranent.....121 B7
Tranmere.....85 F4
Trantlebeg.....157 D11
Trantlemore.....157 D11
Tranwell.....117 F7
Trapp.....33 C7
Traprain.....121 B8
Traquair.....121 F6
Trawden.....94 F2
Trawsfynydd.....71 D8
Trealaw.....34 E4
Treales.....92 F4
Trearddur.....82 D2
Treaslane.....149 C8
Trebanog.....34 E4
Trebanos.....33 D8
Trebartha.....5 B7
Trebarwith.....8 F2
Trebetherick.....4 B4
Treborough.....22 F2
Trebudannon.....4 C3
Trebullett.....5 B8
Treburley.....5 B8
Trebyan.....5 C5
Trecastle.....34 B2
Trecenydd.....35 F5
Trecwn.....44 B4
Trecynon.....34 D3
Tredavoe.....2 D3
Treddiog.....44 C3
Tredegar.....35 D5
Tredegar = Newydd
 New Tredegar.35 D5
Tredington Glos.....37 B6
 Warks.....51 E7
Tredinnick.....4 B4
Tredomen.....48 F3
Tredunnock.....35 E7
Tredustan.....48 F3
Treen.....2 D2
Treeton.....88 F5
Trefaldwyn
 = Montgomery.60 D2
Trefasser.....44 B3
Trefdraeth
 = Newport.....45 F2
Trefecca.....48 F3
Trefechan.....58 F2
Trefeglwys.....59 E6
Trefenter.....46 C5
Treffgarne.....44 C4
Treffynnon
 = Holywell.....73 B5
Trefgarn Owen..44 C3
Trefil.....35 C5
Trefilan.....46 D4
Treflach.....60 B2
Trefnanney.....60 C2
Trefnant.....72 B4
Trefonen.....60 B2
Trefor Anglesey.....82 C3
 Gwyn.....70 C4
Treforest.....34 F4
Trefriw.....83 E7
Tref-y-Clawdd
 = Knighton.....48 B4
Trefynwy
 = Monmouth.....36 C2
Tregadillett.....8 F4
Tregaian.....82 D4
Tregare.....35 C8
Tregaron.....47 D5
Tregarth.....83 E6
Tregeare.....8 F4
Tregeiriog.....73 F5
Tregele.....82 B3
Tregidden.....3 D6
Treglemais.....44 C3
Tregole.....8 E3

Tregonetha.....4 C4
Tregony.....3 B8
Tregoss.....4 C4
Tregoyd.....48 F4
Tregroes.....46 E3
Tregurrian.....4 C3
Tregynon.....59 E7
Trehafod.....34 E4
Treharris.....34 E4
Treherbert.....34 E3
Trekenner.....5 B8
Treknow.....8 F2
Trelan.....3 E6
Trelash.....8 E3
Trelassick.....4 D3
Trelawnyd.....72 B4
Trelech.....45 F4
Treleddyd-fawr..44 C2
Trelewis.....35 E5
Treligga.....8 F2
Trelights.....4 B4
Trelill.....4 B5
Trelissick.....3 C7
Trellech.....36 D2
Trelleck Grange..36 D1
Trelogan.....85 F2
Tremadog.....71 C6
Tremail.....8 F3
Tremain.....45 E4
Tremaine.....8 F4
Tremar.....5 C7
Trematon.....5 D8
Tremeirchion.....72 B4
Trenance.....4 C3
Trenarren.....3 B9
Trench.....61 C6
Treneglos.....8 F4
Trenewan.....5 D6
Trent.....12 C3
Trentham.....75 E5
Trentishoe.....20 E5
Trent Vale.....75 E5
Treoes.....21 B8
Treorchy = Treorci.34 E3
Treorci = Treorchy.34 E3
Tre'r-ddôl.....58 E3
Trerulefoot.....5 D8
Tresaith.....45 D4
Tresawle.....3 B7
Trescott.....62 E2
Trescowe.....2 C4
Tresham.....36 E4
Tresillian.....3 B7
Tresinwen.....44 A4
Treskinnick Cross.8 E3
Tresmeer.....8 F4
Tresparrett.....8 E3
Tresparrett Posts.8 E3
Tressait.....133 C5
Tresta Shetland.....160 D8
 Shetland.....160 H5
Treswell.....77 B7
Tre-Taliesin.....58 E3
Trethosa.....4 D4
Trethurgy.....4 D5
Tretio.....44 C2
Tretire.....36 B2
Tretower.....35 B5
Treuddyn.....73 D6
Trevalga.....8 F2
Trevalyn.....73 D7
Trevanson.....4 B4
Trevarren.....4 C4
Trevarrick.....3 B8
Tre-vaughan.....32 C2
Trevaughan.....32 B4
Treveighan.....5 B5
Trevellas.....4 D2
Treverva.....3 C6
Trevethin.....35 D6
Trevigro.....5 C8
Treviscoe.....4 D4
Trevone.....4 B3
Trewarmett.....8 F2
Trewassa.....8 F3
Trewellard.....2 C2
Trewen.....8 F4
Trewennack.....3 D5
Trewern.....60 C2
Trewethern.....4 B5
Trewidland.....5 D7
Trewint Corn.....8 E3
 Corn.....8 F4
Trewithian.....3 C7
Trewoofe.....2 D3
Trewoon.....4 D4
Treworga.....3 B7
Treworlas.....3 C7
Tre-wyn.....35 B7
Treyarnon.....4 B3
Treyford.....16 C2
Trezaise.....4 D4
Triangle.....87 B8
Trickett's Cross..13 D8
Triffleton.....44 C4
Trimdon.....111 F6
Trimdon Colliery.111 F6
Trimdon Grange.111 F6
Trimingham.....81 D8
Trimley Lower
 Street.....57 F6
Trimley St Martin.57 F6
Trimley St Mary.57 F6
Trimpley.....50 B2
Trimsaran.....33 D5
Trimstone.....20 E3
Trinafour.....132 C4
Trinant.....35 D6
Tring.....40 C2
Tring Wharf.....40 C2
Trinity Angus.....135 C5
 Jersey.....17
Trisant.....47 B6
Trislaig.....130 B4
Trispen.....4 D3
Tritlington.....117 E8
Trochry.....133 E6
Trodigal.....143 F7
Troed-rhiwdalar.47 D8
Troedyrhiw.....34 D4
Tromode.....84 E3
Trondavoe.....160 F5
Troon Corn.....3 C5
 S Ayrs.....118 F3
Trosaraidh.....148 G2
Trossachs Hotel.126 D4

Troston.....56 B2
Trottiscliffe.....29 C7
Trotton.....16 B2
Troutbeck Cumb.....99 B5
 Cumb.....99 D6
Troutbeck Bridge.99 D6
Trow Green.....36 D2
Trowbridge.....24 D3
Trowell.....76 F4
Trowle Common.24 D3
Trowley Bottom..40 C3
Trows.....122 F2
Trowse Newton..68 D5
Trudoxhill.....24 E2
Trull.....11 B7
Trumaisgearraidh
 .....148 A3
Trumpan.....148 B7
Trumpet.....49 F8
Trumpington.....54 D5
Trunch.....81 D8
Trunnah.....92 E3
Truro.....3 B7
Trusham.....10 F3
Trusley.....76 F2
Trusthorpe.....91 F9
Trysull.....62 E2
Tubney.....38 E4
Tuckenhay.....7 D6
Tuckhill.....61 F7
Tuckingmill.....3 B5
Tuddenham
 St Martin.....57 E5
Tudeley.....29 E7
Tudhoe.....111 F5
Tudorville.....36 B2
Tudweiliog.....70 D3
Tuesley.....27 E7
Tuffley.....37 C5
Tufton Hants.....26 E2
 Pembs.....32 B1
Tugby.....64 D4
Tugford.....61 F5
Tullibardine.....127 C8
Tullibody.....127 E7
Tullich Argyll.....125 C7
 Highld.....138 B2
Tullich Muir.....151 D10
Tulliemet.....133 D6
Tulloch Aberds.....135 B7
 Aberds.....153 E8
 Perth.....128 B2
Tulloch Castle.....151 E8
Tullochgorm.....125 F5
Tulloes.....135 E5
Tullybannocher.127 B6
Tullybelton.....133 F7
Tullyfergus.....134 E2
Tullymurdoch.....134 D1
Tullynessle.....140 C4
Tumble.....33 C6
Tumby Woodside.79 D5
Tummel Bridge.132 D4
Tunga.....155 D9
Tunstall E Yorks.....97 F9
 Kent.....30 C2
 Lancs.....93 B6
 Norf.....69 D7
 N Yorks.....101 E7
 Stoke.....75 D5
 Suff.....57 D7
 T&W.....111 D6
Tunstead Derbys.75 B8
 Gtr Man.....87 D8
 Norf.....81 E8
Tunworth.....26 E4
Tupsley.....49 E7
Tupton.....76 C3
Turgis Green.....26 D4
Turin.....135 D5
Turkdean.....37 C7
Tur Langton.....64 E4
Turleigh.....24 C3
Turn.....87 C6
Turnastone.....49 F5
Turnberry.....112 D2
Turnditch.....76 E2
Turners Hill.....28 F4
Turners Puddle..13 E6
Turnford.....41 D6
Turnhouse.....120 B4
Turnworth.....13 D6
Turriff.....153 C7
Turton Bottoms..86 C5
Turves.....66 E3
Turvey.....53 D7
Turville.....39 E7
Turville Heath.....39 E7
Turweston.....52 F4
Tushielaw.....115 C6
Tutbury.....63 B6
Tutnall.....50 B4
Tutshill.....36 E2
Tuttington.....81 E8
Tutts Clump.....26 B3
Tuxford.....77 B7
Twatt Orkney.....159 F3
 Shetland.....160 H5
Twechar.....119 B7
Tweedmouth.....123 D5
Tweedsmuir.....114 B3
Twelve Heads.....3 B6
Twemlow Green..74 C4
Twenty.....65 B8
Twerton.....24 C2
Twickenham.....28 B2
Twigworth.....37 B5
Twineham.....17 C6
Twinhoe.....24 D2
Twinstead.....56 F2
Twinstead Green.56 F2
Twiss Green.....86 E4
Twiston.....93 E8
Twitchen Devon..21 F6
 Shrops.....49 B5
Two Bridges.....6 B4
Two Dales.....76 C2
Two Mills.....73 B7
Twycross.....63 D7
Twyford Bucks.....39 B6
 Derbys.....63 B7
 Hants.....15 B5
 Leics.....64 C4
 Lincs.....65 B6
 Norf.....81 E6
 Wokingham.....27 B5
Twyford Common.49 F7

Twyning.....50 F3
Twyning Green..50 F4
Twynllanan.....34 B1
Twynmynydd.....33 C7
Twyn-Sheriff.....35 D8
Twywell.....53 B7
Tyberton.....49 F5
Tyburn.....62 E5
Tycroes.....33 C7
Tycrwyn.....59 C8
Tyddewi
 = St David's.....44 C2
Tydd Gote.....66 C4
Tydd St Giles.....66 C4
Tydd St Mary.....66 C4
Tyddyn-mawr.....71 C6
Ty-draw.....83 F8
Tye Green Essex..41 D7
 Essex.....42 B3
 Essex.....55 F6
Ty-hen Carms.....32 B4
 Gwyn.....70 D2
Tyldesley.....86 D4
Tyler Hill.....30 C5
Tylers Green.....40 E2
Tylorstown.....34 E4
Tylwch.....59 F6
Ty-mawr.....82 C4
Ty Mawr.....46 E4
Ty Mawr Cwm.....72 E3
Ty-nant Conwy.....72 E3
 Gwyn.....59 B6
Tyncelyn.....46 C5
Tyndrum.....131 F7
Tyneham.....13 F6
Tynehead.....121 D6
Tynemouth.....111 C6
Tyne Tunnel.....111 C6
Tynewydd.....34 E3
Tyninghame.....122 B2
Tynron.....113 E8
Tyn-y-celyn.....73 F5
Tyn-y-coed.....60 B2
Tyn-y-fedwen.....72 F5
Tyn-y-ffridd.....72 F5
Tynygongl.....82 C5
Tynygraig.....47 C5
Tyn-y-graig.....48 D2
Ty'n-y-groes.....83 D7
Ty'n-y-maes.....83 E6
Tyn-y-pwll.....82 C4
Ty'n-yr-eithin.....47 C5
Ty'r-felin-isaf.....83 E8
Tyrie.....153 B9
Tyringham.....53 E6
Tythecott.....9 C6
Tythegston.....21 B7
Tytherington
 Ches E.....75 B6
 S Glos.....36 F3
 Som.....24 E2
 Wilts.....24 E4
Tytherleigh.....11 D8
Ty-uchaf.....59 B7
Tywardreath.....5 D5
Tywyn Conwy.....83 D7
 Gwyn.....58 D2

U

Uachdar.....148 C2
Uags.....149 E12
Ubbeston Green..57 B7
Ubley.....23 D7
Uckerby.....101 D7
Uckfield.....17 B8
Uckington.....37 B6
Uddingston.....119 C6
Uddington.....119 F8
Udimore.....19 D5
Udny Green.....141 B7
Udny Station.....141 B8
Udston.....119 D6
Udstonhead.....119 E7
Uffcott.....25 B6
Uffculme.....11 C5
Uffington Lincs.....65 D7
 Oxon.....38 F3
 Shrops.....60 C5
Ufford Pboro.....65 D7
 Suff.....57 D6
Ufton.....51 C8
Ufton Nervet.....26 C4
Ugadale.....143 F8
Ugborough.....6 D4
Uggeshall.....69 F7
Ugglebarnby.....103 D6
Ughill.....88 E3
Ugley.....41 B8
Ugley Green.....41 B8
Ugthorpe.....103 C5
Uidh.....148 J1
Uig Argyll.....145 E10
 Highld.....148 C6
 Highld.....149 B8
Uigen.....154 D5
Uigshader.....149 D9
Uisken.....146 K6
Ulbster.....158 F5
Ulceby Lincs.....79 B7
 N Lincs.....90 C5
Ulceby Skitter.....90 C5
Ulcombe.....30 E2
Uldale.....108 F2
Uley.....36 E4
Ulgham.....117 E8
Ullapool.....150 B4
Ullenhall.....51 C6
Ullenwood.....37 C6
Ulleskelf.....95 E8
Ullesthorpe.....64 F2
Ulley.....89 F5
Ullingswick.....49 E7
Ullinish.....149 E8
Ullock.....98 B2
Ulnes Walton.....86 C3
Ulpha.....98 E3
Ulrome.....97 D7
Ulsta.....160 E6
Ulva House.....146 H7
Ulverston.....92 B2
Ulwell.....13 F8
Umberleigh.....9 B8
Unapool.....156 F5
Unasary.....148 F2
Underbarrow.....99 E6
Undercliffe.....94 F4
Underhoull.....160 C7

Underriver.....29 D6
Underwood.....76 D4
Undy.....35 F8
Unifirth.....160 H4
Union Cottage.....141 E7
Union Mills.....84 E3
Union Street.....18 B4
Unstone.....76 B3
Unstone Green..76 B3
Unthank Cumb.....108 F4
 Cumb.....109 E6
Unthank End.....108 F4
Upavon.....25 D6
Up Cerne.....12 D4
Upchurch.....30 C2
Upcott.....48 D5
Upend.....55 D7
Up Exe.....10 D4
Upgate.....68 C4
Uphall.....120 B3
Uphall Station.....120 B3
Upham Devon.....10 D3
 Hants.....15 B6
Uphampton.....50 C3
Up Hatherley.....37 B6
Uphill.....22 D5
Up Holland.....86 D3
Uplawmoor.....118 D4
Upleadon.....36 B4
Upleatham.....102 C4
Uplees.....30 C3
Uploders.....12 E3
Uplowman.....10 C5
Uplyme.....11 E8
Up Marden.....15 C8
Upminster.....42 F1
Up Nately.....26 D4
Upnor.....29 B8
Upottery.....11 D7
Upper
 Affcot.....60 F4
Upper
 Ardchronie.....151 C9
Upper Arley.....61 F7
Upper Arncott..39 C6
Upper Astrop.....52 F3
Upper Badcall.....156 E4
Upper Basildon..26 B3
Upper Beeding..17 C5
Upper Benefield.65 F6
Upper Bighouse.157 D11
Upper Boddington 52 D2
Upper Borth.....58 F3
Upper Boyndlie.153 B9
Upper Brailes.....51 F8
Upper Breakish.149 F11
Upper Breinton..49 E6
Upper Broadheath 50 D3
Upper Broughton.64 B3
Upper Bucklebury 26 C3
Upper
 Burnhaugh.....141 E7
Upperby.....108 D4
Upper Caldecote.54 E2
Upper Catesby..52 D3
Upper Chapel.....48 E2
Upper Church
 Village.....34 F4
Upper Chute.....25 D7
Upper Clatford..25 E8
Upper Clynnog..71 C5
Upper
 Cumberworth.88 D3
Upper Cwmbran.35 E6
Upper Dallachy.152 B3
Upper Dean.....53 C8
Upper Denby.....88 D3
Upper Denton..109 C6
Upper Derraid.151 H13
Upper Dicker.....18 E2
Upper Dovercourt 57 F6
Upper Druimfin.147 F8
Upper Dunsforth.95 C7
Upper Eathie.....151 E10
Upper Elkstone.75 D7
Upper End.....75 B7
Upper Farringdon 26 F5
Upper Framilode.36 C4
Upper Glenfintaig 137 F5
Upper Gornal.....62 E3
Upper Gravenhurst 54 F2
Upper Green Mon.35 C7
 W Berks.....25 C8
Upper Grove
 Common.....36 B2
Upper Hackney.76 C2
Upper Hale.....27 E6
Upper Halistra.148 C7
Upper Halling.....29 C7
Upper Hambleton 65 D6
Upper Hardres
 Court.....31 D5
Upper Hartfield.29 F5
Upper Haugh.....88 E5
Upper Heath.....61 F5
Upper Hellesdon.68 C5
Upper Helmsley.96 D2
Upper Hergest..48 D4
Upper Heyford
 Northants.....52 D4
 Oxon.....38 B4
Upper Hill.....49 D6
Upper Hopton..88 C2
Upper
 Horsebridge.18 D2
Upper Hulme.....75 C7
Upper Inglesham.38 E2
Upper
 Inverbrough.151 H11
Upper Killay.....33 E6
Upper
 Knockando.....152 D1
Upper Lambourn 38 F3
Upper Leigh.....75 F7
Upper Lenie.....137 B8
Upper Lochton.141 E5
Upper Longdon.62 C4
Upper Lybster.158 G4
Upper Lydbrook.36 C3
Upper Maes-coed 48 F5
Upper Midway.63 B6
Uppermill.....87 D7
Upper Milovaig.148 D6
Upper Minety.....37 E7
Upper Mitton.....50 B3
Upper North Dean 39 E8
Upper Obney.....133 F7
Upper Ollach.149 E10
Upper Padley.....76 B2
Upper Pollicott.39 C7

Upper Poppleton . . 95 D8
Upper Quinton 51 E6
Upper Ratley 14 E3
Upper Rissington . . 38 C2
Upper Rochford . . . 49 C8
Upper Sandaig . .149 G12
Upper Sanday . . .159 H6
Upper Sapey 49 C8
Upper Saxondale . . 77 F6
Upper Seagry 37 F6
Upper Shelton 53 E7
Upper
  Sheringham 81 C7
Upper Skelmorlie 118 C2
Upper Slaughter . . 38 B1
Upper Soudley . . . 36 C3
Uppersound 160 J6
Upper Stondon . . . 54 F2
Upper Stowe 52 D4
Upper Stratton . . . 38 F1
Upper Street Hants . 14 C2
  Norf 69 C6
  Norf 69 C6
  Suff 57 B6
Upper Strensham . . 50 F4
Upper Sundon 40 B3
Upper Swell 38 B1
Upper Tean 75 F7
Upperthong 88 D2
Upperthorpe 89 C8
Upper Tillyrie . . .128 D3
Upperton 16 B3
Upper Tooting 28 B3
Upper Tote 149 B10
Uppertown Derbys . 76 C3
  Highld 158 C5
  Orkney 159 J5
Upper Town 23 C7
Upper Treverward . 48 B4
Upper Tysoe 51 E8
Upper Upham 25 B7
Upper Wardington 52 E2
Upper Weald 53 F5
Upper Weedon . . . 52 D4
Upper Wield 26 F4
Upper
  Winchendon 39 C7
Upper Witton 62 E4
Upper Woodend . .141 C5
Upper Woodford . . 25 F6
Upper Wootton . . . 26 D3
Upper Wyche 50 E2
Uppingham 65 E5
Uppington 61 D6
Upsall 102 F2
Upshire 41 D7
Up Somborne 25 F8
Upstreet 31 C6
Up Sydling 12 D4
Upton Cambs 56 B3
  Ches W 73 C8
  Corn 8 D4
  Dorset 12 F5
  Dorset 13 E7
  Hants 14 C4
  Hants 25 D8
  Leics 63 E7
  Lincs 90 F2
  Mers 85 F3
  Norf 69 C6
  Northants 52 C5
  Notts 77 B7
  Oxon 39 F5
  Pboro 65 D8
  Slough 27 B7
  Som 10 B4
  W Yorks 89 C5
Upton Bishop 36 B3
Upton Cheyney . . . 23 C8
Upton Cressett . . . 61 E6
Upton Cross 5 B7
Upton Grey 26 E4
Upton Hellions . . . 10 D3
Upton Lovell 24 E4
Upton Magna 61 C5
Upton Pyne 10 E4
Upton
  St Leonard's 37 C5
Upton Scudamore . 24 E3
Upton Snodsbury . 50 D4
Upton upon
  Severn 50 E3
Upton Warren 50 C4
Upwaltham 16 C3
Upware 55 B6
Upwell 66 D4
Upwey 12 F4
Upwood 66 F2
Uradale 160 K6
Urafirth 160 F5
Urchfont 24 D5
Urdimarsh 49 E7
Ure 160 F4
Ure Bank 95 B6
Urgha 154 H6
Urishay Common . 48 F5
Urlay Nook 102 C1
Urmston 87 E5
Urpeth 110 D5
Urquhart Highld . .151 E10
  Moray 152 B2
Urra 102 D3
Urray 151 F8
Ushaw Moor 110 E5
Usk = Brynbuga . . 35 D7
Usselby 90 E4
Usworth 111 D6
Utkinton 74 C2
Utley 94 E3
Uton 10 E3
Utterby 91 E7
Uttoxeter 75 F7
Uwchmynydd 70 E2
Uxbridge 40 F3
Uyeasound 160 C7
Uzmaston 44 D4

V

Valley 82 D2
Valleyfield 106 D3
Valley Truckle 8 F2
Valsgarth 160 B8
Valtos 149 B10
Van 59 F6
Vange 42 F3
Varteg 35 D6
Vatten 149 D7
Vaul 146 G3
Vaynor 34 C4
Veensgarth 160 J6
Velindre 48 F3
Vellow 22 F2
Veness 159 F6
Venn Green 9 C5
Vennington 60 D3
Venn Ottery 11 E5
Venny Tedburn . . . 10 E3
Ventnor 15 G6
Vernham Dean . . . 25 D8
Vernham Street . . 25 D8
Vernolds Common . 60 F4
Verwood 13 D8
Veryan 3 C5
Vicarage 11 F7
Vickerstown 92 C1
Victoria Corn 4 C4
  S Yorks 88 D2
Vidlin 160 G6
Viewpark 119 C7
Vigo Village 29 C7
Vinehall Street . . . 18 C4
Vine's Cross 18 D2
Viney Hill 36 D3
Virginia Water . . . 27 C8
Virginstow 9 E5
Vobster 24 E2
Voe Shetland 160 E5
  Shetland 160 G6
Vowchurch 49 F5
Voxter 160 F5
Voy 159 G3

W

Wackerfield 101 B6
Wacton 68 E4
Wadbister 160 J6
Wadborough 50 E4
Waddesdon 39 C7
Waddingham 90 E3
Waddington Lancs . 93 E7
  Lincs 78 C2
Wadebridge 4 B4
Wadeford 11 C8
Wadenhoe 65 F7
Wadesmill 41 C6
Wadhurst 18 B3
Wadshelf 76 B3
Wadsley Bridge . . 88 E4
Wadworth 89 E6
Waen Denb 72 C3
  Denb 72 C5
Waen Fach 60 C2
Waen Goleugoed . . 72 B4
Wag 157 G13
Wainfleet All
  Saints 79 D7
Wainfleet Bank . . . 79 D7
Wainfleet St Mary . 79 D8
Wainfleet Tofts . . . 79 D7
Wainhouse Corner . .8 E3
Wainscott 29 B8
Wainstalls 87 B8
Waitby 100 D2
Waithe 91 D6
Wakefield 88 B4
Wake Lady Green .102 E4
Wakerley 65 E6
Wakes Colne 42 B4
Walberswick 57 B8
Walberton 16 D3
Walbottle 110 C4
Walcot Lincs 78 F3
  N Lincs 90 B2
  Shrops 60 F3
  Swindon 38 F1
  Telford 61 C5
Walcote Leics 64 F2
  Warks 51 D6
Walcot Green 68 F4
Walcott Lincs 78 D4
  Norf 69 A6
Walden 101 F5
Walden Head 100 F4
Walden Stubbs . . . 89 C6
Waldersey 66 D4
Walderslade 29 C8
Walderton 15 C8
Walditch 12 E2
Waldley 75 F8
Waldridge 111 D5
Waldringfield 57 E6
Waldringfield
  Heath 57 E6
Waldron 18 D2
Wales 89 F5
Walesby Lincs 90 E5
  Notts 77 B6
Walford Hereford . . 36 B2
  Hereford 49 B5
  Shrops 60 B4
Walford Heath . . . 60 C4
Walgherton 74 E3
Walgrave 53 B6
Walhampton 14 E4
Walkden 86 D5
Walker 111 C5
Walker Barn 75 B6
Walkerburn 121 F6
Walker Fold 93 E6
Walkeringham . . . 89 E8
Walkerith 89 E8
Walkern 41 B5
Walker's Green . . . 49 E7
Walkerville 101 E7
Walkford 14 E3
Walkhampton 6 C3
Walkington 97 F5
Walkley 88 F4
Walk Mill 93 F8
Wall Northum 110 C2
  Staffs 62 D5
Wallaceton 113 F8
Wallacetown
  S Ayrs 112 B3
  S Ayrs 112 D2
Wallasey 85 E4
Wall Bank 60 E5
Wallcrouch 18 B3
Wall Heath 62 F2

Wallingford 39 F6
Wallington Hants . 15 D6
  Herts 54 F3
  London 28 C3
Wallis 32 B1
Walliswood 28 F2
Walls 160 J4
Wallsend 111 C5
Wallston 22 B3
Wall under
  Heywood 60 E5
Wallyford 121 B6
Walmer 31 D7
Walmer Bridge . . . 86 B2
Walmersley 87 C6
Walmley 62 E5
Walpole 57 B7
Walpole Cross
  Keys 66 C5
Walpole Highway . 66 C5
Walpole Marsh . . . 66 C5
Walpole
  St Andrew 66 C5
Walpole St Peter . . 66 C5
Walsall 62 E4
Walsall Wood 62 D4
Walsden 87 B7
Walsgrave on
  Sowe 63 F7
Walsham le
  Willows 56 B3
Walshaw 87 C5
Walshford 95 D7
Walsoken 66 C4
Walston 120 E3
Walsworth 54 F3
Walters Ash 39 E8
Walterston 22 B2
Walterstone 35 B7
Waltham Kent 30 E5
  NE Lincs 91 D6
Waltham Abbey . . 41 D6
Waltham Chase . . 15 C6
Waltham Cross . . . 41 D6
Waltham on the
  Wolds 64 B5
Waltham
  St Lawrence 27 B6
Walthamstow 41 F6
Walton Cumb 108 C5
  Derbys 76 C3
  Leics 64 F2
  Mers 85 E4
  M Keynes 53 F6
  Pboro 65 D8
  Powys 48 D4
  Som 23 F6
  Staffs 75 F5
  Suff 57 F6
  Telford 61 C5
  Warks 51 D7
  W Yorks 88 C4
  W Yorks 95 D6
Walton Cardiff . . . 50 F4
Walton East 32 B1
Walton-in-
  Gordano 23 B6
Walton-le-Dale . . . 86 B3
Walton-on-
  Thames 28 C2
Walton on the Hill
  Staffs 62 B3
  Sur 28 D3
Walton-on-the-
  Naze 43 B8
Walton on the
  Wolds 64 C2
Walton-on-Trent . . 63 C6
Walton West 44 D3
Walwen 73 B6
Walwick 110 B2
Walworth 101 C7
Walworth Gate . . .101 B7
Walwyn's Castle . . 44 D3
Wambrook 11 D7
Wanborough Sur . . 27 E7
  Swindon 38 F2
Wandsworth 28 B3
Wangford 57 B8
Wanlockhead 113 C8
Wansford E Yorks . . 97 D6
  Pboro 65 E7
Wanstead 41 F7
Wanstrow 24 E2
Wanswell 36 D3
Wantage 38 F3
Wapley 24 B2
Wappenbury 51 C8
Wappenham 52 E4
Warbleton 18 D3
Warblington 15 D8
Warborough 39 E5
Warboys 66 F3
Warbreck 92 F3
Warbstow 8 E4
Warburton 86 F5
Warcop 100 C2
Warden Kent 30 B4
  Northum 110 C2
Ward End 62 F5
Ward Green 56 C4
Wardhill 159 F7
Wardington 52 E2
Wardlaw 115 C5
Wardle Ches E 74 D3
  Gtr Man 87 C7
Wardley 64 D5
Wardlow 75 B8
Wardy Hill 66 F4
Ware Herts 41 C6
  Kent 31 C6
Wareham 13 F7
Warehorne 19 B6
Warenford 117 B7
Waren Mill 123 F7
Warenton 123 F7
Wareside 41 C6
Waresley Cambs . . 54 D3
  Worcs 50 B3
Warfield 27 B6
Warfleet 7 D6
Wargrave 27 B5
Warham 80 C5
Warhill 87 E7
Wark Northum . .109 B8
  Northum 122 F4
Warkleigh 9 B8
Warkton 53 B6

Warkworth
  Northants 52 E2
  Northum 117 D8
Warlaby 101 E8
Warland 87 B7
Warleggan 5 C6
Warlingham 28 D4
Warmfield 88 B4
Warmingham 74 C4
Warmington
  Northants 65 E7
  Warks 52 E2
Warminster 24 E3
Warmlake 30 D2
Warmley 23 B8
Warmley Tower . . 23 B8
Warmonds Hill . . . 53 C7
Warmsworth 89 D6
Warmwell 13 F5
Warndon 50 D3
Warnford 15 B7
Warnham 28 F2
Warninglid 17 B6
Warren Ches E 75 B5
  Pembs 44 F4
Warren Heath . . . 57 E6
Warren Row 39 F8
Warren Street . . . 30 D3
Warrington
  M Keynes 53 D6
  Warr 86 F4
Warsash 15 D5
Warslow 75 D7
Warsop 77 C5
Warter 96 D4
Warthermarske . . 94 B5
Warthill 96 D2
Wartling 18 E3
Wartnaby 64 B4
Warton Lancs 86 B2
  Lancs 92 B4
  Northum 117 D6
  Warks 63 D6
Warwick 51 C7
Warwick Bridge . .108 D4
Warwick on Eden .108 D4
Wasbister 159 E4
Wasdale Head . . . 98 D3
Washaway 4 C5
Washbourne 7 D5
Wash Common . . . 26 C2
Washfield 10 C4
Washfold 101 D5
Washford 22 E2
Washford Pyne . . . 10 C3
Washingborough . 78 B3
Washington T&W .111 D6
  W Sus 16 C5
Wasing 26 C3
Waskerley 110 E3
Wasperton 51 D7
Wasps Nest 78 C3
Wass 95 B8
Watchet 22 E2
Watchfield Oxon . . 38 E2
  Som 22 E5
Watchgate 99 E7
Watchhill 107 E8
Watcombe 7 C7
Watendlath 98 C4
Water Devon 10 F2
  Lancs 87 B6
Waterbeach 55 C5
Waterbeck 108 B2
Waterden 80 D4
Water End E Yorks . . 96 F3
  Herts 40 C3
  Herts 41 D5
Waterfall 75 D7
Waterfoot E Renf . .119 D5
  Lancs 87 B6
Waterford Hants . . 14 E4
  Herts 41 C6
Waterhead Cumb . . 99 D5
  Dumfries 114 E4
Waterheads 120 D5
Waterhouses
  Durham 110 E4
  Staffs 75 D7
Wateringbury 29 D7
Waterloo BCP 13 E8
  Gtr Man 87 D7
  Highld 149 F11
  Mers 85 E4
  N Lanark 119 D7
  Norf 68 C5
  Perth 133 F7
  Shrops 74 F2
Waterloo Port . . . 82 E4
Waterlooville 15 D7
Watermeetings . . .114 C2
Watermillock 99 B6
Water Newton . . . 65 E8
Water Orton 63 E5
Waterperry 39 D6
Waterrow 11 B5
Watersfield 16 C4
Waterside Aberds .141 B9
  Blackburn 86 B5
  Cumb 108 E2
  E Ayrs 112 D4
  E Ayrs 118 E4
  E Dunb 119 B6
  E Renf 118 D5
Water's Nook 86 D4
Waterstock 39 D6
Waterston 44 E4
Water Stratford . . 52 F4
Waters Upton 61 C6
Water Yeat 98 F4
Watford Herts 40 E4
  Northants 52 C4
Watford Gap 62 D5
Wath N Yorks 94 C4
  N Yorks 95 B6
  N Yorks 96 B3
Wath Brow 98 C2
Wath upon
  Dearne 88 D5
Watlington Norf . . 67 C6
  Oxon 39 E6
Watnall 76 E5
Watten 158 E4
Wattisfield 56 B4
Wattisham 56 D4
Wattlesborough
  Heath 60 C3
Watton E Yorks . . . 97 D6
  Norf 68 D2
Watton at Stone . . 41 C6

Wattston 119 B7
Wattstown 34 E4
Wauchan 136 F2
Waulkmill Lodge .159 H4
Waun 59 D5
Waunarlwydd 33 E7
Waunclunda 47 F5
Waunfawr 82 F5
Waungron 33 D6
Waunlwyd 35 D5
Waun-y-clyn 33 D5
Wavendon 53 F7
Waverbridge 108 E2
Waverton Ches W . .73 C8
  Cumb 108 E2
Wavertree 85 F4
Wawne 97 F6
Waxham 69 B7
Waxholme 91 B7
Way 31 C7
Wayfield 29 C8
Wayford 12 D2
Waymills 74 E2
Wayne Green 35 C8
Way Village 10 C3
Wdig = Goodwick . 44 B4
Weachyburn 153 C6
Weald 38 D3
Wealdstone 40 F4
Weardley 95 E5
Weare 23 D6
Weare Giffard 9 B6
Wearhead 109 F8
Weasdale 100 D1
Weasenham All
  Saints 80 E4
Weasenham
  St Peter 80 E4
Weatherhill 28 E4
Weaverham 74 B3
Weaverthorpe . . . 97 B5
Webheath 50 C5
Wedderlairs 153 E8
Wedderlie 122 D2
Weddington 63 E7
Wedhampton 25 D5
Wedmore 23 E6
Wednesbury 62 E3
Wednesfield 62 D3
Weedon 39 C8
Weedon Bec 52 D4
Weedon Lois 52 E4
Weeford 62 D5
Week 10 C2
Weeke 26 F2
Weekley 65 F5
Week St Mary 8 E4
Weel 97 F6
Weeley 43 B7
Weeley Heath . . . 43 B7
Weem 133 E5
Weeping Cross . . . 62 B3
Weethley Gate . . . 51 D5
Weeting 67 F7
Weeton E Yorks . . . 91 B7
  Lancs 92 F3
  N Yorks 95 E5
Weetwood Hall . . 117 B6
Weir 87 B6
Weir Quay 6 C2
Welborne 68 D3
Welbourn 78 D2
Welburn N Yorks . . 96 C3
  N Yorks 102 F4
Welbury 102 D1
Welby 78 F2
Welches Dam 66 F4
Welcome 8 C4
Weld Bank 86 C3
Weldon 117 E7
Welford Northants . 64 F3
  W Berks 26 B2
Welford-on-Avon . 51 D6
Welham Leics 64 E4
  Notts 89 F8
Welham Green . . . 41 D5
Well Hants 27 E5
  Lincs 79 B7
  N Yorks 101 F7
Welland 50 E2
Wellbank 134 F4
Welldale 107 C8
Well End 40 F1
Wellesbourne . . . 51 D7
Well Heads 94 F3
Well Hill 29 C5
Welling 29 B5
Wellingborough . . 53 C6
Wellingham 80 E4
Wellingore 78 D2
Wellington Cumb . . 98 D2
  Hereford 49 E6
  Som 11 B6
  Telford 61 C6
Wellington Heath . 50 E2
Wellington Hill . . . 95 F6
Wellow Bath 24 D2
  IoW 14 F4
  Notts 77 C6
Wellpond Green . . 41 B7
Wells 23 E7
Wellsborough . . . 63 D7
Wells Green 74 D3
Wells-next-the-
  Sea 80 C5
Wellswood 7 C7
Well Town 10 D4
Wellwood 128 F2
Welney 66 E5
Welshampton . . . 73 F8
Welsh Bicknor . . . 36 C2
Welsh End 74 F2
Welsh Frankton . . 73 F7
Welsh Hook 44 C4
Welsh Newton . . . 36 C1
Welshpool
  = Y Trallwng . . . 60 D2
Welsh St Donats . . 22 B2
Welton Cumb 108 E3
  E Yorks 90 B3
  Lincs 78 B3
  Northants 52 C3
Welton Hill 90 F4
Welton le Marsh . . 79 C7
Welton le Wold . . 91 F6
Welwick 91 B7
Welwyn 41 C5
Welwyn Garden
  City 41 C5

Wem 60 B5
Wembdon 22 F4
Wembley 40 F4
Wembury 6 E3
Wembworthy 9 D8
Wemyss Bay 118 C1
Wenallt Ceredig . . 47 B5
  Gwyn 72 E3
Wendens Ambo . . 55 F6
Wendlebury 39 C5
Wendling 68 C2
Wendover 40 D1
Wendron 3 C5
Wendy 54 E4
Wenfordbridge 5 B5
Wenhaston 57 B8
Wennington Cambs . 54 B3
  Lancs 93 B6
  London 41 F8
Wensley Derbys . . . 76 C2
  N Yorks 101 F5
Wentbridge 89 C5
Wentnor 60 E3
Wentworth Cambs . 55 B5
  S Yorks 88 E4
Wenvoe 22 B3
Weobley 49 D6
Weobley Marsh . . 49 D6
Wereham 67 D6
Wergs 62 D2
Wern Powys 59 C6
  Powys 60 C2
Wernffrwd 33 E6
Wernyrheoldd . . . 35 C7
Werrington Corn . . 8 F5
  Pboro 65 D8
  Staffs 75 E6
Wervin 73 B8
Wesham 92 F4
Wessington 76 D3
Westacott 20 F4
West Acre 67 C7
West Adderley . . . 52 F2
West Allerdean . . .123 E5
West Alvington 6 E5
West Amesbury . . 25 E6
West Anstey 10 B3
West Ashby 79 B5
West Ashling 16 D2
West Ashton 24 D3
West Auckland . . .101 B6
West Ayton 103 F7
West Bagborough . 22 F3
West Barkwith . . . 91 F5
West Barnby 103 C6
West Barns 122 B2
West Barsham . . . 80 D5
West Bay 12 E2
West Beckham . . . 81 D7
West Bedfont 27 B8
West Benhar 119 C8
West Bergholt . . . 43 B5
West Bexington . . 12 F3
West Bilney 67 C7
West Blatchington . 17 D6
Westborough 77 E8
Westbourne BCP . . 13 E8
  Suff 56 E5
  W Sus 15 D8
Westbrook W Berks . 26 B2
West Buckland
  Devon 21 F5
  Som 11 B6
West Burrafirth . . 160 H4
West Burton
  N Yorks 101 F5
  W Sus 16 C3
Westbury Bucks . . 52 F4
  Shrops 60 D3
  Wilts 24 D3
Westbury Leigh . . 24 D3
Westbury-on-
  Severn 36 C4
Westbury on Trym . 23 B7
Westbury-sub-
  Mendip 23 E7
West Butterwick . . 90 D2
Westby 92 F3
West Byfleet 27 C8
West Caister 69 C8
West Calder 120 C3
West Camel 12 B3
West Challow 38 F3
West Chelborough . 12 D3
West Chevington . 117 E8
West Chiltington . . 16 C4
West Chiltington
  Common 16 C4
West Chinnock . . . 12 C2
West Chisenbury . . 25 D6
West Clandon 27 D8
West Cliffe 31 E7
Westcliff-on-Sea . . 42 F4
West Clyne 157 J11
West Clyth 158 G4
West Coker 12 C3
Westcombe 23 F8
West Compton
  Dorset 12 E3
  Som 23 E7
Westcote 38 B2
Westcott Bucks . . . 39 C7
  Devon 10 D5
  Sur 28 E2
Westcott Barton . . 38 B4
West Cowick 89 B7
West Cranmore . . 23 E8
West Cross 33 F7
West Cullery 141 D6
West Curry 8 E4
West Curthwaite . 108 E3
West Darlochan . . 143 F7
Westdean 18 F2
West Dean Wilts . . 14 B3
  W Sus 16 C2
West Deeping . . . 65 D8
Westdene 17 D6
West Derby 85 E4
West Dereham . . . 67 D6
West Didsbury . . . 87 E6
West Ditchburn . . 117 B7
West Down 20 E4

West Drayton
  London 27 B8
  Notts 77 B7
West Ella 90 B4
West End Bedford . . 53 D7
  E Yorks 96 F5
  E Yorks 97 F7
  Hants 15 C5
  Lancs 86 B5
  Norf 68 D2
  Norf 69 C8
  N Som 23 C6
  Oxon 38 D4
  S Lanark 120 E2
  Suff 69 F7
  Sur 27 C7
  S Yorks 89 D7
  Wilts 13 B7
  Wilts 24 B4
West End Green . . 26 C4
Wester
  Aberchalder 137 B8
Wester Balgedie . .128 D3
Wester
  Culbeuchly 153 B6
Westerdale Highld . 158 E3
  N Yorks 102 D4
Wester
  Dechmont 120 C3
Wester Denoon . .134 E3
Westerfield
  Shetland 160 H5
  Suff 57 E5
Westergate 16 D3
Wester Fintray . . .141 C7
Westerham 28 D5
Westerhope 110 C4
Wester Lealty 151 D9
Westerleigh 23 B9
Wester Milton . . .151 F12
Wester Newburn . 129 D6
Wester Quarff . . .160 K6
Wester Skeld 160 J4
Westerton Angus . 135 D6
  Durham 110 F5
  W Sus 16 D2
Westerwick 160 J4
West Farleigh 29 D8
West Felton 60 B3
West Fenton 129 F6
West Ferry 134 F4
Westfield Cumb . . . 98 B1
  E Sus 18 D5
  Hereford 50 E2
  Highld 158 D2
  N Lanark 119 B7
  Norf 68 D2
  W Loth 120 B2
Westfields 12 D5
Westfields of
  Rattray 134 E1
West Firle 17 D8
Westgate Durham .110 F2
  N Lincs 89 D8
  Norf 80 C4
Westgate on Sea . 31 B7
West Ginge 38 F4
West Grafton 25 C7
West Green 26 D5
West
  Greenskares 153 B7
West Grimstead . . 14 B3
West Grinstead . . 17 B5
West Haddlesey . . 89 B6
West Haddon 52 B4
West Hagbourne . . 39 F5
West Hagley 62 F3
Westhall Aberds . .141 B5
  Suff 69 F7
West Hall 109 C5
West Hallam 76 E4
West Halton 90 B3
Westham Dorset . . 12 G4
  E Sus 18 E3
  Som 23 E6
West Ham 41 F7
Westhampnett . . . 16 D2
West Handley 76 B3
West Hanney 38 E4
West Hanningfield . 42 E3
West Hardwick . . . 88 C5
West Harnham . . . 14 B2
West Harptree . . . 23 D7
West Hatch 11 B7
Westhay 23 E6
Westhead 86 D2
West Head 67 D5
West Heath Ches E . 74 C5
  Hants 26 D3
  Hants 27 D6
West Helmsdale . .157 H13
West Hendred . . . 38 F4
West Heslerton . . 96 B5
Westhide 49 E7
Westhill Aberds . .141 D7
  Highld 151 G10
West Hill Devon . . 11 E5
  E Yorks 97 C7
  N Som 23 B6
West Hoathly 28 F4
West Holme 13 F6
Westhope Hereford . 49 D6
  Shrops 60 F4
West Horndon . . . 42 F2
Westhorpe Lincs . . 78 F5
  Suff 56 C4
West Horrington . . 23 E7
West Horsley 27 D8
West Horton 123 F6
West Hougham . . . 31 E6
Westhoughton . . . 86 D4
West Houlland . . .160 H4
Westhouse 93 B6
Westhouses 76 D4
West Humble 28 D2
West Huntington . 96 D2
West Hythe 19 B8
West Ilsley 38 F4
Westing 160 C7
West Itchenor . . . 15 D8
West Keal 79 C6
West Kennett 25 C6
West Kilbride 118 E2
West Kingsdown . . 29 C6
West Kington 24 B3

West
  Kinharrachie 153 E9
West Kirby 85 F3
West Knapton . . . 96 B4
West Knighton . . . 12 F5
West Knoyle 24 F3
West Kyloe 123 E6
Westlake 6 D4
West Lambrook . . 12 C2
West Langdon . . . 31 E7
West Langwell . . .157 J9
West Lavington
  Wilts 24 D5
  W Sus 16 B2
West Layton 101 D6
West Lea 111 E7
West Leake 64 B2
West Learmouth . .122 F4
Westleigh Devon . . 11 C5
  Devon 9 B6
  Gtr Man 86 D4
West Leigh 9 D8
Westleton 57 C8
West Lexham 67 C8
West Lilling 96 C3
Westlington 39 C7
West Linton 120 D4
West Liss 15 B8
West Littleton . . . 24 B2
West Looe 5 D7
West Luccombe . . 21 E7
West Lulworth . . . 13 F6
West Lutton 96 C5
West Lydford 23 F7
West Lyng 11 B8
West Lynn 67 B6
West Malling 29 D7
West Malvern 50 E2
West Marden 15 C8
West Markham . . . 77 B7
Westmarsh 31 C6
West Marsh 91 C6
West Marton 93 D8
West Meon 15 B7
West Mersea 43 C6
Westmeston 17 C7
Westmill 41 B6
West Milton 12 E3
Westminster 28 B4
West Minster 30 B3
West Molesey 28 C2
West Monkton . . . 11 B7
West Moors 13 D8
West Morriston . .122 E2
Westmuir 134 D3
West Muir 135 C5
Westness 159 F4
West Ness 96 B2
West Newham . . .110 B3
Westnewton Cumb 107 E8
  Northum 122 F5
West Newton
  E Yorks 97 F7
  Norf 67 B6
West Norwood . . . 28 B4
Westoe 111 C6
West Ogwell 7 B6
Weston Bath 24 C2
  Ches E 74 D4
  Devon 11 F6
  Dorset 12 G4
  Halton 86 F3
  Hants 15 B8
  Herts 54 F3
  Lincs 66 B2
  Northants 52 E3
  N Yorks 94 E4
  Shrops 61 B5
  Shrops 61 E5
  Staffs 62 B3
  W Berks 25 B8
Weston Beggard . . 49 E7
Westonbirt 37 F5
Weston by
  Welland 64 E4
Weston Colville . . 55 D7
Westoncommon . . 60 B4
Weston Coyney . . 75 E6
Weston Favell . . . 53 C5
Weston Green
  Cambs 55 D7
  Norf 68 C4
Weston Heath . . . 61 C7
Weston Hills 66 B2
Westoning 53 F8
Weston-in-
  Gordano 23 B6
Weston Jones 61 B7
Weston Longville . 68 C4
Weston
  Lullingfields 60 B4
Weston-on-the-
  Green 39 C5
Weston-on-Trent . 63 B8
Weston Patrick . . . 26 E4
Weston Rhyn 73 F6
Weston-sub-Edge . 51 E6
Weston-super-
  Mare 22 C5
Weston Turville . . 40 C1
Weston under
  Lizard 62 C2
Weston under
  Penyard 36 B3
Weston Underwood
  Derbys 76 E2
  M Keynes 53 D6
Westonzoyland . . 23 F5
West Orchard . . . 13 C6
West Overton . . . 25 C6
Westow 96 C3
Westport Argyll . .143 F7
  Som 11 C8
West Putford 9 C5

West Quantoxhead 22 E3
West Rainton 111 E6
West Rasen 90 F4
West Raynham . . . 80 E4
West Retford 89 F7
Westrigg 120 C2
West Rounton . . .102 D2
West Row 55 B7
West Rudham 80 E4
West Runton 81 C7
Westruther 122 E2
Westry 66 E3
West Saltoun 121 C7
West Sandwick . .160 E6
West Scrafton . . .101 F5
West Sleekburn . . 117 F8
West Somerton . . 69 C7
West Stafford 12 F5
West Stockwith . . 89 E8
West Stoke 16 D2
West Stonesdale . .100 D3
West Stoughton . . 23 E6
West Stour 13 B5
West Stourmouth . 31 C6
West Stow 56 B2
West Stowell 25 C6
West Strathan . . .157 C8
West Stratton . . . 26 E3
West Street 30 D3
West Tanfield 95 B5
West Taphouse 5 C6
West Tarbert 145 G7
West Thirston . . . 117 E7
West Thorney 15 D8
West Thurrock . . . 29 B6
West Tilbury 29 B7
West Tisted 15 B7
West Tofts Norf . . 67 E8
  Perth 133 F8
West Torrington . . 90 F5
West Town Hants . 15 E8
  N Som 23 C6
West Tytherley . . . 14 B3
West Tytherton . . 24 B4
Westville 77 E5
West Walton 66 C4
West Walton
  Highway 66 C4
Westward 108 E2
Westward Ho! 9 B6
Westwell Kent . . . 30 E3
  Oxon 38 D2
Westwell Leacon . . 30 E3
West Wellow 14 C3
West Wemyss . . . 128 E5
Westwick Cambs . . 54 C5
  Durham 101 C5
  Norf 81 E8
West Wick 23 C5
West Wickham
  Cambs 55 E7
  London 28 C4
West Williamston . 32 D1
West Willoughby . . 78 E2
West Winch 67 C6
West Winterslow . . 25 F7
West Wittering . . . 15 E8
West Witton 101 F5
Westwood Devon . . 10 E5
  Wilts 24 D3
West Woodburn . .116 F4
West Woodhay . . . 25 C8
West Woodlands . 24 E2
Westwoodside . . . 89 E8
West Worldham . . 26 F5
West Worlington . 10 C2
West Worthing . . . 16 D5
West Wratting . . . 55 D7
West Wycombe . . 39 E8
West Wylam 110 C4
West Yell 160 E6
Wetheral 108 D4
Wetherby 95 E7
Wetherden 56 C4
Wetheringsett . . . 56 C5
Wethersfield 55 F8
Wethersta 160 G5
Wetherup Street . . 56 C5
Wetley Rocks 75 E6
Wettenhall 74 C3
Wetton 75 D8
Wetwang 96 D5
Wetwood 74 F4
Wexcombe 25 D7
Wexham Street . . 40 F2
Weybourne 81 C7
Weybread 68 F5
Weybridge 27 C8
Weycroft 11 E8
Weydale 158 D3
Weyhill 25 E8
Weymouth 12 G4
Whaddon Bucks . . 53 F6
  Cambs 54 E4
  Glos 37 C5
  Wilts 14 B2
Whale 99 B7
Whaley 76 B5
Whaley Bridge . . . 87 F8
Whaley Thorns . . . 76 B5
Whaligoe 158 F5
Whalley 93 F7
Whalton 117 F7
Wham 93 C7
Whaplode 66 B3
Whaplode Drove . 66 C3
Whaplode
  St Catherine . . . 66 C3
Wharfe 93 C7
Wharles 92 F4
Wharncliffe Side . 88 E3
Wharram le Street . 96 C4
Wharton Ches W . . 74 C3
Wharton Green . . 74 C3
Whashton 101 D6
Whatcombe 13 D6
Whatcote 51 E8
Whatfield 56 E4
Whatley Som 11 D8
  Som 24 E2
Whatlington 18 D4
Whatstandwell . . 76 D3
Whatton 77 F7
Whauphill 105 E8
Whaw 100 D4
Wheatacre 69 E7

Wheatcroft ... 76 D3
Wheathampstead . 40 C4
Wheathill ... 61 F6
Wheatley Devon .. 10 E4
  Hants. 27 E5
  Oxon 39 D5
  S Yorks. 89 D6
  W Yorks 87 B8
Wheatley Hill. 111 F6
Wheaton Aston .. 62 C2
Wheddon Cross ... 21 F8
Wheedlemont .. 140 B3
Wheelerstreet... 27 E7
Wheelock..... 74 D4
Wheelock Heath .. 74 D4
Wheelton..... 86 B4
Wheen.... 134 B3
Wheldrake 96 E2
Whelford..... 38 E1
Whelpley Hill..... 40 D2
Whempstead.. 41 B6
Whenby ...-96 C2
Whepstead..... 56 D2
Wherstead..... 57 E5
Wherwell 25 E8
Wheston 75 B8
Whetsted..... 29 E7
Whetstone..... 64 E2
Whicham..... 98 F3
Whichford..... 51 F8
Whickham....110 C5
Whiddon Down...9 E4
Whigstreet.... 134 E4
Whilton..... 52 C4
Whimble..... 10 E5
Whim Farm....120 D5
Whimple 10 E5
Whimpwell Green. 69 B6
Whinburgh.... 68 D3
Whinnieliggate. 106 D4
Whinnyfold...153 E10
Whippingham.... 15 E6
Whipsnade..... 40 C3
Whipton..... 10 E4
Whirlow..... 88 F4
Whisby..... 78 C2
Whissendine..... 64 C5
Whissonsett..... 80 E5
Whistlefield
  Argyll.....145 D10
  Argyll.....145 D11
Whistley Green.. 27 B5
Whiston Mers.. 86 E2
  Northants 53 C6
  Staffs..... 62 C2
  Staffs..... 75 E7
  S Yorks..... 88 F5
Whitbeck..... 98 F3
Whitbourne..... 50 D2
Whitburn T&W... 111 C7
  W Loth..... 120 C2
Whitburn
  Colliery.....111 C7
Whitby Ches W... 73 B7
  N Yorks..... 103 C6
Whitbyheath.. 73 B7
Whitchurch Bath.. 23 C8
  Bucks..... 39 B7
  Cardiff..... 35 F5
  Devon 6 B2
  Hants..... 26 E2
  Hereford..... 36 C2
  Oxon 26 B4
  Pembs..... 44 C2
  Shrops..... 74 E2
Whitchurch
  Canonicorum .. 11 E8
Whitchurch Hill.. 26 B4
Whitcombe..... 12 F5
Whitcott Keysett .. 60 F2
Whiteacen....152 D2
Whiteacre Heath .. 63 E6
Whitebridge....137 C7
Whitebrook..... 36 D2
Whiteburn..... 121 E8
Whitecairn....105 D6
Whitecairns....141 C8
Whitecastle....120 E3
Whitechapel..... 93 E5
Whitecleat....159 H6
White Coppice .. 86 C4
Whitecraig....121 B6
Whitecroft..... 36 D3
Whitecross Corn...4 B4
  Falk..... 120 B2
  Staffs..... 62 B2
Whiteface....151 C10
Whitefarland....143 D9
Whitefaulds....112 D2
Whitefield Gtr Man.87 D6
  Perth..... 134 F1
Whiteford....141 B6
Whitegate..... 74 C3
Whitehall Blackburn .86 B4
  W Sus..... 16 B5
Whitehall Village .159 F7
Whitehaven..... 98 C1
Whitehill..... 27 F5
Whitehills Aberds .153 B6
  S Lanark....119 D6
Whitehough..... 87 F8
Whitehouse
  Aberds....140 C5
  Argyll....145 G7
Whiteinch....118 C5
Whitekirk....129 F7
White Lackington . 12 E5
White Ladies
  Aston..... 50 D4
Whitelaw....119 E6
Whiteleas....111 C6
Whiteley Bank... 15 F6
Whiteley Green.. 75 B6
Whiteley Village. 27 C8
White Lund..... 92 C4
Whitemans Green. 17 B7
White Mill..... 33 B5
Whitemire....151 F12
Whitemoor....4 D4
Whitemore..... 75 C5
Whitenap..... 14 B4
White Ness....160 J5
White Notley.. 42 C3
Whiteoak Green. 38 C3
Whiteparish.. 14 B3

White Pit..... 79 B6
White Post..... 77 D6
Whiterashes....141 B7
White Rocks..... 35 B8
White Roding.. 42 C1
Whiterow....158 F5
Whiteshill..... 37 D5
Whiteside
  Northumb....109 C7
  W Loth..... 120 C2
Whitesmith..... 18 D2
Whitestaunton .. 11 C7
Whitestone Devon... 10 E3
  Devon.....20 E3
  Warks..... 63 F7
Whitestones....153 C8
Whitestreet Green. 56 F3
Whitewall Corner . 96 B3
White Waltham.. 27 B6
Whiteway Glos.. 37 C6
  Glos..... 37 C6
Whitewell Aberds .153 B9
  Lancs..... 93 E6
Whitewell Bottom. 87 B6
Whiteworks..... 6 B4
Whitfield Kent.. 31 E7
  Northants 52 F4
  Northumb....109 D7
  S Glos..... 36 E3
Whitford Devon.. 11 E7
  Flint..... 72 B5
Whitgift..... 90 B2
Whitgreave..... 62 B2
Whithorn....105 E8
Whiting Bay....143 F11
Whitkirk..... 95 F6
Whitland..... 32 C2
Whitletts..... 112 B3
Whitley N Yorks... 89 B6
  Reading..... 26 B5
  Wilts..... 24 C3
Whitley Bay....111 B6
Whitley Chapel....110 D2
Whitley Lower.. 88 C3
Whitley Row..... 29 D5
Whitlock's End... 51 B6
Whitminster.. 36 D4
Whitmore..... 74 E5
Whitnage..... 10 C5
Whitnash..... 51 C8
Whitney-on-Wye. 48 E4
Whitrigg Cumb....108 D2
  Cumb..... 108 F2
Whitsbury..... 14 C2
Whitsome....122 D4
Whitson..... 35 F7
Whitstable..... 30 C5
Whitstone..... 8 E4
Whittingham...117 C6
Whittingslow.. 60 F4
Whittington Glos... 37 B7
  Lancs..... 93 B6
  Norf..... 67 E7
  Shrops..... 73 F7
  Staffs..... 62 F2
  Staffs..... 63 D5
  Worcs..... 50 D3
Whittlebury..... 52 E4
Whittle-le-Woods. 86 B3
Whittlesford.. 55 E5
Whittlestone Head. 86 C5
Whitton Borders..116 B3
  N Lincs..... 90 B3
  Northumb....117 D6
  Powys..... 48 C4
  Shrops..... 49 B7
  Stockton.. 102 B1
  Suff..... 56 E5
Whittonditch.. 25 B8
Whittonstall....110 D3
Whitway..... 26 D2
Whitwell Derbys.. 76 B5
  Herts..... 40 B4
  IoW..... 15 G6
  N Yorks..... 101 E7
  Rutland..... 65 D6
Whitwell-on-the-
  Hill..... 96 C3
Whitwell Street.. 81 E7
Whitwick..... 63 C8
Whitwood..... 88 B5
Whitworth..... 87 C6
Whixall..... 74 F2
Whixley..... 95 D7
Whoberley..... 51 B8
Whorlton Durham .101 C6
  N Yorks....102 D2
Whygate....109 B7
Whyle..... 49 C7
Whyteleafe.. 28 D4
Wibdon..... 36 E2
Wibsey..... 88 A2
Wibtoft..... 63 F8
Wichenford.. 50 C2
Wichling..... 30 D3
Wick BCP..... 14 E2
  Devon..... 11 D6
  Highld....158 E5
  S Glos..... 24 B2
  Shetland....160 K6
  V Glam.....21 B8
  Wilts..... 14 B2
  Worcs..... 50 E4
  W Sus..... 16 D4
Wicken Cambs.. 55 B6
  Northants 52 F5
Wicken Bonhunt. 55 F5
Wickenby..... 90 F4
Wicken Green
  Village..... 80 D4
Wickersley..... 89 E5
Wickford..... 42 E3
Wickham Hants.. 15 C6
  W Berks..... 25 B8
Wickham Bishops. 42 C4
Wickhambreux. 31 D6
Wickhambrook.. 55 D8
Wickhamford.. 51 E5
Wickham Market. 57 D7
Wickhampton.. 69 D7
Wickham St Paul. 56 F2
Wickham Skeith. 56 C4
Wickham Street
  Suff..... 55 D8
  Suff..... 56 C4
Wickhurst..... 27 D6
Wicklewood.. 68 D3

Wickmere....81 D7
Wick St Lawrence. 23 C5
Wickwar..... 36 F4
Widdington.. 55 F6
Widdrington....117 E8
Widdrington
  Station.....117 E8
Widecombe in the
  Moor.....6 B5
Widegates..... 5 D7
Widemouth Bay.. 8 D4
Widewall....159 J5
Widford Essex.. 42 D2
  Herts..... 41 C7
Widham..... 37 F7
Widmer End.. 40 E1
Widmerpool.. 64 B3
Widnes..... 86 F3
Wigan..... 86 D3
Wiggaton..... 11 E6
Wiggenhall
  St Germans.. 67 C5
Wiggenhall St Mary
  Magdalen .. 67 C5
Wiggenhall St Mary
  the Virgin.. 67 C5
Wigginton Herts.. 40 C2
  Oxon..... 51 F8
  Staffs..... 63 D6
  York..... 95 D8
Wigglesworth.. 93 D8
Wiggonby....108 D2
Wiggonholt.. 16 C4
Wighill..... 95 E7
Wighton..... 80 D5
Wigley..... 14 C4
Wigmore Hereford.. 49 C6
  Medway..... 30 C2
Wigsley..... 77 B8
Wigsthorpe.. 65 F7
Wigston..... 64 E3
Wigthorpe.. 89 F6
Wigtoft..... 79 F5
Wigton....108 E2
Wigtown....105 D8
Wigtwizzle.. 88 E3
Wike..... 95 E6
Wike Well End.. 89 C7
Wilbarston..... 64 F5
Wilberfoss..... 96 D3
Wilberlee..... 87 C8
Wilburton..... 55 B5
Wilby Norf..... 68 F3
  Northants 53 C6
  Suff..... 57 B6
Wilcot..... 25 C6
Wilcott..... 60 C3
Wilcrick..... 35 F8
Wilday Green.. 76 B3
Wildboarclough.. 75 C6
Wilden Bedford.. 53 D8
  Worcs..... 50 B3
Wildhern..... 25 D8
Wildhill..... 41 D5
Wildmoor..... 50 B4
Wildsworth.. 90 E2
Wilford..... 77 F5
Wilkesley..... 74 E3
Wilkhaven....151 C12
Wilkieston....120 C4
Willand..... 10 C5
Willaston Ches E.. 74 D3
  Ches W..... 73 B7
Willen..... 53 E6
Willenhall W Mid.. 51 B8
  W Mid.....62 E3
Willerby E Yorks.. 97 F6
  N Yorks..... 97 B6
Willersey..... 51 F6
Willersley..... 48 E5
Willesborough.. 30 E4
Willesborough
  Lees..... 30 E4
Willesden..... 41 F5
Willett..... 22 F3
Willey Shrops.. 61 E6
  Warks..... 63 F8
Willey Green.. 27 D7
Williamscott.. 52 E2
Willian..... 54 F3
Willingale..... 42 D1
Willingdon.. 18 E2
Willingham.. 54 B5
Willingham by
  Stow..... 90 F2
Willington Bedford. 54 E2
  Derbys..... 63 B6
  Durham....110 F4
  T&W..... 111 C6
  Warks..... 51 F7
Willington Corner. 74 C2
Willisham Tye.. 56 D4
Willitoft..... 96 F3
Williton..... 22 E2
Willoughbridge. 74 E4
Willoughby Lincs .. 79 B7
  Warks..... 52 C3
Willoughby-on-the-
  Wolds..... 64 B3
Willoughby
  Waterleys.. 64 E2
Willoughton.. 90 E3
Willows Green.. 42 C3
Willsbridge.. 23 B8
Willsworthy..... 9 F7
Wilmcote..... 51 D6
Wilmington Devon.. 11 E7
  E Sus..... 18 E2
  Kent..... 29 B6
Wilminstone..6 B2
Wilmslow..... 87 F6
Wilnecote..... 63 D6
Wilpshire..... 93 F6
Wilsden..... 94 F3
Wilsford Lincs....78 E3
  Wilts..... 25 D6
  Wilts..... 25 F6
Wilsill..... 94 C4
Wilsley Pound.. 18 B4
Wilsom..... 26 F5
Wilson..... 63 B8
Wilsontown....120 D2
Wilstead..... 53 E8
Wilsthorpe..... 65 C7
Wilstone..... 40 C2
Wilton Borders....115 C7
  Cumb..... 98 D2

Wilton continued
  N Yorks.....103 F6
  Redcar.....102 C3
  Wilts..... 25 C7
  Wilts..... 25 F5
Wimbish..... 55 F6
Wimbish Green.. 55 F7
Wimblebury.. 62 C4
Wimbledon.. 28 B3
Wimblington.. 66 E4
Wimborne Minster 13 E8
Wimborne St Giles 13 C8
Wimbotsham.. 67 D6
Wimpson..... 14 C4
Wimpstone.. 51 E7
Wincanton.. 12 B5
Wincham..... 74 B3
Winchburgh....120 B3
Winchcombe.. 37 B7
Winchelsea.. 19 D6
Winchelsea Beach. 19 D6
Winchester.. 15 B5
Winchet Hill.. 29 E8
Winchfield.. 27 D5
Winchmore Hill
  Bucks..... 40 E2
  London.....41 E6
Wincle..... 75 C6
Wincobank.. 88 E4
Windermere.. 99 E6
Winderton.. 51 E8
Windhill..... 151 G8
Windhouse....160 D6
Windlehurst.. 87 F7
Windlesham.. 27 C7
Windley..... 76 E3
Windmill Hill
  E Sus..... 18 D3
  Som..... 11 C8
Windrush..... 38 C1
Windsor N Lincs.. 89 C8
  Windsor.....27 B7
Windsoredge.. 37 D5
Windygates.. 128 D5
Windyknowe....120 C2
Windywalls....122 F3
Wineham..... 17 B6
Winestead..... 91 B6
Winewall..... 94 E2
Winfarthing.. 68 F4
Winford IoW.. 15 F6
  N Som..... 23 C7
Winforton..... 48 E4
Winfrith
  Newburgh.. 13 F6
Wing Bucks..... 40 B1
  Rutland..... 65 D5
Wingate..... 111 F7
Wingates Gtr Man.. 86 D4
  Northumb....117 E7
Wingerworth.. 76 C3
Wingfield S Beds.. 40 B2
  Suff..... 57 B6
  Wilts..... 24 D3
Wingham..... 31 D6
Wingmore.. 31 E5
Wingrave..... 40 C1
Winkburn..... 77 D7
Winkfield..... 27 B7
Winkfield Row.. 27 B6
Winkhill..... 75 D7
Winklebury.. 26 D4
Winkleigh..... 9 D8
Winksley..... 95 B5
Winkton..... 14 E2
Winlaton....110 C4
Winless....158 E5
Winmarleigh.. 92 E4
Winnal..... 49 F6
Winnall..... 15 B5
Winnersh..... 27 B5
Winscales..... 98 B2
Winscombe.. 23 D6
Winsford Ches W.. 74 C3
  Som..... 21 F8
Winsham..... 11 D8
Winshill..... 63 B6
Winskill..... 109 F5
Winslade..... 26 E4
Winsley..... 24 C3
Winslow..... 39 B7
Winson..... 37 D7
Winson Green.. 62 F4
Winsor..... 14 C4
Winster Cumb.. 99 E6
  Derbys..... 76 C2
Winston Durham.. 101 C6
  Suff..... 57 C5
Winstone..... 37 D6
Winston Green.. 57 C5
Winswell..... 9 C6
Winterborne
  Clenston.. 13 D6
Winterborne
  Herringston. 12 F4
Winterborne
  Houghton.. 13 D6
Winterborne
  Kingston.. 13 E6
Winterborne
  Monkton.. 12 F4
Winterborne
  Stickland.. 13 D6
Winterborne
  Whitechurch. 13 D6
Winterborne
  Zelston.. 13 E6
Winterbourne
  S Glos..... 36 F3
  W Berks.... 26 B2
Winterbourne
  Abbas..... 12 E4
Winterbourne
  Bassett..... 25 B6
Winterbourne
  Dauntsey.. 25 F6
Winterbourne
  Down..... 23 B8
Winterbourne
  Earls..... 25 F6
Winterbourne
  Gunner..... 25 F6
Winterbourne
  Monkton.. 25 B6
Winterbourne
  Steepleton.. 12 F4
Winterbourne
  Stoke..... 25 E5

Winter Gardens. 42 F3
Winteringham.. 90 B3
Winterley..... 74 D4
Wintersett..... 88 C4
Wintershill.. 15 C6
Winterton..... 90 C3
Winterton-on-Sea 69 C7
Winthorpe Lincs.... 79 C8
  Notts..... 77 D8
Winton BCP.. 13 E8
  Cumb..... 100 C2
  N Yorks....102 E2
Wintringham.. 96 B4
Winwick Cambs.. 65 F8
  Northants 52 B4
  Warr..... 86 E4
Wirksworth.. 76 D2
Wirksworth Moor. 76 D3
Wirswall..... 74 E2
Wisbech..... 66 D4
Wisbech St Mary.. 66 D4
Wiseton..... 89 F7
Wishaw N Lanark..119 D7
  Warks..... 63 E5
Wispington.. 78 B5
Wissenden.. 30 E3
Wissett..... 57 B7
Wistanstow.. 60 F4
Wistanswick.. 61 B6
Wistaston..... 74 D3
Wistaston Green. 74 D3
Wiston Pembs.. 32 C1
  S Lanark.... 120 F2
  W Sus..... 16 C5
Wistow Cambs.. 66 F2
  N Yorks..... 95 F8
Wiswell..... 93 F7
Witcham..... 66 F4
Witchampton.. 13 D7
Witchford..... 55 B6
Witham..... 42 C4
Witham Friary.. 24 E2
Witham on the Hill 65 C7
Withcall..... 91 F6
Withdean..... 17 D7
Witherenden Hill. 18 C3
Witherhurst.. 18 C3
Witherley..... 63 E7
Withern..... 91 F8
Withernsea.. 91 B7
Withernwick.. 97 E7
Withersdale Street 69 F5
Withersfield.. 55 E7
Witherslack.. 99 F6
Withiel..... 4 C4
Withiel Florey.. 21 F8
Withington Glos.... 37 C7
  Gtr Man.....87 E6
  Hereford..... 49 E7
  Shrops..... 61 C5
  Staffs..... 75 F7
Withington Green. 74 B5
Withleigh..... 10 C4
Withnell..... 86 B4
Withybrook.. 63 F8
Withycombe.. 22 E2
Withycombe
  Raleigh..... 10 F5
Withyham..... 29 F5
Withypool..... 21 F7
Witley..... 27 F7
Witnesham.. 57 D5
Witney..... 38 C3
Wittering..... 65 D7
Wittersham.. 19 C5
Witton Angus.. 135 B5
  Worcs..... 50 C3
Witton Bridge.. 69 A6
Witton Gilbert....110 E5
Witton-le-Wear.. 110 F4
Witton Park....110 F4
Wiveliscombe.. 11 B5
Wivelrod..... 26 F4
Wivelsfield.. 17 B7
Wivelsfield Green. 17 C7
Wivenhoe..... 43 B6
Wivenhoe Cross.. 43 B6
Wiveton..... 81 C6
Wix..... 43 B7
Wixford..... 51 D5
Wixhill..... 61 B5
Wixoe..... 55 E8
Woburn..... 53 F7
Woburn Sands.. 53 F7
Wokefield Park.. 26 C4
Woking..... 27 D8
Wokingham.. 27 C6
Wolborough.... 7 B6
Woldingham.. 28 D4
Wold Newton
  E Yorks.....97 B6
  NE Lincs.....91 E6
Wolfclyde....120 F3
Wolferton..... 67 B6
Wolfhill....134 F1
Wolf's Castle.. 44 C4
Wolfsdale..... 44 C4
Woll..... 115 B7
Wollaston
  Northants 53 C7
  Shrops..... 60 C3
Wollaton..... 76 F5
Wollerton..... 74 F3
Wollescote.. 62 F3
Wolsingham....110 F3
Wolstanton.. 75 E5
Wolston..... 52 B2
Wolvercote.. 38 C4
Wolverhampton.. 62 E3
Wolverley Shrops.. 73 F8
  Worcs..... 50 B3
Wolverton Hants.. 26 D3
  M Keynes..... 53 E6
  Warks..... 51 C7
Wolverton
  Common.. 26 D3
Wolvesnewton.. 36 E1
Wolvey..... 63 F8
Wolviston....102 B2
Wombleton.. 102 F4
Wombourne.. 62 E2
Wombwell.. 88 D4
Womenswold.. 31 D6
Womersley.. 89 C6
Wonastow..... 36 C1
Wonersh..... 27 E8

Wonson.....9 F8
Wonston..... 26 F2
Wooburn..... 40 F2
Wooburn Green.. 40 F2
Woodacott..... 9 D5
Woodale..... 94 B3
Woodbank....143 G7
Woodbastwick.. 69 C6
Woodbeck..... 77 B7
Woodborough
  Notts..... 77 E6
  Wilts..... 25 D6
Woodbridge Dorset 12 C5
  Suff..... 57 E6
Woodbury
  Salterton.. 10 F5
Woodbury..... 10 F5
Woodchester.. 37 D5
Woodchurch Kent.. 19 B6
  Mers..... 85 F3
Woodcombe.. 21 E8
Woodcote..... 39 F6
Woodcott..... 26 D2
Woodcroft..... 36 E2
Woodcutts..... 13 C7
Wood Dalling.. 81 E6
Woodditton.. 55 D7
Woodeaton.. 39 C5
Woodend Cumb.. 98 E3
  Northants 52 E4
  W Sus..... 16 D2
Wood End Herts.. 41 B6
  Warks..... 51 B6
  Warks..... 63 E6
Woodend Green.. 52 F4
Woodfalls..... 14 B2
Woodford Corn.. 8 C4
  Devon 7 D5
  Glos..... 36 E3
  Gtr Man..... 87 F6
  London..... 41 E7
  Northants 53 B7
  Soton..... 14 C5
  Warr..... 86 F4
Woodford Bridge. 41 E7
Woodford Halse.. 52 D3
Woodgate Norf.. 68 C3
  Oxon.....38 F2
  W Mid..... 62 F3
  W Sus..... 16 D3
Woodgreen.. 14 C2
Woodhall Herts.. 41 C5
  Involyd.....118 B3
  N Yorks..... 100 E4
Woodhall Spa.. 78 C4
Woodham..... 27 C8
Woodham Ferrers. 42 E3
Woodham
  Mortimer.. 42 D4
Woodham Walter. 42 D4
Woodhaven....129 B6
Wood Hayes.. 62 D3
Woodhead....153 E7
Woodhey..... 87 C5
Woodhill..... 61 F7
Woodhorn....117 F8
Woodhouse
  Leics..... 64 C2
  N Lincs..... 89 D8
  S Yorks..... 88 F5
  W Yorks..... 88 B4
  W Yorks..... 95 F5
Woodhouse Eaves. 64 C2
Woodhouselee.. 120 C5
Woodhouselees. 108 B3
Woodhouse Park. 87 F6
Woodhouses.. 63 C5
Woodhurst.. 54 B4
Woodingdean. 17 D7
Woodkirk..... 88 B3
Woodland Devon.. 7 C5
  Durham..... 101 B5
Woodlands Aberds 141 E6
  Dorset..... 13 D8
  Hants..... 14 C4
  Highld..... 151 E8
  N Yorks..... 95 D6
  S Yorks..... 89 D6
Woodlands Park. 27 B6
Woodlands
  St Mary..... 25 B8
Woodlane..... 62 B5
Wood Lanes.. 87 F7
Woodleigh..... 6 E5
Woodlesford.. 88 B4
Woodley Gtr Man.. 87 E7
  Wokingham..... 27 B5
Woodmancote Glos 36 E4
  Glos..... 37 B6
  Glos..... 37 D7
  W Sus..... 15 D8
  W Sus..... 17 C6
Woodmancott.. 26 E3
Woodmansey.. 97 F6
Woodmansterne. 28 D3
Woodminton.. 13 B8
Woodnesborough 31 D7
Woodnewton.. 65 E7
Wood Norton.. 81 E6
Woodplumpton.. 92 F5
Woodrising.. 68 D2
Wood's Corner.. 18 C3
Woodseaves Shrops 74 F3
  Staffs..... 61 B7
Woodsend.. 25 B7
Woodsetts.. 89 F6
Woodsford.. 13 E5
Wood's Green.. 18 B3
Woodside
  Aberdeen....141 D8
  Aberds.....153 D10
  Brack.....27 B7
  Fife..... 129 D6
  Hants..... 14 E4
  Perth..... 134 F2
Woodside of
  Arbeadie....141 E6
Woodstock Oxon.. 38 C4
  Pembs..... 32 B1
Wood Street Norf.. 69 C6
  Sur..... 27 D7
Woodthorpe Derbys 76 B4
  Leics..... 64 C2
  Lincs..... 91 F8
  York..... 95 E8
Woodton..... 69 E5

Woodtown Devon..9 B6
  Devon.....9 B6
Woodvale..... 85 C4
Woodville..... 63 C7
Wood Walton.. 66 F2
Woodyates..... 13 C8
Woofferton..... 49 C7
Wookey..... 23 E7
Wookey Hole.. 23 E7
Wool..... 13 F6
Woolacombe.. 20 E3
Woolage Green.. 31 E6
Woolaston.. 36 E2
Woolavington.. 22 E5
Woolbeding.. 16 B2
Wooldale..... 88 D2
Wooler..... 117 B5
Woolfardisworthy
  Devon.....8 B5
  Devon 10 D3
Woolfords
  Cottages....120 D3
Woolhampton.. 26 C3
Woolhope..... 49 F8
Woolhope
  Cockshoot.. 49 F8
Woolland..... 13 D5
Wollaton..... 9 C6
Woolley Bath.. 24 C2
  Cambs.....54 B2
  Corn.....8 C4
  Derbys..... 76 C3
  W Yorks..... 88 C4
Woolmer Green.. 41 C5
Woolmere Green. 50 C4
Woolpit..... 56 C3
Woolscott..... 52 C2
Woolsington....110 C4
Woolstanwood.. 74 D3
Woolstaston.. 60 E4
Woolsthorpe Lincs .65 B6
  Lincs..... 77 F8
Woolston Devon..6 E5
  Shrops..... 60 B3
  Shrops..... 60 F4
  Soton..... 14 C5
  Warr..... 86 E4
Woolstone
  M Keynes..... 53 F6
  Oxon.....38 F2
Woolton..... 86 F2
Woolton Hill.. 26 C2
Woolverstone.. 57 F5
Woolverton.. 24 D2
Woolwich..... 28 B5
Woolwich Ferry.. 28 B5
Woonton..... 49 D5
Wooperton....117 B6
Woore..... 74 E4
Wootten Green.. 57 B6
Wootton Bedford.. 53 E8
  Hants..... 14 E3
  Hereford..... 48 D5
  Kent..... 31 E6
  N Lincs..... 90 C4
  Northants 53 D5
  Oxon..... 38 C4
  Oxon..... 38 D4
  Shrops..... 49 B6
  Shrops..... 60 B3
  Staffs..... 62 B2
  Staffs..... 75 E8
Wootton Bridge.. 15 E6
Wootton Common. 15 E6
Wootton
  Courtenay.. 21 E8
Wootton Fitzpaine. 11 E8
Wootton Rivers.. 25 C6
Wootton
  St Lawrence.. 26 D3
Wootton Wawen.. 51 C6
Worcester..... 50 D3
Worcester Park.. 28 C3
Wordsley..... 62 F2
Worfield..... 61 E7
Work..... 159 G5
Workington.. 98 B1
Worksop..... 77 B5
Worlaby..... 90 C4
World's End.. 26 B2
Worle..... 23 C5
Worleston..... 74 D3
Worlingham.. 69 F7
Worlington.. 55 B7
Worlingworth.. 57 C6
Wormald Green.. 95 C6
Wormbridge.. 49 F6
Wormegay.. 67 C6
Wormelow Tump.. 49 F6
Wormhill..... 75 B8
Wormingford.. 56 F3
Worminghall.. 39 D6
Wormington.. 50 F5
Worminster.. 23 E7
Wormit..... 129 B5
Wormleighton.. 52 D2
Wormley Herts.. 41 D6
  Sur.....27 F7
Wormley West
  End..... 41 D6
Wormshill.. 30 D2
Wormsley..... 49 E6
Worplesdon.. 27 D7
Worrall..... 88 E4
Worsbrough.. 88 D4
Worsbrough
  Common.. 88 D4
Worsley..... 86 D5
Worstead..... 69 B6
Worston..... 93 E7
Worswell....6 E4
Worth Kent.. 31 D7
  W Sus..... 28 F4
Wortham..... 56 B4
Worthen..... 60 D3
Worthenbury.. 73 E8
Worthing Norf.. 68 C2
  W Sus..... 16 D5
Worthington. 63 B8
Worth Matravers. 13 G7
Worting..... 26 D4
Wortley S Yorks.. 88 E4
  W Yorks..... 95 F5
Worton N Yorks.. 100 E4
  Wilts..... 24 D4
Wortwell..... 69 F5
Wotherton.. 60 D2

Wotter..... 6 C3
Wotton..... 28 E2
Wotton-under-
  Edge..... 36 E4
Wotton
  Underwood.. 39 C6
Woughton on the
  Green..... 53 F6
Wouldham.. 29 C8
Wrabness..... 57 F5
Wrafton..... 20 F3
Wragby Lincs.. 78 B4
  W Yorks..... 88 C5
Wragholme.. 91 E7
Wramplingham.. 68 D4
Wrangbrook.. 89 C5
Wrangle..... 79 D7
Wrangle Bank.. 79 D7
Wrangle Lowgate. 79 D7
Wrangway..... 11 C6
Wrantage..... 11 B8
Wrawby..... 90 D4
Wraxall Dorset.. 12 D3
  N Som..... 23 B6
  Som..... 23 F8
Wray..... 93 C6
Wraysbury.. 27 B8
Wrayton..... 93 B6
Wrea Green.. 92 F3
Wreay Cumb.. 99 B6
  Cumb..... 108 E4
Wrecclesham.. 27 E6
Wrecsam
  = Wrexham.. 73 D7
Wrekenton....111 D5
Wrelton..... 103 F5
Wrenbury..... 74 E2
Wrench Green.. 103 F7
Wreningham.. 68 E4
Wrentham..... 69 F7
Wrenthorpe.. 88 B4
Wrentnall..... 60 D4
Wressle E Yorks.. 96 F3
  N Lincs..... 90 D3
Wrestlingworth.. 54 E3
Wretham..... 68 F2
Wretton..... 67 E6
Wrexham
  = Wrecsam.. 73 D7
Wrexham Industrial
  Estate..... 73 E7
Wribbenhall.. 50 B2
Wrightington Bar. 86 C3
Wrinehill..... 74 E4
Wrington.. 23 C6
Writhlington.. 24 D2
Writtle..... 42 D2
Wrockwardine.. 61 C6
Wroot..... 89 D8
Wrotham..... 29 D7
Wrotham Heath.. 29 D7
Wroughton.. 37 F8
Wroxall IoW.. 15 G6
  Warks..... 51 B7
Wroxeter..... 61 D5
Wroxham..... 69 C6
Wroxton..... 52 E2
Wyaston..... 75 E8
Wyberton..... 79 E6
Wyboston..... 54 D2
Wybunbury.. 74 E4
Wychbold..... 50 C4
Wych Cross.. 28 F5
Wyck..... 27 F5
Wyck Rissington. 38 B1
Wycoller..... 94 F2
Wycomb..... 64 B4
Wycombe Marsh. 40 E1
Wyddial..... 54 F4
Wye..... 30 E4
Wyesham..... 36 C2
Wyfordby.. 64 C4
Wyke Dorset.. 13 B5
  Shrops..... 61 D6
  Sur.....27 D7
  W Yorks..... 88 B2
Wykeham N Yorks.. 96 B3
  N Yorks..... 103 F7
Wyken..... 63 F7
Wyke Regis.. 12 G4
Wykey..... 60 B3
Wylam..... 110 C4
Wylde Green.. 62 E5
Wyllie..... 35 E5
Wylye..... 24 F5
Wymering.. 15 D7
Wymeswold.. 64 B3
Wymington.. 53 C7
Wymondham Leics 65 C5
  Norf..... 68 D4
Wyndham..... 34 E3
Wynford Eagle.. 12 E3
Wyng..... 159 J4
Wynyard Village .. 102 B2
Wyre Piddle.. 50 E4
Wysall..... 64 B3
Wythall..... 51 B5
Wytham..... 38 D4
Wythburn.. 99 C5
Wythenshawe.. 87 F6
Wythop Mill.. 98 B3
Wyton..... 54 B3
Wyverstone.. 56 C4
Wyverstone Street. 56 C4
Wyville..... 65 B5
Wyvis Lodge....150 D7

Y

Yaddlethorpe.. 90 D2
Yafford..... 14 F5
Yafforth..... 101 E8
Yalding..... 29 D7
Yanworth..... 37 C7
Yapham..... 96 D3
Yapton..... 16 D3
Yarburgh..... 91 E7
Yarcombe..... 11 D7
Yard..... 22 F2
Yardley..... 62 F5
Yardley Gobion.. 53 E5
Yardley Hastings. 53 D6
Yardro..... 48 D4
Yarkhill..... 49 E8
Yarlet..... 62 B3
Yarlington..... 12 B4

Yarlside..... 92 C2
Yarm..... 102 C2
Yarmouth.. 14 F4
Yarnbrook.. 24 D3
Yarnfield..... 75 F5
Yarnscombe......9 B7
Yarnton..... 38 C4
Yarpole..... 49 C6
Yarrow..... 115 B6
Yarrow Feus....115 B6
Yarsop..... 49 E6
Yarwell..... 65 E7
Yate..... 36 F4
Yateley..... 27 C6
Yatesbury.. 25 B5
Yattendon.. 26 B3
Yatton Hereford..... 23 C6
  N Som..... 23 C6
Yatton Keynell.. 24 B3
Yaverland.. 15 F7
Yaxham..... 68 C3
Yaxley Cambs.. 65 E8
  Suff..... 56 B5
Yazor..... 49 E6
Y Bala = Bala.. 72 F3
Y Barri = Barry.. 22 C3
Y Bont-Faen
  = Cowbridge.. 21 B8
Y Drenewydd
  = Newtown.. 59 E8
Yeading..... 40 F4
Yeadon..... 94 E5
Yealand Conyers. 92 B5
Yealand
  Redmayne.. 92 B5
Yealmpton...6 D3
Yearby..... 102 B4
Yearsley..... 95 B8
Yeaton..... 60 C4
Yeaveley..... 75 E8
Yedingham.. 96 B4
Yeldon..... 53 C8
Yelford..... 38 D3
Yelland..... 20 F3
Yelling..... 54 C3
Yelvertoft.. 52 B3
Yelverton Devon.....6 C3
  Norf..... 69 D5
Yenston..... 12 B5
Yeoford..... 10 E2
Yeolmbridge.... 8 F5
Yeo Mill..... 10 B3
Yeovil..... 12 C3
Yeovil Marsh.. 12 C3
Yeovilton..... 12 B3
Yerbeston.. 32 D1
Yesnaby....159 G3
Yetlington....117 D6
Yetminster.. 12 C3
Yettington.. 11 F5
Yetts o'Muckhart .128 D2
Y Felinheli.. 82 E5
Y Fenni
  = Abergavenny.. 35 C6
Y Fflint = Flint.. 73 B6
Y Ffôr..... 70 D4
Y-Ffrith..... 72 A4
Y Gelli Gandryll
  = Hay-on-Wye.. 48 E4
Yieldshields....119 D8
Yiewsley..... 40 F3
Y Mwmbwls
  = The Mumbles. 33 F7
Ynysddu..... 35 E5
Ynysgyfflog.. 58 C3
Ynyshir..... 34 E4
Ynyslas..... 58 E3
Ynys-meudwy.. 33 D8
Ynystawe.. 33 D7
Ynysybwl.. 34 E4
Yockenthwaite.. 94 B2
Yockleton.. 60 C3
Yokefleet.. 90 B2
Yoker..... 118 C5
Yonder Bognie..152 D5
York..... 95 D8
Yorkletts.. 30 C4
Yorkley..... 36 D3
York Town.. 27 C6
Yorton..... 60 B5
Youlgreave.. 76 C2
Youlstone..... 8 C4
Youlthorpe.. 96 D3
Youlton..... 95 C7
Young's End.. 42 C3
Young Wood.. 78 B4
Yoxall..... 62 C5
Yoxford..... 57 C7
Y Pil = Pyle.. 34 F2
Yr Hôb = Hope.. 73 D7
Y Rhws = Rhoose. 22 C2
Y Rhyl = Rhyl.. 72 A4
Yr Wyddgrug
  = Mold..... 73 C6
Ysbyty-Cynfyn.. 47 B6
Ysbyty Ifan.. 72 E2
Ysbyty Ystwyth. 47 B6
Ysceifiog..... 73 B5
Yspitty..... 33 E6
Ystalyfera.. 34 D1
Ystrad..... 34 E3
Ystrad Aeron.. 46 D4
Ystradfellte.. 34 C3
Ystraddraffi.. 47 E6
Ystradgynlais.. 34 C1
Ystradmeurig.. 47 C6
Ystrad-mynach.. 35 E5
Ystradowen Carms 33 C8
  V Glam.....22 B2
Ystumtuen.. 47 B6
Ythanbank....153 E9
Ythanwells....153 E7
Ythsie..... 153 E8
Y Trallwng
  = Welshpool....60 D2
Y Waun = Chirk... 73 F6

Z

Zeal Monachorum. 10 D2
Zeals..... 24 F2
Zelah..... 4 D3
Zennor..... 2 C3